D1559272

RUSSIA'S FIRST CIVIL WAR

Frontispiece "The Rebel Siege of Moscow in 1606." Drawn circa 1607. The Hague, Koninklijke Bibliotheek, 78 H 56 (Isaac Massa's Album Amicorum). Courtesy of the National Library of the Netherlands.

RUSSIA'S FIRST CIVIL WAR

The Time of Troubles and the Founding of the Romanov Dynasty

Chester S. L. Dunning

The Pennsylvania State University Press
University Park, Pennsylvania

Library of Congress Cataloging-in-Publication Data

Dunning, Chester S. L., 1949–
Russia's first civil war: the Time of Troubles and the founding of the Romanov
dynasty / Chester S. L. Dunning.
p.   cm.
Includes bibliographical references and index.
ISBN 0-271-02074-1 (alk. paper)
1. Russia—History—Time of Troubles, 1598–1613.   I. Title

DK111 .D86 2001
947'.045—dc21

00-028817

It is the policy of The Pennsylvania State University Press to use acid-free paper for
the first printing of all clothbound books. Publications on uncoated stock satisfy the
minimum requirements of American National Standard for Information Sciences—
Permanence of Paper for Printed Library Materials, ANSI Z39.48–1992.

for
ELSIE
and
STEPHEN

CONTENTS

LIST OF ILLUSTRATIONS AND MAPS

Frontispiece: "The Rebel Siege of Moscow in 1606." Drawn circa 1607. The Hague, Koninklijke Bibliotheek, 78 H 56 (Isaac Massa's Album Amicorum).

Figures

Maps

When I started this book project twelve years ago, my intention was merely to correct many glaringly obvious errors in Soviet scholarship concerning popular uprisings that occurred during Russia's nightmarish "Time of Troubles"—the severe state crisis that nearly destroyed the country in the decade before the founding of the Romanov dynasty in 1613. During the past several years, however, the many blows delivered to various aspects of the traditional interpretation of the Time of Troubles by a handful of revisionists have effectively demolished the old paradigm. Upon close inspection, it turns out that Russia at the dawn of the seventeenth century did not, as long thought, face a social revolution against serfdom. Instead, the country endured and barely survived its first civil war—an extremely violent conflict that split Russian society vertically instead of horizontally. Because of such a dramatic and fundamental shift in our basic understanding of the Time of Troubles, I eventually decided to undertake a far more ambitious book project: the first comprehensive, post-Marxist survey and interpretation of "Russia's First Civil War."

Some readers may object to the title of this book, claiming that there were civil wars in Russia before the Time of Troubles. It is certainly true that there were many civil wars fought among the princes of ancient Rus, and Muscovy's long and bloody dynastic struggle (1425–53), which took place during the reign of Grand Prince Vasilii II, has often been somewhat imprecisely referred to as a civil war. Whatever the exact nature of those early conflicts among the East Slavic princes, however, all of them were confined to relatively small populations and geographic areas, and all of them occurred before the great watershed experience separating medieval from modern Russian history—the unification of Russia presided over by the powerful Rus principality of Muscovy at the end of the fifteenth and beginning of the sixteenth century. Despite significant elements of continuity from the medieval period, the birth of a powerful, autocratic early modern state centered around Moscow marked an entirely new phase in Russian history. The new state swiftly transformed itself into the well-known, multiethnic empire of the tsars and expanded meteorically to become Europe's largest country in the decades before the Time of Troubles. In fact, much of what we think of today when we think of Russia had its origins in the sixteenth century. Not only can we link many of the long-term origins of the Time of Troubles directly back to the rapid emergence of an extremely coercive early modern Russian state and the military ambitions of its ruling elite, but it is also well known that much of the peculiar nature (as well as many of the chronic problems) of later imperial Russia and even the Soviet Union can be traced back not to the Middle Ages but to the powerful influences of the basic structures and unique political culture of the huge Russian empire born in the sixteenth century. In many ways, therefore, it is no exaggeration to say that "Russian" history (as opposed to "Rus" history) really began in the sixteenth century. One may, of course, profitably compare the civil wars of all eras of Russian history; but, on balance, Russia's First Civil War has far more in common with later rebellions and revolutions against the tsars and with Russia's horrific twentieth-century civil war (1918–21) than it does with any of the parochial conflicts among the princes of medieval Rus.

Initial research for this book was made possible by a generous fellowship from the Harvard University Russian Research Center (now the Davis Center for Russian Studies) and by a faculty development leave from Texas A & M University. Since then the Office of the Vice President for Research and the Office of the Assistant Provost for International Programs at Texas A & M University have provided me with critically important financial support for travel and research related to this project. Several colleagues went out of their way to encourage my work, to support my applications for funding, and to offer extremely valuable advice at various stages during the conceptualization and development of this book project. I am especially indebted to Robert O. Crummey, Edward L. Keenan, Ruslan Skrynnikov, Aleksandr L. Stanislavskii, and Richard Hellie. I am also grateful for the valuable assistance I received from Paul Avrich, L. Scott Van Doren, Samuel H. Baron, A. A. Iskenderov, J. Arch Getty, Daniel Rowland, Hugh Graham, Michael Khodarkovsky, Georg Michels, John T. Alexander, Valerie Kivelson, Peter Kenez, Norman Evans, Aleksa Djilas, David Goldfrank, Ann Kleimola, A. P. Pavlov, Aleksandr S. Lavrov, Daniel Bornstein, Rachel Robbins, Wilco van den Brink, Sandra Kroupa, Brad Oftelie, Margaret Glover, Arnold Krammer, Thomas Woodfin, Stephen K. Dunning, Karen Hillier, Stephen M. Shirrell, Mary Petrusewicz, Cherene Holland, Terry Anderson, Patricia Mitchell, Steve Kress, Roger Beaumont, R. J. Q. Adams, Cynthia Bouton, Larry Yarak, Matt Shanks, Jonathan Coopersmith, and (last but not least) Peter J. Potter. I also wish to thank V. Ia. Klimenko for producing the beautiful illustration of the town of Tula that is reprinted in this book and for a detailed drawing of early modern Tula's streets published in

Gradostroitel'stvo Moskovskogo gosudarstva XVI–XVII vekov (Moscow: Stroiizdat, 1994), which strongly influenced the design of my map of the town.

I wish to acknowledge the incredibly generous and timely assistance I received from the staff of the Russian State Library (Rossiiskaia gosudarstvennaia biblioteka) and the Library of the Russian Academy of Sciences (Biblioteka Rossiiskoi Akademii nauk). I also received valuable assistance from the staff of the Russian National Library (Rossiiskaia natsional'naia biblioteka), the Russian State Archive of Ancient Acts (Rossiiskii gosudarstvennyi arkhiv drevnikh aktov), the National Library of the Netherlands (Koninklijke Bibliotheek), the British Library, the Public Record Office, Widener Library (Harvard University), Houghton Library (Harvard Univesity), the Fogg Museum, the New York Public Library, the James Ford Bell Library (University of Minnesota), the University of Washington Libraries, and the interlibrary services division of the Sterling C. Evans Library at Texas A & M University.

It would have been impossible for me to finish this book without the tireless and cheerful assistance of the professional staff of the Department of History, Texas A & M University. Judy A. Mattson did a superb job typing my huge manuscript and keeping track of myriads of endnotes. Robyn C. Konrad, Jude K. Swank, Mary Johnson, and Barbara Dawson efficiently typed many letters, kept my computer running, handled travel and funding documents, and performed a thousand other important tasks over the course of many years. My thanks to all of them is deep and heartfelt. Finally, I wish to acknowledge the incredibly important help I received from my wife, Elsie Kersten. Her guidance during the two months I spent designing and drafting the maps for this book was extremely valuable; but it was her unflagging support and sound advice during many years of research and writing that, more than anything else, made it possible for me to complete this big project.

Russian words and names in the text are spelled using a modified version of the Library of Congress transliteration system. All dates, unless otherwise indicated, are given in Old Style (Julian calendar), which in the seventeenth century was ten days behind the New Style (Gregorian) calendar. Because the old Russian new year began on September 1, in some cases documentary references to a specific year cannot be rendered in the text any more precisely than, for example, 1601–2 or 1612–13.

C.S.L.D.
College Station, Texas
September 2000

INTRODUCTION

Since the formation of the unified Russian state nearly five hundred years ago, its unhappy subjects have rebelled in large numbers surprisingly few times. Besides the well-known 1905 and 1917 Revolutions, the short list of major uprisings in Russia includes famous early modern revolts led by Stepan Razin in 1670–71 and Emilian Pugachev in 1773–74. A much less well known but extremely powerful early modern uprising was the so-called Bolotnikov rebellion of 1606–7, which occurred during Russia's catastrophic and confusing "Time of Troubles" or "Troubles." That rebellion was the highpoint of Russia's first civil war, the largest and most powerful uprising in Russian history before the twentieth century and the first time the Russian people rose against their tsar. The purpose of this study, the first English-language book on the subject, is to bring Russia's first civil war out of the shadows of obscurity and misinterpretation and to place it squarely in the category of the most important uprisings in Russian history.

By the end of the sixteenth century the newly formed Russian state faced its first severe crisis, known ever since as the Time of Troubles (1598–1613).[1] The Troubles began when the ancient ruling dynasty died out and Boris Godunov defeated rival aristocrats to become tsar. Many questioned the legitimacy of the new ruler, whose sins supposedly included having Ivan the Terrible's youngest son Dmitrii killed in 1591 in order to clear a path to the throne for himself. During Tsar Boris's reign Russia suffered a horrible famine (1601–3) that wiped out up to a third of the population. The effects of the famine, coupled with serious long-term economic, social, demographic, fiscal, and political problems, contributed to the delegitimization of the new ruler in the eyes of many Russians. Then in 1604 the country was invaded by a small army headed by a man who claimed to be Tsarevich Dmitrii, miraculously saved from Godunov's plot. Many towns, fortresses, soldiers, and cossacks of the southern frontier quickly joined Dmitrii's forces in the first popular uprising against a tsar. When Tsar Boris died suddenly in April 1605, resistance to the "pretender Dmitrii" (also known as "False Dmitrii") broke down and he became tsar—the only tsar ever raised to the throne by means of a military campaign and popular uprisings. Tsar Dmitrii ruled for about a year before he was assassinated by a small group of aristocrats, triggering a powerful civil war. The usurper Tsar Vasilii Shuiskii denounced the dead Dmitrii as an impostor, but the former tsar's supporters successfully put forward the story that Dmitrii had once again miraculously escaped death and would soon return to punish the traitors. So energetic was the response to the call to arms against Shuiskii that civil war raged for many years and produced about a dozen more pretenders claiming to be Dmitrii or other members of the old ruling dynasty. Russia's internal disorder prompted Polish and Swedish military intervention, resulting in even greater misery and chaos. Eventually, an uneasy alliance was forged among Russian factions and the Time of Troubles ended with the establishment of the Romanov dynasty in 1613. Tsarist Russia's first great state crisis, its worst before the twentieth century, had been so severe that it nearly destroyed the country and left very deep scars.[2]

The Time of Troubles, coming as it did about midway between the unification of Russia and the reign of Peter the Great, has long fascinated and puzzled the Russian people as well as many scholars, poets, and even musicians.[3] Nonetheless, it was so complex and sources about it are so fragmentary and contradictory that to this day the Time of Troubles defies simple recitation of its basic facts, let alone satisfactory explanations of its nature, causes, and significance. To many Russians who lived through the Troubles, it was nothing more or less than divine retribution for the sins of Russia's rulers or its people.[4] Others studying the period sought more secular explanations, noting that at the center of the Time of Troubles was the most powerful uprising in Russian history prior to the twentieth century—the so-called Bolotnikov rebellion, named after the principal rebel commander, Ivan Bolotnikov.[5] Claiming that Tsar Dmitrii had escaped assassination, Bolotnikov's forces occupied nearly half of the country and were able to lay siege to Moscow in the fall of 1606 before being driven back and temporarily defeated in 1607. In terms of threats to the existing regime, Bolotnikov achieved far more than the later and much better known Razin and Pugachev. The Bolotnikov rebellion struck terror into the hearts of the usurper Shuiskii and his supporters, whose desperate propaganda campaign against the rebels painted them in the darkest colors as lower-class rabble intent upon social revolution.[6]

Unfortunately, the traditional interpretation of the Time of Troubles was derived primarily from the usurper Tsar Vasilii Shuiskii's misleading propaganda campaign against his opponents. Because of confusion in sources and disarray in scholarship, such false assessments by a terrified elite were accepted at face value by many Russian historians, who long ago concluded that at the heart of the Troubles was Russia's first social revolution of the oppressed masses against serfdom.[7] The rather frightening notion that rebels in the early seventeenth century were fighting against serfdom was, over the years, also greatly reinforced by elite fear of later rebellions led by Razin and, especially, Pugachev. Likening the Bolotnikov rebellion to those smaller and less successful uprisings, Russian and Soviet scholars lumped them all together as social revolutions or "peasant wars."[8] In the Soviet era, the entire period of the Time of Troubles became known as the "First Peasant War."[9] In studying its causes, Marxist scholars emphasized the subjection and radicalization of Russian peasants and slaves by the beginning of the seventeenth century and focused on long-term social causes—usually linking the Time of Troubles back to the tumultuous reign of Tsar Ivan IV (r. 1547–84) and the enserfment of the Russian peasants.[10]

The traditional image of revolutionary masses fighting for their freedom in the Time of Troubles has had a powerful impact upon the historical imagination. Most Russian and Western studies of the history of early Russia, the development of serfdom, popular rebellions, and the "revolutionary tradition" and its origins have reflected this class war interpretation. Western scholars have sometimes scoffed at doctrinaire Marxist models of the "First Peasant War," but their own work either echoed Soviet scholarship or merely fell back on similar prerevolutionary interpretations.[11] The awkward paradox that within two generations of the Time of Troubles Russia grew to be the largest country in the world and within three generations produced Peter the Great—all with what is generally acknowledged as a "high degree of acceptance" by the same Russian people simultaneously viewed as failed rebels against serfdom—is usually passed over in silence.[12]

Upon reflection, it is clear that scholars have done a poor job so far of fathoming early modern Russian popular consciousness or the motives of Russian rebels.[13] Among other things, in early modern Russia, as elsewhere, social class is generally not the best tool of analysis for studying revolts. Tracking an individual's primary loyalties turns out to be not just a simple matter of determining his or her social class.[14] Instead, the fierce antagonisms observable in early modern Russia and elsewhere were usually not between social classes, but were instead the result of complex tensions among multiple layers of the social hierarchy and competing status groups within the elite. In addition, personal loyalties or regional bonds frequently transcended class differences in forming the basis for revolts.[15] In fact, some scholars seriously doubt that class war or social revolution was even possible in the early modern period, noting that early modern rebellions lacked the goal of fundamental transformation of societies and were dominated by conservative ideologies looking to the past rather than the future.[16] In light of these observations, there is a real need to reexamine many long-held views of Russia's Time of Troubles.

Fortunately, in recent years the traditional interpretation of the Troubles has come under sharp attack. During the last decade and a half, Ruslan Skrynnikov, the late Aleksandr Stanislavskii, and the author of this book have challenged virtually every aspect of the Marxist model of the First Peasant War.[17] Instead of a "peasant war" or social revolution, we have found a complex civil war, Russia's first—that occurred in two phases: 1604–5 and 1606–12.[18] That upheaval produced not horizontal class division but a vertical split through several layers of Russian society.[19] Some observant contemporaries actually recognized that they were witnessing a regional rebellion and civil war that cut across class lines.[20] Gradually, however, most writers about the subject adopted the view of popular uprisings in the Time of Troubles as a social revolution. Complicating the issue somewhat was the fact that several Soviet scholars, inspired by Lenin's pronouncement that "peasant wars" were the civil wars of the feudal period and the highest form of class struggle against serfdom, applied the term "civil war" to the Time of Troubles. Despite the use of the term, however, they still regarded the uprisings of that period essentially as a multifaceted social revolution.[21] The same is true for Western scholars who have written about "civil war" in the Time of Troubles.[22]

It is time to state categorically that Russia's first civil war, while destabilizing in impact, was definitely not a social revolution. It was instead a popular uprising in support of the pretender Dmitrii's claim to the throne, one that united diverse elements of Russian society.[23] There is no evidence that any rebels fought against serfdom, and the abolition of serfdom was never a rebel goal. In fact, serfs did not actively participate in the civil war, and peasants—with the exception of wealthy ones from the Komaritsk district (*Komaritskaia volost*)— were only marginally involved.[24] The bulk of the rebels supporting Dmitrii or later rising in his name were cossacks, petty gentry, lower status military servicemen, military slaves, and townsmen.[25] Even though the largest and most active rebel group, the cossacks, were mostly of peasant origin, they did not think or act like peasants and were not at all interested in championing the cause of the lower classes or in establishing "cossack democracy" in rebel-held areas.[26] Slaves participating in the civil war were not, as Soviet scholars contended, radicalized menials, but were instead elite military slaves with no interest in social revolution.[27] Rebels in the Time of Troubles were also not, as long believed, motivated by "social utopian" legends about Dmitrii as the "returning deliverer" of the masses from serfdom.[28] Instead, they were primarily devout

Orthodox Christian subjects whose religious beliefs helped push them to risk challenging a tsar they regarded as illegitimate.[29] Close analysis also reveals that the origins of the civil war were very complex and not merely the result of enserfment. Serfdom did, of course, play a role in causing the Time of Troubles, but it operated in ways that differ from traditional Marxist explanations.[30] In fact, it turns out that many old preconceptions about the social composition, motivation, and consciousness of rebel forces and about the origins, nature, impact, and significance of the Time of Troubles need to be abandoned.

Before charting a post-Marxist methodology for interpreting Russia's first civil war, it will be useful for many reasons to survey briefly the development of the traditional view that has long dominated scholarship and is still found in many textbooks. The first historian to connect the Time of Troubles directly to the enserfment of the Russian peasants at the end of the sixteenth century was Vasilii Tatishchev (1686–1750).[31] A similar view was held by Mikhail Shcherbatov (1733–90), who also emphasized that the extinction of the ancient ruling dynasty in 1598 helped produce rebellions in the Time of Troubles because of the doubtful legitimacy of Russia's new rulers and the yearning of the people for a lawful tsar related to the old ruling family.[32] In the early nineteenth century Nikolai Karamzin (1766–1826) laid much of the blame for the Time of Troubles on the power-hungry Boris Godunov's murder of Tsarevich Dmitrii in 1591. Karamzin recognized social discontent as a factor in the Troubles, but he did not regard Bolotnikov as the leader of the oppressed masses. Instead, he emphasized foreign interference in Russia's domestic problems as the principal cause of the Troubles, seeing Poland as the main source of the pretender Dmitrii's campaign for the throne and later rebellions in Dmitrii's name.[33] Sergei Solovev (1820–79) was one of the first historians who viewed the Time of Troubles specifically as a class struggle and was the first to refer to the Bolotnikov rebellion as a "peasant war."[34] Nonetheless, he correctly regarded the various pretenders during the Troubles as manifestations of domestic rather than foreign forces, and he focused especially on the rise of the cossacks as the principal cause of popular disturbances. In the context of Russia's dynastic crisis, according to Solovev, cossacks managed to rouse the lower classes against the landed elite.[35] Mykola (Nikolai) Kostomarov (1817–85), imperial Russia's foremost "populist" historian, also downplayed foreign interference in Russia's Time of Troubles and emphasized the role of cossacks legitimately fighting for their freedom under the banner of Bolotnikov and others. Kostomarov was quite sympathetic to the struggle of the "popular masses" and was particularly interested in those periods of Russian history such as the Time of Troubles "where the common people took part in the political process." At the same time, however, he blamed the cossacks for inadvertently producing much of the chaos of the Troubles.[36]

The eminent historian Vasilii Kliuchevskii (1841–1911) attempted to explain the Time of Troubles as a social conflict related to serfdom. He claimed that the Troubles began with an elite political struggle in the aftermath of Tsar Fedor's death in 1598, a struggle that gradually pulled other layers of Russian society into the conflict until eventually the lower classes rose up and transformed it into a social struggle intended to eliminate the upper classes. Thus, he regarded the Bolotnikov rebellion as a class war. According to Kliuchevskii, it took nothing less than foreign intervention to get the warring domestic factions to put an end to the Troubles in order to preserve their country.[37] The foremost historian of the Time of Troubles, Sergei Platonov (1860–1933), developed Kliuchevskii's ideas further, regarding the Troubles as a complex political and social struggle growing out of Russia's late sixteenth-century social crisis and the development of serfdom. According to Platonov's famous model of the period, the first phase of the Troubles was a dynastic crisis sparked by the death of Tsar Fedor in 1598, a phase that lasted through the short reign of Tsar Dmitrii (r. 1605–6). The second phase was a period of "social crisis" during which Bolotnikov and others waged class war in a vast, chaotic social revolution (1606–10). Finally, the last phase of the Troubles was the successful struggle for national survival against foreign intervention. Platonov's model of the Time of Troubles became the dominant interpretation in Western scholarship in the twentieth century and was extremely influential in the development of Soviet historiography once Marxist scholars settled some disagreements among themselves about the nature and periodization of early Russian history.[38]

Early Marxist scholarship on Russian history struggled with the theoretical issue of the role of peasant rebellions in the "feudal era." In general, Karl Marx and others regarded peasants as being incapable of developing revolutionary consciousness on their own—trapped as they were by "naïve monarchism."[39] Some Marxist scholars, therefore, came to view the Bolotnikov rebellion as a genuine social protest of the lower classes, but one that was incapable of achieving revolution because of the immature political consciousness (or "tsarist psychology") of the peasant masses.[40] A few orthodox Marxist scholars even went so far as to describe the Bolotnikov rebellion as "reactionary," which provoked a harsh response from Lenin.[41] Others noted that many of the rebels were gentry and townsmen and saw in the Time of Troubles a confusion of classes, interests, and goals.[42] A few Marxist scholars even went so far as to claim that Bolotnikov was not the leader of peasant revolutionaries but was instead a leader of gentry cavalrymen rebelling against the usurper aristocrat-tsar, Shuiskii.[43]

Seriously complicating Marxist analysis of early Russian history was Friedrich Engels's book (written in 1850) about the "Peasant War" in sixteenth-century Germany, which he described as a kind of bourgeois revolution marking the transition from feudalism to capitalism.[44] Naïve efforts to apply Engels's model to Russia's Time of Troubles were significantly reinforced by Lenin's statement that a prerequisite for "peasant wars" was a new period in Russian history in which capitalism began to develop—a period that he believed began approximately in the seventeenth century.[45] Under the influence of Engels and Lenin, Mikhail Pokrovskii (1868–1932) and several other early Soviet historians developed ideas about the Time of Troubles as some kind of bourgeois revolution (or "cossack revolution" or "peasant revolution") that ushered in a new period in Russian history. According to this romantic interpretation, the pretender Dmitrii was a revolutionary "cossack-tsar" who led the lower classes in a full-scale assault on the "feudal" lords. The famine-weary masses, convinced that Tsar Boris Godunov was a usurper, supposedly hungered for the appearance of Dmitrii as their savior, as a kind of "people's tsar." Rebel goals supposedly included the establishment of a primitive bourgeois democracy or "cossack democracy." In its most extreme form, this interpretation amounted to a crude modernization in which peasants and workers joined forces in demanding a socialist society.[46] Pokrovskii himself forcefully rejected the theories of Kliuchevskii and Platonov that the Time of Troubles started with an elite political struggle and only later pulled the masses into the conflict. He stated categorically that the Troubles started from below, not from above. Pokrovskii went on to reject even the concept of the "Time of Troubles" as a bourgeois label used to mask class war in the early seventeenth century. In like fashion, he and others also rejected the notion of Dmitrii as a Polish puppet, seeing that interpretation as just one more effort by bourgeois historians to mask the radicalism of the "cossack-tsar" Dmitrii and the Russian masses.[47] Many of Pokrovskii's ideas were quickly dismissed by other Soviet scholars, but his rejection of the label "Time of Troubles" became a standard feature of Soviet scholarship on the subject.

Gradually, the romantic view of "cossack revolution" and "peasant revolution," along with the idea of Dmitrii as a cossack-tsar or peasant-tsar, was abandoned. In the 1930s Dmitrii once again came to be viewed as a tool of Polish intervention and a cynical adventurer who manipulated naïve rebels for his own purposes. Nonetheless, his supporters were still seen as fighting not so much for Dmitrii as against the evil Boris Godunov and serfdom, but with misplaced faith in the "good tsar" Dmitrii that prevented them from bringing about revolutionary change.[48] As scholarly interest in Dmitrii's campaign for the throne declined, interest in the Bolotnikov rebellion increased, resulting in an artificial distinction in Soviet scholarship between the two phases of the civil war. While acknowledging that Dmitrii had drawn strong cossack support and had stirred the masses, it was increasingly asserted that the lower classes rebelled in force only later with Bolotnikov in a social, rather than political, struggle against serf owners.[49] Soviet scholars soon returned to a focus on the Bolotnikov rebellion as the defining event of the period—as a peasant war that, according to Lenin, marked the highest form of class struggle in the feudal era.[50] Not surprisingly, Stalin also took an interest in the subject. He personally admired the Bolotnikov rebellion, although he regarded it as doomed to failure because of the naïve monarchism of Russian peasants and the lack of proletarian support.[51] In part because of Stalin's admiration (as well as Lenin's positive comments about peasant wars and his strong interest in the seventeenth century), during the Stalin era it was decided that the Bolotnikov rebellion should not be dismissed as naïve or reactionary, but instead should be praised as a progressive, spontaneous rebellion of the oppressed masses that "shook" feudal society and delivered a severe blow to the serf system—speeding up the eventual transition from feudalism to capitalism.[52]

The first detailed study of the Bolotnikov rebellion was produced in the Stalin era by Ivan Smirnov, who declared that the rebellion was indeed Russia's first peasant war—the most significant peasant war in Russian history. According to Smirnov, the rebels (mostly peasants and slaves) fought to destroy serfdom and feudal oppression.[53] He basically denied any connection between the Bolotnikov rebellion and the pretender Dmitrii, whom he dismissed as a tool of foreign intervention; and he also deemphasized the role of the cossacks. Over the course of the 1950s, Aleksandr Zimin and others responded to Smirnov's work and put forward the idea that the Bolotnikov rebellion was only the culmination of the "First Peasant War." In their view, Khlopko's rebellion of hungry slaves during the famine in 1603, the Bolotnikov rebellion, and cossack unrest up to 1614 all belonged to one large peasant war. Although Smirnov never accepted that interpretation and repeatedly declared that the peasant war was limited to the Bolotnikov rebellion, the expanded definition came to be accepted by a majority of Soviet historians.[54] For the next two generations Marxist scholars argued endlessly about which exploited group—peasants, slaves, or urban plebes—played the most significant role in the First Peasant War; but all agreed that the conflict was essentially some form of lower class vengeance against the elite.[55]

During the 1960s and 1970s Vadim Koretskii made important archival discoveries related to the Bolotnikov rebellion and the timing of the arrival of serfdom in Russia. Koretskii placed the critical step in the development of serfdom—suspension of the St. George's Day privilege of peasant departure—in the 1590s. That decade also saw a sharp decline in the legal status of many townsmen and certain types of slaves. Thus, Koretskii and others felt confident in their assessment of the First Peasant War as the first massive popular rebellion against de facto serfdom.[56] Accepting the framework of the First Peasant War but keying on the participation of many towns in the various uprisings of the Time of Troubles, D. P. Makovskii in 1967 attempted to revive Pokrovskii's view of the period as an early bourgeois revolution or cossack revolution and Dmitrii as a peasant-tsar or cossack-tsar.[57] That view was, however, summarily dismissed by most Soviet historians, who continued to place the events of the period squarely in the feudal era, who still regarded Dmitrii as a tool of the Poles and a cynical manipulator of the masses, and who still viewed the Bolotnikov rebellion as a peasant war—even though they increasingly acknowledged the participation of gentry cavalrymen and other elite groups within rebel forces.[58] Underscoring the key role that cossacks had played in the First Peasant War, Vladislav Nazarov went so far as to boldly declare that the cossacks actively fomented, ideologically formulated, and to a considerable degree actually organized an "open class struggle."[59] Somewhat more sensitive to problems of evidence and the absence of a clearly defined social program in the Bolotnikov rebellion, a few Soviet historians argued that the naïve monarchism of the rebels interfered with their conscious (or unconscious) social goals and thus helped doom the uprisings.[60]

Eventually, an elaborate model of the First Peasant War developed and became standard fare in Soviet historical literature. According to the expanded official description, the first period of the peasant war lasted from 1603 to 1605. The central event of that period was the Khlopko rebellion of 1603. After the rebels were defeated, there was a temporary decline in the peasant war. The second stage of the first period was a mass rising of the lower classes that coincided with the pretender Dmitrii's campaign for the throne in 1604–5. The adventurer Dmitrii, a tool of the Poles, supposedly made many rash "antifeudal" promises in order to take advantage of the peasant uprising, which was not so much pro-Dmitrii as it was antifeudal. In the view of Kirill Chistov and others, a popular "social utopian" legend about Dmitrii's escape from assassination in 1591 and return as the deliverer of the masses from serfdom grew up before Dmitrii's campaign started and explains the mass support for his struggle against Boris Godunov. Once Dmitrii succeeded in becoming tsar, there was another temporary decline in the peasant war. The second period of the First Peasant War lasted from 1606 to 1607; that was the Bolotnikov rebellion. The third period stretched from 1608 to 1614, during which the class struggle merged with the national liberation movement against foreign intervention.[61] In the end, without admitting it, Soviet scholars writing about the First Peasant War managed to reconstruct a politically acceptable version of the Time of Troubles.[62]

During the 1980s some Soviet scholars began to rehabilitate the term "Time of Troubles" while still adhering to the model of the period as a social revolution or peasant war.[63] Others simply chose to ignore the rising tide of criticism of the traditional Marxist interpretation. After the breakup of the Soviet Union, however, it has no longer been possible to ignore the blows of revisionist scholarship that have shattered hundreds of years of misinterpretations.[64]

Even though recent revisionist scholarship has effectively destroyed the traditional interpretation of the Time of Troubles as a social revolution, that fact is still not well known for several reasons: revisionist scholars have until now only challenged aspects of the Marxist model in piecemeal fashion, and the results of our work have been scattered across many different publications. Until now there has been no systematic presentation of an alternative interpretation of the origins and nature of the Time of Troubles, rebel consciousness, or the impact of Russia's first civil war. Until now there has also been no published narrative of the period devoid of the traditional model or tendentious Marxist interpretations of sources. As a result, many readers still turn to outdated studies of the Time of Troubles (especially the works of S. F. Platonov), and most students of Russian history have not yet been exposed to the new scholarship about the subject. Even in Skrynnikov's English-language study, *The Time of Troubles: Russia in Crisis, 1604–1618*, published in 1988, in which he acknowledged that the events of the period were interrelated and worthy of a new, comprehensive approach, the author was still operating within the traditional interpretation and carefully avoided making any generalizations or offering any conclusions at variance with the peasant war model. That book is also extremely weak on background, causes, significance, impact, and the first few years of the Troubles.[65] After Skrynnikov broke with the peasant war model, he continued to call for a comprehensive study of Russia's first civil war;[66] however, he limited his research to extremely important but narrower topics and, in the process, did not always escape the insidious effects of the traditional interpretation.[67] In addition, Skrynnikov's hastily written biography of Tsar Dmitrii, although devoid of the peasant war interpretation, unfortunately perpetuated many old stereotypes about Dmitrii as a conscious impostor and tool of the Poles; it offered no real insights into why so many Russians supported Dmitrii before and after his assassination.[68] Aleksandr Stanislavskii, before his untimely death in 1990, focused primarily on cossacks in the later years of the Time of Troubles but never managed to free himself completely from the traditional Marxist interpretation of the early years of the Troubles.[69] Finally, Maureen Perrie's very useful book, *Pretenders and Popular Monarchism in Early Modern Russia: The False Tsars of the Time of Troubles* (1995), devastates aspects of Marxist scholarship on rebel consciousness. Unfortunately, Perrie was unable to free herself completely from the traditional interpretation of Dmitrii as a conscious impostor, adventurer, and possibly even a sorcerer; and that severely limited the value of her analysis of Tsar Dmitrii's reign and why so many Russians willingly endured unimaginable hardships in the civil war fought in his name.[70]

One of the main purposes of this book is to respond to the call made by Ruslan Skrynnikov and Paul Avrich to provide a new comprehensive study of Russia's Time of Troubles, its origins, nature, impact, and significance.[71] By moving beyond a narrow social interpretation of the topic it will be possible not only to gain a better understanding of the Troubles but also to gain insights into the structures and destabilizing forces at work in Russian history, the relationship of the state to society, the nature of Russian political culture, and the development of popular and elite consciousness.

Introductory chapters will explore the nature of the diverse forces that plunged Russia into crisis by the end of the sixteenth century and triggered civil war in the early seventeenth century. Because Russia's first civil war was the result of the conjuncture of many different causes and preconditions, in order to detect them it will be essential both to mine the rich and provocative literature of comparative history and to look deeply into the unique historical experience of early modern Russia. A comparative approach to the problem of origins will help demonstrate the destabilizing impact on early modern Russia of the "military revolution," the growth of the "fiscal-military state," population and price increases, international competition, and changes in climate. A detailed historical analysis of the background to the Time of Troubles will demonstrate some of the unique structures and destabilizing forces operating in early modern Russia and help us move beyond simplistic views of culture, popular consciousness, and the historical role of serfdom. Attention will also be focused on the background and conditions of all the various groups participating in the civil war. Because Russia's first civil war was, at least on some level, the first powerful popular response to exploitation associated with the rapid growth of the state and state power, it will also be necessary to explore the development of Russian autocracy and the breathtaking expansion of Russia's empire in the sixteenth century. Along the way, how that country's newly acquired southern frontier became increasingly alienated from the heartland and why it emerged as the center of the civil war will be demonstrated. To help explain what finally triggered the civil war it will again be necessary to make use of new research in comparative history and social science. In addition, new research on the poorly understood pretender Dmitrii and his crucial role as the trigger and the driving force in the civil war will be presented, and new ideas about rebel consciousness and the meaning of popular support for Dmitrii will be explored.

The main text provides a detailed narrative and analysis of the participants and events of the civil war. These chapters reveal the nature of that conflict, explore the diversity of social forces involved and what united them, and attempt to overcome a host of problems related to contradictory sources, confused chronology, and hundreds of years of flawed interpretations of the subject. Details about military strategy, tactics, weapons, and battles are also included without apology. Besides being inherently interesting and difficult to extract from tendentious sources and flawed traditional studies of the period, such material helps demonstrate a basic fact about the civil war: the sharp contrast between the poor condition and morale of the tsar's military forces and the incredible energy, tenacity, and skill of the first Russians who dared to rebel against their tsar. Finally, the concluding chapter will explore the complex and poorly understood legacy of Russia's first civil war, once again making use of new research in social science and comparative history.

1

Russia's first civil war (1604–5, 1606–12) was extraordinarily complex and presents scholars seeking to explore its nature and causes with some serious challenges. Fortunately, it turns out to be extremely useful simply to focus on those ways in which Russia's experience was similar to other early modern state crises, rebellions, and civil wars.[1] A comparative approach to the problem of origins of those traumatic events can shed considerable light on the material forces that destabilized many early modern agrarian-based monarchies and helped push them into crisis.[2] In fact, comparative historians have produced some important generalizations that apply directly to the Russian case.

Russia's first civil war was in many ways similar to other civil wars of the early modern period. Of all the forms of early modern collective violence, civil wars were notable for plunging states into the lengthiest and most severe conflicts, for splitting the traditional political order most deeply, and for producing rebel forces capable of defying or defeating temporarily even the most powerful monarchies. Social participation in them was very broad, involving to some extent all social strata and at least enough elite participation to signify serious defection from the regime. Political and geographic space occupied by the rebels resulted in conflict in many parts of the state, not in just one region. Goals and targets of the insurrectionists often revealed a massive societal reaction to the growth of state power and the burdens it imposed on its subject. There was usually a high degree of organization among rebel forces, with leadership and mobilization being national in scale. Early modern civil wars generally produced broad movements creating well-developed ideologies and political and military organizations to facilitate resistance. They were long-lasting primarily because of the participation of a significant percentage of the elite, who provided essential political and social leadership capable of legitimizing revolt and drawing the masses into rebellion against royal authority.[3] In fact, the strength of early modern civil wars was significantly enhanced by the *absence* of radical demands for alteration of the social structure or for significant redistribution of power and wealth.[4] Early modern civil wars often included strong

elements of both agrarian and urban rebellion, which were usually characterized by cooperation among social groups against an unpopular regime rather
than by class antagonism and were provoked by conjunctures of circumstances
rather than simply by social inequality.[5] Early modern civil wars also often
included, grew out of, and were profoundly affected by provincial rebellions—
uprisings in newly acquired territories not yet fully integrated into the state
structure. Provincial rebellions themselves were usually characterized by broad
social participation, including local elites in leadership roles, and by fierce resistance to the growth and intrusion of state power in the region that violated traditional liberties and customary lifestyles.[6]

Equally complex were the causes of early modern civil wars. Comparative
study of those popular upheavals quickly yields the insight that no monocausal
explanation is satisfactory and that it may be impossible to develop a general
causal theory for such complex phenomena in which so many major and minor
variables are at work.[7] Instead, a multicausal explanation is called for. Several
different factors operated simultaneously and sometimes synergistically to
increase the likelihood of revolt or revolution, and the tabulation of a number
of these factors may be the only way to explain complex early modern upheavals.[8]

It turns out that many of the tasks and dilemmas facing post-Marxist historians of the Time of Troubles are, not surprisingly, the same as those facing revisionist scholars studying early modern Western revolutions. There is currently
a certain degree of disarray in the historiography of the French and English
Revolutions produced by the decline of traditional interpretations that focused
on long-term social, economic, and structural processes and that emphasized
the primacy of "absolutism," capitalism, and class conflict as explanatory factors. Revisionist scholars studying those early modern revolutions now emphasize such things as short-term causes, historical contingencies, ideas, belief
systems, and other unique social, cultural, and institutional characteristics of
each country.[9] Similar approaches can help us understand some of the causes
of Russia's first civil war. For example, historians have long focused on the dynastic crisis produced by the death of Tsar Fedor in 1598 as a principal cause of
the Time of Troubles. That crisis sharpened the split within the ruling elite and
contributed to the pretender Dmitrii's success in 1605.[10] The terrible famine
of 1601–3 was also a contributing factor to the civil war, sharpening Russia's
already developing social crisis and contributing to the delegitimization of Tasr
Boris Godunov.[11] The existence and activities of the pretender Dmitrii were
obviously of great significance, as was his assassination in 1606.[12] Russian
Orthodox culture itself provided rebels with motivation and a powerful tool to
use in the struggle against the usurper Tsar Vasilii Shuiskii.[13]

What about long-term causes or preconditions? Perhaps trying to avoid the pitfalls of developing comprehensive interpretive theories to replace the Marxist paradigm, some revisionist scholars of early modern Western revolutions have gone so far as to argue against searching for any long-term causes.[14] That strikes me as too extreme, as an unfortunate and unsatisfactory leap from sociological determinism to what might be called the "contingent and unforeseen" school of history. As will be demonstrated in later chapters, there is certainly much to be gained by a focus on short-term causes or immediate triggers, but exploring long-term causes or preconditions can also be valid and useful.[15] According to Michael Kimmel, neither long-term preconditions nor short-term triggers on their own are sufficient for adequate analysis; both are needed.[16] Focus on long-term causes can help place short-term causes in perspective and demonstrate the significance of long-term social, economic, and structural changes in a non-Marxist framework. With no claim to theoretical significance, Perez Zagorin has suggested the essentially practical idea of distinguishing long-range causes or preconditions of state crises from their immediate precipitants, which are likely to be unique and not susceptible to generalized causal formulation.[17] For something as complex as Russia's first civil war, that approach seems wise and this book will follow it.

Although there is no longer a consensus that the Time of Troubles was caused primarily by serfdom, there is still general agreement that a principal contributing factor was the catastrophic decline of the Russian economy by the 1570s, which led to massive flight of peasants and urban taxpayers, many of whom sold themselves as slaves, became bandits, or ran away to the southern frontier. The result was a huge loss of state revenue and a steep decline in the gentry's peasant labor force. Eventually, the Russian government (dominated by Boris Godunov) was forced to take drastic steps to shore up the declining militia and to rebuild the tax base.[18] In the 1590s the peasants were enserfed, townspeople were bound to their taxpaying communities, and short-term contract slavery changed to real slavery. All these harsh measures failed to solve the problems of the government and the gentry, but they did help turn Russia into a rigidly stratified, caste-like society and contributed to the outbreak of civil war.[19] Serfdom, for example, increased the status of the gentry cavalry force, which emerged as something like a warrior caste.[20] Unfortunately, serfdom also ossified the economy.[21] A number of scholars believed that Boris Godunov was able to straighten out state finances and that Russia underwent a period of "recovery" in the 1590s.[22] In fact, Russia did not emerge from the crisis that actually deepened in the 1590s, leading to even more empty villages and vacant land in much of central Russia. Although some peripheral areas showed signs of increased activity, continued depopulation and decline of the agricultural economy kept Russia in crisis at the end of the sixteenth century.[23] Some so-called signs of recovery, such as a decline in grain prices, were actually because of a decline in demand and a reversion to a natural economy. That in turn proved disastrous for many already depopulated and hard-pressed towns that lost rural markets at the same time that urban taxes were rising and the tax-paying population was shrinking. Hit by so many forces, trade in almost all Russian towns withered, which pushed even more townspeople to flee from the plummeting economy and rising taxes. Many Russian towns became ghost towns in the 1590s.[24] At the same time, a sharp increase in labor demands on some serfs, the growth of land-based taxes, and the lack of innovation in agriculture acted as a brake on any possible recovery of the agricultural economy. Many more peasants fled from the tax rolls, and huge amounts of land continued to fall out of production, devastating an already failing agricultural economy.[25] Among other things, that meant the government faced an increasingly critical shortage of land with peasants to distribute to already hard-pressed, land-hungry gentry and their sons. That in turn deepened a developing crisis of the gentry militia service system that Ruslan Skrynnikov has identified as one of the main preconditions of Russia's first civil war.[26] The continuing economic crisis also sharply reduced state income, and the fiscal crisis lasted right into the Time of Troubles.[27]

What caused the catastrophic decline of the Russian economy in the late sixteenth century that provoked such a severe crisis? It was due to many factors, some unique to Russia. For example, the constant threat of Tatar attacks and slave raids contributed to the militarization of Russian society and an increase in social stratification by the end of the sixteenth century.[28] Unique characteristics of Russian autocracy and Russian Orthodox culture produced a service state that greatly imposed on its subjects and that exacerbated most of the problems common to early modern agrarian absolute monarchies.[29] Russian autocracy certainly facilitated the culturally driven imperialism of Ivan IV, Boris Godunov, and others.[30] That in turn produced the staggering expansion of Russia, which tripled in size during the sixteenth century.[31] Such expansion far outstripped the country's resources and greatly overburdened its people and economy along the way. It is also well known that Ivan IV's costly and disastrous Livonian War (1558–83) contributed to the catastrophic decline of the economy and the destabilization of Russian society.[32] Tsar Ivan's dreaded *oprich-nina* (a state within the state, under the tsar's personal control) and the devastation associated with it also contributed to the crisis.[33] On the other hand, too much focus on Ivan IV's personality and policies can lead to a gross underestimation of the impact on Russia of forces not unique to that society such as weather-related crop failures, famines, and terrible epidemics.[34] It is worth noting, for example, that remarkably similar problems developed at the same time in neighboring Lithuania.[35] Even though a case can be made for blaming Tsar Ivan for actions that helped precipitate serfdom and a severe state crisis, it is important to remember that the development of serfdom throughout Eastern Europe was due at least in part to the same destabilizing factors that were operating inside Russia: population increases, price inflation, famines and epidemics, and primitive agricultural technology and low grain yields in an era of increasingly unreliable weather.[36] As it turns out, a number of important causes or preconditions contributing to Russia's severe crisis may be detected by comparative study of early modern Eurasian societies.

Historians have long been puzzled by the waves of revolutions, rebellions, and civil wars observable across Eurasia in the early modern period. Comparative study of those crises reveals common patterns that cannot be explained away simply as coincidences.[37] The existence of those common patterns led in the 1950s to the development of the very popular theory of a "general crisis" of the seventeenth century.[38] Unfortunately, proponents of the general crisis theory have been better at identifying the existence of crises than at explaining them. In fact, a significant amount of their work was based upon Marxist assumptions, and there is still no consensus about the nature of the general crisis, its chronology, or its causes.[39] Nonetheless, scholarship on this topic has produced some interesting ideas about the basic and deep-seated destabilizing influences that were at work on all Eurasian societies in the early modern period. Among those influences were a doubling of the overall population of Eurasia during the sixteenth century and a correspondingly severe period of price inflation—often called a "price revolution."[40] Some crisis theory proponents focused on the significance of a sharp increase in wars and the growth of armies and war-related taxation in a era of price inflation.[41] Others focused on the growth of state power and the unprecedented increase in fiscal demands placed on populations, demands that could and sometimes did precipitate revolts.[42] Still other crisis theory proponents have focused on the general cooling of the global climate in the early modern period (the "little ice age"), relating it to a widespread subsistence crisis marked by famines, mass migrations, and peasant revolts.[43]

Russia has rarely been included in general crisis studies even though it was subject to similar pressures in the same period.[44] In Roland Mousnier's comparative study of early modern Eurasian revolts, he focused on Russia's Time of Troubles using an essentially Marxist framework and the traditional social revolutionary interpretation of the period. Nonetheless, he offered useful com-

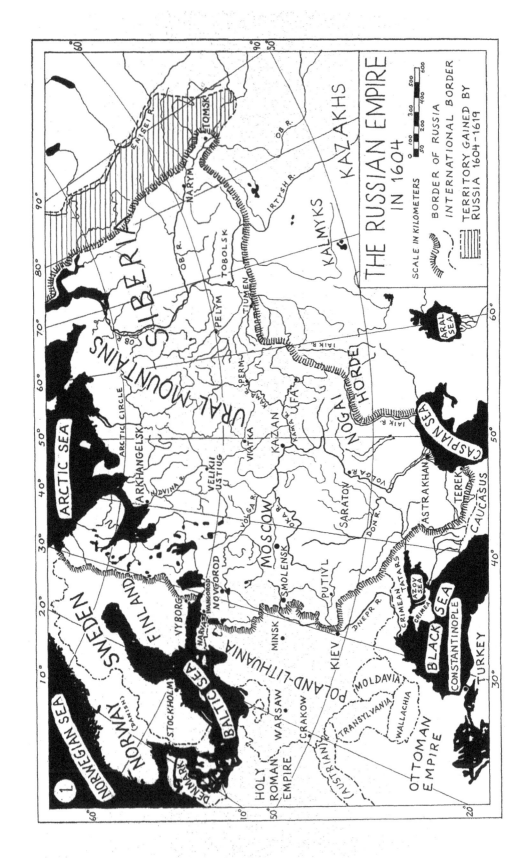

THE RUSSIAN EMPIRE
IN 1604

SCALE IN KILOMETERS

0 100 300 500
50 200 400 600

BORDER OF RUSSIA
INTERNATIONAL BORDER
TERRITORY GAINED BY
RUSSIA 1604–1619

NORWEGIAN SEA

NORWAY

DENMARK

(DANISH)

SWEDEN

STOCKHOLM

BALTIC SEA

FINLAND

VYBORG

NARVA
IVANGOROD
NOVGOROD

ARCTIC SEA

ARKHANGELSK

DVINA R.

ARCTIC CIRCLE

VELIKII
USTIUG

SIBERIA

URAL MOUNTAINS

ENISEI R.

TOMSK

NARYM

OB R.

IRTYSH R.

TOBOLSK

PELYM

TIUMEN

PERM

KAMA R.

VIATKA

KAZAN

KAMA R. UFA

VOLGA R.

IAIK R.

KAZAKHS

KALMYKS

NOGAI HORDE

ARAL SEA

IAIK R.

CASPIAN SEA

ASTRAKHAN

TEREK R.

CAUCASUS

MOSCOW

SMOLENSK

MINSK

WARSAW

CRAKOW

POLAND-LITHUANIA

KIEV

DNEPR R.

PUTIVL

SARATOV

DON R.

VOLGA R.

CRIMEAN TATARS

CRIMEA

AZOV SEA

BLACK SEA

CONSTANTINOPLE

TURKEY

OTTOMAN EMPIRE

MOLDAVIA

WALLACHIA

TRANSYLVANIA

(AUSTRIAN)

HOLY
ROMAN
EMPIRE

1

ments. In Mousnier's view, revolts in the Time of Troubles were directly related to the growth of state power and military expenses beyond the resources of Russian society. The development of state power was the "basic reason" for the revolts, which were reactions to the drive for centralization and uniformity.[45] A later study by Peter B. Brown also emphasized the likelihood of crisis growing out of the Russian ruling elite's military ambition and the consequent growth of state power, taxes, and a royal bureaucracy.[46] That is a good beginning, but we need to take a closer look at the issues raised by crisis theory proponents and other recent scholarship in comparative history in order to gain a better understanding of the origins of the Time of Troubles.

Michael Roberts developed the idea of a "military revolution" of the early modern period—a revolution in military technology, tactics and strategy, the size of armies, and the cost of war—that resulted in greatly increased burdens on governments and taxpayers. Subsequent scholarship on this topic has focused on its profound, even "revolutionary" impact on governments and societies.[47] War was the single greatest expense of the early modern state and forced rulers and bureaucrats to seek revenues with zeal. That affected the economy and eventually almost everyone in society; it helped increase the power of central state authority and could, on occasion, trigger crises or rebellions.[48] Acknowledging the importance of the military revolution but dubious of how its impact has been incorporated into studies of the vague concept of "absolutism," John Brewer and Nicholas Henshall have identified the growth of a "fiscal-military state" geared to war and survival. Development of such a state meant imposition and collection of more taxes, government interference in the economy in an effort to increase revenues, and the creation and development of bureaucracies independent of existing elites. The result was the same whether ruling groups wished to expand their state or were forced to build up their military forces because of international competition and the aggression of neighboring states. In either case, excessive military spending could trigger a fiscal crisis.[49] Brian Downing developed similar ideas about military modernization and the mobilization of domestic resources leading to the emergence of what he referred to as "military-bureaucratic absolutism," a highly bureaucratized and militarized central state that in effect subjugated even the elites and pushed royal power far beyond its customary limitations. A more centralized and coercive state emerged to extract resources from an unwilling population.[50]

A good case can be made that the unified Russian state that emerged in the early sixteenth century was a somewhat primitive but highly effective version of the fiscal-military state geared to war and survival.[51] It is well known that early modern Russia was a service state in which the performance of duties that directly or indirectly bolstered the country's security were required from virtually everyone. Nowhere else in Europe was the principle of service to the state pressed so far as in Russia.[52] In addition, the tsar's bureaucrats were free to extract domestic revenues with no concern about or understanding of the impact of their actions on the economy. Among other things, they imposed taxes with zeal, which the lords then ruthlessly collected. For many Russians taxes rose six hundred percent (adjusted for inflation) over the course of the sixteenth century, almost all due to increases in military-related expenses. In assessing the overall impact of the development of Russian state power in the era of the military revolution, Richard Hellie concluded that it led to increasing social stratification and the emergence of a near-caste society. The process of stratification was already developing before the Time of Troubles and helped push Russia into crisis.[53]

The growth of the fiscal-military state in an era of price inflation might have been sufficient to provoke a state crisis, but it came in conjunction with a widespread subsistence crisis caused primarily by a change in the global climate. The "little ice age," a term for the cooling trend from approximately 1550 to about 1740, has been associated with crop failures, food shortages, astronomical food prices, increasing poverty, famines, pandemics, mass migration, and even peasant revolts—all of which were commonplace during that period.[54] The causal connection between cold, wet weather and crop failures is not in doubt. It is also known that the danger of famine associated with bad weather is especially intense after periods of long, sustained population growth (such as the sixteenth century) have reduced per capita agricultural output to subsistence levels even in good years.[55] Although historians of the French *Annales* school have long been fascinated by the impact of climate on history, they have been reluctant to explore the climate's connection to "surface" events such as famines. For example, Fernand Braudel and others noticed the conjuncture of bad weather and food shortages at the end of the sixteenth century but were reluctant to draw conclusions about it.[56] That has drawn criticism from scholars interested in the link between patterns of the *longue durée* and "short-term events" of great trauma and impact.[57] In fact, although the actual connection between famines and popular unrest is difficult to prove, it is highly probable.[58] By studying that connection, a number of scholars have keyed on the "little ice age" to refine their ideas about a seventeenth-century (or late sixteenth to mid-seventeenth century) "general crisis" to a more sharply focused theory of a "crisis of the 1590s."[59] The second half of the sixteenth century was a time of rising population, prices, taxes, state budgets, and bad weather as well as increasing crop failures, poverty, famines, plagues, mortality levels, war, banditry, mass migrations, and popular uprisings throughout much of Europe. All of these problems were strongly present in the catastrophic 1590s, which saw the conjuncture of the most severe weather, the worst food crises, and the largest number of rebellions of the entire early modern period.[60] Glacial advances and dense volcanic dust veils also peaked at the very end of that decade.[61] Northern Europe suffered the brunt of the crisis of the 1590s, with weather-related crop failures, epidemics, and widespread starvation occurring in England (1594–98), Scotland (1595–98), France (1597), Ireland (1601), Norway (1596–98), Sweden (1596–1603), Prussia (1602), Livonia (1601–3), Poland-Lithuania (1602–3), and Russia on the eve of its civil war (1601–3).[62] Under such conditions it is no surprise that the 1590s saw so many uprisings. Those rebellions peaked in the late 1590s, which were years of revolt in Austria, Hungary, Ukraine, and Finland, followed soon thereafter by the most important popular upheaval of the period, Russia's first civil war (1604–5, 1606–12).[63]

The growth of the fiscal-military state and the "little ice age" both played important roles in destabilizing early modern agrarian absolute monarchies. Other factors were also important. Recently Jack A. Goldstone developed a "demographic/structural" model that attempts to account for the waves of state crises that swept across Eurasia in the early modern period. Goldstone views the crises of large agrarian absolute monarchies mainly as the result of a single basic process: prolonged population growth in the context of relatively inflexible economic and social structures, eventually resulting in rapid price inflation, sudden shifts in resources, and rising social demands on a scale most agrarian-based bureaucratic states found overwhelming. Simply put, long-term population increases helped push fragile political, economic, and social institutions into crisis.[64] Other scholars before Goldstone have focused on demography, of course. In particular, historians of the *Annales* school have long been interested in how population shifts affect long-term social and economic change. Proponents of the *Annales* school, however, have generally avoided relating demographic patterns of the *longue durée* to "surface" events such as rebellions and civil wars. Goldstone is one of the first scholars to make use of the insights of the "new" social history in scholarship focusing on great political events such as a state crises and revolutions. A key insight Goldstone brings from demography is that the approximate doubling of the population of the temperate regions of Eurasia over the course of the sixteenth century had some surprising results. For example, younger sons of elite families (who lacked positions to inherit and who therefore sought new positions at court, in the military, or in the bureaucracy) increased much more rapidly than the increase in the overall population. That had a destabilizing effect, increasing intra-elite competition and conflict. Just as elite competition for scarce resources and suitable positions became sharpest, the state had less ability to respond to demands placed on its services because of the other result of long-term population increase—a rise in prices that, in those societies unable to cope with inflation through increased production or other economic activity, eventually precipitated a fiscal crisis.[65] Many states were unable to overcome the traditional rigidity of their tax system and were simply overwhelmed by the combined impact of inflation, increased demands on state services, and the extraordinary increase in the cost of war and defense. They were thus unable to alleviate the growing misery of many members of a rapidly growing elite. Attempts by governments to raise taxes often further alienated subgroups of the elite yet failed to resolve fiscal crises. For many, especially marginal elites, income erosion, competition with newcomers, and displacement from positions of prestige caused great frustration and intensified intra-elite competition. Competing factions fragmented the elite and led to increasing criticism of the existing regime.[66]

Simultaneously, the impact of rising population and prices on ordinary people was also destabilizing; the combination of increases in taxes, food costs, rents, poverty, fragmentation of landholdings, and the undermining of popular traditional rights led to rising grievances, popular agitation, and urban and rural unrest. As with elites, the impact of population growth on marginal groups such as landless peasants and the young was far out of proportion to the overall population increase, resulting in a huge increase in unhappy plebeians susceptible to anger against the injustice of the regime. Associated with that was a rise in banditry and a large-scale movement of rootless young men and entire families to the periphery or frontier, which in turn made that area more unstable. There was also a rise in folk criticism of the regime and a loosening of bonds of allegiance. All of these things together undermined the stability of society on multiple levels.[67] Goldstone sees the likelihood of revolution or civil war growing out of the combination of financial crises, elite struggle for position and survival, and misery of the masses when they were combined with a "high potential for mobilizing popular groups." According to Goldstone, although sudden events may trigger a revolution or civil war, they are not its true causes. Instead, the key is a shift in elite and popular attitudes toward the state, which is directly related to the impact of long-term population and price increases.[68]

Even though one may quibble with various aspects of Goldstone's model, his basic observations appear to be directly applicable to Russia even though he did not focus on it.[69] Indeed, Jerome Blum and Richard Hellie have already identified population and price increases as significant factors in precipitating Russia's late sixteenth-century economic crisis and increasing social stratification.[70] In light of those observations, let us take a closer look at how well Goldstone's model fits the Russian case. While there is no agreement among historians about the size of Russia's population, there is general agreement that it grew, and possibly doubled, during the sixteenth century.[71] The population increased during the first half of the century at a rate of approximately one percent per year.[72] It increased at a slower rate during the second half of the century.[73] Some contemporaries noted a population decline in central Russia in the late sixteenth century; however, Hellie has pointed out that migration to the frontier may have contributed to a sense of population decline in central Russia, and R. E. F. Smith has raised serious doubts about the extent of the depopulation of the heartland.[74] In any case, the population of Russia may have risen from approximately 5.8 million to more than 10 million over the course of the sixteenth century.[75] Prices in Russia are also subject to debate, but they did rise during the sixteenth century and shot up dramatically during the famine of 1601–3.[76] N. Rozhkov stated that the inflationary trend started in the 1530s and became much stronger in the second half of the sixteenth century.[77] A. G. Mankov also detected sharp inflation in the second half of the century and calculated an overall price increase during the sixteenth century of three hundred to four hundred percent for grain and two hundred percent for meat and livestock. He regarded Russia's inflation as analogous to the "price revolution" of Europe.[78] Paul Bushkovitch also detected a sharp rise in Russian prices in the second half of the sixteenth century and related it to Europe's price revolution.[79] Other scholars, however, have firmly rejected the idea of a significant connection between Russia's price inflation and Europe's, correctly emphasizing the relative isolation of the Russian market from the West.[80] Significantly, they related Russia's price inflation instead directly to Russia's population increase during the sixteenth century.[81] On balance, therefore, population and price trends in Russia make Goldstone's model appear to be directly applicable.

Goldstone argued that the rapid multiplication of younger sons of the elite would put increasing pressure on their government to find them land and good jobs just as the government faced a fiscal crisis because of the effects of price inflation and the astronomical costs of war. That was certainly true for Russia, both for the aristocracy and for the gentry cavalry force. The rapid growth of Russian aristocratic families in the sixteenth century led to the constant subdivision of estates among inheritors. As those holdings became smaller and smaller, they could no longer support the growing elite population, forcing many young lords to look for additional land and income.[82] An increasing number of aristocrats found themselves competing with each other at court and in the military for a share of the limited rewards available. The inevitable result was constant intra-elite intrigue and conflict and a growing sense of insecurity among many Russian aristocrats.[83] That insecurity was significantly increased during Tsar Ivan IV's struggle against real or perceived enemies among the boyars and princes.[84] Toward the end of the sixteenth century, intra-elite competition in the form of court rivalries and the ambition of Boris Godunov sharpened, and it greatly intensified with the death of Tsar Fedor in 1598, the traditional date for the start of the Time of Troubles.[85] In this period there were also many loud complaints about newcomers gaining influence and rewards while old aristocratic families were being shoved aside.[86] Growing aristocratic frustration with the new Tsar Boris definitely helped precipitate Russia's first civil war.[87]

As for the Russian gentry, the sixteenth century also saw their numbers grow rapidly. Large families with several sons became the norm, and the government was able to provide only modest holdings for the new cavalrymen. As the ranks of the gentry militia swelled, the fund of available land and peasant labor for the tsar's cavalry force declined, leading to smaller and smaller land grants (with fewer peasants) and a general impoverishment of the lowest ranks of the militia. As the century progressed, the average size of service land grants shrank significantly, and it gradually became harder and harder for gentry sons to find any land and labor to support themselves.[88] Competition for scarce resources became increasingly sharp in the second half of the sixteenth century, when many cavalrymen could not even afford to show up for military service.[89] The catastrophic decline of the Russian economy and massive peasant flight starting in the 1570s made matters much worse for the gentry. Many cavalrymen were ruined as a result. Those unhappy souls were forced to serve as low-status infantry or, in extreme cases, to sell themselves into slavery or to join the cossacks on the southern periphery of the state.[90] Faced with such prospects, many cavalrymen resorted to desperate measures. Hellie speaks of "a jungle-like atmosphere in which each serviceman was always at war with every other one in a struggle for survival."[91] In this period the beleaguered and frustrated gentry not only fought with each other but repeatedly attempted to close their ranks to newcomers.[92] They also came to look down on their unfortunate fellow cavalrymen who were stuck in lower-status southern frontier service where conditions were much worse, morale was low, and a smoldering resentment against more successful members of the gentry was growing.[93] The anxiety and frustration of these declining marginal elites continued to grow right into the Time of Troubles. The economic decline of the cavalrymen, combined with the state's fiscal problems, definitely precipitated the dangerous gentry militia crisis mentioned above, which in turn played a major role in destabilizing society and preparing Russia for civil war.[94]

By the late sixteenth century Russia certainly faced a severe fiscal crisis that severely limited the government's ability to respond to the demands of increasingly desperate elite groups. The drastic decline in peasant and urban taxpayers in the 1570s caused tax revenues to shrink, and the treasury suffered huge losses.[95] Sharp price inflation made matters worse.[96] As noted earlier, the erosion of the tax base and the chronic shortage of land with peasant labor eventually led the government to the drastic steps of enserfing the peasants and binding the townsmen.[97] Just as Goldstone predicted, however, such measures not only failed to solve the problems faced by the government and the gentry but actually made them worse. Certain subgroups of the elite were alienated by the government's harsh policies that favored others and hurt them.[98] Those policies themselves also slowed down any possible economic recovery.[99] The fiscal crisis continued to deepen right into the Time of Troubles. It was made significantly worse by the famine of 1601–3, because of the double blow of declining revenues and costly government efforts to alleviate the misery of the Russian people.[100] Attempts to shore up the gentry financially in 1605–6 so utterly depleted the treasury that it was essentially empty when civil war broke out against the usurper Vasilii Shuiskii.[101]

According to Goldstone, the general impact of population increases and rising prices on the overall population was also destabilizing. The factors he cites were certainly at work on Russian peasants and townspeople in the second half of the sixteenth century: huge tax increases,[102] sharp increases in the price of food,[103] and increases in rent and labor obligations along with the undermining of traditional rights.[104] Starting in the 1570s, such things contributed to the poverty and ruin of many peasants and townsmen and to massive flight from gentry estates and urban tax rolls.[105] Just as Goldstone's model predicts, such pressures on the lower classes also contributed to a sharp rise in banditry in Russia by the late sixteenth century.[106] Government efforts in the 1580s to recoup lost revenue by increasing taxes on the remaining peasants and townsmen aggravated the situation, leading to deeper poverty and further abandonment of the land and towns.[107] Boris Godunov's harsh solution—enserfing the peasants and binding the townsmen—greatly increased the burdens on an unstable and resentful population.[108] As a result, there were sporadic outbreaks of popular unrest in the following years.[109] Even though the Time of Troubles did not produce an open struggle of peasants against serfdom, the social and economic breakdown caused by the enserfment of millions of Russians was an important precondition of the civil war.[110]

Goldstone argued that sustained population and price increases produced a "high potential for mobilizing popular groups" and movement to the periphery of the country by large numbers of rootless young men. That certainly applies to Russia. The social and economic crisis of the late sixteenth century led to large-scale migration to the frontier by impoverished gentry, peasants, slaves, and townsmen. It also led to the rise of the cossacks. Serfdom, binding townspeople to the tax rolls, and changes in slave law led to further depopulation of the center of the state and to the rise of large and disaffected groups on the southern frontier.[111] In the midst of the growing economic and demographic crisis (and in part to recapture the lost labor supply), the Russian government attempted an overly ambitious program of extending the state south. New towns were built and an attempt was made to transfer the already overstrained service landholding system to the southern frontier. Almost anyone was accepted into southern military service, even cossacks and peasants. Life was hard for these new "lords" who were forced to plow the land for themselves. Collectively this group was poor and differed sharply from the gentry of central Russia. They were a dissatisfied lot and became important participants in the civil war.[112] Many other Russians avoided onerous southern military service and fled farther south to join the cossacks, a communistic brotherhood of social bandits and mercenary soldiers whose numbers and power grew rapidly toward the end of the sixteenth century as a direct result of Russia's social and economic crisis. Cossack freedom acted as a magnet not only for runaway peasants and slaves but also for impoverished gentry. Although the cossacks did not regard themselves as peasants or peasant leaders, and the destruction of serfdom was never proclaimed as a cossack goal, Boris Godunov understood that serfdom could not triumph in Russia while the cossack frontier remained free. He therefore tried to subordinate the cossack lands and encountered stiff resistance. Cossacks helped destabilize the frontier and became extremely important participants in the civil war.[113]

Russia's sharp population decline caused by the terrible famine of 1601–3, far from ameliorating the situation, deepened the fiscal crisis and increased the already sharp competition for peasant labor.[114] It also added many more impoverished Russians to an already seething frontier population that now included well-organized and armed groups of cossacks, gentry, and lower status military servicemen.[115] All that was needed to trigger a civil war, according to Goldstone, was a shift in elite and popular attitudes toward the state. Boris Godunov's ruthless climb to power, his enserfing policies, his tax policies, his treatment of southern military servitors, and his struggle to harness the cossacks all combined to undermine his legitimacy in the eyes of many Russians even before he managed to become tsar in 1598. In addition, many commoners were deeply suspicious of boyars in general and for that reason did not warm to the idea of a mere aristocrat becoming tsar.[116] Once on the throne, Tsar Boris's purge of political enemies alienated many members of the aristocracy.[117] The tsar's decision during the great famine to sacrifice the interests of weaker elements of the gentry in order to protect stronger ones from economic ruin alienated a sizable portion of the gentry militia.[118] The famine itself also contributed to the delegitimization of the tsar. Many Russians came to see it as God's punishment of Russia for the sins of Boris Godunov and for that reason turned against him. The sudden appearance of the pretender Dmitrii provided a convenient way to channel elite and popular anger against Tsar Boris and the state.[119]

Upon close inspection, it appears that Goldstone's model does indeed apply to early modern Russia. Combined with other insights from comparative history such as the growth of the fiscal-military state in an era of price inflation and the impact of the "little ice age," Goldstone's work helps explain why on so many levels things began cascading into crisis in Russia at the end of the sixteenth century. In fact, the severe fiscal crisis facing the central government on the eve of the Time of Troubles can properly be viewed as a powerful sign of the conjuncture of several long-term destabilizing forces.[120] In order to better understand those forces and to detect additional ones contributing to Russia's serious problems by the end of the sixteenth century, the next several chapters will explore that country's unique historical experience leading up to the civil war within the context provided by comparative history. Along the way, these chapters will also provide ample evidence of the significant role played by historical contingency in early modern Russia.[121]

2

Long-Term Origins: The Growth of Autocracy and Imperialism

In the age of the military revolution the princes of Moscow unified Russia, quickly transformed their country into a highly effective fiscal-military state geared to war and survival, and expanded their realm with dizzying speed. In the process, however, they ended up subjugating virtually all elements of Russian society and grossly overburdened the bulk of the population.[1] That contributed to a downturn in the economy, the emergence of a highly stratified society, and the development of a serious state crisis by the beginning of the seventeenth century. It is possible, therefore, at least on some level, to regard Russia's first civil war as the first powerful (if unconscious) popular reaction against the growth of the burdensome state and the policies of its expansionist rulers.[2] For that reason it will be useful to examine briefly the unique combination of forces contributing to Russia's unification and the swift emergence of autocracy, a coercive central state bureaucracy, and powerful military forces capable of satisfying the tsars' imperial ambitions.

Unified by Moscow's Grand Prince Ivan III (r. 1462–1505) and his son Vasilii III (r. 1505–33), Russia quickly emerged as a major military power, and its dramatic growth startled Europe and Asia. Over the course of the sixteenth century Russia's expansion created an empire as well as Europe's largest state. That development puzzled and frightened many contemporaries. Although early modern Russia was in reality structurally similar to other fiscal-military states then emerging, it did not appear to resemble the obviously more "modern" consolidating monarchies.[3] Instead, even though Russia was a new and vigorous country with a rapidly developing national culture, it retained so many antique characteristics that it more closely resembled Western societies in the Middle Ages than those of the early modern period.[4] As a result, many Westerners felt superior to the "barbarous" Russians, but there was no denying that "backward" Russia had arrived on the scene with a remarkable ability to extract domestic resources and to wage war successfully against its neighbors—powers still well beyond the capabilities of some of its more "modern" counterparts in the West.[5] How was that possible? At least a partial explanation may be found by examining the origins and nature of early modern Russia's unique political culture and the remarkable system it produced.

Students of Russian and Soviet history have long studied and debated the development of Russian "autocracy" (political authority resting on a claim of divine right and unencumbered by significant traditional or constitutional limits). Russian autocracy spawned a huge empire that for several centuries inhibited its subjects' social, economic, political, and cultural evolution by requiring onerous service from them, by tolerating no dissent from any groups or institutions, and by systematically draining the economy and society of resources in order to support the imperial ambitions of the ruling elite. That peculiar system did manage to produce the world's largest country but also, from time to time, provoked powerful uprisings against its oppression. In trying to make sense out of Russia's curious historical development, some writers have appropriately applied the terminology of Max Weber to prerevolutionary Russia, seeing it essentially as a "patrimonial regime" in which the political structure from the very beginning was more or less identical with the landed estate of the prince of Moscow, who regarded the entire country and all its people as part of his patrimony (and therefore completely at his disposal). Instead of rights, the prince's subjects had only duties to perform. As a result, Russian society was structured and developed in service to the autocratic state and failed to develop or liberalize along the lines of Western societies.[6] The origins of Russian autocracy are complex and controversial, but they certainly date back at least to the unification of Russia and its rapid development as a fiscal-military state. Russian autocracy was the synergistic result of at least three powerful influences: the Mongols, Orthodox Christianity, and a "grand bargain" struck by the Rus princes after the terrible dynastic wars of the early fifteenth century.

One of the most popular and controversial explanations for the development of Russian autocracy has been to trace it back to the influence of the Mongols.[7] That influence has often been exaggerated, but it was important. The Russian monarchy founded by Ivan III was a direct outgrowth of the principality of Muscovy that grew up under the influence of the "Golden Horde" (khanate of Kipchak) during the period of Mongol domination of the Rus lands (1240–1480). Descendants of Grand Prince Aleksandr Nevskii's youngest son Daniil, the princes of Moscow gained the favor of the khans early on and by the fourteenth century managed to become grand princes of Rus, which in practical terms meant chief tax collectors and enforcers of Mongol policies in the conquered Rus lands. The Moscow princes quickly introduced certain successful Mongol administrative and military institutions into Muscovy in order to more efficiently collect tribute for the khans and to defeat Muscovy's rivals among the other Rus principalities. According to Donald Ostrowski, as early as the four-teenth century, Muscovy's tax-collection system and army were already closely modeled on those of the Mongols.[8] The Mongol taxation system, "far more exploitative than any known in Russia before," allowed the Muscovite princes to grow immensely wealthy and powerful. Even after they stopped paying trib-ute to the Golden Horde, they continued "to collect the full amount of tribute from Russia," keeping it for themselves.[9] The Mongols also provided Muscovy with numerous other administrative, bureaucratic, and diplomatic tools—includ-ing a rapid postal communication system.[10] Most important, perhaps, was the Mongol contribution to Muscovy's military forces. Not only was the Muscovite army modeled directly on the effective Mongol cavalry—down to its tactics, maneuvers, and organization on campaigns; but the Muscovite, and later Russian, cavalry force used Mongol horses, helmets, saddles, sabres, quivers, and bows well into the seventeenth century.[11]

So successful at war, diplomacy, and statecraft were the Moscow princes that their tiny principality grew rapidly in size and prestige, even becoming the home of the metropolitan—the spiritual leader of the Russian Orthodox Church. As Mongol power waned, the Moscow princes, with built-in advan-tages, successfully struggled with their rivals for undisputed leadership of the northeast Rus lands, eventually taking the lead in overthrowing the "Tatar yoke" (Mongol domination) itself. Service at the Muscovite grand prince's court or in his army came to carry more prestige and access to wealth for noble warriors than service for any other Rus prince. Finally, in a major turning point in Russian history, Grand Prince Vasilii II of Moscow (r. 1425–62) decisively defeated his opponents in bitter dynastic wars; in the last years of his reign the grand prince's power and prestige grew enormously. He was able to eradicate the old, dysfunctional political system of Rus and to lay the foundation for the unification of Russia and the establishment of autocracy by his son, Ivan III, and grandson, Vasilii III.[12] The rise of Muscovy obviously owed much to the Mongols. Among other things, Mongol imperialism and the awesome power of the khan, who was called "tsar" by the Russians, certainly influenced the Muscovite rulers as they created their own autocracy and empire. A trace of Mongol-style political organization and leadership can be detected in Muscovite Russia; after the Golden Horde collapsed, Russia's rulers were certainly eager to assert their own claims to the vast territories formerly ruled by their one-time masters.[13] Nevertheless, Mongol influence did not on its own produce Russian autocracy. The Mongols provided some effective tools but not the motivation for the unification of Russia. When the Russians looked for ideo-logical justification for the establishment of autocracy, they did not look to the Moslem Golden Horde; instead, they sought it within the world of Orthodox Christianity.

Without doubt, an extremely important source of Russian autocracy and the imperial ambition of the tsars was Orthodox Christianity itself. During Grand Prince Vasilii II's reign, the fall of the Byzantine empire left Muscovy as the only significant remaining Eastern Orthodox state. The now-autocephalous Russian Orthodox Church quite naturally looked to the grand prince for protection and began to consider him as a possible successor to the Byzantine emperors and as the only truly Orthodox prince remaining on earth. Recognizing that the fate of their church was now closely tied to the fate of Muscovy, Russian ecclesiastics began to refer to Vasilii II as "tsar" and "autocrat."[14] In the next generation, Vasilii's son, Ivan III, the founder of the Russian monarchy, worked tirelessly to promote an image of himself as the sovereign of Russia and as the champion of Orthodox Christianity.[15] Formally ending the "Tatar yoke" in 1480, he went on to claim, at least tentatively, the role of successor to the Byzantine emperors.[16] Ivan was occasionally called "tsar" and regarded his status as similar to that of the Holy Roman emperor.[17] Ivan's son, Grand Prince Vasilii III, was also exalted as the protector of Orthodox Christianity and was even more frequently referred to as "tsar." In 1547, his son, Ivan IV, became the first ruler formally crowned as tsar of Russia. Throughout the process of unification, the Russian Orthodox Church actively supported the pretensions of the grand princes, making use of Byzantine political theory to justify the absolute power of Russia's "divinely-appointed" rulers.[18] The actual impact of such theological justification outside church circles may have been relatively modest, however. It is not clear that Russia's rulers or leading statesmen were familiar with Byzantine political culture even though the court now affected Byzantine (or "pseudo-Byzantine") style.[19] The church did produce a few writers who emphasized Moscow's emergence as a "third Rome," and many scholars have seized upon the "third Rome" theory as a principal source for Russian autocracy.[20] In fact, however, the use and influence of that theory in the sixteenth century has been greatly exaggerated.[21] Despite the introduction of superficial Byzantine trappings, Russia's rulers were not particularly interested in the prospect of becoming universal emperors responsible for the welfare of all Orthodox Christians.[22] Instead, they were content to be sovereigns and autocrats of Russia.

In Russia's traditional society, where there was simply no concept of a secular state, the ruler and the church were just about the only concrete expressions of the Russian nation. The power of the ruler came to be seen as an extension of the power of God.[23] The grand princes and tsars claimed to be protectors of the one true faith, and the Russian Orthodox Church actively promoted the idea that it was the duty of all Russians to obey and serve their pious, divinely-appointed rulers. What emerged by the sixteenth century was a somewhat typical medieval European version of sacred kingship.[24] To the Russians, the title "tsar," although derived from "Caesar" and associated with both "emperor" and "khan," really meant divinely-appointed king.[25] It is true that some efforts were made to trace the lineage of Russia's rulers back to Rome and the emperor Augustus;[26] however, it was really the Old Testament kingdom of Israel that stirred the imagination of early modern Russian statesmen and ecclesiastical writers.[27] Within the context of the fall of the Byzantine empire and the widespread expectation of the Apocalypse sometime soon after the Orthodox calender came to an end in the year 7000 (A.D. 1492), the image of Russia as the New Israel and of Moscow as the New Jerusalem became far more powerful than any notion of Moscow as the Third Rome.[28] The idea of the Russians as God's chosen people and of the tsars as the spiritual descendants of Abraham, whose mission it was to lead the faithful to salvation in an uncertain future, became an important element in the development of Russian autocracy in the sixteenth century. In addition to exalting the tsar, that idea promised divine protection and a unique role in world history for Russia. The imagery of the tsar's army as a heavenly host (or as the reembodiment of the army of ancient Israel) appealed to the religiously-oriented military elite at the same time that it sanctified Russian expansion.[29] Metropolitan Makarii specifically cited King David as a model for Tsar Ivan IV (r. 1547–84) during his lavish coronation ceremony. According to the metropolitan, it was Tsar Ivan's duty not only to rule Russia piously but also to lead a crusade against Islam, Catholicism, and other enemies of the true faith. Partly as a result, the young tsar soon came to see himself and his country as destined to carry out a divinely-ordained conquest of the khanates of Kazan and Astrakhan (successors of the Golden Horde). In a heady mix, Ivan the Terrible's Russia was envisioned simultaneously as a sanctified Christian empire and as the New Israel.[30]

It is clear that the religious aspect of the Russian monarchy was extremely important in legitimizing the new state and its rulers. In fact, defense of the faith and loyalty to the tsar became synonymous.[31] Service to the monarch became not only the prerequisite for advancement but also the sacred duty of all subjects.[32] Even the highest ranking princes and boyars made a great show of humble service to "God's viceroy on earth" and carefully fostered the image of the all-powerful, pious tsar.[33] It is possible that the ruling elite itself may not have believed all the religious rhetoric associated with autocracy, merely finding it useful in cementing their own privileges and promoting social control.

Many ordinary Russians, however, came to believe that the tsar truly was God's viceroy on earth and their protector in a hostile world. Scholars have speculated that the internalization of this religious view of the tsar by the Russian masses was completed by the mid-seventeenth century;[34] but, as we shall see, that element of popular consciousness may be detected at least as early as Russia's first civil war.[35]

The third important source for Russian autocracy was a grand bargain struck by many of the Rus princes in the aftermath of the destructive dynastic conflicts of the early fifteenth century. The new political system erected by Grand Prince Vasilii II and his allies was based on a widely perceived need for a single, undisputed royal dynasty (and the principle of primogeniture) in the Rus lands in order to fend off Tatars and other aggressive neighbors and to avoid slipping back into the chaos and nightmare of dynastic wars. The idea of a strong ruler and of the concentration of administrative and military authority in Moscow was also widely regarded as essential in order to govern and garrison the thinly populated and far-flung Russian lands.[36] In this important matter, the pretensions of the princes of Moscow were supported not only by their own nontitled boyars (aristocratic servitors) and the Russian Orthodox Church, but also by several important princely clans who came to Moscow to share the glory and profit of service to the "sovereign" of Russia. As additional Rus territories were added to the state, their ruling elites were in turn usually integrated into the court and army command of Muscovy and eventually came to share the spoils of real power with earlier arrivals. Princely clan leaders settled down to live in Moscow and joined the ranks of the Muscovite boyars who were already informally organized as the grand prince's main advisers in his *sinklit* (sometimes called the "boyar council" or the "boyar duma"). Those men became a truly national Russian aristocracy actively involved in running the country and commanding the ruler's powerful army. They gradually lost contact with their native regions and any desire to return to the political fragmentation of earlier Rus history.[37]

Boyars and princes, along with the church, exalted the grand prince of Moscow as a sovereign and an autocrat, but the actual political system they invented may have been, at least in the beginning, far more collegial and oligarchic than any of them ever admitted to foreigners or even to Russians outside the highest court circles.[38] Some scholars maintain that a "facade of autocracy" was maintained to mask oligarchic rule, a deception actively promoted by the courtiers of the new Russian monarch who publicly went out of their way to exaggerate their own "slavish" servility to him. The image of an all-powerful autocrat who overawed and demanded service even from boyars and princes was supposedly quite useful to perpetrators of the myth, in part because it helped legitimize and sanctify the political order, thereby justifying their own status and benefits, and in part because it helped convince the Russian people that they too had to serve the tsar with their own blood, sweat, and taxes.[39] Not all scholars accept the notion of the facade of autocracy. Arguments against it range from the traditional view of autocracy as very real, managing to subjugate the elite along with everyone else, to the idea of a constantly shifting balance of power between tsar and boyars depending upon the ruler's capabilities and ambitions.[40] Whether or not the Russian autocrat's power was a facade to the ruling elite, it certainly presented itself as an incredibly absolute and overbearing force to the Russian people and to Russia's neighbors. Contemporary observers in the sixteenth and seventeenth centuries regarded the tsar of Russia as the most absolute ruler of Europe, with the possible exception of the sultan of the Ottoman empire.[41]

The potent combination of ingredients that went into the creation of Russian autocracy resulted in the rapid development of a service state (or "liturgical state") in which the performance of duties that directly or indirectly bolstered the country's security were required from virtually everyone. Russia's tsarist system became "one of the most compulsory in Europe," and there existed "no autonomous social estates or other public bodies" to act as a check on its onerous demands.[42] To protect the tsar and to satisfy his military ambitions, all elements of Russian society were harnessed, and royal power was pushed far beyond its customary limits. In no way did Ivan the Terrible's creation of the *zemskii sobor* (Assembly of the Land), a kind of sounding board composed of various social strata and convened at the government's pleasure, represent a limit on Russian autocracy—even though that "rubber stamp" assembly came to play an important role in choosing a new tsar in 1613.[43] In fact, no group or institution was capable of challenging Russian autocracy. Even with high status, most of the aristocracy actually functioned as an "unfree" group of elite servitors.[44] A whole new class of noble military servitors loyal to and totally dependent upon the crown was also created.[45] Peasants and townspeople found their obligations increasing dramatically, and the whole national economy was subordinated to the needs of the state (and suffered badly as a result).[46] Even the Russian Orthodox Church came to be dominated by and put to work for the tsar.[47] What emerged was a highly militarized society primarily dedicated to the service and greater glory of its autocratic and imperialistic ruler.[48] Or to put it another way, the early modern Russian service state quickly became a highly effective fiscal-military state.

A key element in the development of Russian autocracy and its success in military expansion was the creation of a loyal, centralized, and coercive state administration capable of mobilizing domestic resources and directing the complex tasks of administering a large army and a newly unified country.[49] Starting with a small, Mongol-influenced rudimentary bureaucracy, Ivan III and Vasilii III placed a premium on developing an administrative apparatus capable of bringing newly annexed regions under firm control and making sure that all subjects fulfilled their duties as servitors or taxpayers.[50] The result was the rapid development of a system of centralized administrative offices, or *prikazy* (singular: *prikaz*), and the rise of a hereditary "service bureaucracy" dedicated to meeting the needs of the growing state.[51] By the mid-sixteenth century, the service bureaucracy had made great strides in centralization and rationalization of the tsar's regime, and by the 1570s Russia's prikaz system was largely in place.[52] It was staffed by incredibly loyal and hardworking "secretaries" (*d'iaki;* singular: *d'iak*). High ranking state secretaries (*dumnye d'iaki*), ordinary secretaries (*d'iaki*), and even lowly clerks (*pod'iachie*) received generous rewards for lifelong service. Their families tended to intermarry, and their offices were usually passed down to their sons. They emerged as a powerful caste of bureaucrats who succeeded admirably at imposing the tsar's will.[53] From the very beginning, the bureaucracy was primarily oriented to the task of raising, financing, and supplying the army; and the prikaz system expanded sharply in response to the military revolution and Russia's territorial expansion.[54] Among the various prikazy concerned with military matters, the dominant one was the Military Affairs Office (*Razriadnyi prikaz*), formed in the 1550s. Consisting of about ten departments, it supervised all military appointments, oversaw annual musters, maintained service rosters, coordinated supplies and transport, and provided intelligence about the enemy to military commanders. Its clerks also traveled with the army to provide logistical support. The Military Affairs Office maintained an excellent archive and employed hundreds of people.[55]

The tsar's bureaucrats were not hampered by the concerns of bankers, merchants, or industrialists (a problem for Western monarchies) and were, therefore, basically free to extract resources from the Russian economy in order to pay for the costs of war.[56] They performed that task with zeal—introducing new taxes, increasing existing ones, and eliminating exemptions. By the mid-sixteenth century, almost the entire population owed substantial obligations to the state, and revenues poured in for costly fortress construction and military expansion. Military construction fees, gunpowder fees, harquebusier (an early version of the musketeer) fees, frontier defense fees, and very heavy communication and postal fees were levied. Nonmilitary taxes changed very little over the course of the sixteenth century, but there was a dramatic rise in the overall level of taxation (a six hundred percent increase, adjusted for inflation) due to the increase in military-related taxation—which rose from approximately thirty percent of all taxes collected in 1500 to more than eighty percent by the 1580s.[57] Contemporary observers duly noted that the Russians were heavily taxed.[58] In addition to taxation, the tsar's government aggressively sought revenue by establishing crown monopolies on many profitable commodities. Overall, the service bureaucracy provided the funds necessary to support the tsar's military ambitions with little or no concern about the impact of their actions on individuals or the country's economy.[59] Although the Russian empire expanded rapidly as a result, that short-sighted fiscal policy ended up contributing to serious problems by the end of the sixteenth century.[60]

The creation of large armies owing loyalty directly to their kings was an essential ingredient in the growth of royal power in early modern Europe, and Russia was no exception. The unification of Russia and the growth of autocracy depended to a significant degree on the development and use of a loyal military force.[61] Funding and fielding that army became the main activity of the country. It is no exaggeration to say that, more than any other contemporary European society, early modern Russia was "organized for warfare."[62] War had been the principal activity of Muscovy; after unification, it continued to be the main activity of the new Russian monarchy.[63] With the longest frontiers in Europe and an ambitious ruling elite, Russia quickly developed one of the largest and most powerful armies of northeastern Europe. During the sixteenth century that army was at war with at least one of Russia's western neighbors, on and off, for nearly fifty years; on the Tatar front, to the south and east, warfare was almost constant.[64] All that military activity helped Russia emerge as a major power by the time Vasilii III died in 1533.[65] It also led to the rapid expansion of Russia, which tripled in size over the course of the sixteenth century.[66] The formation of the Russian empire, which almost instantly became the largest country in Europe, greatly enhanced the prestige of the tsars even as it grossly overburdened their subjects.[67]

Because Russia's military forces played the dominant role in creating the empire and a crucial role in its first civil war, it will be useful to examine briefly the nature and development of those military forces. During the process of unifying Russia, Ivan III built up Muscovy's own strong army and converted it into something like a national army.[68] In part due to the existing Rus tradition of lifetime service for aristocratic warriors, Ivan was also remarkably successful at subordinating and putting to use the ruling elites of the principalities he annexed, incorporating them into his own growing administrative and military structure.[69] Together with his own boyars, this expanded group became the "crucial nucleus" of Russia's military force.[70] An informal boyar council advised the monarch on all important matters related to war and foreign policy. Its members, often collectively referred to as "boyars," actually consisted of three distinct ranks. These very high-status aristocratic servitors (in descending rank: boyars, *okol'nichie,* and *dumnye dvoriane*) also functioned as commanders (*voevody*) of royal armies and as military governors of important towns. Just below the boyars were high-ranking courtiers who held similar but somewhat less prestigious posts in the military and administration, and below them were lesser courtiers who functioned as the tsar's entourage. Between two and three thousand courtiers lived in Moscow; they were highly paid and held hereditary and service estates near the capital. Altogether, this group of courtiers (the "sovereign's court") constituted the power elite of early modern Russia; when called upon to do so, they formed part of the tsar's personal regiment on military campaigns.[71]

The bulk of early modern Russia's military forces consisted of most of the secular landholding class mobilized as cavalry. Already strongly imbued with a commitment to serve their various princes, hereditary noble warriors of Rus were enticed or coerced along with their masters into Muscovite service, thereby swelling the ranks of Ivan III's military forces and speeding up Russia's unification.[72] Service to the new Russian monarch soon became the duty, the very reason for being, for Russia's hereditary military servitors.[73] In addition to creating something like a national army, Ivan III launched what Richard Hellie has called Russia's "first service class revolution" when he annexed Novgorod in 1478—a "revolution" that created a much larger army and that had a profound effect on the stratification of Russian society.[74] In order to garrison Novgorod's extensive territories, Ivan settled over two thousand loyal military servitors there. Out of the huge fund of land confiscated from Novgorod's elite, individual plots of land were assigned to support each warrior. Peasants on those lands then paid rent to keep the cavalrymen in military service.

Unlike a hereditary estate (*votchina*), which was the closest thing to private property in early modern Russia,[75] the Novgoradian land assigned to support each warrior was given as a conditional service grant (*pomest'e*) and could be confiscated if the cavalryman failed to show up for service. The pomeste system reduced the costs to the royal court of maintaining its military forces and allowed great expansion of an army dependent upon and extremely loyal to the crown. The pomeste system worked so well, in fact, that it quickly became the basic form of landholding for Russia's cavalry force, spreading from Novgorod throughout most of the country (except northern Russia, which was considered safe from military threat). Lands converted into pomeste estates came largely from newly annexed territories, property confiscated from traitors, and land

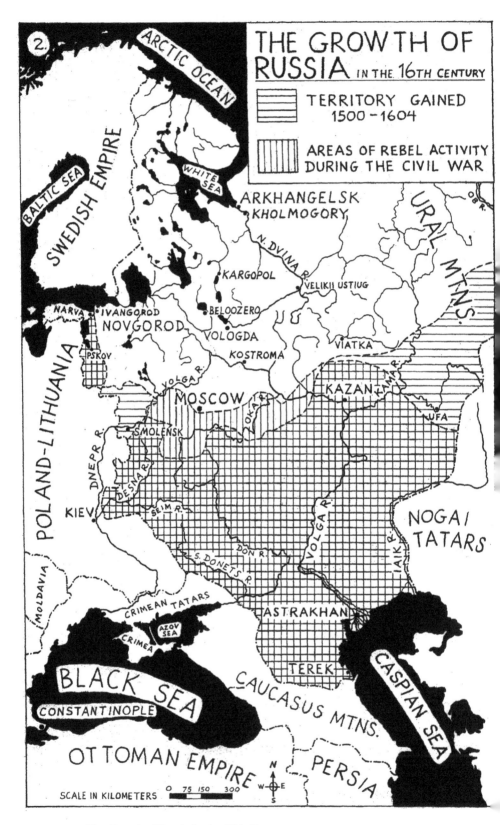

Map 2 The Growth of Russia in the 16th Century.

cultivated by unfortunate free peasants.[76] The pomeste system enabled Ivan III to field an army three or four times the size of his father's and allowed him eventually to move beyond focusing on the unification of Russia to successful military expansion at the expense of neighboring Lithuania. Thus, in 1505 the founder of the pomeste system was able to pass on to Vasilii III a large army and a realm four times the size of the one he had inherited.[77] In similar fashion, Vasilii III used his large army of *pomeshchiki* (holders of pomeste estates) to complete the unification of Russia and, in 1514, to capture the mighty Lithuanian fortress of Smolensk, which firmly secured Russia's western flank and gave Russia control of the upper Dnepr River. By the time Ivan the Terrible came to power, the pomeste-based cavalry force had become the "backbone of the Russian army."[78] Following in the footsteps of his father and grandfather, Tsar Ivan quickly put his cavalrymen to work to create the Russian empire. It is certainly no exaggeration to say that over the course of the sixteenth century the pomeshchiki contributed greatly to the rapid expansion of Russia and the growing power and prestige of the Russian autocrat.[79]

Some scholars have been reluctant to view the *pomeshchiki* as noble warriors or as a landed gentry; and, indeed, their lives bore little resemblance to that of the aristocracy residing in Moscow.[80] It is certainly true that the pomeshchiki were a group of landholders created by and existing at the sufferance of the state. They were not part of the "ruling class," were slow to develop a corporate consciousness, and had no real independent existence. Failure to serve could result in the sudden loss of both pomeste estate and status as a military servitor.[81] Nonetheless, the pomeshchiki were classified as lifelong hereditary military servitors (*sluzhilie liudi po otechestvu*), just like the aristocracy and not like lower status military servitors (*sluzhilie liudi po priboru*) such as artillerymen, fortress guards, and fortification specialists.[82] That distinction was critical in an extremely status-conscious society. Russia's warrior elite, which may be defined as those military servitors who held land and had the right to exploit the peasant labor force on it, included the pomeshchiki and stood far above social inferiors such as ordinary soldiers.[83] It is therefore not inappropriate to refer to the pomeshchiki as a somewhat crude "gentry" (or protogentry). Europeans who visited early modern Russia certainly had no trouble recognizing that the pomeshchiki had the status of "gentlemen." Foreigners frequently referred to them as "gentry" even though the tsar's cavalrymen had few, if any, of the rights and privileges of their Western counterparts. It is also worth noting that, according to several European observers, military service on horseback in many ways defined "nobility" in Russia.[84] That may help to explain why pomeshchiki were so reluctant to adapt to the gunpowder revolution even though that reluctance ultimately doomed them to obsolescence. They preferred the bow and sabre to the harquebus (an early version of the musket) at least in part because one had to dismount in order to fire the gun, thereby lowering one's status. By the end of the sixteenth century the pomeshchiki were becoming increasingly vulnerable to infantry with guns; but, in spite of that, they were treated increasingly favorably by the Russian government and emerged as something like an exclusive "warrior caste."[85] As we shall see, Russia's first civil war strongly reinforced in the pomeshchiki a growing awareness of their identity as important members of the warrior elite and of the acute need to actively protect their status.

The tsar's gentry cavalry force was based in the provinces in which they held pomeste lands. Many of them lived in the countryside in log cabins, much like peasants; but most of them also maintained a residence in the town that was their district headquarters.[86] In addition to their land grants, which on average were inhabited by five or six peasant households, the gentry received modest (and irregular) salaries from the central government.[87] They did not constitute a standing army, but their part-time service was mandatory for life. Starting at about age fifteen and ending only when death, illness, wounds, or old age prevented service, pomeshchiki had to report fully equipped for an annual muster in order to determine their readiness for combat and to correct any shortcomings. Fines were exacted if they did not show up properly mounted or outfitted, and failure to appear at muster could result in the loss of part or all of one's pomeste. By the second half of the sixteenth century, a pomeshchik could pass his status and service lands to his son (or other relative) provided that the recipient was then available for annual military service. Because there was constant conflict on the Tatar front, which was Russia's most dangerous frontier until the seventeenth century, the Russian cavalry force was largely oriented to steppe warfare. Except during emergencies or major military campaigns, about half of the pomeshchiki served along the southern frontier each year from the beginning of April to the beginning of July. Then they went home and were replaced by the other half who guarded against Tatar raids until the beginning of October. During emergencies both halves of the gentry cavalry force were summoned to duty simultaneously. Military service on the frontier was tedious and onerous even for generals, and many soldiers tried to avoid it. Absenteeism was a serious and chronic problem, and commanders often used brutal means, including beatings, to enforce service. Wounded or old pomeshchiki were sometimes exempted from rigorous duty and were instead given relatively easy assignments such as garrisoning fortresses.[88]

The bulk of the pomeshchiki, or gentry cavalry force, were called *deti boiarskie* (singular: *syn boiarskii*). By the mid-sixteenth century these men occupied the

Fig. 1 "Three Russian Cavalrymen." Published in Sigismund von Herberstein, *Rerum Moscovitcarum commentarij Sigismundi liberi baronis in Herberstein, Neyperg, & Guettenhag* (Basileae: per Ionnem Oporinum, 1556). Courtesy of the James Ford Bell Library, University of Minnesota.

bottom rung of the hereditary military service ladder.[89] Significantly higher in status than the deti boiarskie were the *dvoriane* (singular: *dvorianin*), the provincial elite. References to "pomeshchiki" or to the "dvoriane" in general usually mean both dvoriane and the far more numerous deti boiarskie; both groups were part of the gentry cavalry force. Only a few fortunate dvoriane were selected for the top category of provincial service. These *vybornye dvoriane* (chosen dvoriane) could expect to serve for three years in Moscow. While there the vybornye dvoriane were called *zhiltsy* (singular: *zhilets*), or "residents." There were two or three hundred zhiltsy in the capital at any given time. They did not serve at court but did perform some ceremonial duties and occasionally acted as the tsar's bodyguards. They also served in the tsar's regiment if that elite unit was mobilized for military action. After three years, most zhiltsy returned to their provinces to make way for a new group of vybornye dvoriane rotating to Moscow; but a few of them who had impressed their superiors were instead permanently stationed in the capital as *Moskovskie dvoriane* (Moscow dvoriane). This was a really big step for members of the provincial elite. There were several hundred Moscow dvoriane, including courtiers' sons just starting out in service. Although they did not hold court rank, they had high status, performed many important military and administrative duties, and served in the tsar's regiment.[90] Overall, Russia's gentry cavalry force (or gentry militia) consisted of approximately twenty to twenty-five thousand men in the sixteenth century.[91] Higher estimates exist, but John Keep's statement that there were eighty thousand men in the "service elite" at the end of the sixteenth century is absolutely unacceptable.[92] He mistakenly lumped together all of the tsar's military forces in making his estimate. There were, in fact, several other categories of military servitors in early modern Russia, but they were not part of the hereditary military service elite.

The military revolution itself was responsible for the introduction of several new types of specialists and warriors into the Russian army. Ivan III and his successors, in addition to unifying Russia and fighting against Tatar cavalry forces, faced the daunting task of responding to the early stages of the military modernization of their European neighbors. Russia's first steps in response to the gunpowder revolution included rebuilding and strengthening Western border fortifications against possible artillery attacks and the full-scale introduction of artillery into fortresses and military operations in general.[93] An incredible amount of fortress construction occurred in Russia over the course of the sixteenth century; more than thirty major fortresses were completed. During the reign of Ivan the Terrible alone, more than one hundred fifty fortresses or forts were built and equipped, although many of them were nothing more than small, wooden outposts on the southern frontier. Refortification of Smolensk, Russia's

Fig. 2 "Russian Artillery and Artillerymen." Drawn circa 1674 by a Swedish ambassador. Published in Erich Palmquist, *Några widh sidste Kongl: Ambassaden till Tzaren Muskou giorde observationer öfwer Russlandh, des wager, pass meds fästningar och brantzer* (Stockholm: Generalstabens Litografiska Anstalt, 1898). Courtesy of the James Ford Bell Library, University of Minnesota.

largest fortress and the key to the entire western defense system, was undertaken at great expense by Boris Godunov and became "the greatest construction project in the world in the sixteenth century."[94] The Russians also produced a huge quantity of good artillery, quickly mastering the skills taught to them by Westerners. By the beginning of the seventeenth century, Russia had approximately thirty-five hundred artillery weapons, including siege guns and lighter field artillery.[95] Some lead and gunpowder was still imported, along with a few weapons; but Russia was well on its way toward military self-sufficiency.[96] Among the new groups of military specialists emerging in Russia were artillerymen. Like most other lower status military servitors (*sluzhilie liudi po priboru*), artillerymen were a relatively closed corps of privileged townsmen who received a cash salary and often lived in special settlements outside the towns in which they served. They also collectively received lands for gardens, pasture, and hay production. Drawn from the ranks of townsmen and peasants, artillerymen had no right to peasant labor and tilled the land for themselves. They performed their military duties part-time for life, often supplementing their meager income by engaging in commerce or handicraft production. Their officers were drawn from the hereditary service nobility.[97]

Starting in the late fifteenth century, some Russian soldiers began using harquebuses (heavy matchlock guns fired from a stand). By the early sixteenth century there were as many as a thousand harquebusiers in the Russian army who were able to deliver massed firepower in combat.[98] The utility of infantry armed with firearms as a complement to the gentry cavalry force was increasingly recognized as the Russian army clashed with Polish and Swedish troops. Infantry with guns were, in fact, far superior to cavalry in conducting siege warfare. Soon the idea took hold of having a regular standing infantry force that could be called into service on short notice to go on campaign or to protect the tsar. In 1550 Ivan IV established Russia's first standing infantry corps of three thousand experienced volunteers, who came to be called *streltsy* (singular: *strelets*). Although the term is derived from the Russian word for "arrow" and literally means "shooters," the original streltsy were harquebusiers and became "musketeers" only with the introduction of the musket in the seventeenth century. The streltsy wore special red uniforms and were initially settled as a group in their own community just outside Moscow. There they built homes, planted gardens, and supplemented their irregular salaries by engaging in tax-exempt commercial or artisanal activity. They typically ran shops and stables or worked as blacksmiths, butchers, or cobblers. Like other lower status military servitors, the streltsy were a somewhat closed corps who served for life and whose replacements often came from their own families. They were privileged townsmen whose duties were not too onerous in peacetime. They were called upon to perform ceremonial duties, escort ambassadors, fight fires, chase fugitives, stand guard for twenty-four hours at a time, and run errands for their commanders. Streltsy were usually organized in units of five hundred, headed by a *golova* (head or colonel), and subdivided into units of one hundred, headed by a *sotnik* (centurion). Their officers were drawn from the hereditary nobility. The service provided by the streltsy proved to be extremely useful both on campaigns and in garrison duty. As a result, streltsy units were gradually set up in many towns. By 1600 there were approximately twenty to twenty-five thousand streltsy in Russia. The seven to ten thousand settled in Moscow were considered elite, in part because about two hundred of them at a time served as a mounted bodyguard for the tsar. By contrast, streltsy serving on the southern frontier led harder lives and had relatively low status.[99]

The development of autocracy, an energetic bureaucracy, and powerful military forces led to the rapid growth of early modern Russia and the formation of an impressive empire. Yet the costs associated with Russia's survival and expansion in the age of the military revolution were astronomical. Higher and higher taxes had to be imposed in order to pay for such things as fortifications, artillery, and infantry with firearms. The tax levied to pay for the streltsy, for example, was the most onerous of all in the sixteenth century and seriously overburdened the small percentage of Russians who lived in towns.[100] In fact, although the zealous subordination of the entire economy and all social classes to the needs of the fiscal-military state successfully fueled the imperial expansion of Ivan the Terrible and his successors, as noted earlier, it also led to a downturn in the economy and increasing stratification of society. That in turn helped produce a serious and destabilizing state crisis out of which emerged the Time and Troubles and Russia's first civil war.[101]

3

Ivan the Terrible and Russia's Slide into Crisis

During the reign of Russia's first tsar, Ivan IV (d. 1584), his military forces decisively defeated their fierce Tatar rivals and created the Russian empire; but Ivan's
reign also saw the development of an internal crisis that helped prepare Russia
for its first civil war. The traditional view of the period and of Ivan the Terrible
has been that the erratic and cruel policies of the tsar were largely responsible
for the catastrophic decline of his country. Ivan's long and unsuccessful Livonian
War (1558–83), fought to gain access to the Baltic Sea, and the establishment
of the *oprichnina* (the tsar's state within the state under his personal control)
are usually cited as principal causes of Russia's decline, the increasing stratification of Russian society, the development of serfdom, and—of course—the
Time of Troubles.[1] In fact, the "terrible" tsar's policies and personality did play
a part in the development of Russia's late-sixteenth century crisis. Yet, upon
close inspection, it turns out that many of the problems facing the country
during Ivan's reign were shared by Russia's neighbors and cannot reasonably
be blamed solely on the "half-mad" tsar. Among other things, Ivan's reign saw
the beginnings of a conjuncture of the effects of the development of the fiscal-military state, sustained upward population and price pressures, and the
"little ice age."

War and the appropriation of domestic resources needed to meet Russia's
international challenges and to satisfy the imperial dreams of its ruling elite
played crucial roles in Russia's slide into crisis during Ivan the Terrible's reign.
Although Ivan III and Vasilii III, by acquiring Novgorod and Smolensk and by
building up Russia's military power, had managed to secure Russia's western
flank, the greatest danger to the country until the seventeenth century came
from remnants of the Golden Horde to the east and south.[2] The menace posed
by the relentless and powerful Tatars was, in fact, so great that it must be considered a major reason for the centralization of Russia as a "garrison state" and
the subsequent emergence there of a near-caste society.[3] Tatar slave and booty
raids had long been a terrifying feature of life in Russia, and hundreds of thousands of Russians were captured and sold into slavery by the Tatars during the

course of the sixteenth century alone.[4] As a consequence, Russia's military forces were primarily designed to meet the Tatar threat, and low-intensity warfare was almost continuous on the country's southern and eastern frontiers.[5]

With the strong support of his people and buttressed by the work of his father and grandfather, Tsar Ivan initially pursued an extremely active policy of military expansion against the Tatars. From the beginning of his reign, he focused on what many believed to be his divinely-ordained mission, a crusade against those tormentors of Russia. Making good use of the gentry militia and his new streltsy units, Ivan conquered the khanate of Kazan in 1552 and the khanate of Astrakhan in 1556. As a result of those campaigns, the tsar gained control of the entire Volga River, which opened up Caspian Sea trade to the Russians, secured Russia's eastern flank, and paved the way for the rapid colonization of Siberia and the somewhat slower colonization of the southern frontier. Overall, Russia doubled in size during Ivan's reign. Conquest of the Tatar realms increased the prestige of the tsar enormously and created the Russian empire.[6] It gave the tsar control over tens of thousands of non-Slavic peoples—not just the Islamic Tatars but also many of the native tribes of the Volga region, including the Cheremis (Mari) and the Mordvians (Mordva), both of Finnish origin. All these new subjects were quickly put to work either as laborers and taxpayers or as military servitors. Many of them resented the loss of independence and the ever-increasing pressure from Moscow, and they periodically caused trouble for their new masters in the late sixteenth century and during the Time of Troubles.[7] On the other hand, many Tatars, Cheremis, and Mordvians willingly joined the Russian army. As many as twenty-seven thousand of them served the tsar (primarily in cavalry units) by the early seventeenth century.[8]

In the context of Tsar Ivan's great victories over the Tatars, a number of important reforms were implemented to improve the effectiveness of Russia's fighting forces. To increase the size of the army without significantly raising government expenses, Ivan in 1556 issued a new military service code that formally extended the requirement to serve to all landowners. Privileged owners of votchina (hereditary) estates were now required to show up for military service alongside the pomeste-based gentry. In addition, holders of both votchina and pomeste lands were now required to provide an additional cavalryman (fully equipped) for approximately every four hundred acres of land they held. That significantly increased the size of the tsar's army, but the additional burden on the gentry militiamen was not easily met even in good times by the poorer ones; in times of hardship, the requirement proved ruinous to many.[9] Tsar Ivan's reforms at that time also focused on developing local self-government. Among other things, tax collectors were now to be drawn from the local population.

Carefully supervised by the tsar's bureaucrats, these new and more honest tax collectors significantly increased the revenues flowing to Moscow. Another reason for the increase in revenue was that in return for the "privilege of taxing themselves," Ivan's subjects were now required to pay taxes at "twice the previous rate."[10] As a result of his reforms, the tsar's enlarged and better-funded army was well prepared to further extend his realm.

After Tsar Ivan's triumph over the khanates of Kazan and Astrakhan, his subjects expected him to follow up those victories with an assault on the last major remnant of the Golden Horde, the Crimean Tatars—who were then vassals of the Turkish sultan. Just as Russians were being encouraged to colonize newly acquired and pacified lands to the east and the south, however, Ivan rather suddenly changed his mind. Against the advice of many people, instead of invading Crimea, he chose to turn west to seek an outlet to the Baltic Sea, which was then blocked by Russia's western neighbors. In 1558, the Russians invaded Livonia, quickly captured the port of Narva, and began trading directly with Western merchants. Eventually, however, Poland and Sweden intervened to drive Russia back from the Baltic. For Tsar Ivan the long and drawn-out Livonian War (1558–83) proved to be a humiliating disaster. Not only was Russia forced to wait until Peter the Great to regain its position as a Baltic power, but the impact of the Livonian War and its very high costs contributed significantly to the catastrophic decline of Russia's economy and the serious dislocation of its society.[11]

In the midst of the unfortunate Livonian War, Tsar Ivan established his dreaded oprichnina (1565–72) by splitting Russia into two parts—one ruled by the traditional, Moscow-based administration (including the boyar council), and the other under Ivan's personal control. The result was one of the most traumatic episodes in early modern Russian history. The oprichnina contributed to the sharp decline in Russia's economy "which led to the establishment of serfdom" and was a significant factor in the development of the Time of Troubles.[12] Many scholars regard Ivan's oprichnina as completely irrational.[13] Others have discerned in that bloody episode a seriously flawed plan to increase the power of the tsar by making him independent of the boyar council and senior bureaucrats.[14] In either case, during the oprichnina the tsar unleashed overwhelming coercive force with great brutality on many of his subjects with absolutely no regard for their rights—a type of abuse of power that some scholars associate with the emergence of the fiscal-military state.[15] In an apparent effort to create a new, more loyal and subservient elite, Tsar Ivan coopted some nobles into the oprichnina and promoted many men of undistinguished birth into its leadership. The resulting split in the nobility, coupled with the privileges received by the hated *oprichniki* (Ivan's new courtiers and his private army based in the oprichnina) and Ivan's erratic use of violence against his aristocrats, created a long-lasting factional struggle among the boyars.

Most magnates, even before the oprichnina, had been locked in fierce competition with one another for status, appointments, and rewards; starting in the 1560s, that competition became much more fierce and deadly. Moreover, it did not end with the oprichnina or even with Tsar Ivan's death.[16] The split in the administration and nobility destabilized Russia's political structure for many years, as did the use of terror by the bloodthirsty tsar. Ivan actively encouraged denunciations by rivals and underlings of persons he wished to destroy, and he ruthlessly cut down any real or perceived opposition within the nobility, the church, and the bureaucracy. The resulting horror and dislocation traumatized the elite, seriously weakened many princely families, and increased the nobility's dependence on the monarch. Ominously, it also promoted popular distrust of boyars and other officials as potential enemies of the tsar.[17] There was, surprisingly, actually very little elite resistance to Ivan's tyranny, and many of the survivors profited from the downfall of others.[18] Nonetheless, the oprichnina was long remembered with horror by the nobility. After all, the tsar was supposed to preserve the general order and traditional hierarchy of the realm, not upset the system. Ivan the Terrible severely shook elite faith in the crown.[19] That was undoubtedly an important precondition of Russia's first civil war. As Goldstone and others have demonstrated, early modern state crises often stemmed in part from reckless government actions that alienated elites.[20]

Tsar Ivan's oprichniki not only terrorized his opponents and many innocent bystanders, but they also ruthlessly exploited their pomeste estates and the peasants living on those lands. Many peasants, already facing increasing taxes, fled from these "locusts" to boyar or monastic estates where they were treated somewhat better, or to the new frontier lands beckoning to the south and east. The resulting loss of labor undermined the ability of the oprichniki and others to provide military service, seriously weakening Russia's defenses during a time of war on two fronts.[21] When the Crimean Tatars launched a devastating invasion of Russia in 1571, the oprichniki performed miserably. Partly as a result, Tatar forces reached Moscow, burned much of the capital, and returned to the Crimea with more than one hundred thousand prisoners. The somewhat chagrined tsar immediately began making plans to abolish the oprichnina, which he did in 1572.[22] Even so, Ivan's leading oprichnina courtiers who had survived were merely integrated into the old administration and boyar council, an action that did nothing to promote elite stability.[23] In fact, Tsar Ivan managed to sow much hatred among the nobility in his realm.[24] That certainly was one of the causes of the Time of Troubles. The tsar's cruel tyranny and the deep-seated animosities and factional struggles among the boyars caused by the oprichnina actually led one late sixteenth-century observer to predict that Russia would soon plunge into civil war.[25]

There is no doubt that the oprichnina did great damage, and Ivan the Terrible deserves harsh criticism for it. Nonetheless, it is impossible to determine just exactly where damage caused by the oprichnina stopped and that caused by such things as war, taxes, population and price pressures, disease, and climate began. All were factors in the downturn of Russia's economy and the development of its state crisis. Quite apart from the oprichnina, for example, Tsar Ivan imposed much heavier taxes on his people than his predecessors and was not at all concerned about the impact of his exactions.[26] Oprichnina terror also coincided with terrible famines and plagues that killed hundreds of thousands of Russians.[27] Upon close inspection, it is also clear that the Russian economy was already beginning to experience severe shocks when the oprichnina came along, and it only made things worse.[28] Russia's slide into crisis, therefore, cannot simply be attributed to the oprichnina and the personality of the "terrible" tsar.

By the 1570s Russia began to show unmistakable signs of economic decline and social dislocation. Basic reasons for the developing crisis were complex, but they definitely included long-term population growth, increasing price inflation, and the "little ice age." As discussed in Chapter 1, Goldstone has shown that in the early modern period the rapid multiplication of younger sons of the elite put increasing pressure on the government to find them lands and good jobs just as the government was beginning to face a fiscal crisis due to price inflation and the astronomical costs of war. That was certainly true for Russia, both for the aristocracy and the gentry. Over the course of the sixteenth century, elite holders of votchina estates divided their lands among their children again and again until those ancestral holdings were subdivided into units too small to support all the inheritors, forcing subsequent generations to seek additional land and peasant labor through state service in order to survive.[29] The tsarist regime took advantage of the situation by requiring service from votchina estates and by keeping the elite in a constant state of rivalry with one another and with newly promoted parvenues—all feverishly competing for status, positions, and scarce resources. Russian autocracy came to be supported by a more numerous but increasingly weak aristocracy who fought among themselves for the privilege of advising the tsar or commanding his armies and who never seriously contemplated resistance to the arbitrary and demanding regime.[30] In some ways, Ivan's oprichnina is a particularly striking example of this phenomenon.

Dvoriane and deti boiarskie families also multiplied at a high rate during the sixteenth century, and their sons expected positions in the militia as well as pomeste estates with peasants to support them. At first, there was plenty of land for all pomeshchiki, but during the second half of the sixteenth century, the growth in the reserves of service lands slowed down while the gentry birth rate remained very high. It became increasingly difficult to find land for each new generation of military servitors.[31] Tsar Ivan could meet only about half of the demand he faced for inhabited service lands, so the average size of a pomeste grant (and the income it produced) began to decline drastically.[32] The result was fierce competition among the gentry for survival, with the government gaining even more control over them as a result.[33] There was a rapid turnover of pomeste estates in the second half of the sixteenth century as many pomeshchiki, unable to adjust to declining income, simply dropped out of the gentry militia and were quickly replaced by new men.[34] Increasingly, pomeshchiki were also forced to provide for their landless kinsmen, which increased the pressure on their modest resources and on the peasants living on their service lands. As matters grew worse, in many cases no lands were available for younger members of gentry families until their landholding relative died.[35] For its part, the government did seek new estates for the pomeshchiki, often by massive expropriation of state lands occupied by heavily taxed but otherwise free peasants.[36] Such lands virtually disappeared in central Russia during the second half of the sixteenth century as taxes on them more than doubled and as they were increasingly and arbitrarily converted into pomeste estates.[37] Quite naturally, peasants who lived on those lands and had regarded them as their own property were extremely upset at suddenly being forced to work for a lord, especially a pomeshchik.[38]

Peasants paid dearly for the tsar's wars and to support his military servitors. Originally free agriculturalists, by the beginning of the sixteenth century many Russian peasants found themselves on newly created pomeste estates granted to gentry warriors. In addition to paying ordinary taxes, those peasants were now required to help provide resources to outfit their local pomeshchik and to maintain him in the field for several months each year. Because pomeshchiki were often not paid their annual salary by the state, they came to depend totally on the labor of their peasants in order to continue to perform military service.[39] In a subsistence farming economy such as Russia's, as such pressures increased (along with taxes), it became difficult even in reasonably good years for peasants to meet them; in years of crop failure or other disasters it was virtually impossible.[40] Ivan III introduced the first broad restriction on the peasants' right to move probably in order to keep the tax base stable and to assure that

Fig. 3 "Russian Peasants." Published in Adam Olearius, *Voyages très-curieux & tres-renommez faits en Moscovie, Tartarie et Perse* (Leide, 1719). Courtesy of Special Collections, University of Washington Libraries.

peasants completed the harvest needed to sustain their masters in the army. Starting in 1497, peasant movement was restricted to a two-week period around St. George's Day (November 26). That was a big step toward increasing social stratification and serfdom.[41] At first, however, peasants did not strenuously object to the burdens placed on them, probably because Russia prospered in the early sixteenth century and the burdens—kept at traditional levels—were not too onerous. Pomeshchiki were not allowed to interfere with their peasants' lives and instead received their rent from the government. Labor obligations for peasants on pomeste lands in the early sixteenth century may have averaged no more than one or two days a week, and many who wished to do so paid the St. George's Day exit fee and moved in search of a better life. Even though burdens on Russian peasants steadily increased, they remained free for most of the century.[42] Starting in the reign of Ivan the Terrible, however, large-scale peasant abandonment of pomeste lands in response to rapidly increasing taxes, poor harvests, famines, exploitation by lords, and the attraction of newly acquired territories to the south and east became a severe problem for the state and for the gentry—ultimately with drastic consequences for the peasants.

A principal explanation for the decline of the Russian economy in the second half of the sixteenth century centers on the peasantry whose labor was so essential to the gentry militia. As already noted, by the time of Tsar Ivan's reign there was not enough land inhabited by peasants to meet the needs of the rapidly growing warrior class. Sharp competition for land and peasant labor became the norm, and many pomeshchiki bitterly complained about the loss of income and peasants needed to sustain their military service.[43] In this context, during the time of the oprichnina Tsar Ivan began permitting pomeshchiki to control their service lands directly and to collect rent from peasants in person. Giving the gentry direct control over their lands proved to be an unmitigated disaster for the peasants, who now faced increased exploitation or outright plunder from lords desperately trying to squeeze additional revenue from their estates. Peasants came to regard the pomeshchiki as greedy parasites, and many peasants simply ran away from increasingly intolerable conditions. That, of course, placed an even greater burden on those peasants who remained on pomeste estates. Hellie correctly assessed the tsar's policy change as "one of the greatest mistakes Ivan made in his long reign."[44]

In addition to increasing exploitation at the hands of the pomeshchiki, Russian peasants faced significant price inflation and a rapid rise in military-related taxation during the second half of the sixteenth century. Taxes increased three hundred percent over the course of Ivan the Terrible's reign and grossly overburdened his subjects.[45] Such fiscal demands contributed significantly to increasing peasant flight from taxpaying communities. Because taxes were assessed collectively in each district, the remaining peasants were initially forced to pay taxes for the fugitives and for land no longer in production. Such a heavy and unrealistic burden was more than many peasants were able or willing to bear and led to even more peasant flight and a spiraling down of production, peasant income, tax revenues, and the overall economy.[46] Increasingly, any visible surplus was likely to be confiscated, so many peasants simply hid from the authorities any surplus or stopped working. Partly as a result, even though the pomeshchiki desperately needed peasant labor, the number of landless peasants (*bobyli*) increased rapidly.[47] The loss of even one peasant was a serious setback for most members of the increasingly impoverished gentry who were already being asked to make do with smaller holdings and fewer peasants. Often not paid by the government for years at a time and facing significant price inflation, many poor pomeshchiki could no longer afford to show up for military service or showed up lacking the required weapons, armor, and horses.[48] An increasing number preferred to stay at home in order to manage their fragile economies and tried to escape military service altogether. The number of pomeshchiki showing up for service began to decline in the 1560s, and that decline became a serious problem by the 1570s.[49]

An additional source of misery for the overburdened Russian peasants and others was the rising tide of bad weather, crop failures, famines, and epidemics associated with the "little ice age"—made even worse by a growing population and chronically low agricultural productivity.[50] Starting in the 1550s, unusually cold, wet weather and a series of crop failures, famines, and epidemics hit Russia. In the 1560s, some regions of the country saw serious depopulation because of crop failures and epidemics. Many people died, and many others ran away to less affected provinces or to the southern frontier.[51] By the early 1570s, famine and epidemics spread over much of Russia, and the scale of the disaster was huge. Loss of life was very high, much land was abandoned, and agricultural production declined significantly as a result. The country teetered on the brink of a severe crisis.[52] There is no doubt that Tsar Ivan's oprichnina and the devastating Crimean Tatar raid on Moscow in 1571 contributed to the problem; but since famine and plagues also devastated neighboring Lithuania at the same time,[53] it is probable that the "little ice age" was the main culprit— greatly assisted by inflation, high taxes, pomeshchik exploitation, and the Livonian War.

Russia's steep decline during the 1570s was due to the conjuncture of many factors.[54] The most striking feature as well as a major cause of the decline was the massive depopulation of Russia's heartland. That demographic disaster led to a severe crisis for both government and society.[55] In some areas (including the Moscow region), population and land under cultivation declined as much as ninety percent by the end of the decade.[56] Where did all those people go? Some of them moved north of the Volga River, but many overtaxed and disgruntled Russians headed to the southern or eastern frontier. At first, the government itself had actively sponsored colonization of newly acquired territories, and tales of the high productivity of steppe soil brought many eager settlers. Soon they were joined by a steady stream of escapees from famine, plague, war, high taxes, and exploitation by lords.[57] Less adventurous souls simply moved to nearby church, boyar, or crown lands where conditions were often much better than on pomeste estates; or they became landless peasants or sold themselves into slavery in order to pay their debts.[58] Significant numbers of desperate men became outlaws and roamed the countryside in gangs. They tended to receive some sympathy from ordinary Russians and fit the general pattern of "social bandits" described by Eric Hobsbawm.[59] Not surprisingly, the sharp rise in banditry forced the government to increase its police activities against them.[60]

Central Russia's demographic disaster also led to the rapid rise of the cossacks—large bands of social bandits and part-time mercenary soldiers who roamed the southern frontier. (They will be discussed in Chapter 5.) The overall impact of the developing crisis was enormous. Many peasants who had remained on the land were ruined economically, which led to even more peasant flight.[61] Most of the already financially distressed pomeshchiki lost peasants, and, at least in the Moscow district, the pomeste-based economic system collapsed completely.[62] A large number of deti boiarskie were utterly ruined and were no longer able to show up for military service. The morale and fighting ability of the tsar's cavalry force declined seriously, and the crisis threatened the very existence of the entire gentry militia system.[63] Tax revenues shrank precipitously just as the tsar came under increasing pressure to rescue the gentry. Unable to offer significant amounts of money or land with peasants, the beleaguered government did try to aid impoverished pomeshchiki with numerous small remedies, including tax concessions.[64] Such measures, however, failed to halt the decline of the militiamen. Many of them ended up with no peasants and no income. Some desperate pomeshchiki simply gave up and headed to the frontier, which still offered the prospect of survival either in low-status military service or among the cossacks; others instead took the drastic step of selling themselves as elite military slaves to magnates and rich dvoriane.[65]

Slavery had a long history in Russia. In the sixteenth century about ten percent of the population were slaves. Most were household lackeys, but about five percent of agricultural workers were also slaves.[66] The various forms of slavery in Russia declined during the first half of the century but revived as the country's economy and society fell into crisis during Ivan the Terrible's reign.[67] About one percent of the population sold itself into slavery in any given year; but in famine years that number increased to five or even ten percent.[68] During the perilous late sixteenth century, Russian peasants increasingly resorted to selling themselves as slaves in order to survive the declining agricultural economy and to escape the crushing burden of taxes. Vast numbers of peasants sold themselves into slavery during the demographic disaster and the famines of the 1570s and 1580s. They became servants, lackeys, farmers, and even military slaves of the elite. Meanwhile, the loss of their labor contributed significantly to the impoverishment of the pomeshchiki while the loss of their taxes contributed to the state's growing fiscal problems. During the late sixteenth century, all too many impoverished townsmen also sold themselves into slavery, contributing to the decline of both the economy and the tsar's tax receipts.[69] During the same period, large numbers of distressed pomeshchiki, usually to repay debts, sold themselves as elite military slaves—who had much higher status than agricultural slaves or household lackeys, and who often received privileges, land, and other assistance from their owners.[70]

The enslavement of militiamen was, understandably, officially discouraged. Starting in the 1550s, Ivan the Terrible attempted to prohibit his petty gentry from selling themselves into slavery; but self-sale by impoverished warriors remained a serious problem until the late seventeenth century.[71] Tsar Ivan's own policies inadvertently boosted the enslavement of poor pomeshchiki. His 1556 decree, which required holders of pomeste and votchina estates to bring additional soldiers with them on campaigns, resulted in a significant number of combat slaves being added to the gentry militia. Especially prized were competent warriors, including impoverished deti boiarskie.[72] A down-and-out pomeshchik or the son of a poor syn boiarskii who reached age fifteen could now sell himself into slavery and remain in military service as a well-equipped and well-fed retainer of some prosperous magnate or *dvorianin* (singular form of *dvoriane*). The price for such an elite slave was five times higher than for an agricultural or household slave.[73] As the tsar's government became increasingly concerned about the number of impoverished militiamen selling themselves or being forced into slavery, several measures were taken to stop it—including restricting the petty gentry's access to credit and attempting to prevent the abuse of slavery laws (and ruined pomeshchiki) by unscrupulous magnates.[74] Those measure, however, failed to halt the practice.

There are varying estimates of the number and duties of military slaves serving in the gentry militia. Aleksandr Zimin believed that by the late 1550s up to two-thirds of the entire militia force were slaves;[75] but that figure is too high.[76] Richard Hellie studied Russian slavery carefully and distinguished between elite combat slaves who fought on horseback alongside their owners and "baggage train" slaves who took care of the militiamen's horses and supplies but did not fight.[77] The latter group probably consisted mostly of self-sold peasants whose price was far lower than that of combat slaves.[78] Some scholars incorrectly regarded all military slaves as baggage train slaves and denied that any were combatants. In fact, many military slaves were not only combat slaves but were also "armed better than their owners."[79] By the late 1570s, for example, many combat slaves carried harquebuses.[80] Hellie estimated that in the 1550s, almost every militiaman had a slave with him while on duty. Obviously, the impoverishment of the pomeshchiki by the 1570s changed the picture somewhat. In some devastated regions, only twenty percent of the gentry were still able to appear for service with mounted slaves. Overall, by the late 1570s the percentage of militiamen owning any kind of slave had slipped to about seventy percent. Of those slave owners, almost all had a baggage train slave but only about half still had a combat slave. That means that in the late sixteenth century approximately one fourth of the entire gentry militia force consisted of combat slaves.[81] Many of them were excellent, courageous soldiers.[82] Hellie estimated that the total number of military slaves (baggage train and combat) by the beginning of the seventeenth century was about twenty-five thousand. In other words, there were just about as many slaves as militiamen in the tsar's army.[83]

Toward the end of the sixteenth century, the many different forms of Russian slavery declined to two basic types: hereditary slavery and "limited service contract slavery" (*kabal'noe kholopstvo*). It was limited service contract slavery that became increasingly popular among the petty gentry as a survival tool during hard times—at least in part because it appeared to be slavery for only one year in return for a loan. Distressed peasants and townsmen also gravitated toward contract slavery as a temporary tax dodge. Failure to repay the loan at the end of the year, however, resulted in default and doomed the contract slave (and his offspring) to perpetual, hereditary slavery.[84] In spite of that ominous prospect, Russia's economic and social crisis pushed more and more unfortunate deti boiarskie, peasants, and townsmen to take the drastic step of becoming contract slaves. In fact, so many of them sold themselves into slavery that, starting in the 1580s, slave prices dropped and remained depressed right into the Time of Trouble.[85] Because slave ownership carried high status in early modern Russia, rich magnates took advantage of the situation and glutted themselves on relatively cheap slaves—especially during the reign of Ivan the Terrible's son, Tsar Fedor (r. 1584–98).[86] The government became so alarmed at the loss of militiamen and taxpayers to slavery, however, that it began to contemplate drastic steps to stop the hemorrhage.[87]

Russian towns, echoing the mounting problems of peasants and pomeshchiki, also suffered a catastrophic decline in the late sixteenth century. During the first half of the century, the towns had grown rapidly along with a general rise in Russia's internal trade and manufacturing. The number of towns also grew— from about one hundred sixty in 1500 to about two hundred thirty by 1600.[88] Russia's urban population peaked at about two percent of the overall population in the mid-sixteenth century, and they were heavily taxed. Ordinary townspeople lived in a town's *posad,* the taxpaying suburb spreading out from the walls of the *gorod* (inner fortress). The posad included dwellings, the marketplace, warehouses, bakeries, and shops where merchants, traders, craftsmen, artisan manufacturers, apprentices, and laborers lived and worked. During the reign of Ivan the Terrible, Russian towns suffered just as much as the countryside from war, taxes, famine, plagues, Tatar raids, and the erratic policies of the tsar. Trade declined catastrophically, and a number of towns disintegrated.[89] Famine struck several Russian towns in the 1560s, and by the early 1570s epidemics and famine combined to depopulate many more.[90] The loss of life was staggering, but the sharp population decline was also because many townspeople simply ran away to avoid natural disasters and high taxes. Because taxes were assessed collectively in each posad, the remaining townspeople were forced to pay taxes even for those who had fled. That grossly overburdened the urban economy, which declined sharply as tax rates increased. The number of urban poor also increased dramatically as more and more financially distressed townsmen disappeared from the posad tax rolls.[91] Overall, there was a huge decline in the number of urban taxpayers by the 1580s (up to ninety percent in some towns).[92] Many townspeople moved to nearby nontaxed lands; others sold themselves into slavery or headed to the southern frontier.[93]

With such a drastic decline in the number of peasant and urban taxpayers, revenues shrank dramatically and the tsar's treasury suffered huge shortfalls.[94] Sharp price inflation in the 1570s and 1580s made matters worse for everyone.[95] The fiscal crisis became so acute and the decline in the size and readiness of the gentry militia so steep that Tsar Ivan could no longer afford to fight the Livonian War, which finally ended in 1583 on terms unfavorable to Russia.[96] In spite of the end of the war and the death of the "terrible" tsar in 1584, however, the crisis deepened in many parts of the country. As discussed in Chapter 1, by the 1590s, a few peripheral areas recovered somewhat, but much of Russia— especially the heartland—remained in deep crisis. The economic "depression" continued to reduce state revenue and the size of the tsar's army, and an unrealistic tax policy continued to hinder any possible recovery of either the rural or the urban economy.[97] That dangerous situation eventually forced Tsar Ivan's successor to make dramatic policy changes. During the reign of Ivan's mentally retarded son, Fedor, the new tsar's brother-in-law, Boris Godunov, became the de facto ruler of Russia and worked energetically to shore up the gentry militia and state income.[98] His heavy-handed policies failed to resolve the crisis, however, and on the eve of the Time of Troubles actually made things much worse.

4

Boris Godunov (1552–1605) stands out as one of the most famous or infamous characters of early modern Russian history. His personality, policies, and controversial political career have long fascinated people. More than a dozen biographies of him have been written—often presenting radically different interpretations and frequently based on myth or propaganda. He has been portrayed as a brilliant statesman and one of Russia's first tragic heroes; more often, he has been described as an evil tyrant whose ambition and crimes were largely responsible for the Time of Troubles.[1] In fact, Godunov came to dominate Russia at an unfortunate time. As Tsar Fedor's regent, he faced the thankless task of trying to cope with the country's developing crisis. The harsh policies he came up with were controversial and failed to solve Russia's problems; instead, they made matters worse and helped ruin the reputation of the tsar's ruthless brother-in-law. A careful review of Godunov's early career and policies as regent will help us move beyond distorted interpretations of the man and better understand his role in preparing Russia for its first civil war.

Boris Godunov's enemies rather unfairly accused him of being low-born. In fact, Boris's ancestors had been boyars at the Muscovite court in the fourteenth century.[2] Family fortunes declined over the years, however; Boris's father was a mere provincial pomeshchik when his son was born in 1552. It was Boris's uncle, Dmitrii Godunov, who helped establish his nephew's career after the boy's father died prematurely. Dmitrii Godunov joined Ivan the Terrible's oprichnina guard as soon as it was formed and quickly became one of Ivan's courtiers. He also brought his family to the oprichnina court. As a result, Boris Godunov grew up in the tsar's palace, and his sister Irina became the playmate of Tsar Ivan's mentally retarded son, Fedor. Maliuta Skuratov, then the all-powerful oprichnina boss, formed an alliance with Dmitrii Godunov and arranged for his daughter Mariia to marry Boris, who was then serving as a member of the oprichnina guard. That marriage made the young Godunov the son-in-law of the most hated and feared man in Russia.[3] When Tsar Ivan abolished the oprichnina, surviving members of its elite became members of the tsar's personal "court"—

including the Godunovs. Dmitrii Godunov was quickly promoted to the rank of okolnichii, and Ivan even allowed Boris's sister to marry Tsarevich Fedor. The tsar came to regard Boris as one of his own sons and promoted him to the rank of boyar by 1581.[4] Nonetheless, as long as Ivan's eldest son and heir, Ivan Ivanovich, lived, Boris could only hope to be a relatively minor courtier. When the tsar accidentally killed Ivan Ivanovich in the fall of 1581, however, that tragic event opened up a path to power for Boris Godunov, the brother-in-law of Ivan's new heir.[5]

Tsar Ivan knew perfectly well that Fedor could not rule on his own; before his own death in 1584, he set up a council of regents to govern in his son's name. Ivan named as regents two leading boyars: Fedor's uncle, Nikita Romanovich Zakharin-Iurev (head of the Romanov clan), and Prince Ivan F. Mstislavskii (Fedor's second cousin and the senior member of the boyar council); he also named two leading members of his own court: a premier prince of the blood, the popular and heroic Prince Ivan Petrovich Shuiskii (a Suzdal prince who, like the tsar, claimed descent from Aleksandr Nevskii), and Fedor's brother-in-law, Boris Godunov.[6] When Fedor was crowned, Boris carried the tsar's scepter in the procession; Boris's uncle Dmitrii carried one of Fedor's crowns. On the day of the coronation, Boris was named *koniushii boiarin* (master of the horse or equerry)—a title that immediately identified him as the most powerful member of the boyar council.[7] In the early years of Tsar Fedor's reign there occurred a series of sharp conflicts within the ruling elite; in those struggles for power, Boris Godunov triumphed over all his enemies. Nonetheless, the conflict was so bitter that some contemporary observers predicted it would lead to civil war.[8]

At the outset of Tsar Fedor's reign, Boris Godunov and other regents moved against a threat emanating from the court faction supporting Ivan the Terrible's youngest son, Dmitrii—the child of Ivan's sixth and last wife, Mariia Nagaia. The Nagoi clan and its supporters were agitating to have little Dmitrii (born in 1582) recognized as the heir apparent of the incapable Fedor, and they may even have been making plans to thrust Dmitrii onto the throne.[9] Just to be safe, the regents ordered the arrest of Tsaritsa Mariia's uncle, the formerly powerful oprichnik and court leader, Afanasii F. Nagoi, and exiled him to Iaroslavl.[10] Mariia, her brothers, and little Dmitrii were then unceremoniously shipped off to Dmitrii's inheritance, the small principality of Uglich, which was far from Moscow.[11] At about the same time, Dmitrii's guardian and godfather, the notorious former oprichnik Bogdan Belskii (Tsar Ivan's last favorite and a close associate of Afanasii Nagoi), made a desperate bid for power in Dmitrii's name, but he was easily forestalled by the regents and temporarily exiled from the capital.[12]

Trouble soon developed within the council of regents itself. Prince Ivan Mstislavskii made a bid for power in 1585. He was stopped by the other regents, especially Boris Godunov and Nikita Romanovich, and was forced to become a monk—which in Russia was an irreversible step. Mstislavskii's son-in-law, Simeon Bekbulatovich (Tsar Ivan's one-time puppet ruler of Russia), was deprived of his "independent" principality and exiled; he blamed Godunov personally for his misfortune. Mstislavskii's son, Fedor, was not allowed to marry but was allowed to inherit his father's estates as well as his position as senior member of the boyar council.[13] Real power, however, continued to rest in the hands of the remaining three regents. Out of this episode grew a tacit alliance between the Godunovs and the Romanovs to protect their families' interests. When old Nikita Romanovich died he may even have entrusted care of his children to his "ally" Boris.[14] Soon thereafter, the two remaining regents fought it out. Ivan Petrovich Shuiskii, who regarded himself as the most high-born prince in Russia, deeply resented the power of the "low-born" Boris Godunov and intrigued against him. In 1586, Shuiskii took the lead in staging an anti-Godunov riot in Moscow and organized a powerful group of boyars, the metropolitan, and some Moscow merchants who boldly demanded that Tsar Fedor divorce the "barren" Irina. In this matter, however, Shuiskii grossly miscalculated. Fedor loved his wife, refused to divorce her, and authorized Boris to suppress the opposition. Godunov struck hard at his enemies. He had several merchants executed and arranged for the metropolitan to be dethroned, replacing him with Boris's own candidate, his friend Iov.[15] Ivan Petrovich Shuiskii and his son Andrei were formally disgraced, had their property confiscated, and were exiled from Moscow. Aged Prince Ivan Shuiskii was forced to become a monk and kept under heavy guard.[16] Also temporarily banished from the capital were Prince Vasilii Ivanovich Shuiskii and his three younger brothers—Dmitrii, Aleksandr, and Ivan. Many scholars have assumed that they were also sons of Ivan Petrovich Shuiskii.[17] It is far more likely, however, that Vasilii and his brothers were sons of Ivan Petrovich's cousin, Prince Ivan Andreevich Shuiskii (d. 1573).[18] With the downfall of Ivan Petrovich and his son Andrei, Vasilii Shuiskii emerged as the senior member of the temporarily eclipsed clan.

Boris Godunov was now Tsar Fedor's sole regent and the most powerful man in Russia.[19] By 1588, he openly accused the Shuiskii and Nagoi clans of making common cause in a conspiracy against him, and he may have been right.[20] A general purge of Godunov's enemies was launched, with the tsar's brother-in-law using techniques reminiscent of Ivan the Terrible's oprichnina.[21] Ivan Petrovich Shuiskii (d. 1588) and his son Andrei (d. 1589) both died while in confinement, probably murdered quietly on Godunov's orders.[22] Many people at the time blamed Boris for those very convenient deaths. Such suspicions, coupled with Godunov's active persecution of several other opponents (including Fedor Sheremetev, Ivan Kriuk-Kolychev, and members of the Morozov, Vorotynskii, Golitsyn, Kurakin, and Buturlin clans), seriously hurt the regent's reputation. Any more mysterious deaths of his enemies would automatically be blamed on Boris by many nobles.[23] The Nagoi clan, sensing Godunov's temporary vulnerability, began circulating rumors that he was planning to murder Tsarevich Dmitrii in Uglich. In response, the regent ordered the arrest of the disgraced Afanasii Nagoi's son, increased security around members of the Nagoi clan already in exile, and had the church prohibit priests from mentioning the "illegitimate" tsarevich during services (in Orthodox canon law, the child of a man's fourth marriage, let alone his sixth, was not considered to be legitimate).[24] Godunov did not, however, make any immediate move against Dmitrii, although he may have encouraged the spread of rumors about the tsarevich as bloodthirsty and cruel in order to dampen any potential enthusiasm for the little boy.[25] In fact, just when many feared that the regent would unleash a new oprichnina, he managed to defeat all his rivals and then relaxed the pressure on them.[26] And why not? As the unchallenged ruler of his brother-in-law's realm, Godunov could now afford to try to repair his reputation among the elite by appearing as a clement prince.

Another reason for Godunov to relax the political struggle was the serious, multidimensional crisis descending on Russia at that time. In addition to the cascading effects of the demographic disaster, the "little ice age" produced increasingly severe weather and a terrible famine in 1588. Partly as a result, there was a very sharp increase in prices in the period 1589–91. Hunger and the high cost of food pushed more and more desperate peasants and townsmen to depart for the southern frontier, to sell themselves as slaves, or to turn to begging or banditry. That in turn forced many more impoverished pomeshchiki to abandon their estates either to become slaves or to strike out for the frontier.[27] On top of everything else, during the 1580s taxes more than doubled on the tsar's already overburdened subjects, further contributing to the depopulation of villages and towns. Many blamed Boris Godunov personally for Russia's intolerable taxes, regarding him as "an oppressor of the entire country."[28] In spite of steep tax increases, however, state revenues continued to shrink, resulting in a serious fiscal crisis—made much worse by the government's ambitious construction projects and relentless efforts to expand the state to the south. By the late 1580s, the tsar's treasury had been hit hard and the number and quality of gentry militia units had declined sharply. The crisis deepened going into the 1590s.[29] Throughout this period, there were a number of minor outbreaks of rural and urban violence which had to be suppressed, and periodic military action was also required to stop roving gangs of bandits.[30] Moscow itself witnessed several incidents of unrest caused by high taxes, the cost of food, and the machinations of Godunov's political opponents. Such tensions, added to a genuine fear of foreign invasion, caused the regent to place Moscow on military alert in the spring of 1591. Under such circumstances, Godunov may have felt that, temporarily at least, he could not afford to struggle openly with any remaining opponents.[31]

Just about the time Godunov placed Moscow on military alert, disturbing news arrived from Uglich. In May, 1591, Tsarevich Dmitrii was reported to be dead. The Nagoi clan openly accused Godunov's hand-picked Uglich administrator of murder and incited a riot, during which Godunov's agent and his young son were lynched, offices and homes of certain officials hated by the Nagoi clan were plundered, and numerous people were terrorized. Moscow immediately responded by sending a detachment of streltsy to restore order in Uglich and a commission of inquiry to find out what had actually happened. The commission was headed by Prince Vasilii Ivanovich Shuiskii, recently returned from exile and now back in the boyar council. Choosing an able adversary of the unpopular Godunov to head the investigation was done, at least in part, to assure that the commission's findings would not be dismissed as a cover-up of the notorious regent's alleged crimes.[32] On the basis of testimony from several eyewitnesses, the commission concluded that Dmitrii had accidentally slit his own throat during an epileptic seizure that came on while he was playing with a knife. The commission further determined that members of the Nagoi clan were responsible for inciting the riots and lynchings, planting evidence against Godunov, and even torturing individuals in order to force them to say that the tsarevich had been murdered.[33] Dmitrii was hastily buried without fanfare in Uglich. Neither Tsar Fedor nor the head of the Russian Orthodox Church, Patriarch Iov (Russia's first patriarch, elevated in 1589), attended the funeral service or even bothered to visit the grave of the illegitimate tsarevich who was believed to have technically committed the sin of suicide.[34] Two days after Dmitrii was buried, a terrible fire broke out in Moscow, leaving thousands of people homeless. Agents of the Nagoi clan, trying to take advantage of tensions in Moscow and the unpopularity of Boris Godunov, spread rumors that the regent had ordered the capital set on fire in order to distract the tsar and others from the murder of Dmitrii. When the arsonists were caught, however, they confessed (under torture) that the Nagoi clan had put them up to it.[35] On the basis of an investigation into the Moscow fire and the Uglich commission's report, Patriarch Iov and leading boyars convinced Tsar Fedor to order the arrest of the entire Nagoi clan. Tsaritsa Mariia was immediately forced to become the nun Marfa, and she and her relatives were held in close confinement in exile.[36] At this time the Uglich rioters were also punished. Many of them were exiled to Pelym in Siberia where they continued to circulate the story that Boris Godunov was responsible for Dmitrii's death.[37] Such stories had little immediate effect, however. Although many people suspected that the regent was guilty, there was no outburst of sympathy for the dead tsarevich or the fallen Nagoi clan. Instead, Dmitrii was quickly forgotten as Boris Godunov consolidated his power.[38]

It was only after Tsar Fedor died without an heir in 1598, triggering a dynastic crisis, that people recalled the Uglich tragedy. Boris Godunov's rivals for the crown quickly revived the rumor that he had been responsible for killing Tsarevich Dmitrii in order to clear a path to the throne for himself, and many people were quite willing to credit the rumor.[39] Stories also circulated again about Godunov causing the Moscow fire in 1591 and even about him inviting the Crimean Tatars to invade Russia that year in order to distract attention from his crime in Uglich.[40] The regent, of course, managed to overcome his enemies' efforts to deny him the throne, but many Russians continued to believe that he had been responsible for Dmitrii's death. Tsar Boris's reputation suffered even more when a "resurrected" Tsarevich Dmitrii appeared in Poland-Lithuania in 1603, claiming to have miraculously escaped from Godunov's henchmen in 1591. When the pretender Dmitrii then launched an invasion of Russia to overthrow the "usurper" Boris Godunov and even managed to become tsar in 1605, that seemed to prove to many observers that Tsar Boris must have been guilty as charged of attempted assassination in 1591. From then on, Godunov's reputation was permanently ruined. The myths and propaganda about him as a usurper grew to include, in addition to the attempted murder of Dmitrii, the far-fetched notion that he had killed Tsar Fedor.[41] When Tsar Dmitrii was himself assassinated in 1606 and Vasilii Shuiskii seized power, the new ruler desperately needed to "prove" that the real Dmitrii had died in 1591 and that the dead tsar had been an impostor, so he arranged to elevate Tsarevich Dmitrii of Uglich to sainthood as a "martyr" at the hands of the evil Boris Godunov—forever locking into official Russian government and church views the fixed idea of Godunov as the murderer of little Dmitrii.[42] Contemporaries who lived through Russia's first civil war often recalled the Uglich tragedy, and many of them pointed to Godunov's assassination of the tsarevich as one of the most important causes of the Time of Troubles.[43] Others regarded the horrors of the Troubles as nothing less than God's punishment of Russia for Godunov's sins.[44] As Sergei Platonov observed, in a very real sense the tragedy of both Boris

Godunov and Russia began with the death of the tsarevich in 1591.[45] Stories about Uglich became a powerful psychological factor in the civil war.[46]

For many generations following the Time of Troubles, the image of an evil Boris Godunov continued to grow, and it strongly influenced early scholarship on the subject. Most nineteenth-century historians tended to accept at face value the propaganda and myths about him.[47] Careful study of the relevant documents in the early twentieth century finally led historians such as Platonov to argue strongly against the traditional, negative interpretation of Tsar Boris.[48] Among other things, Platonov and others pointed out that the story of the murder of the tsarevich was not put forward by anyone actually present at the time of his death.[49] Moreover, Dmitrii's death came at a very bad time for Boris Godunov and was undesirable and dangerous to him.[50]

Curiously enough, attempts have been made in the late twentieth century, by Aleksandr Zimin and Maureen Perrie, to return to the earlier view of Godunov as the person responsible for the death of the tsarevich.[51] Zimin and Perrie have argued that the Uglich commission report covered up Godunov's crimes. Their indictment of the regent, however, is based only on one controversial English source and some seventeenth-century chronicles and tales that had been strongly influenced by anti-Godunov propaganda generated during the Time of Troubles (especially the tendentious Romanov-era "New Chronicle").[52] In addition, in her effort to explain why Jerome Horsey's colorful account of Boris's crime should be preferred to the Uglich commission report and scholarly interpretations that exonerate Godunov, Perrie conveniently ignored the implications of Horsey's extremely close relationship to the Nagoi clan and his personal grudge against the regent for having expelled him from Russia in 1589. Other scholars regard Horsey as an untrustworthy source and little more than an apologist for the Nagoi clan.[53] Curiously, Perrie also took the Uglich commission to task for not including "several important witnesses, including Tsaritsa Mariya herself."[54] In fact, the tsaritsa was not a witness to her son's death, but eyewitnesses were interrogated by the commission in her intimidating presence. The tsaritsa herself also made several statements at the time that seemed to support the commission's judgment about how the tsarevich died.[55] Finally, Perrie argued that Boris Godunov had reason to get rid of Dmitrii in 1591 because the boy was the "heir presumptive" to Tsar Fedor.[56] Her statement that Dmitrii would have become tsar if Fedor died childless is not shared by many other scholars, however. Instead, historians often point out that Boris's sister, Tsaritsa Irina, had a much stronger claim to the throne than did the illegitimate tsarevich whose funeral was ignored by Tsar Fedor.[57] All things considered, it is highly probable that Boris Godunov did not order the death of Dmitrii. Instead, the Uglich affair was most likely part of a desperate Nagoi plot to get rid of the regent.[58]

During the 1590s, Boris Godunov faced no serious opposition from his rivals; he remained unchallenged until the death of Tsar Fedor. Boris's alliance with the Romanovs remained intact, and he helped advance the career of Nikita's eldest son, Fedor Nikitch Romanov, the new head of the Romanov clan.[59] At the same time, Godunov made peace with the Shuiskii family. Dmitrii Shuiskii was promoted to the rank of boyar in 1591, and Vasilii Shuiskii and his brothers emerged as powerful and fairly cooperative members of Tsar Fedor's boyar council.[60] Calm was at least temporarily restored at court, and Boris Godunov ran the government so efficiently that even many of his critics praised the regent's excellent administrative skills.[61] Those skills were certainly put to the test by Russia's deepening crisis. The continuing disappearance of urban and rural taxpayers, coupled with the obvious failure of Godunov's heavy taxes either to resolve the state's fiscal problems or to shore up the declining militia, eventually forced the regent to take drastic action that was guaranteed to make him even more unpopular in the eyes of the Russian people. He made plans to restrict the mobility of the shrinking taxpaying population.[62]

The development of serfdom is one of the most controversial topics in Russian history, but there is no doubt that it was due to state action in response to the crisis of the late sixteenth century.[63] Sometime during the 1580s, the government began occasionally issuing decrees temporarily suspending the peasants' right of departure in certain regions. Scholars have long assumed that the introduction of such "forbidden years" (suspension of the St. George's Day privilege) began in the final years of the reign of Ivan the Terrible.[64] Ruslan Skrynnikov, however, has forcefully challenged that idea, arguing that "forbidden years" began only under Tsar Fedor and were the direct responsibility of Boris Godunov.[65] After some experimentation, in 1592 the St. George's Day privilege was finally suspended for all peasants in Russia, who were "temporarily" bound to the land where they had been registered as taxpayers. That drastic step effectively enserfed millions of peasants, many of whom blamed Boris Godunov for their fate.[66] Although Marxist scholars have long exaggerated and distorted the impact of the government's action, the "forbidden years" certainly did provoke some minor peasant unrest.[67] Far more serious, the government's harsh new policy caused many peasants to run away from already sparsely populated villages, and since the children of serfs had not yet been tied to the land and could still legally move, many of them also departed. The resulting depopulation, on top of the demographic disaster of the previous two decades, became an extremely serious problem for the state and for the gentry.[68] The government initially established a five-year time limit for the recovery of runaway peasants, after which the fugitives became free. That was probably done to reduce the workload of bureaucrats handling disputes over ownership of peasants. Such a policy also definitely favored rich magnates who could afford to search for runaways. Petty pomeshchiki, by contrast, favored no time limit for the recovery of peasants, but they had to wait until 1649 to gain that privilege.[69]

There are numerous theories about exactly what drove the Russian government to take the drastic step of enserfing the bulk of the population. Most scholars agree that a primary motivation was concern about the security of the realm in light of the decline of the gentry militia.[70] Richard Hellie maintained that the government was reacting to pressure from militiamen anxious to retain (or regain) their peasants, and that Boris Godunov responded favorably to their requests to bind the peasants in order to gain gentry support for his quest for the throne.[71] Ruslan Skrynnikov also acknowledged gentry pressure on the government but rejected Hellie's ideas about Godunov's primary motive. Instead, he argued that the regent was most anxious to solve the immediate fiscal problem of declining state revenue. Skrynnikov noted, for example, that gentry petitions themselves harped on the danger to the tax base posed by runaway peasants.[72] Other scholars agree that the fiscal crisis was a major motivation for enserfing the peasants.[73] Hellie, who acknowledged that the concerns of the pomeshchiki were not always uppermost in the government's mind, nonetheless rejected emphatically the idea that the peasants were enserfed "to aid the fisc," arguing that the government was basically indifferent to where peasants lived since they could be taxed anywhere.[74] That is not true, however. Peasants could and did move to nontaxed lands, became slaves, and fled to the southern frontier; tax revenues had been shrinking for years because of the steady decline in the number of taxpayers. Moreover, the move to enserf the peasants came in the midst of other initiatives by the regent that were specifically designed to shore up the tax base.[75]

At about the same time Boris Godunov enserfed the peasants, he also took steps to bind the taxpaying population of Russian towns. His goal was to rebuild the tax base of depopulated towns and to build up the taxpaying population in new towns being constructed on the southern frontier.[76] In addition to prohibiting the movement of townspeople away from taxpaying districts, Godunov launched investigations in order to recover former townsmen from lay and clerical estates and to force virtually all persons involved in trade and manufacturing onto posad tax rolls. That greatly angered those lords who, as a result, lost profits and valuable labor, and it undermined elite support for the regent.[77] Godunov's policy also greatly angered many townsmen, both long-term residents and recent conscripts who were new to the posad tax rolls and the occasional labor duties demanded of townsmen by the state.[78] The regent's decision to place lower status military servitors (*sluzhilie liudi po priboru*) such as streltsy, gatekeepers, fortification specialists, and artillerymen on the urban tax rolls at this time was a particularly drastic step. Those formerly somewhat privileged men were extremely displeased to find themselves, in effect, enserfed.[79] Their morale and fighting spirit suffered badly as a result. In fact, their sudden loss of status made them begin to think more and more like other heavily taxed townsmen; during the civil war those two groups often acted together in support of the rebel cause. On the other hand, Godunov's drastic move undoubtedly pleased the beleaguered gentry, whose superior status to taxpaying low status military servitors was thereby enhanced. Additional tax concessions to the gentry at this time also served to underline that status distinction.[80] In similar fashion, Godunov's generosity to Russia's leading merchants, the *gosti*, prompted by a sincere desire to restore the economy, served to widen the gulf between elite merchants and ordinary, heavily taxed townsmen. In addition to increasing the stratification of Russian society, such favoritism on the part of the regent helped lead to increasing plebeian resentment of the privileged gosti—resentment that was periodically displayed during the civil war.[81]

Because of the severe economic crisis of the late sixteenth century, there was a significant rise in the number of peasants, townsmen, and ruined pomeshchiki who sold themselves as contract slaves.[82] Ominously, increasingly large numbers of them were unable to repay their loans after a year and were, as a result, converted into permanent, hereditary slaves. That so alarmed the government that it finally took dramatic steps to halt the resulting loss of taxpayers and warriors. In 1597, a new slave law was issued that changed contract slavery completely. From then on, a contract slave was forbidden to repay his loan and was thereby legally converted from a slave for a year into a slave for life. Immediately following the death of his owner, however, that same slave was to be set free and returned to the tax rolls.[83] The new law instantly reduced many marginally employed artisans and craftsmen to slavery.[84] As intended, it also slowed down the disturbing practice of distressed pomeshchiki surviving a bad year by selling themselves as military slaves. Those former deti boiarskie who were unfortunate enough to be serving as contract slaves in 1597, however, suddenly found themselves forced to remain slaves for life.[85] Boris Godunov had chosen to sacrifice the interests of ruined pomeshchiki and other contract slaves in pursuit of fiscal stability and military security (and possibly to please slave-hungry magnates). When one recalls that there were significant numbers of former pomeshchiki among the thousands of military slaves serving in Russia at the end of the sixteenth century, the law of 1597 seems just as drastic and potentially dangerous as the "enserfment" of low status military servitors had been in 1592. Military slaves, formerly a somewhat privileged group, now found themselves trapped forever in low status. It should be no surprise, therefore, that they became increasingly unreliable soldiers—a development that played an important role in Russia's first civil war.[86]

Collectively, all the harsh, enserfing measures taken by the Russian government at the end of the sixteenth century failed to end Russia's fiscal and gentry militia crises. As Richard Hellie observed, those measures did, however, help produce a highly stratified, near-caste society.[87] Serfdom, for example, increased the status of the gentry cavalry force who emerged as something like a warrior caste. Boris Godunov, probably in response to gentry pressure, took measures to limit access to the ranks of the gentry solely to the heirs of existing pomeshchiki. In theory, at least, no longer would the children of slaves, peasants, or the clergy be allowed into the warrior caste. In Russia's very status-conscious society, such a measure no doubt pleased the pomeshchiki almost as much as serfdom did.[88] Autocracy itself provided some legitimization for the increasing stratification of Russian society;[89] however, it did not stop some of the tsar's subjects from grumbling about being perpetually stuck in their home town or village and in their inherited rank or status. Even more galling to many Russians, in order to overcome their own economic problems, the gentry quickly increased the labor obligations on their newly enserfed peasants.[90] As a direct result, there were some minor peasant disturbances in the decade before the Time of Troubles. Though often portrayed as outbreaks of social revolution leading up to the "peasant war," those incidents were actually just isolated protests by desperate, overburdened peasants during hard times.[91] Many more Russians registered their protests by simply running away—either hiding out, joining bandit gangs, or heading to the frontier. Such flight was both a symptom of Russia's continuing crisis and a further cause of the downward spiral of the economy.[92]

The draconian measures of Boris Godunov helped to ossify Russia's economy as well as its society.[93] As noted in Chapter 1, in spite of claims to the contrary, Russia did not "recover" in the 1590s. Instead, its crisis continued to deepen, leading to even more empty villages and vacant land in much of central Russia. In many hard-hit areas, there was a reversion to a natural economy and a sharp decline in market demand; that, in turn, depressed the economies of already depopulated and overtaxed towns. Hit by lost markets and increasing taxation, most towns continued to see their taxpaying population shrink; many, in fact, became virtual ghost towns by the end of the century.[94] Meanwhile, the potent combination of sharply increased labor demands on serfs, growing taxation, and lack of innovation in agriculture acted as a powerful brake on any possible recovery of Russia's economy. Instead, as many more peasants abandoned the tax rolls, huge amounts of land continued to fall out of production, and the agricultural economy, like the urban economy, remained in steep decline right into the Time of Troubles.[95] Among other things, that meant the government faced an increasingly critical shortage of land with peasants to distribute to already hard-pressed pomeshchiki and their sons. That, in turn, deepened the developing crisis within the gentry militia, one of the main preconditions of the civil war.[96] Russia's severe economic problems also sharply reduced already declining state revenues, and the fiscal crisis continued to worsen right into the Time of Troubles. All things considered, Boris Godunov's tax policy and the drastic step of effectively enserfing most of the tsars' subjects not only failed to solve Russia's problems but greatly aggravated the situation and helped prepare the country for civil war.[97]

Enserfment has, of course, long been regarded as one of the most significant causes of the Time of Troubles.[98] In fact, it was an article of faith among Soviet historians that serfdom was the main cause of the "First Peasant War."[99] Because of the collapse of the Marxist interpretation of the period as a social revolution against serfdom, however, the actual relationship of enserfment to the Troubles needs to be carefully reexamined. Noting the vertical rather than horizontal split in Russian society produced by the Time of Troubles, Richard Hellie expressed some healthy uncertainty about the connection between enserfment and such things as the "Bolotnikov rebellion."[100] At the same time, however, it should be remembered that even though Russia's first civil war was definitely not a struggle of peasants against serfdom, enserfment itself was a product of the same crisis that helped to produce the Time of Troubles and the civil war. Enserfment was, in fact, such a drastic response to that crisis that it helped deepen and prolong it, thereby hastening the advent of the Troubles.

Ruslan Skrynnikov, although a strong critic of the "peasant war" model of the period, still regarded the social breakdown produced by enserfment of the peasants as an important precondition of the civil war. He also expressed doubt that any genuine popular movement in Russia was possible without peasant participation.[101] In a very general sense, Skrynnikov was correct. (He would actually have been on stronger ground had he focused on townsmen and lower status military servitors, the enserfment of whom may well help to explain their tendency to support the rebel cause during the civil war.) Obviously, the misery produced by the Russian empire's hunger for taxes even as its economy slipped into severe decline made many people angry, and it is no exaggeration to state that by the end of the sixteenth century, millions of Russian peasants found themselves reduced to virtual slavery.[102] Although the civil war did not see much peasant participation and the abolition of serfdom was never put forward as a rebel goal, enserfment did contribute significantly to the further decline of the Russian economy, and peasant flight from serfdom deprived the gentry of much of its labor force and income. That, in turn, contributed directly to the rising discontent of the gentry and the deepening of the destabilizing gentry militia crisis. In addition, many runaway peasants who flocked to the frontier joined the ranks of hard-pressed military servicemen or became cossacks, and large numbers of those former peasants eventually fought on the rebel side during the civil war.[103] In some ways, then, the key to understanding the impact of enserfment on the Time of Troubles may be to look at the southern frontier. As the next chapter will demonstrate, it was there that many of the destabilizing effects of enserfment, combined with the state's ruthless treatment of the frontier population and its own military forces, produced a powderkeg ready to explode in the unpopular Boris Godunov's face.

5

The Southern Frontier and the Cossacks

Russia's steppe frontier played a unique and important role in that country's early history; it produced the cossacks and was the launchpoint for all the great popular rebellions of the seventeenth and eighteenth centuries. By studying the development of the steppe frontier in the decades leading up to the Time of Troubles, it is possible to gain important insights into the nature and participants of Russia's first civil war and the causes of that long and bloody conflict. Early modern Russia's southern frontier was populated mainly by overworked and underpaid military garrisons and by people who were drawn to its rich soil or who had been forced to flee from serfdom, taxes, or other hardships. With all of its dangers and its simultaneous allure of freedom, the frontier differed from the older, central part of Russia in many ways—not the least of which were the predominance of steppe grassland over forests, the constant threat of Tatar attacks, and the existence of something like a genuine "frontier spirit."[1] It has been claimed that Russia's southern frontier acted as a kind of safety valve, attracting the more restless and energetic population not willing to endure oppression in the heartland and keeping the older, forested part of the country relatively quiet even as the frontier periodically erupted in rage against the relentless expansion of the oppressive state.[2]

Russia's first civil war began on the southern frontier, and that region provided the strongest support and the main fighting force for the rebel cause. At the height of the civil war (1606–7), virtually the entire southern frontier fought on the rebel side. In fact, during much of the civil war, rebel front lines did not penetrate very far north into the forest zone. For the purpose of analysis, therefore, one may consider Russia's first civil war as a provincial rebellion that quickly grew into a much wider conflict. As discussed in Chapter 1, provincial rebellions were not at all uncommon in early modern Europe. Newly acquired regions imperfectly integrated into the developing fiscal-military state where local traditions and solidarities still predominated often proved to be potentially explosive and capable of fiercely resisting the intrusion of state power into the area. Cooperation among diverse social elements in resisting the government was typical of early modern provincial rebellions, and revolts were often endemic to certain regions—especially military borderlands.[3] Early modern Russia's steppe frontier fits this pattern very well. Moreover, according to Goldstone's model, as population and price pressures overwhelmed state finances and provoked a crisis, there was a rise in the number of rootless young men (and banditry) and a marked increase in migration away from the center of the state to the periphery—which, as a result, became less stable and more susceptible to anger directed against the government.[4] Russia on the eve of the Time of Troubles also fits that model very well. Its southern frontier grew rapidly in the sixteenth century as the state expanded to the south and east against the Tatars. When the heartland fell into deep economic and social crisis during the second half of the sixteenth century, many Russians made their way to the frontier, which offered the possibility of prosperity and less onerous demands. The frontier population grew steadily while the population of the older part of the country shrank alarmingly.[5] As a result, by the end of the sixteenth century, Russia's southern frontier was seething with energetic, armed and dangerous men who were unhappy with the policies of Boris Godunov.[6]

As noted earlier, the greatest danger to Russia until the seventeenth century came from remnants of the Golden Horde. Even after the conquests of Kazan and Astrakhan, the southern frontier continued to be the focus of an almost never-ending struggle with the Crimean Tatars. Throughout the sixteenth century, Russian military forces made strenuous efforts to protect that frontier from Tatar slave raids—in part by relentlessly advancing Russia's southern border farther into the steppe. The annexation by Vasilii III of the old frontier principalities of Riazan in 1521 and Severia (or Seversk) in 1523 greatly extended the newly unified Russia's borders south and brought the country's entire southern frontier under a single political authority.[7] The inhabitants of both of those old frontier regions had long been accustomed to fighting Tatars and had gained reputations as fierce and warlike defenders of their lands.[8] In order to better protect Russia's forest heartland from Tatar raids, new frontier towns were built and a series of fortified lines linking those towns was constructed out of a combination of natural obstacles such as rivers and forests and man-made earthworks, trenches, felled trees, and palisades. Each of those fortified lines was known as a *zasechnaia cherta* or *zaseka*. Over the course of the sixteenth century, hundreds of kilometers of these zaseka lines were constructed to block the usual Tatar invasion routes, and special taxes were levied to pay for them. The old town of Tula, located about 180 kilometers south of Moscow on the southern boundary of Russia's more densely settled central region and guarding it from the Tatars' most direct raiding route, was built up as the major southern

Map 3 *Russia's Steppe Frontier.*

frontier defense coordinating center. The zaseka line at Tula came to be seen as the dividing line between the southern frontier and the heartland. Starting in the 1550s, in the context of the struggle against Kazan and Astrakhan, Ivan the Terrible had work begun on zaseka lines farther to the south and east. On the southwest frontier, Seversk towns such as Putivl, Novgorod Severskii, and Rylsk were linked up to new south-central frontier towns such as Orel and Novosil, which had been constructed specifically to protect the approaches to central Russia. Those south-central towns were, in turn, linked up with the south-eastern towns, rivers, and forests of Riazan. The resulting new zaseka line, over one thousand kilometers long, blocked many major and secondary Tatar invasion routes. Regular patrolling along that new fortified frontier and annual mustering of the gentry militia at Serpukhov or other places along the Oka river (only eighty kilometers south of Moscow and long considered the capital's principal line of defense against the Tatars) slowed down slave and booty raids into Russia's central, forested provinces but did not stop them entirely.[9]

It was the devastating Crimean Tatar raid on Moscow in 1571 that prompted Tsar Ivan and his advisers to completely reorganize the southern defense system. More frequent patrols along the entire southern frontier, improvements in defenses, a reorganization of the personnel and duties of southern military servitors, and efforts to attract more people into southern military service combined to make the frontier defense system much more effective in the 1570s, in spite of Tatar raids almost every year.[10] In the southeast, Riazan militiamen were freed from static guard duty and incorporated into regular militia service. In their place were settled "fortress cossacks" (also known as "town cossacks" or "service cossacks"), to be discussed below.[11] In the southwest, the old defense system based upon hiring the warlike local peasant population (*muzhiki-sevriuki*) was abolished. They were replaced by fortress cossacks settled in towns such as Putivl, Rylsk, and Starodub.[12] Tsar Ivan also promoted the settlement of the steppe by pomeshchiki. Volunteers from the ranks of militiamen serving from such places as Tula and Kashira were resettled somewhat farther south in the underpopulated districts of Venev and Epifan in order to strengthen frontier defenses.[13] Throughout the 1570s and 1580s, many peasants also moved to the now-somewhat-safer frontier zone—fleeing from taxes, lords, or economic distress and hoping for a better life. The frontier population grew rapidly at the expense of the heartland, and the region did not suffer the same degree of economic decline as did central Russia. The population shift helped extend the frontier farther south but its impact on the rest of the country (especially on the pomeshchiki) eventually forced the government to try to halt peasant movement to the frontier through the use of "forbidden years" and enserfment.[14]

Tsar Ivan attempted to extend Russia's pomeste system to the southern frontier, in part to find land and labor for his economically distressed pomeshchiki
and in part to push the frontier farther south; however, he ran into serious problems. First of all, service on the southern frontier carried less status than service in the regular gentry cavalry force, so it was difficult to attract sufficient
numbers of militiamen to guard the frontier.[15] Throughout this period, the
frontier zone lacked the stabilizing influence of boyars and rich dvoriane; instead,
poorer, more desperate deti boiarskie predominated.[16] Service lands on the
southern frontier tended to be small and to have few, if any, peasants living on
them.[17] Southern militiamen also usually had trouble obtaining their full land
allotments, were often not paid any salary at all, and seldom received opportunities for advancement.[18] Many southern "lords," with no serfs or slaves, were
actually forced to work the land themselves in order to survive.[19] Their morale
was low, and they often failed to report for duty.[20] Many of them could not
afford to show up for service fully equipped and were, therefore, forced to serve
as deti boiarskie infantry armed with harquebuses—a militarily useful new type
of pomeshchiki who still rode to battle but had to dismount in order to fire
their weapons. The advent of deti boiarskie infantry represented a serious loss
of status for the petty gentry, dampened their enthusiasm for joining frontier
service, and was another sign of the developing gentry militia crisis. Deti boiarskie
infantry soon came to greatly outnumber traditional pomeshchik cavalrymen
in frontier service and by the end of the sixteenth century were often the largest
single group of warriors stationed in frontier towns and forts.[21] In many ways,
the hybrid military service system developing on the southern frontier differed
radically from that of central Russia, failed to yield the results desired by the
ruling elite, and played an important role in preparing the region for civil war.[22]

Although the government had trouble recruiting pomeshchiki into southern military service, the pacification of the steppe and the economic crisis in
central Russia drove many peasants, slaves, and townsmen to the frontier. Usually
careful to avoid settling on the estates of desperate pomeshchiki, these men
found immediate employment as farmers, hunters, and honey gatherers.[23] More
important, they were also recruited by labor-hungry officials into the ranks of
lower status military servitors stationed in southern towns and forts. Grateful
commanders asked few questions about their background. Instead, these new
arrivals were offered small land allotments and immediately put to work as
streltsy, artillerymen, gatekeepers, guards, blacksmiths, stoneworkers, and carpenters. Lower status military servitors were often the single largest group in
southern towns, and sometimes they were almost the only inhabitants. Life was
hard for these men, and they were especially unhappy with Boris Godunov's

decision to bind them to the tax rolls. On the other hand, for many runaways, lower status military service was still preferable to the available alternatives in crisis-struck Russia and occasionally even offered a few of them unique opportunities for advancement. For example, former runaways serving as low status military servitors were, from time to time, recruited into the ranks of the frontier deti boiarskie, which must have pleased them very much. Such promotions, however, provoked many complaints from "real" pomeshchiki whose own status was thereby eroded.[24] Meanwhile, a significant percentage of runaways from central Russia did not seek employment in southern towns; instead, large numbers of fugitive peasants, slaves, townsmen, and bandits made their way even farther south and joined the cossacks, whose numbers increased dramatically in the late sixteenth century.[25]

Cossacks played such an important role in Russia's first civil war that it has occasionally been referred to as a "cossack revolution," and for a long time it was claimed that the "revolutionary cossacks," as champions of the lower classes, actively fomented an open class struggle during the Time of Trouble. Neither assertion is correct, and the demise of the peasant war interpretation of the period finally provides us with an opportunity to gain a better understanding of the strange and fierce cossacks and the crucial role they played in the Russia's first civil war.[26] The Russian term for cossack (*kazak*) was borrowed from an Arabic and Turkic term for "adventurer," "nomad soldier," "free and independent person," "guard," or even "vagrant."[27] The first cossacks in Russia were Tatars who, during the fifteenth century, roamed the steppe as robber bands and occasionally served in the cavalry of the grand prince of Moscow. Some of them settled down permanently to help the Russians guard the Oka River frontier line against Tatar attacks.[28] Slavic cossacks, students of the Tatar freebooters, also began to appear in the dangerous no-man's land between the forests of Russia and the steppe during the fifteenth century. Gathering together in gangs for self-protection, these wandering soldier-adventurers often spent part of the year "cossacking" (hunting, fishing, and banditry) and part of the year living in Russian border towns.[29] By the early sixteenth century, Slavic cossacks began to greatly outnumber their Tatar brethren on the steppe, but one's nationality was basically of little interest to the cossacks. Over the course of the sixteenth century, Ukrainian cossacks developed the earliest and largest predominantly Slavic cossack settlements on the steppe, eventually forming the famous Zaporozhian cossack community on the lower Dnepr River. By the end of the sixteenth century, up to four thousand Ukrainian cossacks were regularly employed in the tsar's service; and many of them also joined rebel forces during Russia's first civil war.[30] Russian cossacks began operating between the Don and Volga Rivers in the early sixteenth century and their numbers grew rapidly in the second half of the century.[31] As Russia expanded south and east, some of these native cossacks were recruited as frontier guards. In response to the Crimean Tatar attack on Moscow in 1571, many more Russian cossacks were recruited for service in dozens of new fortified frontier watchposts along the expanding zaseka lines. They settled down as permanent, state-employed border guards or "fortress cossacks." These warriors were much sought after as guardians of the frontier because they showed more initiative and combativeness than many of the sullen pomeshchiki posted there.[32]

During the second half of the sixteenth century, large numbers of mostly Russian "free" cossacks, who admitted no lord over them, lived in bands of up to one hundred on the steppe beyond Russia's southern frontier. Each separate free cossack band had its own *stanitsa* (settlement), usually located in an easily defended place hidden away in one of the river valleys of the steppe. Inside the cossack stanitsa, most important decisions were made by a quasi-democratic assembly known as a *krug* (circle); however once an *ataman* (chieftain) was chosen by the krug, his fellow cossacks would obey him scrupulously on campaigns. Cossack stanitsas maintained strong contact with one another and frequently joined together in emergencies or to carry out daring booty raids. According to Aleksandr Stanislavskii, cossacks were a new social phenomenon: a new military class in the process of formation. They were a communistic brotherhood of social bandits and part-time mercenary soldiers whose organizational model was that of an army. Hardships and booty were shared equally among all members of the community. The free cossacks were superb horsemen and ferocious warriors; they were extremely bold and brave, often displaying great martial skill. They quickly adapted to gunpowder technology and became expert marksmen. Cossacks preferred attacking to defending and would frequently leave even safe defensive positions in order to fight an enemy. They were skilled at moving and attacking at night, at quick retreats, and at psychological warfare. They frequently unnerved potential adversaries by shrieking and ululating, and they had a well-deserved reputation for cruelty.[33] Cossacks consistently emphasized their uniqueness and separation from other groups in Russian society and were basically indifferent to class origin. New arrivals among the cossacks usually gave up their old names and swore an oath that signified their transfer to a new social order.[34] Cossacks were fiercely proud and protective of their independence and status as "free" men, sharply contrasting themselves to the "unfree" pomeshchiki in the tsar's service. Cossacks came to be associated with the concept of freedom itself, and that attracted many newcomers to their ranks as the Russian state placed increasing burdens on its subjects in the late sixteenth century.[35] Most of the Russians who joined the cossacks were fugitive peasants, slaves, bandits, or escaped convicts, but there were also destitute former pomeshchiki in cossack ranks as well.[36] The rowdy free cossacks were often a nuisance to the Russian government; but in the struggle against the Crimean Tatars they proved useful. They effectively acted as the leading edge of Russian pacification of the southern frontier, and by the 1570s Tsar Ivan began to encourage free cossacks from the Don and Volga to send contingents to serve as scouts and cavalry in the Russian army.[37] When directly employed by the Russian military, free cossacks always insisted on keeping their own atamans and stubbornly resisted all attempts to impose commanders on them or to reduce their freedoms.[38] Even so, service to the tsar quickly became an extremely important—perhaps the most important—source of income for the free cossacks.[39] When not directly sanctioned by the government, cossack harassment of the Crimean Tatars could always be disavowed by the tsar. For that very reason, relations with the free cossacks were handled by Russia's Foreign Affairs Office (*Posolskii prikaz*)—a useful ruse that, of course, fooled no one.[40]

A serious problem for the Russian government in dealing with its cossack "allies" was that in the late sixteenth century more and more Russians "went cossack." The southern frontier (and cossack freedom) acted as a magnet to paupers, soldiers, dispossessed landowners, and runaway peasants and slaves. Displeased by this development, Tsar Ivan tried to stop the flow of his dwindling human capital to the cossacks by closing the borders and prohibiting cossacks from visiting border towns on pain of death (thereby ending "seasonal cossacking").[41] Free cossacks were pressed by the government to give up their nomadic ways and to settle down as fortress cossacks. (A similar process was going on at the same time in Poland-Lithuania through "registration" of Ukrainian cossacks.) Many free cossacks chose instead to strike out even farther into the "wild steppe." Since even the closed border was a sieve, large numbers of Russians followed them and soon there were thriving cossack communities on the Don and the Volga; by 1600, cossack stanitsas were also established on the Terek and Iaik Rivers.[42] During the 1590s, free cossack ranks grew rapidly due to increasing flight from Russia's central provinces by escapees from enserfment and slavery. At the same time, many of the sons of newly enserfed peasants legally left their unfree parents' homes and, if they managed to avoid being stopped by the border authorities, made their way to cossack stanitsas and freedom. On the eve of the Time of Troubles there were at least eight to ten thousand free cossacks operating on Russia's southern frontier who were occasionally employed by the tsar in return for gunpowder, lead, food, and money. Whenever Boris Godunov needed their assistance, he would allow

Fig. 4 "A Cossack with a Harquebus." Woodcut circa 1622. Published in D. A.
Rovinskii, *Materialy dlia Russkoi Ikonografii,* part 3 (St. Petersburg, 1884). Courtesy of
Houghton Library, Harvard University.

them to trade in frontier towns, where the cossacks were usually welcomed as friendly neighbors and customers.

The rapid growth of cossack forces in the late sixteenth century was similar to developments all along the no-man's land between Christian Europe and the Islamic world. As discussed in Chapter 1, proponents of the theory of a crisis of the 1590s and Jack Goldstone focused attention on the rise of large numbers of rootless young men and bandits who gravitated toward the frontier. What happened in Russia and Ukraine was echoed by a sharp rise in banditry all across southern Europe during the late sixteenth century—a clear sign of crisis.[43] Russia and Poland-Lithuania were also not the only countries to try to make use of these unruly frontier ruffians. For example, Habsburg military frontier settlers called *Grenzer* were remarkably similar to the cossacks.[44] So were the *haiduks* of Hungary and the Balkan peninsula.[45] The *uskoks* of Senj, operating on the shores of the Adriatic Sea, were also strikingly similar to the cossacks.[46] Many of these hardy, freedom-loving adventurers regarded themselves as free Christian knights helping the Christian world by plundering the Islamic world.[47] That romantic self-image captured the imagination of many people, and in Russia it contributed to the idealization of the cossacks in the nineteenth and twentieth centuries—a view that has been emphatically rejected as hopelessly unrealistic by many scholars.[48] Nevertheless, most cossacks on Russia's southern frontier considered themselves to be at least nominally Orthodox, and they were always willing to fight as allies of the tsar against the Islamic Tatars and Turks if the pay was good.

Those cossacks who were enticed into Russian service and became fortress cossacks did not retain the autonomy of the free cossacks. Sometimes they lost their ataman and came under the command of a pomeshchik. Sometimes their ataman was settled with them as their commander. In that case, he was usually treated as a member of the gentry, was granted pomeste lands with peasants and slaves, and received a salary.[49] The majority of fortress cossacks, on the other hand, were regarded as lower status military servitors akin to streltsy and artillery-men. They were paid a small salary, given land to work collectively, and were usually exempt from taxes. Their duties were hard and dangerous. Tsar Ivan and his successors occasionally allowed exiled criminals to join the ranks of the versatile and effective fortress cossacks, whose service was becoming increasingly indispensable. At the same time, the beleaguered frontier pomeshchiki were becoming so poor and vulnerable that in many places fortress cossacks were doing just about as well as those "lords" with respect to pay and workload. In fact, there was considerable overlapping between the two groups and more than a few cases of wholesale promotions of fortress cossacks into the ranks of the deti boiarskie—events that must have deeply disturbed "real" pomeshchiki stuck in frontier service. On the other hand, appeals by some fortress cossacks for pay and land equal to that of the deti boiarskie they had replaced sometimes resulted in official reviews that confirmed the status of most petitioners as low status military servitors and rewarded only the "better" cossacks with the rank and income of pomeshchiki. But even those decisions must have upset the frontier gentry who did not relish the thought of sharing their rank with cossack atamans. Such blurring of the distinctions among southern military servitors was potentially destabilizing and was yet another sign of the gentry militia crisis. There were inevitable conflicts and rivalries between the pomeshchiki and the fortress cossacks, but they shared discomfort, poor morale, and a general dissatisfaction with their situation.[50]

The use of fortress cossacks intensified in the 1580s after Russia extricated itself from the Livonian War and began a bold imperial thrust to the south and east. Because of the exhaustion of Russian society and the severe crisis developing at the time, such a strenuous effort to expand the state was certainly unwise. It proved to be extremely burdensome to the country's already overloaded taxpaying population and contributed to the decline of the economy, increasing stratification, and enserfment. It was also very hard on the frontiersmen harnessed to the task of pushing Russia's borders farther into the steppe and helped to create an explosive situation there by the end of the sixteenth century.[51] Russia's energetic expansion at that time was driven in part by the strong desire to prevent any future devastating raids into the heartland, in part by the desire to provide more land for needy pomeshchiki, and in part by a strong impulse to overtake as many Russians as possible who had fled to the frontier in order to put them back to work either directly or indirectly in support of the imperial ambition of the ruling elite.[52]

The man responsible for the expansion of Russia at the end of the sixteenth century was Boris Godunov. To the east, he sent forces, including cossacks, to build and garrison fortresses in strategic locations such as Tiumen (1586) and Tobolsk (1587), thereby gaining control of the Ob River and its tributary, the Irtysh River, which effectively gave the tsar control of western Siberia and set the stage for Russian expansion all the way to the Pacific Ocean by the mid-seventeenth century. Native Siberian peoples such as the Ostiaks were quickly subjugated but remained restless and actually rebelled against their new masters during Russia's first civil war.[53] To the southeast, the Russians consolidated their control over the Volga River basin by constructing new towns and by putting the native population to work. Some towns were specifically constructed in order to maintain control over the lands of the Cheremis and the Chuvash peoples. Cheremis, Chuvashi, and Tatars who converted to Christianity were accepted into frontier military service on the same terms as Russian warriors. Many became pomeshchiki and were settled in the Middle Volga region on lands inhabited by their own kinsmen who were now required to support these new "lords." In this way enserfment, then being implemented in central Russia, was extended to the natives of the Volga basin.[54] It should come as no surprise, therefore, that large numbers of Tatars, Cheremis, and Chuvashi eventually fought, at least indirectly, against Russian imperialism by joining rebel forces during Russia's first civil war.

Farther south down the Volga, construction of several new strategically located towns was ordered by Boris Godunov in order to protect Volga River commerce from cossack pirates and the Nogai Tatars (a powerful remnant of the Mongols who lived east of the Volga River). At the mouth of the Volga, the city of Astrakhan's defenses were greatly strengthened by the construction of a new stone fortress. Upstream from Astrakhan, Samara was founded in 1586, Tsaritsyn in 1588, and Saratov in 1590. The founding of Ufa farther to the east in 1586 directly threatened the Nogai Tatars, who repeatedly but unsuccessfully protested against growing pressure from the Russians. In fact, Boris Godunov even managed to intervene successfully in the turbulent internal affairs of the Nogai horde and temporarily gained the upper hand in dealing with them. By 1600, he was actually able to put his own candidate, Prince Ishterek, in power among the Nogai Tatars.[55] Nevertheless, turmoil continued within the Nogai horde right into the Time of Troubles, and many Nogai Tatars displayed their unhappiness with Godunov's meddling and Russian imperialism during the civil war.

At the same time Russia was expanding rapidly to the east, on the southern frontier there was literally a frenzy of town and fortress construction. Between 1584 and 1599, the border of Russia moved south more than five hundred kilometers. Towns were built in strategic locations in the valleys of the Seversk Donets, the Oskol, and the Don Rivers (as well as their tributaries). They were quickly surrounded with palisades and earthworks and became formidable guardians of the frontier. New towns such as Voronezh (1585–86) and Livny (1586–87) pushed the frontier far south and became very important military outposts. After the Crimean Tatars raided the Moscow suburbs again in 1591, Tsar Fedor and Boris Godunov speeded up construction on the southern frontier. In a burst of activity, the ancient town of Elets was refounded and Belgorod, Kromy, Kursk, and Valuiki were founded. Finally, in 1599, Tsarev-Borisov was boldly constructed over seven hundred kilometers south of Moscow. Many of these new "towns" were, of course, nothing more than forts populated almost exclusively by military servitors. Nevertheless, the Russians managed by this activity to complete most of a third zaseka line protecting the country's central provinces from invasion from the south. Overall, Godunov's frontier construction program proved to be highly effective against the Crimean Tatars. With Russian forts blocking all their preferred routes, the Tatars were no longer able to devastate Russia's heartland. As a direct result, by the early seventeenth century the Tatar frontier stopped being Russia's most dangerous borderland.[56]

The rapid development of southern frontier defenses and the construction of so many new towns had as its main purpose making the border safe from Crimean Tatars; but the impact of the construction program on the free cossacks was also great and conscious. The mass spontaneous migration of peasants, slaves, and others to the frontier had certainly helped push the border south, but the government was determined to recapture the labor of those individuals. Among other things, Boris Godunov knew that serfdom could not triumph completely in central Russia while the free frontier existed.[57] Therefore, toward the end of the sixteenth century, Godunov moved beyond trying to entice free cossacks into becoming fortress cossacks and tried instead to outflank and subordinate the free cossack lands. By then, the rapid expansion of Russia south and east had already had a profound impact on the Volga cossacks. The conquest of Kazan and Astrakhan and the development of a fortified line across the Volga seriously disrupted cossack pirate activity. Many Volga cossacks were forced to retreat to the Don or to move into the Caucasus Mountains (settling on the Terek River) or farther east (settling on the Iaik River).[58] Toward the end of the century, Russian commanders responded to that movement by ordering construction of a new fort on the Terek. In the meantime, construction and fortification of Saratov, Samara, and Tsaritsyn cut in two the lands of the Volga cossacks and harassed their communications with the Don. Fortress construction on Russia's southern frontier simultaneously advanced deep into the heart of cossack territory and truly alarmed the Don cossacks. The new fortress of Tsarev-Borisov, for example, was only a short journey from the Don cossack "capital" of Razdory. Thus, within just a few years, free cossack territory began slipping behind Russia's zaseka lines and border towns. The frontier was rapidly shrinking, and the cossacks were not at all happy about it.[59]

The free cossacks were well aware that Boris Godunov was their enemy. His periodic withholding of grain from them and his on-again, off-again attempts to cut off their contact with frontier towns by forbidding all trade with them may have been intended to force the free cossacks into government service, but instead it made them more stubborn and angry with him.[60] Godunov's stern measures to stop destitute pomeshchiki from joining the free cossacks also failed, and many of those experienced warriors became cossack leaders. Former military slaves who managed to slip past border guards to join the cossacks also brought valuable military skills and weapons with them and ended up playing a leading role in the ranks of the cossacks.[61] In 1597, Boris Godunov ordered the torture and execution of many free cossacks, ostensibly for harming his Nogai Tatar allies. Such a harsh measure reflected Moscow's growing frustration in dealing with the "cossack menace," but it only served to harden cossack hatred of the tsar's brother-in-law.[62] When Godunov became tsar in 1598, he continued to harass the free cossacks. For example, in the context of the construction of Tsarev-Borisov in 1599, the new tsar's commander there ordered all free cossacks from the Seversk Donets, the Oskol, and other nearby rivers to gather at the new town. There they were informed that Tsar Boris would generously permit them to retain their lands without being taxed and that they could continue to serve under their own atamans; however, they were now to consider themselves servants of the tsar. The free cossacks were not pleased by this development, and they stoutly resisted the government's subsequent efforts to carry out a census of the cossack stanitsas.[63] The cossacks were certainly not going to give up their freedom voluntarily and were more than ready to fight to defend it. Boris Godonov's cossack policy stirred up bitter resentment on the southern frontier and was an important precondition of the civil war.[64] In addition to alienating the Don, Volga, Terek, and Iaik cossacks, Godunov also managed to stir the hatred of many Ukrainian cossacks who had fled to Russia's southern frontier in the aftermath of the failure of their rebellions in Poland-Lithuania during the 1590s. Godunov ordered the Don cossacks to drive all the newly arriving Ukrainian cossacks away from their own rivers, woods, and grasslands. That policy was not popular on the Don, where Russian cossacks regarded Ukrainian cossacks as their brothers, and it contributed to the later willingness of many Ukrainian cossacks to fight against Tsar Boris during Russia's first civil war.[65]

At least in part because of Boris Godunov's stormy relationship with the free cossacks, the Russian government faced increasing difficulty recruiting them— even with generous offers—into the ranks of the extremely useful fortress cossacks. In order to recruit more of them into service associated with the rapid construction program on the southern frontier in the 1590s, proclamations were issued declaring that anyone who wished to join the ranks of the fortress cossacks would be allowed to do so. As a direct result, runaways from enserfment, sons of poor peasants, and exiled criminals moved to the frontier to become fortress cossacks. Not only did many of them thereby escape from bondage, but they also gained a few privileges as low status military servitors.[66] Godunov's new policy inevitably brought howls of protest from the pomeshchiki

of central Russia who lost income and labor as serfs ran away to seek employment and higher status as fortress cossacks. Some gentry beat, withheld food
from, or even imprisoned peasants in order to prevent their departure to the
southern frontier. They also put pressure on the reluctant government to carefully scrutinize the background of newly recruited fortress cossacks. In fact,
pressure from militiamen and tax collectors was strong enough to force occasional and half-hearted official investigations that resulted in the return of some
fortress cossacks to serfdom and the tax rolls. Such investigations quite naturally stirred up fear and resentment among many southern military servitors.[67]
The conditions and morale of fortress cossacks soon became poor enough that
their use in large numbers on the southern frontier posed a high risk for the
government. If pressed too hard, they might flee to the free cossacks, or—as
often occurred during Russia's first civil war—they might make common cause
with the cossacks and with fellow low status military servitors in resisting
Moscow. Beatings, imprisonment, and even executions to prevent fortress cossacks from running away to the Don only embittered these men even more.[68]
Boris Godunov's frightening investigations and occasional harsh treatment of
the fortress cossacks had another unintended effect as well; many runaways
from central Russia now knew that they would no longer be safe working as
fortress cossacks. To avoid the possibility of being returned to bondage, those
desperate men had to ride farther south to the free cossack stanitsas, where they
were welcomed as brothers and swelled the ranks of Boris Godunov's foes.[69]

Overall, Boris Godunov's frontier policy resulted in very large numbers of
unhappy military servitors and free cossacks as well as a blurring of the line
between hereditary military service and lower status military service. Further
blurring that line, Godunov imposed yet another onerous burden on southern
frontier military servitors in the 1590s that made them furious—plowing additional land for the state in order to produce enough grain to feed those servicemen busy constructing new towns and fortresses, those stationed in places
where they were unable to produce enough food for themselves, and cossack
atamans the government regarded as friendly. That labor obligation was known
as *gosudareva desiatinnaia pashnia,* which may be loosely translated as "the tsar's
tenth."[70] The financially strapped government had often imposed the same
obligation on peasants living on crown lands during the sixteenth century, especially in wartime;[71] but now, in order to continue the government's ambitious
imperial drive south in the midst of Russia's severe crisis, Godunov resorted to
the extremely drastic step of imposing that onerous burden not only on lower
status frontier military servitors but also on frontier pomeshchiki. Suddenly, in
addition to all their regular duties, disgruntled lower status military servitors

(who had only recently been bound to their towns as taxpayers) and poor pomeshchiki (who already worked their own land without the help of serfs) found themselves being treated like ordinary peasants—forced to labor long and hard for the state on large tracts of land for no pay.[72] Godunov's new policy provoked widespread indignation among frontier military servitors; it showed contempt for their status and the vital contributions they were already making. There is no doubt that it contributed significantly to the overwhelming tendency on the part of southern frontier military servitors of all kinds to support the rebel cause once civil war broke out.[73]

When things finally did reach the breaking point in 1604, most frontier pomeshchiki, lower status military servitors, and townsmen enthusiastically cooperated with the free cossacks in challenging Tsar Boris. That is not surprising if one remembers that among the ranks of the southern pomeshchiki were many newly-promoted lower status military servitors and cossacks; among the lower status military servitors were many cossacks, runaway peasants, slaves, and townsmen; and among the free cossacks were many former peasants, slaves, townsmen, lower status military servitors, and ruined pomeshchiki. The blurring of the distinctions between social groups on the southern frontier was a major cause of protest among pomeshchiki anxious to protect their status, but it also promoted bonds among the various groups of the tsar's warriors whose shared misery produced some solidarity and provoked remarkably similar complaints against Boris Godunov and the central government. Those southern frontier warriors also tended to regard the free cossacks (who were often from the same social background as themselves and were sometimes even former comrades) as friendly neighbors. Southern towns suffered almost as much as the free cossacks did from Boris Godunov's efforts to forbid cossacks from trading at border outposts, and frontier military servitors did not in general approve of Godunov's efforts to harass and harness the free cossacks. When the civil war broke out, most southern frontier towns did not hesitate to join forces with the free cossacks in support of the pretender Dmitrii. When one recalls that many of those towns were populated almost exclusively by disgruntled deti boiarskie mounted infantry and lower status military servitors, their nearly unanimous rebellion against Tsar Boris makes sense. Participation of those towns in the civil war was, in fact, directly related to the gentry militia crisis, which was most strongly felt on the southern frontier.[74]

One of the unexpected ironies associated with the development of Russian autocracy, with its extreme concentration of power in Moscow, was the impact of such a system in the provinces. The traditional view has been that the concentration of power in the capital led to the "atomization" of annexed areas and

to the complete absence of any remaining regional power capable of challenging the center.[75] In fact, in order to create absolute monarchies and to extract
revenues needed to fund them, early modern national leaders invariably found
it necessary to cut deals with local provincial elites—thereby increasing the latter's functional autonomy at the local level. That was a fundamental characteristic of the emerging fiscal-military state, and Russia was certainly no
exception.[76] Starting with Ivan the Terrible, the pomeshchiki were allowed to
"reign supreme in the provinces."[77] In central Russia, such a system worked reasonably well for Moscow because of the loyalty of the gentry who directly benefited from state service. On the southern frontier, however, things were
dramatically different. Southern pomeshchiki were—as we have seen—underpaid and exploited; they also had little status and no voice in Moscow. Their
chances to rise in Russian military service were extremely limited. In fact, government policy discouraged the emergence of local leaders among the motley
southern gentry. Instead, frontier commanders were usually drawn from other
regions. That inevitably led to resentment and growing frustration among the
ranks of the frontier deti boiarskie. Newly arriving commanders ordinarily made
arrangements with the richer local pomeshchiki (those with a significant stake
in the system) to help cement their own power, but that was possible only if
there were any local gentry doing reasonably well. On the southern frontier,
those men were rare; in fact, many frontier towns had no gentry cavalrymen
stationed in them at all. Instead, the beleaguered frontier pomeshchiki were
mostly deti boiarskie infantry with no chance for any significant improvement
of their conditions or status. They had more in common with each other and
with local low status military servitors than with their commanders, especially
after those "outsiders" began forcing them to plow for the tsar. Among the hard-
pressed frontier deti boiarskie there was growing anger both with local commanders and with Moscow.[78] For all its appearance of great power, then, the
Russian government's grip on its southern provinces was actually rather tenuous.[79] On the frontier, the connections among the various layers of military
servitors along with their shared grievances created a dangerous situation for
the autocratic regime. Interestingly enough, the fact that the Russian gentry
was not a closed corporation (in spite of efforts to turn the pomeshchiki into
a warrior caste) but was instead at least partially open to some limited upward
social mobility has long been regarded by some scholars as a "major weakness"
of the Russian gentry "in its relationship to the Crown."[80] At the same time,
however, at least in the case of Russia's southern frontier on the eve of the Time
of Troubles, that somewhat fluid and unstable social structure worked against
the interests of Moscow and created a powerful coalition of armed men angry
with Boris Godunov.[81]

6

The Beginning of the Time of Troubles and the Great Famine

Russia was in crisis at the end of the sixteenth century, suffering from the conjuncture of many destabilizing forces. By coincidence, the country's ruling dynasty died out at that time as well, triggering a sharp political struggle that significantly deepened the crisis. The eminent historian Sergei Platonov long ago noted the potent combination of social, economic, and political problems descending on Russia by 1598 and correctly regarded that combination as the primary cause of the Time of Troubles.[1] According to Platonov, Tsar Fedor's death triggered the first phase of the Troubles, the period of dynastic struggle between Boris Godunov and his rivals.

By the 1590s, Russia's developing crisis was severe enough to cause many people to fear for the future of their country even before Tsar Fedor passed away;[2] but the "Time of Troubles" as such was regarded by contemporaries as being caused by and beginning with Fedor's death in January, 1598.[3] The tsar's death without an heir brought to an end the only ruling dynasty Moscow had ever known. The grand princes who unified Russia had generally practiced primogeniture but did not bother to develop any law of succession. As a result, the extinction of the ruling dynasty in 1598 precipitated an immediate political crisis; but it also set in motion a more profound cultural and psychological crisis. During the process of unifying Russia and forming a Russian national culture, the ruling elite had actively fostered the myth of the divine ordination of the dynasty of Moscow princes.[4] Over the course of the sixteenth century, the concept of sacred kingship grew rapidly in Russia, and the Daniilovich dynasty (descendants of Aleksandr Nevskii's youngest son Daniil who founded the line of Moscow princes) was increasingly seen as chosen by God to lead the Russian Orthodox population to salvation in an era of uncertainty about His plan for the future of the world.[5] In fact, the God-chosen tsar became the one essential element in early modern Russia's completely religious political culture.[6] Tsar Fedor, despite his mental incapacity, was loved and venerated for his piety and for his legitimacy as a member of the sacred ruling dynasty.[7] His death in 1598 without an heir was a severe shock to pious Russians, many of whom wondered why God had apparently withdrawn His favor from Russia. In all likelihood, even in the midst of its developing crisis, Russia would not have faced either the Time of Troubles or its first civil war without Fedor's demise. It was the tsar's death that ushered in an era of sharp political conflicts, succession crises, and tsars who had great difficulty establishing their legitimacy—starting with Boris Godunov.[8]

In the political struggle unleashed by the extinction of the old dynasty, Boris Godunov's critics accused him of aspiring to the throne from the very beginning of Tsar Fedor's reign, or from 1591 at the latest. All the regent's activities, it was claimed, had been aimed at gaining the throne; all his achievements and various good deeds were described as nothing more than cynical moves to gain the good will of the Russian people, especially the nobility, in order to facilitate his bid for power.[9] When did Boris Godunov actually begin to aspire for the throne? It was certainly not as early as his enemies claimed. For example, in 1592, Tsaritsa Irina gave birth to a daughter, Feodosiia. Even though the girl died in 1594, for two years after that Irina and Fedor still appeared to be capable of producing additional children. Skrynnikov correctly determined that Boris Godunov began to contemplate the crown for himself only after it became obvious that Fedor would not produce an heir. By 1597, that point had been reached, and relations between Boris Godunov and Fedor Romanov quickly deteriorated as both men began maneuvering to succeed the ailing, childless tsar.[10]

By the time Fedor died, Boris Godunov had accumulated enormous advantages over any potential rivals for the throne. He had been a competent and effective ruler of Russia for a decade; the bureaucracy was basically loyal to him; the Russian Orthodox Church was headed by his protégé, Patriarch Iov, who—along with much of the clergy—was devoted to him; and Godunov was one of the richest men in Russia.[11] The regent had earned the gratitude of much of the gentry by enserfing the peasants and freeing the lords' personal estates from taxation. He also worked tirelessly to gain the support of other key groups. A common view has been that Boris Godunov based his power on the gentry, consciously building up pomeshchik support for himself because he lacked support among the boyars.[12] That is simply not true. Boris Godunov was himself, first and foremost, one of the leading boyars. He actively sought the support of many other boyar clans and carried out a number of policies strongly favored by aristocrats that were decidedly not in the interests of the pomeshchiki.[13] Contrary to the traditional interpretation of his struggle for power, the bulk of the Russian aristocracy did not oppose Godunov's accession. He had the support of a majority of the boyars, which was a clear reflection of his predominance in government and his clever use of resources and patronage.[14] Nonetheless, he did have to fight for the throne.

When Tsar Fedor died, so did the legitimate dynasty. According to a Russian proverb, "Without the tsar the land is a widow; without the tsar the people are an orphan."[15] In that profoundly troubling moment, Boris Godunov was forced to play a cautious game. Patriarch Iov declared that Tsar Fedor had intended for Tsaritsa Irina to rule after him, and the Russian people quickly swore allegiance to her.[16] In fact, in an unprecedented move, Fedor had formally made his wife coruler with him in the 1590s, allowing her to take part in state affairs. As the tsar's lawful wife and coruler, Irina had a very real claim to the throne.[17] She immediately proclaimed a general amnesty for all prisoners. Within a few days, however, Irina entered a convent and abdicated the throne in favor of the boyar council. She was working in support of her brother but could not simply transfer the mantle of legitimacy directly to him.[18] At that point, the boyars decided to convene a zemskii sobor as soon as possible for the important and unprecedented task of choosing a new tsar, but Godunov temporarily prevented that from happening. He faced serious opposition from a small number of boyars and could not yet control the outcome of an election. Although a majority of the boyars favored his candidacy, the council was badly split on the issue. Boris's potential rivals for the throne included Fedor Mstislavskii, Fedor Romanov, Vasilii Shuiskii, and Bogdan Belskii. The prestigious princes Mstislavskii and Shuiskii, perhaps mindful of the fates of members of their own families who had stood in Godunov's way, declined to campaign against him; and it appears that Vasilii Shuiskii and his brother Dmitrii (by then related by marriage to Boris Godunov) may actually have tried to help the regent's cause somewhat in the boyar council.

Godunov's principal rival for the throne from the very outset of the struggle was Fedor Romanov.[19] The Romanovs and their allies (including Belskii) tried to discredit Godunov by way of a rumor campaign denouncing him for the Uglich tragedy and accusing him of poisoning Tsar Fedor.[20] That strategy put Godunov on the defensive, and he had to maneuver for the throne with extreme caution for several months.[21] Eventually, Fedor Romanov, Bogdan Belskii, and others were forced to seek a compromise candidate to oppose Godunov; they settled on Fedor Mstislavskii's brother-in-law, old and blind Simeon Bekbulatovich.[22] Nonetheless, Godunov outmaneuvered his opponents in the context of a massive military build-up against an alleged Crimean Tatar invasion threat.

With strong support in many quarters (including most boyars, most of the church hierarchy, most bureaucrats, and the bulk of the gentry militia), Godunov soon prevailed over all his opponents and was crowned at the beginning of September, 1598.[23] Tsar Boris made extravagant promises in order to build support for his legitimacy. He promised townsmen and peasants living on state and crown lands lower taxes; he promised to reduce the abuse of serfs; he promised soldiers more pay; he promised to provide relief to the needy, to widows, and to orphans; and he even promised to try to rebuild Russia's declining economy and eliminate poverty.[24] The new tsar also promised to restore peace among the boyars and to make peace with his own opponents. He dissolved the tsar's separate court (a relic of the oprichnina) so that the boyar council was fully restored to its former prestige and function. Although he promoted his family and friends, Tsar Boris was also generous to most boyars—including his old rivals. The Romanovs and the Belskiis were especially honored.[25] The new tsar still had enemies, of course; but his opponents were acutely aware of the potential danger of an open, protracted struggle for the throne. According to Edward L. Keenan, Russia's political culture ultimately obliged them to end at least their open conflict and to join the other boyars in publicly conferring legitimacy on Tsar Boris.[26] Even so, Godunov had a very difficult time establishing his legitimacy in the eyes of many Russians; and, of course, he still had enemies. Many spoke ill of him from the moment he became tsar.[27]

To help calm any discontent and to cement his claim to the throne, the new tsar had himself "elected" after the fact by a sham zemskii sobor.[28] The decision of that zemskii sobor was then represented as the voice of God, and it was claimed that Tsar Boris had, in effect, been "God-chosen." Documents were also falsified to indicate that Tsar Fedor had chosen Boris to be his successor.[29] For many Russians those assertions were good enough to make Godunov appear legitimate; however, if God stopped smiling on Tsar Boris's realm, the question of legitimacy would inevitably return. For other Russians, the crisis caused by the extinction of the sanctified ruling dynasty was not so easily resolved. No matter how hard he tried, an elected tsar simply could not command as much reverence and respect as the Daniilovichi; and his election would be regarded as unnatural by many Russians.[30] Furthermore, Russian political culture sharply differentiated between boyars and tsars; boyars were supposed to advise tsars, not become tsars.[31] In fact, since at least the time of Ivan the Terrible, boyars were also regarded with suspicion by many as oppressors of the people and as potential traitors and regicides.[32] By 1598, there were probably very few Russians who had not heard at least some of the terrible rumors spread about Godunov by his enemies, and few, if any, could forget that the new tsar had been responsible for very high taxes and enserfment. Suffice it to say, not all of Tsar Boris's subjects were cheered by his accession. Nonetheless, in spite of lingering rumors and resentment, Tsar Boris had no real difficulty consolidating his power as Russia's first "elected" ruler. The new tsar was feared and obeyed by the powerful and the humble.[33]

Boris Godunov has been called one of Russia's greatest rulers. Handsome, eloquent, energetic, and extremely bright, he brought greater skill and experience to the tasks of governing than any of his predecessors and was an excellent administrator.[34] Tsar Boris was respected in international diplomacy and managed to make peace with Russia's neighbors, temporarily putting an end to ruinous and costly wars.[35] At home, he worked tirelessly to improve justice for all his subjects and to rid the government of bribery and corruption. He was a zealous protector of the Russian Orthodox Church, a great builder and beautifier of Russian towns, and extremely generous to the needy.[36] He devoted himself to the task of restoring the country's battered economy, especially to reviving towns and trade. To that end, he instituted some modest tax relief for overburdened townsmen. There was no tax relief for peasants, however, who were groaning under the weight of fiscal oppression.[37]

For most Russians, the reign of Tsar Boris was not a happy one. At that time the developing state crisis reached its deepest stage, and a sharp political struggle within the ruling elite undermined Tsar Boris's legitimacy in the eyes of many of his subjects and set the stage for civil war. Of course, most of the forces at work destabilizing Russia at the beginning of the seventeenth century were not well understood by contemporaries. That is one of the reasons why they placed so much emphasis on the political struggle between Tsar Boris and his enemies as the principal cause of Russia's descent into nightmare. Nonetheless, that political struggle did contribute significantly to the outbreak of civil war.[38] In spite of his coronation promise to make peace with his opponents, Tsar Boris began harassing some of them by 1599. That deeply disturbed an already troubled situation; after all, in theory at least, a good tsar was supposed to live in harmony with his boyars.[39] Many members of the boyar council were already unhappy with Tsar Boris's promotion of "unsuitable" people and his failure to heed their own advice.[40] Soon, the new tsar was being secretly condemned by contemporaries for openly persecuting the aristocracy.[41] Boris's tactics reminded some of Ivan the Terrible's oprichnina, but Godunov was actually mild by comparison.[42] He exiled his erstwhile opponent for the throne, old Simeon Bekbulatovich. He also prohibited certain leading boyars from marrying, including Fedor Mstislavskii and Vasilii Shuiskii.[43] It should be noted, however, that rulers of Russia back to Ivan III had occasionally resorted to that particular tactic in dealing with political opponents.[44]

Far more alarming to contemporaries, Tsar Boris revived the time-honored technique of encouraging the denunciation of his political foes by their relatives, associates, servants, and even slaves. Ever since Ivan III, the "duty to denounce" enemies of the ruler had been growing in Russian political culture.[45] Ivan the Terrible used it repeatedly against his opponents, terrifying his elite by rewarding slaves who denounced their masters. The boyars had been so upset by that dangerous tactic that they successfully petitioned Tsar Ivan to halt the practice in 1582.[46] In fact, it had encouraged popular hostility against the boyars as potential traitors to the tsar.[47] Tsar Boris's revival of the practice greatly embittered many aristocrats who regarded it as a grave threat to the social hierarchy as well as a potent technique for destroying Godunov's political foes.[48] The tsar also revived Ivan the Terrible's use of the charge of witchcraft against his opponents.[49] For example, one of Ivan Shuiskii's slaves denounced his master for practicing witchcraft, and Tsar Boris ordered the boyar to stand trial. Some members of the Shuiskii family were confined to their homes, some were exiled, and some persons visiting the Shuiskiis were tortured.[50] Ivan Shuiskii was eventually kicked out of the boyar council, but Vasilii Shuiskii and his brother Dmitrii avoided any charge of treason and remained at least publicly loyal to Tsar Boris.[51] Many boyars must have shuddered in fear that they might be next.

Tsar Boris's harshest measures were taken against the Romanovs.[52] In 1600, the tsar fell ill, and many people expected him to die. His political opponents began making plans to supplant his dynasty as soon as Boris died; the tsar's son, Fedor, was only eleven years old at the time. As soon as Tsar Boris began to recover and found out what was happening, he struck back hard at his enemies. Some scholars believed he did so in order to protect his son;[53] others saw it as revenge against Boris's chief opponents in the struggle for the throne.[54] It may very well have been the former; the Romanovs really had begun concentrating large numbers of their own military retainers (mostly elite slaves) in the capital, thereby alarming Godunov's agents.[55]

In October 1600, Aleksandr Nikitich Romanov (Fedor Romanov's brother) was accused by an employee of using witchcraft against the tsar's family. Tsar Boris ordered one of the Romanov residences in Moscow burned, and all four Romanov brothers were seized and eventually charged with attempted regicide.[56] The Romanovs accused their enemies in the boyar council of plotting against them, and, in fact, some boyars did urge harsh measures against the "traitor" Romanovs and profited from their downfall.[57] The entire Romanov faction was summarily purged from court, and the failure of the boyars to prevent that from happening was seen by some contemporaries as a major cause of the Troubles.[58] The Romanov brothers and their relatives were exiled to remote places, their estates were confiscated, and their military retainers were dispersed.

Fedor Romanov, the eldest brother, was forcibly tonsured, becoming the monk (and future patriarch of the Russian Orthodox Church) Filaret. Two of his younger brothers soon died under mysterious circumstances.[59] Also arrested at about the same time was Bogdan Belskii, who had worked with Fedor Romanov against Godunov in 1598 and may also have been involved in the Romanov conspiracy in 1600. Tsar Boris had Belskii's beard torn out; then he confiscated his estates, freed his slaves, and exiled him in disgrace to Siberia.[60]

After the fall of the Romanovs, the political struggle against Tsar Boris seemed to recede. The rest of the boyars remained at least publicly loyal to the new dynasty.[61] Nonetheless, Tsar Boris grew increasingly isolated and fearful. He now seldom appeared in public, and when he did it was "with much more ceremony and reluctance than any of his predecessors."[62] The reason for his change in behavior? Boris suspected that his political enemies were active behind the scenes. He was especially concerned about rumors circulating since 1600 that Tsarevich Dmitrii had escaped death in Uglich and was planning revenge against him. Tsar Boris and his agents quietly made every effort to track down the source of those rumors. As a precautionary measure, Dmitrii's mother, the nun Marfa, was exiled to Vologda in the far north. Widespread use of torture, denunciations by slaves, exile, and even threats of death by poisoning or drowning failed to uncover the source of the stories about Dmitrii; but such measures made the boyars and others increasingly nervous about the tsar's tyranny.[63]

In fact, Godunov's heavy hand in dealing with his political foes had disastrous consequences for his dynasty and for Russia. It apparently drove the remaining Romanovs, Bogdan Belskii, and possibly the Nagoi clan into a secret alliance against him—an alliance that soon produced a "resurrected" Tsarevich Dmitrii prepared to challenge the "regicide" and "usurper" who sat on the tsarist throne.[64] The end result was civil war. At the end of 1600, however, that civil war certainly did not appear to be imminent. By then, Tsar Boris appeared to have triumphed over all his political rivals. Feared and respected at home and abroad, he applied himself diligently to the tasks of trying to restore Russia's economy and state finances and trying to shore up the gentry militia. At the same time, however, he continued Russia's imperial expansion to the south and east and attempted to tame the cossacks, in the process grossly overstraining his resources and creating serious unrest on the frontier.

All of Tsar Boris's activities and ambitions were soon overwhelmed by a terrible famine—perhaps the worst one in all of Russian history—that wiped out up to a third of Russia's population and left much of the country in ruins.[65] By the time the famine was over, Tsar Boris's reputation (already suffering due to the persecution of his enemies) was ruined in the eyes of many Russians. The famine contributed significantly to the delegitimization of the new dynasty, deepened Russia's developing crisis, and was one of the major causes of the civil war.[66]

We have already seen how the "little ice age" contributed to Russia's developing crisis during the second half of the sixteenth century. Coming on top of chronically low yields in cereal grains and growing population pressure on food supplies, the increasingly cool and unreliable weather depressed agricultural production to subsistence levels and led to increasingly frequent food shortages and famines.[67] The development of serfdom in the 1590s further complicated the situation by significantly reducing any agricultural surplus remaining in the hands of the peasants, thereby giving them less margin of safety to survive lean years.[68] At the very end of the sixteenth century, the most severe weather descended on northern Europe and—as noted earlier—was closely associated with the worst food crises and the largest number of rebellions in all of early modern history.[69] Russia at the dawn of the seventeenth century suffered more than any of its neighbors from the impact of the "little ice age."

During the summer of 1601, across much of Russia there was abnormally cool and rainy weather for more than two months, preventing grain from ripening. As early as late July, parts of Russia were hit by serious frosts; by mid-August, a severe frost killed many still-unripe crops. Winter came early that year, and much of the fall planting, done with frozen or immature seeds, failed to germinate.[70] By the end of 1601, food shortages began to occur, and Tsar Boris's government was forced to take some emergency measures to relieve the suffering. Making things worse, the winter of 1601–2 was extremely cold and severe.[71] Then real catastrophe struck; much of the spring grain crop was destroyed by terrible frosts before it could mature.[72] By that point, many peasants lacked enough old grain to resow their fields, and mid-summer frosts and snow in central Russia ruined most of what little grain had been replanted.

Terrible famine descended on the land in 1602.[73] Food prices skyrocketed to twenty-five times prefamine levels or even higher, and many hungry people could no longer afford the price.[74] They were quickly reduced to eating horses, dogs, cats, and other food proscribed by the church as "unclean." Many of them also ate hay, grass, bark, and roots. The horror of the famine was overwhelming; there was massive starvation and widespread reports of cannibalism. Bodies piled up along the roadsides and were gnawed by wild animals.[75] Prolonged famine destroyed family ties; men abandoned their wives and mothers abandoned their children. Banditry and other crimes increased to epidemic levels.[76] Many peasants and struggling pomeshchiki were forced to sell themselves into slavery in order to survive. Peasants on crown lands were allowed to indenture themselves in return for grain. Not surprisingly, slave sales increased to approximately nine times that of normal years.[77] Although some lords were generous to their dependents, many slaves and military retainers were turned out by their masters to fend for themselves even though those same masters often had food and money in reserve. As a result, large numbers of homeless, unemployed people starved to death.[78] Many peasants, slaves, and other desperate and hungry people migrated to the southern frontier where famine was not as severe as in northern and central Russia.[79]

In the fall of 1602, attempts to plant damaged seeds failed; most of the grain did not grow. Because of that, severe famine continued into 1603. Spring and summer weather in that year was satisfactory for cereal grain production, but many peasants no longer had any seed grain left to plant, so widespread hunger continued.[80] Epidemic diseases spread rapidly among the famine-weakened population.[81] By the time good harvests in 1604 put an end to the famine, much of Russia had been devastated. Contemporaries estimated that famine deaths in the north reached two-thirds of the total population, whereas contemporary estimates put the loss in the south at about one third of the total population.[82] Overall, the famine multiplied the effects of the country's developing crisis and was especially cruel to rural inhabitants and the poor. It delivered a shattering blow to peasant agriculture, contributed to the severe problems already facing Russia's declining towns and villages, reduced already dwindling tax revenues, and sharpened the gentry militia crisis. The famine greatly weakened the Russian empire.[83]

Throughout the famine, Tsar Boris tried desperately to help his suffering people, but the dimensions of the disaster were such that he could not actually do very much. Even before the famine struck, Godunov had publicly committed himself to poor relief; as hunger began to spread across the land, the tsar declared that the poor had a right to eat. He took unprecedented steps to aid the starving and to control food prices.[84] As early as November 1601, Tsar Boris tried unsuccessfully to end speculation and profiteering in the grain market by officially setting grain prices at low rates and by threatening grain hoarders with fines, beatings, and imprisonment. During the famine, he opened up tsarist grain reserves, selling his surplus at half the market price and giving small loaves of bread away to the poor.[85] Much of the grain the tsar sold at low prices, however, ended up in the hands of speculators, and soon even the tsar's reserves were depleted. The greed and dishonesty of officials supervising grain sales and distribution aggravated the problem, as did hoarding by the public. A few petty traders were beaten or executed for profiteering, but such measures did not end the practice or bring any relief.[86]

In fact, there was no way to provide meaningful relief to millions of Russian peasants. That was one reason why Tsar Boris concentrated his efforts on the towns. He spent huge amounts of money providing coins and small loaves of bread daily to the Moscow poor. Similar programs were set up in Smolensk, Novgorod, and Pskov. The problem with such a program was that many hungry people in the countryside heard of the tsar's generosity and flocked to the towns, especially to Moscow. Tens of thousands of people crowded into the capital, depopulating the countryside for more than two hundred kilometers in all directions. Whole families that might have survived in the country now wandered the streets of Moscow where price inflation and scarcity made even the tsar's alms inadequate to live on.[87] Each day in the capital alone, Tsar Boris's agents distributed food and money to about seventy thousand people (nearly equal to the capital's prefamine population), but that was still not enough.[88] Because of the length of the famine, price inflation, dishonesty, greed, and the continued arrival of more and more people in Moscow, the situation grew steadily worse. Starving people died in the streets and on the roads to the capital every day. More than one hundred thousand people died in Moscow during the famine (fifty thousand in just seven months during 1602) and were buried in three huge common graves. Tsar Boris paid for shrouds for each one of them.[89]

Eventually, the tsar was forced to stop distributing alms because of the depopulation of the countryside, severe overcrowding in Moscow, and a depleted treasury. That made the situation temporarily much worse. Hunger riots became commonplace. The market almost ceased functioning because it became dangerous for merchants to try to sell their goods. It also became dangerous just to walk the streets, and anyone foolish enough to be seen giving anything away in public ran the serious risk of being trampled to death by a hungry mob.[90] The situation in Moscow became extremely tense, worse than in the provinces. It was not unusual in the capital to see hungry people grab food or accost lords, speculators, the rich, or anyone who looked well-fed. Many homes were pillaged, and many wealthy individuals were terrorized by desperately poor people. The government tried to control the streets with streltsy units; during the worst days of 1602 and the spring of 1603, boyars personally took command of streltsy units throughout Moscow in order to prevent starving people from robbing the homes of the well-to-do. Robbers were summarily executed when caught, but it became extremely difficult to maintain public order in the midst of such misery.[91] Ugly rumors circulated that rich merchants, lords, monks, bishops, and even Patriarch Iov had huge amounts of grain but refused to release it in hopes of making an even higher profit as prices soared.[92] In fact, the patriarch and bishops gave away much of their grain. Nonetheless, the perception grew that rich lords and monks were withholding grain and making the famine much worse. That, coupled with increased obligations imposed on serfs living on monastic estates during the famine years, eroded the reputation of the patriarch and other church leaders and generally undermined the authority of all well-fed leaders of famine-struck Russia.[93]

During the famine brigands infested the roads approaching Moscow and periodically seized food shipments headed to the capital—thereby intensifying the misery of many people. In order to assure Moscow's food supply from the provinces, it was frequently necessary to send out small gentry detachments to cleanse the main roads of those desperate men. Ordinarily, that was easily and quickly accomplished.[94] On occasion, however, large bands of brigands fought fiercely against government forces. Many Marxist scholars thought they detected in such conflicts the beginning of a massive peasant rebellion. That view is incorrect but has had a powerful impact upon overall assessments of the Time of Troubles. Let us take a closer look at the issues involved.

Tsar Boris tried to ameliorate the traumatic situation in the countryside, which had been made especially serious because of enserfment. Anticipating many problems and widespread mass movement in response to food shortages already developing by the fall of 1601, Tsar Boris issued a controversial decree on November 28, 1601.[95] That decree temporarily authorized the movement from the estate of any pomeshchik to that of another of up to two peasant households. Such transfer was to occur in the same two-week period around St. George's Day (November 26) during which peasants had previously been allowed to move before the advent of the "forbidden years." Probably for that reason, a few contemporaries and several historians incorrectly assumed that Godunov was at least temporarily restoring the peasants' right to move freely on St. George's Day. Some scholars with overheated imaginations have even conjured images of a tsar so fearful of a massive movement against serfdom that he was forced to grant freedom to the restive peasants.[96] In fact, that is not at all what happened. The tsar simply attempted to regulate the inevitable flow of peasants away from the estates of ruined pomeshchiki where there was little food. He hoped to direct those peasants toward functioning estates with food and an economy capable of generating taxes. That would satisfy hungry peasants, generate revenue, and shore up the sturdier elements of the gentry militia. Godunov's decree stopped pomeshchiki from charging their departing peasants' exit fees but was careful not to exempt migrating peasants from any of their tax obligations to the state. In this way, the tsar consciously sacrificed the interests of the weakest pomeshchiki (who were not of much use for military service, anyway) in his effort to shore up state finances and to relieve the misery of the masses.[97] It is important to remember that Boris Godunov was in no way a "gentry tsar" but stood firmly with the magnates and state interests.[98] To that end, no peasants were authorized to move from state and crown lands, from ecclesiastical and boyar estates, or from lands in Moscow province (held primarily by courtiers and bureaucrats). Holders of those estates were powerful or useful, and revenues from those lands—although somewhat reduced—still flowed to the treasury; so there was no reason to allow peasant movement from them.[99] Tsar Boris did, however, temporarily reduce the amount of taxes demanded from crown and state peasants.[100] Nonetheless, serfdom remained basically unchanged except on pomeshchik estates far from the capital. There the story was dramatically different. Large numbers of peasants lived on gentry estates covered by the tsar's decree, and because of it many of those serfs gained the chance to save themselves or to try to improve their situation by moving. They took immediate advantage of the opportunity. Meanwhile, the decision not to let peasants in the Moscow district move inadvertently contributed to the glut of starving people in the streets of the capital.[101]

Many peasants moved legally in response to the tsar's decree—especially impoverished peasants and landless rural workers. Pomeshchiki were generally willing to let those poor souls go without much trouble because the emigrants usually had no grain or animals and were regarded merely as extra mouths to feed in hard times. Some lords had plenty of food but let menials and agricultural slaves go anyway in order to save money—expecting those who were dismissed to feed themselves and then to return after the famine. Pomeshchiki gaining those peasants promised to feed them and to collect taxes from them.[102] In this way, the tsar's expedient did provide relief to many people, and peasants generally favored his decree. On the other hand, it appears that many not-so-desperate peasants also used the tsar's decree simply as an excuse to get away from certain lords or to improve their conditions. Since the loss of even one or two productive peasants could spell ruin for most pomeshchiki, that development alarmed many of them. Understandably, those lords hated Tsar Boris's decree.[103] Increasingly desperate gentry tried various means of coercion in order to retain departing peasants: restraining them by force, charging outrageous (and illegal) exit fees, robbing them, and threatening them with violence. When continuation of the famine forced the tsar to reissue his decree about peasant movement in 1602, he specifically prohibited such coercion and violence. Nonetheless, those practices continued. In addition, serious fighting among the gentry broke out over control of peasants and their belongings. Despite the tsar's efforts to prevent rich lords from taking advantage of the situation, some did entice peasants to their estates, in the process greatly embittering desperate petty pomeshchiki and leading to much bloodshed and ruin.[104] During the famine years, some magnates were also able to coerce ruined deti boiarskie into slavery, which stirred up even more resentment.[105] While the great lords remained loyal to the Godunov regime, the frustration and anger of impoverished pomeshchiki began building against Tsar Boris himself.[106] That was the real cost of the tsar's attempt to help his starving subjects in rural Russia.

It has been claimed that Tsar Boris was finally forced by the angry gentry to put an end to all peasant movement in 1603, but there is no evidence of that. The tsar's temporary measure was not repeated in the fall of 1603 because the famine was ending. It has also been claimed that the reimposition of serfdom in 1603 angered the peasants and made massive rebellion inevitable.[107] Close study of the subject shows how untenable that point of view really is. As noted earlier, in the chaotic years of the famine there was a sharp increase in banditry and in the number of bandits roving the countryside. Many scholars have mistakenly assumed that most of those bandits were angry peasants who had been victims of serfdom and gentry coercion during the famine. Furthermore, it has been rashly assumed that the activities of those bandits represented a rising tide of popular unrest against serfdom and Tsar Boris, one that eventually broke out in some kind of peasant war.[108] As we shall see, that was definitely not the case.

Primarily to assure grain supplies to the capital, but also to restore order, Tsar Boris sent out numerous small detachments of gentry and streltsy to clear the roads of bandits—which they usually accomplished in short order.[109] Because of the frequency of those expeditions, some Soviet scholars believed the tsar was reacting to a widespread, unified movement of peasants and slaves against serfdom as early as 1601–2.[110] That is simply not true. Godunov was actually employing the same methods against robbers that he had used in the 1590s.[111] In fact, he went out of his way to avoid alarming his subjects by treating the epidemic of brigands as a serious problem but not as a national emergency. Regular procedures for suppressing robbery were used, including raising occasional levies of peasants to fight them. (Robbery victims included peasants, not just the elite.) There was no hint of a mass movement or a class war that had to be suppressed by a frightened gentry. In fact, many of the bandits were themselves ruined pomeshchiki and unemployed elite military slaves.[112] Because of the severity and duration of the famine, however, those brigands became a serious problem that did not go away.

In 1603, while the capital still faced a severe food shortage and hordes of aggressive paupers still roamed its streets, gentry units continued to be routinely dispatched throughout central Russia to combat robber bands.[113] The problem became serious enough to prompt a tsarist decree in August 1603, promising freedom to those slaves who had been turned out by their masters during the famine. That decree was specifically intended to pacify desperate, unemployed military slaves—the most dangerous of all the brigands infesting the countryside. Every effort was made to spread the word about the decree to all towns and villages, and it is known that a number of slaves were freed under its terms.[114] In spite of those efforts, however, by September 1603, a large band of robbers menaced the Moscow area and proved to be extremely difficult to suppress. The so-called "Khlopko rebellion"—named after the leader of the bandits—has been regarded by many scholars as the beginning of a mass revolt by the lower classes, either as a harbinger of the Bolotnikov rebellion or as the beginning of the First Peasant War.[115] That interpretation is simplistic and misleading.

The Soviet historian Ivan Smirnov recognized that most of the bandits with Khlopko were slaves, not serfs; but he claimed that they were plow slaves and menials similar to other peasants. Therefore, he still regarded the Khlopko rebellion as a class war. In fact, Smirnov tried to prove that the Khlopko rebellion was part of a huge mass movement covering most of the regions of central Russia by arbitrarily linking all the reports of the routine suppression of banditry in the countryside with the Khlopko rebellion. Nonetheless, Smirnov was never willing to accept the view of many of his colleagues that the Khlopko rebellion was actually the beginning of the First Peasant War—continuing instead to see it as an ominous harbinger of the Bolotnikov rebellion.[116] Vadim Koretskii and some other Soviet scholars also noted that most bandits in 1603 were slaves, not peasants; but they were nonetheless convinced that there must have been large-scale peasant participation in all that bandit activity. Therefore, they saw the Khlopko rebellion as the opening round of the First Peasant War.[117] Other Soviet scholars insisted that most of Khlopko's forces must have been peasants and serfs, and for years they searched the archives for proof of their theory of a huge peasant war beginning in 1603.[118] Their search was in vain. There is no evidence of peasant rebellion in 1603, and there is no reason to view the Khlopko rebellion as the start of a peasant war. The largest group with Khlopko were former elite military slaves—that is to say professional soldiers. Most had been turned out by their masters during the famine, but among the brigands were also some slaves who had been dismissed from the service of such disgraced boyars as the Romanovs.[119]

Virtually nothing is known about the bandit leader Khlopko. According to Richard Hellie his name meant "slave," and it is probably correct to assume that he had been an elite military slave.[120] Khlopko may have come from the southwestern frontier province of Severia (or Seversk), perhaps from the Komaritsk district.[121] That does not, however, justify the assertion that the Khlopko rebellion originated on the southern frontier, as some Soviet scholars suggested.[122] The bulk of Khlopko's forces were probably from the Moscow region.[123] Khlopko's band of approximately five hundred brigands was the largest group the government had to contend with during the famine; they menaced the roads west of the capital. In September 1603, okolnichii Ivan F. Basmanov was dispatched from Moscow with one hundred select streltsy to suppress the bandits; no gentry cavalry were deemed necessary for the operation.[124] Forewarned and greatly outnumbering Basmanov's force, Khlopko set up an ambush in a narrow pass between two groves of trees. His men managed to kill Basmanov and most of the streltsy.[125] Tsar Boris immediately dispatched a much larger force that defeated the bandits in bitter fighting. Khlopko was wounded several times before being captured. Some of the bandits were immediately hanged from trees near the site of the battle; others were secretly hanged at a later time.[126] Many of the brigands escaped, fleeing south to the frontier. One chronicler claimed that they were eventually caught and hanged, but Sergei Platonov was wisely skeptical about the reliability of that source.[127] Many brigands probably did escape to the frontier, possibly to Severia or to the cossacks. Later, some of those bandits may very well have participated in the civil war, but their numbers would certainly have been small compared to rebels drawn from southern military servitors and from the flood of peasants, slaves, townsmen, and ruined pomeshchiki who moved south to escape the famine without ever having participated in a mythical class war in 1603.

Robbery declined as the famine eased, and even proponents of the notion that the Khlopko rebellion was the start of a peasant war were forced to admit that there was a sharp decline in "revolutionary activity" after 1603.[128] Attempts to discern a nascent collective revolutionary consciousness developing among the masses during the famine and attempts to explain the apparent decline in that revolutionary fervor after Khlopko was captured (by citing such things as the immaturity of the rebel movement, poor leadership, or the lack of a coherent ideology) are not at all convincing.[129] The famine did, in fact, produce many desperate people and flashes of violence on the part of the poor and hungry directed against the rich and well-fed. That is not, however, the same thing as social revolution or even civil war. Bandits during the famine had no revolutionary plans.[130]

Overall, the famine had a devastating impact, delivering a severe blow to an already weakened economy. As noted earlier, it shattered peasant agriculture and Russia's already dwindling urban trade, and it greatly increased the poverty of the Russian people. The number of taxpayers declined sharply, as did the income of the lords, the church, and the state. The famine depleted Tsar Boris's treasury, weakened his already traumatized military classes, and reduced the military power of Russia.[131] The famine also caused massive demographic disruption. Beyond the high mortality, there was widespread migration away from famine-struck areas by landless workers and slaves turned out by their masters. Large numbers of desperate people headed south and southwest in search of food. They crowded into southern towns and districts, competing with locals for jobs and resources and disrupting the lives of already unhappy southern military servitors. They also joined the cossacks in large numbers.[132] It has been claimed that the flight of peasants south was profitable for southern pomeshchiki who gained a valuable labor supply as a result. That is inaccurate. As Hellie has shown, runaways avoided the estates of southern pomeshchiki, who had few, if any, peasants and were actually in serious economic distress.[133] Runaways were far more likely to seek employment as low status military servitors or to join the cossacks. The famine actually led to a dramatic increase in the number of military slaves—with their weapons and skills—who became cossacks. One contemporary estimated that twenty thousand slaves fled south during the famine, and many of them soon swelled the ranks of the cossacks. The resulting sharp rise in the number of free cossacks led to their consolidation into larger units of up to five or even six hundred.[134] During the famine, those larger, better armed, and better led cossack hosts (armies) launched powerful raids on merchants that seriously disrupted trade on the Volga and other rivers and that detachments of southern frontier streltsy proved utterly incapable of stopping.[135] Such increased cossack activities prompted a redoubling of Tsar Boris's efforts to subordinate the free cossacks even in the midst of the famine, efforts that stirred great animosity among the now larger and better armed hosts. The sharp rise in food prices during the famine had hit the cossacks hard, and many of them were by then already dependent on Russian grain supplies. (Some had even previously received grain from the government at no cost.) In 1602, when Tsar Boris once again outlawed trade with all free cossacks not cooperating with his officials, his decision cut many of those men off from vital supplies of Russian grain, gunpowder, lead, and weapons. Under those circumstances, it should be no surprise that by 1604 many cossacks were willing and eager to fight against their old nemesis, Boris Godunov.[136]

As already noted, the famine seriously weakened Russia's military strength. Nonetheless, Tsar Boris continued his aggressive imperial expansion in spite of inadequate funding and a crisis-stricken gentry. During the famine, Godunov had good success to the east; the population of Siberia, also hard hit by the famine, was unable to resist Russian expansion.[137] Unwise expeditions against the Turks and Tatars in the Caucasus Mountains, however, failed miserably—with heavy losses.[138] Eventually, Russia's severe crisis slowed down its imperial drive. As one might expect, the tsar's already weakened military forces had been badly hurt by the famine—especially the petty pomeshchiki who were vulnerable because of their chronic shortage of land with peasant labor and chronic arrears in their salaries. The tsar's temporary and partial restoration of peasant movement in response to the famine truly devastated many of his already distressed militiamen. Increasing numbers of petty gentry were so impoverished that they were unable to report for duty. Others became so desperate that they sold themselves as slaves or ran away to join the cossacks. Rising pomeshchik resentment focused not just on wealthy magnates who took advantage of them, but increasingly on the tsar himself. In light of this, it is not surprising that so many of the tsar's militiamen joined the rebel cause during the civil war.[139] The conjuncture of the developing state crisis, Boris Godunov's policies, and the famine made the situation on the southern frontier especially volatile. Among other things, during the famine, the already relatively small number of high status warriors serving on the frontier declined sharply while the number of lower status military servitors continued to increase. More and more of the tsar's southern military forces now consisted of unhappy fortress cossacks and large numbers of impoverished pomeshchiki forced to serve as deti boiarskie infantry.[140] Such demoralized forces became the predominant, often the only, military personnel in such southern towns as Kursk, Elets, Orel, and Putivl. As noted earlier, they got along reasonably well with the free cossacks and, not surprisingly, were quick to cooperate with them when civil war broke out in 1604.[141]

Probably the most serious impact of the famine was the decline in the legitimacy of the oppressive state, predatory Russian elites, the church, and the elected tsar in the eyes of many desperate and miserable people. Tsar Boris lost popularity not just because he sacrificed the weak pomeshchiki in the famine years. The tsar's legitimacy itself—never fully accepted by supporters of his rivals or by many victims of his policies—was seriously undermined by the famine. In Russia's God-centered, tsar-centered political culture, the tsar was supposed to be the protector of his Orthodox flock. The fact that Boris Godunov had been a boyar and was held responsible for enserfment, heavy taxes, the 1597 slave law, and the harassment of cossacks combined with ugly rumors circulating about his rise to power and contributed to his problems after 1598; but it was really the magnitude, horror, and duration of the famine that caused many Russians to begin wondering about Tsar Boris's legitimacy. Some readers may be skeptical about such a claim. Scholars have often declared that there is an inadequate source base to understand popular consciousness in early modern

Russia.[142] Nonetheless, the bankruptcy of Marxist views about the social revolutionary consciousness produced by the Time of Troubles (often echoed in Western historiography) clearly demonstrates the need for historians to try harder to understand what Tsar Boris's subjects were thinking. Here, once again, insights from comparative history can be of help.

Scholars studying the impact of the Black Death of the fourteenth century have noted that the trauma and horror of that massive catastrophe caused many survivors to wonder how such events fit into God's plans for humanity.[143] The plague was viewed by many as the work of God and a clear sign that something was wrong with the established religious and political order. The result was, among other things, a loss of prestige, honor, and respect for the Catholic Church and priests. At the same time, there was a growth in religious fervor among many of the survivors. Popular consciousness in the years after the Black Death was also notably "neurotic" and extremely gloomy. Survivors lived in constant fear and anticipation of further disaster. Emotional disturbance and even hysteria were never far below the surface of consciousness in the late fourteenth century.[144] In general, famines and the horrible sights and experiences associated with them have historically produced similar results: terror, confusion, hallucinations, hysteria, fear of divine punishment, revival of religiosity, and the search for scapegoats.[145] In particular, famines associated with the "little ice age" often produced the belief that God was angry with secular politics, and such ideas contributed to riots, rebellions, and civil wars.[146] Also closely linked to those famines and increasing social stress during the late sixteenth century was a growing fear of witchcraft and increased persecution of "witches."[147] All of this is highly relevant to Russia in the early seventeenth century when famine killed up to a third of the population and seriously disrupted the lives of most people.

In his coronation activities and after, Tsar Boris made every effort to transfer the mantle of legitimacy from Russia's extinct sanctified dynasty to himself and to reinforce the idea that he too had been chosen by God to rule and protect the Russian people. That was an important step in Godunov's consolidation of power within a political culture in which God was seen to be actively involved in the fate of Orthodox Christians and in which the God-chosen tsar was to be obeyed and honored almost as a god himself.[148] It was generally believed that as long as the tsar was good, pious, and legitimate, he and Russia would flourish. It was also widely believed, however, that if the tsar was evil and illegitimate, God would inevitably punish the ruler and Russia.[149] Many people came to view the famine as a clear sign of God's anger with the Russian people and their ruler.[150] It was then just a short leap for them to conclude that Tsar

Boris (already suspect in the eyes of many) was an illegitimate and evil ruler who brought down God's punishment in the form of the famine.[151] If Tsar Boris was not favored by God, many famine-weary and sometimes hysterical people reasoned, then he must be in league with the devil.[152] The Russian people were already rather superstitious, and fear of witchcraft had grown in Russia during the sixteenth century and increased strongly during the Time of Troubles.[153] Even the tsars were superstitious (especially Tsar Boris) and took precautions against sorcerers and witches.[154] The fear that witches caused natural calamities was widespread and very old in Russia,[155] so when suspicion increased that Tsar Boris was not favored by God and rumors circulated that he was actually a sorcerer, the tsar's legitimacy was seriously undermined.[156] If Godunov had been a member of the old sacred ruling dynasty, he might not have been so badly damaged by the famine; but, as his divine aura dissipated, Tsar Boris was increasingly held responsible for the misery of his people. Such a decline in the ruler's legitimacy was an important factor in preparing Russia for civil war.[157] Nonetheless, it is important not to exaggerate the weakness of Boris Godunov's position.

Tsar Boris after the famine has traditionally and inaccurately been portrayed as a weak and despised ruler who was falling from power because he had been rejected by the enserfed masses.[158] It has even been suggested (without any evidence) that the famine-weary masses produced from their collective consciousness a "social utopian" legend about a returning deliverer, Tsarevich Dmitrii, who would save them from serfdom and the evil usurper Boris Godunov.[159] In fact, Tsar Boris did not face a massive popular rebellion against serfdom. Instead, he faced popular uprisings in support of Dmitrii's claim to the throne, and there were certainly no legends about Dmitrii circulating in Russia before someone claiming to be the tsarevich actually appeared in Poland-Lithuania. The masses did not look for or think to invent an alternative to Tsar Boris; Godunov's powerful political foes saw to that.[160] Even the appearance of Dmitrii, however, did not automatically signal the end to the Godunov dynasty. Social scientists have demonstrated that a morally weakened and unpopular ruler regarded by many as illegitimate can still survive as long as key elites remain loyal and as long as the tools of governing and coercion remain more or less intact.[161] That certainly proved to be the case with Boris Godunov.

7

What Triggered the Civil War?

By 1604, in spite of moderate weather and prospects for good harvests, Russia and the Russians had been badly traumatized by the two-year famine and a profound state crisis. Tsar Boris faced many groups alienated by his policies and politics, and a significant number of Russians doubted his legitimacy. However, those things were not sufficient to trigger a rebellion against the sitting ruler of Europe's largest country. Something more was needed. In previous chapters, we have reviewed the long-term and intermediate destabilizing forces that helped push Russia into crisis and brought it to the threshold of civil war. What were the immediate preconditions or causes that triggered the conflict?

Social scientists and comparative historians have identified a number of immediate preconditions that were common to most early modern upheavals. They include times of great hardship;[1] a severe fiscal crisis facing the state;[2] a short-term decline in the revenue and power of the government;[3] the recent imposition of onerous obligations on the ruler's subjects;[4] elites in crisis and decline;[5] intra-elite conflict;[6] elite disaffection with the crown;[7] a discredited regime perceived by many as illegitimate and held responsible for crisis and misery;[8] mobilized, disgruntled elite groups with resources;[9] large numbers of impoverished, landless minor nobles, disbanded soldiers, and young men;[10] and the existence of a militarized frontier zone with a recently-annexed population resentful of the central government's infringement on their land and autonomy.[11] All of those immediate preconditions existed in Russia by 1604. Nonetheless, as serious as the situation was, Tsar Boris was not personally threatened until the arrival on the scene of a charismatic and credible claimant to the throne. In the political culture of early modern Russia, Tsar Boris's enemies would never have dared to risk confrontation with him without the existence of the pretender Dmitrii. It took Dmitrii's invasion of Russia and his campaign for the throne to trigger the civil war.

Russia's first civil war came about as a direct result of the bold invasion of the country by a man claiming to be Tsarevich Dmitrii, somehow "miraculously" rescued from the "usurper" Boris Godunov's alleged assassination attempt in 1591 and now returning to claim the throne from the illegitimate "false tsar" Boris. The pretender Dmitrii quickly generated a broad coalition of supporters from all social strata. The fanatical, quasi-religious support he received and the unprecedented intrusion of the masses into high politics during his military campaign seriously frightened Dmitrii's opponents and have puzzled historians ever since. Misunderstanding of Dmitrii's popular support has contributed to gross misinterpretations of the pretender, his campaign for the throne, his reign, the civil war fought in his name after his assassination, and the very meaning of the Time of Troubles itself. In addition, as in the case of other early modern Russian popular uprisings, faulty views of rebel consciousness during the Troubles have led to significant errors in assessing early modern Russian popular consciousness in general.[12]

As noted earlier, for a long time historians assumed that the outbreak of rebellion against Tsar Boris in 1604 was a spontaneous rising of the Russian people against serfdom. As a result, relatively little attention was paid to Dmitrii or his campaign for the throne as possible triggers. That approach to the topic corresponded with traditional social science theories about popular uprisings that basically ignored "incidental triggers" as mere indicators of deeper social conflicts.[13] Unfortunately, such an interpretation of the beginning of Russia's first civil war ignored much important evidence and was based almost exclusively upon the misleading propaganda generated by Dmitrii's enemies during his lifetime and after his assassination. Starting even before Dmitrii's invasion, Tsar Boris's regime launched an unsuccessful propaganda campaign identifying the "false tsarevich" as a debauched runaway monk who was a tool of the Catholic Poles and the devil.[14] Dmitrii's supporters were simultaneously portrayed as hopelessly naïve or as having darker motives.[15] After Dmitrii's victory, short reign and murder, the usurper Tsar Vasilii Shuiskii faced a powerful civil war against him in Tsar Dmitrii's name that raged for years and nearly destroyed the country. Just like Tsar Boris, a surprised and frightened Shuiskii felt compelled to launch a major propaganda campaign against the unworthy "false Dmitrii" he had assassinated and against Dmitrii's angry supporters who were taking the field against him in large numbers. The Shuiskii regime falsely denounced the rebels as brigands and social revolutionaries determined to overthrow the ruling elite and to seize their property, wives, and daughters.[16]

The combination of the Godunov and Shuiskii propaganda campaigns strongly influenced later historical assessments of Dmitrii and rebels in the Time of Troubles. Historians generally came to regard Dmitrii as a fraud and had difficulty crediting him with the ability to generate powerful popular support. Instead, they looked elsewhere for explanations of popular uprisings during the

Troubles. Some writers concluded that rebellions in Dmitrii's name were nothing more than "senseless," elemental outbursts of the suffering masses entirely devoid of political content but cleverly manipulated by the evil monk or his henchmen. Others focused on Shuiskii's propaganda against Dmitrii's supporters, concluding that the rebellions may have lacked true political content but had a definite social goal—revolution of the masses. Proponents of both the "senseless" and social revolutionary interpretations often tried to explain Dmitrii's popular support with the same vague concept of "naïve monarchism" (strong faith in the benevolence of the ruler toward the common people). Those interpretations are badly flawed, and each in its own way has seriously distorted the meaning of Dmitrii's popular support and contributed to a faulty understanding of early modern Russian popular consciousness. Let us take a closer look at the issues involved.

The erroneous notion that early modern Russian popular rebellions were "senseless" outbursts became a fixed idea among many Russian writers from the seventeenth century right into the twentieth century.[17] Because there was officially no room in imperial Russian political culture for any kind of popular participation, some historians felt more comfortable explaining Dmitrii's widespread support as the spontaneous, unthinking response of the people to their plight or as the result of cynical manipulation of the apolitical masses by Dmitrii and his associates. As in the "naïve monarchist" interpretations of other early modern Russian rebellions, this perspective was due to wishful thinking on the part of a conservative elite badly frightened by the periodic outbursts of fanaticism and unmistakably political activity of the overburdened Russian people, and to the persistence of a faulty view that the masses were too immature to make rational choices and to act upon them.[18] The sharply contrasting but equally erroneous notion that rebels in the Time of Troubles were conscious social revolutionaries began to gain momentum in the late nineteenth century. As we have seen, early Soviet scholars went so far as to describe Dmitrii as the radical leader of a cossack or peasant revolution.[19] Gradually, the role of Dmitrii was deemphasized in favor of a focus on class war in the Time of Troubles, and Soviet scholars eventually settled on a view of the pretender as an unprincipled adventurer who rode to power on a wave of social revolution against enserfment.[20] First Peasant War scholars viewed the popular uprisings that helped propel Dmitrii to power not so much pro-Dmitrii as "antifeudal" to which the "false Dmitrii" merely attached himself. The pretender was supposedly forced to make rash antifeudal promises to the masses in order to gain support.[21] In the view of Kirill Chistov and many others, a popular "social utopian" legend about Dmitrii's escape from Uglich in 1591 and return as the deliverer of the masses from serfdom grew up before Dmitrii's campaign and explains the mass support for his struggle for the throne.[22] Unfortunately, this widely-held interpretation is just as faulty as the notion that those rebellions were senseless. No doubt Dmitrii did benefit from Russia's profound social crisis and the misery of its masses, but it is important to remember that his campaign for the throne united the most varied social strata, and he was brought to power by popular rebellions in support of his claim to be Ivan the Terrible's son, not a promise to abolish serfdom. There was, in fact, no popular social utopian legend circulating about Dmitrii in Russia before his invasion in 1604.[23] Moreover, none of Dmitrii's supporters fought against serfdom, and Dmitrii was never forced to foment social revolution or to make promises to abolish serfdom in order to win power.[24] His vague promises of rewards to his supporters did not include the abolition of serfdom and were not even aimed primarily at the lower classes.[25] Serfs did not actively participate in Dmitrii's campaign for the throne, and peasants—with the exception of relatively wealthy ones from the Komaritsk district—were only marginally involved. The bulk of the rebels supporting Dmitrii were cossacks, petty gentry, lower status military servitors, and townsmen.

Some Soviet scholars acknowledged the cooperation among rebels of differing social groups and the lack of a distinctly "antifeudal" program on the part of Dmitrii in 1604–5 and on the part of Bolotnikov and others who rose against Shuiskii in 1606, conveniently explaining that awkward fact away as a product of naïve monarchism.[26] Many rebels, it was argued, were ready to bring down the "feudal order" and serfdom but were simply unable to conceive of any other political system besides tsarism. By supporting the rebellion in the name of the "good tsar" Dmitrii, peasants and slaves were supposedly hoping for liberation, but their naïve monarchism actually interfered with their conscious (or unconscious) social goals.[27] That is actually an extremely weak argument that has no evidence to support it. Dmitrii's campaign for the throne and the civil war fought in his name after his assassination united the most varied social strata— including many serf owners. No doubt some of Dmitrii's supporters were "naïve monarchists," but that vague term used so freely by scholars with such dramatically different interpretations of popular consciousness in the Time of Troubles does not, on its own, really help us understand the devotion and endurance of Dmitrii's diverse followers.

Daniel Field has argued that the concept of naïve monarchism itself is not only rather condescending but artificially distinguishes the nature of popular veneration of monarchs from that of literate elites, and Robert Crummey has noted that many of Dmitrii's supporters were far from naïve and had their own agenda.[28] Maureen Perrie rightly preferred the term "popular monarchism" to characterize the remarkably strong faith in the benevolence of the tsar on the part of Russians of all social classes. Far more useful than "naïve monarchism," Perrie's term has the virtue of not excluding elites from consideration and not automatically passing anachronistic judgment on the level of sophistication of early modern monarchists.[29] In previous chapters, we have seen that by 1604 many groups at all levels of Russian society had serious grievances against Tsar Boris that made them more receptive to Dmitrii. For example, seeking relief from taxation, the burdens of southern military service, or hated local officials have been plausibly cited as possible motives for joining Dmitrii's cause.[30] Many cossacks may have supported Dmitrii in order to oppose the state's encroachment on their territory and freedom; others may have been naïve monarchists simply seeking status and salary from the "good tsar."[31] None of those possible motives, however, can really explain the dramatic and dangerous step taken by so many different social groups of breaking with the existing tsarist regime—backed as it was by shrill church propaganda denouncing all rebels as tools of a foreign power and Satan. Neither can those possible motives explain the fervor of Dmitrii's diverse supporters, many of whom were willing to fight for years and to endure horrible fates in the name of the "good tsar." The rapid formation of a broad coalition of rebels and the enduring, quasi-religious fanaticism of Dmitrii's supporters are crucial facts that traditional interpretations have failed to explain but that must be accounted for if we are to understand the true nature of Russia's first civil war.

There is an extensive body of theoretical social science literature concerning revolutions and collective violence. Some of the models and theories of general social stress, individual stress and discontent, systemic imbalances, and crises of legitimacy seem plausible in the abstract;[32] however, they are not particularly helpful in dealing with specific historical problems such as the Time of Troubles. Most are explanations of people's psychological motivations for political violence.[33] As it turns out, much of that work has been powerfully influenced by traditional views of early modern rebellions as unthinking responses to material conditions and class tensions, and few of the models ever treat rebels as rational beings capable of making conscious choices.[34] Fortunately, such approaches have drawn criticism from at least some researchers, and several social scientists have acknowledged the critical need for more careful examination of what actually triggers rebellions.[35]

In a very useful study of what caused popular upheavals, Charles Tilly emphasized that, despite attempts to "psychologize" or "sociologize" the subject, the factors that hold up under close scrutiny are political ones.[36] Michael Kimmel has also keyed on the political motivation of coalitions of social groups involved in rebellions.[37] According to several researchers, those coalitions needed the participation of alienated members of the elite, and they did not need to propose any radical alteration of the social structure.[38] What those rebel coalitions did need, however, was awareness of a possible alternative to the existing regime and to their own unhappy conditions; in short, they needed hope.[39] That was provided by the arrival on the scene of a credible challenger to the existing, discredited ruler.[40] The charismatic authority of such a rebel leader could rest on his heroism and ability to inspire and sustain loyalty and devotion among his followers, his hereditary connection to the old ruling dynasty, or his sense of mission.[41] According to Deborah Stone, the success of such a rebel leader depended upon the communication of a credible "causal story" that demonstrated that the people's problems were due to an evil ruler and that the rebel leader had the right to challenge that person. The successful rebel leader portrayed not just the people but also himself as a victim of the bad ruler's conspiracy and carefully avoided any radical prescription involving the redistribution of power or wealth. In this way, the causal story created new political alliances among a wide variety of victims.[42] The causal story could be especially powerful if the rebel leader was able to portray himself as the long-hidden, innocent hereditary heir to the throne returning to challenge a usurper.[43] His legitimacy could also be significantly enhanced by the widespread belief that God had abandoned the existing ruler and favored the rebel leader.[44] In fact, the strength of any rebel movement was directly related to its sense of religious as well as political mission. All of the most powerful and memorable revolts in which rebel fighting spirit was very high contained a religious element—a sense of the purifying function of rebellion.[45] Whatever the long-term causes were, in the final analysis it was ideas, political culture, and religion that played important roles in triggering rebellion.[46]

The above insights apply directly to Russia's first civil war and can help us do a better job analyzing the pretender Dmitrii and the poorly understood popular support generated by his invasion of Russia. Dmitrii's campaign for the throne triggered a powerful rebellion that had a genuine political and religious purpose—to purify the realm polluted by the evil usurper, Boris Godunov, and to restore the old sacred ruling dynasty to the throne in the person of Ivan the Terrible's youngest son. As we shall see, Dmitrii played his part very well, managing to create a broad and lasting coalition of supporters by a combination of determination, personal charisma, heroism, modest behavior in victory, and especially his remarkable story of divinely-aided escape from Godunov's plot to assassinate him in 1591. For the remainder of this chapter, we shall take a closer look at the forces that helped shape the political and religious consciousness of Dmitrii's supporters and that triggered the civil war; then in the next chapter we shall take a closer look at the remarkable pretender Dmitrii himself.

As previously noted, some historians believe there is an inadequate source base for understanding Russian popular consciousness in the sixteenth and seventeenth centuries; however, the persistence of extremely tendentious traditional scholarly views of the motivation of early modern Russian rebels requires that we at least make an effort to better understand those angry people. In order to have any chance of success—as Boris Mironov warned us—it will be absolutely necessary to end the isolation of the study of rebellions and rebel consciousness from the study of ordinary, everyday early modern Russian culture, religion, morality, and consciousness.[47] Since that related area of research is still in its pioneering stage, however, we must proceed with caution.[48] What often gets overlooked in assessing popular support for Dmitrii is that, to a great extent, the rebels were operating within an entirely religious political culture shaped by Russian Orthodox Christianity.[49] An identifiably popular Orthodox Christian consciousness developed in Russia by the sixteenth century and was closely associated with the emergence of the unified Russian state.[50] The traditional assumption in scholarship has been that Russian popular religion must have differed sharply from elite religious consciousness.[51] That view has been the source (or byproduct) of a number of faulty interpretations of allegedly unique characteristics of peasant (or mass) religiosity in early modern Russia and the Time of Troubles, interpretations that attempted to link popular religiosity to such things as naïve monarchism, pretenderism, social utopias, and even millenarianism.[52] Fortunately, that traditional view has recently begun to give way to a more realistic one that sees fewer differences and more in common between early modern elite political-religious consciousness and popular religious consciousness and political culture.[53]

Most Russians of all classes in the sixteenth and early seventeenth centuries lacked a clear concept of a secular state and regarded the tsar as nothing less than the sacred ruler chosen by God to lead and protect his flock of faithful Christians.[54] As a result, religiously-based popular monarchism was remarkably strong in early modern Russia.[55] As we have seen, the religious aspect of the Russian monarchy was important in legitimizing the new state, its ruling dynasty, and the crushing burdens being placed on the Russian people.[56] In the emerging political culture, the tsar was God's viceroy, and it was the duty of all subjects to serve and obey him. Ideally, the tsar ruled and there was no room for the masses to participate in politics; instead, they were supposed to be "as mute as fish."[57] At the same time, however, early modern Russian popular religion was characterized by the assumption of a personal connection between each individual and God, by a surprising degree of independent thinking, and by a belief in personal responsibility for the avoidance of sin.[58] Therefore, when things went wrong, as they surely did in the Time of Troubles, the Russian people could not sit idly by; instead, they were forced to make choices, sometimes dangerous choices, during the civil war years. In that context, the almost cult-like popular veneration of the tsar proved to be politically destabilizing.[59] The extinction of the sacred ruling dynasty in 1598 shocked many Russians who were understandably uncertain about the possible legitimacy of an elected tsar in general and a certain boyar-tsar specifically.[60] In fact, the Time of Troubles forced the issue on the Russians of how to tell a legitimate tsar from a false tsar, and the absence of an unquestionably legitimate ruler allowed discontent to get out of control.[61]

It is now possible, thanks especially to the stimulating research of Daniel Rowland and Valerie Kivelson, to discern that in the God-centered, tsar-centered political culture of early modern Russia, pious Orthodox subjects could legitimately (in their own minds at least) reject a tsar perceived as evil—that is to say, one who violated his obligations to God and his people and destroyed the holy mission of the state. Indeed, the removal of such a "tsar-tormentor" (*tsar'-muchitel*) was apparently encouraged, and many God-fearing Russians took the matter seriously enough to be willing to risk rebellion against an "evil" tsar.[62] Some scholars have dated the emergence of such potentially destabilizing religious-political views to the mid-seventeenth century;[63] but that date is too late. As we have seen, to many of his subjects Boris Godunov appeared to be just such an evil "false tsar" and tool of Satan. When given the opportunity, many pious Orthodox Russians rejected Tsar Boris and turned to Dmitrii in the hope that he was the true tsar—the legitimate, hereditary ruler who could restore Russia to God's grace.[64] When Dmitrii invaded Russia and accused Godunov of being a usurper, he gave Tsar Boris's wavering subjects an alternative who represented at the same time a living rebuke to Godunov as a failed regicide and a miraculous return to the old sacred ruling family. Dmitrii gained rapid support not only because Tsar Boris was unpopular, but also because Dmitrii's claim to be the legitimate, God-chosen ruler of Russia appeared strong. By representing himself as the living link to the extinct dynasty, Dmitrii was able to provoke just about the only type of rebellion possible in early modern Russia—rebellion in the name of the "true tsar" against an illegitimate "false tsar."[65] In such an uprising, the rebels saw themselves as crusaders in a holy war to restore divine order and as Christ's legions fighting against the forces of Satan.[66] It should come as no surprise, therefore, that Dmitrii was regarded by many of his adherents as a sacred figure and as the defender of the true faith.[67] The popular monarchist support he generated had fanatical religious overtones.[68]

The uprisings in support of Dmitrii provide tantalizing evidence to support the conclusions of Rowland and Kivelson concerning the dynamics of religious and political consciousness of ordinary, pious Orthodox subjects of the early tsars. There were, however, at least two additional factors operating in the Time of Troubles to enhance popular monarchist support for Dmitrii: the reputation of Ivan the Terrible and the remarkable "causal story" of Dmitrii's miraculous rescue and return to claim the throne of his father.

A characteristic of early modern Russian popular monarchism and popular-monarchist inspired rebellions was the idealization of certain sacred rulers as "good tsars."[69] Dmitrii benefited from just such a popular retrospective idealization of Russia's first tsar.[70] Ivan the Terrible was, believe it or not, regarded as the first "good tsar" in Russian folklore.[71] This idealization was due to many factors: distaste for the horrifying events of the Time of Troubles;[72] nostalgia for the old dynasty;[73] nostalgia for, if not a golden age, then at least better times (before enserfment, extinction of the Daniilovichi, and the famine);[74] and the memory of a glorious reign when the empire was founded and ruled by a fully legitimate, God-chosen tsar.[75] Ivan IV, in spite of his historical reputation, was strongly supported by most of his subjects and, in general, had a good popular image as a pious Christian ruler.[76] In fact, Ivan was actually an "image monger" who consciously promoted his own reputation among his subjects.[77] His stern and highly public punishment of boyars and bureaucrats who had been found guilty of treason or corruption enhanced his own reputation as a champion of the common people against members of the elite widely regarded as oppressors.[78] Tsar Ivan's propensity for encouraging slaves to denounce their traitorous masters also reinforced popular monarchist hostility toward greedy and corrupt boyars as potential enemies of the tsar.[79] That in turn later aided Dmitrii's cause against the "usurper" and "boyar-tsar" Boris Godunov. Dmitrii actively cultivated and capitalized on the positive image of "good tsar" Ivan IV in his struggle against the "false tsar" Boris.[80] In fact, Dmitrii's campaign itself actually helped inspire the strong popular image Ivan the Terrible gained by the early seventeenth century and was, therefore, at least partially responsible for the development of early modern Russian popular monarchism as an historical force.[81] Dmitrii was able to stimulate and put to good use the popular monarchist idealization of his putative father among many Russians—including soldiers, townspeople, and cossacks.[82] In this context, it is worth noting that the positive memory of Tsar Ivan was especially strong in the same southern provinces that rose for Dmitrii in 1604–5 and rose again in his name in 1606.[83]

In the Time of Troubles, when many people worried about God's anger and punishment of Russia, Dmitrii's causal story about the role of divine providence in rescuing him from Boris Godunov's assassins in 1591 was highly effective at generating popular support. Dmitrii began to circulate that story months before he launched his invasion of Russia.[84] To the Orthodox Christian population Dmitrii consistently emphasized the religious and miraculous element in his escape from death in Uglich. God saved him, he told the Russians, in order to topple the evil usurper, Godunov.[85] His assertion, it should be pointed out, came within the context of a rapidly growing and widespread belief in miracles in early modern Russia.[86] Many of Dmitrii's supporters believed that he had indeed been saved by a miracle of providence in order to help them return to God's grace.[87] Their strong faith in the pretender as God-chosen emboldened them on the battlefield and even gave them the strength to endure torture at the hands of Boris Godunov's agents.[88] In fact, popular support for Dmitrii assumed the form of a "quasi-religious" movement.[89] Dmitrii was well aware of this, so it should come as no surprise that he was careful to demonstrate his piety, humility, and religiosity while campaigning for the throne.[90]

For some Russians, Dmitrii's story was probably reminiscent of ancient stories about the first famously innocent political martyrs of early Rus, Saints Boris and Gleb, who were killed by their half-brother, Sviatopolk the Accursed, in his lust for the throne of Kiev.[91] For many others, however, the "resurrection" of Dmitrii—long assumed to have died or been killed in 1591—was probably more reminiscent of Jesus Christ, the prototypical "returning king."[92] Some scholars, while accepting the idea of Jesus as the ultimate source for the myth of the "returning king," have unconvincingly emphasized the "purely secular character" of most early modern popular "messianic" hopes associated with Dmitrii and others like him.[93] Maureen Perrie, however, has effectively demonstrated that the sacralization of the Russian monarchy in the sixteenth century facilitated the acceptance of Dmitrii as "the true tsarevich, miraculously risen, Christ-like, from the grave."[94] From the outset of his campaign for the throne, Dmitrii's supporters used solar imagery associated with Jesus Christ to describe the tsarevich—the same imagery that had been applied earlier to Russian rulers.[95] According to Perrie, much of Russia's southern and southwestern frontier population—including townspeople, nobles, and monks—quickly came to accept the idea of the resurrection of the tsarevich; and the quasi-religious, popular monarchist rebellion in Dmitrii's name spread rapidly.[96] According to Isaac Massa, a Dutch merchant who lived in Russia during the Time of Troubles, the Russian rebels believed they were "getting back their lawful hereditary ruler, and so the undertaking could not fail; it was bound to succeed."[97] Sure enough,

Dmitrii was eventually welcomed to Moscow by joyful crowds who truly believed he was their miraculously preserved, hereditary tsar and that once again God was smiling on Russia.[98]

As noted earlier, since many scholars regarded Tsar Dmitrii as a fraud, they had difficulty crediting him with the ability to generate powerful popular support. Instead, they looked elsewhere for explanations of the quasi-religious fanaticism of Dmitrii's supporters and in the process misinterpreted early modern Russian popular consciousness and the dynamic forces at work in Russian history.

One last important scholarly effort to account for Dmitrii's immense popularity remains to be discussed: the concept of "pretenderism" or impostorism as the explanation for his success. It has been said that, with Dmitrii "the phenomenon of pretenderism in Russia at once began and reached its zenith."[99] That statement inadvertently points out a serious problem with this interpretive framework. Scholarship on pretenderism as it relates to Russia's original "pretender," Tsar Dmitrii, has been greatly complicated by the not always acknowledged fact that his remarkable and unprecedented story of miraculous rescue and return to claim the throne (not to mention his victory and coronation) struck the imagination of a great many people and actually helped produce the phenomenon of pretenderism. After Tsar Dmitrii's assassination in 1606, his supporters successfully put forward the story that he had, once again, escaped death and would return to punish the traitors. They quickly raised a large, highly motivated army drawn from all social classes that was able to lay siege to Moscow and nearly toppled the usurper Vasilii Shuiskii—all while waiting patiently for the reappearance of their beloved Tsar Dmitrii. One consequence of the dramatic stories of the first and second "resurrection" of Dmitrii was the appearance of a dozen copy-cat pretenders claiming to be Dmitrii or other members of the extinct sacred ruling dynasty. Some of those pretenders were able to generate enough popular support to greatly prolong the civil war.[100]

Once pretenderism became a common political device used by rebels in the Time of Troubles, it took on a life of its own and became a chronic problem in Russian history. After the Troubles, opponents of various tsarist regimes produced about a dozen more pretenders in the seventeenth century and at least forty-four in the eighteenth century, culminating in one of the most famous cases of all—the rebel leader Emilian Pugachev claiming to be Tsar Peter III.[101] The frequency of the appearance of pretenders in early modern Russia is an historical phenomenon worthy of study, and it has generated a considerable amount of literature.[102] Scholars with some justification came to see pretenderism as the traditional and virtually the only means for Russian rebels to attract significant support within a political culture dominated by autocracy and characterized by strong popular monarchism.[103] Unfortunately, those same scholars looked back at Dmitrii through the lens of Pugachev, a conscious impostor who really did challenge serfdom. The result has been serious misinterpretation of Dmitrii, his campaign for the throne, and rebel consciousness in the Time of Troubles. Efforts to place the phenomenon of pretenderism within the context of existing scholarship about early modern Russian rebellions resulted in explanations of Dmitrii and other pretenders that were based upon the same flawed interpretations we have already reviewed. For example, some writers saw all Russian pretenders as manipulators of the gullible masses who managed to push them into essentially meaningless uprisings.[104] Others saw Russian pretenders as the leaders of social revolution or as the product of the social utopian longings of the masses for liberation.[105] Still others sought an explanation in the concept of naïve monarchism.[106] None of those explanations is satisfactory with respect to Dmitrii.

More recently, some scholars have focused on the sacralization of the Russian monarchy in the sixteenth century, seeing it as the source of the Russian people's susceptibility to the phenomenon of pretenderism once the sacred dynasty died out in 1598 and the newly elected ruler was regarded by many as a "false tsar." According to this interpretation, the main attraction of pretenderism was to legitimize opposition to unpopular rulers within a culture in which rebellion in the name of the tsar (or the true tsar) was the only possible form an uprising could take. Still caught up in the traditional interpretation of the Time of Troubles, however, Boris Uspenskii unfortunately related pretenderism to the alleged social utopian yearnings of the masses.[107] Partially breaking with the traditional interpretation of the Troubles, Ruslan Skrynnikov and Maureen Perrie correctly saw pretenderism as a potent weapon for mobilizing all social classes, including elites. According to them, the success of Dmitrii demonstrated the effectiveness of pretenderism as a political device.[108] While their work represents an improvement over previous interpretations, it is still an inadequate explanation—one advanced by historians who accepted traditional views of Tsar Dmitrii as an unsavory, conscious impostor who could not possibly have generated such powerful popular support on his own.[109] Thus, their interpretation turns out to be just another effort to explain away Dmitrii's strong popular support by means of faulty generalizations and categories rather than by careful study.

The attempt to fit Dmitrii into the mold of later Russian pretenders fails to make the critical distinction between the unique and remarkable story of the original pretender and later copy-cats, and it fails to explore how Dmitrii's own story and the fanatical, long-lasting support he was able to generate helped create the historical phenomenon being studied. Dmitrii was no more a product of pretenderism than he was a product of nonexistent social utopian legends. In reality, the only fundamental insight produced by scholarship on Russian pretenders has been nothing more than an affirmation of the need for a "true tsar" in order to legitimize rebellion—something that was already a well-known aspect of early modern Russian political culture. Scholarship on pretenderism has not yet produced any real explanation of why some pretenders were able to generate powerful popular monarchist support while others could not. Even Maureen Perrie, who had considerable faith in the explanatory value of pretenderism, could not come up with any other generalizations that applied to all Russian pretenders. She admitted that there are enough variations in Russian pretenderism that "the precise relationship of pretence to popular monarchism has to be established empirically for each individual occurrence of the phenomenon."[110] That, at least, is good advice with respect to Dmitrii.

An empirical study of Russia's first pretender is precisely what is called for at this point. Far from being a mere figurehead under whom Russian rebels could pursue their own agenda, Dmitrii turns out to have been a remarkable character who seems to have truly believed he was the son of Ivan the Terrible and would, with God's help, win the throne of Russia. He proved to be an intelligent, charismatic, pious, brave warrior-prince who inspired fierce courage in others and amazed the Russian people by his generosity in victory and his genuine concern for their welfare.[111] Dmitrii really did seem to loom larger than life, and his sense of personal mission inspired many people to fight for him with religious zeal.[112] As one astonished and exasperated contemporary foe of Dmitrii observed, he somehow managed to draw "all hearts to himself."[113]

In the final analysis, the pretender Dmitrii himself provided the crucial trigger for Russia's first civil war. His causal story and personal conduct and character had profound effects upon his contemporaries, on the course of the Time of Troubles, and on early modern Russian history. To many people, the Christlike resurrection of Tsarevich Dmitrii "proved" that miracles do occur and that God was on his side. That belief not only stimulated fanatical support for Dmitrii in his struggle against Boris Godunov, but it also resulted in the rapid and widespread belief in a second "resurrection" of Tsar Dmitrii after his assassination in 1606—a development that instantly rekindled the civil war in which the rebels, certain that they were once again struggling against Satanic forces, fought with zeal for the "true tsar." As previously noted, the startling resurrections of Dmitrii were directly responsible for the emergence of about a dozen more pretenders in the later years of the Troubles and were also largely responsible for the development of the tradition of pretenderism in the decades following the

Time of Troubles. Famous rebel leaders and pretenders such as Stepan Razin and Emilian Pugachev also came to be regarded as immortal, Christ-like champions of the faithful Orthodox masses—for which reason they commanded zealous, quasi-religious support.[114] The real source of that popular image of Russian rebel leaders was not, as long suspected, millenarianism or social utopian yearnings of the masses. Instead, it was the remarkable story of Tsar Dmitrii. Careful analysis of all the great rebellions of early modern Russia also shows just how essential popular monarchism was as a motivational force, and Dmitrii was—as we have seen—an important contributor to the growth of that phenomenon as well. Thus, in the case of Tsar Dmitrii we have a curious paradox: he helped strengthen popular monarchism in Russia while at the same time he helped create the destabilizing tradition of pretenderism.[115] No wonder there is so much confusion about him.

Dmitrii's amazing and complex story captured the imagination of his contemporaries in Russia and throughout Europe and has fascinated many generations since then.[116] Unfortunately, scholarship on Dmitrii has been extremely poor and has greatly impeded the task of accurately assessing the pretender and those he inspired to fight for him. In order to overcome that problem, the next chapter will take a close look at the identity, personality, and early activities of the remarkable man who caused so much trouble.

8

The Pretender Dmitrii Ivanovich

The young man who launched an invasion of Russia in 1604 claiming to be Tsarevich Dmitrii Ivanovich became the first and only tsar ever raised to the throne by means of a military campaign and popular uprisings. For that very reason Boris Godunov and other enemies vilified him as an evil impostor and as a tool of foreign powers and of Satan. Unfortunately, their propaganda campaigns against the pretender have profoundly affected appraisals of Tsar Dmitrii and his activities ever since the Time of Troubles. Even recent studies of Dmitrii are still mired in faulty views of the man and his activities.[1]

In spite of all the propaganda against Dmitrii, both before and after his death, and in spite of historians' prejudices against him as an impostor, tool of the Poles and Jesuits, evil monk, or sorcerer, he brilliantly acted the part of the true tsarevich determined to topple the evil usurper Godunov. Far from being a tool of others, Dmitrii proved to be a very charismatic twenty-two year old who could inspire his followers. He was not impressive to look at: mediocre height, dark complexion with a wart next to his nose under his right eye, and one arm slightly longer than the other. However, he was incredibly strong and agile, a skilled horseman, and a courageous warrior. He was also extremely intelligent and resourceful, well-read, reform-minded, and very advanced in his thinking for a Russian lord. In addition to being able to read and write Russian, he had a good command of Polish and even studied some Latin (though he still made obvious errors). His eloquence was an incredibly important asset, along with his magnanimous disposition, forgiving nature, and boldness. He was an attractive, dynamic character who inspired confidence in his claim to the throne and in his ability to fight his way to power.[2]

Who was the man who claimed to be Ivan the Terrible's youngest son? At the time of his appearance in the early seventeenth century most people believed that the real Tsarevich Dmitrii had died or been killed in 1591. The traditional view of the pretender was that he was an impostor—most commonly identified as a runaway defrocked monk named Grigorii (Grishka) Otrepev.[3] He has also generally been regarded as a political adventurer and tool of Polish Catholic intervention in Russia.[4] Some contemporaries and even some scholars in the twentieth century believed he might have been a sorcerer.[5] Because of Tsar Boris's propaganda denouncing him and the massive campaign to discredit him after his assassination, it is still difficult to get at the truth about the strange person who fought his way to power and became one of the only truly enlightened rulers Russia ever had.[6] Complicating the task even further, the Russian Orthodox Church and the Romanov dynasty locked in an official view of the pretender that h for centuries was politically unwise for scholars to challenge.[7] Russians investigating Tsar Dmitrii were also repelled by his connection to Poland-Lithuania and his secret "conversion" to Catholicism. For these reasons, most historians of the Time of Troubles adopted a negative view of Dmitrii, a view strongly reinforced by the behavior of other men pretending to be Tsar Dmitrii after his assassination in 1606.[8] The overall result has been an extremely distorted interpretation of the man and his role in the Time of Troubles.

Because of the conjectures of some contemporary foreigners, for a long time there was a heated debate over whether or not the pretender was even a Russian;[9] in fact, he was.[10] It is well known that Tsar Dmitrii maintained good relations with the Zaporozhian cossacks who had a history of supporting pretenders to the throne in Moldavia and elsewhere in Eastern Europe.[11] Because of that, some believed Dmitrii was originally a low-born cossack.[12] As we have already seen, the weakness of historiography and source criticism concerning Dmitrii eventually allowed the development of even more erroneous views of him as the leader of revolutionary cossacks and as a cossack-tsar.[13] Of course, Soviet scholars later modified that romantic interpretation and came to view Dmitrii as a cynical manipulator of the masses rising against serfdom who quickly sold out his supporters as soon as he managed to become tsar.[14] That faulty view continues to haunt scholarship about the man responsible for Russia's first civil war.

In spite of many long-held assumptions about Dmitrii, he was not the product of a Polish plot or a Jesuit conspiracy. Although Dmitrii launched his campaign for the Russian throne from Poland-Lithuania, King Sigismund III, the Jesuits, and self-serving Polish lords were not the source of the pretender scheme; they merely took advantage of it.[15] The source of the pretender scheme was a conspiracy among Russian lords. The resurrection of the tsarevich was definitely tied to Boris Godunov's struggle against his boyar opponents.[16] After rumors of Tsarevich Dmitrii's survival began to circulate in Russia, Tsar Boris adopted harsh and tyrannical measures against suspected opponents.[17] When Dmitrii finally revealed himself in Poland-Lithuania in 1603, Tsar Boris openly accused the boyars of organizing the pretender scheme.[18] There is, in fact, quite a bit of evidence linking the pretender to the Romanov clan.[19] There is also some evidence of a link between the pretender scheme and Bogdan Belskii,[20] and the Nagoi clan may also have been involved.[21] All of those boyar families had suffered at the hands of Boris Godunov, and surviving members probably entered into some kind of secret alliance against Tsar Boris. It was, of course, extremely dangerous to challenge the tsar. Denunciations, trials, torture, exile, and death awaited those suspected of harboring ill will toward the Godunov dynasty. Therefore, another method to oppose Tsar Boris was needed, and secrecy was extremely important. Because of the conservative nature of Russian Orthodox culture, the only way the conspirators could hope to challenge Godunov was by demonstrating that he was a false tsar and that there was a legitimate alternative.[22] Tsar Boris's enemies were well aware of the ugly rumors about him as a regicide and the general decline of his legitimacy because of the famine. By resurrecting Dmitrii, the tsar's opponents hoped simultaneously to "prove" that Tsar Boris was a usurper and to provide an acceptable alternative in the person of the "miraculously preserved" tsarevich.

Who was chosen to play the role of Dmitrii? Tsar Boris and Patriarch Iov sought maximum impact for their propaganda campaign against the pretender by loudly denouncing him as a notorious runaway defrocked monk and dabbler in the black arts named Grigorii Otrepev.[23] (In Orthodox Russia, defrocked monks had an extremely odious reputation.) Dmitrii's opponents before and after his death took up Godunov's accusation that the pretender was Otrepev,[24] and to this day, the most common scholarly view of the pretender is that he was the unsavory monk.[25] Many complex "proofs" have been offered; but it is, in fact, not at all clear that the pretender was Otrepev. Let's take a closer look at that theory and its problems.

Tsar Boris's officials were unable to prove that the pretender was Otrepev, but they made extensive use of Otrepev's relatives (loyal and trusted supporters of the Godunovs) in order to assemble evidence against Dmitrii. However, that official propaganda was filled with contradictions and errors.[26] Over the course of several years, Tsar Boris's government, the Russian Orthodox Church, and then the regime of Vasilii Shuiskii produced several different versions of the biography of one Iurii Bogdanovich Otrepev, the son of a streltsy sotnik (centurion), who became the monk Grigorii and later fled to Poland-Lithuania where he assumed the identity of Tsarevich Dmitrii. One version of this propaganda has the teenager Iurii disobeying his parents, running away from home, and falling into wickedness and heresy—for which he was forcibly tonsured.[27] Another version has Iurii voluntarily becoming a monk at age fourteen.[28] A number of sources mention the young monk Grigorii traveling from one remote monastery to another for months, or even for several years.[29] Eventually, his widowed mother sent him to Moscow where relatives pulled strings to get him admitted to the prestigious Miracles (Chudov) Monastery in the Moscow Kremlin, where his grandfather was a monk.[30] Otrepev's intelligence and writing skills led to his appointment as a deacon within a year. He soon caught the attention of Patriarch Iov, entered the patriarch's service, and performed his duties with distinction. Iov personally testified that Otrepev accompanied him to meetings of the church hierarchy and, occasionally, even to meetings of the boyar council. Otrepev acquired great renown as the patriarch's secretary.[31]

In 1602, in the midst of the famine, a small group of "monks," including the future pretender Dmitrii, fled from Moscow to Poland-Lithuania; Otrepev was definitely one of those runaways. The flight of those "monks" greatly upset Patriarch Iov who made strenuous but unsuccessful efforts to prevent them from crossing the border.[32] After the pretender announced his presence in Poland-Lithuania and began seeking assistance to claim the Russian throne, Patriarch Iov's staff fabricated ingenious stories about why Otrepev had fled across the border and was now the person posing as Dmitrii. One version they produced held that, while in the patriarch's service, Otrepev had dabbled in the black arts and disavowed God. He was supposedly condemned to exile and confinement for life by the patriarch and an assembly of bishops but somehow managed to escape to Poland-Lithuania.[33] Such a false story of heresy and sorcery was specifically designed to discredit the pretender.[34] Different versions of Otrepev's "official" biography were also produced by Tsar Boris's officials, the church, and later by Vasilii Shuiskii's accomplices. Those stories asserted that before Iurii became a monk he had entered the service of the Romanov clan where he fell into wickedness, was condemned to death, and escaped that fate by agreeing to be tonsured.[35] Many scholars studying the contradictory evidence about Otrepev took much of it at face value and settled on the view that the young Otrepev entered Romanov service as a teenager, served with distinction, and was forced to become a monk only when the Romanov clan was accused of treason in 1600.[36] There are, however, serious problems with that interpretation. First, it requires compressing of the amount of time the young monk spent wandering among remote monasteries after he was tonsured. Second, it requires that Otrepev's well-documented brilliant career at the Miracles Monastery be compressed into a year or so. As a result, scholars such as Ruslan Skrynnikov were forced to praise Otrepev's exceptional abilities that allowed him to rise so meteorically. We are told that Otrepev's career was like a "fairy tale" and that in just months "he mastered what others took a lifetime to comprehend."[37] Even Maureen Perrie, who shared Skrynnikov's view that the pretender really was Otrepev, balked at that interpretation, declaring that Otrepev must have become a monk several years earlier.[38] However, if he became a monk as a teenager, he could not have achieved distinction in Romanov service before being tonsured. The problems of attempting to merge the biographies of the monk and the tsarevich are not easily overcome.

After Dmitrii revealed himself in Poland-Lithuania, Tsar Boris produced very unimpressive "witnesses" who claimed that the pretender was actually Otrepev. One of those "witnesses" was Otrepev's uncle Smirnoi, a man trusted by the tsar who had thrived in Godunov service.[39] Two others were itinerant monks who claimed to have accompanied Otrepev to Lithuania and had knowledge of his transformation into the tsarevich. Their stories were not even believable enough for the patriarch and bishops to make use of, and they were quickly dismissed as vagrants.[40] In fact, while Tsar Boris lived no reliable witnesses came forward to denounce the pretender as Otrepev. The propaganda campaign against Dmitrii consisted of shameless, contradictory lies.[41] Several years after Tsar Dmitrii's assassination, it was alleged that during his reign one of his envoys to King Sigismund secretly informed the Poles that the tsar was really Otrepev and that the boyars were ready to overthrow him in favor of Sigismund's son, Prince Wladyslaw. That envoy, Ivan Bezobrazov, supposedly claimed to have known and even to have played with Otrepev as a child.[42] Unfortunately, scholars who seized on that "proof" never bothered to note the highly partisan Polish source of this apocryphal story; nor did they ever bother to ask themselves how likely an impostor would be to employ an old acquaintance for a delicate diplomatic mission. Such is the unhappy state of scholarship on Dmitrii.

After Tsar Dmitrii was assassinated in 1606, the usurper Tsar Vasilii Shuiskii desperately needed to "prove" that Dmitrii had been an impostor. One technique he used was to coerce testimony from Tsar Dmitrii's secretary, Jan Buczynski, that the dead tsar was really the evil monk, Grishka Otrepev.[43] Curiously, however, Tsar Vasilii made no effort to produce Otrepev's mother, uncle, or brother to help build his case. Shuiskii's agents studied Tsar Boris's propaganda against Dmitrii but were unable to find much of value in it, so they decided to manufacture new documents to "prove" that the dead tsar was Otrepev. The only evidence of any significance that they produced was the story of Otrepev's transformation into the tsarevich as described by a monk named Varlaam Iatskii.[44] Varlaam claimed to have accompanied Otrepev to Lithuania. He described the places they visited together and recounted how Otrepev had a fellow monk, Leonid, assume Otrepev's identity when Grishka decided to play the role of the tsarevich.[45] Because the final version of Varlaam's story was doctored by Shuiskii's agents, scholars long ago regarded it as a hoax.[46] However, in the late nineteenth century, when Paul Pierling studied the pretender's own version of his flight to

Lithuania and his activities leading up to declaring himself to be the tsarevich, Pierling was struck by the remarkable parallels between Tsar Dmitrii's story and Varlaam's story about Otrepev. He was already suspicious of the pretender because Tsar Dmitrii's own story—told to Prince Adam Vishnevetskii in 1603—of escape from Uglich and growing up incognito was so vague that many in Poland-Lithuania at the time had been quite skeptical about him.[47] Pierling concluded that Varlaam could not have known the pretender's story told to Prince Adam so he must have been telling the truth. The fact that Varlaam's story included precise and accurate information about the capture and execution of Iakov Pykhachev, one of Tsar Boris's agents sent to assassinate the pretender in Poland-Lithuania, helped convince Pierling of the authenticity of Varlaam's story that Otrepev was indeed playing the role of Dmitrii.[48] Pierling's findings were viewed skeptically by Sergei Platonov and others, but when Soviet scholars discovered an earlier version of Varlaam's tale without obvious doctoring, as well as a reference to his interrogation by Shuiskii officials, the result was widespread acceptance of Pierling's conclusions.[49] There are, however, a number of serious problems with Varlaam's story that, in their rush to judgment, scholars have ignored. Let us take a closer look at the issues involved.

First of all, there is no real mystery about why Varlaam was able to name the places Otrepev (or Dmitrii) visited in Poland-Lithuania; Varlaam was one of the monks who fled across the border with Otrepev and the other "monks" in 1602.[50] (Skrynnikov even went so far as to identify Varlaam as the mastermind of the plan to have Otrepev assume the identity of the tsarevich.)[51] Since even persons who ardently believed Tsar Dmitrii was genuine openly admitted that he had been accompanied by Otrepev on his flight to Poland-Lithuania, it should not be any surprise that they traveled to the same places at the same time, nor should it be a surprise that their companion monk, Varlaam, would be able to recall details of the journey.[52] It also turns out that Varlaam was one of the monks whose testimony in Poland-Lithuania that Dmitrii was genuine helped convince King Sigismund to grant the tsarevich an audience.[53] The fact that Varlaam also admitted that he had been a friend of Iakov Pykhachev, the Godunov agent who tried to kill the pretender in Poland-Lithuania, makes it easier to understand why he had precise knowledge of that episode—knowledge that deeply impressed some historians.[54] At the same time, however, it should be noted that Varlaam's admission makes his testimony about Otrepev appear to be untrustworthy. I. A. Golubtsov has also demonstrated that precise details about the pretender's activities abroad were also known by several people in Smolensk who were connected to Varlaam and may have supplied information to him.[55] Another troubling problem with Varlaam as a source is his close association with none other than Tsar Vasilii's brother, Ivan Shuiskii. That, plus the fact that Varlaam's story was reworked as propaganda seriously undermines its credibility. Suffice it to say, Varlaam's story contained many lies about Otrepev and Dmitrii that were noted as such even by supporters of Varlaam's claim about the identity of the pretender.[56]

Many scholars have focused on Dmitrii's "naïve" story of how he escaped from Uglich and grew up in obscurity. As Pierling noted, neither Dmitrii nor his supporters could offer skeptical Polish lords any proof to back up his claims.[57] The pretender has even been taken to task by scholars for not telling the Poles clever lies that might have linked him to long-dead boyar opponents of Tsar Boris.[58] What those scholars overlooked, however, was the possibility that revealing details about the pretender's childhood might very well have endangered his Russian supporters who were still subject to Godunov reprisals. It has also been claimed that several people saw Otrepev assume the identity of Dmitrii in Poland-Lithuania;[59] however, those sources are contradictory and were all clearly part of the propaganda campaign against the pretender.[60] In addition, historians who combined the biographies of Dmitrii and Otrepev—assuming that they were the same person—sometimes failed to note that sources about Dmitrii's activities in Poland-Lithuania did not necessarily identify him as Otrepev.

There are also chronological problems with sources about Otrepev assuming Dmitrii's identity. For example, the prestigious Prince Janusz Ostrozhskii apparently knew the pretender as Dmitrii, not Otrepev, even before the monk supposedly assumed the identity of the tsarevich.[61] Finally, there are a number of other, even less impressive arguments in favor of identifying the pretender as Otrepev: someone wrote "tsarevich of Muscovy" under Otrepev's name in a book he received in Poland-Lithuania in 1602.[62] Both Dmitrii and Otrepev were literate and had good handwriting.[63] It has also been claimed that Otrepev was about the same age as Dmitrii.[64] In reality, there are no surviving records of Otrepev's birth; he could easily have been many years older than Dmitrii, as some sources indicate.[65] It has been claimed that the pretender feared being recognized as Otrepev during his campaign for the throne, and for that reason felt the need to have the monk Leonid assume the identity of Otrepev.[66] The basis for that claim is nothing more than Godunov propaganda. In fact, Tsar Boris really did send three monks to expose Dmitrii as Otrepev (or to assassinate him) during his invasion of Russia. At least one, possibly all three, however, ended up declaring that the pretender really was Dmitrii.[67] It has also been repeatedly claimed that many people recognized Otrepev when he entered Moscow in triumph, for which reason numerous of his opponents were secretly killed.[68] There is absolutely no truth to those rumors, something even admitted by Skrynnikov, the most recent biographer to assert that Otrepev was the pretender.[69] A number of contemporaries openly scoffed at the clumsy propaganda identifying the pretender as Otrepev. Although often dismissed by scholars as victims of Otrepev's clever use of the monk Leonid as a "false Otrepev," several contemporaries claimed outright to have seen Otrepev during Dmitrii's lifetime or after his assassination, and that Dmitrii was definitely not that monk.[70] Captain Jacques Margeret, a French soldier who lived in Russia for many years and held high positions under both Tsar Boris and Tsar Dmitrii, posed significant challenges to the theory of Otrepev as the pretender. In a book he wrote in 1607, Margeret claimed that Otrepev was older than Dmitrii and was still alive after Dmitrii's assassination. In addition, Margeret pointed out that Tsar Dmitrii did not behave like an impostor fearful of exposure even after he became aware of plots against him. Margeret also noted that in order to get rid of Tsar Dmitrii, the usurper Shuiskii was forced to assassinate him because there was no way to make the absurd charges the assassins leveled against him believable to the public.[71] Margeret's arguments against identifying Otrepev as the pretender actually dominated the scholarly debate on the issue for a long time and helped convince some historians that Tsar Dmitrii was not Otrepev.[72] At the very least, his eyewitness testimony made other scholars less certain about the traditional identification.[73]

Historians have failed to prove that Otrepev played the role of Dmitrii. In fact, it is difficult to imagine Tsar Boris's opponents choosing the highly visible secretary of Patriarch Iov to play the role of the tsarevich, a point that has been ignored by historians already convinced that the pretender was Otrepev. Propaganda about the pretender had him dabbling in the black arts and assuming the identity of Dmitrii on his own initiative (under Satan's influence).[74] Unfortunately, in their exploration of the pretender's psychology, Boris Uspenskii and Maureen Perrie both took much of that propaganda at face value and came to regard him as a self-starter and possibly even a sorcerer whose deliberate imposture was motivated by his alienation from the Russian Orthodox Church.[75] Fortunately, however, Ruslan Skrynnikov recognized that the charges of heresy and black magic were nothing more than propaganda designed to discredit the pretender in the eyes of his potential supporters.[76] We have already seen how Tsar Boris effectively used charges of witchcraft against his boyar opponents. It was, in fact, a common tool used in early modern Europe to destroy political opponents and especially to distract people from rebellion.[77] The Russian government itself continued to rely on such tactics against rebels long after the Time of Troubles.[78] According to Skrynnikov, the pretender was not a dissipated youth dabbling in the black arts but instead a young warrior and courtier who made a good name for himself by honorable service to the Romanov clan.[79] Skrynnikov believed that Otrepev assumed the identity of Dmitrii only as a young man in 1600 or 1601. He, therefore, shared the view of Uspenskii and Perrie that the pretender was a conscious impostor. There are, however, serious problems with the theory of Dmitrii as a deceiver. Let's take a closer look at the issues involved.

Many contemporary observers and historians noted that the pretender played the role of Dmitrii so convincingly that he must have been raised from childhood to believe that he was the tsarevich; he certainly managed to convince many others that he was the true Dmitrii.[80] Sergei Solovev, who believed Tsar Dmitrii was actually Otrepev, carefully studied the evidence concerning his character and behavior and was forced to conclude that he had not been a conscious pretender.[81] The evidence of that, in fact, is so compelling that even Maureen Perrie, another firm believer that Tsar Dmitrii was really Otrepev, had to admit that Otrepev may actually have believed he was the son of Ivan the Terrible.[82] Since the pretender, whoever he was, acted the part so convincingly, when was he chosen to play the role? A later date is unlikely because the pretender would have been old enough to be conscious of his deception, which does not appear to have been the case.[83] An early date also presents problems. If, as seems likely, he was raised to believe he was Dmitrii, how can that be explained? Few were interested in Dmitrii in the 1590s, and no one could have predicted that Tsar Fedor would die without an heir.

There is a possible solution to this mystery: the powerful historical image of Boris Godunov as a regicide and usurper has distracted scholars from the fact that the Uglich affair was part of a Nagoi clan plot against the regent. Perhaps the Nagois, failing to topple Godunov in 1591, secretly raised a child to believe he was the tsarevich in the hope that there would eventually be an opportunity to use him to regain their position at court. [84]After the Romanovs felt the wrath of Tsar Boris in 1600, they may have been brought into a secret alliance against Godunov that centered around the young pretender. That may help to explain how the Romanovs and others came up with a well-trained pretender on such short notice; the Nagois may have had a candidate waiting in the wings. When the pretender declared himself in Poland-Lithuania, he was already a self-assured, well-educated Russian nobleman who was well-versed in statecraft, an excellent horseman, and a courageous warrior who inspired confidence in his supporters.[85] His carriage and manner, plus several persons coming forward to identify him as Dmitrii, helped convince King Sigismund III and the Jesuits that he was authentic.[86] Although many scholars have scoffed at the possibility that the pretender really was Tsarevich Dmitrii, loose ends concerning the Uglich affair led no less a scholar than Sergei Platonov to conclude that, even though it would be difficult to prove, we cannot be certain that Dmitrii died in 1591.[87]

The possibility that the tsarevich survived and later came to the throne has over the years been supported by a small number of investigators of the subject.[88] There is actually some evidence to back up that astonishing claim. For example, there were suspicious irregularities associated with the Uglich affair (including an uncanonical delay in burying the tsarevich, a four-day watch over the body by the Nagois who would not allow anyone else to approach it, and the investigating commission's inability to recognize the body as that of Dmitrii).[89] Several sources claimed that another boy was substituted for Dmitrii before the tsarevich's "death."[90] Captain Margeret specifically suggested that the Nagois and the Romanovs were responsible for the switch.[91] A contemporary English source claimed that the Nagois and Bogdan Belskii were involved.[92] Belskii, who was Tsarevich Dmitrii's godfather, had tried to seize power in the name of Dmitrii shortly after Tsar Ivan died. Later, in 1605, while participating in the popular uprising in Moscow in support of Dmitrii, Belskii swore on a cross that the pretender was truly his godson and that he and others had known about the tsarevich's survival in 1591 and had sheltered him from Boris Godunov for years.[93]

Whoever the pretender was, he played his part convincingly in Poland-Lithuania, on his campaign for the throne, and as tsar. Tsar Dmitrii may have been the real son of Ivan the Terrible; at least he was convinced that he was. Dmitrii probably fled to Poland-Lithuania in 1602, disguised as a monk and accompanied by Otrepev and others.[94] Fearing a developing boyar plot against him, Tsar Boris unsuccessfully tried to stop Dmitrii's departure by closing the border.[95] The pretender's activities at this point are not well-known and have often been confused with Otrepev's. By late 1602, local Lithuanian authorities became aware of a man claiming to be Dmitrii.[96] The pretender or his boyar supporters chose wisely in seeking patrons for Dmitrii in Poland-Lithuania; the young man developed ties with Orthodox Christians, Antitrinitarians (Arians), and Calvinists, not just Catholics.[97]

In 1603, Dmitrii revealed his identity to Prince Adam Vishnevetskii—a powerful Ukrainian magnate, adventurer, and champion of Orthodox Christianity in Poland-Lithuania who was a distant relative of Ivan the Terrible and the son of the largest landowner in the Dnepr region bordering the Russian province of Severia. Prince Adam was at that time involved in a nasty border dispute with Tsar Boris, whose troops had recently burned some of Vishnevetskii's towns near the Seversk frontier.[98] Significantly, the Vishnevetskii clan already had a

Fig. 5 "The Pretender Dmitrii Ivanovich." Woodcut by Franciszek Sniadecki.
Printed in Stanislaw Grochowski's Wedding Brochure, 1605. From D. A. Rovinskii,
Materialy dlia Russkoi Ikonografii, part 2 (St. Petersburg, 1884). Courtesy of Houghton
Library, Harvard University.

well-known history of involvement in pretender affairs in Eastern Europe during the sixteenth century.[99] Prince Adam had good reason to recognize Dmitrii as part of his family's struggle against Tsar Boris, and Vishnevetskii's recognition was extremely important for the pretender as well.[100] At first, Prince Adam had been skeptical, but when many Russians showed up who "recognized" Tsarevich Dmitrii he began to show interest.[101] Prince Adam was also influenced by Tsar Boris's strenuous efforts to denounce the pretender or to have him killed; Godunov even offered Vishnevetskii land, money, and a truce if he would turn the "traitor" over to Russian authorities. Because of the tsar's interest and threats to use force to get hold of the pretender, Vishnevetskii moved Dmitrii away from the border zone and began treating him as an honored guest. Together, they began making plans to put Dmitrii on the Russian throne.[102]

The Vishnevetskii clan had strong ties to Ukrainian cossack leaders, and Prince Adam felt confident enough about Dmitrii's ability to plead his own case to send him to negotiate directly with the Zaporozhian cossacks for military assistance. Dmitrii was honorably and favorably received by them.[103] Dmitrii also made efforts in this period to appeal to the Don cossacks, sending messages promising them the freedom Boris Godunov had taken away. The result was not at all surprising. The Don cossacks quickly recognized Tsarevich Dmitrii "resurrected like Lazarus;" and in November 1603, they sent ataman Andrei Korela and others to Lithuania to cement their alliance with Dmitrii and to make war plans.[104] By January 1604, Prince Adam began gathering small numbers of troops on his own estates for possible service in Dmitrii's campaign for the throne. The activities of Vishnevetskii, the pretender, and the cossacks quickly came to the attention of Polish and Lithuanian officials who became concerned about the possibility of a private war against Russia that might hurt their government's interests and that might even trigger another major cossack rebellion in Ukraine.[105] Prince Adam was first urged, then ordered, to explain what was going on to King Sigismund and to send the putative tsarevich to court.[106] Sigismund was initially somewhat enthusiastic about the pretender scheme as a way to secure eventual Russian assistance for his plans to regain the throne of Sweden.[107] Most of the powerful Polish lords, including Chancellor Jan Zamoyski, however, were hostile to the idea of supporting Dmitrii, arguing that it could bring disaster to Poland-Lithuania. In the end, they managed to force the king to retreat from any official recognition of the pretender.[108]

In the meantime, the Vishnevetskii clan sought help from a relative by marriage, the powerful Catholic lord, Jerzy Mniszech, who was the palatine of Sandomierz—commander of both Lvov and Sambor. From the outset, Mniszech was enthusiastic because he saw in the pretender affair an opportunity to end his own serious financial problems. Dmitrii was moved to Mniszech's home in Sambor, and the palatine helped him gain the important, if temporary, support of the Lithuanian Chancellor Leo Sapieha.[109] Together, Mniszech and Sapieha soon produced a number of "witnesses" who swore that the pretender was indeed Tsarevich Dmitrii.[110] That development favorably impressed King Sigismund, but the continuing opposition of Polish lords limited the king's options.[111] Mniszech was only able to secure a small sum from him for Dmitrii's expenses; and even that sum was merely deducted from what the palatine already owed the king, so no money actually changed hands.[112]

King Sigismund, Polish Catholic leaders, and the Jesuits soon took great interest in reports that Dmitrii was considering conversion to Catholicism. They dreamed, among other things, of converting all of Russia and of then using the Russians against Sweden.[113] Dmitrii was brought before the king for an audience, during which Sigismund made very stiff demands for territorial concessions once Dmitrii became tsar in return for nothing more than informal recognition and extremely limited support. Sigismund insisted that Dmitrii cede the rich Chernigov-Seversk lands and half of the rich border province of Smolensk—territories formerly belonging to Lithuania. During his audience, Dmitrii may have promised the king that once he became tsar, he would eventually convert Russia to Catholicism and provide an army to aid Sigismund's war against Sweden.[114] Dmitrii soon thereafter met with Catholic leaders and promised them that he would lead a crusade against the Turks. He then secretly "converted" to Catholicism.[115] Dmitrii's "conversion" was, when discovered, used by his enemies after his assassination to "prove" that he had been an evil tool of Polish Catholic intervention in Russia. In fact, Dmitrii's conversion was simply a necessary political ploy in order to secure even limited support in his struggle against the powerful Boris Godunov. His conversion was probably insincere. This "secret Catholic" continued to maintain an outward appearance of being Orthodox on his campaign and once he became tsar. As tsar, he also maintained close ties to radical Protestants (Arians) and Calvinists, preferring them to the Jesuits and other Catholics and completely frustrating all Catholic hopes for the conversion of Russia.[116] In the spring of 1604, however, King Sigismund and the Jesuits were still hopeful. Despite their enthusiasm, though, skeptical Polish lords prevented the king from actively supporting Dmitrii's campaign for the throne.[117] That forced Sigismund to work behind the scenes, secretly encouraging Mniszech, the Vishnevetskiis, and others to pursue the pretender affair as a private venture while the king publicly remained silent.[118] In fact, because of continuing pressure from Polish lords, Sigismund's government at least "officially" tried to stop Mniszech and Dmitrii from raising an army in order to avoid provoking a general war with Tsar Boris.[119] To the confusion of historians, Sigismund also later loudly and falsely proclaimed that he never had anything whatsoever to do with the pretender affair and had actively tried to put a stop to it.[120] Probably the most important thing the king really did, however, apart from turning a blind eye, was to order the release of ataman Korela and his Don cossack associates, who had been arrested by Lithuanian officials, and to allow them to visit Dmitrii and cement their alliance with him.[121]

In the meantime, Jerzy Mniszech had been busy making plans to put Dmitrii on the Russian throne and to personally become immensely wealthy in the process. The palatine had no difficulty securing Dmitrii's promise to marry his daughter Marina, pay him a huge sum of money, and cede border territories to him. Severia and the Smolensk lands were apparently to be split between Mniszech and King Sigismund once Dmitrii's campaign for the throne succeeded.[122] Again, as in the case of the pretender's conversion, his willingness to cede Russian-held territory to his future father-in-law and the king of Poland was used by his enemies after his assassination to "prove" that he had been an evil tool of Polish intervention. It has also strongly influenced negative historical opinion about Dmitrii. In fact, his agreement with Mniszech was a necessary political ploy in order to secure much-needed support. Tsar Dmitrii never took a single step to dismember Russia in order to fulfill that insincere bargain, frustrating the palatine and Sigismund alike.

Because the king and the Jesuits did not provide much assistance to Dmitrii, those Polish lords hoping for gain by championing his cause were forced to use their own money and men while at the same time avoiding a collision with government officials hostile to their enterprise. Mniszech, always broke, gathered a small force of unemployed, rather seedy veteran mercenary soldiers by the summer of 1604, but he was unable to pay them. As a result, they terrorized and robbed Lvov merchants. The palatine, coming under increasing pressure from officials, contemplated bowing out of the campaign; but the rowdy mercenaries threatened to ransack his own estates if he did not lead them into Russia.[123] Mniszech then reluctantly agreed to continue as commander-in-chief of the planned invasion force. Nonetheless, the combination of the lack of official support, Mniszech's own unsavory reputation, the predation of his mercenaries, and a fear that Tsar Boris was well informed and prepared for the invasion caused a number of important Polish and Lithuanian lords at this point to withdraw their earlier offers of military support for Dmitrii's campaign.[124] In fact, Tsar Boris did follow events across the border closely, and one of his assassins made it all the way to Sambor during the summer of 1604 before being stopped.[125]

By September 1604, Mniszech and his associates managed to gather together a force of approximately twenty-five hundred men, about eleven hundred of whom were cavalry and infantry forces drawn from men in service to the magnates and approximately fourteen hundred of whom were so-called "cossacks." About two-thirds of the latter group were, in fact, Ukrainians; but the Zaporozhian cossacks declined to participate at this time, and only about five hundred of Dmitrii's "cossacks" were true Ukrainian cossacks. The rest were either fortress cossacks or were simply peasants and others dressed as cossacks. There were also a few Don cossacks in Dmitrii's invasion force and about two hundred or so Russians who had crossed the border to join his cause. By the time Dmitrii's small army invaded Russia, Don cossack arrivals had increased the number of cossacks to at least three thousand and brought the army's overall size up to more than four thousand.[126] That army was obviously too small to succeed on its own, but Dmitrii also counted on cossacks all along Russia's southern frontier to support his campaign in force. He sent his banner to his new Don cossack allies and coordinated military planning with a delegation from the Don that arrived in his camp during August 1604.[127] The Don cossacks were instructed to bring their forces as soon as possible to the Russian southwestern border province of Severia (or Seversk), which was to be the starting point of Dmitrii's invasion.[128] The palatine and the pretender had long been aware of the potential for strong support from Tsar Boris's subjects in Severia, and they sent numerous letters to Seversk towns that were very effective at convincing people that Dmitrii was genuine and deserved their support.[129] The time to strike was at hand.

Before invading Russia, Dmitrii's small army first had to make its way east to the Dnepr River, cross it, and reach the border. That proved to be somewhat tricky. Mniszech received several warnings from Polish-Lithuanian officials that his private army was illegal and would not be allowed to cross the Dnepr. In fact, a large Polish army was hastily gathered south of Kiev in part to prevent Dmitrii's forces from continuing and in part to prevent possible looting of Kiev by Mniszech's men.[130] All ferry boats were also ordered away from Dnepr crossings in the region, temporarily stranding Dmitrii's army. At that point, a remarkable thing happened. Simple Orthodox Christian subjects of King Sigismund who lived in the Kiev area, no doubt fascinated by all the news and stories about Dmitrii, showed up without authorization from anyone to ferry the tsarevich and his men across the Dnepr, for which Dmitrii was extremely grateful.[131] Such a spontaneous popular response to the resurrected "true tsar" was a good omen. Once Dmitrii and his men were across the mighty Dnepr, Mniszech led them to the banks of the Desna River, the border between Russia and Poland-Lithuania. In October 1604, Dmitrii boldly crossed that border to claim the throne of his father.

9

Dmitrii's Invasion and the Beginning of the Civil War

Dmitrii's invasion in October 1604 triggered the first phase of Russia's first civi
war—a massive rebellion of southwestern and southern frontier province.
towns, garrisons, and cossacks that grew into a much wider conflict that top
pled the Godunov dynasty. Dmitrii's campaign for the throne and the rebel
lions in favor of the resurrected tsarevich are worth close study because the
anticipated in many ways the rekindled civil war of 1606–12 in terms of issue.
geography, towns and groups involved, and rebel consciousness as well as mi
itary operations, commanders, and personnel. The study of Dmitrii's campaig
for the throne and the zealous popular support he generated will shed consid
erable light on the origins, nature, and course of the later, more destructiv
phase of the civil war.

Dmitrii's cause was greatly assisted by Russia's severe multidimensional cri
sis and by the decline in legitimacy of Tsar Boris in the eyes of many of his sub
jects. In addition, during the famine the southern frontier population, alread
disgruntled and hostile to many of Tsar Boris's policies, received large numbe
of desperate and hungry people from central Russia.[1] Many of the new arriva
were also angry about the actions and policies of the Godunov regime, makir
the southern frontier extremely susceptible to Dmitrii's appeals. In launchir
his invasion, Dmitrii counted on the hostility toward Tsar Boris of the fronti
population and the cossacks. In the months before his invasion, he sent coun
less messages to cossack stanitsas and Russian frontier towns urging them
take up his just cause, and he was greatly encouraged by the responses he receivec
The Don cossacks enthusiastically spread news of the return of the "true tsa
far and wide along the southern frontier all the way east to the Ural Mountair
managing to generate much support for Dmitrii. They also gathered togeth
a potent military force eager to link up with his small army.[3] Reports receive
by Dmitrii from Russia's western border provinces also showed strong pote
tial support from townspeople, garrisons, and the local population.[4]

In choosing their invasion route, Dmitrii and Jerzy Mniszech avoided t
most obvious roads to Moscow such as the one via Smolensk. They had neith

the manpower nor the ordnance to attempt an assault on Russia's strongest fortress, and they could not afford to leave strong points still loyal to Tsar Boris behind them. In addition, the Smolensk region, still suffering from the after-effects of the famine, did not have much food available for purchase or seizure by an invading army.[5] Dmitrii and his commander-in-chief looked for a route with plenty of available provisions and one that would be difficult for Tsar Boris's army to block. They also needed to achieve some quick victories in order to gain momentum and to give the cossacks time to link up with them. For those reasons, they chose to invade Russia's large and vulnerable southwestern wooded-steppe province of Severia (or Seversk).[6] In addition to its convenient location near the place Dmitrii's forces had been organized, Severia shared the same general grievances and misery common across Russia's southern frontier. Severians, in fact, had even more reasons than most of the frontier population to be hostile to Boris Godunov and receptive to Dmitrii.

One of the first regions to be incorporated into ancient Kievan Rus, Severia was a relatively wealthy province with reasonably fertile soil, some cereal grain production, and an abundance of natural products such as honey, wax, fish, and small animal furs.[7] For centuries, Severians fought almost continuously against steppe nomads, and for that reason the Seversk frontiersmen developed a well-deserved reputation as fierce warriors. The martial skills of the relatively prosperous free peasant population were akin to those of the free cossacks, many of whom actually lived near Severia and maintained strong contact with the region's townspeople. The ferocity of the Severians, who were predominantly Ukrainians, and the region's unbroken woodlands and river networks made it hard even for the powerful Crimean Tatars to invade.[8] Severia long enjoyed semiautonomy under Lithuanian administration until it was acquired by Grand Prince Ivan III of Moscow at the beginning of the sixteenth century. The region was not fully incorporated into Russia until 1523, however, and even after that its prosperous free peasant population continued to enjoy considerable auton-omy while they guarded Russia's southwestern frontier.[9] Votchina estates and even pomeste land grants and grasping pomeshchiki were rare in Severia through-out most of the sixteenth century.[10] The region's wealth and relative freedom gradually attracted many Russians searching for a better life or fleeing from taxes, lords, or the law. New arrivals were quickly infected by the "free" spirit of Severia, and the populous region and its rowdy inhabitants were difficult for Moscow to govern.[11]

In addition to several important towns with glorious histories such as Putivl, Novgorod Severskii, and Chernigov, Severia contained large districts of palace lands in which state peasants occupied a relatively favorable position, even hav-

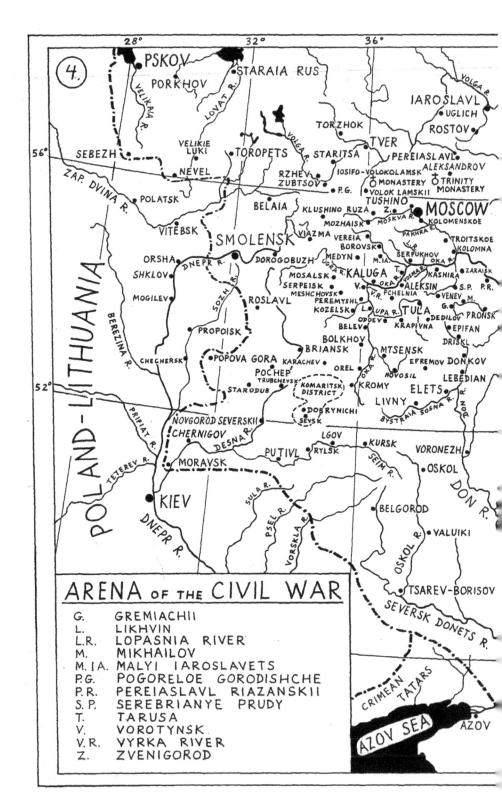

Map 4 Arena of the Civil War.

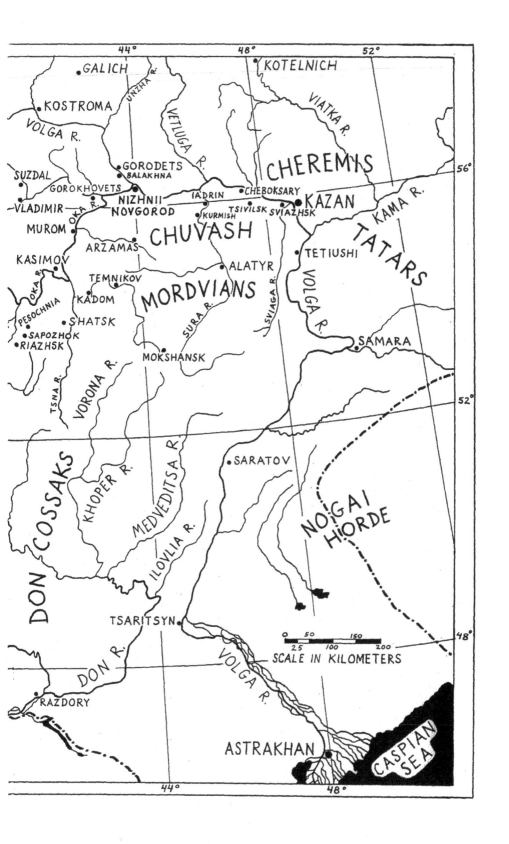

ing the privilege of electing their own canton administrators.[12] Local units of those palace lands were responsible as a whole—not as individuals—for meeting tax obligations, and the central government had little interest in who lived there as long as taxes were paid and the local population helped defend the frontier.

The most important of those palace land districts was the rich and populous Komaritsk district, located on the divide between the Desna-Dnepr and Oka-Volga basins.[13] There were more than a thousand taxpaying households in the Komaritsk district by the beginning of the seventeenth century.[14] The district's inhabitants were relatively prosperous, fiercely independent, and accustomed to defending themselves. Those muzhiki-sevriuki were extremely displeased by Tsar Ivan IV's decision after the devastating Crimean Tatar invasion of 1571 to reorganize the Seversk frontier's defenses by replacing locals with relocated low status military servitors (mostly fortress cossacks) and pomeshchiki.[15] Some of those new arrivals were pardoned criminals; others were militiamen sent to perform low-status frontier duty as punishment.[16] Even worse, at the end of the sixteenth century, Boris Godunov imposed very unpopular mandatory plowing for the state (*gosudareva desiatinnaia pashnia,* or the tsar's tenth) on the population of Severia in order to feed newly arriving servicemen; he even began sporadically assigning palace lands to pomeshchiki and to groups of lower status military servitors. Thus, by the beginning of the seventeenth century, many Seversk peasants found themselves being enserfed or displaced.[17] That was a heavy blow to relatively wealthy individuals who were fiercely proud of their freedom and who considered the land they worked and paid taxes on to be essentially their own property. Their attitude was, in fact, similar to that of other state peasants. Russian peasants living on taxable state land were accustomed to buying, selling, and inheriting those properties—which the government had long tolerated. When such state land was suddenly assigned to a lord, unhappy peasant occupants understandably regarded it as confiscation.[18] In Severia, growing popular anger increasingly focused directly against Boris Godunov, who had not only been responsible for the local inhabitants' misery through his enserfment and frontier policies but, when he was regent, had also been given huge tracts of land in the Komaritsk district and elsewhere in the province by Tsar Fedor—lands yielding a very high income to the tsar's brother-in-law. When Godunov became tsar, many Seversk peasants naturally expected nothing good to come from the new ruler who had deprived them of their freedom and who was—at the same time—their personal, greedy local lord.[19]

It is not necessary, as some writers have done, to conclude that many Komaritsk district peasants became serfs owned directly by Boris Godunov. Most were still free and prosperous palace land peasants whose declining position was still far superior to that of ordinary serfs.[20] Nonetheless, during the famine, Tsar Boris's 1601 and 1602 decrees allowing the movement of some peasants from one pomeste estate to another specifically excluded from movement all peasants living on state and crown lands. That meant large numbers of peasants in Severia—especially in the Komaritsk district—found themselves, in effect, temporarily bound to the land.[21] In addition, desperate people arriving from central Russia during the famine who sought food on crown lands in Severia and elsewhere received grain only if they were willing to indenture themselves.[22] As a result, a very tense situation developed in the region. During the famine years, Komaritsk peasants also occasionally struggled with monasteries over control of property. Those monasteries, backed by the central government, gained the upper hand and stirred deep resentment among the peasants.[23] The discontent of the native Seversk population and new arrivals to the region was well known to Dmitrii, and he counted on being able to exploit it. He used all possible means to attract Severians to his cause, and months of wooing them proved to be very effective.

Surprisingly enough, despite the numerous reports Tsar Boris received about Dmitrii's activities, the Russian government was not expecting his invasion when it finally came. No measures had been taken to fortify western border garrisons, and the tsar did not place his army in the field in anticipation of Dmitrii, hoping instead that the hostility of Polish lords to the pretender's plans would put a stop to them before any invasion took place.[24] Tsar Boris did, however, sign a treaty with King Karl IX of Sweden in August, 1604, in part to avoid the possibility of a two-front war.[25] Other than that, he took no special precautions. Had he done so, Tsar Boris's forces could easily have crushed Dmitrii's invasion at the border, and Russia might not have been forced to endure its first civil war.

On October 13, 1604, Dmitrii crossed the Russian border with more than four thousand men. So began the civil war.[26] While Dmitrii's main force trekked though heavily wooded terrain in order to maintain the element of surprise and to avoid open battle with larger Russian armies, a detachment of cossacks under ataman Beleshko headed straight to a small Russian border fortress, Moravsk (*Monastyrevskii ostrog*), carrying a letter from Dmitrii addressed not to the fortress' *voevodas* (commanders) but to the streltsy sotnik (centurion). That letter warned of Dmitrii's approach with a large army and urged recognition of his claim to the throne. Dmitrii had been correctly forewarned of sentiment in his favor in Moravsk, and after brief negotiations the fortress declared for him without a fight. The inhabitants of Moravsk, almost all military servitors, simply took their voevodas captive and turned them over to Dmitrii's cossacks. On October 21, the fortress formally surrendered when a delegation went to pay homage to the "true tsar" carrying the traditional Russian hospitality gifts of bread and salt. The Moravsk voevodas, B. Lodiagin and M. Tolochanov, were treated honorably as prisoners of war.[27] News of Dmitrii's first victory spread like wildfire. Throughout the region the tsarevich was hailed as the "rising sun." Not just Seversk peasants but military garrisons and Severians of all social classes were prepared to believe Dmitrii really was the true tsar fighting against an evil usurper.[28] Tsar Boris's regime was quick to claim that much of the popular support Dmitrii generated came from slaves who fled to the southwestern frontier during the famine.[29] As we have seen, that unfortunately convinced some Soviet scholars that Dmitrii's campaign for the throne was a social revolution.[30] In fact, many of the slaves in question were elite military slaves who were not the least bit interested in revolution, and the number of them settling in Severia has been exaggerated in any case. (Many of those men actually joined the cossacks.) No doubt there were some slaves who ended up in Severia and later rallied to Dmitrii's cause; however, the bulk of the pretender's support came from the native Ukrainian population of the region and from military garrisons unhappy with Tsar Boris.[31]

News of Dmitrii's progress spread quickly to the ancient town of Chernigov, located approximately 70 kilometers northeast of Moravsk. Chernigov had a sizable garrison and a small but significant civilian population living in its posad and actively engaged in trade.[32] The excited townspeople and much of the garrison immediately wished to submit to Dmitrii; but one of the voevodas, Prince I. A. Tatev, and some trusted streltsy retreated to the citadel to resist. Immediately upon arriving before the town walls, ataman Beleshko's cossacks tried to storm it, but they were driven back by streltsy gunfire. Soon Mniszech's mercenary forces arrived before Chernigov, whereupon the townsmen and mutinous fortress cossacks, streltsy, and other low status military servitors threw open the gates in the name of Dmitrii. Mniszech's men then entered the town and began to plunder it. In the meantime, the Chernigovites themselves captured their commanders—Tatev, Prince P. M. Shakhovskoi, and N. S. Vorontsov-Veliaminov. When Dmitrii arrived the next day to receive the oath of obedience from the town's inhabitants, the voevodas were turned over to him. Tatev and Shakhovskoi readily agreed to recognize Dmitrii as their lawful ruler and were taken into honorable captivity, but Vorontsov-Veliaminov refused and was immediately put to death as a traitor to the true tsar.[33] It was at this point that Dmitrii publicly expressed great indignation that his soldiers had plundered the loyal population of Chernigov.[34] Demanding recognition of his claim to the throne but also posing as the protector of the Russian people instead of an angry conqueror proved to be a very successful strategy for Dmitrii. His commander-in-chief,

Jerzy Mniszech, was very impressed by the reception the clement tsarevich received during the campaign. Throughout Severia rose the cry: "God save Dmitrii Ivanovich, Tsar of all the Russias."[35]

As Dmitrii's army was approaching Chernigov, the Don cossack ataman Korela arrived as planned with reinforcements.[36] Due primarily to Mniszech's misleading propaganda and to the traditional interpretation of Dmitrii's campaign, there has been considerable exaggeration in scholarly literature about the type, size, and activities of the cossacks joining Dmitrii's cause at this time. Platonov erroneously concluded that, in addition to Korela's Don cossack detachment, another Zaporozhian cossack army of several thousand men operated independently farther south and, in effect, opened up a second front. Platonov believed the Zaporozhian cossacks were responsible for the surrender of the fortresses of Tsarev-Borisov and Belgorod before linking up with Dmitrii's army.[37] That is simply not true. The Zaporozhian cossacks did not actively participate in the first phase of Dmitrii's campaign.[38] However, exaggerated reports of up to ten thousand Don cossacks traveling with ataman Korela gave rise to the false impression of a huge cossack movement in favor of Dmitrii in the fall of 1604, a movement that supposedly swept up large numbers of southern townspeople in a violent social protest or open class war.[39] In fact, a majority of even the friendly Don cossacks did not participate in the opening round of Dmitrii's invasion, and Korela's forces certainly did not trigger class war in southern Russia as they rode to Dmitrii's aid. Close examination of sources reveals that Korela's Don cossack detachment actually had only about five hundred men in it.[40] Nonetheless, Korela's detachment was a very significant addition to Dmitrii's army. Those superb horsemen and extremely brave and stubborn warriors, many armed with harquebuses, were true heroes in the cause of Dmitrii and made an extraordinary contribution to his success.[41]

Because of the ease of their initial victories and the arrival of Korela's reinforcements, Dmitrii and Mniszech altered their original plan, which had been to continue advancing under cover of dense woodlands. Instead, they decided to proceed straight up the Desna River to the ancient town of Novgorod Severskii, located approximately 150 kilometers east northeast of Chernigov. Novgorod Severskii, after Putivl, was the most important fortress in Severia. Strategically located on a direct road north to Moscow, the town had a significant civilian population as well as a sizable garrison.[42] If Dmitrii could win it over, Novgorod Severskii would be a great prize. Two hundred cossacks under the command of Jan Buczynski rode ahead of Dmitrii's army and attempted to negotiate with the residents of the town, threatening the voevodas if they failed to surrender. This time, however, that tactic failed to work, primarily because of the energetic defense preparations made by one of Tsar Boris's best voevodas, okolnichii Petr F. Basmanov.

Under orders from Moscow to stop Dmitrii, Basmanov had already tried unsuccessfully to personally reinforce the Chernigov garrison with an elite Moscow streltsy detachment, which was only 15 kilometers away from Chernigov when that town declared for Dmitrii. Basmanov immediately returned to Novgorod Severskii more determined than ever to block Dmitrii's path to Moscow. He quickly surrounded the town with solid defense works and reinforced its garrison.[43] Fortunately for Basmanov, Novgorod Severskii already had more than twenty artillerymen tending its cannons at this time.[44] To the town's three hundred or so deti boiarskie, fortress cossacks, streltsy, and other servicemen, Basmanov added his detachment of Moscow streltsy and ordered the quick transfer of troops from other fortresses. About sixty pomeshchiki came from Briansk, and about six hundred Moscow streltsy and fortress cossacks came from Kromy, Belev, and Trubchevsk. Other troops may also have come from Rylsk and Pronsk.[45] Although those transfers to Novgorod Severskii made the other fortresses vulnerable, they gave Basmanov more than a thousand men to help him resist Dmitrii's army. Tsar Boris's commander also ordered the conscription of recruits (*datochnye liudi*) from the local population to aid in the defense of Novgorod Severskii. About five hundred peasants from the nearby Komaritsk district, located about 50 kilometers to the northeast, were quickly added to Basmanov's forces.[46]

Now reasonably well fortified and reinforced, Basmanov was able to drive back Mniszech's initial attempts to storm the fortress. Dmitrii's army then settled down to invest the town. A full-scale storming was attempted on the night of November 17–18, complete with the use of a moveable siege tower made of prefabricated log panels and filled with straw and brush, which Dmitrii's men intended to use to set fire to the wooden walls of the fortress. Basmanov was well informed about the enemy's plans, however, and succeeded in driving the besiegers back. This first major failure of Dmitrii's army provoked a near-mutiny among Mniszech's mercenaries, who now wished to return home; but, just as they were making plans to abandon the siege and leave Dmitrii in the lurch, exciting news arrived in camp: the great fortress of Putivl had voluntarily declared for Dmitrii. That development quieted down Mniszech's men and immediately changed the strategic situation in Severia.[47]

Stone-walled Putivl, located on the Seim River (a tributary of the Desna) approximately 100 kilometers south southeast of Novgorod Severskii, was a large, rich city—the most important and most heavily fortified town in Severia.[48] It was the key point in the defense of the entire southwestern frontier. Dmitrii knew full well that possession of Putivl would greatly aid his cause, but he had harbored no illusions about capturing it with his small army—which did not even have any siege guns. Now Putivl fell into his lap. Why?

Putivl had a long and glorious past and a truculent frontier spirit. Unlike most southern frontier towns, Putivl had a sizable civilian population; by 1600, Putivl had a relatively large posad with seven hundred taxpaying households.[49] Its inhabitants did not particularly welcome Moscow's expansion into the region or its policies of enserfment, binding townsmen, high taxes, and plowing for the tsar. Even though it was the deti boiarskie of Putivl who initiated the rebellion in favor of Dmitrii, the townspeople quickly made common cause with the militiamen.[50] The Putivl deti boiarskie were, of course, like most other southern militiamen, a poor and discontented lot. Back in 1594, when Tsar Fedor had ordered the strengthening of the Putivl garrison by the addition of a new five hundred-man detachment of relatively low-status deti boiarskie infantry, only about one hundred local militiamen showed up for service, so the rest of the detachment was filled in by promoting fortress cossacks and streltsy. When Boris Godunov's terrifying investigations of southern frontier garrisons in search of runaway taxpayers came to Seversk towns such as Putivl and Rylsk in 1597, they provoked genuine bitterness within those beleaguered garrisons. During the famine years, the already small number of sturdy pomeshchiki in Putivl declined still further while there was an increase in the number of lower status deti boiarskie infantry and low status military servitors. By the time Dmitrii invaded Russia, therefore, in Putivl—as in many other southern frontier towns—disgruntled deti boiarskie infantry were the predominant military force.[51]

As elsewhere on the frontier, the garrison and townspeople of Putivl had also maintained close ties to the free cossack stanitsas located nearby.[52] They all shared a common discontent with the policies of Tsar Boris, and most were willing to believe Dmitrii was indeed the true tsar. When news of Dmitrii's presence in Severia and his early victories reached Putivl in mid-November, most of the garrison—led by two local deti boiarskie, Iurii Bezzubtsev and S. Bulgakov—joined the townspeople in declaring for Dmitrii. Also taking up Dmitrii's cause at that time were Putivl's two voevodas, okolnichii Mikhail M. Saltykov and Prince V. M. Mosalskii, along with a Moscow treasury official, B. I. Sutupov, who had just arrived in town with a large sum of money intended as the payroll for the Seversk garrisons.[53] The only active resistance to the town's break with Tsar Boris came from about two hundred Moscow streltsy stationed there; they held out for two days before surrendering to the rebels.[54] Even the monks at the local monastery showed enthusiasm for Dmitrii, for which reason he later granted them additional land as a reward.[55]

The rebellion of Putivl was of immense importance to Dmitrii's cause and helped trigger many more rebellions in his favor. Putivl soon became the temporary "capital" of Dmitrii's government, hosting his war council and judiciary. Not only was Putivl a strong fortress, but its citizens and its garrison significantly augmented Dmitrii's forces; Putivl's abundance of food and munitions was also extremely important to his war effort. As soon as the town surrendered, secretary Sutupov personally delivered the payroll he brought to Putivl to Dmitrii, who used part of it to pay Mniszech's disgruntled mercenaries. Sutupov then immediately became one of Dmitrii's principal advisers. Voevodas M. M. Saltykov and V. M. Mosalskii also swore oaths to Dmitrii and became important courtiers of the "true tsar."[56] The transfer of allegiance by the high-ranking, prestigious okolnichii Saltykov—a member of Tsar Boris's boyar council—was an especially significant boost to Dmitrii's cause. In fact, Dmitrii's conscious policy of treating gently those voevodas and others surrendering to him became another important magnet that attracted more towns and garrisons to his cause.[57]

Soon after Putivl declared for Dmitrii, agitation on his behalf and rebellions in his name spread rapidly throughout the southwestern frontier to places such as Rylsk, situated up the Seim River about 70 kilometers northeast of Putivl, and Kursk—located farther up the Seim River about 75 kilometers east of Rylsk. Rylsk was an important fortress that had been reinforced by three hundred Moscow streltsy at the beginning of Dmitrii's campaign. Nonetheless, its voevoda, A. Zagriazhskii, was unable to stop the garrison from declaring for Dmitrii, and his men sent him to Dmitrii as a prisoner in late November. At about the same time, the Kursk garrison declared for Dmitrii and arrested its voevoda, Prince G. B. Roshcha-Dolgorukii, and his streltsy golova (colonel), Ia. Zmeev. Those two men were taken to Dmitrii, agreed to recognize him as tsar, and were immediately appointed as Dmitrii's new voevodas in Rylsk. Also taken into custody at Kursk was an important dvorianin, Prince Grigorii P. Shakhovskoi, who also agreed to recognize Dmitrii as tsar and was later appointed as Dmitrii's new voevoda in Belgorod when it rebelled against Tsar Boris. It is worth noting that Dmitrii's supporters were consistently willing to serve under commanders who had opposed him once those officers recognized Dmitrii as the true tsar.[58]

In addition to towns and fortresses, many peasant villages in Severia rose in the name of Dmitrii in the fall of 1604. Those uprisings constituted the first massive peasant rebellion in Russian history. Soviet scholars incorrectly regarded those revolts as an on-going peasant war that had begun even before Dmitrii's invasion.[59] They were, in fact, rebellions in favor of Dmitrii and not against serfdom. The muzhiki-sevriuki, even though they were relatively wealthy state peasants, had reasons to resent the policies of Tsar Boris, and conscription of those proud Seversk peasants as recruits in order to shore up fortress defenses against Dmitrii led to even greater resentment. The first to rise against Tsar Boris were inhabitants of the huge, populous Komaritsk district. At the end of November, after very brief resistance, the entire district—including the town of Sevsk and its small garrison of low status military servitors—declared for Dmitrii. The Sevsk garrison delivered its two voevodas to Dmitrii as prisoners on December 1, 1604.[60]

The Komaritsk uprising quickly spilled into other nearby palace and state land districts and helped trigger a rebellion in early December of the small garrison in Kromy, a strategically important fortress located just northeast of the Komaritsk district.[61] The Kromy garrison usually contained several hundred soldiers, but at least two hundred had been transferred to Novgorod Severskii and elsewhere to fight against Dmitrii. When Kromy rebelled, therefore, it had relatively few troops. The garrison commander, dvorianin Grigorii Akinfiev, joined his men in declaring for Dmitrii.[62] The inhabitants of the Kromy region then quickly pushed the rebellion toward Karachev, a little more than 50 kilometers to the northwest, and toward Orel, about 30 kilometers to the northeast. In response, Tsar Boris's alarmed commanders rushed reinforcements to Karachev, but they were too late; the town declared for Dmitrii anyway, soon followed by the nearby town of Briansk and several villages and towns in the Orel region.[63] The loss of Kromy was a severe blow, but Tsar Boris's commanders could not afford to lose Orel. If they did, a clear path to Moscow would open up for Dmitrii's army. For that reason, they quickly transferred reinforcements to Orel from towns farther north. That was an intelligent move since Orel's garrison had consisted primarily of demoralized lower status deti boiarskie infantry. Enough sturdy dvoriane and deti boiarskie cavalry were transferred to Orel to keep the fortress loyal and to drive away rebels operating nearby. Nevertheless, widespread rebellion throughout Severia and the acquisition of many towns there secured Dmitrii's grip on the region.[64] As a result, he was able to turn his attention back to the siege of Novgorod Severskii.

News of the surrender of Putivl and of uprisings throughout Severia quickly reached Novgorod Severskii and set off a week-long struggle between townspeople wishing to surrender to Dmitrii, and Basmanov's troops who were determined to resist. Basmanov ordered the burning of Novgorod Severskii's posad and herded all willing inhabitants into the palisaded and fortified town center. Many inhabitants fled instead—some straight to Dmitrii. Valiant Basmanov, five hundred streltsy, and others, however, offered such a spirited defense that they managed to prevent capture of the town.[65] (It should be noted here that early modern Russian soldiers had a well-deserved reputation for being excellent defensive fighters, especially in protecting fortresses.)[66] In early December 1604, Dmitrii's forces were augmented by the arrival of eight siege guns and six light cannons from Putivl that immediately began an almost continuous bombardment of Novgorod Severskii, inflicting heavy losses on Basmanov's garrison and destroying much of what was left of the town. Basmanov and his men were soon reduced to eating their horses but continued stubbornly to hold out. In a play for time, Basmanov began negotiations with Dmitrii and requested a two-week truce; he was actually hoping that Tsar Boris's army would arrive in time to save him from surrendering. To Basmanov's surprise and relief, Dmitrii and Mniszech readily agreed to the truce, having already tried by every means at their disposal to capture the town and by then facing increasingly disgruntled Polish mercenaries among their own forces.[67] As it turned out, the two-week delay did, in fact, give Tsar Boris's army time to approach Novgorod Severskii in order to break the siege.

Even though Russia's western border had not been reinforced prior to Dmitrii's invasion, Tsar Boris responded quickly to the threat once Dmitrii's army crossed the border. At first, only small detachments were available to send to Severia to slow down Dmitrii's progress. For example, to protect the main road to Moscow, voevoda Fedor I. Sheremetev (a boyar) and a small detachment advanced to Orel, from which they ineffectively harassed rebels in nearby Kromy after it rebelled.[68] Once Dmitrii invaded, Tsar Boris ordered an immediate emergency mobilization of all available forces; boyars, gentry, low status military servitors, non-Russian troops, and all others trained in fighting were required—on pain of death—to report to Moscow within two weeks (by October 28, 1604). But, of course, the gentry militia was not a standing army, and mobilization actually took well over a month. Among other things, rainy fall weather turned many roads to mud and slowed down the movement of troops.[69] Far more serious, successful mobilization of the tsar's cavalry force was directly dependent upon the condition of the gentry's agricultural economy. By 1604, the gentry militia was, as we have seen, in severe crisis. In addition to all their chronic problems, the famine had reduced the numbers and effectiveness of the pomeshchiki and prevented many of the poorer ones from showing up for service.[70] Since militiamen were required to provide their own weapons and food for campaigns, many of the deti boiarskie who did manage to show up were poorly equipped and hungry. Even on short campaigns the provisions of those impoverished cavalrymen usually ran out very quickly. As a result, large numbers of pomeshchiki were typically forced to fast for days at a time while on active duty.[71] Their salaries, often in arrears even when they were outfitting for a campaign and desperately needed money, were also completely inadequate to purchase additional provisions while on duty—especially in war zones where prices were always inflated.[72]

In 1604, Tsar Boris's cash-strapped government could do very little to alleviate the severe problems of his miserable pomeshchiki. Since Russian commanders, even in good years, ordinarily did not have the means to provide for their men, campaigns often outlasted supplies and resulted in pomeshchiki being distracted from their duties while foraging for food—usually seizing it from local villages and doing much harm in the process. Eventually, the desertion of hungry soldiers would force the dismissal of the army. In fact, it was almost impossible, even in times of affluence, to keep the militia on campaign for many months, and 1604 was by no means a good year, although the famine had abated.[73] The half of the militia that had already been mobilized for routine service during the spring and early summer of 1604 proved to be so miserable and hungry that their commanders had been forced to let them return home early.[74] That group was certainly not in good condition for remobilization in the fall, and there were serious problems getting them to return to active duty. It was also not easy getting the other half of the militia mobilized. Absenteeism was very high, forcing Tsar Boris to adopt harsh measures to insure adequate numbers of troops. He ordered those pomeshchiki who failed to report for duty to be tracked down and delivered to their muster points under guard. He threatened no-shows with death and ordered confiscation of pomeste and votchina estates, prison terms, and public beatings in order to frighten his reluctant soldiers into showing up for duty.[75] Ordinarily, the size of the gentry militia in this era was somewhere between twenty and twenty-five thousand men. Because of the militia crisis, the famine, and many other factors, however, Tsar Boris was able to mobilize fewer than fifteen thousand militiamen to fight against Dmitrii, and many of them were forced to serve as low-status infantry rather than as cavalry.[76]

Tsar Boris was realistic enough to know that his pomeshchiki were having a hard time meeting their obligations. Earlier in 1604, he had reduced by half the number of mounted slaves armed with harquebuses that holders of pomeste estates and owners of votchinas were required to field during emergencies (from approximately one man per 400 acres held to one man per 800 acres).[77] Although many militiamen had great difficulty meeting even that reduced obligation, it did result in large numbers of combat slaves being mobilized in the fall of 1604. Tsar Boris also decreed that old or sick pomeshchiki, or those with important duties, could send in their place a mounted, armed, and fully supplied military slave substitute for every 800 acres of land they held.[78] Many took the tsar up on his offer, which resulted in a significant increase in the number of military slaves being mobilized compared to previous years.[79] Ordinarily, the ratio of combat slaves to pomeshchiki was about 1:3; therefore, when they were combined with baggage train slaves, the overall number of slaves in the army was usually about the same as the number of gentry cavalrymen.[80] However, even

Fig. 6 "A Russian Cavalryman." Drawn circa 1674 by a Swedish ambassador. Published in
Erich Palmquist, *Någre widh sidste Kongl: Ambassaden till Tzaren Muskou giorde observationer
öfwer Russlandh, des wager, pass meds fastningar och brantzer* (Stockholm: Generalstabens
Litografiska Anstalt, 1898). Courtesy of the James Ford Bell Library, University of
Minnesota.

though the numbers of pomeshchiki mobilized in 1604 was lower than usual, the policy of allowing masters to send combat slaves as substitutes resulted in a higher than normal numbers of combat slaves in the emergency mobilization—at least fifteen thousand men, perhaps as many as twenty thousand. That means there were more combat slaves than pomeshchiki being mobilized, and the total number of slaves in the army (combat and noncombatant) greatly outnumbered the gentry cavalry force in the fall of 1604.[81] In addition, since combat slaves were required to be outfitted with harquebuses, they also commanded far more firepower than the gentry militia.[82] Many of the combat slaves were former pomeshchiki who were excellent soldiers, and no doubt some of them were still angry about Boris Godunov's 1597 slave law. On the other hand, in the midst of the militia crisis, many pomeshchiki could no longer afford to field relatively expensive combat slaves, so they sent armed peasants, household lackeys, old slaves, and day laborers instead.[83] Thus, among the very large group of slaves mobilized in 1604, many were demoralized former deti boiarskie and many more were poorly trained peasants lacking discipline or any kind of fighting spirit. Those military slaves often had even less to eat than the hungry cavalrymen. Under such circumstances, it should be no surprise that slaves proved to be the most unreliable element in Tsar Boris's army.[84]

Streltsy units were also mobilized at this time, and—like the pomeshchiki— were expected to provide food for themselves while on campaign. Their salaries were really too low to afford that even in peacetime and were certainly inadequate to sustain them on long campaigns. Most streltsy simply could not afford the high-priced food available in a war zone.[85] In 1604, there were between seven and ten thousand elite Moscow streltsy and anywhere between twelve and twenty thousand regular streltsy who served primarily in town and fortress garrisons.[86] Not all of them were available for duty against Dmitrii, however. Some garrisons were stripped for that purpose, but streltsy were also needed to defend other frontiers. In addition, many of them had been sent on campaign to the Caucasus Mountains in the summer of 1604 and were not available for service on the western front.[87] Other low status military servitors were also mobilized for service against Dmitrii. By 1604, Russia had up to thirty-five hundred artillerymen; many of them were mobilized for the campaign, but many others remained at their posts on other frontiers.[88] Tsar Boris had between five and six thousand fortress cossacks; some were sent to the western border in 1604, but others remained at their posts guarding against Crimean Tatar invasions.[89]

Ordinarily, the tsar could also count on up to ten thousand free cossacks being willing to fight in his campaigns, but the free cossacks hated Boris Godunov and few were willing to serve him. Tsar Boris was also unable to attract the usual three or four thousand Ukrainian cossacks into his service in the fall of 1604 because of their interest in Dmitrii. (That was true even though earlier in the year he had been able to employ some Zaporozhian cossacks against the Crimean Tatars and Turks.)[90] The tsar could usually count on large detachments of fierce Asian and other non-Russian native troops drawn from the Tatars, Mordvians, Cheremis, and Chuvashi—sometimes up to twenty-seven thousand or more. Those Asian troops were often used as a kind of terror weapon on the western front.[91] Because of the famine and resentment against Tsar Boris's imperial policies, however, the number of those exotic troops in his army was significantly lower in 1604. Finally, by the beginning of the seventeenth century, the tsar's forces also regularly included small numbers of Western foreign troops. Primarily Germans, Livonians, and Poles, those mercenary forces included Swedes, Danes, Greeks, Flemings, Dutch, French, English, and Scots as well. Tsar Boris had about twenty-five hundred of them available for service against Dmitrii. Those soldiers were often the best fighters in the tsar's army and were usually well-provisioned.[92] Overall, however, Russia's military servitors of all types had great difficulty enduring long campaigns or conducting protracted sieges. It is no exaggeration to state that the average soldier in Tsar Boris's army sent against Dmitrii was malnourished while on active duty.[93]

In addition to all the regular military forces available to the tsar, in emergencies virtually all segments of Russian society were required to provide recruits to serve as a labor force for military construction work; for transportation of supplies, artillery, and munitions; and for many other tasks. Those recruits—primarily peasants—were required to bring carts, digging tools, and draft animals furnished by their own communities, which was a heavy burden for many of the tsar's subjects. One of the more important tasks recruits performed on campaigns was service in engineering battalions that preceded the tsar's army in order to prepare roads and river crossings for easier passage.[94]

In extreme emergencies, as in the case of Dmitrii's invasion, all landholders in Russia were also required to provide, in addition to combat slaves, a recruit for every 400 acres of land they held.[95] In 1604, of course, not all militiamen could afford that extra burden, but many did provide recruits. In addition, monasteries were also required to provide recruits at the same rate of one man per 400 acres, although church officials sometimes provided horses and wagons or sleds instead.[96] Merchants were also required to furnish recruits during emergency mobilizations.[97] Most recruits performed manual labor, but some were outfitted for combat.[98] Purposely dressed to resemble cossacks, many combat recruits were equipped with harquebuses; others were outfitted with bow and arrows, a scimitar, or a boar spear. Combat recruits drawn from the peas-

Fig. 7 "A Russian Infantryman." Drawn circa 1674 by a Swedish ambassador. Published in Erich Palmquist, *Några widh sidste Kongl: Ambassaden till Tzaren Muskou giorde observationer öfwer Russlandh, des wager, pass meds fastningar och brantzer* (Stockholm: Generalstabens Litografiska Anstalt, 1898). Courtesy of the James Ford Bell Library, University of Minnesota.

antry and lacking any training were not very effective militarily, but that did not stop Tsar Boris from using them against Dmitrii.[99] He needed all the soldiers he could get. There is no way to accurately estimate the number of recruits mobilized by the tsar in 1604, but there were certainly more than ten thousand of them, perhaps many more. Not surprisingly, recruits were treated poorly by Russian commanders, and they suffered even more privation than most other elements in the tsar's army.[100] Armed, hungry, and demoralized combat slaves and peasant recruits often mixed with each other on campaigns. Many of them did not remain under the watchful eye of their own lords but instead served in separate detachments.[101] That foolish policy created a potentially dangerous situation for the outnumbered and to some extent outgunned gentry militia and Tsar Boris's loyal commanders.

Estimating the overall size of the forces mobilized against Dmitrii is not easy. By the end of the sixteenth century, the tsar theoretically had a total of about 110,000 soldiers available for service—including frontier garrisons and hired cossacks, but not counting recruits.[102] That represented approximately two percent of the male population of Russia before the famine or about three percent by 1604, a not unexpected figure in such a highly mobilized and militarized early modern state.[103] When recruits are added in, the size of the army could be much larger. Very high overall estimates of the size of the tsar's military forces made by contemporaries probably included recruits and referred to full-scale emergency mobilizations. Some scholars have accepted contemporary estimates of a total force of one hundred fifty thousand men.[104] Other contemporary estimates of two hundred thousand or even three hundred thousand men in the Russian army were quite common, and incredible estimates of five hundred thousand or even 1.5 million men also circulated in early modern Europe.[105]

Because of the gentry militia crisis and the famine, in 1604 there were undoubtedly fewer men in Tsar Boris's army than usual. (The number of pomeshchiki was about ten thousand less than normal.) When one factors in the need to keep garrisons on other frontiers, the overall force available for service against Dmitrii is further reduced. In addition, just before Dmitrii's invasion, Tsar Boris sent one of his best voevodas, okolnichii I. M. Buturlin, with about ten thousand men (mostly streltsy and fortress cossacks) on an ill-fated expedition into the Caucasus Mountains. Buturlin lost more than seven thousand men in battle far from the western front.[106] So how many troops did Tsar Boris actually mobilize against Dmitrii? Estimates by a participant in the campaign, a merchant living in Moscow at the time, and other contemporaries put the total number of men Tsar Boris was able to field by late November 1604 at about two hundred thousand men.[107] That estimate is too high, but even using conservative figures for each of the above-mentioned categories yields an over-all total of about ninety thousand men—not counting recruits. Reducing that figure by the numbers necessary to account for men remaining in garrison duty or campaigning in the Caucasus yields a number that is still more than fifty thousand, and by adding recruits to that number, the overall size of the army opposing Dmitrii comes to more than seventy thousand men. That figure is credible and is supported by Military Affairs Office records and the testimony of the co-commander of Tsar Boris's Western mercenary troops, Captain Jacques Margeret, who participated in the campaign against Dmitrii.[108]

In time of war, senior Russian field commanders were chosen from members of the boyar council. Technically, all aristocrats had to have field command experience before being promoted into the council, but only a small percentage of the boyars concentrated on military duties and had any real expertise in military affairs.[109] Unfortunately for Tsar Boris, those few experts were not always chosen to command the army. Instead, voevodas were usually chosen on the basis of family background rather than competence. Such officers often became more preoccupied with maintaining their family's honor and their place in the service hierarchy's pecking order than with their military duties. Their *mestnichestvo* (precedence-ranking system) disputes with one another frequently caused serious problems on campaigns.[110] Even worse, those poorly trained voevodas, no matter how lofty their status, often performed miserably in the field.[111] Further complicating matters, in 1604 Tsar Boris was forced to carefully choose only boyars he considered loyal to his dynasty or, at least, those he believed were not secretly involved in the conspiracy to put Dmitrii on the throne.[112] As a result, to fight against Dmitrii, Godunov chose two of his highest-ranking boyars, Fedor Mstislavskii and Dmitrii I. Shuiskii, neither one a good field commander. The Military Affairs Office mobilized two armies for Mstislavskii and Shuiskii. One of the regiments formed in Moscow was immediately placed under Shuiskii's command and began marching to Severia by November 12. Shuiskii's intention was to gather additional forces on the way, to bypass Dmitrii's army, and to concentrate on recapturing rebel-held Chernigov. Meanwhile, even before being brought up to full strength, the main army—commanded by Mstislavskii—moved forward to Briansk, through which a major road connected Severia to Moscow. Pomeshchiki continuing to drift into Moscow from outlying areas were quickly sent forward to beef up those forces. Fedor Mstislavskii served as the senior commander for the entire campaign against Dmitrii, and his basic instructions were simple: attack the army besieging Novgorod Severskii as soon as possible.[113]

Tsar Boris was extremely concerned about Dmitrii's progress in Severia. At first, he tried to hide the invasion from his subjects and his soldiers, claiming that the emergency mobilization was due only to a cossack mutiny and incursion into Severia. No one was fooled; almost everyone knew that Tsarevich Dmitrii's campaign for the throne was the real cause of the mobilization. When that fact became obvious to the ruling elite, they shifted tactics and began loudly denouncing Dmitrii as an evil runaway monk and notorious sorcerer.[114] Tsar Boris also employed informers to report any and all mention of Dmitrii's name by his subjects; if caught, the punishment was death, sometimes of entire families. "Constantly, night and day, they gave victims to torture, burning them alive on slow fires, or pushing them under the ice." No one dared to speak the truth, and a dark and fearful mood settled over Moscow. Tsar Boris withdrew even farther from public view. Many people believed he was secretly afraid that Dmitrii might somehow succeed in his quixotic campaign for the throne.[115]

By December 1604, Mstislavskii had assembled an army of forty to fifty thousand men near Briansk, about 180 kilometers northeast of his objective—Novgorod Severskii. His force consisted of more than twenty-five thousand pomeshchiki and lower status military servitors, plus additional military slaves and recruits.[116] Mstislavskii's army was divided into the traditional, Mongol-inspired five regiments: advance guard, left wing, right wing, rear guard, and main regiment in the center. Each regiment was commanded by a voevoda and was usually divided into detachments of one hundred men commanded by a *sotnik* (centurion). Senior voevoda Mstislavskii led the main regiment. While on the march, the five regiments traveled separately but maintained close contact with the senior voevoda; each regimental commander had to be prepared on very short notice to quickly join forces with the main regiment.[117] Secretaries and clerks from the Military Affairs Office accompanied the army and provided centralized logistical support, military intelligence, and overall strategy—leaving very few key decisions to field commanders.[118] Because the campaign against Dmitrii was conducted during the winter, travel was actually easier than it would have been during the fall or spring. Mstislavskii's army moved toward Dmitrii's at approximately 15 kilometers per day.[119] A detachment of one hundred men was sent ahead to help Basmanov defend Novgorod Severskii; they arrived at the besieged town on December 14. Mstislavskii's army arrived in the area the next day and set up camp about 10 kilometers from Dmitrii's forces. Because he was still waiting for reinforcements, Mstislavskii delayed attacking for a few days.[120]

On December 20, 1604, Tsar Boris's army approached Dmitrii's much smaller army, which was forced to abandon the siege of Novgorod Severskii in order to face the approaching enemy.[121] Even though Dmitrii's forces had been growing as more and more towns and villages of Severia took up his cause, he probably still had fewer than ten thousand men at this point.[122] To make matters worse, as soon as Mstislavskii's army approached Novgorod Severskii, Basmanov ordered the continuous bombardment of Dmitrii's forces with all of his remaining artillery and dispatched frequent sorties to harass and tie down some of Dmitrii's cossacks. Isaac Massa, a Dutch merchant who lived in Moscow at the time, described Basmanov's clever ruse of pretending to surrender the fortress only to unleash a terrible artillery salvo from hidden positions as Dmitrii's soldiers came rushing through an open gate. Basmanov's men inflicted heavy casualties and, in the resulting confusion, were even able to make a bold sortie to capture some of Dmitrii's supplies. Caught between Mstislavskii and Basmanov, Dmitrii was in a very difficult position. Fortunately for him, Mstislavskii did not seize the initiative.[123]

The battle between Dmitrii's army and Mstislavskii's occurred on December 21, 1604. On the surface, it appeared to be a complete mismatch, with Dmitrii's forces outnumbered by more than three to one. However, there were several factors working in the pretender's favor: In addition to the lack of military skill and constant squabbling over rank and status on the part of Tsar Boris's commanders, the tsar's gentry cavalry force suffered from serious problems related not only to the militia crisis and the famine but also to outdated military organization and tactics. Even though Russian soldiers were extremely hardy, the severe conditions of camping in wintertime with inadequate shelter and meager rations inevitably produced sullen and demoralized troops.[124] Rich noblemen, of course, kept warmer and ate well. They wore fine armor with chain mail shirts and conic helmets and carried good lances or costly sabres in addition to their bows and arrows; they also rode on good horses. Much of the militia, on the other hand, suffered from exposure, could barely afford to provide its own food, and had to cut costs wherever possible. As a result, many pomeshchiki wore poor armor or, more often, cheap and ineffective quilted hemp or flax clothing with sewn-in iron plates and a poor cloth hat with a metal nosepiece. They usually carried a scimitar in addition to bows and arrows, and they rode sturdy small horses that were remarkably inexpensive.[125] Militiamen strongly preferred bows and arrows to harquebuses. In addition to higher status, the bow was also still superior in accuracy and rate of fire to gunpowder weapons—and it was cheaper.[126]

The tsar's gentry cavalry force consisted of excellent horsemen able to shoot arrows accurately from the saddle, but they had no formal military training. Among militiamen, there was little pretension to expertise and almost no specialization. In general, they suffered from poor morale and lacked discipline and courage on the battlefield. Organized for steppe warfare, the gentry cavalry force operated in a relatively unsophisticated way. There were no officers below the rank of sotnik, and detachments did relatively little coordinated maneuvering together. Instead, the militia was somewhat horde-like, trusting in sheer numbers to overwhelm an opposing force. Pomeshchiki were supposed to keep an eye on their voevoda's large battle standard during any conflict and to listen for signals. One brass kettle drum gave the signal to mount up or to dismount. Several other drums, trumpets, and shawms signaled attacks and retreats. There was little actual planning or order in attacks or in defense. The militia was generally poor at offensive warfare and quick to retreat in the face of stiff opposition. Even after winning a battle, they usually had trouble following up their victory by pursuing the retreating enemy. Instead, disorder and looting by hungry and miserable militiamen often reduced the value of battlefield successes. Overall, the gentry militia, despite its size, was increasingly anachronistic in the age of the gunpowder revolution and could not be counted upon to overwhelm even much smaller forces of highly motivated opponents.[127] One of Tsar Boris's most senior Western officers, Captain Margeret, referred to the pomeshchiki as "a multitude of men badly mounted, without order, courage, or discipline" who "often do more damage to the army than good."[128]

The battle before Novgorod Severskii lasted only three hours and consisted mostly of minor skirmishing. Because of Mstislavskii's timidity, Dmitrii's commander-in-chief, Jerzy Mniszech, was able to seize the initiative. He sent three Polish cavalry companies on a lightning-quick strike against the enemy's right wing regiment, which wavered and began to retreat in disorder into the main regiment, which in turn began to waver and retreat. During all this time, the tsar's commanders made no effort to turn the tide of battle against the small attacking force. Captain Margeret, an eyewitness, remarked famously: "In fact, one might have said that the Russians had no arms to strike with, although there were forty or fifty thousand of them."[129] The immobility of the tsar's army was due at least in part to one of the Polish cavalry companies accidentally stumbling across senior voevoda Mstislavskii himself, who was thrown from his horse and wounded, receiving several blows to his head. Mstislavskii would have been captured except for the timely arrival of a dozen Russian harquebusiers who forced the Poles to retreat and even managed to capture an impetuous Polish captain, Mateusz Domoracki.[130] Nonetheless, with the tsar's entire army except the left wing beginning to retreat in disorder, Mstislavskii's subordinate voevodas, Princes Vasilii V. Golitsyn and Andrei A. Teliatevskii, ordered a full retreat from the battlefield.[131] That left Dmitrii's men holding the field and able to declare victory.

News of that victory quickly spread throughout the frontier and convinced many more of Tsar Boris's subjects to join the cause of the "true tsar." During

the battle, Dmitrii had personally inspired courage in his troops, and his bravery was noted by many people. His overall losses that day were minimal, perhaps as few as one hundred twenty Polish cavalrymen.[132] In fact, had Dmitrii's
commanders been more experienced and struck at the tsar's retreating forces,
the victory could have been decisive.[133] Instead, the tsar's army remained intact
and continued to block the path to Moscow. Mstislavskii's forces did suffer a
few thousand casualties, but only a small number of pomeshchiki had been
killed.[134] Large numbers of wounded soldiers were sent to Moscow, and med-
ical teams were sent from the capital to Severia to care for the remaining sick
and wounded.[135] The tsar's army avoided any further contact with Dmitrii's
forces and, for the time being, withdrew north about 65 kilometers to Starodub
to await reinforcements and a new senior voevoda to assist the wounded
Mstislavskii.[136]

Tsar Boris was, of course, shocked and disappointed by his army's setback,
which was not revealed to the public partly out of fear that it might lead some
of them to take up Dmitrii's cause. Instead, the first of several fake "victory"
parades was held in the capital, and Tsar Boris sent congratulations to Mstislavskii
for his efforts.[137] Keeping up appearances was also important in foreign affairs.
By the end of 1604, Karl IX of Sweden was eyeing Russian territory and demanded
that Tsar Boris surrender Ivangorod and other towns to him in return for a
vague promise of aid against Dmitrii and Poland-Lithuania.[138] It was essential,
therefore, to show the Swedes that the tsar was not desperate. In fact, in strictly
military terms, Dmitrii's victory before Novgorod Severskii had not really
changed the strategic situation very much. Although some southern frontier
deti boiarskie switched to Dmitrii's side after the battle, he still faced a large
Russian army.[139] He also faced increasing unrest among his Polish mercenaries,
who grew tired of losing men in repeated failures to storm Novgorod Severskii
and did not relish another encounter with Tsar Boris's much larger army. Even
the welcome arrival of up to four thousand Zaporozhian cossacks in Dmitrii's
camp on the day after the battle with Mstislavskii's forces did not really alter
the situation much.[140] In spite of heroic efforts, Basmanov's stubborn garrison
could not be dislodged from the smoldering town. As a result, Dmitrii reluctantly lifted the siege on December 28—withdrawing his army east, deeper into
Russia and toward the fertile and friendly Komaritsk district where he hoped
to find rest, provisions, and additional men before his next confrontation with
Tsar Boris's army.[141]

10

Tsar Boris Strikes Back and the Civil War Widens

By the end of 1604, Dmitrii's forces were growing, were better supplied, and were operating in friendly territory. In spite of that, serious unrest broke out again among the Polish mercenaries in his army, who continued to complain loudly about Dmitrii's policy against looting. Tired of campaigning, they demanded all money that had been promised to them, and by January 1, 1605, they openly mutinied and plundered their own army's baggage train. Mniszech and Dmitrii were powerless to stop them. Some of the Polish mercenaries even tore up Dmitrii's banner and cursed him before departing for the border on January 2. Two days later, the deserting Poles were joined by Dmitrii's commander-in-chief; Mniszech had also decided that the campaign was hopeless and too dangerous to continue. Claiming poor health and pressing business in Warsaw, he and his two principal lieutenants crossed the border with about eight hundred Polish soldiers.

Ruslan Skrynnikov claimed that Mniszech deserted because he was frightened by growing lower class support for Dmitrii. Actually, when Tsar Boris's boyars wrote a threatening letter to Mniszech, they did mention the danger of rebellious masses to "men of quality." It is possible that they may have been genuinely frightened by the growth of Dmitrii's popular support, but they were also continuing Tsar Boris's propaganda campaign against Dmitrii's supporters.[1] Dmitrii did manage to retain the support of a few of his Polish captains and their men, but his army was now no longer dominated by Polish troops or officers. Instead, faithful cossacks and Russians came to predominate. The Polish mercenary forces had helped Dmitrii survive during the first few months of his campaign, but the decline of the Polish presence in his army actually aided Dmitrii's cause. As he advanced into the Komaritsk district, more and more Russians flocked to his banner and more towns and fortresses of the southwestern and southern frontier declared for him.[2]

Dmitrii set up his winter camp in the Komaritsk district about 10 kilometers from Sevsk and very near the small fort of Chemlyzhskii ostrog. The local townspeople and villagers welcomed him with open arms, the peal of church bells, and the traditional offerings of bread and salt. They were truly astonished by the extraordinary behavior of Tsarevich Dmitrii and his army. Instead of seizing supplies from local peasants (the usual practice of a Russian army), Dmitrii took only what was offered by the generous and friendly population. He did not allow his army to plunder any villages and kept his soldiers from causing harm to civilians. The impact of that strategy was enormous. Local legends about Dmitrii's humanity, kindness, informality, and sense of humor survived for centuries. Severians and other subjects of Tsar Boris flocked to his banner in large numbers.[3]

Despite the desertion of the Polish mercenaries, during early 1605 Dmitrii's army grew larger every day. In addition to his remaining several hundred Polish cavalrymen and infantrymen, plus more than a thousand Ukrainians and about two hundred Russians who had crossed the border with him, by the beginning of 1605 Dmitrii's forces had been augmented by at least four thousand Zaporozhian cossacks and hundreds of Don cossacks, who even brought some light field artillery with them.[4] Dmitrii's forces had also been growing steadily during the first few months of his campaign because of the stream of Severians and Russian deti boiarskie and low status military servitors joining his army. The deti boiarskie of Putivl and other towns provided new leadership and élan for Dmitrii's cause, and Seversk townsmen and peasants practiced at arms (muzhiki-sevriuki) formed numerous detachments.[5] Arming Seversk peasants stirred indignation and lasting resentment among Tsar Boris's commanders and helped produce the faulty view of Dmitrii's campaign as a social revolution or peasant war.[6] Likewise, a contemporary source's reference to Dmitrii arming slaves at this time led to all sorts of faulty interpretations of the meaning and nature of the popular support he inspired. Many Russian slaves were, of course, professional soldiers who had no interest in fighting against serfdom, and the reference to Dmitrii arming slaves may actually have been about cossacks.[7] In fact, every day more and more of Tsar Boris' subjects of all social classes, anxious to join the cause of the true tsar, made their way toward Dmitrii's camp.

For several weeks following the battle before Novgorod Severskii in December 1604, the commanders of Tsar Boris's army carefully avoided approaching Dmitrii's growing forces for a decisive battle. That was due in part to Mstislavskii's wounds, the timid and poor generalship of his subordinates, and a wait for reinforcements; but the lack of aggressive campaigning against Dmitrii may also have been due to growing ambivalence on the part of Russian commanders about fighting for Tsar Boris against the highly motivated supporters of Dmitrii.[8] Eventually, however, news of Dmitrii's growing forces prodded Tsar Boris's main army to advance against Dmitrii before the entire frontier rose up in his name.

By early January 1605, significant reinforcements arrived in the camp of Mstislavskii's army from Briansk and Moscow, including three regiments commanded by Dmitrii Shuiskii that had been operating independently in Severia since November.[9] A number of southern frontier fortress garrisons were also thinned out to beef up the tsar's main army; from Voronezh came one hundred streltsy, from Livny came two hundred fortress cossacks (cavalry), and from Elets came one hundred streltsy and four hundred cossack infantrymen armed with harquebuses.[10] Prince Vasilii Shuiskii also arrived from Moscow to serve as Mstislavskii's second-in-command, bringing with him many elite warriors from court—members of the "tsar's regiment." Shuiskii had been chosen not because he was a good general (he was not), but simply because the high-ranking boyar was not suspected of involvement in Dmitrii's activities.

By the time of the Shuiskii brothers' arrival in camp, Mstislavskii's army—including slaves and recruits—had approximately forty thousand men. Exaggerated reports of its size as reinforcements swelled its ranks in early January hit one hundred thousand or even two hundred thousand men.[11] More cautious estimates of seventy or eighty thousand are still too high; that was actually the approximate size of all forces available for operations against Dmitrii. Nonetheless, Mstislavskii's army, even at only about fifty thousand men, still dwarfed Dmitrii's forces.[12] Once the bulk of the reinforcements arrived, senior voevodas Mstislavskii and Vasilii Shuiskii decided to advance into the Komaritsk district in order to destroy Dmitrii's forces. While the main army prepared to confront Dmitrii, a smaller one—with siege guns—was sent under the command of Fedor Sheremetev to invest rebel-held Kromy, located to the northeast of the Komaritsk district. That action was taken in part to cover the flank of the main army as it advanced, but it was also deemed necessary because of the strategic significance of Kromy, which guarded the route to Moscow.[13]

Tsar Boris's main army advanced into the Komaritsk district at slow pace, unsure of the size or location of Dmitrii's army but fully aware of the sympathies of the local population, who strongly supported the pretender and acted as spies for him. By this time, the tsar's army had been on campaign for months and was growing increasingly hungry as supplies dwindled. That prompted the tsar's commanders to dispatch a force of at least four thousand horsemen on a foraging expedition within the Komaritsk district. Such authorized expropriations by hungry soldiers were ordinary in early modern Russia but contrasted sharply with the behavior of Dmitrii's army.[14] At the time, Mstislavskii and Shuiskii believed Dmitrii was encamped about 45 kilometers away. In fact, his army was much closer to them than they suspected, and Dmitrii was well informed about the movements of their foraging expedition. He sent his remaining Polish cavalry to fall on those forces in a surprise attack. They succeeded brilliantly, inflicting more than five hundred casualties; many of the tsar's sol-diers simply fled at the first sign of battle. The routing of the foraging force struck fear into the tsar's army, operating as it was in hostile territory with faulty intelligence about the enemy's whereabouts.[15] That defeat also provoked deep and lasting anger among Tsar Boris's commanders toward the population of Komaritsk district.

On January 20, 1605, the tsar's army pitched camp in the large village of Dobrynichi, located on a flat plain surrounded by many hills, approximately 18 kilometers northwest of Sevsk and quite near Dmitrii's headquarters (close to Chemlyzhskii ostrog). The tsar's forces crowded into the village until they were barely able to move; they were completely unaware that Dmitrii's army had advanced to within 5 kilometers of them. Dmitrii, assured of the support of the region's population, decided to strike boldly before the enemy became aware of his presence.[16] By this time, Dmitrii's army had swollen to as many as fifteen thousand soldiers.[17] Still outnumbered by more than three to one, Dmitrii's men were overconfident after their success before Novgorod Severskii. The few remaining Polish officers urged caution, even negotiations; but Dmitrii listened instead to his cossack atamans who favored an immediate attack.[18]

During the night of January 20–21, local peasants loyal to Dmitrii were sent forward to Dobrynichi with the intention of setting fire to the crowded camp of the tsar's army. They were detected by guards, however, and Mstislavskii ordered the entire army to remain on alert all night. Just after dawn, the two armies began to approach each other, and battle began with skirmishing and cannon play on both sides. Dmitrii and his new commander-in-chief, Hetman Adam Dworzicki, decided to repeat the successful flanking maneuver employed at Novgorod Severskii. About six thousand men—Dmitrii's Polish cavalry units, bolstered by Ukrainian, Belorussian, and Russian cavalry forces—attacked the right wing of Mstislavskii's army. Their intention was to cut between the tsar's army and Dobrynichi; then Dmitrii's cossack cavalry was supposed to hit Mstislavskii's main force, with infantry being held in reserve to screen Dmitrii's artillery and to mop up after the expected victory. Because of the terrain, it was possible to hide the bulk of the forces being employed in the attack behind low hills so that, at first, it appeared that only a relatively small force was involved.

Mstislavskii, warned of the enemy's approach, sent forward his right wing regiment, commanded by Vasilii Shuiskii, and two companies of foreign mercenaries under Captain Margeret and Walther von Rosen to engage the noisy and overconfident Polish cavalry. As those forces converged, from behind nearby hills came many more Polish and cossack cavalry units, catching Shuiskii completely by surprise. The Poles led such a furious and brave attack on the right wing of the tsar's army that, after brief resistance, the tsar's troops—seized with fear—broke ranks and scattered, dissolving the right wing entirely. As usual, Mstislavskii's main force did not quickly come to the aid of their comrades. Instead, according to Captain Margeret, they "stood there as if in a trance, as motionless as if dead," giving Dmitrii's Polish cavalry access to the village, at the entrance to which were located most of Mstislavskii's infantry and some cannon.[19] Meanwhile, the rest of Dmitrii's army, especially the cossacks, seeing the breach being made in the enemy's lines, rushed forward to claim victory. Instead, they met a rude surprise.

It was customary for the tsar's commanders to concentrate artillery and streltsy units within the main regiment.[20] That was certainly the case at Dobrynichi. The streltsy were, of course, the tsar's best infantrymen. Dressed in bright red uniforms and wearing no armor, the streltsy's task was not to engage in hand-to-hand combat but to deliver massed firepower from their harquebuses while being protected by cavalry units. Streltsy often took up position behind a *guliai gorod,* a wall or screen composed of prefabricated panels made of logs and mounted on carts or sleds for quick and easy positioning. Each panel was about 1.5 meters wide and 2 meters high and joined to adjacent panels by iron chains. The guliai gorod, with small openings for shooting through, provided very good cover and was virtually impossible for cavalry to break through. Such protection was essential for the vulnerable streltsy with their unwieldy weapons.[21] Harquebuses weighed about 10 kilograms and had to rest on a stand when fired. Loading and firing those guns was slow work, so streltsy units were usually positioned in deep echelons. After the first row fired a volley and retreated to reload, the second row would move forward to shoot. Their harquebuses had a range of about 300 meters, but volleys were so imprecise that their effective range was closer to 50 meters.[22]

In addition to approximately six thousand streltsy, many of whom were stationed behind the guliai gorod, Mstislavskii had five or six thousand other less-skilled harquebusiers at Dobrynichi—deti boiarskie infantry, some fortress cossacks, military slaves, and recruits.[23] Those men were not positioned in the traditional manner but instead in a long line, which made them vulnerable but also increased their firepower significantly. That excellent defensive tactic, a recent innovation in the West, was first seen in Russia at the battle of Dobrynichi and may have been introduced to the Russians by Captain Margeret, co-commander of the tsar's mercenary forces, who was credited with the victory over Dmitrii at Dobrynichi by several sources.[24] Wherever the new idea came from, it was a wise precaution in case Dmitrii's army attempted to repeat the tactics they had employed at Novgorod Severskii—which, of course, they did.

Just as Dmitrii's forces approached Dobrynichi at top speed, Mstislavskii's men let loose a general volley from more than ten thousand harquebuses and three hundred cannon. Scores of Dmitrii's men were killed or wounded. Even worse, the noise and the smoke so startled and unnerved Dmitrii's cavalry and horses that they turned back in confusion, creating great disorder as they retreated right into Dmitrii's other advancing cavalry units. The result was chaos. Dmitrii's entire army was forced to flee from the battlefield, hotly pursued by the tsar's foreign cavalry, led by Captain Margeret, who cut down as many of the fleeing rebels as possible. The courage and energy of the foreigners quickly inspired several Russian cavalry units to join the pursuit, and up to six thousand cavalrymen pursued the enemy for 7 or 8 kilometers.[25] In the meantime, the tsar's army advanced across the battlefield, and discipline broke down as soldiers fought like dogs over booty—a chronic problem in the Russian army made even worse by the especially poor conditions of Tsar Boris's hungry troops.[26] The breakdown of discipline in Mstislavskii's army may have influenced the decision to recall the cavalry pursuing Dmitrii, although the official reason given was to celebrate the great victory.[27] Each soldier participating in the battle received a gold coin as a reward; the foreign mercenaries were especially rewarded, receiving many rubles in cash, salary increases, and larger land allotments.[28]

Not surprisingly, after the battle of Dobrynichi, Dmitrii's Polish officers falsely blamed the catastrophe on the Zaporozhian cossacks, claiming that they had been frightened by the great clouds of smoke drifting across the battlefield and ran away—pursued by the Polish cavalry who urged them to return to continue the fight.[29] For a while, at least, Dmitrii was inclined to believe the Poles and blamed his cossack infantry for running away from the battlefield.[30] In reality, however, it was the Polish cavalry leading the forces that encountered the tsar's streltsy who were the first to turn back in confusion.[31] During the retreat, several hundred cossack infantry had actually refused to leave their posts, choosing instead stubbornly and heroically to guard Dmitrii's artillery until they were finally overwhelmed and cut down by Mstislavskii's advancing cavalry.[32] Despite the self-serving comments of Polish officers, the cossacks were excellent fighters and ferociously loyal to Dmitrii; they never contemplated abandoning him in battle.[33] Because of the disorderly retreat, however, Dmitrii himself barely escaped capture. His horse was shot out from under him, and only the quick thinking and bravery of Dmitrii's new ally, the Putivl voevoda Vasilii M. Mosalskii, saved him from certain death.[34] As it turned out, Dmitrii lost nearly all his infantry and more than a dozen junior officers at Dobrynichi; he also lost all his artillery. At least five thousand of his soldiers, mostly cossacks and Komaritsk peasants, had been killed; and many thousand were taken prisoner.[35] The tsar's commanders divided the prisoners into two groups: Poles, whose lives were spared and who were sent to Moscow to be displayed in a victory parade; and all others—including deti boiarskie, cossacks, streltsy, and Seversk townsmen and peasants—who were immediately executed. Military Affairs Office records show a total of eleven thousand five hundred rebels killed or executed at Dobrynichi. Mstislavskii's own losses during the battle had been surprisingly high, perhaps as many as six thousand casualties; but he had achieved an important victory.[36]

After the battle of Dobrynichi, the tsar's commanders believed that Dmitrii would not be able to recover and that the campaign was almost over, so Mstislavskii's army began an unhurried pursuit of the enemy. Vasilii Shuiskii and a smaller army were left behind in the Komaritsk district to rest and to punish the local population for supporting Dmitrii. For his part, Dmitrii fled south to Rylsk and then to Putivl. Had Mstislavskii and his associates pursued him with vigor, Dmitrii might easily have been expelled from Russia at this point; but, as usual, the tsar's commanders did not take full advantage of their success. Instead, even when they periodically caught up with Dmitrii's retreating forces, Mstislavskii's troops were more interested in booty than battle and repeatedly failed to deliver the final blow to the enemy. Those lost opportunities were not due to treachery, as some have suspected, but to the lack of talented commanders and to the exhaustion of the tsar's militiamen after campaigning for several months. Many of the soldiers were sullen, cold, and hungry. At the same time, Tsar Boris's voevodas were slow and timid, fearful of operating in a region with an openly hostile civilian population.[37] They were, in fact, far more interested in harshly punishing the Seversk population, especially the inhabitants of the Komaritsk district, for having dared to support Dmitrii. Tsar Boris and his commanders were extremely angry about the rebellion of Severia, and once Dmitrii had been defeated, it was deemed necessary to neutralize the region and to make an object lesson out of the first group of the tsar's subjects who rose against him. With Tsar Boris's approval, a terror campaign was launched against the Komaritsk district and adjacent lands.[38]

The army that carried out the punitive campaign in Severia was commanded by Mstislavskii's second-in-command, Prince Vasilii Shuiskii.[39] The Komaritsk district was singled out for the most cruel treatment. About four hundred fifty Kasimov Tatars, extremely loyal supporters of the tsars and masters at such reprisals, led the assault on the local population—soon followed by large numbers of other soldiers (mostly Tatars) "who ravaged the country to such an extent that not a hedge or a stalk was left standing."[40] The region was completely plundered and burnt; everything possible was destroyed—homes, barns, crops, livestock, and humans. Shuiskii's men killed thousands of people by the most despicable means. Men were hanged by one foot from trees, then burned alive or used for target practice. Women were raped, tortured, and then impaled. Little boys and babies were drowned, and older girls and young women were sexually assaulted and then carried off to be sold as slaves.[41] Other areas of Severia were subjected to similar treatment. Many more innocent people were slaughtered; many more women and girls were raped and enslaved.

Because of the wealth of the region and the fact that Dmitrii had seized nothing from the local population, the booty gained by Shuiskii's troops was enormous. His men glutted themselves by theft and pillage for many days, enraging the surviving local population but accomplishing nothing significant militarily.[42] In fact, the immediate impact of Shuiskii's terror campaign was to galvanize fanatical, quasi-religious support for Dmitrii throughout the entire region. The local population now openly repudiated the "false tsar" Boris Godunov and looked to Dmitrii as their only salvation. Support for Dmitrii grew rapidly among those who had previously stayed on the sidelines, and even Severians who were tortured by Shuiskii's men stubbornly refused to their dying breath to denounce Dmitrii as an impostor.[43] A contemporary was "amazed by the joyful manner in which innocent people endured torment and torture for the sake of Dmitrii, whom they had never seen, considering death itself a blessing if they perished for his sake!"[44]

News of the atrocities being committed by Tsar Boris's army spread rapidly throughout the region and beyond, and it had a serious impact. Neighboring populations, learning of those horrors, felt they had no recourse but to throw themselves into the arms of the pretender; according to a contemporary, "all those who could reach Dmitrii or join his army hurried to swear allegiance to him."[45] Severians headed in large numbers to Putivl to join Dmitrii's forces.[46] Even more alarming to the tsar's commanders was the rapid spread of rebellion along the southern frontier during early 1605, opening up a new front, adding large numbers of soldiers to Dmitrii's cause, and changing the entire strategic situation in the country. One after another important steppe frontier fortress declared for Dmitrii. Attempts to view those uprisings as class war are completely unsupportable. Unlike Severia, the southern frontier had few peasants and nonmilitary townsmen. Instead, the local population usually consisted entirely of disgruntled military servitors and cossacks who shared a common dislike for Tsar Boris. During the first months of 1605, the overwhelming majority of southern military servicemen rose in the name of Dmitrii, and they were joined by large numbers of free cossacks. Local commanders who resisted were overthrown as traitors to the true tsar, but the majority of frontier town and fortress commanders also declared for Dmitrii. That allowed them to retain their rank as they entered Tsar Dmitrii's service.[47]

What triggered the rebellions in those southern frontier towns that widened the civil war? Throughout the fall of 1604 and during the winter months, cossacks spread news of Dmitrii's progress and agitated on his behalf all along the frontier. Dmitrii's victory before Novgorod Severskii also had an impact. In addition to stirring more support for the pretender among the frontier population, Mstislavskii's defeat prompted the tsar's commanders to transfer significant numbers of military servitors from southern towns and fortresses to Severia, which weakened those frontier garrisons.[48] Recognizing that such transfers would weaken their southern defenses generally, Tsar Boris's commanders simultaneously ordered the reinforcement of the most important southern fortress, Tsarev-Borisov, a strongpoint located very far south (more than 400 kilometers southeast of Putivl). To accomplish that, they transferred troops there from Belgorod, a town with over one hundred deti boiarskie and a small posad population (located 260 kilometers east southeast of Putivl) that was commanded by voevoda A. Izmailov and his colonel (golova) B. Khrushchev. That transfer seems to have triggered the rebellion of Belgorod in January 1605, during which at least one stubborn dvorianin was killed by his companions for refusing to kiss the cross for Tsar Dmitrii.[49] The reinforcement of Tsarev-Borisov also failed to have its intended effect. To that large garrison were transferred five hundred elite Moscow streltsy who became indignant at being forced to serve indefinitely on the low-status southern frontier. Early in 1605, along with a large number of deti boiarskie and low status military servitors, the Moscow streltsy in Tsarev-Borisov declared for Tsar Dmitrii. That was a major blow to Boris Godunov, and by late winter streltsy units and deti boiarskie from Tsarev-Borisov began to appear among Dmitrii's forces in Putivl.[50] Also joining Dmitrii by then were the former voevodas of Belgorod and Tsarev-Borisov, Princes Boris M. Lykov and Boris P. Tatev; and from Belgorod to Putivl were transferred up to one hundred fifty pieces of artillery.[51] News of Dmitrii's kind treatment of commanders surrendering to him greatly helped his cause, especially when he showed confidence in those former foes. There was, for example, considerable propaganda value in the appointment of Prince Grigorii Shakhovskoi, who had been taken prisoner at Kursk, as Tsar Dmitrii's voevoda in newly acquired Belgorod.[52]

As news of rebellions in Tsarev-Borisov and Belgorod spread, it triggered uprisings in other southern frontier towns. Soon, the new fortresses of Oskol (with one hundred fifty deti boiarskie) and Valuiki—both located not far from Belgorod—declared for Dmitrii. Valuiki's voevoda, Dmitrii V. Turenin, was arrested by his rebellious soldiers. Even more alarming to Tsar Boris, uprisings began to spread north to important fortresses that had only recently been stripped of many soldiers in order to reinforce Mstislavskii's army. The strong fortress of Voronezh (only 140 kilometers south of Elets), with two hundred deti boiarskie and a significant posad population, rose for Dmitrii next. Then the very important fortress of Elets (located 200 kilometers east of Kromy and only 200 kilometers south of Tula)—which by then had one hundred fifty deti boiarskie, one hundred streltsy, and two hundred fortress cossacks—declared for Dmitrii. That was soon followed by the rebellion of Livny (located just 80 kilometers downstream from Elets) and its garrison of several hundred deti boiarskie and low status military servitors.[53] During the uprisings in those towns, only a few dvoriane were punished for resisting; in fact, a majority of commanders eventually joined their garrisons in declaring for Dmitrii. By March 1605, senior officers from Oskol, Valuiki, and Voronezh joined Dmitrii's inner circle of military advisers in Putivl. The rebellion of the bulk of Russia's southern military servitors and a majority of frontier fortress commanders abruptly changed the strategic situation and widened the civil war.[54] As rebellion spread rapidly across a very large area and added many more troops to Dmitrii's army, it forced a sharp change in the strategy of the tsar's commanders who had been pursuing Dmitrii with little success.

After the disaster at Dobrynichi, Dmitrii retreated to Rylsk, some 70 kilometers northeast of Putivl, followed slowly by Mstislavskii's forces. Having lost most of his army, Dmitrii was almost in despair by then. Rylsk, which had declared for him just after Putivl did, was an important rebel stronghold. However, even though its garrison strongly supported Dmitrii, the town did not appear to be capable of resisting Mstislavskii's large army. For that reason, Dmitrii entrusted its defense to Prince G. B. Roshcha-Dolgorukii (taken prisoner during the Kursk uprising and reassigned once he swore an oath to Dmitrii) and a few hundred streltsy and cossacks; while Dmitrii, along with his remaining men (mostly cossacks), retreated to the relative safety of well-fortified Putivl, the most important town in the region which was then serving as Dmitrii's temporary capital.[55]

In the meantime, Tsar Boris's commanders, with more than twenty thousand troops at their disposal, thought to make short work of the siege of Rylsk. They failed to take into account, however, the fierce loyalty to Dmitrii of the town's garrison and the local population. Siege operations were also conducted sluggishly. For two weeks, Mstislavskii's artillerymen bombarded the town and tried to set its wooden walls on fire, but cannon fire from inside the fortress prevented the tsar's army from getting very close. According to Captain Margeret,

Mstislavskii's army remained before Rylsk "without doing anything." Eventually, a general storming of the town was ordered, but that too failed. The sturdy defense of Rylsk by voevoda Roshcha-Dolgorukii eventually earned him a promotion to the rank of okolnichii and membership in Tsar Dmitrii's war council.[56] While in Putivl, Dmitrii heard numerous reports about Mstislavskii's growing difficulties. Large numbers of his fatigued and demoralized men were beginning to desert—some to go home, some to join Dmitrii. Many of the remaining soldiers were too busy foraging for food to fight. In dispatches to Moscow, the tsar's commanders despaired of success and begged for additional reinforcements to compensate for the soldiers who were running away. As noted earlier, the gentry militia was notoriously ineffective at conducting sieges, especially after their supplies ran out. Distracted by the search for food and increasingly diverted to the task of hunting down deserters, the tsar's army was unable to continue the siege of Rylsk.[57]

Operating in hostile territory with unreliable communications and frequently losing precious supply trains to bands of local rebels, the tsar's frustrated commanders decided to break off the siege of Rylsk and to retreat back to the Komaritsk district where Vasilii Shuiskii's army was located.[58] A major reason for that plan was the perilous situation developing at the strategically-located fortress of Kromy just northeast of the Komaritsk district. Tsar Boris's forces had been ineffectively besieging that rebel-held town on and off since early December 1604 and were in some danger of defeat, which would simultaneously open the road to Moscow to Dmitrii's supporters and bring together the two regions in rebellion—the southwestern and the southern frontiers. It was imperative, therefore, to prevent that defeat from occurring. As they were retreating from Rylsk, however, Mstislavskii's rear guard was attacked by the Rylsk garrison, which managed to put it to flight and to capture many supplies. One contemporary source put the number of Mstislavskii's men killed in that battle at two thousand, with two hundred men captured.[59] News of the defeat of the tsar's army spread quickly, bringing joy to Dmitrii and the citizens of Putivl and inspiring still others to join Dmitrii's cause. It was at this point that Tsar Boris's commanders, seeing their army melting away, bowed to the inevitable. Admitting that their men were exhausted, they dismissed much of the army to go home and rest up for a planned summer campaign.[60]

When Tsar Boris learned about the dismissal of the army, he became very angry. He sent a delegation to his senior field commanders who upbraided them for breaking off the siege of Rylsk and warned them not to dismiss any more soldiers. Tsar Boris also sent along a small detachment of reinforcements composed of elite Moscow dvoriane and courtiers drawn from the "tsar's regiment."[61]

The tsar's stern orders provoked grumbling within the remainder of the exhausted army; those soldiers now faced a rapidly spreading civil war and were being asked to fight against their former comrades who had once guarded Russia's southwestern and southern frontiers. In spite of the exhaustion and low morale of the tsar's troops, however, the growing strategic danger to Tsar Boris urgently required that his remaining forces concentrate on the task of capturing Kromy.

In the meantime, Dmitrii had been very active in Putivl. Legend has it that, upon arrival there after the disaster of Dobrynichi, he feared that all was lost and prepared to flee to Poland—only to be confronted by the townspeople who had so strongly supported him and now feared retribution from Tsar Boris. They supposedly threatened to turn him over to the tsar unless he remained in Putivl to rally support for his cause.[62] The story is probably apocryphal, but Dmitrii did stay in Putivl. There he formed a war council composed of Russian commanders who had willingly switched to his side and even a few who had surrendered to him but only later swore an oath of loyalty. By spring 1605, his principal advisers included Tsar Boris's former commanders Boris Lykov, Boris Tatev, Dmitrii Turenin, Artemii Izmailov, and Vasilii Mosalskii, along with dvorianin Petr Khrushchev (who had been captured in September 1604). Secretary Bogdan Sutopov became Dmitrii's chancellor and keeper of the seal. Together, these men made plans for a renewed military campaign.[63] Dmitrii now held court as "Tsar Dmitrii," dropping the use of "tsarevich" to describe himself.[64] He continued to reward generously all captured voevodas and officers being brought to him from towns and fortresses rising in his name if those men were willing to join his service. It is worth noting that Dmitrii was not forced to use coercion or terror in order to entice many of Tsar Boris's noblemen to join his cause.[65] Only when spies or assassins were discovered in Putivl did Dmitrii turn them over to the townspeople—who stripped the traitors naked, tied them to a post in the main square, and shot them to death. As noted in Chapter 8, Tsar Boris tried to expose Dmitrii as an impostor by sending monks to Putivl to denounce him as Grishka Otrepev, but the plan backfired when at least one of the monks—possibly to avoid torture—recognized Dmitrii as the "true tsar" instead.[66] While in Putivl, Dmitrii also gained an unexpected new ally, Prince Ishterek of the Nogai horde east of the Volga River, formerly a puppet of Tsar Boris, who now recognized Dmitrii as tsar and pledged to send men to aid his campaign for the throne.[67]

While in Putivl, Dmitrii raised a large sum of money, especially from refugees fleeing Shuiskii's terror campaign in the Komaritsk district. Artillery from southern frontier fortresses was also concentrated in Putivl, and Dmitrii formed a new army around the remnants of his old one and the Putivl garrison—which was now headed by Iurii Bezzubtsev, who had been instrumental in the transfer of the town's loyalty to Dmitrii. The new army's ranks soon swelled with the addition of troops from towns and fortresses joining Dmitrii's cause and ordinary townsmen and well-armed Seversk peasants who flocked to Putivl in large numbers. Dmitrii made generous promises to those who joined his army, and it certainly did not hurt his cause that the men who did so were then no longer required to pay heavy taxes to Tsar Boris or to plow for the state.[68] By spring 1605, Dmitrii had few Polish soldiers left in his army, and efforts to raise additional troops in Poland-Lithuania were not very successful—primarily because of horror stories told by the Poles who had deserted Dmitrii in January and news of the debacle at Dobrynichi.[69] The timely arrival of large numbers of Don cossacks in Putivl, however, greatly increased the size and effectiveness of Dmitrii's new army. One contemporary estimated that four thousand Don cossacks reached Putivl in February 1605.[70] Skrynnikov regarded that number as too high and estimated that no more than a thousand cossacks, led by ataman Lunev, arrived at Putivl at that time. Even that smaller number, however, meant that about half of the entire Don cossack population had entered Dmitrii's service by late winter 1605.[71] The total number of cossacks of all types in Dmitrii's army now stood at between four and five thousand.[72] Those brave and skilled warriors played a decisive role in Dmitrii's campaign for the throne.

With growing popular support, according to a contemporary, Dmitrii "took courage again" and "put a fine army back into the field."[73] Tsar Dmitrii, as he now called himself, may have received secret letters from some of Tsar Boris's enemies at court or in the army that encouraged him to persevere. Dmitrii himself sent countless letters from Putivl all over Russia, even to Moscow, recounting his childhood escape from the evil usurper, Boris Godunov, and calling upon the Russian people to end their resistance to their "legitimate sovereign." He promised to reward those who surrendered and threatened those who persisted in supporting Godunov. As a result of his propaganda, Russians deserted Tsar Boris in large numbers, recognizing Dmitrii as their tsar; and many of them made their way to Putivl.[74] As his situation improved, according to a contemporary, Dmitrii used "great modestie" instead of tyranny, terror, or vengeance—a sharp contrast to Tsar Boris. He acted the part of the clement prince very effectively. Forgiving, kind "Tsar Dmitrii" even wrote conciliatory letters to Patriarch Iov and Tsar Boris, offering them amnesty and fair treatment if they would recognize him as tsar.[75] Dmitrii made no attempt to stir the masses against their lords or to promote class war; instead, he merely called for punishment of traitors who resisted the "true tsar" and offered generous rewards to those lords and commoners willing to join his ranks.[76]

In this period, Dmitrii also made a public display of his Orthodox Christian faith, probably at least in part to counter Godunov propaganda about him as the evil defrocked monk and Polish puppet, Grishka Otrepev.[77] Interestingly enough, some contemporary sources claimed that the real Otrepev was brought to Putivl at this time and "everyone who wanted to could see him."[78] (As noted in Chapter 8, sources hostile to Dmitrii claimed that he found a substitute to play the role of Otrepev and even threw him into prison in Putivl.)[79] Overall, Dmitrii carried himself with such piety, authority, and courage that he made a strong impression on many Russians as their true, clement Orthodox tsar. So openly confident was he in the justice of his cause that, according to a contemporary Englishman, his public prayers before battling Tsar Boris's army ran something like this:[80] "O most just Judge, kill me first with a Thunderbolt, destroy me first, and spare this Christian bloud, if unjustly, if covetously, if wickedly I goe about this Enterprize which thou seest. Thou seest mine innocencie, help the just cause. To thee O Queen of Heaven, I commend myself and these my Souldiers." By spring 1605, with growing popular support, Dmitrii had fully recovered from his winter defeat and was ready to resume active campaigning. By then, Tsar Boris's commanders were busy concentrating all their efforts on capturing strategically-located Kromy at any cost. As it turned out, that strategy proved to be the undoing of Godunov dynasty.

The long siege of Kromy had begun in December 1604, right after its garrison declared for Dmitrii.[81] The strategic location of that ancient town (founded in 1147), situated just northeast of the Komaritsk district near the source of the Oka River, was the main reason it had been fortified with a new outer oak palisade in 1595. Kromy's fortress was situated on a hill, with its narrow approach protected for much of the year by marshes. Several roads from the south joined at Kromy, which guarded the route to Moscow from the south and southwest.[82] The small rebel garrison holding the town fiercely defended it and interfered with communications between Moscow and Tsar Boris's forces arrayed against Dmitrii; they also constituted a menacing forward base for an assault on Moscow should rebel forces sweep north and converge on Kromy. So strategic was the town's location that in January 1605, voevoda Fedor Sheremetev was sent with siege guns to speed up its capture at the same time Mstislavskii engaged Dmitrii's army at Dobrynichi.[83] Sheremetev's forces, however, were not able to dislodge the small rebel garrison. A principal reason for that was the timely arrival of a Don cossack detachment led by the brilliant and energetic ataman Korela.

A contemporary source claimed that Korela reached Kromy just after Dmitrii's defeat at Dobrynichi (January 21, 1605).[84] There are various estimates of the size of his cossack detachment, but it was probably only between four and five hundred men.[85] Because Kromy was then under siege, Korela had to fight his way past Tsar Boris's forces to reach the town. To do so, the ataman employed a typical cossack mobile defense formation known as a *tabor*. Fortifying his supply sleds and arranging them in a rectangle (with its open side facing Kromy) so that his flanks and rear were covered, Korela stationed half his men inside the moving rectangle with the other half—carrying harquebuses—acting as an escort while the sleds moved rapidly up the hill toward the fortress. Gunfire and arrows from the tsar's army besieging the town had almost no impact, and Korela's detachment quickly reached the fortress.[86] Ataman Korela's men immediately set to work to dig a series of interconnected trenches all around and within the battered fortifications of Kromy, throwing up earthworks in front of the trenches with many small openings through which to shoot at the enemy. Thus, according to a contemporary, they were soon able to advance and retreat "like mice" in stealth and relative safety while under fire. Even if they lost the outer earthworks, they could quickly retreat to their inner defenses and fire deadly volleys at any advancing force foolish enough to rush in after them.[87] Once they were ensconced in Kromy, Korela's men feared no force arrayed against them. Cossacks were not only excellent and brave soldiers, but they were extremely skilled at fortifications and defense.[88] Ataman Korela was described by a contemporary as a "mangy little man, all covered with scars" whose "great bravery" led to his selection as a cossack chieftain. Korela's men energetically defended Kromy, and—according to a contemporary—the mere mention of the ataman's name made his enemies besieging the fortress "tremble."[89]

In February 1605, Mstislavskii sent several hundred men from his army to reinforce Sheremetev's as yet unsuccessful siege of Kromy.[90] That force proved inadequate, and Sheremetev continued to suffer heavy losses at the hands of Korela. In despair, he appealed to Moscow for additional reinforcements.[91] Tsar Boris and his commanders were well aware of the danger to Moscow that would be posed by a rebel victory at Kromy—especially in light of Mstislavskii's lack of success in pursuit of Dmitrii and the rising tide of rebellion sweeping north across southern and southwestern Russia. Therefore, no further thought was given to laying siege to Dmitrii in Putivl. Instead, Mstislavskii's army retreated north into the Komaritsk district, linked up with Shuiskii's army, and proceeded directly to Kromy, arriving at Sheremetev's siege camp on March 4, 1605.[92] To supplement the forces besieging Kromy, Tsar Boris also managed to raise large numbers of additional troops from the monasteries and towns of north Russia—although there is evidence of increasing resistance to additional levies of recruits in many towns. Thus was assembled a siege army "formidable" in size if not in fighting spirit or capability.[93] One contemporary estimated that by April 1605, the siege force contained about sixty thousand men.[94] Orders were also given that all available siege guns were to be sent as soon as possible to aid in the capture of Kromy.[95]

Following direct orders from Moscow, senior commanders Mstislavskii and Vasilii Shuiskii attempted to storm Kromy before most of the additional artillery arrived. An advance regiment of infantrymen under the command of boyar Mikhail G. Saltykov managed to sneak up to the outer wall of the fortress under cover of darkness and set fire to it, forcing the defenders to retreat into the palisaded inner fortress. From there Korela's well-protected men concentrated harquebus fire on the attacking force and inflicted very heavy casualties. That forced voevoda Saltykov to recall his men from the burning outer wall of the fortress. From then on, the tsar's commanders were understandably reluctant to try such a frontal attack again.[96] The arrival of more siege guns eventually allowed the tsar's commanders to bombard Kromy day and night. By spring, a large percentage of Russia's three thousand five hundred artillerymen and several thousand cannon of various sizes were now concentrated in the siege camp before Kromy. By using incendiary shells, the tsar's artillerymen were soon able to burn the entire citadel to the ground. Nonetheless, the cossacks only dug in deeper, endured the constant shelling, and quickly emerged to fight whenever the tsar's commanders sent men forward to capture the ruined fortress; casualties were heavy on both sides.[97] Korela had early on sent word to Dmitrii begging for reinforcements.[98] Eventually, Dmitrii sent a leader of the Putivl garrison, Iurii Bezzubtsev, to relieve Kromy with about five hundred Don and fortress cossacks and about one hundred sleds filled with food, gunpowder, lead, and other supplies.[99] In a disastrous error, Bezzubtsev's force was mistaken by Tsar Boris's soldiers as a relief column coming to their aid, so the cossacks managed to slip past the guards in broad daylight and delivered those critically important supplies to Kromy.[100]

Reinforcements and fresh supplies greatly emboldened Korela's cossacks. They began making daily sorties in detachments of two or three hundred men with harquebuses, taking up positions near enemy lines. When the tsar's commanders sent gentry cavalry to attack the cossacks, those men met withering and accurate gunfire. Dozens of outgunned pomeshchiki were killed in each encounter; mounted pomeshchiki with bows and arrows were simply no match for the cossacks. Korela kept his men constantly active, using a new stratagem each day to catch the enemy off guard and to wear him out. Frequently, Korela's men harangued the besiegers or threw messages to them calling them traitors to the true tsar Dmitrii and listing the many crimes of Boris Godunov. If the Dutch merchant Massa is to be believed, Korela even had naked women appear on Kromy's ruined ramparts to hurl gross insults and to sing satirical ditties about the tsar's commanders. Massa claimed that constant combat and the use of such psychological warfare "pushed the besiegers to the limit."[101] Of course, the tsar's exhausted army, with its chronic shortage of food, was also pushed to the limit by hunger and exposure to the cold weather—which greatly diminished its fighting power.[102]

The tsar's commanders continued to send forays into the Komaritsk district to find food and to continue the punishment of its remaining inhabitants for supporting Dmitrii.[103] However, those forays provided insignificant relief to the troops besieging Kromy. Efforts were also made to shore up the morale and loyalty of the gentry before Kromy by increasing the size of their pomeste estates; but that, of course, had little practical effect. Attrition due to battle losses, untreated wounds, hunger, and disease began taking a toll. Many of the tsar's troops simply melted away in search of food or to return to their homes. Others slipped away in order to join forces loyal to Dmitrii.[104] To make matters worse, starting in March 1605, the Military Affairs Office, as a precaution, began ordering the removal of many units from the shrinking siege army in order to reinforce important garrisons north and northeast of Kromy—including Tula, Epifan, Novosil, Odoev, and about a dozen other fortresses—which were being threatened by the rising tide of rebellion sweeping north.[105]

The misery of the tsar's siege army was relieved briefly when ataman Korela was wounded and the cossacks stopped making sorties for awhile. Even so, the tsar's commanders made no serious effort to storm Kromy, content instead merely to continue the ineffective bombardment of the ruined fortress until they used up most of their gunpowder and shot.[106] Soon, cossack activity inside Kromy was back to normal. The valor and endurance of Korela's men was extraordinary, while arrayed against them were hungry troops "chilled to the bone" who had little interest in risking their lives for any cause.[107] When spring rains began to melt the ice, the resulting flooding turned the siege camp into a sea of mud, and as the marshes surrounding Kromy thawed, they turned back into a nearly impenetrable moat protecting Korela's position. The recovering cossack ataman correctly regarded the spring weather as helping to "dissipate and destroy" the besieging army. Soon, dysentary broke out in the tsar's siege camp, and many gentry units deserted for home.[108] In the end, the tsar's army lost large numbers of men, wasted an enormous amount of powder and lead, and accomplished nothing during the long siege of Kromy. According to Captain Margeret, "they only made fools of themselves" until Tsar Boris died in April.[109]

A number of contemporary sources mentioned treason among the tsar's troops as a factor contributing to the failure of the siege of Kromy. In addition to simple desertion to join Dmitrii's forces, Massa claimed that traitors often secretly brought gunpowder right up to Korela's position or sometimes shot arrows into Kromy with letters telling Dmitrii's ataman about what was happening in the tsar's army or in Moscow.[110] A few fairly reliable sources spoke of treason among the tsar's commanders, some of whom may have secretly contacted Dmitrii or his representatives with information about troop movements. In addition to his policy of treating surrendering officers and men with kindness, Dmitrii also made a concerted effort to woo senior voevoda Mstislavskii with letters "full of benevolence and friendship," various proofs of his identity, and offers to pardon any commanders willing to recognize him as tsar. Such appeals had no effect on Mstislavskii; but reports and rumors of the treason of other commanders, news of the desertion of large numbers of gentry militiamen, and the fact that Mstislavskii had received letters from Dmitrii helped undermine the Godunov regime's faith in its unlucky senior field commander.

While many of Tsar Boris's soldiers eventually became persuaded of Dmitrii's authenticity and simply bided their time or actually deserted to join the "true tsar's" service, even among Godunov's skeptical voevodas there was growing respect for Dmitrii—viewed increasingly by many of them as a "rising sun."[111] Dmitrii's forces were, in fact, growing every day. The rapid spread of rebellions in his name, the desertion of more and more troops to his side, and the creation of a new army in Putivl made him a formidable foe.[112] That is in sharp contrast to propaganda and historical assessments of a down-and-out pretender who was on the ropes and only saved by the sudden death of Tsar Boris. In fact, by spring 1605, large numbers of cossacks, most southern frontier military servitors, and more than half of Tsar Boris's frontier commanders had joined Dmitrii's cause.[113] The tsar's alarmed voevodas before Kromy informed Moscow of growing treason in the ranks, daily desertions, and a shrinking siege army at the very same time that Dmitrii's army was growing more numerous and stronger.[114] The situation was becoming extremely perilous to the Godunovs, which made a successful outcome of the siege of Kromy one of Tsar Boris's highest priorities. For his part, Dmitrii became so confident of the eventual outcome of the siege of Kromy that he saw no need to launch another impetuous attack on the tsar's army besieging Korela's men.[115] Events soon demonstrated that his assessment of the strategic situation was correct.

Throughout the winter of 1604–5, Tsar Boris waited anxiously for news from the front. Except for the heroic defense of Novgorod Severskii by Petr Basmanov and the victory at Dobrynichi, the tsar had little to celebrate. Disturbing news kept reaching him of growing rebellion on the frontier, failed sieges, desertions from and deterioration of his exhausted army, the loss of more and more towns, garrisons, and commanders, and the flocking of many of his soldiers and sub-jects to Dmitrii's banner. There were also reports that many people in Moscow were increasingly inclined to believe that Dmitrii was indeed Dmitrii.[116] The tsar's uncle, Semen Godunov, now the head of the secret police, suspected trea-son everywhere, spied on everyone, and made much use of denunciation and torture in pursuit of "traitors."[117] In reality, except for the conspirators involved in launching Dmitrii's challenge to Boris Godunov, most of the tsar's boyars and courtiers remained loyal to him. There was, however, growing resentment against Semen Godunov's heavy hand and what was perceived to be the malig-nant influence on Tsar Boris of his suspicious wife Mariia—the daughter of one of Ivan the Terrible's most notorious oprichnina henchmen.[118] Tsar Boris him-self, who was seriously ill again, began to despair and came to believe that he was in great danger. His circle became smaller and smaller as he hid in his Kremlin palace and refused to hear petitions from his people. He sent assassins to kill Dmitrii, but they failed. He also had Patriarch Iov excommunicate every-one who favored Dmitrii, but that did not check popular enthusiasm for Godunov's nemesis.[119]

In spite of the tsar's growing anxiety, every effort was made to make it appear that things were going well, but few people were deceived. Periodic fake "vic-tory parades" and the frequent movement of large detachments of new military forces through Moscow barely masked the growing sense of crisis.[120] The authen-tic victory parade for the heroic and popular Petr Basmanov was an exception. Never before had a voevoda been so honored by a tsar. Tsar Boris heaped trea-sure and honors on Basmanov and promoted him to the rank of boyar, and Basmanov very quickly emerged as a leading figure in the ailing and beleaguered tsar's court.[121] Basmanov was a good enough general to recognize the grave dan-ger to Tsar Boris posed by the failing siege of Kromy, and he begged to be sent there as senior commander before it was too late.[122] The competence and even the loyalty of Mstislavskii and Shuiskii were increasingly questioned at court, and there was some discussion about replacing them; but the upstart boyar Petr Basmanov had many jealous rivals with higher mestnichestvo status, so he did not get his wish while Tsar Boris lived.[123]

11

The Death of Tsar Boris and Dmitrii's Triumph

By early spring 1605, Tsar Boris had been gravely ill for a long time. Even so, his sudden death on April 13 came as a shock to everyone. Rumors circulated that he had committed suicide in despair, having come to believe that his enemy was the true Dmitrii.[1] Other rumors suggested that he had been poisoned by his enemies or secret supporters of Dmitrii.[2] In fact, Tsar Boris probably died of natural causes.[3] Even his death was questioned by some; there were reports that he had been seen by many people attempting to flee the country.[4]

Without doubt, the death of Tsar Boris was a principal reason for Dmitrii's success in becoming tsar. While Boris Godunov lived, most of his boyars and courtiers remained loyal to him. and immediately upon his death, the boyars moved swiftly to enthrone his son as Tsar Fedor Borisovich. Documents were even faked to make it appear that the new tsar had been chosen by a zemskii sobor.[5] Nonetheless, Tsar Boris's death also unleashed the conspirators who had been responsible for Dmitrii in the first place, and it provoked great division among the lords, many of whom had no love for the sinister figures who dominated the regime of Tsar Fedor Borisovich—the hated Semen Godunov and the dowager Tsaritsa Mariia. Others may have simply sensed opportunities for themselves in recognizing Dmitrii as tsar.[6] Boris Godunov's intelligent and able son, Fedor, was only sixteen years old at the time of his father's death, and he was unable to retain the loyalty or even the passive acceptance of the Russian elite for very long. From the very beginning, according to a contemporary, the young tsar's court "was gripped by intense fear."[7] Aware of the weakness of the Godunov dynasty's claim to legitimacy, Tsar Fedor Borisovich's officials sternly warned Russian towns and lords not to have anything to do with either the so-called "Dmitrii" or the blind and aged Simeon Bekbulatovich, who had been the compromise candidate for tsar put forward by Boris Godunov's opponents in 1598. The Godunovs by this time had become isolated from and had alienated many of the great lords, and by 1605 lots of people really did believe Tsar Boris was a regicide and usurper who had managed to bring down the wrath of

God on Russia. For many of them, his death was seen as a sign of God's punishment and of Dmitrii's authenticity.

In sharp contrast to sentiment about the Godunovs or Tsar Fedor Borisovich, enthusiasm for Dmitrii was growing fast—even in Moscow. The population of the capital grew bolder each day, gathering together to demand the return of persons wrongly exiled by Tsar Boris—including Dmitrii's mother, the nun Marfa. The new tsar's hurried distribution of seventy thousand rubles in alms to the Muscovites did little to calm the populace.[8] Even the oath of loyalty to Tsar Fedor administered to the people, which failed to denounce Dmitrii as the impostor Otrepev, gave some the impression that the court suspected Dmitrii really was the son of Ivan the Terrible.[9] There were also damaging rumors floating around that young Tsar Fedor, terrified of the wrath of the people and the true Dmitrii, was secretly planning to flee to England.[10] For his part, Dmitrii made every effort to attract the Russian people in general, and he sent messages specifically to the common people of Moscow urging them to overthrow the Godunovs and to recognize him as tsar. Dmitrii also wooed Tsar Boris's courtiers and commanders with offers of amnesty and high positions in his service.[11] Within a few weeks, the combination of the rising tide of popular support for Dmitrii and the abandonment of Tsar Fedor Borisovich by many great lords and soldiers doomed the Godunov dynasty.

One of the very first decisions made by the new Tsar Fedor, his mother, and his great-uncle Semen proved to be fatal: the recall to Moscow of senior voevodas Mstislavskii and Vasilii Shuiskii from the army besieging Kromy and the dispatch of newly-promoted boyar Petr Basmanov to inform the army of Tsar Boris's death, to administer the loyalty oath to the soldiers, and to help bring the siege to a successful conclusion. That decision set the stage for the defection of several boyars to Dmitrii and the rebellion of the army—a major turning point in the civil war.[12] The main reason for the recall of Mstislavskii and Shuiskii was probably the need for the stabilizing influence of the two most prestigious boyars in disorderly Moscow and at court. The fact that they had not been successful in the campaign against Dmitrii and the many rumors of treason among the tsar's voevodas may also have been factors in the decision. According to one contemporary, they "returned in shame and secrecy to Moscow."[13] Vasilii Shuiskii, upon arrival in the capital, tried to calm the city's restive crowds by—once again—publicly declaring that the real Dmitrii had died in 1591.[14] Fedor Mstislavskii, however, made no such public statement. Semen Godunov was deeply suspicious of Mstislavskii's possible involvement in treason and may even have planned to assassinate him.[15] For his part, ambitious Petr Basmanov was, of course, hoping to be named commander-in-chief to replace Mstislavskii at Kromy, but his mestnichestvo status was not high enough; he was forced to settle for the position of deputy commander under a higher ranking boyar, Prince Mikhail Petrovich Katyrev-Rostovskii, who was not a good general but was a loyal supporter of the Godunovs.[16]

Senior voevodas Katyrev-Rostovskii and Basmanov arrived at the Kromy siege camp on April 17, 1605, and administered the oath of allegiance to the tired, hungry, and demoralized army. The new tsar sent a very favorable message to the soldiers assuring them of generous rewards for their continued loyalty.[17] Basmanov and his spies quickly discovered, however, that many soldiers were reluctant to swear an oath to Tsar Fedor and were favorably inclined toward Dmitrii.[18] A contemporary described the situation in the siege army this way: "they held to their oath as long as a hungry dog keeps a fast."[19] The crisis developing in the tsar's army was brought to a head by the arrival on April 20 of new orders from Moscow, promoting Mstislavskii's former deputy commander, boyar Prince Andrei Teliatevskii, to the position held by Basmanov—thereby lowering the status of the latter. A precedence quarrel erupted immediately, during which voevodas Z. I. Saburov and Mikhail F. Kashin-Obolenskii joined Basmanov in rejecting what seemed to be an affront to their honor.[20] Such mestnichestvo disputes, all too common among Russian commanders, could become very serious problems. In this case, it proved to be fatal to the young Tsar Fedor. Basmanov loudly protested that the sinister Semen Godunov, Teliatevskii's son-in-law, was responsible for the outrage of making him a "slave to Teliatevskii." According to a contemporary, the demoted boyar "wept for an hour" claiming that he preferred death to dishonor; he then secretly joined a developing conspiracy against the Godunovs.[21] Basmanov was motivated to take that drastic step not only by his grudge against Semen Godunov; Basmanov's father and grandfather had both been victims of the dowager tsaritsa Mariia's father during the oprichnina, and Petr Basmanov himself was a close relative of allies of the Romanov clan.[22]

Many commanders participated in the conspiracy to transfer the army's loyalty to Dmitrii. Even before Basmanov's dispute with Teliatevskii pushed him to betray Tsar Fedor Borisovich, there were several other voevodas waiting for the opportunity to switch sides. Among them were two very high-ranking brothers, Princes Vasilii and Ivan V. Golitsyn. The Golitsyns had not been trusted by Boris Godunov, and some members of the family had even been persecuted by him. However, Vasilii Golitsyn had been given high rank by Tsar Boris. It is probable that Vasilii Golitsyn was the real ringleader of the conspiracy developing among the officers in the Kromy siege camp.[23] After the departure of Mstislavskii and Shuiskii from the tsar's army, Golitsyn's authority and influence increased. Two of his relatives had earlier surrendered to Dmitrii and had become "Tsar Dmitrii's" courtiers—Princes Boris Tatev and Boris Lykov.[24] They may have made secret contact with Vasilii Golitsyn to renew an old plot against the Godunovs the three of them had been accused of (by Prince Dmitrii M. Pozharskii) back in 1602.[25] The Golitsyns were also related to the Romanovs and were closely related to Petr Basmanov—their half-brother;[26] Basmanov had been raised in the household of Prince Vasilii Iurevich Golitsyn, his mother's second cousin.[27] Petr Basmanov was accused by some of corresponding with Dmitrii and of instigating the plot to transfer the army's loyalty to him.[28] However, it may well have been Vasilii Golitsyn who brought the angry Basmanov into an already developing conspiracy. In any case, those two men led the rebellion of the army against Tsar Fedor.[29]

Also active in the developing conspiracy among the tsar's commanders in the Kromy siege camp were the prestigious and influential Liapunov brothers, vybornye dvoriane from the old southeastern frontier province of Riazan.[30] When the moment for rebellion came, they brought virtually all of the Riazan nobility and gentry with them in the transfer of loyalty to Dmitrii. In effect, they led a rebellion of the militiamen and towns of that province that essentially duplicated the earlier transfer of loyalty to Dmitrii of the commanders, garrisons, and townspeople of the southwestern and southern frontiers. Their movement against the Godunovs also immediately triggered rebellions of townspeople and gentry in areas neighboring Riazan province all along the old frontier region south of the Oka River—including Tula, the most important southern defense coordinating center (180 kilometers south of Moscow), and Kashira, located right on the Oka (the "border of the frontier") only 110 kilometers south of the capital. Thus, the rebellion led by the Liapunovs constituted in many ways a huge provincial rebellion and completed the uprising of the entire southern frontier against the Godunovs.[31]

How did that come about? First, it should be remembered that Riazan province had only been incorporated into the Moscow-centered state in 1521. Like the Severians, the inhabitants of Riazan province were frontiersmen long accustomed to fighting the Tatars and fending for themselves; also like Severians, Riazan men had long before earned a reputation for being proud, fiercely independent, and warlike. Riazan, like other southern provinces, had been hit hard by the crisis that descended on Russia in the late sixteenth century, which increased discontent throughout the region. As elsewhere, Riazan's pomeshchiki saw their income and landholdings decline.[32] Just like other frontier regions, Riazan province also saw the blurring of the distinction between pomeshchiki and fortress cossacks and the wholesale promotion of cossacks into the ranks of the deti boiarskie. Impoverished Riazan deti boiarskie were also often forced to serve as lower-status infantry—just like the unhappy pomeshchiki elsewhere on the frontier. For understandable reasons, therefore, morale was not high in Riazan province and adjacent areas.[33] In some ways, however, Riazan was not like other southern frontier provinces. The proud Riazan nobility were generally not prominent in Moscow's service; instead, many of them stayed at home. In fact, the province had significantly more gentry living in it than other southern provinces.[34] The Riazan nobility was much better connected to rank-and-file militiamen in the region than was the case elsewhere on the frontier. The functional autonomy of local elites within Russia's autocratic system was more pronounced in Riazan, where Moscow's grip was somewhat tenuous and the relative independence of the local nobility could become quite dangerous to an unpopular ruler.[35]

Among the most prominent members of the Riazan elite were the Liapunovs and the Izmailovs who owned huge estates there. Prokofii Liapunov and his brothers were arrogant self-promoters and adventurers who had participated in the disorder in Moscow after Ivan the Terrible's death. Later, in 1603, Tsar Boris ordered Zakhar Liapunov beaten with a knout for daring to trade illegally with the free cossacks of the Don.[36] Not only did that incident infuriate the Liapunovs and their allies, but it further cemented the complex symbiotic relationship between the Riazan townspeople and pomeshchiki (increasingly of cossack origin) on the one hand and the Don cossacks on the other—all of whom shared a deep resentment against Boris Godunov. At the siege of Kromy, such bonds that potentially linked Korela's cossacks to the Riazan gentry in the tsar's army proved to be more powerful than any oath of loyalty to Tsar Fedor Borisovich.[37]

During Dmitrii's campaign for the throne, one of the Liapunov brothers' friends, dvorianin Artemii Izmailov, was captured and quickly became a member of Dmitrii's war council in Putivl. The newly-promoted Izmailov may have secretly contacted the Liapunovs as well as other members of his own family serving in the Kromy siege camp and urged them to switch sides. Another one of Dmitrii's new courtiers, Boris Tatev, who was related to the Golitsyns and may have secretly assisted them in planning the rebellion of the army, also owned huge estates in Riazan province and may have helped to persuade the Liapunovs to act.[38] Other officers in the Kromy siege camp who were also probably involved in the conspiracy included Prince Luka O. Shcherbatyi and vybornyi dvorianin Zakhar Bibikov—both of whom were later rewarded by Tsar Dmitrii for their activities.[39] Although often accused of being one of the conspirators, okolnichii Mikhail Glebovich Saltykov was actually captured during the rebellion and only agreed to join Dmitrii's service later.[40] Several other high-ranking dvoriane in the tsar's siege camp, perhaps sensing the critical situation developing there or just anxious for some rest, conveniently chose to return to Moscow for Tsar Boris's funeral in the days leading up to the rebellion.[41]

The conspiracy among Tsar Fedor Borisovich's commanders was greatly facilitated by low morale, hunger, disease, breakdown of discipline, and rising sentiment in favor of Dmitrii among the soldiers in the Kromy siege camp. Many of the remaining gentry units were still bitter that Tsar Boris had forbidden them to go home to rest; and by spring 1605, in small groups and large they simply deserted and went home. Others secretly defected, carrying messages to Korela or to Putivl about how strong the sentiment in favor of Dmitrii was among Tsar Fedor's troops.[42] Enthusiasm for Dmitrii was growing throughout the siege camp, but especially among Riazan gentry units and detachments from Tula, Aleksin, Kashira, and other old frontier towns; by April 1605, it just so happens that those forces constituted a dangerously high percentage of the troops remaining in the Kromy siege camp. Even though high-ranking commanders organized the rebellion, it was the participation by the siege army's poor and dispirited pomeshchiki that played the decisive role in the uprising and more or less completed the rebellion of the entire southern frontier against the Godunov dynasty.[43]

Lower class participation in the rebellion of the tsar's army before Kromy has often been grossly distorted by the mistaken notion that risings in Dmitrii's name were part of a social revolution against serfdom. Many common soldiers, military slaves, and recruits did favor Dmitrii and participated in the rebellion; but it was planned and led by the gentry, not the lower classes. As noted earlier, a large percentage of the tsar's army consisted of military slaves and recruits armed with harquebuses, often organized into units operating separately from their lords. The sheer number and firepower of those men made them a significant military force, although many of them were not professional soldiers but were instead poorly trained peasants. In fact, the increasing intrusion of nonprofessional soldiers into the ranks of combat slaves had the effect of lowering the status of the group as a whole and further humiliating many elite military slaves whose lives had already been upset by Boris Godunov's 1597 slave law. Needless to say, among the ranks of military slaves and recruits at Kromy were many oppressed and unhappy men who played a significant role in the success of the rebellion in the tsar's army.[44] Among the recruits in the Kromy siege camp, of particular interest are those from the Komaritsk district. At least five hundred, maybe many more, of them had been added to the tsar's army during the winter of 1604–5. Astonishingly, many of those same recruits were retained in service even after Vasilii Shuiskii's sickening punitive raids on their relatives, neighbors, and friends. In fact, they were still in the Kromy siege camp when Tsar Boris died. It is safe to assume that many of these men became active supporters of the rebellion of the tsar's army.[45]

Conspirators among the officers in the Kromy siege camp secretly coordinated plans with ataman Korela's men and agreed to act on May 7.[46] The approach of Dmitrii's army may have been the signal for rebellion. While in Putivl, Dmitrii's forces had been growing steadily as more and more southern frontier military servitors, townspeople, and Seversk peasants flocked to his banner. Dmitrii also had between four and five thousand Don cossacks under his command.[47] By the beginning of May, five hundred Belorussian cavalrymen also arrived in Dmitrii's camp from Lithuania.[48] Some scholars believed Dmitrii's forces were still too weak to fight the tsar's army at this time. Contemporary sources, on the other hand, emphasized that Dmitrii was able to field a "fine army" by spring 1605. Polish sources indicated that he had more than thirteen thousand men by then.[49] By the end of April, Dmitrii decided to take advantage of the crisis in the Kromy siege camp and ordered a small force of three hundred men under the command of Jan Zaporski to proceed to Kromy; they were joined by at least eight hundred Don cossacks on the way. As they approached Kromy, they clashed with loyalist Tatar forces covering the siege army, dispersed them, and managed to capture about one hundred fifty prisoners. News of the approach of Dmitrii's forces provoked great anxiety in the tsar's army. In order to frighten and demoralize those men even more, Zaporski and Korela spread disinformation that forty thousand troops and three hundred siege guns were on their way from Putivl.[50]

At dawn on May 7, 1605, the rebellion began by prearranged signal. By then the conspirators had already managed to halt the usual posting of combat-ready guards units. Conspirators set fire to several places in the siege camp, and Korela's cossacks swiftly and silently infiltrated the tsar's army without firing any weapons. Their plan was to sow panic and chaos and to join with mutineers to quickly capture those voevodas still loyal to Tsar Fedor.[51] At the same time, the Liapunovs and their companions led a rebellion of all the gentry detachments from Riazan province, Tula, Aleksin, Kashira, and several other towns of the old frontier— the troops of which were spread throughout the siege army.[52] As a result of so many things happening everywhere simultaneously, there was immediate panic and confusion throughout the siege camp. Soldiers fled in all directions, leaving behind their clothes and weapons.[53] The advance regiment that had been conspirator Vasilii Golitsyn's old detachment and that contained one thousand dvoriane and deti boiarskie from Riazan and two hundred from Aleksin, took the lead in the uprising. With the help of Korela's cossacks, they quickly captured their commander, Tsar Fedor's uncle, Ivan I. Godunov. Another four hundred Riazan pomeshchiki served under voevoda Godunov's still-loyal deputy, Mikhail G. Saltykov, and they quickly arrested him as well.[54] The left wing regiment's commander, Z. I. Saburov, who had earlier sided with Basmanov in his mestnichestvo dispute, was ill that day; but his deputy, Prince Luka O. Shcherbatyi, probably joined many of his own troops—which included seven hundred deti boiarskie from Tula—in declaring for Dmitrii.[55] The newly appointed commander of the right wing regiment, conspirator Vasilii Golitsyn, ran into serious problems. His deputy, Mikhail F. Kashin-Obolenskii, refused to join the rebellion, and more prosperous gentry units from Suzdal and Nizhnii Novgorod remained loyal to Tsar Fedor.[56] A panicky Golitsyn had his slaves tie him up so he would not look like a traitor if the rebellion failed.[57] In the main regiment, Basmanov's efforts to arrest senior voevoda Katyrev-Rostovskii and his loyal deputies also failed. At least three hundred deti boiarskie from Kashira served in the main regiment and had quickly joined the rebellion, but the artillery commander, okolnichii Vasilii P. Morozov, and others—including dumnyi dvorianin Vasilii B. Sukin—remained loyal to the tsar.[58] Only some of the hundreds of pomeshchiki from Novgorod and Pskov serving in the main regiment joined the rebels; others remained loyal to Tsar Fedor.[59] The entire rear guard regiment, composed of more prosperous pomeshchiki from Vladimir, Pereiaslavl, Mozhaisk, and Uglich, remained firmly under the control of voevoda Teliatevskii and did not join the rebellion.[60]

In spite of the stubborn loyalty to Tsar Fedor of senior commander Katyrev-Rostovskii, voevoda Teliatevskii, and others who eluded capture, the panic and confusion within the siege army prevented the loyalists from organizing effective opposition to the rebellion. In fact, those commanders had no way of telling trustworthy troops from the mutineers, who in general refrained from firing their weapons or killing anyone.[61] In the midst of the chaos, a large number of soldiers tried to cross a makeshift bridge spanning the Kroma River, either to escape the siege camp or to link up with Korela's forces in order to demonstrate their loyalty to Dmitrii. The weight of the crowd broke the bridge, plunging hundreds of men into the river; some drowned but most made it to shore and fled to their homes.[62]

It has been argued that voevoda Teliatevskii and other loyalist commanders could have used their artillery to disrupt the attack from Kromy and to kill many of Korela's cossacks and many of the mutineers, but that they hesitated to be the first to open fire and to start bloodletting.[63] That is possible; but it is more likely that loyalist commanders were not well positioned to fight back and were confused about just exactly who was on which side. Also, ataman Korela was well informed about which voevodas and which gentry units were likely to resist, and he knew exactly where their artillery was located. His cossacks concentrated their attacks on those places, thereby greatly reducing Tsar Fedor's commanders' chances of organizing any effective resistance.[64]

There were more than a thousand Western mercenary troops stationed in the Kromy siege camp who remained in good order and might have been used to turn the tide against Korela's men and the mutineers, but Teliatevskii and other loyalist commanders failed to make use of them. Some sources claimed that Basmanov and Vasilii Golitsyn had parleyed before the revolt with the commander of those mercenary troops, von Rosen, which supposedly resulted in some mercenaries choosing to remain on the sidelines during the rebellion and later joining Dmitrii's cause.[65] That is remotely possible but not likely. At least seventy German mercenaries remained loyal to Tsar Fedor and retreated from Kromy to Moscow, where they received high praise from the young tsar; and when Dmitrii came to power, he also praised the loyalty of the Western mercenaries to Tsar Fedor, enrolled them in his own service, and encouraged them to show the same loyalty to him.[66]

The insurrection in the Kromy siege camp was basically bloodless, which is truly remarkable. That shows just how weak the loyalty of the tsar's soldiers to the Godunov dynasty really was, but it is also testimony to good planning and restraint on the part of the conspirators and Korela's men. Panic-struck troops still loyal to Tsar Fedor hastily abandoned the siege camp in complete disorder, throwing down their weapons and leaving all their artillery, munitions, and other supplies behind. The Don cossacks chased them for many kilometers—not to kill them but to humiliate them, whipping the fleeing soldiers and shouting insults at them.[67] Several thousand of those defeated and demoralized men passed through Moscow on their way home, unwilling or unable to explain why they had abandoned the siege of Kromy. Princes Katyrev-Rostovskii and Teliatevskii, along with a few other loyal commanders, also retreated to Moscow.[68]

In assessing the rebellion in the Kromy siege camp, some scholars have argued that a majority of the tsar's troops remained loyal to the Godunovs but were simply overwhelmed by the chaos and fled in terror.[69] In fact, a majority of troops in the siege camp switched sides and recognized Dmitrii as the true tsar.[70] Others have argued that a majority of the gentry militiamen remained loyal to the Godunovs but were overwhelmed by the rebellion of lower class soldiers, slaves, and recruits within the tsar's army.[71] That is also false. Loyal pomeshchiki were overwhelmed by a conspiracy among their own commanders and the defection of large numbers of dvoriane and deti boiarskie. Although it is true that most of the southern frontier pomeshchiki who joined the rebellion were not as well off as the gentry of Russia's central provinces, their participation represented the entire southern frontier's rejection of the Godunovs—not some lower class movement against serfdom. Participation in the uprising by boyars and most of the leading gentry from the Riazan and Tula regions clearly shows that even members of the tsar's court and rich lords joined Dmitrii's cause.[72] Although many of the better-off gentry from central and northern provinces fled from Kromy toward Moscow, it should be noted that many of the sturdy deti boiarskie belonging to the detachments from Novgorod and Pskov joined the rebellion. In fact, large numbers of gentry in those very same units who supposedly remained "loyal" to Tsar Fedor were really completely indifferent to the fate of the Godunovs; instead of rallying in Moscow to defend their tsar, they hastily retreated north to their homes.[73]

It is no exaggeration to say that the mutiny of the tsar's army before Kromy was the decisive event in Dmitrii's campaign for the throne. At Kromy, the revolt of the southern frontier reached its zenith, and when several of Tsar Fedor's boyars and their men joined that powerful regional rebellion it represented a sharp expansion of the civil war and doomed the Godunov dynasty.[74] As Charles Tilly has reminded us, when substantial coalitions develop between well-armed challengers and defecting members of an existing regime's elite, and when mass defections from that regime's army effectively neutralize its military forces, a rapid transfer of power is likely to occur.[75] In fact, the shock of news about the rebellion of the tsar's army and the momentum that gave to Dmitrii's cause proved overwhelming to the Godunovs, who were soon swept from power. One contemporary soldier noted that Dmitrii had been extremely pleased to learn of the events at Kromy "which freed and opened up all the highways and byways, all the doors and windows, to good fortune."[76]

Immediately following the rebellion in the tsar's army, Basmanov, the Golitsyns, and other mutinous commanders contacted Dmitrii and made plans to hasten the overthrow of Tsar Fedor.[77] They sent secret messages to boyar opponents of the Godunovs in Moscow and dispatched several prominent individuals to help persuade the capital's population to recognize Dmitrii.[78] On May 12, 1605, Ivan Golitsyn arrived before Putivl to formally surrender the tsar's army to Dmitrii. Golitsyn's retinue included about five hundred courtiers, dvoriane, and other leaders from the Kromy siege army.[79] Dmitrii graciously received them and personally set out for Kromy on May 16. He left approximately ten thousand soldiers in Putivl and was accompanied on the journey by only about two thousand men—mostly cossacks, some Russian troops, and about six hundred Polish and Belorussian cavalry. He arrived at Kromy on May 19.[80] Before then he sent word ahead ordering the remnant of the Kromy siege army surrendering to him to move toward Orel, 35 kilometers to the northeast. Orel was a strategically important town guarding the road to Moscow; its garrison, commanded by Fedor Sheremetev, had remained stubbornly loyal to Tsar Fedor despite widespread popular rebellion in the area.[81]

Dmitrii sent Prince Boris Lykov (a Golitsyn cousin) ahead to administer the oath of loyalty to former members of the Kromy siege army, to thank the soldiers for their loyalty, and to dismiss from service for a month's refreshment all those pomeshchiki who held lands south of Moscow and wished to go home. Many streltsy and cossacks were also allowed to go home at this time. A large number of men, perhaps half of the remainder of the army, took advantage of the offer and returned home singing the praises of Tsar Dmitrii.[82] When those exhausted soldiers got home, many of them triggered rebellions in favor of Dmitrii in their own towns; that happened almost immediately in Aleksin, Kashira, Shatsk, and Pereiaslavl-Riazanskii (later known as Riazan). The archbishop of Riazan, Ignatii, became the first bishop to recognize Dmitrii as tsar. He was probably influenced by the Liapunovs and other Riazan gentry returning home from Kromy.[83] Throughout the old frontier zone, from the Tula region to Riazan province and farther east to the Volga, soldiers returning from Kromy brought news of the triumphant progress of Tsar Dmitrii. Leading gentry and simple soldiers convinced their fellow townspeople and villagers to recognize Dmitrii, and soon there was a stream of fortress commanders, officers, and leading townsmen making their way toward Kromy to pay homage to Tsar Dmitrii. As usual, he graciously received his new subjects and immediately pressed them into service.[84] Dmitrii's willingness to appoint former opponents to his war council and as his voevodas went a long way toward lowering elite anxiety about him. Rumors and news of his trust in the Russian people spread rapidly. Dmitrii remained in Kromy for several days receiving delegations of well-wishers while his soldiers gathered together all the supplies abandoned during the rebellion of the tsar's army—including many artillery pieces, seventy big siege guns, large quantities of munitions, and many horses.[85]

As Dmitrii advanced from Kromy to Orel, huge crowds gathered along the route to see the new tsar. They greeted him as the true son of Tsar Ivan and as the "rising sun" of Russia.[86] Voevodas and prominent townsmen from as far away as Tsaritsyn on the lower Volga came to pay homage to him.[87] By the time Dmitrii reached Orel, its obstinate voevoda, boyar Fedor Sheremetev—now surrounded by the remnant of the Kromy siege army—transferred the town's allegiance to Dmitrii without any bloodshed.[88] The commanders of the rebellious army, Petr Basmanov and Vasilii Golitsyn, along with two recent converts, voevodas Mikhail G. Saltykov and Fedor Sheremetev, thereupon greeted Dmitrii on the road before Orel with an entourage of two hundred dvoriane.[89] An informal delegation from Moscow also apparently met with Dmitrii at this time and assured him that many in the capital were ready to recognize him as tsar.[90] In Orel, Dmitrii had a few stubborn enemies who were unwilling to swear an oath of loyalty to him thrown into the town's dungeon.[91] He chose not to combine the small army accompanying him with the remnant of the Kromy siege force; instead, he kept those two armies a few kilometers apart and posted vigilant guards as a security measure.[92] From Orel, he sent the old Kromy siege force north, under the command of Vasilii Golitsyn, to cut off Moscow's supply routes.[93] Units of that army proceeded to strategically located Tula, whose dvoriane had already switched to Dmitrii's side at Kromy. Tula's voevoda, Prince Ivan S. Kurakin, and the townspeople opened the town's gates to Dmitrii's men without incident. Other units of Golitsyn's army advanced to the important town of Kaluga, which immediately surrendered, and then on to strategically located Serpukhov, located on the Oka River only 90 kilometers south of Moscow.[94]

Dmitrii and his two thousand troops advanced north slowly, pausing in Krapivna, about 40 kilometers southwest of Tula. By the time he reached Krapivna, his small army received reinforcements from the Volga cossacks and from Prince Ishterek's Nogai Tatars.[95] Dmitrii was careful not to unleash the Tatars on the Russians, however, no doubt mindful of the powerful negative impact of Tsar Boris's recent use of Tatar troops to punish the Severians.[96] At this point, Dmitrii sent proclamations to most towns and villages throughout Russia announcing his success and urging his subjects to recognize his lawful authority. Many, but not all, towns wavered; in only a few places were Dmitrii's couriers put to death.[97] While some lower Volga towns and many Volga and Terek cossacks rushed to join Dmitrii's cause, Astrakhan's voevoda, Mikhail Saburov, remained loyal to Tsar Fedor and bravely fought off numerous cossack assaults and efforts to stir the town's inhabitants to rebel in the name of Dmitrii.[98] In June 1605, once it became apparent that Dmitrii would succeed in becoming tsar, Astrakhan's population rose in his name. In doing so, they openly defied their archbishop but managed to convince voevoda Saburov to join them—for which reason Tsar Dmitrii later not only forgave him for holding out so long but even promoted him.[99] While in Krapivna Dmitrii on several occasions sent couriers with letters to Moscow, both to the boyars and to the common people, assuring them of his clemency if they would recognize him as tsar and, according to a contemporary, "admonishing them that God first and then he would punish them for their obstinacy and rebellion if they should continue to resist."[100]

Moscow had, of course, been in turmoil ever since the death of Tsar Boris, but the rebellion of the tsar's army before Kromy provoked panic at the court of Tsar Fedor.[101] It emboldened the opponents of the Godunovs and brought the young tsar's short reign to a quick end. At about the same time the Godunovs made the fatal error of offending Petr Basmanov's honor by demoting him, they also foolishly yielded to popular demands and pressure from the boyars to recall from exile Tsar Boris's old enemy, Bogdan Belskii. Upon his return to Moscow, Belskii immediately began to intrigue against Tsar Fedor among the boyars. By then many of them were already in contact with Vasilii Golitsyn and other turncoat voevodas in Dmitrii's camp.[102] Such disarray and treason among the boyars in Moscow effectively paralyzed the Godunov regime. The execution of couriers from Dmitrii who were caught trying to stir the people to rebel did nothing to slow down growing sentiment in Dmitrii's favor.[103] Tsar Fedor's efforts to raise another army to send against Dmitrii also failed completely. Those few units mustered in Moscow and sent against the enemy simply faded away—going home or actually joining Dmitrii's forces.[104]

Tsar Fedor did manage to dispatch several thousand loyal Moscow streltsy to Serpukhov to block the advance of Dmitrii's men before they could cross the Oka River. Those streltsy units beat back Golitsyn's attempt to cross the river on May 28.[105] That incident showed Dmitrii just how exhausted his newly-acquired gentry militiamen from the old Kromy siege army really were. Even though Dmitrii's overall strength now stood at approximately thirty thousand men, many of his soldiers were tired, hungry, or ill.[106] Altering his plans somewhat, Dmitrii now advanced with his own small force to Tula and ordered ataman Korela and his Don cossacks to bypass Tsar Fedor's Oka defense line and to make haste to Moscow. By May 31, Korela's men were camped only 10 kilometers from the capital.[107]

The approach of Korela's cossacks provoked widespread panic in the capital, where support for Dmitrii had been growing steadily. According to a contemporary, crowds ran about like a "swarm of bees." Some immediately made ready to open the gates to Korela. Although that effort was temporarily stopped, defense preparations in general were haphazard and minimal. While loyal authorities tried to reinforce the city's defenses with additional artillery, the rich took time to hide their valuables and others made ready to greet the new tsar with the traditional offerings of bread and salt.[108] For his part, ataman Korela concentrated on cutting Moscow off from supplies still coming in from the northeast through Krasnoe Selo—a large village populated by wealthy merchants and goldsmiths that occupied a strategic position from which to attack the capital.[109] Korela sent a courier to read a letter from Dmitrii to the inhabitants of Krasnoe Selo, who immediately declared for Tsar Dmitrii. Perhaps accompanied by some of Korela's cossacks, several thousand townspeople then boldly escorted two of Dmitrii's couriers to Moscow. Those two men, Gavrila Pushkin and Naum Pleshcheev, had earlier surrendered to Dmitrii and had been immediately put to work in his service.[110] Troops hastily sent to stop those couriers turned back in fear at the sight of such a large and determined crowd.[111] By midmorning on June 1, 1605, as the couriers and their escort approached Red Square intending to read Dmitrii's proclamation to the people of Moscow, thousands of not-at-all unfriendly Muscovites came out to greet them and to listen to Dmitrii's words.[112] The Godunovs had obviously lost control of the situation as more and more of the capital's population, from lords to commoners, warmed to the prospect of a new ruler.[113]

Dmitrii's conciliatory proclamation was read to a huge crowd drawn from all classes.[114] In it Dmitrii addressed all ranks, from Mstislavskii and the Shuiskii brothers to lesser boyars, courtiers, bureaucrats, merchants, and ordinary townspeople. He declared his desire to claim the throne without further bloodshed. He offered a full pardon to those who had fought against him if they would immediately arrest, but not kill, the Godunovs and recognize him as their tsar. In the proclamation he recounted his escape from Uglich, giving credit to God for saving him from the traitor Boris Godunov. He forgave the Russian people for being misled and misinformed about him and listed the many crimes of Tsar Boris—including laying waste to Severia, persecution of many noble families, spilling Christian blood, allowing the gentry militiamen to be ruined economically, restricting the movement of townsmen, high taxes, and the execution of Dmitrii's couriers. Dmitrii then promised to reward his new subjects for their loyalty to him. To the boyars and nobles he promised honors, preferment, retention of existing estates, and prospects for more. The merchants and traders were promised tax reductions, and ordinary citizens were promised peace and prosperity. To encourage the Muscovites to act, he reminded them that he possessed a large army and that many towns had already declared for him. If they failed to recognize him, he declared, they would feel "God's anger and his own."[115] Dmitrii's proclamation had an immediate and powerful effect on the crowd, triggering the rebellion that overthrew the Godunov dynasty.[116]

Not surprisingly, Soviet scholars incorrectly regarded the rebellion in Moscow as a class struggle against the ruling elite, as a simple manifestation of urban lower class unrest.[117] While it is true that the common people of Moscow were involved in the rebellion, it was not a social revolution; it was a popular uprising in support of Dmitrii's claim to the throne—one which united elements from all levels of society. Just as had been the case in many of the towns joining his cause earlier, leadership in the Moscow uprising was provided by boyars, dvoriane, deti boiarskie, and leading townsmen, and Dmitrii's promises that provoked the rebellion were aimed primarily at those elites, not commoners.[118] Contemporary sources stated that virtually the entire population of Moscow rose against the Godunovs.[119]

The exact role of the boyars in the Moscow uprising is not easy to determine. Some boyars—especially Belskii—were, of course, actively involved in the toppling of the Godunovs.[120] There were, in fact, boyars on Red Square when Dmitrii's proclamation was read. Either the crowd demanded that more senior boyars appear publicly to explain the conduct of the Godunovs, or else leading boyars were sent from the Kremlin by Tsar Fedor and his mother in order to calm the crowd. In either case, Mstislavskii, Vasilii Shuiskii, Belskii, and others soon arrived on Red Square.[121] Some boyars then apparently attempted to entice Dmitrii's couriers into the Kremlin but were forestalled by the crowd, which began to demand information about the fate of the previous messengers Dmitrii had sent to Moscow. At that moment—and the timing here appears too good to have been coincidental—unknown persons opened the Moscow jails and released all political prisoners, including Dmitrii's previous couriers.[122] Their timely arrival on Red Square and their horrific accounts of torture at the hands of the Godunovs "inflamed the people further," according to a contemporary.[123] One source claimed that at this point Vasilii Shuiskii declared that Dmitrii had in fact escaped from Uglich and was alive.[124] Some sources claimed that Bogdan Belskii took the lead in inciting the crowd to riot.[125] Whatever the case, the multitudes on Red Square rioted in support of Dmitrii, shouting: "God grant that the true sun will once again arise over Russia."[126]

The crowd divided into two parts. More than a thousand people—including nobles—invaded the Kremlin, plundered the Godunov's palace, and arrested Tsar Fedor and his mother.[127] The palace guard fled; nowhere did any guards, courtiers, troops, or boyars put up any resistance—a clear indication that the Godunovs had completely lost control of the Kremlin as well as Moscow and that high-born princes were deeply involved in the uprising.[128] Some rebels may have wished to treat their royal captives harshly, but Dmitrii had clearly urged his supporters to arrest, not kill them. If possible, no blood was to be spilled during the rebellion. Popular leaders such as Belskii were able to prevent a bloodletting rampage by the crowds, who instead contented themselves with looting Godunov properties and arresting and roughing up members of the Godunov clan and their few remaining loyal supporters.[129]

The bulk of the rebels spent much of the day pawing through possessions taken from the residences of those "traitors" and getting drunk on the liquor they found.[130] Although some of the "traitors" were beaten, no one was killed—just as Dmitrii had requested. In the chaos that day, many rich lords and merchants became targets of poor rebels, were roughed up, and had their property plundered; but none of them was killed.[131] The only serious casualties were among the rioters themselves, of whom more than fifty died from overdrinking or fighting with one another over the spoils.[132] That is nothing less than astonishing. Just like the rebellion in the Kromy siege army, the Moscow uprising was virtually bloodless. Boyars involved in the rebellion understandably worked to keep the crowd's ominous assaults on rich people from getting out of control; but such restraint also demonstrates careful planning and a general respect for Dmitrii's wishes.[133]

The rebellion died down in the afternoon as boyars rode through the streets urging the restoration of order. All Godunov clan members were rounded up and held prisoner.[134] Later the same day the boyar council, under Belskii's influence, declared Tsar Fedor deposed and proclaimed its support for Tsar Dmitrii.[135] The council purged only Godunov clan members from its ranks. All other boyars were by then willing to support Tsar Dmitrii—at least publicly. Of course, the boyar council did not grant power to Dmitrii. Some of its members had been involved in the uprising, but the council's decision to support Dmitrii was only a confirmation of a fait accompli and a prudent act of self-protection. Dmitrii was not raised to the throne by the boyars. He was, instead, the only tsar in Russian history to come to power by means of a military campaign and popular rebellions.[136] By the end of that fateful day, Dmitrii's putative godfather, Bogdan Belskii, had emerged as the master of Moscow and began making preparations to send a delegation to Dmitrii in order to formally surrender the city to him.[137] So ended the first phase of Russia's first civil war.

Dmitrii was, of course, delighted to hear the news from Moscow. Advancing to Tula on June 5, he was now able to dismiss most of the remainder of the exhausted Kromy siege army to go home for much needed rest—but not before rewarding those men with money, food, and horses brought from the capital.[138] For the final march to Moscow, Dmitrii would need only the small army (mostly cossacks and Belorussian cavalry) that had accompanied him from Putivl. At this point, another large force of about two thousand Don cossacks arrived in Dmitrii's camp and was received with honor.[139] While in Tula, Dmitrii also sent messengers throughout the country to inform the Russian people of his victory and to receive their oaths of allegiance. Most of his new subjects willingly swore an oath to the new tsar, and many went to church to pray for him.[140] Dmitrii also sent greetings to exiled members of the Nagoi clan, recalling his relatives to court and restoring their ranks.[141]

In Tula, Dmitrii was presented with bread and salt by the first delegation arriving from Moscow, which was headed by several second-tier boyars—

including Andrei Teliatevskii—and included important bureaucrats, dvoriane, and leading merchants. Probably at the urging of Petr Basmanov, Dmitrii angrily denounced Teliatevskii, allowed the cossacks to rough him up, and temporarily threw him into prison.[142] While Dmitrii was in Tula, most members of the Godunov clan and their supporters were led from captivity in Moscow to exile in various places throughout the country. The hated Semen Godunov was imprisoned and starved to death.[143] The boyars also ordered the removal of Tsar Boris's body from the Kremlin's Archangel Cathedral and had it reburied in a small monastery.[144] From Tula, Dmitrii next advanced to Serpukhov accompanied by his small army and his principal advisers—including Vasilii Golitsyn, Petr Basmanov, Ivan Golitsyn, Mikhail G. Saltykov, Fedor Sheremetev, Boris Tatev, Boris Lykov, Vasilii M. Mosalskii, Grigorii B. Roshcha-Dolgorukii, Aleksei G. Chertenok-Dolgorukii, Ivan S. Kurakin, Artemii I. Izmailov, and Dmitrii V. Turenin.[145]

At Serpukhov Dmitrii was met with great honor by a large delegation headed by Russia's leading boyar, Fedor Mstislavksii. Among those greeting the new tsar were Dmitrii Shuiskii, most of the remaining courtiers, Moscow dvoriane, bureaucrats, gosti, and other merchants. The delegation brought along the tsar's carriage and two hundred horses for the final stage of Dmitrii's journey, and more than five hundred people attended a banquet in Serpukhov celebrating Tsar Dmitrii's victory.[146] A number of details concerning the transition of power were also worked out at this time—probably including negotiations over the addition of Dmitrii's supporters to the boyar council. A decision was made to send a delegation headed by Vasilii Golitsyn and Petr Basmanov to Moscow in order to receive the Muscovites' oath of allegiance to the new tsar and to prepare the capital for Dmitrii's triumphal entry. Many pomeshchiki and some cossacks accompanied Dmitrii's emissaries in order to prevent any mishaps.[147]

As soon as the delegation arrived in Moscow, the deposed Tsar Fedor and his mother were strangled to death and it was falsely announced that they had committed suicide.[148] Vasilii Golitsyn personally presided over the assassination of Fedor Borisovich Godunov.[149] Most sources suggested that Dmitrii had ordered those deaths.[150] Although some propagandists angrily accused Dmitrii of the brutal murder of young Fedor Godunov, the incredibly passive response of the public to the news of his death was a clear sign that the Godunov dynasty had been delegitimized in the eyes of many. No one had been willing to defend Tsar Fedor during the rebellion of Moscow, and his assassination did not trigger a public outcry or even so much as a hint of popular resistance to the new regime. As we shall see, that was a remarkable contrast to the general reaction to Tsar Dmitrii's assassination in 1606—which rekindled the civil war.

In order to complete the relatively narrow and mild purge of Dmitrii's enemies in Moscow, Golitsyn brought with him an official letter from Dmitrii addressed to church leaders in which he denounced Patriarch Iov as a traitor and demanded his removal from office.[151] Jesuits who accompanied Dmitrii's invasion of Russia fully expected the patriarch, who had been one of Dmitrii's fiercest enemies, to be put to death.[152] In fact, Dmitrii had already written to Iov, urging him to recognize his claim to the throne and to retire in dignity.[153] Iov may actually have replied in a letter to Dmitrii while the latter was still in Tula. In that letter Iov supposedly recognized Dmitrii as tsar and urged him to ignore Iov openly since the patriarch was by that time extremely unpopular and many people had already threatened to kill him.[154] Iov was, of course, very unpopular not just because of his close association with Boris Godunov; he was also still hated by many for allegedly failing to share his grain with hungry people during the famine.[155] In a carefully choreographed scene in Moscow, Petr Basmanov ordered Patriarch Iov to go to Uspenskii Cathedral in the Kremlin. There the patriarch was denounced as Dmitrii's enemy before a large crowd, after which the crowd seized him while he was still inside the cathedral, roughed him up, and dragged him to Red Square. Some spoke of killing him, but Dmitrii's boyars prevented that. Instead, Iov was banished to a small, remote monastery. The crowd on Red Square was then allowed to plunder the patriarch's palace as a sort of consolation prize.[156]

With Moscow now cleared of Dmitrii's main enemies and with his supporters in firm control, the new tsar made plans to enter the city.[157] He advanced slowly toward the capital. Each day, huge crowds came from all directions to see and to cheer him. From Moscow came a constant stream of lords, bishops, priests, and monks with presents as well as hundreds of servants with food and drink for the tsar and his entourage. On his short journey, Dmitrii made frequent speeches to his new subjects, recounting his adventures to delighted audiences who were, in the words of one of Dmitrii's enemies, "prepared to believe everything he told them."[158] Dmitrii advanced to a suburb of Moscow, Kolomenskoe, where a camp was set up for him in a meadow just a few kilometers from the gates of the capital. There, for three days he received large numbers of boyars, courtiers, and others who expressed joy at his safe arrival and gave him—along with the traditional gifts of bread and salt—valuable presents of gold, silver, gemstones, pearls, and fine liquor. Dmitrii repeatedly forgave his former opponents who were now willing to recognize him as tsar.[159] Also coming to Dmitrii at this time was a delegation of the Western mercenaries who had been in Tsar Fedor's service and had fought bravely against the new tsar. Rather than scolding them, he praised their steadfastness to the oath they had sworn to Tsar Fedor and their skill and valor. He then formally accepted them into his own service, admonishing them to show the same zeal for him that they had shown for the Godunovs. In this way, Captain Margeret entered Dmitrii's service and retained his position as commander of the tsar's foreign troops.[160]

Some sources hostile to Dmitrii falsely claimed that he delayed his entry into the capital because he still feared that he would be recognized as the monk Otrepev by many Muscovites. According to those sources, Dmitrii ordered a wave of secret arrests, tortures, executions, and exiles of monks and others both before and after his entry into the city.[161] That was decidedly not the case. Dmitrii proved to be a consistently clement prince who was extremely reluctant to spill blood, and he was by this time quite popular. He faced no open opposition and certainly did not instigate any secret purge of monks and other alleged opponents.[162] In fact, the general atmosphere surrounding Dmitrii's entry into Moscow was one of exultation at the return of the "true tsar."

On June 20, 1605, Moscow was at last ready for Tsar Dmitrii's formal entry into the city. The boyars first brought him beautiful garments to wear and asked him to receive his father's inheritance in the name of God. Dmitrii then made a triumphal entry into Moscow as a conquering hero. He rode with the boyars at his side and was preceded and followed by dozens of beautifully attired courtiers, hundreds of his loyal Belorussian cavalry in full armor, and several thousand cossacks and Russian troops. Up to eight thousand men participated in the parade, and the procession took hours to complete. The crowds along the path were huge and well-attired for the occasion. The incredible noise of scores of kettle drums and trumpets in the tsar's parade was matched by the ceaseless pealing of the city's church bells and deafening shouts such as: "you are the true sun shining over Russia."[163] Dmitrii was met on Red Square by a large delegation of bishops, priests, and monks carrying crosses, icons, banners, and holy relics. Dmitrii stopped briefly, wept openly, and publicly thanked God for his success. Then the bishops led him into the Kremlin to the sound of bells and shouts of "Long live our Dmitrii Ivanovich, Tsar of all the Russias."[164]

Once inside the Kremlin, Dmitrii was accompanied to Archangel Cathedral and wept over the coffins of his father, Ivan the Terrible, and his brother, Tsar Fedor Ivanovich. Following that, he was greeted in the Cathedral of the Assumption as the sacred ruler and defender of the Russian Orthodox Church. Archpriest Terentii lavishly praised the new tsar and admonished him "to imitate Christ in his mercy towards the people."[165] Then the boyars led Dmitrii to the palace, seated him on the throne of his father, and paid homage to him.[166] Once Tsar Dmitrii's spectacular entry into the capital was completed, several boyars, bureaucrats, and others emerged from the Kremlin onto Red Square.

There Bogdan Belskii called upon the assembled crowd to thank God for the new ruler and to be faithful to him—the true Dmitrii Ivanovich. The crowd roared in approval.[167] Moscow then gave itself over to celebration for the return of the "miraculously resurrected" tsar. Tsar Dmitrii was formally crowned in a traditional ceremony on July 21, 1605.

12

The Short Reign of Tsar Dmitrii

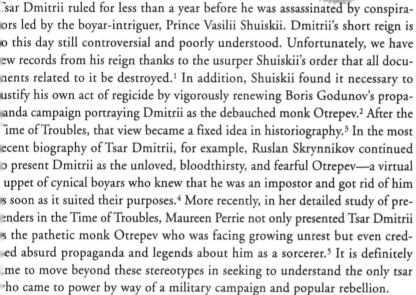

Tsar Dmitrii ruled for less than a year before he was assassinated by conspirators led by the boyar-intriguer, Prince Vasilii Shuiskii. Dmitrii's short reign is to this day still controversial and poorly understood. Unfortunately, we have few records from his reign thanks to the usurper Shuiskii's order that all documents related to it be destroyed.[1] In addition, Shuiskii found it necessary to justify his own act of regicide by vigorously renewing Boris Godunov's propaganda campaign portraying Dmitrii as the debauched monk Otrepev.[2] After the Time of Troubles, that view became a fixed idea in historiography.[3] In the most recent biography of Tsar Dmitrii, for example, Ruslan Skrynnikov continued to present Dmitrii as the unloved, bloodthirsty, and fearful Otrepev—a virtual puppet of cynical boyars who knew that he was an impostor and got rid of him as soon as it suited their purposes.[4] More recently, in her detailed study of pretenders in the Time of Troubles, Maureen Perrie not only presented Tsar Dmitrii as the pathetic monk Otrepev who was facing growing unrest but even credited absurd propaganda and legends about him as a sorcerer.[5] It is definitely time to move beyond these stereotypes in seeking to understand the only tsar who came to power by way of a military campaign and popular rebellion.

Accurately assessing Tsar Dmitrii is incredibly difficult. Almost every wild tale about the evil monk has been credited by some historians, and almost every action or policy of Tsar Dmitrii has been discounted. The "impostor" has been accused of seducing or raping many women, including Boris Godunov's daughter, Kseniia. Otrepev supposedly impregnated thirty nuns and also had sex with monks and handsome young courtiers.[6] He has been accused of profaning Orthodox Christianity, icons, and crosses, and of practicing black magic and communicating with Satan.[7] The impostor supposedly lived in terror of being discovered, for which reason he allegedly became less and less accessible to his people.[8] The bloodthirsty monk also supposedly ordered many secret tortures and executions of persons who could identify him as Otrepev or who opposed his evil plans.[9] His most fiendish plot, it was claimed, was a plan to kill all the boyars and clergy in order to convert Russia to Catholicism.[10] In short, Tsar Dmitrii was seen as the Antichrist.[11]

Before evaluating this lurid evidence, it should be noted that branding an assassinated ruler as a tyrant, usurper, and heretic was a common and effective strategy employed by usurpers in early modern Europe.[12] The demonization of Dmitrii was, of course, absolutely essential in order to legitimize Shuiskii's coup d'état in 1606 because Tsar Dmitrii was a popular ruler regarded by many of his subjects as a sacred, Christ-like figure.[13] Due primarily to Shuiskii's efforts to discredit him, there developed a faulty historical image of Tsar Dmitrii as a frivolous, despised heretic who quickly lost the respect and support of his people and was toppled by an angry population led by a popular patriot and champion of Orthodox Christianity, Vasilii Shuiskii.[14] In fact, nothing could be further from the truth; Tsar Dmitrii was a secure and confident ruler who was not facing rebellion at the time of his assassination.

Greatly complicating any evaluation of Dmitrii's reign is the fact that some scholars came to regard him as the leader of the revolutionary masses, either as a cossack-tsar or as a cynical adventurer whose policies favoring the lower classes enraged the boyars and provoked his assassination.[15] A variation on that erroneous theme has been that, once he rode to power on a wave of social revolution, Dmitrii abandoned the masses and ruled in the interests of the lords.[16] Some have claimed that the rebellion against serfdom died down when Dmitrii became tsar, but the frivolous new ruler was unable to maintain boyar support and, by spring 1606, also faced growing popular unrest. In a desperate bid to maintain or regain the support of the masses, Dmitrii supposedly planned to abolish serfdom and possibly to renew class war against the lords, but he was killed by the angry boyars before he could implement such radical policies. His assassination, however, far from securing the ruling elite's position, supposedly provoked a massive social revolution led by Ivan Bolotnikov.[17] These interpretations of Tsar Dmitrii's reign are, as we shall see, utterly false.

Tsar Dmitrii's triumphal entry into Moscow in June 1605 was a joyous occasion. He was welcomed by many of his subjects as the true tsar who had been rescued by divine providence in order to restore God's favor to Russia. Sources mentioning open opposition to the new tsar and widespread recognition of him as Otrepev were strongly influenced by Vasilii Shuiskii's later propaganda campaign and are not accurate. Equally false are hostile sources referring to the fearful and bloodthirsty monk immediately ordering secret executions of scores of his opponents who knew he was an impostor.[18] In fact, during Tsar Dmitrii's first days in Moscow, thousands of people came forward to swear that he was the true tsar.[19] Dmitrii was actually supremely confident and very reluctant to spill the blood of his opponents. Despite centuries of scholarly denial, he was from the very beginning of his reign a popular ruler.[20] That is an essential point to keep in mind when trying to make sense out of the plots against him, his assassination, and the civil war fought in his name that raged for many years and nearly destroyed Russia. Once the propaganda and legends about Dmitrii are stripped away, what is truly noteworthy was his strikingly smooth transition to power.

Contrary to the traditional interpretation, the new tsar did not seem too radical or too Westernized to most of the Russian elite. He was able to reach swift accord with most boyars, church officials, bureaucrats, voevodas, and others, and he continued many of the same general policies of his predecessors—including those of Tsar Boris. There was never any discussion of convening a zemskii sobor in order to legitimize his claim to the throne, and, except for Vasilii Shuiskii's foolish plot against him in the new tsar's first days in Moscow—which was quickly discovered and crushed—Dmitrii faced no rebellions during his short reign. He certainly did not feel the need to hide his true identity, carry out major purges, or launch a terror campaign in order to stay in power. Instead, he confidently played the part of the good, wise, and just tsar who was accessible to his subjects.[21] Contrary to traditional interpretations, his realm was a strong absolute monarchy feared and respected by its neighbors. According to Richard Hellie, Tsar Dmitrii was actually "one of the few really enlightened rulers Russia has ever had."[22]

Contemporaries, even some of his enemies, judged Tsar Dmitrii to be an exceptional person. The victorious young warrior-prince who "loved honor" was not only brave and bold;[23] he was an extremely intelligent and resourceful person. He was extraordinarily well educated for a Russian tsar, well-versed in statecraft, advanced in his thinking, and very reform-minded.[24] He was an excellent speaker who carried himself with "majesty and grandeur."[25] He was determined to rule as a wise and clement prince, not as a tyrant, and he wished to make his subjects feel that they lived in a "free country."[26] His manifestos displayed great care and concern for his people, and he obviously strove to gain their affection.[27] Those efforts were more than marginally successful. Many of his subjects loved him, and he was the very first Russian ruler to be idealized as a "just tsar."[28] He introduced the practice of receiving petitions directly from the people twice a week in order to speed up and assure justice for ordinary Russians, and he attempted to eliminate bribery among public officials.[29] He lowered the tax burden and labor demands on the war-torn southern provinces that had supported him during his campaign for the throne. (In fact, his tenyear tax exemption for Putivl and Severia closely followed Boris Godunov's earlier example of a ten-year tax exemption for war-torn Karelia.)[30] Dmitrii responded to his subjects' economic distress by attempting to set taxes at affordable rates.[31]

According to contemporaries, he promulgated excellent laws and planned a new law code.[32] He also made plans for promoting education and science in Russia.[33] Tsar Dmitrii definitely had lofty military ambition; he was also the first tsar to call himself "emperor."[34] He worked hard to improve the effectiveness of the Russian army, and he often practiced with his soldiers—who tended to adore him.[35] More than one scholar has seen in Tsar Dmitrii a forerunner of Peter the Great.[36]

The eminent historian Sergei Platonov suspected that much of Tsar Dmitrii's remarkable reputation was simply due to his servants' attempts to justify working for him.[37] That is incorrect; even Dmitrii's enemies praised the same virtues. Ruslan Skrynnikov regarded Dmitrii's reforms and other actions which made him appear to be a "good tsar" as nothing more than insincere demagogery.[38] That is also incorrect. As Maureen Perrie has observed, "we have no reason to doubt Dimitry's sincerity" about intending "to rule with justice and mercy." She also noted the existence of "evidence that he was able to implement some positive measures of reform."[39] Nonetheless, Tsar Dmitrii must have been quite a shock to many of his subjects. Not raised in the claustrophobic and tradition-bound Russian court, he did not behave in the usual manner of the tsars. Dmitrii proved to be an unconventional ruler who challenged many court and cultural norms. He upset some conservatives by breaches of tradition and his neglect of elaborate court ceremonies and religious rites. That aroused suspicions about him which Vasilii Shuiskii and others were able to exploit.[40]

To begin with, Tsar Dmitrii dressed and acted in informal, "Western" ways.[41] He was also a highly literate, independent thinker who did not conceal his disdain for the low level of education among his boyars.[42] He preferred to surround himself with educated courtiers such as Mikhail Molchanov, Mikhail Tatishchev, Ivan T. Gramotin, and Ivan D. Khvorostinin instead of high-born aristocrats.[43] According to Captain Margeret, Tsar Dmitrii also "sometimes showed a bit too much familiarity toward the lords" who had been "brought up in such subjection and fear that they would almost not dare to speak" in the presence of the tsar "without command."[44] Dmitrii trusted some very intelligent and well-educated foreigners with important posts in government—especially the Polish Protestant Buczynski brothers, Jan and Stanislaw.[45] He also failed to observe and occasionally ridiculed some Russian customs.[46] For example, he had no interest in attending church services for many hours each day.[47] While he was careful to observe Orthodox Christian rituals in general, Tsar Dmitrii shocked some people by riding on horseback while on pilgrimages.[48] He also "kept a joyful table" and dispensed with some of the seemingly endless religious rituals associated with dining at court. He did not fast zealously and

Fig. 8 "Tsar Dmitrii." Engraved by Lucas Kilian in 1606. From D.A. Rovinskii, *Materialy dlia Russkoi Ikonografii,* part 2 (St. Petersburg, 1884). Courtesy of Houghton Library, Harvard University.

occasionally ate food deemed "unclean" by the Russian Orthodox Church.[49] He did not rest after dinner, as was customary. Instead, he often wandered around the Kremlin or Moscow alone or with just one or two guards—rejecting the custom of being surrounded by a crowd of boyars and courtiers wherever he went.[50]

More shocking to many Russians were his interactions with and toleration of Protestants, Catholics, and Jews.[51] Especially scandalous was his decision to allow Catholics, even Jesuits, to have a church of their own in Moscow.[52] Although Tsar Dmitrii kept his own contact with the Jesuits in low profile, for Russians brought up to regard the "Latin faith" as a Satanic heresy, Dmitrii's religious toleration must have been a shock. The tsar's enemies never tired of trying to link him to some kind of Catholic plot to destroy the Russian Orthodox Church. In fact, the mere presence of Poles and other Westerners in Moscow and at court was so disturbing to some xenophobic Russians that they did not bother to distinguish between Tsar Dmitrii's inner circle of foreign Protestant advisers and the hated Catholics found wandering around the capital during his reign. All of them were regarded by unsophisticated Russians as suspicious heretics.[53] It is a noteworthy aspect of early modern Russian political culture that much of the criticism leveled against Tsar Dmitrii by his enemies was remarkably similar to conservative complaints about that later "Antichrist," Peter the Great. Peter's enemies also complained that he was a tyrant, a heretic, a tool of Satan, an immoral blasphemer, and a "Latinizer" whose Western-style dress and habits, preference for foreigners who scorned the backward Russians, and mockery of sacred Orthodox Christian rituals "proved" that he was an "impostor" and "false tsar."[54] Unlike Tsar Dmitrii, however, Peter the Great set up an elaborate and effective mechanism to detect and punish potential traitors.[55]

Tsar Dmitrii did not face significant opposition at the outset of his reign; instead, the general atmosphere was one of celebration. There were some dark rumors, however, spread by Vasilii Shuiskii—one of the losers in the newly emerging power structure.[56] It has been claimed that Tsar Dmitrii faced formidable boyar opposition from the very beginning of his reign and that Shuiskii's faction was strong and planned to strike against the false tsar before he could entrench himself in power.[57] That was definitely not the case. Close examination of sources and the issues involved reveals that most boyars were loyal supporters of the new tsar and that the intriguer Shuiskii was isolated and acting, more or less, on his own.

Tsar Dmitrii's nemesis, Prince Vasilii Shuiskii, was one of the most senior and prestigious boyars whose family of Suzdal princes traced their ancestry back to Riurik, the legendary founder of the ancient Rus state. Short, stocky, balding, and unattractive, Vasilii Shuiskii was extremely nearsighted and looked vaguely ridiculous; yet he was a cunning and dangerous intriguer.[58] Like Boris Godunov's rival, Ivan Shuiskii, before him, Prince Vasilii firmly believed he was far more worthy to occupy the Russian throne than anyone else and was more than willing to shed blood to get it. He had dreamed of becoming tsar after Boris Godunov's death only to be forestalled by Dmitrii. In desperation at losing out, Shuiskii tried to organize a hasty conspiracy against the new tsar. Within a few days of Dmitrii's entry into the capital, Vasilii and his two younger brothers, Dmitrii and Ivan, were arrested for spreading a rumor that Dmitrii was Grishka Otrepev, a tool of the Jesuits who planned to destroy the Russian Orthodox Church.[59] The Shuiskii brothers had apparently approached some lords, merchants, priests, and others with their claims and had actually begun to assemble a small group of trusted individuals in a plot to distract the Kremlin guards by means of arson so they could assassinate Tsar Dmitrii.[60] Because of Shuiskii's lofty status and Dmitrii's desire to appear to be a just ruler rather than a tyrant, an extraordinary public state trial was held in which "persons chosen from all estates" listened to the evidence in the case.[61] The new tsar may actually have convened a zemskii sobor for the occasion.[62] It has been claimed that Dmitrii was forced to do this because he could not count on the boyar council, on its own, to condemn a high-born prince and that, in any case, the tsar's real motive was not to seek the truth in the matter but to make a preemptive strike against a clan with a strong claim to the throne and strong support among the boyars.[63] In fact, that was not at all the case. The Shuiskii brothers were not particularly popular among their fellow boyars. Dmitrii's real motive in convening such a high-profile investigation of Vasilii Shuiskii's charges against himself was to refute decisively the rumor campaign that some conservative boyars, clergymen, and others had been inclined to credit.[64]

During Vasilii Shuiskii's trial, Tsar Dmitrii personally acted as prosecutor. He stunned his subjects by his eloquent refutation of the traitor's lies and by his testimony about how the Shuiskii clan had always been disloyal subjects.[65] Dmitrii's performance was so effective that the boyars immediately declared their love for the new tsar and shouted that Shuiskii deserved execution.[66] Shuiskii thereupon made a full confession and fell to his knees, declaring that by his actions he had offended God. He was then upbraided by the new patriarch, Ignatii.[67] Shuiskii was swiftly convicted of lese majesty and condemned to death. Not many days later he was taken to Red Square and prepared for the executioner's ax. At the last minute, Tsar Dmitrii commuted his sentence to exile, along with his brothers, in faraway Viatka. Some contemporaries noted that this was Dmitrii's greatest mistake since Shuiskii eventually did manage to assassinate him.[68] Why did Tsar Dmitrii let the traitor live? It has been claimed that the false tsar's "mother," the nun Marfa, secured the reprieve either because she knew that Dmitrii was an impostor or because she did not want her "son" to begin his reign by spilling the blood of a high-born prince. Some sources stated that the tsar's secretary, Jan Buczynski, secured the reprieve by arguing that Dmitrii should go out of his way to pardon Russian lords and to treat them with kindness. Another source claimed just the opposite—that Buczynski argued against clemency for such a dangerous traitor. Still another source credited the state secretary Afanasii Vlasev for stopping the execution. Finally, Ruslan Skrynnikov has pointed to the precedent for last-minute reprieves set by Tsar Boris. Suffice it to say, the truth about the tsar's ultimately fatal decision is not known.[69] Only a minor courtier named Petr Turgenev and a merchant named Fedor Kalachnik were executed in connection with Shuiskii's plot; Kalachnik was taunted as a traitor deserving death by the crowd gathered on Red Square.[70]

Skrynnikov boldly asserted that Tsar Dmitrii's two close associates, Bogdan Belskii and Petr Basmanov, urged Shuiskii's execution to get the powerful boyar out of the way in order to secure their own positions but that the high-born princes objected to their bid for power and stood by one of their own. Supposedly, the Golitsyns, Boris Lykov, and Boris Tatev were alarmed by the rise of the "low-born" Belskii and Basmanov and convinced other high-born nobles and church leaders to join with them in forcing Dmitrii to spare Shuiskii's life. According to Skrynnikov, "the false tsar was rapidly becoming a prisoner of the Moscow nobility."[71] There are a number of problems with that interpretation. Although it is true that some aristocrats resented being shoved aside by "lesser" men who were close to the new tsar, there is certainly no evidence that the minor princes Tatev and Lykov pleaded for clemency for Shuiskii. In fact, they both owed their careers to Tsar Dmitrii. Prince Boris Tatev had joined Dmitrii's cause in 1604 and had been promoted to the rank of boyar by him. Prince Boris Lykov also joined Dmitrii's cause during his campaign for the throne and had been promoted to a prestigious position at court by him.[72] Although Tatev eventually joined Shuiskii's later, successful conspiracy against Dmitrii, Skrynnikov himself wrote that the boyars involved in Shuiskii's first aborted assassination plot were quick to denounce him as a traitor once their plan was uncovered.[73] Would those compromised men really have pressed for clemency?

Skrynnikov also believed that Bogdan Belskii's departure from Moscow to take up his important position as governor of Novgorod was somehow related to his "defeat" in a power struggle with the high-born princes over the issue of clemency for Shuiskii. For unclear reasons, Skrynnikov believed his own unproven hypothesis constituted evidence that the "false tsar" was not in control but had become a captive of the boyars.[74] Actually, sending the trusted Belskii to Novgorod was more likely connected to Tsar Dmitrii's plans for military action against Sweden later that year. Or it could have been the result of a feud between Belskii and Petr Basmanov, each angling to become Tsar Dmitrii's most trusted ally and eyeing the other as the chief obstacle to that goal.[75] It should also be remembered that Dmitrii had repeatedly shown himself to be a clement prince during his campaign for the throne. The tsar himself may have wished to appear as a gentle, forgiving ruler. One contemporary wrote that Tsar Dmitrii thought the conviction of Shuiskii, on its own, without execution, would send a cautionary message to all wavering lords and that the tsar felt himself to be in no further danger after the exile of the Shuiskiis.[76]

The idea that Tsar Dmitrii did not control his own boyar council but was a virtual captive of it has been put forward several times by Skrynnikov.[77] This notion appears to be derived both from the tradition of not taking the "impostor" seriously and from the intriguing theory that Russian autocracy was itself an illusion masking effective control by the boyars. A similar perspective on both issues has been advanced by Edward L. Keenan.[78] In the case of Tsar Dmitrii, however, there is considerable evidence to dispute Skrynnikov's claim. A closer look reveals that Dmitrii had strong allies on the boyar council and that he was nobody's puppet. As noted earlier, Dmitrii had negotiated with the boyars before entering the capital about such things as the distribution of ranks and offices, the purging of the Godunovs from the boyar council, and the retention of estates. Only close relatives of Tsar Boris lost their positions and property; all others had their status and holdings—even if received from Tsar Boris—confirmed by the new tsar.[79] Dmitrii was quite mild and generous to his boyars, preferring to woo them with rewards rather than to cow them by resorting to tyranny.[80] Following customary practice in early modern Russia, however, a few lords who had worked closely with the Godunovs and were not considered particularly trustworthy (or who had been enemies of the new tsar's inner circle) may have been "demoted" by being shipped off to become voevodas in remote towns.[81]

Tsar Dmitrii had many supporters on the boyar council. His initial allies included members of his own family, participants in the plot to make him tsar, other lords who had been exiled or otherwise mistreated by Tsar Boris, and those voevodas who joined his cause during his campaign for the throne. Of course, Dmitrii was especially generous to the Nagoi clan. In addition to returning his mother to exalted status in the Kremlin, Dmitrii appointed Marfa's three brothers and two cousins to high positions on the boyar council and gave them rich rewards—including former estates of Boris Godunov.[82] Bogdan Belskii was also richly rewarded and placed on the boyar council by Dmitrii.[83] The new tsar also brought Ivan Nikitich Romanov back from exile, richly rewarded him, restored his estates, and made him a boyar.[84] The monk Filaret (Fedor Nikitich Romanov) could not, of course, become a boyar again; but Tsar Dmitrii did promote him to the prestigious position of metropolitan of Rostov.[85] The Romanovs were unquestioningly loyal to Tsar Dmitrii.[86] Other great lords who had been disgraced, exiled, and impoverished by Tsar Boris were also readmitted to the boyar council by Dmitrii. For example, Ivan Vorotynskii had his estates restored and was promoted to the rank of boyar.[87] The brothers I. P. and V. P. Golovin were both restored to favor and promoted to the rank of okolnichii. Vasilii Shchelkalov, an important bureaucrat out of favor with Tsar Boris, was also promoted to the rank of okolnichii, and newly-promoted okolnichii Prince Ivan A. Khvorostinin became a member of the tsar's inner circle.[88]

Tsar Dmitrii went out of his way to arrange marriage alliances between those lords returning from exile and the Nagoi clan in order to secure their firm support.[89] Dmitrii also generously rewarded and promoted those voevodas and other officers who had joined him during his campaign for the throne—including his closest ally, Petr Basmanov, along with Ivan Golitsyn, Vasilii M. Mosalskii, Boris Tatev, Boris Lykov, Mikhail G. Saltykov, Petr and Grigorii Shakhovskoi, Fedor Sheremetev, Artemii Izmailov, Grigorii Mikulin, and Dmitrii V. Turenin. Many of those men became energetic supporters of the new tsar.[90] A few other men who had not been out of favor under Tsar Boris but were promoted to the boyar council by Dmitrii also became his strong allies. A good example of this is state secretary Afanasii Vlasev, who was promoted to the rank of okolnichii by Tsar Dmitrii.[91] From the very beginning of his reign, Dmitrii also made strenuous efforts to gain the support of the senior member of the boyar council, Fedor Mstislavskii—who was related to the old dynasty, had been kept from marrying by Tsar Boris, and had been suspected of pro-Dmitrii sympathies at the Godunov court.[92] Dmitrii quickly forgave Mstislavskii for fighting against him and let him retain his chairmanship of the boyar council. The new tsar restored Mstislavskii's property which Boris Godunov had confiscated and heaped honors and gifts on him—including one of Tsar Boris's palaces. Dmitrii's "exaltation" of Mstislavskii included an immediate marriage alliance with the Nagoi clan.[93] The tsar's efforts paid off; Mstislavskii became a loyal supporter of Dmitrii. Dmitrii also restored to favor Fedor Mstislavskii's brother-in-law, Simeon Bekbulatovich, who had been badly treated by Tsar Boris.[94]

Tsar Dmitrii's allies dominated the boyar council, but they did not dominate the tsar. Skrynnikov has asserted that the "false tsar" was, in effect, a terrified prisoner of the boyars and that they forced the impostor to carry out policies against his wishes or his own best interests.[95] Skrynnikov's perspective is tantalizingly similar to Edward Keenan's controversial view of early modern Russian autocracy as an illusion masking boyar rule.[96] Nevertheless, the fact that Tsar Dmitrii had many allies on the boyar council makes it essential to scrutinize Skrynnikov's arguments carefully. He claimed that, at the outset of Dmitrii's reign, the new tsar was forced by the boyars to dismiss his unruly cossacks and the Polish military forces that had helped him gain the throne.[97] Dmitrii did, in fact, dismiss those men from his service, but there is no evidence that it was done under boyar pressure. Instead, it seems more likely that the new commander-in-chief of the entire Russian army no longer needed those men. He thanked and richly rewarded those faithful soldiers before sending them home—which was the usual and customary practice after military campaigns in that era.[98] More significant evidence that Dmitrii was a captive of the boyars, according to Skrynnikov, were his decisions—made soon after exiling or imprisoning opponents—to pardon them and allow them to return to his service.[99] In particular, Skrynnikov believed the boyars prevented Vasilii Shuiskii's execution in the summer of 1605 and then, in late fall, managed to force the tsar to pardon Shuiskii and allow him to return to court despite protests from Dmitrii's advisers that Shuiskii was a very real danger to the throne. The boyars must have forced this upon the tsar, Skrynnikov argued, because it was obviously not in Dmitrii's own interest and Shuiskii immediately resumed plotting against the tsar, albeit more cautiously than before.[100]

There is, in fact, no evidence of boyar pressure to pardon Shuiskii, and one contemporary source actually claimed Dmitrii's secretaries, the Buczynski brothers, were the ones who repeatedly urged the tsar to forgive the traitor and allow him to return to Moscow.[101] It is worth noting that at about the same time Tsar Dmitrii also pardoned several members of the Godunov clan, put them back to work as voevodas, and even promoted one of Tsar Boris's relatives to the rank of boyar. Vasilii Shuiskii himself was returned to the boyar council, and Dmitrii actually arranged for him to marry a relative of the Nagoi clan.[102] Tsar Dmitrii was a clement and forgiving prince, and he may very well have naïvely decided to pardon Shuiskii on his own.[103] For what it is worth, the periods of time spent in exile during Tsar Boris's reign also tended to be remarkably short.[104] Suffice it to say, Skrynnikov has not proven that Tsar Dmitrii was a puppet of the boyars. Maureen Perrie has expressed healthy skepticism about Skrynnikov's assertion, reminding us that the traditional interpretation was that Dmitrii was overthrown by the boyars precisely because they resented his independent policies and assertion of authority.[105] Contemporary observers of the tsar, even one of his opponents, confirmed that Dmitrii dominated his boyar council, that he was much better educated in the art of government than his boyars, that his speeches were learned and wise, that his proposed policies easily prevailed, and that the tsar was personally responsible for making good laws.[106]

No doubt some boyars grumbled about Tsar Dmitrii's unconventional behavior and contact with foreigners. More troubling to at least a few high-born princes was their inability to break into the tsar's inner circle. Some of those proud men had gladly abandoned the Godunovs, hoping to be able to dominate the new tsar's government.[107] As it turned out, Tsar Dmitrii, by his appointments to the boyar council and by his choice of close advisers, seemed to be shoving those princes into the background in favor of the Nagoi clan and pushy, well-educated upstarts. Some aristocrats deeply resented the rise of "unworthy" and "low-born" men in Tsar Dmitrii's service.[108] It may even have appeared to some aging survivors of Ivan the Terrible's reign that Dmitrii was reconstructing Tsar Ivan's personal court aristocracy. In fact, many of the men in the new tsar's inner circle did come from families which had been active in the hated oprichnina.[109] Of course, Tsar Dmitrii had no intention of reinstituting his father's terror campaign, but the hatred some princes felt for the likes of Basmanov and others close to the new tsar was very real.[110] It is likely that painful memories of the oprichnina were conjured up by Dmitrii's enemies as they quietly sought allies among the nobility.

Conspirators plotting against Tsar Dmitrii were able to find some sympathizers among the Russian Orthodox clergy.[111] Unfortunately, Skrynnikov jumped to the conclusion that all "princes of the church" joined with the boyars to prevent Dmitrii from executing Shuiskii.[112] Not only is that interpretation wrong about the relationship of the boyars to Tsar Dmitrii, but it is also wrong about the relationship of the clergy to the unconventional new tsar. Dmitrii had no trouble imposing his will on the Russian Orthodox Church, whose leaders were in no position to dictate terms to the tsar. It should be remembered that in this period the church was effectively controlled by the "secular political elite" dominant in the Kremlin.[113] Tsar Dmitrii also had allies among the church leaders who praised the new tsar, actively participated in celebrating his accession to the throne, and tried to get along with him even though many of them were scandalized by his religious toleration and contact with foreign "heretics."[114] As noted earlier, the unpopular Patriarch Iov was removed from office and replaced by Tsar Dmitrii's choice, the well-educated Greek Cypriot, Ignatii, who (as bishop of Riazan) had been the first church leader to recognize Dmitrii as tsar. Tsar Dmitrii's enemies, of course, regarded the toppling of Iov as an arbitrary action taken in violation of church rules.[115] They vividly portrayed the new patriarch as an evil man hated by the Russian people but forced upon them by the "false tsar" who was also busy raping nuns and ordering the secret torture and execution of monks and other clergymen every night.[116] In fact, church leaders—including Iov—recognized that as Boris Godunov's friend, Iov was no longer a viable patriarch. He was convinced to resign and offered as an excuse his advanced age and blindness.[117] Skrynnikov found that excuse to be unconvincing, but Iov really was nearly blind by then and certainly had no interest in trying to cling to his office against the wishes of the new tsar and the hostile population of Moscow.[118] Apparently, some clergymen who had been very close to Patriarch Iov and were therefore considered untrustworthy also lost their positions when he left office. No doubt, they became potential recruits in the plot against Tsar Dmitrii.[119]

Propaganda against Tsar Dmitrii made him out to be a tool of the Jesuits who planned to destroy the Russian Orthodox Church and convert the country to Catholicism. Once he became tsar, however, Dmitrii showed no interest whatsoever in converting Russia and little interest in working with or even having contact with Catholics. He clearly preferred the company of Protestants and educated Russians.[120] (Of course, it should be noted that, to many xenophobic Orthodox Christians, Protestants were just as bad as the "heretic" Catholics.)[121] Wild tales about "Otrepev" as an evil tool of Satan who delighted in spilling Orthodox Christian blood in order to hide his true identity have made it extremely difficult for historians to look objectively at Tsar Dmitrii's relationship to the Russian Orthodox Church.[122] In fact, church leaders cooperated with the new tsar. False rumors about the secret executions of monks were really just part of a propaganda campaign secretly promoted by Shuiskii and by the Swedish government at a time when King Karl IX rightly feared Tsar Dmitrii was planning a war against him.[123]

Far from being hostile to the Russian Orthodox Church, Dmitrii actually confirmed and even issued new charters of immunities to some monasteries.[124] He also had some churches decorated.[125] He went on pilgrimages and otherwise tried to observe the basic rituals of the Orthodox Christian faith.[126] He did, however, encounter criticism for ordering a survey of all monastic holdings in order to gain sorely needed revenue with which to shore up his impoverished gentry militiamen in preparation for a planned crusade against the Crimean Tatars and the Turks.[127] Dmitrii did, in fact, borrow money from rich monasteries.[128] He also confiscated a few pieces of church property in Moscow, which resulted in the eviction of some priests from lodgings convenient to the Kremlin.[129] According to Skrynnikov, that relatively modest confiscation and Dmitrii's taxation of the church's wealth pushed an exasperated clergy into opposition to him.[130] That is not at all clear; other tsars before and after Dmitrii, including Boris Godunov and Vasilii Shuiskii, occasionally imposed emergency taxes on the church and even seized church property without provoking any such dramatic reaction.[131] Beyond Shuiskii's disinformation campaign and Swedish-inspired propaganda, Skrynnikov has provided no evidence of such a reaction on the part of church leaders during Tsar Dmitrii's reign.

What really stirred serious opposition within the Russian Orthodox Church and elsewhere was Dmitrii's decision in the fall of 1605 to marry a Polish Catholic princess, Marina Mniszech—the daughter of his one-time military commander, Jerzy Mniszech, the palatine of Sandomierz.[132] Some fanatic church leaders flatly opposed the marriage; others, including the zealous metropolitan of Kazan, Hermogen, demanded that Marina convert to Orthodoxy before the wedding.[133] Marina, however, insisted on remaining a Catholic, and Tsar Dmitrii backed her up. In the end, after senior clergymen made several unsuccessful attempts to talk the tsar out of the marriage, Patriarch Ignatii blessed the union and Tsar Dmitrii ordered disgrace and exile for any church leaders who refused to go along. Metropolitan Hermogen refused to bless the marriage and was immediately sent back to Kazan and shut up in a monastery. The rest of the clergy quickly quieted down and, at least publicly, bowed to the tsar's will.[134] Except for Hermogen, all metropolitans, archbishops, bishops, abbots, and leading clergymen joined Patriarch Ignatii and Tsar Dmitrii's boyars in signing off on the marriage agreement and the plan to dispatch an embassy to Poland-Lithuania to make the necessary arrangements. Even Metropolitans Isidor of Novgorod and Pafnutii of Krutitsa, both future allies of the intriguer Vasilii Shuiskii, signed the document approving the royal marriage.[135]

The lone holdout (and future patriarch), seventy-five year old Metropolitan Hermogen, was a most atypical religious leader. He had lived among the Don cossacks for many years and had joined the clergy only at the age of fifty. He was an excellent speaker and very well educated for that era, and he managed to rise to the lofty rank of metropolitan of Kazan within just ten years. In Kazan, he displayed a "rare fanaticism" in his missionary work and was merciless to his enemies. Hermogen took severe measures against Islamic subjects of the tsar and even harassed many Tatars who had at least nominally converted to Christianity. The aged metropolitan was a religious fanatic who fought against any perceived threat to the Russian Orthodox Church. He was afraid of no one and was exceedingly forthright in expressing his views. Even his friends often found him "too blunt in word and deed."[136] Long before the issue of Dmitrii's marriage came up, Hermogen had already defied Patriarch Iov and Tsar Boris by refusing to sign Godunov's coronation charter.[137] By late 1605, he was once again in disgrace. It is not known whether Vasilii Shuiskii, newly returned from exile himself, contacted the old metropolitan—who became his future ally and patriarch. Because of the fact that both men were known opponents of Dmitrii, a more cautious Shuiskii was probably not in a hurry to approach Hermogen. Instead, he may have been content to begin working secretly with sympathetic church officials who were not in disgrace. Shuiskii's contacts may have included Metropolitans Pafnutii and Isidor, both of whom emerged as his allies once he managed to seize the throne. Nonetheless, even those two church officials' possible involvement in Shuiskii's plot is mere conjecture, and there is certainly no evidence to support the claim that the entire clergy opposed Tsar Dmitrii.[138]

As soon as Vasilii Shuiskii returned to Moscow in late 1605, he began secretly conspiring to assassinate Tsar Dmitrii, presenting himself to carefully chosen ultra-Orthodox individuals as the champion of the Russian Orthodox Church and the "first sufferer" for the faith at the hands of "Otrepev." He promised to halt the "flood of heresy" the false tsar had introduced to Russia.[139] Shuiskii found some willing supporters among monks and priests, and he may have found additional recruits among resentful, low-ranking courtiers who had served Tsar Boris and had then been dismissed when Dmitrii came to power. Shuiskii may also have been able to recruit a few secretaries and clerks in the tsar's bureaucracy who had been dismissed as unreliable, had opposed Dmitrii's policies, or—more likely—had been punished for corruption or had at one time or another been on the receiving end of one of the tsar's periodic outbursts against his bureaucrats for stupidity and arrogance.[140] In any case, Shuiskii's small group of conspirators made their first feeble attempt to assassinate the tsar in the Kremlin in January 1606. Three persons were apprehended and executed without naming their accomplices. One contemporary was astonished that Shuiskii's involvement in the plot was not discovered. At that time, Moscow was filled with false rumors about secret executions of monks who opposed the "false tsar."[141] Tsar Dmitrii responded to the incident by increasing Kremlin security. Among other things, he created an elite bodyguard of several hundred foreign mercenaries led by the intelligent and trustworthy Captain Jacques Margeret.[142] Dmitrii's enemies later portrayed this as an "heretical innovation" that greatly upset the Russian lords.[143] That is an exaggeration. The persons really disturbed by this wise precaution were potential assassins. It is worth noting that after Tsar Dmitrii's murder, the usurper Vasilii Shuiskii—who dismissed many of the foreign troops Tsars Boris and Dmitrii had recruited over the years—did not feel any great pressure to dismiss the captain of Tsar Dmitrii's foreign bodyguard. Instead, Shuiskii attempted to retain him in his own service.[144]

In the early months of 1606, Shuiskii's conspirators concocted several more assassination plots in an attempt to kill Dmitrii before his bride-to-be arrived in the country or the traitors themselves were discovered.[145] With access to the tsar in the Kremlin now more carefully guarded, they temporarily switched tactics and planned to assassinate Dmitrii during one of the many winter military exercises in which the bold tsar took active part and exposed himself to great risk. The assassins were unable to find an opportune moment in the field, however, and were soon forced to turn to yet another strategy.[146] By then, the conspirators had managed to gain a few supporters among the Moscow streltsy, but seven of those men were indiscreet enough to be discovered. In March 1606, before an assembly of the entire Moscow streltsy detachment, Tsar Dmitrii—flanked by Petr Basmanov (who served as the head of the streltsy prikaz), Fedor Mstislavskii, and the Nagois—made an impassioned speech in which he assured his soldiers that he was indeed the son of Ivan the Terrible. His speech made a strong impression; the streltsy immediately tore the traitors in their ranks to pieces.[147] After that dramatic and bloody incident, opposition to the tsar temporarily quieted down. The conspirators had to be extremely cautious as they made new plans and sought additional allies.[148]

According to tradition, by early 1606 the Shuiskii brothers were able to count on wide support in their struggle against the "false tsar." Because of various assassination attempts, lurid propaganda, and a lingering prejudice against Tsar Dmitrii, historians have often taken at face value the assertions by Dmitrii's enemies that he had basically been abandoned by most Russians—even his former allies—in the months before his assassination.[149] There are, however, a number of problems with that interpretation. For example, historians have usually credited evidence that during the winter of 1605–6 the Shuiskiis were joined in their conspiracy by the Golitsyns, other disillusioned boyars, and even Dmitrii's mother. It is alleged that the false tsar angered the nun Marfa by contemplating the desecration of the real Tsarevich Dmitrii's grave in Uglich, and that Marfa then secretly aided the Shuiskiis and Golitsyns in making secret contact with King Sigismund to complain about the impostor and to offer the throne to Sigismund's son, Prince Wladyslaw, in return for assistance in overthrowing "Otrepev."[150] In fact, it is very likely that the Golitsyns did join Shuiskii's conspiracy, but the basis for the colorful story of Marfa and the boyars contacting the king of Poland is extremely weak. It consists of the Polish general Stanislas Zolkiewski's memoirs, written many years later, in which he credited a dubious Swedish source's absurd tale about treason in Moscow.[151] Historians should have been more skeptical about this information, especially since the king of Sweden was at that time actively pursuing a propaganda campaign to undermine Tsar Dmitrii.[152] Scholars have also taken at face value a story about Tsar Dmitrii's ambassador to Poland, Ivan Bezobrazov, secretly informing Sigismund that the Shuiskiis, the Golitsyns, and others wished to get rid of the impostor in favor of Prince Wladyslaw.[153] Again, the source of this story is the same Swedish propaganda-influenced Polish general's memoirs.[154] In fact, historians have been so anxious to credit Zolkiewski's information that they have ignored obvious problems with it. For example, Zolkiewski claimed that the recently-pardoned Vasilii Shuiskii was the person who recommended Bezobrazov for the embassy to Poland—which is extremely unlikely. Bezobrazov also supposedly told the Poles that he grew up as a neighbor and playmate of Otrepev and recognized him as the man playing the role of Tsar Dmitrii.[155] Why would a false tsar send such an ambassador?

Other evidence has also been distorted in order to fit the traditional interpretation of Tsar Dmitrii. For example, in December 1605, Dmitrii sent his secretary, Jan Buczynski, to Poland; in January 1606, Buczynski sent the tsar a letter stating that King Sigismund was aware that his own internal foes hoped to make use of Tsar Dmitrii in a plan to topple the king.[156] That information has been erroneously interpreted to mean that Dmitrii himself planned to topple Sigismund, which in turn supposedly forced Sigismund to join in a conspiracy with Dmitrii's boyar opponents. It has also been alleged that Buczynski's letter convinced the tsar that some of his boyars must be traitors who had secretly informed the Poles of his intentions.[157] In fact, all that is pure conjecture. The case against Dmitrii on this particular point is not helped by the fact that rumors circulating in Poland maintained that the tsar planned to send against Sigismund an army commanded by one of the Shuiskii princes![158] Nor is the case against Dmitrii aided by Skrynnikov's erroneous notion that the large sum of money Dmitrii sent to his future father-in-law, an ardent Catholic, was actually intended to finance a rebellion against Sigismund by Protestant and Orthodox noblemen.[159] Skrynnikov was also utterly convinced that King Sigismund became involved in the plot against Dmitrii.[160] However, there is no proof of that. For what it is worth, Sigismund later denied any involvement; and the pope was at the time actually urging Sigismund to cooperate with Tsar Dmitrii, not to try to topple him for being slow to convert Russia to Catholicism.[161]

The eminent historian Sergei Platonov boldly declared that by January 1606, Dmitrii's secretary Buczynski warned him of a rumor that "Moscow was completely convinced that Dimitry was not the real tsar."[162] A serious problem with that assertion is that Buczynski was in Poland when he supposedly informed Dmitrii of that startling rumor. In fact, historians have frequently made use of the lies Buczynski was coerced into telling by Shuiskii's henchmen after his master had been assassinated.[163] Skrynnikov even went so far as to credit the story about the return to Russia at the beginning of 1606 of one of the Russians who had earlier identified Dmitrii as Dmitrii to Polish authorities. Supposedly, the renegade Khripunov met at the border one of Dmitrii's Polish officers who was then on his way home and informed the officer that Moscow knew Tsar Dmitrii was an impostor and would soon be rid of him.[164] The problem with that source, which Skrynnikov neglected to mention, is that Khripunov, whatever he may have said, had by then been living in Poland-Lithuania for several years. What would he really know about popular sentiment in Moscow? We are told by historians of similar discussions about the false tsar in taverns and virtually everywhere in Russia, but no credible sources have ever been cited. In fact, scholars have been so eager to credit the idea that Dmitrii was widely regarded as an impostor that they have often made use of the extremely dubious story told by the Saxon mercenary Conrad Bussow about the tsar's closest ally, Petr Basmanov. Supposedly, Basmanov casually admitted to some of his soldiers that Dmitrii was an impostor.[165] It is, however, absurd to think that Basmanov ever committed such a foolish act of lese majesty.

The difficult truth for historians to accept is that in early 1606 Tsar Dmitrii was still a popular ruler while the conspirators represented only a relatively small group of disgruntled and ambitious individuals.[166] Nevertheless, Shuiskii's allies busied themselves by spreading false rumors, and they were secretly joined by at least a few boyars and other lords. The motivation to commit treason at this time for princes such as the Golitsyns, far from being a function of Orthodox fervor, may simply have been the closing off of any further opportunities for advancement at Tsar Dmitrii's court. Edward Keenan has reminded us that one of the only paths to power in early modern Russia was by marriage alliances with the tsar and that sharp political struggles at court over royal marriages sometimes resulted in murder. Furthermore, according to Keenan, the tsar was not free to marry whomever he pleased but was forced to take into account the wishes of his boyars and the balance of power among the boyar clans. Foreign marriages were supposedly "taboo" for the tsars because they cut off opportunities for Russian aristocrats to advance at court.[167] Keenan may have exaggerated somewhat in declaring tsarist foreign marriages taboo.[168] Nonetheless, his point is well taken, and with respect to Tsar Dmitrii is supported by at least two contemporary sources. Conrad Bussow declared that the tsar's planned wedding displeased Russian lords because "he was disregarding the daughters of the magnates," and Isaac Massa bluntly stated after Dmitrii's assassination that he would still have been in power had he, among other things, chosen to "marry a Muscovite princess."[169]

Vasilii Shuiskii probably gained an ally or two among the boyars and other Russians for gently rebuking the tsar for serving "unclean" veal at a banquet in April 1606. Mikhail Tatishchev, previously assumed to be greatly favored by

Dmitrii, stood up for Shuiskii on that occasion and was extremely rude to the tsar. Dmitrii immediately banished him from court—much to the alarm of the conspirators. It is probable that one of the traitors, Vasilii Golitsyn, somehow managed to convince his half-brother, Petr Basmanov, to prevail upon Dmitrii to forgive Tatishchev and return him to court in time for the tsar's wedding. Captain Margeret noted that everyone suspected Tatishchev was already involved in a plot against the tsar and stated that his "recall was a mistake approaching that of recalling Shuiskii, for Tatishchev was known to have a malicious temperament and to be incapable of forgetting any injury."[170] Tsar Dmitrii really was foolhardy not to be more cautious. This particular incident may have convinced Shuiskii and his co-conspirators that it was too dangerous to postpone their strike against the tsar much longer. To deflect suspicion from themselves, however, they encouraged a rumor that some lords wished to replace Dmitrii with Simeon Bekbulatovich. It is possible that, because of those rumors, Dmitrii may have ordered Simeon tonsured;[171] however, there is no evidence that the blind old man became a monk against his own wishes, and he had actually been treated very well by Tsar Dmitrii.

In spite of the defection of a few great lords, the majority of Tsar Dmitrii's boyars remained loyal to him. It was therefore necessary for the aristocratic conspirators to be extremely careful and publicly to continue to appear to be friendly to the tsar.[172] It has often been incorrectly asserted that Dmitrii, faced with growing opposition among the boyars, turned to the gentry for support.[173] In fact, Tsar Dmitrii was very popular among his troops, and he did focus much attention and resources on the pomeshchiki, but he did not do that in order to counterbalance wavering boyars. It is important to remember that the tsar was a warrior-prince with military ambition. He had personally tested the mettle of the Russian army in combat and found it wanting. In order to improve the fighting capability of his military forces, he decided it was necessary to shore up the battered, demoralized gentry militiamen.[174]

Contemporaries were struck by Dmitrii's love for and generosity to his military forces.[175] Shortly after coming to power, he ordered a general survey of the conditions of his cavalrymen to make sure they had adequate salaries and landholdings. Many, of course, did not, so the tsar lavished resources on them. He raised their salaries and, in the process, depleted an already shrinking treasury.[176] Dmitrii's enemies later claimed that he squandered the treasury frivolously;[177] but the lion's share of his expenditures were made to strengthen his military forces.[178] The tsar went out of his way to find out directly from his pomeshchiki what their problems were, and he promised to help solve them and to improve their lives.[179] Dmitrii distributed a huge amount of land to his pomeshchiki and constantly sought more for them.[180] He continued and refined Boris Godunov's policy of excluding the sons of the nongentry from the ranks of pomeste estate holders by adding sons of townsmen to the list of persons ineligible to join the militia.[181] Dmitrii also confiscated the estates of some former slaves who had been promoted into the ranks of the gentry by Tsar Boris.[182] Some historians of the peasant war school saw the removal of such "dangerous" lower class elements from the militia as an attempt to suppress a mythical "antifeudal" movement developing in the country.[183] Actually, the poor performance and unreliability of such forces, vividly demonstrated at the siege of Kromy in 1605, affected the tsar's decision far more than any alleged fear of the lower classes. Dmitrii wanted a first-rate military force and wished to set it apart from the rest of Russian society. In many ways, his "warrior caste" in formation was the logical culmination of the increasing stratification of Russian society in the late sixteenth century.[184]

In addition to shoring up the economies of the gentry, Tsar Dmitrii sharpened their martial skills by requiring his men to receive active training, especially in siege warfare. According to a contemporary, the tsar personally "took part in these exercises as a common soldier, and spared nothing to instruct the Muscovites in the science of war."[185] He also ordered the production of a large quantity of new artillery, especially mortars built to fire grenades. Dmitrii personally tested some of the new cannons.[186] In addition, the tsar ordered the construction of new ships for transporting his army and its supplies.[187] Dmitrii was also always on the lookout for foreign military specialists, and he and Captain Margeret may have introduced some basic reforms concerning infantry maneuvers in battle.[188]

Initially, Tsar Dmitrii planned possible military action against Sweden, intending to regain the port of Narva (lost to the Swedes by Ivan the Terrible) and to aid Sigismund III in his long struggle against Karl IX. By September 1605, Petr Basmanov was reported to be gathering large forces near the Swedish border.[189] The king of Poland was soon informed that up to forty thousand Russian troops were available for action against Sweden. Sigismund's great victory over Karl's forces at the battle of Kirkholm in September 1605, however, changed the strategic situation in Livonia; soon Dmitrii's offers of military aid to Poland turned into financial assistance instead.[190] It has been asserted that Tsar Dmitrii changed his mind about war with Sweden because of boyar opposition at home.[191] In fact, he really was worried about appearing to be too pro-Polish at the very same time he was making plans to marry a Polish princess. By then rumors were circulating about Dmitrii's secret promise of territorial concessions to Sigismund, and the tsar tried to scotch them by publicly quarreling over the titles the Polish king used in addressing him. At the same time, a worried King Karl was offering to recognize all of Dmitrii's titles and proposed a peace treaty with Russia.[192] What really influenced the tsar's decision to change his military plans, however, was the arrival in Moscow late in 1605 of a group of Don cossacks with the captured commander of the strategically important Tatar fortress of Azov. Dmitrii soon became extremely enthusiastic about leading a Christian crusade against the Crimean Tatars and the Turks.[193]

Tsar Dmitrii dreamed of achieving a great victory over Islam, undoubtedly influenced by Ivan the Terrible's conquest of Kazan and Astrakhan.[194] He was probably also influenced by the need to find additional lands for his gentry and the desire to pacify the southern frontier—especially the Astrakhan region, where there was continuing cossack unrest. The tsar's militiamen shared his enthusiasm about the plan.[195] Dmitrii attempted to enlist the aid of Sigismund III, the pope, and others in the crusade; he received encouraging replies but no offers of military assistance. Sigismund actually urged him to lead his army to victory over the Tatars and Turks in order to earn the title "tsar."[196] In fact, Dmitrii did plan to personally lead his army in a major campaign against the Crimean Tatars once his wedding festivities (planned for spring 1606) were completed. During the winter of 1605–6, he had huge quantities of food, munitions, and artillery, along with siege engines and a large number of troops forward based to the strategically located southern frontier fortress of Elets.[197] He also sent a sizable military force, including many streltsy, to Astrakhan under the command of Fedor Sheremetev.[198] By spring 1606, Dmitrii had reportedly massed up to one hundred thousand men in the Elets region.[199] Additional troops levied in the spring were to move south with the tsar from Moscow soon after the royal wedding. Months earlier, Tsar Dmitrii had sent a large sum of money to his future father-in-law, Jerzy Mniszech, asking him to bring with the wedding party those Polish, Belorussian, and Lithuanian veterans from Dmitrii's campaign for the throne who wished to rejoin the tsar's service for the planned crusade against Islam. More than a thousand well-armed men took him up on the offer and accompanied Marina and the wedding party to Moscow for just that purpose.[200] In preparation for the upcoming military campaign, Tsar Dmitrii apparently sent a letter to the Crimean khan in which he repeated an insulting message Ivan the Terrible had sent to the khan's predecessor many years earlier.[201]

Vasilii Shuiskii and his small group of co-conspirators decided they had to act before the tsar departed on campaign, where he would be more carefully guarded and more difficult to kill than in Moscow. They chose the tsar's upcoming wedding celebration as the time to strike and began making careful preparations. According to the flawed traditional interpretation of Tsar Dmitrii's reign, by the time his fiancée arrived in Moscow in late spring 1606, the "false tsar" was trembling in fear of boyar plots.[202] In reality, Dmitrii was well aware of rumors about plots but did not take them seriously. Instead, he remained serene and self-confident, displaying no fear of his subjects.[203] In assessing Dmitrii's last days, historians have, in general, been overly influenced by Shuiskii's propaganda campaign to discredit him once the tsar was dead. Dmitrii's enemies claimed that the trapped impostor had felt the need to take desperate measures to protect himself, and they hurled the most ridiculous charges at him.[204] For example, he was falsely accused of wanting to give land away to the Crimean Tatars or of wanting many Russian soldiers to die on his planned crusade against Islam in order to facilitate Polish Catholic colonization of Russia.[205] He was also accused of planning to massacre the boyars, the clergy, and even the inhabitants of Moscow.[206] And, of course, he continued to be accused of vile heresy, sorcery, and wild sexual misconduct. Furthermore, it has even been claimed that Dmitrii was so terrified that he planned to move the capital of Russia away from Moscow or to flee from the country in order to save his life.[207]

One of the most outrageous and enduring charges against Dmitrii was the accusation that he encouraged the cossacks to raid Russian merchants along the Volga and even invited the cossack pretender "Tsarevich Petr" to come to Moscow in order to intimidate the "false tsar's" opponents.[208] That absurd accusation has been the source of great confusion in scholarship and eventually grew into a complex "peasant war" interpretation of the desperate "Otrepev's" problems in the spring of 1606. In fact, the Terek cossacks, frustrated by their inability to shoot their way into Astrakhan during the winter of 1605–6, took their cue from Dmitrii and created their own copy-cat pretender to the throne as a pretext for raiding merchants on the Volga and possibly to gain entry into Astrakhan itself.[209] "Tsarevich Petr," represented as the son of Tsar Fedor Ivanovich, and up to four thousand Terek cossacks proceeded up the Volga and caused enough harm to gain Tsar Dmitrii's attention by April 1606.[210] In an attempt to neutralize the brigands, Dmitrii wrote to Tsarevich Petr, knowing full well that he was dealing with an impostor. According to Captain Margeret, in his letter Tsar Dmitrii invited Petr to Moscow, promising that "if he were the true son of his brother Fedor he would be welcome." However, Dmitrii added, "if he were not the true son of Fedor, he should withdraw from the emperor's lands."[211] Petr understood completely the meaning of the tsar's letter and did not ride toward Moscow. Instead, he and his men stayed safely out of Tsar Dmitrii's way.[212] Nonetheless, after Dmitrii's assassination, his enemies spread the rumor that Dmitrii had really intended to invite Petr to the capital.[213] One contemporary expressed uncertainty about the rumor's meaning, seeing in it either an expression of friendship on Dmitrii's part or as a ruse to capture the brigands.[214] Adding to the confusion, one faulty and reworked source actually had Petr writing to Dmitrii, calling him an impostor and demanding the throne for himself.[215] Those propaganda-influenced versions of events have been credited by scholars who came to view Dmitrii as a desperate impostor who hoped to use Petr against his boyar opponents.[216] In fact, Tsar Dmitrii would never have considered an alliance with Petr, and if Petr had been foolish enough to go to Moscow he would surely have been arrested and executed.[217] Part of the problem in interpreting this episode has been that historians have incorrectly assumed that Tsarevich Petr's intention from the beginning was to travel to Moscow.[218] That was clearly not the case. His goal was booty, and his path did not lead toward the capital. Petr and his cossacks may very well have been, as Margeret put it, "discontented with Dmitrii, reckoning that they had not been recompensed by him as they had hoped to be."[219] Those brigands were in no position, however, to threaten Tsar Dmitrii. Among other things, the tsar had a large army advancing down the Volga toward Astrakhan at that very same time.[220]

The most extreme interpretation of the Tsarevich Petr episode was put forward by Vadim Koretskii, a major contributor to the Marxist model of the First Peasant War. Whereas most scholars—correctly—viewed the Bolotnikov rebellion as being triggered by Tsar Dmitrii's assassination;[221] Koretskii and a few other scholars have asserted that Tsar Dmitrii was himself facing an impending peasant rebellion before his assassination and, in desperation, suddenly changed his policies in the spring of 1606 in order to appease cossacks and peasants.[222] According to Koretskii, Tsar Dmitrii was caught between a growing boyar conspiracy and a mass revolt against serfdom and the entire feudal order. In desperation he turned to Tsarevich Petr in a bid to shore up his position with the masses. Supposedly, if Dmitrii had not agreed to placate the cossacks and peasants, or perhaps even begin some kind of class war against the boyars, his own authority over the southern frontier would have evaporated—he would no longer be considered the "true tsar" by Tsarevich Petr and others. Therefore, Dmitrii was forced to seek an alliance with Petr and to make plans to fulfill the social utopian dreams of his lower class supporters. Koretskii described a terrified Dmitrii making hasty plans to restore the St. George's Day privilege of peasant departure and being assassinated by the boyars before he could implement such a radical policy. But the assassination, we are told, only served to intensify the developing peasant war.[223]

Koretskii's fantastic theory, which demands the suspension of many of the most basic assumptions of early modern Russian political culture, was based upon incredibly shaky evidence. Koretskii cited growing unrest in southern Russia during the winter of 1605–6. It is, however, by no means clear that the winter disturbance on the southern frontier should have been of any real concern to Tsar Dmitrii. Even Koretskii was forced to admit that it was not aimed against Dmitrii but rather naïvely against some unpopular local administrators who had acted unfairly and without the tsar's consent or knowledge. Indeed, in the spring of 1606, just when he was supposedly most fearful of revolt, Tsar Dmitrii ordered punishment for those men responsible for the disturbance. Whatever one makes of this incident, Dmitrii's response to it certainly does not lend much support to Koretskii's view of the period. Koretskii also tried to portray Tsarevich Petr as a social revolutionary whose very existence was a symptom of a growing peasant rebellion and around whom the disgruntled population of the southern frontier supposedly began gathering in a menacing mass movement.[224] There is, in fact, very little evidence of burning class consciousness and commitment to class war operating in Petr's mind in the spring of 1606. For all his later representation as a social revolutionary, at that time Petr was just an adventurer; brigandage, not revolution, was uppermost in the minds of Petr's followers.[225] Even if Petr had been a true revolutionary in the spring of 1606, he probably would not have found all that many supporters to join him in rebellion against Tsar Dmitrii. Many southerners, after all, had fought for Dmitrii in 1604–5 and later had their tax burden lowered by him. Koretskii certainly did not prove that the southern provinces were on the verge of rebellion against Tsar Dmitrii.

Koretskii assumed that, by the time of Petr's appearance, Tsar Dmitrii had already made up his mind to change his policies in order to placate the masses. The plots in Moscow against the tsar were cited as evidence that Dmitrii was probably ready to turn against the Russian aristocracy. Actually, there is no evidence that Dmitrii took any of those plots seriously or ever considered a radical change in his policies. What evidence did Koretskii cite to show that Dmitrii was about to change his social policies in the spring of 1606? He was able to cite only one undated, unsigned document concerning the restoration of the peasants' right to move after the fall harvest. Koretskii believed that this controversial document (the *Svodnyi sudebnik*) was a rough draft of Tsar Dmitrii's new law code and represented the tsar's desperate attempt to placate the masses, an attempt that virtually guaranteed his assassination by the lords.[226] However, Koretskii provided a weak case at best for Dmitrii needing to placate the masses, and the Svodnyi sudebnik by itself does not provide enough additional evidence to prove his theory. It is worth noting that not all Soviet historians were convinced that the Svodnyi sudebnik in any way represented Dmitrii's thinking or even belonged to the period of his reign.[227]

Despite all the confusion in sources and historiography, it is clear that Tsar Dmitrii ruled in the interests of the lords and never contemplated the abolition of serfdom.[228] His peasant policy was actually more conservative than Boris Godunov's.[229] Dmitrii's decrees on slaves and fugitive peasants, made in early 1606, have been somewhat misleadingly described as "concessions" to his lower class supporters in order to maintain his appearance as a "good tsar."[230] It is true that the tsar did prevent lords from using loopholes in the law to retain a slave who legally sought freedom after his master's death.[231] Dmitrii also prevented lords who had forced their peasants to flee during the famine (by not feeding them) from being able to forcibly return those miserable souls to bondage.[232] Nonetheless, Tsar Dmitrii clearly ruled in the interests of the lords. Serfs not returned to their old masters were not freed; they were merely tied to the land of the lords who had fed them.[233] Some scholars, recognizing the enserfing nature of Tsar Dmitrii's social policies, claimed that Dmitrii's peasant policy specifically favored the gentry of southern provinces who had supported him during his campaign for the throne.[234] Richard Hellie, however, has effectively countered that faulty notion.[235] Tsar Dmitrii actively supported his entire gentry, not just southern pomeshchiki, and the Russian gentry strongly approved of his social policies.

Close analysis of Tsar Dmitrii's reign reveals that, despite Shuiskii propaganda and historians' hostility toward him, Dmitrii was a popular ruler who was not facing an impending social revolution or any kind of rebellion when he fell victim to Shuiskii's conspiracy during the tsar's wedding celebration in May 1606.[236] It was the regicide and usurper, Vasilii Shuiskii, who faced the "Bolotnikov rebellion." In many ways, it is the assassination of Tsar Dmitrii that provides the key to understanding the real Time of Troubles, the rekindled civil war that raged in Russia from 1606 to 1612.

13

Assassination of the Tsar

On May 2, 1606, Tsar Dmitrii's fiancée, Marina Mniszech, arrived in Moscow in the grandest procession seen in the capital since the entry of Ivan III's bride-to-be, the Byzantine princess Zoe Paleologue, in 1472.[1] According to the traditional interpretation of the Time of Troubles, by that time the "false tsar" had already lost the respect and support of his people, and the arrival of the Catholic princess and many unruly Polish wedding guests only served to bring matters to a head. Vasilii Shuiskii supposedly led an aroused Orthodox Christian population in a deadly assault on the heretic Otrepev and his Catholic friends, after which the highly popular and patriotic Shuiskii was chosen to be the new tsar. In fact, that is not at all what happened. Instead, the popular tsar's murder and Shuiskii's seizure of power rekindled the civil war. For that reason, it is necessary to take a close look at the tsar's assassination and its immediate aftermath.[2]

It had taken half a year, but by the time of Marina Mniszech's arrival in Moscow, Vasilii Shuiskii managed to stitch together a relatively small group of conspirators who were determined to assassinate Tsar Dmitrii. Shuiskii and his co-conspirators regarded the approaching royal wedding celebration as their last and best chance to get rid of the tsar before he uncovered their plot or departed on his campaign against the Crimean Tatars. By spring 1606, Shuiskii could count on the support of some individuals at court, in the church, and among the merchant elite. In fact, his allies in treason were remarkably similar to those assembled by his kinsman, Prince Ivan Petrovich Shuiskii, in the latter's unsuccessful coup against Boris Godunov during the 1580s. In addition to a few boyars, church officials, and his family's own trusted friends and servitors, Vasilii Shuiskii was able to gain the support of several disgruntled merchants.[3]

The Shuiskiis traditionally enjoyed the support of rich merchants in Moscow and other leading towns such as Novgorod, Pskov, and Smolensk.[4] Russia's leading merchants had, of course, sworn an oath of loyalty to Tsar Dmitrii and remained publicly loyal to him.[5] Nonetheless, during the Time of Troubles (a period of serious economic dislocation) the nervous gosti felt compelled to become increasingly involved in political activity in order to protect their inter-ests.[6] Although Dmitrii was sympathetic to their needs, many Russian mer-chants were frightened by the tsar's active pursuit of free trade with the West—which may have reminded them of Ivan the Terrible's unpopular policy of favoring foreign merchants.[7] Shuiskii took note of that anxiety and arranged many secret meetings with unhappy merchants.[8] Some Smolensk merchants were not only ardently anti-Polish and fearful of being overwhelmed by the loss of their exclusive trade privileges; they were also, along with other members of the local military and bureaucratic elite, upset that one of Tsar Dmitrii's favorites, Vasilii M. Mosalskii, acquired some of the best Smolensk lands for himself and was getting rich at their expense. Quietly, Shuiskii managed to gain the sup-port of several Smolensk merchants and dozens of Smolensk-based militiamen.[9] The Shuiskii clan had long had close ties to Novgorod and Pskov, and Vasilii Shuiskii could also count on the support of several merchants and more than a hundred pomeshchiki from those two towns.[10] Novgorod, in particular, had no fond recollections of Dmitrii's father, Ivan the Terrible.[11] In addition to bad memories of the oprichnina and the apparent threat posed by Dmitrii's trade policy, Shuiskii benefited to a considerable extent from King Karl IX's constant bombardment of Novgorod and other northwestern Russian towns with pro-paganda about Dmitrii as a tool of the Jesuits who planned to hand over Novgorod, Pskov, and Smolensk to Sigismund III.[12] Also working to Shuiskii's advantage, Tsar Dmitrii had borrowed money from his leading merchants to support his planned campaign against the Crimean Tatars. In addition, some Moscow merchants were forced to provide accommodations for the tsar's numer-ous wedding guests arriving from Poland—which apparently made them angry.[13]

The fact that Tsar Dmitrii was marrying a Catholic princess did not settle well with many conservative Orthodox Russians, and the arrival of her large entourage provided many opportunities to spread rumors about the "false tsar's" evil plans. In the first place, among the several thousand Polish wedding guests and attendants were nearly two thousand veterans of Dmitrii's campaign for the throne who planned to join his crusade against the Crimean Tatars—for which reason they brought their weapons, armor, and provisions with them to Moscow. The sight of all those foreign soldiers and their weapons entering the capital, as if in another victory parade, made many Russians nervous and played right into the hands of conspirators who whispered about heinous Polish plots.[14] Skrynnikov claimed that a frightened "Otrepev" had summoned those Polish troops to Moscow to shore up his eroding position. That is not true; the tsar was not frightened, and his situation was far from desperate.[15] There were so many wedding guests arriving in Moscow, however, that they had to be lodged all over the city and not concentrated near the Kremlin. Some were quartered in the homes of rich merchants, bishops, and courtiers who may very well have resented the imposition.[16] A far more serious problem was the behavior of many of those guests during the two weeks of wedding festivities. In addition to being arrogant and condescending to the less sophisticated Russians, they stole things, assaulted their hosts, and destroyed property. Some drunken Poles got involved in minor quarrels with the local population, and there were even a few violent confrontations on the streets. The misbehavior of the wedding guests greatly disturbed the Muscovites, and Shuiskii was able to feed their growing anger and to make use of it. His agents may actually have staged a few of the confrontations in order to make the Poles look especially odious to the Russians.[17]

Part of the growing resentment against the "Latin heretics" in Moscow was because the arrogant and unruly Polish guests received special treatment and access to the tsar during the wedding festivities, privileges not extended to most of the population of the capital.[18] That Tsar Dmitrii actually allowed Polish Catholics into Orthodox cathedrals also must have outraged some religious conservatives.[19] Unfortunately, the combination of Shuiskii propaganda and historians' own prejudices against Tsar Dmitrii has produced a grossly inaccurate picture of angry boyars and bishops forced by an evil "Otrepev" to participate in a scandalous and sacrilegious marriage ceremony—a ceremony so shocking in its violation of Orthodox customs that it greatly helped Shuiskii stir the outraged population of Moscow against the heretic tsar and his Catholic friends.[20] That was exactly what Shuiskii wanted everyone to believe, but it is far from the truth.

As noted in the last chapter, Tsar Dmitrii did face some initial opposition to his plan to marry a Catholic, but in the end his boyars and all but one of his bishops signed off on the marriage agreement, including the provision for Marina to remain a Catholic.[21] It was necessary, as a result of that agreement, to make some changes in the wedding ceremony that normally required the bride and groom to take Orthodox communion together. The issue was resolved to the satisfaction of the patriarch by substituting the anointment and crowning of Marina as tsaritsa for the communion ceremony.[22] Solely on the basis of accusations made by Shuiskii after Dmitrii's assassination (based on testimony coerced from Dmitrii's secretary), Platonov claimed that "those experienced in canon law" were angered by that innovation and that Shuiskii's agents explained its significance to the crowds and stirred the mood of the capital to a "revolutionary boil."[23] Skrynnikov also credited the same propaganda about clerical opposition to the wedding arrangements and Dmitrii's fear that church leaders might balk at the last minute.[24] In fact, there is no credible evidence for such sim-

Fig. 9 "Tsaritsa Marina Mniszech." Printed in Stanislaw Grochowski's Wedding
Brochure, 1605. From D. A. Rovinskii, *Materialy dlia Russkoi Ikonografii,* part 2
(St. Petersburg, 1884). Courtesy of Houghton Library, Harvard University.

mering opposition to the improvised wedding plans. Boyars and church leaders actively participated in all parts of the wedding and coronation ceremonies.[25] Even Vasilii Shuiskii played a prominent role, demonstrating that the clement and naïve Tsar Dmitrii had restored him to favor.[26] Some supporters of the traditional interpretation have adamantly refused to credit eyewitness reports of the Russian elite kissing Marina's hand because of their erroneous belief that a powerful rebellion against the "false tsar" was then developing.[27] As hard as it may be to accept, however, most of the Russian elite and the common people were not outraged by violations of Orthodox customs in the tsar's wedding ceremonies, and there was no powerful rebellion brewing against Dmitrii. In fact, the residents of Moscow welcomed Marina and a large crowd applauded the bride-to-be on her wedding day.[28]

Shuiskii propaganda claimed that Tsar Dmitrii was severely criticized by his subjects for scheduling his wedding ceremony on an Orthodox holy day, an action which supposedly greatly upset the boyars, church officials, and the common people.[29] In fact, the tsar wanted the wedding held four days earlier but was somehow overruled by the boyars who planned the event. Perhaps his secret enemies were responsible for the delay.[30] On the other hand, it should be remembered that no bishop or boyar objected to the timing of the unorthodox wedding celebration, and the overwhelming majority of Muscovites were not the least bit angry with their tsar.[31]

Muscovites did grow increasingly outraged by the continued misbehavior of some of the Polish wedding guests. Those Poles inadvertently aided Shuiskii's conspiracy by stirring the capital's population to a near boil. Shuiskii's whispering campaign against the tsar emphasized that the impostor condoned or was at least unwilling to stop the misconduct of the "Latin heretics," and by May 12, that rumor campaign was in high gear.[32] It culminated in the absurd claim that the tsar intended to massacre his boyars, clergy, and merchants during an artillery display being prepared for the wedding guests just outside Moscow.[33] The fact that Dmitrii's father, Ivan the Terrible, had dealt cruelly with Novgorod, his boyars, and church officials and was reported to have once threatened to kill all the inhabitants of Moscow may have influenced the content of Shuiskii's absurd rumor and its credulous reception in certain quarters.[34] Based on a comment made by Isaac Massa, Skrynnikov once wrote that in this particular case Shuiskii's agitation was successful and led to a large-scale popular disturbance on the night of May 14, during which thousands of conspirators supposedly armed themselves and prepared to strike against Dmitrii but were forestalled by the timely arrival of forces loyal to the tsar at key points in the city.[35] In more recent publications, Skrynnikov came to doubt Massa's faulty information and acknowledged that the popular disturbance on the night of May 14 was aimed against the unruly Poles, not against Tsar Dmitrii, and that the plot against the tsar really was "strictly conspiratorial" and did not involve large numbers of people. Indeed, Skrynnikov also came to acknowledge that, even as late as May 1606, Tsar Dmitrii had no reason to worry about the devotion of the overwhelming majority of his subjects.[36]

The serious disturbance on the night of May 14 was actually caused by the death of a Russian at the hands of one of the Polish wedding guests. Approximately four thousand Russians, many of them armed, descended on the residence where the death occurred and demanded the surrender of the guilty man. The alarmed Poles reacted by arming and barricading themselves and then randomly firing their weapons all night long. Upon learning of the developing confrontation, Tsar Dmitrii correctly feared the Muscovites might launch an assault on all the Polish wedding guests and quickly dispatched thousands of streltsy to restore order. He also summoned all his guards and put them on twenty-four hour duty. The potentially dangerous incident quickly passed, but the tsar's officials were now constantly besieged by complaints about the misconduct of the wedding guests. Just as Shuiskii hoped, Moscow had become a powderkeg filled with seething Russians itching to teach the Poles a lesson.[37]

It has been said that the tsar was completely distracted by his new bride and therefore failed to take seriously numerous reports he received of plots against his life. It is actually more likely that the rising tide of indignation against the Poles diverted his attention. In Tsar Dmitrii's final days, he was warned repeatedly by his father-in-law, his secretary Jan Buczynski, Petr Basmanov, and the officers of his foreign guard of a conspiracy against him. Dmitrii authorized the seizure of some indiscreet agitators but did not take any of the rumors seriously. His guards also rounded up a few suspicious characters who admitted that there was a plot against the tsar; but, somehow, treacherous boyars—probably the Golitsyns—successfully encouraged Dmitrii to ignore the evidence as just one more groundless rumor and to dismiss the warnings of his foreign officers as nervous overreactions.[38] Dmitrii himself was utterly fearless and extremely confident of the devotion of his subjects. He therefore insisted that Basmanov and others concentrate on protecting the Polish wedding guests from danger, and he even reproached his father-in-law for faintheartedness. The tsar actually ordered half of his own weary foreign guard to stand down from the alert of May 14–15 in order to get some much-needed rest.[39] No doubt Dmitrii could easily have prevented his assassination by taking the rumors circulating in Moscow seriously and by increasing his personal security. He was a popular ruler and would have immediately prevailed over any unmasked conspirators, including Vasilii Shuiskii.[40] By failing to heed the repeated warnings of his closest advisers, Tsar Dmitrii committed a fatal error.

On the night of May 15–16, six assassins managed to slip into the Kremlin before they were detected. Three were immediately killed; the other three were tortured but did not reveal Shuiskii's involvement or plans.[41] Even at that point, Tsar Dmitrii still did not show much concern or take any special precautions. The fact that the captain of his bodyguard, Jacques Margeret (who had been warning Dmitrii about the plots against him), suddenly fell seriously ill (or was poisoned) and could not show up for work may help to explain the lack of adequate security just before the tsar was assassinated.[42] Some historians incorrectly credited a report by Isaac Massa that, on the day before the tsar was killed, an ultra-Orthodox secretary named Timofei Osipov was sent to the Kremlin by the conspirators to martyr himself by openly denouncing Dmitrii as the heretic Otrepev. According to Skrynnikov, after being tortured, Osipov revealed the conspirators' plans, which in turn alarmed Shuiskii and forced him to act without delay.[43] In fact, Massa's chronology was confused, and Skrynnikov misread his sources. Osipov's denunciation probably occurred in January 1606, and he did not reveal Shuiskii's plot. Nor was he martyred; instead, he was sent into exile.[44] May 16 actually passed without serious incident, but after the six assassins had been caught in the Kremlin, Shuiskii and his co-conspirators could not afford to wait any longer. Instead, they devised an ingenious plan and set it in motion very early on the morning of May 17, 1606.

After Dmitrii's assassination, the usurper Vasilii Shuiskii falsely claimed that he had led the entire Orthodox population of Moscow against the evil "Otrepev."[45] Instead of thousands, Shuiskii actually led a few hundred persons. He was acutely aware of the narrowness of his base of support and the popularity of Tsar Dmitrii, and for that reason he was forced to resort to a ruse in order to distract the population of Moscow during the assassination.[46] Some historians have erroneously credited later propaganda about the involvement in the conspiracy of persons close to the tsar—the false tsar's "mother," members of the Romanov clan, Prince Mstislavskii, and Captain Margeret.[47] There is also confusion in sources and in scholarship about the exact whereabouts and involvement of other boyars such as Petr Sheremetev.[48]

Skrynnikov boldly and incorrectly asserted that Sigismund III and his ambassador to Russia, Alexander Gosiewski, were among Shuiskii's co-conspirators.[49] On the basis of incredibly poor sources, Skrynnikov concluded that the Polish king became so angry because of Dmitrii's failure to cede territory to him or to promptly convert Russia to Catholicism that he joined the boyars in the conspiracy to kill the tsar—hoping to place his son Wladyslaw on the Russian throne.[50] As noted in the last chapter, Skrynnikov also conjectured that Dmitrii was actively working with Polish rebels, thereby virtually forcing Sigismund to join Shuiskii's plot against him.[51] In fact, there is no evidence of any involvement by Sigismund in Dmitrii's assassination, just as there is no evidence of Dmitrii supporting Polish rebels. It is true, however, that Sigismund and the Jesuits were frustrated by the tsar's lack of interest in converting Russia to Catholicism and by his association with Protestants.[52] It is also true that in May 1606 Dmitrii quarreled with Ambassador Gosiewski over Sigismund's continued unwillingness to recognize all of Dmitrii's titles. In frustration, Dmitrii informed the Jesuits that he might be forced to delay his planned crusade and to use force against the king because of the dispute over titles.[53] By doing this, the tsar was not planning to attack Poland; he was actually continuing his strategy of public quarrels with the Poles in order to counter sentiment that he was too friendly to those "Latin heretics." Dmitrii was also applying strong diplomatic pressure to get his titles recognized; he knew full well that the Jesuits would report his comments to King Sigismund and to the pope—both of whom very much wanted Dmitrii to lead his crusade against Islam. Despite Catholic frustration with Dmitrii, the pope appealed to Sigismund in April 1606 to work out his problems with the tsar, assuring the king that Dmitrii loved him and would help expel the Turks from Europe.[54] That certainly did not amount to a papal sanction to topple Dmitrii. For what it is worth, after the tsar's assassination, the usurper Shuiskii did not rush to thank Sigismund for aid in getting rid of Dmitrii but instead accused the king of meddling in Russia's internal affairs by having supported the dead tsar.[55]

Who was involved in Shuiskii's conspiracy? Some members of the boyar council were participants, but not many.[56] Vasilii Shuiskii's brothers, Dmitrii and Ivan, along with his nephew, okolnichii Mikhail Skopin-Shuiskii, were definitely involved; so too were Vasilii and Ivan Golitsyn. Vasilii Shuiskii's friend, okolnichii Ivan Kriuk-Kolychev, and the recently pardoned okolnichii Mikhail Tatishchev were also active participants, along with Boris Tatev.[57] Some monks and priests were involved and possibly a few high-ranking clerics as well.[58] A significant number of merchants from Novgorod, Pskov, Smolensk, and Moscow participated in the conspiracy.[59] The Saxon mercenary Conrad Bussow erroneously wrote that Shuiskii gathered all the leaders of the Moscow posad together to discuss plans to arouse the entire population of the capital against Dmitrii.[60] Shuiskii did, in fact, attract some posad leaders to his cause but certainly not the mass of the city's population.[61] The Moscow garrison and militiamen in general were also definitely not involved in the coup.[62]

Somehow Shuiskii managed to arrange, without causing alarm, for the convenient arrival in the Moscow suburbs of about two hundred trusted dvoriane and deti boiarskie from Novgorod, Pskov, and Smolensk—who were ostensibly on their way to join the tsar's army at Elets as soon as the royal wedding celebration was finished.[63] Under cover of darkness during the night of May 16–17, those men were secretly brought into the city to carry out the assassination.[64]

In a carefully coordinated operation just before dawn on Saturday, May 17, 1606, armed horsemen led by the Shuiskiis and Golitsyns approached the Kremlin's Frolov gate, which linked the Kremlin to Red Square. The streltsy on guard there recognized the powerful boyars and suspected nothing. They were taken completely by surprise in an assault led by Vasilii Golitsyn and Mikhail Tatishchev. As soon as the assassins secured the gate, they let about two hundred armed warriors and a few merchants into the Kremlin who immediately made their way to Dmitrii's palace.[65] At that very moment, other conspirators began sounding the tocsin to rouse the population of Moscow. Bells in the district occupied by merchants from Novgorod and Pskov started the clamor, soon followed by bells in the Kremlin's Cathedral of the Assumption (Uspenskii Sobor) and then everywhere throughout the capital.[66] At that point, Vasilii Shuiskii sent heralds out in all directions to shout the same electrifying message: "Brothers, the Poles want to assassinate the tsar! Do not let them into the Kremlin!" Shuiskii himself swiftly rode from the Frolov gate across Red Square toward a crowd of merchants and artisans who had been preparing for the day's business. Pretending to be concerned about the tsar's safety, he quickly stirred the crowd against the hated Polish wedding guests.[67] The misdeeds of some Poles during the previous two weeks made Shuiskii's lies easy to believe. Soon, Moscow's streets overflowed with angry Russians who completely blocked access to the Kremlin and paralyzed attempts by the tsar's foreign guard and streltsy units to return there to protect Dmitrii. As Isaac Massa described it, "by this ruse, the Poles, seized with terror and armed in their houses, were pinned down by the multitude outside" who were "eager to pillage and murder all of them."[68] The population of Moscow fell on the Poles and other foreigners in a bloodthirsty rage, and there was a terrible massacre. Even monks, priests, and children participated in the carnage.[69] Foreign merchants were singled out for beatings and looting, just as they had been during the riot which helped topple Fedor Godunov the year before. Most of those men survived, but many lost their entire fortunes.[70] During six or seven hours of rioting, the Russians killed approximately four hundred twenty Poles, mostly guards and servants. Many other foreigners also perished, and hundreds of Russians were killed by the spirited defense put up by some Poles. One Polish lord's retainers killed nearly three hundred rioters.[71] Contemporary estimates of the total number of dead that day ranged from five hundred to three thousand five hundred.[72]

Meanwhile, as the tocsin first sounded, the assassins quickly made their way to Tsar Dmitrii's palace. As already noted, Dmitrii had dismissed half his guards from duty on May 15; by the morning of May 17, his bodyguard was still not back up to full strength. Instead of the usual one hundred guards, there were fewer than fifty on duty—perhaps as few as thirty—and not even a single officer.[73] The assassins killed a few of the guards as they forced their way into Dmitrii's palace. At that point, the tsar sent Basmanov from his chambers to find out what the alarm was about, and as soon as he emerged Tatishchev killed him.[74] Then, as the assassins crowded into the palace, the tsar and a few guards retreated to an inner room and locked the doors. While the attackers broke the doors down, Dmitrii shouted a quick warning to his bride and her ladies-in-waiting, who were in an adjacent room, and then he attempted to jump from a window to a nearby building. But he slipped and fell to the ground far below, which broke his leg.[75] Had he made it to the other building and managed to reach the crowd pouring into the Kremlin to save him, there is little doubt that he would have survived. As Massa put it, "the townspeople would have massacred the lords and conspirators."[76] As it turned out, the dazed tsar was temporarily rescued by a few nearby streltsy who opened fire on the assassins as they rushed forward to finish their task. The streltsy managed to kill one or two traitors before being overwhelmed by them. Tsar Dmitrii pleaded with the assassins to ask his mother if he was the real Dmitrii or to take him to Red Square and let him speak.[77] The assassins, however, could not afford to bring him before the people.[78] Fearing the rapid approach of crowds of Tsar Dmitrii's loyal subjects, the traitors quickly killed the tsar. Under the gaze of Vasilii Golitsyn, a merchant named Mylnikov denounced Dmitrii as a heretic and shot him.[79] Then the assassins hacked the tsar to death, leaving at least twenty one wounds and smashing in his skull.[80] So ended the life of a remarkable person.

The traitors had succeeded in killing the tsar, but their work was far from done. They were well aware of Dmitrii's popularity and of the need to quickly justify their outrageous actions. While plotting Dmitrii's murder, Shuiskii and his co-conspirators had carefully planned a whole series of maneuvers to make their victim appear odious to the people and to sever the powerful bond between him and the masses.[81] From the very moment the assassins killed Dmitrii, they falsely shouted to the confused crowd gathering around them that the tsar had admitted that he was Otrepev before his death. Vasilii Golitsyn added another bold lie: that Dmitrii's mother had already declared him an impostor.[82] The bodies of the tsar and Petr Basmanov were stripped naked. A cord was tied around Dmitrii's genitals, another around his feet, and a third around Basmanov's feet. Then they were dragged out of the Kremlin to Red Square.[83] The assassins passed Marfa's residence on the way and asked her if the dead tsar was really her son. Obviously in shock, she replied that they should have asked her while he was still alive.[84] It actually took the Nagoi clan more than a week to recover from the assassination and to decide on their best survival strategy in light of Dmitrii's death. Once Vasilii Shuiskii managed to become tsar, however, the Nagois wisely joined his propaganda campaign to denounce the "impostor" and "heretic"—thereby preserving their lives, their freedom, their property, and much of their status at court.[85]

The principal technique Shuiskii chose to justify the assassination was an elaborate attempt to demonize Tsar Dmitrii. Since Dmitrii was widely regarded as a sacred figure who had restored God's grace to Russia, it was deemed essential to desacralize him by demonstrating that he had been an evil impostor and heretic whom Shuiskii and others had been forced to kill in order to protect the Russian Orthodox Church and the Russian people.[86] Tsar Dmitrii was denounced as a tool of the devil and as the Antichrist;[87] but Shuiskii chose to focus primarily on a dramatic propaganda campaign asserting that the false tsar had been a sorcerer who had profaned icons and crosses and had communicated with unclean spirits.[88] In fact, Dmitrii himself may have given Shuiskii the idea by his own denunciation of Tsar Boris as a sorcerer, by having Godunov's "unclean" palace razed, and by ordering the removal of Tsar Boris's body from the Kremlin.[89] If Shuiskii could successfully demonstrate that Dmitrii had been a sorcerer in league with Satan, the Russian people would then be released from their sacred oath to him and the assassination would be justified.[90] Shuiskii dreamed that a grateful population would then want him, their savior, to be the next tsar.

Within the context of early modern Russian culture, one of the most obvious and convenient ways for the assassins to demonstrate that Tsar Dmitrii had been a sorcerer was simply to associate him with the controversial *skomorokhi*, Russian minstrels who were then generally feared and respected as magicians. Church leaders hated the minstrels and their musical instruments, which they associated with witchcraft. During the sixteenth century, the Russian Orthodox Church had launched a major campaign against the minstrels as tools of the devil and of the Antichrist,[91] and none other than Ivan the Terrible himself had established the precedent of humiliating an opponent by dressing him up as a minstrel, complete with bagpipes.[92] The idea of repeating that technique to humiliate and demonize Tsar Dmitrii appealed to Shuiskii, who choreographed a most bizarre spectacle for the residents of Moscow.[93]

Early in the afternoon of May 17, as the Muscovites' bloody assaults on the

Poles were just beginning to calm down, the rioters on Red Square were dumb-founded by the horrible spectacle of the dead and naked tsar being dragged toward them from the Kremlin. Before and behind Dmitrii's corpse went con-spirators carrying masks used by Russian minstrels and shouting to the crowd: "Here are the gods whom he adored!"[94] Dmitrii's body was unceremoniously placed on a small table with his feet resting on the corpse of Petr Basmanov. One of the conspirators then placed a minstrel's bagpipe in Dmitrii's mouth and a minstrel's mask on his belly. That was done specifically to show that the tsar had been immoral and in league with the devil.[95] Shouts about the mask being the false tsar's god were followed by a list of complaints about Tsar Dmitrii as a spendthrift and heretic who had planned to destroy the Russian Orthodox Church as well as the boyars and other innocent Orthodox Christian subjects.[96] Among the charges leveled against the dead tsar was that minstrels' masks instead of icons hung on his walls, while holy icons were shoved under his bed;[97] that was especially indicative of sorcery to many Russians.[98] Another charge was that Tsar Dmitrii and Tsaritsa Marina preferred to go to the bathhouse instead of to church;[99] bathhouses and such impious behavior were also closely associated with sorcery in early modern Russia.[100] The assassins also referred to the dead tsar as a "pagan" and as a "Polish minstrel."[101]

The people of Moscow were stunned by the assassination of Tsar Dmitrii and by the grotesque display of his body. The corpse lay on Red Square for three days for all to see; Dmitrii was even denied the dignity of a Christian burial. A few Shuiskii supporters came forward from time to time to curse the dead tsar, to subject his body to further humiliation, or to make lewd jokes about him.[102] Many other puzzled and upset Russians examined Dmitrii's mutilated and dirty body and wondered what had really happened. Vasilii Shuiskii was, of course, hoping that his efforts to demonize Dmitrii would prove effective and that things would quickly calm down in the capital—just as they had after Fedor Godunov was toppled the year before. That would then allow him to concen-trate on the upcoming struggle against his boyar opponents for the vacant throne. But, even as Shuiskii turned his attention to becoming tsar, his oppo-nents were already actively spreading rumors that—once again—Dmitrii had miraculously escaped assassination and would soon return to punish the trai-tors. Just hours after Dmitrii's body had been placed on public display, a rumor began to circulate in Moscow that a foreigner who resembled the tsar had been killed in his place.[103] Soon, a syn boiarskii dramatically rode up to the corpse, inspected it, and shouted: "You have not killed the true Dmitrii—he has escaped!"[104] A French merchant well acquainted with the tsar also examined the body and expressed doubt that it was really Dmitrii.[105] The corpse was by then not easy to identify, but several observers continued to remark on differences between it and Tsar Dmitrii.[106] Rumors of the tsar's escape snowballed within a few days into a potent weapon against Shuiskii, fanned by members of the dead tsar's inner circle then being held prisoner—including his secretaries, his chamberlain, his widow, his father-in-law, and several Russian lords.[107] Most sophisticated Russians and foreigners did not believe those rumors and correctly regarded them as part of a plot against Shuiskii.[108] However, many ordinary Russians were quite willing to believe that Dmitrii had somehow managed to cheat death again—no doubt with God's help.[109]

The assassination of Tsar Dmitrii opened the path for Vasilii Shuiskii to become tsar, but he was never able to put Dmitrii's ghost to rest. Within weeks of his seizure of power, Tsar Vasilii was confronted by a full-scale civil war once again fought in the name of the miraculously rescued "true tsar" Dmitrii. That rekindled civil war raged for years and eventually toppled Shuiskii from the throne, but it also very nearly destroyed the country.[110]

14

Vasilii Shuiskii Seizes Power and Rekindles the Civil War

During the afternoon of May 17, 1606, as news of Tsar Dmitrii's assassination spread throughout Moscow and as rumors began to circulate that he had some-how managed to escape death once again, leading boyars rode around the capital calming people down and restoring some semblance of order to the streets. Rioting and looting gradually died down and gave way to drinking plundered liquor.[1] Some people celebrated the day's bloody events; many others were in shock because of the tsar's assassination and wept bitter tears.[2] That evening the boyars locked themselves in the Kremlin for a tense all-night session to deal with the crisis brought on by the assassination and riot and to begin delibera-tions on choosing a new tsar.[3] Just because Vasilii Shuiskii had successfully con-spired to kill Dmitrii did not automatically mean he could count on becoming tsar. In trying to establish his claim, Shuiskii painted Dmitrii in the darkest colors and tried to present himself as a fierce defender of the Russian Orthodox Church and as the chief sufferer at the hands of the evil "false tsar."[4] Shuiskii was portrayed by his supporters as the most popular man in Moscow who had heroically led the people against the heretic "Otrepev" and was, therefore, worthy of the crown.[5] In truth, however, many Muscovites would gladly have killed Shuiskii as a traitor, and they worked actively to prevent him from becoming tsar.

The boyar council was, of course, in turmoil. Tsar Dmitrii had many friends and supporters on the council who were outraged by his assassination and were resolved to seek revenge against Shuiskii, but the very fact of Tsar Dmitrii's death greatly complicated their plans. Taken by surprise, none of them felt him-self to be in a strong enough position to risk immediate, open confrontation with Shuiskii and his shrill propaganda campaign against the dead tsar. Such a confrontation would have swiftly and inevitably ended in bloodshed because Shuiskii and his coconspirators were guilty of regicide and would obviously fight for their lives. In addition, since Tsar Dmitrii had no heir or powerful Russian clan of in-laws around whom to rally, his allies at first lacked a strong leader or even a coherent strategy.

In sharp contrast, Shuiskii had worked out a clear plan. He gained great tactical advantage by presenting the coup and demonization of the "false tsar" as a fait accompli to the population of Moscow and to his fellow boyars. Making it even harder for Shuiskii's opponents to object to his portrayal of Tsar Dmitrii, the assassins rather conveniently found a handful of compromising documents in the Kremlin that they declared proved that Dmitrii was a secret Catholic involved in a diabolical plot with the Poles to destroy Russia. Shuiskii made sure that "Otrepev's" alleged evil intentions were given maximum publicity.[6] As a result, Dmitrii's supporters on the boyar council were uncertain of the outcome of an open confrontation with Shuiskii. In addition to being personally dangerous, such a breach might plunge the country into civil war. The political culture of early modern Russia's ruling elite militated strongly against such a risk and virtually dictated that some kind of compromise be worked out, at least temporarily.[7] Reluctantly, therefore, the dead tsar's supporters among the boyars decided at least publicly to accept Shuiskii's demonization of Dmitrii as the necessary price to restore order, to avoid civil war, and to protect their own lives, property, and status at court. That did not mean, however, that they would support Shuiskii's claim to the throne. He was forced to maneuver for the crown.

All factions on the boyar council could at least agree on one thing: none of them wanted Patriarch Ignatii to play the role of kingmaker that Patriarch Iov had tried to play in 1598. Even Tsar Dmitrii's allies accepted the logic of getting rid of Ignatii once they had agreed not to publicly challenge the demonization of the dead tsar. Moreover, choosing a new patriarch presented opportunities not just for Shuiskii but also for his opponents. After meeting all night long, the boyar council announced on the morning of May 18 that Patriarch Ignatii had been deposed; he was accused of knowing that Tsar Dmitrii had been a secret Catholic.[8] Selection of a new patriarch was then put off until a new tsar had been chosen. But how should a new tsar be chosen? Some boyars urged the convocation of a zemskii sobor in order to elect the new ruler, but that proposal was blocked by Vasilii Shuiskii (who wisely feared that Tsar Dmitrii's popularity in the country would jeopardize his own chances of being elected), by other boyars who were not anxious to share power with any other group, and by those who believed the issue needed to be resolved quickly.[9]

Vasilii Shuiskii was not the only candidate for tsar; other boyars also hoped for the crown.[10] Shuiskii's challengers could count on support from Tsar Dmitrii's former allies and any boyars who had favored Shuiskii's execution in June 1605 and feared retaliation. Even some of Shuiskii's fellow conspirators, especially Vasilii Golitsyn, now dreamed of becoming tsar.[11] Among Tsar Dmitrii's supporters, members of the Romanov clan hoped for the crown although the family's very popular leader, Filaret, was not eligible because he had been tonsured on Boris Godunov's orders. Filaret's brother Ivan did not have a realistic chance, either; he was unpopular and seriously ill in 1606. Filaret's nine-year-old son, Mikhail, however, was apparently briefly considered by the boyar council but rejected as too young. In the end, the widespread rumors at the time that a Romanov would become tsar proved to be inaccurate.[12] The struggle for the throne quickly came down to just two candidates—Shuiskii and Fedor Mstislavskii, chairman of the boyar council. The prestigious Mstislavskii became the reluctant candidate of those not involved in Dmitrii's assassination and those who owed their careers to the dead tsar.[13] In effect, Mstislavskii became the candidate of the stop-Shuiskii movement and was strongly supported by the Nagoi and Romanov clans.[14] Opposition to Shuiskii badly divided the boyar council. In such a tense situation, not all opponents of Shuiskii kept their struggle inside the confines of the Kremlin. Dmitrii had many angry supporters in Moscow who wished to take revenge against Shuiskii, and some boyars secretly became involved in plots against the regicide.[15]

Unfortunately for Shuiskii's opponents, Prince Mstislavskii was not particularly interested in a potentially deadly struggle with Shuiskii. While the divided council debated the merits of convening a zemskii sobor to choose a new tsar and possibly a new patriarch, Mstislavskii became increasingly uncomfortable as Shuiskii's main opponent. Contemporaries noted that had a zemskii sobor been convened, Mstislavskii would have been chosen tsar.[16] However, he did not push for a zemskii sobor, and he did not even work actively to stop Shuiskii. In fact, Mstislavskii soon withdrew his name from consideration and threatened to become a monk if his supporters persisted in pushing his candidacy. His decision left a vacuum; most boyars still refused to vote for Shuiskii, but no alternate candidate emerged, either. With the boyars at loggerheads, Shuiskii's nervous supporters seized the initiative and bypassed the boyar council in order to elevate their candidate to the throne. They were determined to make Shuiskii tsar at any cost in order to guarantee that they would not eventually be punished for regicide. As a result, Shuiskii was not duly elected tsar but, according to contemporaries, achieved that office by means of "intrigues and scheming."[17] Once Shuiskii had seized the throne, he tried to make it appear that he had been elected by a zemskii sobor or at least by the boyar council in cooperation with a broad cross-section of the population of Moscow.[18] Nothing could be further from the truth. Many eyewitnesses and other contemporaries knew better,[19] and at least some historians since then have avoided the trap of Shuiskii propaganda concerning this issue.[20] Other scholars have incorrectly credited Shuiskii's version of events.[21] The result has been a serious overestimation of

Shuiskii's popular support and a serious underestimation and misunderstanding of the nature of opposition to him. In fact, Shuiskii's bold seizure of power reignited the civil war.

On May 19, 1606, a meeting was held at Vasilii Shuiskii's townhouse that-was attended by his two brothers, his nephew Mikhail V. Skopin-Shuiskii, and his close friend, okolnichii Ivan F. Kriuk-Kolychev, and other coconspirators—including the assassin Mylnikov and several other merchants. Very few members of the boyar council attended. Even the Golitsyns, Shuiskii's former coconspirators, did not participate.[22] Shuiskii had a narrow group of supporters, but it did include some pomeshchiki from Novgorod and Smolensk.[23] Mikhail Tatishchev took the lead in organizing the meeting and planning the announcement of Shuiskii's accession.[24] At the meeting documents were prepared to help Shuiskii become tsar. His pedigree was slightly altered to make him a direct descendant of Aleksandr Nevskii.[25] He also signed a pledge to respect the boyar council and not to execute courtiers or to confiscate their property without a trial before the council. In addition, he pledged not to listen to slander and to severely punish false witnesses and informers.[26] (Such a pledge must have been difficult for Shuiskii, who loved nothing more than malicious gossip about his real or potential enemies.)[27] The offer of these voluntary "limitations" on his autocratic powers as tsar was an election ploy, and it has been variously interpreted ever since. Some writers have anachronistically described it as one of the earliest attempts by the boyars to impose "constitutional" limits on autocracy, but it is far more likely that the desperate usurper himself wished to appear less arbitrary in dealing with the elite than Boris Godunov (or Ivan the Terrible) had been.[28] Shuiskii was obviously trying to reassure his opponents that they and their property, especially that which had been given to them by Tsar Dmitrii, would not be in jeopardy during his reign. Such a ploy probably helped Shuiskii's cause, but it is important to remember that the boyar council was not directly involved in Shuiskii's accession.

Once Shuiskii's coconspirators completed their preparations at his residence, they led him to Red Square to proclaim him tsar. Bells sounded throughout Moscow, and a crowd gathered to watch the spectacle. Shuiskii propaganda claimed that at *Lobnoe mesto* (a platform on Red Square from which decrees were read) a broadly representative assembly of boyars, clergymen, Moscow dvoriane, and merchants presented two candidates to the assembled masses—Shuiskii and Mstislavskii. Shuiskii, it was claimed, was much more popular because he had been the leader of the struggle against the false tsar and the hated Poles. The crowd allegedly roared its approval of "Tsar Vasilii" before Shuiskii was escorted to the Cathedral of the Assumption (Uspenskii Sobor) in the Kremlin where his close confidant, Pafnutii, the metropolitan of Krutitsa, proclaimed him tsar.[29] In fact, that is not what really happened. The assembly that presented Shuiskii to the masses at Lobnoe mesto was much narrower and less illustrious than Shuiskii supporters claimed. Most boyars did not participate in that event.[30] The crowd was also carefully chosen to support Shuiskii. According to a contemporary, Shuiskii was chosen by his accomplices in murder and treason—merchants, pie sellers, cobblers, and a few boyars. The eminent historian Solovev wrote that Shuiskii was not so much chosen as he was "shouted tsar" by his accomplices.[31] The narrowness of the group supporting him, his reputation as a liar, his act of regicide, his hasty seizure of power without the approval of a zemskii sobor, and his lack of any serious effort to gain the support of the common people all combined to undermine Tsar Vasilii's credibility and to destabilize his reign from the outset.[32] Hatred for the "boyar-tsar" was so great that a large percentage of the country's population soon rose against the usurper and plunged Russia into a long and terrible civil war. Tsar Vasilii was never able to exercise his authority over more than half the country, and he was eventually driven from the throne he had so brazenly seized.[33]

Even before news of Shuiskii's seizure of power spread across Russia and galvanized opposition to him, the new tsar faced serious problems establishing his authority in Moscow. In that context, Tsar Dmitrii's corpse continued to play a macabre role. During the night after Dmitrii's assassination, a very severe frost hit the Moscow region and killed many crops and even some trees. The unseasonably cold weather lasted a week and provoked widespread fear and wonderment about Tsar Dmitrii and his assassination.[34] Some people suspected that God was punishing Russia for the murder of the tsar. Shuiskii supporters, however, were quick to claim that it was proof the false tsar had been a sorcerer. Additional "proof" was provided by the wide circulation of Shuiskii-sponsored rumors about the mysterious appearance at night of fires around Dmitrii's corpse accompanied by the sounds of devilish minstrel music.[35] By that time, of course, doubts were already being expressed openly about the identity of the mutilated corpse lying on Red Square, and Shuiskii's enemies had begun circulating rumors that, once again, Dmitrii had miraculously escaped assassination and another had been killed in his place.[36] Such doubts and rumors, coupled with the unseasonably cold weather, probably influenced one of the very first decisions made by the new Tsar Vasilii on May 19, which was to order Dmitrii's corpse removed to a graveyard for paupers and suicides located just outside Moscow. A story quickly circulated that as the body was being dragged from the city a great, icy wind knocked the gates down.[37] That rumor caused further anxiety among an already upset population. Dmitrii's body was locked in the paupers' cemetery overnight but was found outside the locked doors the next morning. Monks working for Shuiskii also reported other strange and frightening events and music associated with the corpse, including the appearance of devils at the cemetery. The troublesome body was subsequently cast into a ditch and covered with dirt.[38] By such means Tsar Vasilii's supporters continued to try building their case for identifying Tsar Dmitrii as an evil sorcerer and Shuiskii as the savior of Russia.

In the meantime, the boyar council made no public objection to Shuiskii's unorthodox accession to the throne. By their inaction, the boyars made civil war against the regicide "boyar-tsar" inevitable. Only by immediately throwing down the gauntlet, declaring Shuiskii a traitor, and trying to take him prisoner could his opponents possibly have prevented civil war. But they lacked an alternate candidate and thought more about their own comfort and safety than about taking chances. They were, after all, risk-aversive inside players more inclined to intrigue at court for power and advantage than to break longstanding tradition by moving their political struggle into the public arena. Shuiskii's pledge to respect the boyars' lives, positions, and property slowed down any move against him. In addition, at least a few aristocrats were apparently dreaming of a devolution of power back to the provinces, princes, and boyars. It was said at the time that some wished to divide the country into principalities and expected the new tsar to share his state revenues with them. Several boyars did work behind the scenes against Shuiskii, however, and the new tsar's first days in power were very difficult for him.[39]

Tsar Vasilii's opponents on the boyar council were able to prevent him from naming his first or even his second choice to the office of patriarch. Neither Metropolitan Pafnutii nor Metropolitan Hermogen received enough votes. Instead, the council voted to promote Shuiskii's rival, Metropolitan Filaret Romanov, to the rank of patriarch.[40] Why did the boyars choose an ally of Tsar Dmitrii? It was probably because there were many former supporters of Dmitrii on the council who were anxious to prevent Shuiskii from gaining so much power that it might threaten their positions and safety. Tsar Vasilii was extremely displeased by the boyars' decision and looked for the first opportunity to get rid of Patriarch Filaret.[41] For his part, the new patriarch seems to have immediately gotten involved in intrigues to delay the new tsar's coronation—intrigues associated with the "resurrection" of Tsar Dmitrii. On Sunday, May 25, 1606, there was a sharp popular disturbance in Moscow. Shuiskii's opponents had tacked broadsheets from "Tsar Dmitrii" on the gates of several boyar residences that declared that the tsar had escaped assassination and that Shuiskii and his coconspirators were traitors. The broadsheets provoked the appearance of a large and ugly crowd that agitated against the "regicide" Shuiskii. As a result, the unpopular new tsar was nearly toppled from his throne at the outset of his reign. Shuiskii was saved from an uncertain fate only by early warning and fast action by his supporters in calming down and dispersing the crowd. Tsar Vasilii came to believe Patriarch Filaret was behind this plot and began quietly planning to remove him from office as soon as possible.[42]

In an attempt to put an end to the rumors about Tsar Dmitrii escaping assassination, Shuiskii came up with an ingenious plan that once again made use of Tsar Dmitrii's corpse. On May 27, Dmitrii's body mysteriously and conveniently surfaced again in a churchyard far from the ditch it had been left in the week before. News of the corpse's movement frightened many people in Moscow. On that same day, Tsar Vasilii had word put out that the reappearance of the corpse was due to the earth's refusal to receive such an evil sorcerer.[43] Orders were given to dispose of the body as that of a sorcerer in an informal ceremony intended to drive away an agent of Satan.[44] On May 28, Dmitrii's corpse was taken to the small Kotel River just outside Moscow and placed inside a mobile wooden fortress that, months earlier, had been constructed on Tsar Dmitrii's orders. Because of the frightening images painted on it the Russians had nicknamed the contraption the "monster from hell." Dmitrii's body, therefore, was burned in "hell," and his ashes were scattered.[45] Legend has it that his ashes were fired from a cannon in the direction from which he had come to Moscow.[46]

In a superbly timed announcement on the same day, the Kremlin circulated the astonishing news that the true Tsarevich Dmitrii's body had been discovered miraculously preserved in Uglich and that the nun Marfa had given permission to transfer his remains to Moscow's Cathedral of the Archangel.[47] Faced with boyar intrigue and popular disturbances, Tsar Vasilii had decided very early on that the only way to end the "false and insane belief in Dmitrii's existence" was to send a high-profile delegation to Uglich to transfer the martyred tsarevich's remains to Moscow where the body could be canonized. Shuiskii hoped such a spectacle would simultaneously "prove" that Tsar Dmitrii had been an impostor and that Boris Godunov had the real tsarevich murdered in 1591.[48] Patriarch Filaret was chosen to lead the delegation, but Mikhail Tatishchev and Dmitrii Shuiskii accompanied him just to make sure things worked out according to plan.[49] Shuiskii's henchmen in Uglich, in the meantime, somehow managed to procure the body of an innocent lad who had just died or was killed for the purpose. Precisely on cue, upon reaching Uglich, the delegation reported to Moscow that the relics of the martyr Dmitrii had been discovered intact. News of that stunning discovery, along with a bold lie that miracles had been reported at the tsarevich's grave, was widely circulated throughout Russia along with long denunciations of the many crimes committed by the evil "Otrepev" and accounts of the heroism of the new tsar and his fellow patriots.[50] Preparations were made for a highly publicized holy procession to bring the tsarevich's sacred relics back to Moscow.

On May 30, 1606, shortly after the delegation had been chosen to go to Uglich, the inhabitants of Moscow were summoned to Red Square to hear articles of condemnation of the impostor "Otrepev" and additional justifications for his assassination.[51] Apparently, Tsar Vasilii was still nervous about popular sentiment and the maneuvering of his enemies. He may have been disturbed by rumors that Dmitrii's corpse had been burned because Shuiskii did not want it seen or by persistent gossip that the assassins had killed the wrong man.[52] In any case, dangerous new plots against Shuiskii really were being hatched. At about this time, another writing appeared one night on the doors or gates of many of the nobles and foreigners living in Moscow that commanded the people in the name of Tsar Vasilii to ransack these houses because traitors lived in them. Many of the common people assembled, hoping for booty; they were appeased and dispersed only with considerable difficulty.[53] Shuiskii thought he discerned Patriarch Filaret's hand in this plot, but he was not certain. Already on May 29, Tsar Vasilii had taken measures to protect himself from any possible conspiracy involving Mstislavskii's brother-in-law, Elder Stefan—the perennial candidate for tsar, formerly known as Simeon Bekbulatovich. Shuiskii ordered him transferred to the remote Solovetskii monastery.[54] Probably for similar reasons, the tsar also decided not to wait for the spectacle of the return of the "true" Tsarevich Dmitrii from Uglich before having himself crowned. Instead of waiting for Patriarch Filaret to perform the ceremony, Shuiskii decided to have himself crowned on June 1.[55]

Because of the haste in organizing Tsar Vasilii's coronation, very few lords and others from outside Moscow participated in the glum ceremony presided over by Metropolitan Isidor of Novgorod.[56] Shuiskii claimed that he had Patriarch Filaret's blessing for the ceremony, which was a lie.[57] Claiming that Tsar Dmitrii had looted the treasury, Tsar Vasilii did not follow the tradition of generously rewarding the participants in the coronation ceremony or his subjects generally—for which reason he quickly gained a reputation for stinginess.[58] He did not even attempt to promote many of his own supporters to the boyar council. Shuiskii was, in fact, very wary of his fellow boyars and gathered around himself favorites of lower rank who owed everything to him.[59] Following the precedent set by Tsar Dmitrii, the new tsar refused to live in his predecessor's luxurious mansion, claiming to be afraid of the ghost of the dead sorcerer. Instead, Shuiskii had a rather modest house built for himself.[60]

Immediately following his coronation, Tsar Vasilii sent couriers all over the country to administer the sacred oath of loyalty to all his subjects.[61] The couriers gathered people together in local churches where all the charges against the impostor "Otrepev" were repeated and even embellished. Tsar Dmitrii, it was alleged, had not merely been planning to kill the boyars, church officials, and important dvoriane, but also the bureaucrats, gosti, other merchants, and tradesmen. The false tsar, it was alleged, had planned to use "Tsarevich Petr's" cossacks to massacre all his opponents, and only the swift action of the pious Vasilii Shuiskii, the entire church leadership, and all the boyars saved the Russian people and the Orthodox Church from disaster. Finally, couriers reassured the people that "Otrepev" had admitted that he was an impostor before he died. Then they administered the oath of allegiance to Tsar Vasilii.[62] For good measure, the new tsar apparently ordered the inclusion in some oaths to him of a prohibition against witchcraft or occult measures that might harm the ruler.[63] Shuiskii's intention was, of course, to get the population of Russia to swear an oath to him as soon as possible in order to divert his subjects from possible rebellion in the name of the "good tsar" Dmitrii. He failed to achieve his objective, however. Many people still believed Dmitrii was alive and were poised to rebel against the regicide "boyar-tsar." Even in Moscow, Shuiskii's enemies on the boyar council remained active, and new plots against him were organized within days of his coronation.[64]

In the meantime, the spectacle took place that was supposed to be Shuiskii's "master-stroke" to put an end to the maddening rumors about Tsar Dmitrii's survival.[65] Three days after Tsar Vasilii's coronation, Patriarch Filaret returned to Moscow at the head of a grand procession conveying the body of the "martyred" Tsarevich Dmitrii from Uglich. The public was informed that the "true Dmitrii's" body had been discovered miraculously preserved and that his coffin emitted a wonderful fragrance. Tsar Vasilii's confederates even thought to put nuts in the hand of the corpse in order to counter the official story of accidental suicide that even Shuiskii had supported in 1591. As soon as the tsarevich's body was discovered, Shuiskii propaganda claimed, it performed miracles—in Uglich and along the road to Moscow.[66] When the procession neared the capital, Tsar Vasilii, the nun Marfa, boyars, bishops, priests with icons, and a large crowd went on foot to greet the tsarevich's relics. By then Tsar Vasilii had already decreed that little Dmitrii should be declared a saint. Contrary to some interpretations, however, the crowd drawn to the procession did not all naïvely assume the body in the coffin was really that of the tsarevich. Many people knew that Vasilii Shuiskii had lied repeatedly about the subject in the past and suspected that he had ordered the murder of a child in order to perpetrate a ruse. The crowd was particularly restive that day, and Captain Margeret wrote that Tsar Vasilii came close to being stoned to death by his own subjects.[67] The unruly crowd was denied the opportunity to gaze upon the tsarevich's body. Instead, his sealed coffin was quickly escorted into the Kremlin to the Cathedral of the Archangel accompanied only by the highest ranking boyars and bishops. Nevertheless, the cathedral was soon surrounded by huge crowds of the curious, the sick, the lame, and others. Guards held them back and admitted only a preselected group of unfortunates—each of whom was immediately "cured," recovered his sight, or was able to walk again after touching St. Dmitrii's casket. Bells were rung throughout the Kremlin and the city each time such a "miracle" occurred.[68] Some gullible people truly believed in St. Dmitrii's miracles; many others recognized the spectacle as a fraud. According to a contemporary, Shuiskii's enemies took immediate advantage of the situation in order "to stop this vulgar show." They arranged to have a very ill man die in the cathedral, which raised a few eyebrows despite frantic efforts by Shuiskii supporters to claim that the sick man's faith had faltered and he therefore had deserved to die. Very soon the stench of the decaying flesh of "St. Dmitrii" became a serious problem, especially since the bodies of dead saints were supposed to give off fragrant smells. In spite of burning massive quantities of incense, the cathedral had to be temporarily closed and the rotting corpse quietly interred.[69] So ended a bizarre episode, although "miracles" associated with St. Dmitrii continued to be proclaimed in the capital's churches for several days.[70] Even some ardent Shuiskii supporters were embarrassed by this spectacle. Isaac Massa, for example, wrote: "These miracles did not last long, and they did not end any too soon."[71]

Tsar Vasilii had reason to believe his enemies were working actively against him. He may have suspected Mstislavskii, but he certainly suspected Patriarch Filaret, whose usefulness once he had presided over the transfer of St. Dmitrii to Moscow was at an end in any case. As already noted, after Shuiskii's coronation new plots had been hatched against him. They were probably in favor of, but perhaps without the knowledge of, Mstislavskii.[72] Things came to a head on Sunday, June 15, 1606.[73] On that day Shuiskii's enemies once again managed to convene the common people on Red Square in the name of Tsar Vasilii. Muscovites were led to believe the tsar wished to speak to them. Several thousand people stood before the Kremlin carrying rocks and weapons because Shuiskii's opponents had encouraged the commoners to believe Tsar Vasilii wanted them to plunder and kill all foreigners in the city. The tsar, on his way to church when informed of the gathering of his subjects on Red Square, was astonished and fearful. He ordered an immediate investigation and the dispersal of the crowd—which proved difficult. Shuiskii did not personally go out to address the crowd. According to Captain Margeret, who was at the tsar's side at that moment, Shuiskii might have been in grave danger had he ventured out of the Kremlin.[74] The masses were not yet happy with the regicide "boyar-tsar."

Shuiskii immediately accused his enemies on the boyar council of responsibility for the incident and threatened to abdicate unless the guilty ones were found and punished. Soon, five men were arrested and convicted as conspirators; then they were whipped through the streets of the capital and exiled. When their sentence was pronounced, it was publicly proclaimed that Mstislavskii—earlier accused of involvement—was innocent. Guilt fell on Petr Nikitich Sheremetev. Because he was related to the Romanov and Nagoi clans, suspicion also fell on them. The tsar demoted the Nagois and some Romanov kin who sat on the boyar council.[75] In fact, many of Tsar Dmitrii's favorites were demoted at this time and (following the customary practice) were "banished" to minor positions as voevodas of remote towns.[76] Tsar Vasilii took his primary revenge against Patriarch Filaret, accusing him of plotting against the Shuiskii regime by secretly declaring that Tsar Dmitrii was still alive. Filaret was driven from his palace and stripped of his holy office.[77] In this way, Tsar Vasilii more or less gained control of the situation on the boyar council and in Moscow. Nonetheless, he made a dangerous enemy in Filaret Romanov, who eventually participated in the civil war against Shuiskii by resuming his position as patriarch in the court of a resurrected Tsar Dmitrii.

As soon as Patriarch Filaret had been toppled, Tsar Vasilii swiftly arranged for Metropolitan Hermogen to become patriarch. In Hermogen he gained a strong, intelligent, and energetic ally who became a fanatic opponent of Shuiskii's enemies. Not only did the new patriarch rail against "godless" rebels and supporters of the dead "heretic Otrepev," but he imposed strict discipline on the Russian Orthodox Church and turned it into an extremely useful instrument for propping up Tsar Vasilii's regime. Many clergymen had been shocked by the assassination of Tsar Dmitrii and especially by the irregular removal of Patriarchs Ignatii and Filaret, and they were also none too pleased by Vasilii Shuiskii's usurpation of the throne. Patriarch Hermogen, however, relentlessly and successfully fought against any dissension within the church, calling down curses on unruly priests or anyone else questioning Tsar Vasilii's legitimacy.[78] Hermogen made maximum use of the story of St. Dmitrii to combat Shuiskii's foes, who were accused of great sin and sacrilege for their attachment to the "heretic Otrepev." Not surprisingly, when the civil war against Tsar Vasilii broke out, it was repeatedly blamed on Satan by the Russian Orthodox Church, and all rebels were demonized.[79] Patriarch Hermogen's tireless efforts did help Shuiskii gain effective control of Moscow although there continued to be many unsettling rumors and sporadic unrest in the capital throughout the summer.[80] Elsewhere in Russia the situation was dramatically different.

Outside Moscow, belief in Tsar Dmitrii's survival and opposition to Shuiskii's coup spread like wildfire. Tsar Vasilii had been well prepared for the necessary propaganda campaign against the dead tsar in order to justify his assassination, but Shuiskii was completely unprepared to fight against an enemy who would not stay dead. How did the stories of Tsar Dmitrii's escape from assassination spread so quickly and become such a potent weapon in the hands of Shuiskii's enemies? At least part of the answer lies in an extremely clever rumor campaign launched by Tsar Dmitrii's allies immediately after his assassination.

Within a few days of Dmitrii's murder, the following story circulated in Moscow and elsewhere: someone had gone to the tsar's stable around midnight before the assassination and, in the name of Tsar Dmitrii, fetched several horses. Those horses were not returned, and no one knew what became of them. Tsar Dmitrii, it was said, had secretly departed from Moscow accompanied by one of his close associates, dvorianin Mikhail Molchanov, and some others in a dangerous test of the loyalty of his subjects and in order to discover who the traitors were who had been plotting against him.[81] There were just enough facts in this rumor to make it plausible, and Tsar Vasilii was wise to be concerned about it. For example, twenty-five horses really were missing from the tsar's stable. More important, Molchanov had been seized by the conspirators on the day of the assassination, accused of helping the false tsar practice witchcraft, and nearly beaten to death;[82] yet he somehow managed to escape Shuiskii's clutches, stole Tsar Dmitrii's state seal and favorite Turkish horse, and fled from Moscow incognito.[83] Tsar Vasilii had the stable hand who delivered the horses to Molchanov's accomplices tortured in order to make him confess what had really happened, but the man died without revealing anything. A search for Molchanov and his confederates was quickly staged. One of Tsar Dmitrii's close advisers was caught riding one of the tsar's horses a few kilometers from Moscow, but Molchanov got away.[84]

Molchanov made his way to Putivl (Tsar Dmitrii's "capital" during his campaign for the throne) and then to Poland-Lithuania, managing to spread word far and wide that Tsar Dmitrii had escaped assassination. His technique was a bold one; from the very beginning it seems that Molchanov decided at least temporarily to play the role of Tsar Dmitrii himself.[85] As he and his companions fled from the capital, Molchanov was represented as the tsar traveling in disguise to a ferryman at the Oka River and to others in Serpukhov and at several inns along the way to Putivl.[86] Rumors quickly circulated that an innkeeper and several others recognized and spoke with Tsar Dmitrii and that the angry tsar had written a letter reproaching the traitors for the assassination attempt and promising swift revenge. Several notes and letters allegedly written by Dmitrii were also found along the roadsides.[87] By such means, according to an English contemporary, did Molchanov draw "manie Gentlemen and soldiers" into opposition to the usurper Vasilii Shuiskii.[88] His clever ploy had a powerful effect in the provinces and even to some extent in Moscow; it nearly toppled Tsar Vasilii. Many Russians hoped and were quite willing to believe that Dmitrii had once again miraculously escaped assassination.[89]

Mikhail Molchanov was well suited for the task of temporarily playing the role of Tsar Dmitrii. Although he did not strongly resemble the dead tsar, he knew Dmitrii very well and could imitate him.[90] A scion of a family that had served in Ivan the Terrible's hated oprichnina, Molchanov had apparently been somewhat of an operator and shady character in his youth. He was accused of theft by a secretary in 1604 and had been forced to petition Tsar Boris in order to clear himself of that charge.[91] There is no evidence that he was imprisoned for practicing witchcraft at that time;[92] however, he may have been accused of sorcery and subjected to a beating sometime during Tsar Boris's reign.[93] The Soviet historian Ivan Smirnov believed Molchanov may actually have been a secret accomplice of the pretender Dmitrii during Tsar Boris's lifetime—which might help to explain the Godunov regime's harsh treatment of him.[94] In any case, Tsar Dmitrii's enemies accused Molchanov of sinister and promiscuous behavior in addition to joining the false tsar in acts of sorcery.[95] Molchanov was even accused of participating in the assassination of Tsar Fedor Borisovich, an act that a source hostile to Dmitrii claimed endeared him to "Otrepev."[96] Molchanov did become one of Tsar Dmitrii's close associates; an English merchant referred to him as Dmitrii's "speciall favorite."[97] Nevertheless, he certainly was not a mere "stooge" of Tsar Dmitrii, as some have contended.[98] Molchanov was bright, energetic, and very well educated; he was fluent in Polish and could read and write some Latin.[99] His spontaneous and timely "resurrection" of Tsar Dmitrii was extremely effective. More than any other individual, Molchanov was responsible for the immediate and widespread belief that Tsar Dmitrii was still alive—a belief that quickly mobilized a full-scale civil war against Shuiskii.[100]

When he arrived in Putivl, Molchanov stayed out of sight and did not try to act the part of Tsar Dmitrii, probably because many people in that city were well acquainted with the tsar they had helped put on the throne. Molchanov had time to gauge the reactions of the residents of Putivl to news of the assassination of "Otrepev," Shuiskii's accession to the throne, and rumors that Tsar Dmitrii was still alive and had even been seen in various places. Molchanov was heartened by the attitude of the local population and by news that some ser-vicemen from Putivl who were in Moscow at the time of the assassination had refused to swear an oath of loyalty to Tsar Vasilii.[101] Molchanov quickly con-cluded that it really was possible to fight against Shuiskii by means of the ghost of Dmitrii and that Putivl could once again serve as a base of operations for the rebels. By the time Tsar Vasilii's newly-appointed voevoda of Putivl, Grigorii Shakhovskoi, arrived from Moscow in June, Molchanov had already made secret contact with him. Those two former close associates of Tsar Dmitrii decided that Putivl was ripe for rebellion. While Shakhovskoi made plans to lead the local population in an uprising against Shuiskii, Molchanov stayed out of sight and made plans to travel to Poland-Lithuania in order to play the role of Tsar Dmitrii.[102]

It has often been asked why Tsar Vasilii was so foolish as to send Shakhovskoi, a strong supporter of Tsar Dmitrii, to serve as voevoda in strategically located Putivl where support for the dead tsar had been so strong. Most of Tsar Dmitrii's close associates who had been similarly "exiled" from Moscow were appointed to far less sensitive posts, and Shuiskii was well aware of Shakhovskoi's back-ground and loyalties. Grigorii Shakhovskoi, a member of an impoverished princely family, had reached the rank of vybornyi dvorianin under Tsar Boris. He had a reputation for being a quick-witted and honorable man.[103] Grigorii and his father, Petr M. Shakhovskoi, had been active supporters of the pre-tender Dmitrii. As voevoda of Chernigov, Petr Shakhovskoi had deserted Tsar Boris for Dmitrii; Grigorii also joined Dmitrii's service early on and was sent by him to precipitate rebellion against the Godunovs in Belgorod. The younger Shakhovskoi was later named voevoda of Kursk by Tsar Dmitrii, and his father was promoted to the rank of boyar (but soon died).[104] Grigorii Shakhovskoi was recalled to Moscow in 1606 and participated in Tsar Dmitrii's wedding cere-mony.[105] Contrary to Conrad Bussow's assertion, Shakhovskoi did not flee from Moscow at the time of Dmitrii's assassination. Instead, he was appointed by Tsar Vasilii to replace the old voevoda of Putivl, Prince Andrei I. Bakhteiarov-Rostovskii.

We can only speculate about why Tsar Vasilii decided to make Shakhovskoi voevoda of Putivl. Was the new tsar so concerned about opposition in the cap-ital that he neglected to consider seriously the potential for opposition in the provinces? Was he hoping that his propaganda campaign against Tsar Dmitrii and the invention of "St. Dmitrii" would suffice to calm the country down? It is possible that one of Shuiskii's secret enemies on the boyar council maneu-vered to get Shakhovskoi posted in Putivl. Many hasty compromises were made in the aftermath of Dmitrii's assassination. Whatever influenced Tsar Vasilii's decision, it was surely one of his dumbest.[106] Shuiskii would have been far wiser to retain the old voevoda in Putivl, who—although appointed by Tsar Dmitrii—proved to be extremely loyal to the new tsar. When Tsar Vasilii's courier came to Putivl to administer the oath of loyalty, Bakhteiarov-Rostovskii (still voevoda at the time) not only credited the courier's lies about the evil "Otrepev" but also reacted positively to Shuiskii's pledge to the residents of Putivl to greatly favor them and his generous invitation to the local population to send a few of their "best" townsmen to Moscow to discuss their needs and desires. The old voevoda then led the somewhat unenthusiastic townspeople in swearing loyalty to Tsar Vasilii.[107]

As soon as the new voevoda, Grigorii Shakhovskoi, arrived in Putivl, he assembled the townspeople and electrified them with a speech in which he denounced Shuiskii as a traitor and declared that Tsar Dmitrii had escaped assassination and was at that very moment in Poland-Lithuania gathering an army for a new campaign to restore himself to the throne. Shakhovskoi told them that Tsar Dmitrii had instructed him to ask the residents of Putivl to help raise troops for that purpose. The townspeople, in the words of a contemporary, "listened to this news with great rejoicing." Shakhovskoi also declared that Shuiskii was preparing reprisals against the inhabitants of Putivl because of their past devotion to Tsar Dmitrii. Then he led the townspeople in swearing a new sacred oath of loyalty to Tsar Dmitrii and another oath to seek vengeance against the usurper in Moscow.[108] The old veovoda, Bakhteiarov-Rostovskii, was killed on the spot for refusing to swear an oath of loyalty to Tsar Dmitrii.[109] In that way did "bloodthirsty" Prince Grigorii Shakhovskoi begin the civil war against Tsar Vasilii.[110] Contrary to the traditional interpretation of events in Putivl, it was not just the lower classes who responded favorably to Shakhovskoi's speech. The entire population of the town, including fortress cossacks and streltsy, stood up for Tsar Dmitrii, and the deti boiarskie of the Putivl district rose en masse against Shuiskii. It was, in fact, the deti boiarskie of the district—not peasants or the urban poor—who took the initiative in helping Shakhovskoi reignite Russia's first civil war. Those fighting men provided crucial military expertise, weapons, and leadership which turned popular anger against the usurper Shuiskii into the powerful armed struggle often referred to as the "Bolotnikov rebellion."[111]

Putivl was swiftly joined by many other towns of the southwestern and southern frontier in declaring for Tsar Dmitrii. The events of 1604–5 seemed to be repeating themselves. Many of the same men who had fought for Dmitrii the year before quickly reorganized their old units in order to resume the struggle against Moscow. The region that had so strongly supported Dmitrii's campaign for the throne once again took the lead in fielding armies for the "true tsar."[112]

Within five months, more than eighty towns and nearly half the country stood in the rebel camp, and Tsar Vasilii found himself besieged in his own capital. At first, the alarmed tsar tried to deny that any uprising had taken place, hiding it as best he could from his subjects in Moscow and even from the first army he sent against the rebels.[113] When it was no longer possible to hide the fact of the rebellion, Shuiskii propaganda tried to portray it as the result of Polish meddling in Russia's internal affairs.[114] The rebels themselves were initially dismissed as mere brigands, criminals, slaves, urban poor, and other riffraff.[115] As the civil war rapidly spread and threatened Moscow itself, Tsar Vasilii finally tried to frighten his wavering subjects into remaining loyal by portraying the insurgents as social revolutionaries—as have-nots determined to overthrow the Russian elite and seize their property, their wives, and their daughters.[116] It was that "official" view of Tsar Vasilii's opponents that so strongly influenced historians and led to the traditional social revolutionary (or peasant war) interpretation of the so-called "Bolotnokov rebellion."[117] Nevertheless, Russia's first civil war was definitely not a social revolution. Just as in its first phase (1604–5), the rekindled civil war (1606–12) produced not class division but a vertical split through several layers of Russian society. The bulk of the rebels were cossacks, petty gentry, lower status military servitors, and townspeople; just as in 1604–5, they were driven by their zealous support of Tsar Dmitrii as the legitimate, sacred ruler.[118] As we shall see, however, unlike the first phase of the civil war, the second phase lasted long enough to mobilize on the rebel side significant numbers of non-Slavic native peoples from areas only recently added to the Russian empire. Their participation was probably more anticolonial than pro-Dmitrii, although it is worth noting that Tsar Dmitrii had established a reputation for dealing fairly and sympathetically with their grievances.[119]

Due at least in part to the refusal to believe Tsar Dmitrii was capable of generating strong popular support, scholars have long been puzzled by the speed of the development of the rebellion against Vasilii Shuiskii, by the fanaticism of the rebels fighting in Tsar Dmitrii's name, and especially by the persistence and endurance of those men. They fought relentlessly against Shuiskii for four years; even after he was deposed, they kept the civil war going for two more years by fighting just as hard against foreign intervention. In the search for an explanation of this noteworthy phenomenon that did not focus on Tsar Dmitrii, many historians found it easy to credit Shuiskii propaganda and concluded that most participants in the Bolotnikov rebellion were members of the lower classes struggling against serfdom and feudal oppression. Emphasis was usually placed on "revolutionary" peasants, cossacks, slaves, and urban plebes.[120] There are, however, many serious problems with such an interpretation. Most important, there is no evidence that any rebels fought against serfdom or for the rights of peasants.[121] As in 1604–5, peasants did not provide the initiative for the renewed civil war and were not the main force supporting the "resurrected" Tsar Dmitrii. In fact, very few serfs even participated in the "Bolotnikov rebellion."[122] Once again, as in 1604–5, the most significant peasant participation was by the relatively wealthy crown peasants of the Komaritsk district.[123]

Cossacks provided the largest and most important rebel military force in the renewed civil war, just as they had done during Dmitrii's campaign for the throne; but, once again, they were not interested in championing the cause of the lower classes and pursued their own nonrevolutionary agenda.[124] According to some writers, large numbers of radical slaves participated in the Bolotnikov rebellion and played a leading role.[125] Actually, the number of slaves involved has been greatly exaggerated, and most of those who did participate were military slaves (often former deti boiarskie who had fallen on hard times) with no interest in the abolition of serfdom.[126] Some writers have emphasized the involvement in the rebellion against Shuiskii of low status military servitors and urban plebes, seeing that as a sign of social revolution.[127] In fact, soldiers and townspeople of all types enthusiastically participated in the civil war in the name of Tsar Dmitrii and on occasion provided initiative and leadership, but they did not pursue a radical social agenda. In most cases, leadership in getting towns and districts to declare against Shuiskii and in organizing rebel forces was provided, just as it had been in 1604–5, by local gentry militiamen.[128] Such elite and marginal elite participation, which resulted in broad coalitions among rebel forces and which denied Shuiskii control over a large part of his army, was the main reason his opponents were as successful as they were.[129]

Rebels from all social classes were united by their opposition to Vasilii Shuiskii and their commitment to the cause of Tsar Dmitrii.[130] Such broad popular support for Dmitrii in 1606, as in 1604–5, has been explained away as the result of the "naïve monarchism" of the Russian masses whose utopian dreams associated with Dmitrii allegedly survived his short reign and produced a huge rebellion against the assassins of the putative "tsar-liberator."[131] The weakness of that line of analysis has already been discussed in Chapter 7, and the fact remains that there is no credible evidence of any social utopian content in the consciousness of Russian rebels in 1604–5 or in 1606.[132] Some Soviet scholars acknowledged these problems with the traditional interpretation and came to the not very helpful conclusion that the rebels were trapped in a world view imposed on them by the elite. According to Vadim Koretskii's extremely weak argument, the "naïve" rebels still struggled "objectively" against serfdom but—

Map 5 Russia's First Civil War.

due to their political immaturity—merely wished to modify rather than over-throw it.[133] Such an interpretation offers no useful insight into the reignited civil war.

Close analysis of rebel territory and rebel forces by summer 1606 reveals that they were virtually the same as in 1604–5. Many of the same soldiers and com-manders who had fought for Dmitrii just over a year earlier rose once again in support of his claim to the throne.[134] For that reason, it should come as no sur-prise that, in an era of deep social, economic, and political crisis, many of the preconditions of the Bolotnikov rebellion were virtually identical to the pre-conditions of the first phase of the civil war. Those preconditions included intra-elite conflict; elite disaffection with the crown; a discredited regime seen by many as illegitimate and responsible for the current crisis; large numbers of impoverished, landless petty nobles, disbanded soldiers, and young men; and a militarized frontier zone with a provincial population resentful of the central government's infringement on their land and freedom.[135]

In 1606, as in 1604–5, almost all social groups had serious grievances and were represented in the ranks of rebel forces. A noteworthy exception were the boyars. Several of them sided with Dmitrii in 1604–5, but very few joined rebel forces in 1606. That was certainly not due to any radical rebel agenda. Instead, it had more to do with the boyar tradition of residing in the capital, partici-pating in council meetings almost daily, and believing that it was necessary to maintain a constant presence at court in order both to protect one's family sta-tus and possessions and to be in line for new rewards, assignments, and oppor-tunities.[136] In addition, the renewed civil war developed so quickly that it preempted the usual boyar maneuvering and involvement in plots. It is also important to remember that the boyars, like many inhabitants of Moscow, were fairly certain that Tsar Dmitrii really had been assassinated and were, therefore, uncertain about what forces or individuals were behind the dead tsar's "resur-rection." Shuiskii propaganda denouncing the rebels as evil brigands intent upon overturning the established order and seizing the property and women-folk of the ruling elite may actually have had some impact on the conservative boyars.

Even without boyars, the rebels in 1606 had from the outset a broad social base. One of the main reasons for that was precisely because—Shuiskii propa-ganda to the contrary—the insurgents did not seek radical redistribution of land, wealth, or power.[137] Instead, they were united by their opposition to the usurper, Vasilii Shuiskii. In fact, it is worth emphasizing that, without the assas-sination of Tsar Dmitrii, there would have been no Bolotnikov rebellion or renewed civil war. Just as it took the existence of Dmitrii to trigger civil war against the Godunov regime in 1604, it took the assassination of Tsar Dmitrii to reignite that conflict.

Vasilii Shuiskii brought the civil war on himself by killing Russia's charismatic and popular ruler.[138] Of course the ambitious and wily Shuiskii had already been suspect in the eyes of many Russians even before he managed to seize the throne. In addition, the simple fact that he was a boyar, like Tsar Boris before him, definitely worked to his disadvantage. Many Russians were deeply suspicious of boyars in general and regarded "boyar-tsars" as inherently illegitimate.[139] Among other things, it was almost universally assumed that Shuiskii would rule exclusively in the interests of his fellow boyars.[140] Considering the extent of Tsar Dmitrii's efforts to shore up his gentry militiamen, Shuiskii's coup must have been deeply offensive to many of them. Not only was Tsar Vasilii not very interested in the condition of his military forces, but it was also widely assumed that the boyar-tsar and his inner circle would cut off opportunities for advancement for men of "lesser birth" and prefer only the high-born aristocracy.[141] In this context, it is worth noting that social scientists tell us to expect an especially violent reaction when individuals have been led to believe that the government is concerned about their condition and is about to help them only to have those hopes suddenly shattered.[142]

The fact that Vasilii Shuiskii led the coup against Tsar Dmitrii and then seized power himself triggered a strong negative reaction from many suspicious Russians. They objected both to the overthrow of a tsar without a public inquiry into the charges against him and to the coronation of a new tsar—a regicide at that—without consulting representatives from the provinces. Many Russians who joined the rebellion in 1606 were resolved to call Shuiskii to account for those actions.[143] As Captain Margeret put it, "and must all the country believe, without any other proof, the word of four or five men who were the principal conspirators?"[144]

Southern frontiersmen, in particular, must have been disturbed by Shuiskii's seizure of power. It was widely assumed that the usurper would cancel the ten-year tax exemption Tsar Dmitrii had bestowed on the war-torn southern provinces that had propelled him to power and that Tsar Vasilii would also reinstitute the hated practice of plowing for the state (the tsar's tenth) that had not been performed since Dmitrii launched the civil war in 1604.[145] Rebel leaders in 1606 also spread a rumor that Shuiskii planned to punish the southern provinces for having supported Dmitrii in 1604–5.[146] That possibility must have seemed very real to the inhabitants of Severia, and especially the Komaritsk district, which had been terrorized by one of Tsar Boris's armies in 1605. To understand why those same areas were the first to rebel against Tsar Vasilii and the first to organize and fund military forces to oust the usurper, one need look no further than the region's memory of just exactly who had been the commander of Tsar Boris's punitive expeditions—none other than Vasilii Shuiskii himself.[147] News of the despised Shuiskii's seizure of power produced energetic opposition to him on the part of many inhabitants of the southern frontier.

Vasilii Shuiskii stirred up bitter hatred and opposition on the part of many Russians, not just southerners, by what a contemporary called his "wolf-like" advance to the throne.[148] Tsar Vasilii's apologists, of course, claimed that he was a good and pious ruler.[149] Many sources from the period, however, painted a completely negative picture—accusing the new tsar of being a regicide, liar, usurper, complete moral failure, drunkard, fornicator, homosexual, and even a sorcerer who dissipated the state treasury, threw the country into turmoil, and was responsible for the deaths of countless innocent people.[150] Most important, Shuiskii was widely regarded as an evil, false tsar—a "tsar-tormentor" (*tsar'-muchitel'*).[151] All that was needed to galvanize opposition to him, therefore, was widespread awareness of a possible legitimate alternative to his discredited regime and the arrival on the scene of that credible charismatic challenger.[152]

Tsar Dmitrii certainly qualified as a credible charismatic challenger to Vasilii Shuiskii. We have already seen that Dmitrii had been accepted by many Russians as the legitimate ruler who had risen, Christ-like, from the dead.[153] Such cult-like popular veneration of the tsar proved to be politically destabilizing.[154] Dmitrii's supporters had fought for him in 1604–5 with quasi-religious fervor, regarding themselves as crusaders in a holy war to restore the legitimate tsar to the throne.[155] Dmitrii's subsequent victory over the Godunovs served to confirm his status as the God-chosen, true tsar.[156] It also inadvertently validated popular rebellion as a means to pursue such a holy end. Although Tsar Dmitrii faced some minor opposition during his short reign, he was generally regarded as a sacred ruler who had restored God's grace to Russia.[157] His assassination, therefore, had a traumatic effect upon many faithful Orthodox Christian Russians who had trouble accepting Shuiskii's coup and his self-serving propaganda about the dead tsar. As a result, Tsar Vasilii had great difficulty establishing his own legitimacy in the eyes of many Russians. He immediately lost control over the southern part of the country and was never able to exercise authority over more than half of Russia.[158] Rumors that Tsar Dmitrii had once again escaped assassination served to quickly unify Shuiskii's enemies and to legitimize rebellion against him.[159] Such rumors were easy for Russians of all social classes to believe for several reasons. First, it was an age of strong belief in miracles.[160] Second, even unloved tsars such as Boris Godunov were typically rumored to have survived their reported deaths.[161] Third, and most important, Dmitrii's prior escape from Uglich was widely regarded as having been divinely assisted. Many Russians were therefore quite prepared to believe God had once again saved the true tsar who would soon return to punish the traitors.[162]

Widespread belief that Tsar Dmitrii was still alive proved to be an extremely potent "causal story" which triggered a powerful rebellion against Tsar Vasilii. Not only did Dmitrii have an obvious right to challenge Shuiskii; but, once again, as in 1604–5, he appeared to be a victim along with everyone else of an illegitimate ruler's evil deeds. Furthermore, as in 1604–5, rebels championing Dmitrii's cause in 1606 were not associated with radical prescriptions for redistributing power or wealth.[163] Rumors about Tsar Dmitrii's survival were especially potent because, once again, as in the first phase of the civil war, they portrayed him as the hidden legitimate ruler who would soon emerge to restore justice.[164] Thus, just like the rebels who fought against Tsar Boris, the insurgents rising against Vasilii Shuiskii in the name of the "true tsar" were really conservatives, not radicals, and their goal was as much religious as political: to restore the God-chosen ruler to the throne.[165] The strength of the rebel movement was, in fact, directly related to its religious, purifying mission.[166] So powerful was the motivation of Ivan Bolotnikov and other crusaders in the cause of Tsar Dmitrii that they were able to quickly organize a powerful army that defeated Tsar Vasilii's military forces and laid siege to Moscow—all while waiting in vain for Tsar Dmitrii to reappear. Shuiskii's allies were shocked and deeply impressed by the valor and endurance of the dead tsar's fanatical supporters. And, as we shall see, Tsar Dmitrii himself remained so utterly essential to the rebel movement that more than one impostor bearing his name emerged to greatly prolong the nightmare of Russia's first civil war.[167]

15

The Beginning of the "Bolotnikov Rebellion"

Civil war against the usurper Vasilii Shuiskii began in mid-June 1606 in Putivl and spread with dizzying speed to many other towns and regions of the southwestern and southern frontier.[1] Prince Grigorii Shakhovskoi was incredibly active in organizing opposition to Shuiskii and in converting Putivl once again into the capital of an armed struggle in support of the "true tsar" Dmitrii. He sent couriers in all directions who falsely reported that Dmitrii had escaped assassination and was in Poland-Lithuania organizing an army. News filtered into Moscow by late June that the inhabitants of five or six principal towns on the southern frontier had revolted—seizing, robbing, and imprisoning their voevodas and other Shuiskii loyalists and declaring their steadfast loyalty to Tsar Dmitrii.[2] According to Isaac Massa, in each of these towns the pattern was usually the same: "The manifestos of the tsar of Moscow were burned, and he was denounced as a scoundrel and a traitor. The inhabitants of these lands and towns swore an oath to fight to their last drop of blood. They demanded to know why the Muscovites had dared, without consulting them at all, assassinate a crowned tsar for no reason." Soon, according to a contemporary, the entire southern frontier all the way to the Volga and Astrakhan "formed a league sworn to avenge" Tsar Dmitrii. Rebel towns corresponded with one another, began to coordinate their efforts, and tried to determine just exactly where the "true tsar" was located.[3]

Within the first month of the renewed civil war, at least fourteen southern towns and fortresses joined the rebellion. Besides Putivl they included Elets, Kromy, Rylsk, Chernigov, Starodub, Livny, Valuiki, Kursk, Orel, Belgorod, Tsarev-Borisov, and probably Oskol and Novgorod Severskii.[4] In some cases, Shuiskii supporters were robbed, tortured, or thrown from towers to their death.[5] In Orel, Starodub, Belgorod, and Tsarev-Borisov, Shuiskii's voevodas were killed by the townspeople. The voevoda of Livny fled, and in Valuiki, voevoda Mikhail F. Aksakov joined the rebels in swearing an oath to Tsar Dmitrii. In Chernigov, voevoda Prince Andrei Teliatevskii led the rebellion of his garrison.[6]

Almost all of Severia quickly and enthusiastically followed Putivl's lead, including the fertile crown peasant districts of Komaritsk and Samovsk.[7] The Komaritsk district, in particular, became one of the main bases of the rebellion alongside Putivl and provided many soldiers, much money, and vast quantities of food for the war effort.[8] Shakhovskoi also sent couriers to cossack stanitsas nearby and far away, which resulted in thousands of free cossacks once again joining the cause of the "true tsar." As we have seen, the cossacks tended to adore Dmitrii and to despise boyars and boyar-tsars. They had been extremely upset by reports of Tsar Dmitrii's assassination and responded enthusiastically to false news of his escape from death. Just as in 1604–5, in the period 1606–12 the cossacks became the main rebel fighting force.[9] In Putivl, Shakhovskoi set up a "great council" to supervise the rebellion.[10] While he and others organized military forces and made plans, they anxiously awaited some kind of official statement from "Tsar Dmitrii." In the meantime, Shakhovskoi sent numerous couriers to Moscow with false news of Tsar Dmitrii's activities and plans, which provoked sporadic unrest in the capital throughout the summer.[11]

As noted in the last chapter, Shakhovskoi and Mikhail Molchanov had already agreed that the latter was to make his way to Poland-Lithuania to continue playing the role of Tsar Dmitrii. While Shakhovskoi set about stirring up rebellion, Molchanov crossed the border and made his way to Sambor (in Galicia), the home of Tsar Dmitrii's father-in-law, Jerzy Mniszech, who was then being held prisoner by Shuiskii. Along the way, Molchanov once again made sure as many people as possible learned about Tsar Dmitrii's "escape."[12] In Sambor Molchanov was very well received by Lady Mniszech who was able to facilitate secret communications with her husband and daughter—both of whom were extremely pleased to hear of Tsar Dmitrii's "resurrection."[13] Molchanov quickly sent a letter from "Tsar Dmitrii" to Shakhovskoi that was read to the people of Putivl. The letter filled them with enthusiasm for gathering money and military forces to expel the usurper Shuiskii from Moscow.[14] Molchanov also sent letters from "Tsar Dmitrii" elsewhere throughout Russia's southern frontier that were similarly effective, in part because they bore the authentic stamp of Dmitrii's state seal.[15]

Meanwhile, Lady Mniszech helped Molchanov set up a "court" in Sambor and gathered approximately two hundred soldiers for the "tsar."[16] She sent letters to Polish lords stating categorically that Dmitrii was alive.[17] Thus, word was spread far and wide that Tsar Dmitrii was well and looking for supporters to help him reclaim his throne. Soon, veterans of Dmitrii's earlier campaign and some disgruntled Polish lords involved in a developing mutiny against Sigismund III began to gravitate toward Sambor. The build-up of such untrustworthy Polish military detachments in Sambor made the king nervous, so he urged Chancellor Leo Sapieha to watch events there closely. Rumors also spread that an important boyar had joined Tsar Dmitrii in Sambor along with many other Russians, Poles, Belorussians, and Lithuanians. In fact, few important lords traveled to Sambor.[18] The most famous of the new arrivals from Russia was a dvorianin named Zabolotskii, whose adherence to "Tsar Dmitrii" cost his family dearly; two of his relatives were thrown in prison by Tsar Vasilii and their names were struck from the list of Moscow dvoriane.[19] Molchanov appointed Zabolotskii as his chief voevoda and sent him off to Putivl with some troops, but he never arrived. Chancellor Sapieha had Zabolotskii and his men detained as a possible threat to King Sigismund and to peace between Poland-Lithuania and Russia. An official investigation into the resurrected tsar was then ordered by Sapieha. Despite Shuiskii propaganda, the Polish government had nothing to do with the Sambor intrigue and actually feared it.[20]

Only a small number of people, none of whom had ever met Tsar Dmitrii before, were allowed to see "Dmitrii" in Sambor sitting on his makeshift throne. Indeed, Molchanov's lack of close resemblance to Tsar Dmitrii was a real problem in Poland where Dmitrii had been seen by many great lords. The new "Dmitrii" was understandably not presented at the Polish court, and he rarely saw visitors in Sambor.[21] A rumor circulated by August 1606 that Tsar Dmitrii was living in the Bernardine monastery in Sambor wearing a monk's garb. The monks, however, denied the rumor and declared that they had not seen Dmitrii since 1604. In October, 1606, the priest who had received Dmitrii's confession when he "converted" to Catholicism in 1604 tried to visit "Tsar Dmitrii" in Sambor but was rebuffed.[22] Chancellor Sapieha also sent someone to examine "Dmitrii" at about the same time, but his agent was also turned away with the excuse that the tsar was living in a monastery and not appearing to anyone.[23]

Molchanov himself must have been frustrated by having to hide from most visitors. He was well aware that the Poles were skeptical about his identity. At one point he seems to have contemplated abandoning the pretense and returning home under his own name as one of Tsar Dmitrii's voevodas.[24] Molchanov was convinced that the rebels needed "Tsar Dmitrii" to appear at some point, but he also fully understood that he could not personally play the role of the tsar in Putivl because many people there knew Dmitrii by sight. As a result, despite Shakhovskoi's pleas, "Tsar Dmitrii" kept failing to appear in Russia. Eventually, some anxious rebels began to search for him on their own. A delegation traveled to Poland in August 1606 but could not find their tsar.[25] Tsar Vasilii's envoys, however, were able to surmise that Molchanov was playing the role of Dmitrii in Sambor, and they denounced him to Polish authorities. The Russians described Molchanov's physical features in great detail, even down to the lash marks on his back inflicted on him in Moscow.[26] By then, however, it really did not matter because Lady Mniszech had died and Molchanov was unable to find another protector. As a result, "Tsar Dmitrii's" court in Sambor simply disappeared.

In 1607 or 1608 Molchanov made his way back to Russia under his own name and joined the court of yet another resurrected "Tsar Dmitrii" in Tushino where he continued to struggle against Shuiskii. Molchanov was, in fact, at least partially responsible for the intimate knowledge of Tsar Dmitrii, the Nagois, and life in the Kremlin that the Tushino impostor (sometimes called the "second False Dmitrii") was able to display.[27] Eventually, according to a contemporary, Molchanov became one of the prominent lords involved in overthrowing Tsar Vasilii in 1610. Probably for that reason, he was subsequently allowed to join the boyar council.[28] Although Molchanov's short stint as "Tsar Dmitrii" had not been especially successful, it did stimulate and help sustain belief in the resurrection of Tsar Dmitrii during the crucial opening phase of the renewed civil war. Perhaps most important, while playing the role of "Tsar Dmitrii" Molchanov found a brilliant commander for the rebel army in Ivan Bolotnikov.

Ivan Isaevich Bolotnikov has long been portrayed as a conscious social revolutionary who led the masses in a struggle against serfdom and feudal oppression.[29] That was definitely not the case. Bolotnikov's biography has also been distorted by scholars who naïvely credited Isaac Massa's faulty information about him instead of Conrad Bussow's much more reliable, first-hand knowledge of his own commander.[30] Ivan Bolotnikov was a Russian by birth.[31] The year of his birth and even his approximate age in 1606 are unknown, however. He was no longer a young man by the time of Tsar Dmitrii's death; a contemporary English source referred to him as an "olde Robber or borderer."[32] The Bolotnikov family of deti boiarskie had settled on the southern frontier in Krapivna (not far from Tula). There is a reference in Russian records of the late sixteenth century to "Ivan Bolotnikov," who was then a petty pomeshchik.[33] Like so many other southern frontier militiamen in that period, Ivan seems to have fallen on hard times. No doubt due to nagging financial problems, he indentured himself as an elite military slave to boyar Prince Andrei Teliatevskii.[34]

At some point, Bolotnikov—also like so many others in his situation—ran away to join the cossacks. It has long been assumed that he rose to the rank of ataman (chieftain) among the Don cossacks.[35] That is certainly possible but there is no evidence of such a promotion. Later references to him as a cossack ataman may actually have been part of an effort by Tsar Vasilii and others to demean him, and careful study of sources reveals that Bolotnikov may actually have joined the Volga cossacks instead of the Don cossacks.[36] In either case, at some point he was taken prisoner by the Crimean Tatars and sold into slavery in Turkey, another all-too-common fate for Russians in that era. According to one of his own soldiers, while in Turkish slavery Bolotnikov "was chained to the galleys and for several years had to fulfil hard and menial tasks." He was eventually freed by "Germans," who defeated the Turks at sea, and he was then taken to Venice. From there he made his way back to Russia by way of Poland-Lithuania.[37]

Isaac Massa erroneously stated that Bolotnikov had gone on military campaigns in Hungary and Turkey and then joined the rebellion against Shuiskii at the head of ten thousand veteran cossacks.[38] Some scholars seized upon those comments as evidence that Bolotnikov was an ataman elected by cossacks and that his army was a foreign (Zaporozhian) cossack host intent upon spreading social revolution in Russia.[39] A few peasant war scholars even asserted that Bolotnikov arrived in Sambor with that large cossack force and that the presence of those men was the main reason "Tsar Dmitrii" chose Bolotnikov to be commander-in-chief of the rebel army.[40] It has also long been incorrectly argued that peasants and slaves joining Bolotnikov's rebel forces were organized along cossack lines into democratic, self-ruling units that fought actively against serfdom.[41] It is time to move beyond such inaccurate stereotypes of Ivan Bolotnikov and the remarkable campaign he waged in the name of Tsar Dmitrii.

While traveling without an armed escort through Poland-Lithuania, Bolotnikov heard about Shuiskii's coup and rumors that Tsar Dmitrii had escaped assassination and was living in Sambor. He decided to go there to see if the rumors were accurate.[42] In Sambor "Tsar Dmitrii" (Molchanov) warmly received Bolotnikov, interviewed him at length, and immediately chose him to be commander-in-chief of the rebel army being organized in Putivl. It has been claimed that Bolotnikov was chosen simply because he did not know Molchanov was an impostor and the latter only wanted supporters who were completely dependent upon him and believed he was Dmitrii.[43] That is extremely unlikely. Bolotnikov was an experienced warrior with many good qualities acknowledged even by his enemies.[44] A Shuiskii supporter referred to him as "a big, strong, and very courageous man" distinguished in war "by his bravery and boldness."[45] One of Tsar Vasilii's archbishops referred to Bolotnikov as a "worthy man and knowledgeable in military affairs."[46] Bolotnikov accepted his charge and swore a sacred oath of loyalty to "Tsar Dmitrii." In return, the "tsar" gave him a sabre, a fur coat, and a small sum of money to help him get to Putivl. More important, he also gave him a letter to Prince Shakhovskoi in what appeared to be Tsar Dmitrii's own handwriting and that was sealed in red wax by Dmitrii's state seal. The letter authorized Bolotnikov's appointment as commander-in-chief of the tsar's military forces and commanded the Putivl voevoda to give him money and control over the troops being raised to fight against Shuiskii. Molchanov also instructed Bolotnikov to tell everyone he met that he had seen and spoken with Tsar Dmitrii and had received his letter of appointment from the tsar's own hand. Ivan Bolotnikov was utterly convinced that the young man he met in Sambor really was Tsar Dmitrii.[47]

Bolotnikov departed from Sambor without the mythical army of ten thousand cossacks. As we have already seen, Molchanov's first commander-in-chief, Zabolotskii, had been detained by nervous Polish authorities for traveling with a much smaller force, and Bolotnikov would never have been allowed to move about freely with such an army.[48] Bolotnikov arrived in Putivl not with ten thousand cossacks but with something just as powerful—Tsar Dmitrii's official appointment of him as commander-in-chief of all his military forces. By the time he showed up, the rebels had already tasted defeat at the hands of Shuiskii's army and were eager for an experienced voevoda chosen directly by Tsar Dmitrii. Bolotnikov's arrival was greeted warmly, and under his direction—according to a contemporary—the rebels "struggled yet more valiantly."[49]

Before Bolotnikov appeared on the scene, Shakhovskoi and others had already hastily organized military forces to struggle against Shuiskii. The Putivl district's large gentry detachment (mostly deti boiarskie infantry) played a prominent role, as did the newly promoted golova (colonel) of the Putivl fortress cossacks, Iurii Bezzubtsov—the former sotnik (centurion) of the Putivl cossacks who had served Tsar Dmitrii so well during his campaign for the throne.[50] Thousands of free cossacks joined forces with the Putivl garrison, the garrisons of several other southern frontier towns, and most of the region's pomeshchiki to form "Tsar Dmitrii's" army. Shuiskii propaganda falsely claimed that the rebels were all lower class brigands.[51] In fact, many of those men were veterans of Dmitrii's campaign for the throne in 1604–5 who quickly reactivated their old units in order to serve the "true tsar" once again. Otherwise, Shakhovskoi would never have been able to organize and field an army with such speed.[52]

While awaiting the arrival of "Tsar Dmitrii's" commander-in-chief, Shakhovskoi needed an interim commander to perform a very important task: to link up with and help defend the rebels in the fortress of Elets (350 kilometers east northeast of Putivl). Elets was of enormous strategic value because, in an unprecedented move, Tsar Dmitrii had stored massive quantities of food, gunpowder, lead, and artillery there in preparation for his planned campaign against the Crimean Tatars.[53] The Elets garrison of about one thousand men (mostly deti boiarskie infantry and fortress cossacks, beefed up by units sent there in anticipation of action against the Crimean Tatars) had rejected Shuiskii's coup from the very beginning.[54] Thus, Elets, almost overnight, became a principal rebel stronghold. As such, its recovery by Tsar Vasilii became a high priority. If the rebels could hold onto Elets they would have enough supplies not only to sustain themselves for more than a year but also to support a large and rapid assault on Moscow itself.[55]

Prince Shakhovskoi chose Istoma Pashkov to command the relief force. He was ordered to advance to Elets, to spread news that Tsar Dmitrii was still alive, and to capture as many towns and fortresses as possible in preparation for the march against the usurper in Moscow.[56] Pashkov has traditionally been portrayed as a prominent nobleman—as the spokesman for the "lords" who found themselves in an uneasy alliance with the revolutionary masses.[57] Actually, he was a mere pomeshchik with cossack connections.[58] Although later represented as a gentry leader who eventually rejected the radical agenda of Bolotnikov, Pashkov was referred to by Tsar Vasilii's officials in 1606 as the "brigand of Epifan."[59] Pashkov had been born about 1583 into a petty pomeshchik family near the town of Epifan. His father had a nominal pomeste entitlement of approximately 400 acres but actually held less than 300 acres by the time of his death in 1603. Istoma thereupon petitioned Tsar Boris to obtain his father's holdings; by then the younger Pashkov had served in the tsar's militia for five years but still had not received pomeste land anywhere. Tsar Boris granted his request, making Pashkov the lord of two villages—one near Venev and the other near Serpukhov.[60] Tsar Dmitrii later promoted Pashkov to the rank of sotnik and gave him command of one hundred Epifan deti boiarskie.[61]

The pomeshchiki Pashkov commanded are worth a closer look. In 1585, in a decision typical of the Russian government's efforts to shore up southern frontier defenses, three hundred fortress cossacks of Epifan were promoted en masse into the ranks of the deti boiarskie and received small land allotments (in reality, mostly just the conversion of their collectively held dachas to pomeste estates). Of course, that promotion did not quite turn those men into "true" gentry. Most of them continued to work the land themselves, and as a group they did not prosper. By the time Istoma Pashkov became their sotnik, the majority of his one hundred deti boiarskie still had very small holdings of less than 100 acres each.[62] Because of the social background and relative poverty of his marginal pomeshchiki, it is not surprising to find Pashkov occasionally referred to by contemporaries as a "cossack ataman." Pashkov maintained close ties with his men who in turn remained fiercely loyal to him.[63] Together they joined the rebel cause within just a few weeks of Tsar Dmitrii's assassination.

Pashkov's role in the early stage of the civil war has been overlooked in some studies due primarily to poor use of sources.[64] A number of scholars believed Pashkov joined the rebels only at the end of summer 1606, along with the Tula and Riazan gentry.[65] In fact, he was the first rebel commander chosen by Shakhovskoi, and he led the first rebel army into action against Shuiskii's forces. Along with Ivan Bolotnikov, Istoma Pashkov was regarded as a principal rebel commander by Tsar Vasilii and other contemporaries.[66]

At about the same time Pashkov's army was making its way from Putivl toward Elets, exciting news about events in the great lower Volga port town of Astrakhan reached Prince Shakhovskoi. Astrakhan was one of the largest towns in Russia; the population inside its mighty stone walls probably stood at ten thousand in the early seventeenth century. The town was a critically important fortress guarding southeastern Russia and access to the Volga River from the Caspian Sea. Many of its merchants prospered by a brisk trade with Persia, the Caucasus, Central Asia, and Russian towns up the Volga.[67] Astrakhan had a large garrison, beefed up by Tsar Dmitrii, consisting of more than a thousand men—including pomeshchiki (mostly deti boiarskie infantry), streltsy, artillery-men, and guards.[68]

Because of faulty sources and the traditional social revolutionary interpreta-tion of the Bolotnikov rebellion, historians have long been understandably con-fused about the details of just how Astrakhan joined the rebel cause in 1606.[69] It actually started when the town received word from Moscow about the over-throw of the evil "Otrepev" and the accession of Tsar Vasilii. Many of the towns-people swore an oath of loyalty to the new tsar; others did not and wondered aloud about the true fate of Tsar Dmitrii.[70] Within a few days, on June 17, 1606, a soldier arrived in Astrakhan with an outdated letter from the now-dead Tsar Dmitrii authorizing him to travel to the lower Volga region. The fact that the letter was old was completely lost on the town's population. Many of them rejoiced at the "news" that Tsar Dmitrii was alive and immediately rebelled in the name of the "true tsar."[71] Suddenly, the Astrakhanites who had embraced Shuiskii's coup with enthusiasm now found themselves in serious trouble. A few of them were thrown from Astrakhan's towers to the cheers of the rebel crowd. Others were shut up in prison or fled from the town. Many of them had their homes ransacked and their slaves set free.[72] The fact that some of the town's rich merchants were sympathetic to Tsar Vasilii inevitably meant they were subjected to looting or worse at the hands of the rebels or were forced to flee without their possessions.[73] Largely because of that, peasant war scholars incorrectly called the rebellion in Astrakhan a class war.[74] It was actually a popular uprising in which most of the garrison and townspeople joined voevoda Prince Ivan D. Khvorostinin in swearing an oath of loyalty to Tsar Dmitrii.[75] Prince Khvorostinin, a supporter of Dmitrii who had been named by him as voevoda of Astrakhan, led the town's struggle against the usurper Shuiskii for several years.[76]

Soon after the rebellion in Astrakhan, boyar Fedor Sheremetev and his army (which Tsar Dmitrii had sent down the Volga to prepare for military operations against the Crimean Tatars) arrived before the gates of the town. Sheremetev had been instructed by Tsar Dmitrii to replace Khvorostinin as voevoda of Astrakhan. Before reaching the town, however, he had received word of Shuiskii's coup and new instructions from Tsar Vasilii. Shuiskii had mistakenly assumed that Sheremetev would already be in Astrakhan by the time he received his orders, and the new tsar had decided to retain him as voevoda there. As a result, Sheremetev arrived before Astrakhan with Tsar Vasilii's official blessing just a few days after the town had declared for Dmitrii. Because of that, Khvorostinin refused to open the gates of the town to the army of the "traitor Shuiskii." Shut out of the fortress and facing a hostile local cossack population, Sheremetev and his men were forced to retreat north about 15 kilometers to Balchik Island, where they constructed a wooden fort and remained for more than a year.[77]

Sheremetev tried repeatedly to blockade Astrakhan from Volga River traffic and made occasional forays against the town. In response, Khvorostinin first had the townspeople dig new trenches outside the fortress walls to forestall possible siege operations. Then, toward the end of summer 1606, military units from Astrakhan along with Don, Volga, Terek, and Iaik cossacks began periodically attacking Sheremetev's semipermanent camp. In the meantime, rebellions in the Sviazhsk and Nizhnii Novgorod regions farther up the Volga cut off easy communications between Sheremetev's army and Moscow.[78] According to Isaac Massa, almost fifteen hundred newly impoverished merchants from Astrakhan and other towns near the Caspian Sea flocked to Sheremetev's camp on Balchik Island for protection, where they endured terrible siege conditions and perished in large numbers from hunger and cold.[79] Massa's figure for the number of merchants on Balchik Island is wildly exaggerated, but his estimate may be close to the total number of persons who sought protection from voevoda Sheremetev.[80] For what it is worth, Sheremetev himself stated that merchants had abandoned the dangerous Volga region altogether because it was unsafe and because they had no goods left to trade.[81]

One of the tasks Tsar Vasilii had assigned to Fedor Sheremetev was to conduct negotiations on his behalf with the Nogai Tatar Prince Ishterek and other powerful Nogai leaders, large numbers of whose subjects ("yurt Tatars") were settled in the Astrakhan region.[82] Unfortunately for Sheremetev, Molchanov sent a letter from "Tsar Dmitrii" to Prince Ishterek, and voevoda Khvorostinin also negotiated with the Tatar leader in Dmitrii's name. As a result, many local Nogai Tatars joined the rebellion against Shuiskii.[83] In fact, they took maximum advantage of the chaos produced by the civil war, mustered thousands of men, and—according to a contemporary—began to "ravage all the areas they could reach."[84] Soon, other non-Slavic native peoples of the Volga region also rebelled against Shuiskii and generally against the heavy hand of Russian imperial expansion.[85] Try as he might, Tsar Vasilii was never able to gain control over southeastern Russia.

For years Astrakhan itself remained an important rebel anchor and magnet for free cossacks wishing to join "Tsar Dmitrii's" service. Over the course of the civil war, voevoda Khvorostinin was able to field a total of as many as twenty thousand men for military service against the hated usurper in Moscow.[86] During the civil war, the Astrakhan region also produced a number of copy-cat pretenders claiming to be sons of Ivan the Terrible or Tsar Fedor Ivanovich. Tsar Dmitrii was, of course, their model and inspiration. Some of those "tsareviches" actually managed to gain the support of large numbers of Don, Volga, and Terek cossacks who actively cooperated with Astrakhan against Sheremetev's beleaguered army. Although the cossack "tsareviches" were merely attempting to legitimize their own banditry by means of such pretense, the fact that they attracted numerous supporters was yet another sign of the widespread popular rejection of Vasilii Shuiskii's legitimacy and of the power of the lingering hope for the miraculous appearance of a resurrected member of the defunct sacred ruling dynasty.[87] The most important of those cossack pretenders was Tsarevich Petr (already mentioned in Chapter 12), whose activities during the civil war will be discussed in future chapters.

"Tsar Vasilii IV," as Shuiskii vainly hoped he would be remembered by posterity, had been truly stunned by the news reaching Moscow of the rapid revolt of town after town and garrison after garrison on the southern frontier. The widespread belief that Tsar Dmitrii had escaped assassination and the amazing speed with which the rebels fielded an army against Shuiskii, not to mention the periodic disturbances in Moscow sparked by the arrival of rumors about Dmitrii's whereabouts and activities, almost completely unnerved the shaky new tsar. A contemporary in Moscow at the time wrote: "The tsar desired with all his heart to become a monk and enter a monastery, but the magnates prevented him."[88] Instead, Shuiskii was forced to make vigorous preparations to resist the rebellion.

Despite rebel gains, Shuiskii held powerful advantages. Even unloved by many of his subjects, Tsar Vasilii had been accepted at least nominally by most of the central and northern parts of the country, by the court and the bureaucracy, by the top military leadership, and by much of the army.[89] In addition to holding the capital, he could count on the support of members of the elite in the important towns of Novgorod, Smolensk, and Nizhnii Novgorod. Even though the civil war split the country in two and disrupted tax revenues and ordinary military planning, operations, and recruitment; Tsar Vasilii still had a vast area and considerable resources to draw upon. Overall, enough of the tools of governing and coercion remained intact for Shuiskii to survive for a long time despite being regarded as illegitimate by many of his subjects.[90] In one of his smarter moves made shortly after he seized power, Tsar Vasilii sent representatives to the Don cossack stanitsas with gifts of money, lead, and gunpowder in order to convince them to swear an oath of loyalty to him—hoping thereby to neutralize a powerful force that had fought valiantly for Tsar Dmitrii in the past. Shuiskii's strategy was partially successful; some Don cossacks decided to stay on the sidelines during the renewed civil war.[91]

Because of Tsar Dmitrii's preparations for his planned campaign against the Crimean Tatars, Shuiskii had at his immediate disposal, on paper at least, many fully mobilized militia regiments to send against the rebels. Unfortunately for the new tsar, many of those soldiers refused to swear an oath of loyalty to him and simply melted away, heading for home or for rebel-held towns.[92] In addition, many militiamen and streltsy who remained nominally loyal to Shuiskii were, nonetheless, regarded by him as untrustworthy. For that reason, some of them were foolishly dispatched to other towns and forts for lower status garrison duty, which many of them regarded as punishment. Not surprisingly, large numbers of these men later rebelled against Tsar Vasilii and greatly aided the cause of "Tsar Dmitrii."[93] Because Shuiskii had demonized Tsar Dmitrii's foreign troops in his whispering campaign against "Otrepev," the new tsar felt compelled to dismiss many of the several thousand skilled mercenary troops in Russian service. Given no severance pay, many of those men were reduced to begging and robbery by the time they reached the border.[94] Many others, however, made their way to rebel-held towns and reentered "Tsar Dmitrii's" service. Among them, according to a contemporary, were "valiant and determined men" (including the Scottish captain Albert Wandmann) who performed extremely valuable service to the rebel cause as "commanders of cavalry, captains, or governors of captured towns."[95] A number of foreign officers Tsar Vasilii tried to retain in his service, such as Captain Margeret, soon found excuses to leave Russia; a few of them later returned to fight against Shuiskii in the service of "Tsar Dmitrii."[96]

Tsar Vasilii made a concerted effort to retain the loyalty of his remaining troops and to gain additional forces and money from towns and monasteries.[97] Fearing the effects of admitting that he was fighting against the ghost of Tsar Dmitrii, however, at first he tried to hide the fact of the rebellion. Shuiskii issued a fairly plausible emergency proclamation that the Crimean Tatars had invaded Russia with fifty thousand men, had already captured thousands of Russians and carted them off to the Turkish slave auctions, and were still rampaging around the country. He called upon all towns to rush military recruits (datochnye liudi) to Moscow in order to resist the invaders. By July, new detachments of recruits arrived in the capital almost daily, and preparations for a possible siege of the city were begun.[98] By then financial aid from rich monasteries was also forthcoming.[99] Because of the continuing effects of Russia's severe economic and social problems, the gentry militia crisis, and the popularity of Tsar Dmitrii among Russian soldiers, however, there were many no-shows among recruits as well as pomeshchiki in Shuiskii's army.[100] Some unenthusiastic towns also failed to send any men or money, claiming that they had no resources left after years of famine and civil war.[101]

Despite all his problems, Tsar Vasilii still commanded a large army. He confidently turned down self-serving offers of military aid from the ambitious and land-hungry Swedish and Polish kings, declaring that he needed no foreign assistance in order to keep his throne.[102] As soon as he could, Shuiskii sent the bulk of his available military forces south to suppress the rebellion. Nervous about the loyalty of his own troops, however, the tsar's official explanation for transferring the army to the Serpukhov area was to stop the alleged Crimean Tatar invasion.[103] Only when Tsar Vasilii's soldiers actually clashed with rebel forces near Elets did many of them learn that they were fighting against their fellow countrymen and against "Tsar Dmitrii."[104] The shock of that discovery helps to explain many of the problems Shuiskii's commanders faced in the field.

Tsar Vasilii's offensive against the rebels began by early July 1606.[105] Initially, the main army, once again under the command of senior boyar Prince Fedor Mstislavskii, did not concentrate all its strength at Serpukhov. Instead, units were spread out in various fortresses along the Oka River while the tsar's commanders discussed their strategic options.[106] Mstislavskii's forces totaled somewhere between fifty and sixty thousand men.[107] The senior voevoda was most concerned about two towns in rebel hands, Elets and Kromy. Because of the huge supply depot in Elets, its recovery was considered a higher priority than Kromy. For that reason, Mstislavskii sent a relatively small force under the command of Prince Iurii N. Trubetskoi and Mikhail A. Nagoi against Kromy.[108] The military significance of that fortress had, of course, been amply demonstrated during Dmitrii's campaign for the throne; it was the strategic gateway between the southwestern frontier and central Russia, and it was there that the rebellion of Tsar Fedor Borisovich's army had doomed the Godunov dynasty. Nervousness about the loyalty of their troops and bad memories of the siege of Kromy in 1605 caused Shuiskii's commanders to take the precaution of sending against that fortress only the most loyal units from Novgorod, Pskov, Velikie Luki, and the Moscow region. Voevoda Trubetskoi established his headquarters in Karachev, 50 kilometers northwest of Kromy, and sent Nagoi ahead to start the siege while he organized recruits arriving from the north into new detachments.[109] Upon learning of the enemy's approach, the rebels in Kromy sent word to Prince Shakhovskoi in Putivl asking for help and then dug in to withstand the siege.

In the meantime, Mstislavskii sent a larger army under the command of Prince Ivan M. Vorotynskii toward Elets, which quickly became the focal point of bitter conflict lasting all summer.[110] At first, voevoda Vorotynskii tried to win over the fortress garrison by diplomacy. A letter from Tsar Dmitrii's mother was presented to the fortress commander by none other than boyar Grigorii F. Nagoi, Tsar Dmitrii's uncle. In the letter, the nun Marfa denounced her putative son as Otrepev and appealed to the inhabitants of Elets to give up the struggle against the legitimate Tsar Vasilii. Grigorii Nagoi also brought along an icon depicting the newly canonized St. Dmitrii to show the rebels. Despite such an impressive display of Nagoi clan loyalty to the new tsar, Elets did not yield. Thereupon, Vorotynskii laid siege to the fortress.[111] The rebels in Elets had, of course, maintained close contact with Putivl, and, as already noted, Shakhovskoi quickly dispatched the first rebel army commanded by Istoma Pashkov to help defend that fortress. Pashkov's small army probably advanced to Elets via friendly Rylsk and Kursk, gaining additional troops along the way. He was able to lead approximately seven to eight thousand men into battle against Vorotynskii's much larger army.[112] According to legend, Pashkov defeated Vorotynskii in one of the earliest engagements of the renewed civil war and put Tsar Vasilii's army to flight.[113] In reality, Vorotynskii defeated Pashkov in a major battle and then continued besieging Elets.[114] Voevoda Vorotynskii and all his officers and men were soon rewarded with gold coins by a grateful Tsar Vasilii.[115] They were unable, however, to make any progress in their siege operations. As a result, by August, additional military units were—with considerable difficulty—concentrated in Vorotynskii's hands in order to speed up the siege.[116]

Sometime during the sieges of Kromy and Elets, "Tsar Dmitrii's" commander-in-chief, Ivan Bolotnikov, arrived in Putivl from Sambor. When did Bolotnikov arrive in Russia? Because he led rebel forces to victory at Kromy in the late summer, many historians assumed he arrived in Russia (along with his mythical Zaporozhian cossack army) only at the end of summer and immediately won his first great battle.[117] That is not what really happened. Bolotnikov actually arrived in Putivl sometime in July, 1606.[118] Shakhovskoi immediately gave him command of an army of twelve thousand men and sent him north, across the friendly Komaritsk district, to relieve besieged Kromy.[119] There, sometime in July, Bolotnikov was defeated in his first encounter with voevoda Mikhail Nagoi and was forced to retreat.[120] He apparently returned briefly to Putivl after that defeat and, along with Iurii Bezzubtsev, organized new rebel military units.[121] Bolotnikov also spent a few weeks in and around the Komaritsk district, adding new recruits, regrouping and training his men, and ousting from the region some stray supporters of Tsar Vasilii. There is some evidence that Bolotnikov's men saw military action at Novgorod Severskii at this time, and at least one of Shuiskii's voevodas was captured in battle by Bolotnikov somewhere in the area.[122]

"Tsar Dmitrii's" commander-in-chief may have established his own temporary headquarters in the village of Bordakovka, in the southern part of the Komaritsk district.[123] Of course, the population of the Komaritsk district and the neighboring Samovsk district responded enthusiastically to Bolotnikov's appeals for more troops, food, supplies, and money. Towns in the area joining the rebel cause by August included Trubchevsk, Sevsk, Pochep, Lgov, Moravsk, and Popova Gora—along with the southern fortress of Voronezh and probably Oskol as well.[124] The only towns in the zone Bolotnikov was operating in whose garrisons remained loyal to Shuiskii were Briansk and Karachev; despite Tsar Vasilii's efforts to fortify those towns, their inhabitants rebelled by September 1606, killed their voevodas, and declared for Tsar Dmitrii.[125] In fact, so many men eagerly flocked to Bolotnikov's banner that, according to a contemporary, throughout southwestern Russia "only women remained" in most towns and villages.[126] By August, with a larger and somewhat better trained army, Bolotnikov was able to move north again to attempt to relieve Kromy. Before he arrived there, Mikhail Nagoi's siege army had been reinforced by three regiments, and his superior, voevoda Iurii Vorotynskii, had assumed overall command of the siege operations.[127] Trubetskoi, however, was no more successful than Nagoi had been. Like Elets, Kromy stubbornly resisted Shuiskii's forces while waiting for assistance from Putivl.

As summer wore on, Tsar Vasilii's siege armies grew increasingly weary. The rebels were at this time generally better provided for than the tsar's forces, and they fought with much greater zeal.[128] Shuiskii's commanders also had great difficulty operating in a region in which Tsar Dmitrii had been very popular and over which the tide of revolt was once again spreading rapidly. For example, the voevoda of Livny (70 kilometers west of Elets), okolnichii Mikhail B. Shein, was ordered to transfer his forces to Elets in order to reinforce Vorotynskii's siege; but the inhabitants of Livny chose instead to rise in rebellion in the name of Tsar Dmitrii, and Shein was forced to flee—in the process abandoning all his supplies and possessions.[129]

News of the loss of Livny and the lack of progress in the sieges of Elets and Kromy prompted a frustrated Tsar Vasilii to order a thorough review of the campaign, his commanders, and their strategy. At the beginning of August 1606, courtiers were sent into the field to review the situation and to make recommendations about the military forces fighting the rebels as well as those protecting central Russia and Moscow from possible rebel advances. As a result of that strategic review, additional military units were ordered to reinforce the siege of Elets.[130] Soon, regiments from the Riazan district commanded by boyar Prince Vasilii K. Cherkasskii and Grigorii F. Sunbulov joined the siege. Troops from Serpukhov and Novosil were also ordered to advance to Elets.[131] Even with additional forces arriving before that rebel stronghold, however, voevoda Vorotynskii was unable to capture the fortress.[132] In fact, the transfer of boyar Prince Mikhail F. Kashin's regiment from Novosil (70 kilometers northwest of Elets) unleashed a sharp struggle in that town. Novosil's garrison, composed mostly of deti boiarskie infantry, immediately led a rebellion of the townspeople in the name of Tsar Dmitrii.[133] Shuiskii's commanders were then forced to send Kashin's regiment back to Novosil, but to no avail; the rebels would not open the town's gates to those returning soldiers.[134] As a result, Tsar Vasilii's siege armies now found themselves facing a rebel stronghold behind them as well as in front of them. That seriously threatened their lines of communication, supply, and reinforcement, and it lowered the morale of their weary troops even further.

Sometime in late August, Bolotnikov made his second attempt to relieve beleaguered Kromy.[135] In addition to large numbers of troops from Seversk towns and a sizable force of Komaritsk peasants, his army now included detachments of Don cossacks (but not Bolotnikov's mythical ten thousand Zaporozhians). The wily golova (colonel) Iurii Bezzubtsev led the rebel army's main contingent of deti boiarskie infantry.[136] Bolotnikov's forces advanced rapidly against Trubetskoi's much larger army. By then, some of Trubetskoi's troops, mobilized in the spring, had already participated in the siege of Kromy for two months and had exhausted their meager provisions. As noted earlier, it was almost impossible even in good years to keep the tsar's army on campaign for many months; and in the early seventeenth century, in the midst of a severe gentry militia crisis, prolonged sieges were almost impossible to sustain. Many of Trubetskoi's men were hungry, demoralized, and distracted by foraging for provisions. Making matters worse, the cost of food in siege camps—always high—was even higher than usual in 1606 due to the severe freeze that occurred just after Tsar Dmitrii's assassination. Many of Tsar Vasilii's soldiers simply could not afford to pay for food. As a result, there was growing malnutrition and discontent in the siege camps before Kromy and Elets.[137] In light of this, it is no real surprise that Bolotnikov's men were able, without great difficulty, to fight their way through the enemy's lines to bring badly needed supplies and rein- forcements to besieged Kromy. That further demoralized Trubetskoi's disgrun- tled men.

In an early display of his energetic tactical skills, Bolotnikov immediately ordered repeated forays from Kromy to keep up pressure on his wavering oppo- nents. Very soon, Trubetskoi and Nagoi were forced to begin a general retreat of their exhausted forces. The retreating army very quickly began to disinte- grate. Even Shuiskii's most trustworthy detachments (from the regions of Novgorod, Pskov, Smolensk, and Moscow) began to abandon Trubetskoi's army and headed for home, complaining about the spread of rebellion throughout the entire frontier.[138]

To support the rebel cause, Tsar Dmitrii's father-in-law, then being held pris- oner in Iaroslavl, spread a false rumor that eight thousand of Shuiskii's men had been badly beaten at Kromy, driven from the field, and pursued for 10 kilo- meters by rebel forces.[139] That rumor was credited by some people at the time and led some historians to write about a great "victory" achieved at Kromy by Bolotnikov (and his mythical ten thousand Zaporozhian cossacks).[140] Even with- out such a great victory, however, Bolotnikov's men were able to hold the field while the enemy retreated north. For his part, voevoda Trubetskoi tried to keep his army together by withdrawing to nearby Orel (40 kilometers to the north- east of Kromy). There he attempted to make a stand, but his own retreat had changed the strategic situation in the area and opened a path to the heartland for the rebels. While Trubetskoi and his men tried vainly to hold the line at Orel, rebellion swept through the region. Inside Orel itself, loyal gentry units from Novgorod witnessed the wavering of the townspeople and the local gar- rison (mostly deti boiarskie infantry). Fearing the consequences of remaining there, the Novgorodians simply abandoned the town and began retreating north. That prompted the Orel garrison and the entire town to declare for Dmitrii. Shuiskii's commanders, aware of the dangerous situation developing in Orel, had hastily dispatched one thousand five hundred streltsy under voevoda Prince Danila I. Mezetskii in order to try to persuade the town's garrison to remain loyal; but Mezetskii's men, who encountered the Novgorodians running away from Orel, were unable to recover the town for Tsar Vasilii. Almost immedi- ately, Bolotnikov's forces occupied Orel, from which they were able to pursue and harass the remainder of the tsar's army that was now rapidly retreating north toward Kaluga—the main hub of the upper Oka defensive lines (located 70 kilometers north of Orel).[141]

The passage of Bolotnikov's army through the region triggered many more rebellions among garrisons and townspeople. In short order, the inhabitants of Bolkhov, Belev, Odoev, Kozelsk, Peremyshl, Meshchovsk, Serpeisk, and probably Likhvin and Vorotynsk as well, declared for Tsar Dmitrii and opened their gates to Bolotnikov's forces. Many of those new rebels also quickly signed up to help carry the struggle all the way to Moscow.[142] In Odoev and Bolkhov, a few unfortunate Shuiskii supporters were robbed, tortured, and thrown from towers to their deaths.[143]

By the time Bolotnikov managed to break up the siege of Kromy, Tsar Vasilii's commanders besieging Elets were facing the very same problems that had overwhelmed Trubetskoi. The two-month siege of Elets had accomplished nothing useful, and Shuiskii's frustrated and weary troops were subjected to a constant barrage of demoralizing reports about rebel victories elsewhere and the rebellion of more and more towns.[144] By late summer, food was becoming scarce and too expensive for many of Tsar Vasilii's militiamen.[145] When news reached Elets about Bolotnikov's success at Kromy and about the hasty retreat of Trubetskoi's army, it had a powerful demoralizing effect on the besiegers. Some deti boiarskie began to desert the siege camp for home. Morale among the remaining troops sank even further when badly needed supplies were captured by rebel forces.[146] Voevoda Vorotynskii himself, short on supplies and facing mounting desertions, grew increasingly afraid of being trapped behind a rapidly advancing line of rebel troops and rebellious towns. He therefore chose to break off the siege of Elets and retreated north toward the large town of Tula—a major fortress and coordinating center of southern defenses located 180 kilometers northwest of Elets.[147] The retreat of Tsar Vasilii's siege army prompted many rumors that Vorotynskii's forces had been smashed in a large battle by a rebel army arriving from Putivl.[148] On the basis of those rumors, some scholars later wrote colorful accounts of a great rebel "victory" at Elets.[149] In fact, there is no more truth to the myth of the catastrophic defeat of Tsar Vasilii's army before Elets than there is to the mythical defeat of Shuiskii's forces before Kromy.[150] So confused are the sources and the scholarship on this subject that even the name of the "victorious" rebel commander at Elets has been hotly disputed.[151] In fact, just as in the first attempt to relieve Elets in July, the commander of the returning rebel army was Istoma Pashkov.[152] Even without a great victory, Pashkov's men held the field as Vorotynskii's army retreated north, and news of the retreat of the tsar's forces from Elets had a similar effect to news of Trubetskoi's retreat from Kromy—inspiring the rebels and demoralizing Shuiskii's supporters. And just like Bolotnikov, Pashkov quickly pursued the retreating army and applied enough pressure on it to keep

Vorotynskii from being able to regroup his forces in order to prevent the rebel tide from sweeping north.[153]

As Vorotynskii's army retreated, his subordinate voevoda, Mikhail Kashin, still unable to retake Novosil, abandoned that effort and also retreated north to Tula. There, Vorotynskii planned to regroup his forces and to hold out in Tula's impressive fortress that guarded the road to Moscow. Unfortunately for Vorotynskii, many of his militiamen hastily abandoned him at this time, including gentry detachments from Riazan and Kashira. Most of those weary men went home, but some of them joined the rebel cause. Vorotynskii, faced with the disintegration of his army and unsure of the loyalty of the inhabitants of Tula, was forced to make a hasty retreat to Moscow. That drastic move opened up a direct path to the capital for the supporters of "Tsar Dmitrii." It also triggered the further disintegration of Vorotynskii's army and a powerful uprising of the population of Tula and most of the region's dvoriane and deti boiarskie.[154] This was the first time large numbers of sturdy and even prosperous gentry joined rebel forces in the renewed civil war. The shock of the loss of Tula and the retreat and disintegration of both armies sent to crush the rebellion inspired fear in the hearts of Shuiskii supporters as well as dumbfounded admiration for the valiant and successful rebel soldiers. One contemporary who lived in Moscow claimed that Tsar Vasilii's forces had been "so badly beaten by the rebels in all encounters that fewer than half returned."[155] Repeating the pattern of Bolotnikov's advance, Pashkov's army took advantage of the situation and advanced rapidly from Elets toward Tula, triggering rebellions in several towns and fortresses along the way—including Mtsensk (where one Shuiskii loyalist survived being thrown from a tower only to sit in prison for a year), Dedilov, and Krapivna.[156] Pashkov then entered and occupied Tula itself.[157]

The rebellion of Tula marked a new phase in the renewed civil war. Up to that time, the bulk of the rebel leadership had come from petty deti boiarskie of the southern provinces. But in the older, more settled frontier zones such as the Tula and Riazan districts were settled many relatively prosperous gentry with large holdings and many serfs. In fact, the most prestigious Tula dvoriane typically served in Moscow and even at court. When these men led the defection of Tula from Tsar Vasilii, followed by a similar rebellion of their peers in the Riazan district, it marked a significant split within the ruling elite and doomed Russia to many years of ruinous civil war.[158] The Tula and Riazan dvoriane, as noted earlier, had long resented the boyars for closing off career opportunities to them and for unfair economic competition.[159] Many pomeshchiki from the old frontier region had, of course, joined Dmitrii's cause in 1605 and helped tip the balance of power decisively away from the Godunovs toward Dmitrii. Now, once again, they rejected a "boyar-tsar" who had usurped the throne.

At first, the Riazan gentry, witnessing the Tula elite's revolt against Shuiskii, merely disobeyed voevoda Vorotynskii's orders and abandoned Tula for home.[160] Their arrival home, however, sparked rebellions in several Riazan towns—including Zaraisk and Mikhailov. The rebels killed the voevoda of Mikhailov and shipped the Zaraisk voevoda off to Putivl, where he was later put to death.[161] While the senior voevoda of Pereiaslavl-Riazanskii (later known as Riazan), Vasilii K. Cherkasskii, remained loyal to Shuiskii, his associate voevoda, Grigorii F. Sunbulov, threw his support to the rebels and declared himself Tsar Dmitrii's voevoda of Pereiaslavl-Riazanskii. Cherkasskii, taken by surprise, was arrested and shipped off to Putivl where he was eventually executed.[162] One of the Riazan lords who had been most active in helping Dmitrii gain power in 1605, the prestigious dvorianin Prokofii Liapunov, once again declared for Tsar Dmitrii. In the process, he captured one of Shuiskii's voevodas (Prince G. S. Karkadinov) and shipped him off to Putivl where he was also later executed.[163] Soon, the entire Riazan region rose in the name of Tsar Dmitrii—including the towns of Pereiaslavl-Riazanskii, Serebrianye Prudy, Pronsk, Venev, Riazhsk, Sapozhok, Pesochnia, Shatsk, and Epifan.[164] In Gremiachii, Shuiskii loyalists were thrown from a tower to their deaths by the town's fortress cossacks.[165] Contrary to the views of peasant war scholars, the rebel armies' advance into the more settled regions of the country that had sizable gentry estates worked by peasants did not stimulate a widespread uprising by privately owned serfs.[166] It was, in fact, the enthusiastic embrace of Tsar Dmitrii's cause by large numbers of dvoriane, deti boiarskie, lower status military servitors, and townspeople that marked this phase of the civil war; serfs barely participated, if at all.

Tsar Vasilii was, of course, mortified by reports of rebel gains and the retreat and disintegration of his armies. Even before the worst news about the collapse of the sieges of Elets and Kromy reached him, Shuiskii ordered preparations for a possible siege of the capital.[167] Tsar Vasilii was also understandably still nervous about his popularity inside Moscow. Despite the gradual decline of dangerous incidents, on or about July 22, new broadsheets from "Tsar Dmitrii" appeared on the streets of the capital and once again provoked a minor disturbance. Officials responded by carefully screening the handwriting of all bureaucrats and clerks in Moscow in an unsuccessful effort to find the forger.[168] At about the same time, Tsar Vasilii took the extraordinary precaution of ordering the dismantling of two bridges across the moat protecting the Kremlin as well as the stationing of cannon at the Kremlin gates. In early August, there was a huge gunpowder explosion in Moscow; no serious damage was done, but it frayed nerves. At about the same time, news arrived in the capital about great rebel "victories" in the south, and still more letters from "Tsar Dmitrii" appeared that announced that he would return at the beginning of September. Shuiskii responded to these disturbing developments by staying inside the Kremlin and ordering its gates locked.[169]

Once it became obvious that there was a powerful civil war going on, Tsar Vasilii dropped all pretense about a Crimean Tatar invasion and launched a bitter propaganda campaign against "Otrepev" and the rebel "brigands." He made a passionate, if misleading, appeal to his subjects—urging them to fight against evil, Polish-backed heretics who had "plundered churches, torn out icons, alters, and gospels, smashed holy images, murdered nobles, merchants, and townsmen, and raped their wives and daughters."[170] Patriarch Hermogen assisted in the campaign to demonize the rebels and to portray Shuiskii as a pious, legitimate tsar.[171] Their strategy was partially effective, but the rebellion kept growing and the belief in Tsar Dmitrii's "resurrection" continued to spread—even in Moscow. Prisoners and suspected rebels were brought into the capital almost every day; maddeningly, even under torture they swore that Dmitrii was alive. By the dozens, fanatic partisans of the dead tsar were drowned in the river, almost all claiming with their dying breath that Dmitrii was once again marching on Moscow to reclaim his throne and punish the traitors.[172] Witnessing such ardent faith in Tsar Dmitrii and hearing constant reports of rebel victories had a sobering effect on many people in the capital, even some courtiers. For example, it was rumored that, toward the end of August, Tsar Vasilii felt compelled to order the arrest and exile to Siberia of a member of the boyar council for advising him to find out if Dmitrii was in fact still alive and, if so, to return the throne to him immediately in order to avoid a destructive civil war.[173]

Tsar Vasilii did not have to wait long for Tsar Dmitrii's angry supporters to arrive in central Russia. By the end of summer 1606, with Bolotnikov's army approaching Kaluga and Pashkov's army already in Tula, the rebels had effectively expelled Shuiskii's forces from the southwestern and southern frontier. By then, virtually all towns and fortresses south of the Oka River had sworn allegiance to Tsar Dmitrii.[174] The rebels were now rapidly advancing through the old frontier zone to directly challenge Shuiskii for control of the important fortified towns along the Oka River, towns that protected the heartland and the approaches to Moscow itself.[175]

16

The Civil War Widens and the Rebels Advance to Moscow

By early fall 1606, as "Tsar Dmitrii's" main voevodas, Ivan Bolotnikov and Istoma Pashkov, led their armies into central Russia and approached Moscow, rebellion swept from the frontier through the central Volga region and into the heartland itself. Because of contradictory sources about this phase of the civil war, there has been considerable confusion among scholars concerning chronology, the composition of rebel forces, the routes they took, when and where battles occurred, and even who won or lost. For those reasons, it is necessary to take a careful look at the weeks leading up to the siege of Moscow.

As Tsar Vasilii and his military advisers studied the developing strategic situation at the end of the summer, they decided to concentrate on stopping Bolotnikov's advance to Kaluga. Because that important town screened the capital from the south, they feared a breakthrough there more than anywhere farther east where Pashkov was operating. Spies were sent to the Kaluga region to gain as much information as possible about Bolotnikov's forces, plans, and activities.[1] Since voevoda Trubetskoi's army had fallen to pieces, it was necessary to form a new army to face the rebels at Kaluga. All available troops were to be used for this purpose. The plan was to combine the remnants of Trubetskoi's army with former members of the Kromy and Orel garrisons who had not joined those towns in declaring for Dmitrii. Tsar Vasilii sent officials to try to persuade those dispirited soldiers to stop their disorganized retreat and to rally at Kaluga in order to protect the capital.[2] Meanwhile, the tsar's brothers, Ivan and Dmitrii, formed the nucleus of the new army out of the "tsar's regiment" and advanced to Kaluga in early September. Many courtiers, Moscow dvoriane, zhiltsy, and some provincial gentry were in that elite force.[3]

Bolotnikov's army attempted to cross the Ugra River at its confluence with the Oka River, about 7 kilometers west of Kaluga. The Shuiskii brothers were waiting for him.[4] Although Ivan Shuiskii has been described as a mediocre commander, on September 23, in a bitter battle he stopped the rebels from crossing the Ugra and pushed them back. Many of Bolotnikov's men were killed in that confrontation.[5] For this victory, Tsar Vasilii sent his commanders and soldiers hearty congratulations, pieces of gold, and notification of salary increases.[6] Legend has it that Bolotnikov won the battle.[7] Even though he did not, there are good reasons for the widespread belief that he had been victorious. Ivan Shuiskii was unable to profit from his victory due to the rebellion of Kaluga itself, which had long had very strong trade ties with Severia and the Komaritsk district.[8] The timing of that rebellion is unclear. Shuiskii was unable to enter Kaluga because of the uprising, and that may be why he met Bolotnikov's army outside the town. Or Kaluga may have rebelled as Bolotnikov's forces approached or possibly during the battle at the Ugra River crossing.[9] In any case, Ivan Shuiskii's victorious army was unable to use Kaluga as a base and, as a result, began retreating toward Moscow.[10] Images of the tsar's army in disorderly flight may or may not be an accurate reflection of its retreat from Kaluga, but the myth about a "victorious" Bolotnikov crossing the river and advancing northward to Serpukhov virtually unopposed is completely without foundation.[11]

After the battle at the Ugra River, Bolotnikov retreated eastward toward Aleksin. The approach of his army provoked an uprising in that town in favor of Tsar Dmitrii. Many members of the Aleksin garrison and gentry from that district immediately joined Bolotnikov's growing army. From Aleksin, Bolotnikov crossed the Oka River and returned to Kaluga where he was welcomed and where many men from the town's garrison and the district's gentry joined his forces.[12] Operating out of Kaluga, Bolotnikov then made a serious effort to cut Moscow off from the west. According to a contemporary, "He brought every locality through which he passed back to its allegiance to Dmitry, who was about to arrive, and by this means he progressively increased his army."[13]

While Tsar Vasilii concentrated on stopping Bolotnikov southwest of Moscow, opportunities opened up for the rebels farther east. From Tula, Pashkov sent a small force east through the Riazan district toward Riazhsk and possibly on to the central Volga region—areas then in the process of rebelling against Shuiskii.[14] In the meantime, Pashkov and the main part of his army advanced north in hot pursuit of Vorotynskii's forces; they crossed the Oka River and by mid-September made it all the way to Serpukhov—only 90 kilometers south of Moscow.[15] By then, Pashkov's army was swollen by the addition of new recruits from several garrisons and districts joining the rebel cause at about this time. The inhabitants of Serpukhov, seeing the approach of the large rebel army, declared for Tsar Dmitrii and opened their gates.[16] Pashkov entered Serpukhov and immediately gained many more recruits. Like Bolotnikov, wherever Pashkov went he brought villages, towns, and fortresses back to the cause of Dmitrii with little or no resistance.

Not surprisingly, news of the rebel occupation of Serpukhov caused panic in Moscow. Many lords and their wives fled from the capital because of it.[17] To prevent Pashkov from approaching Moscow, a small detachment under voevoda Prince Vladimir V. Koltsov-Mosalskii was hastily sent from the capital along the Serpukhov road to the Lopasnia River—the first real barrier north of Serpukhov. There Koltsov-Mosalskii tried to stop the rebels but was unsuccessful, suffering heavy losses in the process.[18] He was forced to retreat north all the way to the Pakhra River, only 18 kilometers south of Moscow, where his exhausted men were quickly reinforced.[19] In the meantime, Pashkov's forces paused at the Lopasnia River long enough for Tsar Vasilii's close friend, Metropolitan Pafnutii, to be able to send two spies there to gain information about the enemy.[20] Taking no chances, Shuiskii ordered his brilliant nephew, Prince Mikhail Skopin-Shuiskii, to take command of the forces guarding the Pakhra River, providing him with an additional cavalry detachment from Ivan Shuiskii's army located farther to the west. Sometime after September 23, Skopin-Shuiskii's army defeated Pashkov's attacking forces in a fierce battle. Pashkov suffered heavy casualties and was forced to retreat.[21]

The battle at the Pakhra River was a significant but fleeting victory for Tsar Vasilii. He ordered some salaries increased but sent his men no gold.[22] Skopin-Shuiskii's victory did at least relieve the immediate threat to the capital. Nonetheless, before his defeat, Pashkov managed to send a small scouting detachment all the way to the Moscow suburbs. Those men advanced to Kolomenskoe and, by September 17, reached the village of Kotly, just a few kilometers south of the capital.[23] Only Skopin-Shuiskii's victory at the Pakhra forced them to retreat.

There is considerable confusion in the sources and in the literature concerning Pashkov's next move.[24] In fact, he retreated to Serpukhov.[25] While there, he learned of a rebellion in the important town of Kashira, just 50 kilometers to the east, and of repeated but unsuccessful efforts by Tsar Vasilii's brother, Dmitrii, to retake that town with a small army.[26] Pashkov immediately led his men to Kashira, which he quickly occupied and secured from the threat posed by Dmitrii Shuiskii's forces. Troops from the town's garrison and local militiamen flocked to join Pashkov's now-sizable army.[27] From Kashira, Pashkov made his way along the Oka River northeast about 50 kilometers to the fortified town of Kolomna, a key position in the defense of Moscow. The rebel army quickly occupied Kolomna.[28] There is much absurdity in some sources and in the literature concerning Pashkov's arrival there, which must have been by very early October. Tsar Vasilii's propagandists represented events at Kolomna as a fierce siege, ending with the rebels going on a killing, looting, and burning spree that destroyed the town.[29] Other dubious sources claimed that the voevoda, streltsy, and inhabitants of Kolomna declared their support for Tsar Dmitrii simply to avoid being killed.[30] In fact, if there was any siege at all, it was a short one.

Kolomna's voevoda S. Kokhanovskii opened the gates to the rebels and swore an oath of loyalty to Tsar Dmitrii.[31] The Soviet historian Ivan Smirnov regarded Kokhanovskii as a typical adventurer in the "peasant war"; but Skrynnikov correctly noted that he was a high-ranking vybornyi dvorianin who remained steadfastly loyal to the rebel cause until the fall of Tula in late 1607.[32] It is also known that units of Moscow streltsy, which had been recently transferred to Kolomna by Tsar Vasilii, willingly joined forces with Pashkov.[33] It has been claimed that the rebels promised not to loot the property of the wealthy in Kolomna but then broke that promise. That is pure speculation. In fact, Pashkov did persecute local gentry and merchants who remained loyal to Tsar Vasilii, and that may have included allowing their property to be looted.[34]

The fall of Kolomna (located about 100 kilometers southeast of Moscow) terrified Tsar Vasilii and his supporters. With the military situation sharply deteriorating, they gathered together all available remaining forces and planned to move them toward Kolomna in order to stop Pashkov's approach to the capital. Meanwhile, in Kolomna, Pashkov was joined by sizable units of Riazan district gentry led by Prokofii Liapunov and Grigorii Sunbulov. Despite their superior social status, those gentlemen had little choice but to recognize the incredibly successful Pashkov as the senior voevoda of their combined forces.[35] Pashkov now advanced against Moscow with a large army. In the capital, rumors spread that Tsar Dmitrii himself was in Kolomna. Many pomeshchiki chose to desert Shuiskii, either going home or quietly joining the rebels.[36]

Contrary to assertions made by some scholars, Pashkov did not link up with Bolotnikov at this time. The two armies did not join forces at Kolomna for the final assault on the capital.[37] There is another myth about the two rebel armies that has permeated traditional interpretations of the "Bolotnikov rebellion." According to Platonov and others, Bolotnikov led an army consisting primarily of lower class social revolutionaries while Pashkov's army consisted primarily of conservative gentry who found themselves in an uneasy alliance with their radical social inferiors. Pashkov himself was supposedly a prominent spokesman for the lords supporting "Tsar Dmitrii," and, while on campaign, his army allegedly treated surrendering gentry "lawfully" by keeping them in captivity or even letting them go. Bolotnikov's army, on the other hand, supposedly carried out a wave of executions of gentry opponents and was determined to exterminate the "lords."[38] In fact, there is no truth to the traditional class war interpretation of the two rebel armies. As noted earlier, rebel forces included representatives of all social classes (but very few serfs). The two rebel armies were formed in the same region at about the same time and contained heterogeneous elements.[39] Many rebels in both armies were veterans of Dmitrii's campaign for the throne in 1604–5.[40] Skrynnikov carefully studied the insurgent forces in 1606 and concluded that there were basically no significant distinctions in the social composition of the two rebel armies.[41] There were also no real distinctions in their behavior. Pashkov's army carried out just about as many acts of vengeance against Shuiskii supporters as did Bolotnikov's army.[42] For the dvoriane and deti boiarskie in both rebel armies, those violent acts against Shuiskii supporters were not seen as ominous signs of class war but as well-deserved reprisals against their enemies.[43]

Although the armies of Bolotnikov and Pashkov did not join forces at this time, Pashkov's bold thrust toward Moscow effectively screened Bolotnikov's activities west of the capital. From Kaluga Bolotnikov's men fanned out into the regions southwest, west, and even northwest of Moscow. They made a serious effort to cut the capital off from the western provinces, especially Smolensk. Some of that large border city's elite had supported Shuiskii's coup, and Tsar Vasilii was counting on military aid from Smolensk.[44] The Soviet historian Ivan Smirnov believed that Bolotnikov personally led his men on those expeditions, but the name of the rebel commander-in-chief is not mentioned in any sources concerning his army's activities west of the capital.[45] At least several rebel detachments were involved, and those forces included dvoriane, deti boiarskie, and cossacks. Their commander may have been one of Bolotnikov's lieutenants, the cossack ataman Soloma Kazak.[46] Those rebel units were extremely successful and met virtually no resistance. As they approached many towns, they stimulated rebellions in them in the name of Tsar Dmitrii.[47] In short order, Bolotnikov's men brought a large territory over to the rebel side. Shuiskii propaganda claimed those uprisings were motivated only by the townspeople's fear of being sacked and killed by rebel soldiers.[48] It is more likely that those civilian populations and garrisons rebelled for the same reason so many others had up to this point—opposition to the usurper in Moscow.[49]

The two main fortresses on the Smolensk road, Viazma and Mozhaisk (110 kilometers west of Moscow) declared for Dmitrii and seriously disrupted communications between Moscow and the western provinces.[50] Other towns southwest, west, and even northwest of the capital quickly followed suit and joined the rebel cause—including Medyn, Dorogobuzh, Roslavl, Vereia, Ruza, Pogoreloe Gorodishche, Zvenigorod, Malyi Iaroslavets, Borovsk, Rzhev, Zubtsov, Staritsa, and Selo Borisovo Gorodishche.[51] So successful were Bolotnikov's troops that by the time the siege of Moscow began in late October, rebels were operating in large numbers as far north as the roads linking the capital to towns in northwest Russia. They did not succeed in their attempts to entice the important town of Tver into rebellion; but many towns, villages, and servicemen in that region did join the rebel cause, and communications between Moscow and Tver were disrupted.[52] One monastery located 60 kilometers west of the capital that insisted on remaining loyal to Tsar Vasilii, the Savvina-Storozhevsk monastery in Zvenigorod, was apparently looted and burned.[53] Rebel forces also menaced the heavily fortified and extremely wealthy Iosifo-Volokolamsk monastery northwest of Moscow and actually managed to occupy the nearby town of Volok Lamskii (90 kilometers from Moscow) by mid-October. To prevent them from looting the monastery's well-provisioned villages, the monks paid a bribe of more than eight rubles to two of the rebel commanders.[54]

Despite the success of Bolotnikov's forces, they failed to encircle Moscow completely. Roads connecting the capital to the northeast remained open. That meant some supplies and men could still reach Moscow from north Russia even as the rebels closed in on Shuiskii from three sides. Nonetheless, rebel victories to the southeast, south, southwest, west, and northwest of Moscow had a powerful effect. Among other things, the capital was now cut off from its usual sources of grain. Grain prices in the city rose to three or four times normal, which was beyond the ability of many to pay. While the boyars grumbled about "unlucky" Tsar Vasilii, the Muscovites were increasingly unhappy with both the tsar and his advisers. Many people expected Moscow to fall to the rebels.[55] Panic-struck and hungry people fled from the capital, and the stream of lords and soldiers abandoning Tsar Vasilii for the rebel camp or for home became much larger.[56] That left the tsar in Moscow with relatively few soldiers.[57] In fact, by this time Shuiskii was having extreme difficulty recruiting or even maintaining military forces.[58] Many servicemen were reluctant to oppose the rebels, and the tsar was unable to find enough money to pay the financially distressed ones who were still willing to fight for him.[59] Cavalrymen in the capital could no longer find or afford fodder for their horses.[60] In order to keep his hard-pressed soldiers from starving or abandoning their posts, Tsar Vasilii began a daily distribution of food to them and their families.[61]

By this time Shuiskii's treasury was almost empty. Compounding the problem, the rebellion had seriously interrupted the ordinary flow of taxes to Moscow. Even some areas not directly threatened by the rebels were slow to send money to Tsar Vasilii's government.[62] Adding insult to injury, several West Siberian tribes (Ostiaks, Voguls, and Samoeds) chose this time to resist Russian imperial pressure by menacing the town of Tobolsk and by withholding their tax payments—resulting in the loss of yet another significant source of revenue for Tsar Vasilii.[63] As a result of all these problems, Shuiskii became increasingly desperate for cash and manpower. Even in the relatively quiet region of northeast Russia, the tsar had great difficulty raising troops or money. For example, recruits gathered in Perm in September for service in Moscow rebelled while marching to the capital, strongly influenced by the attitude of people they met in the village of Kotelnich (near Viatka). There local leading citizens, streltsy, and a priest invited the recruits to drink to Tsar Dmitrii's health in their tavern and announced that the true tsar had already captured Moscow.[64] In the far north, efforts to raise money and even to administer the oath of loyalty to Tsar Vasilii were sometimes met with threats of violence; in a few cases, Shuiskii supporters were robbed and killed.[65]

Any hope Tsar Vasilii may have had about getting money or soldiers from the central Volga region to the east of Moscow was also shattered by September. Probably in association with the rebellions in the Riazan region and the activities of the small military force Pashkov sent toward Riazhsk, the entire central Volga area was in turmoil.[66] Town after town, district after district, and people of all social classes—natives and Slavs alike—rose in the name of Tsar Dmitrii. Towns and fortresses in the region joining the rebel cause at this time included Murom, Arzamas, Tsivilsk, Alatyr, Kurmysh, Iadrin, Cheboksary, and Sviazhsk.[67] Among other things, those rebellions severed normal communications between Moscow and the strategically important city of Nizhnii Novgorod, the entire Volga region, and Sheremetev's beleaguered army bivouaced north of Astrakhan.[68]

Why did the central Volga region join the rebel cause? Like the southern and southwestern frontier zones, the central Volga region had been the focus of intense colonization in the second half of the sixteenth century; however, unlike those other areas, the region was densely populated by non-Slavic natives, and large numbers of Russian peasants were among the early colonists. Rebellions in the central Volga region in 1606 in some ways resembled uprisings on the southern frontier but with many more peasants and large numbers of non-Russian natives joining the struggle. To some extent, participation in the second phase of the civil war by tribes such as the Cheremis (Mary), Mordvians, and Chuvash, as well as various Tatar groups, was more of a protest against Russian imperial control, taxation, and overall pressure than a particularly strong attachment to Tsar Dmitrii; but, as noted in Chapter 14, Dmitrii did have a positive reputation among those peoples.[69]

One can gain a better understanding of the dynamics of rebellion in the central Volga region by taking a closer look at the well-studied case of Arzamas, located on a tributary of the Oka River about 100 kilometers south of the important Volga city of Nizhnii Novgorod. The Arzamas region became the focus of spontaneous, voluntary colonization soon after the Russians captured Kazan in 1552, but significant government-sponsored colonization came only after the reorganization of southern frontier defenses in the 1570s. Thus, before many pomeshchiki arrived in the area, large numbers of Russian peasants migrated there seeking freedom and economic opportunity in the relatively rich, heavily wooded region. They immediately encountered the native Mordvians, a people of Finnish extraction who had centuries before settled in the area between Nizhnii Novgorod and Kazan. Many Mordvians were Islamic, and large numbers of them served as cavalry in the tsar's army.[70] Other Mordvians (and Chuvashi), however, tried to defend tribal pagan cults from the pressures of Orthodox Christian missionaries who posed an external threat which helped unify the natives in opposition to Moscow.[71] Russian peasants voluntarily settling among the Mordvians, by contrast, did not treat the natives as inferiors and did not try to convert them to Orthodoxy. Instead, they worked on the lands of the Mordvians and helped them develop a mutually profitable business gathering the incredibly abundant local honey.[72]

As the region came increasingly under pressure from government-sponsored colonization, the Russian honey farmers frequently made common cause with the Mordvians in resisting Moscow's imperial drive and enserfing policies.[73] The local population, Mordvian and Russian, was increasingly deprived of its lands as the government promoted large-scale colonization by pomeshchiki. Although some peasants were imported with the militiamen to serve as their labor force, in many cases Russian peasant honey farmers already settled in the region were coerced into laboring on the new pomeste estates. That created a very tense situation. As the gentry population in the region grew steadily (increasing 40% between 1585 and the 1620s), so too did the population of servile peasants (increasing 200% in the same period) and especially the number of landless agricultural workers (up 1000%).[74] Already by the 1590s, the impoverished and overburdened local population expressed its unhappiness in periodic disturbances.[75]

Many other Russian peasants in the region also rose in the name of Tsar Dmitrii—the first large group of peasants to rebel against Shuiskii since the inhabitants of the Komaritsk district. Some of those Russian rebels were long-time residents, formerly free peasants who had been forced to work on the lands of newly arriving pomeshchiki; many others were more recent arrivals who had crossed the Oka and entered the central Volga region to escape famine or serfdom only to find themselves quickly reenserfed and assigned to work for new lords.[76] It is, therefore, no real surprise to find these men resisting pressure from Moscow alongside the native population. In fact, all layers of local society, Slav and non-Slav, elite and commoner, participated in the decision by the Arzamas district to rebel against Shuiskii and to send troops to support the rebel siege of Moscow.[77] Many Arzamas pomeshchiki, like gentry militiamen throughout the central Volga region and the southern frontier, enthusiastically supported Tsar Dmitrii.[78] Among other things, they shared a common distaste for the Moscow ruling elite's disdain for them as unworthy petty provincials and a common anger at the boyars' unwillingness to share honors and rewards with them. Two sons of a former Arzamas voevoda (who had been appointed by Dmitrii but ousted by Shuiskii) provided leadership and helped legitimize the local uprising against Tsar Vasilii.[79] Obviously influenced by events in Arzamas, the entire central Volga region remained a hotbed of rebel activity throughout the long civil war.[80]

The story was much the same farther east in Alatyr, located on the Sura River about halfway between Arzamas and the Volga River. There, however, the rebels were forced to drown one voevoda and to throw the other in prison before the town declared for Dmitrii.[81] Another major center of resistance to Shuiskii was the region surrounding Kurmysh, also located on the Sura about 150 kilometers south of Nizhnii Novgorod. In addition to Tatars and Mordvians, a large percentage of the local population there consisted of Cheremis people, another native group of Finnish extraction who often provided large numbers of cavalrymen for the tsar's army. For many of the same reasons as the Mordvians, the Cheremis resisted Russian imperialism and even rebelled against Moscow briefly in the 1590s.[82]

In 1606, in Kurmysh the newly baptized Tatar prince Andrei B. Kazakov convinced the townspeople and the district's population to declare for Tsar Dmitrii. The rebels then incited Tatars and Cheremis in the neighboring Iadrin area to rebel against Shuiskii. They also seriously disrupted communications between Moscow and the Volga region by robbing and killing Tsar Vasilii's couriers.[83] Some of the rebels rode off to Moscow to participate in the siege. Kazakov stayed behind and managed to stir up the whole region, helping to push yet another native central Volga tribe of settled agriculturalists, the Chuvashi, to rebel against Tsar Vasilii. Soon the town of Cheboksary, located on the Volga in the heart of Chuvash territory, declared for Dmitrii; its Shuiskii-loyalist voevoda was killed.[84] Rebels in Cheboksary were well positioned to disrupt the already dwindling Volga trade to wealthy Nizhnii Novgorod, which was the usual starting place for the Volga boatmen and the main point of departure for the region's overland carrying trade to Moscow.

Gradually, a large and motley array of Russian pomeshchiki, honey farmers, and peasants, along with Tatars, Cheremis, Mordvians, and Chuvashi coalesced into a significant military force. They marched against Nizhnii Novgorod, which, in addition to being a major trade center, was Tsar Vasilli's main administrative and political headquarters for the entire central Volga region. Soon pomeshchiki and others from the Nizhnii Novgorod district itself joined rebel forces arriving from as far away as Murom and laid siege to the heavily fortified city. Among the rebel commanders were two wily Mordvian elders who played many "dirty tricks" on the besieged city but were unable to capture it.[85] The besiegers of Nizhnii Novgord maintained only loose ties with the rebel armies marching on Moscow but occasionally sent captured Shuiskii supporters to Putivl.[86]

In faraway Moscow, Tsar Vasilii was extremely upset by the news arriving from the central Volga region, but he had more immediate problems on his hands and could not afford to weaken his already thin forces by sending regiments away from the capital. Instead, he ordered his loyal voevoda in Sviazhsk (near Kazan), who had so far managed to fend off rebel attacks, to gather together local garrisons and members of the remaining loyal population in his district in order to recapture Kurmysh and Iadrin, and especially to capture the "traitor" Prince Andrei Kazakov.[87] Shuiskii's plan failed completely, however; Kurmysh remained in rebel hands. In fact, soon after the Sviazhsk voevoda stripped his town of troops in order to carry out Tsar Vasilii's orders, rebels approached Sviazhsk with news of the siege of Moscow and triggered a rebellion of the entire population of that town, from gentry to commoners, who then immediately swore an oath to fight for Tsar Dmitrii. When Shuiskii heard of this development, all the beleaguered tsar could do to retaliate was to have church leaders place Sviazhsk under interdiction.[88]

In spite of all the bad news coming in from the central Volga region, Tsar Vasilii could at least take heart in the fact that the rebels there were unable to sweep into the area northeast of Moscow, which would have threatened the capital's only remaining open roads and its access to vital supplies and recruits. Instead, the Moscow-Vladimir-Nizhnii Novgorod-Kazan line more or less held even as virtually all Russian territory south of that line fell into rebel hands. There are several reasons why northeastern Russia remained loyal to Tsar Vasilii. It has been plausibly argued that emigration from that area by the more desperate and restive souls who ended up on the southern frontier kept the north relatively quiet throughout the entire early modern period. Another reason offered has been the sturdiness of north Russian peasant economies and their relative independence from the pressures of greedy pomeshchiki.[89] More important perhaps, that region had not participated in Dmitrii's campaign for the throne in 1604–5, and therefore it had no former rebel military units available for quick remobilization. In addition, no cossacks lived in the area. In another sense, though, Shuiskii was able to hold onto the region in 1606 only by default. Had rebel units penetrated into northeastern Russia, there is no reason to believe the local population would have resisted joining the cause of Tsar Dmitrii. Tsar

Vasilii was not especially popular in the area, and rebel forces had been successful in turning local populations to their cause wherever they went. In the case of northeast Russia, the rebels simply ran out of time—in part because the region was protected by difficult terrain and dense forests and had relatively few towns and roads, and in part because of the stubborn resistance of Nizhnii Novgorod and Kazan.

Nizhnii Novgorod remained true to Shuiskii primarily because of the loyalty of its voevoda and garrison and because—like Novgorod, Pskov, and Smolensk—it had a strong contingent of successful and influential merchants who worked closely with Moscow merchants and were generally sympathetic to Tsar Vasilii, especially after the rebels virtually shut down Volga trade and hurt Nizhnii Novgorod's economy. Merchants in Kazan also lost money when Volga trade was disrupted, but Kazan's steadfast loyalty to Shuiskii was due more to the charisma and attitude of its voevoda, Bogdan Belskii.[90] Belskii, Tsar Dmitrii's godfather who had been "exiled" by Tsar Vasilii to become governor of Kazan, probably could have persuaded the inhabitants of that town to declare for Dmitrii, but he was well aware that his godson was really dead and had no interest in supporting some unknown impostor.

Despite the relatively good news Tsar Vasilii received from Kazan and Nizhnii Novgorod, there was no denying that Shuiskii was in deep trouble. During the first five months of his reign, he endured staggering setbacks and lost control of nearly half of the country and its people. By the time the siege of Moscow began in late October 1606, rebels controlled at least eighty towns (more than one third of all Russian towns and about half of those significant enough to have voevodas) as well as a very large number of villages.[91] To Shuiskii's great surprise and chagrin, what had started out as a rebellion of the southwestern and southern frontiers had rapidly developed into a potent civil war extending from the steppe across the old frontier zone right into the forests and woodlands of central Russia and even to Moscow's suburbs. Rebel territory was huge and growing larger every day. Rebel forces, including more and more of Tsar Vasilii's own gentry militiamen, were growing rapidly, were highly motivated, and were reasonably well supplied.[92] Under these circumstances, it is no surprise that Shuiskii was frightened and that Moscow was in turmoil.

To rally his demoralized forces and to keep Moscow's terrified and wavering inhabitants loyal, Tsar Vasilii's propaganda now began to falsely claim that the satanic rebels wished to exterminate the entire population of the capital—not just the tsar and his close associates—because the Muscovites were all guilty of murdering Tsar Dmitrii.[93] Tsar Vasilii took the additional precaution of having the population of the capital swear another oath of loyalty to him; his officials emphasized in the process that they were all in great danger and must stick together.[94] Patriarch Hermogen also moved his propaganda campaign into high gear. In addition to his usual tirades about the rebels intending to destroy the Russian Orthodox Church, he had Shuiskii order the inhabitants of Moscow to visit churches and to pray for divine assistance against the evil supporters of "Tsar Dmitrii." Special services were conducted in which bishops and priests admonished their parishioners not to surrender to the forces of Satan.[95]

Next, the patriarch had it announced that on October 12, 1606, a certain clergyman had a vision in which Holy Mother Mary pleaded with Jesus to spare the Russian people whom He was planning to punish for their sins by means of the heretic rebels. In the end, it was said, Mary managed to persuade Jesus to relent, and the clergyman was told to tell the Russian people about his vision.[96] Hermogen immediately ordered a strict and extremely convenient six-day fast, complete with constant bell ringing and prayer throughout the hungry capital (October 14–19), in order to avert the wrath of God, and the clergyman's "vision tale" was read to large crowds in the Cathedral of the Assumption (Uspenskii Sobor) and in most of the other churches in Moscow on October 16. Tsar Vasilii, Patriarch Hermogen, and many people went to church, wept openly, and carefully observed the fast. Since a large percentage of the capital's population was truly frightened by the approach of the rebels as a possible sign of God's anger, this cleverly staged event was regarded by many of them as a genuine miracle, and that really did help Shuiskii's cause.[97]

It turns out that Tsar Vasilii's propagandists had cynically reworked the text of a "vision tale" fortuitously produced in mid-September by a former zealous supporter of Tsar Dmitrii, Archpriest Terentii of the Kremlin's Cathedral of the Annunciation. Ironically, the original text was actually hostile to Shuiskii, but with only minor revisions it became a potent propaganda tool against the rebels.[98] Not surprisingly, such "vision tales" became more and more commonplace during the dark days of the Time of Troubles.[99]

In addition to waging psychological warfare, Tsar Vasilii and his supporters prepared militarily as best they could for a possible siege of the capital. That task was not an easy one due to the critical shortage of troops and supplies on the one hand and the problem of trying to defend a huge, sprawling city that was larger in area than Paris on the other. Ordinarily, more than seventy thousand people lived in Moscow in that era. The Kremlin and the inner city were surrounded by two rings of stone and brick walls and were further protected on the south side by the Moskva River; however, the vulnerable outer wall of the capital—which enclosed 4,600 acres and was more than 15 kilometers in circumference—was made of nothing but wood and earth.[100] Only the roads to the north and northeast, especially the heavily used route through the sub-urb of Krasnoe Selo, remained open or unmenaced by rebel units.

Shuiskii's military engineers concentrated almost exclusively on reinforcing the city's weak outer wall at the southern entrance to the city because that was the direction from which the main rebel army would undoubtedly approach the capital. The banks of the Moskva River to the east and west of that approach would inevitably box in any advancing army and force it to attack the south-ern entrance of the city along either the Kaluga or the Serpukhov road. There Moscow's outer wooden wall, with its periodic watchtowers, offered only min-imum protection to the city's trans-river district (*zamoskvorech'e*) known as "wooden town." Directly in front of the highly vulnerable Kaluga and Serpukhov gates, therefore, Tsar Vasilii's engineers quickly constructed an elaborate maze of temporary fortifications. They built a large guliai gorod composed of mov-able prefabricated panels of logs (each about 1.5 meters wide and 2 meters high) chained together to create a wall invulnerable to cavalry attacks. Openings in the panels allowed harquebusiers and archers to stand and shoot at the enemy and artillerymen to discharge their cannons without exposing themselves to enemy fire. This particular guliai gorod had a large quantity of artillery sta-tioned behind it and was big enough to contain campgrounds for many sol-diers, pens for a large number of horses, and supply depots.[101]

In a final effort to fend off the siege, Tsar Vasilii ordered the hasty forma-tion of five regiments to march south and stop Pashkov's advance. By this time, however, the bulk of Shuiskii's pomeshchiki had already dispersed to their homes and were not available. As a result, the tsar's commanders were only able to field three regiments. Even that required pressing into service nearly all able-bodied men sixteen years and older who lived in or near the capital.[102] Under the over-all command of Fedor Mstislavskii and his associates (Dmitrii Shuiskii, the Golitsyn brothers, and Ivan Vorotynskii), many high-ranking courtiers, mem-bers of the tsar's household staff, palace officials, and even secretaries and clerks joined the bulk of the remaining Moscow dvoriane, zhiltsy, and streltsy for the campaign. This small army departed from Moscow along the Kolomenskoe road on October 23 and was reinforced by detachments of Skopin-Shuiskii's troops and additional units of Moscow streltsy at Domodedovo, near the Pakhra River. From there the army advanced to the village of Troitskoe (or selo Troitsko-Lobanov), located about 30 kilometers north of rebel-held Kolomna.[103]

The battle of Troitskoe occurred on or about October 25. It has been alleged that by then Mstislavskii and the Golitsyns were so unhappy about Tsar Vasilii that they fought for him with little enthusiasm and that many of their soldiers were actually sympathetic to Tsar Dmitrii. Whether that is true or not,

Fig. 10 "A Bird's-Eye View of Moscow in the Early Seventeenth Century." Printed

Mstislavskii's army was decisively defeated by Pashkov's men in bloody fighting. The tsar's forces then fled north in panic.[104] Many pomeshchiki and courtiers were captured and later sent to Putivl.[105] Some retreating soldiers spoke of seven thousand men killed and nine thousand men robbed and chased for a great distance while being taunted and beaten with knouts.[106] In fact, Shuiskii's army disintegrated as it was retreating, and the tsar's troops hastily abandoned all their possessions. Only disorganized and demoralized remnants of the defeated army made it back to Moscow, which now braced itself for an inevitable siege.[107]

One contemporary interpreted the flogging and dispersal of Shuiskii's men as gentle treatment, as a sign of Pashkov's sympathy for the poor clerks and others who had been dragooned into defending Tsar Vasilii. That led some scholars (as we have already seen) to the mistaken conclusion that Pashkov's "gentry" force was showing class solidarity with Shuiskii's gentry militia.[108] Actually, Pashkov's immediate goal was Moscow, not prisoners. By dispersing retreating enemy forces he was not being slowed down or unnecessarily burdened by large numbers of captives.[109] It is also worth noting that it was not at all unusual after a battle for victorious cavalry to pursue an enemy for up to 30 kilometers. Pashkov's men chased, lashed, and insulted their terrified opponents for two days (October 26–27) in much the same way ataman Korela's cossacks had tormented, humiliated, and dispersed Tsar Boris's fleeing troops in 1605 at Kromy. Hot pursuit of Shuiskii's retreating forces probably brought cossack units of Pashkov's army to Kolomenskoe by October 27. The opening round of the siege of Moscow began the next day.[110] Contrary to legend, Bolotnikov's army had not yet combined forces with Pashkov's, and Bolotnikov himself did not arrive in time to see the start of the siege.[111]

By October 28, 1606, the day the siege began, Tsar Vasilii commanded only small, relatively weak forces and was no longer able to wage an active struggle to prevent rebel armies from approaching the capital. Already running dangerously low on men and supplies, Shuiskii's voevodas at the outset of the siege could not afford to risk a major battle in the suburbs. Instead they were forced to retreat behind the barricades of the guliai gorod just south of Moscow's Serpukhov and Kaluga gates and to a few other fortified locations east and southeast of the city.[112] Contemporaries at this point likened the beleaguered Tsar Vasilii to an eagle that no longer had any feathers, beak, or talons—a pathetic and defenseless bird now trapped in a cage.[113] Many people fully expected Moscow and Tsar Vasilii to quickly fall into rebel hands.[114] Those expectations, however, failed to take into account Shuiskii's energetic and ingenious efforts to retain control of the capital and to frustrate his enemies.

Those believing the end was near for Tsar Vasilii also failed to take into account two fundamental weaknesses of the "Bolotnikov rebellion." First, in many ways, it was not so much a centralized movement with unified leadership as it was a series of powerful local responses to false news of Tsar Dmitrii's survival or to the arrival of rebel troops in the neighborhood. In different places the renewed civil war assumed somewhat different forms. Local conditions often dictated those forms, some of which were more radical than others.[115] Sometimes the initiators of rebellion against Tsar Vasilii were petty gentry, lower status military servitors, cossacks, or ordinary townspeople; at other times, the local voevoda or important dvoriane took the lead. The haphazard formation of rebel forces and the great distances involved also contributed to relatively limited contact or coordination among various rebel groups. Instead, the rapid retreat of Shuiskii's armies propelled the rebellion forward with dizzying speed, widening and deepening it along the way. As that occurred, the real nerve center of the rebellion quickly shifted from Putivl to the commanders of the two rebel armies, who maintained—at best—only haphazard contact with each other. The only glue that really bound them together was the burning desire to expel the usurper from Moscow. Pashkov and Bolotnikov did not have a coordinated plan to accomplish their goals, nor had they even worked out who should assume overall command of the siege of the capital. Such basic strategic weaknesses make it all the more astonishing that the rebels were able to accomplish so much so quickly with nothing more than the ghost of Tsar Dmitrii to unite them.

That brings us to the second basic weakness of the rebel movement—the fact that Tsar Dmitrii was really dead. Obviously, if he had survived the assassination attempt there would not have been any civil war in Russia in 1606; Shuiskii and his accomplices would have been dealt with in short order. As it turned out, however, the dead tsar's failure to appear in the rebel camp to inspire his forces ultimately doomed the siege of Moscow.[116]

17

The Siege of Moscow

The siege of Moscow began on October 28, 1606. The first detachments of Pashkov's army to approach the capital were the cossacks and militiamen who had chased Tsar Vasilii's army from the battlefield at Troitskoe. Up to ten thousand rebels quickly occupied the village of Zabore, located near the Danilov monastery less than two kilometers south of Moscow's Serpukhov gate.[1] That advance guard quickly dug in and fortified Zabore cossack-style. They established a very sturdy defense perimeter by arranging hundreds of sleds in a rough circle around the village, stacking them on top of one another, and ingeniously binding them all together. Then the rebels poured water over the sleds. As soon as the water froze, they had—in the words of a contemporary—an "improvised rampart as strong as stone."[2] In this and other acts of military engineering, the rebels received high praise even from their enemies.[3] The advance guard was now secure, well-provisioned, and prepared to hold out for weeks, if necessary, while waiting for Pashkov's main army to arrive.[4] Their fortified enclave, so near the Serpukhov gate, immediately became a major concern for Shuiskii's commanders because rebels in Zabore could attack at any time and, if successful, set fire to the wooden outer wall of the capital. The only thing that stood between them and Moscow was the large guliai gorod into which was crowded much of the remainder of Tsar Vasilii's army. That meant any time Shuiskii's troops wished to advance, they would have to go past Zabore and leave the enemy enclave behind their own lines and dangerously close to the city's walls.

Pashkov's main army arrived in the general vicinity of Moscow within a few days and established a strong fortified camp, complete with earthworks and palisades, in the village of Kolomenskoe—about 13 kilometers south of the capital.[5] Pashkov himself probably occupied a mansion Tsar Dmitrii had built there. From Kolomenskoe the rebel commander sent word to Moscow demanding the immediate surrender of the city to "Tsar Dmitrii's" army and the extradition of Vasilii Shuiskii and his two brothers as the instigators of the plot to kill the "true tsar." Many Muscovites, fully expecting a successful siege, at this point secretly abandoned the capital to join the rebels or simply to get out of harm's

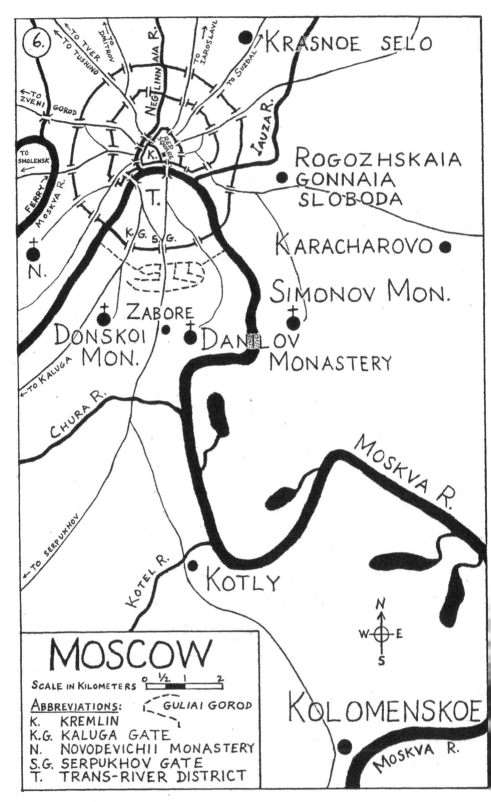

Map 6 Moscow.

way.[6] Within just a few days, in early November, Bolotnikov's army also arrived in Kolomenskoe (probably via Serpukhov).[7] With the joining of the two rebel armies, Tsar Vasilii was in serious trouble. Since Shuiskii commanded relatively small forces at this time, it is completely understandable that his soldiers did not immediately advance to do battle with the large rebel army. Instead, those men remained encamped in the guliai gorod and other defensive positions for more than two weeks while waiting for desperately needed reinforcements.[8] The rebels may well have been able to force the surrender of the capital at this stage, but they failed to press their advantage.[9]

Why did the rebels delay their attack, which allowed Tsar Vasilii time to recover and to gain additional troops? It was due in part to confusion, lack of coordination, and the relative independence of the various rebel units descending on Moscow. It was also due to the conflict developing between Bolotnikov and Pashkov. When Bolotnikov arrived in Kolomenskoe, he insisted that, as Tsar Dmitrii's commander-in-chief, he should occupy the "most comfortable quarters" there—meaning Tsar Dmitrii's mansion. That forced Pashkov to evacuate Kolomenskoe. In status-conscious early modern Russia, Pashkov and his lieutenants felt deeply dishonored by this episode and began secretly plotting their revenge against Bolotnikov.[10] That eventually led Pashkov to betray the rebel cause during the siege of Moscow. He undoubtedly believed that his victories over Shuiskii's forces and his early arrival before the capital had entitled him to better treatment; and, like Petr Basmanov at Kromy in 1605, his "honor" was more important to him than the cause he claimed to be fighting for. In the end, Bolotnikov's arrogant treatment of Pashkov had terrible consequences for the rebels. In the meantime, however, he concentrated real power in his own hands. Once Bolotnikov's army joined the siege, everyone acknowledged that he was, indeed, the commander-in-chief of all rebel forces.[11] A sullen Pashkov was forced to move his own forces north from Kolomenskoe to the village of Kotly, only a few kilometers south of Moscow.[12] The approach of that large rebel force alarmed residents of the capital and disheartened many of Tsar Vasilii's soldiers.[13]

In the literature on the Bolotnikov rebellion there is a great deal of nonsense about the rift between Bolotnikov and Pashkov. According to the traditional interpretation, the radical social goals of Bolotnikov's "democratic" forces eventually forced a fearful Pashkov and his "gentry" army to switch sides to Tsar Vasilii.[14] In reality, there was little difference in the social composition of the two rebel armies, and Pashkov was definitely not the spokesman for conservative gentry nervous about a temporary alliance with dangerous social revolutionaries.[15] Pashkov arrived in the vicinity of the capital with a core force of approximately seven to eight thousand men who had been mobilized at Putivl at the outset of the rebellion. Although that small army was officially labeled by Tsar Vasilii's government as nothing more than brigands, cossacks, slaves, peasants, and urban plebes, it was actually made up primarily of southern frontier military servitors and cossacks. Leadership and initiative were provided by the deti boiarskie of the Putivl district, and the army was virtually identical to the one raised by Dmitrii during his campaign for the throne.[16] As Pashkov's army advanced, it grew in size due to additional towns and garrisons joining the rebel cause—not just the lower classes of those towns but virtually all military servicemen, including deti boiarskie. The garrison of Elets, in particular, significantly strengthened Pashkov's forces. By the time Pashkov occupied Tula, there began a virtual stampede of deti boiarskie, lower status military servicemen, and townspeople of the old frontier region rushing to join "Tsar Dmitrii's" army. Pashkov was able to advance into central Russia with large detachments from Tula, Kashira, and Venev. By the time the Riazan district gentry forces joined him at Kolomna, Pashkov's army was quite large and socially diverse—composed predominantly of deti boiarskie, lower status military servitors, townsmen, and cossacks.[17]

Ivan Bolotnikov started out from Putivl with some 12,000 men—a diverse force similar to Pashkov's and drawn from the Seversk region's deti boiarskie, lower status military servitors, cossacks, townsmen, and peasants.[18] Bolotnikov and his army were falsely denounced by Tsar Vasilii's government as brigands and social revolutionaries—as nothing more than peasants, slaves, radical cossacks, and urban plebes.[19] As we have seen, Bolotnikov has also long been falsely accused of bringing 10,000 Ukrainian cossacks with him to Russia. In fact, he did have large numbers of cossacks in his army, but they were Russian fortress cossacks and free cossacks from the stanitsas adjacent to Severia as well as the Don and the Volga.[20] Peasant war scholars boldly asserted that Bolotnikov was a cossack ataman who led an army of social revolutionaries and organized radical slaves and peasants into cossack-style "democratic" units while on the march to Moscow.[21] That is absolutely untrue. The dominant element in Bolotnikov's socially diverse army were deti boiarskie; in fact, his forces were quite similar to Pashkov's.[22] Bolotnikov's army probably did have a larger peasant component than Pashkov's due to his recruitment of Komaritsk district peasants; but, as discussed earlier, those relatively rich peasants were definitely not social revolutionaries. Bolotnikov's army gained additional forces from the garrison of Kromy and from the garrisons and townspeople of several more towns declaring for Dmitrii as his army marched north to the Oka River. Bolotnikov was also able to bring before Moscow detachments from Kaluga and Aleksin.[23] In addition, while he was in Kaluga, Bolotnikov sent forces west of Moscow that succeeded in bringing large numbers of Smolensk and Tver district military servicemen, including deti boiarskie, over to the rebel side.[24]

Rebel forces descending on Moscow were socially diverse. The strength of the rebel movement was, in fact, as noted earlier, its capacity to unite various strata of Russian society on the side of the "legitimate" Tsar Dmitrii.[25] Under the loose overall command of Ivan Bolotnikov, many different groups participated in the siege of Moscow. Some of them maintained their cohesion (e.g., Aleksin servicemen, the Moscow streltsy from Kolomna, and the Riazan district detachments of Liapunov and Sunbulov) and operated somewhat independently. That was certainly true of Istoma Pashkov's forces.[26] As will be demonstrated, the existence of such relatively independent units proved to be a serious problem for the conduct of the siege; in the end, a few of them betrayed the rebel cause and saved Tsar Vasilii from almost certain defeat. Most rebel forces, however, remained steadfastly loyal to "Tsar Dmitrii," and Bolotnikov had extremely loyal lieutenants as well as disgruntled ones. For example, Iurii Bezzubtsev served with distinction as one of Bolotnikov's principal voevodas.[27] Because of the continuous arrival of individuals and small groups joining rebel forces and to very sporadic communications among the rebel commanders, Bolotnikov and Pashkov did not even know the size of their own siege army; but it was definitely very large and powerful.[28] The rebels also had plenty of food and munitions, thanks especially to holding Elets; but they did not have much artillery, and what they did have was not adequate to lay siege to a large, fortified city. They placed their hopes instead on defeating Tsar Vasilii's army or convincing the hungry and frightened inhabitants of the capital to overthrow the usurper.

How large was the rebel army? The high estimate among contemporary sources was 187,000 men.[29] The low contemporary estimates were between 20,000 and 30,000 men.[30] There are problems with both the high and low estimates. Since the two rebel armies started out with almost 20,000 men and were joined by thousands more as nearly half the country rose in rebellion against Shuiskii, 20,000 to 30,000 men seems too low. In fact, at least 20,000 rebels participated in a single engagement during the siege of Moscow, and there are contemporary estimates that by the end of the siege 20,000 rebels had been killed, up to 21,000 had been captured, and more than 10,000 had escaped.[31] Conrad Bussow gave an overall figure for rebel forces of 100,000 men—60,000 with Bolotnikov and 40,000 with Pashkov. Even though that overall number is also found in another contemporary source, Bussow's figure has often been dismissed as unbelievable.[32] Nevertheless, his estimate is worth a closer look.

Isaac Massa wrote that Pashkov's advance guard amounted to 10,000 men and that his main force totaled 30,000 men. That is virtually the same as Bussow's estimate.[33] An English eyewitness to the siege estimated rebel forces at 60,000 men.[34] That is certainly a plausible number.

At the outset of the siege, Tsar Vasilii had a relatively small army at his disposal, but he urgently sought additional forces. Camped before the Serpukhov gate were the remnants of his armies that had been beaten by the rebels and forced to retreat. Many of the tsar's militiamen had melted away, but there were still thousands available to defend the capital. Many of those miserable souls, however, had to be fed at Shuiskii's expense.[35] There were also still hundreds of Moscow and Pskov streltsy left in the capital.[36] Shuiskii could also count on hundreds of courtiers, Moscow dvoriane, and zhiltsy who made up the "tsar's regiment."[37] There were probably still hundreds of military slaves remaining in Shuiskii's army, but there is no information about them in any surviving documents. Tsar Vasilii was desperate enough to arm the population of Moscow even though he was not certain of their loyalty. All men sixteen years old and up were pressed into siege duty. They were armed with harquebuses, sabres, spears, and axes, and they probably manned the city walls whenever a battle appeared imminent. Merchant loyalists helped direct this general conscription that Skrynnikov estimated may have yielded more than ten thousand men.[38] In addition, up to a thousand soldiers from the Moscow region drifted into the capital by mid-November.[39]

Recruits were also actively sought everywhere the rebels had not overrun or cut off. So important was the task of bolstering Moscow's forces that the tsar's brother Ivan was sent to oversee the recruitment of fresh troops (as well as the forced return of those who had prematurely gone home) from towns, monasteries, and estates north and northeast of the capital. Prince Ivan received a generally cool reception but did manage to return to Moscow after mid-November with a small number of additional soldiers.[40] For example, from the Northern Dvina region (Kholmogory) about a hundred streltsy were sent to aid in Moscow's defense.[41] Prince Shuiskii was also able to mobilize some servicemen in Galich, but he also complained that many of them failed to show up and, instead, ran away or hid from his recruiters.[42] Several towns such as Novgorod remained loyal to Tsar Vasilii but could not send troops because they were cut off from the capital by rebel forces. On the other hand, many Novgorodians were decidedly unenthusiastic about Tsar Vasilii. In fact, many "loyal" towns equivocated about sending aid to Moscow. Significant numbers of northern and central Russian townspeople and servicemen were simply unwilling to help Shuiskii defend himself.[43]

Tsar Vasilii's propaganda machine worked overtime at this point to hide the weakness of his position. Whenever even modest forces arrived in the capital, their size and strength was greatly exaggerated. Muscovites were told that large numbers of troops were on their way from Novgorod, Pskov, Smolensk, and other loyal towns. It was even reported that thousands of Kasimov Tatars were speeding to Tsar Vasilii's defense. In fact, none of these things was true, and many inhabitants of Moscow became quite skeptical of such reports as they noted that the tsar's army was not growing in size while the rebel army grew daily.[44] To encourage wavering subjects, Shuiskii's recruiters in the northern provinces told the same stories about large numbers of troops rushing to Moscow to protect Tsar Vasilii. Official letters were also sent to "loyal" towns and read publicly in which it was boldly declared that the tsar had already utterly destroyed the rebel armies. Many people did not believe those lies, however, and they were in no hurry to prove their loyalty by joining Shuiskii's army.[45]

During the two-week period of relatively minor skirmishing between the arrival in the Moscow vicinity of Pashkov's forces and the start of large-scale fighting, Tsar Vasilii's commanders prepared as best they could for the siege. The principal siege voevodas, Prince Dmitrii V. Turenin and Ivan M. Pushkin, commanded the force in the guliai gorod before the Serpukhov gate. Their task was to defend the city's vulnerable walls and, whenever possible, to harass the enemy enclave in Zabore.[46] The tsar's brilliant nephew, the newly promoted boyar Prince Mikhail Skopin-Shuiskii, was named "sortie voevoda" and commanded a second, probably larger army stationed just east of the capital along the Iauza River. From there Skopin-Shuiskii's men could attack enemy positions, but their primary purpose was to prevent rebel forces from crossing the Iauza and making their way north to surround the capital.[47] Skopin-Shuiskii's army included most of the "tsar's regiment," and he was assisted by Prince Andrei V. Golitsyn-Bulgakov and Prince Boris P. Tatev.[48] South of the Iauza River a small force of Tsar Vasilii's Moscow streltsy occupied the Simonov monastery, a strongpoint that also blocked rebel forces from being able to surround the city and cut it off from the stream of men and supplies still coming in from the northeast.[49]

The first significant battles during the siege of Moscow occurred in early November. Over the course of three days, Tsar Vasilii's siege voevoda Turenin sent several expeditions against Zabore. Even with strong artillery support, however, those attacks failed. Zabore's improvised fortifications were too strong, and the rebels energetically defended themselves. Amazingly enough, they succeeded in quickly extinguishing fires caused by incoming incendiary mortar rounds simply by smothering them with damp hides.[50] Toward mid-November

the rebels counterattacked; they reached the wooden wall of Moscow and managed to set fire to parts of it and to several buildings in the vulnerable trans-
river ("wooden town") district of the capital before being driven back.[51] From
then on, skirmishing around Zabore became a daily routine. The rebels also
attempted to capture the Simonov monastery but were beaten back by the
Moscow streltsy units stationed there. Repeated efforts by small detachments
of rebel forces to cross the Iauza River also failed.[52]

As the siege of the capital progressed, the inhabitants of Moscow became
increasingly hungry and impatient. The city's food supply had been badly disrupted by a combination of the rebellion of the Riazan district and other grain-
producing areas; by rebel detachments menacing the roads west, south, and east
of Moscow; and by the generally poor harvest of 1606. As noted earlier, many
people had abandoned the capital because of hunger and the high price of food
even before the siege began. By November, grain in Moscow—when it could
be found—cost three or four times its normal price, and there was no fodder
for horses anywhere to be found.[53] During the siege, many people continued
to leave the capital in search of food. Those who remained in the city faced real
hardships. By mid-November, angry and hungry crowds periodically gathered
before the Kremlin and shouted their disapproval of the Shuiskii regime. There
was, briefly, a real possibility of insurrection.[54] As the eminent historian S. M.
Solovev so eloquently put it: "Who would go hungry for Shuiskii?"[55]

Throughout the siege the rebels managed to send a stream of letters into
the city encouraging disgruntled Muscovites to give up and declare for Tsar
Dmitrii. Those letters had some effect; many in the capital were willing to surrender. As noted earlier, upon his arrival before Moscow Pashkov had demanded
the extradition of the Shuiskii brothers. Once Bolotnikov showed up, both
rebel commanders continued to send letters urging the surrender of the capital. According to an English contemporary, in those letters the rebels now
demanded that, in addition to handing over the Shuiskiis, the inhabitants of
Moscow also had to deliver up other specifically named individuals—several
of Tsar Vasilii's aristocratic accomplices and "some 70 principall Cittizens"—
who were denounced as the "cheefe Actors" in Shuiskii's coup. Bolotnikov and
Pashkov urged the Muscovites to overthrow those traitors, and Tsar Vasilii's
supporters became increasingly nervous about growing sympathy for the rebel
cause inside the capital.[56]

The letters sent by the rebels to the Muscovites have been cited by historians as the most important evidence that Bolotnikov was leading a social revolution and making radical demands that frightened Pashkov and other lords
into switching sides during the siege.[57] There are serious problems with that

interpretation. In fact, none of the rebel letters have survived. What has survived is Shuiskii propaganda about the letters, propaganda that understandably cast the rebels in the worst possible light in order to frighten wavering subjects into remaining loyal to the tsar.[58] There is no reason, however, for us to accept at face value Patriarch Hermogen's assertion that the "satanic" rebels urged Moscow's slaves and rogues to kill the merchants and tradesmen and steal their property. Nor should we be in a hurry to credit his claim that the rebels planned to give the Moscow poor the wives and daughters of prosperous citizens as well as the high offices of Shuiskii loyalists.[59]

Shuiskii propaganda is reflected in two other surviving documents that repeat and even enhance Hermogen's official views of the radical demands and intentions of the rebels. On top of everything else, the Muscovites were repeatedly told that the rebels intended to exterminate the entire population of the capital.[60] According to one contemporary, Hermogen's scare tactics had some effect— convincing the "Nobles and better sort of Citizens" to strongly support Tsar Vasilii.[61] Despite Shuiskii propaganda (and contrary to peasant war scholars' conclusions), there is no reason to believe the accusation that the rebels sent letters only to the poor of Moscow. Skrynnikov, with reason, believed that letters were sent to all inhabitants of the capital. He also pointed out that those letters were clearly authorized by both Pashkov and Bolotnikov, not just the "radical" Bolotnikov.[62]

Sometime before mid-November, a group of citizens from Moscow boldly appeared in the rebel camp with the demand that, if Tsar Dmitrii was still alive, he should show himself. The Muscovites stated that if they could see Dmitrii with their own eyes they would immediately surrender to him. Bolotnikov, of course, could not produce Tsar Dmitrii. He told the delegation that he had received his commission directly from Dmitrii, but the Muscovites flatly contradicted him. They declared that Bolotnikov must have received his command from an impostor because, in their own words, "we killed Dmitrii." The Muscovites went on to say that if Bolotnikov would stop fighting for the dead tsar and give himself up, Tsar Vasilii would "make him a great man." Bolotnikov refused their offer, citing his sacred oath to Dmitrii. Then he warned the delegation: "If you do not surrender of your own free will, I and my lord will do as we see fit and will soon visit ourselves upon you." Once the Muscovites returned to the capital, Bolotnikov immediately dispatched an urgent plea to Prince Shakhovskoi in Putivl, begging him to convince Tsar Dmitrii to come quickly to Moscow. Bolotnikov mentioned his conversation with the Muscovites and said no additional troops were needed to gain victory—just the presence of the tsar himself.[63]

It is quite possible that the visit by the delegation from Moscow slowed down decisive military action early in the siege—in effect, giving Shuiskii a reprieve. The Muscovites also probably used the occasion of their visit to the rebel camp to begin secret negotiations with lords such as Liapunov and Pashkov. The Muscovites were, of course, working for Tsar Vasilii. In fact, the head of the delegation may have been the same merchant named Mylnikov who helped kill Tsar Dmitrii. Another delegate, a servant of the Izmailov family (old friends of the Liapunovs), was specifically sent to the rebel camp in order to appeal to the Riazan dvoriane, and Military Affairs Office records clearly show that certain documents were to be secretly given to the Riazan district gentry leaders.[64]

The failure of the negotiations with the delegation from Moscow convinced the rebel commanders that the boyars, courtiers, and leading citizens of the capital were still loyal to Shuiskii. From that point on their letters to the people of Moscow began to urge immediate action against the traitors among Shuiskii's elite supporters.[65] Those letters so alarmed Tsar Vasilii that he apparently had all the scribes and clerks in Moscow rounded up again in order to compare their handwriting to that found on the inflammatory messages—but to no avail.[66] By then, the capital was in turmoil. Patriarch Hermogen tried to help Tsar Vasilii by urging Muscovites to pray for deliverance from the evil rebels who were planning to "exterminate" all of them. At the same time, however, captured rebel prisoners—even under torture—kept declaring that Tsar Dmitrii was alive and ready to forgive the Muscovites if they would just surrender to his army. Many of Tsar Vasilii's supporters grew fearful of the hunger, unrest, anger, and talk about Tsar Dmitrii's survival among the common people of Moscow. Even among the lords, not just the lower classes, there was extreme nervousness and some wavering. Shuiskii's advisers eventually urged the tsar to risk battle soon— before scarcity and high prices brought him down internally.[67]

Skirmishes had been occurring daily between Shuiskii's forces and the rebels entrenched in Zabore. Because of the continuing failure of Tsar Dmitrii to appear in the rebel camp, some of Tsar Vasilii's troops began to take courage and fought bravely for him in those encounters.[68] Many others, however, remained confused and unsure what to think or do. In addition to increased fighting before the Serpukhov gate, the second theater of battle east of Moscow also heated up. There Skopin-Shuiskii's army had been skirmishing almost daily with small rebel forces attempting to cross the Iauza and surround the capital.[69] The rebel goal was the large, rich village of Krasnoe Selo located just northeast of Moscow. That village not only controlled the only roads by which men and supplies could still reach Tsar Vasilii, but Krasnoe Selo's geographic setting would also allow the rebels to dominate the capital if they could occupy it.

Sometime around mid-November, the rebels fiercely attacked Skopin-Shuiskii's forces and tried to cross the Iauza in very large numbers, but they were thrown back with great losses.[70] As a result, Moscow remained open to a trickle of recruits and supplies. The rebels were severely criticized by one contemporary observer for not attempting to capture Krasnoe Selo earlier. That criticism appears to be valid; by the time the rebels made their last major effort to capture the village (in late November), it was heavily manned and fortified.[71] Tsar Vasilii had become so concerned about the potential loss of Krasnoe Selo that when six hundred streltsy and three hundred recruits arrived from the north, they were given harquebuses and plenty of gunpowder and lead and were immediately stationed in that village under the command of Nikita Mikhailovich Pushkin.[72] That effectively ended the threat of Moscow being surrounded and cut off by rebel forces.

As noted earlier, Tsar Vasilii was facing growing unrest and a potential full-scale insurrection inside the capital by mid-November. At that critical moment, Shuiskii was saved by a combination of the timely arrival of reinforcements from north Russia and Smolensk and by the betrayal of the rebel cause by Prokofii Liapunov. Not surprisingly, the actions of Prokofii Liapunov and Grigorii Sunbulov have long been regarded as an indication of a widening rift between gentry elements in the rebel army and Bolotnikov's "social revolutionary" masses. According to the traditional interpretation, the combination of reprisals against lords loyal to Shuiskii, Bolotnikov's letters inciting the lower classes of Moscow to overthrow their masters, and a few weeks of rubbing shoulders with their social inferiors in the siege camp was enough to convince Liapunov and other lords that, as bad as Shuiskii and the boyars were, they were better than the prospect of social revolution that would threaten the gentry itself.[73] We have already reviewed the weakness of this entire line of interpretation. Let's take a closer look at the specific case of Prokofii Liapunov's betrayal of the rebel cause.

Secret contact between Tsar Vasilii, eager to stir up trouble in the rebel camp, and the Riazan lords was established during the negotiations between the delegation from Moscow and "Tsar Dmitrii's" commander-in-chief.[74] The Liapunovs and Sunbulovs were, in fact, among the most prestigious families of the Riazan district.[75] Shuiskii's representatives offered the proud and ambitious Prokofii Liapunov and Grigorii Sunbulov great rewards if they would switch sides. Since Tsar Dmitrii had not appeared and the prospects for rewards and high positions in the rebel camp were slight, the offer from Tsar Vasilii—even though he was generally detested by the Riazan gentry—looked good to those gentlemen.[76] There may well have been some element of elite distaste for his socially inferior senior commanders and rank-and file rebels involved in Liapunov's decision; it has also been claimed that he may have been influenced by reports of a developing peasant rebellion sweeping across the Riazan district.[77] In any case, secret preparations were made to facilitate the transfer of allegiance to Shuiskii when it would have the greatest chance to cause maximum damage to the rebels—during a major battle.[78]

On November 15, Bolotnikov and Pashkov attempted to storm the Serpukhov gate. The weather was bad and visibility was poor. Moving as separate regiments, rebel forces approached the capital. At that point, Liapunov, Sunbulov, and up to five hundred troops under the Riazan voevodas' command moved very close to Shuiskii's lines and, by prearranged signal, indicated their submission to Tsar Vasilii. Other rebel forces saw what was happening; nevertheless, they threw themselves against the guliai gorod before the Serpukhov gate. However, after skirmishing with Shuiskii's troops and, at one point, cutting some of them off from their companions, most of the rebels retreated to their fortified camps.[79]

It has been claimed that Liapunov's defection resulted in the loss of many of the rebels' most formidable warriors. Some peasant war scholars boldly declared that Liapunov led five hundred pomeshchiki over to Shuiskii's side—a clear indication of class division in the rebel camp.[80] In fact, Tsar Vasilii's propaganda did emphasize that many Riazan dvoriane and deti boiarskie joined Liapunov and Sunbulov's defection.[81] However, Liapunov's regiment was not especially large, and even the Soviet historian Ivan Smirnov saw the need to caution against crediting Shuiskii propaganda that exaggerated the significance of Liapunov's defection and the forces he took with him.[82] Let us take a closer look at the five hundred men who supposedly joined Liapunov's treachery. Skrynnikov has pointed out that the sources do not actually specify their social origin. There were, in fact, not that many militiamen holding the relatively high rank of dvorianin in the defecting forces; and, even after Liapunov's defection, there were still a great many pomeshchiki remaining in the rebel army.[83] One Riazan district pomeshchik who participated in the siege of Moscow wrote that only forty persons went over to Tsar Vasilii's side with Liapunov. Vadim Koretskii suggested that was a reference only to the number of elite dvoriane switching sides on that occasion.[84] Skrynnikov, however, countered that the number probably referred to deti boiarskie and that Liapunov succeeded in bringing with him only forty deti boiarskie and a couple of hundred lower status military servitors and slaves from Liapunov's and Sunbulov's own detachments. Skrynnikov also believed that two hundred Moscow streltsy, who had joined the rebels in Kolomna, switched sides with Liapunov—bringing the total number with him to approximately five hundred.[85] However, the defection to Shuiskii of at least fifty of the streltsy Skrynnikov referred to actually occurred on November 17, two days later.[86] In any case, Liapunov's treachery did not cause severe problems in the rebel camp in spite of Patriarch Hermogen's claim that many rebels ran away at this point.[87] Most of the deti boiarskie in the rebel army remained loyal to "Tsar Dmitrii," as did the overwhelming bulk of the rebel forces. In fact, the rebel camp continued to grow even after Liapunov's betrayal.[88]

Tsar Vasilii was, of course, delighted by news of Liapunov's defection. The next morning (Sunday, November 16) there was a loud celebration in Moscow. Bells pealed and cannon were fired as Liapunov and Sunbulov formally led their men into the city. The noise and commotion frightened some Muscovites, who grabbed their weapons and rushed to the Kremlin before they found out that it was a happy occasion.[89] Tsar Vasilii went to great lengths to show his appreciation to Liapunov and Sunbulov, praising them highly and immediately making them voevodas in his own army. Liapunov was eventually promoted to the rank of dumnyi dvorianin and rewarded with land in the Riazan district from the tsar's own palace estates.[90] Both men were rewarded with gold, along with their fellow defecting dvoriane and deti boiarskie. The rank-and-file streltsy who joined them were rewarded with gilded silver coins.[91] Liapunov pleased his new master very much by publicly declaring that Tsar Dmitrii really was dead and, therefore, not to be feared.

The next day, November 17, in the late morning Pashkov and Bolotnikov again advanced from their camps toward Moscow. Tsar Vasilii's entire army, headed by the tsar's brother Dmitrii and his nephew Skopin-Shuiskii, went out to meet the rebels. Battles occurred several kilometers south of the capital and at the Simonov monastery to the southeast of the city. During one of those engagements, about fifty Moscow streltsy deserted the rebels and switched sides. Shuiskii's forces also captured one distinguished dvorianin and some prisoners who were coerced into talking. Tsar Vasilii's propagandists made the most of his army's apparent success that day and the defection of the streltsy. Soon they were telling everyone that the deserters had informed the tsar's authorities that the rebel camp was in disarray and shrinking in size and that half of the rebel forces had been forced to fight and were more than willing to switch sides. According to a contemporary, that bold lie "somewhat comforted simple people" in the capital.[92] In fact, the battles on November 17 were inconclusive. The rebels, somewhat shaken, remained intact. Many of them, however, did wonder where Tsar Dmitrii was and when he would show himself. Meanwhile, Shuiskii's luck began to change. On November 18, up to a thousand men, mostly peasant recruits from Moscow area villages, arrived to bolster the capital's defenses. On the other hand, on the same day, the inhabitants of Moscow presented a petition to Tsar Vasilii declaring that the people could no longer afford the price of food and other goods. The petitioners begged the tsar to take immediate, decisive action against the rebels.[93]

While Shuiskii celebrated the combination of Liapunov's treachery, the arrival of additional troops even of mediocre quality, and his army's minor successes, he kept a close watch on events west of the capital. The rebels had, of course, more or less cut Moscow off from loyal Novgorod, Tver, and Smolensk. Communication with those towns was extremely difficult, and there did not seem to be any way for troops from their garrisons to march to the aid of Tsar Vasilii. In the early days of the siege of the capital, however, Shuiskii and his advisers boldly decided to attempt to reopen the roads to Smolensk, Tver, and other loyal towns to the west in order to gain critically important additional troops. Their strategy was risky because it involved sending away some of the precious forces then guarding Moscow; but, as it turned out, the gamble paid off.

The city of Smolensk, boasting Russia's mightiest fortress, had a population of about 20,000 at the beginning of the seventeenth century. Up to 1,200 dvoriane and deti boiarskie lived in the Smolensk district, and the fortress itself was garrisoned by 1,800 lower status military servitors.[94] Soon after Smolensk was cut off from Moscow by Bolotnikov's army, the garrison and inhabitants of the town—with the blessing of their voevoda and archbishop—gathered forces in order to clear the rebels from nearby towns and roads and go to the aid of Tsar Vasilii. For some unknown reason, command of the Smolensk forces sent into action at this time was given to an "ordinary" pomeshchik, Grigorii I. Poltev, instead of to a higher ranking officer. Poltev led a force of 640 men (deti boiarskie, lower status military servitors, and novices) while the bulk of the local pomeshchiki and ordinary soldiers remained behind to defend Smolensk.[95]

Moscow was with some difficulty informed of Poltev's intentions, and Tsar Vasilii's commanders made their own plans accordingly. Two detachments of men were sent west from the capital to open up the roads to loyal towns and to meet with the Smolensk forces then working their way east. Since the rebel-held towns of Mozhaisk and Volok Lamskii controlled access and communications between Moscow and western and northwestern Russia, Prince Danila I. Mezetskii was ordered to lead his men from the capital along the Smolensk road directly to Mozhaisk; at the very same time, the tsar's friend, okolnichii Ivan F. Kriuk-Kolychev, was ordered to lead his forces northwest toward Volok Lamskii. Kriuk-Kolychev was instructed to clear the rebels from that town and the roads in the area, to reestablish contact with the Iosifo-Volokolamsk monastery, and then—if all went well—to unite with Mezetskii's men and Poltev's Smolensk detachment at Mozhaisk. That combined force was then to hurry back to Moscow. Until those men returned to the capital, Tsar Vasilii's commanders planned to refrain from risking a major battle with the large rebel army.[96]

Poltev's Smolensk detachment quickly cleared the rebels out of Dorogobuzh and Viazma.[97] Then they advanced to the fortress of Mozhaisk, arriving there by mid-November—at about the same time Prince Mezetskii's detachment reached the town from Moscow. The siege of Mozhaisk lasted about a week. The fortress was manned by vybornyi dvorianin Petr Zekziulin, local deti boiarskie and lower status servicemen who had declared for Tsar Dmitrii, and cossacks led by ataman Ivan Goremykin.[98] During the course of the siege, Mezetskii entered into negotiations with the rebel leaders. Goremykin gathered his men in a cossack circle, discussed the matter, and agreed to Mezetskii's terms. The ataman's willingness to surrender was strongly influenced by the bribe he was paid and by the land, salary, and employment in Tsar Vasilii's service also promised to him.[99] No doubt the arrival before Mozhaisk of Kriuk-Kolychev's detachment also had some effect on the rebels' decision to surrender.

During the time Kriuk-Kolychev's detachment was marching to Volok Lamskii from Moscow, the monks of the Iosifo-Volokolamsk monastery helped Tsar Vasilii's cause by means of a stratagem. Elder Dionisii (the former boyar Prince Andrei Ivanovich Golitsyn) invited the rebel commander Soloma Kazak, who was then holding Volok Lamskii, to the monastery and gave him a large sum of money. At the monastery, Dionisii managed to get the rebel ataman and his associates drunk, had the monks seize them, and later sent them as prisoners to Moscow.[100] When the rebels learned of their ataman's fate, they attacked the monastery furiously, but its fortifications were much too strong for them. In addition, the local peasants and others from the monastery's estates stood by their masters instead of running away or joining the rebel cause—for which reason they were later generously rewarded.[101] Kriuk-Kolychev's detachment arrived in time to defeat the rebels and put an end to the siege of the monastery. By November 9, soldiers wounded in that action were being sent back to Moscow along an open road that had been cleansed of rebels.[102] At that point, Kriuk-Kolychev then raced to Mozhaisk just in time to accept the surrender of ataman Goremykin. As early as November 24, some of the former rebels in Mozhaisk, newly recruited into Tsar Vasilii's service, began entering Moscow—including deti boiarskie, townsmen, and military slaves.[103] With the western blockade of the capital now broken, Kriuk-Kolychev combined the forces of Poltev, Mezetskii, and his own men with servicemen from Viazma. He then headed back to Moscow with 1,500 more men than he and Mezetskii had started out with. Kriuk-

Kolychev had been ordered to return to the capital no later than November 29; he managed to return by November 28.[104]

At about the same time the Smolensk road was being cleared of rebels, the archbishop of Tver was conducting an active struggle against them in the Tver region. The archbishop gathered together deti boiarskie and other servicemen from his own estates and elsewhere, combined them with volunteers from Tver itself, and attacked rebel forces vigorously. According to Patriarch Hermogen, those loyal forces defeated the "damned traitors" and "heretics," cleared the roads (including the one to Novgorod), and sent rebel prisoners to Moscow.[105] In addition to that good news coming from the northwest, by November 24 Tsar Vasilii received word that the gentry, posad leaders, and "better" people of Kolomna, 100 kilometers southeast of the capital, had decided to transfer their allegiance back to him. The revolt in favor of Shuiskii was led by dvorianin Vladimir T. Dolgorukii, and a grateful tsar later rewarded the Kolomna loyalists with a gift of furs.[106] Further cheering Tsar Vasilii's supporters, by late November small groups of soldiers began drifting into the capital from the northeastern towns of Iaroslavl, Rostov, and Vladimir by way of the open road through Krasnoe Selo; most of those men had been recruited by Ivan Shuiskii.[107]

Probably in response to reports of the success of Tsar Vasilii's forces west of the capital and news of the arrival of more Shuiskii loyalists from the northeast in late November, Bolotnikov and Pashkov decided to try one more time to force their way across the Iauza River in order to seize Krasnoe Selo. They attacked Tsar Vasilii's forces on November 26. There is much confusion in the sources and in the literature concerning the events of November 26–27. Some scholars have portrayed the battle as a great Shuiskii victory; others vividly described the rebel capture of Krasnoe Selo; and many wrote that Pashkov's betrayal of the rebel cause occurred at this time. In fact, none of those things actually happened in that encounter. Let us take a closer look at the battle in order to separate legend from fact.

On November 26, rebel infantry numbering some 2,000 men crossed the Moskva River southeast of the capital and headed north. Long before they could reach the Iauza River, however, they were detected by voevoda Skopin-Shuiskii who sent two or three regiments forward to stop them. A battle soon developed east of the capital in and around the villages of Karacharovo and Rogozhskaia gonnaia sloboda. Skopin-Shuiskii's men forced many of the rebels to take cover in Karacharovo, where—under the command of the former Kolomna voevoda S. Kokhanovskii—they stubbornly resisted the tsar's army. Nevertheless, by the end of the day about one hundred rebels had been taken prisoner. Those men were taken to Moscow to be interrogated. After that, they were stripped naked and forced to remain outside all night long; by morning, half of them had died of exposure to the severe cold. So ended the November 26 rebel attempt to seize Krasnoe Selo.[108] Unfortunately, a few sources and some historians erroneously claimed the rebels actually managed to reach the village.[109] One unreliable source, "Inoe skazanie," stated that the rebels were unable to capture Krasnoe Selo due to the timely arrival of two hundred "frightening" streltsy from the Northern Dvina region.[110] Some historians believed Pashkov himself captured Krasnoe Selo after fierce fighting, in what amounted to a great rebel victory.[111] Others believed Pashkov captured the village only to surrender to Tsar Vasilii the next day.[112] It is, in fact, possible that an advance guard of rebels did approach Krasnoe Selo on November 26 but made no effort to storm it.[113] Krasnoe Selo was by then heavily garrisoned, and there was certainly no battle there on November 26 or 27. However, in Moscow there was great alarm at this point due to vague reports that the rebels had captured some roads into the city and had diverted provisions intended for the hungry Muscovites.[114] Once again, Tsar Vasilii was urged to take immediate, decisive action against the rebels.

On the morning of November 27, 1606, a huge parade and muster took place in Moscow. Tsar Vasilii himself appeared on his war horse holding his scepter and orb. The patriarch, bishops, and many clergymen carrying icons and the coffin of "St. Dmitrii" sang prayers and blessed the soldiers with holy water. Then the tsar and his senior voevodas, Mstislavskii and Vorotynskii, led their regiments out of the capital through the Kaluga and Serpukhov gates and through the guliai gorod. The tsar's army then advanced into the field in battle formation. By this time, the arrival of soldiers and peasant recruits from the north and northeast, plus the transfer of allegiance of Liapunov's men, allowed Tsar Vasilii to field a fairly large force. One source claimed that Shuiskii's army poured out of the gates like water and, united in spirit, went into battle.[115] In fact, Tsar Vasilii's plan that day was not to engage in a major battle. Shuiskii was well aware that at some point he personally needed to appear in "battle" against the rebels or risk being forever labeled a coward. Still waiting for Kriuk-Kolychev's arrival with more soldiers, however, Shuiskii's plan was to delay the real battle and to use the mass deployment of his army on November 27 as a kind of dress rehearsal. He did this for three basic reasons: first, by slowly advancing in force toward the rebel camp at Kolomenskoe, Shuiskii's army would automatically force Bolotnikov and Pashkov to give up any further plans to capture Krasnoe Selo; the rebels would be too busy defending themselves to try such a maneuver. Second, Tsar Vasilii would be able to claim that he had participated in a battle against the hated rebels, but the tsar would not actually be in any real danger. Third, by letting Mstislavskii and Vorotynskii serve as senior commanders on November 27, Tsar Vasilii allowed those two men to restore their pride after the humiliating defeat they had suffered at the battle of Troitskoe. Then Shuiskii would be free to appoint more competent commanders for the real battle he was planning.

On November 27, as the tsar's army began its march toward the enemy's main camp, rebel forces numbering about twenty thousand men moved north from Kolomenskoe to meet them. The two armies skirmished with each other on and off until early evening, but the tsar's forces remained in the field (along with their artillery) all night long—making the battle appear more important and more decisive than it really had been.[116] Tsar Vasilii was now able to return to Moscow as a "victor." His propagandists declared that the tsar had been "bold and brave," that his army had suffered no losses, and that the exhausted rebels had been forced to flee. It was also falsely claimed that many rebels had switched sides to join Tsar Vasilii's cause. In reality, Shuiskii's forces suffered heavy casualties, and the tsar's "victory" was in name only.[117]

The Soviet historian Ivan Smirnov noted the exaggeration in Shuiskii propaganda about the events of November 27, but he nonetheless regarded the battle as a significant victory for Shuiskii because—according to Smirnov—that was when Pashkov and his men switched sides.[118] That is not true; Pashkov actually betrayed the rebels during a battle on December 2.[119] In fact, even though Tsar Vasilii claimed "victory" on November 27, in Moscow there was still alarm and great dissension. Many people expected the hungry capital to fall to the rebels at any time, and some still talked of surrender.[120] Shuiskii knew that he had no choice but to risk a general battle with the rebels very soon, but he wanted that battle to be on his own terms. To that end, the dress rehearsal on November 27 had served its purpose well, and Shuiskii's gamble to open up a path to Smolensk had also paid off. Advance units of Kriuk-Kolychev's detachment, with 1,500 additional troops from Smolensk and other western towns, began to arrive in Moscow by November 28; and they were immediately deployed in preparation for a general battle.[121] It took a few more days (up to December 1) for all the Smolensk troops and returning Moscow detachments to reach the capital. The day after all those forces were in place, December 2, Tsar Vasilii finally risked a major battle with the rebels.[122] As one might expect, there is considerable confusion in sources and historiography concerning the final round of the siege of Moscow. Let us take a close look at that conflict.

Before December 2, Tsar Vasilii's officials secretly contacted Pashkov and made careful plans to use his betrayal during the upcoming battle to maximum advantage. The tsar had also been convinced to bring up all his artillery to deal with rebel-held Zabore, and in the days before December 2 a well-planned

Fig. 11 "Tsar Vasilii Defends Moscow Against the Rebel Attack." Detail from "The Rebel Siege of Moscow in 1606," drawn circa 1607. The Hague, Koninklijke Bibliotheek, 78 H 56 (Isaac Massa's Album Amicorum). Courtesy of the National Library of the Netherlands.

assault on that rebel stronghold was attempted in order to improve the tactical position of Shuiskii's army at the outset of the general battle with Bolotnikov's forces.[123] Probably on November 29, advance units of Kriuk-Kolychev's forces began setting up camp near the Novodevichii monastery, located west of Zabore across the Moskva River. The first to arrive there were Smolensk troops under the command of dvorianin Voin Divov and three colonels.[124] On November 30, Ivan Shuiskii and his newly recruited regiments from northern and northeastern Russia also arrived at the Novodevichii monastery. Other troops trickled in on December 1. Because of Ivan Shuiskii's high rank, he became the senior commander of this force; his associates included voevodas Ivan V. Golitsyn, Mikhail B. Shein, Ivan Kriuk-Kolychev, and Grigorii I. Poltev. From Novodevichii monastery, on November 30, Ivan Shuiskii's men quickly marched east, crossed the frozen Moskva, passed the small Donskoi monastery, and began the siege of Zabore.[125] For two days (November 30–December 1), Ivan Shuiskii's forces vigorously attacked the rebel stronghold without success. Simultaneously, there was an intense artillery bombardment of Zabore, but also to no avail. The rebels stubbornly resisted all efforts to capture their position, and Shuiskii's forces suffered heavy casualties in fierce fighting.[126] On December 2, the third day of the frustrating siege of Zabore, a general battle developed south of Moscow.

In preparation for a major battle, a large army had been formed in the guliai gorod in front of Serpukhov gate. It was commanded by Mikhail Skopin-Shuiskii; his associates included voevodas Andrei Golitsyn-Bulgakov, Boris Tatev, and okolnichii Vasilii P. Morozov, who was in charge of artillery.[127] Their immediate goal was the Danilov monastery (just south of Moscow), from which they hoped to add elements of Ivan Shuiskii's detachments before engaging Bolotnikov's main army. On December 2, Skopin-Shuiskii led his forces from the guliai gorod to the Danilov monastery with no great difficulty; then he paused to allow some of Ivan Shuiskii's newly arriving units to join him. In the meantime, Bolotnikov had been watching developments around besieged Zabore closely; and when informers tipped him off about Skopin-Shuiskii's planned sortie in strength, the rebel commander-in-chief quickly moved most of his men north from Kolomenskoe to meet the tsar's army. He also sent orders to Pashkov to attack the enemy's flank while he boldly engaged Skopin-Shuiskii's forces head on.[128] As the two opposing armies converged, a very large battle developed near the village of Kotly.[129] While Bolotnikov's forces fiercely attacked Skopin-Shuiskii's army, Pashkov moved his corps into position—pretending to relieve the siege of Zabore. However, he and his senior officers had carefully arranged their troops so that, upon closing with the enemy, Pashkov and several hundred of his most trusted men quickly transferred their allegiance to

Shuiskii and even joined the tsar's forces in attacking the rebels during the battle. The result was predictable: the rebel army, stunned by the betrayal of a senior commander, began to waver in confusion and panic. At that point, Skopin-Shuiskii and Ivan Shuiskii hit the disoriented rebels hard. Soon, their lines began to break up as hundreds of them fled from the battlefield in terror; Bolotnikov was soon forced to order a hasty retreat to Kolomenskoe.[130]

Skopin-Shuiskii's forces moved forward rapidly, pressing their advantage and inflicting heavy casualties. Many rebels, separated from their units, quickly surrendered. Many others, attempting to elude the tsar's army by hiding, were discovered and slaughtered like "swine."[131] In their chaotic retreat from Moscow, Bolotnikov's remaining forces were unable to make a stand in Kolomenskoe. To avoid being trapped there, Bolotnikov reluctantly ordered a general retreat south toward Serpukhov. Skopin-Shuiskii was then able to occupy Kolomenskoe, capturing Bolotnikov's camp and large quantities of supplies. The tsar's army was unable to pursue the fleeing enemy in force immediately, however, because the rebel stronghold of Zabore still menaced the gates of Moscow. Therefore, after taking Kolomenskoe, Skopin-Shuiskii and Ivan Shuiskii threw most of their forces against Zabore.[132] It is no exaggeration to say that the heroic struggle of the cossacks in Zabore prevented the complete destruction of Bolotnikov's army. Because of their stubborn resistance, many other rebels were able to flee from Moscow holding onto their weapons; and Bolotnikov himself was able to retreat in good order with more than ten thousand men still determined to continue the struggle in Tsar Dmitrii's name.[133]

To contemporaries, there was no doubt that Pashkov's treachery caused the defeat of Bolotnikov and forced him to break off the siege.[134] What motivated Pashkov's drastic step? We have already dismissed the traditional interpretation of Pashkov as a gentry leader who came to fear Bolotnikov's radical forces as a threat to the lords.[135] The bad blood between Pashkov and the rebel commander-in-chief had more to do with the former's sense of "honor" and Bolotnikov's arrogant insistence on displacing him from Kolomenskoe. Tsar Vasilii found out early on about the conflict between the rebel commanders and made a special effort to heat up that rivalry. In secret negotiations with Pashkov, the tsar's representatives may have played on elite fears of armed and angry masses, and they may have reminded Pashkov that he should expect no reward for his loyal service to a dead tsar; but they certainly informed him just how well rewarded Liapunov and others had been for joining Tsar Vasilii's cause. Pashkov was promised a high position in Shuiskii's service, and a large sum of money was secretly delivered to him on the eve of the battle during which he betrayed the rebel cause.[136] After the siege of Moscow was broken, Pashkov became a colonel in Tsar Vasilii's service and was rewarded with very large estates in the Venev and Serpukhov areas.[137]

Who joined Pashkov's treachery? Because of Shuiskii propaganda and the traditional interpretation of the Bolotnikov rebellion, there is some confusion about this issue. The unreliable "New Chronicle" claimed that Pashkov was joined by all the dvoriane and deti boiarskie in the rebel army.[138] Two other sources said Pashkov was joined by thousands of men but did not specify who they were.[139] Two sources specifically claimed Pashkov was joined by 500 of his own men.[140] Still another source claimed that he was joined by 400 cossacks.[141] In fact, it is extremely likely that Pashkov's own Epifan servicemen (many of whom were former cossacks) formed the core of his turncoat faction. There is no reason to believe the "New Chronicle's" version of events even though many peasant war scholars were quick to credit that grossly inaccurate source. Whatever the exact number of men joining Pashkov may have been, one thing is absolutely clear: The overwhelming bulk of Pashkov's own army—including a majority of the deti boiarskie under his command—remained loyal to the rebel cause. Those men were either killed, captured, or escaped along with Bolotnikov on December 2. The rebels who fled to fight another day were certainly not just lower class brigands as Shuiskii propaganda portrayed them.[142]

By the time Bolotnikov's army had been defeated and put to flight, the rebel stronghold of Zabore had been under continuous siege and bombardment for more than two days. Now, Tsar Vasilii's entire army concentrated on destroying it.[143] Surrendering rebels were paid to reveal the secrets of Zabore's defenses—especially how the rebels were able to extinguish incoming incendiary mortar rounds. Tsar Vasilii's commanders then put that information to good use.[144] Voevoda Morozov's artillerymen came up with incendiary rounds that could not be easily extinguished and very quickly managed to set fire to the rebel stronghold. By then the three-day siege and the defeat of Bolotnikov had demoralized many of the rebels, and their hopeless situation provoked dissent inside Zabore. Some wished to surrender; others were in favor of fighting to the death. Tsar Vasilii's representatives offered rewards to those willing to give up, and soon a large number of rebel gentry and cossacks decided to take Shuiskii up on his offer. In the confusion caused by their actions and by the relentless bombardment of Zabore, however, the tsar's soldiers managed to break through and took the stronghold by storm.[145] Many rebels were killed at that time, and a very large number surrendered. Many of those who voluntarily surrendered and subsequently swore an oath of loyalty to Tsar Vasilii were offered positions in Shuiskii's service. (He excluded only those cossacks known to be recent runaway serfs or slaves; they were returned to their masters.) In fact, the tsar managed to recruit large numbers of former rebel cossacks by generous offers of food, shelter, and employment. It is worth noting that Tsar Vasilii certainly displayed no fear of cossacks as social revolutionaries in making that offer. Instead, he was glad to have additional soldiers and arranged for his new cossack troops to be fed and billeted in Moscow. Ordinary townspeople were forced to house two or three of them at a time, and orders were issued not to harm the tsar's newest recruits.[146]

The siege of Moscow ended in disaster for the rebels. They had suffered a crushing defeat, and Tsar Vasilii's army returned to the capital in triumph with many prisoners. Bells pealed, prayers of thanksgiving were said, and Shuiskii's supporters celebrated their great victory.[147] A very happy Tsar Vasilii heaped rewards on his loyal warriors—including land grants, slaves, salary increases, and promotions. Every soldier who had killed a rebel or had been wounded in battle was rewarded. The tsar bestowed the highest honors on his nephew, Mikhail Skopin-Shuiskii, and others whose service had been especially important. He immediately promoted to the rank of boyar his friend Ivan Kriuk-Kolychev, okolnichii Mikhail B. Shein, and the hero of the Kolomna revolt in favor of Shuiskii—Vladimir T. Dolgorukii.[148]

It is difficult to estimate the number of rebels killed, wounded, captured, or surrendering in the final battle of the siege of Moscow. The tsar's commanders had definitely tried to kill as many of them as possible on the battlefield. According to a contemporary, trapped rebels were "slaughtered like pigs"; others were ambushed by the tsar's troops who inflicted "hideous carnage" on enemy forces.[149] The intense bombardment of Zabore also inflicted extremely heavy casualties. Thousands of rebels were probably killed; however, estimates of the total number of rebels killed are complicated by the inclusion in records of battlefield casualties of thousands of surrendering cossacks who were actually executed at a later time. Estimates of the number of men captured are also complicated by the inclusion in official counts of prisoners taken of thousands of cossacks who voluntarily surrendered. A contemporary source claimed that Skopin-Shuiskii's army killed 2,000 rebels and captured 700.[150] Conrad Bussow claimed that 10,000 cossacks in Zabore had been forced to surrender, and Isaac Massa claimed that 6,000 prisoners were taken during the final battle. Other contemporary estimates of Bolotnikov's losses ranged from more than 10,000 to more than 20,000.[151] One source estimated the overall number of casualties on both sides during the siege at 40,000 and the number of rebels surrendering or captured at 15,000; another source claimed that 21,000 rebels were captured.[152]

Very large numbers of rebels were thrown into overcrowded prisons and dungeons. Those men were almost all Russians, and many were cossacks. Most of them did not stay incarcerated in Moscow for long. According to a contemporary, hundreds of them were brought out each night, lined up near the Iauza

River, and "butchered like cattle with cudgel blows to the forehead, then thrust under the ice."[153] Hundreds of prisoners were also sent from Moscow to fill the jails of other towns such as Novgorod and Pskov. In Novgorod, newly arriving prisoners suffered the same fate as those in Moscow; they were cudgeled and put under the ice of the Volkhov River. In Pskov, on the other hand, the 400 prisoners sent from Moscow received sympathy, food, and clothing from ordinary townspeople—an evil portent for Tsar Vasilii.[154] Overall, the number of rebel prisoners executed after the siege of Moscow was estimated by contemporaries to be as high as 15,000.[155] Rebel leaders who were considered particularly obnoxious were publicly impaled. Even near death, however, many still professed stubborn loyalty to Tsar Dmitrii. One impaled ataman even named Tsar Vasilii's brother Dmitrii as the traitor responsible for the rebellion. That caused such a stir that the tsar and several boyars were forced to make a hasty appearance before the people to declare the dying man's statement to be utterly false.[156]

Not all captives were killed, of course. Some rebel cossacks were given as slaves to heroic and distinguished warriors, who were allowed to inspect cossack prisoners and claim many of them as their own runaway slaves and serfs without having to produce any documentation whatsoever. Not surprisingly, that inevitably led to disputes with the original owners of those poor souls.[157] Thousands of other rebels were simply left to languish in prison. Months later, when Tsar Vasilii desperately needed all the men-at-arms he could get his hands on, many of those same prisoners were set free on the condition that they fight against their onetime comrades.[158]

What was the point of Shuiskii's highly publicized large-scale executions of rebel prisoners, especially cossacks? The tsar's officials boldly claimed that the rebels who had laid siege to Moscow were all brigands, serfs, and slaves who deserved execution for rising against their masters.[159] Obviously, Shuiskii was still trying to convince wavering subjects that his enemies were dangerous social revolutionaries. Beyond that motive, as well as simple revenge, the executions were definitely intended to intimidate and dampen the enthusiasm of rebels still at large. The use of terror did not produce the desired effect, however; the struggle against Tsar Vasilii continued unabated. Fanatic belief in Tsar Dmitrii's survival persisted, and rumors of his imminent return continued to circulate. Try as he might, Shuiskii was unable to put the ghost of the "true tsar" to rest. Tsar Vasilii's use of terror on such a large scale against captured rebels also set an evil precedent in the civil war. It deeply embittered his opponents, especially the cossacks, who, as a result, fought even harder for "Tsar Dmitrii" and increasingly resorted to similar terror tactics against supporters of the bloodthirsty usurper who still sat on Dmitrii's throne.

18

Retreat from Moscow, the Siege of Kaluga,
and the Rise of Tsarevich Petr

Once Tsar Vasilii had finished celebrating his great victory, he and his advisers reviewed their strategic situation, which was still perilous. Belief in Tsar Dmitrii's survival remained strong everywhere in Russia, and the southern half of the country was still in rebel hands. Bolotnikov and part of his army had retreated in good order, were reported to be quickly regrouping, and were gaining new recruits every day. To the east, Nizhnii Novgorod was still under siege. Obviously, it was going to be very difficult and time-consuming for the tsar to destroy the rebels and end the civil war. Nonetheless, the failure of the siege of Moscow dramatically changed the strategic situation, giving the initiative to Shuiskii.

Even as the smoke cleared from the last battle of the siege and as rebel cossacks were being executed by the hundreds, Tsar Vasilii's propagandists attempted to maximize the impact of the victory over Bolotnikov and to intimidate and sow doubt among rebels and their potential sympathizers. On December 5, 1606, proclamations went out to all parts of the country falsely claiming that the rebellion was over and that only a few brigands had escaped in disarray. The "capture" of the rebel commander Pashkov was announced, and a phony list of thirteen towns that had supposedly "cleansed" themselves of traitors and submitted humbly to Tsar Vasilii was also included. The gentry and townspeople of most rebel areas, it was claimed, had seen the error of their ways and now bowed to Shuiskii.[1] Those were bold lies, indeed. Most of the towns named in the proclamations were still in rebel hands (Tula, Kaluga, Kashira, Aleksin, Likhvin, Kozelsk, Meshchovsk, Belev, and Bolkhov), although Medyn and Borovsk many actually have been cleansed of rebels during the siege of the capital. At least Shuiskii's proclamations finally acknowledged that many pomeshchiki and towns had actually participated in the rebellion against him—an admission that had been carefully avoided in all previous announcements and decrees issued by Tsar Vasilii.[2]

The primary task facing Shuiskii and his voevodas was, of course, the destruction of Bolotnikov's army; but, in order to take advantage of the new strategic situation created by the rebel retreat, Tsar Vasilii also launched several other minor military campaigns in early December for the purpose of ending the siege of Nizhnii Novgorod and outflanking the rebels to the southeast and southwest. The situation to the east and southeast of Moscow was particularly dangerous. Tsar Vasilii recognized that and was determined to quickly break up the siege of Nizhnii Novgorod and suppress rebellion throughout the critically important central Volga region. Sources about those military operations are confusing, but it is clear that Shuiskii sent an army to the central Volga region immediately after Bolotnikov's retreat from Kolomenskoe.

The first objective of the tsar's army was the strategically located town of Murom. Voevodas Grigorii G. Pushkin and S. G. Ododurov, with troops from Vladimir and Suzdal, approached Murom by December 11, at which point the town voluntarily switched back to Shuiskii's side and swore an oath of loyalty to him. Rebel leaders in the town were rounded up and thrown in prison.[3] Pushkin's forces then proceeded to Arzamas and Alatyr. Both towns temporarily submitted to Tsar Vasilii, and the Alatyr voevoda was killed; however, after the tsar's army left the area both towns later rejoined the rebellion against Shuiskii.[4] News of the progress of the tsar's army at the end of 1606, however, sent shockwaves throughout the central Volga region and forced the rebels to break off the siege of Nizhnii Novgorod.[5] Sviazhsk also switched back to Shuiskii at this time.[6] Although small groups of rebels remained active in the area, the tsar's army greatly reduced the danger emanating from the central Volga region. In fact, in the aftermath of the break-up of the siege of Nizhnii Novgorod, many local rebel gentry switched sides to support Tsar Vasilii and later participated in the campaign against Bolotnikov.[7] Another somewhat delayed result of the progress of Shuiskii's army was the decision made by many Tatars, Cheremis, and Chuvashi to abandon the rebel cause and to join Tsar Vasilii's army.

More is known about Shuiskii's campaign in the Riazan region. Many rebels from that area had participated in the siege of Moscow where, as we have seen, two of the more important Riazan lords, Liapunov and Sunbulov, betrayed the rebel cause. Both of those men immediately became high-profile voevodas of Tsar Vasilii and joined the struggle against supporters of "Tsar Dmitrii." As soon as Bolotnikov had retreated from Moscow, Shuiskii dispatched Liapunov and Sunbulov with a small military force and artillery to suppress rebellion in Riazan province.[8] Rebel activity in that area has long been viewed by scholars (influenced by Shuiskii propaganda) as a social revolution of the local peasants. In reality, Riazan rebels came from all social classes and developments in the area during the winter of 1606–7 were not part of a peasant war. Liapunov quickly succeeded in returning the towns of Pereiaslavl-Riazanskii (Riazan) and Zaraisk to Tsar Vasilii's side.[9] However, efforts to win over the population of the small towns of southern Riazan province and those in the neighborhood of Tula failed at this time; those areas remained firmly in rebel hands.[10] Most of Riazan province, by contrast, quieted down enough to allow Liapunov and Sunbulov to join the campaign against Bolotnikov in early 1607. Once their forces left the Riazan area, however, rebel activity there began to increase again. By summer 1607, Pereiaslavl-Riazanskii came under repeated attacks from local rebels of all types—including deti boiarskie, lower status military servitors, and townsmen. For about 20 kilometers in all directions around Pereiaslavl-Riazanskii, peasants and others championing the cause of "Tsar Dmitrii" prevented Shuiskii supporters from rallying to protect the town. Virtually under siege, Pereiaslavl-Riazanskii's voevoda was forced to admit his complete inability to cope with the problem.[11]

In general, fanatic peasant rebels in the region badly frightened much of the local gentry by struggling against them for several years—either actively in the name of Tsar Dmitrii or passively by refusing to pay taxes or to perform duties for them. In fact, many local lords simply sat out the civil war in Pereiaslavl-Riazanskii because they were afraid to visit their estates. In essence, those men had been exiled by their own peasants and neighbors; and, as a result, they ended up imposing a heavy burden on the voevoda of Pereiaslavl-Riazanskii and his beleaguered town's resources.[12] The activity of the Riazan area peasants cannot be described as a social revolution; those fanatic rebels did not take aim at serfdom, only at certain lords. A probable explanation for their behavior was the fierce anger the local population felt about the betrayal of "Tsar Dmitrii" by Liapunov, Sunbulov, and other Riazan area gentry who joined them in switching sides during the siege of Moscow.

To areas south and southwest of Moscow, Tsar Vasilii dispatched small military detachments in order to win over wavering rebel towns and to isolate Bolotnikov's forces that had retreated to Kaluga. In late December, Shuiskii also boldly sent proclamations to the rebels holding ten towns and two crown peasant districts in which he exaggerated the success of his voevodas since the siege of Moscow and appealed to the rebels to lay down their weapons. For a number of reasons, a cossack and a peasant were chosen to carry those messages to the rebel-held frontier.[13] Of course, real victory for Tsar Vasilii in the civil war required outfitting and fielding a large army in order to smash Bolotnikov and mop up rebels throughout a vast territory. Not surprisingly, therefore, once the immediate threat to Moscow had passed, Shuiskii busied himself trying to raise more troops and revenue for that gargantuan task.

Raising troops to fight against "Tsar Dmitrii" continued to be extremely difficult for the unpopular Tsar Vasilii. Not only did the rebels still hold almost half of the country, but belief in the survival of Tsar Dmitrii simply would not die down. For Shuiskii, it was essential, of course, to build up his cavalry forces. As noted earlier, many pomeshchiki had failed to show up for service (or ran away) during the fall of 1606 and the siege of Moscow. Even though Ivan Shuiskii had some limited success recruiting soldiers for the final battles of the siege, there were still not enough cavalrymen in service to go on the offensive against the rebels with any degree of confidence. Not surprisingly, bringing stay-at-home gentry back into service proved to be a difficult task. In the months following Bolotnikov's retreat from Moscow, a significant percentage of pomeshchiki, even from areas considered very loyal to Shuiskii, continued to fail to report for duty; in some areas the number of "no-shows" was as high as thirty percent. In general, there was widespread reluctance on the part of the gentry to save the usurper. Even threats to confiscate their property and the actual incarceration of their peasants in order to force reluctant warriors to serve proved to be ineffective recruiting techniques.[14] To put the best face possible on a bad situation, Tsar Vasilii issued an exemption from service for the militiamen of the Perm district who had openly refused to serve and had returned home instead. In a bold lie, the tsar declared that their service was not needed because all the rebels had already been killed or captured.[15] Later, in the spring of 1607, a realistic assessment of the dismal prospects for any further recruiting in Perm led to the pragmatic decision to offer those reluctant pomeshchiki an exemption from service in return for a cash fee that could be used to pay other, less unwilling soldiers.[16]

Because of the extreme difficulty in recruiting additional pomeshchiki, Tsar Vasilii turned increasingly to recruiting datochnye liudi. Such low quality military forces had proven invaluable in the defense of Moscow, so Shuiskii began experimenting with wider use of them. He turned for help especially to the rich monasteries whose estates and villages could yield very large number of recruits.[17] Tsar Vasilii received several levies of recruits from the Iosifo-Volokolamsk monastery during the period 1606–7; he also received levies of men from the Velikii Ustiug monastery and the Kirillo-Belozersk monastery.[18] Those poorly trained men were not particularly reliable, however. Like much of the gentry, peasant recruits were not enthusiastic about serving Shuiskii.[19]

Tsar Vasilii's desire to have eager pomeshchiki and recruits may have kept him from harshly punishing no-shows and runaways.[20] He also tried to motivate his soldiers by providing them with more generous salaries. After Bolotnikov's retreat from Moscow, Shuiskii significantly increased the salaries of pomeshchiki fighting against the rebels and even the salaries of those cavalrymen abandoning the rebel camp and joining his service. He also offered a bounty for every rebel killed.[21] Such generosity cost money, of course, and Shuiskii spared no effort to raise funds to pay his soldiers. As already noted, however, he had faced sharply declining revenues since long before the siege of Moscow and was essentially broke by then.[22]

The tsar's financial situation did not improve after the siege ended, and he had great difficulty raising money for a major campaign to crush the retreating rebel forces. Not only did the rebels still occupy much of Russia, but the civil war had seriously disrupted the country's economy. Tax revenues, even from regions safely under Shuiskii's control, became irregular. Constant reminders to pay arrears and the dispatch of bureaucrats to straighten out chaotic provincial finances failed to yield much revenue.[23] As a result, Tsar Vasilii was forced to turn increasingly to wealthy monasteries for money.[24] Yet even there he faced resistance. For example, the elders of the Iosifo-Volokolamsk monastery had to be reminded twice to come up with 3,000 rubles to pay for recruits.[25] Eventually, the desperate tsar was forced to seize money from monasteries, which did not improve his image or popularity.[26] During the winter of 1606–7, Shuiskii also "borrowed" money from Russian merchants and began selling off old clothing, furs, and precious objects found in the treasury in order to pay his soldiers.[27] Another technique used to shore up his gentry militia was the confiscation of the estates of pomeshchiki remaining in the rebel camp (and some persistent no-shows) in order to redistribute them to land-hungry cavalrymen who showed up to fight.[28] Tsar Vasilii also continued to provide food and other necessities to the families of ruined pomeshchiki who remained loyal to him.[29] However, in spite of all his efforts, Shuiskii faced chronic fiscal problems and manpower shortages until he was eventually deposed in 1610. Russia's continuing economic and gentry militia crises, the impact of the civil war, and Shuiskii's image as a usurper all combined to frustrate his energetic attempts to crush rebel forces decisively and rid himself of Tsar Dmitrii's ghost.

As mentioned in the last chapter, after the breakup of the siege of Moscow, more than ten thousand armed rebels retreated south in good order. Bolotnikov and Iurii Bezzubtsev managed to rally many of those weary troops in Serpukhov.[30] Other rebel forces retreated to Kolomna, which had just recently switched back to Shuiskii's side; there they were actively fought by the local garrison and suffered serious casualties. After being rebuffed at Kolomna, those rebels were forced to retreat farther south to Venev, where they rallied and fought against Tsar Vasilii's forces in early 1607.[31] In the meantime, Shuiskii quickly rewarded the townspeople of Kolomna for their loyalty and fighting spirit; on December 12, 1606, he sent them a fairly large sum of money.[32]

Serpukhov, on the other hand, remained loyal to "Tsar Dmitrii" and gave

Bolotnikov and his men a warm reception and a helping hand. Bolotnikov contemplated making a stand in Serpukhov while waiting for Tsar Dmitrii to show up, but the local authorities convinced him that their town did not have adequate provisions to feed all his men for long. To avoid being trapped there by rapidly advancing enemy forces, the rebel commander-in-chief abandoned Serpukhov and led his forces farther south, first to Aleksin and then to Kaluga—which boasted the best fortifications in the region.[33] Not long after Bolotnikov pulled out of Serpukhov, advance regiments of an army commanded by Ivan Shuiskii arrived there. By December 13, the Iosifo-Volokolamskii monastery also sent men and supplies to support voevoda Shuiskii's operations at Serpukhov.[34] On the basis of a totally inaccurate report about the defeat of the tsar's army near Serpukhov in December, the Soviet historian Ivan Smirnov erroneously concluded that the tsar's brother Dmitrii had been soundly defeated by the rebels near Kaluga, after which he had shamefully retreated and was defeated again before Serpukhov.[35] Many scholars have with good reason rejected Smirnov's reconstruction of those events, and even Smirnov himself later admitted that Serpukhov had probably been captured by Ivan Shuiskii's forces in their initial advance against the retreating Bolotnikov.[36]

Legend has it that Dmitrii Shuiskii led an army against Bolotnikov and suffered a catastrophic defeat before Kaluga by December 12. Shuiskii supposedly lost 14,000 men and was forced to retreat in humiliation; news of the disaster supposedly stirred fear in Moscow.[37] In fact, Bolotnikov did not win a great victory over Dmitrii Shuiskii at Kaluga; the tsar's incompetent brother was not even on campaign at this time. He was so unpopular and such a poor military leader that he had been left in Moscow to work as a low-profile bureaucrat. Dmitrii Shuiskii was described by a contemporary as a craven, effeminate man who loved beauty and food but not military matters.[38] It was, in fact, Ivan Shuiskii who led the army that chased Bolotnikov to Serpukhov and beyond.

Two of Ivan Shuiskii's subordinates, Ivan V. Golitsyn and Danila I. Mezetskii, leading a detachment that included Smolensk troops, were the first to reach Serpukhov in hot pursuit of Bolotnikov. Although they arrived too late to trap him, they did manage to kill or capture a small number of rebels. Other rebel stragglers retreating from there froze to death in the woods.[39] Golitsyn and Mezetskii continued to pursue Bolotnikov's men to Aleksin; and from there, Mezetskii's regiment followed Bolotnikov's retreating forces to Kaluga and battled with the rebels near that town.[40] Apparently, that confrontation did not go well for Mezetskii. Rumors of his defeat probably stimulated the legend of Dmitrii Shuiskii's crushing defeat. Mezetskii's lack of success soon prompted Tsar Vasilii to dispatch larger forces to Kaluga. It was at this point that Ivan

Shuiskii's main force advanced to Kaluga from Serpukhov and began the siege of the rebel stronghold.[41] As the tsar's army approached, Bolotnikov's forces retreated inside the Kaluga fortress, where they were enthusiastically received by the townspeople and had plenty of food and munitions for a protracted siege.[42]

While Bolotnikov's men prepared for a siege, the tsar's forces concentrated on trapping the rebels in Kaluga.[43] Prince Ivan M. Vorotynskii was sent from Moscow with a large force to capture Aleksin and thereby shut the door to the east from Kaluga.[44] Contrary to the conclusion of many scholars, Vorotynskii succeeded in taking the town, which soon became a base of operations against the rebels.[45] At about the same time, Tsar Vasilii's forces captured Kashira, which also became a base of operations against the rebels.[46] In the meantime, Prince Nikita Andreevich Khovanskii had been sent from Moscow with a detachment of troops to try to isolate Kaluga from the west and return the towns of Serpeisk, Mosalsk, and Meshchovsk to Shuiskii's side. Khovanskii succeeded in getting the population of Meshchovsk to switch sides and swear an oath of loyalty to Tsar Vasilii—an achievement that was hailed as a military triumph.[47] Khovanskii was then ordered to advance to Kaluga with new recruits from Meshchovsk in order to bolster Ivan Shuiskii's siege army.[48] The tsar's commanders also scoured the entire country under their control for additional troops to aid the siege; the Kirillo-Belozersk monastery, among others, sent recruits for service there.[49] Artillery was also concentrated in Ivan Shuiskii's hands, and gradually Kaluga was surrounded on three sides by the tsar's forces.[50]

Kaluga was an important town with a large trading and artisan population as well as a sizable garrison. It was still a very significant strongpoint of the old frontiers's Oka River defense line against the Crimean Tatars. The town also enjoyed strong economic ties with Severia, and much Oka River trade routinely passed through the hands of Kaluga's merchants. The town was extremely well-provisioned, and most of its population (especially young townsmen) enthusiastically supported the cause of Tsar Dmitrii.[51] Only a few rich merchants supported Shuiskii, and they suffered at the hands of the rebels.[52] Kaluga's most serious problem as it came under siege was the absence of a stone citadel and stone walls. For that reason, while voevoda Ivan Shuiskii was still moving his men into position, Bolotnikov ordered the quick repair and reinforcement of Kaluga's fortifications. The town was at that time surrounded by two wooden palisades, complete with towers and gates. Bolotnikov not only strengthened those palisades, but he also had a ditch dug (or deepened) outside the outer wall and another ditch dug between the two palisades. Earth removed from the inner ditch was piled up on the inside of the outer wall—turning it into breastworks and fortifying it against artillery and battering rams.[53]

The siege of Kaluga began on December 20, 1606.[54] Ivan Shuiskii's army attacked the town for weeks but accomplished almost nothing.[55] Artillery and harquebus salvos proved to be virtually useless against Bolotnikov's improved fortifications. Even worse, the rebel commander-in-chief dispatched lightning-fast sorties almost every day, which often surprised Shuiskii's forces in one place or another and inflicted serious casualties. The rebels would then quickly retreat behind the palisade, having suffered almost no losses. One contemporary compared Bolotnikov's successful tactics to those of ataman Korela at the siege of Kromy in 1605. Kaluga's artillerymen also proved to be extremely useful in fending off the enemy. In spite of its size, voevoda Shuiskii's army seemed utterly powerless, and soon his soldiers gave themselves over to drinking and gambling to pass the time.[56] In January 1607, Ivan Shuiskii wrote to Tsar Vasilii begging for reinforcements because the hated rebels were "daily increasing their forces and supplies by reason of their great courage despite all the efforts" of the tsar's army. In fact, Kaluga was not completely blockaded and continued to receive men and supplies from Severia.[57]

Tsar Vasilii, hoping to avoid a repeat of Tsar Boris's disastrous siege of Kromy, responded to his brother's request by sending all available forces to Kaluga. A new army commanded by Fedor Mstislavskii (which included detachments led by Mikhail Skopin-Shuiskii, Boris Tatev, Ivan N. Romanov, and Vasilii P. Morozov) joined the siege but acted independently of Ivan Shuiskii. The arrival of Mstislavskii's forces made the total number of soldiers besieging Kaluga very large.[58] Nonetheless, sharp mestnichestvo quarrels among Tsar Vasilii's commanders stirred dissension and weakened the siege. These precedence disputes came to the attention of Bolotnikov's men, who loudly mocked the over-proud, self-important enemy voevodas from the safety of Kaluga's fortifications. Even with additional troops, the tsar's siege force continued to have no success against the energetic rebels.[59]

Eventually, Mstislavskii and Skopin-Shuiskii came up with what seemed to them a good plan to destroy Kaluga's fortifications. They decided to construct a special type of movable siege tower known as a *primët* or *podmët*. Large numbers of local peasants were put to work chopping trees; and hundreds of sleds brought logs, firewood, and straw to the tsar's siege camp every day. Soon, there was a "mountain of wood" outside Kaluga. Carpenters quickly constructed many log panels virtually identical to those used in a guliai gorod (1.5 meters wide and 2 meters high, complete with arrow slits) that were then fastened together to form open-ended boxes or cages. In the meantime, fierce and sustained artillery fire and great battering rams allowed the tsar's forces to cross Kaluga's outer ditch in one place and approach the palisade. Then the prefabricated boxes (or modular units) were skidded or rolled on logs toward Kaluga's outer wall where several of those boxes were joined together, and then additional units were stacked on top of the first row. This technique offered protection to construction workers and to soldiers shooting at the rebels while the siege tower was being built. Gradually, the tower grew in height and length. Once it was completed, the stacked boxes were to be filled with straw and firewood in the hope that setting the tower on fire would burn down the palisade and smoke out the rebels. As the tower was being built, Bolotnikov's men recognized the danger but were unable to do much to slow down the construction work.[60] By the beginning of February 1607, the tower was nearly completed, and Kaluga could expect the worst.

On the night before the last section was to be put in place and preparations were being made to set it afire, Bolotnikov struck back with a brilliant plan. Deserters from the tsar's army may have tipped him off about the besiegers' intentions, but the enemy operation was easy enough for the rebels to understand and counter. For several days Bolotnikov had his troops secretly dig tunnels under the outer palisade in order to place mines under the siege tower. At a time of his choosing, Bolotnikov ordered the mines set off. The result was a huge explosion that lifted earth, logs, and soldiers high into the air and rained lethal debris onto the besiegers' camp. Many were killed and the siege camp fell into total confusion. The impact of the explosion was greatly increased by a well-timed rebel sortie in strength from Kaluga during which Bolotnikov's men killed and wounded many besiegers. When the wind shifted, the rebel commander also ordered the remaining piles of wood set afire, which sent smoke billowing into the dazed and choking enemy camp. This amounted to a brilliant victory for Bolotnikov, and it saved Kaluga. According to a chronicler, "Much blood was spilled but Kaluga was not taken." Unable to capture the rebel stronghold, Tsar Vasilii's commanders settled down to blockade Kaluga, hoping to starve it into submission while they tried to capture other rebel towns.[61]

Elsewhere, Tsar Vasilii's forces were equally unsuccessful in military operations. A detachment of 500 men commanded by Prince Andrei V. Khilkov was sent from Kashira (which had just recently switched back to Shuiskii's side) against rebel-held Venev in January 1607. Some rebels were captured in skirmishing, but Khilkov's men were unable to capture the town. In late January or early February, rebel forces suddenly emerged from Venev, defeated the tsar's troops, and forced Khilkov to retreat to Kashira.[62] At about the same time, not far from Venev, the rebel-held town of Mikhailov was placed under siege by Prince Ivan A. Khovanskii. Small rebel detachments from Putivl aided the townspeople in fending off the tsar's forces. Eventually, the rebels emerged in strength from Mikhailov and forced Khovanskii's detachment to break off the siege and retreat to beleaguered Pereiaslavl-Riazanskii.[63] South of Kaluga, Tsar Vasilii's voevodas tried to build on their recent success at Meshchovsk by laying siege to Kozelsk. The Kirillo-Belozersk monastery sent many recruits for service in that operation, but some of those men ran away. Voevoda Artemii V. Izmailov's persistent but unsuccessful siege of Kozelsk lasted for months and was only abandoned when the tsar's forces hastily withdrew from the Kaluga area in the spring of 1607. At that point, Izmailov led his men and artillery back to Meshchovsk without incident, for which he was promoted to the rank of okol-nichii.[64] Farther to the west, Prince Grigorii B. Dolgorukii had been sent by Tsar Vasilii to harass rebels in the Briansk region but he also failed to accomplish much.[65]

Altogether, in early 1607 things were not going very well for the tsar's forces. Reports of rebel victories and the failure of various sieges had a negative effect on the morale of Shuiskii's soldiers, the tsar's supporters, and the population of Moscow. Disturbing rumors of Tsar Dmitrii's survival and imminent return continued to circulate. In January 1607 Tsar Vasilii ordered the execution of a priest in Moscow for distributing satirical letters announcing that Dmitrii was still alive, and spies sent to gather information about rebel forces encountered several people who swore not only that Dmitrii was alive but that they had seen him with their own eyes.[66] Feeling somewhat vulnerable, Tsar Vasilii attempted to shore up his position by recalling former Patriarch Iov from exile. In February 1607, the aged Iov and Patriarch Hermogen together examined the documents associated with Shuiskii's "election" and reported their approval. Then, once again, they both denounced Dmitrii as an impostor and threatened the rebels with perdition unless they immediately surrendered to the "legitimate" Tsar Vasilii.[67] Even with the strong endorsement of two patriarchs, however, Shuiskii could not put an end to frightening reports about rebel movements and plans. The rumor circulating in Moscow that seven thousand Ukrainian cossacks were advancing from Putivl to break up the siege of Kaluga was bad enough;[68] but unsubstantiated reports that thirty thousand rebels led by "two great lords who had gone over to the other camp" were on their way to aid Bolotnikov or to attack Moscow itself caused widespread panic in the capital.[69] In fact, those two "great lords," boyar Prince Andrei Teliatevskii and Vasilii M. Mosalskii, while waiting for Tsar Dmitrii to show up, had temporarily become voevodas of the unsavory cossack pretender Tsarevich Petr, whom we have met before and whose rise within the leadership of the rebel movement marked an ominous new phase in the civil war—one in which the role of cossacks rose dramatically.

Both before and during the siege of Moscow, Bolotnikov had written to

Prince Shakhovskoi in Putivl urging him to find Tsar Dmitrii and bring him to Moscow. Unable to comply, Shakhovskoi instead at some point made contact with the large group of cossacks on the southern frontier who were headed by the self-styled "Tsarevich Petr," the mythical son of Tsar Fedor Ivanovich who had supposedly been hidden from the evil Boris Godunov as a child and had grown up in obscurity. Shakhovskoi knew perfectly well that no such person existed, but he nevertheless invited Petr and his cossacks to hurry to Putivl to help restore Tsar Dmitrii to the throne.[70]

"Tsarevich Petr" started out as Ilia (or Ileika) Korovin, the illegitimate son of a poor woman of Murom and a petty trader or cobbler named Ivan Korovin.[71] Ileika grew up in poverty and in his youth traveled briefly to Moscow. He later worked as a shop assistant in Nizhnii Novgorod and then as a cook on a merchant vessel operating on the Volga River. After several other odd jobs, he ended up in Astrakhan selling leather goods in the marketplace. Eventually, he joined the crew of a ship carrying voevoda S. Kuzmin to the fortress of Terek, north of the Caucasus Mountains. There Ileika met many Terek River cossacks but seems to have first served in a local streltsy detachment before deciding to became a cossack.[72] He participated in the ill-fated Caucasus campaign of voevoda Ivan Buturlin; but when Buturlin's army was destroyed, Ileika managed to make his way back to Terek where, in late 1604, he sold himself as a slave to syn boiarskii Grigorii Elagin.[73] That lifestyle did not appeal to him, however, and by late winter he ran away to Astrakhan where he joined (or rejoined) the cossacks. At that time robbery on the lower Volga River by Volga and Terek cossacks was becoming a very serious problem. Merchant ships and caravans were frequently attacked by those brigands who stole huge sums of money and trade goods.[74] By early spring 1605, Terek and Volga cossacks were also boldly besieging Astrakhan itself—possibly as allies of the pretender Dmitrii but more likely as opportunistic bandits. During the siege, young Ileika managed to get inside the city as a spy. In the end, however, voevoda Mikhail Saburov succeeded in pushing the cossacks back; in frustration, they eventually broke off the siege and dispersed.[75] During summer 1605, after more wandering, the cossacks Ileika rode with happened to meet Tsar Dmitrii's new voevoda of Astrakhan, Ivan D. Khvorostinin, on his way to take up his post.[76]

The winter of 1605–6 found Ileika Korovin back on the Terek River in a large cossack host (army). He was by then a "young companion" or apprentice (chur), first of an old cossack named B. Semenov (himself a runaway slave) and then of ataman Fedor Nagiba. As an apprentice, Ileika occupied a low position and did not even have the right to speak during meetings of the cossack circle.[77] At those meetings, the Terek cossacks discussed their economic plight and what they might do to improve their situation. They contemplated piracy against Turkish ships on the Caspian Sea or becoming mercenary troops of the Persian shah. Some of the cossacks were still angry about their failure to capture Astrakhan. According to a statement made under duresss by Tsarevich Petr after the rebel surrender of Tula in late 1607, those Terek cossacks claimed Tsar Dmitrii had wished to reward them for their service but had been prevented from doing so by greedy, "evil boyars."[78] Not surprisingly, Petr's coerced recollection has often been cited as evidence of social revolution in the Time of Troubles.[79] In fact, early modern Russian folk culture and cossacks did hold boyars in low regard, but far too much weight has been given to Petr's unreliable testimony in evaluating his role in Russia's first civil war. As noted in Chapter 12, there is no evidence of burning class consciousness among the Terek cossacks in 1605; booty, not class war, was on their minds.[80]

At some point, a group of about 300 Terek cossacks—commanded by ataman Fedor Bodyrin—decided to copy Tsar Dmitrii's dramatic success by putting forward a pretender to the throne of their own as a pretext for raiding on the lower Volga.[81] At first, Ileika's comrades chose another young man named Mitka to play the role of tsarevich; but when they discovered that he had never even visited Moscow, they turned to Ileika.[82] He was proclaimed to be the mythical "Tsarevich Petr." There was, of course, no Tsarevich Petr; Tsar Fedor Ivanovich had no sons. Tsaritsa Irina only gave birth to one child, a girl named Feodosiia (1592–94) who died before the age of two. Nevertheless, because of the Uglich affair in 1591 and rumors that Boris Godunov had been responsible for Tsarevich Dmitrii's death, many people were suspicious of the regent's possible involvement in Feodosiia's death. Accounts, legends, and folklore about "Tsarevich Petr" were strongly influenced by rumors about Godunov's possible involvement in Feodosiia's death. Not surprisingly, most of the versions of Tsarevich Petr's escape from Boris Godunov also closely paralleled Tsar Dmitrii's account of his childhood experience.[83]

Soviet scholars believed that the poorest, most radical cossacks (or even the "young companions" themselves) took the lead in promoting the cause of Tsarevich Petr. That is not true. Ataman Bodyrin and his senior cossacks made the decision, which was not initially supported by the majority of Terek cossacks.[84] Bodyrin's 300 men separated from the main body of cossacks and headed downstream to the town of Terek to link up with fortress cossacks and others. Terek's voevoda, Petr Golovin, hearing about the pretender scheme, tried his best to put a stop to it. He sent a cossack colonel to demand that Bodyrin hand over the "tsarevich" and to warn him of the gravity of the pretense. The cossacks did not give up Ileika, however; instead, they went by boat to the mouth of the Terek River and stayed for awhile on an island just off the coast. Soon, news of their activity prompted many more Terek cossacks to join the ranks of "Tsarevich Petr." Voevoda P. Golovin's appeal to some of those cossacks to remain in Terek to defend it fell on deaf ears. The prospect of booty under Petr's banner was simply too appealing to most of the Terek cossacks.[85] Sometime in early 1606 Tsarevich Petr's forces, growing daily, headed straight for Astrakhan.[86] After Astrakhan's voevoda wisely refused to allow them to enter the city, Petr's detachment proceeded up the Volga robbing merchants. By then, about four thousand men rode with the "tsarevich," and they caused enough harm that word of their activities reached Tsar Dmitrii in late April 1606.[87]

It is at this point that Shuiskii propaganda and peasant war scholarship have complicated the story somewhat. A few Soviet historians believed that as soon as the Terek cossacks chose Ileika as Tsarevich Petr, they intended to go to Moscow to meet Tsar Dmitrii.[88] That is not true. The Terek cossacks' goal was booty, not social revolution, and their path did not lead toward Moscow. Nor did Tsar Dmitrii urge them to come to the capital. The tsar's letter to Tsarevich Petr made it abundantly clear that Dmitrii wanted the impostor to leave the country, not come to his aid. Dmitrii's trusted courier Tretiak Iurlov delivered that message to Petr near Samara. Instead of hurrying to Moscow, Petr and his army continued moving up the Volga—staying safely out of the tsar's way.[89] Petr and his men were in the area of Sviazhsk when they learned about Tsar Dmitrii's assassination.[90] It has been generally accepted that news of the tsar's death caused Petr to turn south and vanish into the steppe—heading to the Don or Seversk Donets River; however, it is just as likely that the approach of voevoda Sheremetev's army on its way to Astrakhan caused the Terek cossacks to turn south.

Petr's men retraced their route along the Volga, robbing and killing more merchants and others along the way.[91] According to Captain Margeret, they sacked three castles on the Volga and captured some light artillery and munitions. Then they separated, most of them going into the steppe. Others withdrew to a fort about halfway between Kazan and Astrakhan, hoping to continue robbing merchants.[92] According to Tsarevich Petr, those cossacks stopped at the small Kamyshenk River (200 kilometers north of Tsaritsyn) where they made plans to depart for the Don.[93] No doubt those plans were influenced by the movements of Sheremetev's army and developments in Astrakhan. In mid-June 1606, Astrakhan rebelled against Vasilii Shuiskii in the name of Tsar Dmitrii, and local cossacks played an active role in the uprising. One source specifically connected the robbery of rich merchants' houses in Astrakhan at that time with Tsarevich Petr.[94] As noted in Chapter 15, by September 1606 detachments of free cossacks from the Don, Volga, and Terek—operating out of Astrakhan—were busy attacking Sheremetev's army north of the city; but Petr and his four thousand men were not among them. According to a contemporary source, Petr's army departed from the Astrakhan area before August with the intention of marching to Moscow in order to restore Tsar Dmitrii to his throne.[95] Petr's actual intentions at that time are unknown, but the route he chose did not take him in the direction of Moscow.

Tsarevich Petr and his small army departed from the Volga and headed for the Don River, but they did not stay there for long. They paused at Monastyrevskii gorodok near Azov and then went by boats to the Seversk Donets River. They traveled 100 kilometers up the Seversk Donets to the cossack stanitsas located just southeast of Tsarev-Borisov, their ranks swelling as they proceeded.[96] Although the exact timing is unknown, it was there that Prince Shakhovskoi's courier met up with them and proposed that Petr lead his men in haste to Putivl. Shakhovskoi urged Petr to raise as many cossacks as possible to assist Tsar Dmitrii's army (which was supposedly then on its way to Putivl from Poland-Lithuania) in regaining the throne from Shuiskii. According to Conrad Bussow, Petr was offered rich rewards, including the "best principality"; Shakhovskoi also told him that if Tsar Dmitrii failed to show up, then "Petr could be tsar, since he was the true born son of Fedor Ivanovich and therefore the lawful heir to the realm."[97]

Now acting as official allies of Tsar Dmitrii and cooperating with Shakhovskoi's Putivl headquarters, Tsarevich Petr's army immediately approached the big fortress of Tsarev-Borisov. Its voevoda, the same Mikhail Saburov who had frustrated the Terek cossack siege of Astrakhan in 1605, tried to keep the garrison loyal to Tsar Vasilii with the assistance of the elder of the local monastery. However, Tsarev-Borisov's inhabitants demanded that Petr's men be allowed entry and threatened the elder's life. Declaring for Tsar Dmitrii, the soldiers forced open the fortress gates. Voevoda Saburov and Prince Iurii Priimakov-Rostovskii were killed in the process, either by their own men or by Petr's cossacks. The rebellion of Tsarev-Borisov occurred no later than August 1606.[98] From there Petr's army made its way to Putivl. They may have advanced by way of Valuiki; its voevoda, Mikhail F. Aksakov, and the entire garrison declared for Tsar Dmitrii at about that time.[99] Petr's army did pass through Belgorod, which quickly joined the rebel cause. Belgorod's voevoda, Petr Buinosov-Rostovskii, was killed during the pro-Dmitrii uprising of his garrison.[100] It is also probable that on their way to Putivl Petr's army passed through Livny, where at least one dvorianin was killed during the successful uprising of that garrison.[101]

Tsarevich Petr arrived in Putivl with many more than the four thousand cossacks he had started out with. He actively recruited men before and after his arrival in the "capital" of the rebellion by offering great rewards once Tsar Dmitrii was restored to the throne. Petr not only succeeded in bringing Terek, Volga, and Don cossacks with him but was also able to recruit streltsy from Astrakhan and other frontier garrisons. Conrad Bussow estimated that Petr arrived in Putivl with ten thousand men.[102] When did they arrive? Because of the faulty assumption by scholars that Shakhovskoi did not contact Petr before the siege of Moscow, Petr's arrival in Putivl has usually been placed in November or December 1606.[103] In fact, Petr could easily have reached Putivl by the end of August. One contemporary source claimed that he did so, and other sources make it clear that he was in Putivl during the fall of 1606.[104]

The arrival of Petr and his army in Putivl caused quite a commotion. Prince Shakhovskoi had been actively spreading phony stories about the "tsarevich's" childhood escape from the evil Boris Godunov and issuing reports that Petr intended to put his "uncle," Tsar Dmitrii, back on the throne.[105] Tsarevich Petr's entry into the "capital" of the rebellion at the head of a small army stirred the hopes of many people who had been frustrated by Dmitrii's continued failure to appear. Most of the inhabitants of Putivl greeted Tsarevich Petr with joy and quickly swore an oath of loyalty to him as their "protector" until Tsar Dmitrii's return.[106] Some historians characterized Petr's arrival in Putivl as nothing less than a revolution in which the townspeople and Petr's cossacks pushed aside Shakhovskoi and other members of the Putivl elite and began to pursue a far more radical social agenda.[107] That is not true. Petr did usher in a new phase in the civil war, one associated with a steady increase in the number of cossacks fighting against Tsar Vasilii; in fact, the cossacks soon became the principal rebel fighting force.[108] That does not mean, however, that rebel goals changed dramatically.

Because he was of "tsarist" birth, Petr quite naturally took over the war council Shakhovskoi had formed and transformed it into a makeshift boyar council. However, he did not shove aside Shakhovskoi, who stayed on the council and continued to maintain considerable power and influence within the rebel leadership. Petr also promoted several dvoriane to membership on his boyar council. Although it is possible that the tsarevich's atamans and sotniki wielded real power in Putivl, Petr did not allow any of them to sit on the council. Instead, under his leadership, the influence of the gentry actually increased in the rebel "capital." Far from being a social revolutionary, Petr had become somewhat of a snob, preferring titled gentlemen as his advisers and voevodas. In addition to Prince Shakhovskoi, his principal retainers now included boyar Prince Andrei Teliatevskii (Bolotnikov's old master), at least two Mosalskii princes, Prince Mikhail Aksakov, Prince Fedor Zasekin, S. Kokhanovskii, and the brilliant and wily golova Iurii Bezzubtsev.[109] Acting the part of a tsar, not a champion of the masses, Petr held court, distributed lands and promotions, issued decrees in the names of both Tsar Dmitrii and himself, and even planned an embassy to the Polish king Sigismund III.[110] There is no evidence whatsoever that Petr pursued a radical social agenda in Putivl. On the other hand, Petr quickly proved that he was no Dmitrii. The "tsarevich" was, after all, from the lower class and had not been raised to act or speak like a lord; nor did he have Dmitrii's forgiving nature. Instead, Petr proved to be bloodthirsty and vengeful in dealing with recalcitrant supporters of Vasilii Shuiskii. He was also accused of raping the daughters of Tsar Vasilii's captive voevodas.[111] If Prince Shakhovskoi had any misgivings about the boorish, cruel, and arrogant Petr, however, he kept them to himself.

The rise in the use of violence against "traitors" that was associated with the ascendancy of Petr has often been cited as evidence of the social revolutionary character of the "Bolotnikov rebellion." Scholars have asserted that Petr "launched a reign of terror" in Putivl and that the lords on his boyar council were powerless to prevent the mass executions of gentry.[112] That is extremely unlikely. In fact, just as in the case of the treatment of Shuiskii loyalists by Bolotnikov and Pashkov, there is no evidence of a split between elite and common rebels in Putivl on the issue of the use of violence against their opponents. Instead, gentry in the rebel camp as well as commoners strongly approved the executions of men who had betrayed Tsar Dmitrii. There is no evidence that those executions signified social revolution or class war. However, dispassionate analysis of the subject has been seriously complicated by uncertain chronology and by Shuiskii's active propaganda campaign that exaggerated the terror unleashed by Petr and his radical, lower class supporters.[113] Let us take a closer look at what really happened.

Very soon after Petr's arrival in Putivl, he was denounced as an impostor by Father Superior Dionisii of the local Bogoroditskii Molchinskii monastery. The monks of that monastery had been strong supporters of the pretender Dmitrii and had been rewarded with more land once he became tsar. When Vasilii Shuiskii seized the throne, he confirmed Tsar Dmitrii's grant to the monastery and sent Father Superior Dionisii back to Putivl with a new confirmation charter and a "miracle-working" icon. Dionisii tried to convince the inhabitants of Putivl that Tsarevich Petr, their new "protector," was nothing but a fraud, but the townspeople turned against Dionisii instead. Tsarevich Petr had the monk beaten and thrown from a tower to his death. In the process, Tsar Vasilii's charter was publicly ripped up.[114] Soon after that, according to a hostile chronicler, Petr "spilled much blood" as he put to death captured boyars, dvoriane, and deti boiarskie.[115] One source stated that Petr had seventy men executed in one day. Skrynnikov wisely doubted the accuracy of that particular document, but the execution of captured lords did become almost a daily occurrence on the Putivl town square.

Shuiskii propaganda and some scholars lumped together as victims of Petr in Putivl many of the commanders who had actually been killed when their towns declared for Tsar Dmitrii; nevertheless, over time, dozens of well-known dvoriane were put to death to the cheers of the rebel capital's townspeople.[116] It has long been assumed that the executions of captured voevodas, boyars, courtiers, and dvoriane who had been sent to Putivl by Bolotnikov and Pashkov began as soon as Petr arrived there. In fact, the drift into wider use of terror and reprisals by the rebels was gradual, and the exact timing of the Putivl executions is not known. Some scholars have suggested that Shuiskii's mass executions of rebel cossacks after the siege of Moscow were a disproportionate response to reports of Petr's use of terror in Putivl;[117] but it is just as likely that news of Shuiskii's slaughter of cossacks and his offer of a bounty for every rebel killed hardened attitudes in the rebel camp and stirred Petr to increase the level of violence against stubborn supporters of Tsar Vasilii who were crowded into the prisons of Putivl.[118] Whereas Dmitrii had often shown favor to captive lords, hoping to gain their support, Tsarevich Petr began to execute some of them. Those lords were not killed because of their social class, however; they were put to death for refusing to swear an oath of loyalty to Tsarevich Petr.[119]

It has been plausibly claimed that the boorish, lower-class "tsarevich" had trouble securing the obedience of captive lords because he was such an obvious hoax. Skrynnikov went so far as to credit Shuiskii propaganda that some prisoners recognized their runaway slaves among the rebel commanders.[120] Was that true? Close examination of the evidence suggests otherwise. For example, the chronicle reference to doomed lords dramatically denouncing the impostor tsarevich as the bastard son of a shoemaker and as the slave of Grigorii Elagin contained information about Petr that could not possibly have been known by any of the prisoners in Putivl and appears instead to have been based upon documents composed several months later by Tsar Vasilii's government.[121] On the other hand, the execution of boyar Prince Vasilii Cherkasskii may well have been influenced by the fact that he had been the former owner of B. Semenov, the old cossack Petr had originally been apprenticed to and who now served as one of his atamans.[122]

The public executions of stubborn Shuiskii loyalists not only drew popular support but may also have been intended to imitate Tsar Ivan IV's popular public executions of elite "traitors." Tsar Ivan had almost always made a point of asking gathered crowds if the guilty persons deserved execution; inevitably, the response was a loud "yes." Then the tsar, as the pitiless dispenser of justice, would subject his doomed prisoners to cruel public humiliation and ritualistic torture and execution. Such shocking spectacles were very popular in early modern Russia and actually served to strengthen the bond between Ivan the Terrible and his ordinary subjects.[123] Virtually the same thing happened in Putivl. Unrepentent Shuiskii supporters were denounced as traitors to the crowds and put to death in a variety of horrible ways. Some were beaten or hacked to death; some were crucified. Others were pushed off towers and bridges or scalded to death. A few were hung upside down and then shot; others were dismembered or impaled.[124] The cruelest torture appears to have been reserved for those who denounced Petr as an impostor.[125]

The similarity between Tsar Ivan's ritualized cruelty to traitors and that of rebels in the Time of Troubles was not accidental. Ivan the Terrible shared a positive folkloric image with cossack bandits in part, at least, precisely because their cruelty was perceived by supporters as appropriate and as serving a purifying function.[126] In fact, the cossacks actively cultivated their reputation for being cruel to enemies and for seeking harsh revenge. It simultaneously intimidated their opponents and stirred widespread fear and respect for them as dispensers of rough justice.[127] As we have seen, cossacks and other rebels had occasionally resorted to similar humiliations and executions of Shuiskii loyalists before Petr became a rebel leader, and similar rituals continued to be carried out on a smaller scale in later stages of the civil war.[128] It should also be noted that many of the forms of torture and execution used in Putivl were remarkably similar to the horrible punishments Tsar Vasilii, then one of Tsar Boris's voevodas, had inflicted upon the population of the Komaritsk district back in 1605 for daring to support Dmitrii. Revenge for those despicable actions cannot be ruled out as a motive for the cruel executions in Putivl.

The increasing use of terror by Petr and others was definitely linked to disarray in rebel leadership and goals in light of the failure of Bolotnikov's siege of Moscow and the continued failure of Tsar Dmitrii to appear in the rebel camp; it was also clearly linked to the emergence of the cossacks as the principal rebel fighting force. Although most rebels strongly approved of the executions in Putivl, Tsar Vasilii's propagandists were eventually able to stir indignation and fear among members of the gentry by issuing vivid reports of Petr's activities.[129] Putivl came to have a fearful reputation in the minds of Shuiskii's gentry supporters, and Tsarevich Petr came to be regarded as their most bloodthirsty opponent.[130] By summer 1607, a Polish envoy in Moscow reported that Petr was generally viewed as an impostor and that, due to his executions, a majority of the Seversk gentry had deserted his camp and switched sides to support Tsar Vasilii.[131] Even though that report was somewhat exaggerated, it demonstrates that Tsarevich Petr, even without being a social revolutionary, proved to be an unworthy stand-in for Tsar Dmitrii. Petr had much greater difficulty attracting gentry to the rebel camp; and, as the cossack role in the civil war increased under his leadership, terror against elite "traitors" reached a wider sweep and frightened at least some otherwise sympathetic pomeshchiki away from the rebel cause.

No later than early December 1606, Petr departed from Putivl intending to meet with King Sigismund and also to search for Tsar Dmitrii.[132] On his way to the Polish-Lithuanian border he passed through and may have captured some villages and towns near rebel-held Briansk; in fact, the voevoda of Briansk, T. Bolobanov ended up working closely with Petr in this period.[133] Sometime in December 1606, Petr crossed the border and reached the town of Orsha, where he met with the local commander, Andrzej Sapieha, and quickly discovered that he could not count on King Sigismund to provide military aid to the rebels. Learning that, Petr declined Sapieha's offer of an escorted procession to meet the king and quickly left Orsha.[134] He concentrated on trying to find Tsar Dmitrii and recruiting soldiers for the rebel cause. In the process, Petr quickly managed to secure the assistance of some Polish and Belorussian soldiers who had been in Tsar Dmitrii's service—including a lord (pan) named Zenowicz, who was then the governor (starosta) of the bordertown of Chechersk. Pan Zenowicz not only helped Petr recruit soldiers; several months later he also found someone to play the role of Tsar Dmitrii and accompanied him across the border—a development that had a great impact on the civil war.[135] In early January 1607, Petr left the capable pan Zenowicz in charge of recruiting foreign soldiers and returned to Russia. Nevertheless, the colorful tsarevich in just a short time managed to make such an impression in Belorussia that a legendary version of his life story was written down there at the beginning of 1607.[136]

Petr returned to Putivl sometime in January 1607 and continued his efforts to raise troops to relieve Bolotnikov's men in beleaguered Kaluga.[137] To his great joy, up to seven thousand Zaporozhian cossacks arrived in Putivl that same month to join his forces.[138] Bolstered by those reinforcements, in February 1607, Tsarevich Petr moved the rebel army of up to thirty thousand men and his entire court north to the large fortified town of Tula, only about 90 kilometers from Kaluga. It was news of that army's advance that caused such panic in Moscow.[139] It may be recalled that Tula had been an active supporter of the rebel cause for a long time, and some rebels escaping from the failed siege of Moscow had retreated there.[140] Beyond the attraction of its ardently pro-Dmitrii population and its location (closer than Putivl to both Kaluga and Moscow but still easily accessible from the steppe frontier), Tula appealed to Tsarevich Petr and Prince Shakhovskoi (who had been a junior voevoda there ten years earlier) because it was a strong fortress deemed to be "better than Kaluga"; among other things, it had an impressive stone citadel or "kremlin" (*kreml'*). Tula also contained a large civilian population and a marketplace with many shops; by this time it was also a well-developed armament manufacturing center.[141]

Once Petr's army was ensconced in Tula, those forces immediately became a serious menace both to Shuiskii's army besieging Kaluga and to Moscow itself. Tsar Vasilii sent word far and wide denouncing Tsarevich Petr as a bloodthirsty impostor and ordered his commanders at all costs to prevent Petr from breaking up the siege of Kaluga.[142] Just as Shuiskii feared, in Tula Petr and his boyar council made plans for the immediate relief of Bolotnikov's tired men because of reports that Kaluga's food supplies were dwindling and that hunger was becoming a serious problem in that stubborn rebel stronghold.

19

Collapse of the Siege of Kaluga and the Beginning of Tsar Vasilii's Offensive

In February 1607, from the new rebel headquarters in Tula, Tsarevich Petr dispatched a large army with a huge supply train to aid Bolotnikov's hungry men in Kaluga. Prince Vasilii F. Aleksandrov-Mosalskii was chosen to command the relief force of 26,000 men.[1] The rebel army was slowed down somewhat by hundreds of sleds loaded with food, gunpowder, lead, and light artillery; but it made good progress. At the Vyrka River (a tributary of the Oka), just 7 kilometers south of Kaluga, they encountered Tsar Vasilii's forces. The battle at the Vyrka River occurred on or about February 23, 1607.[2]

The three regiments opposing the rebels were commanded by Ivan N. Romanov, Danila I. Mezetskii, and Mikhail A. Nagoi.[3] When the rebels saw the enemy regiments blocking their path, they attempted to force their way past them by means of the typical cossack mobile defense formation known as a *tabor*—an open-ended rectangle of horses and sleds (carts in summer) tied together so that the bulk of the army could advance under the cover provided by the sleds on both flanks and to the rear. Unfortunately for the rebels, the huge supply train was extremely cumbersome and as a result the tabor lacked maneuverability and made flight virtually impossible. On their own, the rebel cossacks probably could have broken through the enemy position and reached Kaluga; but, tied down by their intertwined carts and horses, the rebel forces quickly got bogged down in battle. Shuiskii's troops took advantage of the situation by attacking the tabor furiously and smashing some of the sleds. That brought the rebel advance to a complete standstill. Although they resisted enemy attacks with great courage for "a day and a night," the rebels were defeated and suffered great losses. Many prisoners and most of the supply train—including artillery—fell into the hands of Shuiskii's forces. Large numbers of prisoners were thrown in the river and drowned. Voevoda Aleksandrov-Mosalskii himself was wounded in battle and captured; he died later in Moscow.[4] As the battle of Vyrka was ending, some rebel cossacks, seeing the hopeless position they were in, chose death over captivity. They denied Shuiskii's forces much of the rebel gunpowder supply by perching themselves on the carts laden with powder barrels and igniting them. The resulting explosion was tremendous; according to a contemporary, up to 3,000 men perished almost instantly.[5]

The battle of Vyrka was a great victory for Tsar Vasilii. Prince Mezetskii, who had been seriously wounded in combat, was recalled to Moscow as a hero by a grateful and greatly relieved tsar.[6] Good news soon reached Shuiskii from elsewhere as well. At about the same time as the battle of Vyrka, the tsar's commanders were making plans to move against Tula. Because that rebel stronghold was screened to the north by several smaller towns still in rebel hands, those towns quickly became targets of Shuiskii's forces. However, the rebels in Venev and Mikhailov stubbornly and successfully resisted. As a result, the tsar's commanders shifted the focus of their efforts to Serebrianye Prudy—a smaller, less well-fortified town in the Tula region, the capture of which would greatly facilitate operations against Tula.

Voevoda Andrei Khilkov, after his frustrating retreat from before Venev to Kashira, was sent to capture Serebrianye Prudy. He commanded a mixed regiment of soldiers from Kashira, Iaroslavl, Uglich, and Tula. Joining Khilkov's offensive after their successful campaign in the central Volga region, voevodas Grigorii Pushkin and S. G. Ododurov brought with them not only their own troops but also some gentry from Nizhnii Novgorod who had recently switched sides to support Tsar Vasilii.[7] With those reinforcements, Khilkov made a vigorous assault on Serebrianye Prudy under cover of darkness. He may have been in a hurry due to intelligence reports concerning a rebel relief force being sent from Tula by Tsarevich Petr. Khilkov's troops met sharp resistance at first, and casualties were high on both sides. Eventually, however, the greatly outnumbered rebels realized that they were not going to be able to hold out much longer and decided to surrender. They admitted Khilkov's men into the town and swore an oath of loyalty to Tsar Vasilii.[8] The very next day Khilkov set up an ambush about 4 kilometers from Serebrianye Prudy in order to trap the relief force coming from Tula. That rebel army, which included many Zaporozhian cossacks, was commanded by Prince Ivan D. Klubkov-Mosalskii and I. Starovskii.[9] The rebels were taken completely by surprise and utterly defeated. Many of them were captured, including both of their commanders who were sent to Moscow in chains. The battle of Serebrianye Prudy was a significant victory for Tsar Vasilii. Taken together with the almost simultaneous rebel defeat at the Vyrka River, it sharply eroded the strategic situation of Shuiskii's foes. In Moscow panic gave way to celebration, and optimistic plans were made for capturing Tula and pressing the siege of Kaluga.[10]

In early March 1607, a more confident Tsar Vasilii and the boyar council approved new laws concerning slaves and peasants. In addition to being a continuation of the tsar's previous efforts to aid his hard-pressed gentry, Shuiskii's new laws also aimed at influencing wavering subjects and even some groups of rebels. On March 7, a generous new slave law was promulgated that overturned Boris Godunov's hated 1597 law that had trapped many elite warriors—then serving as contract slaves—in permanent slavery. Shuiskii now promised freedom to those slaves who had been forced into involuntary slavery. His goal was probably to woo such unfortunate but well-armed and experienced warriors from the rebel camp and to convince other military slaves not to join the cause of "Tsar Dmitrii."[11] Shuiskii's slave law can definitely be viewed as a clever propaganda measure, especially in conjunction with his exaggerated reports of Tsarevich Petr's cossack terror and the widespread announcement of recent victories achieved by his commanders.[12]

In sharp contrast to his slave law, on March 9, 1607, Shuiskii issued a harsh decree on runaway peasants that favored the gentry and strongly reinforced serfdom.[13] Many scholars have assumed that Tsar Vasilii's draconian law was intended as some kind of revenge against peasant rebels.[14] In fact, the decree was really a sop to the beleaguered gentry militia who had lost many peasants during the famine and civil war. Shuiskii was specifically trying to put an end to the sharp conflict between gentry and aristocrats over peasant labor, conflicts that threatened his own regime's survival. By tilting in favor of the gentry instead of the aristocrats on the issue of recovering runaway peasants, the tsar was simultaneously trying to shore up his vulnerable pomeshchiki to prevent any further gentry defections to the rebel cause and trying to entice rebel gentry back to his side.[15] Because of the chaos of the civil war, however, Shuiskii was actually unable to strictly enforce his new decree on runaway peasants.[16] Upon reflection, that may have been what he had in mind all along. The new law had definite propaganda value, portraying Tsar Vasilii as a friend of the gentry, while in practical terms it had no real negative impact on his greedy aristocratic supporters who, of course, had no interest in returning runaway peasants living on their estates to their original gentry masters. In addition to new laws, Shuiskii continued his strenuous efforts to raise more money and troops for what he hoped would be the final round of the civil war—assaults on Kaluga and Tula.

The rebels in Kaluga were beginning to run out of supplies by this time; the loss of the supply train at the Vyrka River had really hurt them. In spite of that, Bolotnikov and his men did not lose their resolve. When the tsar's soldiers in the Kaluga siege camp shouted news of their victory at Vyrka and called upon the rebels to surrender, Bolotnikov supposedly laughed at them, once again swore an oath to Tsar Dmitrii, and hanged a few suspected traitors—

including his own cook—in full view of the besiegers.[17] Conrad Bussow penned an improbable story about a Baltic adventurer named Friedrich Fiedler who, during the siege of Kaluga, had supposedly been paid by Tsar Vasilii to poison Bolotnikov but instead revealed the plot to the rebel commander-in-chief and was rewarded by him.[18] On the other hand, it is not impossible to imagine efforts by Shuiskii to kill Bolotnikov by means of assassins; Tsar Vasilii really did want to get rid of the energetic rebel leader.[19]

In the meantime, the tsar's voevodas greatly intensified the bombardment of Kaluga. Continuous artillery fire, day and night, including incendiary mortar rounds, killed many rebels. Bolotnikov's men did not passively endure the bombardment, however; instead, they pursued an active defense. Cossack detachments made sorties from Kaluga continually, and Bolotnikov's men constantly fired their weapons at the besiegers. As a result, casualties were also high among Shuiskii's forces.[20] On at least one occasion, some of Bolotnikov's cossack troops (including a Don cossack ataman) were taken by surprise and captured by the besiegers. Those rebel prisoners were transported to Moscow to be put on public display, but they ended up embarrassing Tsar Vasilii by swearing that they had seen Tsar Dmitrii alive. Not surprisingly, the prisoners were then thrown in the river and drowned.[21] Meanwhile, back in Kaluga, the hungry rebels were reduced to eating their horses and grew steadily weaker; nonetheless, they continued to stubbornly resist Shuiskii's forces.[22]

After the rebel surrender of Serebrianye Prudy, Tula was more vulnerable; and, by late March, Tsar Vasilii's commanders launched an offensive against that rebel stronghold.[23] Prince Ivan Vorotynskii advanced to Tula from Aleksin along with Semen R. Alferev and a new colonel, Istoma Pashkov. Other regiments were sent from Moscow to bolster their forces.[24] Seeing the enemy approach Tula, Prince Andrei Teliatevskii made a sortie in force from the fortress, quickly defeated Vorotynskii, and dispersed the enemy army. Vorotynskii, Alferev, and Pashkov fled—barely making it back to Aleksin.[25] This defeat was a severe blow to Tsar Vasilii, coming so soon after his much-celebrated victories.[26]

At about the same time—and connected to Vorotynskii's campaign—voevodas Khilkov, Ododurov, and Pushkin (fresh from their victory at Serebrianye Prudy) circled around Tula to the south and attacked Dedilov in late March, hoping that its capture would isolate Tsarevich Petr's headquarters. Instead, rebel forces inflicted a terrible defeat on the tsar's army. Voevoda Ododurov was killed, and Khilkov's troops fled—abandoning most of their weapons and supplies in the process. Many of the tsar's soldiers were killed, and many more drowned in the Shat River as they tried to escape. Khilkov managed to retreat to Kashira with only a few troops and even fewer weapons.[27] He was immediately recalled to Moscow and relieved of command; boyar Prince Andrei V. Golitsyn was sent to Kashira to replace him. Tsarevich Petr's forces took immediate advantage of the situation and relieved several towns near Tula then under siege. They also managed to retake Serebrianye Prudy and began making plans to try again to aid Bolotnikov in Kaluga.[28] The defeats suffered by Vorotynskii and Khilkov undid the results of Tsar Vasilii's commanders' earlier victories at Vyrka and Serebrianye Prudy. Shuiskii's joy suddenly gave way to anxious concern. Trying to prevent further defections to the rebels, the tsar's propagandists sent dispatches all over the country announcing fictitious victories. But in Moscow there was growing fear once again. To make matters worse, at about this time the clapper of the "great Moscow bell" fell down one night—an event regarded by many as an evil omen.[29]

Rumors of rebel victories and possible intervention by troops from Poland-Lithuania made Tsar Vasilii's supporters very nervous. Many fully expected that the Polish king would eventually seek revenge for the massacre of the Polish wedding guests during Shuiskii's coup d'état and for the continued incarceration of the Polish ambassador. When eight of the ambassador's men escaped (dressed as peasants) and managed to return home by March 1607, Shuiskii suspected treason and some kind of developing plot. Several guards were tortured, additional sentries were posted at the ambassador's residence, and some Moscow city gates were closed.

Reports also came in that Tsar Dmitrii's father-in-law, Jerzy Mniszech (who, along with his daughter Marina, had been incarcerated in Iaroslavl), was in communication with the rebels and that his wife and Mikhail Molchanov were already at the border with 30,000 soldiers. In addition, news reached Moscow at about this time of serious unrest in Iaroslavl, Kostroma (where Jerzy Mniszech's son was being held), and Rostov (where other Polish lords were incarcerated). That greatly alarmed Tsar Vasilii. Apparently, Mniszech's men planned and executed a coordinated rampage of looting and arson in Iaroslavl, Kostroma, and Rostov. They hoped to use that diversion to escape and join the rebels, but their plot was discovered. Most of them were prevented from escaping; many were treated very harshly, and some were executed. Security around all Polish prisoners was significantly tightened. Some of the Poles were separated from the others and sent into more distant exile. Mniszech's personal retinue was also greatly reduced. After a tense stand-off with Russian authorities, seventy of his men were detached from him with the promise that they would be repatriated to Poland-Lithuania. According to Isaac Massa, those poor souls were probably put to death instead. The suspicious Tsar Vasilii also refused to release the Crimean Tatar ambassador to return home in early April; nor would he allow

Polish, Armenian, or Tatar merchants to depart from Moscow—fearing that they might provide information to the rebels.[30]

Throughout this period, the siege of Kaluga continued without success. Bolotnikov's men were very hungry, but Shuiskii's forces were also beginning to suffer from hunger, cold, and exhaustion due to the lengthy siege. Frequent sorties by Bolotnikov's troops also inflicted high casualties on the tsar's soldiers, and morale in the siege camp was low.[31] By early April, the ice on the Oka River began to break up, and Shuiskii's commanders became concerned that Bolotnikov might make use of the large number of sailboats and barges (some of which were up to 24 meters in length) located in Kaluga to escape down river. To prevent that from happening, they ordered the construction of large rafts to hold troops and artillery and stationed them below the town. That tactic proved to be very successful. Shuiskii's commanders also attempted to use river craft in conjunction with ground detachments from the Kaluga siege camp in operations against other rebel towns in the area; however, those campaigns were not successful. As Massa put it, the tsar's forces were "everywhere defeated."[32]

By late April, Tsarevich Petr and his commanders felt they were finally ready to try again to relieve Kaluga. In preparation for that campaign, Petr sent a small detachment to relieve Kozelsk (located 60 kilometers southwest of Kaluga), which had been under siege for months by voevoda Artemii V. Izmailov. A breakthrough at Kozelsk would open the road to Kaluga. Unfortunately for the rebels, Izmailov's men crushed the relief force, for which their commander was promoted to the rank of okolnichii by Tsar Vasilii.[33] In spite of that, voevoda Teliatevskii decided to attempt to reach Kaluga and departed from Tula with a large army of cossacks, soldiers from southern frontier garrisons, and troops from the Tula and Riazan regions. Chosen to be his subordinate commanders were Iurii Bezzubtsev and S. Kokhanovskii. They advanced to within 40 kilometers of Kaluga and encountered the tsar's army at a village near the small Pchelnia River.[34] Because Shuiskii's commanders laying siege to Kaluga took the threat from Tula very seriously, they sent forward three regiments under the command of Prince Boris Tatev to stop Teliatevskii. From Aleksin, Prince Iurii P. Ushatyi, Semen Alferev, and Istoma Pashkov also advanced with additional troops to reinforce Tatev's regiments. Altogether, the tsar's forces awaiting the rebels at Pchelnia stood at 17,000 men.[35] That was a fairly large army; however, many of those soldiers were former rebel cossacks who had surrendered at Zabore after the siege of Moscow and agreed to enter Shuiskii's service. Those men proved to be extremely unreliable; more than once, many of them betrayed their new employer.[36]

The battle of Pchelnia occurred on or just before May 3, 1607.[37] The tsar's forces engaged in a furious and bloody struggle with Teliatevskii's large army. Casualties were heavy on both sides, but the battle ended in disaster for Tsar Vasilii's men. Prince Tatev was killed, along with two of his subordinate commanders; Prince Ushatyi was wounded; and a large number of Shuiskii's gentry and other soldiers were captured. The defeat was total and overwhelming.[38] One contemporary estimate put Tsar Vasilii's losses at a staggering 14,000 men; another source claimed that all 17,000 men were lost.[39] What actually happened? There is a legend that the defeat was due to the betrayal of Shuiskii by voevoda Tatev and one of his associates, who allegedly led virtually all of their men over to the rebel side during the battle (as Pashkov had done during the siege of Moscow).[40] More reliable sources, however, do not mention any betrayal by Tatev, and the legend has rightly been questioned by some scholars.[41] It is far more likely that it was not Tatev but the Zabore cossacks in his army who switched sides during the battle. One source claimed that 15,000 men switched sides that day; another source mentioned that "many people" switched sides and identified them as "simple soldiers." Isaac Massa, somewhat confused about the details, nonetheless confirmed that Tatev's Zabore cossacks asked to join the rebel army and were accepted. Massa declared that "their defection made them the cause of the whole army's defeat."[42]

Tsarist forces escaping from the battle of Pchelnia fled in disorder back to the Kaluga siege camp, but they did not stay there for long. Instead, many of them simply kept retreating toward Moscow. In fact, the crushing defeat of Shuiskii's forces at Pchelnia had a catastrophic effect on the hungry and weary army camped before Kaluga. Learning of the deaths of their commanders and comrades, many of the demoralized soldiers in the siege camp panicked and began to abandon their posts.[43] Bolotnikov took immediate advantage of the situation by leading a sortie of all his forces against the disorganized besiegers. The rebels inflicted a stinging defeat on the enemy, set fire to the siege camp, and put the tsar's soldiers to flight. Shuiskii's commanders barely had time to get out of their tents before terror overwhelmed their troops, who abandoned most of their provisions, munitions, and heavy artillery. So ended the siege of Kaluga.[44]

While several of Tsar Vasilii's commanders fled in panic, others—including Skopin-Shuiskii and Pashkov—tried to organize an orderly retreat to Aleksin and Serpukhov in order to reduce the loss of men, weapons, and supplies and in order to prevent the retreat from becoming a total rout. Their efforts were only partially successful, however. The tsar's forces remained widely scattered and their paths of retreat were littered with abandoned weapons, artillery, and clothing.[45] Under the circumstances, Mstislavskii and Skopin-Shuiskii quickly gave up on the plan to halt the retreat at Aleksin and, instead, pulled back all the way to Serpukhov. Skopin-Shuiskii managed to save some artillery by that action; but, as a result, Aleksin became too vulnerable to hold. Vorotynskii wisely chose to abandon the town and also retreated north to Serpukhov, whereupon Aleksin was immediately reoccupied by rebel forces. The abandonment of the Kaluga siege also forced voevoda Izmailov to break off the siege of Kozelsk and retreat to Meshchovsk.[46]

Embarrassed and frustrated by his failure to capture Kaluga, Prince Mstislavskii led some of his men and artillery to rebel-held Borovsk (only about 80 kilometers southwest of Moscow), linked up with a small siege force there, and stormed the town. He then put all rebel defenders and all inhabitants of Borovsk to the sword. After that, while Vorotynskii attempted to reorganize his forces in Serpukhov, Mstislavskii and Ivan Shuiskii rallied their own army only 10 kilometers south of Moscow. That was done in order to calm down the alarmed ruler and the fearful population of the capital, who fully expected a renewed rebel attack at any time—and not without reason. In fact, the road to Moscow from Kaluga and Tula was now open again. So demoralized and disorganized were Shuiskii's forces and so unpopular at this point was Tsar Vasilii that, according to Isaac Massa, if the rebels had had an army with which to strike Moscow they "would have taken it without resistance." Not surprisingly, Tsar Vasilii was greatly disappointed at the failure of his commanders. In spite of Mstislavskii's minor victory at Borovsk, he did not dare show his face in the capital. Even the tsar's brother, Ivan, felt compelled to sneak into Moscow unnoticed. Their demoralized troops who had fled to the capital after the disasters at Pchelnia and Kaluga were carefully questioned by government clerks to sort out fact from rumor about the failed campaign. Asked why they had fled from the rebels, some of the tsar's soldiers replied: "Go on campaign with the tsar and see for yourselves!"[47]

The battle of Pchelnia and the collapse of the siege of Kaluga were powerful blows to Tsar Vasilii. It was impossible to hide the setback, which some contemporaries likened to the catastrophic collapse of the siege of Kromy in 1605. Instead of acknowledging the power of the rebel forces, however, Shuiskii's commanders blamed their failure on mestnichestvo quarrels among the tsar's voevodas and the alleged "treason" of Boris Tatev and other officers, whose deaths in battle allowed their reputations to be conveniently smeared by Shuiskii's living but humiliated commanders.[48] The truth was far more difficult to accept.

In trying to explain the catastrophic defeat of the tsar's forces, Platonov emphasized the difficulty of winter campaigning. Smirnov strongly disagreed, correctly stressing that the hardships faced by the rebels were greater than those facing Shuiskii's forces. As expected, however, Smirnov's own explanation for the rebel victory emphasized lower class support for Bolotnikov's "social revo-lution" and class division among Tsar Vasilii's own forces.[49] A more accurate assessment would have to take into account the continuing effects of the gen-try militia crisis and the consistent inability of the tsar's weary and hungry army to sustain sieges for many months. Of course, the desertion of the Zabore cos-sacks at Pchelnia also played a major part in the disaster. Nonetheless, whether those cossacks acted spontaneously or had secretly planned all along to desert Shuiskii's army at a critical moment, it should be remembered that most of Tsar Vasilii's other troops were also not anxious to fight or die for him. In sharp con-trast, rebel forces were highly motivated. Even in the worst of conditions, Bolotnikov's men remained active, brave, and stubborn; their faith in Tsar Dmitrii was unshaken, and their opposition to the tsar-usurper still burned white hot.[50]

Why didn't the rebels follow up their victories with a quick campaign against Moscow? After decisively defeating the tsar's forces at Pchelnia, Teliatevskii did not proceed either to Kaluga or to Moscow. Instead, he returned to Tula with many captives.[51] Contemporaries and historians criticized the rebel comman-der for not taking advantage of a good opportunity to march on Moscow again.[52] However, Teliatevskii had suffered high casualties in battle and may have felt that his army was too weak to continue advancing, or he may have been bogged down by too many captives. He may also have wanted to savor a victory instead of immediately risking another battle and possible defeat. It is not likely—as some have suggested—that he was somewhat reluctant to join up with Bolotnikov at Kaluga because his former slave might push him aside and insist on assum-ing overall command of his army. Whatever his reasons, Teliatevskii's decision to return to Tula forced Bolotnikov to retreat to Tula also.

Once the siege of Kaluga had been broken, Bolotnikov's men were too tired, hungry, and decimated to resume an active offensive against Moscow without the assistance of another large rebel army. Instead, Bolotnikov led his battered forces from Kaluga to Tula to rest and to plan the next rebel offensive.[53] He left behind a small garrison commanded by an experienced and trustworthy Scottish merce-nary captain named Albert Wandmann, who continued to stoutly defend Kaluga for several more years. Supplies seized from the tsar's abandoned siege camp kept the garrison well fed and well armed, and most of the artillery that had been left behind was also carefully stored in Kaluga in anticipation of a future campaign against Moscow.[54] Even though Bolotnikov's move to Tula may be regarded as a retreat, the rebel commander-in-chief nevertheless issued proclamations announc-ing the recent successes of "Tsar Dmitrii's" forces against the evil usurper in Moscow and encouraging Russians of all classes to join the rebel cause.[55]

Looking at the overall strategic situation after the battle of Pchelnia, Shuiskii had clearly suffered a major setback; but, in fact, both sides had suffered appalling casualties by the end of winter 1607—estimated by one contemporary at 40,000 men.[56] In addition, both sides could point to successes and failures in what was becoming a chaotic and protracted civil war. Tsar Vasilii's forces had been successful in clearing the Moscow area and much of the central Volga region of rebels; the Kasimov Tatars continued to work for Shuiskii and periodically disrupted rebel supply lines; and several important lower Volga towns remained steadfastly loyal to Shuiskii. Fedor Sheremetev's army on Balchik Island also kept the Volga cossacks and the rebels in Astrakhan tied down. Even though the Nogai Tatars broke with Tsar Vasilii in this period, they devoted most of their energy to attacking their neighbors rather than aiding the rebel cause.[57] To the south, even after the battle of Pchelnia and the loss of Aleksin and Serebrianye Prudy, Shuiskii's forces continued to hold many important towns along the old Oka frontier defense line. On the other hand, by spring 1607 Tsar Vasilii faced very serious problems, and there was genuine panic in Moscow because of recent rebel gains and the consequent renewed threat to the capital.

The rebels still held a huge territory—about a third of the entire country. Virtually all of Russia below the Oka frontier line remained in their hands, including several agriculturally rich provinces and many important fortresses and towns with sturdy garrisons. Belief in the survival of Tsar Dmitrii and hatred for the tsar-usurper continued to unite rebels of all social classes and kept their morale from slipping even as they endured great hardships.[58] By the spring of 1607 small detachments of mercenaries from Poland-Lithuania began arriving in Tula and elsewhere to bolster rebel forces. Shuiskii propaganda greatly exaggerated the numbers of evil foreigners joining the rebels at this time and represented the entire civil war as the product of Polish intervention. King Sigismund did, in fact, permit some untrustworthy lords he was anxious to get rid of to seek their fortune in Russia, but he did not contemplate military action of his own at this time.[59] Rebel forces remained overwhelmingly Russian, with cossacks forming the largest contingent. Shuiskii propagandists claimed that most rebels were peasants, and many scholars since then have credited that lie; but contemporaries knew better.[60] Not counting town garrisons, the rebel army in Tula once Bolotnikov arrived there contained more than 20,000 battle-hardened soldiers with plenty of food, weapons, and munitions.[61] Also aiding the rebel cause in the spring of 1607 was an uprising against Shuiskii by West Siberian tribes, especially the Ostiaks, who killed many of the tsar's soldiers, disrupted the flow of revenue to Moscow, and pillaged the entire region for many months.[62]

The failure of the rebels to follow up their victories at Pchelnia and Kaluga with a quick strike against Moscow gave Tsar Vasilii a much-needed breathing spell, but he was in serious trouble and knew it. The mood in much of the country and in the capital was one of fear and growing opposition to the "unlucky" tsar. Demands that Shuiskii abdicate were voiced, and anonymous letters continued to appear that denounced him as a usurper. One unreliable contemporary report claimed that ten boyars called upon the tsar to become a monk in order to prevent any further disasters, whereupon they were all arrested for treason. In any case, Tsar Vasilii did feel the need to seek broader input about what to do next.[63] He held either a special meeting with the boyars and the higher clergy or a meeting with even wider membership to discuss his options. During that meeting, the patriarch and others convinced Shuiskii that, in order to save his crown, he had to personally lead a campaign against the rebels.[64] To his credit, Tsar Vasilii wasted no time preparing for that campaign. He immediately called for a general mobilization of all available forces and made plans to field the largest army possible. He also launched a major new propaganda campaign in order to frighten the residents of Moscow; once again, it was claimed that the rebels intended to exterminate the entire population of the capital, including all women and children. Apparently, Shuiskii's fear tactic worked; according to a contemporary, the Muscovites regained their courage and prepared to defend the capital and Tsar Vasilii "to the last drop of blood."[65] Patriarch Hermogen ordered special prayers for victory and, once again, sent letters to all towns denouncing Tsar Dmitrii as an impostor and heretic and branding the rebels as traitors and brigands—bloodthirsty enemies of Christ who plundered estates, raped women and children, and sought to destroy the Russian Orthodox Church.[66]

Couriers from Moscow blanketed the country with Tsar Vasilii's decree commanding all remaining gentry to show up for military service with any able-bodied men still left on their estates. Recalcitrants were threatened with forced recruitment, physical punishment, and confiscation of their possessions.[67] A special review of available weapons and servicemen was conducted in the Kremlin, and word got out that this time the tsar was deadly serious. As a result, many previously reluctant gentry militiamen flocked to Moscow out of fear of punishment.[68] It is even possible that news of the tsar's stern command influenced some wavering Seversk gentry to desert the rebel cause.[69] Shuiskii also continued his on-going efforts to shore up the economies and morale of his militiamen and other soldiers by increases in land allotments and salaries, by generous rewards for service against the rebels, and by the rapid promotion of heroic individuals.[70] In addition to fully mobilizing his servicemen, Tsar Vasilii again demanded large numbers of low-quality datochnye liudi (recruits) for military service from all categories of nonservice lands—including property held by townsmen, state and crown peasants, the patriarch, the metropolitans and bishops, monasteries, and even property held by ordinarily exempt gentry widows and minors.[71] There was considerable grumbling about such heavy demands, and there were many no-shows; but Shuiskii did manage to gain large numbers of recruits.[72] Unfortunately, stripping the productive labor from much of the land had a negative impact on the country's overall economy, which was already reeling from the chaos of civil war and the disruption of Volga trade.[73] Not surprisingly, Tsar Vasilii faced increasingly severe financial problems as the civil war continued, and special taxes had to be levied to help pay for the planned campaign against the rebels. As usual, church lands were heavily assessed for that task by the financially embarrassed tsar.[74]

By late May 1607, Tsar Vasilii and his commanders had more or less prepared for a major offensive and for what was expected to be a difficult siege of Tula. Because of Shuiskii's emergency mobilization measures, a very large army was assembled at Serpukhov. Contemporary estimates placed its size at somewhere between one hundred thousand and one hundred fifty thousand men.[75] Many of the soldiers and recruits had been recently gathered from central and northern Russia. They were joined by large numbers of Kazan Tatars, Chuvashi, and Cheremis—clear evidence of the progress Tsar Vasilii's voevodas had made in pacifying the central Volga region. At Serpukhov, most of those non-Slavic native troops were organized as a separate detachment commanded by the Tatar Prince Petr Urusov, who was married to the widow of Tsar Vasilii's cousin, Andrei I. Shuiskii.[76]

The core of the army formed at Serpukhov was composed of the remnants of the tsar's forces who had fled from Kaluga. Smaller detachments were added from various town garrisons, and a significant force arrived from Riazan province under the command of Prokofii Liapunov and Grigorii F. Sunbulov.[77] Artillery was stripped from several fortresses and added to that which Skopin-Shuiskii and others had managed to save after the disaster at Kaluga. The tsar's close friend, Ivan Kriuk-Kolychev, brought most of the heavy siege guns and incendiary mortars from Moscow to Serpukhov. At the staging area, all the artillery was concentrated in the tsar's regiment. Only when the army reached Tula were those guns transferred to the main regiment under the watchful eye of artillery voevoda Vladimir T. Dolgorukii.[78]

Tsar Vasilii departed from Moscow for Serpukhov at noon on May 21, 1607, after praying in several churches and—according to Massa—visiting briefly with a prophetess. Once Shuiskii was mounted on his horse and received his quiver and bow, he led the tsar's regiment (consisting of several thousand courtiers, Moscow dvoriane, and zhiltsy), most of the staff of the Military Affairs Office, and some palace and treasury officials to his field headqarters. Although many boyars accompanied Shuiskii on this campaign, the tsar left his militarily incompetent brother Dmitrii behind in charge of the capital and routine government business.[79] During the campaign the tsar was able to choose from nearly two dozen boyars and okolnichie to serve as his commanders. Although Prince Mstislavskii was the senior boyar, he and other top-ranking courtiers had not been very successful in operations against rebel forces. For that reason, effective command of the tsar's army was probably given to more successful and energetic relatives such as Skopin-Shuiskii or to trustworthy and able friends such as Kriuk-Kolychev, who had only recently been named to the important post of *dvoretskii* (majordomo or chief steward).[80] The arrival of Tsar Vasilii and his impressive entourage in Serpukhov provided an immense psychological boost to his troops, who counted on the tsar's presence on the campaign to strike fear into the hearts of the rebels.[81] Shuiskii, too, fully understood the significance of his own actions. At Serpukhov, before his huge army, the tsar vowed not to return to Moscow except as a victor. Failing that, he declared, he was prepared to die fighting against the evil rebels.[82]

Tsar Vasilii had seized the initiative by swiftly preparing and launching a major offensive against the rebels. Meanwhile, Tsarevich Petr—for good or ill—had also been very active in Tula. The crude behavior and terror against stubborn Shuiskii supporters that he had displayed in Putivl continued unabated in his new headquarters. As time wore on, Petr's sadistic streak, combined with Tsar Dmitrii's failure to reappear after almost a year, alienated significant numbers of rebels, especially gentry, who nervously watched as their own fates became increasingly intertwined with that of the bloodthirsty and obviously fraudulent "tsarevich."[83] As noted in the last chapter, Petr had also become a snob and now preferred the company of titled gentlemen. For that reason, Skrynnikov conjectured that Bolotnikov must have been effectively demoted upon his arrival in Tula because, as a former slave, he could not have aspired to sit on Tsarevich Petr's boyar council.[84] That is hopelessly inaccurate. Bolotnikov was undoubtedly the most charismatic and trusted figure in the entire rebel leadership, and he retained his position as commander-in-chief of all rebel forces while in Tula. Contemporary sources noted that honors and gifts were heaped on Bolotnikov after the siege of Kaluga was broken and that he was involved in all important military decisions made in Tula.[85] Documents from the time referred to Bolotnikov as Tsarevich Petr's "boyar" and "chief general."[86] "Tsar Dmitrii's" commander-in-chief may have had some misgivings about the sadistic "tsarevich," but they shared the same basic objectives and apparently got along well enough.

Evaluating Tsarevich Petr's use of terror in Tula is just as complicated as it was in the case of Putivl. The traditional interpretation, of course, based on Shuiskii propaganda, held that Petr was waging class war on Russian lords as part of a vast social revolution.[87] In fact, as we have already seen, the occasional use of terror against stubborn Shuiskii supporters began before the "tsarevich" emerged as a rebel leader; and, while in Putivl, Petr had men executed for refusing to swear an oath to him—not because of their social background. Furthermore, there is evidence of considerable popular support for the harsh treatment of unrepentant supporters of Tsar Vasilii. It is difficult, however, to separate reality from the relentless Shuiskii propaganda that successfully demonized Tsarevich Petr in the minds of many pomeshchiki.[88] Just as in the case of Putivl, the timing of the executions in Tula is a significant issue. It appears that violence against captured Shuiskii loyalists gradually increased as the rebels lost important battles and as the situation in Tula became increasingly desperate. In fact, out of frustration and anger, both sides resorted to greater use of violence and terror against their foes by the summer of 1607. In addition, Tsar Vasilii's decision during the campaign against Tula to continue the practice of having large numbers of captured cossacks executed undoubtedly contributed to the rising violence against Shuiskii loyalists in the besieged rebel stronghold.[89]

In Tula, some of the first victims of Tsarevich Petr's wrath were captives brought back by voevoda Teliatevskii from the successful battle of Pchelnia. Dozens of those men were tortured to death.[90] If one recalls that thousands of Zabore cossacks switched to the rebel side during that battle, it is not difficult to imagine the angry tales they told in Tula about the mass executions of their comrades ordered by Tsar Vasilii back in December 1606. No doubt such tales inflamed passions among all rebels, but especially among the cossacks. Nonetheless, contemporary sources also reveal that, as in Putivl, some pomeshchiki were put to death in Tula simply for refusing to swear a loyalty oath to Tsarevich Petr.[91] Also as in Putivl, rebel crowds in Tula were given the chance to approve or disapprove of the punishment of captured enemies. Although they usually approved, at least one fortunate soldier in Tula was saved from execution by the shouts of the people.[92] Some other captives were beaten or tortured and then thrown into prison where they grew hungry but managed to stay alive.[93] Gentry from the Tula region who continued to fight for Shuiskii received special attention from Petr. They lost their residences, family papers, and other property in Tula, and their estates were subjected to devastating raids. Local inhabitants were also occasionally charged with hiding grain from the rebels and then tortured and imprisoned. At least one prominent Tula pomeshchik who tried to expose Petr as a fraud was tortured to death; then his nearby estate was plundered and burned.[94] In supervising executions in Tula, as he did in Putivl, Tsarevich Petr not only instilled terror but also provided crude entertainment. Again echoing Ivan the Terrible's horrifying spectacles, Petr was particularly fond of placing his victims in a confined space with an angry bear.[95]

News of Tsarevich Petr's sadism spread far and wide, and not just because of Shuiskii's shrill propaganda. Many rebels, especially among the gentry, were put off or frightened by the cruel "tsarevich" and his cossack supporters. Although most of them remained loyal to the rebel cause, others gradually lost hope for the return of the true tsar or the success of their rebellion and began deserting the camp of Tsarevich Petr. By June 1607, as Shuiskii's forces closed in on Tula, dozens of rebel pomeshchiki quietly slipped away. Some of them simply went home; others joined Tsar Vasilii's cause since he then appeared to be gaining the upper hand in the civil war. In the end, Tsarevich Petr proved to be an altogether unworthy substitute for the charismatic Tsar Dmitrii. As a result, by summer 1607, even some militiamen from Severia—long the backbone of the rebel army—began to desert. That, in turn, caused rebel forces to gradually become more and more cossack in appearance and character. It would still be a gross error to regard them as a social revolutionary army of the lower classes, as Shuiskii propaganda proclaimed. Even with the problem of Tsarevich Petr, the rebels still had a large army dedicated to toppling Shuiskii, not to overthrowing the social order or serfdom. A Polish envoy at the time duly noted the increasing gentry defection from Petr but bluntly rejected Tsar Vasilii's claim that all that remained in the rebel camp were "simple peasants." Instead, it was obvious to him that the rebels still commanded powerful military forces who were completely dedicated to the cause of "Tsar Dmitrii."[96] Indeed, as the rebels endured both Shuiskii's offensive and the coarse behavior of Tsarevich Petr, they longed for Dmitrii to appear and made every effort to find him.

Tsar Vasilii has often been criticized for remaining in Serpukhov for two weeks before advancing against Tula. Isaac Massa somewhat unfairly attributed the delay to the tsar's fear, stating that Shuiskii was "forever apprehensive lest he be betrayed" and for that reason "did not wish to go far from the environs of Moscow."[97] In fact, the delay was not due to the tsar's cowardice; it took six weeks to gather his huge army in Serpukhov.[98] In addition, Shuiskii had many other things to think about besides the Tula campaign. For example, the tsar was growing increasingly concerned about events on the lower Volga. Astrakhan had by then become a powerful rebel center that attracted large numbers of free cossacks from the Volga, Don, Terek, and Iaik Rivers. Not only was Tsar Vasilii's voevoda, Fedor Sheremetev, unable to capture the city, but his own base on

Balchik Island came under repeated attacks by cossacks. Sheremetev grimly reported to Shuiskii that Astrakhan would not yield.[99] (In fact, it did not surrender until the very end of the civil war.) In the spring of 1607, after two rebel couriers carrying manifestos from "Tsar Dmitrii" were caught stirring up trouble near Tsaritsyn, Tsar Vasilii ordered "strong reinforcements" from Saratov sent down the Volga to bolster Sheremetev's forces.[100] Up river from Balchik Island, however, rebel cossacks with false manifestos from "Dmitrii" soon managed to provoke an uprising of the Tsaritsyn garrison.[101] News of that loss disturbed Tsar Vasilii and may have prompted his dispatch of a totally false announcement to all towns in which he boldly declared that Sheremetev had succeeded in ending the rebellion in Astrakhan and Terek; Shuiskii even instructed his subjects to conduct solemn church services in celebration of this "victory."[102] In fact, very real danger continued to emanate from Astrakhan.

The rebel voevoda in Astrakhan, Ivan D. Khvorostinin, played a role similar to that of Prince Shakhovskoi in Putivl. Faced with no prospect of Tsar Dmitrii ever showing up, Khvorostinin eventually entered into negotiations with a local copy-cat pretender who led a large detachment of Volga and other cossacks. "Tsarevich Ivan-Avgust" claimed to be the son of Ivan the Terrible and his fourth wife, Anna Koltsovskaia—who actually produced no heirs and was confined to a convent after Ivan divorced her. Ivan-Avgust thus falsely claimed to be the "elder brother" of Tsar Dmitrii as well as the uncle of Tsarevich Petr. Khvorostinin set up a makeshift court for Ivan-Avgust in Astrakhan, and the "tsarevich" apparently exercised some real authority; however, it is possible that Khvorostinin's public deference to him may actually have been merely for show. Probably a former slave, this pretender had visited Moscow and knew a thing or two about life at the tsar's court. In Astrakhan, however, he proved to be—like Petr—a coarse and terrifying figure. Ivan-Avgust and Khvorostinin sent a judge to Tsaritsyn to investigate captured Shuiskii loyalists after the town joined the rebellion. Some of those men were put to death and some were beaten and released. Others were brought back to Astrakhan for trial. There not only did Ivan-Avgust order the execution of the former Tsaritsyn voevoda, F. P. Chudinov-Akinfov; but his cossacks also apparently tortured Chudinov-Akinfov's loyal subordinates to death, possibly with the inhabitants of Astrakhan involved in determining the fates of those unfortunate souls. Khvorostinin may have shuddered to himself about his new ally, but Ivan-Avgust provided a significant number of troops with which to harass Sheremetev's army on Balchik Island and a useful "tsarist" individual around whom to rally additional forces to the banner of "Tsar Dmitrii."[103] Even as Tsar Vasilii tried to focus on the Tula campaign, he knew that he could not afford to ignore the threat posed by Astrakhan.

Troubling news from the lower Volga put the tsar in a very cautious mood. During the time Tsar Vasilii was supposedly cowering in Serpukhov, rumors spread throughout Russia of many clashes between his regiments and the rebels. According to those rumors, the rebels usually managed to surprise Shuiskii's voevodas and were "victorious in all encounters."[104] One spectacular but completely false report had Bolotnikov advancing against the tsar's army, winning a major battle, and capturing sixteen pieces of heavy ordnance and many small arms. Supposedly, Tsar Vasilii thereupon refused the demands of his commanders to retreat to Moscow, citing his oath to remain in the field until victory.[105] A gullible Isaac Massa even chided the rebels for not knowing how to profit from their mythical "victories."[106] In fact, the rebels were not at all successful at this time, although they did attempt to stir up trouble wherever possible in order to slow down Shuiskii's offensive against Tula. Toward the end of May, for example, Tsarevich Petr attempted to organize a campaign to recapture Meshchovsk (160 kilometers west of Tula) by ordering rebels from Roslavl to link up with colonel Tretiak Bolobanov's Briansk forces for an attack; but the plan failed miserably.[107]

Far worse for the rebel cause was the fate of the campaign launched from Tula at the beginning of June. A very large rebel army with artillery appeared to be headed straight for Serpukhov but then suddenly turned toward Kashira (located 75 kilometers northeast of Tula). Some sources claimed the rebel goal had been Serpukhov but that the presence of Shuiskii's large army there forced the rebels to alter their plans. That is not true. The rebels were well aware of the size of the tsar's forces in Serpukhov and intended from the outset to try to retake Kashira, which would allow them to bypass the tsar's big army and directly threaten weakly-defended Moscow.[108] Despite efforts to conceal the rebels' intentions, Shuiskii's commanders learned about their goal from scouts and spies and rushed hundreds of pomeshchiki from Serpukhov to Kashira in order to bolster Prince Andrei V. Golitsyn's garrison.[109] To Kashira from Riazan province also hurried another detachment of gentry commanded by Boris M. Lykov, Prokofii Liapunov, and F. Bulgakov.[110] (That left very few Shuiskii loyalists remaining in the entire Riazan region.) Bolstered by those forces, voevoda Golitsyn advanced from Kashira southwest about 14 kilometers to the confluence of the little Vosma River and the Besputa River, near the village of Vosma. There he arrayed his forces in battle formation to await the enemy.[111] The rebel army advancing against him was commanded by Prince Teliatevskii and Prince Mikhail F. Aksakov.[112] Two sources hostile to the rebels named Bolotnikov as Teliatevskii's second-in-command, but it is not at all clear that Bolotnikov accompanied Teliatevskii on this campaign.[113] The rebel army was very large, containing between 30,000 and 40,000 men. It was composed of large numbers of free cossacks and troops from many fortresses of the old and new frontier provinces.[114] On June 5, the rebel army approached the Vosma River and clashed with the tsar's forces.[115]

Perhaps inspired by the size of his army or his recent victory at Pchelnia, Teliatevskii foolishly chose to make a frontal attack on the tsar's forces. Golitsyn's main regiment was stationed on the southern shore of the Vosma River in the direct path of the rebel army; only the Riazan cavalry had been held back as a reserve force north of the little river. The battle of Vosma began just after dawn and lasted about four hours.[116] At the outset of the fighting, a large rebel detachment of cossacks on foot pushed their way past Golitsyn's main force, crossed the river, and lodged themselves in a gully near the Riazan cavalry. From that sheltered position the cossacks unleashed accurate harquebus volleys at the Riazan pomeshchiki, killing and wounding many men and horses and forcing Golitsyn's reserve force to retreat.[117] Liapunov and his fellow officers did not panic, however; instead, they managed to maneuver around the entrenched cossacks, crossed the Vosma, and joined Goilitsyn's main force just as it was reeling from heavy blows delivered by Teliatevskii's army. Inspired by the arrival of those reinforcements, the tsar's soldiers did not retreat but stood their ground with shouts such as "Better to die here!"[118] At that point, one of the rebel detachments composed of between three and four thousand men suddenly switched sides; that frightened and disoriented the other rebels and proved to be the turning point in the battle.[119] There is no evidence to support the traditional interpretation that the turncoats were mostly pomeshchiki frightened by the radical agenda of rebel peasants, slaves, and cossacks; but those men—whoever they were—may well have been disgusted with Tsarevich Petr and tired of waiting for Tsar Dmitrii to appear.[120] In any case, now coming under heavy blows from Golitsyn's army, Teliatevskii's forces were decimated and retreated in disorder toward Tula. They lost their entire supply train, all their artillery, drums, and banners. A very large number of Teliatevskii's men were killed or captured, and Golitsyn's cavalry chased the fleeing rebels for more than 30 kilometers.[121]

In the aftermath of the battle of Vosma, the cossack detachment that had been entrenched north of the river was quickly surrounded by the tsar's forces. Shuiskii's commanders repeatedly encouraged the rebels to surrender on favorable terms, even promising them liquor; but the stubborn cossacks dug in and quickly improvised makeshift defenses in what was really an impossible position to defend. Remarkably, they withstood a withering siege for two days and inflicted severe casualties on the attackers. Finally, on June 7, their position was stormed by Golitsyn's entire regiment. The cossacks held them off until they literally ran out of gunpowder. Most of them were then cut down by enemy cavalry, and many were captured. The total number of rebel losses in the disastrous battle of Vosma was enormous. One contemporary estimated that 16,000 rebel cavalry and 3,600 rebel infantry had been killed.[122] Shuiskii propagandists bragged about capturing 5,000 rebels, but that figure needs analysis. Another, more reliable source put the number of men captured at 1,700. It seems likely that the higher number included the several thousand rebels who had switched sides during the battle.[123]

The fate awaiting the 1,700 real captives was a grim one. Out of about a thousand cossacks who had been captured on June 7, all but seven were hanged the next day. The seven lucky ones were spared only because of a petition submitted to the tsar's voevodas by several honorable central Volga pomeshchiki who requested mercy for those individuals who had prevented fellow rebels from killing the petitioners back in 1606.[124] Golitsyn sent the remaining 700 captives (probably from Teliatevskii's main force) to Serpukhov. There some were imprisoned and others were bailed out by favored gentry who took them as slaves—just as had been done after the siege of Moscow.[125]

The battle of Vosma was a catastrophe for the rebel cause. Not only did it put a stop to the immediate threat to Moscow but it greatly enhanced the chances for success of Tsar Vasilii's offensive. After that battle the decimated rebels were put sharply on the defensive and were forced to endure the long siege of Tula. The defeat at Vosma also contributed to the decline of rebel gentry enthusiasm for continuing the civil war. As news of the battle spread it caused more and more servicemen of the frontier provinces to contemplate abandoning the odious Tsarevich Petr and what looked increasingly like a lost cause. Some of those servicemen actually drifted back into Shuiskii's service in time to participate in the siege of Tula.

20

The Siege of Tula and the Resurrection of "Tsar Dmitrii"

After the battle of Vosma, Tsar Vasilii did not immediately lead his entire army to Tula. Even though Shuiskii's primary goal was to lay siege to that rebel stronghold, the cautious tsar recognized the dangers that still lurked in the region. Shuiskii's commanders were especially nervous about the prospect of leaving the rebel-held fortresses of Kaluga and Aleksin behind (and to the north of) the tsar's army. In order for the Tula siege to be successful, they reasoned, it would first be necessary to pacify the surrounding area to prevent rebel attacks on the siege army at inopportune times. Therefore, a decision was made in early June 1607 to allow the victors at the battle of Vosma to pursue the defeated rebels to Tula (which would effectively cut that town off from Kaluga) while other forces attempted to recapture Aleksin before the tsar's main army and siege guns advanced to Tula.

To implement this strategy, the Kashira and Riazan regiments that had fought at Vosma were sent in pursuit of the retreating rebels and ordered to join up with three additional regiments that were advancing from Serpukhov under the command of Skopin-Shuiskii. The rendezvous point chosen was the village of Pavshino, about twenty-five kilometers northwest of Tula. After those forces joined together, Skopin-Shuiskii and Andrei Golitsyn caught up with the rebel army on June 12, at the small Voronia River just a few kilometers northwest of Tula.[1] There the swampy Voronia dumped into the Upa River and would have to be forded by the tsar's army advancing along the Kaluga road. For that reason, the rebels chose to make a stand at the Voronia in order to prevent the tsar's army from approaching Tula. They hastily gathered reinforcements but were still definitely outnumbered by the tsar's army. Nevertheless, the Voronia crossing was part of the old Tula zaseka system of defense against the Tatars, and it had several fortified positions and plenty of hazards to slow down advancing forces; there were also thick stands of trees providing good cover for anyone defending the position.[2]

The rebel commanders (Teliatevskii, Bolotnikov, and Kokhanovskii) stationed large numbers of cavalry and infantry on a broad front all along the

Voronia in order to block the tsar's forces. For two days the rebels successfully withstood innumerable direct attacks on their positions, but on June 14 the tsar's forces outflanked them to the west and managed to cross the river in several places. At that point Skopin-Shuiskii threw his main force into the fray, and the rebels were soon forced to retreat rapidly to Tula itself. Rebel losses were very heavy, with up to 4,500 men killed or captured. Some tsarist troops hotly pursued the enemy right into Tula where those impetuous men were quickly cut off and killed by the rebels.[3] Voevodas Skopin-Shuiskii and Golitsyn began mopping up the area immediately surrounding the rebel headquarters and making preparations for a siege. They sent word to Tsar Vasilii that the rebels were now trapped in Tula.[4]

The tsar remained in Serpukhov for more than a week after receiving news of the victory at the Voronia River and the start of the siege of Tula. Only when he received word of the impending capture of Aleksin (then under siege by Prince Vorotynskii) did Shuiskii advance to Aleksin with the tsar's regiment and most of his heavy artillery. He arrived before that town on June 28, 1607. As noted in the last chapter, Aleksin—only 40 kilometers northwest of Tula—had been abandoned by Tsar Vasilii's forces in early May, following the disastrous battle of Pchelnia. The town had then been immediately reoccupied by the rebel voevoda L. A. Kologrivov. He and his garrison, along with many townsmen and deti boiarskie from the area, managed to resist Vorotynskii's siege until late June. Then, on June 29, the day after Tsar Vasilii arrived in the neighborhood, Aleksin was "captured" by the tsar.[5] Some sources claimed that Shuiskii took the town by storm.[6] Other sources claimed the beleaguered townspeople, seeing themselves hopelessly outnumbered and outgunned, surrendered to the tsar and begged his forgiveness; the kindly and pious ruler supposedly immediately pardoned them and sent them food and drink.[7] Smirnov was skeptical of the story of voluntary surrender, but Skrynnikov found it to be plausible.[8] In fact, the "capture" of Aleksin was carefully stage-managed so that Tsar Vasilii would have a victory to proclaim. With Aleksin secured, Shuiskii and the tsar's regiment immediately advanced at high speed toward Tula, arriving in the siege camp the very next day, June 30.[9]

Tsar Vasilii's announcement of his capture of Aleksin also claimed great successes by his voevodas in cleansing other towns and villages in the area of traitors. In fact, the rebels in Riazhsk (southeast of Tula), including voevoda Ivan L. Mosalskii, did surrender to Shuiskii's forces in June. Tsar Vasilii's voevoda, N. Pleshcheev, immediately occupied Riazhsk and from there campaigned against neighboring towns. Soon Pesochnia and nearby Sapozhok surrendered to the tsar's forces. Also in June, Tsarevich Petr's voevodas in Mikhailov (90 kilometers east of Tula), Fedor Zasekin and Lev Fustov, surrendered to Shuiskii's troops then besieging the town. Those two turncoats claimed that many of the inhabitants of Mikhailov were also ready to surrender, but efforts by Shuiskii's forces to occupy the town were not successful. In general, in spite of a few successes and some misleading propaganda, Tsar Vasilii's commanders failed to suppress rebellion in the old frontier region, which greatly complicated the task of besieging Tula.[10] At least the siege itself prevented Tula from continuing its role of directing rebel operations and prevented its inhabitants from seizing opportunities to harass Shuiskii's forces. In fact, once the siege began, rebel activity throughout southern Russia became more disconnected and local in nature, which was easier for the tsar's commanders to cope with. On the other hand, by concentrating his forces around Tula, Shuiskii freed up rebels elsewhere. For example, the tsar pulled so many loyal troops away from the Riazan region that rebel activity there intensified. By the summer of 1607 rebel peasants and others in the Riazan area waged war actively against Shuiskii supporters and terrorized many of them.[11]

Reports from the lower Volga region also continued to make Tsar Vasilii nervous as he tried to concentrate on the siege of Tula. By the time Shuiskii arrived in the siege camp, for example, he learned that the small army of seven thousand men he had ordered to advance from Saratov to aid voevoda Sheremetev in his struggle against "Tsarevich Ivan Avgust" and Astrakhan had unwittingly approached Tsaritsyn shortly after its garrison joined the rebel cause. Scouts from Shuiskii's army were seized and killed by the rebels, and soon the tsar's relief army itself came under surprise attack from the Tsaritsyn garrison (assisted by four hundred soldiers from Astrakhan and several large cossack detachments). Under such pressure, the tsar's army was forced to hastily retreat across the Volga. The rebels tried but were unable to dislodge them from that new position by force, so they tricked the enemy into thinking ten thousand more rebel troops were about to arrive from Astrakhan. That prompted Shuiskii's army to retreat rapidly up the Volga in disorder.[12] Not surprisingly, that retreat then allowed Tsarevich Ivan-Avgust to sail up the Volga with about seven thousand men. His forces reached Tsaritsyn by July, cruelly putting to death all traitors to Tsar Dmitrii they met along the way.[13]

Ivan-Avgust's goal at that point may have been Moscow;[14] but in late summer his forces were stopped at Saratov by voevoda Z. I. Saburov, whose garrison inflicted such severe losses on the "tsarevich's" forces that Ivan-Avgust immediately decided to retreat to Astrakhan. That ended the immediate threat to the central Volga region posed by the "tsarevich's" cossacks; more importantly, the rebel defeat suffered at Saratov put on end to the possibility of Ivan-

Avgust marching to the aid of Bolotnikov and Tsarevich Petr in beleaguered Tula.[15] At the time of his arrival in the siege camp, however, Tsar Vasilii still feared the threat coming from Astrakhan.

Upon arrival in the Tula siege camp, the tsar discovered to his annoyance that rebels in the vicinity were still defiant and very active. Among other things, they plundered and burned the estates of militiamen who had switched back to Shuiskii's side.[16] The tsar ordered a response in kind, authorizing his troops to plunder the civilian population of all areas still in rebel hands, to destroy all crops and livestock, and to wage a cruel war against all traitors; but punitive raiders were carefully instructed not to attack Shuiskii loyalists or their property.[17] Such raids may have marginally helped Tsar Vasilii by rewarding his soldiers with booty and by frightening a few wavering rebels. Inevitably, however, the increase in violence by the tsar's army prompted an increase in violence against Shuiskii supporters held in captivity in Tula and elsewhere. It also made the rebels in general more determined than ever to resist the tsar-usurper.

The siege of Tula lasted four months. The town contained a large, well-supplied civilian population and impressive fortifications. Built on the southern bank of the Upa River, Tula was defended by a large citadel (*kreml'* or kremlin) that had been constructed in the early sixteenth century. The base of the kremlin walls was composed of stone (5 meters high) on top of which brickwork raised the walls to anywhere between 10 and 18 meters high. The kremlin also had plenty of towers and openings from which to shoot at attackers. Tula's streets radiated out from the kremlin to an oak palisade (with at least fourteen towers and five gates) that surrounded the town. Both ends of the palisade went right up to the Upa River, which protected the town to the north. The town was also somewhat protected to the west by marshes and to the east by a small tributary of the Upa, the Khomutovka River.[18]

It would obviously take a large army to capture Tula, and Tsar Vasilii had assembled the largest one he could for the task. Contemporary estimates of one hundred thousand or even one hundred fifty thousand soldiers in his siege army should be viewed skeptically, but the tsar probably did concentrate more than thirty thousand troops, very large numbers of recruits, and thousands of peasant laborers before Tula's walls. Shuiskii's army was certainly much larger than the rebel force it was besieging.[19] Inside Tula, however, despite terrible losses at the battles of Vosma and Voronia, the rebels still had a relatively large army that continued to display skill, determination, and energy. By this time, of course, cossacks had become the largest group in the rebel army; but there were also still large numbers of deti boiarskie, lower status military servicemen from southern fortresses, and many townsmen. There were also some Tula area peasants, former members of Tsar Dmitrii's bodyguard, and a small number of foreign mercenaries under the command of a Lithuanian lord named I. Starovskii. Altogether, rebel forces in Tula exceeded twenty thousand well-armed men.[20]

Tsar Vasilii established his headquarters in a small village owned by one of his courtiers that was located next to the Voronia River near its confluence with the Upa, just a few kilometers west of Tula.[21] The tsar's senior commanders placed the main part of their siege army to the west of Tula on the south side of the Upa River, thereby cutting the town off from the Kaluga and Krapivna roads. A relatively small detachment was stationed north of the Upa River, blocking the roads from Tula to Aleksin, Venev, and Moscow. Batteries of siege guns commanded by voevodas Vladimir Dolgorukii, I. O. Ododurov, and G. Kologrivov were set up on both sides of the river in order to sweep the town from two sides; and constant artillery barrages killed or wounded many rebels. Under the circumstances, Tsar Vasilii expected to make short work of the siege.[22]

As many as twenty-two attempts were made to take Tula by storm during the first several weeks, but they failed completely and cost Shuiskii about two thousand casualties.[23] The rebels not only stubbornly resisted but used their abundance of harquebuses and gunpowder to very good effect. Every day dozens of small rebel bands emerged from all sides of Tula either to repair damage done by Shuiskii's siege guns or to shoot at the enemy. They killed or wounded many of the tsar's soldiers.[24] The incredibly wily and energetic rebels greatly frustrated Tsar Vasilii, who had not planned to spend all summer sitting in a peasant village near mosquito-infested marshes. The rebel commander-in-chief, Ivan Bolotnikov, proved to be an extremely worthy opponent whose bravery and cleverness in defending Tula matched his earlier defense of Kaluga.[25] For a long time the tsar and his commanders remained confused and unable to come up with a viable plan for capturing Tula. Most Russian sources are remarkably silent about the first phase of the siege, perhaps not wishing to draw attention to the tsar's lack of success.[26] One foreign contemporary, however, ridiculed Shuiskii's inability to capture an "insignificant fortress" during the course of an entire summer.[27] Wild and false rumors spread across the land about Tsar Vasilii's humiliating retreat to Moscow, his possible dethronement, his capture in a great battle before Tula, and even his death.[28] In fact, Shuiskii grew increasingly angry about the slow siege and began taking it out on the small numbers of rebels his men were able to capture, ordering them to be tortured.[29] At some point he also grimly vowed to put all rebels in Tula to death.[30]

As the siege dragged on, the tsar's commanders continued to dispatch detachments to capture rebel towns in the area and to further isolate Tula from potential relief forces and supplies.[31] About 60 kilometers to the east, the tsar's voevodas

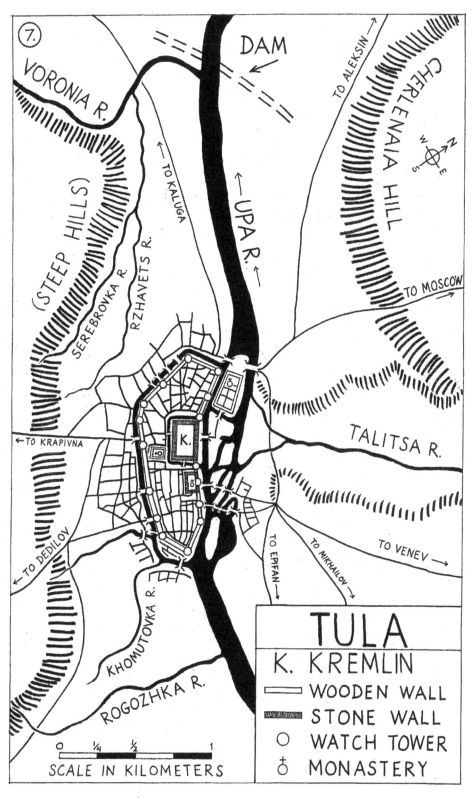

Map 7 Tula.

attempted to capture Gremiachii, a town that dominated the road connecting the Tula region to turbulent Riazan province; they were trying to follow up on their recent successes at Riazhsk, Pesochnia, and Sapozhok. Voevodas Prokofii Liapunov and F. Bulgakov laid siege to Gremiachii, but it is not clear from surviving sources that they succeeded in capturing the town.[32] Tsar Vasilii also sent voevodas A. Dolgorukii and I. O. Ododurov against Dedilov, located about 30 kilometers southeast of Tula. They quickly succeeded in capturing the town; and nearby Epifan was also temporarily cleared of rebels.[33]

The tsar's commanders wisely focused considerably more attention on rebel-held Krapivna (40 kilometers southwest of Tula), which controlled the roads connecting Tula to the southern and southwestern frontier zones. In order to cut off that potential avenue for rebel troops and supplies headed for Tula, Shuiskii sent voevodas Iurii Petrovich Ushatyi, S. Kropotkin, and Petr Urusov to capture Krapivna and to devastate the rebel-occupied area. Prince Urusov and his Tatar and Cheremis troops were specifically ordered to wage a campaign of terror throughout the region and to kill and plunder all traitors to Tsar Vasilii.[34] However, while Shuiskii's voevodas laid siege to Krapivna, Prince Urusov became convinced that rumors of Tsar Dmitrii's survival were true, for which reason he and his Tatar detachment abruptly broke with Tsar Vasilii. Thousands of them rode east and crossed the Volga to link up with Urusov's father in the Nogai horde, after which they waged war against Shuiskii's frontier towns in the name of Tsar Dmitrii.[35] Prince Urusov's departure was a great blow to Shuiskii, who already feared treason among his commanders. The tsar and his advisers were also alarmed by the failure of the siege of Krapivna. As long as that town and nearby Odoev remained in enemy hands, there was no way to prevent rebel relief forces from approaching Tula. Determined to remove that threat, Tsar Vasilii immediately dispatched another detachment under Prince Danila Mezetskii, who quickly captured Krapivna and then took Odoev as well.[36]

In the same region, other tsarist forces succeeded temporarily in retaking Belev and Bolkhov, probably through negotiations rather than battle. Shuiskii's troops also managed to retake Likhvin, located 90 kilometers west of Tula. These successes accomplished their purpose—to hinder any possible relief of Tula. About 35 kilometers west of Likhvin, the stubborn rebel garrison of Kozelsk (which had already withstood several months of siege during the winter and spring) was once again besieged by a detachment of Shuiskii's soldiers under the command of Prince Vasilii F. Mosalskii.[37] The tsar contemplated following up his commanders' victories during the summer with military operations even farther to the west, focusing on rebel-held Briansk; but the arrival on the scene of someone claiming to be Tsar Dmitrii interrupted Shuiskii's plans.

If Tsar Vasilii had been cheered by the progress made by many of the detachments sent out from the Tula siege camp, he was still frustrated by Tula's stout resistance. As usual during a long siege, the tsar's army began to run low on supplies and morale slipped badly. As early as July, large numbers of the tsar's hungry and discouraged soldiers simply abandoned the siege camp for home. The defection of Prince Urusov also led to the departure of many non-Russian troops.[38] At this point, although Tsar Vasilii had been primarily concerned about the threat he faced to the east, he received disheartening news of the appearance of "Tsar Dmitrii" to the west. Rumors quickly circulated that Shuiskii would have to retreat to Moscow in order to forestall the unexpected new threat, but Tsar Vasilii was actually more concerned that breaking off the siege of Tula would be a disaster from which he might never recover.[39] At the same time, however, he recognized that his siege was now clearly in a race against time and the progress of "Dmitrii." The tsar nervously urged his commanders to speed up their efforts to capture Tula.

In late July, a syn boiarskii from Murom named Ivan S. Krovkov proposed to one of Tsar Vasilii's Military Affairs Office secretaries a method to force the surrender of Tula: build a dam on the Upa River below (to the west of) Tula and flood the town. Krovkov's plan was immediately presented to the tsar. At first Shuiskii and the boyars laughed at the idea, but when Krovkov offered to forfeit his life if he failed, the tsar ordered him to carry out the audacious project.[40] By early August, a very large number of recruits and peasants were put to work constructing the dam.[41] It was an amazing piece of engineering, possible only because of the geography of the Tula area.

Tula sat on the southern bank of the Upa River, which flowed from the southeast to the northwest at that point (on its way to the Oka). Hills sloping up on the northeastern side of the river and hills to the southwest of the town created a shallow valley where, at or near Tula, several small rivers and streams flowed into the Upa and created numerous marshes. Krovkov figured out that by damming the Upa downstream from Tula, there was just enough slope to the land that the water would back up and flood the town. The slope was so gentle that there was real hope that the rising water would inundate the town before simply washing around and eroding the dam. Krovkov and others chose a perfect location, just below the confluence of the Voronia River and the Upa, one and a half kilometers northwest of Tula (see Figure 12). That site was far enough away from the town to avoid constant harassment of workers by the rebels and also assured the rapid flooding of the valley floor once the dam was completed. Thousands of workers (many from monasteries) brought logs, straw, and sacks of dirt to the construction site.[42] In order to impound enough water to flood Tula, the dam needed to be nearly a kilometer in length and fairly high. That ambitious goal required a huge labor force and more than two months to accomplish. The work was not completed until the beginning of October.[43]

In the first stage of construction, workers concentrated on building a long and sturdy log and earth causeway from the gently sloping and marshy northern bank of the Upa. Only after that heavy, slow work was nearly finished did they turn their attention to the opposite shore. On the steeper southern bank it was possible to construct a much shorter causeway fairly rapidly by having workers simply pile up thousands of sacks of dirt, sand, and gravel. In the last phase of construction, when speed was essential, all of the tsar's soldiers took turns hauling sacks of dirt right alongside the peasant recruits. The project was an enormous undertaking; the amount of earth moved was staggering. A century and a half later the ruins of the dam were still visible and impressive.[44]

During all this time, of course, the rebels continued daily to inflict damage to the tsar's army. As Tsar Vasilii's siege force sustained more and more casualties and as food supplies dwindled, the grumbling among his soldiers grew as did rumors of "Tsar Dmitrii's" return to Russia. By September, large numbers of Shuiskii's wounded or sick troops were sent home; and many healthy but hungry militiamen and common soldiers continued to slip away from the siege camp. The tsar never stopped making strenuous efforts to raise additional forces for the Tula campaign, but even offers of great rewards failed to produce satisfactory results.[45] By the end of summer, Tsar Vasilii became quite concerned that the siege of Tula would last well into the fall and that—due to the decline of his own forces and the progress of the new "Dmitrii"—the outcome of the siege he was hoping for was not at all assured. The tsar with reason came to fear that he might lose his army and maybe even his throne.[46]

The appearance of someone playing the role of Tsar Dmitrii and the beginning of his military campaign against Tsar Vasilii by late summer 1607 ushered in a new phase in the civil war just as the siege of Tula was coming to a close. The new "Dmitrii" was able to gather large forces and to greatly expand rebel-held territory; he eventually set up his own capital and court in Tushino and laid siege to Moscow on and off for eighteen months. Ever since his arrival on the scene, the man often referred to as the "second false Dmitrii" or as the "brigand of Tushino" has stirred interest and provoked strong opinions about his identity and significance. Not surprisingly, since he came from Poland-Lithuania and counted among his supporters a number of Polish, Lithuanian, and Belorussian captains and soldiers, some contemporaries regarded him simply as a pawn of a foreign power—either King Sigismund III or a group of Polish

Fig. 12 "A View of Tula from Tsar Vasilii's Dam." Illustration by V. Ia. Klimenko published in *Russkoe gradostroitel'noe iskusstvo: Gradostroitel'stvo Moskovskogo gosudarstva XVI–XVII vekov*, edited by N. F. Gulianitskii (Moscow: Stroiizdat, 1994).

lords determined to profit personally from Russia's civil war.[47] Of course, the same thing had been said, wrongly, about Tsar Dmitrii himself; and it turns out to be just as inaccurate an assessment of the "second false Dmitrii." That erroneous view was really more a reflection of Shuiskii propaganda and Russian xenophobia than anything else, but many historians have written about the "resurrected" tsar under the influence of that flawed perspective.[48] The image of the "second false Dmitrii" in historiography has also been seriously distorted by the traditional interpretation of the Time of Troubles as a period of social revolution.[49]

Who was the "second false Dmitrii"? To this day no one knows for sure. Tsar Vasilii's agents made a concerted effort to discover his true identity but failed.[50] The man was about the same height as Tsar Dmitrii but only vaguely resembled him.[51] The impostor was fairly well-educated; he wrote Russian and Polish fluently and when "discovered" was employed as a teacher.[52] Many sources identified him as a Russian who had lived for several years in Belorussia before assuming the identity of Tsar Dmitrii.[53] Several sources specifically identified him as a baptized Jew named Bogdan. The Romanov dynasty, when established in 1613, concurred with that identification, basing its conclusion on Patriarch Filaret's personal acquaintance with the "second false Dmitrii" at Tushino and the alleged discovery of a copy of the Talmud and other Hebrew writings among "Dmitrii's" papers after he was killed in 1610.[54] Skrynnikov was perhaps too quick to credit that identification.[55] Maureen Perrie has wisely pointed out that branding the impostor as a Jew may have been just a useful device to discredit him and the entire rebel movement. On the other hand, Perrie also acknowledged that the Tushino impostor may actually have been a baptized Jew.[56]

Only one faulty source identified the Tushino impostor as the son of a highborn aristocrat; other sources flatly denied him such an exalted birth.[57] A few sources identified him as a member of the petty gentry Verevkin family of Severia or specifically as the son of a priest from that family.[58] Most sources, however, claimed that the "second false Dmitrii" lacked the polish of a gentleman and was definitely from the lower class. He did, in fact, have many vile habits and, like the coarse Tsarevich Petr, was frequently crude in behavior. Contemporary sources identified him variously as the son of a blacksmith or a coach driver, as an apprentice, a common laborer, a peasant, or a cossack.[59] He was most frequently identified as a priest's son. The impostor was quite well-versed in Orthodox priestly matters and occasionally displayed the mannerisms of a cleric. According to one source, Tsar Vasilii's agents tortured a captured rebel commander who finally admitted that the new "Dmitrii" was really a priest's son from Moscow, a stable boy named Mitka, who had been sent away from the capital in 1601 by one of the Mosalskii princes.[60] Some sources identified the impostor as a former servant or secretary of Tsar Dmitrii who had an intimate knowledge of his former master's secrets and mannerisms that allowed him to play the role of the tsar.[61] Maureen Perrie credited those sources and came to regard the "second false Dmitrii" as a self-starter who either initiated the pretense on his own or was a willing participant from the beginning.[62] In fact, the impostor did manage to impress many people with his intimate knowledge of Tsar Dmitrii's life; even what was represented as his handwriting strongly resembled Dmitrii's. However, those things can easily be explained by the presence at the Tushino court of such clever former close associates of Tsar Dmitrii as Mikhail Molchanov, Pan Miechowicki, and Captain Margeret.[63] Evidence against Perrie's conclusion also includes the many sources that categorically stated that the future "tsar" was not Tsar Dmitrii's servant but had actually been living in Belorussia for a long time before being "discovered."[64] Sources claiming that the impostor was extremely reluctant at first to assume Tsar Dmitrii's identity and had to be carefully trained led Skrynnikov to conclude that the "second false Dmitrii" was far from being a self-starter. He plausibly regarded him instead as a cowardly individual with a weak personality who was a virtual puppet of his handlers.[65]

Who was behind the creation of the "second false Dmitrii"? As stated earlier, it was definitely not the Polish government. At that time King Sigismund was facing serious unrest at home and opposed any activities that might provoke conflict with Tsar Vasilii. That forced the creators of the impostor to work quietly. In fact, when Sigismund's officials learned about the involvement of several of his subjects in this effort to aid the Russian rebels, local authorities were immediately ordered to put a stop to those illegal activities.[66] On the other hand, the rise of the Tushino impostor was definitely associated with the increasing participation in Russia's civil war by Polish and Belorussian adventurers. Because he was "discovered" in Belorussia by those "foreigners," a number of contemporaries and some scholars since then regarded him as the willing or reluctant creation of self-serving lords from Poland-Lithuania.[67] Close examination of the sources, however, led Skrynnikov to reject the idea of the impostor as a product of foreign intervention. Instead, Skrynnikov correctly pointed to the rebel camp inside Russia as the source of the initiative for the resurrection of Tsar Dmitrii.[68] Perrie argued strongly against what she saw as Skrynnikov's selective use of evidence to support his conclusion; but her own attempt to detach the creation of the Tushino impostor from Tsarevich Petr is completely unconvincing, as is her effort to deny the conclusion of several scholars that the Pan Zenowicz who worked with Petr was the same Pan Zenowicz who helped produce the "second false Dmitrii."[69]

Prince Shakhovskoi and Ivan Bolotnikov had, of course, long been aware of the need to produce someone to play the role of Tsar Dmitrii in order to defeat Tsar Vasilii. The effort by Mikhail Molchanov to pose as Dmitrii helped stir widespread belief that the tsar was still alive and helped to mobilize the rebellion against Shuiskii; but by the fall of 1606 that pretense had been abandoned, and rebel scouts from Putivl searched in vain in Poland-Lithuania and elsewhere for their beloved tsar. Those efforts were redoubled during the siege of Moscow but still to no avail.[70] After the siege was broken and the rebels retreated to Kaluga, there was a renewed sense of urgency in the search for Dmitrii. At the end of December 1606, Tsarevich Petr personally searched for the "true tsar" in eastern Belorussia. While abroad, Petr employed a number of Polish and Belorussian lords, including Pan Zenowicz, to raise troops for the rebel cause and to produce someone to play the role of Dmitrii. Zenowicz and a fellow nobleman, Pan Sienkiewicz, immediately got started on their assignments.[71] The rebels, in the meantime, continued to seek official Polish military cooperation as well, but with no success. Instead, it was Petr's agents who managed to hire soldiers in eastern Belorussia. Despite Polish government efforts to prevent it, small numbers of soldiers began crossing the border and migrating toward rebel-held territory in Russia by the spring of 1607.[72] During the time in which Tsarevich Petr's allies abroad searched for and trained someone to play the role of Dmitrii, the rebels ended up in Tula. After Bolotnikov arrived there, he continued to send couriers in search of the "true tsar." Eventually, after receiving encouraging news, the rebel commander-in-chief dispatched from Tula one of his able lieutenants, Ivan Martynovich Zarutskii, with letters to be presented to "Tsar Dmitrii." Zarutskii made a beeline for Starodub, near the border of Poland-Lithuania, where he remained for some time waiting for the "tsar" to show up. By then, Zarutskii was well aware that Pan Zenowicz and others had finally located a suitable pretender.[73]

According to tradition, the future "Tsar Dmitrii" was at the time of his "discovery" a priest's servant and teacher who had lived for some time in the town of Shklov in Belorussia. From Shklov he eventually moved a short distance to a village near Mogilev, entered the service of a priest named Fedor Nikolskii, and taught children to read. He was so poor that he dressed in rags and needed to supplement his meager income by doing odd jobs in Mogilev. At some point during the winter of 1606–7, Nikolskii caught the future "tsar" in bed with his wife, beat him soundly, and drove him out of his home. The unemployed beggar wandered the streets of Mogilev with no food or shelter until he was spotted by an accomplice of Tsarevich Petr's allies. Pan Miechowicki, a veteran of Tsar Dmitrii's campaign for the Russian throne, noticed that the beggar looked vaguely like Dmitrii and approached him with an offer of food, clothing, and a chance for glory.[74] The beggar at first refused the offer and fled Mogilev for Propoisk. However, Pan Miechowicki just happened to have several influential friends in Propoisk at that time, including the town's governor, Pan Ragoza, and the very same Pan Zenowicz who had agreed to help Tsarevich Petr find someone to play the role of "Dmitrii." They supposedly tossed the beggar in jail for a week, threatened him with execution as a spy, and eventually prevailed upon him to assume Dmitrii's identity. Pan Miechowicki was put in charge of training the impostor. When he was ready, the "tsar" was accompanied to the Russian border by Pan Zenowicz and Pan Ragoza. By then, whoever he really was, he had accommodated himself to his new role. If not brave, he was now at least willing to play his part. Before crossing the border, he issued his handlers a wide-ranging decree from "Tsar Dmitrii" authorizing the recruitment of soldiers abroad. The plan was for active recruitment of mercenaries to begin once the impostor had been recognized as Tsar Dmitrii by several Russian towns; "Dmitrii" offered to pay two or three times as much as those soldiers could earn at home.[75]

The impostor crossed the border in late May, 1607, near the town of Popova Gora. He brought with him no foreign troops and was accompanied only by his two aides, Grigorii Kashnets and a scribe named Aleksei Rukin. They quickly made their way to nearby Starodub and set in motion the carefully choreographed resurrection of Tsar Dmitrii. Starodub was chosen as the launch point for the pretense because of its proximity to the Polish-Lithuanian border and because, unlike Putivl, most of its inhabitants had not personally seen Tsar Dmitrii. For security reasons, the impostor traveled incognito as "Andrei Andreevich Nagoi," Tsar Dmitrii's "kinsman." He arrived in Starodub on June 12.[76] There he and his two companions revealed to local authorities that Tsar Dmitrii was alive and would soon arrive with Pan Miechowicki and many soldiers. As Dmitrii's "kinsman," "Andrei Nagoi" promised rich rewards in return for supporting Tsar Dmitrii's struggle against the usurper Vasilii Shuiskii. That story caused quite a stir and revealed the strong rebel sympathies of the local population. Eventually, however, after several frustrating weeks of waiting for Dmitrii's army to arrive, people began to question the fantastic stories told by "Prince Andrei." At that point, in a carefully staged event, the local authorities arrested "Nagoi" and his companions and questioned them publicly on July 10, 1607.[77]

The interrogation was designed to convince the inhabitants of Starodub and other towns that Tsar Dmitrii was indeed alive and had finally returned home to resume his struggle for the throne. Before the town's entire population, "Prince Andrei" and his companions were threatened with torture to make them reveal the truth. Scribe Aleksei Rukin was stripped of his shirt and allegedly beaten with the knout, at which point he shouted that he would show them where Tsar Dmitrii was if he was released. He then revealed to a shocked crowd that "Andrei Nagoi" was none other than Tsar Dmitrii himself, traveling incognito to test their loyalty before revealing his identity. When "Nagoi" acknowledged that he really was "Tsar Dmitrii," the townspeople fell at his feet, promising to fight and die for him. At some point, the emissary from Tsarevich Petr and Bolotnikov, Ivan Zarutskii, stepped forward, also "recognized" the tsar, and presented him with letters from the Tula rebel leadership. The effect was to doubly convince the people of Starodub that Dmitrii was alive and standing before them. Conrad Bussow told the tale that "Tsar Dmitrii" then immediately ordered Zarutskii to joust with him outside the gates of the town. In a carefully orchestrated battle, Zarutskii knocked the "tsar" off his horse, whereupon the angry townspeople seized and beat Zarutskii as a "traitor" and brought him bound with rope to the "tsar" for judgment. "Dmitrii" laughed and ordered the release of the bruised Zarutskii, telling the people that this was just another test of their loyalty. The crowd roared its approval and "Tsar Dmitrii" was conducted with great honor into the best lodgings in the fortress. On the very same day, probably by prior arrangement, Pan Miechowicki arrived in Starodub with a detachment of foreign mercenaries expecting high pay in the service of "Tsar Dmitrii." The appearance of that force silenced any remaining doubters in Starodub.[78]

After the "tsar" revealed himself in Starodub, he sent agents to all the towns of Severia and adjacent provinces announcing his escape—with God's help— from Shuiskii's assassins and recounting his experiences since then. He called upon his subjects to help him build an army to retake his throne. At first, the cautious authorities in Putivl and Chernigov held the "tsar's" agents for questioning and sent their own people to Starodub to check up on "Dmitrii." Once they were satisfied that he was indeed the "true tsar," the response throughout Severia was extremely enthusiastic, and very soon ordinary Russians and free cossacks began flocking to Starodub to aid the resurrected "tsar."[79] Over the course of the next two months, the "second false Dmitrii" managed to assemble a small army with which to challenge Shuiskii and possibly relieve Tula.

To some extent, at least, the appearance of the "second false Dmitrii" stalled the trend of frontier gentry drifting away from the rebel cause because of Tsarevich Petr. Nevertheless, since by that time there were relatively few professional soldiers left in the region, the bulk of "Dmitrii's" recruits consisted of three thousand poorly-trained Russians (many of them peasants), supplemented by foreign mercenaries and a small number of cossacks. The presence of so many peasants and other members of the lower class in the army of the "second false Dmitrii" caused Soviet scholars to suggest that the impostor was continuing Bolotnikov's mythical social revolution against serfdom. That is absolutely false.[80] It has also been claimed that Pan Miechowicki brought five thousand foreign mercenaries with him to Starodub but that only a small number were well-armed gentry. Skrynnikov with good reason challenged that high figure. In fact, a contemporary source mentioned only seven hundred cavalrymen joining "Tsar Dmitrii" as soon as he proclaimed himself; that was probably a reference to Miechowicki's mercenaries. The rest of "Dmitrii's" army consisted of native Russians.[81] Only after King Sigismund's loyal troops decisively defeated his rebel subjects in battle in July 1607 and many detachments of soldiers involved in the Polish civil war were disbanded did significant numbers of foreign troops begin drifting into Russia. Sigismund was glad to see the backs of those troublemakers and willingly granted permission for them to join "Tsar Dmitrii's" army. By late summer those mercenaries significantly bolstered the impostor's forces as he began to challenge Tsar Vasilii.[82]

"Tsar Dmitrii" formed a very modest boyar council in Starodub. Among his closest advisers was syn boiarskii Gavrila Verevkin, one of the principal initiators of the town's embrace of the resurrected "tsar." Another close adviser was Drugoi T. Ryndin, a former bureaucrat who had served Tsar Dmitrii; he was promoted to the rank of dumnyi diak (state secretary) by the impostor.[83] Probably the most influential adviser was Ivan Zarutskii. This man, a Ukrainian born in Tarnopol, had led an active life. Captured by the Crimean Tatars in his youth, Zarutskii escaped from Crimea to become a cossack leader. Later he joined the rebellion against Vasilii Shuiskii and quickly rose to become one of Bolotnikov's most trusted lieutenants. Zarutskii has been badly misunderstood by scholars caught up in the traditional interpretation of the Time of Troubles as a period of social revolution. Variously described as a revolutionary democrat, a crusader against the "feudal lords," and a tool of Polish intervention, Zarutskii was actually an incredibly smart and charismatic opportunist as well as an excellent military commander. It is possible that he was accompanied from Tula by two princes of the Zasekin family who also joined the impostor's boyar council.[84]

In Starodub the "tsar" and his advisers spent several weeks presiding over the build-up of their small army and planning their campaign. They were motivated to act as soon as possible not only because of the siege of Tula but also because they did not have enough money to pay the foreign troops already in Starodub and others who were on their way there. By late August, Colonel Jozef Budzilo arrived with a substantial detachment of soldiers from Belorussia. With other foreign troops scheduled to arrive soon thereafter, the "second false Dmitrii" decided to launch his campaign against Shuiskii on September 10, 1607. His first objective was strategically located Briansk, from which he could either attempt to relieve Tula or head for poorly-defended Moscow. According to Bussow, "Tsar Dmitrii" stated that his objective was to relieve Tula and Kaluga. By September 15, the "tsar's" army reached Pochep (75 kilometers southwest of Briansk) where the local population welcomed "Dmitrii" with joy. By September 20, the impostor's army approached Briansk.[85]

Tsar Vasilii had been receiving ominous reports about the appearance of "Tsar Dmitrii" since July. He was deeply disturbed by news of the impostor's plan to advance to Briansk. Shuiskii was forced to act quickly to counter that grave threat to the siege of Tula and to his own crown; he therefore rushed troops there to forestall "Dmitrii." Tsar Vasilii ordered his voevoda in Meshchovsk, Grigorii F. Sunbulov, to send forces immediately to Briansk and to capture the town or burn it down if necessary. Sunbulov dispatched E. Bezobrazov (a former Briansk voevoda who had been booted out by the rebels) with two hundred fifty soldiers to take Briansk. Much to the delight of Tsar Vasilii, Bezobrazov quickly captured the town and sent word of his victory to the Tula siege camp.[86] Shuiskii then ordered reinforcements to be sent to Briansk as quickly as possible. Sunbulov was instructed to advance from Meshchovsk with all available forces, and other detachments under the command of Mikhail F. Kashin and Andrei N. Rzhevskii rushed there from the Tula siege camp. Smolensk authorities were also ordered to send all available deti boiarskie and streltsy to Briansk.[87]

Unfortunately for Tsar Vasilii, "Tsar Dmitrii's" approach to Briansk triggered a strong positive response from the local population. "Dmitrii" camped for about a week in Svenskii monastery near the town, and many people from Briansk and the surrounding area came to greet him. Some of the townspeople informed the "tsar" that Shuiskii's newly-installed voevoda in Briansk, Mikhail Kashin, had figured out that he did not have enough men to hold the town until the arrival of reinforcements. In fact, in desperation Kashin's men burned the town and retreated. After the fires were put out and clean-up crews did their work, "Tsar Dmitrii" entered Briansk no later than September 25. Before that he dispatched troops under the command of voevoda Ryndin and Colonel Budzilo to harass Kashin's retreating forces.[88]

Tsar Vasilii was bitterly disappointed by the news from Briansk. To make matters even worse, scouts from "Tsar Dmitrii" made it all the way to Tula and informed the besieged rebels that the "true tsar" was on his way to rescue them. Other scouts approached Shuiskii's siege army itself and urged the soldiers and construction workers to abandon the usurper. On September 24 or 25, a courier from "Dmitrii" (a syn boiarskii from Starodub) boldly emerged from Tula to deliver a letter from his master to Tsar Vasilii in front of all of Shuiskii's boyars and commanders. The brave rebel publicly declared that Tsar Dmitrii had returned to recover his crown but that too much blood had already been spilled. Therefore, Shuiskii would be shown mercy if he surrendered immediately. The outraged tsar ordered the courier burned at the stake; but while the man could still speak, he kept repeating that he had been sent by the "true tsar." Those words made quite an impression.[89] Shuiskii was now terrified that time was running out for the siege of Tula. Not only was his army incredibly weary, but by then soldiers were melting away from the siege camp in large numbers. While the resurrection of "Tsar Dmitrii" had galvanized the rebels, it instilled fear and wonder among Shuiskii's soldiers. Tsar Vasilii grew increasingly nervous about the loyalty of his own troops as well as the loyalty of the construction workers building the dam on the Upa. He therefore ordered work on the dam speeded up. As noted earlier, Shuiskii went so far as to order all of his troops to take turns helping to construct the last section of the dam.[90]

In the meantime, "Tsar Dmitrii" was having problems of his own. On September 26, his foreign troops staged a rebellion due to lack of pay. Many of them abandoned the impostor and made their way back across the border.[91] That forced the "tsar" and his loyal commanders to improvise somewhat. They abandoned smoldering Briansk, crossed the Desna River, and headed southeast. They reached rebel-held Karachev by October 2. There they were joined by a large detachment of Zaporozhian cossacks. By October 4, "Dmitrii" felt confident enough to send Pan Miechowicki and Colonel Budzilo to relieve beleaguered Kozelsk, then under siege by as many as eight thousand men led by Prince Vasilii F. Mosalskii and Captain Matias Mizinov.[92]

At dawn on October 8, the rebel army attacked Shuiskii's siege force. Mosalskii had been warned of their approach and had encircled his camp with extra guards; but those men were quickly driven back, and the rebels managed to burst right into the panic-struck enemy camp. Many of Shuiskii's soldiers, including Prince Mosalskii, fled; but many others, including Captain Mizinov, were captured along with all their supplies. After the battle, the inhabitants of Kozelsk (who had successfully repulsed Shuiskii's forces on and off for many months) came out to greet the rebel army with the traditional offering of bread and salt. Shouts of joy about the return of the "good tsar" could be heard everywhere. On October 11, Dmitrii ceremonially entered Kozelsk—one day after the fall of Tula.[93] The impostor has been criticized for not advancing quickly and aggressively to relieve Tula. It has even been suggested that he intentionally stalled his campaign in order to let Shuiskii capture all rebel leaders not under "Dmitrii's" control. In reality, the impostor's small army faced a daunting task; thousands of Tsar Vasilii's troops were assigned to slow it down. All things considered, the timid "second false Dmitrii" did about as well as he could under the circumstances.

The arrival in Tula of couriers from "Tsar Dmitrii" in late September cheered the tired and hungry rebels somewhat, but most of them realized that there was little hope that "Dmitrii's" forces would reach them before the dam on the Upa was completed. Grumbling among the cossacks and townsmen eventually led to a sharp confrontation with the rebel leadership. Angry that no help was immediately forthcoming, many began to openly question the story of Tsar Dmitrii's survival. They called Prince Shakhovskoi a "liar" and the author of their current misery, and they threatened to turn him and Bolotnikov over to Shuiskii. Bolotnikov was able to calm them down temporarily by recounting his own meeting with "Tsar Dmitrii" in Poland-Lithuania and his sincere belief that the man he met really was Dmitrii. He urged his men to hold out for a few more days, telling them that Dmitrii's army was advancing to Tula and would arrive in a week or so. He stated that he fully expected aid from his sovereign, to whom he had written urgent appeals to hurry to their rescue. If Tsar Dmitrii did not arrive in time to save them, Bolotnikov said, they could eat his (Bolotnikov's) body. By such speeches he kept his men from surrendering for many days even though they had already slaughtered all the horses in Tula and were beginning to get very hungry. The brave commander-in-chief maintained his standing among rank-and-file rebels, but those unhappy men did throw Shakhovskoi in prison, telling him that he would be released when Tsar Dmitrii arrived. If Dmitrii failed to appear, the rebels said, he would be turned over to Shuiskii as a deceiver and as the "initiator of this war and bloodshed."[94] As it turned out, the situation in Tula only worsened.

By the end of September the final phase of damming the Upa began, and after a furious week's work of hauling heavy sacks of dirt, sand, and gravel around the clock, the project was completed. The water immediately began to flood the shallow river valley. Within a day Tula was flooded, and its inhabitants were forced to camp out on the roofs of their homes and to go about town on rafts.[95] Already hungry and exhausted, the beleaguered rebels now faced even more severe hardships. Water flooded all the storehouses and ruined most of what little grain and salt was left. Few could afford the incredibly high prices for the little food which remained unspoiled. By the beginning of October, many poor souls were reduced to eating "unclean" food—cats, mice, hides, and even carrion. Many of them died of starvation, disease, or exhaustion.[96]

Bolotnikov attempted to hold out in spite of the hunger and the flood. The rebels hoped something would go wrong with Shuiskii's dam and that the water might subside enough to permit them to make a sortie in strength from Tula for the purpose of breaking through the siege camp to escape and link up with "Tsar Dmitrii's" forces. Bussow told the story of a sorcerer monk who offered for a large sum of money to swim underwater to the dam and destroy it. After failing in the task, the monk allegedly told the rebel leaders that Shuiskii had built the dam with the aid of twelve thousand devils and that he (the monk) had only succeeded in winning over half of them; the rest of the devils were still defending the dam.[97] In fact, there was nothing the rebels could do to stop the water from rising.

Despite Bolotnikov's best efforts to hold out, the situation in Tula quickly became unbearable. In despair, many talked openly of surrender. The rebel commander-in-chief even lost his ability to communicate with and control all his forces, let alone the townspeople, because parts of the town were cut off from one another by the flood. In their extreme misery and without authorization from the rebel leaders, small groups of soldiers and townspeople began to abandon Tula. Soon, a hundred, two hundred, even three hundred people left each day. By the end of the first week in October, representatives of the Tula citizenry who had covertly departed from the town began discussions with Tsar Vasilii's commanders about terms of surrender, including the possibility of handing over the rebel leaders.[98]

There can be no doubt that the flooding of Tula forced its surrender, but sources are confused and contradictory about the end of the so-called "Bolotnikov rebellion." That is not surprising considering all the misleading Shuiskii propaganda and the widespread rumors of treachery and betrayal among the rebels. News of the surrender of Ivan Bolotnikov stunned most rebels and prompted numerous theories to account for the fall of Tula. Almost every possible explanation can be found in contemporary sources, and the subject has been further complicated by the traditional interpretation of the Time of Troubles as a period of social revolution. Not surprisingly, there are untrustworthy sources favorable to Shuiskii that claimed he captured Tula and seized the rebel leaders.[99] Most sources, however, spoke about a deal struck between the citizens of Tula and the tsar. Still other sources mentioned a deal between Bolotnikov and Shuiskii. Isaac Massa, hearing the various versions, wrote this about the rebel commander-in-chief: "Some said that he had surrendered voluntarily, others that he was captured through treachery."[100] Let us try to sort out the sources and the issues involved in order to determine what actually happened.

One version of the surrender of Tula that was initially promoted by Tsar Vasilii was that everyone in the town—all townspeople, all rebels, and all commanders, including Bolotnikov and Tsarevich Petr—surrendered to Shuiskii.[101] A more refined version quickly emerged: all rebels and commanders except Petr surrendered, and they turned the false tsarevich over to Tsar Vasilii.[102] True or not, the latter version was at least partly designed to undermine the rebel cause and Bolotnikov's incredible reputation by making it appear that he and others had betrayed the rebellion. The rebel commander-in-chief was represented as being repentant about fighting against Tsar Vasilii. The subsequent, carefully staged special treatment of Bolotnikov while in captivity, contrasting sharply with the torture and execution of Petr, was consciously designed to hurt Bolotnikov's reputation among rebels and waverers in order to blunt the rebellion and the rising threat posed by the "second false Dmitrii."[103] That strategy was somewhat successful; the notion that the surrender of Tula was the result of treachery became very widespread, and propaganda about Bolotnikov's betrayal of the rebel cause was accepted by at least a few gullible people.[104]

The most common version of the surrender of Tula found in contemporary sources was that the townspeople, or at least the leading townsmen, betrayed the rebels, including Bolotnikov, in order to save themselves.[105] This plausible version has attracted the support of several historians.[106] Unfortunately, supporters of this version have neglected to note that it would have been necessary for the townsmen to include rebel troops in their conspiracy. It was not possible to betray the whole rebel army and to have that result in a peaceful surrender of those soldiers—which is precisely what occurred; nor was it possible for the leading townsmen to act alone in this matter.

Some more plausible variants of this version have the townsmen and rank-and-file rebels ready to surrender no matter what their officers thought. Scholars have even speculated that a cossack circle or a general meeting of ordinary townspeople must have been held to reach a collective decision.[107] That is not at all likely. In fact, this version requires us to believe both that such a meeting could be held secretly and that every single one of Bolotnikov's own men was willing to betray him. Another variation of this version of the surrender put forward by a few scholars was that the townspeople and the rebel soldiers were joined in their treachery by one of Bolotnikov's fellow commanders, either Teliatevskii or Shakhovskoi, or perhaps both of them.[108] That is pure speculation, however, and is based solely on the mild treatment Teliatevskii and Shakhovskoi received at the hands of Tsar Vasilii after the surrender of Tula. It is also extremely unlikely. Bolotnikov was far more popular than the other rebel leaders. It is ridiculous to assume that there was unanimous agreement among the conspirators to seize the brave commander-in-chief and that all of Bolotnikov's soldiers were willing to go along with such a plan. Skrynnikov has rightly challenged this version of the surrender, pointing to sources that included Shakhovskoi and Teliatevskii among those who were betrayed along with Bolotnikov. However, Skrynnikov noted that Iurii Bezzubtsev was the one rebel commander who entered Tsar Vasilii's service after the fall of Tula and speculated that he may have betrayed Bolotnikov. At that time, Bezzubtsev's son, a captive at the siege of Moscow, was being held by Shuiskii; and, according to Skrynnikov, his fate may have influenced his father's actions.[109] As we shall soon see, however, this is also not a plausible interpretation of what happened.

A powerful underlying assumption in most Soviet historians' attempts to sort out what happened at Tula was that the heroic Bolotnikov remained true to his "revolutionary" cause to the end and could not possibly have betrayed the radical masses; therefore, he must have been betrayed.[110] Indeed, Soviet scholars who dared to credit sources about Bolotnikov himself negotiating the surrender with Tsar Vasilii were punished in the Stalin era and severely reproached in the following decades.[111] That unsubtle external influence made it extremely difficult to get at the truth.

In fact, Bolotnikov was certainly intelligent enough to observe the growing desertions from Tula, and no doubt he heard that some townsmen were negotiating with Shuiskii. He was also deeply aware of the misery of the inhabitants of Tula and his own troops and knew that no relief from "Dmitrii" would arrive in time to save them. Therefore, it should come as no surprise to anyone that the rebel commander-in-chief himself joined the negotiations with Shuiskii with the goal in mind of preserving the lives of his men and possibly their freedom as well.[112] Bolotnikov's decision to parley with the enemy was definitely not the result of a psychological crisis brought on by a sense of betrayal or abandonment by the "second false Dmitrii."[113] In fact, one contemporary specifically claimed that Bolotnikov's negotiations amounted to some kind of trick to deceive Shuiskii and save the rebel army.[114]

Tsar Vasilii was well aware that he could not take Tula by storm. Because of the very real danger posed by the "second false Dmitrii's" campaign against him and the rapid decline of his siege army, the tsar was more than willing to cut a deal with the inhabitants of Tula in order to end the siege and return to Moscow as soon as possible; but Shuiskii's prestige was also on the line because he had sworn to stay in the field until he achieved victory. The tsar, therefore, welcomed contacts from the Tula citizenry and especially from the rebel commanders. The actual negotiations are difficult to follow because it was not in the interest of Tsar Vasilii's propagandists to mention them. It appears that Bolotnikov reluctantly agreed to surrender but insisted on negotiating the best terms possible: pardons for all the rebels and complete freedom for them to depart from Tula with their weapons and to go wherever they wished.[115] Bolotnikov informed Tsar Vasilii that such a pardon was essential; otherwise, the rebels would hold out until the last man. Shuiskii was probably also informed that many of the rebels were willing to rejoin his service if they were forgiven. Since Shuiskii was himself in a difficult position, he readily agreed to those remarkable demands in order to be able to declare "victory" at Tula.[116] The tsar also swore a solemn oath to spare the lives of the rebels.[117] Appearing magnanimous at this point was a wise strategy on Shuiskii's part considering the available alternatives. There were also precedents in that era for pardoning enemy troops and for allowing besieged forces to go free in order to end sieges.[118]

Shuiskii's propagandists represented his decision as a demonstration of the pious tsar's mercy, and they may even have used the extraordinary bravery demonstrated by the misguided rebels as justification for letting them go instead of executing or jailing them.[119] Rank-and-file rebels were officially allowed to depart for "home" from Tula with their weapons; those who desired to serve Tsar Vasilii were offered salaries and positions in his army.[120] There is good reason to believe Shuiskii was also forced to promise the rebels that he would not launch investigations into their backgrounds in order to identify and return former serfs and slaves to their owners.[121] The price the rebels had to pay for this remarkable agreement appears to have been the surrender of their leaders, especially Bolotnikov and Tsarevich Petr, who were to be paraded as trophies and as proof that Tsar Vasilii had really "captured" Tula. Shuiskii did, however, solemnly promise to spare the lives of those men.[122]

A number of sources and historians insisted that Tsar Vasilii seized the rebel leaders at Tula through treachery.[123] One version had Shuiskii cutting a deal with the townsmen and rebel troops who then seized their leaders and delivered them to the tsar.[124] Another version had the tsar cutting a deal with Bolotnikov to allow all the rebels to go free, only to treacherously seize him and Tsarevich Petr at the last moment.[125] A third version was that the rebel leaders surrendered voluntarily (or were offered by their troops) to Shuiskii on the condition that their lives would be spared, but that Tsar Vasilii later broke his word by having them put to death.[126] The tsar was certainly treacherous enough to break his own oath, but there is good reason to doubt that he seized Bolotnikov upon the surrender of Tula. The precariousness of Tsar Vasilii's own position and his willingness to let the armed rebels go (and even to receive them into his own service) makes it extremely unlikely that he would risk the peaceful end of the siege of Tula that he so greatly desired by pulling a stupid stunt guaranteed to outrage the still-intact and well-armed rebel army. Instead, the surrender or seizure of Bolotnikov and Tsarevich Petr must have been one of the conditions for the generous terms offered to rank-and-file rebels. However, betrayal of the rebel commanders seems improbable because so many sources emphasized Tsar Vasilii's oath not to harm Bolotnikov or Petr; if the townsmen and soldiers were betraying their commanders, how much concern would they have shown for the well-being of those men?

Upon reflection, it seems far more likely that Bolotnikov himself cut the very best deal possible for his men by sacrificing his own freedom. By surrendering to Shuiskii, the rebel commander-in-chief made certain that his forces remained intact and would soon be available to bolster the "second false Dmitrii's" campaign against Tsar Vasilii. That may well have been the "trick" one contemporary thought Bolotnikov was playing on Shuiskii. Through his own heroic action, Bolotnikov once again guaranteed that the civil war against the tsar-usurper would continue.

Tula capitulated to Tsar Vasilii on October 10, 1607.[127] After the tsar's solemn oath to abide by the agreed upon terms, his friend Kriuk-Kolychev led a small detachment into Tula without incident in order to occupy it. Bolotnikov, Tsarevich Petr, Prince Shakhovskoi, Prince Teliatevskii, voevoda Bezzubtsev, voevoda Kokhanovskii, ataman Nagiba, and a few other atamans then surrendered and were escorted to Tsar Vasilii's camp.[128] Also taken into custody were approximately fifty foreign mercenaries from Tsar Dmitrii's old bodyguard.[129] Even though there was no truth to the rumors that Bolotnikov was taken prisoner by surprise and against his will, many sources clearly indicated that Tsarevich Petr did not surrender willingly. It is entirely possible that Bolotnikov or others were forced to tie up the fearful Petr in order to fulfill the agreement made with Tsar Vasilii.[130]

There are some colorful stories in the sources about Bolotnikov riding out of Tula to Shuiskii's pavilion, having an audience with the tsar, offering him his sword, and prostrating himself before the tsar—apologizing for his sincere but misguided belief in Tsar Dmitrii.[131] Such a meeting may have occurred. Tsar Vasilii was certainly curious about the rebel commander who had nearly toppled him from the throne, and a meeting with Bolotnikov would also have facilitated Shuiskii propagandists' efforts to undermine the rebel cause by portraying Bolotnikov as a turncoat. Conrad Bussow's assertion that Bolotnikov offered to enter Shuiskii's service in return for showing mercy to the rebels is not credible.[132] But, as a prisoner, Bolotnikov was a great prize for Tsar Vasilii, and he was very carefully guarded. Tsarevich Petr was also kept under very close watch. Shuiskii had definite plans for those two troublemakers and wanted no slip-ups. By contrast, Prince Shakhovskoi was simply disgraced and shipped off to a remote monastery; but he soon managed to escape and made his way to the camp of the "second false Dmitrii" where he resumed his role as a senior rebel commander and one of the "tsar's" most trusted advisers.[133] Prince Teliatevskii was also quickly exiled and not even deprived of his rank or any of his prop-

erty. Voevoda Kokhanovskii was exiled to Kazan without punishment, and ataman Nagiba and other cossack chieftains were similarly exiled to north Russia.
The mild treatment those leaders received fueled erroneous speculation that
they had betrayed the rebel cause at Tula.[134]

As noted earlier, the one rebel voevoda who did enter Shuiskii's service at
this time was Iurii Bezzubtsev; he was immediately given command of four
thousand rebel cossacks who also took the tsar up on his offer of food, shelter,
and employment. In November, Bezzubtsev and his men were sent to Kaluga
(attached to a large detachment with siege guns) to try to convince the rebel
garrison there to surrender or, failing that, to help capture the town. Although
Skrynnikov has identified Bezzubtsev as a possible traitor to Bolotnikov, events
at Kaluga proved him wrong. There Bezzubtsev and his cossacks turned on the
other soldiers accompanying them, forcing the tsar's loyal officers and men to
abandon all their artillery and munitions and to retreat in disarray. Thereupon,
Bezzubtsev handed the supplies over to Kaluga's defenders, and he and his men
rode off to join up with the "second false Dmitrii." Bezzubtsev subsequently
became a significant player in the rebel "capital" of Tushino.[135]

What about the more than ten thousand rebels who were allowed to freely
depart from Tula, supposedly to go home or to return to their frontier garrisons?
In fact, a very large percentage of them joined the army of "Tsar Dmitrii" instead
and resumed the struggle against Shuiskii.[136] That makes Tsar Vasilii's "victory"
at Tula look very hollow, indeed; but at least the siege was over, and Shuiskii
had avoided disaster.

Having achieved his "victory," Tsar Vasilii was anxious to dismiss his exhausted
siege army and to return to Moscow in triumph. Some detachments still in reasonably good shape were sent west to bolster efforts to stop the "second false
Dmitrii," but the rest of the siege army was sent home to rest.[137] So ended the
siege of Tula. However limited Tsar Vasilii's victory had been, it did, in fact,
mark the end of the Bolotnikov rebellion and the beginning of a new phase in
the civil war. Unfortunately for Shuiskii, the new phase included another wave
of enthusiasm for "Tsar Dmitrii" and another frightening siege of Moscow.

21

The capitulation of Tula allowed Tsar Vasilii's nervous commanders to turn their attention to stopping the advance of the "second false Dmitrii." "Dmitrii" had managed to reach Kozelsk, only 130 kilometers west of Tula, by the time Bolotnikov surrendered. In order to block the impostor's path north to Moscow, the garrison of Meshchovsk was quickly and heavily reinforced. Blocking his path to the east proved to be more difficult. News of "Tsar Dmitrii's" progress triggered rebellions during the fall of 1607 in several towns south of Tula that had only recently been "cleansed" of rebels by Shuiskii's forces—Dedilov, Krapivna, and Epifan. In order to prevent the impostor from linking up with those towns and in order to block his path to Tula, Tsar Vasilii sent a detachment commanded by Prince T. F. Seitov and Ivan M. Pushkin to "cleanse" the strategically-located towns of Belev, Bolkhov, and Likhvin and to occupy an old zaseka defense line that stretched from Likhvin to Bolkhov. (One of that line's most heavily fortified points was very near Belev.) Soldiers stationed in the region who were due to be relieved were ordered to remain at their posts, and the tsar's forces quickly reinforced them all along the zaseka line. The tsar's commanders also succeeded—if only temporarily—in inducing Belev, Bolkhov, and Likhvin to switch back to Shuiskii's side.[1] In spite of those efforts, "Dmitrii's" small army fought its way into Belev by October 16.[2]

As soon as "Tsar Dmitrii" entered Belev, he learned of Bolotnikov's surrender at Tula. Panic-struck, the impostor and his demoralized army departed from Belev the very next day—retreating southwest all the way to Karachev. There "Dmitrii" was abandoned by the Zaporozhian cossacks who had only recently joined his service. In addition, he faced another mutiny by his foreign troops, who seized all the booty picked up in Kozelsk and Belev and departed for Poland-Lithuania. In late October, the terrified "tsar" abandoned his own camp; taking only thirty trusted Russians with him, he headed toward Putivl in the hope of passing the winter in friendly territory.[3] News of the impostor's difficulties greatly relieved Tsar Vasilii, who foolishly concluded that the threat posed by "Dmitrii" was now passing. Shuiskii failed to seize the opportunity to actively pursue and destroy his enemy. Instead, he merely ordered another punitive raid in southwestern Russia to be carried out by his remaining Tatar and Mordvian cavalrymen. According to Platonov, that was one of Shuiskii's greatest mistakes, one that significantly prolonged the civil war. It saved the "second false Dmitrii" and gave him time to recover.[4]

At the same time Tsar Vasilii's forces were rushing west to stop "Tsar Dmitrii," Shuiskii's commanders were confronted by widespread rebellion in the Riazan region. Frantic appeals for help from the beleaguered voevoda of Pereiaslavl-Riazanskii (Riazan) pushed Shuiskii, once Tula had capitulated, to dispatch a detachment commanded by Prokofii Liapunov to resume the task of suppressing rebellion in his home province.[5] Liapunov was given a free hand to restore order and to secure the obedience of the entire region—which had been in turmoil for almost a year. He was merciless in punishing rebel towns and villages, burning them and taking many prisoners. As a result, he quickly pacified the province by sheer brutality. In fact, Tsar Vasilii at one point was actually forced to order him to be less indiscriminate in punishing the area's inhabitants. The people of the region long remembered Liapunov's reign of terror. Many of them remained covert rebel sympathizers and continued to regard him and other local lords who supported Shuiskii as traitors. Until the very end of the Time of Troubles, large numbers of the region's somewhat cowed inhabitants continued to resist local authorities passively by sullenly refusing to pay taxes to or to work for the enemies of "Tsar Dmitrii."[6] While conducting his pacification campaign, Liapunov made a concerted effort to placate disgruntled gentry and to build links between the Riazan elite and Tsar Vasilii.[7] For his work, he was soon promoted to the rank of dumnyi dvorianin. Tsar Vasilii also lavished estates and villages on him and issued a special decree thanking Liapunov for his innumerable services.[8]

After the siege of Tula, Tsar Vasilii was once again able to focus some attention on the troubled Volga region. He sent nine former rebels (streltsy and Terek cossacks) to Astrakhan to inform the townspeople of Bolotnikov's capitulation and to offer them similarly favorable terms if they would end their rebellion. Astrakhan bluntly refused to surrender; its inhabitants by then were filled with excitement about rumors of the return of "Tsar Dmitrii" to Russia.[9] By the time Bolotnikov surrendered, Shuiskii was well aware that Tsarevich Ivan-Avgust had been stopped cold at Saratov in the late summer and had been forced to retreat all the way back to Astrakhan. Partly because of that, in early October, following instructions received from the Tula siege camp, Shuiskii's voevoda on Balchik Island, Fedor Sheremetev, finally abandoned his position just north of Astrakhan and marched his men up the Volga to rebel-held Tsaritsyn. Sheremetev's army stormed the town on October 24, killing and capturing many men. Large numbers of rebel cossacks fled into the steppe. Tsar Vasilii was extremely pleased by news of that victory, coming so soon after the fall of Tula. He ordered Sheremetev to remain in strategically-located Tsaritsyn where for several months he fought off cossack attacks coming from Astrakhan. Eventually, Sheremetev was ordered to retreat farther up the river to Kazan so that his army would be available for operations against the "second false Dmitrii."[10]

Believing that he had gained the upper hand against the rebels, Tsar Vasilii returned to Moscow very soon after the surrender of Tula, arriving home by October 18.[11] There he celebrated the capture of Tula and finally got married after more than a year and a half of delays and postponements. Shuiskii made no plans whatsoever to resume active campaigning against "Dmitrii" until the following spring. The tsar's celebration of his "complete victory" over the rebels was regarded at the time by some observers as premature, to say the least.[12] Even Tsar Vasilii's close ally, Patriarch Hermogen, questioned the extent of the victory achieved at Tula and blamed Shuiskii's premature triumphal return to Moscow on the tsar's "crafty companions."[13] Nevertheless, Tsar Vasilii was in a good mood. He announced only a few promotions but rewarded his soldiers for the Tula campaign with generous salary increases.[14]

Shuiskii's victory celebration also included showing off his prizes, Tsarevich Petr and Ivan Bolotnikov, who were conducted—along with fifty-two former members of Tsar Dmitrii's foreign guard—past crowds of curious spectators into the capital. The foreigners were soon released from custody, only to be rounded up again within a few months when Shuiskii became fearful of the progress of the "second false Dmitrii." Most of those poor souls ended up in Siberia, where some of them remained for many years. Not surprisingly, the rebel commander-in-chief and the "tsarevich" were not released or exiled but were instead kept under close guard.[15] Although Tsar Vasilii had sworn an oath to spare the lives of those two men, he did not keep his word.[16] However, in order to perpetuate propaganda about Bolotnikov's betrayal of the rebel cause and to prevent him from becoming a martyr, the prisoners Bolotnikov and Petr were treated very differently in public, starting with their journey from Tula to Moscow. Several sources mentioned that Petr was tied up on the tsar's orders and traveled bareheaded all the way to the capital.[17] Bolotnikov, on the other hand, was not subjected to that humiliation.[18] The fates of the two men were also quite different.

The hated false tsarevich was tortured repeatedly and coerced into producing a confession about his humble origins and treasonous activities.[19] One source indicated that Tsar Vasilii then ordered Petr executed "on the advise the entire realm." A few scholars have seen this as an indication that Shuiskii convened some kind of zemskii sobor to judge the putative tsarevich, much as Tsar Dmitrii had done in the treason case of Vasilii Shuiskii. It is doubtful that the tsar needed to bother with such a meeting, and there is no record of it; on the other hand, such an entity could have been convened in order to release the tsar from his oath to spare Petr's life.[20] The impostor was hanged publicly just outside Moscow next to the Serpukhov road near the Danilov monastery. Some contemporaries criticized Tsar Vasilii for breaking his oath, and there were, of course, rumors that Petr had escaped death and was living in Lithuania; but there was no noticeable public reaction to the sadistic "tsarevich's" death. Any potential sympathizers were by then far more interested in news of "Tsar Dmitrii's" return to Russia.[21]

In sharp contrast to the treatment of Petr, Shuiskii kept Bolotnikov in close confinement in Moscow for many weeks. There would be no public execution of the former rebel commander-in-chief, who was too highly respected even by his enemies to allow Tsar Vasilii the luxury of openly breaking his vow to spare the man's life. It took the threat of a rebel offensive against Moscow in February 1608 to prompt the tsar to order Bolotnikov relocated to Kargopol in the far north, well away from the forces of the "second false Dmitrii." By the end of February, Bolotnikov and his guards reached Iaroslavl, where the local gentry were shocked to see this dangerous rebel traveling unfettered. According to a contemporary, when they chided the guards for not tying him up, Bolotnikov himself replied to them: "I will soon have you in chains and sewn into bearskins."[22] Smirnov, of course, interpreted this as a sign of Bolotnikov's continued antagonism toward his class enemies, which was definitely not the case.[23] Bolotnikov was actually well aware of "Tsar Dmitrii's" progress and dreamed of escape or liberation. Once he reached Kargopol, he was thrown into prison. Some time later, as the "second false Dmitrii" approached Moscow, a panicky Tsar Vasilii ordered Bolotnikov secretly killed. First his eyes were put out, and then he was drowned.[24] Also put to death at about this time were the other cossack atamans who had surrendered with Bolotnikov and had also been exiled to the far north. In addition, the fearful tsar suddenly resumed the mass executions of thousands of cossack prisoners who had been crowding his jails ever since the end of the siege of Moscow over a year before.[25] Interestingly enough, when word of Bolotnikov's death got out, foreigners and Russians alike were upset. Tsar Vasilii, it seems, had been wise to be cautious and secretive in dealing with the charismatic rebel commander. One of Shuiskii's archbishops wrote that many people were indignant about the tsar breaking his oath to spare the brave man's life.[26] Bolotnikov had by then earned the respect of friend and foe alike. As one contemporary simply but eloquently put it, "Bolotnikov had the common people with him."[27] The rebel cause lost its most talented, energetic, and attractive leader when it lost Ivan Bolotnikov. Even so, Shuiskii's problems were far from over.

The "second false Dmitrii," demoralized and abandoned during the fall of 1607, never reached Putivl. Instead, on October 29, in the Komaritsk district he met up with a group of Polish lords leading one thousand eight hundred mercenaries (both cavalry and infantry) they had gathered abroad to serve "Tsar Dmitrii." Some of those men were relatives of the Polish wedding guests killed or taken prisoner when Shuiskii carried out his coup d'état in 1605; others were veterans of Dmitrii's campaign for the throne.[28] Cheering the impostor even more, in November yet another group of Polish lords with mercenary soldiers joined his forces at Starodub. Also joining him at about this time was another copy-cat pretender, "Tsarevich Fedor Fedorovich," who claimed to be Tsarevich Petr's younger brother. Tsarevich Fedor brought three thousand Don cossacks with him and served his "uncle Dmitrii" loyally.[29] Thus reinforced, "Tsar Dmitrii" was able to resume the offensive against Shuiskii. He advanced to Briansk, which had just recently switched to Shuiskii's side.[30] Sources about the battle of Briansk are contradictory, but there was much skirmishing before the rebels eventually gave up and moved on to friendly Orel. Arriving before that town in December, cautious "Dmitrii" waited until early 1608 before entering it.[31] To the north of Orel, in Bolkhov, sat a large detachment of Tsar Vasilii's soldiers. At the end of 1607, Shuiskii sent his luckless brother Dmitrii to Bolkhov to take charge of efforts to stop the impostor's progress. Voevoda Dmitrii Shuiskii remained there until spring 1608. Heavy snows and extremely cold weather that winter prevented much fighting, but small detachments of the opposing forces skirmished with each other and carried out occasional raids for supplies and booty.[32]

During the winter, "Dmitrii's" army grew rapidly due to the arrival of more foreign mercenaries, cossacks, and large numbers of Bolotnikov's men from Tula. In and around Orel were now massed more than seven thousand Polish and Belorussian troops as well as at least eight thousand Don and Zaporozhian cossacks commanded by Ivan Zarutskii.[33] Because of active recruiting, more and more rebels continued to flock to "Tsar Dmitrii." Even faraway Astrakhan raised detachments of cossacks and Tatars for service in Orel.[34] When Prince Roman Rozynski (a poor Ukrainian magnate) arrived in April at the head of four thousand foreign mercenaries, he was able to impose himself as "Dmitrii's" senior commander. The "tsar" himself was not at all respected by the mercenaries, who treated him harshly. Although "Dmitrii" was an essential figurehead, real power in his camp came to rest in the hands of the commanders of the rebel forces, not with the impostor.[35] Under those circumstances, it is easy to understand why some contemporaries and historians regarded the "second false Dmitrii" as part of Polish intervention in Russia's civil war.[36] In fact, this phase of the Time of Troubles did see the decline or disappearance of the earlier rebel commanders, who had either been taken prisoner or had been shoved aside by newcomers.

One notable exception was Bolotnikov's lieutenant, Ivan Zarutskii, who became one of the most important figures in the court of "Tsar Dmitrii." Zarutskii was promoted to the rank of boyar and received rich rewards and large estates; he worked closely with the new commander-in-chief, Rozynski, helping to plan military operations. Zarutskii imposed strict discipline on rebel cossack forces and was put in charge of a special prikaz (office) for cossack affairs. When Iurii Bezzubtsev showed up with several thousand cossacks who had turned against Shuiskii and disrupted the siege of Kaluga, that wily commander immediately became one of Zarutskii's atamans.[37] Zarutskii's cossack detachments also swelled in size in this period as large numbers of runaway peasants and slaves from central Russia joined the ranks of the "free cossacks" and were allowed to serve side by side with new arrivals from the Don and Volga. Many more Ukrainian cossacks also drifted into "Tsar Dmitrii's" service in this period. Not surprisingly, cossacks continued to be the main rebel fighting force.[38]

There is an enormous amount of misinformation in historical literature about cossacks in the rebel army during the later stages of the Time of Troubles. Many past scholars insisted on viewing them as a monolithic force of social revolutionaries who were determined to spread "cossack democracy."[39] Nothing could be further from the truth. To start with, much of the Don cossack population stayed at home and did not even participate in the civil war. Although many free cossacks did join in the struggle against Tsar Vasilii, a large percentage of the "second false Dmitrii's" cossacks had never been to the Don and had only recently "gone cossack." Contrary to the views of Soviet scholars, cossacks in "Dmitrii's" service also did not form a united cossack host. They served instead in many different detachments that had little contact with one another. If they managed to preserve their quasi-democratic form of self-government at all, it was only at the smallest unit level. These men were not even allowed to elect their own atamans; Zarutskii and other boyars appointed the cossack commanders who served "Tsar Dmitrii." There was certainly no attempt made to impose cossack organization or customs on the rebel army as a whole or on areas liberated from Shuiskii's forces. Another faulty conclusion reached by Soviet scholars was that there was a gradual separation of atamans from rank-and-file cossacks in the impostor's service that resulted in a decline in radicalism on the part of the atamans—who supposedly began thinking more and more like gentry. In fact, there is no evidence of any such stratification or consciousness shift occurring among "Dmitrii's" cossack forces. Some atamans did receive pomeste estates, but that followed well-established precedents and did not change their status or behavior; groups of ordinary rebel cossacks also received towns and villages to exploit. It was actually Tsar Vasilii who tried to separate "better" cossacks in his service from rank-and-file cossacks in this period, and his efforts may have influenced the faulty view of increasing differentiation among the cossacks in "Dmitrii's" service. For cossacks in the rebel army, however, that differentiation actually came much later, after the Time of Troubles, and then as the direct result of a deliberate policy pursued by the new Romanov dynasty. Attempts to offer the incredibly atypical example of rich boyar Ivan Zarutskii as proof of growing differentiation among the cossacks in "Dmitrii's" service are completely without merit.[40]

Tsar Vasilii took steps to slow down the alarming movement of runaway peasants and slaves becoming cossacks in "Tsar Dmitrii's" service. On February 25, 1608, he issued an unprecedented new law guaranteeing those men their freedom if they would abandon the rebel cause. Shuiskii also offered amnesty and generous rewards to pomeshchiki and other soldiers who were willing to rejoin his service. For similar reasons, the tsar also made concessions to townsmen and possibly even to crown peasants.[41] Still camped in Orel at that time, the impostor quite naturally took similar steps. He sent a manifesto far and wide offering clemency for all those willing to switch to his side; and, just like Shuiskii, he promised freedom to all runaway peasants and slaves willing to join his service.[42] The impostor's decree proved to be a powerful magnet. However, the growing enthusiasm of the lower class for "Tsar Dmitrii's" promises of freedom to them, added to the large numbers of foreign troops in "Dmitrii's" army, deeply disturbed many rebel pomeshchiki from Severia and the Briansk region, who quickly lost interest in continuing the rebellion; those men now rushed to Moscow to take advantage of Tsar Vasilii's generous amnesty.[43] Seeing that happening, "Dmitrii" took an extraordinary step to prevent waverers from abandoning his service. He declared that the gentry switching to Shuiskii's side would have their property confiscated and redistributed to any of their servants who were willing to join his service. Even slaves were promised the lands, possessions, womenfolk, and titles of their traitorous former masters. "Dmitrii" actually followed through on his ominous threat in at least a few cases, which—of course—led to indignation and fear on the part of many lords and helped Shuiskii's cause.[44]

The "second false Dmitrii's" radical new policy has often been seen by scholars as a sign of social revolution of the masses, but all "Dmitrii" was really doing was trying to frighten lords into remaining loyal to him and trying to attract the military slaves of Shuiskii loyalists. Far from being revolutionary, this tactic was quite similar to Tsar Boris's practice of rewarding slaves with the property of the disgraced lords they had denounced.[45] In any case, if the impostor was generous to his lower class supporters, it is important to remember that he was even more generous to lords joining his service. "Tsar Dmitrii's" courtiers and commanders received lands confiscated from Shuiskii loyalists complete with serf labor. The impostor made no effort to abolish serfdom; instead, peasants on the estates he distributed were required to remain there. They could not leave on their own or be transferred. Even runaways had to be returned to their new lords. No doubt that helps to explain why large numbers of Russian gentry were attracted to "Tsar Dmitrii's" service.[46] There was certainly no social revolution emanating from the camp of the "second false Dmitrii." In fact, by spring 1608, the impostor attempted to appeal to "respectable" townsmen by distancing himself from the excesses of Tsarevich Petr and other cossack "tsareviches," by apologizing for past rebel terror and bloodshed, and by promising that he would restrain all his soldiers—including cossacks and foreigners— from looting and unnecessary violence. Appeals were also sent to Moscow to try to convince the boyars that they had nothing to fear by surrendering to the "true tsar."[47]

By the spring of 1608, the army of "Tsar Dmitrii" was large enough to begin an offensive against Shuiskii's forces. The rebel plan was to advance against Bolkhov with twenty-seven thousand men and, if successful there, to continue on to Moscow. In anticipation of that move, over the course of several months Dmitrii Shuiskii managed with considerable difficulty to concentrate about thirty thousand men in and around Bolkhov in order to stop the rebel offensive. The tsar's brother actively recruited cossacks and pulled many soldiers away from border fortresses, including Smolensk; in addition, more than a thousand pomeshchiki from northern Russia came to Bolkhov to help stop "Tsar Dmitrii's" progress. The rebel army approached Prince Shuiskii's position in late April.[48] A battle soon developed that lasted four days and was a disaster for the tsar's brother. Shuiskii apparently lost his nerve and began to retreat; that retreat very quickly degenerated into a panic-stricken flight toward Moscow. Many pieces of artillery and large quantities of supplies fell into rebel hands. Moscow reacted to news of the defeat and the arrival of the retreating troops with a mixture of terror and grief. Many people, including soldiers, began to believe that Tsar Vasilii was fighting a losing battle against the real Tsar Dmitrii.[49]

After achieving victory at Bolkhov, the impostor's army advanced toward Moscow—meeting almost no resistance. Tsar Vasilii tried to steady the population of the capital, declaring once again that the enemy planned to kill every-one in the city, including women and children. He also emphasized the par-ticipation of large numbers of hated Catholic mercenaries from Poland-Lithuania in the rebel movement. Far more important, the tsar replaced voevoda Dmitrii Shuiskii with his much-more competent and popular nephew, Mikhail Skopin-Shuiskii. Even the brilliant Skopin-Shuiskii, however, was unable to defeat the rebel army; he was also forced to waste time crushing a minor conspiracy against Tsar Vasilii among disgruntled lords. Nonetheless, he managed by the begin-ning of June to set up some hasty defense lines to protect the approaches to the capital. At this point, Tsar Vasilii made an extraordinary speech to his troops, offering to let them depart without punishment but encouraging them to stay to defend Moscow and his crown. Of course, all of them vowed to stay and fight for him. Soon, however, many changed their minds and defected to "Tsar Dmitrii."[50] In the meantime, the impostor's army settled in Tushino, a strate-gically located village only twelve kilometers northwest of Moscow that con-trolled several roads linking the capital to the west. "Dmitrii" set up his court there and stayed in Tushino for a long time. Gradually, an untidy, muddy, stink-ing suburb of tents and log huts sprang up into which was crowded a large pop-ulation of soldiers, courtiers, bureaucrats, and others. There were constant arrivals and departures and a feverish buzz of activity in Tushino. "Dmitrii's" new "capital" was too far away from Moscow to act as the operational base for the siege of that city, but it did have the advantage of being an easily defended position.[51]

The approach to Moscow by the rebel army and the presence of large num-bers of Polish troops in it finally convinced Tsar Vasilii to speed up peace nego-tiations with an envoy from King Sigismund. Shuiskii hastily agreed to release all Polish subjects who had been held captive since Tsar Dmitrii's assassina-tion—including Tsar Dmitrii's widow and father-in-law as well as the Polish ambassador, Alexander Gosiewski. The former prisoners, once released, were instructed to head straight for Poland-Lithuania; Marina Mniszech was specif-ically ordered not to refer to herself as "tsaritsa" and, under no circumstances, was she to recognize the Tushino impostor as her husband or to join him. In return for Shuiskii's display of good faith, the Polish envoy made a false promise that King Sigismund would recall his subjects from "Tsar Dmitrii's" camp.[52] Tsar Vasilii was so pleased by this arrangement that his military forces took no action for two weeks; many people thought the war must be over. Shuiskii even offered the impostor's commander-in-chief, Rozynski, a chance to participate in peace talks and a large sum of money for his troops as soon as they departed for home from Tushino. Rozynski took advantage of the situation and, on June

25, attacked Skopin-Shuiskii's army by surprise and so furiously that it was forced to retreat to the very gates of Moscow before finally stopping the enemy advance.[53] Just three days later, another rebel army that had approached Moscow from the south was also defeated and forced to retreat. Thanks primarily to Skopin-Shuiskii, the capital was now at least reasonably secure from direct, frontal attacks. That, unfortunately, set the stage for a very long, drawn-out and ruinous siege that lasted for a year and a half.[54]

"Tsar Dmitrii's" forces dug in at Tushino. For over a year Russia experienced the bizarre spectacle of having two tsars, two courts, and two armies. In Tushino a rudimentary bureaucracy carried out many normal government activities around the clock. "Tsar Dmitrii's" principal advisers quickly grew beyond Rozynski, Zarutskii, and Bezzubtsev to include several prominent Russian lords who abandoned Moscow for Tushino and were quickly rewarded with high positions, land, and peasants. Some of those lords—derisively called "migratory birds" by a contemporary—later brazenly returned to Moscow in search of even more rewards; but quite a few aristocrats stayed on in the Tushino impostor's service. Those Russian lords were no more impressed by "Tsar Dmitrii" than the Poles were, but they were nevertheless determined either to fight against Shuiskii or to profit from the civil war. On the Tushino impostor's boyar council sat such powerful men as Mikhail G. Saltykov and Dmitrii Trubetskoi. They were soon joined by several of Tsar Dmitrii's former courtiers, including Grigorii Shakhovskoi and Mikhail Molchanov. The Saltykov and Romanov families were by far the most influential Russians in Tushino. Members of the Romanov clan, in particular, as bitter foes of Tsar Vasilii, flocked to Tushino—including the Troekurovs, the Sitskiis, and the Cherkasskiis. Filaret Romanov himself, then serving as metropolitan of Rostov, was "captured" by the rebels in October 1608 and brought to Tushino where he was graciously received by the "tsar" and quickly resumed his old title of patriarch of the Russian Orthodox Church. The Tushino boyars secretly corresponded with friends and relatives in Moscow and enticed many of them into "Dmitrii's" service. When some of those lords later became dissatisfied and returned to Moscow, Tsar Vasilii did not have them executed as traitors. Instead, the beleaguered tsar treated them gently and tried, with little success, to use their testimony to help prove that "Dmitrii" was a fraud.[55]

Much to the alarm of Tsar Vasilii, in September 1608, Tsaritsa Marina (who did not wish to go home and was desperate to hold onto her crown) and her father were both "captured" by the rebels and brought to Tushino. After intense secret negotiations, Marina "recognized" the impostor as her husband. That news spread rapidly and electrified the nation. Many people were convinced by her action that Tsar Dmitrii must still be alive. As a result, even more gentry and aristocrats made their way to Tushino.[56] Eventually, several members of Tsar Dmitrii's foreign bodyguard also turned up there, including Captain Margeret—whose military expertise and intimate knowledge of Dmitrii proved to be quite valuable.[57]

The Tushino impostor and his court, far from being radical, projected a conservative, aristocratic image and jealously guarded the exalted status of the resurrected tsar. However, because of the amazing story of Tsar Dmitrii and the subsequent activities of Tsarevich Petr and the "second false Dmitrii," Russia was virtually inundated by a wave of opportunistic copy-cat tsarist pretenders during the later stages of the civil war. Up to ten more pretenders, usually of slave or peasant background, were produced by various cossack groups. We have already seen how Tsarevich Ivan-Avgust, operating on the Volga, had caused serious problems for Tsar Vasilii during the summer of 1607; but with the establishment of the snobbish court of "Tsar Dmitrii," Ivan-Avgust and other cossack pretenders came to be viewed by the Tushinites as potential rivals or as sources of embarrassment. "Tsar Dmitrii" eventually ordered even his extremely loyal "nephew," "Tsarevich Fedor Fedorovich," put to death to please his new courtiers and to attract more Russian lords to his cause. After extremely useful service against Tsar Vasilii, Tsarevich Ivan-Avgust also made the mistake of traveling to Tushino to join his "younger brother." There he was unceremoniously hanged. "Tsar Dmitrii" also sent out manifestos stating that all false tsareviches were to be seized and brought before him for judgment, and he offered great rewards for their capture.[58] The Tushino impostor, it seems, would tolerate no others.

Throughout the summer of 1608, Tushinite forces tried without success to capture Moscow or to blockade it completely; elsewhere they met little resistance because of Shuiskii's unpopularity and growing enthusiasm for "Tsar Dmitrii." Even in Moscow, although Tsar Vasilii remained defiant, the capital's besieged population grew increasingly nervous and hungry, and many merchants and others abandoned the city to avoid being trapped there or killed.[59] The arrival in Tushino of Jan-Piotr Sapieha (a kinsman of Lithuanian Grand Chancellor Lew Sapieha) with seven thousand cavalrymen in August speeded up rebel military activity and clearly demonstrated that King Sigismund was not abiding by his agreement with Shuiskii to prevent his subjects from raising troops for "Dmitrii." Although Sapieha and Rozynski did not particularly like one another, their uneasy alliance marked the complete triumph of foreign officers within the rebel high command.[60] Under their influence, a new strategy was developed for occupying the area around the capital and invading the northern provinces.

So confident were the rebel commanders of their own strength and Tsar Vasilii's weakness that they decided to split up their forces for those operations. In September, Rozynskii's detachments concentrated on the area west and south of Moscow while Sapieha led about fifteen thousand troops north of the capital. Sapieha quickly seized many roads and villages and cut Moscow off from the north; he then laid siege to the wealthy and strategically located Trinty-St. Sergius monastery (approximately 70 kilometers north of Moscow).[61] Tsar Vasilii responded by sending his brother Ivan with fifteen thousand troops to dislodge Sapieha, but the collision of those forces resulted in disaster for Prince Shuiskii. Thousands of his men were killed or wounded, and only a small number of them managed to get back to Moscow. Many others simply disappeared; a few may have joined the rebels but most of them just went home.[62]

The Tushino court was by then facing serious financial problems trying to pay its mercenary soldiers and trying to fund an active war against Tsar Vasilii, but Shuiskii's own forces were now so utterly depleted that he could no longer field an army against "Dmitrii" without resorting to his enemy's strategy of importing foreign military assistance. After haughtily dismissing offers of Swedish military assistance in 1606, Tsar Vasilii now entered into serious negotiations with King Karl IX. The tsar sent his popular nephew Skopin-Shuiskii to Novgorod for the important task of concluding an agreement with the Swedes. In the meantime, Sapieha's forces, in spite of their victory over Ivan Shuiskii's army, were completely frustrated in their attempts to capture the Trinity-St. Sergius monastery by storm or by stratagem. The fortress-monastery, actively supplied by the local population, heroically and successfully resisted the siege for sixteen months.[63]

During the fall of 1608, Rozynski's troops tried to close the blockade around Moscow by concentrating on Kolomna, which controlled the road between the capital and the grain-producing Riazan region. The rebels were unable to capture the town, however. They were stopped by the brilliant Prince Dmitrii Pozharskii in his first action as a commander. Thanks to Pozharskii's men, Moscow retained its lifeline to the southeast; grain and small gentry detachments from the Riazan area continued to reach the beleaguered Tsar Vasilii.[64] Almost everywhere else, however, the Tushinites were incredibly successful due primarily to the absence of any opposing military forces capable of challenging them and to renewed—if temporary—popular enthusiasm for "Tsar Dmitrii."

Despite the claims of Shuiskii propaganda, the rebels faced no significant resistance in most towns in the Moscow region or in the northern and northeastern districts that had previously been untouched by the civil war. Many towns were, in fact, greatly attracted by "Dmitrii's" lavish promises of gentle treatment and tax exemptions. Tushinite forces were thus able to fan out over a vast territory in central and northern Russia. They quickly occupied Vladimir, Suzdal, Arzamas, Balakhna, Vologda, Pereiaslavl Zalesskii, Iaroslavl, Kostroma, and Galich. Rostov's large clerical population, however, did resist the rebels and attempted to keep the townspeople from recognizing "Tsar Dmitrii"; the end result was that Rostov was destroyed. Events in Pskov were just as dramatic. Many of the Pskov region's villages and soldiers responded enthusiastically to the progress of "Tsar Dmitrii," and it was difficult for Shuiskii loyalists to keep Pskov's inhabitants from joining the rebel cause. Couriers from Tushino caused quite a stir among the town's population, who grew indignant when those men were thrown in prison by voevoda Petr Sheremetev. Already angry about Tsar Vasilii's heavy tax levies and fearful that he was planning to hand Pskov to the Swedes, in September 1608 soldiers and townsmen suddenly arrested their voevoda, opened the gates to local rebel forces, and swore an oath to "Tsar Dmitrii." Then they released the four hundred rebel prisoners who had been detained in Pskov since December 1606. Those rebels, along with many townsmen and peasants from all over central and northern Russia, made their way to Tushino to join "Tsar Dmitrii's" forces while a small number of Pskov's wealthier citizens (especially merchants) fled in terror to Novgorod. As soon as officials from Tushino arrived in Pskov, stubborn Shuiskii loyalists—including Petr Sheremetev—were put to death in horrible ways. Pskov became an ardent supporter of "Tsar Dmitrii." Neither Shuiskii's Novgorodian troops nor Swedish soldiers were ever able to recapture the town. Even though there was at least one more bloody revolt by Pskov's merchants and some clergymen sympathetic to Tsar Vasilii, that was not enough to overcome popular support for "Tsar Dmitrii." Pskov simply would not yield to Shuiskii.[65]

So successful was the rebel offensive that by late 1608 more than half of Russia recognized "Tsar Dmitrii." To follow up that campaign, the impostor's commanders sent forces from Balakhna to lay siege to Nizhnii Novgorod in an effort to open up a path to the central and lower Volga where enthusiasm for "Tsar Dmitrii" was strong and growing. That bold move was probably influenced by reports of new uprisings against Shuiskii among the Tatars, Mordvians, Chuvashi, and Cheremis.[66] However, Nizhnii Novgorod stubbornly resisted the rebel siege and even drove the besiegers away. Another rebel detachment sent against the city was also defeated and its commander was captured and hanged by Shuiskii loyalists. Nizhnii Novgorod continued to defy rebel forces and to provide desperately needed funds to Tsar Vasilii. Its troops also helped recapture Murom and Vladimir in early 1609.[67]

Elsewhere, troops from loyal Kazan and from voevoda Fedor Sheremetev's army also scored some minor successes against rebel forces to the east, and Liapunov continued waging his terror campaign against rebel villages in the Riazan area.[68] But there was no denying that Tushino was gaining the upper hand. Tsar Vasilii found himself stuck in Moscow surrounded by rebel forces and receiving reports almost daily about "Dmitrii's" army gaining control of another part of his realm. In despair, Shuiskii supposedly turned to sorcery to defeat the ghost of Tsar Dmitrii. Increasingly cut off from his revenue sources, the tsar also continued to demand large sums of money from wealthy monasteries. Meeting considerable resistance, he eventually ordered the confiscation of precious silver objects from churches and monasteries in order to melt them down to mint coins to pay his soldiers. Some clerics never forgave Shuiskii for that radical act.[69]

Just when it appeared that Tsar Vasilii was doomed, he was unwittingly granted a reprieve by the Tushinites. What saved him was the debt, arrogance, greed, corruption, and excessive violence of "Tsar Dmitrii's" commanders. Because the Tushino court could not actually afford to pay or even properly maintain its own soldiers, they were soon forced to forage for themselves. Willingly or not, rebel cossacks had to become robbers, which quickly alienated many potential supporters of "Tsar Dmitrii."[70] In much the same way, the foreign mercenaries from Tushino threw away much of the good will toward "Dmitrii" that had developed in relatively prosperous north Russia. By raiding towns and villages for booty, food, and horses, those men turned many Russians into angry opponents of the Tushino impostor. For example, the town of Iaroslavl had been so enthusiastic about "Dmitrii" that it sent treasure and supplies to Tushino and promised to equip one thousand cavalrymen for the "true tsar." The Tushino authorities foolishly responded by demanding even more and began to confiscate merchandise from many of Iaroslavl's petty traders. Not surprisingly, that provoked extreme anger among the local population who quickly lost enthusiasm for "Dmitrii."[71]

Everywhere else the story was much the same. Even if one of the Tushino commanders was diplomatic enough not to steal everything from a community, another commander would soon come along and confiscate what was left. Friendly towns were overassessed and overtaxed, and the protests of local leaders were ignored or were met with threats of violence. In this way, the Tushinites in very short order caused an indescribable amount of misery and provoked much anger throughout central and northern Russia. (Severia and the Komaritsk district—long in rebel hands—were left undisturbed and enjoyed peace and good harvests at this time.)[72]

"Tsar Dmitrii's" commanders also stirred opposition when they installed themselves on lands confiscated from "traitors" and indiscriminately seized other properties as well, claiming those estates as their "patrimonies." Not surprisingly, they ruthlessly exploited their new holdings and overworked and abused their serfs. Because unpaid rebel cossacks who had turned to banditry also wreaked havoc and stirred enormous hostility, the Tushino authorities eventually attempted to placate both their wavering subjects and the grumbling cossacks by granting individual cossack units the right to collect food (and possibly even taxes) from certain specific towns (e.g., Vladimir) and villages. This high-status form of maintenance, known as *kormlenie,* was usually reserved for high-ranking officials; the novel idea of extending it to the rebel cossacks may have been imported from Ukraine. The first hint of the use of kormlenie by rebels in the civil war occurred in 1607, but it became a regular part of the Tushino court's attempt to control and feed its cossack troops. In fact, even cash-strapped Tsar Vasilii occasionally resorted to this unprecedented method of maintaining cossack forces in his own army. Cossack kormlenie fell on palace lands, monastic property, privately-owned estates, and even taxable state lands. Cossack kormlenie quickly came to be viewed by the gentry on both sides during the civil war as a serious threat to their own status; they grew incensed at increasing cossack competition for income, labor, land, and military significance. Even more alarming, some Tushino cossacks were also granted pomeste estates, which they ruthlessly exploited. Members of the gentry and other professional soldiers came to fear the rebel cossacks for their rising status as well as their violence and greed. Since more and more peasants and slaves relatively unskilled at warfare "went cossack" during this stage of the civil war and swelled the ranks of "Tsar Dmitrii's" army, the privileges received by those new arrivals were especially disturbing to members of the gentry, who complained bitterly to "Tsar Dmitrii" about the pushy new cossack recruits.[73]

In general, the Tushinite commanders and troops threw away a great opportunity by foolishly behaving as if they were occupying enemy territory rather than liberating it from the usurper Shuiskii. Any protest against or opposition to rebel predation was savagely punished. Swiftly and inevitably, that led many people to break with "Tsar Dmitrii." Since there was no hope that Tsar Vasilii would come to their rescue, however, those unhappy men and women were forced to organize their own active resistance to the cruel Tushinite oppressors.

A popular movement against the Tushino impostor and his greedy and violent foreign mercenaries and cossacks began in late November 1608 in the north Russian town of Galich. Angry townsmen organized a makeshift militia in order to protect themselves from the Tushinites, and in the name of "the entire realm" they called upon other towns in the region to join their struggle. Soon Vologda,

Kostroma, and many other towns and villages also rose in rebellion. Townspeople and peasants from crown lands and taxable state lands worked together to throw off the Tushino yoke. Within just a few months, rebellion against "Tsar Dmitrii" swept across a huge part of northeastern Russia.[74]

Vologda, the most important town in the region, quickly emerged as the nerve center of the resistance movement. Many Russian merchants who had abandoned besieged Moscow were settled in Vologda, and most of the European merchants who still traded with war-torn Russia via the White Sea also chose to conduct their business in that relatively peaceful town. As we have already seen, Russian merchants tended to favor Tsar Vasilii during the civil war, and the merchants of Vologda proved to be no exception. They became energetic foes of the Tushino impostor. They also had such a high opinion of the Dutch and English traders they did business with that they used those foreigners as advisers and to maintain contact with Prince Skopin-Shuiskii in Novgorod. Vologda's ordinary townspeople and neighboring free peasants were also quick to join the resistance movement because of the ruthless exploitation they experienced at the hands of the Tushinite lords who had installed themselves in the area. Prompted by Galich, during the winter of 1608–9, fed-up and angry Vologda area peasants and townspeople rebelled against the local Tushinite authorities, cut off their heads, and swore an oath to Tsar Vasilii. In Vologda, a regional council of defense was set up, regular communications were established and maintained with other towns, and volunteers and supplies were gathered for the resistance movement. Soon, the town was awash in relatively cheap food and other supplies for the conflict. A largely-peasant militia was formed, and a small-scale war against the Tushinites quickly developed.

Led by Vologda, the area's towns attempted to coordinate all their resistance activities with Prince Skopin-Shuiskii. Much to the surprise of the Tushino court, by early 1609, a full-scale popular rebellion against "Tsar Dmitrii" was raging in north Russia. Many towns and thousands of peasants and townsmen fought aggressively against the Tushinites, managing to clear them out of a large portion of the region surprisingly quickly. In response, Sapieha sent military forces under the command of the particularly cruel and ruthless Alexander Lisowski to reoccupy the area and to punish the rebels. After some initial success, however, by spring 1609 even Lisowski's forces were driven away by local militia units. There is no doubt that in this phase of the civil war "Tsar Dmitrii's" forces might very well have prevailed over Tsar Vasilii if it had not been for the energetic actions of north Russian townspeople and free peasants. In Moscow, the beleaguered tsar was surprised but very pleased by the news coming from Vologda.[75]

Tsar Vasilii was initially unable to offer any meaningful assistance to or to profit militarily from the growing rebellion against the Tushino impostor. Shuiskii still faced large enemy forces just outside the gates of the capital, was still unable to raise a new army, and continued to be an unpopular ruler. In fact, at this point his enemies in Moscow attempted a coup d'état. The ringleaders included Grigorii Sunbulov, Mikhail Molchanov (who came into the capital secretly from Tushino), and Shuiskii's old companion in regicide, Mikhail Tatishchev. In February 1609, the conspirators, numbering about three hundred, managed to enter the Kremlin and stormed into a boyar council meeting demanding the overthrow of the "stupid, indecent and obscene tsar." Most boyars quickly retreated to their homes, but treacherous Prince Vasilii Golitsyn accompanied the conspirators to Red Square. Along the way, the troublemakers came across Patriarch Hermogen, roughed him up, and dragged him to Red square with them. There the conspirators called upon the inhabitants of Moscow to rise against Tsar Vasilii—the unelected ruler responsible for thousands of deaths and Moscow's current misery. An appeal to recognize "Tsar Dmitrii," however, had no effect whatsoever on the gathered crowd, which soon began to break up. In a panic, the conspirators themselves left Red Square in a hurry. Tsar Vasilii, who had locked himself up in his palace, managed to survive primarily due to Patriarch Hermogen's support. In retaliation, he had Tatishchev put to death but correctly felt that he was in no position to move against Golitsyn or anyone else.[76] The unloved tsar, now being deserted by some of his former allies, began to place all his hopes on his nephew's negotiations to secure Swedish military assistance.

Even as good news reached Tsar Vasilii from north Russia, trouble continued to pop up everywhere else. In the spring of 1609, the Tushinites renewed the siege of Kolomna in order to complete the blockade of Moscow. Although the Kolomna road was closed only briefly during the siege, that was enough to affect the hungry capital. Food prices there, already high, suddenly skyrocketed. Moscow's already siege-weary population suffered a great deal—especially the poor, who now starved to death by the hundreds each day. Hungry Muscovites frequently gathered on Red Square to express their dissatisfaction, and more plots against Tsar Vasilii were hatched. This time, however, Shuiskii's investigation of treason produced a surprising conspirator—Tsar Vasilii's close friend and principal ally in achieving the crown, boyar Ivan Kriuk-Kolychev. He was tortured and then beheaded by command of the now-friendless and increasingly paranoid usurper.[77]

The news from southeastern Russia was also alarming. It seems that Prokofii Liapunov, who had probably been involved in the failed February coup against Shuiskii, now began to maneuver for power himself. Falsely claiming descent from Riurik, the legendary ninth-century founder of the ruling dynasty of Rus, Liapunov gained the allegiance of a few towns and began to fight against both

Tsar Vasilii and "Tsar Dmitrii." Briefly styling himself the "white tsar," Liapunov caused enormous damage and killed many people.[78] During the summer of 1609, the Crimean Tatars also invaded Russia, inflicted much damage, and took many captives back to their slave markets. Shuiskii, too embarrassed to admit his utter inability to oppose them, at first foolishly tried to claim that he had invited the Crimean Tatars to come help him in the struggle against Tushino. When the Tatars crossed the Oka and carried out merciless attacks on Shuiskii's own realm (menacing Serpukhov, Borovsk, and Kolomna), however, the tsar's reputation suffered badly.[79] In fact, Riazan area support for the "white tsar" may well have been greatly boosted by the apparent betrayal of the region by Tsar Vasilii. By September, Shuiskii was so weak and discredited that his boyars were able to force him to rescind his generous 1607 decree promising freedom to involuntary slaves and to return to Boris Godunov's extremely unpopular and draconian 1597 slave law. Once again, the greedy lords were given permission to enslave unfortunate men against their will. Even viewed charitably as a sincere effort to cut off a significant source of the rebel cossacks, this unpopular decision only served to convince many people that they had no choice but to continue fighting against the boyar-tsar in Moscow.[80]

The news from north Russia was far more encouraging to Tsar Vasilii. Just three days after the failed February coup, Prince Skopin-Shuiskii concluded an agreement with King Karl IX's representatives in Vyborg. In return for the transfer to Sweden of the fortress of Korela and its surrounding towns and villages as well as the tsar's renunciation of any claims to Livonia, the Swedes agreed to provide up to five thousand soldiers to be paid by Tsar Vasilii.[81] The agreement was extremely unpopular in the border area being transferred to Sweden, but Shuiskii gambled that the foreign troops would help him save his crown.

The Swedes actually managed to raise only three thousand mercenaries (mostly Germans, English, Scots, and French) for Russian service, and those men joined Prince Skopin-Shuiskii in Novgorod. The tsar's nephew, after carefully coordinating his planned offensive with the militias of north Russia then liberating the region from the Tushinites, advanced against the enemy from Novgorod on May 10, 1609, along with the newly-hired mercenaries and three thousand Russian troops of his own. Skopin-Shuiskii quickly drove the Tushinites from Tver, immediately after which his unpaid mercenaries rebelled against their own greedy officers. Most of those soldiers departed for the border, robbing villagers and townspeople along the way; only a few hundred foreigners remained in Skopin-Shuiskii's army.

To the surprise of many, popular uprisings against "Tsar Dmitrii" in north

Russia, not foreign military assistance, turned the tide at this point. Detachments of peasants and townsmen from Iaroslavl, Kostroma, and elsewhere soon joined Skopin-Shuiskii's forces, as did about three thousand soldiers from Smolensk. The tsar's nephew was thus able to quickly build his army back up to about fifteen thousand men; even a few cossacks joined him. Skopin-Shuiskii's army became powerful enough to cleanse the Tushinites from his path as he marched south. When he reached Aleksandrov, he had his forces build fortifications and dig in to await the arrival of voevoda Fedor Sheremetev's army, then advancing from Nizhnii Novgorod. That excellent strategy was designed to close north Russia off completely to the Tushinites. Sapieha immediately perceived the danger to his own forces which were then still bogged down in the siege of Trinity-St. Sergius monastery. For that reason, he advanced against Skopin-Shuiskii in August but was defeated in a two-day battle. After that the brilliant Skopin-Shuiskii systematically beat back Tushinite forces wherever he could, all the while carefully fortifying the strong points that guarded the roads north to the large territory already liberated from "Tsar Dmitrii's" forces. Eventually, Sapieha and Rozynski combined their armies in a desperate attempt to destroy the powerful threat posed by Skopin-Shuiskii, but they were decisively defeated. After that, Tushino's power declined rapidly.[82]

"Tsar Dmitrii's" court was by this time deeply in debt, and most of the impostor's soldiers went unpaid. Bad news from north Russia and elsewhere caused "Dmitrii's" boyar council to begin falling apart. Even worse, some of his Polish commanders began to negotiate with King Sigismund, who had invaded Russia in September 1609 and laid siege to the great fortress of Smolensk. Only Sigismund's lack of ready cash to pay those officers prevented them from immediately departing from Tushino for Smolensk. "Tsar Dmitrii" himself grew increasingly desperate as news of Skopin-Shuiskii's relentless advance provoked desertions and fights among his remaining advisers. As rumors circulated of treason, the Tushino court spun completely out of control. The suspicious and violent Rozynski eventually put the "tsar" under close watch and threatened to behead him for plotting with Rozynski's enemies (meaning other Tushino commanders). However, with the aid of some loyal cossacks, "Dmitrii" managed to flee in disguise to Kaluga in late December 1609.

The "tsar's" departure caused the entire Tushino camp to break up in disarray. Some Tushinites followed the impostor to Kaluga while others began serious negotiations with King Sigismund.[83] Once again, friendless Tsar Vasilii was saved—but only temporarily. Foreign intervention soon overwhelmed him and transformed the civil war into a bitter, chaotic struggle for the very survival of an independent Russia.

22

*Foreign Intervention and the Formation of the
National Liberation Movement*

In the final years of the Time of Troubles the struggle between Tsar Vasilii and
"Tsar Dmitrii" was overwhelmed by foreign intervention. Russia's neighbors
took advantage of the civil war to grab territory and, in the process, pushed the
country into chaos. For a time, Russia had no tsar, and its very survival as an
independent state was in serious doubt. It proved to be extraordinarily difficult
to get the factions that had been struggling against each other to cooperate
against foreign aggression, but that powerful external threat eventually pushed
many Russians to set aside their differences in a desperate effort to regain control of their destiny and to restore order in their war-torn land.

Despite faulty scholarship blaming much of the civil war on Poland, King
Sigismund had actually been careful to avoid provoking conflict with Russia
up to this point. Allowing some of his subjects to enter Tushinite service had
more to do with the king's desire to get rid of those unruly men than it did with
his dreams of Polish expansion eastward. Nevertheless, Russia's internal distress
stirred Sigismund's interest. At first, the king's hands were tied by the truce he
had signed with Boris Godunov, which had been reconfirmed after Vasilii Shuiskii
seized power. Sigismund was also understandably reluctant to get involved in
a foreign conflict while he was facing a growing rebellion at home. By the summer of 1607, a huge mutiny against the king peaked with open combat between
the mutineers and royalist forces under the command of crown hetman (commander) Stanislas Zolkiewski; but Zolkiewski's men won a decisive victory at
the battle of Guzów on July 6, 1607 (New Style). As a result, many mutineers
(e.g., Pan Mikolaj Miechowicki) drifted across the border into the service of
"Tsar Dmitrii" searching for employment and riches. The king encouraged them
to go, thereby simultaneously ridding himself of troublemakers and further
weakening Russia. Later, Sigismund also encouraged some of his allies to lead
their private detachments into Tushinite service in the hope that those men
might create opportunities for Poland-Lithuania. Sigismund even managed to
convince himself that the boyars, exasperated by Tsar Vasilii's failures and unpopularity, were ready to hand him the Russian throne. At one point, the king made

secret plans to seize Chernigov and Novgorod Severskii but was blocked by opposition from Zolkiewski and other Polish aristocrats. Forced to sit on the sidelines, Sigismund searched for a plausible pretext for direct military intervention in Russia. He did not have to wait long.[1]

The pretext the Polish king needed was provided by Tsar Vasilii's agreement with King Karl IX (February 1609), which ceded territory to Sweden in return for mercenary forces. Not only was Karl Sigismund's hated cousin who had deposed him as king of Sweden and usurped the throne, but the Treaty of Vyborg that Skopin-Shuiskii had negotiated with Karl committed Russia to an eternal alliance with Sweden aimed against Poland-Lithuania and transferred territory to Sweden that directly threatened Sigismund's newly acquired Livonian possessions.[2] As a result, the Polish king's advisers stopped objecting and began helping him make plans for military intervention in Russia. Their immediate goal was the great fortress of Smolensk (lost by Lithuania to the Russians in 1514), which Sigismund's commanders were certain would submit without much of a struggle. The king took personal charge of the siege in September 1609, calling upon all his subjects in Tushinite service to rally to him and help capture Smolensk. As noted in the last chapter, only Sigismund's lack of ready cash prevented many soldiers from immediately abandoning Tushino. Without the prospect of regular pay at Smolensk, however, some of them ended up following "Dmitrii" to Kaluga, instead. As a result, the king had at his disposal in the Smolensk siege camp only twelve thousand men and a few big guns—a completely inadequate force to capture the huge, state-of-the-art fortress. An attempt to take Smolensk by storm in October failed, forcing Sigismund to carry out a frustrating and expensive twenty-month siege that slowed down Polish intervention considerably.[3]

If King Sigismund had problems, they were not nearly as severe as those facing the Russian opponents of Tsar Vasilii. After "Tsar Dmitrii" fled to Kaluga, the Tushino camp quickly broke up and the siege of Moscow ended. In early 1610, Sapieha was forced to abandon the siege of Trinity-St. Sergius monastery, and Rozynski burned Tushino to the ground; both commanders then retreated to the west. News of the collapse of the Tushino camp reverberated across Russia. In Pskov, for example, the opponents of "Tsar Dmitrii" clashed again with his supporters. For several months there was much bloodshed and disorder in the town. Finally, in the spring of 1610, Shuiskii supporters, temporarily in the ascendancy, tried to force the inhabitants of Pskov to swear an oath to Tsar Vasilii. Instead, the Shuiskii-loyalist voevoda ended up being expelled from the town, and about two hundred citizens were imprisoned as traitors to "Dmitrii."[4] Nonetheless, even though Pskov continued to support the "second false Dmitrii," most Russian lords in the collapsing Tushino court came to believe that rebellion in the name of "Tsar Dmitrii" was now a lost cause. Unwilling to follow the impostor to Kaluga but still strongly opposed to Tsar Vasilii, they had few options left open to them. Not surprisingly, they chose to negotiate with Sigismund III. Patriarch Filaret, other members of the Romanov clan, boyar Mikhail G. Saltykov, and Mikhail Molchanov were ready to support Sigismund's son, Wladyslaw, as tsar.

After two weeks of intense negotiations in the Smolensk siege camp, the Russians produced a treaty on February 4, 1610, which they hoped would help end the civil war and restore order in Russia. It stipulated that Wladyslaw was to convert to Orthodoxy before becoming tsar, that serfdom was to be preserved (any peasant movement that might hurt the lords was to be forbidden), that Wladyslaw was not to free any slaves or allow them into his military service, that impoverished gentry were to be given small holdings to support their military service, and that the new tsar was to rule in the traditional way—by conferring with the boyars and the patriarch on important matters. Vague promises to pay the cossacks for their faithful service were also included. It has been asserted that this treaty represented an attempt by the boyars to impose "constitutional" restrictions on autocracy. It is far more likely, however, that it was merely an attempt by those desperate men to protect themselves from powerful favorites who might emerge in the court of Tsar Wladyslaw. The Russian lords negotiating with the Polish king probably did not dream of altering the basic structure of their government.[5] In any case, Sigismund did not guarantee that his son would abide by the treaty's conditions, but he was genuinely pleased to gain prestigious Russian allies. The king began to dream quietly of the complete conquest of Russia, which would, among other things, then allow him to crush Karl IX and regain the Swedish crown. Prospects for successful intervention soon improved even more; by March 1610, a large percentage of the Tushino Poles were finally enticed into Sigismund's service. In the same period, boyar Ivan Zarutskii repeatedly attempted to convince the Tushino cossacks to break with "Tsar Dmitrii" and join the Poles, but many of them refused. About two thousand cossacks openly defied their commander and set out for Kaluga; but Zarutskii and Rozynski had them ambushed, and many were killed. Ambitious and ruthless Zarutskii then led his remaining cossacks into Polish service—but only temporarily.[6]

The shock of the cold-blooded slaughter by Zarutskii of cossacks loyal to "Dmitrii" and the entry of the Tushino boyars into alliance with King Sigismund marked a turning point in the civil war for many rebels. Patriotic elements among the former Tushinite forces objected to aiding foreign intervention. Iurii

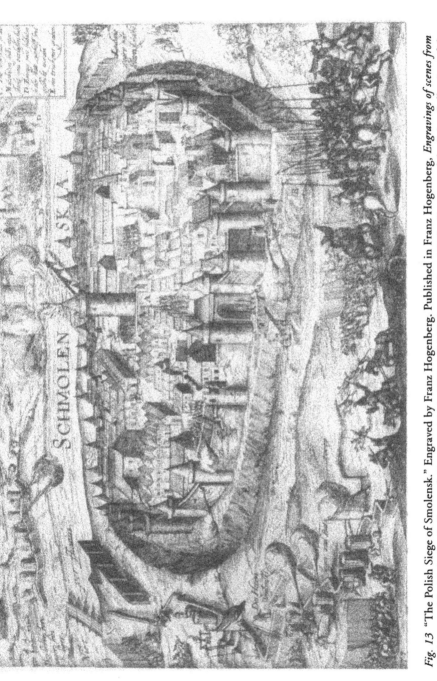

Fig. 13 "The Polish Siege of Smolensk." Engraved by Franz Hogenberg. Published in Franz Hogenberg, *Engravings of scenes from the history of the Netherlands, France & Germany 1535, 1558–1622* (Cologne, circa 1624). Courtesy of the Print Collection of the Miriam and Ira D. Wallach Division of Art, Prints and Photographs, The New York Public Library, and of the Astor, Lenox and Tilden Foundations.

Bezzubtsev and others broke decisively with those "traitors," and Bezzubtsev's cossacks began actively fighting against the interventionists without attempting to coordinate their activities with "Tsar Dmitrii" in Kaluga. In fact, many patriotic cossacks who eventually did go to Kaluga were deeply offended by Jan-Piotr Sapieha's obvious control over the "tsar" and regarded that as virtually the same thing as Polish intervention. As a result, many cossacks abandoned the cause of "Dmitrii" altogether. Some of them returned home but most chose to fight against the interventionists.[7] Even without those patriotic cossacks, however, "Tsar Dmitrii" somehow managed to stage a comeback.

After his flight from Tushino, the "tsar" had been warmly received in Kaluga, and its inhabitants agreed to help him fight against both Tsar Vasilii and Polish intervention. "Dmitrii" called upon his supporters to kill the hated foreign interventionists and to confiscate their possessions to aid the cause of the "true tsar." Many foreigners, not just Poles, were indiscriminately killed as a result. The impostor soon received a big boost when, in February 1610, Tsaritsa Marina (with the aid of Sapieha) made her way to Kaluga accompanied by a small detachment of cossacks and foreign mercenaries. She was very well received by her "husband" and the townspeople. Word soon went out far and wide that "Tsar Dmitrii" was alive and well and building a new army with which to regain his throne. By spring 1610, "Dmitrii's" army was growing rapidly. Prince Shakhovskoi brought thousands of Tushinite cossacks to Kaluga, and Jan-Piotr Sapieha brought a sizable detachment of foreign troops. Those forces were more than a match for the Crimean Tatars Tsar Vasilii induced to strike at the impostor's growing strength. By summer 1610, "Tsar Dmitrii's" army stood at ten thousand men; and, much to the surprise of his enemies, he was ready to march on Moscow.[8]

Meanwhile, Tsar Vasilii had been trying to make sense out of the conflicting reports coming in from all quarters and to plan his next moves. In March 1610, his brilliant nephew Skopin-Shuiskii made a triumphal entry into the capital widely hailed as the hero who had ended the siege of Moscow and eliminated the longstanding threat posed by Tushino. Skopin-Shuiskii was by this time far more popular than Tsar Vasilii and was being secretly promoted by Prokofii Liapunov and others as the next tsar. Although Skopin-Shuiskii immediately rejected the radical idea of toppling his uncle, the paranoid tsar learned about his nephew's flirtation with treason. Tsar Vasilii thereupon invited Skopin-Shuiskii to a private audience during which Shuiskii was reportedly urged to abdicate. Less than a month after that meeting, the popular commander died mysteriously. Many people claimed that he had been poisoned by a jealous relative, either the tsar himself or his brother Dmitrii—who was, in fact, hoping to succeed the childless ruler some day. Skopin-Shuiskii's death, whatever its cause, proved to be a disaster for the unpopular Tsar Vasilii. Few people believed the tsar sincerely mourned the loss of his nephew, and many suspected him of involvement in murder. To make matters worse, Skopin-Shuiskii's significant efforts to modernize and improve the fighting capacity and morale of the tsar's army also abruptly ended with his death.[9] Tsar Vasilii chose his militarily incompetent and extremely unpopular brother Dmitrii, now one of the only boyars he trusted, to replace Skopin-Shuiskii as his main commander; that appointment provoked strong protests among officers and soldiers alike. Prokofii Liapunov, who had already openly broken with Shuiskii and had tried to raise Riazan province and adjacent territories against him, now loudly called for the overthrow of the "murderer" of valiant Skopin-Shuiskii.[10]

King Karl, at least, did not break his self-serving alliance with the unpopular Tsar Vasilii. In 1610 he sent ten thousand mercenary troops to assist Shuiskii against Polish intervention. By then the tsar's spring levy of militiamen and recruits had boosted the size of his own army to thirty thousand men. Many cavalrymen, it seems, were strongly attracted to Shuiskii's offer of very high salaries. In early June, Dmitrii Shuiskii's assistant, voevoda Grigorii Valuev, advanced westward along the Smolensk road with six thousand men, cleared the area of rebels and interventionists, and set up a fortified camp near the village of Klushino (150 kilometers west of Moscow) in order to block any Polish offensive until additional forces arrived from Moscow. Hetman Zolkiewski, learning of Valuev's actions, swiftly advanced with a small army and surrounded the enemy's camp before Dmitrii Shuiskii or the Swedish general, Jacob de la Gardie, could arrive to assist the outnumbered Russian forces.

By June 23, Shuiskii and de la Gardie managed to reach Klushino and camped there with the intention of attempting to relieve Valuev the next day. Instead, Zolkiewski's somewhat smaller army (which contained many former Tushinites, including Zarutskii's cossacks) boldly advanced against Klushino and won a decisive battle in about four hours. As a result of secret negotiations, most of the mercenary forces were induced to abandon their Russian allies. (Captain Margeret, who entered Polish service along with Zarutskii, was probably responsible for the successful negotiations with the opposing mercenaries—for which he received rich rewards from King Sigismund.) De la Gardie, to save himself, concluded a hasty truce with Zolkiewski, as a result of which half of his men went over to the Polish side. The actions of the mercenaries plus Dmitrii Shuiskii's own cowardice quickly turned defeat and a somewhat chaotic retreat by the Russian army into a complete rout. Shuiskii's army broke up completely, and even Valuev was induced to switch sides upon receiving assurances that King

Sigismund would lift the siege of Smolensk as soon as his son became tsar. Zolkiewski now advanced to Viazma virtually unopposed and began making plans to march on Moscow. In the meantime, "Tsar Dmitrii's" small army also advanced from Kaluga against Moscow. That was enough to provoke successful uprisings in "Dmitrii's" name in Kashira and Kolomna. Soon, the impostor occupied Serpukhov and advanced all the way to Kolomenskoe, where he set up camp in preparation for a possible assault on the capital.[11]

The beleaguered and unpopular Tsar Vasilii no longer had an army. He unsuccessfully sought Crimean Tatar assistance; and he ordered an emergency gentry levy, which yielded very few men, to help prepare Moscow for yet another siege. Not surprisingly, Shuiskii's enemies became very active at this time. Large crowds flocked to Red Square to denounce unlucky Tsar Vasilii, who was forced to remain in hiding. In the meantime, Prokofii Liapunov, Vasilii Golitsyn, and others made plans to depose Shuiskii. Golitsyn dreamed of the crown for himself, but Mstislavskii and other boyars were more interested in the idea of "Tsar Wladyslaw" and the prospect of ruling Russia in his name. The extremely popular Filaret Romanov (who had been captured by Valuev and sent to Moscow as a "prisoner") also began quietly lobbying on behalf of Wladyslaw's candidacy. Tsar Vasilii was utterly powerless to put a stop to the plots, which now included some of the same leading merchants who had been among Shuiskii's strongest allies in the past. On July 16, 1610, one of "Tsar Dmitrii's" principal voevodas, Prince Dmitrii Trubetskoi, in a ruse, approached the capital and urged Moscow to get rid of Shuiskii while he, Trubetskoi, eliminated "Tsar Dmitrii." Then, he proposed, both sides could join forces, elect a new tsar, and put an end to the civil war. The very next day, July 17, thanks especially to the efforts of the Liapunovs and Golitsyns, a huge crowd assembled on Red Square demanding the overthrow of Tsar Vasilii. On cue, the boyars at this point finally arrested Shuiskii in spite of strong protests from Patriarch Hermogen.[12] They offered to grant the deposed tsar a virtually independent province centered at Nizhnii Novgorod if he would cooperate, but he sullenly refused. In frustration, the boyars took Shuiskii to his residence, beat him up, and had him forcibly tonsured as the monk Varlaam. He was then placed under close guard in a Kremlin monastery.[13]

The end of the reign of "Tsar Vasilii IV" marked the end of another phase in the civil war, but it did not end Russia's misery. Polish intervention continued, "Tsar Dmitrii" still had an army in the suburbs of the capital, and several Russian boyars now vied with one another for the crown. Moscow by then actually exercised little control over most of Russia; instead, chaos reigned in the land as small armies scoured the countryside for food and as thousands of displaced persons wandered around. Many people longed for a tsar capable of restoring order, but each group supported a different candidate. As a result, Russia disintegrated into near-collapse. In the end, however, anger against foreign intervention and the strong desire to have a native tsar saved the country from complete destruction.

In the days following the coup against Tsar Vasilii, Prokofii Liapunov, Patriarch Hermogen, and others tried to put Prince Vasilii Golitsyn on the throne, but that was blocked by the other boyars. Filaret Romanov, with the patriarch's approval, then proposed his fourteen-year-old son, Mikhail, as a candidate for tsar, but neither he nor anyone else could gain a majority during the boyar council deliberations. For that reason, the boyars voted to convene a zemskii sobor for the important task of choosing a new tsar. In the meantime, a council of seven boyars was appointed to rule (Mstislavskii, Vasilii Golitsyn, Ivan Romanov, Fedor Sheremetev, Ivan Vorotynskii, Andrei Trubetskoi, and Boris Lykov). Before a zemskii sobor could be convened, however, Zolkiewski's army quickly approached Moscow unopposed, and the hetman began extensive negotiations with the "council of seven" about Prince Wladyslaw becoming tsar. The Moscow boyars, whose interest in Wladyslaw's candidacy had been growing for several months, were at that time especially anxious to get rid of "Tsar Dmitrii's" forces then menacing the capital; and Zolkiewski cleverly offered to help them. In fact, the Russians were very impressed by the Polish commander's speeches, by the apparent willingness of Wladyslaw to convert to Orthodoxy, and by King Sigismund's lavish promises to grant "freedom" to the Russian gentry if they chose his son as tsar. Up to five hundred courtiers, gentry, bureaucrats, and others traveled to Zolkiewski's camp to negotiate final details. The council of seven was even prepared to welcome back without recrimination or punishment all of the Tushino lords who had joined forces with Zolkiewski except for one man—Ivan Zarutskii, Bolotnikov's old lieutenant who was of non-noble birth. Zolkiewski, who was running out of time and money, proved to be more than willing to sacrifice Zarutskii in order to close the deal. Learning of the betrayal, Zarutskii fled with his cossacks; news of his departure caused celebration among the lords in Moscow. The council of seven now quickly agreed to invite Wladyslaw to rule, and on August 17, about ten thousand Russians swore an oath of loyalty to Tsar Wladyslaw. Several towns immediately followed suit.[14]

The controversial decision by the council of seven to select Wladyslaw was always represented by them as the will of many layers of Russian society. Platonov and others interpreted the tendentious documents the boyars produced to mean that some kind of rump zemskii sobor had been hastily convened to approve Wladyslaw's election.[15] Other scholars doubted that any kind of zemskii sobor ever met for that purpose.[16] In fact, the key documents associated with Wladyslaw's selection were not signed by the boyar council (as was customary) nor even by all members of the council of seven. Those documents were also far more conservative and less conciliatory to the gentry than the agreement Sigismund had made with the former Tushino boyars several months earlier.[17]

Although many courtiers, bureaucrats, and merchants approved of Wladyslaw's selection, a number of boyars and Patriarch Hermogen flatly rejected the idea of a foreign tsar. Indeed, the council of seven's choice alienated many patriotic Russians, and popular suspicion of the boyars as greedy traitors grew much stronger as a result of that decision. As early as August 18, monks from the Simonov monastery made contact with "Tsar Dmitrii," and by August 20 many people began to quietly abandon Moscow for "Dmitrii's" camp. News of the "election" of Tsar Wladyslaw was also extremely unpopular in the provinces. Pskov refused to accept the decision, remaining steadfastly loyal to "Tsar Dmitrii." Soon, the inhabitants of Tver, Vladimir, Rostov, and Suzdal also broke with the "traitors" in Moscow and sent representatives to meet with "Tsar Dmitrii." In the meantime, Zolkiewski's forces quietly surrounded the suddenly more popular impostor's camp in Kolomenskoe. The hetman, in Sigismund's name, offered "Dmitrii" large estates in Poland-Lithuania if he would stop interfering in the king's business. Even though he seemed to be trapped, the "tsar" haughtily rejected the offer and somehow managed to flee to Kaluga. Unfortunately for "Dmitrii," Sapieha's forces defected from him at this time due to a large bribe paid by the council of seven. At least partially compensating for that loss, however, was the reentry of Zarutskii and his cossack troops into "Tsar Dmitrii's" service.[18]

Having rid the Moscow area of "Dmitrii's" forces, Zolkiewski then cleverly organized a grand embassy of Russian dignitaries to visit King Sigismund in the Smolensk siege camp, ostensibly to discuss Wladylaw's accession. What Zolkiewski actually had in mind, though, was the removal of all potential Russian candidates for the throne and others around whom opposition to Polish intervention might be organized. He had been secretly informed by Sigismund that the king did not intend to let his son become tsar but instead planned to conquer Russia himself. Keeping that news to himself, Zolkiewski managed to convince Vasilii Golitsyn and Filaret Romanov to join the embassy, and he briefly contemplated sending young Mikhail Romanov as well. The former Tsar Vasilii, now called Varlaam, and his two brothers were also included in the delegation going to Smolensk. Once the embassy reached Sigismund's camp, after much ceremonial stalling by the Poles, they were eventually informed of the king's plan to rule Russia in his own name. Quite naturally the Russians rejected that idea out of hand, whereupon they were all arrested and taken to Poland under guard. In that way, the Poles removed from Moscow for many years the men who might have been able to put a stop to Polish intervention. While in exile, the monk Varlaam and his brother, Dmitrii Shuiskii, died under mysterious circumstances in September 1612. Prince Golitsyn also died while in Polish captivity.[19]

The Poles made sure that Moscow only slowly learned of King Sigismund's real intentions. Even the council of seven was kept in the dark about the king's plans. For several months the unpopular boyars continued to labor under the illusion that Wladyslaw would eventually show up and share power with them. Those unhappy men were, therefore, at a loss to explain why Polish troops began a series of devastating raids on Russian towns (e.g., Kozelsk) and why Sigismund renewed siege operations against Smolensk (which had been temporarily suspended during the negotiations concerning Wladyslaw's candidacy). The council of seven, never popular, not only proved to be incapable of bringing peace to Russia but also ended up being double-crossed by the Poles. As that reality sank in, the capital began to seethe with discontent. King Sigismund received a report that many people in Moscow now regarded the boyars as traitors and wished to surrender to "Tsar Dmitrii." The council of seven, fearing the anger of its own subjects, at this point took the incredibly drastic and extremely unpopular step of inviting Zolkiewski's troops into the capital to restore order.

Real power in Moscow quickly came to rest in the hands of the Polish garrison commander, Alexander Gosiewski, and his Russian accomplices—especially boyar Mikhail G. Saltykov. A long-time associate of Saltykov's, Captain Margeret, was appointed to be one of the commanders (and paymaster) of the elite detachment of eight hundred mercenaries (mostly Germans) who formed the core of the occupation force. Those Russian lords who cooperated with the interventionists were greatly rewarded. Prince Mstislavskii, for example, received the exalted title of "master of the horse." Those lords who resisted were severely punished. The increasingly brutal Polish military dictatorship actually shoved aside most members of the council of seven, but those humiliated and basically irrelevant boyars—by remaining in the capital and not openly breaking with the hated Polish interventionists—now appeared to be traitors to most patriotic Russians who were horrified to see those greedy boyars allow the occupation of their capital by a foreign army bent on rape and pillage. King Sigismund's lavish gifts of titles and lands even nudged the confused and unpopular council of seven to order Smolensk to surrender to the Poles. That radical and unpatriotic command was, of course, ignored by the defenders of Smolensk; but it finally stirred Patriarch Hermogen and many others to step forward to openly denounce the council's "treason." In the resulting confusion, agents of "Tsar Dmitrii" openly agitated against the Poles on the streets of the capital. In reaction, Moscow's stern rulers arrested several prominent individuals, including Patriarch Hermogen—who was accused of unauthorized contact with "Dmitrii." Once again, the people of Moscow heard solemn warnings about the impostor "Dmitrii's" intention to murder the well-to-do of the capital and to confiscate their wives and property. Of course, most Muscovites did not believe that shopworn propaganda and instead came to deeply loathe Moscow's brutal foreign rulers and the Russian traitors who assisted them.[20]

During the summer and fall of 1610, Polish military forces and Russian detachments still loyal to the council of seven successfully cleared the Moscow area of soldiers loyal to "Tsar Dmitrii." After that, they cleansed Serpukhov and Tula of the impostor's supporters and began to threaten Kaluga itself. Zarutskii, quickly emerging as the real leader of "Dmitrii's" army, managed to inflict a serious defeat on those forces in November 1610—eliminating the immediate danger to Kaluga. The impostor's supporters were also cheered at that time by the news that Kazan's population had rebelled against voevoda Belskii, killed him, and sworn an oath to "Tsar Dmitrii." In spite of the good news, however, the "second false Dmitrii" grew increasingly fearful of treason and began foolishly to alienate his key supporters. He arbitrarily ordered arrests, confiscations, and executions, which increasingly outraged Tsaritsa Marina, the "tsar's" boyars, his foreign mercenaries, and many others. A clever undercover Polish effort to topple "Dmitrii" at this time resulted in forged documents that appeared to compromise the Kasimov Tatars who then made up the bulk of the paranoid tsar's bodyguard. In a fit of anger, "Dmitrii" had fifty of them detained briefly, beaten, tortured, and then released—including the captain of his bodyguard, the proud and high-born Prince Petr Urusov. In revenge, on December 11, 1610, while "Dmitrii" was sleighriding outside Kaluga, Urusov killed him.[21]

The shock of "Tsar Dmitrii's" death produced turmoil in Kaluga. In the midst of the town's mourning and animated discussions about what to do next, Tsaritsa Marina gave birth to "Tsarevich Ivan Dmitrievich" and begged the citizens of Kaluga and the cossacks to protect him as the rightful claimant to the throne. There was actually very little enthusiasm for the "whore Marina" and the "illegitimate baby brigand" among the Kaluga boyars, who seriously doubted that "Dmitrii" had fathered little Ivan and, in any case, were now anxious to reach some kind of agreement with the Moscow government. But the common people of Kaluga strongly opposed negotiations with the traitors who had let Polish troops occupy the capital, and the powerful Ivan Zarutskii—already scorned by Moscow—stood by Marina and her son, at least for the moment.

Kaluga's population swore an oath of loyalty to heir "Ivan Dmitrievich." There is considerable confusion in the sources about what happened next. Zarutskii, Marina, and Ivan soon departed from Kaluga, and boyar Dmitrii Trubetskoi quickly emerged as the senior commander of "Tsar Dmitrii's" former soldiers (mostly cossacks) who remained in that town. Marina and Ivan eventually settled in Kolomna where they were treated very well as legitimate claimants to the throne. Zarutskii, however, briefly flirted with rejoining Polish service before making contact with Prokofii Liapunov and other patriotic Russians to offer the service of his cossack forces for the daunting task of liberating Moscow from the interventionists and the traitors who supported them.[22]

The death of the "second false Dmitrii" caused rejoicing in Moscow among the members of the council of seven and their adherents, but his demise actually removed the chief obstacle to unifying the Russian people against foreign intervention. A powerful but still disjointed patriotic movement slowly began to develop throughout the land and even in Moscow. The capital was by this time once again growing hungry, and its people were tired of the escalating violence and greed of the Polish occupation forces—who had so much booty by this time that they occasionally loaded their guns with pearls and jewels instead of lead. Many fights broke out between Muscovites and interventionists, several foreigners were murdered, and the propaganda campaign against the Poles and their accomplices grew bolder. Retaliations were swift and fierce, and a smoldering, undeclared war developed over the course of several months. More sentries were posted, larger and more frequent patrols were conducted, attempts were made to disarm the townspeople, all movement by civilians was prohibited after dark, and entry into the city was severely restricted. More ominously, artillery was moved from Moscow's outer defenses to the Kremlin walls and aimed at the city's own streets. The council of seven and the Polish interventionists rightly felt themselves to be under a kind of slow-motion siege. Even under arrest, Patriarch Hermogen managed to send secret appeals to the citizens of Nizhnii Novgorod urging them to find a way to expel the heretics from the country. Hermogen revealed to them King Sigismund's plan to conquer and rule Russia, and he warned all Orthodox Christians to fight against Polish Catholic domination and the possible destruction of the Russian Orthodox church. Not surprisingly, his appeals were quite effective.[23]

Outside Moscow, opposition to Polish intervention developed spontaneously in several different areas. In many ways, it was a reprise of the powerful opposition to the oppressive Tushinites that had burst forth and swept across much of north Russia two years earlier. As former supporters of "Tsar Dmitrii" were now forced to make hard choices, many of them responded to the patriarch's appeal to their patriotism. In part for self-protection, in part for religious and national survival, some Russian commanders began ignoring the orders they received from the unpopular council of seven and instead clashed with Polish interventionists. They also began reaching out to other patriots.

Prince Dmitrii Pozharskii, the voevoda of Zaraisk, contacted Zarutskii and helped convince him to commit his forces to the national liberation movement. Some lords, including Prokofii Liapunov in Riazan province, openly declared war on the council of seven and Polish intervention. Liapunov summoned all patriots throughout the land to help him liberate Moscow. In retaliation, the council of seven ordered the arrest and torture of Liapunov's supporters in the capital and prevailed upon King Sigismund to send a detachment of Zaporozhian cossacks to raid Liapunov's home territory. Those cossacks quickly captured Tula and burned Aleksin. Liapunov himself came under siege in Pereiaslavl-Riazanskii by Moscow-loyalist forces under the command of Grigorii Sunbulov, but the beleaguered voevoda managed to dispatch an appeal to Pozharskii to help him. The brilliant Pozharskii quickly drove Sunbulov's forces away and inflicted a stinging defeat on King Sigismund's Zaporozhian cossacks. At about the same time, Zarutskii's Don cossacks managed to drive the interventionists out of Tula.

Almost overnight Pozharskii, Liapunov, and even Zarutskii gained enormous prestige and popularity for fighting against the hated foreigners. Very soon a loose-knit national liberation army began to form around Pozharskii and Liapunov. The patriotic movement grew very rapidly and spread all over the country—from Kaluga and Severia to Kazan in the east and Vologda in the north. Concerned citizens often crowded into their local church's refectory to discuss strategy, and it is clear that townspeople and peasants regarded their own unprecedented activism as part of a life-or-death religious struggle. Town after town joined the liberation movement with enthusiasm. Peaceful coups against the council of seven occurred with dizzying speed in Murom, in Vladimir, and—most importantly—in Nizhnii Novgorod and Iaroslavl.[24]

There were very good reasons why Patriarch Hermogen had appealed specifically to Nizhnii Novgorod to begin organizing opposition to Polish intervention. Not only was the town's religious life administratively under the direct supervision of the patriarch, but that prosperous central Volga trade and administrative center had stubbornly supported Tsar Vasilii (and Hermogen) against rebel forces on many occasions. Nizhnii Novgorod boasted strong fortifications and a garrison of five hundred streltsy. The town's wealth grew directly out of its strategic location at the intersection of several important trade routes. Nizhnii Novgorod's population of about eight thousand was primarily oriented to trade and maintained close ties with the inhabitants of many other towns on the Volga, in central and northern Russia, and even in Siberia. Nizhnii Novgorod's trade fairs were extremely famous and drew people from very far away. Its merchants, shopkeepers, blacksmiths, and boatbuilders were respected everywhere. Even though the civil war had shut down much Volga River traffic, Nizhnii Novgorod itself had suffered only a relatively modest decline in trade activity and profits. Nonetheless, the town's wealthy merchants and sturdy shopkeepers were nervous about the future and certainly had enough money to help finance the creation of an army of patriots to rid their land of foreign interventionists. Patriarch Hermogen was not disappointed by the powerful response of Nizhnii Novgorod's inhabitants to his appeal. The town's merchants soon emerged as the most important financiers of Russia's national liberation movement.[25]

In January 1611, Nizhnii Novgorod informed Prokofii Liapunov that the town, on the advice of Patriarch Hermogen and "the entire realm," had resolved to raise forces to liberate Moscow. Murom immediately sent a detachment of gentry and fortress cossacks to help with the task; Vladimir and Suzdal did likewise. Iaroslavl also began making military preparations at this time. When the rulers of Moscow sent five hundred streltsy to Vologda to put a stop to such activities, those soldiers were wooed into switching sides and immediately joined Iaroslavl's growing force of armed patriots.

Prokofii Liapunov sent agents to Nizhnii Novgorod to begin coordinating activities with them, and he also started aggressively recruiting cossacks formerly in "Tsar Dmitrii's" service. Liapunov made important concessions to those cossacks, offering them not only food, gunpowder, lead, and salaries if they would join the "national militia" but also promising freedom to any former slaves among them willing to fight against foreign intervention. The response was overwhelming. Thousands of "cossacks" came forward to serve. Some were, indeed, free cossacks from the Don and Volga; but many others were former slaves, serfs, and urban plebes from the Moscow region who had "gone cossack" while the Tushino impostor waged war against Tsar Vasilii or who became "cossacks" only in response to Liapunov's appeal. By early February 1611, Kaluga (under the control of boyar Dmitrii Trubetskoi) began cooperating actively with Liapunov's forces, as a result of which Kolomna was captured. When Serpukhov rebelled against the council of seven soon thereafter, Zarutskii's cossacks went to their aid along with five hundred streltsy from Vologda and Riazan province sent by Liapunov. The patriots very quickly consolidated their position near Moscow, and Liapunov sent letters to many towns outlining plans for the liberation of the capital. Although the rapid growth of the national liberation forces clearly demonstrated the unpopularity of the council of seven, personal rivalries among the leaders of the patriot movement, the wariness of many of them to cooperate with cossacks, and occasional clashes with detachments loyal to Moscow frustrated Liapunov's own ambitious plans at this time. The result was an uncoordinated advance against Moscow.[26]

In the capital, news of the approach of patriot forces stirred the city's population to action. Arms and soldiers were smuggled in and plans were made to coordinate a popular uprising with the patriot militia's attack. On March 19, 1611, however, a clash between townsmen and the hated Polish occupation force provoked a premature battle. Even without coordinated militia support, the Muscovites—soon joined by the Moscow streltsy—pressed the occupying forces so hard they were in danger of annihilation. Only the daring and ferocious assaults by Captain Margeret's German mercenaries saved the Polish garrison.

By March 21, elements of the "national militia" managed to force their way into Moscow's suburbs. In heavy fighting, however, Prince Pozharskii was seriously wounded, and his troops were forced to retreat. The Polish commander Gosiewski then immediately ordered much of the outer city burned. The fires raged for days and gave the Poles time to crush the uprising inside Moscow. In that bloody work they were actively assisted by Mikhail G. Saltykov, members of the council of seven (especially Fedor Mstislavskii, Fedor Sheremetev, and Ivan Romanov), other nobles, and rich merchants who greatly feared their own countrymen and knew what fate awaited them if the insurgents were successful. For the time being, at least, the "national militia's" efforts to liberate the capital had been blocked. Nevertheless, the Poles now held only the inner city (the Kremlin and the Kitaigorod district); the rest of Moscow was in ashes. Many of the city's inhabitants had perished in the fire; many others soon froze to death; and large numbers abandoned the capital in search of shelter and food or to join the resistance movement. The Polish garrison now began wholesale looting, in the process robbing and killing some of the same rich merchants who had just helped them crush the uprising. Gosiewski at this point dropped all pretense of cooperation with the council of seven. The dictator of Moscow abused several council members and began arbitrarily and violently cutting down any perceived opposition. After the uprising, Gosiewski also threw Patriarch Hermogen in prison. Even from there Hermogen still managed to continue stirring up the patriot cause by writing incendiary letters to Russian towns right up to his death by starvation in February 1612.[27]

The burning of Moscow profoundly shocked the Russian people and helped galvanize opposition to Polish intervention, but there was actually a long pause in patriot military operations during the spring of 1611. Pozharskii was temporarily out of action, and the imperious and arrogant Liapunov faced many difficulties trying to organize the "national militia." He and Zarutskii did manage to cooperate; they both administered an oath to their forces to fight against the Poles and to serve a tsar to be chosen by the "entire realm." Liapunov also proclaimed a general mobilization of Russia's entire gentry militia and warned all cavalrymen to appear before Moscow by May or risk losing their estates. Many pomeshchiki responded to his call. Liapunov and others also managed to set up a highly representative "national militia council" with members drawn from the "entire realm"—including dvoriane, deti boiarskie, common soldiers, and free cossacks. Unfortunately, there was constant bickering among the senior commanders over control of the patriot movement, and Liapunov had no choice but to reduce the high salaries some pomeshchiki had received during Tsar Vasilii's last desperate year in power. In addition, most national militia units lacked discipline, supplies, and heavy artillery. Zarutskii's and Trubetskoi's cossacks, however, did manage to dig in and fortify positions in Moscow's suburbs, and they gradually closed all paths to the capital except for the Smolensk road. As a result, supplying the Polish garrison in Moscow became extremely difficult and perilous.

Along the Smolensk road cossack raids and partisan activity kept increasing, even after the great fortress of Smolensk finally fell to King Sigismund on June 3, 1611. Patriotic soldiers arriving before Moscow from Kazan helped Zarutskii's men occupy Novodevichii monastery, from which they could constantly menace the all-important Smolensk road. The brilliant rebel commander Iurii Bezzubtsev and his cossack detachment also arrived from Severia to help capture Moscow. Polish attempts to neutralize the cossacks by offering them large rewards were flatly rejected; the cossacks declared that they were firmly committed to a Russian Orthodox tsar and to the expulsion of foreign interventionists. Irregular detachments of patriots (including Tatars, Mordvians, and Chuvashi) also arrived almost every day to bolster the forces arrayed before Moscow. Despite its growing strength, however, the loosely coordinated national militia was still not capable of taking the capital by storm. An effort to do just that was thrown back with heavy losses on July 5, 1611.[28]

To no one's surprise, the great city of Novgorod had balked at the council of seven's acceptance of Polish intervention in 1610. As a result, Mikhail G. Saltykov's son, Ivan, was sent there to enforce obedience to the council's controversial decision. Nervous city officials reluctantly admitted him only after he promised not to introduce foreign troops into Novgorod—as had happened in Moscow. Saltykov's regime was unpopular, especially after he ordered the executions of several hundred cossack rebels who had been languishing in the city's jails since the failure of Bolotnikov's siege of Moscow. Polish troops also terrorized the region around Novgorod, stirring great bitterness against the council of seven and voevoda Saltykov. At about the same time as the failed uprising in Moscow, a patriotic rebellion also broke out in Novgorod during which Ivan Saltykov was impaled. Novgorod's sudden decision to join the national liberation movement was big news in the camps before Moscow, but Swedish military intervention in Russia actually prevented that wealthy city from sending much aid to Liapunov.

Ever since the collapse of Tsar Vasilii's regime and the council of seven's agreement to have a Polish prince as tsar, King Karl felt that he had a good excuse to grab Russian territory for himself. As Polish military intervention in Russia gained momentum, Sweden's direct intervention in north Russia also picked up speed. Swedish forces briefly laid siege to Novgorod in August 1610. In September, they besieged the fortress of Korela (which had resisted Tsar Vasilii's agreement to turn it over to the Swedes in 1609), and it finally fell to them in March 1611. Unsuccessful Swedish campaigns were also launched in Russia's far north during the winter of 1610–11.

By late spring 1611, Novgorod again came under siege by a Swedish army commanded by Jacob de la Gardie. In June, de la Gardie began intense secret negotiations with representatives from the city who (in quiet coordination with Liapunov and other national militia leaders) requested military assistance against the Poles and secretly offered the Russian throne to one of the Swedish king's sons if he would be willing to convert to Orthodoxy. In the meantime, Novgorod itself was to be placed under the protection of Sweden, and de la Gardie was to be allowed in to serve as its military governor. Even though Liapunov and Novgorodian officials regarded this drastic step as a necessary sacrifice in order to liberate Moscow, they had no illusions about how ordinary Russians would react to it. Because of the fierce hatred of the Swedes by the common people of Novgorod, the gates of the city had to be secretly opened to Swedish occupation forces. Once done, that resulted in the immediate surrender of the city on July 17, 1611. In sharp contrast to the hated regime of Ivan Saltykov, however, Novgorod's new rulers from the very beginning went out of their way to placate former rebel cossacks and even managed to entice some of them into joining the city's garrison. Soon, Russian cossacks were also helping the Swedes in military operations elsewhere, including the far north.

King Karl was, of course, delighted by the news from Novgorod; and, just like his cousin Sigismund, he now began to behave as a conqueror—completely disregarding all the solemn agreements made with the Russians by his representatives. No Swedish prince hurried to become tsar, and Sweden failed to assist the Russians against the Poles. Instead, de la Gardie quickly seized complete control of Novgorod and the surrounding area and began Sweden's systematic conquest and annexation of many border towns and fortresses (including Kopore, Iama, Ivangorod, Oreshek, Gdov, Porkhov, Staraia Rusa, Ladoga, and Tikhvin), completely cutting Russia off from the Baltic Sea by early 1612. De la Gardie failed, however, to capture Pskov. Swedish troops also renewed their attempt to conquer Russia's far north, fully intending to capture the old port town of Kola (Murmansk) and Russia's extremely important new White Sea port town of Arkhangelsk in order to close them both to European ships. The plan was for Sweden to gain control of all of Russia's exports and to force merchants to buy those products at Sweden's Baltic ports. Fortunately for the Russians, even with cossack allies the Swedes failed to capture or shut down those northern ports—which became indispensable for Russia in the seventeenth century due to Sweden's successful conquest of Russia's entire Baltic coastline during the Time of Troubles.

Karl's aggressive policies were inherited by his son, Gustav Adolf, who succeeded him in late 1611. King Gustav Adolf, like Sigismund, contemplated becoming the ruler of Russia in his own name. He was therefore in no hurry to send his younger brother, Prince Karl Filip, to become tsar in spite of de la Gardie's constant reminders that some Russian commanders and lords were more than ready to swear an oath to him. Like Sigismund, the new king of Sweden ended up overplaying his hand in Russia. In late 1612, Gustav Adolf proudly announced that more than two hundred Russian towns had acknowledged Karl Filip as tsar; but Sweden's greatest king still dreamed of having those towns—and even more Russian territory—for himself. Swedish intervention was a powerful shock to the beleaguered Russians, and it greatly complicated and slowed down their efforts to expel the Poles from Moscow.[29]

In the final years of the Time of Troubles, news of Russia's misery and of Polish and Swedish military intervention spread far and wide. Hearing of the capture of Moscow, Smolensk, and Novgorod, many people doubted that Russia would be able to survive as an independent country. Intermittent efforts were made in the West to provide mercenary soldiers to counter Polish and Swedish interventionists; some Protestant contemporaries especially stressed the need to stop Catholic Poland from conquering Russia. Even King James of England came to dream of intervention in north Russia and the acquisition of Arkhangelsk in order to prevent the Swedes or the Poles from threatening English merchants' direct access to and accumulated privileges in the Russian marketplace. James, Russia Company merchants, and others also fantasized about pulling the trade of Persia and the entire Orient through Russia to England. The archbishop of

Map 8 Foreign Intervention.

Canterbury himself got involved in the king's half-baked plan to stop the Catholics in Russia and to profit from an English monopoly on Russia's export trade. There was even loose talk of sending the future King Charles I to Russia as a candidate for tsar or as the "protector" of north Russia. King James became so interested in the plan that he eventually sent an ambassador to negotiate the details with the Russians. Arriving shortly after the election of Mikhail Romanov as tsar in 1613, the tardy English envoys first made certain that the young man was secure on the throne before giving up on the king's mad dream. It seems that Russia's internal misery went to the heads of several kings before the Russian people finally put an end to the civil war.[30]

23

The End of the Civil War and the Election of Mikhail Romanov

The massing of patriotic forces preparing to expel the Polish garrison from Moscow seemed to be proceeding well during the spring and early summer of 1611, but for a number of reasons that effort stumbled. As a result, Russia continued to suffer from foreign intervention and descended into near chaos before competing domestic factions eventually joined forces to save their homeland and elect a new tsar. The incredible difficulty the various groups had cooperating with each other even in the face of foreign military intervention has traditionally been explained in terms of class conflict between the cossacks and the gentry—in other words, as a continuation of the mythical "First Peasant War."[1] That was definitely not the case.

By late spring 1611, Prokofii Liapunov, Dmitrii Pozharskii, and other militia leaders succeeded in mobilizing sizable forces of gentry militia and cossacks for the purpose of liberating Moscow. Pozharskii was the first national militia commander to reach out to Zarutskii's cossacks and to urge them to join the struggle against foreign intervention. Liapunov subsequently took the important step of sending manifestos far and wide promising freedom to all cossacks who joined the national militia even if those men had only recently been slaves or serfs. There was, understandably, a strong positive response from "cossacks" old and new. Thousands of men claiming to be cossacks flocked to the camps of the national liberation movement. Some were, in fact, free cossacks from the Don and Volga, but most had "gone cossack" more recently, including many refugees from smoldering Moscow. The bulk of those men had been in Tushino service, but others had seen very little military action before joining the national militia.[2]

Power within the militia leadership quickly came to rest in the hands of Liapunov, Dmitrii Trubetskoi, and Ivan Zarutskii. Liapunov made strong efforts to forge and maintain cooperation between gentry units and the cossack forces of the two former Tushino boyars. He treated the cossack commanders as equal partners in the struggle against the interventionists since their men provided the national militia with its main fighting force. In fact, the cossacks fought with a frenzy against Polish troops. No doubt there were awkward moments whenever noble warriors came across their former slaves among the cossack patriots, but social tension was not allowed to interfere with the important task at hand. Indeed, the "council of the entire realm" set up by the national militia leaders deliberately included representatives from the dvoriane, deti boiarskie, common soldiers, and free cossacks. That highly representative agency—which in many ways resembled a zemskii sobor—met almost constantly and resolved many of the minor conflicts that emerged among the diverse forces camped before Moscow. A rudimentary bureaucracy was also set up, staffed mainly by incredibly dedicated secretaries and bureaucrats who had deserted the ruined capital; and Liapunov and his fellow senior commanders began to administer the territories under the control of their provisional government.[3]

At the end of June 1611, the "council of the entire realm" issued a famous decree sometimes referred to as the "constitution" of the "first militia" (or of the "first national host").[4] In addition to laying the foundation for a temporary national government, the decree focused on shoring up the patriotic forces fighting against the interventionists—both gentry and cossacks. The council's proclamation has traditionally been viewed as a conservative reaction to the presence of radical or revolutionary cossacks within the national militia—as an attempt to control those unruly men, to preserve the serf system, and generally to benefit the gentry at the expense of their former slaves and serfs serving in the cossack detachments. Viewed as a response to angry gentry petitions, the decree has been interpreted as a sharp jab at the patriotic cossacks.[5] In fact, that is an extremely faulty interpretation. Like the treaty signed by the Tushino boyars at King Sigismund's Smolensk siege camp in February 1610, the decree of June 30, 1611, focused on shoring up ruined deti boiarskie who were the backbone of the gentry militia. Those men were to receive land allotments—especially from estates confiscated from boyar traitors collaborating with the Polish interventionists. The decree's twenty-third article, which required the return to their old masters of runaway or abducted peasants and set no time limit for finding them, has been correctly interpreted as an expression of the gentry's desire to put a stop to unfair and damaging competition by the boyars (who were not strongly represented in the national militia).[6] The decree thus clearly indicated that serfdom was to remain sacrosanct.

Some scholars thought they discerned in the decree's language concerning the return of runaways a direct attack on "radical" cossacks in the national militia, either as an attempt to dry up the source of those forces or as a repudiation of Liapunov's promise of freedom to them. Supposedly, a large percentage of the patriotic cossacks camped before Moscow were suddenly confronted with the prospect of being claimed by their old masters and forced back into serf-dom. Platonov went so far as to argue that Liapunov felt that his own forces had grown strong enough to allow him to throw down the gauntlet to the motley cossack detachments.[7] According to the traditional interpretation, the cossacks became so upset by the "council of the realm's" decree and its insistence on maintaining serfdom that the national militia inevitably broke down over the issue.[8] That was definitely not the case. In fact, the decree was in direct response to cossack as well as gentry petitions and was signed by cossack representatives of the "council of the realm." Runaway serfs and slaves mentioned in the decree were specifically those who fled to towns, other estates, or elsewhere—not those who had become cossack patriots serving in the national militia. Upon reflection, the traditional interpretation of the intent of the council's decree makes no sense at all because it would obviously have destroyed at the outset the fragile coalition Liapunov and others had so painstakingly assembled. In fact, no attempt whatsoever was made to investigate cossacks in the national militia in order to return runaways among them to bondage. That entire group of critically important soldiers were declared to be free men. Much to the confusion of many scholars, those patriotic cossacks had no objection to enslaving or enserfing other men who did not fight for their country.[9]

According to the June 30 decree, cossack atamans and veteran fortress cossacks in the national militia were scheduled to receive pomeste estates or a salary; no such privileges were extended to rank-and-file cossacks or newcomers among them. The distinction made between the two groups in the decree has led to serious misinterpretations. Many scholars have seen it as an indication of growing separation between ordinary cossacks and their leaders, who supposedly began to think and act more like gentry in this phase of the Time of Troubles. Indeed, Skrynnikov has pointed out that many of the cossack atamans were former deti boiarskie who still possessed gentry viewpoints.[10] No doubt some cossack leaders did dream of becoming gentry; but Stanislavskii has convincingly challenged the view of growing differentiation between cossacks and their atamans in the national militia. He has also pointed out just how extremely rare the distribution of pomeste estates to cossack leaders was in the period 1611–12. There really was no growing rift between rank-and-file cossacks and their atamans. Cossack commanders were certainly not growing rich at this time, and they had little incentive to separate themselves from the proud men they had to work with every day.[11]

It has long been rashly and incorrectly assumed that cossacks in the national militia formed a monolithic host and acted as champions of democracy or of the peasants in their struggle against serfdom. Nothing could be further from the truth. There were no elected atamans in the national militia who commanded more than a hundred men; cossack forces before Moscow were under the overall command of boyars Zarutskii and Trubetskoi, who appointed their own subordinate commanders. Patriotic cossacks preserved their quasi-democratic self-government only at the smallest unit level. Cossack detachments in the national militia also acted independently and maintained only very loose contact with one another. Those men had no interest in spreading democracy, and they did not regard themselves as peasants or as peasant leaders. Instead, as Stanislavskii has pointed out, they were a new military class in formation— a communistic brotherhood of professional soldiers. They consistently emphasized their uniqueness and separation from all other groups in Russian society and were basically indifferent to class origin. It is a mistake to regard cossacks as peasants, even if they came from the peasantry. Moreover, in spite of the fantasies of many Soviet scholars, the destruction of serfdom was never proclaimed as a cossack goal during the Time of Troubles. In fact, peasants did not always get along with cossacks and occasionally fought bitterly against them.[12]

Even though cossacks in the national militia were not a "revolutionary host," they did fight for their interests. They regarded themselves as a special corporation deserving certain privileges in return for military service. They jealously guarded those privileges and constantly strove to improve their position relative to other groups through rewards and a regular salary. In this way they were quite similar to Ukrainian cossacks of the same era.[13] Cossacks in Russia sought a status similar to that of the gentry and demanded similar rewards. It was, of course, critically important for the national militia leaders to provide the cossacks with a reliable food supply and to meet the other, strictly military needs of that all-important military force. The alternative was cossack banditry, which experience had shown only generated chaos, misery, and great hostility.[14] As noted in chapter 21, the policy of granting cossack units high-status kormlenie (the right to collect food, and possibly taxes, from a designated area) became routine in the Tushino camp. It was also experimented with by the north Russian towns in their struggle against Tushino.[15] By the time of the formation of the national militia, the cossacks had become better organized and had emerged as a powerful force quite capable of lobbying on their own behalf in direct competition with the gentry; and by then many cossacks were used to having the privilege of high-status kormlenie as a reward for their vital military service. Significantly, in response to cossack petitions, the June 30 decree issued by the "council of the realm" placed the cossacks in the national militia under the same administrative authority as the gentry and not under a separate "cossack affairs" office, as had been the case in Tushino. Cossacks, like all other patriotic soldiers, were provided with at least some food and a small salary by the new makeshift government; but, in part to redirect their foraging away from tax-paying lands, cossacks in the national militia were also granted generous korm-lenie privileges in certain areas—primarily crown and palace villages that, because of the civil war, no longer produced for the tsar. Cossack *pristavstvo*, as it was called, amounted to a given cossack unit's temporary collective control of a spe-cific place and the right to collect a fixed amount of rent or supplies from it.[16] Of course, even the most patriotic peasants did not appreciate being forced to support the wild and fierce cossacks.

Pomeshchiki in the national militia, already uneasy about the presence of former serfs and slaves within the ranks of the cossacks, grew increasingly alarmed by sharp cossack competition for resources and military significance. National militia cavalrymen complained to their commanders about the activities of the cossacks in much the same way that the rebel gentry had complained to Tushino authorities about those same unruly soldiers.[17] In fact, in many ways the cos-sacks really did think of themselves by this time as a viable alternative to the relatively ineffective gentry militia (with its allergy to adopting gunpowder tech-nology). The cossacks did not wage class war against the gentry, but the two groups were competitors for scarce resources; and there is no denying that cos-sack kormlenie was perceived as a serious threat to gentry landholding.[18] Nevertheless, it was regarded as a necessary evil by the national militia com-manders who had no other way to sustain the cossacks—recognized by all of them as the most important military force in the struggle against Polish inter-vention. Many lords were unhappy about cossack activities, privileges, and grow-ing arrogance; but Liapunov, Zarutskii, and Trubetskoi wisely focused on unifying and fortifying their forces, not on destroying the fragile coalition they had forged in order to liberate their homeland.

Cossack foraging for food and booty stirred protests from the gentry and from villagers in the area around Moscow. Within a very short time, predatory cossack activities began to harm the national militia's reputation and the cohe-sion of its forces. In response, Liapunov severely cracked down on those men. He imposed harsh restrictions on cossack food gathering that quickly made him very unpopular among those soldiers, who were facing extreme hardships at this time while most of the gentry units were reasonably well supplied. When one militia commander ordered twenty-eight cossacks drowned for illegal loot-ing, other cossacks quickly rescued their guilty comrades. Tensions grew on both sides. Cossack forces in the national militia now felt boxed in—receiving inadequate supplies and yet facing increasing restrictions on obtaining any more. They blamed Liapunov directly for their plight. He was, by his own admission, unable to supply the cossacks except by means of kormlenie, and now he was backing away from that earlier arrangement. When Liapunov authorized the summary execution of some cossack thieves in July 1611, many cossacks howled in protest at what they perceived to be an attack on their privileges as well as a blow to their ability to survive. Liapunov's foolish attempt to end the collection of supplies by the cossacks themselves without having a realistic and acceptable alternative logistical system in place inevitably provoked a sharp response. The cossacks invited him to a cossack circle to debate the issue. There, on July 22, 1611, the imperious commander behaved so arrogantly that angry cossacks killed him. The assassination of Liapunov was intended as much to protect cossack status as it was to protect their food supplies.[19]

The traditional interpretation of Liapunov's death as the symbolic manifestation of class tensions within the national militia that doomed it to failure in 1611 is inadequate. In addition to the complex issue of cossack status and maintenance, many cossacks already hated Liapunov for having betrayed Bolotnikov during the siege of Moscow and for his subsequent bloodthirsty rampage of terror against rebels in Riazan province. Another reason for tension between the cossacks and the national militia commander concerned Liapunov's support for a Swedish candidate for tsar, which ruined his reputation among the cossacks and many other patriots.[20] Liapunov was also deeply resented by several highborn aristocrats who felt that he had risen too high and that he dealt too haughtily with other boyars. Some of those lords entered into multiple conspiracies against him (including Shakhovskoi and other former Tushinites). In addition, Liapunov was simultaneously the focus of a conspiracy by wily Polish interventionists who forged a letter in his name calling for the death of the cossacks. That letter was produced by the cossacks as evidence of Liapunov's evil intentions during their fatal meeting with the national militia commander.[21]

Liapunov's death was certainly a blow to the patriot cause, but it was not the result of class war. With him gone, however, the problems of getting cossack forces and gentry detachments to cooperate grew even more intractable, primarily due to the grandiose ambitions of Zarutskii and Trubetskoi. The traditional view of this phase of the Time of Troubles has been that, once Liapunov was murdered, the cossacks declared open war on the gentry, forcing the latter to flee and causing the collapse of the national militia. With only cossacks and Tushino lords left before Moscow, the cossacks supposedly gave themselves over to an orgy of plunder that slammed the door on the possibility of liberating the capital in 1611.[22] That is not what really happened. Liapunov's murder did not lead to gentry flight from the national militia. Even Liapunov's own son felt safe among the patriotic cossacks after his father's death, and gentry units continued to arrive in the camps before Moscow for the rest of the summer of 1611. The "council of the realm" and the patriots' small bureaucracy continued to function—and not just in the interests of the cossacks. Cossack kormlenie did continue, of course, and—in at least one case—was extended to a group of 350 Moscow streltsy who joined the national militia. Bureaucrats continued to supervise the distribution of resources, and militia authorities continued to deal with such internal problems as robbery and murder.[23]

Zarutskii emerged as the effective head of the militia; and under his supervision patriotic forces (mostly cossacks) very effectively stopped the Polish hetman Jan Karol Chodkiewicz's large-scale offensive during the summer of 1611 and continued to tighten the blockade around hungry Moscow. In a major effort to capture the city in the fall, however, the patriots failed and suffered many casualties. Soon, gentry forces within the national militia began to disappear. What eventually led to the breakup of the militia forces in the fall of 1611 was definitely not class war; it was instead primarily what always led to the dissolution of the gentry militia in that era—exhaustion and lack of provisions after several months of active duty. Indeed, famine descended on the entire Moscow region by late 1611—not due to cossack banditry so much as to the disruption of war and the concentration in one place of too many mouths to feed. In addition, the national militia had assigned remote estates to a large percentage of the gentry, and many of them were anxious to visit those lands in order to claim them and to rest there for the winter. The departure of those cavalrymen in large numbers meant the decline of the militia's strength. Efforts to storm Moscow in December 1611 failed again, and many cossacks were killed. Because of increasing frustration and hunger, many of the cossacks themselves began drifting off in search of food and better shelter for the winter. As a result, active patriot military operations around Moscow were suspended until the spring of 1612.[24]

Another problem that contributed to the dissolution of the national militia by the end of 1611 was Zarutskii's increasing agitation on behalf of Tsaritsa Marina's son Ivan as the future tsar. Zarutskii, not surprisingly, came to dream of putting Ivan Dmitrievich (the "little brigand") on the throne with himself acting as regent. He tried with little success to stir up popular support for "heir Ivan" as a counter to Liapunov's interest in a Swedish tsar. Once Liapunov was dead and Zarutskii became the de facto commander of the national militia, he continued to promote the "little brigand's" candidacy. Although many laymen and some church leaders urged continued cooperation between gentry and cossack forces in order to expel the foreigners, Patriarch Hermogen (in prison in Moscow) managed to send another letter to Nizhnii Novgorod warning against cooperation with Zarutskii's cossacks and urging the repudiation of "Marina's accursed son." There was a quick and powerful response to his message. In August 1611, Nizhnii Novgorod and Kazan entered into an agreement against Zarutskii and his cossacks (as well as against the Poles and the Swedes), declaring that they would reject any cossack candidate for tsar chosen without the consent of the entire realm. Furthermore, they would refuse to allow Zarutskii's cossack forces into their towns. Thus began a rapidly growing split between patriotic towns led by Nizhnii Novgorod and the increasingly cossack-dominated national militia. Serious efforts were made by Nizhnii Novgorod's authorities from this point on both to check the growing influence of cossacks within the national liberation movement and to reorganize Russia's struggle against foreign intervention so that it was no longer dependent upon those unruly men.[25]

Greatly accelerating the developing split between Nizhnii Novgorod and Zarutskii's forces—and therefore seriously threatening the very existence of the national liberation movement—was the appearance at this time of yet another pretender masquerading as "Tsar Dmitrii" who managed to temporarily attract considerable cossack support. The identity of the man sometimes referred to as the "third false Dmitrii" is unknown. Possibly a deacon or a petty trader from Moscow or Kaluga, "Matiushka" or "Sidorka" ended up as a beggar in Novgorod where he revealed his identity as "Dmitrii" and managed to attract a few supporters. They soon moved to Ivangorod, which was then under siege by the Swedes. On March 23, 1611, the beleaguered town enthusiastically welcomed the resurrected tsar. "Dmitrii" was apparently a good speaker, and news of the "true tsar's" return to claim his throne and to fight against Swedish intervention spread like wildfire. Several other towns trying to fend off the Swedes quickly recognized "Dmitrii"—including Gdov, Iama, and Kopore.

In Pskov, a detachment of former Tushinite cossacks who had been living there for many months took up the new impostor's cause and invited him to move to that town in early July 1611. However, Pskov's administrators balked and refused to admit the "tsar." "Dmitrii" hung around the area for several weeks and then suddenly disappeared when a combined Swedish and Russian army from Novgorod arrived and laid siege to Pskov for about five weeks. Not surprisingly, the national militia forces hurriedly sent to relieve Pskov contained many cossacks who had long supported one "Dmitrii" or another. Although Zarutskii's efforts to interest those men in little Ivan Dmitrievich had failed to stir them, rumors that "Dmitrii" himself was alive in the Pskov region provoked great enthusiasm. Once the siege of Pskov was broken by patriot forces, the town (including its streltsy garrison) and the national militia units there at the time formally welcomed "Tsar Dmitrii," who arrived in Pskov on December 4, 1611.[26]

The impostor immediately sent out manifestos declaring his miraculous survival and calling upon patriots to rally to him. There was a dramatic response. Several northern towns took up his cause immediately, and some cossacks from Novgorod joined his growing forces. Many southern frontier towns (including Zaraisk, Tarusa, Vorotynsk, and Bolkhov) soon swore oaths of obedience to the "tsar" in Pskov as well. To the east, "Dmitrii" was also recognized as tsar in Alatyr, Kurmysh, and Arzamas. In those districts, crown and palace peasants—extremely angry about national militia efforts to enserf them in order to provide for impoverished gentry—took up the cause of "Dmitrii" with a vengeance and were joined by many local streltsy units. Those men terrorized local pomeshchiki unwilling to swear an oath to the "true tsar" and forced them to flee. Very quickly, patriot forces all over Russia split decisively into supporters of "Dmitrii" and opponents of any cossack candidate for tsar.[27]

The Swedes tried by various means to neutralize or to come to terms with the new impostor, but those efforts failed. It was clearly in the interest of "Dmitrii" to identify himself closely with the patriot cause so he urged his supporters to attack Swedish occupation forces at every opportunity.[28] For obvious reasons, "Dmitrii" made a special appeal to the Tushinite veterans encamped before Moscow. Some sources claimed that he initiated contact with them; other sources claimed that the excited cossacks in the national militia heard rumors about him and initiated the contact on their own. Whatever the case, a cossack delegation from the national militia soon journeyed to Pskov to meet with the "tsar."[29] There they apparently quickly figured out that he was an impostor but were intimidated into sending a report back to the national militia that "Tsar Dmitrii" was alive. That message caused a sensation. On March 2, 1612, at a huge conclave before Moscow a large majority of cossacks declared for "Dmitrii." Although many patriots fled in protest, both Zarutskii and Trubetskoi felt they had no choice but to join their excited men in swearing an oath of loyalty to "Tsar Dmitrii."[30] Most towns in the Moscow area, however, quickly rejected the reincarnated tsar. Even more important, the immediate and strident hostility of the powerful, newly-emerging commander-in-chief of patriot forces, Prince Dmitrii Pozharskii, to the link being forged between Zarutskii and Trubetskoi on the one hand and "Tsar Dmitrii" on the other was enough to force Trubetskoi and Zarutskii to begin making extremely polite overtures to Pozharskii in which they apologized profusely for having been forced by their men to swear an oath to the latest "Dmitrii."[31]

Zarutskii actually regarded the newest "Dmitrii" as a serious rival to himself and began making plans to have him eliminated as soon as possible. Taking matters into his own hands, Zarutskii organized a delegation from the national militia to travel to Pskov, ostensibly to forge a stronger link to the "tsar." In fact, Zarutskii's agent, Ivan Pleshcheev, quickly became one of "Dmitrii's" close advisers. Pleshcheev's real mission, however, was to seize the impostor at the first available opportunity. Because of "Dmitrii's" reign of rape and terror in Pskov, Pleshcheev soon found several secret allies—including the town's voevoda, Prince Ivan F. Khovanskii, and other leading citizens fed up with the cruel impostor. The conspirators took advantage of the approach of a Swedish army to send the bulk of the ardently pro-Dmitrii forces out of Pskov to fight the enemy. While those men were away, an attempt was made to arrest "Dmitrii," but he managed to escape. The extremely anxious conspirators finally captured him on May 20, 1612. Several weeks later he was sent in chains under heavy escort to the national militia camps before Moscow. There, the "third false Dmitrii" was put on public display for a long time for the amusement of the soldiers. Only much later was he hanged.[32] Although Zarutskii again apologized to Prince Pozharskii for having temporarily backed "Dmitrii" and even pledged to stop working on behalf of Tsaritsa Marina and little Ivan Dmitrievich, the cossack boyar actually continued to intrigue against opponents of the "little brigand," including Pozharskii.[33]

In spite of all the problems created by ambitious and unscrupulous militia commanders and by the "third false Dmitrii," by the fall of 1611 in Nizhnii Novgorod a new patriotic movement and a new military force capable of salvaging Russia's national sovereignty were beginning to take shape. Chosen by his fellow citizens to heed Patriarch Hermogen's call, an eloquent and energetic local butcher named Kuzma Minin convinced his fellow citizens to raise money for an army to cleanse Russia of foreign interventionists and to restore order in the realm. Minin was granted broad powers to impose extraordinary taxes on the population of Nizhnii Novgorod as well as on local monasteries and crown peasant villages; and he raised a lot of money very quickly. Next, Minin chose the brilliant and self-effacing Prince Pozharskii, then recovering from his wounds on a nearby estate, to be commander-in-chief of the new militia being formed. That choice shocked and annoyed a number of ambitious aristocrats who pointed out that Pozharskii was, after all, only a minor prince and not even a boyar. But Minin rightly concluded that the honest and unflappable Pozharskii was just the man for the incredibly difficult task of getting various patriot factions to work together. Pozharskii, in turn, insisted that Minin continue as the patriotic movement's treasurer with very broad powers. Together, those two men quickly put together a detachment of gentry cavalry, cautiously reached out to some patriotic cossack atamans with offers of pomeste grants and salaries, and spread word far and wide of their intentions. Repeating their successful strategy against Tushino, patriotic towns exchanged letters about local decisions to cooperate with Minin and Pozharskii in order to oppose foreigners and unruly cossacks. The region's recent bitter experience at the hands of the greedy Tushinites stirred many people to enthusiastically join the new patriot movement.

The news that Minin and Pozharskii could actually pay troops a regular salary caused many soldiers of all types (as well as armed peasants) to flock to Pozharskii's banner. Within a few months, most of the major towns of the middle and upper Volga joined the new patriot movement, including Iaroslavl, Kostroma, and Vologda. Militia units from Kolomna and Riazan province, detachments of streltsy, and even some local cossacks quickly swelled the ranks of Pozharskii's new army, which has often been referred to as the "second militia." Minin and Pozharskii cautiously organized their forces to struggle against both the Poles in Moscow and Zarutskii and the "little brigand." They also declared their intention to convene a zemskii sobor to choose a new tsar. Not surprisingly, that produced something akin to open warfare between remnants of the old national militia and the new one. Zarutskii and Trubetskoi immediately recognized the potential threat to their own status and ambition posed by Pozharskii's army. For that reason, in early 1612 they blocked Minin and Pozharskii's plans to use Suzdal as a base of operations against Moscow. That action forced the new national militia leaders to choose Iaroslavl as the base of their operations, which worked out well. Iaroslavl was still a rich town with wide commercial contacts even though its trade had suffered during the civil war. The town also boasted a strong fortress and had already proven its worth during the struggle against the oppressive Tushinites. Zarutskii tried desperately to prevent Pozharskii from occupying strategically located Iaroslavl, which linked the upper Volga region to the far north, but Pozharskii's forces beat him back. Iaroslavl thereupon enthusiastically opened its gates to Minin and Pozharskii and quickly emerged as the headquarters of the national liberation movement and as the seat of the new provisional government.[34]

At first, the merchants of Iaroslavl balked at Minin's unprecedented demand for up to thirty per cent of their net worth. That forced him to coerce those stingy and greatly surprised men with armed streltsy. Meanwhile, Pozharskii's forces, unable to approach Moscow due to the temporary flirtation of old national militia elements there with the "third false Dmitrii," spent their time clearing Zarutskii loyalists out of a wide region—including Tver, Rostov, and Vladimir. Iaroslavl soon became a powerful magnet attracting more and more towns fed up with both rampaging cossacks and foreign interventionists. Troops and supplies poured into Iaroslavl from the Volga region and the far north. Within just a few months a very large area of north and central Russia had once again spontaneously organized itself against an external threat, virtually duplicating what the region had done in response to the aggression of the Tushinites. No doubt the progress of the relentless Swedish interventionists in north Russia also influenced the rapid emergence of the national liberation movement.

The new provisional government in Iaroslavl functioned reasonably well. In addition to gathering food and supplies, it distributed estates to impoverished gentry and cossack atamans, minted coins, and invited representatives from towns, monasteries, and even prosperous peasant villages to come to Iaroslavl and remain there as advisers. The provisional government enrolled large numbers of townsmen and streltsy in the new national militia and also attracted many pomeshchiki away from the old militia forces then still flirting with the Pskov impostor. The arrival in Iaroslavl of a few wealthy aristocrats caused some friction, but Prince Pozharskii dealt diplomatically with them—wisely regarding those extremely arrogant men as essential for the pacification and reconstruction of the country. Pozharskii was equally diplomatic in negotiating with the unruly but still-essential cossacks. By June 1612, he managed to attract seventeen atamans and their detachments away from the declining Moscow-area militia forces—much to the alarm of Zarutskii and, to a lesser extent, Trubetskoi. In general, Pozharskii worked extremely well with the cossacks; he made good use of them and earned their respect and trust. Minin and Pozharskii also succeeded in drawing many more towns, nobles, gentry, cossacks, Tatars, Mordvians, Chuvashi, and others into Iaroslavl service by the summer of 1612. In fact, the only group offering to serve that Pozharskii rejected was a small contingent of Protestant foreign mercenaries who had arrived in north Russia to help stop Polish intervention. Foreign troops were not at all popular in Russia at that time, and Pozharskii did not trust or need those men. Instead, he repeatedly emphasized the need for the Russian people themselves to liberate their homeland. With patience and determination, Pozharskii managed to build a strong army and looked for the first available opportunity to put it to good use. By summer 1612, his forces in Iaroslavl stood at more that ten thousand men and may have numbered as many as twenty thousand soldiers.[35]

The provisional government in Iaroslavl was strongly committed to liberating the country and convening a zemskii sobor to choose a new tsar. Minin and Pozharskii wisely avoided publicly picking a favorite candidate, but they did loudly and adamantly oppose "heir Ivan Dmitrievich" and the Pskov impostor. Several leading Russian candidates for tsar were, of course, still in Polish captivity. In spite of that, Filaret Romanov's close relatives were quite active in Iaroslavl and floated the prospect of his fifteen-year-old son, Mikhail, as a candidate for the throne. Since young Mikhail was at that time still in Polish-occupied Moscow living with his uncle Ivan (a member of the despised council of seven), there was understandably very little enthusiasm in Iaroslavl for his candidacy. Prince Pozharskii himself cleverly hinted at the possibility of a Swedish tsar in negotiations with the Swedish interventionists—who were then holding Novgorod and many other Russian towns. The Swedes, in turn, displayed considerable interest in the prospect of "Tsar Karl Filip"; and, as a result, Pozharskii was able to negotiate a critically-important truce with them in June 1612 that secured his northern base and allowed him to move his army toward Moscow to concentrate on liberating the capital from the Polish interventionists.[36]

During the spring of 1612, Polish hetman Chodkiewicz once again launched an offensive from the west in order to clear patriot forces from the Smolensk road and to link up with the Polish garrison in Moscow. His soldiers were constantly harassed by Russian partisans and, in retaliation, brutally terrorized the countryside. Chodkiewicz, however, even with the active assistance of the Moscow garrison, failed to dislodge Zarutskii's forces. The bloodthirsty dictator of Moscow, Alexander Gosiewski, sensing the approaching end, wisely chose this moment to remove his mercenary detachment from Moscow, replacing those weary but well-paid men with fresh troops. On his way out of the capital, he looted what was left of the Kremlin treasury. (Among the items stolen was the tsar's "unicorn horn" staff that was cut into little pieces and distributed to the mercenaries; the Russians complained bitterly about its loss for many decades.) Once Gosiewski and Chodkiewicz departed from the Moscow area, Zarutskii made yet another attempt to storm the inner city but failed, suffering staggering losses.[37] By then he was desperate to achieve victory before the arrival of Pozharskii's army in the vain hope of retaining his position of leadership and of promoting Ivan Dmitrievich as a candidate for tsar. Publicly, however, Zarutskii and Trubetskoi had already both been forced to renounce the "little brigand" as well as the Pskov pretender in their negotiations with the provisional government and the increasingly powerful Prince Pozharskii. Even so, many people in Iaroslavl warned against cooperating with Zarutskii, correctly fearing that he would attempt to assassinate Pozharskii. Zarutskii was at this time loudly denounced as the author of Liapunov's murder and as a greedy and corrupt self-promoter. Under the circumstances, Pozharskii wisely refused to have anything more to do with Zarutskii, even though the latter continued to make soothing overtures to him and denounced all charges against himself as false.

Rebuffed and frustrated, Zarutskii reportedly resorted to witchcraft and hired assassins to get rid of the new national militia commander-in-chief. However, those plots not only failed but backfired. Zarutskii was personally implicated in them and as a result lost the support of Trubetskoi and others, who quickly abandoned him to work with Pozharskii. Isolated and increasingly desperate, Zarutskii briefly flirted with the Polish interventionists again, but that act of "treason" was discovered by Trubetskoi. In a panic, just as Pozharskii's army began arriving before Moscow, on July 28, 1612, Zarutskii abruptly departed. By then, however, he had lost much of the support of his own rank-and-file cossacks, who were still hungry and ill-clad while their rich commander remained completely indifferent to their suffering. Many of those men also did not appreciate Zarutskii's careless sacrifice of cossack lives while hurriedly attempting to capture Moscow, and some of them were still angry about Zarutskii's massacre of their brothers back when the Tushino camp broke up. Therefore, when Zarutskii ordered his men to join him in abandoning the siege of Moscow, most of them flatly refused. Only about twenty-five hundred cossacks accompanied him on his flight. Zarutskii's detachment made a beeline for Kolomna, picked up Marina and Ivan, looted the town, and then headed into Riazan province—causing enormous damage along the way. Zarutskii set up his new headquarters and "heir Ivan's" court in Mikhailov. Although Trubetskoi, Pozharskii, and many other patriot leaders were glad to be rid of him, Zarutskii and Marina continued to be a thorn in the side of the Russians for about two more years.[38]

Prince Pozharskii had been anxious to work out an agreement about unified command with Trubetskoi, who still commanded three or four thousand cossacks, in advance of the arrival of Pozharskii's own forces in the Moscow vicinity; but Trubetskoi looked down on Pozharskii as a low-born prince and was not at all helpful. In fact, Trubetskoi was not the only Russian commander who felt superior to the national militia's commander-in-chief. Several great lords had already deserted Iaroslavl when Pozharskii refused to step aside in favor of one of them; and by the time the bulk of Pozharskii's army finally reached the environs of Moscow in early August, very few high-born nobles were among its officers. Pozharskii commanded at least ten thousand men (dvoriane, deti boiarskie, streltsy, cossacks, native and Asian troops, townsmen, and peasants); but his motley forces—armed with many lances, pole-axes, and spears but few harquebuses—provoked premature derision from the new garrison in Moscow. The Russian commander-in-chief was urged by the enemy to send his men back home to plow the fields. Far worse, a haughty and disdainful Trubetskoi kept his own cossack forces on the sidelines when Pozharskii's men fought their first battle with hetman Chodkiewicz, who approached the capital from the west again in August with about eight thousand Zaporozhian cossacks and Polish troops. During that bloody confrontation, several cossack units ignored their inactive commander (Trubetskoi) and joined Pozharskii's men.

The patriotic decision by those soldiers to join forces with the new national militia helped decide the outcome of the battle. Chodkiewicz was eventually forced to retreat. He then tried one more time to approach the capital with fresh supplies for the garrison, but fanatic attacks by the cossacks again forced him to withdraw his forces from the Moscow area—which ultimately doomed the Polish garrison. King Sigismund personally invaded Russia in the fall of 1612 in a last-ditch effort to resupply and reinforce his beleaguered troops in Moscow and to conquer additional territory. His army actually managed to reach Tushino and Volok Lamskii before national militia cossacks and local partisan activity stopped them and forced the king to retreat.[39]

Although Trubetskoi's cossacks played a decisive role in the struggle against Polish interventionists before Moscow, it was no thanks to their ruthlessly ambitious commander. Even as he failed to provide crucial support to Pozharskii, Trubetskoi tried to stir his cossacks against the gentry in the national militia. It was desperate need, not class war, which drove those cossacks—urged on by their commander—to complain bitterly about their own suffering and sacrifice during the previous year and a half while Pozharskii's army by contrast looked well-fed, well-clothed, and well-supplied. No doubt there was some smoldering class antagonism and envy among Trubetskoi's cossacks, but it is important to remember that it was only their commander's ambition that kept the two armies from joining forces sooner. In early September, Trubetskoi attempted to storm the capital on his own and failed. By then, even he recognized that the quick unification of all patriot forces was going to be necessary in order to achieve victory. In a major diplomatic step to end Russia's long and nightmarish civil war, Pozharskii announced that the two forces were combining into a single national militia under the nominal control of Trubetskoi. In fact, boyar Prince Trubetskoi had finally been defeated. Pozharskii and Minin were now firmly in charge of all militia forces and immediately speeded up the siege.[40]

The garrison in Moscow, now shrunken to about fifteen hundred men, was desperately hungry due to the failure of Chodkiewicz's campaign. Famine forced them to allow many Russians to leave the Kremlin by October 1612. Prince Mstislavskii, the president of the council of seven, personally sent a delegation to Pozharskii to inform him of the desire of the Russian lords who had cooperated with the Polish interventionists to leave Moscow and to beg for an honorable reception. Cossacks in the militia were extremely angry with those traitors and called for their deaths or, at the very least, the confiscation of their property. Pozharskii, however, regarded those compromised boyars as necessary for the restoration of order in the country. In return for renouncing their oath to "Tsar Wladyslaw," he allowed them to keep their estates and agreed to credit the lie that they had been held in Moscow against their will. For his part, a grateful Mstislavskii wrote a letter to the entire realm in which he apologized for having supported Wladyslaw. On October 26, Mstislavskii—his head prominently bandaged to cover and draw attention to an injury inflicted by a member of the Polish garrison—led Ivan Romanov, Mikhail Romanov, and other sheepish aristocrats out of the Kremlin. Many cossacks derided them as traitors as they filed out of the ruined city. The next day, October 27, the Polish garrison surrendered unconditionally, and national militia forces entered the capital. Much work remained to be done, but at least the Russians controlled Moscow again and, except for the problem of Zarutskii and Tsaritsa Marina, the civil war was now at an end.[41]

To the great surprise of many contemporaries, by late 1612 the Russian people at long last and with extraordinary difficulty had put aside their differences in order to save their country from chaos and foreign intervention. As Pozharskii, Minin, and Trubetskoi contemplated the difficult tasks of rebuilding the destroyed Russian state and restoring order, they knew full well that the recent military victory at Moscow had to be followed up immediately by the convocation of a zemskii sobor truly representing the entire realm for the critically important task of choosing a new tsar who would be regarded as legitimate in the eyes of most of the nation. As soon as Moscow was liberated, therefore, they sent urgent and unprecedented messages throughout the country calling for representatives of all groups of free men (dvoriane, deti boiarskie, streltsy and other low status soldiers, townspeople, clergy, peasants from crown and taxable state lands, and cossacks) to come as quickly as possible to Moscow. Many local administrators and voevodas initially balked at the idea of allowing commoners to participate in the election of a tsar; but Minin and Pozharskii insisted that their involvement was necessary to restore order to the realm, and their will prevailed. By January 1613, several hundred delegates arrived in the capital—the broadest cross-section of Russian society ever assembled to choose a tsar. In an extraordinary move that demonstrated just how strong patriotic sentiment had become, Pozharskii and Trubetskoi were forced by the representatives of the towns to order the "traitors"—meaning Mstislavskii and other former members of the council of seven—to leave Moscow during the zemskii sobor's deliberations. It was widely believed that those deeply compromised boyars wished to have a foreign tsar who would rule solely in the interests of the aristocracy. Prince Mstislavskii and the others bowed to popular pressure by announcing their immediate departure on a short pilgrimage, but those high-born lords must have been deeply incensed by being shoved aside by men of lesser birth.[42]

While waiting for the delegates to arrive, Pozharskii dismissed more than half of the national militia's gentry detachments in order to reduce pressure on food supplies in the Moscow area. That left fewer than two thousand gentry militiamen near the capital, along with approximately one thousand streltsy and other soldiers, and at least six thousand free cossacks.[43] Some gentry and national militia leaders were anxious to remove thousands of cossacks from the vicinity of the capital as soon as possible, but the prudent commander-in-chief still regarded those men as a necessary defense against possible Polish advances. In fact, Sigismund's army had been stopped in November 1612 only 90 kilometers west of Moscow, and those same cossacks had played a crucial role in turning him back. Prince Pozharskii was by this time extremely grateful to the patriotic cossacks for the essential role they had played in defeating and pushing back the Polish interventionists. Pozharskii appealed to the Russian towns to overcome their fears and prejudices and to voluntarily feed those heroic men. He also gave national militia cossack atamans the right to continue collecting food in certain districts. Senior cossacks in the militia received a salary; rank-and-file cossacks received a two-year exemption from debts and taxes, the promise of housing in Moscow and other towns, and a guarantee of freedom to all former serfs and slaves among them who had fought to liberate their homeland.[44] Many pomeshchiki, who detested and feared the cossacks, did not approve of those measures, but their commander-in-chief regarded them as no more than a just and fair reward for the liberators of Moscow. Far more annoying and alarming to the gentry and the aristocrats, however, was the decisive role those same cossacks came to play in the election of the new tsar.

The idea of a foreign tsar, once championed by several boyars, quickly faded as the election approached. Cossacks and other patriots would simply not tolerate any further consideration of Prince Wladyslaw.[45] On the other hand, the candidacy of Karl Filip still had some support in Swedish-controlled Novgorod, and he was definitely preferred to Wladyslaw by Russian Orthodox church leaders. According to some writers, Pozharskii himself may have favored the Swedish prince, although the traditional view has always been that his negotiations concerning Karl Filip were merely insincere plays for time.[46] As it turned out, after many delays, the tardy Karl Filip finally arrived at the Russian border in July 1612 to await the outcome of the clash between the Poles and the Russian patriots before Moscow. By that time, many towns of northwest Russia officially supported Karl Filip as tsar, but since they were then under the heel of Swedish interventionists, their declarations were probably coerced and not sincere.[47] In addition, whatever support among Russian aristocrats the Swedish prince may have enjoyed at one time quickly vanished as the boyars themselves began once more to dream of occupying the throne and as Pozharskii and others came under irresistible pressure from the cossacks to choose a native Russian tsar.[48]

During several weeks of maneuvering for the election, the Romanov faction was extremely active. Ivan Romanov very much wanted to become tsar but was unpopular for having actively collaborated with the hated Polish interventionists. However, the candidacy of his nephew, Mikhail, drew some gentry and merchant support and was enthusiastically embraced by much of the remaining national militia forces (then serving as the Moscow garrison) as well as by the cossack delegates to the zemskii sobor. Mikhail's father, Filaret Romanov, was popular among the cossacks for having been the patriarch of the Russian Orthodox Church in Tushino, for having been a strong supporter of Tsar Dmitrii, and for being related to the old sacred ruling dynasty. It is also possible that former Romanov military slaves who had been forced to join the cossacks after Tsar Boris moved against the Romanov clan in 1600 may have influenced their brothers' attitudes in 1613. Some cossacks in Moscow also—rather naïvely—hailed Mikhail Romanov as the "anti-boyar" candidate for tsar insofar as support for him might block the candidacy of Fedor Mstislavskii, Ivan Golitsyn, Ivan Romanov, or even Dmitrii Trubetskoi—who was busy at this time grabbing property for himself and acting like he had already been anointed tsar.[49]

Although the Romanov faction joined some of the others in spreading money around to influence the election, the zemskii sobor initially rejected Mikhail Romanov as a candidate, and the delegates were temporarily deadlocked.[50] On cue, some cossacks from Trubetskoi's detachments then proposed their own arrogant and obnoxious commander as tsar. Trubetskoi did everything he could to advance his candidacy at this point but was strongly resisted by Pozharskii and the aristocrats.[51] For a brief time after that impasse, some cossacks gravitated toward another militia commander who had also previously served at Tushino, Prince Dmitrii M. Cherkasskii, who was related by marriage to the Romanovs and the old ruling dynasty. But his candidacy was also quickly blocked by the boyars.[52]

Throughout this period, young Mikhail Romanov's candidacy kept gaining support as Romanov agents made quiet appeals behind the scenes to block Trubetskoi and as some cossacks openly pleaded Mikhail's case and not-too-subtly threatened supporters of other candidates. Eventually, cossack delegates in the zemskii sobor supporting Mikhail Romanov prevailed in a vote held on February 7, 1613. Continued resistance on the part of Trubetskoi and Pozharskii resulted in the virtual siege of their residences. Both were accused of plotting to put a foreign tsar on the throne so they could continue to dominate the new government and steal state revenues. The cossacks loudly demanded a native tsar who would reward them for their sacrifices and for liberating Moscow. In a last ditch effort to derail Mikhail Romanov's candidacy, the boyars pushed forward Mikhail's unpopular uncle, Ivan, who immediately declared his own preference for Prince Mstislavskii. But both of those men were widely regarded as traitors and were truly hated for their past support of Polish intervention. Crowds in Moscow ignored the pleas on behalf of those aristocrats and demanded Mikhail Romanov as tsar.[53]

In the end, the boyars were forced to accept the fact that the young Romanov and not one of them was going to become the ruler of Russia. There was, understandably, considerable grumbling about it. The sixteen-year-old boy did not impress the boyars at all; he was poorly educated and not particularly intelligent.[54] Nonetheless, those great lords consoled themselves with the knowledge that Trubetskoi would not become tsar and that Mikhail's ambitious and highly intelligent father, Filaret, was still in Polish captivity. That meant that the boyars still had an excellent opportunity to dominate and profit from the new government. One of the boyars allegedly said at the time, "Let us have Misha Romanov for he is young and not yet wise; he will suit our purposes."[55] But, of course, the boyars really did not have the final word. They merely bowed to irresistible popular pressure and tried to make the best of a situation that they certainly did not control. After a three-day fast to seek divine guidance and to allow Mstislavskii and other absent dignitaries to return to Moscow, on February 21, 1613, the cossack-dominated zemskii sobor finally proclaimed Mikhail Romanov as the new tsar.[56]

Tsar Mikhail was crowned in Moscow on July 21, 1613, in a ceremony intended to show unity among the various factions that had joined together to end the civil war. Some contemporaries noted, however, that since the troublesome cossacks had put Romanov on the throne, Russia's Time of Troubles was bound to continue. They need not have worried. Mikhail Romanov actually feared and detested the cossacks. In fact, under the strong influence of reactionary boyars, even in preparation for his coronation, the deeply conservative new tsar revealed his true feelings about his subjects by snubbing many patriots simply because they were mere commoners. It is one of the great and tragic ironies of Russian history that the founder of the Romanov dynasty quickly put an end to the Troubles in part by crushing the very same patriotic cossacks who saved the country and brought him to power.[57]

24

Tsar Mikhail and the End of the Time of Troubles

Tsar Mikhail Fedorovich Romanov (r. 1613–45) was chosen by his subjects to restore God's grace to Russia and to lead the country out of civil war. For a long time the traditional interpretation of the Time of Troubles as a period of social revolution caused scholars to focus only on the emergence of elite support for the restoration of autocracy—supposedly out of fear of the aroused lower classes.[1] In fact, bitter memories of the horrors of the civil war pushed most Russians, regardless of social position or sides taken in years past, to support the new Romanov regime in the hope that Tsar Mikhail would be able to reimpose order. Russia's first civil war produced a very broad consensus across class lines in support of restoring as much as possible of the form and content of the tsarist system of the old sacred ruling dynasty.[2] That powerful consensus gave the young tsar, his mother, and their principal advisers the time and support needed to assert the new regime's authority, to preside over the rebuilding of the Russian government, to mop up the last traces of the civil war, and to confront Polish and Swedish interventionists. Even so, the problems produced by a decade of extraordinarily bitter conflict were so severe that, in spite of the traditional designation of Mikhail Romanov's election as the end of the Time of Troubles, it actually took several years for the new tsar to put an end to the destabilizing forces unleashed by the civil war.

As one might expect of a new dynasty with a relatively weak claim to legitimacy, the Romanovs worked assiduously to promote Tsar Mikhail as the "God-chosen," sacred ruler of Russia and his family as the natural successors of the ancient ruling dynasty that had died out in 1598. False electioneering propaganda to the effect that Tsar Fedor Ivanovich had intended for the crown to pass from him directly to Tsar Mikhail's father, Fedor (later Filaret), was refined and became part of the official Romanov version of the Time of Troubles.[3] The relationship of the new tsar's family to the old dynasty was emphasized while its adherence to Tsar Dmitrii, to the "second false Dmitrii," and to Prince Wladyslaw was carefully covered up. The new government brazenly and falsely proclaimed that Patriarch Filaret had opposed Wladyslaw's plans to become tsar

Fig. 14 "Tsar Mikhail Romanov." Engraved circa 1633. Published in Adam
Olearius, *Des Welt-berühmten Adami Olearii colligirte und vermehrte Reise-
Beschreibungen: bestehend in der nach Musskau und Persien* . . . (Hamburg, 1696).
(Frequently misidentified as a portrait of Tsar Mikhail's son, Tsar Aleksei.) From
D. A. Rovinskii, *Materialy dlia Russkoi Ikonografii,* part 1 (St. Petersburg, 1884).
Courtesy of The British Library.

while delicately avoiding any mention of just exactly how Filaret had managed to become head of the Russian Orthodox Church while he was in Tushino.[4] The new regime also revised Tsar Mikhail's own embarrassing personal history so that during the two years he lived in the Polish-occupied Kremlin, instead of being just a low-profile nephew of the collaborator Ivan Romanov, Mikhail was falsely portrayed as a "captive" who was respected even by the hated Poles for his family's connection to the old ruling dynasty and for his personal piety and dignity.[5] The new tsar was also repeatedly and misleadingly described as prudent, judicious, and capable.[6] Even the fact of Mikhail's election by the zemskii sobor, which was celebrated during his coronation, was gradually deemphasized or ignored in favor of a portrayal of the new tsar as the God-chosen successor of the defunct sacred dynasty whose accession had been approved not by the people but by the high clergy and the boyars.[7]

In the aftermath of Russia's first civil war, the Romanov regime attempted to enhance its own legitimacy as well as that of the political order it represented by placing great emphasis on the autocratic and sacred nature of Tsar Mikhail's office. As discussed earlier, to most Russians in the early modern period the salvation of all Orthodox Russians (and perhaps the whole world) depended on the piety of the tsar. In that spirit, the new tsar began to wear a pectoral cross over his robes—a former practice of the Muscovite grand princes but never before seen on a tsar.[8] Mikhail and his advisers also insisted that since a legitimate, God-chosen tsar once again ruled Russia, it was time for the Russian people themselves to withdraw from involvement in matters of state and once again to become as "mute as fish." In fact, Tsar Mikhail was deeply afraid of his own subjects, and those fears were fanned by his conservative relatives, close friends, and the boyars.[9] As noted earlier, the Russian elite had been taken by surprise and badly frightened by the powerful popular support Tsar Dmitrii generated during his campaign for the throne; and they were even more confused and terrified by the fanatical and relentless popular support for pretenders claiming to be "Dmitrii" during the period 1606–12. Many aristocrats at Tsar Mikhail's court deeply resented the unprecedented role ordinary Russians ended up playing in politics and military affairs during the Time of Troubles, activities traditionally reserved for the tsar and the nobility. The new ruler was therefore strongly urged to put an end to such unseemly popular encroachments on the ruling elite's exclusive privileges. Tsar Mikhail was advised that he had to take stern measures in order to survive and to cement his authority, including the suppression of all popular activism—which was widely regarded at court as a principal cause of the civil war in the first place.[10]

Because of the threats posed by the continued presence of foreign troops in

Russia and smoldering unrest associated with Zarutskii, Tsaritsa Marina, and little Ivan Dmitrievich, the strategy adopted for restoring domestic order by the insecure Romanov regime included brutally lashing out at any and all hints of opposition to Tsar Mikhail's legitimacy; and there were, in fact, some people who questioned that legitimacy.[11] Unlike the ill-fated Tsar Dmitrii, however, the Romanovs quickly set up machinery to investigate and severely punish any comments or actions, no matter how trivial, which threatened or even slighted the ruling family.[12] There were, of course, precedents for such heavy-handed measures.[13] Nevertheless, the speed and zeal with which the paranoid Romanovs pursued their real or perceived enemies was completely without precedent. Not surprisingly, there were many investigations of possible treasonable activity among the population of the southern frontier and relatively few in such "loyal" towns as Nizhnii Novgorod.[14]

The Romanovs were particularly nervous about nostalgia for Tsar Dmitrii, and from the outset of Tsar Mikhail's reign anyone who claimed Dmitrii was still alive or who even dared to remember him fondly was brutally punished.[15] Others were tortured or imprisoned for comments favorable to any pretender or past ruler whose legitimacy the new regime disputed.[16] At one time Marxist scholars caught up in the traditional interpretation of the Time of Troubles viewed these harsh measures of the early Romanovs as "state terror" or class war aimed primarily against the lower classes, "terror" that supposedly resulted in hundreds of executions and exiles. In fact, that was a misinterpretation and gross exaggeration of the new regime's ruthless efforts to stamp out pretenderism and to enforce its own claims to legitimacy.[17] Tsar Mikhail's boyars played a prominent role in investigating such cases of "treason." Edward Keenan believed that their vigorous prosecution of even the most petty political crimes was intended to overawe Tsar Mikhail's subjects and to secure the boyars' own position as the effective rulers of Russia by sustaining the "myth" of the weak new tsar's autocracy.[18] Richard Hellie has reminded us, however, that the situation at the end of the Time of Troubles was still unstable and dangerous. Armed opponents of the Romanovs still operated inside Russia, and many of Tsar Mikhail's subjects continued to harbor "romantic notions" about Tsar Dmitrii.[19] Under those circumstances, the very unpopular boyars probably had little choice but to embrace and promote the new tsar's legitimacy as the best means to secure their own futures and to avoid any reckoning for their inconsistent and unpatriotic activities during the civil war.[20]

From the very beginning of Mikhail's reign, the aristocracy—of which the Romanovs had been a part—dominated and set the reactionary tone of his regime.[21] Curiously, the traditional interpretation of the outcome of the Time of Troubles placed the boyars squarely in the category of "losers." Despised for accommodating foreign intervention, they were supposedly replaced by a new Romanov aristocracy.[22] That is not what really happened. Tsar Mikhail, like all grand princes and tsars before him, added some family members to the ruling circle. Nonetheless, due at least in part to the weakness of the new tsar's legitimacy, he emphasized his connection to the pre-1598 regime by restoring as much as possible of the old aristocracy and court. Mikhail was extremely generous to boyars and courtiers who had survived the Time of Troubles.[23] For understandable reasons, few questions were asked about which sides they had supported during the civil war. Almost all of the great lords were encouraged to help the tsar restore order and, in effect, the old regime. As a result, the new boyar council looked a lot like it had been before the Time of Troubles. Not surprisingly, Fedor Mstislavskii (one of the richest aristocrats) resumed his position as the senior boyar.[24] To ensure the boyars' loyalty, the new tsar showered those already rich men with more lands and gifts.[25]

A small number of the Romanovs, their in-laws, and other leading aristocrats emerged as a self-serving ruling elite who ruthlessly exploited their positions in order to increase their personal holdings. They pursued policies that served only the interests of the aristocracy, and they did not hesitate to seize the property of others in their quest for more wealth.[26] Those greedy and arrogant lords ignored, shoved aside, or even humiliated honorable patriots such as Kuzma Minin and Dmitrii Pozharskii who dared to urge the government to live up to the promises that had been made to the cossacks and other heroic commoners. In fact, Minin and Pozharskii were regarded with jealousy and contempt by many of the new tsar's courtiers. Those two men were somewhat reluctantly rewarded for their past service (Minin became a dumnyi dvorianin and Pozharskii became a boyar), but they were both quickly removed from any meaningful involvement in the operation of the new government.[27] It must have been disheartening to many supporters of Tsar Mikhail to see the new regime so quickly fall under the influence of corrupt men who had done little or nothing to help their country in its time of need. Isaac Massa wrote in 1614 that Tsar Mikhail required wise counselors to help restore order to Russia but was instead surrounded by "young and ignorant men"; even the tsar's most honest officials were "ravening wolves, who pluck and pillage the common people most of all." Massa also noted that no one received justice from the young tsar and nobody was able to petition him without paying someone at court a large bribe.[28]

Aristocrats at court constantly pressured the young tsar for large rewards, including much crown land (e.g., in Severia and the Vologda region) occupied by taxpaying peasants whose status the greedy lords boldly wished to reduce to that of serfs. Understandably, those peasants resisted—sometimes violently. They were occasionally assisted by free cossacks who were also angry at attempts by the aristocrats to "enslave" them. Such outbreaks of popular violence terrified Tsar Mikhail and his courtiers, and they were dealt with very harshly. Scholars have traditionally regarded the unrest in the early years of Mikhail's reign as a continuation of the mythical social revolution of the Time of Troubles.[29] That is an extremely faulty interpretation. Most rebels at the time were not serfs but free men resisting new pressure being applied by greedy courtiers. Cossack resistance in this period was also not due to class war but instead to the desperate attempts by those hard-pressed soldiers to retain their status. Those patriots reacted in horror and indignation as the nobility and the church successfully lobbied the tsar to authorize the tracking down of all fugitive peasants—including those who had bravely served against the Poles—in order to return them to servile status.[30] Rebellions among the Volga Tatars, the Cheremis, and other non-Slavic nationalities early in Mikhail's reign were also not part of a social revolution or peasant war; instead, they were revolts against the extraordinary fiscal pressures that were being applied by the corrupt new regime without any consideration of the impact those exactions had on the tsar's ordinary subjects.[31] In retrospect, the infuriating activities of young Tsar Mikhail's courtiers appear to have been extremely short-sighted considering the fact that the Romanov regime was still confronted by Polish and Swedish armies operating inside Russia and by thousands of cossacks and other supporters of Tsaritsa Marina and the "little brigand." The greedy and thoughtless reactionaries at Mikhail Romanov's court greatly complicated the tsar's task of ousting foreign troops, pacifying the realm, and building support for the new dynasty.

In the early years of his reign, Tsar Mikhail wisely asked the members of the zemskii sobor that had elected him to remain in Moscow in order to help him rebuild the shattered Russian state. In fact, Mikhail Romanov made far more extensive use of the zemskii sobor than any other tsar, and he was wise to do so. The energetic and experienced patriots in that assembly maintained ongoing contact with the towns and provinces they represented, and they provided the central government with valuable information about conditions far from the capital. Unlike some of the young tsar's greedy courtiers, however, the zemskii sobor delegates actually helped with the difficult tasks of restoring the state administration and renewing the flow of taxes to fund the day-to-day operations of government and to maintain military forces capable of challenging foreign interventionists and the renegade Zarutskii.[32]

The civil war had, of course, disrupted much ordinary economic activity, wiped out many taxpayers, and put many of the survivors several years behind in paying their bills. As a result, relatively high taxes now had to be levied on whatever goods and profits remained. The zemskii sobor delegates helped the tsar's officials locate potential sources of revenue and legitimized the new regime's heavy taxation and other unpopular emergency revenue-generating measures, which fell primarily on the towns. So great a burden falling on such a small part of the Russian population (townspeople made up less than three percent of the total population of Russia in the seventeenth century), however, inevitably slowed down the country's economic recovery from the Time of Troubles. By 1616, grumbling among his overtaxed subjects forced Tsar Mikhail to seek additional legitimization for his extraordinary revenue measures. In that year he wisely appointed the popular and much-trusted Prince Pozharskii as head of a new agency set up to collect yet another onerous and unpopular tax amounting to twenty percent of everyone's income.[33] Despite such extraordinary measures, Tsar Mikhail's government remained chronically short of cash long after the Time of Troubles was over. In fact, fiscal problems related to the destruction caused by the civil war continued to haunt the early Romanovs throughout the seventeenth century.

Although it was actually the domination of the new tsar by aristocrats that led some historians to accurately characterize the period between Mikhail's election and Patriarch Filaret's return to Russia in 1619 as the "non-tsar period," the unprecedented activity and duration of the zemskii sobor led Platonov and others to an extremely faulty view of that institution. During the Time of Troubles, the townsmen who played such a critically important role in organizing and funding the national militia supposedly gained a sense of themselves as members of an emerging "nation-state" and after 1613 attempted to modify the tsarist system into a kind of constitutional monarchy in which those newly politicized commoners in some way shared power with the tsar. Through their participation in the zemskii sobor, which worked closely with Tsar Mikhail, the townsmen allegedly came to view the state as something distinct from the person of the tsar and themselves as representatives of the "will of the people."[34] That still-influential view is, in fact, hopelessly anachronistic and inaccurate.

There is no evidence that early modern Russian townsmen ever viewed themselves as having any constitutional right to participate in the central government or that they came to see the state in secular terms as something distinct from the tsar. Far from it! The townsmen, like other Russians in the early seventeenth century, still regarded themselves as subjects of a God-chosen autocrat. While there certainly were very real religious and moral restraints on the exercise of tsarist power, there was no budding constitutionalism or constitutional monarchy in seventeenth-century Russia. The zemskii sobor was an incredibly useful tool for speeding up Russia's recovery, but it had no autonomy from the tsar and sought none. As noted earlier, the zemskii sobor was a government-created and government-summoned consultative assembly with no legislative prerogatives. It was essentially a sounding board with strong links to the state's chief revenue sources—the towns. Its members were content to act as advisers and, in fact, were extremely pleased with themselves for having been asked to help the tsar restore order. Instead of regarding themselves as the emerging voice of Russian "citizens," they willingly and actively helped rebuild autocracy and asked few questions about whose interests were being served by the restoration of the sacred old regime.[35] In the end, with the active support of the zemskii sobor delegates, incredibly resilient bureaucrats, and many other patriotic Russians, much of the administrative structure of autocracy was quickly rebuilt, and the new regime gained sufficient resources to deal with the lingering problems of foreign military intervention and the "little brigand," Ivan Dmitrievich.[36]

King Sigismund and Prince Wladyslaw, despite the loss of Moscow in 1612 and the election of Tsar Mikhail, still dreamed of conquering Russia. They even made plans to personally lead Polish military forces against the new tsar in 1613.[37] However, the king faced too many fiscal and political problems at home to carry out an energetic invasion. That respite gave the fragile new Romanov regime time to recover and to begin making its own plans to liberate Polish-occupied Russian territory. The tsar, Prince Mstislavskii, and others regarded such a campaign as a good opportunity to send most of the remaining cossacks in the national militia—whom they feared and hated—away from the Moscow area. As a result, in 1613, Russian forces (primarily cossacks) under the command of Dmitrii Cherkasskii drove Polish troops out of Kaluga, Viazma, Dorogobuzh, and Belaia, and then laid siege to Smolensk. Before that mighty fortress soon arrived an additional two thousand cossacks who had recently abandoned Zarutskii to join Tsar Mikhail's service. By 1614, the siege produced hunger in Smolensk and high hopes among the Russians for its imminent capture. With fewer than twelve thousand men in the siege army, however, the Russians were unable to recapture the fortress; and concentrating additional forces there to end the stalemate was not a realistic option because of the ongoing struggle against the Swedes to the north and Zarutskii and Tsaritsa Marina to the south.[38]

In 1613, Tsar Mikhail and his advisers sent Dmitrii Trubetskoi with almost all of the remaining cossacks stationed in the Moscow vicinity, plus additional gentry detachments, to confront Swedish forces in northwest Russia.[39] The Russians quickly managed to liberate a few towns and weakened the Swedes' overall strategic position somewhat. King Gustav Adolf, who briefly contemplated turning Swedish-occupied Russia into a buffer state to be ruled by his younger brother, Karl Filip, still held many important strongholds in the region but was increasingly disheartened by the complete lack of support for his ambitious military plans among the Russians themselves—even in Swedish-dominated Novgorod. Continuing partisan warfare in the region, the exhaustion of Swedish troops, and severe fiscal problems at home also threatened to reverse many of Sweden's gains made in Russia during the Time of Troubles. That prompted the king personally to lead a military campaign into north Russia during 1614. After some initial success against voevoda Trubetskoi, Gustav Adolf's forces got bogged down in a siege of the strategically and economically important town of Pskov. The heavily outnumbered and outgunned Pskov garrison stubbornly and heroically resisted the Swedes throughout all of 1615 and early 1616. By then, fiscal and domestic political pressures on the frustrated king forced him to begin serious negotiations to end the war in Russia.

After many months of complex diplomacy in which Prince Pozharskii played an important role, both countries agreed to sign the Treaty of Stolbovo in 1617. By the terms of the treaty, Sweden restored Novgorod, Ladoga, Staraia Rusa, and Porkhov to Russia but retained the strategically located lands and towns it had acquired along the coast of the Gulf of Finland (including Korela, Ivangorod, Iama, Kopore, and Oreshek)—thereby cutting Russia off completely from the Baltic Sea. Since the Swedes had failed to capture Arkhangelsk during the Time of Troubles, however, the Russians during the seventeenth century were still able to bypass Sweden and trade directly with the West via the White Sea even though that far northern trade route was inconvenient and dangerous. The Russians remained angry about Swedish military intervention, of course, and dreamed of regaining access to the Baltic; but relations between the two countries rapidly improved after the signing of the treaty. In fact, Sweden became the first country to maintain a permanent diplomatic representative in Moscow.[40]

Gustav Adolf personally regarded the Treaty of Stolbovo as a great triumph; and, in fairness, it did produce a buffer zone that secured his country's eastern borders and allowed the king to turn his attention elsewhere. As is well known, Gustav Adolf soon intervened in the Thirty Years War and established a sizable Baltic empire for Sweden. Nevertheless, Swedish military intervention in Russia failed to produce the total domination of that country's trade with the West that the Swedes had greatly desired and that may, in fact, have been their only real hope for sustaining Sweden's short-lived imperial adventure.[41]

One of Tsar Mikhail's first military actions was to send an army south against Ivan Zarutskii—the last serious domestic rival to the new Romanov regime.[42]

Not surprisingly, the traditional interpretation of the activities of Zarutskii's cossack forces in the period 1612–14 linked them to the mythical social revolution of the Time of Troubles.[43] As we have already seen, however, Zarutskii was by no means a revolutionary; he was instead just an energetic opportunist. In fact, after Zarutskii abandoned the siege of Moscow, he and more than two thousand cossacks still loyal to Tsaritsa Marina and Ivan Dmitrievich ruthlessly plundered estates along the southern frontier during late 1612 and early 1613. By June 1613, Tsar Mikhail's forces caught up with Zarutskii at Voronezh, and, after a fierce battle, many rebel cossacks deserted their commander and the "little brigand"—choosing instead to enter Tsar Mikhail's service. Zarutskii was reduced to leading only Marina, Ivan, and a few hundred loyal cossacks to Astrakhan.[44] At first, that great rebel stronghold welcomed them with open arms; city officials recognized little Ivan as "tsar" and Marina and Zarutskii as his regents.[45]

Soon after their arrival, however, Zarutskii launched a reign of terror during which many of the town's leading citizens—including voevoda Ivan D. Khvorostinin, the head of the streltsy garrison, and several monks and merchants—were put to death. The archbishop's residence was also sacked, and hundreds of townspeople and Zarutskii's cossacks divided up the possessions of their victims.[46] This incident has traditionally been regarded as evidence of class war.[47] In fact, Zarutskii—as we have seen before—was a desperate and extremely wreckless individual; and his frantic negotiations seeking Persian or Turkish aid to support "Tsar Ivan Dmitrievich" quickly alienated many Orthodox Christians in Astrakhan and among local cossacks. As a direct result, a conspiracy soon developed to seize Zarutskii that he found out about and managed to forestall only by means of his terror campaign. There is some evidence that Zarutskii was prompted to move against Khvorostinin when he did because he learned of the voevoda's secret plans to recognize Mikhail Romanov as tsar.[48]

During the time Zarutskii was negotiating with foreign powers, Tsar Mikhail's commanders concentrated troops and supplies along the Volga as far south as Samara in preparation for an assault on Astrakhan and to prevent Zarutskii and his men from heading north.[49] In order to hold Tsar Mikhail's forces back and to increase his own options, Zarutskii attempted to gain alliances with local cossacks, Nogai Tatars, and even the Crimean Tatars. In response, diplomats from Moscow successfully petitioned the Don and Terek cossacks to reject Zarutskii's offers and to recognize Tsar Mikhail instead. They also convinced the sultan not to allow the Crimean Tatars to aid Zarutskii.[50] Only by taking the son of Prince Ishterek hostage was the desparate and increasingly isolated Zarutskii able to gain the temporary and reluctant support of the Nogai Tatars.

About five hundred of them became his personal bodyguard in Astrakhan.

By spring 1614, Zarutskii's support among the population of Astrakhan began to wane rapidly as word spread that Tsar Mikhail's commanders were preparing to march on the city. Rumors that Zarutskii intended to allow five hundred newly arriving Volga cossacks to loot the city prompted a powerful uprising by the townspeople. A surprised Zarutskii and about eight hundred men (mostly Volga cossacks) were temporarily forced to retreat to the citadel where they were besieged for days by more than three thousand men. In May 1614, Zarutskii, Marina, Ivan, and a dwindling number of loyal cossacks managed to escape from Astrakhan—which was immediately occupied by Tsar Mikhail's forces. The tsar's troops entering the city were greeted by the sounds of church bells and loud cheers.[51] Streltsy units were quickly dispatched to track down Zarutskii and Ivan, which they managed to do by mid-June. In a remote area along the Iaik River, Zarutskii's cossacks, realizing at last that their situation was hopeless, suddenly seized their commander and handed him—along with Tsaritsa Marina and the "little brigand"—over to Tsar Mikhail's men.[52]

The captives, in chains, were quickly taken to Moscow under very heavy guard. There, by command of Tsar Mikhail and the zemskii sobor, Zarutskii was impaled and Ivan Dmitrievich, then almost four years old, was hanged outside the city gates.[53] Tsaritsa Marina was locked up in a tower in Kolomna and died soon thereafter. Sources differ on whether she starved to death or died of natural causes. Not surprisingly, according to one legend, she managed to escape—by using witchcraft to transform herself into a magpie and then flying away.[54] According to Maureen Perrie, the executions of Zarutskii and the "little brigand" in 1614 "effectively marked the end of the Time of Troubles" even though social unrest, banditry, and war with Sweden and Poland-Lithuania continued for a few more years.[55] Of course, rumors persisted for a long time that Tsar Dmitrii or Ivan Dmitrievich still lived and would someday return to claim the Russian throne; however, those rumors were due primarily to continuing cossack nostalgia and on-going Polish efforts to destabilize the new Romanov regime. None of those rumors, nor the pathetic pretenders sometimes associated with them, gained any significant support in Russia; and they gradually faded away once Wladyslaw abandoned his claim to the Russian throne in 1634 and stopped subsidizing his own personal false "Ivan Dmitrievich."[56]

Once Zarutskii and the "little brigand" had been eliminated, Tsar Mikhail felt secure enough to begin dealing harshly with the free cossacks still serving in the national militia. As noted earlier, Mikhail Romanov was no friend to the cossacks who had liberated Moscow and put him on the throne. Having endured the siege of the capital inside the Kremlin for two years, he had grown to share the council of seven's hatred for the patriotic cossacks in the national militia. Even before he was crowned, the new tsar began to echo boyar and gentry denunciations of cossack banditry and violence; and, just as soon as they could, Tsar Mikhail and his advisers speeded up the transfer of cossack forces away from Moscow. Although free cossacks made up at least half of the national militia and were still indispensable for operations against the Poles, the Swedes, and Zarutskii, the reactionary court shared the gentry's fear of the cossacks' military prowess, independence, and emergence as serious competitors to the gentry cavalry force.[57] Bent on restoring as much as possible of the pre-civil war old regime, Tsar Mikhail and his advisers made it a priority to shore up the shattered and foundering gentry militia as Russia's principal fighting force and began pushing the cossacks aside. Because of cossack support of Tsar Dmitrii and other pretenders during the Time of Troubles, as well as day-to-day difficulties getting cossack troops to cooperate with gentry detachments, it was easy for the frightened Russian elite to credit ten years of their own propaganda as well as countless hysterical gentry claims about the cossacks as dangerous social revolutionaries. (In this same period, Ukrainian magnates also genuinely but wrongly feared the Zaporozhian cossacks as social revolutionaries.) That was a seriously flawed perception, but in truth the cossacks really were a threat to the traumatized gentry's role in Russian society; and, unlike the gentry, the free cossacks did not easily fit into the new regime's plans for the restoration of the old regime and the development of a rigidly stratified society.[58]

Once Zarutskii was out of the way, the tsar and his boyars began seriously—and somewhat prematurely—to heed the gentry's calls for the outright elimination of the "cossack menace." Emphasis was placed on cossack banditry and the need to restore order by suppressing them even though Russia continued to face Polish and Swedish military intervention as well as powerful raids by the Nogai and Crimean Tatars.[59] In fact, banditry really did become a chronic problem in the aftermath of the civil war and required serious measures to suppress it. Some cossacks (and displaced peasants and townsmen) had become bandits in order to survive; others, however, were falsely accused of banditry simply because they resisted government attempts to suppress their independence and freedom. It turns out that most of the cossacks the Romanov regime took stern measures against were not bandits at all; instead, they were loyal, patriotic soldiers who foolishly believed the new tsar would live up to the promises made to them by Prince Pozharskii.[60] Tsar Mikhail not only failed to reward them but launched a series of menacing investigations into their social background. Employing techniques similar to those used by the Polish government in Ukraine, the tsar's officials attempted simultaneously to co-opt cossack atamans into the ranks of the petty gentry, to liquidate cossack self-rule at the small unit level, to stop newcomers from joining the tsar's cossack detachments, and to return all runaway serfs and slaves in those detachments either to their former masters or to new ones. Not surprisingly, those measures provoked serious unrest among the patriotic cossacks, who were well aware that the new tsar was dominated by greedy and unscrupulous boyars who were now boldly trying to enslave many of the heroic liberators of Moscow.[61]

In their analyses of the Romanov regime's harsh cossack policy, Soviet scholars often exaggerated the degree of differentiation between the cossack elite and rank-and-file cossacks that had developed over the course of the Time of Troubles, incorrectly discerning a gradual shift in the thinking of the better-off cossasks until they came to resemble and act like pomeshchiki.[62] Stanislavskii, however, has clearly demonstrated that the process of transforming the cossack elite into pomeshchiki actually occurred in the period 1613–19 as the direct result of a conscious government policy designed to harness the free cossacks; it was definitely not the result of natural social development within cossack forces themselves. As members of the cossack elite were enticed into the ranks of the gentry by the new tsar, those men increasingly came to be regarded as traitors by rank-and-file cossacks who continued to stoutly defend their traditions and independence. Former atamans who sided with Tsar Mikhail were not infrequently killed during sporadic outbursts of cossack anger at and violent resistance to the grossly unfair treatment they received from the Romanov regime.[63]

Some cossack units responded to threats of investigation by abruptly abandoning state service. In order to support themselves and to show their displeasure at the betrayal of the promises made to them, they went out of their way to raid the estates of Prince Mstislavskii and even members of the Romanov clan but were always careful to avoid harming Pozharskii's property. Many cossacks attached to Trubetskoi's army, then fighting against the Swedes, also refused to obey orders to proceed to Moscow where menacing investigations awaited them. On their own initiative, some of them organized mixed military units of cossacks, peasants, and streltsy who declared their eagerness to continue fighting against foreign interventionists but only if the Romanov regime would give up its efforts to return runaways among them to their former masters. Tsar Mikhail's court reacted in horror to such developments. In spite of continued military pressure from Sweden and Poland-Lithuania (as well as devastating Tatar raids), the new regime focussed obsessively on eliminating the "cossack menace." During the summer of 1615, some of those upstart cossack leaders (e.g., Mikhail Balovnia) were tricked into traveling to Moscow to negotiate with tsarist officials, where they were seized, briefly jailed, and then executed. Gentry militia units also occasionally attacked disaffected cossack groups without warning, killing or capturing thousands of them. Most of the survivors were eventually hanged or forced into slavery. Such savage reprisals against the essentially loyal free cossacks—whose only real crime was their desire for a fair reward for past service and the chance to continue living as free men—had a powerful, destabilizing psychological effect in the country in addition to dangerously reducing the size and effectiveness of the Russian army. Cossack and, to a lesser extent, popular enthusiasm for Tsar Mikhail temporarily waned just as the country faced a renewed Polish effort to capture Moscow and put Prince Wladyslaw on the Russian throne.[64]

The Romanov regime should not have been surprised to find itself facing serious difficulties fielding sufficient military forces to counter the renewed Polish offensive beginning in 1615. The harsh treatment of the cossacks had provoked such disaffection that many of those patriots lost all interest in defending the new dynasty. Among Russian commanders, only Prince Pozharskii could still inspire the cossacks to fight for their homeland. As a result, a reluctant court was forced to rely increasingly on Pozharskii to raise and command troops to counter the Polish drive toward Moscow. Although he was hated by many high-born courtiers, Prince Pozharskii was still loved and respected by the patriotic cossacks; and he immediately drew their support "like a magnet." The incredibly honorable and brilliant Pozharskii even managed to entice many cossacks away from the Polish invasion force, and he was able to inflict such serious losses on the Poles that their offensive temporarily stalled out.[65]

Starting in 1617, "Tsar Wladyslaw" himself made one final attempt to capture Moscow. Thousands of cossacks in the Russian army at that time openly refused to fight against the Poles under the banners of corrupt and cowardly boyar commanders who not only failed to pay or feed them but who openly planned to enslave or enserf them as soon as their military service was no longer desperately needed. Only after the frantic boyars went into the field personally to negotiate with the rebel cossacks and insincerely agreed to meet their demands were many of those disaffected warriors willing to defend the capital again.[66] It is noteworthy that, even then, the suspicious cossacks were still willing to serve only under the trustworthy Pozharskii, and the reluctant court had no choice but to agree. By then the regime had finally begun to realize the great danger to its survival posed by its own unpopularity. Many patriots who had initially been wildly enthusiastic about Tsar Mikhail were now having second thoughts about him. The treacherous boyars had, of course, never been popular and were at this time widely believed to be secretly negotiating with the hated Poles; a terrified Prince Mstislavskii was even threatened by an armed crowd of angry and suspicious Muscovites. In order to survive, Tsar Mikhail felt compelled at long last to richly reward and publicly exalt Pozharskii and to trust him with the defense of the capital in the fall of 1618. The entire population of the city was summoned for the task of resisting the Poles, and they responded willingly and enthusiastically to the beloved Prince Pozharskii. As a result, the Polish hetman Chodkiewicz and Prince Wladyslaw were stopped decisively and forced to withdraw.[67]

Because Prince Wladyslaw's military campaign had failed to achieve its primary objective, the Polish government was forced by fiscal constraints to immediately enter into serious peace negotiations with the Russians. Nevertheless, the fourteen-year Truce of Deulino that was signed in December 1618 proved to be a harsh one for the Russians. By its terms, Poland-Lithuania gained thirty towns and a considerable amount of territory: the entire Smolensk and Chernigov regions and much of Severia. During the negotiations, Tsar Mikhail hastily ordered the evacuation and transfer to the Poles of several border towns and fortresses that, up to that point, had been actively and successfully resisting enemy forces.

Why did the tsar accept such a one-sided truce that transferred many of his loyal subjects to Lithuanian administration and made many of his remaining subjects extremely unhappy? In part, it was due to the Romanov regime's growing fear of continued cossack unrest (and to the related problem of the weakness of the Russian army) at a time when the tsar and his advisers finally realized that Mikhail had lost some popular support. It may also have been influenced by Polish threats to unleash their own pretender "Ivan Dmitrievich" in order to stir up trouble for the new regime inside Russia. The main reason, however, was simply to assure the prompt return of the tsar's father, Patriarch Filaret, from Polish captivity.[68] Although Prince Wladyslaw continued to dream of conquering Russia and the Russians continued to dream of retaking Smolensk, the two sides did not go to war again until the truce expired in 1632. Then, after a relatively brief, expensive, and fruitless Russian campaign to recapture the great fortress, both sides agreed in 1634 to a permanent treaty that recognized all Polish territorial gains made during the Time of Troubles in return for Wladyslaw's agreement to drop his claim to the Russian throne. In spite of that treaty, the Russians continued to deeply resent the bloody and humiliating results of Polish military intervention in their country's first civil war and looked for an early opportunity to turn the tables on their aggressive western neighbors.

Once the Truce of Deulino was signed, the Romanov regime felt secure enough to resume the grim business of eliminating all remaining free cossacks

Map 9 Russian Territory Lost by Treaty.

in the Russian army. Under such pressure, the cossacks failed to maintain their status as a special service class; and by the end of 1619, there were no more free cossacks in central Russia. Many of them fled to the Don and other places along the frontier; others became bandits. Small numbers of former national militia cossacks were forced to become serfs.[69] Remarkably enough, in spite of its harsh treatment of the patriotic cossacks, the Romanov regime was soon able to make use of many of them as it resumed Russia's colonization and extension of the southern frontier. The government quickly returned to the practice of settling fortress cossacks (including former national militia atamans) along Russia's southern borderlands; and some of them were even given serfs to work their lands.[70] Tsar Mikhail was also able to make use of the free cossacks of the Don and Volga as well. Many of those free men were still looking for employment; and, in fact, large numbers of them had not participated in the civil war and therefore did not feel personally betrayed by any of the regime's broken promises. Tsar Mikhail also cleverly flattered the free cossacks, calling them the "protectors of the Russian land" and "knights of the glorious Don." He granted them many favors in return for harassing the Crimean Tatars and others who stood in the way of Russian imperial expansion.[71] Once again, the foolish cossacks were only too willing to help Russia extend its control southward, eventually closing the frontier and greatly reducing their own independence. Although the cossacks periodically rebelled against the relentless encroachment on their lands and liberty by the Russian state and provided the main fighting force for such powerful uprisings as the Razin and Pugachev rebellions, there is no denying that the cossacks themselves also actively aided the expansion of the Russian empire and the resulting extinction of their own much-vaunted freedom.

In many ways, Patriarch Filaret's return to Moscow in 1619 marked the real end of the Time of Troubles. By then, Russia was well on the road to recovery, the last remnants of the civil war had been eliminated, and the country was once again at peace with its neighbors. Much of the state structure had been rebuilt and was functioning, and a greatly relieved Russian society was willing to accept the Romanov dynasty as legitimate and to work hard to rebuild the devastated country. Patriarch Filaret immediately took charge of his son's regime and became the effective ruler of Russia until his own death in 1633. Under Filaret's firm hand, Russia by the 1620s—superficially at least—appeared to be much like it had been before the civil war. In fact, the early Romanovs made spectacular progress in recovering from the Time of Troubles and resuming the rapid expansion of their realm—much to the surprise and annoyance of their neighbors. Because of that, many people came to believe that the widespread and horrifying reports of the chaos and destruction produced by Russia's first civil war had been greatly exaggerated. Yet, as Robert Crummey wisely pointed out, the nightmarish experience of the Time of Troubles really did leave very deep scars, and Russia "would never be quite the same again."[72]

25

Disturbing Legacy

The Time of Troubles, one of the darkest chapters in Russian history, left deep scars, but its impact has puzzled generations of scholars for at least two reasons. First, historians have usually evaluated the outcome of the Troubles primarily in terms of winners and losers in a mythical class struggle; and, as a result, their conclusions are filled with errors and confusion.[1] Second, the incredibly rapid recovery of the autocratic regime and the spectacular expansion of Russia's empire under the early Romanovs has obscured the impact of Russia's first civil war and led some writers to minimize or even ignore it in their comments about the development of autocracy, increasing social stratification, or the growth of Russia in the seventeenth century.[2] That view is just as mistaken as the class war interpretation. In fact, the Time of Troubles produced a powerful consensus in favor of restoring and even enhancing the power of the tsars. At the same time, however, the extraordinary success of Russian autocracy in the seventeenth century exposed deeply embedded elements of opposition among the tsars' overburdened subjects—opposition that, ironically, found much of its origin, justification, tactics, and vocabulary in the very same civil war that produced the consensus favoring a more powerful autocracy. Such was the troubling and somewhat confusing legacy of the Time of Troubles.

Without doubt, the real winner in Russia's first civil war was the autocratic government represented by the new Romanov dynasty. Writers have, of course, long noted that the Time of Troubles hastened centralization of authority and the strengthening of autocracy, but their explanations were usually tied to a faulty class war interpretation of the period.[3] In fact, that traditional approach cannot explain with any credibility how Russia, devastated by civil war and foreign intervention, could so quickly restore the essential components of its state structure and bureaucratic administration, let alone develop them so breathtakingly far beyond the precrisis old order within just a few decades. Nor can it account for the astonishing growth of Russia in the seventeenth century.

Under Tsar Mikhail the Russian empire reached the Pacific Ocean and became the world's largest country. In the next generation, his son, Tsar Aleksei (r.

1645–76), was able to shift forever the balance of power between Russia and Poland-Lithuania in the Thirteen Years War (1654–67), managing in the process to regain all territory lost to Poland in the Time of Troubles and adding half of Ukraine and the ancient capital city of Kiev to his domain for good measure. Within a century of the Troubles, Aleksei's son, Peter the Great (r. 1689–1725), completed Russia's revenge against Sweden. Peter, of course, not only regained all territory that had previously been lost to the Swedes and once again gave Russia direct access to the Baltic Sea; but, in the process, he also transformed the Russian empire into the "great power" so well-known and feared since the eighteenth century. Although there is clearly no monocausal explanation for the incredible success of the early Romanovs, one of the most important factors was the Time of Troubles itself. In order to demonstrate that and to chart a post-Marxist interpretation of the impact of Russia's first civil war, it will first be useful once again to tap into the insights provided by new research in comparative early modern history that have already proved so helpful in identifying preconditions and long-term causes of that great state crisis.

We have already seen that Jack Goldstone's intriguing model of the long-term causes of early modern state breakdowns applies to Russia. His model also contains useful ideas concerning the outcome of state crises. In remarks that are highly relevant to the study of elite consciousness and the restoration of order under the early Romanovs, Goldstone commented on the conservative nature of both elite and folk "ideologies of rectification" and predicted the strengthening of traditional institutions and a certain degree of cultural stagnation in the postcrisis recovery period. Beyond the not-unexpected strong motivation on the part of frightened rulers, church officials, bureaucrats, and increasingly entrenched aristocrats to restore order and reassert traditional authority and institutions, Goldstone detected in postcrisis early modern Spain, Turkey, and China a powerful nostalgic impulse to rebuild as much as possible of a romanticized image of the precrisis old order. The results included an increase in authoritarianism and rigidly enforced conformity—including increased codification of roles and responsibilities for all subjects and the emergence of much more highly "role-prescriptive" societies in which a principal duty of the exalted ruler was to keep everyone in his or her assigned place. These "closed societies" also became increasingly xenophobic and chauvinistic; and, at least in the Turkish and Chinese cases, all these factors combined to greatly strengthen the power of the state.[4] In many ways, Russia after the Time of Troubles fits Goldstone's model perfectly.

Just as useful in assessing the aftermath of Russia's first civil war is the model of the development of the fiscal-military state discussed earlier. In the age of the gunpowder revolution, Russia became a somewhat primitive but highly effective fiscal-military state geared to war and survival. As we have seen, that development helped precipitate the profound fiscal and economic crisis that led to the Time of Troubles. It turns out that recent scholarship on the subject of "absolutism" and the development of the fiscal-military state is also highly relevant to the study of Russia *after* the Time of Troubles. Valerie Kivelson has demonstrated that Russian autocracy in the seventeenth century rested to a considerable extent on the government's ability to compromise with and accommodate the needs of regional elites and landholders.[5] In fact, influenced by Nicholas Henshall's *The Myth of Absolutism* (1992), Kivelson correctly pointed out that Russian autocracy functioned in many ways like early modern West European regimes, which were far more dependent on compromise with their elites than the outdated concept of "absolutism" implied.[6] But how did that come about? What factors led to such a rapid recreation and even acceleration of the fiscal-military state in the years after the Time of Troubles? What produced such a broad consensus that enabled the early Romanovs to construct such a successful and coercive state and to triple the size of their empire before the reign of Peter the Great? Kivelson did not really focus on those questions, but Henshall's model of the fiscal-military state may provide at least part of the answer.

Henshall was building on the work of John Brewer, who sought to explain how England, which managed to avoid both autocracy and absolutism, nonetheless managed to become a strong state and a great power—complete with a radical increase in military forces, a sharp rise in the level of taxation, and the rapid growth of a coercive bureaucracy devoted to organizing the fiscal and military activities of the state. Brewer found his explanation in the aftermath of seventeenth-century England's severe state crisis (the combination of the Civil War and the Glorious Revolution of 1688), when there emerged a political culture in which cooperation among government officials and elites developed into a powerful on-going consensus not merely for restoration of order but in favor of the creation and maintenance of a powerful state and empire.[7] If, as I suspect, early modern Russia was a fiscal-military state, then not only is Kivelson's comparison of the pomeshchiki to the English gentry appropriate and useful, but Brewer's observations about factors that accelerated elite cohesion to the state and England's rapid emergence as a great power may also apply to Russian autocracy and imperial expansion after the Time of Troubles.

Also potentially useful in evaluating Russia after its first civil war is recent scholarship by Harold G. Brown focusing on the restoration of order after the French Revolution. Brown discovered that, after years of political violence and uncertainty, many French communities were not only willing but anxious to cooperate with state authorities to restore order. In fact, there was surprisingly strong support for even the most draconian measures to suppress banditry and disorder. Furthermore, it seems that the savage repression of lawlessness actually increased support for the Napoleonic regime and, in the process, helped transform the relationship between the state and French society. With considerable popular and elite cooperation, the new government gained unprecedented powers of surveillance and regulatory control over the French people, and this marked the transition from a premodern "organic society" to a more modern police state (or "security state"), increasingly accepted by many people as necessary to maintain public order.[8] Even though it may seem absurd to compare Russia after the Time of Troubles with France at the dawn of the nineteenth century, some of Brown's findings may help us better understand just what did happen in Russia after 1613. Although it is commonly believed that Russia's transition to a "well-ordered police state" did not occur until Peter the Great, the savage repression of cossacks and banditry under Tsar Mikhail—while complicating the task of ending foreign military intervention—was welcomed by many Russians and ushered in an era of unprecedented state surveillance of the tsar's subjects and ruthless repression of any and all potential sources of opposition to the Romanov regime. Such measures as the vigorous prosecution of even trivial cases of lese majesty may actually have enhanced the new dynasty's legitimacy in the eyes of many and helped prepare the Russian people for the more intrusive, modern police state commonly associated with later Romanov history.

It should be apparent by now that there were many factors related to the civil war that contributed to the enhanced power of the autocratic regime of the early Romanovs. We have already seen, for example, that the Time of Troubles did not lead to political innovation or the emergence of any secular notion of a Russian "nation-state" independent of the tsar. Instead, the chaos and destruction of the civil war years produced a sharp political, social, and cultural reaction that rejected innovation in favor of restoring as much as possible of the precrisis old order. As a result, the prestige and authority of the tsar—already very high in Russian political culture—actually increased in the seventeenth century.[9] That, in turn, strengthened and sanctified the imperial ambitions of the early Romanovs and the quick reconstruction and growth of the central state bureaucracy, which soon resumed its coercive and large-scale allocation of Russia's human and capital resources for the purpose of exalting the ruler and expanding the state. The results were profound. As already noted, the empire of the Romanovs tripled in size over the course of the seventeenth century. In the same period, the tsarist bureaucracy grew at an even faster rate and produced a powerful "caste of professional civil servants" accustomed to interfering with the economy and regulating and controlling the lives of the Russian people.[10]

It is well known that, even before the Time of Troubles, Russian culture placed a high value on the preservation of established order and the maintenance of traditional social hierarchy.[11] Not surprisingly, that tendency was strengthened by the violence and uncertainty of the civil war years, and in the decades after the Troubles it combined with a sharp political and cultural reaction, a very weak economy, and zealous bureaucrats to greatly accelerate the regimentation and stratification of Russian society.[12] Russia in the seventeenth century became even more of a "role prescriptive" society than it had been in the late sixteenth century. By the time Tsar Aleksei issued his famous law code, the *Ulozhenie*, in 1649, in which his regime took the final legal step in the enserfment of the peasants, the central government also attempted to force all other subjects into fixed positions in a "highly-stratified, explicitly ordered society."[13] The result was the legal codification of an eerily premodern, near-caste society dedicated to the service of Russia's "God-chosen" ruler.[14] As elite and popular worship of the tsars increased, the emerging "orientalized" Russian political culture severely limited any possible modernization of society even as Russia emerged as a major player on the European and world stage.[15] Although Russia's rather backward system was powerful enough to lay the basis for its emergence as a great power in the eighteenth century, that system also impoverished the country and the Russian people in many ways.[16]

According to the traditional interpretation of the Time of Troubles, the winners included the townsmen.[17] A brief look at the condition of the Russian economy and towns in the seventeenth century will demonstrate very quickly that almost nothing could be further from the truth. Russia lay in ruins by the end of the Troubles. Large parts of the country had been destroyed; many towns and villages stood empty; several important towns had been lost to Poland-Lithuania and Sweden; and an already-declining economy had been seriously disrupted.[18] In many places trade and industry simply disappeared and agricultural activity ceased altogether or continued its late-sixteenth-century slide backward to a low-level focus on self-sufficiency rather than production for the marketplace.[19] Several scholars have emphasized that the huge decline in production and the reversion to a "natural economy" caused by the Time of Troubles, coming on top of the late sixteenth-century economic crisis, delivered the "final blow" to the development of the early modern Russian economy along capitalist lines—with drastic consequences for the Russian people. Among other things, in spite of a return to relatively normal prices by the late 1620s, the "great ruin" contributed significantly to the relative backwardness of the economy and to the already-developing stratification and regimentation of Russian society.[20]

The overall population of Russia recovered relatively quickly after the Time of Troubles; by mid-century, it reached more or less the level of the late sixteenth century.[21] That growth, however, was very uneven and did not favor the towns and taxpaying villages of central Russia.[22] Towns in the far north and along the Volga River, which had been less adversely affected in the civil war years, tended to recover quicker; and some of them saw significant growth in population and economic activity in the seventeenth century.[23] It was a very different story in the heartland, however, where a number of towns and more than half of all peasant villages had been completely abandoned by the end of the civil war.[24] A few towns in central Russia did see a brief population spurt immediately following the Time of Troubles, but that was due primarily to migration there by nontaxpaying churchmen and gentry. By the 1620s even those towns ceased growing.[25] Overall, most Russian towns continued to decline or stagnate in the early seventeenth century.[26]

Although the economic base of the country remained fragile and relatively unproductive, the cash-strapped central government's appetite for revenue grew in the years following the Time of Troubles. Unfortunately, that meant raising taxes on townspeople—still the most important source of revenue for the state's increasing military expenses. Just as the collection of taxes without concern about their impact on the economy had hurt Russian towns and trade activity in the sixteenth century, so too did overtaxing a struggling urban population in the seventeenth century seriously interfere with Russia's recovery from the Time of Troubles. At first, the central government attempted to tax townspeople as if there had been no decline in urban population or economic activity, but the remaining townspeople simply could not meet the government's demands. Strenuous efforts by the early Romanovs to solve the state's fiscal problems by returning runaway taxpayers to their old taxpaying communities and by binding townsmen even more tightly were also not very successful; and, as a result, the government inevitably overburdened the remaining townspeople, which in turn led to a further spiraling down of the urban economy, occasional outbreaks of violence, and further abandonment of towns by desperate, overtaxed subjects.[27] Under those circumstances, it should really be no surprise that over the course of the seventeenth century the percentage of urban taxpayers in Russia relative to the overall population actually declined. Russian towns and commercial activity continued to stagnate for several generations; even a hundred years after the Time of Troubles, many towns had not recovered the population, vitality, and economic growth they had enjoyed in the mid-sixteenth century.[28] Instead, in the towns, as elsewhere, a highly stratified society emerged—a clear sign of economic backwardness and trouble.[29]

It is no exaggeration to state that, in the aftermath of the Time of Troubles, the failure of early modern Russian towns and capitalism to develop significantly until the eighteenth century had drastic consequences. It not only put Russia further behind the West economically, but it also helped push the country down an entirely different, decidedly illiberal path of political, social, legal, and cultural development—one in which wealth actually declined as a status symbol in favor of one's position in an increasingly rigid social hierarchy dedicated to the service of the tsar. While in the early modern West the rise of capitalism, towns, and an increasingly powerful and self-aware middle class laid the basis for the transition to modern states and societies; at the same time in Russia the economy remained extremely weak and the tiny and beleaguered Russian middle class merely constituted another relatively powerless stratum in a backward, highly regimented, near-caste society.[30]

Here it should be noted that some Marxist scholars, bowing to Lenin's faulty pronouncements about the development of the Russian economy in the seventeenth century, boldly declared that the Time of Troubles actually resulted in a great victory for Russia's leading merchants and somehow stimulated economic growth and Russia's eventual transition to capitalism.[31] That is a hopelessly inaccurate pronouncement.[32] It is true that Russia's leading merchants, the gosti (especially those who had helped Minin and Pozharskii and later the Romanovs), were richly rewarded and saw their privileges and status significantly enhanced in the seventeenth century.[33] At the same time, however, their obligations to the state also increased, and they emerged as an elite caste of part-time merchants and part-time agents of the tsar—not as great merchant-capitalists. The high status achieved by the gosti under the early Romanovs was actually another sign of the weakness of the Russian economy and the emergence of a near-caste society.

According to the traditional interpretation of the Time of Troubles, the gentry shared "victory" with the townsmen and were, in effect, a "rising class" during the seventeenth century. Having liberated Russia from foreign intervention, the gentry militiamen supposedly demonstrated their new power and self-awareness by participating in Tsar Mikhail's election and by working closely with him in the zemskii sobor.[34] Even though it is well documented that gentry participation in the activities of the central government quickly faded as autocracy was reconstructed, there still persists a widespread belief among scholars that it was not until the victorious and influential gentry made the decision on their own to deliberately disengage "from matters of central-state politics" that free rein was given "to the bureaucratic forces of the centralizing state."[35] That interpretation is in need of serious revision. There was, in fact, no powerful gentry lobby contending with the tsar's courtiers or bureaucrats in the years immediately following the Time of Troubles. Whatever sense of common identity had been forged among the gentry during the civil war did not in any way mark the emergence of a triumphant new interest group with budding political aspirations. Instead, what developed was a growing realization on the part of the economically and militarily weak gentry of their shared vulnerability to serious threats posed to them by greedy and influential "strong men" at court on the one hand and by competent cossack military forces on the other.[36]

We have already seen that the extraordinary activity of the zemskii sobor in the early years of Tsar Mikhail's reign did not represent the development either of a secular notion of the Russian state as something separate from the person of the tsar or of groups of the tsar's subjects as an emerging force independent of and interested in sharing power with the ruler. On the contrary, the gentry representatives to the zemskii sobor—like the townsmen—were pleased to be invited to help the tsar restore order, and they asked few questions about whose interests were being served in the process.[37] It should also be remembered that it was the government (especially Patriarch Filaret, newly returned from Polish captivity and taking charge of his son's realm) that took the initiative in sending zemskii sobor representatives home and in deciding to convene that institution much less frequently.[38] The recent discovery that the autocracy of the early Romanovs was far more dependent on compromise with and accommodation of the needs of regional elites and landholders than was maintained in traditional scholarship on "absolutism" or autocracy does not justify viewing the gentry after the Time of Troubles as victors, let alone as some kind of emerging, powerful, interest group. On the other hand, looking ahead to the lobbying activities of unhappy pomeshchiki during the 1630s and 1640s, one cannot help but to conclude that the gentry's involvement in the zemskii sobor of Tsar Mikhail's early years did significantly raise their collective consciousness about how autocracy functioned, whose interests it served, and how to go about the task of pragmatically and rationally protecting gentry interests in the future.[39]

It should be remembered that the gentry militia had been in deep crisis on the eve of the Time of Troubles. Needless to say, the destruction and dislocation associated with the famine, a prolonged civil war, and foreign intervention—far from improving the situation—made things much worse. By the end of the Time of Troubles, the ranks of the gentry had been seriously depleted. Many militiamen remaining in service had lost most of their peasant labor force and were barely able to eke out a living. Many others had lost everything and by 1613 were truly desperate men.[40] Perhaps even worse, the battered gentry had proven to be almost useless in the age of gunpowder technology, frequently being humiliated in battle by cossacks and foreign troops. Because of that, the early Romanovs were forced to attempt significant military reforms in order to compensate for the weakness of the gentry and to move beyond reliance on those nearly obsolete forces for defense and expansion of the realm.[41] Nevertheless, Russia's ruling elite shared the gentry's fear of the militarily potent free cossack forces as a threat to an increasingly rigid social hierarchy in which even a badly weakened gentry still had some role to play. Thus, as we have seen, it was Tsar Mikhail and his courtiers who consciously shored up the gentry as Russia's exclusive warrior caste and made common cause with them to purge the Russian army of free cossacks.[42] In addition, and much to the relief of the gentry, the Romanovs more or less put a stop to the use of slaves in combat.[43] The tsar's government also made massive distributions of land to the gentry in the years immediately following the Time of Troubles, cut tax assessments and service obligations on gentry holdings to more realistic levels, and took energetic measures to hunt down runaway peasants who were needed to rebuild the gentry's shattered economies.[44]

In spite of the new regime's efforts to shore up its traumatized gentry, however, the early seventeenth century did not see much improvement in their overall condition. Just as in the late sixteenth century, many gentry militiamen ended up with less land than they were officially entitled to, many failed to retain even a minimal peasant labor force, and large numbers were forced to plow the land for themselves in order to survive. A significant percentage of the impoverished deti boiarskie still failed to show up for annual military service, and thousands of them were forced by economic circumstances to serve as lower status infantry. Some became so desperate that, despite government prohibition, they sold themselves into slavery.[45] Just as in the decades before the Time of Troubles, despite official reassurance that they were Russia's exclusive warrior caste, the gentry under the early Romanovs saw the government return to the policy of using large numbers of cossacks on the southern frontier. Even more demoralizing to the militiamen was the government's return to the practice of accepting into military service, and occasionally into the ranks of the gentry itself, runaway peasants and almost anyone else willing to endure harsh conditions on the southern frontier.[46]

Over the course of the early seventeenth century, the struggling gentry's complaints about their status and conditions grew louder and more frequent. Protests were especially strong against unfair and often illegal competition for land and peasant labor on the part of corrupt and greedy "strong men," but the government usually ignored the gentry's complaints or failed to implement promised remedies.[47] By the 1640s, the gentry still averaged only about five peasant households each at a time when twenty was seen as the necessary minimum for a militiaman to render effective service.[48] By then, many gentry were actually so impoverished and upset at being taken advantage of by the rich and powerful and at being ignored by an obviously corrupt government that they dared to vent their anger and frustration against Tsar Aleksei himself.[49] In 1648, the demoralized gentry profoundly shocked the tsar and his ruling circle by their unwillingness to take the side of the central government against rioters in Moscow and other towns, whose ominous protests about the abuse of power by bureaucrats and "strong men" echoed the gentry's own complaints.[50] It was only then that the Romanov regime finally agreed to make fundamental concessions to the gentry, including specific language in Tsar Aleksei's Ulozhenie that formally codified the enserfment of peasants in ways favorable to the gentry.[51] Thus, it was not at the end of the Time of Troubles but only after 1649 that the Russian gentry began to look and act like real "winners" and members of the "ruling class."[52]

According to the traditional interpretation of the impact of the Time of Troubles, Russia's old aristocracy were to be counted among the losers. Their economies had been ruined by war and chaos, and their reputations had been ruined by accommodating foreign intervention. As a result, they were supposedly replaced by a new Romanov aristocracy and lost power and influence to such "winners" as the townsmen and the gentry.[53] That is an extremely faulty interpretation. As Robert Crummey and others have ably demonstrated, in the generations following the Time of Troubles, aristocrats must surely be counted among the biggest winners. We have already seen that Tsar Mikhail restored as much as possible of the old aristocracy and court and showered gifts and privileges on most of the survivors. From the outset of his reign, the tsar forged a strong alliance with the reactionary aristocracy, and those "strong men" took maximum advantage of their privileged position to secure greater wealth and power for themselves—even to the point of harming the country.[54] Among other things, over the course of the seventeenth century many of them entrenched themselves in the top ranks of the rapidly expanding central state bureaucracy—further enriching themselves. Sometimes those aristocratic servitors performed their jobs well; often they badly misgoverned Russia in the name of the tsar.[55] For a long time, historians caught up in the traditional view of the period claimed that aristocratic landholding must have declined in the early seventeenth century in favor of gentry landholding. In fact, aristocratic landholding remained quite vigorous under the early Romanovs. Russia's "strong men" were actually able to use their power and influence to increase their landholdings and to pull valuable peasant labor away from the struggling gentry, in the process provoking many angry complaints about their predatory ways.[56]

According to the traditional interpretation of the Time of Troubles, the lower classes were the real losers.[57] Even though we have seen that Russia's first civil war was not a social struggle against serfdom, it is impossible to disagree with that general conclusion. Nevertheless, due to the faulty class war interpretation of the period, there is considerable confusion and misinterpretation in the literature assessing the impact of the Bolotnikov rebellion and the Time of Troubles on the status of peasants and the development of serfdom in the seventeenth century.[58] At one time, for example, many scholars believed the Time of Troubles led directly to the formal enserfment of peasants in 1649 as a kind of delayed-reaction reward for the so-called "winners," the gentry.[59] At first, only a few voices objected to that conclusion—pointing out that the peasants were already de facto serfs by the 1590s or that there was little evidence of serf involvement in the uprisings of the Time of Troubles.[60] Most Soviet scholars, on the other hand, were anxious to validate Lenin's vague pronouncement that peasant rebellions in Russian history had been "progressive." Therefore, they boldly declared that the Bolotnikov rebellion dealt a powerful blow to the serf system and frightened the government and the lords into slowing down their efforts to increase tax and labor demands on a potentially violent and rebellious peasantry—with the result being a delay in the final step in enserfment for half a century.[61] Richard Hellie has already expressed healthy skepticism about that faulty conclusion.[62] It is true that officials of the central government did urge masters to show restraint in the treatment of peasants in the decades following the Time of Troubles.[63] However, that had more to do with fear that the critically important labor force would simply run away from harsh conditions than with any imagined fear of peasant violence.[64] As for the delay until 1649 of the final step in enserfing the peasants, it was also not due to fear of peasants but rather to the ruling elite's stubborn resistance to granting laws favoring gentry serfholders rather than themselves.[65]

The most significant impact of the Time of Troubles on the bulk of the Russian people, apart from sheer physical destruction and economic stagnation, may have been the harsh precedent set by Tsar Vasilii Shuiskii's 1607 decree on runaway peasants that strongly reinforced serfdom. In it Shuiskii "introduced a police element into what had largely been a civil matter," making local officials for the first time legally and materially responsible for returning runaway peasants to their rightful owners. Although the beleaguered Shuiskii was unable to enforce his decree in much of the country during the civil war, after the Time of Troubles his coercive approach to enforcement proved to be so successful that it became a permanent part of serf law.[66] Moreover, Shuiskii's decrees began an ominous blurring of the distinction between peasants and slaves, an innovation that was also retained by the Romanovs. In the decades following the Troubles the legal rights of all peasants continued to decline as the government increasingly tended to equate peasants with slaves and began treating both groups less and less as subjects and more and more as mere property.[67] As a result, in the highly stratified, near-caste society codified by Tsar Aleksei's Ulozhenie, not only were the bulk of the Russian people reduced to the status of serfs, but those unfortunate souls by law and custom were also well on their way to becoming something akin to chattel.

There has never been much scholarly controversy about the impact of the Time of Troubles on the Russian Orthodox Church. Instead, there has been general agreement that the church was a big winner. In fact, however, the growth of the church's power and wealth in the early seventeenth century helped set the stage for a traumatic schism among Russia's Orthodox population.[68] During the Time of Troubles, the Orthodox faith, the patriarch, the clergy, and the monasteries had played crucial roles in stirring "patriotic nationalism" and in rallying the Russian people to resist foreign intervention. As a result, Orthodoxy and the Russian Orthodox Church emerged from that period with significantly enhanced stature.[69] That was especially true for the relatively new office of patriarch. Its more exalted status was symbolically and powerfully expressed by the selection of Tsar Mikhail's father for the position and by Patriarch Filaret's immediate emergence as the real ruler of Russia. That was something no mere metropolitan could ever have aspired to, and it inadvertently established an awkward precedent that would later haunt Filaret's grandson, Tsar Aleksei.

The "great sovereign" Patriarch Filaret presided over the development of a powerful clerical bureaucracy, an increase in the power of his own office in both secular and church affairs, and the rapid growth of the church's landholdings and wealth.[70] Just as the enhanced prestige of the tsar sanctified and facilitated the unprecedented growth of the central state bureaucracy's interference in the lives of ordinary Russians, so too did the enhanced prestige and authority of the patriarch sanctify and facilitate the unprecedented growth of the clerical bureaucracy's aggressive, overbearing, and sometimes crude and violent efforts to expand the church's territory, wealth, and influence and to regulate and intrude into the lives of ordinary Russians. Just to cite one example, during the Time of Troubles the church had managed to acquire by various means much additional land, and Filaret and other church leaders made sure it retained all those gains and acquired even more.[71] Like the aristocrats at the tsar's court, the "strong men" of the church took maximum advantage of their positions and influence to increase their holdings and to gain and retain valuable peasant labor. At the outset of Tsar Mikhail's reign, the church was able to secure the government's active assistance in recovering runaway peasants.[72] From then on, powerful and wealthy church officials' successful on-going efforts to acquire even more land and peasants put them in direct but uneven competition with the struggling gentry, who grew just as angry about the greed of spiritual "strong men" as they were about predatory lay magnates.[73] Needless to say, many peasants also deeply resented the church's insatiable appetite for acquiring them and exploiting their labor. It is worth noting that by the time Tsar Aleksei was forced to confront the imperious and unpopular Patriarch Nikon at mid-century, the spiritual leader of the Russian people owned approximately thirty-five thousand serfs.[74]

In the decades following the Time of Troubles, the Russian Orthodox Church followed many of the same general trends that Jack Goldstone detected in the religious establishments of other early modern agrarian societies recovering from severe state crises. In Russia, as elsewhere, as the power and authority of the church was strengthened, traditional religious orthodoxy was reaffirmed and became more rigidly defined and conformist, and major efforts were made to purify a society (and clergy) perceived as corrupt and to purge all deviations from orthodoxy—which were widely regarded as being responsible for the crisis in the first place. As elsewhere, Russian society also became increasingly xenophobic and chauvinistic, and there emerged both elite and folk "ideologies of rectification."[75] It is well known that Patriarch Filaret and his successors jealously guarded the church's control over the spiritual life of the tsars' subjects and in matters of faith demanded obedience from all of them. In addition, during the seventeenth century the church worked tirelessly to shield "true Christians" from evil foreign influences and ended up presiding over one of the more xenophobic and chauvinistic periods in Russian history.[76] After the Time of Troubles the church also launched major efforts to purify a society viewed as corrupt and to reform the intellectual and moral life of the clergy. For many Russians, the resulting changes such as the banning of the extremely popular minstrels or the requirement that the faithful stand for several hours in church were annoying and made the exalted and arrogant leaders of the Russian Orthodox Church almost as unpopular as did those same spiritual strong men's lust to acquire land and peasants.[77]

Historians have traditionally focused on Patriarch Nikon's zealous liturgical reforms as the primary cause of the development during the second half of the seventeenth century of the most traumatic and long-lasting schism in the history of the Russian Orthodox Church. In fact, in that era of extreme xeno-phobia, one group of deeply conservative and suspicious dissenters—known as Old Believers—did reject the patriarch's reforms (his reactionary attempt to "re-Byzantinize" the Russian church) as "foreign cultural innovations" that threatened the purity of their faith and their very souls. The response of the church and the tsarist regime was, not surprisingly, brutal persecution of the Old Believers and harsh imposition of Nikon's unpopular reforms. In the cul-tural and emotional climate of the seventeenth century, there was simply no possible compromise between the radically differing "ideologies of rectifica-tion" represented by the equally stubborn Patriarch Nikon and Archpriest Avvakum. The shock of the resulting collision was profound.[78] Recently, how-ever, Georg Michels has demonstrated that at the heart of the rapidly develop-ing split between the official church and many faithful Orthodox dissenters was not concern about the liturgy at all but instead a growing alienation from the powerful Romanov-era church's unprecedented, acquisitive, and aggressive intru-sion into the countryside, the villages, and the lives of the tsar's ordinary lay and clerical subjects.[79] Although most Russians, at least publicly, refrained from criticizing the brutal suppression of those spiritual dissenters, many Orthodox Christians were deeply impressed by the courage and passion of the schismat-ics, who remained a thorn in the side of the Romanov dynasty until 1917.

One of the most important legacies of the Time of Troubles was to force Russian people at all levels of society to take a closer look at their traditional faith and how it was practiced. In ways somewhat reminiscent of the impact of the Black Death on the fourteenth-century European mind, the Troubles pro-foundly shocked most Russians psychologically, emotionally, and spiritually. Some regarded the Troubles as God's punishment for the sins of the Russian people or their rulers and concluded that, if God allowed the country to sur-vive, there would be need for significant moral and spiritual reform. At the same time, others who fought long and hard against an "evil" regime or against foreign intervention had their traditional faith reaffirmed and strengthened; and many of them became utterly convinced that untainted Orthodox Christianity itself was primarily responsible for the country's survival. Under those circum-stances, it should be no surprise that the early decades of the seventeenth cen-tury produced a resurgence of interest in religion and a considerable variety of official and personal commitments to defend, shore up, or reform Russian Orthodoxy.[80] Many Russians apparently concluded that the Time of Troubles had been caused primarily by the "silence" of the Russian people—that is, by the failure of the Orthodox faithful to oppose an evil or false tsar. As a result, at least some of them resolved not to remain silent in the future if they saw a tsar deviate from or threaten the existence of "true Christianity."[81]

The idea that the Russian people were themselves personally responsible for the fate of the realm and for Christianity itself made very significant progress during the Time of Troubles. The civil war saw tens of thousands of Russians who were willing to stand up to oppose false tsars, setting a powerful precedent and greatly reinforcing the potentially destabilizing aspect of early modern Russian political culture that allowed even lowly Orthodox subjects to oppose erring or evil rulers.[82] According to Paul Bushkovitch, the Time of Troubles actually undermined the older Orthodox notion of complete harmony between tsar and people and contributed to the growing split between the state and the nation.[83] Moreover, when all national institutions failed during the Troubles, Russia's salvation came at the hands of the people themselves, adding to patriotic Russians' growing sense of personal responsibility to defend their homeland as the last refuge of true, untainted Christianity.[84] According to Michael Cherniavsky, the Time of Troubles inevitably led to some separation in the minds of the faithful between the sacred mission of "Holy Russia" and the temporary, sometimes evil occupants of the tsarist or patriarchal thrones.[85]

Scholarship on the intriguing notion of "Holy Russia" has traditionally focused on the sixteenth century or even earlier as its point of origin.[86] The first usage of the term that can be precisely dated, however, is 1619; and it was, significantly, associated with Patriarch Filaret's return from Poland—a joyful event marking the symbolic end to the Time of Troubles.[87] The term actually came into common usage only in the decades after the Time of Troubles and was associated especially with the Don cossacks—those "Christian crusaders" who had played such an important role in the salvation of Holy Russia during the Troubles.[88] All things considered, therefore, it seems highly probable that the term originated in the growing realization during the civil war that the Russian land and its people, not just the tsar, had important roles to play in safeguarding the country's sacred mission. In other words, if Russia was ruled by a sacred shepherd, then his flock and the land were sacred too. Daniel Rowland has demonstrated that the notion of the Russian people as a holy people or God's chosen people was already in play during the sixteenth century.[89] In addition, Nancy Shields Kollmann has charted the increasing use of such terms as the Russian "state" and the Russian "land" during the Time of Troubles and has detected in them an intentional distinction from the tsar's authority and the central government.[90] According to Cherniavsky, what remained in the Time of Troubles "after Tsar and State and Church hierarchy were gone" was nothing less than the "concentrated essence of Russia" or Holy Russia.[91] After the Troubles, much of Russia's religious resurgence was apparently animated by such an idea.[92] The early Romanovs, deeply fearful of such popular attitudes, saw clearly enough the subversive potential of any notion of Holy Russia that was separate from the person of the tsar; it was a dangerous concept that might further empower the ruler's lowly but devout subjects to dare to judge or even to oppose his actions. For that reason, the central government was careful to avoid use of the term.[93]

Over the course of the seventeenth century, as many of the tsars' unhappy subjects periodically challenged the oppressive state and church's growing aloofness, rationalization, and bureaucratization in such outbursts as the 1648 riots, the Russian schism, and the Razin rebellion (1670–71), an increasingly nervous ruling elite came to the conclusion that Russia's traditional, God-centered ideology was responsible for much of the unrest. As a result, starting with Peter the Great's father, Tsar Aleksei, most of the court and aristocracy (followed by the gentry once the Ulozhenie satisfied them) gradually abandoned the traditional ideology in favor of one that would compel the allegiance of all subjects and maintain stability.[94] Not surprisingly, they gravitated toward a more Western-style ideology in which "the ruler was the sole judge alike of God's will and the public good" and in which "to advocate putting God's law above the law of the state" would be treated as "an act of treason."[95]

It was Peter the Great, of course, who completed the transformation of Russia from a sacred realm to a secular empire and, in the process, completely replaced the old, potentially destablizing ideology with his own vision of a "well-ordered police state" based on the impersonal rule of law.[96] The bulk of the ruling elite and gentry saw the utility for themselves of that transition and went along with it without much protest. Try as they might, however, Peter and his successors were unable to eradicate completely all vestiges of the troublesome old nonsecular political culture. Religious dissent became the rallying point for many discontented elements of Russian society and seriously undermined popular loyalty to both church and state. Opponents of the Petrine empire and the very heavy burden it placed on its subjects not infrequently rose in rebellion in the name of the "true faith," the "true tsar," and "Holy Russia." In fact, the term Holy Russia had a very long life as what Cherniavsky called the "myth of enslaved masses."[97]

The rapid reconstruction of a highly effective fiscal-military state in the years following the Time of Troubles further enhanced the status of the tsar and patriarch and led to the dizzying growth of the Russian empire and its secular and clerical bureaucracies. Even more than in the sixteenth century, the ambitious new regime and its church grossly overburdened the Russian people and, in the process, helped produce a rigidly stratified, near-caste society. The rapid growth of state and church power also produced a widening split between the Russian people and the increasingly impersonal central government and church that intruded more and more into the lives of the tsar's subjects. Even before the schismatics broke with the official church and state, there were a number of sharp outbursts of popular violence directed against the growing bureaucratization, corruption, and arrogance of the autocratic government and the Russian Orthodox Church. Especially alarming to many Russians was the Romanov regime's determination to rationalize the state order and to remove the tsar from all vulgar contacts—in effect, abandoning the tsar's traditional role of "merciful ruler" and protector of his people.[98] In such popular disturbances as the 1648 riots and the activities of the spiritual dissenters we can detect many Russian people stubbornly clinging to their "traditional, highly personalized and theocratic ideological system" in spite of the regime's relentless efforts to create a more rational, impersonal, and ultimately secularized state order.[99]

The growing split between the tsarist government and the official church on the one hand and the Russian people on the other, which was noticeable by the mid-seventeenth century, became a permanent feature of the Romanov era and had disastrous consequences, the effects of which were still being felt in the twentieth century. As the state-building of the Romanovs focused increasingly on meeting the needs of an expanding empire, the condition or needs of the tsar's subjects were never seriously taken into account. In addition to overburdening the Russian people and alienating many of them from church and state in the process, Geoffrey Hosking has reminded us that the tsar's government failed utterly to nurture the development of "community associations which commonly provide the basis for the civic sense of nationhood." Instead, the rapid growth of the Russian empire actually increased the huge gap between elite society and the Russian people and impeded the formation of a Russian nation.[100] Some of the origins of that tragic split can be traced back to the sixteenth-century development of autocracy, imperialism, and enserfment.[101] Nevertheless, Russia's first civil war also played a critically important role. In addition to the tremendous boost it gave to the oppressive autocracy and the heavy-handed church of the Romanovs, the traumatic Time of Troubles—ironically—also helped give voice to critics of the path being taken by the central government and the official church. It is no exaggeration to say that the Troubles contributed significantly to the dissenting tradition that produced such things as the 1648 riots and the Russian schism and that continued to haunt the Russian empire until its demise.[102]

Soviet scholars traditionally lumped the events of the Time of Troubles together with later cossack-led frontier uprisings such as the Razin rebellion

(1670–71) and the Pugachev rebellion (1773–74), regarding them all as "peasant wars" or social revolutions against serfdom.[103] That faulty interpretation has, among other things, seriously distorted the study of the relationship of the Bolotnikov rebellion and the Time of Troubles to those later uprisings. A closer look at that relationship is worthwhile in trying to assess the legacy of Russia's first civil war. We have already determined that the civil war was not a social revolution, and Michael Khodarkovsky has demonstrated that the Razin rebellion was also not a "peasant war" or a struggle of the masses against serfdom.[104] The Pugachev rebellion, on the other hand, which occurred at a later time when the overburdened serfs really were treated as little more than chattel, did see significant serf participation and did take aim directly against serfdom and "evil" gentry masters.[105] It contained powerful elements of social revolution and thus was qualitatively different from the earlier uprisings to which it is usually compared. Nevertheless, the Pugachev rebellion did share certain characteristics with and was influenced by both the Time of Troubles and the Razin rebellion.

In ways similar to Russia's first civil war, the Razin and Pugachev rebellions both saw the southern frontier go up in flames as cossacks and non-Russian minorities reacted violently to the relentless pressure of a central government determined to expand its control deeper into the frontier zone and to harness more tightly that region's population.[106] Just as in the Time of Troubles, disgruntled cossacks took the lead in the Razin and Pugachev rebellions, and those uprisings were to some extent anticolonial in nature.[107] Repetition of such patterns tells us something about continuing instability on Russia's southern frontier throughout the early modern period and something about Russian imperialism; but generalizations based on such comparisons have only limited value in assessing the period of the Time of Troubles. Even though Russia's first civil war also started out as a frontier rebellion, it quickly expanded into a huge, long-lasting civil war, whereas the Razin and Pugachev rebellions never overcame their frontier or sectional character, never seriously threatened the heartland, and were ruthlessly suppressed relatively quickly.[108]

A far more revealing point of comparison concerns rebel consciousness. In ways strikingly reminiscent of the Time of Troubles, many Razin and Pugachev supporters were motivated to a great extent by their religious beliefs.[109] We have already observed that the religious revival produced by the Troubles can be regarded as one of the sources of opposition to the Romanovs—from rioters in 1648 to religious dissenters to cossack-led frontier uprisings.[110] Although there are good reasons to be skeptical of the emphasis placed in traditional scholarship on Old Believers as the inciters, organizers, and leaders of the Razin and Pugachev rebellions; there is no denying the presence and energetic activity of

Russian schismatics within the ranks of those powerful movements.[111] Many early modern Russian rebels were undoubtedly just as troubled by the empire's lack of spiritual orientation as they were by corruption and the gross exploitation of the masses presided over by church and state. Some rebels really did regard themselves as representatives of God's "chosen people" who had been betrayed by a wicked ruling elite that casually abandoned Russia's all-important spiritual mission in favor of the fleeting benefits and glory of a secular empire. In this context, it was certainly no coincidence that opponents of the Romanovs rallied so often behind pretenders masquerading as "true tsars" or their representatives.[112]

We have already determined that the real source of Russian pretenderism, which became a chronic problem by the eighteenth century, was the miraculous story of the "true tsar" Dmitrii's multiple "resurrections" during Russia's first civil war.[113] Emilian Pugachev was, of course, the most famous Russian pretender after the Time of Troubles. Interestingly enough, even though he claimed to be Catherine the Great's unfortunate husband, Peter III, some of Pugachev's followers regarded him as nothing less than the "second coming" of Stenka Razin.[114] In fact, both Pugachev and Razin were in a very real sense spiritual reincarnations of Russia's original pretender—Dmitrii. It is quite striking that, just like Tsar Dmitrii, Razin and Pugachev were both regarded by many Russians as immortal, Christ-like deliverers of the people from an overbearing and evil regime; and both were hailed, just as Dmitrii had been, as "resplendent suns" with magical powers who—even if defeated—would return again with God's help to champion the cause of Russia's faithful Orthodox masses.[115]

Early modern Russia's ruling classes reacted in horror and incomprehension to the Razin and Pugachev rebellions and tried to dismiss them—in Aleksandr Pushkin's famous phrase—as "senseless and merciless." As a result, the lords came to fear the Russian people as irrational, uncontrollable, and sometimes even irreligious. To protect themselves from the violent and superstitious masses, much of privileged Russian society not only strongly supported harsh repression of all rebels but also became increasingly reactionary supporters of autocracy and serfdom.[116] Try as they might, most of the Romanov empire's increasingly secularized elite utterly failed to comprehend the Russian people's mystical, nonsecular ideas about the meaning and purpose of the sacred realm they had so bravely defended against false tsars and evil foreigners during the Time of Troubles.

It is, of course, well known that some thoughtful members of imperial Russia's "ruling class" eventually recoiled from the harsh treatment and miserable conditions of the bulk of the tsar's subjects and formed an intellectual, conscience-based opposition to autocracy and serfdom. Ironically, that "revolutionary intelligentsia" also deeply misunderstood the source of much of the anger and alienation of the Russian people whose cause they so ardently championed. Inspired by what they believed had been the heroic resistance of the masses to serfdom under the leadership of Bolotnikov, Razin, and Pugachev, many radicals in the nineteenth century made energetic but ineffective (and very frustrating) efforts to stir the people against the imperial government by conjuring the memory of those past rebel leaders as champions of the lower classes. Fixated on purely secular notions of state, society, materialism, and class conflict, even the most sincere "friends of the people"—from Populists to Socialist Revolutionaries to Marxists—usually failed to bridge the huge gap in consciousness that separated many of them, as members of the elite, from the empire's long-suffering, faithful Orthodox masses. Sadly, that split between the Russian people and their "ruling class," which developed in the era of the Time of Troubles and deepened with each successive popular uprising, did not close in 1917 or during the "dictatorship of the proletariat" that followed the Revolution.[117] In light of that, it really should not be surprising that most Russian and Soviet historians who studied early modern popular uprisings, including the so-called Bolotnikov rebellion, could not bridge that gap, either.

In conclusion, Russia's first civil war left a profound and complex legacy. Even as memories of that nightmarish experience gradually faded away, its impact continued to reverberate for generations. Looking back, it is possible to trace many of the problems associated with Russia's historical "backwardness" and the poverty and oppression of its people under both the tsars and the commissars to the aftermath of the civil war carried out in Tsar Dmitrii's name.

NOTES

ABBREVIATIONS

AAE   *Akty, sobrannye v bibliotekakh i arkhivakh Rossiiskoi imperii Arkheograficheskoiu eks-peditsieiu Imp. Akademii nauk*

AI   *Akty istoricheskie, sobrannye i izdannye Arkheograficheskoiu kommissieiu*

Akty Iushkova   *Akty XIII–XVII vv., predstavlennye v Razriadnyi prikaz*

AMG   *Akty Moskovskago gosudarstva, izdannye Imperatorskoiu Akademieiu Nauk*

AZR   *Akty, otnosiashchiesia k istorii Zapadnoi Rossii*

ChOIDR   *Cheteniia v Imperatorskom Obshchestve Istorii i Drevnostei Rossiiskikh pri Moskovskom Universitete*

DAI   *Dopolneniia k Aktam Istoricheskim*

FOG   *Forschungen zur osteuropäischen Geschichte*

MERSH   *Modern Encyclopedia of Russian and Soviet History*

PSRL   *Polnoe sobranie russkikh letopisei*

RBS   *Russkii biograficheskii slovar'*

RGADA   Rossiiskii gosudarstvennyi arkhiv drevnikh aktov

RIB   *Russkaia istoricheskaia biblioteka*

SGGD   *Sobranie gosudarstvennykh gramot i dogovorov*

S.P.   Public Record Office. State Papers Foreign

SRIO   *Sbornik Imperatorskago Russkago Istoricheskago Obshchestva*

VBDM   *Vosstanie I. Bolotnikova: Dokumenty i materialy*

ZhMNP   *Zhurnal Ministerstva Narodnago Prosveshcheniia*

NOTES TO THE INTRODUCTION

1. Terms such as "Time of Troubles" or "Troubles" (in Russian: *Smutnoe vremia* or *Smuta*) were commonly used by contemporaries to describe the terrible events occurring in Russia at the beginning of the seventeenth century. See, for example, Stanislavskii, "Novye dokumenty," 79; Novombergskii, *Slovo i delo*, 1:12; S. Veselovskii, *Akty podmoskovnykh opolchenii*, 17; Miklashevskii, *K istorii*, 266; N. Veselovskii, *Pamiatniki*, 2:236; Dunning, "Letter," 102; T. Rymer, *Foedera, Conventiones, Literae et Cojuscunque Generis Acta Publica, inter Reges Angliae*, 20 vols. (London, 1726–35), 14:747.

2. The classic study of the Time of Troubles is S. F. Platonov, *Ocherki po istorii Smuty v Moskovskom gosudarstve XVI–XVII vv* (1899); a condensation and popularization of that work is S. F. Platonov, *Smutnoe vremia* (1923). An English translation of Platonov's shorter study was prepared by John T. Alexander: S. F. Platonov, *Time of Troubles* (1970).

3. Stanislavskii, *Grazhdanskaia voina*, 3; Brody, *Demetrius Legend*; Emerson, *Boris Godunov*; Emerson and Oldani, *Modest Musorgsky and Boris Godunov.*

4. See, for example, Timofeev, *Vremennik,* 110–11; Palitsyn, *Skazanie,* 252–53; *Russkaia istoricheskaia biblioteka* [hereafter cited as RIB], 13: cols. 101–5, 224–25; Horváth, "A Bolotnyikovféle," 998–1006.

5. Avrich, *Russian Rebels,* 50; Smirnov, *Vosstanie,* 493, 495; Kamen, *Iron Century,* 384; *Istoriia krest'ianstva,* 2:427.

6. Skrynnikov, *Smuta,* 120–21, 134–35.

7. Kliuchevskii, *Sochineniia,* 3:48; Platonov, *Ocherki,* 305.

8. Buganov, *Krest'ianskie voiny;* idem, "Ob ideologii," 44–60; Smirnov et al., *Krest'ianskie voiny;* Yaresh, "Peasant Wars"; Pronshtein, "Reshennye i nereshennye voprosy"; Mavrodin, "Sovetskaia istoricheskaia literatura"; idem, "Sovetskaia istoriografiia"; Nazarov, "Peasant Wars"; Avrich, *Russian Rebels;* "Soveshchanie po istorii krest'ianskikh voin (konspektivnyi otchet)," *Istoricheskii sbornik* 1 (1934):285–302; V. M. Paneiakh, "Nauchnaia sessiia po istorii krest'ianskikh voin v Rossii," *Voprosy istorii,* 1964, no. 9:140–44; Piontkovskii, "Istoriografiia," 80–119. Cf. Fenomenov, *Razinovshchina i Pugachevshchina.*

9. *Bol'shaia Sovetskaia Entsiklopediia,* s.v. "Krest'ianskaia voina nachala 17 v."; Koretskii, *Formirovanie;* Makovskii, *Pervaia krest'ianskaia voina;* Zimin, "Nekotorye voprosy"; idem, "K itogam."

10. Grekov, *Krest'iane,* 2:310; Koretskii, *Formirovanie,* 364–66; Zimin, *V kanun,* 209–11, 236–40; *Istoriia krest'ianstva,* 2:427–34.

11. See, for example, Hellie, *Enserfment,* 102–3, 107; idem, *Slavery,* 574–76; Avrich, *Russian Rebels,* 10–47; Blum, *Lord and Peasant,* 254–59; Field, *Rebels,* 2–7; Keep, *Soldiers,* 73–74; Longworth, *Cossacks,* 77–79; Billington, *Icon and Axe,* 198–99; Smith, *Peasant Farming,* 108–9, 144–49; Kamen, *Iron Century,* 386; Vernadsky, *Tsardom,* 1:237–40; Mousnier, *Peasant Uprisings,* 153–95; Riasanovsky, *History of Russia,* 157–74; MacKenzie and Curran, *History of Russia,* 176–82; Anderson, *Lineages,* 201–2, 206–8, 210–11, 331–34; Wallerstein, *The Modern World-System,* 315–20; Florinsky, *Russia,* 1:231–32; Hosking, *Russia,* 59; Freeze, *Russia: A History,* 59–63. There have been very few exceptions to this trend in Western scholarship. See the careful comments about the Time of Troubles in Crummey, *Formation,* chapter 8; and in Moss, *A History of Russia,* vol. 1, chapter 9.

12. This paradox is noted in Keep, *Soldiers,* 3–4.

13. See comments about this in Longworth, "Subversive Legend," 17–40; Kivelson, "Devil Stole His Mind," 733–56; Mironov, "Poverty of Thought," 427–35.

14. Elliott, "Revolution and Continuity," 115–17; Zagorin, *Rebels,* 1:11–16; Mousnier, *La plume, la faucille, et le marteau,* 355–68, 373.

15. Forster and Greene, *Preconditions,* 13; Hagopian, *Phenomenon,* 17; Rowland, "Problem," 281–82.

16. Moote, "Preconditions," 138–43; Steensgaard, "Seventeenth-Century Crisis," 48; Elliott, "Revolution and Continuity," 117–19; Forster and Greene, *Preconditions,* 15–16; Billington, *Icon and Axe,* 198–200; Bercé, *Revolt,* 25, 120; Ellul, *Autopsy of Revolution,* 38.

17. Dunning, "Use and Abuse," 357–80; Skrynnikov, *Rossiia v nachale* XVII *v.;* idem, *Smuta;* Stanislavskii, *Grazhdanskaia voina;* Dunning, "Skrynnikov," 71–81; idem, "Cossacks," 57–74; Skrynnikov, "Spornye problemy," 92–110; idem, "Civil War," 61–79; Dunning, "Byla li krest'ianskaia voina," 21–34; idem, "Crisis," 97–119; idem, "Preconditions"; Polikarpov, "V Rossii grazhdanskuiu voinu," 189.

18. Skrynnikov, *Smuta,* 3; idem, *Tsar' Boris i Dmitrii Samozvanets,* 560.

19. Skrynnikov, "Civil War," 70, 77–78.

20. See, for example, La Ville, *Discours sommaire,* 9; Massa, *Short History,* 149, 151–52. Cf. Massa, *Kratkoe izvestie,* 151.

21. See, for example, Smirnov et al., *Krest'ianskie voiny,* 307–9; Nazarov, "Peasant Wars," 115–16, 136–39; Cherepnin, *Voprosy metodologii,* 153, 159, 164–65, 213, 225, 258.

22. See, for example, Vernadsky, *Tsardom,* 234–45.

23. Dunning, "Skrynnikov"; idem, "Crisis"; Skrynnikov, *Rossiia v nachale* XVII *v.*

24. Dunning, "Byla li krest'ianskaia voina," 24; Massa, *Kratkoe izvestie,* 81.

25. Skrynnikov, *Rossiia v nachale* XVII *v.;* idem, *Smuta;* Dunning, "Skrynnikov."

26. Dunning, "Cossacks"; Stanislavskii, *Grazhdanskaia voina.*

27. Hellie, *Slavery,* 574–76; Skrynnikov, *Rossiia v nachale XVII v.,* 206–14, 249–51; Dunning, "Skrynnikov," 73–74.

28. Perrie, "Popular Legends."

29. Dunning, "Byla li krest'ianskaia voina," 31; idem, "Crisis," 114–15; Perrie, *Pretenders,* 63, 87, 245–46.

30. Skrynnikov, "Civil War," 70, 73–74; Dunning, "Crisis," 100–101; idem, "Goldstone's Model," 576–79, 588–89.

31. Tatishchev, *Istoriia,* 7:367.

32. Shcherbatov, *Istoriia,* 7, part 2:147–48, 181–82.

33. Karamzin, *Istoriia,* 11:120; 12:25–27, 53, 94, 125–26, 244.

34. Solov'ev, "Obzor sobytii," 11. The first reference to events in the Time of Troubles as a "revolution" was probably made by a French writer in 1760; see Lacombe, *Histoire,* 77.

35. Solov'ev, *Istoriia,* 4:390–91.

36. Kostomarov, *Smutnoe vremia,* 2:280, 637–38; Thomas Prymak, "Mykola Kostomarov and East Slavic Ethnography," *Russian History* 18 (Summer 1991): 163, 165, 175, 182.

37. Kliuchevskii, *Sochineniia,* 3:29–48, 51, 56–57, 60.

38. Platonov, *Ocherki;* idem, *Smutnoe vremia,* 31–59, 93; idem, *Time of Troubles.* To note the strong and enduring influence of Platonov's model, see Riasanovsky, *History of Russia,* 157–74; MacKenzie and Curran, *History of Russia,* 172–85; and comments by L. V. Ivanov in *Istorik-Marksist* 68, no. 4 (1938): 153–56.

39. Mavrodin, "Soviet Historical Literature," 43.

40. Tkhorzhevskii, *Narodnye volneniia,* 11–13; Pokrovskii, *Russkaia istoriia s drevneishikh vremen,* 2:48–50; 3:50; Firsov, *Krest'ianskaia Revoliutsiia,* 55–56.

41. Mavrodin, "Soviet Historical Literature," 43; Yaresh, "Peasant Wars," 242.

42. Shapiro, "Ob istoricheskoi roli," 63; Pokrovsky, *Brief History,* 1:73; Ladokha, *Razinshchina i Pugachevshchina,* 4.

43. Smirnov, *Vosstanie,* 24–27. Cf. Mavrodin, "Soviet Historical Literature," 44, 49.

44. See Engels, *The Peasant War in Germany.*

45. Pronshtein, "Resolved and Unresolved Problems," 28.

46. Pokrovsky, *Brief History,* 1:71–90; Firsov, *Krest'ianskaia Revoliutsiia,* 61; Dubrovskii, "Krest'ianskie voiny," 44–46, 81–92; Tomsinskii, *Krest'ianskie dvizheniia;* Mavrodin, "Soviet Historical Literature," 49, 53; Yaresh, "Peasant Wars," 250; Stanishevskii, *Narodnoe dvizhenie;* Nechaev, *Bolotnikov;* Aronovich, "Vosstanie," 113–26; Piontkovskii, "Istoriografiia," 80–119.

47. Pokrovsky, *Brief History,* 1:73, 76; Mavrodin, "Soviet Historical Literature," 44.

48. Mavrodin, "Soviet Historical Literature," 50–51; Smirnov, "K kharakteristike vnutrennei politiki Lzhedmitriia I," 186–207; *Ocherki istorii SSSR,* 494–95. See also Savich, *Bor'ba,* 8–20.

49. See, for example, Nechaev, *Bolotnikov,* 76–77; Picheta, *Istoriia krest'ianskikh volnenii,* 26–28; Got'e, *Smutnoe vremia,* 35–59.

50. Smirnov et al., *Krest'ianskie voiny,* 307–9; Nazarov, "Peasant Wars," 115–16, 136–39; Mavrodin, "Soviet Historical Literature," 44–45, 50.

51. I. V. Stalin, "Beseda s nemetskim pisatelem Emilem Ludvigom," *Bor'ba klassov* 4 (1932): 6; Smirnov, *Vosstanie Bolotnikova,* 8–10, 28 n. 1; Yaresh, "Peasant Wars," 241; Aronovich, "Vosstanie Ivana Bolotnikova," 1:113.

52. Yaresh, "Peasant Wars," 247, 252, 258–59. Cf. Shapiro, "Historical Role," 27–28.

53. Smirnov, *Vosstanie,* 9, 493, 495.

54. Zimin, "Nekotorye voprosy," 97–99; Smirnov, "O nekotorykh voprosakh," 116–17; idem, "K istorii," 111–16; Pronshtein, "Reshennye i nereshennye voprosy," 156–57; Nazarov, "Peasant Wars," 118–19; Mavrodin et al., "Ob osobennostiakh," 69–79; Gorfunkel', "K voprosu," 112–18; Ul'ianov, *Krest'ianskaia voina,* 8–13.

55. See, for example, Tikhomirov, "Pskovskie povesti," 186; Indova et al., "Narodnye dvizheniia," 53; Makovskii, *Pervaia krest'ianskaia voina,* 468–72.

56. Koretskii, "Novgorodskie dela," 306–30; idem, "Novoe o krest'ianskom zakreposhchenii," 130–52; idem, *Zakreposhchenie,* 118–19, 145; idem, *Formirovanie,* 364–66; Paneiakh, "Zakreposhchenie,"

157–65; Anpilogov, "K voprosu," 160–77; *Zakonodatel'nye akty,* 2:59–60, 66–97; Zimin, *V kanun,* 209–11; *Istoriia krest'ianstva,* 2:376–78, 424–25. Cf. Grekov, *Krest'iane,* 2:310.

57. Makovskii, *Pervaia krest'ianskaia voina,* 295–97, 470–72, 477, 482.

58. Cherepnin et al., *Krest'ianskie voiny,* 18–19; Skrynnikov, *Sotsial'no-politicheskaia bor'ba,* 8; Koretskii, *Formirovanie,* 8–9.

59. Nazarov, "Peasant Wars," 126; idem, "O nekotorykh osobennostiakh," 120.

60. Koretskii, *Formirovanie,* 366; Pronshtein, "Reshennye i nereshennye voprosy," 154–57; Mavrodin, "Sovetskaia istoricheskaia literatura," 39–40, 45. Cf. V. I. Shunkov, "Retsenziia na knigu I. I. Smirnova *Vosstanie Bolotnikova," Izvestiia AN SSSR* 6, no. 4 (1949), 370.

61. *Bol'shaia Sovetskaia Entsiklopediia,* s.v. "Krest'ianskaia voina nachala 17 v."; Cherepnin, *Voprosy metodologii,* 166–67; Koretskii, *Formirovanie,* 365; Mavrodin, "Sovetskaia istoricheskaia literatura," 39–40; Chistov, *Russkie legendy,* 40–42; Nazarov, "Peasant Wars," 137; Buganov, *Krest'ianskie voiny,* 6–50; Kozachenko, *Razgrom;* Podorozhnyi, *Razgrom pol'skikh interventov;* Shepelev, "Klassovaia bor'ba," 5–48; idem, "K voprosu," 277–322; Picheta, "Krest'ianskaia voina," 91–139; Proskuriakova, *Klassovaia bor'ba;* Dolinin, "Razvitie," 109–37.

62. See Skrynnikov, *Sotsial'no-politicheskaia bor'ba,* 7 n. 17; idem, *Rossiia v nachale XVII v.,* 4–5. Cf. "O krest'ianskoi voine," 102–20.

63. See Skrynnikov, *Time of Troubles;* Dunning, "Skrynnikov," 72–73, 81; *Smuta v Moskovskom gosudarstve,* 6–20.

64. Dunning, "Byla li krest'ianskaia voina," 22. See also Polikarpov, "V Rossii grazhdanskuiu voinu," 189.

65. See Skrynnikov, *Time of Troubles,* xiii, 307 n. 17. Cf. Skrynnikov, *Sotsial'no-politicheskaia bor'ba,* 10. See also Dunning, "Skrynnikov," 80–81; and reviews of Skrynnikov's *Time of Troubles* by Valerie Kivelson (*Slavic Review* 49 [Fall 1990]:446–47) and Brian Davies (*The Russian Review* 49 [October 1990]:199–200).

66. Skrynnikov, *Rossiia v nachale XVII v.,* 4–5.

67. See, for example, Skrynnikov, *Rossiia v nachale XVII v.,* 251; idem, "Civil War," 78.

68. Skrynnikov, *Samozvantsy.* See comments in Dunning, "Skrynnikov," 75–76.

69. See, for example, Stanislavskii, *Grazhdanskaia voina,* 6–25.

70. Perrie, *Pretenders.* See my review of her book in *The Russian Review* 56 (July 1997):465–66.

71. See Avrich, *Russian Rebels,* 7.

NOTES TO CHAPTER 1

1. Bercé, *Revolt,* 1; Zagorin, *Rebels,* 1:39.

2. See Kimmel, *Revolution,* 217–18, 222.

3. Zagorin, *Rebels,* 1:39, 45–46, 183, 218; 2:51–54; Hagopian, *Phenomenon,* 15–17; Mousnier, *Peasant Uprisings,* 319–20; Kimmel, *Absolutism,* 1; idem, *Revolution,* 11.

4. Tilly, *European Revolutions,* 15; Stone, "Causal Stories," 293–95.

5. Zagorin, *Rebels,* 1:175, 178, 197, 233–34. Strong urban participation in Russia's first civil war prompted more than one failed Marxist attempt to classify it as a form of bourgeois revolution marking a transition from feudalism to capitalism (e.g., Pokrovskii and Makovskii). That was decidedly not the case. Russia in the early seventeenth century was not yet on the threshold of such dramatic social and economic transformation. (See Bushkovitch, "Towns," 215–32; Pipes, *Russia,* chapter 8). In fact, a large percentage of Russia's urban population participating in the civil war were military garrisons rather than traditional townsmen. Henry Kamen (*Iron Century,* 365–66) has also pointed out that the theoretical distinction between urban and agrarian rebellion may not always be possible or useful in the early modern period. That is certainly true in the case of Russia's first civil war.

6. Zagorin, *Rebels,* 1:40; 2:1–6; Bercé, *Revolt,* 127–30; Hagopian, *Phenomenon,* 17, 40; Tilly, *European Revolutions,* 189. See also Kimmel, *Revolution,* 218–19; Mousnier, *Peasant Uprisings,* 335.

7. Zagorin, *Rebels*, 1:39; Bercé, *Revolt*, 1. Some students of chaos theory also warn that historical processes are nonlinear and that the complexity of initial conditions makes it impossible to predict outcomes when so many independent variables are operating simultaneously. See, for example, Roth, "Is History a Process?," 197–243; Çambel, *Applied Chaos Theory,* xi–xii, 4–5, 13–14.

8. Tilly, *European Revolutions*, 11; Kimmel, *Revolution*, 9; Zagorin, *Rebels*, 1:54–57, 123–28; Mousnier, *Peasant Uprisings*, xx, 318; Hagopian, *Phenomenon*, 16–17, 123; Skocpol, *States*, 17–18, 117, 289 n. 44; Johnson, *Revolutionary Change*, xi.

9. See, for example, François Furet, *Interpreting the French Revolution* (Berkeley: University of California Press, 1981); Lynn Hunt, *Politics, Culture, and Class in the French Revolution* (Berkeley: University of California Press, 1984); Clifton B. Kroeber, "Theory and History of Revolution," *Journal of World History* 7 (Spring 1996):23.

10. Pavlov, *Gosudarev dvor;* Platonov, *Time of Troubles,* chapter 2.

11. Skrynnikov, "Civil War," 74.

12. Dunning, "Byla li v Rossii," 30–31.

13. Ibid., 31. See also the intriguing comments about Russian Orthodox culture and political instability in Rowland, "Limits," 125–55, and in Kivelson, "Devil Stole his Mind," 733–56.

14. Concerning this trend in revisionist scholarship see critical comments by Jack Goldstone (*Revolution and Rebellion*, 12–15); by Lawrence Stone ("The Revolution Over the Revolution," *The New York Review of Books*, 11 June 1992, 47–51), and by Geoffrey Parker (*The American Historical Review* 97 [December 1992]:1488).

15. See comments on this issue in Larner, *Enemies of God,* 192.

16. Kimmel, *Revolution*, 9–10.

17. Zagorin, *Rebels*, 1:55.

18. Hellie, "Warfare," 82–83; idem, *Enserfment*, 8–10, 16–17, 21, 31, 39, 95, 146–47, 262; idem, "Stratification," 136, 140; Skrynnikov, "Civil War," 72; idem, *Smuta*, 6–7.

19. Hellie, *Slavery,* 4, 16; idem, "Stratification," 119; idem, "Warfare," 81, 83–84; Keep, *Soldiers,* 13; Kolycheva, *Agrarnyi stroi,* 195.

20. Hellie, *Enserfment*, 47, 48–49, 238–41; Keep, *Soldiers*, 37.

21. Mousnier, *Peasant Uprisings*, 331, 346; Crummey, *Formation*, 20–21, 215.

22. Blum, *Lord and Peasant*, 160–61; Veselovskii, *Feodal'noe zemlevladenie*, 35; Zimin, "Osnovnye etapy," 50; Smirnov, *Vosstanie Bolotnikova*, 64; Hellie, *Enserfment*, 99.

23. Kolycheva, *Agrarnyi stroi,* 195–201.

24. Makovskii, *Razvitie*, 32–33, 226, 278–79, 292, 320, 496–97; Smith, *Peasant Farming,* 144–45; Rozhkov, *Sel'skoe khoziaistvo*, 305–10.

25. Hellie, *Enserfment*, 97; Smith, *Peasant Farming*, 226; Kolycheva, *Agrarnyi stroi*, 201.

26. Skrynnikov, "Civil War," 72.

27. Mousnier, *Peasant Uprisings*, 181, 331, 346; Makovskii, *Razvitie*, 226; Smith, *Peasant Farming*, 107, 226.

28. Keep, *Soldiers*, 15; Hellie, *Slavery,* 23.

29. Alef, "Origin," 8–9; Pipes, *Russia*, 73–77, 85, 87, 191–206; Crummey, *Formation*, 91, 96, 132–33, 135–37; Hellie, "Warfare," 76–84; Kleimola, "Up through Servitude," 210–12, 220; Keenan, "Muscovite Political Folkways," 118, 129–32, 135, 140–42, 146–47; Hunt, "Ivan IV's Mythology," 769–70, 772, 776–77; Flier, "Breaking the Code," 226.

30. Alef, "Origin," 8–9; Pipes, *Russia*, 73–77, 85, 87, 191–206; Crummey, *Formation*, 91, 96, 132–33, 135–37; Hellie, "Warfare," 76–84; Kleimola, "Up through Servitude," 210–12, 220; Keenan, "Muscovite Political Folkways,"118, 129–32, 135, 140–42, 146–47; Hunt, "Ivan IV's Mythology," 769–70, 772, 776–77; Flier, "Breaking the Code," 226.

31. Vasilii III inherited 1.7 million square kilometers in 1505; Boris Godunov inherited between 4.3 and 5.4 million square kilometers in 1598. See Hellie, *Enserfment*, 21; Smith, *Peasant Farming*, 103.

32. Hellie, "Warfare," 80; Keep, *Soldiers*, 47–48; Kolycheva, *Agrarnyi stroi*, 177.

33. Skrynnikov, "Civil War," 70–71; Zimin, *Oprichnina*, 389–430.

34. See Kolycheva, *Agrarnyi stroi*, 172–77.

35. Von Loewe, "Juridical Manifestations," 397–98.

36. Wright, "Neo-Serfdom in Bohemia,"242–44; Makkai, "Neo-Serfdom: Its Origin and Nature in East Central Europe," 232–38; von Loewe, "Juridical Manifestations," 396–98; Prodan, "The Origins of Serfdom in Transylvania," 17. See also Shapiro, *Russkoe krest'ianstvo.*

37. Mousnier, *Peasant Uprisings*, xvii–xx; Bercé, *Revolt*, viii; Zagorin, *Rebels*, 1:28–30, 36.

38. Hobsbawm, "The Overall Crisis," 33–53; Aston, *Crisis in Europe*; Rabb, *The Struggle for Stability*, 3–28; Parker and Smith, *General Crisis*, 1–21.

39. Steensgaard, "Seventeenth-Century Crisis," 26–27; Moote, "Preconditions,"134–36; Elliott, "Revolution and Continuity,"110–33; Kamen, *Iron Century*, 339–41; Zagorin, *Rebels*, 1:136–39.

40. See Parker, *Europe in Crisis*, 22–23, 73; Kamen, *Iron Century*, 61–84; Zagorin, *Rebels*, 1:128–30.

41. Steengaard, "Seventeenth-Century Crisis," 37–40; Parker and Smith, *General Crisis*, 14–15.

42. Steensgaard, "Seventeenth-Century Crisis," 42–48; Bercé, *Revolt*, 220; Mousnier, *Peasant Uprisings*, 327–32.

43. Parker and Smith, *General Crisis*, 4–12; Mousnier, *Peasant Uprisings*, 312–18.

44. See Crummey, "Muscovy and the Crisis," 156–80; Dukes, "Russia and the 'General Crisis'," 1–17.

45. Mousnier, *Peasant Uprisings*, 163–65, 331, 348.

46. Brown, "Muscovy," 55–58.

47. Roberts, *Essays*, 195–225; Duffy, *Military revolution*, 1.

48. Hale, *War and Society*, 232, 235–36, 247; Parker, *Military Revolution*, 61–64; Steensgaard, "Seventeenth-Century Crisis," 48. See also Tallett, *War and Society.*

49. See Henshall, *Myth of Absolutism*, 1–5; Brewer, *Sinews of Power*, xvii. Cf. Skocpol, *States*, 14, 25–32, 110–11, 154; Martin, *Feudalism to Capitalism*, 110–12.

50. Downing, *Military Revolution*, 3, 10–11, 56, 77–78.

51. Dunning, "Preconditions," 122–23. See also Richard Hellie, "Russia, 1200–1815," in Bonney, ed., *The Rise of the Fiscal State in Europe*, 481–505; and relevant comments in essays by Robert O. Crummey, David Goldfrank, and Brian Davies in *Forschungen zur osteuropäischen Geschichte* [hereafter cited as FOG], 56 (1999).

52. Keep, *Soldiers*, 1.

53. Zlotnik, "Muscovite Fiscal Policy," 243–58; Alef, "Origin," 7–9, 96, 136; Hellie, "Warfare," 74–99.

54. Parker and Smith, *General Crisis*, 4–12; Mousier, *Peasant Uprisings*, 312–18; de Vries, "Measuring," 42–43; Pfister, "The Little Ice Age," 112–16; LeRoy Ladurie, *Times of Feast*, 224–27, 297, 312.

55. Appleby, "Epidemics and Famine," 77; Kahan, "Natural Calamities," 361, 371.

56. Braudel, *Mediterranean*, 1:270, 275; idem, *Capitalism and Material Life*, 18–20.

57. Arnold, *Famine*, 9–11; de Vries, "Measuring," 42.

58. Arnold, *Famine*, 7–8, 80–85; LeRoy Ladurie, *Times of Feast*, 314; Jütte, *Poverty and Deviance*, 188–89; Gurr, *Why Men Rebel*, 48.

59. Clark, *European Crisis*, 3–4.

60. Ibid., 4–9, 12–13; Appleby, "Epidemics and Famine," 63–83; Steensgaard, "Seventeenth-Century Crisis," 38; Kamen, *Iron Century*, 366–80, 384; Bercé, *Revolt*, 144–47; Jütte, *Poverty and Deviance*, 180–89.

61. LeRoy Ladurie, *Times of Feast*, 142–43, 164, 225, 297; Post, *The Last Great Subsistence Crisis*, xii.

62. Clark, *European Crisis*, 6–7; Kamen, *Iron Century*, 368–75, 383; Leroy Ladurie, *Times of Feast*, 289; Appleby, *Famine in Tudor and Stuart England*, 109, 112, 133–34; idem, *Famine*, 13; Kirby, *Northern Europe*, 150; Koretskii, "Golod," 229–30; Boldakov, *Sbornik*, 17, 46–52.

63. Kamen, *Iron Century*, 366, 370–75, 384; Kirby, *Northern Europe*, 151–53; Zherbin and Shaskol'skii, "Krest'ianskaia voina," 76–90.

64. Goldstone, *Revolution and Rebellion*, xxvi, 4–7, 37, 459.

65. Ibid., 31–35, 102–23, 425. See also Kimmel, *Absolutism*, 6.

66. Goldstone, *Revolution and Rebellion*, 20–21, 24, 109, 460–62. See also Forster and Greene, *Preconditions*, 14–15; Zagorin, *Rebels*, 1:57, 130–32; Bacon, "Seditions," 81–84; Stone, *Causes*, 54, 125, 134.

67. Goldstone, *Revolution and Rebellion*, 7–8, 34, 133–34, 460, 464.

68. Ibid., xxiii–xxiv, 8–11, 24, 35, 70–77, 126, 133, 346, 462.

69. See Dunning, "Goldstone's Model." Cf. Crummey, "Muscovy and the Crisis," 161–69.

70. Blum, "Prices," 198–99; Hellie, "Warfare," 75, 79.

71. Urlanis, *Rost naseleniia*, 190; Kopanev, "Naselenie," 233–54; Vodarskii, *Naselenie*, 27–29.

72. Kopanev, "Naselenie," 241–42; Eaton, "Decline," 227.

73. Vodarskii, *Naselenie*, 27–29.

74. Hellie, "Warfare," 80; Smith, *Peasant Farming*, 127–28.

75. Urlanis, *Rost*, 190; Kopanev, "Naselenie," 245, 254; Keep, *Soldiers*, 88. Even scholars who calculate a more conservative population estimate of approximately eight million in 1600 assume a one-third increase during the second half of the sixteenth century after a sharper rise during the first half of the century. See Goehrke, "Zur Problem," 65–85; Pipes, *Russia*, 13.

76. Abramovich, "Novyi istochnik," 117–18; Blum, "Prices," 182–99; Koretskii, *Formirovanie*, 129, 145, 231–32; Smith, *Peasant Farming*, 143–46.

77. Rozhkov, *Sel'skoe khoziaistvo*, 202–19, 283–86, 495–97.

78. Man'kov, *Tseny*, 6, 32–33, 40–41, 53, 99–101.

79. Bushkovitch, *Merchants*, 52, 54.

80. On the isolation of the Russian economy from the West, see Braudel, *Perspective of the World*, 441–44. On the other hand, Russian trade with the West, although modest, resulted in significant importation of silver (up to 25% of the value of all imports), much of which was then exported to Persia. See Bushkovitch, *Merchants*, 62–63; Attman, *The Bullion Flow*, 77–79, 109–11.

81. Blum, "Prices," 182, 198–99; Boris N. Mironov, "In Search of Hidden Information," *Social Science History* 9 (Fall 1985): 342, 356 n. 1. See also Man'kov, *Tseny*, 33–34.

82. Veselovskii, *Feodal'noe zemlevladenie*, 165–202; Blum, *Lord and Peasant*, 170–74.

83. Zimin, *Reformy*, 223–24; Veselovskii, *Feodal'noe zemlevladenie*, 89, 308–9; Crummey, *Formation*, 104, 109–10; Kleimola, "Up through Servitude," 211–19.

84. Skrynnikov, "Civil War," 70–71; Rowland, "Limits," 133–34, 139, 142, 144–45, 149, 156; Hunt, "Ivan IV's Mythology," 770–71.

85. Zimin, *V kanun*, 104–233; Skrynnikov, *Rossiia v nachale XVII v.*, 28–37, 79–103.

86. See, for example, Timofeev, *Vremennik*, 111–12; Palitsyn, *Skazanie*, 258–59, 269; Rowland, "Problem of Advice," 267–68.

87. Platonov, *Time of Troubles*, 64–68; Pavlov, *Gosudarev dvor*; Margeret, *Russian Empire*, 60–61, 81.

88. Skrynnikov, "Glavnye vekhi," 96, 100; idem, "Civil War," 71–72.

89. Blum, *Lord and Peasant*, 155, 200–202, 211; Hellie, *Enserfment*, 29, 34, 39; Keep, *Soldiers*, 34, 42–45, 48–49.

90. Skrynnikov, "Civil War," 72–73; Zimin, *Reformy*, 356; Skrynnikov, *Rossiia v nachale XVII v.*, 21–22, 51–52; idem, "Glavnye vekhi," 101–4; Dunning, "Cossacks," 60–62.

91. Hellie, *Enserfment*, 37.

92. Ibid., 47, 48–49, 238–39; idem, "Warfare," 83–84.

93. Blum, *Lord and Peasant*, 177–78, 208–9; Keep, *Soldiers*, 32, 34, 42–44, 46–47; Skrynnikov, "Glavnye vekhi," 102; idem, *Smuta*, 5–6, 81–82, 91–92.

94. Skrynnikov, "Civil War," 70; Kolycheva, *Agrarnyi stroi*, 183.

95. Hellie, *Enserfment*, 34, 39, 93–95, 97; Skrynnikov, "Glavnye vekhi," 96, 100–101; Kolycheva, *Agrarnyi stroi*, 172, 174, 176–83, 187, 189.

96. Blum, "Prices," 189–99; Man'kov, *Tseny*, 33–34, 119–20; Smith, *Peasant Farming*, 108.

97. Hellie, "Warfare," 82–83; idem, *Enserfment*, 8–10, 16–17, 21, 31, 39, 95, 146–47, 262; idem, "Stratification," 136, 140; Skrynnikov, "Civil War," 72; idem, *Smuta*, 6–7.

98. Hellie, *Enserfment*, 100–101; idem, "Stratification," 145.

99. Kolycheva, *Agrarnyi stroi*, 195, 201; Mousnier, *Peasant Uprisings*, 331, 346; Crummey, *Formation*, 20–21.

100. Skrynnikov, *Boris Godunov*, 121–22; Margeret, *Russian Empire*, 59.

101. Skrynnikov, *Time of Troubles*, 28; idem, *Smuta*, 52.

102. Zlotnik, "Muscovite Fiscal Policy," 243–58; Veselovskii, *Soshnoe pis'mo*, 2:360–62; Blum, *Lord and Peasant*, 158, 222, 228–29.

103. Smith, *Peasant Farming*, 143–46.

104. Hellie, *Enserfment*, 45, 86, 115–16; Keep, *Soldiers*, 46–47; Makovskii, *Razvitie*, 210, 385; Blum, *Lord and Peasant*, 155–58, 234–36; Smith, *Peasant Farming*, 144, 223.

105. Blum, *Lord and Peasant*, 154–55, 158, 235–43; Kolycheva, *Agrarnyi stroi*, 182–83, 187, 189; Crummey, *Formation*, 7–8; Makovskii, *Razvitie*, 392, 482; Mousnier, *Peasant Uprisings*, 162–63; Zimin, *Oprichnina*, 389–430; Eaton, "Decline," 224, 229.

106. Keep, "Bandits," 201; *Istoriia krest'ianstva SSSR*, 2:423–24.

107. Kolycheva, *Agrarnyi stroi*, 189, 195–201.

108. Skrynnikov, *Boris Godunov*, 79–80, 119; idem, *Smuta*, 179, 183; Mousnier, *Peasant Uprisings*, 181; Hellie, *Enserfment*, 103.

109. See, for example, Smirnov, *Vosstanie Bolotnikova*, 56–61; *Istoriia krest'ianstva*, 2:424–25; Hellie, *Enserfment*, 102; Makovskii, *Razvitie*, 484–85; Zimin, "Osnovnye etapy," 49–50; Koretskii, "Bor'ba krest'ian s monastyriami," 194, 197–200.

110. Skrynnikov, "Civil War," 70, 72–73; idem, *Smuta*, 252; Stanislavskii, *Grazhdanskaia voina*, 7–8, 36, 38, 243–47; Dunning, "Cossacks," 62–65, 69, 71–72.

111. Kolycheva, *Agrarnyi stroi*, 169–204; Stanislavskii, *Grazhdanskaia voina*, 10–14, 19–20.

112. Keep, *Soldiers*, 34, 37–39, 72–74; Skrynnikov, *Smuta*, 6.

113. Stanislavskii, *Grazhdanskaia voina*, 6–45, 243–47; Skrynnikov, *Rossiia v nachale XVII v.*, 51–57, 104–11, 215–22; Dunning, "Cossacks," 57–74.

114. Skrynnikov, *Rossiia v nachale, XVII v.*, 41, 49; Margeret, *Russian Empire*, 58–59; Bushkovitch, "Taxation," 357; Culpepper, "Legislative Origins," 182–83.

115. Stanislavskii, *Grazhdanskaia voina*, 13; Skrynnikov, *Smuta*, 183–84, 186; Keep, *Soldiers*, 73–74; Hellie, "Warfare," 77–84.

116. Perrie, "Popular Image," 279; idem, "Folklore," 133, 139; Keenan, "Muscovite Political Folkways," 140; Kliuchevskii, *Sochineniia*, 3:53.

117. Platonov, *Time of Troubles*, 42–43, 64–68; Skrynnikov, *Boris Godunov*, 108–10; Palitsyn, *Skazanie*, 252–53; Margeret, *Russian Empire*, 81; Pavlov, *Gosudarev dvor*, 65.

118. Skrynnikov, *Rossiia v nachale XVII v.*, 45–50; idem, *Boris Godunov*, 124.

119. Skrynnikov, "Civil War," 64, 70, 72–75; idem, *Smuta*, 7–8, 81–82, 91–92, 112–15, 179, 183, 252; idem, "Glavnye vekhi," 100, 103; Stanislavskii, *Grazhdanskaia voina*, 11, 17–20; Dunning, "Cossacks," 59–63; Hellie, "Stratification," 145; idem, *Enserfment*, 103; Keep, *Soldiers*, 19, 30–32, 62–63, 73–74; Platonov, *Ocherki*, 241–42; idem, *Time of Troubles*, 38–39.

120. See Kimmel, *Absolutism*, 6.

121. See Roth, "Is History a Process?," 197–98; Çambel, *Applied Chaos Theory*, 2–4.

NOTES TO CHAPTER 2

1. Kliuchevskii, *Sochineniia*, 3:8.

2. Mousnier, *Peasant Uprisings*, 163–65, 318, 327–32, 348.

3. See Kivelson, "Merciful Father," 635–36, 641.

4. Keenan, "Trouble," 104–6, 110, 113; Kollmann, *Kinship*, 186–87; Cherniavsky, *Tsar and People*, 33; Bushkovitch, "Formation," 355–56; Rowland, "Ivan the Terrible." The one Western country in the medieval and early modern period that Muscovite Russia loosely resembled was Castile, a militarized crusader state also located on the frontier of Christendom and locked in a struggle to "reconquer" territory previously lost to Islam. By the beginning of the early modern period, the king of Castile was the absolute master of his realm. There he wielded enormous power

over his people, the economy, and even the Catholic church that neighboring monarchs could not imagine for themselves. See Billington, *Icon and Axe,* 69–71; Downing, *Military Revolution,* 40 n. 64; Yanov, *Origins,* 7.

5. Pipes, *Russia,* 85; Esper, "Military Self-Sufficiency," 189–90.

6. See Platonov, *Time of Troubles,* 169–70; Pipes, *Russia,* 22; Rowland, "Limits," 125–26; Alef, "Origin," 9–10.

7. Halperin, *Russia and the Golden Horde,* 87–88, 95–98; Downing, *Military Revolution,* 9, 38–39; Pipes, *Russia,* 73–77; Cherniavsky, "Khan or Basileus," 67–72; Kivelson, "Merciful Father," 641–43.

8. Ostrowski, "Mongol Origins," 525–26, 534–36. See also Donald Ostrowski, *Muscovy and the Mongols: Cross-Cultural Influences on the Steppe Frontier, 1304–1589* (Cambridge: Cambridge University Press, 1998).

9. Halperin, *Russia and the Golden Horde,* 89.

10. Vernadsky, *Mongols and Russia,* 127–30, 222–23, 362–63, 387–88.

11. Ostrowski, "Mongol Origins," 535–36; Halperin, *Russia and the Golden Horde,* 91; Hellie, *Enserfment,* 30–31.

12. Alef, "Origin," 8–9; Blum, *Lord and Peasant,* 135.

13. Halperin, *Russia and the Golden Horde,* 87–88, 97–103; Keenan, "Muscovite Political Folkways," 132; Pipes, *Russia,* 75–76; Cherniavsky, "Khan or Basileus," 67–72; Alef, "Origin," 7–8.

14. Keenan, "Trouble," 106; Crummey, *Formation,* 80–81, 133–34.

15. Crummey, *Formation,* 194–96; Madariaga, "Autocracy," 373.

16. Crummey, *Formation,* 134–35.

17. Kivelson, "Merciful Father," 644; Crummey, *Formation,* 96, 132–33; Szeftel, "Title," 70–71.

18. Cherniavsky, *Tsar and People,* 45–71; Pipes, *Russia,* 72–74; Shevchenko, "Neglected Source," 82–89, 92; Kollmann, "Pilgrimage," 166–67, 179–80; Miller, "Creating Legitimacy"; Raba, "Authority," 323–26.

19. Keenan, "Muscovite Political Folkways," 118; Rowland, "Limits," 125; Ostrowski, "Mongol Origins," 525. See also Savva, *Moskovskie tsari,* 400.

20. See Vernadsky, *Tsardom,* 1:17–19; Cherniavsky, *Tsar and People,* 71; idem, "Khan or Basileus," 66, 71–73; Crummey, *Formation,* 135–37; Hunt, "Mythology," 777; Strémooukhoff, "Moscow the Third Rome: Sources of the Doctrine," 84–101.

21. Alef, "Origin," 7; Bushkovitch, "Formation," 357–58, 361; Rowland, "Moscow," 591–95.

22. Shevchenko, "Neglected Source," 91; Chaev, "Moskva—tretii Rim'," 1–23.

23. Rowland, "Problem," 278; Kivelson, "Devil Stole His Mind," 733, 742. See also Tsimbaev, "Rossiia i Russkie," 23–32.

24. Cherniavsky, *Tsar and People,* 28–29, 33; Hunt, "Mythology," 769–70, 772, 776; Bushkovitch, "Formation," 364–65; Miller, "Creating Legitimacy," 290–92, 294, 300.

25. Margeret, *Russian Empire,* 14–15; Herberstein, *Notes,* 1:33–34; Szeftel, "Title," 70–71.

26. Cherniavsky, *Tsar and People,* 41–42; Crummey, *Formation,* 135, 137–38.

27. Rowland, "Moscow," 591–614; idem, "Problem," 278; Shevchenko, "Neglected Source," 85. See, for example, RIB 13: cols. 183, 224, 525–30; Timofeev, *Vremennik,* 136, 150; N. F. Droblenkova, *Novaia povest' o preslavnom Rossiiskom tsarstve i sovremennaia ei agitatsionnaia patrioticheskaia pis'- mennost'* (Moscow-Leningrad: AN SSSR, 1960), 198.

28. Flier, "Breaking the Code," 226; idem, "Iconology," 53, 68. See also Billington, *Icon and Axe,* 72–76.

29. Rowland, "Biblical Imagery," 183, 187–88, 190, 196–98; Flier, "Breaking the Code," 242.

30. Miller, "Creating Legitimacy," 306–13; Crummey, *Formation,* 135–40, 143, 152–54, 199, 202; Cherniavsky, *Tsar and People,* 51; Pipes, *Russia,* 79; Hosking, *Russia,* 3–4; Keep, *Soldiers,* 1. See also *Polnoe sobranie russkikh letopisei* [hereafter cited as PSRL], 13:150; Hakluyt, *Principal Navigations,* 2:439.

31. Rowland, "Limits," 151–52; idem, "Biblical Imagery," 183, 197–98; Crummey, "Constitutional Reform," 38; Miller, "Creating Legitimacy," 290–93, 314–15.

32. Kleimola, "Up through Servitude," 210.

33. Keenan, "Muscovite Political Folkways," 142, 146–47; Kollmann, *Kinship*, 187.
34. Kivelson, "Devil Stole His Mind," 743; Pipes, *Russia*, 73; Crummey, *Formation*, 138.
35. Even before the Time of Troubles, Tsar Ivan IV seems to have taken the religious aspect of autocracy far more seriously and much further than the ruling elite ever intended, with disastrous results; see Madariaga, "Autocracy," 373–74; Hunt, "Mythology," 769–71, 809; Bushkovitch, *Religion and Society*, 32–33; Kollmann, *Kinship*, 23; Skrynnikov, "Overview," 66–69, 81. See also Al'shits, *Nachalo samoderzhaviia v Rossii*.
36. Keenan, "Muscovite Political Folkways," 129–31, 140–41.
37. Alef, "Origin," 7–9, 96, 136, 176; Hellie, *Enserfment*, 22; Crummey, *Aristocrats*, 3, 215–20; idem, *Formation*, 14, 103–4; Skrynnikov, *Smuta v Rossii*, 5; Bushkovitch, *Religion and Society*, 34; Zimin, *Reformy*, 223–24.
38. Skrynnikov, "Overview," 65–66; Keenan, "Muscovite Political Folkways," 118, 132; Rowland, "Limits," 126; Bushkovitch, *Religion and Society*, 32–33; Weickhardt, "Kotoshikhin: An Evaluation and Interpretation," 152–53.
39. Keenan, "Muscovite Political Folkways," 129, 135, 142, 146–47; Kollmann, *Kinship*, 146–51; Rowland, "Limits," 151–52; Poe, "What Did Russians Mean When They Called Themselves 'Slaves of the Tsar'?," 585–608.
40. Pipes, *Russia*; Kleimola, "Up through Servitude," 210–12, 220; Hellie, "Warfare," 80; idem, "Keenan's Scholarly Ways," 177–90; Crummey, "The Silence of Muscovy," 157–64; Brown, "Anthropological Perspective and Early Muscovite Court Politics," 55–66.
41. See, for example, Herberstein, *Notes*, 1:32; Hakluyt, *Principal Navigations*, 2:439; Fletcher, *Russe Commonwealth*, 20–20v; Margeret, *Russian Empire*, 3, 28; Bodin, *The Six Bookes of a Commonwealth*, 149, 201, 222.
42. Weickhardt, "Pre-Petrine Law," 679; Keep, *Soldiers*, 1; Mousnier, *Les hierarchies sociales*, 106–16; Alef, "Origin," 9.
43. Brown, "Zemskii Sobor," 89–90; Crummey, "Reform under Ivan IV: Gradualism and Terror," 18; Kollmann, *Kinship*, 185–86.
44. Alef, "Origin," 8–9, 96, 136, 176; Kleimola, "Up through Servitude," 210, 212; Hellie, *Slavery*, 712–13; Auerbach, "Der begriff 'Adel'," 73–88.
45. Hellie, "Warfare," 79–80.
46. Blum, *Lord and Peasant*, 158–59; Pipes, *Russia*, 87, 191–206; Hellie, "Warfare," 76–78, 81–84; Braudel, *Perspective*, 444–47.
47. Herberstein, *Notes*, 1:54; Staden, *Land and Government*, 25, 40; Fletcher, *Russe Commonwealth*, 83v; Bond, *Russia*, 179; Possevino, *Moscovia*, 45–47; Vernadsky, *Tsardom*, 1:20; Fedotov, *St. Filipp, Metropolitan of Moscow*, 143–47.
48. See Keep, *Soldiers*, 1, 3–5, 13, 62; Esper, "Military Self-Sufficiency," 185; Tsimbaev, "Rossiia i Russkie," 23–32.
49. Keenan, "Muscovite Political Folkways," 136–37; Skrynnikov, *Smuta*, 4–5; Zlotnik, "Muscovite Fiscal Policy," 258; Hellie, *Enserfment*, 236.
50. Pipes, *Russia*, 66–68, 71, 86; Kollmann, "Pilgrimage," 166; Weickhardt, "Bureaucrats," 332; Keep, *Soldiers*, 1; Hellie, *Enserfment*, 26.
51. Crummey, *Formation*, 105–6, 114; Keenan, "Muscovite Political Folkways," 137; Demidova, *Sluzhilaia biurokratiia*.
52. Zimin, *Reformy*, 328–33, 421–22, 449–60; Hellie, "Warfare," 81; Brown, "Muscovite Government Bureaus," 269–71; Shmidt, "Der Geschäftsgang in den russischen Zentralämtern der zweiten Hälfte des 16. Jahrhunderts, 65–86.
53. Weickhardt, "Bureaucrats," 331–34; Hellie, *Enserfment*, 187; Keep, *Soldiers*, 35–36; Kollmann, *Kinship*, 182; Keenan, "Muscovite Political Folkways," 137–38; Poe, "Elite Service Registry," 251–52.
54. Brown, "Muscovite Government Bureaus," 271; Weickhardt, "Bureaucrats," 332; Zlotnik, "Muscovite Fiscal Policy," 243–44, 258.
55. Keep, *Soldiers*, 35–36; Hellie, *Enserfment*, 187; Smith, "Muscovite Logistics," 61; Chernov, *Vooruzhennye sily*, 98.
56. Hellie, "Warfare," 81.

57. Zlotnik, "Muscovite Fiscal Policy," 243–58. See also Pipes, *Russia,* 115; Blum, *Lord and Peasant,* 228–29; Hellie, *Slavery,* 2.

58. See, for example, Fletcher, *Russe Commonwealth,* 41; Margeret, *Russian Empire,* 34–35. See also Smith, *Peasant Farming,* 144, 232–34, 237–38.

59. Pipes, *Russia,* 194–98; Braudel, *Perspective,* 444–45; Margeret, *Russian Empire,* 39; Bushkovitch, "Taxation," 385, 390, 397–98.

60. See Mousnier, *Peasant Uprisings,* 163–65, 331, 348. Cf. Brown, "Muscovy, Poland, and the Crisis," 55–58.

61. Alef, "Origin," 96, 136, 139; idem, "Muscovite Military Reforms," 73, 107–8.

62. Pipes, *Russia,* 115.

63. Hellie, *Enserfment,* 21; Crummey, *Formation,* 107.

64. Blum, *Lord and Peasant,* 177; Keep, *Soldiers,* 5–6, 15–16; Esper, "Military Self-Sufficiency," 190.

65. Crummey, *Formation,* 114.

66. See Hellie, *Enserfment,* 21; Smith, *Peasant Farming,* 103.

67. Margeret, *Russian Empire,* 3; Pipes, *Russia,* 79, 83; Crummey, *Formation,* 152–54; Vernadsky, *Tsardom,* 1:4.

68. Alef, "Muscovite Military Reforms," 73, 87, 106–8; idem, "Origin," chapters 3–4.

69. Alef, "Origin," chapters 5–6; idem, "Muscovite Military Reforms," 107–8; Hellie, *Enserfment,* 26; Crummey, *Formation,* 8–9, 109–10.

70. Keenan, "Muscovite Political Folkways," 132.

71. Hellie, *Enserfment,* 22–23; Keep, *Soldiers,* 20–22; Skrynnikov, *Rossiia v nachale XVII v.,* 10; Crummey, *Formation,* 9; Bushkovitch, *Religion and Society,* 33–34; Alef, "Origin," 93.

72. Alef, "Muscovite Military Reforms," 73, 87–88; idem, "Origin," 8–9, 96, 136, 139, 176.

73. Keep, *Soldiers,* 1; Crummey, *Formation,* 8–10, 114; idem, "Constitutional Reform," 38.

74. Hellie, "Warfare," 76–78.

75. See Weickhardt, "Pre-Petrine Law," 663–79; Richard Pipes, "Was There Private Property in Muscovite Russia?," 524–30; Weickhardt, "Was There Private Property in Muscovite Russia?," 531–38.

76. Blum, *Lord and Peasant,* 175–78; Hellie, *Enserfment,* 26–28; Crummey, *Formation,* 90, 108–9; Skrynnikov, *Smuta,* 3–4; Veselovskii, *Feodal'noe zemlevladenie,* 281–84, 287–97.

77. Alef, "Origin," 139; idem, "Muscovite Military Reforms," 99, 106–7; Hellie, *Enserfment,* 21; Smith, *Peasant Farming,* 103.

78. Hellie, *Enserfment,* 24, 28, 33–34, 267.

79. Skrynnikov, *Smuta,* 4–5; idem, "Glavnye vekhi," 96; Alef, "Muscovite Military Reforms," 107; Crummey, *Formation,* 114.

80. Richard Hellie, for example, refers to the pomeshchiki as members of the "middle service class" (*Enserfment,* 24).

81. Hellie, "Warfare," 80; idem, *Enserfment,* 33; Keep, *Soldiers,* 37; Auerbach, "Der begriff 'Adel'," 73–88.

82. Keep, *Soldiers,* 22.

83. Stevens, *Soldiers,* 18; Hellie, *Enserfment,* 24; Kivelson, *Autocracy,* 38–39.

84. Fletcher, *Russe Commonwealth,* 53v–55v; Margeret, *Russian Empire,* 30–31, 41, 45–47.

85. Hellie, "Warfare," 77–78; Keep, *Soldiers,* 13, 30, 37; Skrynnikov, *Smuta,* 5–6; idem, "Glavnye vekhi," 101. Cf. Esper, "Military Self-Sufficiency," 204.

86. Keep, *Soldiers,* 28; Crummey, *Formation,* 12; Margeret, *Russian Empire,* 45–46; Hellie, *Enserfment,* 24; Bushkovitch, *Religion and Society,* 34, 47.

87. Hellie, *Enserfment,* 24; Keep, *Soldiers,* 42–44; Blum, *Lord and Peasant,* 179–81, 200.

88. Hellie, *Enserfment,* 21–22, 29–32, 51, 57, 165–66; Keep, *Soldiers,* 15–16, 34, 39–40, 45–46, 52; Storozhev, *Istoriko-iuridicheskie materialy,* 22–23, 177–79, 193; Smith, "Muscovite Logistics," 53; Alef, "Muscovite Military Reforms," 78; Rozhdestvenskii, *Sluzhiloe zemlevladenie,* 297–99.

89. Blum, *Lord and Peasant,* 175–76; Keep, *Soldiers,* 22, 28–29; Hellie, *Enserfment,* 24, 28.

90. Hellie, *Enserfment,* 23; Keep, *Soldiers,* 22, 28, 32–33; Margeret, *Russian Empire,* 41–42.

91. Hellie, *Enserfment*, 24, 28, 267. Bushkovitch (*Religion and Society*, 34) puts the number at 35–40,000.

92. Keep, *Soldiers*, 28.

93. Esper, "Military Self-Sufficiency," 189–90; Hellie, "Warfare," 76; Zlotnik, "Muscovite Fiscal Policy," 243; Alef, "Muscovite Military Reforms," 77–78. Carol Stevens (*Soldiers*, 6, 15–16) implies that Russia did not experience the military revolution until the seventeenth century, but she does at least acknowledge that fortress work done in the sixteenth century was inspired by confrontations with Russia's western neighbors.

94. Hellie, *Enserfment*, 157–59; Skrynnikov, *Time of Troubles*, 79.

95. Razin, *Istoriia*, 2:346; Hellie, *Enserfment*, 155–57; Smith, "Muscovite Logistics," 37.

96. Bond, *Russia*, 189–90; Morgan and Coote, *Early Voyages*, 1:35; 2:237.

97. Hellie, *Enserfment*, 24, 160–61, 210–11; idem, "Warfare," 79; Alef, "Muscovite Military Reforms," 78–81; Keep, *Soldiers*, 60, 75–76; Pallott and Shaw, *Landscape*, 38.

98. Alef, "Muscovite Military Reforms," 80–81; Hellie, *Enserfment*, 160–61.

99. Keep, *Soldiers*, 60–63; Hellie, *Enserfment*, 161–65; Margeret, *Russian Empire*, 40, 49; Berry and Crummey, *Rude and Barbarous Kingdom*, 180; Skrynnikov, *Rossiia v nachale XVII v.*, 65; Nikitin, "K voprosu," 44; Zagorovskii, *Belgorodskaia cherta*, 30.

100. Zlotnik, "Muscovite Fiscal Policy," 246; Hellie, *Enserfment*, 163–64.

101. See Mousnier, *Peasant Uprisings*, 163–65, 331, 348; Blum, *Lord and Peasant*, 158–59; Hellie, "Warfare," 76–78, 81–84.

NOTES TO CHAPTER 3

1. Platonov, *Smutnoe vremia*, 31–59; Grekov, *Krest'iane*, 2:310; Blum, *Lord and Peasant*, 146–47, 159; Avrich, *Russian Rebels*, 10–13; Makovskii, *Razvitie*, 210, 216, 383, 461–68, 471; Hellie, "Foundations," 150–54; idem, *Enserfment*, 22, 102–3; Skrynnikov, "Civil War," 70–71; Zimin, *V kanun*, 7–103, 236–40; Yanov, *Origins*, 13–16; Alef, "Origin," 11; MacKenzie and Curran, *History*, 162–69; Riasanovsky, *History*, 150–53, 157–60.

2. Hellie, "Warfare," 77; idem, *Enserfment*, 21; Skrynnikov, *Time of Troubles*, 79; Smith, "Muscovite Logistics," 53.

3. Hellie, *Slavery*, 23; Keep, *Soldiers*, 15; Anderson, *Lineages*, 201.

4. Vernadsky, *Tsardom*, 1:11–12, 51–52; Keep, *Soldiers*, 15–16.

5. Hellie, *Enserfment*, 21; Keep, *Soldiers*, 5.

6. Crummey, *Formation*, 137, 152–54; Esper, "Military Self-Sufficiency," 190; Flier, "Iconology," 63, 67; Pipes, *Russia*, 79; Keep, *Soldiers*, 18; Braudel, *Perspective*, 442–43; Shaw, "Southern Frontiers," 117; French, "Russian Town," 264.

7. Shaw, "Southern Frontiers," 132–33; Skrynnikov, *Time of Troubles*, 192; Koretskii, *Zakreposhchenie*, 59, 296–97; Smirnov, *Vosstanie*, 346–53; Zimin, "Osnovnye etapy," 51; Massa, *Short History*, 26; Lantzeff and Pierce, *Eastward to Empire*, 110.

8. Margeret, *Russian Empire*, 47. Cf. Berry and Crummey, *Rude and Barbarous Kingdom*, 269; Esper, "Military Self-Sufficiency," 193–94. For a long time it was incorrectly assumed that there were only about ten thousand Tatars, Cheremis, and Mordvians in Russian military service by the late sixteenth century. See, for example, Kliuchevskii, *Skazaniia inostrantsev*, 93–94; Seredonin, *Izvestiia*, 13; Zimin, "Osnovnye etapy," 51; Hellie, *Enserfment*, 267; Keep, *Soldiers*, 77–78.

9. Hellie, *Enserfment*, 28, 37–38; Keep, *Soldiers*, 30, 42–45; Blum, *Lord and Peasant*, 200–201.

10. Crummey, *Formation*, 156–57.

11. Blum, *Lord and Peasant*, 146–47, 158; Yanov, *Origins*, 13–16, 20; Grekov, "Iur'ev den'," 71; Hellie, "Warfare," 80; idem, *Enserfment*, 9–10; Keep, *Soldiers*, 47–48; Kolycheva, *Agrarnyi stroi*, 177.

12. Makovskii, *Razvitie*, 65–72, 210, 216, 461–68, 471; Hellie, *Enserfment*, 93, 95, 282 n.5; Smith, *Peasant Farming*, 108; Blum, *Lord and Peasant*, 159; Zimin, *Oprichnina*, 389–430; Avrich, *Russian Rebels*, 12–13; Skrynnikov, "Civil War," 70–71.

13. Makovskii, *Razvitie*, 468; Sakharov, *Obrazovanie*, 92, 100, 104–5, 108, 112; V. N. Sheviakov, "K voprosu ob oprichnine pri Ivane IV," *Voprosy istorii* 31, no. 9 (1956):71–75; Hellie, "What Happened? How Did He Get Away with It? Ivan Groznyi's Paranoia and the Problem of Institutional Restraints," 199–224.

14. Skrynnikov, "Overview," 62–82; Kollmann, *Kinship*, 23; Alef, "Origin," 11.

15. See Downing, *Military Revolution*, 77.

16. Skrynnikov, "Civil War," 70–71; idem, *Smuta*, 5; Kollmann, *Kinship*, 183; Bond, *Russia*, 163; Kleimola, "Up through Servitude," 219.

17. Skrynnikov, "Overview," 68, 77, 81; Fletcher, *Russe Commonwealth*, 25–26; Hunt, "Ivan IV's Mythology," 770–71; Kleimola, "Reliance," 57; idem, "Up through Servitude," 214–19; Rowland, "Limits," 144–45, 149; Veselovskii, *Issledovaniia po istorii*, 125–26; Pavlov, "Zemel'nye pereseleniia v gody oprichniny," no. 5, 89–104; Perrie, *Image*, 13, 31–32, 45–46, 60–63, 65, 91–93.

18. Kleimola, "Up through Servitude," 220. See also Hellie, "Why Did the Elite Not Rebel?" 155–62.

19. Rowland, "Limits," 133–34, 139, 142, 156; Skrynnikov, *Time of Troubles*, xiii–xiv.

20. Goldstone, *Revolution*, 7–8.

21. Staden, *Land and Government*, 33; Platonov, *Time of Troubles*, 24, 26–27; Zimin, *Oprichnina*, 418; Blum, *Lord and Peasant*, 156; Skrynnikov, "Overview," 73–74; Danilova, "Istoricheskie usloviia," 119; Hellie, "Foundations," 150; idem, *Enserfment*, 45, 100, 115; Keep, *Soldiers*, 18–19.

22. Staden, *Land and Government*, 46–48; Hakluyt, *Principal Navigations*, 3:169–70; Skrynnikov, *Ivan the Terrible*, 132–33; idem, "Overview," 81; Crummey, *Formation*, 171.

23. Kleimola, "Reliance," 57; Kollmann, *Kinship*, 183.

24. Bond, *Russia*, 163, 339.

25. Fletcher, *Russe Commonwealth*, 26.

26. Blum, *Lord and Peasant*, 159; Skrynnikov, *Boris Godunov*, 79–80.

27. Skrynnikov, "Overview," 81; idem, *Time of Troubles*, xv.

28. Kolycheva, *Agrarnyi stroi*, 177.

29. Veselovskii, *Feodal'noe zemlevladenie*, 165–202; Blum, *Lord and Peasant*, 170–74.

30. Kleimola, "Up through Servitude," 211–19; Crummey, *Formation*, 104, 109–10; Veselovskii, *Feodal'noe zemlevladenie*, 89, 308–9; Zimin, *Reformy*, 223–24; Hellie, "Why Did the Elite Not Rebel?" 155–62.

31. Skrynnikov, "Glavnye vekhi," 93–94, 96; idem, "Civil War," 70–73; idem, *Smuta*, 6, 51.

32. Makovskii, *Razvitie*, 180, 189; Keep, *Soldiers*, 42–43, 48–49; Skrynnikov, "Glavnye vekhi," 100.

33. Hellie, *Enserfment*, 37.

34. Blum, *Lord and Peasant*, 182–83, 211.

35. Keep, *Soldiers*, 45–46; Eaton, "Early Russian Censuses," 79.

36. Platonov, *Time of Troubles*, 8–10; Keep, *Soldiers*, 46; Eaton, "Early Russian Censuses," 42.

37. Gnevushev, "Zemlevladenie," 281–82; Smith, *Peasant Farming*, 107; Koretskii, "Pravaia gramota," 194; Alekseev and Kopanev, "Razvitie," 64–69.

38. Gnevushev, "Zemlevladenie," 268; Smith, *Peasant Farming*, 223; Kopanev, "Zakonodatel'stvo." See also Shveikovskaia, "K kharakteristike," 75–86.

39. Hakluyt, *Principal Navigations*, 2:231; Fletcher, *Russe Commonwealth*, 54; Hellie, *Enserfment*, 37.

40. Blum, *Lord and Peasant*, 236; Kahan, "Natural Calamities," 353, 355, 361, 363; Hellie, *Enserfment*, 255.

41. Hellie, *Enserfment*, 84–85; idem, "Warfare," 75, 77–78; idem, *Muscovite Society*, 104–5.

42. Makovskii, *Razvitie*, 179–83; Veselovskii, *Feodal'noe zemlevladenie*, 309–10.

43. Blum, *Lord and Peasant*, 211.

44. Hellie, *Enserfment*, 45, 115–16; Blum, *Lord and Peasant*, 155–58, 234–35; Keep, *Soldiers*, 45, 47.

45. Veselovskii, *Soshnoe pis'mo*, 2:360–62; Koretskii, "Pravaia gramota," 195–96, 206–12; Rozhkov, *Sel'skoe khoziaistvo*, 222–33; Smith, *Peasant Farming*, 144; Blum, *Lord and Peasant*, 158, 222, 228–29; Skrynnikov, *Boris Godunov*, 79–80.

46. Kolycheva, *Agrarnyi stroi*, 187; Crummey, *Formation*, 7–8; Blum, *Lord and Peasant*, 235–39. See also Scott, "Everyday Forms of Resistance," 13–14.

47. Kahan, "Natural Calamities," 361; Blum, *Lord and Peasant,* 239–43; Eaton, "Early Russian Censuses," 101–5.

48. Hakluyt, *Principal Navigations,* 2:231–32; Fletcher, *Russe Commonwealth,* 53v–54; Blum, *Lord and Peasant,* 155, 200–202; Hellie, *Enserfment,* 29, 39; Keep, *Soldiers,* 34, 42–45, 48–49.

49. Hellie, *Enserfment,* 29, 39, 45; Skrynnikov, "Overview," 73–74.

50. Kahan, "Natural Calamities," 353, 355, 363, 365, 371.

51. Staden, *Lord and Government,* 40, 46; Kolycheva, *Agrarnyi stroi,* 172–76.

52. Kolycheva, *Agrarnyi stroi,* 177–79; Staden, *Land and Government,* 29; Sakharov, *Obrazovanie,* 111–12; Morgan and Coote, *Early Voyages,* 2:307–9, 336–40; Novosel'skii, *Bor'ba,* 13–33.

53. Von Loewe, "Juridical Manifestations," 397–98.

54. Kolycheva, *Agrarnyi stroi,* 172, 187; Smith, *Peasant Farming,* 108; Blum, *Lord and Peasant,* 152, 154–60; Keep, *Soldiers,* 47–48; Yanov, *Origins,* 4, 14–16; Hellie, *Enserfment,* 9, 93–94; Crummey, *Formation,* 21–22.

55. Skrynnikov, "Glavnye vekhi," 96; Blum, *Lord and Peasant,* 154–55; Rozhkov, *Sel'skoe khoziaistvo,* 456–58, 467.

56. Fletcher, *Russe Commonwealth,* 46; Rozhkov, *Sel'skoe khoziaistvo,* 166; Makovskii, *Razvitie,* 392, 482; Hellie, *Enserfment,* 94–95; Kolycheva, *Agrarnyi stroi,* 182–83, 189. Smith argued that the actual extent of the depopulation may have been closer to fifty percent, with much of the missing population merely hiding temporarily from tax collectors or working on tax-exempt lands (*Peasant Farming,* 127–28). On this, see also Kolycheva, *Agrarnyi stroi,* 183.

57. Kopanev, "Naselenie," 251; Danilova, "Istoricheskie usloviia," 134–38; Blum, *Lord and Peasant,* 152, 154–57; Hellie, "Warfare," 80; Vernadsky, *Tsardom,* 1:9–10.

58. Hellie, *Enserfment,* 42, 94.

59. Keep, "Bandits," 201; Hobsbawm, *Bandits,* 13–14. See also Scott, *Moral Economy,* 194; idem, "Everyday Forms of Resistance," 27.

60. *Istoriia krest'ianstva,* 2:423–24.

61. Blum, *Lord and Peasant,* 235–43; Eaton, "Early Russian Censuses," 101–5; Mousnier, *Peasant Uprisings,* 162–63.

62. Kolycheva, *Agrarnyi stroi,* 183; Skrynnikov, "Glavnye vekhi," 101; Eaton, "Early Russian Censuses," 80.

63. Fletcher, *Russe Commonwealth,* 59–59v; Skrynnikov, *Rossiia posle oprichniny,* 46; idem, "Overview," 73–74; idem, "Glavnye vekhi," 96; Hellie, *Enserfment,* 34, 39; Keep, *Soldiers,* 34.

64. Veselovskii, *Feodal'noe zemlevladenie,* 101; Hellie, *Enserfment,* 42–44, 46, 48; Alekseev and Kopanev, "Razvitie," 62; Koretskii, "Iz istorii krest'ianskoi voiny," 124; idem, "K istorii vosstaniia Khlopka," 215; Skrynnikov, "Glavnye vekhi," 102; idem, *Boris Godunov,* 37–38.

65. Blum, *Lord and Peasant,* 200–201; Hellie, *Enserfment,* 31, 39.

66. Hellie, *Slavery,* 15, 460, 490, 495, 685, 688.

67. Makovskii, *Razvitie,* 32, 133–35, 140–43, 236, 257, 458–59; Hellie, *Enserfment,* 95.

68. Hellie, *Slavery,* 688.

69. Paneiakh, *Kabal'noe kholopstvo,* 34–47; Hellie, *Enserfment,* 95; idem, "Stratification," 140.

70. Hellie, *Slavery,* 20–21; Skrynnikov, *Smuta,* 182–83; idem, *Rossiia v nachale* XVII *v.,* 52.

71. Hellie, *Slavery,* 78–79.

72. Skrynnikov, *Smuta,* 4; Hellie, *Slavery,* 319; idem, *Enserfment,* 38; Paneiakh, *Kabal'noe kholopstvo,* 77.

73. Hellie, *Slavery,* 80, 468; idem, *Enserfment,* 39; Zimin, *Reformy,* 356; Skrynnikov, *Rossiia v nachale* XVII *v.,* 51–52.

74. See, for example, Skrynnikov, *Smuta,* 178–79; idem, *Rossiia nakanune 'smutnogo vremeni',* 104; Hellie, *Enserfment,* 39.

75. Zimin, *Reformy,* 448; idem, "Nekotorye voprosy," 108.

76. Keep, *Soldiers,* 58; Hellie, *Slavery,* 467.

77. Hellie, *Slavery,* 467–68; idem, *Enserfment,* 165.

78. Keep, *Soldiers,* 58; Skrynnikov, *Smuta,* 183.

79. See Hellie, *Enserfment,* 220–21, 290 n. 119.

80. Hellie, *Slavery,* 470.

81. Keep, *Soldiers,* 58; Hellie, *Slavery,* 468.

82. Massa, *Kratkoe izvestie,* 154.

83. Hellie, *Slavery,* 470–71.

84. Skrynnikov, *Smuta,* 178–79; Hellie, "Warfare," 79, 83; idem, *Slavery,* 50–51, 62.

85. Eaton, "Early Russian Censuses," 94; Hellie, *Slavery,* 326–27, 331.

86. See Hellie, *Slavery,* 690, 691–92; Palitsyn, *Skazanie,* 107, 225; Margeret, *Russian Empire,* 32; Skrynnikov, *Smuta,* 180. Cf. Anderson, *Lineages,* 208.

87. Hellie, "Warfare," 83.

88. Makovskii, *Razvitie,* 77, 223; Blum, *Lord and* Peasant, 118, 120–25; Hellie, "Foundations," 148–49; idem, *Enserfment,* 87–88; Eaton, "Decline," 227; Yanov, *Origins,* 3–4.

89. Makovskii, *Razvitie,* 32–33, 213, 278–79, 292, 320, 496–97; Blum, *Lord and Peasant,* 158; Hellie, "Foundations," 150; Kolycheva, *Agrarnyi, stroi,* 179–80.

90. Kolycheva, *Agrarnyi stroi,* 174, 176–81; Blum, *Lord and Peasant,* 152.

91. Fletcher, *Russe Commonwealth,* 116; Blum, *Lord and Peasant,* 154–55, 158; Eaton, "Early Russian Censuses," 157–58. See also French, "Early Russian Town," 268–70.

92. Fletcher, *Russe Commonwealth,* 46; Eaton, "Early Russian Censuses," 180–81; idem, "Decline," 224, 229; Smirnov, *Goroda,* 2:34, 37–38, 120, 127; Zimin, *Oprichnina,* 389–430; Got'e, *Zamoskovnyi krai,* 162–65.

93. Hellie, "Stratification," 124.

94. Rozhkov, *Sel'skoe khoziaistvo,* 233–34; Skrynnikov, *Boris Godunov,* 77; idem, "Glavnye vekhi," 100; Kolycheva, *Agrarnyi stroi,* 195; Blum, *Lord and Peasant,* 229.

95. Blum, "Prices," 198–99; Man'kov, *Tseny,* 33–34, 119–20; Smith, *Peasant Farming,* 108.

96. Skrynnikov, "Glavnye vekhi," 96; Blum, *Lord and Peasant,* 96, 152; Crummey, *Formation,* 174.

97. Kolycheva, *Agrarnyi stroi,* 189, 195–201.

98. Skrynnikov, *Boris Godunov,* 29–31, 73–74, 77–78.

NOTES TO CHAPTER 4

1. Skrynnikov, *Boris Godunov,* xi–xvii.

2. Platonov, *Boris Godunov,* 215 n. 8; Veselovskii, "Iz istorii," 88; Kollmann, *Kinship,* 35; Morozova, "Boris Godunov," 60–61.

3. Skrynnikov, *Boris Godunov,* 1–5.

4. Veselovskii, "Iz istorii," 90; Bond, *Russia,* 269; Skrynnikov, *Boris Godunov,* 6–7.

5. Zimin, *V kanun,* 90–94; Morozova, "Boris Godunov," 63–64.

6. Pavlov, *Gosudarev dvor,* 3–29; Purchas, *Hakluytus Posthumus,* 14:115; Berry and Crummey, *Rude and Barbarous Kingdom,* 307; Bond, *Russia,* 269; Zimin, *V kanun,* 106–8. Skrynnikov incorrectly claimed that Boris Godunov was not chosen by Tsar Ivan to sit on Fedor's council of regents (*Rossiia nakanune 'smutnogo vremeni',* 11–13), and he therefore completely misinterpreted Godunov's first steps to power.

7. Hakluyt, *Principal Navigations,* 3:413; Purchas, *Hakluytus Posthumus,* 14:116–17; Margeret, *Russian Empire,* 40; Berry and Crummey, *Rude and Barbarous Kingdom,* 144; Veselovskii, "Iz istorii," 90. See also Kollmann, *Kinship,* 95. Morozova ("Boris Godunov," 64–65) argued that Boris Godunov— in spite of his title—was actually overshadowed in the early years of Tsar Fedor's reign by senior members of his own family.

8. Bond, *Russia,* 339; Berry and Crummey, *Rude and Barbarous Kingdom,* 139–40.

9. PSRL 14:35; Vernadsky, *Tsardom,* 1:184–85; Perrie, *Pretenders,* 11–12.

10. Skrynnikov, "Boris Godunov i tsarevich," 183, 188; idem, *Boris Godunov,* 46. There is some confusion concerning Afanasii Nagoi's exact identity. A contemporary Englishman, Jerome Horsey, referred to him as Tsaritsa Mariia's brother, a faulty identification that has been accepted by many.

(See Berry and Crummey, *Rude and Barbarous Kingdom,* 357; Perrie, "Horsey's Account," 38–39.) Afanasii Nagoi was also misidentified as Mariia's "father" in the English translation of Skrynnikov's *Boris Godunov* (11).

11. Margeret, *Russian Empire,* 17; Perrie, *Pretenders,* 11.

12. PSRL 14:35; Bestuzhev-Riumin, "Obzor sobytii," 51. Cf. Vernadsky, *Tsardom,* 1:184–85. Skrynnikov incorrectly regarded Belskii's defeat as a temporary defeat for Godunov as well. See Skrynnikov, "Boris Godunov i tsarevich," 183–84; idem, *Boris Godunov,* 11–14.

13. Margeret, *Russian Empire,* 53, 69; Ischboldin, *Essays,* 116; *Modern Encyclopedia of Russian and Soviet History* [hereafter cited as MERSH], 23:159–60.

14. Margeret, *Russian Empire,* 16; Platonov, *Boris Godunov,* 33–34; Skrynnikov, "Boris Godunov i tsarevich," 185; idem, *Boris Godunov,* 15–20; Crummey, *Formation,* 206. See also Vovina, "Patriarkh Filaret," 56.

15. Platonov, *Boris Godunov,* 35–36; Vernadsky, *Tsardom,* 1:188–90; Skrynnikov, "Boris Godunov i tsarevich," 185–86; idem, *Boris Godunov,* 20, 23–26.

16. Platonov, *Boris Godunov,* 36; Skrynnikov, *Boris Godunov,* 21, 24, 26.

17. See, for example, Vernadsky, *Tsardom,* 1:189; Skrynnikov, *Boris Godunov,* 24; Abramovich, *Kniaz'ia,* 111.

18. See MERSH 35:56, 59, 61.

19. Skrynnikov, *Smuta,* 28.

20. "Puteshestviia v Moskoviiu sera Eremeia Gorseia," *Chteniia v Imperatorskom Obshchestve Istorii i Drevnostei Rossiiskikh pri Moskovskom Universitete* [hereafter cited as ChOIDR], 2 (1907), section 3:61; Skrynnikov, *Boris Godunov,* 32–33.

21. Skrynnikov, *Boris Godunov,* 36; Crummey, *Formation,* 206.

22. Skrynnikov, "Boris Godunov i tsarevich," 187; idem, *Boris Godunov,* 33–34; Koretskii, "Mazurinskii letopisets," 287.

23. Skrynnikov, *Boris Godunov,* 33–34, 36.

24. Fletcher, *Russe Commonwealth,* 98v–99; Margeret, *Russian Empire,* 17; Bond, *Russia,* 255, 365; Berry and Crummey, *Rude and Barbarous Kingdom,* 330; Vernadsky, "Death," 3; idem, *Tsardom,* 1:193–95; Skrynnikov, "Boris Godunov i tsarevich," 188, 191; Chistov, *Russkie legendy,* 33–36; Perrie, *Pretenders,* 14–15.

25. Fletcher, *Russe Commonwealth,* 16v; Bussow, *Moskovskaia khronika,* 80; Thompson, "Legend," 52; Platonov, *Boris Godunov,* 131–33.

26. Crummey, *Formation,* 206.

27. Fletcher, *Russe Commonwealth,* 116; Skrynnikov, *Boris Godunov,* 29–31; Cf. Smith, *Peasant Farming,* 143 n. 2.

28. Skrynnikov, *Boris Godunov,* 37; Fletcher, *Russe Commonwealth,* 46–46v, 90.

29. Kolycheva, *Agrarnyi stroi,* 195.

30. *Istoriia krest'ianstva,* 2:423–25; Blum, *Lord and Peasant,* 258; Koretskii, "Iz istorii krest'ianskoi voiny," 119–22.

31. Hellie, *Enserfment,* 98–99; Skrynnikov, *Boris Godunov,* 29–31, 37; idem, "Boris Godunov i tsarevich,"189–91.

32. Vernadsky, *Tsardom,* 1:194–95; Skrynnikov, *Boris Godunov,* 53; idem, "Boris Godunov i tsarevich," 194.

33. Klein, *Uglichskoe sledstvennoe delo; Akty, sobrannye v bibliotekakh i arkhivakh Rossiiskoi imperii Arkheograficheskoiu ekspeditsieiu Imp. Akademii nauk* [hereafter cited as AAE], 2:78, 81; *Sobranie gosudarstvennykh gramot i dogovorov* [hereafter cited as SGGD], 2:164; Vernadsky, "Death," 14; Skrynnikov, *Boris Godunov,* 62–63; idem, "Boris Godunov i tsarevich,"195–96; Sapunov, "K voprosu o dostovernosti informatsii uglichskogo sledstvennogo dela," 157–74.

34. Platonov, *Boris Godunov,* 148–50; Skrynnikov, *Boris Godunov,* 63.

35. Golubtsov, "Izmena Nagikh," 56–57, 70; Skrynnikov, "Boris Godunov i tsarevich," 192; idem, *Boris Godunov,* 64.

36. Golubtsov, "Izmena Nagikh," 61–62; Platonov, *Boris Godunov,* 138; Skrynnikov, *Boris Godunov,* 65.

37. Vernadsky, *Tsardom*, 1:220; Thompson, "Legend," 51.

38. Platonov, *Ocherki*, 161–62; idem, *Boris Godunov*, 148–50; Thompson, "Legend," 51; Perrie, *Pretenders*, 21.

39. Palitsyn, *Skazanie*, 251; RIB 13: cols. 151, 564; Bussow, *Moskovskaia khronika*, 107; Platonov, *Ocherki*, 181–82; Vernadsky, "Death," 8; Thompson, "Legend," 24; Perrie, "Popular Legends," 225; idem, "Horsey's Account," 33.

40. Massa, *Short History*, 30–32; Bussow, *Moskovskaia khronika*, 204; PSRL 14:42, 44; Purchas, *Hakluytus Posthumus*, 14:147; Berry and Crummey, *Rude and Barbarous Kingdom*, 259, 358; Thompson, "Legend," 56; Rudakov, "Razvitie," 272–73.

41. Margeret, *Russian Empire*, 17–18; Timofeev, *Vremennik*, 218; Massa, *Short History*, 37; Platonov, *Boris Godunov*, 152–53; Skrynnikov, *Boris Godunov*, 88.

42. See AAE 2:110–11; SGGD 2:307, 310–11, 317; RIB 13: col. 151; Palitsyn, *Skazanie*, 251; Platonov, *Boris Godunov*, 139; Skrynnikov, *Boris Godunov*, x–xii, 51; Thompson, "Legend," 50; Nikolaieff, "Boris Godunov," 281–83.

43. See, for example, Bussow, *Moskovskaia khronika*, 107; Timofeev, *Vremennik*, 94.

44. RIB 13: cols. 564, 837–59; Rowland, "Muscovite Political Attitudes," 111–12; Bushkovitch, "Formation," 370.

45. Platonov, *Boris Godunov*, 125–27, 152.

46. Vernadsky, "Death," 1; Thompson, "Legend," 49, 58.

47. Evgenii Belov, "O smerti tsarevicha Dimitriia," *Zhurnal Ministerstva Narodnago Prosveshcheniia* [hereafter cited as ZhMNP], 168 (1873), part 1:1–44; part 2:277–320; Pierling, *La Russie*, 3:24–35; Kliuchevskii, *Sochineniia*, 3:22; Platonov, *Boris Godunov*, 5, 128, 140–41; Thompson, "Legend," 48; Vernadsky, "Death," 9–10; Skrynnikov, *Boris Godunov*, xi–xiii, xvi; idem, "Boris Godunov i tsarevich," 193.

48. Platonov, *Drevnerusskie skazaniia*, 343–53; idem, *Boris Godunov*, 155; Tiumenev, "Peresmotr," 93–135, 323–59; Rudakov, "Razvitie," 254–83; Polosin, *Sotsial'no-politicheskaia istoriia*, 218–45; Vernadsky, "Death," 4–5, 10–13, 19; Skrynnikov, *Boris Godunov*, xiii–xv.

49. Vernadsky, "Death," 18.

50. See Platonov, *Time of Troubles*, 57–58; Skrynnikov, "Boris Godunov i tsarevich," 191; idem, *Boris Godunov*, xv, 55; Thompson, "Legend," 49 n. 3; Crummey, *Formation*, 211.

51. Zimin, "Smert' tsarevicha," 92–111; idem, *V kanun*, 153–82; Perrie, "Horsey's Account," 28–49; idem, *Pretenders*, 18–19.

52. Perrie, *Pretenders*, 19.

53. See Berry and Crummey, *Rude and Barbarous Kingdom*, 252–53, 256–57; Ia. S. Lur'e, "Pis'ma Dzheroma Gorseia," *Uchenye zapiski Leningradskogo gosudarstvennogo universiteta* 73 (1941), seriia istoricheskikh nauk, part 8, 195; Skrynnikov, "Boris Godunov i tsarevich," 196.

54. Perrie, *Pretenders*, 18.

55. Skrynnikov, *Boris Godunov*, 62–63; idem, "Boris Godunov i tsarevich," 196 n. 68.

56. Perrie, *Pretenders*, 16–17.

57. Platonov, *Boris Godunov*, 153–54; idem, *Time of Troubles*, 57–58; Skrynnikov, *Boris Godunov*, xv; Bennet, "Idea of Kingship," 8.

58. Waliszewski, *La Crise*, 39–59; Vernadsky, *Tsardom*, 1:194–96; idem, "Death," 12–13; Polosin, *Sotsial'no-politicheskaia istoriia*, 223; Skrynnikov, "Boris Godunov i tsarevich," 191–92. Skrynnikov noted that the Romanovs, not the Godunovs, were the most likely beneficiaries of the Uglich tragedy; but he did not accuse them of involvement in it. See Skrynnikov, *Boris Godunov*, 55; idem, "Boris Godunov i tsarevich," 197.

59. Skrynnikov, *Boris Godunov*, 66–69.

60. MERSH 35:56, 62; Skrynnikov, *Smuta*, 29.

61. Timofeev, *Vremennik*, 56, 65; RIB 13: col. 147; Massa, *Short History*, 33–34; Platonov, *Boris Godunov*, 145, 147–48; Rowland, "Problem," 264–65.

62. Skrynnikov, *Boris Godunov*, 76–77.

63. See Hellie, *Enserfment*, 1–18.

64. See Platonov, *Time of Troubles*, 29; Hellie, *Enserfment*, 96; Crummey, *Formation*, 174; Koretskii, *Formirovanie*, 71, 76, 80–81; Skrynnikov, *Boris Godunov*, 71–75.

65. Skrynnikov, *Rossiia posle oprichniny,* 167–216; idem, *Boris Godunov,* 77–80; idem, "Zapovednye i urochnye gody," 99–129.

66. Hellie, "Warfare," 82; idem, *Enserfment,* 97–98, 103; idem, *Muscovite Society,* 116–18; Skrynnikov, *Boris Godunov,* 75–77, 79–80; Koretskii, *Formirovanie,* 3–4; idem, *Zakreposhchenie,* 123, 128–34; idem, "Novgorodskie dela," 313; Mousnier, *Peasant Uprisings,* 181.

67. Makovskii, *Razvitie,* 484–85; Zimin, "Osnovnye etapy," 49–50; Koretskii, "Iz istorii krest'ianskoi voiny," 119–21; idem, "Bor'ba," 194, 197, 199, 202.

68. Pavlov-Sil'vanskii, *Sochineniia,* 1:306–7; Hellie, *Enserfment,* 106.

69. Hellie, *Enserfment,* 104–6; idem, "Warfare," 82–83; idem, *Muscovite Society,* 123–28; Skrynnikov, *Boris Godunov,* 78–79. The five-year limit for the recovery of runaway peasants has often been incorrectly portrayed as a favor to southern landowners. (See, for example, Koretskii, *Zakreposhchenie,* 157–58; Zimin, "K voprosu," 278.) In fact, as Hellie pointed out, runaway peasants tried to avoid southern lords (who would have quickly enserfed them), and there were very few serfs working on southern estates. See Hellie, *Enserfment,* 326 n. 14. Cf. Stevens, *Soldiers,* 24–25.

70. Platonov, *Time of Troubles,* 53; Hellie, *Enserfment,* 8–10, 16–17, 21, 146–47, 262; Skrynnikov, *Smuta,* 7; Crummey, *Formation,* 207.

71. Hellie, "Warfare," 81–82; idem, *Enserfment,* 17, 48, 100–101. Cf. Smith, *Peasant Farming,* 144–45. Elsewhere, Hellie acknowledged that binding the peasants helped only those cavalrymen who were already doing well, not those in distress, and that serfdom did not come about because of pressure from poor pomeshchiki (*Slavery,* 671–73).

72. Skrynnikov, *Smuta,* 6–7; idem, *Boris Godunov,* vii–viii, 77–78.

73. Platonov, *Time of Troubles,* 53; idem, *Boris Godunov,* 100–101; Crummey, *Formation,* 206–7.

74. Hellie, *Enserfment,* 41, 241.

75. Skrynnikov, *Boris Godunov,* 76–77.

76. Smirnov, *Posadskie liudi,* 1:172; Skrynnikov, *Smuta,* 6; Hellie, "Stratification," 136; idem, "Warfare," 82.

77. Hellie, "Stratification," 145; Smirnov, *Posadskie liudi,* 1:160–68, 177, 185; Skrynnikov, *Boris Godunov,* 117.

78. Nazarov, "Klassovaia bor'ba," 216–23.

79. Skrynnikov, *Boris Godunov,* 119; Smirnov, *Posadskie liudi,* 1:160–68.

80. Skrynnikov, "Glavnye vekhi," 102–3; idem, *Rossiia nakanune 'smutnogo vremeni',* 71–72; idem, *Boris Godunov,* 37–38; Hellie, *Enserfment,* 48.

81. See Hellie, "Stratification," 124–25, 128; Makovskii, *Pervaia krest'ianskaia voina,* 189, 468; Skrynnikov, *Boris Godunov,* 116–17; Bushkovitch, "Taxation," 392. Cf. Baron, "Gosti Revisited," 2.

82. Eaton, "Early Russian Censuses," 94; Hellie, *Slavery,* 326–27, 331; Skrynnikov, *Smuta,* 178–79.

83. Skrynnikov, *Rossiia v nachale XVII v.,* 53; Hellie, *Slavery,* 50–53, 62, 697; idem, "Warfare," 83; Paneiakh, *Kholopstvo v XVI-nachale XVII veka,* 246–48; *Zakonodatel'nye akty,* 1:65–66.

84. Hellie, *Slavery,* 39–40.

85. Skrynnikov, *Smuta,* 179.

86. Ibid., 183; idem, *Rossiia v nachale XVII v.,* 249–50.

87. Hellie, *Enserfment,* 48–49, 240–41; idem, *Slavery,* 4, 16; idem, "Stratification," 119; idem, "Warfare," 81, 83–84; Keep, *Soldiers,* 13; Mousnier, *Peasant Uprisings,* 165, 331, 346; Pallott and Shaw, *Landscape,* 10.

88. *Akty Moskovskago gosudarstva, izdannye Imperatorskoiu Akademieiu Nauk* [hereafter cited as AMG], 1: no. 40; Hellie, *Enserfment,* 47–49, 238–39, 262–63; idem, "Warfare," 83–84; Keep, *Soldiers,* 13, 37. Cf. Crummey, "Origins," 62.

89. Hellie, "Warfare," 78.

90. Smirnov, *Vosstanie,* 41–42; Koretskii, "Bor'ba," 176, 197; Hellie, *Enserfment,* 48, 101–2, 116–17.

91. Smirnov, *Vosstanie,* 56–61; *Istoriia krest'ianstva,* 2:424–25; Makovskii, *Razvitie,* 485–86; Zimin, "Osnovnye etapy," 49–50; Koretskii, "Iz istorii krest'ianskoi voiny," 119–20; idem, "Bor'ba," 194, 197–200; Hellie, *Enserfment,* 102.

498   Notes to Pages 67–70

92. *Istoriia krest'ianstva,* 2:423–24; Kamen, *Iron Century,* 377–81; Scott, *Moral Economy,* 194; idem, "Everyday Forms of Resistance," 13–14; Hobsbawm, *Bandits,* 17–19.
93. Mousnier, *Peasant Uprisings,* 331, 346; Crummey, *Formation,* 20–21, 215.
94. Rozhkov, *Sel'skoe khoziaistvo,* 305–10; Kolycheva, *Agrarnyi stroi,* 195–201; Tikhomirov, "Monastyr'-votchinnik," 159–60; Makovskii, *Razvitie,* 32–23, 226, 278–79, 292, 320, 469–67; Smith, *Peasant Farming,* 144–45; Hellie, *Enserfment,* 97, 102; Eaton, "Early Russian Censuses," 171, 179.
95. Hellie, *Enserfment,* 97; Kolycheva, *Agrarnyi stroi,* 201; Smith, *Peasant Farming,* 226.
96. Smith, *Peasant Farming,* 107; Skrynnikov, "Civil War," 72.
97. Kolycheva, *Agrarnyi stroi,* 195.
98. See, for example, Tatishchev, *Istoriia,* 7:367; Solov'ev, "Obzor sobytii," 11.
99. Grekov, *Krest'iane,* 2:310; Koretskii, *Formirovanie,* 364–66; Hellie, *Enserfment,* 103.
100. Hellie, "Warfare," 84–85; idem, *Enserfment,* 102–3.
101. Skrynnikov, "Civil War," 70; idem, *Smuta,* 252.
102. Margeret, *Russian Empire,* 32; Shil', "Donesenie," 17; Koretskii, *Zakreposhchenie,* 189; Hellie, *Enserfment,* 117.
103. Skrynnikov, "Civil War," 72–73; idem, *Rossiia v nachale* XVII *v.,* 110–15.

NOTES TO CHAPTER 5

1. Shaw, "Southern Frontiers," 119–20; Tikhomirov, *Rossiia,* 408–9, 411; Sviatskii, *Istoricheskii ocherk,* 35; Avrich, *Russian Rebels,* 26; Keep, *Soldiers,* 16; Stanislavskii, *Grazhdanskaia voina,* 12–13.
2. Solov'ev, *Istoriia,* 7:43–44; Hellie, *Enserfment,* 128–29. See also Bercé, *Revolt,* 145–46.
3. Zagorin, *Rebels,* 1:40; 2:1–6; Bercé, *Revolt,* 127–34; Hagopian, *Phenomenon,* 17, 40; Jütte, *Poverty,* 189.
4. Goldstone, *Revolution,* 33, 126, 133, 346, 464; Jütte, *Poverty,* 180, 189.
5. Rozhdestvenskii, "Sel'skoe naselenie," 61; Tikhomirov, *Rossiia,* 422–29; Koretskii, *Formirovanie,* 83–116; idem, "K istorii formirovaniia," 84; Hellie, *Enserfment,* 94, 179; Shaw, "Southern Frontiers," 138; Eaton, "Early Russian Censuses," 196–97; Crummey, *Formation,* 215; Blum, *Lord and Peasant,* 236; Margeret, *Russian Empire,* 11.
6. Keep, *Soldiers,* 19; Koretskii, *Formirovanie,* 116; *Istoriia krest'ianstva,* 2:428; Stanislavskii, *Grazhdanskaia voina,* 17–20.
7. Shaw, "Southern Frontiers," 22; Kleimola, "Holding on," 130.
8. Solov'ev, *Istoriia,* 4:469; Tikhomirov, *Rossiia,* 407–9; Keep, *Soldiers,* 16; Crummey, *Formation,* 214.
9. Tikhomirov, *Rossiia,* 408, 421–22; Vernadsky, *Russia at Dawn,* 249; idem, *Tsardom,* 1:13; Razin, *Istoriia,* 2:307, 342; Hellie, *Enserfment,* 174–76; Keep, *Soldiers,* 16; Shaw, "Southern Frontiers," 122–24; Kleimola, "Holding on," 131–32; Stevens, *Soldiers,* 19–20.
10. Hellie, *Enserfment,* 176–77; Shaw, "Southern Frontiers," 124, 132; Pallott and Shaw, *Landscape,* 16, 32; Kleimola, "Holding on," 134; Vernadsky, *Tsardom,* 1:10–13; Osipov, *Ocherki,* 11.
11. Kleimola, "Holding on," 134; AMG 1: no. 3.
12. Stanislavskii, *Grazhdanskaia voina,* 12–13.
13. Tikhomirov, *Rossiia,* 407, 410; AMG 2:5–6; P. P. Nekrasov, "Ocherki po istorii riazansk-ago kraia XVI veka," ZhMNP 50 (1914):283–87; Pavlov-Sil'vanskii, *Sochineniia,* 1:98; Blum, *Lord and Peasant,* 169–70.
14. Platonov, *Time of Troubles,* 34; Eaton, "Early Russian Censuses," 196–97; Koretskii, *Formirovanie,* 83–116; Blum, *Lord and Peasant,* 236; Crummey, *Formation,* 215; Hellie, *Enserfment,* 94, 179, 236; Shaw, "Southern Frontiers," 138; Orchard, "Frontier Policy," 113–14; Kolycheva, *Agrarnyi stroi,* 200–201.
15. Hellie, *Enserfment,* 31; Skrynnikov, "Glavnye vekhi," 102; idem, *Rossiia v nachale* XVII *v.,* 10–11, 20.

16. Tikhomirov, *Russiia*, 381, 393–94, 425; Rozhkov, *Sel'skoe khoziaistvo*, 28; Shaw, "Southern Frontiers," 122; Eaton, "Early Russian Censuses," 78, 196; Skrynnikov, *Rossiia v nachale XVII v.*, 11.

17. Tikhomirov, *Rossiia*, 381, 393–409; Rozhkov, *Sel'skoe khoziaistvo*, 28; Blum, *Lord and Peasant*, 177–78, 208–9; Keep, *Soldiers*, 46–47; Pallott and Shaw, *Landscape*, 35, 37; Skrynnikov, "Glavnye vekhi," 102–3.

18. Pavlov-Sil'vanskii, *Sochineniia*, 1:119–20; Smirnov, *Vosstanie*, 131; Hellie, *Enserfment*, 31; Keep, *Soldiers*, 32, 34, 42–44; Kleimola, "Holding on," 137–38; Skrynnikov, *Rossiia v nachale XVII v.*, 10, 20–22; Pallott and Shaw, *Landscape*, 36–37.

19. Blum, *Lord and Peasant*, 208–9; Skrynnikov, *Smuta*, 6, 82; Stevens, *Soldiers*, 24–25.

20. Keep, *Soldiers*, 19, 38–39.

21. *Boiarskie spiski*, 1:41, 232; 2:79; Skrynnikov, *Smuta*, 81–82, 91–92; idem, "Civil War," 72–73. The militarily useful deti boiarskie infantry may be regarded as ancestors of the dragoons who served in the tsar's new formation regiments during the later seventeenth century.

22. Tikhomirov, *Rossiia*, 410, 412; Skrynnikov, *Smuta*, 5–6; idem, "Glavnye vekhi," 101–4; Keep, *Soldiers*, 34.

23. Blum, *Lord and Peasant*, 236; Shaw, "Southern Frontiers," 120; Pallott and Shaw, *Landscape*, 20–21.

24. Vladimirskii-Budanov, *Obzor*, 119; D'iakonov, *Ocherki stroia*, 265; Nikitin, "K voprosu," 44–56; Skrynnikov, *Rossiia v nachale XVII v.*, 21–23, 109; idem, *Boris Godunov*, 119; idem, "Predvestniki," 54; Zagorovskii, *Belgorodskaia cherta*, 29–30; Shaw, "Southern Frontiers," 122, 125–26; Pallott and Shaw, *Landscape*, 37–38; Hellie, *Enserfment*, 28, 52–53.

25. Skrynnikov, *Rossiia v nachale XVII v.*, 110, 249–50; idem, "Civil War," 73; idem, *Boris Godunov*, 115–16.

26. Dunning, "Cossacks," 57–58; Stanislavskii, *Grazhdanskaia voina*, 3–5, 247; Skrynnikov, *Rossiia v nachale XVII v.*, 3, 5, 250–51; idem, *Smuta*, 5–8, 248–52. See also Kornblatt, *Cossack Hero*, 5, 15–21.

27. Longworth, *Cossacks*, 334; Stanislavskii, *Grazhdanskaia voina*, 6–7, 11; Vernadsky, *Russia at Dawn*, 249–50.

28. Hellie, *Enserfment*, 208; PSRL 25:386; Longworth, *Cossacks*, 13–14.

29. Dunning, "Cossacks," 58.

30. Longworth, *Cossacks*, 14; March, "Cossacks," 9, 16–17, 21; Gordon, *Cossack Rebellions*, 64–67, 75–79; Margeret, *Russian Empire*, 47.

31. Stanislavskii, *Grazhdanskaia voina*, 7–8; Longworth, *Cossacks*, 21–23; Hellie, *Enserfment*, 208; Smirnov, *Vosstanie*, 123–24.

32. Longworth, *Cossacks*, 14–15; Zagorovskii, *Belgorodskaia cherta*, 55–64; Keep, *Soldiers*, 16; Skrynnikov, *Rossiia v nachale XVII v.*, 20.

33. Stanislavskii, *Grazhdanskaia voina*, 9–10, 243–47; Longworth, *Cossacks*, 19–21, 31–33, 36–46; Skrynnikov, *Rossiia v nachale XVII v.*, 104; Kornblatt, *Cossack Hero*, 8; Gordon, *Cossack Rebellions*, 79–80, 82–86; Esper, "Military Self-Sufficiency," 204.

34. Dunning, "Cossacks," 71; Kornblatt, *Cossack Hero*, 6.

35. Stanislavskii, *Grazhdanskaia voina*, 7, 10–11, 242; Skrynnikov, *Smuta*, 252; idem, "Civil War," 73; Solov'ev, *Istoriia*, 7:43–44.

36. Stanislavskii, *Grazhdanskaia voina*, 7–8, 26–27; Skrynnikov, *Smuta*, 180–82; idem, *Rossiia v nachale XVII v.*, 108, 110–11; Smirnov, *Vosstanie*, 123–24; Zimin, "Nekotorye voprosy," 104; Dunning, "Letter," 105; Popov, *Izbornik*, 354; Massa, *Kratkoe izvestie*, 77. See also Hobsbawm, *Bandits*, 27; Kamen, *Iron Century*, 377–81.

37. Shaw, "Southern Frontiers," 20; Margeret, *Russian Empire*, 49–50; Stanislavskii, *Grazhdanskaia voina*, 11–14; Longworth, *Cossacks*, 15–18, 33–36.

38. Margeret, *Russian Empire*, 49–50; Skrynnikov, *Rossiia v nachale XVII v.*, 104–6, 108, 114; Stanislavskii, *Grazhdanskaia voina*, 10–11; Hellie, *Enserfment*, 208–9; *Istoriia krest'ianstva*, 2:426; Smirnov, *Vosstanie*, 132–33; Pavlov-Sil'vanskii, *Sochineniia*, 1:306–7.

39. Skrynnikov, *Sibirskaia ekspeditsiia*, 62; Stanislavskii, *Grazhdanskaia voina*, 12.

40. Chernov, *Vooruzhennye sily*, 89; Stanislavskii, *Grazhdanskaia voina*, 10–11, 19–20. Cf. March, "Cossacks," 34.

41. Stanislavskii, *Grazhdanskaia voina*, 242; Skrynnikov, "Civil War," 73; Longworth, *Cossacks*, 18; Smirnov, *Vosstanie*, 123–24.

42. Longworth, *Cossacks*, 20–23; Gordon, *Cossack Rebellions*, 89–96; Kozlov, "O poiavlenii," 92–95.

43. Goldstone, *Revolution*, 33, 126, 346; Gordon, *Cossack Rebellions*, 2–3; Clark, *European Crisis*, 7, 13; Kamen, *Iron Century*, 377–81; Bercé, *Revolt*, 130, 133, 144–48; Bracewell, *Uskoks*, 12; Hobsbawm, *Bandits*, 19.

44. Gunther Rothenberg, *The Austrian Military Border in Croatia, 1522–1747* (Urbana: University of Illinois Press, 1960), 29–30, 125.

45. Hobsbawm, *Bandits*, 61–62, 66, 71.

46. Bracewell, *Uskoks*, 1–4, 8, 10–11, 43–44, 66, 82–83, 162–63, 170–71.

47. Hobsbawm, *Bandits*, 62; Bracewell, *Uskoks*, 12–13, 155, 171; Mousnier, *Peasant Uprisings*, 160.

48. Gordon, *Cossack Rebellions*, 2–3; Longworth, *Cossacks*, 1–3, 7–8; Stanislavskii, *Grazhdanskaia voina*, 4; Kornblatt, *Cossack Hero*, 3–38, 99–106.

49. Tikhomirov, *Rossiia*, 410; Stanislavskii, *Grazhdanskaia voina*, 13–17; Keep, *Soldiers*, 74–75; Skrynnikov, *Rossiia v nachale* XVII *v.*, 108–9; Shaw, "Southern Frontiers," 125; Pallott and Shaw, *Landscape*, 20.

50. Miklashevskii, *K istorii*, 271; Anpilogov, *Novye dokumenty*, 206; Skrynnikov, *Rossiia v nachale* XVII *v.*, 20–21, 23–24, 109; Stanislavskii, *Grazhdanskaia voina*, 12–17; Makovskii, *Razvitie*, 190–91; Hellie, *Enserfment*, 28, 52; Storozhev, "Desiatni," 92–94.

51. Skrynnikov, "Glavnye vekhi," 104; *Istoriia krest'ianstva*, 2:426.

52. Shaw, "Southern Frontiers," 137–38; Skrynnikov, "Civil War," 72; idem, *Boris Godunov*, 27–28; Platonov, *Time of Troubles*, 38.

53. Lantzeff and Pierce, *Eastward to Empire*, 109–10, 112–13, 125, 127–29; Hellie, *Enserfment*, 209; Crummey, *Formation*, 209.

54. Platonov, *Time of Troubles*, 34; Smith, *Peasant Farming*, 203; Lantzeff and Pierce, *Eastward to Empire*, 110; Shaw, "Southern Frontiers," 132–33; PSRL 14:36.

55. Lantzeff and Pierce, *Eastward to Empire*, 110–11; Novosel'skii, *Bor'ba*, 34; PSRL 14:52; Osipov, *Ocherki*, 14–19; Shaw, "Southern Frontiers," 121, 132; Skrynnikov, *Boris Godunov*, 27–28; Orchard, "Frontier Policy," 116–17; Crummey, *Formation*, 207. See also Longworth, *Cossacks*, 18.

56. Keep, *Soldiers*, 62–63; PSRL 14:45; Shaw, "Southern Frontiers," 125; Pallott and Shaw, *Landscape*, 16–19; Lantzeff and Pierce, *Eastward to Empire*, 109–10; Novosel'skii, *Bor'ba*, 44; Skrynnikov, *Boris Godunov*, 48–50; Hellie, *Enserfment*, 175–77.

57. Skrynnikov, *Rossiia v nachale* XVII *v.*, 249; idem, *Boris Godunov*, 115–16; Stanislavskii, *Grazhdanskaia voina*, 11.

58. Keep, *Soldiers*, 16; Longworth, *Cossacks*, 23; Kozlov, "O poiavlenii," 92–95.

59. Skrynnikov, *Boris Godunov*, 27–28; idem, *Smuta*, 7–8, 252; Stanislavskii, *Grazhdanskaia voina*, 18; Shaw, "Southern Frontiers," 124–25; Platonov, *Time of Troubles*, 36–37.

60. Skrynnikov, *Rossiia v nachale* XVII *v.*, 107–8; idem, *Boris Godunov*, 116; Hellie, *Enserfment*, 209.

61. *Istoriia krest'ianstva*, 2:427; Skrynnikov, *Rossiia v nachale* XVII *v.*, 108, 110–11, 167, 249–50; idem, *Smuta*, 181–82; Massa, *Kratkoe izvestie*, 77; Popov, *Izbornik*, 354; Adrianova-Peretts, *Voinskie povesti*, 201.

62. Skrynnikov, "Predvestniki," 55–56; idem, *Boris Godunov*, 119; *Istoriia krest'ianstva*, 2:426–27.

63. Bagalei, *Materialy*, 10; Shaw, "Southern Frontiers," 125; Skrynnikov, *Rossiia v nachale* XVII *v.*, 106–7.

64. Skrynnikov, "Civil War," 70, 72–73; idem, *Smuta*, 252.

65. Stanislavskii, *Grazhdanskaia voina*, 11–12. Cf. Gordon, *Cossack Rebellions*, 208.

66. Skrynnikov, *Rossiia v nachale* XVII *v.*, 110; Stanislavskii, *Grazhdanskaia voina*, 13; Anpilogov, *Novye dokumenty*, 367–68; Keep, *Soldiers*, 73.

67. Anpilogov, *Novye dokumenty*, 307–73; Skrynnikov, "Predvestniki," 54–56; idem, *Rossiia v nachale* XVII *v.*, 110; idem, *Boris Godunov*, 119. Skrynnikov's interpretation of Boris Godunov's "investigation" of fortress cossacks is preferable to that found in the "New Chronicle" (PSRL 14:44) and in most Soviet studies of the topic (e.g., *Istoriia krest'ianstva*, 2:426–27.)

68. Keep, *Soldiers,* 73–74; Skrynnikov, *Rossiia v nachale* XVII *v.,* 167.

69. Skrynnikov, *Rossiia v nachale* XVII *v.,* 110.

70. Platonov, *Ocherki,* 91, 254–55; Smirnov, *Vosstanie,* 132–33; RIB 18: cols. 2–24; Miklashevskii, *K istorii,* 266–68; *Istoriia krest'ianstva,* 2:428; Skrynnikov, "Civil War," 73; idem, *Smuta,* 82; Stevens, *Soldiers,* 50. Cf. Osipov, *Ocherki,* 25–36.

71. Grekov, "Iur'ev den'," 71; Koretskii, *Zakreposhchenie,* 31; Skrynnikov, *Rossiia v nachale* XVII *v.,* 112.

72. Miklashevskii, *K istorii,* 233–34, 266–69; Platonov, *Time of Troubles,* 38–39; Skrynnikov, "Glavnye vekhi," 102; idem, *Rossiia v nachale* XVII *v.,* 112–14.

73. Platonov, *Ocherki,* 241–42; *Istoriia krest'ianstva,* 2:428; Skrynnikov, *Rossiia v nachale* XVII *v.,* 112, 114–15; idem, "Glavnye vekhi," 103.

74. Keep, *Soldiers,* 62–63; Shaw, "Southern Frontiers," 122, 125–26; Pallott and Shaw, *Landscape,* 37–38; Stanislavskii, *Grazhdanskaia voina,* 12–13, 16; Skrynnikov, *Smuta,* 82; *Rossiia v nachale* XVII *v.,* 109; idem, "Civil War," 70; idem, "Glavnye vekhi," 100, 103.

75. See Pipes, *Russia,* 67; Kollmann, "Concepts," 47 n. 26.

76. See Henshall, *Myth of Absolution;* Kivelson, *Autocracy;* Kollmann, "Concepts," 38, 43; Stevens, *Soldiers,* 10, 26–28, 69–70.

77. Hellie, *Enserfment,* 35.

78. Keep, *Solders,* 30–32, 63; *Istoriia krest'ianstva,* 2:428; Skrynnikov, "Civil War," 72–73; idem, *Rossiia v nachale* XVII *v.,* 11.

79. Avrich, *Russian Rebels,* 12–13; Keep, *Soldiers,* 19, 73–74. See also Keenan, "Muscovite Political Folkways," 131.

80. Keep, *Soldiers,* 37.

81. On the theoretical issue of the relationship of rapid social mobility and "status inconsistency" (both of which were quite pronounced all across Europe during the sixteenth century) to rebellions and civil wars, see Zagorin, *Rebels,* 1:130–31; Stone, *Causes,* 19, 54.

NOTES TO CHAPTER 6

1. Platonov, *Time of Troubles,* 42.

2. Platonov, *Ocherki,* 115–16; Presniakov, "Moskovskoe gosudarstvo," 12.

3. Timofeev, *Vremennik,* 26, 75, 112, 160, 164; RIB 13: cols. 547, 854; PSRL 14:18–19. See also Cherniavsky, *Tsar and People,* 44; Bennet, "Idea of Kingship," 105; Kondratieva and Ingerflom, "Bez Carja," 257–66.

4. Keenan, "Muscovite Political Folkways," 141–42; idem, "Trouble," 110–13; Bennet, "Idea of Kingship," 4–5; Perrie, *Image,* 2.

5. Rowland, "Limits," 137; idem, "Moscow," 196–98; idem, "Problem," 278; Bushkovitch, "Formation," 365; Hunt, "Mythology," 770, 776; Flier, "Iconology," 68, 74; Cherniavsky, *Tsar and People,* 28–29; Soloviev, *Holy Russia,* 30.

6. Rowland, "Limits," 130, 135–36; Kivelson, "Devil Stole His Mind," 733, 736, 742–43; Bushkovitch, "Formation," 363–64; idem, *Religion and Society,* 3–4; Cherniavsky, *Tsar and People,* 30, 33; Hunt, "Mythology," 769, 772; Zhivov and Uspenskii, "Tsar' i Bog," 47–61.

7. Rowland, "Muscovite Political Attitudes," 131–32; idem, "Limits," 134–35; Bushkovitch, "Formation," 369. See also Weber, "Routinization of Charisma," 271–72.

8. See relevant comments in Hans J. Torke, "The Significance of the Seventeenth Century," FOG 56 (1999); Rowland, "Limits," 138.

9. RIB 13: cols. 152–53, 565–66, 1282; Timofeev, *Vremennik,* 52–54; Massa, *Short History,* 33–34; Margeret, *Russian Empire,* 16–18; Kashtanov, "Diplomatika kak spetsial'naia istoricheskaia distsiplina," 43–44; Bushkovitch, "Formation," 371.

10. Skrynnikov, *Boris Godunov,* 67–70; Vernadsky, *Tsardom,* 1:204; Morozova, "Boris Godunov," 68

11. Margeret, *Russian Empire*, 59; Massa, *Short History*, 35–36; Fletcher, *Russe Commonwealth*, 28–28v; Skrynnikov, *Boris Godunov*, 45–46.

12. Hellie, *Enserfment*, 44, 48, 92–93, 98; Platonov, *Time of Troubles*, 51–54.

13. See, for example, *Novyi Letopisets*, 24–25; Hellie, *Enserfment*, 105–6; Rowland, "Problem," 280–81; idem, "Muscovite Political Attitudes," 223–24; Skrynnikov, *Boris Godunov*, ix, 124. See also Kobrin, *Vlast' i sobstvennost' v srednevekovoi Rossii*.

14. Pavlov, *Gosudarev dvor*, 50–60.

15. Kondratieva and Ingerflom, "Bez Carja,"257–66; Cherniavsky, *Tsar and People*, 44.

16. SGGD 2:144; PSRL 14:19–20; *Piskarevskii letopisets*, 95, 105; Platonov, *Ocherki*, 170–71.

17. Platonov, *Time of Troubles*, 57–58. Skrynnikov (*Boris Godunov*, 83) erred in accepting anti-Godunov propaganda that Tsar Fedor wanted Irina to take the veil and died in isolation and neglect without naming a successor.

18. Skrynnikov, *Boris Godunov*, 83–86.

19. Platonov, *Time of Troubles*, 62; Skrynnikov, *Boris Godunov*, 87–88; Vernadsky, *Tsardom*, 1:205; Pavlov, *Gosudarev dvor*, 50–60.

20. Platonov, *Ocherki*, 181–82; Perrie, "Legends," 225–27; Ptashitskii, "Perepiska," 210; Skrynnikov, *Boris Godunov*, 88–89.

21. Skrynnikov, "Boris Godunov's Struggle," 330–49.

22. Vernadsky, *Tsardom*, 1:205, 210; Skrynnikov, *Boris Godunov*, 97–98; idem, *Rossiia v nachale XVII v.*, 34.

23. Margeret, *Russian Empire*, 18–20; Skrynnikov, *Boris Godunov*, 98–102.

24. Bond, *Russia*, 277; Massa, *Short History*, 43; Palitsyn, *Skazanie*, 104; Grekov, *Krest'iane*, 2:335–56; Vernadsky, *Tsardom*, 1:210–11; Skrynnikov, *Boris Godunov*, 116–20; idem, *Rossiia v nachale XVII v.*, 40.

25. AAE 2:48; Massa, *Short History*, 44; Bussow, *Moskovskaia khronika*, 208; A. P. Pavlov, "Sostav Boiarskoi dumy v period tsarstvovaniia Borisa Godunova," in *Gosudarstvennye uchrezhdeniia i klassovye otnosheniia v otechestvennoi istorii*, part 2 (Moscow-Leningrad, 1980), 259; idem, *Gosudarev dvor*, 63–65; Skrynnikov, *Rossiia v nachale XVII v.*, 29–30; idem, *Boris Godunov*, 102–7; idem, "Boris Godunov i padenie," 119; Golubtsov, "Izmena Nagikh," 62–63.

26. See Keenan, "Muscovite Political Folkways," 142.

27. Bennet, "Idea of Kingship," 13, 23; Crummey, *Formation*, 211; Rowland, "Limits," 138.

28. Platonov, *Ocherki*, 228, 296–97, 558–65; Skrynnikov, *Boris Godunov*, 103–4; idem, "Boris Godunov's Struggle," 325–53.

29. AAE 2:13–14, 22; Bennet, "Idea of Kingship," 15, 17–22.

30. Kliuchevskii, *Sochineniia*, 3:53.

31. Keenan, "Muscovite Political Folkways," 140.

32. Perrie, "Popular Image," 279; idem, "Folklore," 133, 139.

33. Margeret, *Russian Empire*, 3; RIB 13: col. 567; PSRL 14:2.

34. RIB 13: col. 147; Platonov, *Boris Godunov*, 45–48; Skrynnikov, *Boris Godunov*, xi, xiv, xvi–xvii; idem, "Civil War," 74; Crummey, *Formation*, 206; Rowland, "Problem," 264–65; idem, "Limits," 140.

35. Skrynnikov, *Rossiia v nachale XVII v.*, 78; Bushkovitch, *Religion and Society*, 132.

36. Bond, *Russia*, 276–77; Timofeev, *Vremennik*, 65, 80–81; PSRL 14:6–7; Palitsyn, *Skazanie*, 252; RIB 13: cols. 224, 532, 1282–83; Margeret, *Russian Empire*, 59.

37. PSRL 14:55; 34:202; Bussow, *Moskovskaia khronika*, 90; Skrynnikov, "Civil War," 74; idem, *Boris Godunov*, 116–22.

38. Platonov, *Time of Troubles*, 42–43; Kollmann, *Kinship*, 150–51. See also Palitsyn, *Skazanie*, 252–53; Rowland, "Muscovite Political Attitudes," 160–61, 172.

39. Pavlov, *Gosudarev dvor*, 65; Rowland, "Limits," 153; Bushkovitch, "Formation," 368.

40. RIB 13: cols. 150, 224–25, 567, 580, 1729; Timofeev, *Vremennik*, 56, 75–76, 87, 101; Palitsyn, *Skazanie*, 258–60, 269; Rowland, "Muscovite Political Attitudes," 161, 164–65, 223; idem, "Problem," 267–68; Bushkovitch, "Formation," 369. See also Bacon, "Of Seditions and Troubles," 82.

41. Timofeev, *Vremennik*, 56; RIB 13: cols. 150, 567, 580, 1279; Bushkovitch, *Religion and Society*, 132.

42. Blum, *Lord and Peasant*, 147–48; Skrynnikov, *Time of Troubles*, xv.

43. Margeret, *Russian Empire*, 53, 146 n. 170, 147 n. 172.

44. Berry and Crummey, *Rude and Barbarous Kingdom*, 140–41; Kleimola, "Up through Servitude," 214.

45. Kleimola, "Duty to Denounce," 763–72.

46. Bond, *Russia*, 163; Fletcher, *Russe Commonwealth*, 25; Berry and Crummey, *Rude and Barbarous Kingdom*, 139, 270; Tatishchev, *Istoriia*, 7:362–65; Perrie, *Image*, 92–93.

47. Perrie, *Image*, 12, 31, 47, 60–61, 65, 91–92; idem, "Popular Image," 279–80, 283–85.

48. Margeret, *Russian Empire*, 60; PSRL 14:52; RIB 13: cols. 532, 563, 1283–84; Palitsyn, *Skazanie*, 252–53; Timofeev, *Vremennik*, 75–76; Rowland, "Muscovite Political Attitudes," 156–57, 161, 164–65; idem, "Problem," 267–69; Perrie, *Pretenders*, 29–30; Platonov, *Time of Troubles*, 64.

49. Zguta, "Witchcraft Trials," 1192–93; Kleimola, "Duty to Denounce," 771–72; AAE 2:58–59. See also Purchas, *Hakluytus Posthumus*, 14:162; Levack, *Witch-Hunt*, 125.

50. RIB 13: col. 1279; Margeret, *Russian Empire*, 60; Zolkiewski, *Expedition*, 42–43; Skrynnikov, *Rossiia v nachale XVII v.*, 31; idem, *Boris Godunov*, 107; Pavlov, *Gosudarev dvor*, 65.

51. Pavlov, *Gosudarev dvor*, 78; Vernadsky, *Tsardom*, 1:221–22.

52. Palitsyn, *Skazanie*, 252–53; RIB 13: col. 1284; Skrynnikov, *Boris Godunov*, 108–10.

53. Skrynnikov, "Boris Godunov i padenie," 119–22; idem, *Boris Godunov*, 110–12; idem, *Rossiia v nachale XVII v.*, 33–34.

54. Perrie, *Pretenders*, 28–29; Pavlov, *Gosudarev dvor*, 73–76.

55. Skrynnikov, *Rossiia v nachale XVII v.*, 33.

56. AAE 2:38; Skrynnikov, *Boris Godunov*, 108–9; idem, "Boris Godunov i padenie," 119. See also Zguta, "Witchcraft Trials," 1193.

57. Skrynnikov, "Boris Godunov i padenie," 120.

58. RIB 13: col. 479; Palitsyn, *Skazanie*, 252–53; Bushkovitch, "Formation," 369.

59. RIB 13: col 1284; *Akty istoricheskie, sobrannye i izdannye Arkheograficheskoiu kommissieiu* [hereafter cited as AI], 2:34; Skrynnikov, *Boris Godunov*, 109–10; idem, *Rossiia v nachale XVII v.*, 70.

60. Bussow, *Disturbed State*, 26–27; Berry and Crummey, *Rude and Barbarous Kingdom*, 331; Platonov, *Time of Troubles*, 63; Pavlov, *Gosudarev dvor*, 65, 69, 76–77; Skrynnikov, *Rossiia v nachale XVII v.*, 34–36; Vernadsky, *Tsardom*, 1:221–22; Floria, "Iz sledstvennogo dela," 304–5.

61. Skrynnikov, *Rossiia v nachale XVII v.*, 36–37; Vernadsky, *Tsardom*, 1:222.

62. Margeret, *Russian Empire*, 52. See also Palitsyn, *Skazanie*, 251–60; Platonov, *Time of Troubles*, 64.

63. Margeret, *Russian Empire*, 60–61; Massa, *Short History*, 55–56; Kliuchevskii, *Sochineniia*, 3:31–32.

64. Platonov, *Time of Troubles*, 64–68; idem, *Boris Godunov*, 193–96; idem, *Ocherki*, 234, 561 n. 70; Margeret, *Russian Empire*, 81; Tikhomirov, "Samozvanshchina," 120–21; Vovina, "Patriarkh Filaret," 56; Crummey, *Formation*, 217.

65. Massa, *Short History*, 51; MERSH 14:101–4; Hellie, *Enserfment*, 106–7; idem, *Slavery*, 3; Skrynnikov, *Boris Godunov*, 120–21; idem, *Rossiia v nachale XVII v.*, 38–39, 43; Firsov, *Golod*, 6–7; Gnevushev, *Akty*, 269–72, 280, 287–88, 320–22, 324–26, 329–31, 342–43, 345.

66. Skrynnikov, "Civil War," 70, 74; idem, *Rossiia v nachale XVII v.*, 249; Mousnier, *Peasant Uprisings*, 330–31.

67. Kahan, "Natural Calamities," 353, 355, 361, 365, 371. See also Arnold, *Famine*, 30; Appleby, "Epidemics and Famine," 77.

68. Arnold, *Famine*, 50, 55; Kahan, "Natural Calamities," 361.

69. Kamen, *Iron Century*, 366–80; Clark, *European Crisis*, 3–9; Appleby, "Epidemics and Famine," 63–83; Le Roy Ladurie, *Times of Feast*, 164, 225, 297; Braudel, *Mediterranean*, 1:270–75.

70. PSRL 14:55; 32:187; Palitsyn, *Skazanie*, 105; Tikhomirov, "Maloizvestnye pamiatniki," 94; Popov, *Izbornik*, 190, 219, 414; Koretskii, *Formirovanie*, 118–21; MERSH 14:101; Skrynnikov, *Boris Godunov*, 120–21.

71. Koretskii, "Golod," 221; Popov, *Izbornik*, 219; Skrynnikov, *Rossiia v nachale XVII v.*, 38; Kirby, *Northern Europe*, 150.

72. Tikhomirov, "Maloizvestnye pamiatniki," 94; Veselovskii, *Arzamasskie akty*, 210.

73. PSRL 32:188; MERSH 14:101; Skrynnikov, *Rossiia v nachale XVII v.*, 38; Koretskii, "Golod," 226–27. See also Kahan, "Natural Calamities," 361.

74. Margeret, *Russian Empire*, 58, 149 n. 183. There is considerable controversy over food prices during the famine. Some contemporary estimates had grain prices hitting 80 to 120 times prefamine levels by 1603. (See Popov, *Izbornik*, 219; RIB 13: col 393; *Vosstanie I. Bolotnikova: Dokumenty i materialy* [hereafter cited as VBDM], 68, 71; Kliuchevskii, *Sochineniia*, 7:187, 216, 472; Man'kov, *Tseny*, 111; Smirnov, *Vosstanie*, 64; Koretskii, "Golod," 227.) R.E.F. Smith has plausibly challenged those very high estimates (*Peasant Farming*, 143–46).

75. Margeret, *Russian Empire*, 58; Massa, *Short History*, 51–52; Bussow, *Moskovskaia khronika*, 97; Palitsyn, *Skazanie*, 106; Petreius, *Reliatsiia*, 75; Skrynnikov, *Rossiia v nachale XVII v.*, 39, 41, 69. See also Skripil', "Povest'," 256–323; Kamen, *Iron Century*, 68–69, 383.

76. PSRL 14:55; Massa, *Kratkoe izvestie*, 60; Bussow, *Moskovskaia khronika*, 97; Margeret, *Russian Empire*, 58; Skrynnikov, *Rossiia v nachale XVII v.*, 69. See also Arnold, *Famine*, 86; Hobsbawm, *Bandits*, 17–18; Kamen, *Iron Century*, 377–78; Clark, *European Crisis*, 6–7.

77. Eaton, "Early Russian Censuses," 93; Iakovlev, *Kholopstvo*, 60–64, 66–68, 71–72, 81; Hellie, *Slavery*, 363; Skrynnikov, *Rossiia v nachale XVII v.*, 54; idem, *Smuta*, 180; Culpepper, "Legislative Origins," 183; Polosin, *Sotsial'no-politicheskaia istoriia*, 258–60; Smirnov, *Vosstanie*, 69–71; Palitsyn, *Skazanie*, 108; Paneiakh, "K voprosu," 265–67; Zimin, *Khrestomatiia*, 251–52; Skrynnikov, *Boris Godunov*, 122.

78. Palitsyn, *Skazanie*, 107; Skrynnikov, *Smuta*, 180, 183–84; Stanislavskii, *Grazhdanskaia voina*, 13; MERSH 14:103. See also, Arnold, *Famine*, 82.

79. Dunning, "Cossacks," 61; Palitsyn, *Skazanie*, 108; Skrynnikov, *Smuta*, 180–81; *Istoriia krest'ianstva*, 2:429–30; MERSH 14:103. See also *Pamiatniki russkogo prava*, 4:540–41; Arnold, *Famine*, 91–93.

80. Koretskii, *Formirovanie*, 126; Skrynnikov, *Rossiia v nachale XVII v.*, 39.

81. PSRL 14:61; Massa, *Short History*, 54; Aleksandrenko, "Materialy," 452; Boldakov, *Sbornik*, 17; Koretskii, "Golod," 227–30.

82. Koretskii, *Formirovanie*, 127, 131–32; idem, "Golod," 231.

83. Skrynnikov, *Rossiia v nachale XVII v.*, 54; Koretskii, "Golod," 231–32; Eaton, "Early Russian Censuses," 171; Culpepper, "Legislative Origins," 182–83; Margeret, *Russian Empire*, 59; Arnold, *Famine*, 6, 50.

84. Palitsyn, *Skazanie*, 104; Bussow, *Moskovskaia khronika*, 90; Skrynnikov, *Rossiia v nachale XVII v.*, 40, 43–44; idem, "Zemskaia politika," 169–75; Semevskii, *Istoriko-iuridicheskie akty*, 57; Aleksandrenko, "Materialy," 188.

85. Bussow, *Moskovskaia khronika*, 98; VBDM, 68–73; Koretskii, "Golod," 221–22; *Sbornik Khil'kova*, no. 62; *Zakonodatel'nye akty*, 1:67–69; Skrynnikov, "Zemskaia politika," 183; idem, *Boris Godunov*, 121–22. Massa (*Short History*, 52) was wrong about Tsar Boris not issuing an edict to force the sale of surplus grain.

86. Massa, *Short History*, 54; Skrynnikov, *Rossiia v nachale XVII v.*, 40–42; Semevskii, *Istoriko-iuridicheskie akty*, 55–57; Smith and Christian, *Bread and Salt*, 110–11.

87. Margeret, *Russian Empire*, 58–59; Massa, *Short History*, 53–54; Palitsyn, *Skazanie*, 105; Nemoevskii, "Zapiski," 37; Skrynnikov, "Zemskaia politika," 164–71; idem, *Boris Godunov*, 121–22; idem, *Rossiia v nachale XVII v.*, 40–41; Anpilogov, *Novye dokumenty*, 432.

88. Bussow, *Moskovskaia khronika*, 97; PSRL 34:203; Skrynnikov, *Rossiia v nachale XVII v.*, 40–41; B. N. Morozov," Chastnoe pis'mo nachala XVII v.," in *Istoriia russkogo iazyka. Pamiatniki XI–XVIII vv.* (Moscow, 1982), 290.

89. Massa, *Short History*, 52; RIB 13: col. 481; PSRL, 14:55; Margeret, *Russian Empire*, 58; Palitsyn, *Skazanie*, 106; Tikhomirov, "Maloizvestnye pamiatniki," 94; Kopanev, "Pinezhskii letopisets," 81; Koretskii, "Golod," 228. Conrad Bussow's contemporary estimate of more than five hundred thousand famine deaths in Moscow (*Moskovskaia khronika*, 97) is far too high.

90. Margeret, *Russian Empire*, 59; Massa, *Short History*, 51–52; Bussow, *Moskovskaia khronika*, 222–23; PSRL 14:55; Palitsyn, *Skazanie*, 108–9; Skrynnikov, *Rossiia v nachale XVII v.*, 41, 63, 69. See also Jütte, *Poverty*, 185–86, 188.

91. Skrynnikov, *Rossiia v nachale XVII v.*, 62–63, 69, 259 nn. 22–24, 27; Buganov, *Krest'ianskie voiny*, 18; Smirnov, *Vosstanie*, 84; Karamzin, *Istoriia*, 11: prim. 168. See also Arnold, *Famine*, 83; Gurr, *Why Men Rebel*, 131–32.

92. Massa, *Short History*, 53; Palitsyn, *Skazanie*, 106; Bussow, *Moskovskaia khronika*, 98; Koretskii, "Golod," 235–36; Skrynnikov, "Zemskaia politika," 179; idem, *Boris Godunov*, 122; Smith and Christian, *Bread and Salt*, 111. See also Arnold, *Famine*, 84.

93. Koretskii, "Golod," 236–38, 255–56; Gorfunkel', "Perestroika," 100, 106–7, 110; Skrynnikov, *Rossiia v nachale XVII v.*, 42–43; idem, "Zemskaia politika," 182–83.

94. Massa, *Short History*, 51, 54; Skrynnikov, *Rossiia v nachale XVII v.*, 60, 62–63.

95. AAE 2: no. 20; Hellie, *Muscovite Society*, 130–31; Skrynnikov, *Rossiia v nachale XVII v.*, 41, 45; idem, *Boris Godunov*, 123; Kahan, "Natural Calamities," 362–63.

96. See PSRL 34:240; Koretskii, *Formirovanie*, 187–88, 190; Skrynnikov, *Boris Godunov*, ix, 123.

97. Skrynnikov, *Rossiia v nachale XVII v.*, 45–47; Culpepper, "Legislative Origins," 184–85; Paneiakh, "K voprosu," 267–69; idem, "Materialy," 106.

98. Skrynnikov, *Boris Godunov*, ix, 122–24; idem, *Rossiia v nachale XVII v.*, 45, 47, 50.

99. Culpepper, "Legislative Origins," 184; Skrynnikov, *Rossiia v nachale XVII v.*, 45–46. Koretskii (*Formirovanie*, 190) incorrectly regarded the exclusion of the Moscow region as a response to popular uprisings.

100. Anpilogov, *Novye dokumenty*, 427–30, 432; AAE 2:75; Skrynnikov, "Zemskaia politika," 171; Culpepper, "Legislative Origins," 183.

101. Skrynnikov, *Rossiia v nachale XVII v.*, 46, 48.

102. Palitsyn, *Skazanie*, 107; Koretskii, "Iz istorii zakreposhcheniia," 76, 78, 81–83; Paneiakh, "K voprosu," 265–67; D'iakonov, "Zapovednye leta," 16–18; Iakovlev, *Novgorodskie knigi* 2:124; Skrynnikov, *Rossiia v nachale XVII v.*, 46–48.

103. Culpepper, "Legislative Origins," 185; Skrynnikov, *Boris Godunov*, 124–25; idem, *Smuta*, 185–86.

104. Skrynnikov, *Rossiia v nachale XVII v.*, 46, 49; AAE 2: nos. 23, 24; PSRL 34:240; Koretskii, "Iz istorii zakreposhcheniia," 69, 77–78.

105. Palitsyn, *Skazanie*, 108; Skrynnikov, *Rossiia v nachale XVII v.*, 54.

106. Skrynnikov, "Civil War," 73; idem, *Smuta*, 185–86; Koretskii, *Formirovanie*, 187–88.

107. Skrynnikov, *Boris Godunov*, x, 126; idem, *Rossiia v nachale XVII v.*, 49.

108. Skrynnikov, *Rossiia nakanune smutnogo vremeni*, 167–216; idem, *Boris Godunov*, 124–25, 147–49, 154.

109. Skrynnikov, *Rossiia v nachale XVII v.*, 60, 62, 67–68.

110. Smirnov, *Vosstanie*, 79 n. 2, 82–83; Koretskii, "K istorii vosstaniia Khlopka," 217–19; Zimin, "Nekotorye voprosy," 98.

111. Skrynnikov, *Rossiia v nachale XVII v.*, 59–60; idem, "Predvestniki," 56.

112. Skrynnikov, *Rossiia v nachale XVII v.*, 67–69; idem, "Narodnye vystupleniia," 57–70; Koretskii, "K istorii vosstaniia Khlopka," 219–20; *Boiarskie spiski*, 2:197, 212.

113. PSRL 14:58.

114. *Pamiatniki russkogo prava*, 4:375; AI 2: no. 44; Culpepper, "Legislative Origins," 183; Skrynnikov, *Boris Godunov*, 126; idem, *Rossiia v nachale XVII v.*, 71; Hellie, *Slavery*, 127. See also Koretskii, "Iz istorii krest'ianskoi voiny," 128–33.

115. B. D. Grekov, "Ocherki po istorii feodalizma v Rossii. Sistema gospodstva i podchineniia v feodal'noi derevne," *Izvestiia Gosudarstvennoi Akademii istorii material'noi kultury* 72 (1934): 141–42; Smirnov, *Vosstanie*, 71, 74–83; Avrich, *Russian Rebels*, 15; Zimin, "Nekotorye voprosy," 97–98, 105–9; Koretskii, *Formirovanie*, 364; Nazarov, "Peasant Wars," 118; Skrynnikov, *Boris Godunov*, 125.

116. Smirnov, *Vosstanie*, 71, 77–80, 82–83; idem, "O nekotorykh voprosakh," 116–17.

117. Koretskii, *Formirovanie*, 230–32, 235, 364; idem, "K istorii vosstaniia Khlopka," 210–12;

idem, "Iz istorii krest'ianskoi voiny," 119–22, 129, 134; Makovskii, *Pervaia krest'ianskaia voina,* 275.

118. Zimin, "Nekotorye voprosy," 97–98, 107–8; Nazarov, "Peasant Wars," 118; *Istoriia krest'ianstva,* 2:430–31; Indova et al., "Narodnye dvizheniia," 53; Skrynnikov, *Boris Godunov,* 125.

119. Skrynnikov, *Sotsial'no-politicheskaia bor'ba,* 324–25; idem, *Smuta,* 249–50; idem, *Rossiia v nachale XVII v.,* 58–62, 69, 70–72; Koretskii, "Iz istorii krest'ianskoi voiny," 129; idem, "K istorii vosstaniia Khlopka," 210–11.

120. Hellie, *Slavery,* 38, 574.

121. Sviatskii, *Istoricheskii ocherk,* 37; Piasetskii, *Istoricheskie ocherki,* 14.

122. See, for example, Koretskii, *Formirovanie,* 364; Smirnov, *Vosstanie,* 79.

123. Massa, *Short History,* 65; Makovskii, *Pervaia krest'ianskaia voina,* 275; Koretskii, "K istorii vosstaniia Khlopka," 210–11.

124. Skrynnikov, *Rossiia v nachale XVII v.,* 65. There has been some scholarly confusion about the date of this military expedition, but it was definitely during September, 1603. (See Koretskii, *Formirovanie,* 226–28; idem, "K istorii vosstaniia Khlopka," 218–19; Massa, *Short History,* 65; Kusheva, "K istorii kholopstva," 91.) Weak arguments for a different date may be found in S. Lur'e, "K voprosu,"131–32; idem, " O date," 209–11. Skrynnikov, (*Boris Godunov,* 125) erred in stating that other commanders failed to support Basmanov's expedition due to their concern about unrest in Moscow.

125. Massa, *Short History,* 62; *Sinbirskii Sbornik,* 145.

126. Massa, *Short History,* 65; PSRL 14:58; Margeret, *Russian Empire,* 60–61. Smirnov (*Vosstanie,* 80) erred in crediting the "New Chronicle" about Khlopko's forces defeating detachment after detachment of the tsar's troops. See Skrynnikov, *Rossiia v nachale XVII v.,* 66–67.

127. PSRL 14:58; Platonov, *Ocherki,* 243.

128. Skrynnikov, *Rossiia v nachale XVII v.,* 72; Dunning, "Causes," 99.

129. See, for example, Koretskii, *Formirovanie,* 232–33; Chistov, *Russkie legendy,* 40–42; Skrynnikov, "Narodnye vystupleniia," 57–70; idem, *Sotsial'no-politicheskaia bor'ba,* 88–89.

130. Smirnov, *Vosstanie,* 84–85, 501–3, 506, 512; Koretskii, *Formirovanie,* 238. See also Hobsbawm, *Bandits,* 18, 20.

131. Margeret, *Russian Empire,* 58–59; Culpepper, "Legislative Origins," 182–83; Koretskii, "Golod," 250–54; Makovskii, *Razvitie,* 106–7; Eaton, "Early Russian Censuses," 171; Got'e, *Zamoskovnyi krai,* 214–21; Skrynnikov, "Civil War," 74; idem, *Rossiia v nachale XVII v.,* 41. One of the most important sources of the tsar's income in the early seventeenth century was the revenue derived from state-licensed taverns. During the famine, however, distillation of liquor was forbidden. That contributed to significant shortfalls in treasury receipts. See Bushkovitch, "Taxation," 397; Smith and Christian, *Bread and Salt,* 111, 142.

132. *Istoriia krest'ianstva,* 2:429–30; Piasetskii, *Istoricheskie ocherki,* 14; Dunning, "Cossacks," 61; Skrynnikov, *Smuta,* 180–82.

133. See Koretskii, "Iz istorii zakreposhcheniia," 185; Skrynnikov, *Smuta,* 187. Cf. Hellie, *Enserfment,* 326 n. 14.

134. Palitsyn, *Skazanie,* 107–8; Skrynnikov, *Rossiia v nachale XVII v.,* 104, 110–11; idem, *Smuta,* 180–81, 183–84; Koretskii, *Formirovanie,* 234; Smirnov, *Vosstanie,* 75–76; Stanislavskii, *Grazhdanskaia voina,* 13.

135. Massa, *Short History,* 68; Sbornik Imperatorskogo Russkogo Istoricheskogo Obshchestva [hereafter cited as SRIO] 137:352–53; Rozhdestvenskii, *Akty vremeni Lzhedimitriia,* 139–40; Skrynnikov, *Rossiia v nachale XVII v.,* 72–73; Stanislavskii, *Grazhdanskaia voina,* 19; Belokurov, *Snosheniia,* 446.

136. Skrynnikov has tried to challenge the view of Boris Godunov as an active opponent of the free cossacks in the early seventeenth century, citing evidence of food deliveries to "good cossacks" and the recruitment of free cossacks into military service in 1604. Stanislavskii has correctly challenged that view, reminding us that the cossacks knew perfectly well Godunov was their enemy. The 1604 recruitment of cossacks was an exception related to a feared Crimean Tatar invasion. See Skrynnikov, *Rossiia v nachale XVII v.,* 104–5, 107–8, 111, 249; RIB 18: cols. 248–49; PSRL14:61; *Razriadnaia kniga 1559–1605 gg.,* 349; *Razriadnaia kniga 1550–1636 gg.,* vol. 2, part 1, 216–17. Cf. Stanislavskii, *Grazhdanskaia voina,* 17–20; Sukhorukov, *Istoricheskoe opisanie,* 64; Skliar, "O nachal'nom etape," 91; Smirnov, *Vosstanie,* 126–27; Pronshtein and Mininkov, *Krest'ianskie voiny,* 40.

137. Lantzeff and Pierce, *Eastward to Empire*, 127, 129; Orchard, "Frontier Policy," 118–19; Koretskii, "Golod," 231, 2.

138. Belokurov, *Snosheniia*, 330–37, 353, 404, 431–32; PSRL 14:57; 34:240; Popov, *Izbornik*, 322–23; Massa, *Short History*, 67.

139. Skrynnikov, "Glavnye vekhi," 104; idem, *Rossiia v nachale XVII v.*, 47, 50, 115, 249; Hellie, *Enserfment*, 38.

140. Skrynnikov, *Rossiia v nachale XVII v.*, 21, 24–27, 104, 114; *Istoriia krest'ianstva*, 2:427–28.

141. Skrynnikov, "Glavnye vekhi," 101–3; Dunning, "Cossacks," 60; Keep, 73–74.

142. Cracraft, "Empire Versus Nation," 525; Bushkovitch, *Religion and Society*, 3, 102. Cf. Keep, "Emancipation," 47.

143. Lerner, "The Black Death and Western European Eschatological Mentalities," 533–52.

144. Ziegler, *Black Death*, 260–61, 267, 269–70, 274, 277, 279.

145. Arnold, *Famine*, 6, 8, 15–17, 19, 76–77; Camporesi, *Bread of Dreams*, 8, 14–15, 18, 26, 56, 125–26.

146. Arnold, *Famine*, 8, 15–16; Jütte, *Poverty*, 185–86, 188; Bercé, *Revolt*, 25. See also Gurr, *Why Men Rebel*, 48, 131; Hobsbawm, *Bandits*, 23–24; Cohn, *Pursuit of the Millennium*, 315.

147. Zguta, "Witchcraft Trials," 1188–89, 1205. See also Camporesi, *Bread of Dreams*, 14–15; Clark, *European Crisis*, 12–13; Levack, *Witch-Hunt*, 118, 139–41; Macfarlane, *Witchcraft in Tudor and Stuart England*, 249; Trevor-Roper, *European Witch-Craze*, 91, 93, 155, 183–86. See also Lynn White, Jr., "Death and the Devil," in *The Darker Vision of the Renaissance*, edited by R. S. Kinsman (Berkeley: University of California Press, 1974), 26.

148. See, for example, Rowland, "Muscovite Political Attitudes," 266, 278; idem, "Limits," 130, 135–36; Cracraft, "Empire Versus Nation," 527; Mousnier, *Peasant Uprisings*, 154–55; Kollmann, *Kinship*, 186–87; Hunt, "Mythology," 771–72, 776; Bennet, "Idea of Kingship," 4–5, 13, 15, 17–18, 20–22; Cherniavsky, *Tsar and People*, 33; Flier, "Iconology," 68, 74; Kivelson, "Devil Stole His Mind," 733, 736, 742–43, 755; Zhivov and Uspenskii, "Tsar i Bog," 47–153.

149. PSRL 14:59; Rowland, "Limits," 132, 135–38; idem, "Muscovite Political Attitudes," 129; Cherniavsky, *Tsar and People*, 71.

150. RIB 13: cols. 224–25; PSRL 14:49; Massa, *Short History*, 51, 54; Bennet, "Idea of Kingship," 105; Hellie, *Enserfment*, 102–3.

151. RIB 13: col. 479; Bussow, *Moskovskaia khronika*, 107; Timofeev, *Vremennik*, 92–98; Purchas, *Hakluytus Posthumus*, 14:147; Platonov, *Boris Godunov*, 186–87; Thompson, "Legend," 48, 54, 58; Mousnier, *Peasant Uprisings*, 180, 330–31; Rowland, "Limits," 138; Skrynnikov, "Civil War," 74; Parker, *Empire in Crisis*, 107.

152. RIB 13: cols. 147, 224–25; Bushkovitch, "Formation," 370; Bennet, "Idea of Kingship," 105–9; Avrich, *Russian Rebels*, 46; Rowland, "Muscovite Political Attitudes," 160–61; idem, "Limits," 137; Siegelbaum, "Peasant Disorders," 227, 235.

153. Bussow, *Moskovskaia khronika*, 128, 146; Massa, *Short History*, 166; Skrynnikov, *Time of Troubles*, 44–45; Zguta, "Witchcraft Trials," 1188–89, 1193.

154. AI 1:252; AAE 2:58–59, 102; Zguta, "Witchcraft Trials," 1192–93; idem, "Was there a Witch Craze," 124; Kleimola, "Duty to Denounce," 771–72; Perrie, *Image*, 178; Ivanits, *Russian Folk Belief*, 87–88.

155. See, for example, *The Russian Primary Chronicle*, 134–35, 151–52; Zguta, "Witchcraft Trials," 1205.

156. See Purchas, *Hakluytus Posthumus*, 14:162; Berry and Crummey, *Rude and Barbarous Kingdom*, 362; *Moskovskaia tragediia*, 35–36; Frantsev, "Istoricheskie povestvovanie," 31; Aleksandrenko, "Materialy," 400, 535; Skrynnikov, *Boris Godunov*, 151.

157. See Gurr, *Why Men Rebel*, 207; Hagopian, *Phenomenon*, 11; Zimmerman, *Political Violence*, 203, 206–8, 213. See also Skrynnikov, "Civil War," 74; Hellie, "Warfare," 78; Downing, *Military Revolution*, 13.

158. See, for example, Skrynnikov, *Boris Godunov*, 115, 147, 149–51; idem, "Civil War," 74.

159. Chistov, *Russkie legendy*, 40–41. See also Skrynnikov, *Rossiia v nachale XVII v.*, 82.

160. Perrie, "Legends," 226–31; idem, *Pretenders*, 36–37.

161. Skocpol, *States and Social Revolutions*, 25–27, 31–32; Zimmerman, *Political Violence*, 208, 213.

NOTES TO CHAPTER 7

1. Gurr, *Why Men Rebel,* 48, 131–32; Bacon, "Seditions,"81.
2. Kimmel, *Absolutism,* 6; Zagorin, *Rebels and Rulers,* 1:126; Skocpol, *States and Social Revolutions,* 17; Goldstone, *Revolution,* 26, 102–9.
3. Scott, *Moral Economy,* 228–29; idem, "Everyday Forms," 13–14.
4. Scott, *Moral Economy,* 193–94.
5. Moote, "Preconditions," 155; Forster and Greene, *Preconditions,* 11, 13; Zagorin, *Rebels and Rulers,* 1:131; Stone, *Causes,* 54; Bercé, *Revolt,* 73.
6. Bacon, "Seditions," 79, 82; Forster and Greene, *Preconditions,* 13; Goldstone, *Revolution,* 24–25, 37, 48, 67, 69, 82, 109.
7. Moote, "Preconditions," 155; Bacon, "Seditions," 85; Skocpol, *States and Social Revolutions,* 32; Goldstone, *Revolution,* 70, 93–94, 107, 220, 222–24.
8. Bercé, *Revolt,* 221; Zimmerman, *Political Violence,* 203; Moote, "Preconditions," 155; Forster and Greene, *Preconditions,* 15–16; Gurr, *Why Men Rebel,* 207; Bacon, "Seditions," 79; Hagopian, *Phenomenon,* 11; Krejchí, *Great Revolutions Compared,* 14–15.
9. Skocpol, *States and Social Revolutions,* 9–10, 32.
10. Bercé, *Revolt,* 72–73, 106, 128, 221; Bacon, "Seditions," 82; Goldstone, *Revolution,* 34, 460.
11. Tilly, *European Revolutions,* 189; Hagopian, *Phenomenon,* 17; Zagorin, *Rebels and Rulers,* 2:2, 5; Forster and Greene, *Preconditions,* 11; Bercé, *Revolt,* 127, 130; Goldstone, *Revolution,* 133–34, 464.
12. See Mironov, "Poverty of Thought," 429, 434–35; Kivelson, "Devil Stole His Mind," 736; Longworth, "Subversive Legend," 17.
13. Skocpol, *States and Social Revolutions,* 25.
14. AAE 2:78–79; Massa, *Short History,* 69, 74–75; Palitsyn, *Skazanie,* 110–15; RIB 13: cols. 17, 155–56, 797; SRIO 137:176, 247, 319.
15. RIB 13: col. 724; SRIO 137:414.
16. AAE 2:129; Tikhomirov, "Novyi istochnik," 116. See also Skrynnikov, *Smuta,* 120–21, 134–35, 251; Dunning, "Byla li krest'ianskaia voina," 28.
17. See Avrich, *Russian Rebels,* 1, 7, 258, 270; Kivelson, "Devil Stole His Mind," 735; Field, *Rebels,* 2, 5; Alexander Kerensky, *Russia and History's Turning Point* (New York, 1965), 54.
18. Longworth, "Subversive Legend," 17; Kivelson, "Devil Stole His Mind," 735–36. See also Field, *Rebels,* 1–2.
19. Pokrovsky, *Brief History,* 1:71–73; Firsov, *Krest'ianskaia Revoliutsiia,* 61; Makovskii, *Pervaia krest'ianskaia voina,* 295–97; Solov'ev, *Istoriia,* 7:45.
20. Koretskii, *Formirovanie,* 365; Zimin, "Nekotorye voprosy," 99; Skliar, "O nachal'nom etape," 96; Skrynnikov, *Sotsial'no-politicheskaia bor'ba,* 325–26.
21. Mavrodin, "Sovetskaia literatura," 39–40; Koretskii, *Formirovanie,* 242; *Ocherki istorii SSSR,* 494–95; Skrynnikov, *Boris Godunov,* 147–49.
22. Chistov, *Russkie legendy,* 27–30, 40–42.
23. Perrie, "Popular Legends," 227–28.
24. Dunning, "Byla li krest'ianskaia voina," 24–26; Perrie, *Pretenders,* 63; idem, "Popular Legends," 232.
25. See AAE 2:76, 89, 92–93.
26. Pronshtein, "Resolved and Unresolved Problems," 28–30; Shapiro, "Ob istoricheskoi roli," 63; Longworth, "Subversive Legend," 32.
27. Smirnov, *Vosstanie,* 27–29; Yaresh, "Peasant Wars," 245–46; Mavrodin, "Soviet Historical Literature," 51. Cf. Skrynnikov, *Boris Godunov,* 147–49.
28. Crummey, *Formation,* 217–18. For a discussion of the origins and development of the concept of naïve monarchism, see Field, *Rebels,* 5–6, 9–10. Valerie Kivelson's study of the 1648 Moscow riots led her to doubt the utility of the naïve monarchist interpretation of the Russian people ("Devil Stole His Mind," 746–47). See also Ingerflom, "Samozvanstvo," 99–100.
29. See Perrie, *Image,* 1–2; idem, *Pretenders,* 2–3.
30. Aleksandrenko, "Materialy," 262; Smirnov, *Vosstanie,* 132–35; Avrich, *Russian Rebels,* 16,

24; Skrynnikov, *Rossiia v nachale* XVII *v.*, 166, 175–76; Perrie, *Pretenders,* 71. Cf. Mousnier, *Peasant Uprisings,* 344; Bercé, *Revolt,* 113.

31. Stanislavskii, *Grazhdanskaia voina,* 7–8, 20–21, 243–47. Cf. Zagorin, *Rebels and Rulers,* 2:5.

32. See, for example, Gurr, *Why Men Rebel;* Johnson, *Revolutionary Change;* Zimmerman, *Political Violence;* Neil J. Smelser, *A Theory of Collective Behavior* (New York: Free Press, 1962); Samuel P. Huntington, *Political Order in Changing Societies* (New Haven: Yale University Press, 1968).

33. Zagorin, *Rebels and Rulers,* 1:49–55; Skocpol, *States and Social Revolutions,* 9–12; Parker and Smith, *General Crisis,* 15; Roland Mousnier, "The Fronde," in Forster and Greene, *Preconditions,* 157–58.

34. See Kivelson, "Devil Stole His Mind," 735–36.

35. Kimmel, *Absolutism,* 5; idem, *Revolution,* 9–10.

36. Charles Tilly, "Does Modernization Breed Revolution?" *Comparative Politics* 5(1973):447.

37. Kimmel, *Revolution,* 11; idem, *Absolutism,* 1.

38. Skocpol, *States and Social Revolutions,* 9–10; Tilly, *European Revolutions,* 14–15; Zagorin, *Rebels and Rulers,* 1:269; 2:53–54; Bercé, *Revolt,* 221; Forster and Greene, *Preconditions,* 14–15.

39. Kimmel, *Revolution,* 11–12; Zimmerman, *Political Violence,* 208.

40. Tilly, *European Revolutions,* 10; Skocpol, *States and Social Revolutions,* 11; Bacon, "Seditions," 85, 87; Forster and Greene, *Preconditions,* 16; Moote, "Preconditions," 155; Willner and Willner, "Rise and Role of Charismatic Leaders," 197.

41. Weber, "Routinization of Charisma," 269–72; Willner and Willner, "Rise and Role of Charismatic Leaders," 195.

42. Stone, "Causal Stories," 281–83, 285, 293–94, 295, 300.

43. Bercé, *Revolt,* 32–33; idem, *Le roi caché.*

44. Weber, "Routinization of Charisma," 270.

45. Bercé, *Revolt,* 118, 124; Krejchí, *Great Revolutions Compared,* 15–16; Zagorin, *Rebels and Rulers,* 1:149; Perrie, *Pretenders,* 246.

46. Kimmel, *Revolution,* 222–23; Clifton B. Kroeber, "Theory and History of Revolution," *Journal of World History* 7 (Spring 1996):23.

47. Mironov, "Poverty of Thought," 429, 434–35.

48. See Baron and Kollmann, *Religion and Culture,* 3–8; Keenan, "Afterword," 199–206.

49. See Perrie, *Pretenders,* 65–69, 245–46; Bushkovitch, "Formation," 364; idem, *Religion and Society,* 3–4; Buganov, "Religious ideologies," 207; Bak and Benecke, *Religion and Revolt,* 2–5; Siegelbaum, "Peasant Disorders," 227. See also Baron and Kollmann, *Religion and Culture,* 3–4; Kollmann, "Concepts," 38–39.

50. Bernshtam, "Russian Folk Culture," 40–41; Vlasov, "Christianization," 16, 19–25, 29.

51. See, for example, Vlasov, "Christianization," 31; Keep, "Emancipation," 47–48. See also Scott, "Everyday Forms," 27.

52. See Siegelbaum, "Peasant Disorders," 223–24, 227; Longworth, "Last Great Rising," 13–15, 22–23; Wada, "Inner World," 61–94; Field, *Rebels,* 5–9; Chistov, *Russkie legendy,* 30–32, 42, 64; Perrie, *Pretenders,* 66; Platonov, *Ocherki,* 191–201. See also Cohn, *Pursuit of the Millennium,* 53–60, 282. Cf. Zagorin, *Rebels and Rulers,* 1:41–42, 170.

53. Kivelson, "Devil Stole His Mind," 734; Rowland, "Problem," 281–82; Eve Levin, "Supplicatory Prayers as a Source for Popular Religious Culture in Muscovite Russia," in Baron and Kollmann, eds., *Religion and Culture,* 98–99.

54. Rowland, "Moscow," 596–98, 605, 607, 613; idem, "Limits," 147; Kivelson, "Devil Stole His Mind," 733, 742–43; Zhivov, "Religious Reform," 186–87; Keenan, "Trouble," 110–11, 113; Miller, "Creating Legitimacy," 290–91, 293–94, 314–15; Chistov, *Russkie legendy,* 28; Cherniavsky, *Tsar and People,* 28–29, 33; Hunt, "Mythology," 769–70, 777; Bushkovitch, *Religion and Society,* 3–4; idem, "Formation," 363–65; Billington, *Icon and Axe,* 199–200; Siegelbaum, "Peasant Disorders," 225–26; Uspenskii, "Tsar and Pretender," 260–61.

55. Perrie, *Image,* 1–2.

56. Rowland, "Limits," 151–52; idem, "Biblical Imagery," 183, 197–98; Crummey, "Constitutional Reform," 38; Hellie, "Warfare," 78; Kollmann, "Pilgrimage," 181.

57. Timofeev, *Vremennik*, 109.

58. Bernshtam, "Russian Folk Culture," 42–43, 45.

59. Perrie, "Folklore," 131, 141; Kivelson, "Devil Stole His Mind," 736, 745; Longworth, "Subversive Legend," 28. See also Field, *Rebels*, 10, 12–13, 24–25.

60. Kliuchevskii, *Sochineniia*, 3:53; Keenan, "Muscovite Political Folkways," 140; Perrie, "Popular Image," 279; idem, "Folklore," 127–28, 133, 139.

61. Cherniavsky, *Tsar and People*, 53; Bennet, "Idea of Kingship," 1–2.

62. Rowland, "Limits," 126–27, 130, 137–39, 154–55; Kivelson, "Devil Stole His Mind," 736, 745–48. See also Bennet, "Idea of Kingship," 105. Cf. Bak and Benecke, *Religion*, 3.

63. Crummey, *Formation*, 138; Kivelson, "Devil Stole His Mind," 736.

64. See Perrie, "Folklore," 141; idem, *Pretenders*, 239; Kivelson, "Devil Stole His Mind," 745–48.

65. Perrie, *Pretenders*, 246; Crummey, *Formation*, 217; Rowland, "Limits," 155; Longworth, "Pretender phenomenon," 82.

66. Mousnier, *Peasant Uprisings*, 182; Kivelson, "Devil Stole His Mind," 745–48, 755; Bak and Benecke, *Religion*, 2–5; Zagorin, *Rebels and Rulers*, 1:149; Levack, *Witch-Hunt*, 77; Keep, "Emancipation," 48; Trevor-Roper, *European Witch-Craze*, 117. Attempts to discern irreligiosity among early modern Russian rebels have not been persuasive; see, for example, Klibanov, "Irreligiosity," 214–22.

67. RIB 13: col. 367; Bussow, *Disturbed State*, 46; Pirling, *Dmitrii Samozvanets*, 159; Perrie, *Pretenders*, 65, 78–79, 83, 103. See also Billington, *Icon and Axe*, 199–200; Uspenskii, "Tsar and Pretender," 261.

68. Massa, *Short History*, 77, 81–82; Timofeev, *Vremennik*, 84; Perrie, *Pretenders*, 66–68, 245–46; Buganov, "Religious ideologies," 207; Siegelbaum, "Peasant Disorders," 227. See also Krejchí, *Great Revolutions Compared*, 15–16.

69. Perrie, *Image*, 2; idem, *Pretenders*, 2–3.

70. Perrie, *Image*, ix, 30–31, 59, 62–63, 132, 278; idem, "Popular Legends," 232. Cf. Burke, *Popular Culture*, 170–71.

71. Perrie, "Popular Image," 275.

72. Purchas, *Hakluytus Posthumus*, 14:113; Perrie, *Image*, 34, 65, 279; Skrynnikov, *Rossiia v nachale XVII v.*, 80.

73. Perrie, *Image*, 109–10.

74. Ibid., 30–31, 109; Skrynnikov, *Sibirskaia ekspeditsiia*, 162. See also Kivelson, "Devil Stole His Mind," 749–50.

75. Rowland, "Limits," 133; Skrynnikov, "Civil War," 74.

76. Perrie, *Image*, 12–13; Purchas, *Hakluytus Posthumus*, 14:113. See also Miller, "Creating Legitimacy," 290–91, 300.

77. Perrie, *Image*, 31–32; idem, "Popular Image," 286.

78. Perrie, *Image*, 12–13, 45–47, 91–92; idem, "Popular Image," 275–77, 280–83; Skrynnikov, *Sotsial'no-politicheskaia bor'ba*, 99.

79. Perrie, *Pretenders*, 29–30.

80. Perrie, "Popular Legends," 232.

81. See Perrie, *Image*, ix, 40–41; Wada, "Inner World," 68.

82. Perrie, *Image*, 48, 234, 240–41, 243.

83. I. Khudiakov, "Narodnye istoricheskie skazki," ZhMNP, 1864, no. 3, part IV, 63; Perrie, *Image*, 9–10.

84. Perrie, *Pretenders*, 59.

85. AAE 2:89–90, 92–93; SGGD 2:201; Perrie, "Popular Legends," 227–28, 232, 243; idem, *Pretenders*, 64–65, 68–69, 79.

86. Bushkovitch, *Religion and Society*, 10, 74, 100–102, 106, 111.

87. Bussow, *Disturbed State*, 50; Skrynnikov, *Sotsial'no-politicheskaia bor'ba*, 153–54; Perrie, *Pretenders*, 78–79.

88. Massa, *Short History*, 77, 81, 82; Timofeev, *Vremennik*, 84; Ustrialov, *Skazaniia*, 1:167; Pirling, *Dmitrii Samozvanets*, 159; Billington, *Icon and Axe*, 198.

89. Perrie, *Pretenders,* 66, 245–46.
90. See, for example, Purchas, *Hakluytus Posthumus,* 14:159–60.
91. Besançon, *Tsarevich,* 105, 108–9. See also Cherniavsky, *Tsar and People,* 5–43.
92. On Jesus as the "returning king" see Burke, *Popular Culture,* 152–53.
93. Chistov, *Russkie legendy,* 24, 224–25, 338–39; Bercé, *Le roi caché,* 228–29, 312.
94. Perrie, *Pretenders,* 66, 69, 245.
95. Bussow, *Disturbed State,* 46; Pirling, *Dmitrii Samozvanets,* 159; N. T. Vajtovich, *Barkalabauski letapis* (Minsk, 1977), 198; Uspenskij, "Tsar and Pretender," 261; Perrie, *Pretenders,* 66–67, 74, 83. Cf. Cherniavsky, *Tsar and People,* 106.
96. Perrie, *Pretenders,* 65–66; Golubtsov, "Izmena Smol'nian," 232, 246.
97. Massa, *Short History,* 70.
98. Bussow, *Disturbed State,* 50; Perrie, *Pretenders,* 78–79, 103.
99. Crummey, *Formation,* 217.
100. Perrie, *Pretenders,* 245–46.
101. Longworth, "Pretender phenomenon," 61; Solov'ev, "Zametki," cols. 265–81; Kliuchevskii, *Sochineniia,* 3:27–28.
102. [Shcherbatov], *Kratkaia povest';* Solov'ev, "Zametki;" Mordovtsev, *Samozvantsy i ponizovaia vol'nitsa;* Sivkov, "Samozvanchestvo v Rossii v poslednei treti XVIII v.," 80–135; Tikhomirov, "Samozvanshchina"; Troitskii, "Samozvantsy;" Chistov, *Russkie legendy;* Longworth, "Pretender phenomenon;" Perrie, *Pretenders.* See also Bercé, *Le roi caché.*
103. Longworth, "Pretender phenomenon," 82; Perrie, *Pretenders,* 246.
104. [Shcherbatov], *Kratkaia povest';* Solov'ev, "Zametki."
105. Smirnov, *Vosstanie,* 29, 506; Chistov, *Russkie legendy,* 29; Skrynnikov, *Sotsial'no-politicheskaia bor'ba,* 97–100, 324–26; Nazarov, "Peasant Wars," 131–32, 137.
106. Field, *Rebels,* 1–26. Field was strongly influenced by the work of Kirill Chistov (*Russkie legendy*).
107. Uspenskij, "Tsar and Pretender," 259–60; Perrie, *Pretenders,* 239, 245–46.
108. Skrynnikov, *Civil War,* 74–75; idem, *Rossiia v nachale XVII v.,* 79–80, 249–51; idem, *Smuta,* 251–52; Perrie, *Pretenders,* 2, 5, 245, 247.
109. See Uspenskij, "Tsar and Pretender," 259–92; Skrynnikov, *Samozvantsy;* Perrie, *Pretenders,* 7–106, esp. page 56.
110. Perrie, *Pretenders,* 3.
111. RIB 13: cols. 620–21, 1290; Purchas, *Hakluytus Posthumus,* 14:158–60; Massa, *Short History,* 76–77, 80; Margeret, *Russian Empire,* 75, 88–89; Zolkiewski, *Expedition,* 43.
112. On this aspect of charismatic leadership, see Willner and Willner, "Rise and Role of Charismatic Leaders," 195.
113. Massa, *Short History,* 76.
114. See Avrich, *Russian Rebels,* 121, 251; Longworth, "Subversive Legend," 21–25; idem, "Peasant Leadership," 188, 199, 201; Raeff, "Pugachev's Rebellion,"195;. Sokolova, *Russkie istoricheskie predaniia,* 164–65. Cf. Druzhinin, *Raskol,* 277–81.
115. James Billington (*Icon and Axe,* 200) noted the seemingly paradoxical connection between periodic rebellions in the name of the "true tsar" and the strengthening of Russian autocracy and popular support for the tsars. Daniel Field (*Rebels,* 24–25) also commented on the apparent paradox of the myth of the tsar, which simultaneously contributed to political stability but could also be a source of serious disruption.
116. See, for example, Brereton, *Newes of the present Miseries of Rushia;* Pirling, *Iz Smutnago Vremeni,* 182–88, 190–93; Margeret, *Russian Empire,* xxviii–xxix; Brody, *Demetrius Legend.*

NOTES TO CHAPTER 8

1. Skrynnikov, *Samozvantsy;* Perrie, *Pretenders.* See my reviews of their books in Dunning, "Skrynnikov," 75–76; and *The Russian Review* 56 (July 1977):465–66.

2. Purchas, *Hakluytus Posthumus,* 14:158; Margeret, *Russian Empire,* 75, 83, 85, 88–89; RIB 13: cols. 620–21, 1290; SGGD 2:162, 229; Zolkiewski, *Expedition,* 43; Karamzin, *Istoriia,* 11:165; Solov'ev, *Istoriia,* 4:403; Pierling, *Dimitri et les Jésuites,* 4; idem, *Rome,* 77; Sviatskii, *Istoricheskii ocherk,* 37–38, 42; Mérimée, *Épisode,* 293–97, 303; Vernadsky, *Tsardom,* 1:224, 229; Tikhomirov, "Samozvanshchina," 119; Skrynnikov, *Boris Godunov,* 142–44; Perrie, *Pretenders,* 67.

3. See Skrynnikov, *Samozvantsy;* idem, *Smuta,* 9–10; Graham, "Note," 362; Perrie, *Pretenders,* 44–58; Pierling, *La Russie,* 3:419–20; Ilovaiskii, *Smutnoe vremia,* 324–27; idem, "Pervyi Lzhedimitrii," 636–67; Palitsyn, *Skazanie,* 110–15.

4. Purchas, *Hakluytus Posthumus,* 14:158; Massa, *Short History,* 38, 69, 71; Howe, *False Dmitri,* 66; Shaum, "Tragoedia," 8; Ilovaiskii, *Smutnoe vremia,* 1–10, 259–61, 328; Platon, *Kratkaia istoriia,* 2: ch 65; Solov'ev, *Istoriia,* 4:403–16; Smirnov, *Vosstanie,* 85; Zimin, "Nekotorye voprosy," 99; Savich, *Bor'ba,* 8–20; Kozachenko, *Razgrom,* 23–47.

5. Purchas, *Hakluytus Posthumus,* 14:162; Massa, *Short History,* 144–45; Timofeev, *Vremennik,* 83–84, 88; Uspenskij, "Tsar and Pretender," 273–74; Perrie, *Pretenders,* 56, 242.

6. RIB 13: cols. 620–21; Zolkiewski, *Expedition,* 43; Santich, *Missio,* 128–29; Solov'ev, *Istoriia,* 4:402–3; Pierling, *Rome,* 77; Ikonnikov, *Neskol'ko zametok,* 60–61; Vernadsky, *Tsardom,* 1:229; Hellie, *Enserfment,* 49.

7. Brody, *Demetrius Legend,* 42–43, 46.

8. The eminent seventeenth-century French historian Jacque-Auguste de Thou was the first to note the role of unsavory later "false Dmitriis" in discrediting Tsar Dmitrii's reputation. See de Thou, *Histoire,* 14:503.

9. Bussow, *Moskovskaia khronika,* 93, 132–33; Massa, *Short History,* 147; Ilovaiskii, *Smutnoe vremia,* 328; Kliuchevskii, *Sochineniia,* 3:33; Aleksandrenko, "Materialy," 438, 539; Hirschberg, *Dymitr,* 280–82. Much has been made of the Saxon mercenary soldier Conrad Bussow's alleged conversation with Tsar Dmitrii's close confidant, Petr Basmanov, who supposedly admitted to him that Tsar Dmitrii was a foreign impostor. (See, for example, Solov'ev, *Istoriia,* 4:402; Skrynnikov, *Smuta,* 28; Perrie, *Pretenders,* 86.) In fact, Basmanov had no reason to commit lese majesty, and it is absurd to credit Bussow's colorful story. That it has been accepted without question for so long testifies to the problems of scholarship about Tsar Dmitrii.

10. Margeret, *Russian Empire,* 80, 83–84; Howe, *False Dmitri,* 1; Kostomarov, *Smutnoe vremia,* 642; Pierling, *La Russie,* 3:407–10; Pirling, *Iz Smutnago Vremeni,* 12–20; Solov'ev, *Istoriia,* 4:406; Platonov, *Boris Godunov,* 192; idem, *Stat'i,* 276–77; Troitskii, "Samozvantsy," 135–36; Tikhomirov, "Samozvanshchina," 119; Skrynnikov, *Boris Godunov,* 142–43; Koretskii and Stanislavskii, "Amerikanskii istorik," 244.

11. PSRL 14:60; AAE 2:79; Obolenskii, "Skazanie," 7–8; Kulish, *Materialy,* 24; Longworth, *Cossacks,* 77; March, "Cossacks," 26–27; Vernadsky, *Tsardom,* 1:223; Gordon, *Cossack Rebellions,* 106; Skrynnikov, *Boris Godunov,* 145; idem, *Rossiia v nachale* XVII *v.,* 118; Perrie, *Pretenders,* 41, 46.

12. Mérimée, *Épisode,* 293–97, 301–5; idem, *Mémoires,* 179–81.

13. Solov'ev, *Istoriia,* 7:45; Pokrovsky, *Brief History,* 1:71–73, 76; Makovskii, *Pervaia krest'ian-skaia voina,* 295–97. Cf. *Istoriia krest'ianstva,* 2:433; Skrynnikov, *Boris Godunov,* 146–47; idem, *Rossiia v nachale* XVII *v.,* 79.

14. Koretskii, *Formirovanie,* 365–66; Zimin, "Nekotorye voprosy," 99; Skrynnikov, *Sotsial'no-politicheskaia bor'ba,* 325–26; idem, *Boris Godunov,* 147–49.

15. Margeret, *Russian Empire,* 83–85; Pierling, *Rome,* 149–50; Santich, *Missio,* 113–51, 194–95; Mérimée, *Épisode,* 297–300; Vernadsky, *Tsardom,* 1:223, 225–26; Barbour, *Dimitry,* 168–69, 173–74; Brody, *Demetrius Legend,* 32–34; Skrynnikov, "Civil War," 61; Perrie, *Pretenders,* 63–64.

16. Margeret, *Russian Empire,* 81; Smith, *Voiage,* M2-M3; Kostomarov, *Kto,* 11, 13, 17, 18, 19, 41–63; Solov'ev, *Istoriia,* 4:405–6; Platonov, *Boris Godunov,* 192; idem, *Ocherki,* 186–90, 224–25; Kliuchevskii, *Sochineniia,* 3:31–32; Vernadsky, *Tsardom,* 1:220–21, 227; Nikolaeff, "Boris Godunov,"

281. Skrynnikov's efforts to exonerate the boyars and to identify the source of the pretender scheme as the monks of the Miracles Monastery in the Moscow Kremlin (*Rossiia v nachale XVII v.*, 96–98; idem, *Sotsial'no-politicheskaia bor'ba*, 106–9) is not satisfactory and appears to be based primarily upon Conrad Bussow's statement about monks in general aiding the pretender (*Disturbed State*, 27). Maureen Perrie's assertion that the pretender was acting on his own initiative (*Pretenders*, 55, 57–58) is also unsatisfactory. The pretender was sent to Poland-Lithuania by Tsar Boris's enemies.

17. Margeret, *Russian Empire*, 60–61, 91; Massa, *Short History*, 55–56.

18. Bussow, *Disturbed State*, 37.

19. Margeret, *Russian Empire*, 81; AI 2:64–66; AAE 2:78; SRIO 137: 247, 319, 367; Bussow, *Disturbed State*, 27; Platonov, *Boris Godunov*, 146, 181–83, 193–96; idem, *Time of Troubles*, 64–69; idem, *Ocherki*, 186–87, 233–34; Kliuchevskii, *Sochineniia*, 3:31–32; Tikhomirov, "Samozvanshchina," 120–21; Florinsky, *Russia*, 1:227; Thompson, "Legend," 55; Skrynnikov, *Samozvantsy*, 26–28; idem, *Boris Godunov*, 126–31, 134; Vovina, "Patriarkh Filaret," 56. Skrynnikov (*Samozvantsy*, 40) adopted the unconvincing view that it was not the Romanovs but the Shuiskiis who were involved in the pretender scheme. (See Perrie, *Pretenders*, 52–53.) Skrynnikov probably based his claim on a statement made by the commander of Tsar Dmitrii's bodyguard, Captain Jacques Margeret, that Tsar Boris suspected the Shuiskiis more than the other boyars (*Russian Empire*, 60) and on the connection between the Shuiskiis and the monk Varlaam, which will be discussed below (see Golubtsov, "Izmena Smol'nian," 248). Pavlov also argued against the Romanov connection to the pretender scheme (*Gosudarev dvor*, 78), basing his unconvincing conclusion on an unwarranted acceptance of later claims by the Romanovs to have opposed the pretender and on the softening of the conditions of some family members toward the end of Tsar Boris's reign.

20. Bussow, *Disturbed State*, 26–27; Smith, *Voiage*, M2–M3; AI 2:51; Belokurov, *Razriadnye zapisi*, 5; Kostomarov, *Kto*, 41–49; Vernadsky, *Tsardom*, 1:220; Pavlov, *Gosudarev dvor*, 76; Perrie, *Pretenders*, 79–81.

21. Margeret, *Russian Empire*, 81; Smith, *Voiage*, M2–M3. Cf. Massa, *Short History*, 92. Although they had been exiled and imprisoned by Boris Godunov after the Uglich incident, by the end of the sixteenth century the Nagoi clan's situation improved somewhat. Still spied upon, members of the family were allowed to retain their votchina estates and some even held appointments as military governors in the Volga region. See Golubtsov, "Izmena Nagikh," 61–63.

22. See Rowland, "Limits," 155; Kivelson, "Devil Stole His Mind," 745–47; Crummey, *Formation*, 217. Cf. Kliuchevskii, *Sochineniia*, 3:35.

23. AAE 2:78–79; RIB 13: col. 827; Pierling, *La Russie*, 3:419–20; Barbour, *Dimitry*, 317; Uspenskii, "Tsar and Pretender," 274; Skrynnikov, *Boris Godunov*, 135–37; Koretskii, "Novoe o krest'ianskom zakreposhchenii," 135, 143; Barezi, *Discours merveilleux*, 30–31.

24. Massa, *Short History*, 69; Palitsyn, *Skazanie*, 110–15; Zolkiewski, *Expedition*, 39–40; RIB 13: cols. 155–56, 797; SRIO 137:247, 319; Golubtsov, "Izmena Smol'nian," 235–50; Skrynnikov, *Boris Godunov*, 133–37; Kopanev, "Pinezhskii letopisets," 81–84.

25. Skrynnikov, *Samozvantsy*; idem, *Boris Godunov*, 127–43; idem, *Rossiia v nachale XVII v.*, 79–103; Perrie, *Pretenders*, 44–50; Pirling, *Dmitrii Samozvanets*; Keenan, "Reply," 208; Graham, "Note," 357–62.

26. See Skrynnikov, *Rossiia v nachale XVII v.*, 82, 86, 97; idem, *Boris Godunov*, 127.

27. SRIO 137:176; Skrynnikov, *Boris Godunov*, 127.

28. RIB 13: col. 17.

29. RIB 13: col. 638; PSRL 14:59; 34:111; *Boiarskie spiski*, 2:38; Skrynnikov, *Boris Godunov*, 131–32; Perrie, *Pretenders*, 52.

30. RIB 13: cols. 638–39; Skrynnikov, *Boris Godunov*, 134–35.

31. RIB 13: cols. 17–19, 639, 933; AAE 2:78–79; Margeret, *Russian Empire*, 81; PSRL 14:59; Skrynnikov, *Samozvantsy*, 29–31. The number of years Otrepev served in the Miracles Monastery (between one and four) is not known. See PSRL 34:205; RIB 13: col. 933; Palitsyn, *Skazanie*, 111; SRIO 137:247.

32. Margeret, *Russian Empire*, 81–82; Koretskii, "Novoe o krest'ianskom zakreposhchenii," 143–44. Skrynnikov (*Boris Godunov*, 140) did not credit the sources about Patriarch Iov trying to

stop the monks from escaping and erroneously declared that no one paid any attention to them at the time and that no special guards (*zastavy*) were posted at the border. Cf. RIB 13: col 21; Koretskii, "Golod," 230.

33. SRIO 137:177, 193–94.

34. Barezi, *Discours merveilleux*, 30–31; Skrynnikov, *Boris Godunov*, 135–37; idem, *Rossiia v nachale XVII v.*, 83, 88, 91–92.

35. AAE 2:78–79; SRIO 137:247, 319; Obolenskii, "Skazanie," 3–4; Skrynnikov, *Boris Godunov*, 128–31, 133–34; idem, *Rossiia v nachale XVII v.*, 83–85.

36. Platonov, *Time of Troubles*, 64–69; Skrynnikov, *Samozvantsy*, 26–29.

37. Skrynnikov, *Rossiia v nachale XVII v.*, 91; idem, *Boris Godunov*, 135.

38. Perrie, *Pretenders*, 52.

39. Skrynnikov, *Boris Godunov*, 127–28; idem, *Rossiia v nachale XVII v.*, 82, 97.

40. AAE 2:79; Skrynnikov, *Boris Godunov*, 137–38; idem, *Rossiia v nachale XVII v.*, 92.

41. Skrynnikov, *Boris Godunov*, 127, 137; idem, *Rossiia v nachale XVII v.*, 83–86, 91–92.

42. Zolkiewski, *Expedition*, 45–46.

43. Skrynnikov, *Time of Troubles*, 46.

44. Shchepkin, "Wer war Pseudodemetrius," 20:291–92; Barbour, *Dimitry*, 51.

45. RIB 13: cols. 18–25, 48, 155–56, 797; AAE 2:141–44.

46. See Golubtsov, "Izmena Smol'nian," 249–50; Kostomarov, *Kto*, 20–24; idem, *Smutnoe vremia*, 274–79; Platonov, *Drevnerusskie skazaniia*, 11–14; Ilovaiskii, *Smutnoe vremia*, 334–36.

47. Pierling, *La Russie*, 3:401–6; Pirling, *Iz Smutnago Vremeni*, 2–12; Skrynnikov, *Samozvantsy*, 35–36; Perrie, "Legends," 229–30.

48. Pierling, *La Russie*, 3:414–15; Pirling, *Iz Smutnago Vremeni*, 24–26; Skrynnikov, *Sotsial'no-politicheskaia bor'ba*, 105–6, 170.

49. See Golubtsov, "Izmena Smol'nian," 243–51; Kusheva, "Iz istorii," 58; Cherepnin, "Smuta," 95; Skrynnikov, *Boris Godunov*, 137–39, 141–42; idem, *Sotsial'no-politicheskaia bor'ba*, 105–6, 170; Perrie, *Pretenders*, 50.

50. Skrynnikov, *Samozvantsy*, 33; idem, *Boris Godunov*, 137–38.

51. Skrynnikov, *Sotsial'no-politicheskaia bor'ba*, 107–9.

52. See Margeret, *Russian Empire*, 81–82.

53. SRIO 137:577; Skrynnikov, *Rossiia v nachale XVII v.*, 121–22.

54. Golubtsov, "Izmena Smol'nian," 237–38. Cf. Skrynnikov, *Boris Godunov*, 138–39.

55. Golubtsov, "Izmena Smol'nian," 236–38.

56. Ibid., 244, 246, 248; Skrynnikov, *Rossiia v nachale XVII v.*, 98–99; idem, *Sotsial'no-politich-eskaia bor'ba*, 99; idem, *Boris Godunov*, 143; Perrie, *Pretenders*, 54.

57. SGGD 2:294; Pierling, *La Russie*, 3:401–6; Barbour, *Dimitry*, 7–11, 13; Skrynnikov, *Boris Godunov*, 141–42, 144; Perrie, "Legends," 229–30.

58. Perrie, *Pretenders*, 95. Dmitrii may have named the former head of the Russian Foreign Affairs Office, Vasilii Shchelkalov, as one of his protectors. Shchelkalov had been dismissed by Boris Godunov at about the same time as the purge of the Romanovs and was possibly connected to them. He apparently tried to convince Tsar Boris of his innocence and even appeared in the field ready to fight against Dmitrii's invasion. See Kliuchevskii, *Sochineniia*, 33; Vernadsky, *Tsardom*, 1:220; Skrynnikov, *Boris Godunov*, 108.

59. Skrynnikov, *Boris Godunov*, 143.

60. See, for example, RIB 13: col. 21.

61. See for example, Skrynnikov, *Rossiia v nachale XVII v.*, 100; Perrie, *Pretenders*, 49. Cf. AAE 2:142; Aleksandrenko, "Materialy," 427.

62. A. Dobrotvorskii, "Svedenie o knige Vasiliia Velikogo, prinadlezhashchei nyne Zagorovskomu Monastyriu i sokhranivsheisia na nei nadpisi," *Zapiski Imperatorskago Arkheologicheskago Obshchestva* 8(1856): 57–58; idem, "Kto," 10, 96; Skrynnikov, *Boris Godunov*, 140; idem, *Smuta*, 10; Perrie, *Pretenders*, 49.

63. Skrynnikov, *Boris Godunov*, 142–43.

64. Ibid., 132; idem, *Rossiia v nachale XVII v.*, 88. See also Kopanev, "Pinezhskii letopisets," 84.

65. Margeret, *Russian Empire*, 82; Alekseeva, *Istoricheskie pesni*, 33.
66. RIB 13: cols. 48, 155–56, 797; Skrynnikov, *Rossiia v nachale* XVII v., 177–78; Perrie, *Pretenders*, 69–70.
67. Paerle, "Zapiski," 167–69; Pierling, *Rome*, 204–5; idem, *La Russie*, 3:156–57; Skrynnikov, *Rossiia v nachale* XVII v., 176–77.
68. PSRL 14:67; RIB 13: cols. 578, 652; Popov, *Izbornik*, 329; Massa, *Short History*, 113; Aleksandrenko, "Materialy," 267.
69. Skrynnikov, *Rossiia v nachale* XVII v., 232–33.
70. SRIO 137:580; Purchas, *Hakluytus Posthumus*, 14160; Ustrialov, *Skazaniia*, 1:333; Frantzev, "Istoricheskie povestvovanie," 17; Obolenskii, *Inostrannye sochineniia*, 4:11; Margeret, *Russian Empire*, 81–82. These sources had a significant impact on the research of Kostomarov (*Kto*, 31–34; *Smutnoe vrema*, 120) and Ilovaiskii (*Smutnoe vremia*, 329–31). See also Pierling, *La Russie*, 3:420–21; idem, *Rome*, 59, 204.
71. Margeret, *Russian Empire*, 81–82, 87–91.
72. Levesque, *Histoire de Russie*, 3:306–7; Kostomarov, *Kto;* Shmurlo, *Kurs*, 2:224–55; Pierling, *La Russie*, 3:397–429; Pirling, *Iz Smutnago Vremeni*, 182, 193–94, 229; Platonov, *Stat'i*, 275–77; Brody, *Demetrius Legend*, 40–41; Graham, "Note," 358–59; Alpatov, *Russkaia istoricheskaia mysl'*, 33–34. The historians Nikolai Karamzin and Nikolai Ustrialov, who greatly admired Margeret's book, both struggled to overcome the Frenchman's evidence about the identity of Tsar Dmitrii. See Margeret, *Sostoianie Rossiiskoi Derzhavy i Velikago Kniazhestva Moskovskago*, 220–22; Ustrialov, *Skazaniia*, 1:241.
73. Ilovaiskii, *Smutnoe vremia*, 324–27; Beliaev, "Uglichskoe delo," 1–29; Platon, *Kratkaia istoriia*, 2:167–79; Kliuchevskii, *Sochineniia*, 3:32, 36–37; Platonov, *Stat'i*, 276; idem, *Ocherki*, 189, 447 n. 71; Vernadsky, *Tsardom*, 1:226; Graham, "Note," 357–60; Perrie, *Pretenders*, 44; Brody, *Demetrius Legend*, 39, 45; Skrynnikov, *Rossiia v nachale* XVII v., 79.
74. PSRL 14:59; Palitsyn, *Skazanie*, 111; Purchas, *Hakluytus Posthumus*, 14:159, 162; Timofeev, *Vremennik*, 83–84, 88; Massa, *Short History*, 144–45; SRIO 137:176–77, 193–94.
75. Uspenskij, "Tsar and Pretender," 260, 291 n. 109, 273–74; Perrie, *Pretenders*, 55–58, 242.
76. Skrynnikov, *Rossiia v nachale* XVII v., 83–84, 88, 91–92; idem, *Boris Godunov*, 135–37.
77. Trevor-Roper, *European Witch-Craze*, 189; Levack, *Witch-Hunt*, 138, 141.
78. See, for example, Longworth, "Subversive Legend," 21–22.
79. Skrynnikov, *Rossiia v nachale* XVII v., 88–89.
80. Margeret, *Russian Empire*, 69, 75, 80, 90–91; Purchas, *Hakluytus Posthumus*, 14:149; de Thou, *Histoire*, 14:502; Santich, *Missio*, 119 n. 9; Smith, *Voiage;* Kostomarov, *Kto;* Shmurlo, *Kurs*, 2:182–91; Kliuchevskii, *Sochineniia*, 3:33–34; Barbour, *Dimitry*, 321, 323, 327; Crummey, *Formation*, 217–18; Graham, "Note," 359. Cf. Massa, *Short History*, 69.
81. Solov'ev, *Istoriia*, 4:403.
82. Perrie, *Pretenders*, 57.
83. Barbour, *Dimitry*, 323.
84. Margeret, *Russian Empire*, 17, 80–81; Kostomarov, *Kto*, 35–40.
85. Zokiewski, *Expedition*, 43; Margeret, *Russian Empire*, 69, 75; Purchas, *Hakluytus Posthumus*, 14:158; RIB 13: cols. 620–21; Solov'ev, *Istoriia*, 4:402–3; Pierling, *Rome*, 77; idem, *Dimitri et les Jésuites*, 4; Vernadsky, *Tsardom*, 1:229; Crummey, *Formation*, 217–18. Vernadsky (*Tsardom*, 1:224) believed the pretender had enough time while abroad to learn the ways of a gentleman, and Mérimée (*Épisode*, 293–94) keyed on the pretender's horsemanship and military prowess to assert that he could not have been a monk.
86. SRIO 137:577; Pierling, *Rome*, 176; idem, Pierling, *La Russie*, 3:49–50, 434–35; Skrynnikov, *Rossiia v nachale* XVII v., 121–22; Perrie, *Pretenders*, 67.
87. Platonov, *Stat'i*, 276; idem, *Ocherki*, 189, 447 n. 71. Cf. Kliuchevskii, *Sochineniia*, 3:32, 36–37; Ilovaiskii, *Smutnoe vremia*, 324–27; Graham, "Note," 357–60.
88. See Levesque, *Histoire de Russie*, 3:220–26; Suvorin, *O Dimitrii;* Waliszewski, *La Crise;* Kostomarov, *Kto;* Barbour, *Dimitry*, 317–27.
89. Barbour, *Dimitry*, 323–24.
90. Margeret, *Russian Empire*, 17; Smith, *Voiage*, M2; SGGD 2:294; Ustrialov, *Skazaniia*, 1:154;

2:130; Howe, *False Dmitri*, 90–91; Solov'ev, *Istoriia*, 4:424; Chistov, *Russkie legendy*, 43–45; Perrie, "Legends," 230–31.

91. Margeret, *Russian Empire*, 80–81.

92. Smith, *Voiage*, L2, M2-M3.

93. See *Razriadnye knigi 1598–1638 gg.*, 2:227; Smith, *Voiage*, L2-M3; Purchas, *Hakluytus Posthumus*, 14:151; Bussow, *Moskovskaia khronika*, 109. See also Kostomarov, *Kto*, 35–40.

94. Margeret, *Russian Empire*, 81–82; AAE 2:141–44; RIB 13: cols. 18–25; SRIO 137:193–94; Howe, *False Dmitri*, 2; Pierling, *La Russie*, 3:413–14; Skrynnikov, *Smuta*, 9. Barbour (*Dimitry*, 14) and Vernadsky (*Tsardom*, 1:223) claimed that the pretender left Russia in 1601; Mérimée, (*Épisode*, 293–97, 302–5) incorrectly guessed 1603.

95. Margeret, *Russian Empire*, 82. Skrynnikov (*Boris Godunov*, 140) did not credit the report about Tsar Boris closing the border to stop Dmitrii, but see Koretskii, "Golod," 230; idem, "Novoe o krest'ianskom zakreposhchenii," 143–44; RIB 13: col. 21.

96. Aleksandrenko, "Materialy," 427.

97. Treadgold, *West*, 1:49.

98. Tikhomirov, "Samozvanshchina," 118; Barbour, *Dimitry*, 7–8; Skrynnikov, *Rossiia v nachale XVII v.*, 101–2, 117; Pierling, *La Russie*, 3:46–47; Pirling, "Nazvannyi Dimitrii i Adam Vishnevetskii," 124; Sobieski, *Szkice Historyczne*, 68–79.

99. Golobutskii, *Zaporozhskoe kazachestvo*, 83, 133–35; Sobieski, *Szkice Historyczne*, 51–52, 75; Gordon, *Cossack Rebellions*, 106; McNeill, *Europe's Steppe Frontier*, 47–51; Perrie, *Pretenders*, 39–40.

100. Pierling, *La Russie*, 3:46–47; Pirling, "Nazvannyi Dimitrii i Adam Vishnevetskii," 124; Skrynnikov, *Sotsial'no-politicheskaia bor'ba*, 113–15; idem, *Rossiia v nachale XVII v.*, 102–3.

101. Pirling, "Nazvannyi Dimitrii i Adam Vishnevetskii," 125–26.

102. Bussow, *Disturbed State*, 30–31; *Dopolneniia k Aktam Istoricheskim* [hereafter cited as DAI], 1:255; Cherepnin, "Smuta," 96; Skrynnikov, *Rossiia v nachale XVII v.*, 82, 102, 118.

103. PSRL 14:60; AAE 2:79; Obolenskii, "Skazanie," 7–8; Kulish, *Materialy*, 24; Shchepkin, *Kratkie izvestiia*, 4; Longworth, *Cossacks*, 77; Skrynnikov, *Boris Godunov*, 145–47. Skrynnikov (*Sotsial'no-politicheskaia bor'ba*, 111–12) also noted that the pretender had potential contacts with the Zaporozhian cossacks by means of his connection to the Arians.

104. Aleksandrenko, "Materialy," 413; Stanislavskii, *Grazhdanskaia voina*, 20; Skrynnikov, *Rossiia v nachale XVII v.*, 118, 219.

105. Aleksandrenko, "Materialy," 431; Shambinago, "Pis'ma," 442; Skrynnikov, *Rossiia v nachale XVII v.*, 116–19.

106. *Zapiski Zholkevskago*, prilozhenie, cols. 8–10; Pirling, *Dmitrii Samozvanets*, 63.

107. *Zapiski Zholkevskago*, prilozhenie, cols. 5–10; Sobieski, *Szkice Historyczne*, 88; Hirschberg, *Dymitr Samozwaniec*, 35; Floria, *Russko-pol'skie otnosheniia*, 193–98.

108. RIB 1: cols. 1, 5, 10, 16, 38; Maciszewski, "La noblesse polonaise," 23–48; Skrynnikov, "Civil War," 75; idem, *Rossiia v nachale XVII v.*, 119–20.

109. *Zapiski Zholkevskago*, prilozhenie, col. 2; Floria, *Russko-pol'skie otnosheniia*, 92; Skrynnikov, *Boris Godunov*, 144–45.

110. SGGD 2:294; Pirling, *Dmitrii Samozvanets*, 73–74; Pierling, *La Russie*, 3:49–50, 434–35.

111. *Zapiski Zholkevskago*, prilozhenie, cols. 7–8; SRIO 137:577; RIB 13: cols. 23–24; Ptashitskii, "Despoty," 21:135–36.

112. Skrynnikov, *Rossiia v nachale XVII v.*, 122.

113. Pirling, *Dmitrii Samozvanets*, 82–85; Pierling, *Rome*, 178; Santich, *Missio*, 108–10, 113–51.

114. Chilli, "Istoriia," 17:23–24; Pirling, *Dmitrii Samozvanets*, 98; Pierling, *La Russie*, 3:69–70; Skrynnikov, *Rossiia v nachale XVII v.*, 123–25.

115. Pirling, *Dmitrii Samozvanets*, 101; Pierling, *Rome*, 20–37, 182–83; Santich, *Missio*, 113–15.

116. Wielewicki, "Historici Diarii," 145; Pierling, *Rome*, 142, 150; Graham, "Further Sources," 88–90; Kostomarov, *Kto*, 34; Brody, *Demetrius Legend*, 33; Santich, *Missio*, 147–48; Treadgold, *West*, 1:48–49; Skrynnikov, *Rossiia v nachale XVII v.*, 100–101; Perrie, *Pretenders*, 45–46.

117. Skrynnikov, *Smuta*, 11.

118. *Zapiski Zholkevskago,* prilozhenie, cols. 6–8; Ptashitskii, "Despoty," 21:135; Pierling, *Rome,* 191; Pirling, *Dmitrii Samozvanets,* 98; Maciszewski, *Polska,* 72–73; Davies, *God's Playground,* 1:456; Perrie, *Pretenders,* 43; Skrynnikov, *Rossiia v nachale* XVII *v.,* 123, 127–28.

119. *Zapiski Zholkevskago,* prilozhenie, cols. 18–19; Floria, *Russko-pol'skie otnosheniia,* 92; Skrynnikov, *Rossiia v nachale* XVII *v.,* 127–28, 131–32.

120. Massa, *Short History,* 76; Pirling, *Dmitrii Samozvanets,* 380; Pierling, *Rome,* 39; Brody, *Demetrius Legend,* 32; Skrynnikov, *Smuta,* 69–70.

121. Skrynnikov, *Rossiia v nachale* XVII *v.,* 119.

122. Aleksandrenko, "Materialy," 444; SGGD 2:161–62, 166; Chilli, "Istoriia," 17:25; Skrynnikov, *Rossiia v nachale* XVII *v.,* 122, 124–26.

123. Zolkiewski, *Expedition,* 40; Pirling, *Dmitrii Samozvanets,* 151; Floria, *Russko-pol'skie otnosheniia,* 98–99; Skrynnikov, *Rossiia v nachale* XVII *v.,* 127–28.

124. Floria, *Russko-pol'skie otnosheniia,* 88; Skrynnikov, *Rossiia v nachale* XVII *v.,* 128–29.

125. RIB 13: col. 24; Pirling, *Dmitrii Samozvanets,* 201–2; Golubtsov, "Izmena Smol'nian," 237.

126. RIB 1:cols. 365–67; "Novyi dokument," 13; Ustrialov, *Skazaniia,* 1:156; Skrynnikov, *Rossiia v nachale* XVII *v.,* 101, 129, 217–18; idem, *Sotsial'no-politicheskaia bor'ba,* 231–32; Nazarov, "K istorii nachal'nago perioda," 185. Cf. Vernadsky, *Tsardom,* 1:222, 227. Bussow's estimate (*Disturbed State,* 37) of eight thousand men in Dmitrii's army is too high. Purchas' estimate (*Hakluytus Posthumus,* 14:158–59) of ten thousand troops joined by ten thousand cossacks is completely unacceptable.

127. SGGD 2:173; SRIO 137:178.

128. Massa, *Short History,* 72–73; Aleksandrenko, "Materialy," 430; Pirling, *Dmitrii Samozvanets,* 154; Skrynnikov, *Rossiia v nachale* XVII *v.,* 218–20. Cf. Kulish, *Materialy,* 24.

129. SGGD 2:173–75; Aleksandrenko, "Materialy," 389; Perrie, *Pretenders,* 61.

130. *Zapiski Zholkevskago,* prilozhenie, cols. 21–23; RIB 1: col. 366; Skrynnikov, *Rossiia v nachale* XVII *v.,* 131–32; Floria, *Russko-pol'skie otnosheniia,* 89–90.

131. *Akty, otnosiashchiesia k istorii Zapadnoi Rossii* [hereafter cited as AZR], 4:248.

NOTES TO CHAPTER 9

1. Palitsyn, *Skazanie,* 108; Koretskii, "Golod," 231; Dunning, "Cossacks," 61; Culpepper, "Legislative Origins," 183; *Istoriia krest'ianstva,* 2:429–23; Skrynnikov, *Smuta,* 180–81.

2. SRIO 137:243, 248, 260; Crummey, *Formation,* 216–17.

3. Massa, *Short History,* 72–73; Platonov, *Time of Troubles,* 71; idem, *Boris Godunov,* 197, 200–201; Barbour, *Dimitry,* 106.

4. Aleksandrenko, "Materialy," 389; SGGD 2:173–75.

5. AI 2:62–63; Skrynnikov, *Rossiia v nachale* XVII *v.,* 142–43.

6. See Koretskii, "Golod," 230–31; Petreius, *Istoriia,* 196; Skrynnikov, *Rossiia v nachale* XVII *v.,* 145.

7. Margeret, *Russian Empire,* 62; Massa, *Short History,* 78; Popov, *Izbornik,* 324; Sviatskii, *Istoricheskii ocherk,* 34–35; Tikhomirov, *Rossiia,* 410; Smirnov, *Vosstanie,* 112–13.

8. Tikhomirov, *Rossiia,* 407–10; Vernadsky, *Russia at Dawn,* 152–53, 249; Keep, *Soldiers,* 16; Shaw, "Southern Frontiers," 122; Massa, *Short History,* 153.

9. Rusina, "Istorii vykhodzhennia Chernihovo-Sivershchyny do skladu Rosii," 91–100.

10. Shaw, "Southern Frontiers," 122; Piasetskii, *Istoricheskie ocherki,* 61; Smirnov, *Vosstanie,* 114; Skrynnikov, *Smuta,* 82–83.

11. Tikhomirov, *Rossiia,* 409; Piasetskii, *Istoricheskie ocherki,* 13; Sviatskii, *Istoricheskii ocherk,* 34–35; *Istoriia krest'ianstva,* 2:223.

12. Davies, "Village into Garrison," 492.

13. Popov, *Izbornik,* 324; Belokurov, *Razriadnye zapisi,* 42, 117, 173, 178; Tikhomirov, *Rossiia,* 409; Sviatskii, *Istoricheskie ocherki,* 5, 37; Smirnov, *Vosstanie,* 110–14; Avrich, *Russian Rebels,* 22; Smith, *Peasant Farming,* 100.

14. Smirnov (*Vosstanie,* 112) claimed the number was twenty-five hundred, based upon the mistaken idea that twenty-five hundred Komanitsk district peasant householders were drafted by Tsar Boris's commanders for service against Dmitrii. The actual number recruited was five hundred, but there were certainly many more than five hundred households in the Komaritsk district. (By the 1640s, more than five thousand taxpaying households were located there.) See Skrynnikov, *Rossiia v nachale XVII v.,* 147; Davies, "Village into Garrison," 492.

15. AMG 2:5–6; Tikhomirov, *Rossiia,* 407, 410; Sviatskii, *Istoricheskii ocherk,* 34.

16. Piasetskii, *Istoricheskie ocherki,* 13; Stanislavskii, *Grazhdanskaia voina,* 13.

17. Smirnov, *Vosstanie,* 114–15, 121; Tikhomirov, *Rossiia,* 410–11; *Istoriia krest'ianstva,* 2:426; Skrynnikov, "Civil War," 64; Stanislavskii, *Grazhdanskaia voina,* 12–13.

18. Veselovskii, *Soshnoe pis'mo,* 2:97–98; Makovskii, *Pervaia krest'ianskaia voina,* 132, 135; Hellie, "Foundations," 150; idem, *Enserfment,* 310 n. 75; Kopanev, "Zakonodatel'stvo"; Shveikovskaia, "K kharakteristike," 75–86.

19. Piasetskii, *Istoricheskie ocherki,* 12–13, 22; Sviatskii, *Istoricheskii ocherk,* 41; Fletcher, *Russe Commonwealth,* 28v; Bond, *Russia,* 37; Smirnov, *Vosstanie,* 114–17.

20. Koretskii, *Formirovanie,* 198–99; Skrynnikov, *Samozvantsy,* 78. Cf. Massa, *Short History,* 76; Popov, *Izbornik,* 324; Davies, "Village into Garrison," 492.

21. Culpepper, "Legislative Origins," 184; Skrynnikov, *Boris Godunov,* 123–24.

22. Skrynnikov, *Boris Godunov,* 122.

23. Koretskii, "Golod," 254.

24. Skrynnikov, *Rossiia v nachale XVII v.,* 143.

25. Ul'ianovskii, "Russko-shvedskie otnosheniia," 63.

26. Skrynnikov, *Smuta,* 9; Vernadsky, *Tsardom,* 1:222.

27. RIB 1: col. 367; SGGD 2:169; SRIO 137:260; *Moskovskaia tragediia,* 22; Barbour, *Dimitry,* 76.

28. Pirling, *Dmitrii Samozvanets,* 159; SRIO 137:243, 260; V. I. Koretskii, "Solovetskii letopisets kontsa XVI v.," *Letopisi i khroniki. 1980 g.* (Moscow, 1981): 243.

29. SRIO 137:414.

30. See, for example, Zimin, "Nekotorye voprosy," 99; Ovchinnikov, "Nekotorye voprosy," 82–83; Skliar, "O nachal'nom etape," 91–99; "O krest'ianskoi voine," 111–15.

31. See Skrynnikov, *Smuta,* 180–81; idem, *Rossiia v nachale XVII v.,* 144; Piasetskii, *Istoricheskii ocherk,* 13; Stanislavskii, *Grazhdanskaia voina,* 13.

32. Tikhomirov, *Rossiia,* 413.

33. Ustrialov, *Skazaniia,* 1:156–57; PSRL 14:61–62; "Novyi dokument," 11; RIB 13: col. 724; Margeret, *Russia Empire,* 61; Purchas, *Hakluytus Posthumus,* 14:159; SGGD 2: no. 80; Belokurov, *Razriadnye zapisi,* 191; *Istoriia krest'ianstva,* 2:431; Skrynnikov, *Rossiia v nachale XVII v.,* 146–47.

34. RIB 1: cols. 369–70.

35. SGGD 2: no. 139; Massa, *Short History,* 73.

36. Massa, *Short History,* 73; *Istoriia krest'ianstva,* 2:431; Skrynnikov, *Rossiia v nachale XVII v.,* 220.

37. Platonov, *Ocherki,* 248–49; idem, *Boris Godunov,* 200–201; idem, *Drevnerusskie skazaniia,* 64.

38. Skrynnikov, *Rossiia v nachale XVII v.,* 215, 217–18. Allen (*Ukraine,* 92) correctly noted that most of the Ukrainian cossacks in Dmitrii's army were not Zaporozhian cossacks, but he erred in estimating their number at twelve thousand.

39. See, for example, Pirling, *Dmitrii Samozvanets,* 154; Purchas, *Hakluytus Posthumus,* 14:158–59; Skrynnikov, *Rossiia v nachale XVII v.,* 216–17; Skliar, "O nachal'nom etape," 94; Nazarov, "O nekotorykh osobennostiakh," 120, 123.

40. Skrynnikov, *Rossiia v nachale XVII v.,* 218–20.

41. Margeret, *Russian Empire,* 71; Massa, *Short History,* 80.

42. Tikhomirov, *Rossiia,* 413. Skrynnikov (*Rossiia v nachale XVII v.,* 154) correctly rejected Platonov's faulty claim (*Ocherki,* 246) that Novgorod Severskii lacked a significant civilian population.

43. Massa, *Short History,* 78–79; Skrynnikov, *Rossiia v nachale XVII v.,* 146–47.

44. Tikhomirov, *Rossiia,* 413.

45. AMG 1:66–67, 74; *Razriadnye knigi 1598–1638,* 1:145–46, 164, 166.

46. Due to a mistake in the copying of military records, some scholars concluded that twenty-five hundred Komaritsk peasants were recruited for service at Novgorod Severskii. (See Belokurov,

Razriadnye zapisi, 2; Smirnov, *Vosstanie*, 111–12; Skrynnikov, *Rossiia v nachale* XVII *v.*, 147.) Other scholars erroneously argued that no Komaritsk peasants could have been recruited because of the social revolution then occurring. (See Nazarov, "K istorii nachal'nago perioda," 192 n. 24.) Smirnov completely misinterpreted his sources and concluded (*Vosstanie*, 111, 117–18) that the recruitment of Komaritsk peasants occurred later, toward the end of 1604.

47. PSRL 34:206; RIB 1: col. 372; Paerle, "Zapiski," 158–59; Barbour, *Dimitry*, 84.

48. Tikhomirov, *Rossiia*, 412; Massa, *Short History*, 73; Margeret, *Russian Empire*, 61; SGGD 2:176.

49. P. Smirnov, *Goroda*, 2:41; N. A. Ernst, "Putivl i ego posad v pervoi polovine XVII v.," *Iubileinyi sbornik istoriko-etnograficheskogo kruzhka pri universitete sv. Vladimira* (Kiev, 1914), 75.

50. Skrynnikov, "Civil War," 64; Avrich, *Russian Rebels*, 17–18, 26.

51. Skrynnikov, *Smuta*, 79–80, 82, 91–92; idem, *Rossiia v nachale* XVII *v.*, 21, 104, 114, 149; idem, "Glavnye vekhi," 101–2; *Istoriia krest'ianstva*, 2:426; Tikhomirov, *Rossiia*, 410–12.

52. Bussow, *Moskovskaia khronika*, 359 n. 77.

53. PSRL 14:61–62; RIB 13: col. 724; Barbour, *Dimitry*, 85; Skrynnikov, "Civil War," 64; idem, *Rossiia v nachale* XVII *v.*, 148; Avrich, *Russian Rebels*, 26. Completely unreliable accounts of events in Putivl may be found in Purchas, *Hakluytus Posthumus*, 14:159; and in RIB 13: col. 571. Massa (*Short History*, 78) confused the chronology of Sutupov's arrival in Putivl.

54. Skrynnikov, *Rossiia v nachale* XVII *v.*, 149–50.

55. Skrynnikov, *Smuta*, 155.

56. Massa, *Short History*, 73; Bussow, *Disturbed State*, 37; Skrynnikov, *Rossiia v nachale* XVII *v.*, 150.

57. *Istoriia krest'ianstva*, 2:433.

58. *Razriadnye knigi 1598–1638*, 1:172; PSRL 14:62; Belokurov, *Razriadnye zapisi*, 84, 204; *Boiarskie spiski*, 1:159, 203; Skrynnikov, *Rossiia v nachale* XVII *v.*, 150–51, 179.

59. Skliar, "O nachal'nom etape," 96; *Istoriia krest'ianstva*, 2:431.

60. Piasetskii, *Istoricheskie ocherki*, 15, 61; Smirnov, *Vosstanie*, 114, 116; Skrynnikov, *Rossiia v nachale* XVII *v.*, 151–52.

61. Margeret, *Russian Empire*, 61; *Razriadnye knigi 1598–1638*, 1:149, 173; *Boiarskie spiski*, 2:86; Piasetskii, *Istoricheskie ocherki*, 15; Skrynnikov, *Rossiia v nachale* XVII *v.*, 153.

62. AMG 1:76; Platonov, *Ocherki*, 255; Skrynnikov, *Rossiia v nachale* XVII *v.*, 164.

63. Belokurov, *Razriadnye zapisi*, 232, 238; Margeret, *Russian Empire*, 61; Massa, *Short History*, 78; Sviatskii, *Istoricheskii ocherk*, 37–38.

64. Massa, *Short History*, 79; Belokurov, *Razriadnye zapisi*, 232; Skrynnikov, *Rossiia v nachale* XVII *v.*, 153–54.

65. Margeret, *Russian Empire*, 61; Bussow, *Disturbed State*, 38; RIB 1: col. 371; Paerle, "Zapiski," 157; Platonov, *Ocherki*, 246; Barbour, *Dimitry*, 82–84.

66. Fletcher, *Russe Commonwealth*, 61; Olearius, *Travels*, 43, 152; d'Avity, *Description générale de l'Europe, quatriesme partie du monde*, 3:1143.

67. RIB 1: col. 376; 13: col 29; Paerle, "Zapiski," 170; Massa, *Short History*, 79; Barbour, *Dimitry*, 84–85. Massa incorrectly asserted that Novgorod Severskii surrendered due to starvation (*Short History*, 80).

68. *Boiarskie spiski*, 2:44; Skrynnikov, *Rossiia v nachale* XVII *v.*, 154–55.

69. Massa, *Short History*, 74; Bussow, *Disturbed State*, 37; Belokurov, *Razriadnye zapisi*, 192–93.

70. Skrynnikov, *Boris Godunov*, 146.

71. Margeret, *Russian Empire*, 50–51; Fletcher, *Russe Commonwealth*, 58–59; Herberstein, *Notes*, 1:99; Hakluyt, *Principal Navigations*, 2:230; Keep, *Soldiers*, 30, 38; Skrynnikov, *Rossiia v nachale* XVII *v.*, 21.

72. Hellie, *Enserfment*, 24, 163.

73. Keep, *Soldiers*, 38–39; Smith, "Muscovite Logistics," 41; Hellie, *Enserfment*, 46, 159; Skrynnikov, *Boris Godunov*, 147–49.

74. Skrynnikov, *Rossiia v nachale* XVII *v.*, 142. Cf. Hellie, *Enserfment*, 38–39, 46.

75. Bussow, *Disturbed State*, 37–38; Storozhev, *Istoriko-iuridicheskie materialy*, 24, 201. Cf. Hellie, *Enserfment*, 38.

76. Skrynnikov, *Rossiia v nachale* XVII *v.*, 21, 56.

77. Margeret, *Russian Empire*, 46; Chernov, *Vooruzhennye sily*, 125, 128; Skrynnikov, *Smuta*, 182–83; idem, *Rossiia v nachale* XVII *v.*, 55. Cf. Keep, *Soldiers*, 42–43. Hellie (*Enserfment*, 48) regarded this move by Tsar Boris as a bid to gain pomeshchik support. It was more likely a response to the weakness of the militia forces after the famine.

78. Tatishchev, *Istoriia*, 7:370, 372; Chernov, *Vooruzhennye sily*, 125; Keep, *Soldiers*, 59; Hellie, *Enserfment*, 48; Skrynnikov, *Rossiia v nachale* XVII *v.*, 55–56. Tatishchev erred in dating the new statute 12 June 1604; it was issued in the fall in response to Dmitrii's invasion.

79. See, for example, *Boiarskie spiski*, 1:155, 162, 220, 234, 238; 2:80–81, 83–84. Cf. Seredonin, *Izvestiia inostrantsev*, 13.

80. Hellie, *Slavery*, 467–71; idem, *Enserfment*, 165, 267; Skrynnikov, *Smuta*, 180–81.

81. Skrynnikov, *Sotsial'no-politicheskaia bor'ba*, 325; idem, *Rossiia v nachale* XVII *v.*, 56; Hellie, *Slavery*, 468; A. Vostokov, "Russkie sluzhiloe soslovie po desiatniam 1577–1608 gg.," *Iuridicheskii vestnik* 28 (June–July 1888): 266.

82. Skrynnikov, *Smuta*, 182–83; Hellie, *Enserfment*, 220–21; Keep, *Soldiers*, 59.

83. Margeret, *Russian Empire*, 47, 50; Skrynnikov, *Rossiia v nachale* XVII *v.*, 56–57; Keep, *Soldiers*, 58.

84. Keep, *Soldiers*, 38; Skrynnikov, *Smuta*, 183.

85. Fletcher, *Russe Commonwealth*, 58–59; Hellie, *Enserfment*, 163.

86. Margeret, *Russian Empire*, 49; Seredonin, *Izvestiia inostrantsev*, 13; Hellie, *Enserfment*, 161–63, 267; Keep, *Soldiers*, 61.

87. Allen, *Russian Embassies*, 2:470 n. 1.

88. Keep, *Soldiers*, 75–76.

89. Margeret, *Russian Empire*, 49; Stanislavskii, *Grazhdanskaia voina*, 13–14.

90. Margeret, *Russian Empire*, 47, 49; Aleksandrenko, "Materialy," 291–92; Skrynnikov, *Rossiia v nachale* XVII *v.*, 216–17.

91. Keep, *Soldiers*, 77; Berry and Crummey, *Rude and Barbarous Kingdom*, 286.

92. Margeret, *Russian Empire*, 26, 47, 141 n. 149; Massa, *Short History*, 83. There are estimates of up to nine thousand Western mercenaries in the tsar's army. (See Seredonin, *Izvestiia inostrantsev*, 13; Purchas, *Hakluytus Posthumus*, 14:148; Berry and Crummey, *Rude and Barbarous Kingdom*, 288–89; Kliuchevskii, *Skazaniia inostrantsev*, 93–94; Hellie, *Enserfment*, 169, 267.) However, some of those estimates appear to include Ukrainian cossacks. In any case, Captain Margeret—who commanded those men under Tsar Boris—was the most expert witness, and his numbers are usually reliable.

93. Smith, "Muscovite Logistics," 39 n. 10.

94. Hellie, *Enserfment*, 25, 29; Keep, *Soldiers*, 56–58; Skrynnikov, *Rossiia v nachale* XVII *v.*, 57.

95. Margeret, *Russian Empire*, 46–47, 50; Skrynnikov, *Rossiia v nachale* XVII *v.*, 55.

96. Margeret, *Russian Empire*, 47; Massa, *Short History*, 74; Veselovskii, *Feodal'noe zemlevladenie*, 231–43; Makovskii, *Razvitie*, 275.

97. Margeret, *Russian Empire*, 50; Razin, *Istoriia*, 3:303–13; Zlotnik, "Muscovite Fiscal Policy," 247–48; Hellie, *Enserfment*, 25, 232, 267.

98. Veselovskii, *Feodal'noe zemlevladenie*, 231; Fletcher, *Russe Commonwealth*, 55v; Staden, *Land and Government*, 40; Keep, *Soldiers*, 57–58; Hellie, *Enserfment*, 43; Skrynnikov, *Rossiia v nachale* XVII *v.*, 55.

99. Margeret, *Russian Empire*, 50; *Boiarskie spiski*, 2:44. Cf. Davies, "Village into Garrison," 482, 492.

100. See Keep, *Soldiers*, 57; Chernov, *Vooruzhennye sily*, 93. Cf. Purchas, *Hakluytus Posthumus*, 2:229.

101. Skrynnikov, *Rossiia v nachale* XVII *v.*, 57; idem, *Smuta*, 183; *Boiarskie spiski*, 2:44.

102. Margeret, *Russian Empire*, 143 n. 159; Seredonin, *Izvestiia inostrantsev*, 13; Kliuchevskii, *Skazaniia inostrantsev*, 89–96; Chernov, *Vooruzhennye sily*, 95; Keep, *Soldiers*, 87–88; Hellie, *Enserfment*, 164, 267. Cf. Fletcher, *Russe Commonwealth*, 55–55v; Berry and Crummey, *Rude and Barbarous Kingdom*, 286.

103. See Stevens, *Soldiers*, 7.

104. See Herberstein, *Notes*, 2:254; Zimin, *Reformy*, 445–48.

105. Herberstein, *Notes*, 2:196–97; Hakluyt, *Principal Navigations*, 2:229, 258; Margeret, *Russian*

Empire, 19, 120 n. 51; Mansuy, Le Monde slave et les classiques français aux XVIe–XVIIe siècles, 14; Limonov, Kul'turnye sviazi Rossii, 221.

106. PSRL 14:57; 34:240; Popov, Izbornik, 322–23; Allen, Russian Embassies, 2:470 n. 1, 549–50; Skrynnikov, Rossiia v nachale XVII v., 74–75.

107. Bussow, Disturbed State, 37–38; Massa, Short History, 74; Purchas, Hakluytus Posthumus, 14:141.

108. Margeret, Russian Empire, 62. Cf. Boiarskie spiski, 2:3–95; Purchas, Hakluytus Posthumus, 14:159. Smith ("Muscovite Logistics," 38) believed that no Russian army in the sixteenth century could have been larger than thirty-five thousand men.

109. Margeret, Russian Empire, 42–43; Keep, Soldiers, 26, 41.

110. Keep, Soldiers, 26; Hellie, Enserfment, 32; Eskin, "Smuta i mestnichestvo," 63–124. See also Kollmann, By Honor Bound.

111. Fletcher, Russe Commonwealth, 59. Cf. Massa, Short History, 85.

112. Platonov, Boris Godunov, 194–96.

113. Belokurov, Razriadnye zapisi, 1–2, 192, 193; Bussow, Disturbed State, 37–38; Massa, Short History, 74; Skrynnikov, Rossiia v nachale XVII v., 155. Platonov (Ocherki, 249) misunderstood Tsar Boris's strategy and incorrectly concluded that the choice of Briansk had been a mistake that cost the tsar's army precious time.

114. Massa, Short History, 74–75. Solovev (Istoriia, 4:416) incorrectly claimed that Tsar Boris referred to Dmitrii's invasion as a Crimean Tatar attack. There actually was a Crimean Tatar alert in the spring of 1604. See Razriadnye knigi 1598–1638, 1:160.

115. Massa, Short History, 73.

116. Margeret, Russian Empire, 62; Boiarskie spiski, 2:3–95; Skrynnikov, Rossiia v nachale XVII v., 156. Massa's estimate of one hundred thousand men (Short History, 80) is too high.

117. Margeret, Russian Empire, 42–43; Hellie, Enserfment, 28–29, 43; Ostrowski, "Mongol Origins," 535–36; Halperin, Russia and the Golden Horde, 91; Smith, "Muscovite Logistics," 37.

118. Smith, "Muscovite Logistics," 61; Chernov, Vooruzhennye sily, 98; Hellie, Enserfment, 29, 187.

119. Razin, Istoriia, 2:349; Smith, "Muscovite Logistics," 46, 53; Hellie, Enserfment, 163.

120. Paerle, "Zapiski," 160; Margeret, Russian Empire, 61; Skrynnikov, Rossiia v nachale XVII v., 154–55.

121. Bussow, Disturbed State, 38. Cf. Massa, Short History, 80.

122. There are wild estimates of Dmitrii's army containing up to thirty-eight thousand men. (See Hirschberg, Dymitr Samozwaniec, 75.) Even less wild but still exaggerated estimates (e.g., Purchas, Hakluytus Posthumus, 14:158–59; Barbour, Dimitry, 80–81; Allen, Ukraine, 92) were based on the inaccurate assumption that up to thirteen thousand cossacks joined Dmitrii's army as he approached Chernigov in the fall of 1604. See Skrynnikov, Rossiia v nachale XVII v., 156.

123. Massa, Short History, 79–80; Skrynnikov, Boris Godunov, 147.

124. See Keep, Soldiers, 38. Cf. Herberstein, Notes, 1:99; Hakluyt, Principal Navigations, 2:230; Fletcher, Russe Commonwealth, 59.

125. Margeret, Russian Empire, 46–49; Hellie, Enserfment, 30–31; idem, Economy, 39–46.

126. Esper, "Military Self-Sufficiency," 204; Skrynnikov, Smuta, 183; Hellie, Economy, 202–4, 229–33.

127. Herberstein, Notes, 1:97–100; Margeret, Russian Empire, 43; Fletcher, Russe Commonwealth, 59–59v; Hakluyt, Principal Navigations, 2:230–31; Massa, Short History, 84–85; Keep, Soldiers, 38–39; Hellie, Enserfment, 28–33, 168; Crummey, Formation, 10; Skrynnikov, Smuta, 183.

128. Margeret, Russian Empire, 47.

129. Ibid., 61–62; Skrynnikov, Rossiia v nachale XVII v., 156. This famous passage in Margeret's book was embellished and used by historians (including Karamzin and Solovev) and by Russia's great poet, Aleksandr Pushkin—who had the brave Frenchman speak these lines as a character in his play, Boris Godunov. See Pushkin, Boris Godunov, 7–8, 86–87; Solov'ev, Istoriia, 4:418.

130. Bussow, Disturbed State, 38; Massa, Short History, 80; Margeret, Russian Empire, 62; Skrynnikov, Rossiia v nachale XVII v., 156.

131. RIB 1: cols. 378–80; 13: col. 29; Paerle, "Zapiski," 162; Bussow, Disturbed State, 38.

132. Massa, *Short History*, 80. Skrynnikov (*Rossiia v nachale XVII v.*, 157) doubted the low estimate of casualties suffered by Dmitrii's army, arguing unpersuasively that overall casualty figures for the tsar's army must have included some of Dmitrii's men.
133. Margeret, *Russian Empire*, 61–62. Cf. Bussow, *Disturbed State*, 38.
134. RIB 1: col. 380; *Boiarskie spiski*, 2:4, 10, 11, 14; Margeret, *Russian Empire*, 61; Solov'ev, *Istoriia*, 4:418; Barbour, *Dimitry*, 86–89. Some sources put Mstislavskii's casualties at up to four thousand men. Skrynnikov (*Rossiia v nachale XVII v.*, 157) called that an exaggeration, but contemporaries specifically mentioned "a large number of wounded" and "great damage" inflicted on the tsar's army. See Massa, *Short History*, 80; Bussow, *Disturbed State*, 38.
135. Massa, *Short History*, 80. This is an interesting point. The usual practice in early modern Russia was to provide little help for the wounded. See Keep, *Soldiers*, 39.
136. Margeret, *Russian Empire*, 62.
137. Massa, *Short History*, 80; AAE 2:77.
138. Ul'ianovskii, "Russko-shvedskie otnosheniia," 62–63.
139. Tikhomirov, "Novyi istochnik," 97.
140. "Novyi dokument," 11–12; Skrynnikov, *Rossiia v nachale XVII v.*, 217–18. Cf. RIB 1: col. 383; Paerle, "Zapiski," 162–63. Estimates of up to twelve thousand cossacks joining Dmitrii at this time are too high.
141. Margeret, *Russian Empire*, 62; Skrynnikov, *Rossiia v nachale XVII v.*, 157. Cf. Bussow, *Disturbed State*, 38. Massa (*Short History*, 80) incorrectly reported the surrender of Novgorod Severskii.

NOTES TO CHAPTER 10

1. Skrynnikov, *Rossiia v nachale XVII v.*, 157–58; RIB 1: col. 101; Karamzin, *Istoriia*, 11: prim. 276.
2. Massa, *Short History*, 80; Margeret, *Russian Empire*, 62; RIB 1: cols. 382–83; Pirling, *Dmitrii Samozvanets*, 166; Barbour, *Dimitry*, 89–90; Skrynnikov, "Civil War," 63, 75; idem, *Boris Godunov*, 147.
3. Massa, *Short History*, 76; Sviatskii, *Istoricheskii ocherk*, 37–38; Piasetskii, *Istoricheskie ocherki*, 15. Cf. SGGD 2: no. 139.
4. RIB 1: col. 383; Paerle, "Zapiski," 162–63; Belokurov, *Razriadnye zapisi*, 2, 238; Piasetskii, *Istoricheskie ocherki*, 15; Barbour, *Dimitry*, 90; Pirling, *Dmitrii Samozvanets*, 167; Skrynnikov, *Rossiia v nachale XVII v.*, 158. Some sources incorrectly estimated that by this time Dmitrii had up to twelve thousand Zaporozhian cossacks in his service. Some sources also exaggerated the number of Don cossacks in Dmitrii's army by early 1605, putting it as high as three thousand men.
5. Margeret, *Russian Empire*, 62; Massa, *Short History*, 76.
6. See Koretskii, *Formirovanie*, 365; *Ocherki istorii SSSR*, 494–95; Mavrodin, "Sovetskaia literatura," 39–40.
7. Palitsyn, *Skazanie*, 108, 110; Skrynnikov, *Rossiia v nachale XVII v.*, 206–14, 249–51; idem, *Smuta*, 180–81; Stanislavskii, *Grazhdanskaia voina*, 7–8, 243–47; Dunning, "Cossacks," 61–63, 71–72.
8. Margeret, *Russian Empire*, 62. See also Vernadsky, *Tsardom*, 1:227; Platonov, *Boris Godunov*, 194.
9. Piasetskii, *Istoricheskie ocherki*, 16.
10. Nazarov, "K istorii nachal'nogo perioda," 199; Skrynnikov, *Rossiia v nachale XVII v.*, 168.
11. See, for example, Bussow, *Disturbed State*, 40; Massa, *Short History*, 80; Alpatov, *Russkaia mysl'*, 17.
12. See for example, Barbour, *Dimitry*, 91. Cf. *Boiarskie spiski*, 2:4, 10–11, 14; PSRL 14:62; Belokurov, *Razriadnye zapisi*, 195, 197; Piasetskii, *Istoricheskie ocherki*, 15–16. There is a totally inaccurate report in some Soviet publications that Mstislavskii commanded only twenty thousand men and was actually outnumbered by Dmitrii's forces. See, for example, *Sovetskaia voennaia entsiklopediia*, 3:212.

13. Margeret, *Russian Empire*, 62; Skrynnikov, *Rossiia v nachale* XVII *v.*, 164.

14. See Hellie, *Enserfment*, 38–39. Cf. Sviatskii, *Istoricheskii ocherk*, 37–38; Massa, *Short History*, 76; SGGD 2: no. 139.

15. Massa, *Short History*, 82; Piasetskii, *Istoricheskie ocherki*, 16.

16. Margeret, *Russian Empire*, 62; Massa, *Short History*, 82.

17. Bussow, *Disturbed State*, 40; Sviatskii, *Istoricheskii ocherk*, 39. Exaggerated estimates of Dmitrii's forces ran his numbers up to twenty-three thousand, or even thirty-eight thousand men— partly because of scholarly confusion about inaccurate sources stating that up to thirteen thousand cossacks joined his army. See, for example, Hirschberg, *Dymitr Samozwaniec*, 75; Razin, *Istoriia*, 3:68–83; *Sovetskaia voennaia entsiklopediia*, 3:212.

18. RIB 1: col. 385; Paerle, "Zapiski," 163.

19. Margeret, *Russian Empire*, 63; Massa, *Short History*, 83–84. Bussow (*Disturbed State*, 40) exaggerated the extent of Dmitrii's apparent "victory" at Dobrynichi before his cavalry ran into difficulty.

20. Hellie, *Enserfment*, 164.

21. Razin, *Istoriia*, 3:78; Hellie, "Warfare," 78–79.

22. Hellie, *Enserfment*, 160, 162, 181–82; Razin, *Istoriia*, 2:548; Margeret, *Russian Empire*, 28, 38, 51.

23. Margeret, *Russian Empire*, 63; Massa, *Short History*, 84.

24. See Margeret, *Russian Empire*, xviii, 98 n. 36; Razin, *Istoriia*, 3:68–76; Alpatov, *Russkaia mysl'*, 17, 33; Zhordaniia, *Ocherki*, 1:250, 255, 273–76; Beskrovnyi, *Ocherki*, 61; Hellie, *Enserfment*, 164–65; Massa, *Short History*, 33; Bussow, *Disturbed State*, 40–41.

25. Margeret, *Russian Empire*, 63; Bussow, *Disturbed State*, 40; Massa, *Short History*, 84.

26. Massa, *Short History*, 85; Hellie, *Enserfment*, 32–33; Keep, *Soldiers*, 38–39.

27. Massa, *Short History*, 84. Bussow unconvincingly claimed that the premature recall of the cavalry was the result of treason among Tsar Boris's commanders (*Disturbed State*, 40).

28. Massa, *Short History*, 84; Bussow, *Disturbed State*, 42. Cf. Fletcher, *Russe Commonwealth*, 61v; Alef, "Muscovite Military Reforms," 82; Keep, *Soldiers*, 41.

29. RIB 1: cols. 387–88; Paerle, "Zapiski," 165; Skrynnikov, *Rossiia v nachale* XVII *v.*, 159–60.

30. Pirling, *Dmitrii Samozvanets*, 169–70.

31. Margeret, *Russian Empire*, 63.

32. RIB 1: col. 388; Skrynnikov, *Rossiia v nachale* XVII *v.*, 160. Massa (*Short History*, 84) incorrectly credited five hundred Poles with this heroic deed.

33. Margeret, *Russian Empire*, 28; Massa, *Short History*, 80; Longworth, *Cossacks*, 32–33. Part of the confusion about cossack activity in the aftermath of the battle of Dobrynichi has been due to an inaccurate story that the Zaporozhian cossacks deserted Dmitrii's camp after the battle and were so angry about the loss of many of their comrades that they contemplated killing the pretender. See, for example, RIB 13: col. 726; Paerle, "Zapiski," 166; Perrie, *Pretenders*, 62.

34. Massa, *Short History*, 84; Bussow, *Disturbed State*, 40–41.

35. Margeret, *Russian Empire*, 63; Koretskii, "Novoe o krest'ianskom zakreposhchenii," 144. Other estimates of the number of Dmitrii's men who were killed range from three thousand (Paerle, "Zapiski," 165) to seven or eight thousand (PSRL 14:62; Massa, *Short History*, 85). Dmitrii lost either thirteen or thirty artillery pieces.

36. See Belokurov, *Razriadnye zapisi*, 238; Margeret, *Russian Empire*, 63; Massa, *Short History*, 85.

37. Chilli, "Istoriia," 17:27; Pirling, *Dmitrii Samozvanets*, 171; Skrynnikov, *Rossiia v nachale* XVII *v.*, 163; idem, *Boris Godunov*, 147–49; Sviatskii, *Istoricheskii ocherk*, 40–41.

38. Massa, *Short History*, 76, 81; RIB 13: cols. 34–35; Piasetskii, *Istoricheskie ocherki*, 22; Skrynnikov, *Samozvantsy*, 87; idem, *Rossiia v nachale* XVII *v.*, 161–62.

39. Sviatskii, *Istoricheskii ocherk*, 41.

40. Massa, *Short History*, 76–77; Margeret, *Russian Empire*, 124 n. 73. Cf. Berry and Crummey, *Rude and Barbarous Kingdom*, 180, 286–87; Kliuchevskii, *Skazaniia inostrantsev*, 83–84. Massa claimed that forty thousand Kasimov Tatars were involved in the punitive expedition; however, Military Affairs Office records show that there were only about 450 Kasimov Tatars in the tsar's army at that time

(*Boiarskie spiski*, 2:32). There were, of course, thousands of other Tatar troops in the army who were involved in the punitive raids.

41. Bussow, *Disturbed State*, 41; Massa, *Short History*, 77; RIB 13: cols. 34–35; Popov, *Izbornik*, 265–66. See also Timofeev, *Vremennik*, 84.

42. Massa, *Short History*, 77, 81. Cf. Margeret, *Russian Empire*, 64.

43. Massa, *Short History*, 77, 81, 90–91; Perrie, *Pretenders*, 65–66.

44. Paerle, "Zapiski," 167.

45. Massa, *Short History*, 77; Skrynnikov, *Rossiia v nachale XVII v.*, 161.

46. Massa, *Short History*, 90–91; Piasetskii, *Istoricheskie ocherki*, 22.

47. RIB 1: col. 369; 13: cols. 571–72, 724; PSRL 14:61–62; 31:150; Belokurov, *Razriadnye zapisi*, 1; Purchas, *Hakluytus Posthumus*, 14:160; Pavlov, *Gosudarev dvor*, 79; Skrynnikov, *Rossiia v nachale XVII v.*, 165–69; Perrie, *Pretenders*, 63.

48. Nazarov, "K istorii nachal'nom perioda," 199.

49. *Rodoslavnaia kniga roda Khitrovo* (St. Petersburg, 1867), 361–62, 393; Skrynnikov, *Rossiia v nachale XVII v.*, 165–66, 168–69. See also Zagorovskii, *Belgorodskaia cherta*, 22–24, 33.

50. RIB 1: col. 393; *Boiarskie spiski*, 2:33–34, 51.

51. Belokurov, *Razriadnye zapisi*, 5; Purchas, *Hakluytus Posthumus*, 14:160.

52. See *Boiarskie spiski*, 2:33; Belokurov, *Razriadnye zapisi*, 84, 204.

53. Margeret, *Russian Empire*, 61; *Istoriia krest'ianstva*, 2:431–32; Smirnov, *Vosstanie*, 144–45; Anpilogov, *Novye dokumenty*, 320; Perrie, *Pretenders*, 63; Pirling, *Dmitrii Samozvanets*, 204–5.

54. Pavlov, *Gosudarev dvor*, 79; Skrynnikov, *Smuta*, 250; idem, *Rossiia v nachale XVII v.*, 169; Perrie, *Pretenders*, 63; Pirling, *Dmitrii Samozvanets*, 204; *Istoriia krest'ianstva*, 2:432.

55. Bussow, *Disturbed State*, 41.

56. Margeret, *Russian Empire*, 64; RIB 1: col. 392; PSRL 14:62; Pierling, *Rome*, 203; Skrynnikov, *Rossiia v nachale XVII v.*, 163, 179. I have found no evidence to support Barbour's claim (*Dimitry*, 104) that up to five thousand cossacks from Putivl broke through the siege line and reinforced Rylsk, thereby discouraging Mstislavskii. Indeed, on approaching Rylsk, Zaporozhian cossacks loyal to Dmitrii were fired upon by its nervous garrison. See Skrynnikov, *Rossiia v nachale XVII v.*, 161.

57. Massa, *Short History*, 77–78; Pirling, *Dmitrii Samozvanets*, 171; Platonov, *Ocherki*, 253; Skrynnikov, *Boris Godunov*, 147–49. See also Smith, "Muscovite Logistics," 41; Keep, *Soldiers*, 38; Hellie, *Enserfment*, 32–33, 46, 159.

58. PSRL 14:62–63; Skrynnikov, *Rossiia v nachale XVII v.*, 163–64.

59. Skrynnikov, *Rossiia v nachale XVII v.*, 169; Purchas, *Hakluytus Posthumus*, 14:160; Paerle, "Zapiski," 167; Pirling, *Dmitrii Samozvanets*, 203.

60. Margeret, *Russian Empire*, 64; Massa, *Short History*, 86. Cf. Hellie, *Enserfment*, 46; Smith, "Muscovite Logistics," 41.

61. PSRL 14:62–63; Belokurov, *Razriadnye zapisi*, 3.

62. RIB 13: col. 35; Popov, *Izbornik*, 226; Pirling, *Dmitrii Samozvanets*, 172–73.

63. Skrynnikov, *Rossiia v nachale XVII v.*, 178–80, 191–92; SGGD 2:209; Golubtsov and Rummel', *Rodoslavnyi sbornik*, 614. I have found no evidence of lower class participation in Dmitrii's Putivl government as hypothesized by some Soviet scholars. See, for example, *Istoriia krest'ianstva*, 2:433; Nazarov, "K istorii nachal'nogo perioda," 184–200.

64. AAE 2:76, 89; RIB 13: col. 27; Hirschberg, *Dymitr Samozwaniec*, 87–88.

65. Massa, *Short History*, 73, 78; Belokurov, *Razriadnye zapisi*, 5; Skrynnikov, *Smuta*, 64; idem, *Rossiia v nachale XVII v.*, 168–69, 179–80; Perrie, *Pretenders*, 71.

66. Paerle, "Zapiski," 167–69; Frantzev, "Istoricheskoe povestvovanie," 18; Obolenskii, *Inostrannye sochineniia*, 4:11; Pierling, *Rome*, 59, 204–5; idem, *La Russie*, 3:156–57; Perrie, *Pretenders*, 69–70.

67. Popov, *Izbornik*, 228; Pirling, *Dmitrii Samozvanets*, 150; Novosel'skii, *Bor'ba*, 57–59; Skrynnikov, *Rossiia v nachale XVII v.*, 173.

68. RIB 1: col 393; 13: cols. 35–36; Massa, *Short History*, 85; Piasetskii, *Istoricheskie ocherki*, 22; Skrynnikov, *Rossiia v nachale XVII v.*, 175; *Istoriia krest'ianstva*, 2:433; Perrie, *Pretenders*, 71. Cf. Miklashevskii, *K istorii*, prilozhenie, 266; N. N. Ogloblin, "Eletskaia 'Iavochnaia kniga' 1615–16 gg.," ChOIDR 153 (1890), book 2, part 3:6.

69. SRIO 137:585; RIB 1: cols. 16–17, 39; Maciszewski, *Polska a Moskwa*, 71; Skrynnikov, *Sotsial'no-politicheskaia bor'ba*, 203. Massa's assertion (*Short History*, 85–86) that Dmitrii received "much aid from Poland" was incorrect; that is what Tsar Boris wanted his subjects to believe.

70. Paerle, "Zapiski," 166. Cf. Longworth, *Cossacks*, 77–78.

71. Skrynnikov, *Rossiia v nachale XVII v.*, 218, 220.

72. Bussow, *Disturbed State*, 41.

73. Massa, *Short History*, 86.

74. Bussow, *Disturbed State*, 41–42; Skrynnikov, *Rossiia v nachale XVII v.*, 175.

75. Purchas, *Hakluytus Posthumus*, 14:160; Massa, *Short History*, 88; Pierling, *Rome*, 205.

76. Skrynnikov, *Rossiia v nachale XVII v.*, 175–76; Perrie, *Pretenders*, 63–66, 71.

77. Pirling, *Dmitrii Samozvanets*, 168, 175.

78. Margeret, *Russian Empire*, 82; Ustrialov, *Skazaniia*, 1:333; SRIO 137:580; Pierling, *Rome*, 205.

79. RIB 13: cols. 48, 155–56, 797–98.

80. Purchas, *Hakluytus Posthumus*, 14:159–60.

81. *Boiarskie spiski*, 2:44, 86; *Razriadnye knigi 1598–1638*, 149, 173; Piasetskii, *Istoricheskie ocherki*, 15; Skrynnikov, *Rossiia v nachale XVII v.*, 153–55.

82. Massa, *Short History*, 86; Smirnov, *Vosstanie*, 144–45; Lantzeff and Pierce, *Eastward to Empire*, 110.

83. Margeret, *Russian Empire*, 62; Skrynnikov, *Rossiia v nachale XVII v.*, 164–65.

84. Bussow, *Disturbed State*, 41. Longworth (*Cossacks*, 77–78) plausibly suggested that Korela reached Kromy in February, 1605. On the other hand, Skrynnikov's assertion that Korela arrived there in late December or early January (*Rossiia v nachale XVII v.*, 164–65) is not acceptable.

85. Skrynnikov, *Rossiia v nachale XVII v.*, 164, 220. Bussow (*Disturbed State*, 41) grossly over-estimated the size of Korela's cossack detachment, putting it at four thousand to five thousand men. Massa (*Short History*, 87) also exaggerated it size, guessing that it contained two thousand cossack infantrymen.

86. Massa, *Short History*, 87. Cf. Le Vasseur, *Description*, 56.

87. Bussow, *Disturbed State*, 42–43. See also Razin, *Istoriia*, 3:78; Gordon, *Cossack Rebellions*, 80.

88. Margeret, *Russian Empire*, 28, 49; Longworth, *Cossacks*, 33; Le Vasseur, *Description*, 13.

89. Massa, *Short History*, 87.

90. Belokurov, *Razriadnye zapisi*, 199, 238; Pirling, *Dmitrii Samozvanets*, 203.

91. Skrynnikov, *Rossiia v nachale XVII v.*, 165, 169. Cf. PSRL 14:63.

92. Margeret, *Russian Empire*, 64; Bussow, *Disturbed State*, 42; Skrynnikov, *Rossiia v nachale XVII v.*, 169.

93. Massa, *Short History*, 86, 90. Cf. Hellie, *Enserfment*, 159, 168.

94. Purchas, *Hakluytus Posthumus*, 14:161. Massa's estimate (*Short History*, 89) of three hundred thousand men besieging Kromy is a wild exaggeration.

95. Belokurov, *Razriadnye zapisi*, 4.

96. Skrynnikov, *Rossiia v nachale XVII v.*, 170. There is no truth to the often-repeated chronicler's assertion (PSRL 14:63) that M. G. Saltykov's failure was due to his treachery and desire to help Dmitrii. See Margeret, *Russian Empire*, 158 n. 217.

97. RIB 13: col. 36; Skrynnikov, *Rossiia v nachale XVII v.*, 170. See also Keep, *Soldiers*, 75–76; Hellie, *Enserfment*, 156–57, 268.

98. Massa, *Short History*, 87.

99. Bussow, *Disturbed State*, 43. Cf. Belokurov, *Razriadnye zapisi*, 238; RIB 13: col. 393. Skrynnikov (*Rossiia v nachale XVII v.*, 172, 220) suggested that Bezzubtsev may have led eight hundred cossacks to relieve Kromy.

100. Bussow, *Disturbed State*, 43; Massa, *Short History*, 87; Skrynnikov, *Rossiia v nachale XVII v.*, 170–71.

101. Massa, *Short History*, 88–89; Stanislavskii, *Grazhdanskaia voina*, 21; Koretskii, "Novoe o krest'ianskom zakreposhchenii," 144; Hellie, *Enserfment*, 168.

102. Bussow, *Disturbed State*, 43; Skrynnikov, *Rossiia v nachale XVII v.*, 171. Cf. Hellie, *Enserfment*, 38, 46, 159, 163; Keep, *Soldiers*, 38; Smith, "Muscovite Logistics," 39 n. 41, 41.

103. Piasetskii, *Istoricheskie ocherki*, 23.

104. Massa, *Short History*, 88–89; Bussow, *Disturbed State*, 42–43; Skrynnikov, *Boris Godunov*, 149. See also Hellie, *Enserfment*, 32; Keep, *Soldiers*, 39–40.

105. PSRL 14:63; Nazarov, "K istorii nachal'nogo perioda," 199; *Istoriia krest'ianstva*, 2:432.

106. Massa, *Short History*, 89, 90, 98; Skrynnikov, *Rossiia v nachale XVII v.*, 171.

107. Bussow, *Disturbed State*, 43. This was, of course, a chronic problem in the Russian army even when conditions were far better than they were at Kromy. See Fletcher, *Russe Commonwealth*, 59–59v; Margeret, *Russian Empire*, 47; Hellie, *Enserfment*, 37. Cf. Krejchi, *Great Revolutions Compared*, 15–16.

108. Bussow, *Disturbed State*, 43; Massa, *Short History*, 87, 98; Skrynnikov, *Rossiia v nachale XVII v.*, 170–71; idem, *Boris Godunov*, 149.

109. Margeret, *Russian Empire*, 64; Bussow, *Disturbed State*, 43; Massa, *Short History*, 86.

110. Massa, *Short History*, 89–90, 98. See also Popov, *Izbornik*, 62; RIB 13: col. 36.

111. Massa, *Short History*, 88–89; Bussow, *Disturbed State*, 43.

112. Bussow, *Disturbed State*, 42–43. Massa (*Short History*, 85–86) erred in claiming that Dmitrii received much aid from Poland at this time, and Skrynnikov (*Rossiia v nachale XVII v.*, 220) erroneously claimed that Dmitrii had virtually no army once he sent cossacks to Kromy to reinforce Korela.

113. See RIB 1: col. 369; 13: cols. 571–72, 724; PSRL 14:61–62; 31:150; Belokurov, *Razriadnye zapisi*, 1; Purchas, *Hakluytus Posthumus*, 14:160; *Istoriia krest'ianstva*, 2:432; Pavlov, *Gosudarev dvor*, 79; Skrynnikov, *Rossiia v nachale XVII v.*, 165–69; idem, *Smuta*, 250.

114. Bussow, *Disturbed State*, 43.

115. Massa, *Short History*, 90.

116. Ibid., 90, 93.

117. Margeret, *Russian Empire*, 60–61; Massa, *Short History*, 55–56, 73; Skrynnikov, *Boris Godunov*, 149–51; idem, *Rossiia v nachale XVII v.*, 181.

118. Massa, *Short History*, 59, 91–92; Pavlov, *Gosudarev dvor*, 78; Skrynnikov, *Rossiia v nachale XVII v.*, 179–80.

119. Purchas, *Hakluytus Posthumus*, 14:160; Makarii, *Istoriia*, 10:89–90; Skrynnikov, *Boris Godunov*, 151.

120. Massa, *Short History*, 80, 86.

121. Purchas, *Hakluytus Posthumus*, 14:141–42; Massa, *Short History*, 86, 91; Popov, *Izbornik*, 234; Pavlov, *Gosudarev dvor*, 69.

122. Purchas, *Hakluytus Posthumus*, 14:142.

123. Massa, *Short History*, 91, 97. Cf. Skrynnikov, *Boris Godunov*, 152; idem, *Rossiia v nachale XVII v.*, 189.

NOTES TO CHAPTER 11

1. RIB 13: col. 39; Massa, *Short History*, 91, 93–94; Bussow, *Disturbed State*, 43; Purchas, *Hakluytus Posthumus*, 14:160; Perrie, "Popular Legends,"233.

2. Purchas, *Hakluytus Posthumus*, 14:147; Vernadsky, *Tsardom*, 1:228.

3. Margeret, *Russian Empire*, 64; Skrynnikov, *Boris Godunov*, 151; Perrie, "Popular Legends," 233. Cf. Purchas, *Hakluytus Posthumus*, 14:160.

4. SGGD 2:213–14; Massa, *Short History*, 106–7; Chistov, *Russkie legendy*, 46; Perrie, "Popular Legends," 233–36.

5. Belokurov, *Razriadnye zapisi*, 199; AAE 2:87; Skrynnikov, *Rossiia v nachale XVII v.*, 185. See also Timofeev, *Vremennik*, 85; Rowland, "Muscovite Political Attitudes," 207–8.

6. Massa, *Short History*, 94; Pavlov, *Gosudarev dvor*, 78–79; Platonov, *Boris Godunov*, 27, 189, 203–4; Perrie, *Pretenders*, 71; Skrynnikov, *Rossiia v nachale XVII v.*, 179–80, 184, 250–51.

7. Massa, *Short History,* 97.

8. Skrynnikov, *Rossiia v nachale* XVII *v.,* 186–87; idem, *Boris Godunov,* 152; Massa, *Short History,* 96–97.

9. SGGD 2:196–97; Pierling, *La Russie,* 3:164–65.

10. Smith, *Voiage,* I2–I2v; Perrie, *Pretenders,* 71–72.

11. Bussow, *Disturbed State,* 44–45; Skrynnikov, *Rossiia v nachale* XVII *v.,* 180, 250–51.

12. Pavlov, *Gosudarev dvor,* 78–79; Skrynnikov, *Sotsial'no-politicheskaia bor'ba,* 325.

13. Margeret, *Russian Empire,* 66; Massa, *Short History,* 96. Bussow (*Disturbed State,* 44) claimed that Mstislavskii was recalled to help the young tsar.

14. Massa, *Short History,* 97. Zolkiewski (*Expedition,* 43–44) incorrectly wrote that Shuiskii remained in the Kromy siege force and attempted to prevent the defection of the army.

15. Massa, *Short History,* 91, 97; Skrynnikov, *Boris Godunov,* 152–53.

16. Belokurov, *Razriadnye zapisi,* 200; Skrynnikov, *Rossiia v nachale* XVII *v.,* 189. Margeret (*Russian Empire,* 66) and Massa (*Short History,* 96–97) erred in referring to Basmanov as the commander-in-chief of Tsar Fedor Borisovich's army.

17. Margeret, *Russian Empire,* 66; Bussow, *Disturbed State,* 44.

18. RIB 13: col. 40; PSRL 34:206; Massa, *Short History,* 98; Popov, *Izbornik,* 328.

19. Bussow, *Disturbed State,* 44.

20. Belokurov, *Razriadnye zapisi,* 115–16, 200, 245–46; Bussow, *Disturbed State,* 42–43; Pavlov, *Gosudarev dvor,* 69; Skrynnikov, *Rossiia v nachale* XVII *v.,* 190.

21. Belokurov, *Razriadnye zapisi,* 200; Perrie, *Pretenders,* 72. The English translation of Skrynnikov's *Boris Godunov* (152) contains an error about the new arrangement of ranks which angered Basmanov. See also Eskin, "Smuta i mestnichestvo," 268.

22. Pavlov, *Gosudarev dvor,* 82 n. 85; Skrynnikov, *Rossiia v nachale* XVII *v.,* 193–94.

23. Zolkiewski, *Expedition,* 44; Skrynnikov, *Boris Godunov,* 36, 105; idem, *Rossiia v nachale* XVII *v.,* 190.

24. Belokurov, *Razriadnye zapisi,* 5, 203; Pavlov, *Gosudarev dvor,* 77.

25. Skrynnikov, *Rossiia v nachale* XVII *v.,* 191.

26. Bussow, *Disturbed State,* 77; Pavlov, *Gosudarev dvor,* 69; Likhachev, *Novoe rodoslovie kniazei Golitsynykh,* 14.

27. MERSH 3:156; *Russkii biograficheskii slovar'* [hereafter cited as RBS], 2:560–61.

28. PSRL 14:64; Massa, *Short History,* 98.

29. Margeret, *Russian Empire,* 66.

30. Koretskii, "Novoe o krest'ianskom zakreposhchenii," 145.

31. Belokurov, *Razriadnye zapisi,* 200–201; Skrynnikov, *Rossiia v nachale* XVII *v.,* 196–97, 250–51. See also Zagorin, *Rebels,* 1:40; 2:1–6; Bercé, *Revolt,* 127–34; Hagopian, *Phenomenon,* 17, 40; Jütte, *Poverty and Deviance,* 189.

32. Kleimola, "Holding on," 136–37.

33. Stanislavskii, *Grazhdanskaia voina,* 14–15; Skrynnikov, *Rossiia v nachale* XVII *v.,* 23, 109, 198.

34. Kleimola, "Holding on," 138, 140–41; idem, "Genealogy," 300–301; Skrynnikov, *Rossiia v nachale* XVII *v.,* 196.

35. See Hellie, *Enserfment,* 35; Keep, *Soldiers,* 19, 30, 73–74.

36. Skrynnikov, *Rossiia v nachale* XVII *v.,* 191–92. Cf. Skrynnikov, *Boris Godunov,* 116. See also Kleimola, "Genealogy," 289–91, 295–98.

37. Stanislavskii, *Grazhdanskaia voina,* 17–20; Skrynnikov, *Boris Godunov,* 152; *Istoriia krest'ianstva,* 2:426–27, 431; Keep, *Soldiers,* 62–63.

38. See Belokurov, *Razriadnye zapisi,* 203; *Boiarskie spiski,* 1:208; 2:4; Skrynnikov, *Rossiia v nachale* XVII *v.,* 192.

39. Belokurov, *Razriadnye zapisi,* 203; *Boiarskie spiski,* 1:162; 2:61, 88; *Razriadnaia kniga 1559–1605,* 349–50; Koretskii, Solov'eva, and Stanislavskii, "Dokumenty," 36.

40. Margeret, *Russian Empire,* 66; Belokurov, *Razriadnye zapisi,* 200; Petreius, *Reliatsiia,* 91; Skrynnikov, *Rossiia v nachale* XVII *v.,* 190–91, 200. False accusations against Saltykov may be found in RIB 13: col. 41; PSRL 14:64.

41. SRIO 137:521, 586.

42. RIB 13: col. 40; Popov, *Izbornik*, 328; Massa, *Short History*, 98; Bussow, *Disturbed State*, 43.

43. Belokurov, *Razriadnye zapisi*, 200–201; SRIO 137:437, 521; Skrynnikov, *Rossiia v nachale XVII v.*, 196, 250–51.

44. Margeret, *Russian Empire*, 46–47, 50; Skrynnikov, *Rossiia v nachale XVII v.*, 55–57, 249–50; idem, *Smuta*, 179, 182–83. See also Hellie, *Slavery*, 467–69, 471; Keep, *Soldiers*, 57–59.

45. SRIO, 137:437; Piasetskii, *Istoricheskie ocherki*, 23; Smirnov, *Vosstanie*, 120–21.

46. Massa, *Short History*, 93, 98; Skrynnikov, "Rebellion," 139.

47. See RIB 1: col. 393; 13: cols. 35–36; Massa, *Short History*, 85; *Boiarskie spiski*, 2:33–34, 51; Paerle, "Zapiski,"166; Bussow, *Disturbed State*, 41, 43, 44; Piasetskii, *Istoricheskie ocherki*, 22; Purchas, *Hakluytus Posthumus*, 14:160; Skrynnikov, *Rossiia v nachale XVII v.*, 175, 218, 220–21.

48. RIB 1: col. 390; Paerle, "Zapiski," 169; Ustrialov, *Skazaniia*, 2:169.

49. Massa, *Short History*, 86, 93; Bussow, *Disturbed State*, 42–43; Skrynnikov, *Rossiia v nachale XVII v.*, 195. Cf. Skrynnikov, *Boris Godunov*, 152.

50. RIB 1: col. 395; Purchas, *Hakluytus Posthumus*, 14:161; Pirling, *Dmitrii Samozvanets*, 195; Hirschberg, *Dymitr Samozwaniec*, 114; Skrynnikov, *Rossiia v nachale XVII v.*, 195–96.

51. Belokurov, *Razriadnye zapisi*, 29; Massa, *Short History*, 98–99; Petreius, *Reliatsiia*, 90–91; Skrynnikov, "Rebellion," 139–40.

52. Popov, *Izbornik*, 328; Belokurov, *Razriadnye zapisi*, 200–201; *Razriadnaia kniga 1550–1636*, 1:225.

53. Massa, *Short History*, 99.

54. *Boiarskie spiski*, 2:53; Skrynnikov, *Rossiia v nachale XVII v.*, 197.

55. *Boiarskie spiski*, 2:61, 88; Belokurov, *Razriadnye zapisi*, 203.

56. RIB 13: cols. 42, 576; *Boiarskie spiski*, 1:197.

57. PSRL 14:64.

58. Massa, *Short History*, 98–99; Skrynnikov, *Rossiia v nachale XVII v.*, 197–98.

59. Belokurov, *Razriadnye zapisi*, 200–201; RIB 13: col. 40; *Boiarskie spiski*, 2:27.

60. Belokurov, *Razriadnye zapisi*, 29; *Boiarskie spiski*, 2:69.

61. Massa, *Short History*, 100; RIB 13: col. 44; Skrynnikov, "Rebellion," 140.

62. Massa, *Short History*, 99.

63. Skrynnikov, *Rossiia v nachale XVII v.*, 198–99.

64. Petreius, *Reliatsiia*, 90–91; Massa, *Short History*, 100; Skrynnikov, "Rebellion," 139–40.

65. Skrynnikov, *Rossiia v nachale XVII v.*, 199; Paerle, "Zapiski," 171; Massa, *Short History*, 100.

66. Bussow, *Disturbed State*, 44; Massa, *Short History*, 100; Zhordaniia, *Ocherki*, 1:250–51.

67. Margeret, *Russian Empire*, 66; Petreius, *Reliatsiia*, 91; Massa, *Short History*, 99–100; RIB 13: col. 41.

68. PSRL 34:242; RIB 13: col. 576; Popov, *Izbornik*, 238; Massa, *Short History*, 100.

69. Skrynnikov, *Rossiia v nachale XVII v.*, 198, 199–200.

70. Bussow, *Disturbed State*, 44; Massa, *Short History*, 99–100; Purchas, *Hakluytus Posthumus*, 14:161.

71. Skrynnikov, *Rossiia v nachale XVII v.*, 194, 198; idem, "Rebellion," 138–39.

72. Skrynnikov, *Rossiia v nachale XVII v.*, 200–201, 203.

73. RIB 13: cols. 40–41; PSRL 14:64; *Boiarskie spiski*, 2:27; Belokurov, *Razriadnye zapisi*, 200–201; Skrynnikov, *Boris Godunov*, 152.

74. Pavlov, *Gosudarev dvor*, 78–79; Skrynnikov, *Rossiia v nachale XVII v.*, 200–201.

75. Tilly, *European Revolutions*, 14.

76. Bussow, *Disturbed State*, 44.

77. There is no evidence to support Skrynnikov's assertion that Basmanov and the Golitsyns, once they gained control of the tsar's army, were reluctant to bow to Dmitrii (*Rossiia v nachale XVII v.*, 202).

78. SGGD 2:197.

79. *Razriadnaia kniga 1550–1636*, 1:225; SGGD 2:196–98; SRIO 137:437; Santich, *Missio*, 127 n. 34.

80. Margeret, *Russian Empire,* 66–67; Bussow, *Disturbed State,* 44; Hirschberg, *Dymitr Samozwaniec,* 115. One contemporary estimated the total size of Dmitrii's army at this point to be twelve thousand men (RIB 1: col. 394), which is fairly accurate. Skrynnikov (*Rossiia v nachale XVII v.,* 203) doubted that figure, but he consistently underestimated Dmitrii's military strength throughout the campaign. By the spring of 1605, Dmitrii had the support of more than a third of the country and had more than half of all the Don cossacks in his army.

81. RIB 1: col. 396.

82. Margeret, *Russian Empire,* 67; Massa, *Short History,* 101.

83. Margeret, *Russian Empire,* 66; PSRL 34:243; Pirling, *Dmitrii Samozvanets,* 207.

84. *Razriadnaia kniga 1559–1605,* 342; Belokurov, *Razriadnye zapisi,* 133, 199, 203; *Razriadnaia kniga 1550–1636,* 1:226; Koretskii, "Novoe o krest'ianskom zakreposhchenii," 145.

85. Hirschberg, *Dymitr Samozwaniec,* 114.

86. Frantzev, "Istoricheskoe povestvovanie," 24; Aleksandrenko, "Materialy," 398–99, 533; Perrie, *Pretenders,* 72–73.

87. PSRL 14:64.

88. Belokurov, *Razriadnye zapisi,* 238–39.

89. SRIO 137:587; Petreius, *Reliatsiia,* 91. See also Margeret, *Russian Empire,* 66; Belokurov, *Razriadnye zapisi,* 200.

90. Hirschberg, *Dymitr Samozwaniec,* 166; Skrynnikov, *Rossiia v nachale XVII v.,* 204.

91. PSRL 14:64; Skrynnikov, *Rossiia v nachale XVII v.,* 204.

92. RIB 1: cols. 396–97; Solov'ev, *Istoriia,* 4:424; Skrynnikov, *Rossiia v nachale XVII v.,* 202.

93. Margeret, *Russian Empire,* 67; Solov'ev, *Istoriia,* 4:424.

94. Massa, *Short History,* 101–2; Belokurov, *Razriadnye zapisi,* 133; RIB 1: col. 396.

95. Popov, *Izbornik,* 228; Pirling, *Dmitrii Samozvanets,* 189–90; Novosel'skii, *Bor'ba,* 57–59.

96. See AAE 2:90.

97. Massa, *Short History,* 102.

98. Belokurov, *Razriadnye zapisi,* 202; Massa, *Short History,* 107; Smirnov, *Vosstanie,* 217–18; Skrynnikov, *Rossiia v nachale XVII v.,* 205, 221–22. There is considerable confusion on this point due to Massa's error (*Short History,* 94) about the surrender of Astrakhan in April and to Dmitrii's disinformation about the surrender of that town in May. See AAE 2:90; RIB 13: cols. 44–45; Skrynnikov, *Rossiia v nachale XVII v.,* 205.

99. Massa, *Short History,* 107; Belokurov, *Snosheniia,* 513; idem, *Razriadnye zapisi,* 202; Smirnov, *Vosstanie,* 218; Skrynnikov, *Time of Troubles,* 15; *Kratkaia istoriia Astrakhanskoi Eparkhi,* 40.

100. Margeret, *Russian Empire,* 67; Belokurov, *Razriadnye zapisi,* 72, 201; RIB 13: col. 729; Bussow, *Disturbed State,* 44–45. Cf. Smirnov, *Vosstanie,* 218.

101. Massa, *Short History,* 100.

102. Smith, *Voiage,* L2; Hirschberg, *Dymitr Samozwaniec,* 166; Skrynnikov, *Rossiia v nachale XVII v.,* 187, 204, 224. See also Massa, *Short History,* 96; Skrynnikov, *Boris Godunov,* 153; Perrie, *Pretenders,* 77.

103. Bussow, *Disturbed State,* 44–45.

104. Massa, *Short History,* 101; Skrynnikov, *Boris Godunov,* 152.

105. Massa, *Short History,* 102.

106. Hirschberg, *Dymitr Samozwaniec,* 115.

107. Massa, *Short History,* 103; Skrynnikov, "Rebellion," 142.

108. Bussow, *Disturbed State,* 45; Massa, *Short History,* 102–3.

109. Margeret, *Russian Empire,* 67; Skrynnikov, "Rebellion," 142–43. See also Massa, *Short History,* 162.

110. Bussow, *Disturbed State,* 45; PSRL 34:206, 242; Skrynnikov, "Rebellion," 143–44.

111. PSRL. 14:64–65.

112. Popov, *Izbornik,* 328; PSRL 14:65; 34:206, 242; Massa, *Short History,* 103–4; Purchas, *Hakluytus Posthumus,* 14:148; Margeret, *Russian Empire,* 67; Bussow, *Disturbed State,* 45.

113. Massa, *Short History,* 104; Skrynnikov, *Boris Godunov,* 153.

114. Popov, *Izbornik,* 328.

115. AAE 2:89–91; Belokurov, *Razriadnye zapisi*, 5, 202. Cf. Massa, *Short History*, 104; Purchas, *Hakluytus Posthumus*, 14:148–49.

116. Bussow, *Disturbed State*, 45–46.

117. See *Ocherki istorii SSSR*, 494–95; Smirnov, *Vosstanie*, 85–86; Makovskii, *Pervaia krest'ianskaia voina*, 291; Bakhrushin, *Nauchnye trudy*, 1:219–20; Koretskii, "Golod," 237; Dunning, "Skrynnikov," 75.

118. PSRL 34:206; Skrynnikov, *Sotsial'no-politicheskaia bor'ba*, 275; idem, *Rossiia v nachale XVII v.*, 251.

119. PSRL 14:65; 34:206; Skrynnikov, "Rebellion," 149.

120. Massa, *Short History*, 103–4; Skrynnikov, *Rossiia v nachale XVII v.*, 224.

121. Margeret, *Russian Empire*, 67. Cf. Smith, *Voiage*, K3; PSRL 14:65.

122. Bussow, *Disturbed State*, 46; Aleksandrenko, "Materialy," 533. Skrynnikov speculated that Korela's cossacks opened the prisons ("Rebellion," 148–49).

123. Smith, *Voiage*, L; Purchas, *Hakluytus Posthumus*, 14:150.

124. Petreius, *Reliatsiia*, 91–92. Cf. Skrynnikov, *Smuta*, 19.

125. *Razriadnaia kniga 1550–1636*, 1:227; Bussow, *Disturbed State*, 46–47; Skrynnikov, *Boris Godunov*, 153. Cf. Belokurov, *Razriadnye zapisi*, 5. Skrynnikov with reason adopted the view that Belskii's speech actually came several days later ("Rebellion," 146–47).

126. Bussow, *Disturbed State*, 46; Massa, *Short History*, 105.

127. PSRL 14:65; 34:206; Bussow, *Disturbed State*, 46; Massa, *Short History*, 105; Margeret, *Russian Empire*, 67; *Razriadnaia kniga 1550–1636*, 1:227.

128. Skrynnikov, *Boris Godunov*, 153. Skrynnikov incorrectly claimed that Tsar Fedor was not arrested on that day ("Rebellion," 150–51).

129. Belokurov, *Razriadnye zapisi*, 201; Smith, *Voiage*, L1–L2; Massa, *Short History*, 104; Bussow, *Disturbed State*, 46–47; Purchas, *Hakluytus Posthumus*, 14:149–50; Kopanev, "Pinezhskii letopisets," 82.

130. Popov, *Izbornik*, 329; Belokurov, *Razriadnye zapisi*, 201; Bussow, *Disturbed State*, 46; Massa, *Short History*, 105; PSRL 14:65; Koretskii, Solov'eva, and Stanislavskii, "Dokumenty," 36. Curiously, Skrynnikov had difficulty understanding why the Saburov and Veliaminov clans became targets during the Moscow uprising ("Rebellion," 150; *Rossiia v nachale XVII v.*, 213). In fact, they were close relatives of the Godunov clan. See Margeret, *Russian Empire*, 67.

131. Bussow, *Disturbed State*, 47; Smith, *Voiage*, L1v–L2; Purchas, *Hakluytus Posthumus*, 14:150; Perrie, "Popular Legends," 234; idem, *Pretenders*, 76; Skrynnikov, "Rebellion," 150–51.

132. Massa, *Short History*, 105; Smith, *Voiage*, L2; Skrynnikov, *Sotsial'no-politicheskaia bor'ba*, 282.

133. Massa, *Short History*, 103. Skrynnikov unconvincingly asserted that the reason no one was purposely killed or executed on the day of the uprising was because of a widespread popular view that the Godunovs had not been cruel oppressors ("Rebellion," 151–52; *Rossiia v nachale XVII v.*, 213–14).

134. Massa, *Short History*, 105; Skrynnikov, "Rebellion," 152.

135. Smith, *Voiage*, L2–L2v; Purchas, *Hakluytus Posthumus*, 14:151; Popov, *Izbornik*, 328. Skrynnikov (*Rossiia v nachale XVII v.*, 223–24) incorrectly wrote that the boyars declared for Dmitrii two days later.

136. Skrynnikov, *Samozvantsy*, 211–12; idem, *Smuta*, 12, 18–19.

137. Bussow, *Disturbed State*, 47; Skrynnikov, *Boris Godunov*, 153.

138. Massa, *Short History*, 102, 106; Skrynnikov, *Rossiia v nachale XVII v.*, 205, 224.

139. PSRL 14:65; Skrynnikov, *Rossiia v nachale XVII v.*, 218–20.

140. SGGD 2:191, 200, 202; Massa, *Short History*, 106.

141. Belokurov, *Razriadnye zapisi*, 6; Skrynnikov, *Sotsial'no-politicheskaia bor'ba*, 314.

142. *Razriadnaia kniga 1550–1636*, 1:227–28; Belokurov, *Razriadnye zapisi*, 203–4; PSRL 14:65; Skrynnikov, *Smuta*, 157; MERSH 54:45. Cf. Margeret, *Russian Empire*, 67.

143. Belokurov, *Razriadnye zapisi*, 201; Koretskii, Solov'eva, and Stanislavskii, "Dokumenty," 36; Massa, *Short History*, 108; PSRL 14:66.

144. Margeret, *Russian Empire*, 67; Massa, *Short History*, 106.

145. Belokurov, *Razriadnye zapisi*, 202–3; *Razriadnaia kniga 1550–1636*, 1:187, 226; Hirschberg, *Dymitr Samozwaniec*, 115.

146. Popov, *Izbornik,* 329; RIB 1: col. 397; Tikhomirov, *Klassovaia bor'ba,* 208.

147. Margeret, *Russian Empire,* 67; RIB 13: col. 731; *Letopis' o mnogikh miatezhakh,* 92; PSRL 14:65; Belokurov, *Razriadnye zapisi,* 6, 203; Nazarov "Novyi letopisets," 304.

148. Margeret, *Russian Empire,* 67; Smith, *Voiage,* L2v; Petreius, *Reliatsiia,* 92.

149. PSRL 14:66; Platonov, *Time of Troubles,* 78.

150. Massa, *Short History,* 108–9; Bussow, *Disturbed State,* 47–48; PSRL 14:65; Belokurov, *Razriadnye zapisi,* 6, 203; RIB 13: cols. 534–35. Cf. Purchas, *Hakluytus Posthumus,* 14:151, 157.

151. PSRL 34:242; Dmitrievskii, *Arkhiepiskop Arsenii,* 100.

152. Pirling, *Dmitrii Samozvanets,* 210 n. 1. See also Makarii, *Istoriia,* 10:89–92.

153. Purchas, *Hakluytus Posthumus,* 14:160; Pierling, *Rome,* 205; Koretskii, "Novoe o krest'ian-skom zakreposhchenii," 145–46.

154. AAE 2:92, SGGD 2:200; Santich, *Missio,* 130; Pierling, *La Russie,* 3:178. Some scholars doubted that Patriarch Iov ever acknowledged Dmitrii as tsar, claiming that Dmitrii's boast about Iov's contrition was just a ploy to speed up the transfer of power. See Skrynnikov, *Rossiia v nachale XVII v.,* 229–31; Perrie, *Pretenders,* 77–78.

155. Koretskii, "Golod," 236, 239.

156. AAE 2:154; PSRL 14:65; RIB 13: cols. 732, 935–36, 1293; Massa, *Short History,* 112; Markarii, *Istoriia,* 10:91–94; Platonov, *Drevnerusskie skazaniia,* 282. Koretskii erred in calling Iov a victim of an "anti-feudal" movement of the lower classes ("Golod," 237, 239, 256). Skrynnikov was mistaken about Dmitrii needing Iov out of the way because the patriarch would recognize him as the impostor Otrepev (*Boris Godunov,* 154).

157. Bussow, *Disturbed State,* 48.

158. Massa, *Short History,* 107–8; Purchas, *Hakluytus Posthumus,* 14:161.

159. Bussow, *Disturbed State,* 48–49, 204 n. 1; PSRL 14:64, 66; Skrynnikov, *Rossiia v nachale XVII v.,* 231–32.

160. Bussow, *Disturbed State,* 49; Zhordaniia, *Ocherki,* 1:250–51; Margeret, *Russian Empire,* xviii; Barbour, *Dimitry,* 137–38.

161. PSRL 14:67; Popov, *Izbornik,* 329; Aleksandrenko, "Materialy," 267; Massa, *Short History,* 110, 112–13; RIB 13: cols. 578, 652; Perrie, *Pretenders,* 81.

162. Skrynnikov, *Rossiia v nachale XVII v.,* 232–33.

163. Bussow, *Disturbed State,* 49–50; Massa, *Short History,* 109–10; Santich, *Missio,* 133–34; Hirschberg, *Dymitr Samozwaniec,* 129.

164. Massa, *Short History,* 110; Purchas, *Hakluytus Posthumus,* 14:161. There is no truth to Massa's assertion that Dmitrii was aware of certain monks' "inquisitive looks" that prompted him to have them secretly put to death the next day.

165. AAE 2:383–85; PSRL 14:66; RIB 13: col. 733; Aleksandrenko, "Materialy," 535; Purchas, *Hakluytus Posthumus,* 14:161–62; Dmitrievskii, *Arkhiepiskop Arsenii,* 100–101; Perrie, *Pretenders,* 79.

166. Massa, *Short History,* 110.

167. Bussow, *Disturbed State,* 50–51.

NOTES TO CHAPTER 12

1. Skrynnikov, *Smuta,* 14; Perrie, *Pretenders,* 86.

2. See, for example, SGGD 2:296–324; Massa, *Short History,* 142–43; Purchas, *Hakluytus Posthumus,* 14:186–91; de Thou, *Histoire,* 14:498–502; Howe, *False Dmitri,* 221–39; Gnevushev, *Akty,* 1–3; Skrynnikov, *Time of Troubles,* 46; Perrie, *Pretenders,* 99–103.

3. Palitsyn, *Skazanie,* 110–15; Brody, *Demetrius Legend,* 42–43, 46.

4. Skrynnikov, *Samozvantsy.*

5. Perrie, *Pretenders,* 56, 103–4. Skrynnikov correctly regarded the accusation of sorcery against Dmitrii as utterly baseless propaganda (*Rossiia v nachale XVII v.,* 83, 91–92; *Smuta,* 83–84, 88, 91–92).

6. Massa, *Short History,* 119, 143, 148; RIB 13: col. 580; de Thou, *Histoire,* 14:501; Zolkiewski, *Expedition,* 45; Palitsyn, *Skazanie,* 113.

7. Ustrialov, *Skazaniia,* 2:196, 238; RIB 13: col. 827; Palitsyn, *Skazanie,* 110, 264; Uspenskij, "Tsar and Pretender," 273–74; Perrie, *Pretenders,* 56, 99–104.

8. Massa, *Short History,* 115; Palitsyn, *Skazanie,* 112; Howe, *False Dmitri,* 56–57, 201; de Thou, *Histoire,* 14:501; Skrynnikov, *Smuta,* 22.

9. Massa, *Short History,* 113, 114, 148; RIB 13: cols. 1291–93; Bussow, *Disturbed State,* 54–55.

10. RIB 13: col. 165; Massa, *Short History,* 142–43, 147.

11. Timofeev, *Vremennik,* 83, 84, 88.

12. Mousnier, *Assassination,* chapter 5, especially pages 99, 105; Ford, *Political Murder,* 151.

13. Kulakova, "Vosstanie," 40–41; Perrie, *Pretenders,* 103.

14. Platonov, *Time of Troubles,* 79–82; idem, *Moscow and the West,* 40–42; Skrynnikov, *Time of Troubles,* 28–32, 38–43.

15. Pokrovsky, *Brief History,* 1:72–75; Koretskii, *Formirovanie,* 249–57, 365.

16. Skrynnikov, *Sotsial'no-politicheskaia bor'ba,* 325–26; idem, *Boris Godunov,* 147–49.

17. See *Bol'shaia Sovetskaia Entsiklopediia,* 3d ed., s.v. "Krest'ianskaia voina nachala 17v."; Koretskii, *Formirovanie,* 253–57.

18. Skrynnikov, *Rossiia v nachale XVII v.,* 232–33. Cf. Kulakova, "Vosstanie," 35. Examples of these charges leveled against Tsar Dmitrii may be found in PSRL 14:67; Popov, *Izbornik,* 329; Palitsyn, *Skazanie,* 111–12; Massa, *Short History,* 110, 112–14; RIB 13: cols. 578, 652; Aleksandrenko, "Materialy," 267. Perrie, unfortunately, credited those sources (*Pretenders,* 81). In his earlier writings on the subject, so did Skrynnikov (*Time of Troubles,* 5–7).

19. Bussow, *Disturbed State,* 51.

20. Massa, *Short History,* 135, 138; Palitsyn, *Skazanie,* 115; RIB 13: col. 367; Nemoevskii, "Zapiski," 80, 119; Chistov, *Russkie legendy,* 51; Brody, *Demetrius Legend,* 36; Treadgold, *West,* 1:48; Wada, "Inner World," 68; Abramovich, *Kniaz'ia Shuiskie,* 129.

21. Margeret, *Russian Empire,* 69, 75, 80, 89–91; de Thou, *Histoire,* 14:502; Purchas, *Hakluytus Posthumus,* 14:149; Bussow, *Disturbed State,* 55; Massa, *Short History,* 116, 119, 126, 143; Santich, *Missio,* 119 n. 9, 128–29; Crummey, *Formation,* 217–18; Vernadsky, *Tsardom,* 1:226–27, 229; Solov'ev, *Istoriia,* 4:403; Perrie, *Pretenders,* 87.

22. Hellie, *Enserfment,* 49.

23. Bussow, *Disturbed State,* 55; Margeret, *Russian Empire,* 75, 89; Massa, *Short History,* 116, 119, 126, 143.

24. Margeret, *Russian Empire,* 70, 83, 85; Massa, *Short History,* 116; Bussow, *Disturbed State,* 51; Purchas, *Hakluytus Posthumus,* 14:158; RIB 13: cols. 620–21; Zolkiewski, *Expedition,* 43; SGGD 2:169, 229; Tikhomirov, "Samozvanshchina," 119.

25. Bussow, *Disturbed State,* 51; Margeret, *Russian Empire,* 70.

26. SGGD 2:260; Margeret, *Russian Empire,* 69; Skrynnikov, *Smuta,* 13–14; Perrie, *Pretenders,* 87.

27. Popov, *Izbornik,* 329; Miller, *Istoriia,* 2:193–94; Dmytryshyn et al., *Russia's Conquest,* 51–54; Skrynnikov, *Smuta,* 18. Cf. Nazarov, "Zhalovannaia gramota," 354–68.

28. Palitsyn, *Skazanie,* 115; Wada, "Inner World," 68.

29. Bussow, *Disturbed State,* 52; Skrynnikov, *Smuta,* 14.

30. London: Public Record Office: State Papers Foreign [hereafter cited as S.P.], 91/1, f. 215; Smirnov, *Vosstanie,* 90–91; *Istoriia krest'ianstva,* 2:433; Skrynnikov, *Boris Godunov,* 120.

31. Rossiiskii gosudarstvennyi arkhiv drevnikh aktov [hereafter cited as RGADA], fond 214 (Sibirskii prikaz), kniga 14, list 493; Solov'ev, *Istoriia,* 4:431–32; Skrynnikov, *Smuta,* 17–18.

32. Massa, *Short History,* 116; Skrynnikov, *Samozvantsy,* 160–61; Perrie, *Pretenders,* 89–90.

33. Margeret, *Russian Empire,* 87; Pierling, *Rome,* 77; idem, *Dimitri et les Jésuites,* 4; Treadgold, *West,* 1:48; Barezi, *Discours merveilleux,* 37.

34. Aleksandrenko, "Materialy," 419; Skrynnikov, *Smuta,* 19.

35. RIB 13: cols. 620–21; Nemoevskii, "Zapiski," 65; Palitsyn, *Skazanie,* 114; Howe, *False Dmitri,* 34; Massa, *Short History,* 117, 123, 142; *Reporte,* F4; *La légende,* 8; Margeret, *Russian Empire,* xviii; Hellie, *Enserfment,* 48–49, 167–68; Skrynnikov, *Time of Troubles,* 10, 26–28; idem, *Smuta,* 14–15, 54, 250.

36. Solov'ev, *Istoriia*, 4:403; Ikonnikov, *Neskol'ko zametok*, 60–61; Barbour, *Dimitry*, 160.

37. Platonov, *Time of Troubles*, 79.

38. Skrynnikov, *Samozvantsy*, 157–62, 168–69.

39. Perrie, *Pretenders*, 87.

40. Bussow, *Disturbed State*, 52; Brody, *Demetrius Legend*, 35; Barbour, *Dimitry*, 142, 158–62; Crummey, *Formation*, 219.

41. Bussow, *Disturbed State*, 32; Platonov, *Moscow and the West*, 36; Perrie, *Pretenders*, 86–87.

42. Bussow, *Disturbed State*, 51–52; Skrynnikov, *Smuta*, 20.

43. See, for example, SRIO 137:313; Massa, *Short History*, 59, 66; Margeret, *Russian Empire*, 70; Platonov, *Time of Troubles*, 60–62; idem, *Moscow and the West*, 61–63; Skrynnikov, *Time of Troubles*, 44–45; MERSH 49:108; Treadgold, *West*, 1:49–50; Smirnov, *Vosstanie*, 89–90, 102–3; Rowland, "Muscovite Political Attitudes," 97, 104.

44. Margeret, *Russian Empire*, 69–70.

45. Massa, *Short History*, 110–11, 114; Margeret, *Russian Empire*, 77; Skrynnikov, *Time of Troubles*, 28; idem, *Rossiia v nachale XVII v.*, 101; Treadgold, *West*, 1:49.

46. Margeret, *Russian Empire*, 86; Platonov, *Time of Troubles*, 79.

47. Bussow, *Disturbed State*, 52, 61–62; Crummey, *Formation*, 219.

48. Margeret, *Russian Empire*, 86–87; Bussow, *Disturbed State*, 52.

49. Bussow, *Disturbed State*, 51–52; RIB 13: col. 36.

50. Bussow, *Disturbed State*, 52; Skrynnikov, *Time of Troubles*, 31; idem, *Smuta*, 20; Perrie, *Pretenders*, 86.

51. Palitsyn, *Skazanie*, 112–13; Massa, *Short History*, 119, 124; *Zapiski Zholkevskago*, col. 179; Pirling, *Dmitrii Samozvanets*, 333–34; Platonov, *Moscow and the West*, 35–37; Kulakova, "Vosstanie," 38–39; Crummey, *Formation*, 219; Perrie, *Pretenders*, 87, 101–2.

52. Kulakova, "Vosstanie," 36.

53. Palitsyn, *Skazanie*, 112–14; Skrynnikov, *Time of Troubles*, 28; Lotman and Uspenskij, "Role," 10–11.

54. Cracraft, "Opposition," 22, 30–33.

55. Ibid., 22–30.

56. Skrynnikov, *Rossiia v nachale XVII v.*, 233. Cf. Cracraft, "Opposition," 32.

57. Skrynnikov, *Time of Troubles*, 1, 5.

58. RIB 13: cols. 544–45, 622, 710; Skrynnikov, *Time of Troubles*, 54, 258–59.

59. Nemoevskii, "Zapiski," 115; Santich, *Missio*, 135; Skrynnikov, *Time of Troubles*, 5–6.

60. Massa, *Short History*, 113–14; RIB 1: col. 109; 13: col. 734; Aleksandrenko, "Materialy," 540. Conrad Bussow's chronologically and factually confused version of the plot inaccurately declared that many priests and streltsy were involved and that all of the conspirators, including Vasilii Shuiskii, were subsequently tortured (*Disturbed State*, 55).

61. Margeret, *Russian Empire*, 68.

62. Kliuchevskii, *Sochineniia*, 8:112; Solov'ev, *Istoriia*, 4:428; Platonov, *Ocherki*, 272–74; idem, *Stat'i*, 299–300; Cherepnin, *Zemskie sobory*, 150.

63. Skrynnikov, *Smuta*, 12; idem, *Sotsial'no-politicheskaia bor'ba*, 308–9; idem, *Time of Troubles*, 1.

64. Santich, *Missio*, 135.

65. Nemoevskii, "Zapiski," 114; Santich, *Missio*, 135; Skrynnikov, *Time of Troubles*, 5–6; Brody, *Demetrius Legend*, 41. Cf. Skrynnikov, *Boris Godunov*, 34; idem, *Rossiia v nachale XVII v.*, 30–31.

66. Santich, *Missio*, 135.

67. Skrynnikov, *Time of Troubles*, 6.

68. Margeret, *Russian Empire*, 68–69; Bussow, *Disturbed State*, 54; RIB 1: cols. 398–99; 13: cols. 52, 734–35; Popov, *Izbornik*, 235, 240. The exact dates of the trial and planned execution are uncertain but were sometime in June or July, 1605. Massa (*Short History*, 113–14) and the "New Chronicle" (PSRL 14:67) erred in placing these events in August.

69. See Margeret, *Russian Empire*, 68–69, 163 n. 240; Massa, *Short History*, 114; Skrynnikov, *Smuta*, 13, 22. Cf. RIB 13: col. 1279.

70. PSRL 14:67; Palitsyn, *Skazanie*, 111; Aleksandrenko, "Materialy," 253. Skrynnikov erred

in crediting the accusation that Dmitrii ordered the secret murder of monks involved in the plot. See Skrynnikov, *Time of Troubles*, 7; *Rukopisnye nasledie Drevnei Rusi*, 83.

71. Skrynnikov, *Time of Troubles*, 6–7.

72. *Razriadnaia kniga 1550–1636*, 1:226; Belokurov, *Razriadnye zapisi*, 5, 203; Skrynnikov, *Rossiia v nachale XVII v.*, 191–92, 203.

73. Skrynnikov, *Time of Troubles*, 6.

74. Ibid., 7.

75. On the feud between Belskii and Basmanov, see Skrynnikov, *Rossiia v nachale XVII v.*, 193. Mestnichestvo lawsuits actually declined during Tsar Dmitrii's reign; see Eskin, "Smuta i mestnichestvo," 268.

76. Bussow, *Disturbed State*, 54.

77. Skrynnikov, *Time of Troubles*, 5, 7–8, 14; idem, *Smuta*, 12–13, 20–22.

78. Keenan, "Muscovite Political Folkways," 142–43, 146–47.

79. AAE 2:91; Skrynnikov, *Time of Troubles*, 4–5.

80. SGGD 2:260; Palitsyn, *Skazanie*, 111; Skrynnikov, *Time of Troubles*, 10.

81. Belokurov, *Razriadnye zapisi*, 6, 7, 204; Smirnov, *Vosstanie*, 94, 98–99. The best example of this was the Suzdal prince Petr I. Buinosov-Rostovskii, a Godunov supporter and enemy of the Romanovs. Under Tsar Boris he held the prestigious post of governor of Novgorod. Tsar Dmitrii shipped him off to become voevoda of remote Belgorod—a significant reduction in status. See Pavlov, *Gosudarev dvor*, 56, 65, 71, 154; Skrynnikov, *Boris Godunov*, 94, 105, 109; Sukhotin, *Chetvertchiki*, 41; Bussow, *Disturbed State*, 199 n. 84; SRIO 142:865. There is no truth to Massa's assertion (*Short History*, 112–13) that these lords were "banished" because they knew the tsar was an impostor.

82. AAE 2:92, 94; SGGD 2:200, 202–3; Margeret, *Russian Empire*, 68; Palitsyn, *Skazanie*, 111; Massa, *Short History*, 111; Golubtsov, "Izmena Nagikh," 62; Skrynnikov, *Sotsial'no-politicheskaia bor'ba*, 314; Ul'ianovskii, "Pravoslavnaia tserkov'," 39–40, 59–60.

83. MERSH 4:1–2; Platonov, *Time of Troubles*, 80.

84. Skrynnikov, *Time of Troubles*, 4–5; idem, *Smuta*, 46, 53. Skrynnikov mistakenly concluded that, out of fear, Dmitrii was slow to return the Romanovs to court.

85. RIB 35: cols. 69–70; Skrynnikov, *Smuta*, 47; Perrie, *Pretenders*, 83.

86. Skrynnikov, *Time of Troubles*, 44–45.

87. Skrynnikov, *Smuta*, 53; idem, *Time of Troubles*, 5.

88. Perrie, *Pretenders*, 83; MERSH 49:108.

89. Massa, *Short History*, 118; Margeret, *Russian Empire*, 69.

90. *Drevniaia Rossiiskaia Vivliofika*, 20:76; Massa, *Short History*, 78, 119; *Razriadnaia kniga 1550–1636*, 1:226; Belokurov, *Razriadnye zapisi*, 5, 30, 203; Skrynnikov, *Rossiia v nachale XVII v.*, 191–92, 203; idem, *Smuta*, 78–79; idem, *Time of Troubles*, 5. Smirnov (*Vosstanie*, 92–93, 99) was wrong about Fedor Sheremetev's loyalties.

91. Bussow, *Disturbed State*, 200 n. 89.

92. Massa, *Short History*, 91, 97; Skrynnikov, *Boris Godunov*, 152–53.

93. Massa, *Short History*, 118; Margeret, *Russian Empire*, 69; Barsukov, *Rod Sheremetevykh*, 2:114–15; Santich, *Missio*, 135; Skrynnikov, *Time of Troubles*, 15; idem, *Smuta*, 53.

94. MERSH 23:160; Skrynnikov, *Time of Troubles*, 42; idem, *Smuta*, 50; Margeret, *Russian Empire*, 53, 147 n. 172.

95. Skrynnikov, *Samozvantsy*, 154–74; idem, *Smuta*, 12, 21–22, 27–28.

96. Keenan, "Muscovite Political Folkways," 142–43, 146.

97. Skrynnikov, *Time of Troubles*, 7–8, 11–12; idem, *Smuta*, 12.

98. Skrynnikov, *Time of Troubles*, 24; Stanislavskii, *Grazhdanskaia voina*, 21.

99. Skrynnikov, *Time of Troubles*, 14–15.

100. Ibid., 7, 15; idem, *Smuta*, 13, 20, 22.

101. Massa, *Short History*, 114.

102. Platonov, *Time of Troubles*, 80; Skrynnikov, *Time of Troubles*, 15.

103. Crummey, *Formation*, 219.

104. Skrynnikov, *Boris Godunov*, 110.

105. Perrie, *Pretenders*, 86–87.

106. Bussow, *Disturbed State*, 51–52; Margeret, *Russian Empire*, 70; Massa, *Short History*, 116; Skrynnikov, *Time of Troubles*, 30.

107. Platonov, *Boris Godunov*, 203–4.

108. Timofeev, *Vremennik*, 75, 104, 111–12; Palitsyn, *Skazanie*, 269; Platonov, *Time of Troubles*, 79–80; Rowland, "Problem," 267–68; idem, "Limits," 139–40; Skrynnikov, *Smuta*, 52–53.

109. Skrynnikov, *Time of Troubles*, 5; idem, *Smuta*, 13, 63.

110. Skrynnikov, *Time of Troubles*, 16.

111. Bussow, *Disturbed State*, 53.

112. Skrynnikov, *Time of Troubles*, 6.

113. Keenan, "Afterword," 205.

114. See, for example, AAE 2:224; Massa, *Short History*, 110; Platonov, *Drevnerusskie skazaniia*, 72 n. 1, 444 n. 4; Vasenko, "Zametki," 265; Treadgold, *West*, 1:49; Skrynnikov, *Time of Troubles*, 28–29, 44; idem, *Smuta*, 27; Ul'ianovskii, "Pravoslavnaia tserkov'," 29–62.

115. Massa, *Short History*, 148; *La légende*, 28–29; *Reporte*, F13; Skrynnikov, *Time of Troubles*, 3–4.

116. Palitsyn, *Skazanie*, 112; Massa, *Short History*, 112–14.

117. Dmitrievskii, *Arkhiepiskop Arsenii*, 102.

118. Skrynnikov, *Time of Troubles*, 4. Cf. Massa, *Short History*, 167; Bussow, *Moskovskaia khronika*, 357 n.71.

119. RIB 13: col. 652; Skrynnikov, *Rossiia v nachale XVII v.*, 232.

120. Treadgold, *West*, 1:48–49; Pierling, *Rome*, 150; Pirling, "Nazvannyi Dimitrii i pol'skie ariane," 1–10; *Zapiski Zholkevskago*, cols. 171–72; Platonov, *Time of Troubles*, 81; idem, *Moscow and the West*, 35–36.

121. Palitsyn, *Skazanie*, 112; Lotman and Uspenskij, "Role," 10–11.

122. See, for example, RIB 13: cols. 225, 568–69; Timofeev, *Vremennik*, 83, 89, 101; Massa, *Short History*, 110, 119, 121, 146–48; Palitsyn, *Skazanie*, 110, 112–13; Aleksandrenko, "Materialy," 267; PSRL 14:67; Val'denberg, *Drevnerusskie ucheniia*, 366–67; *Rukopisnye nasledie Drevnei Rusi*, 83.

123. Ul'ianovskii, "Russko-shvedskie otnosheniia," 66–67; idem, "Pravoslavnaia tserkov'," 35–43, 55–62; Skrynnikov, *Rossiia v nachale XVII v.*, 232–33.

124. RIB 14: cols. 170–77; Solov'ev, *Istoriia*, 4:450; Nazarov, "Zhalovannaia gramota," 354–68; Ul'ianovskii, "Pravoslavnaia tserkov'," 38–43.

125. RIB 13: cols. 537–39.

126. Bussow, *Disturbed State*, 52; Margeret, *Russian Empire*, 86–87.

127. Bussow, *Disturbed State*, 54; Barbour, *Dimitry*, 209; Kulakova, "Vosstanie," 36; Skrynnikov, *Time of Troubles*, 28; Ul'ianovskii, "Pravoslavnaia tserkov'," 45–52.

128. *Akty feodal'nogo zemlevladeniia i khoziaistva*, 2: nos. 415–16; Massa, *Short History*, 148, 168; Solov'ev, *Istoriia*, 4:450; Hellie, *Enserfment*, 49; Skrynnikov, *Time of Troubles*, 28.

129. Bussow, *Disturbed State*, 54; Buturlin, *Istoriia*, 1:190; Platonov, *Ocherki*, 221; idem, *Moscow and the West*, 37. Koretskii went so far as to declare that Tsar Dmitrii's actions reflected his Jesuit-influenced secularizing tendencies (*Formirovanie*, 240).

130. Skrynnikov, *Smuta*, 27; idem, *Time of Troubles*, 28.

131. RIB 35: no. 39; Palitsyn, *Skazanie*, 256; *Akty XIII–XVII vv., predstavlennye v Razriadnyi prikaz* [hereafter cited as *Akty Iushkova*], no. 336; Nosov, "Belozerskaia izba,"52; Hellie, *Enserfment*, 43–44, 89–90, 95, 301 n. 148, 342 n. 99; Ul'ianovskii, "Pravoslavnaia tserkov'," 47–48.

132. Howe, *False Dmitri*, 39; Bussow, *Disturbed State*, 53; Platonov, *Time of Troubles*, 80–81; Brody, *Demetrius Legend*, 35; Skrynnikov, *Time of Troubles*, 28, 32; Crummey, *Formation*, 219; Perrie, *Pretenders*, 97.

133. Skrynnikov, *Time of Troubles*, 28.

134. SGGD 2:298; Skrynnikov, *Smuta*, 53. Cf. Massa, *Short History*, 113.

135. Palitsyn, *Skazanie*, 111–12; Skrynnikov, *Smuta*, 43, 46; idem, *Time of Troubles*, 44; Ul'ianovskii, "Pravoslavnaia tserkov'," 60–61.

136. RIB 13: cols. 1314–15; Platonov, *Stat'i*, 211–14; MERSH 14:11–12; Kedrov, *Zhizneopisanie*, 32–36; Skrynnikov, *Time of Troubles*, 49; idem, *Smuta*, 53–54.

137. Skrynnikov, *Boris Godunov*, 100.

138. See PSRL 34:211; Palitsyn, *Skazanie*, 111–12, 116; Platonov, *Time of Troubles*, 80–81. Cf. Skrynnikov, *Rossiia v nachale XVII v.*, 232–33; idem, *Smuta*, 43, 46.

139. RIB 13: cols. 160–61, 168–69, 172; Massa, *Short History*, 114, 120; Howe, *False Dmitri*, 32; Kulakova, "Vosstanie," 35; Platonov, *Time of Troubles*, 81.

140. Bussow, *Disturbed State*, 53; Margeret, *Russian Empire*, 70; Massa, *Short History*, 110–11, 119; RIB 13: cols. 163, 818.

141. Margeret, *Russian Empire*, 70; Bussow, *Disturbed State*, 53–55; Massa, *Short History*, 114, 121–23, 136–37; Palitsyn, *Skazanie*, 113; Howe, *False Dmitri*, 32; Skrynnikov, *Time of Troubles*, 18–19, 137. It is probable that the fanatically Orthodox diak Timofei Osipov was one of the assassins apprehended in January 1605, although the story of his denunciation of the tsar as the heretic Otrepev has often been incorrectly placed in May, just before Dmitrii's assassination. Conrad Bussow's chronology about Shuiskii's activities is seriously confused, and he was certainly wrong about Shuiskii being supported by "all the inhabitants of Moscow."

142. Massa, *Short History*, 116–17, 121; Bussow, *Disturbed State*, 53–54; Margeret, *Russian Empire*, 69; de Thou, *Histoire*, 14:492; Purchas, *Hakluytus Posthumus*, 14:162–63, 176; Howe, *False Dmitri*, 33; Zhordaniia, *Ocherki*, 1:250–55; Barbour, *Dimitry*, 204–8.

143. *La légende*, 6–7; *Reporte*, F4; Bussow, *Disturbed State*, 54; Palitsyn, *Skazanie*, 112; Platonov, *Moscow and the West*, 36–37; Barbour, *Dimitry*, 208.

144. Margeret, *Russian Empire*, xviii–xix, 78–79.

145. Bussow, *Disturbed State*, 54.

146. Massa, *Short History*, 117–18, 126; Bussow, *Disturbed State*, 56; Perrie, *Pretenders*, 102.

147. Massa, *Short History*, 121–22; Skrynnikov, *Smuta*, 26. Cf. Bussow, *Disturbed State*, 54–55; Petreius, *Istoriia*, 212; PSRL 14:68; AAE 2:108–9; RIB 13: cols. 78–79; Platonov, *Ocherki*, 222–23. Skrynnikov, with no supporting evidence, declared that many more streltsy were involved in the assassination plot (*Time of Troubles*, 30).

148. Massa, *Short History*, 122–23; Perrie, *Pretenders*, 97.

149. See, for example, RIB 13: cols. 581, 857–58, 869; Massa, *Short History*, 113, 116–17; Bussow, *Disturbed State*, 52–56, 60; Platonov, *Moscow and the West*, 40–42; Skrynnikov, *Time of Troubles*, 18, 29–30, 43; idem, *Smuta*, 22.

150. Platonov, *Time of Troubles*, 80; Skrynnikov, *Time of Troubles*, 16–18; idem, *Smuta*, 24–25.

151. Zolkiewski, *Expedition*, 46; Petreius, *Istoriia*, 373.

152. Ul'ianovskii, "Russko-shvedskie otnosheniia," 66–67.

153. Skrynnikov, *Time of Troubles*, 17–18; idem, *Smuta*, 25.

154. Zolkiewski, *Expedition*, 44–45.

155. Skrynnikov fully credited this dubious story (*Time of Troubles*, 17–18, 29).

156. SGGD 2:262.

157. Skrynnikov, *Time of Troubles*, 13–14; idem, *Smuta*, 26.

158. See Skrynnikov, *Smuta*, 26.

159. See Skrynnikov, *Time of Troubles*, 13–14, 22–23.

160. Ibid., 32.

161. Pirling, *Dmitrii Samozvanets*, 380; Graham, "Further Sources," 86.

162. Platonov, *Time of Troubles*, 79.

163. See Skrynnikov, *Smuta*, 51; idem, *Time of Troubles*, 46.

164. Skrynnikov, *Time of Troubles*, 79.

165. Bussow, *Disturbed State*, 82; Skrynnikov, *Smuta*, 28; idem, *Time of Troubles*, 29; Solov'ev, *Istoriia*, 4:402; Perrie, *Pretenders*, 86.

166. Palitsyn, *Skazanie*, 115; Massa, *Short History*, 135, 138; Brody, *Demetrius Legend*, 36; Skrynnikov, *Smuta*, 32; Kulakova, "Vosstanie," 35, 40–41; Perrie, *Pretenders*, 103.

167. Keenan, "Muscovite Political Folkways," 144, 160.

168. See Hellie, "Keenan's Scholarly Ways," 184.

169. Bussow, *Disturbed State*, 53; Massa, *Short History*, 149.

170. Margeret, *Russian Empire*, 70; Howe, *False Dmitri*, 45; Skrynnikov, *Time of Troubles*, 30–31.

Bussow (*Disturbed State*, 61) was wrong about the chronology of this incident. There is no evidence to support Skrynnikov's claim that the boyar council forced "Otrepev" to return Tatishchev to court (*Smuta*, 21–22).

171. See Skrynnikov, *Samozvantsy*, 186; idem, *Time of Troubles*, 29–30; Ischboldin, *Essays*, 117. Cf. Platonov, *Boris Godunov*, 174; MERSH 3:194.

172. Bussow, *Disturbed State*, 55.

173. Smirnov, *Vosstanie*, 91; Skrynnikov, *Time of Troubles*, 26–27; idem, *Smuta*, 15.

174. Hellie, *Enserfment*, 167.

175. RIB 13: cols. 620–21; Popov, *Izbornik*, 329; Nemoevskii, "Zapiski," 65; AMG 1: no. 44.

176. See Hellie, *Enserfment*, 49; Skrynnikov, *Time of Troubles*, 10, 26; idem, *Smuta*, 15; Belokurov, *Razriadnye zapisi*, 6, 76, 79, 141; *Akty Iushkova*, no. 226; Storozhev, "Desiatni," 87; Popov, *Izbornik*, 329; PSRL 31:243; Mal'tsev, *Bor'ba*, 343, 376–82, 384–85; Sedov, "Pomestnye oklady kak istochnik," 228–29.

177. RIB 13: cols. 1292–93; Nemoevskii, "Zapiski,"151, 213; SRIO 137:182–83; Palitsyn, *Skazanie*, 112; AZR 4:300.

178. Skrynnikov, *Smuta*, 15. Tax revenues were lower due to the lingering impact of Russia's severe crisis, the famine, and Dmitrii's campaign for the throne.

179. RGADA, fond 214 (Sibirskii prikaz), kniga 11, list 493; *Akty iuridicheskie*, 389; RIB 25: no. 44; AMG 1: no. 44.

180. RGADA, fond 210 (Razriadnyi prikaz), opis' 4 (Dela desiaten'), kniga 124, listy 126 ob, 197; kniga 130, listy 4ob, 18, 19, 200; Vernadsky, *Tsardom*, 1:220; Skrynnikov, *Time of Troubles*, 27; idem, *Smuta*, 250; Koretskii, "Novye dokumenty," 76.

181. AMG 1: no. 44.

182. RGADA, fond 210 (Razriadnyi prikaz), opis' 4 (Dela desiaten'), kniga 98, list 1; Skrynnikov, *Boris Godunov*, 149.

183. Smirnov, "K kharakteristike vnutrennei politiki Lzhedmitriia I," 200–207; Bussow, *Moskovskaia khronika*, 354 n. 62; Skrynnikov, *Smuta*, 250.

184. Hellie, *Enserfment*, 48–49.

185. Massa, *Short History*, 117–18; Bussow, *Disturbed State*, 55–56. Cf. *La légende*, 8; *Reporte*, F4.

186. Howe, *False Dmitri*, 34; Massa, *Short History*, 117.

187. Belokurov, *Snosheniia*, 41–42.

188. See Margeret, *Russian Empire*, xviii, 98 n. 36; Nazarov, "O datirovke," 216–21; Hellie, *Enserfment*, 167–68.

189. Massa, *Short History*, 120; Ul'ianovskii, "Russko-shvedskie otnosheniia," 71, 73; Parker, *Europe in Crisis*, 94–98.

190. Ul'ianovskii, "Russko-shvedskie otnosheniia," 65–66; Aleksandrenko, "Materialy," 444.

191. Massa, *Short History*, 120.

192. Pirling, *Dmitrii Samozvanets*, 318; Ul'ianovskii, "Russko-shvedskie otnosheniia," 66–69, 73. Cf. Skrynnikov, *Time of Troubles*, 12.

193. Massa, *Short History*, 116; Ul'ianovskii, "Russko-shvedskie otnosheniia," 73–74; Skrynnikov, *Time of Troubles*, 27; *Zapiski Zholkevskago*, cols. 171–72; Pierling, *Dimitri et Possevino*, 4–5.

194. See Flier, "Iconology," 63; Wielewicki, "Historici Diarii," 145.

195. Belokurov, *Snosheniia*, 513; Skrynnikov, *Time of Troubles*, 26–28, 31–32.

196. Aleksandrenko, "Materialy," 419; Massa, *Short History*, 131; Bussow, *Disturbed State*, 56; Pirling, *Dmitrii Samozvanets*, 266; Pierling, *Rome*, 111–12, 166–67; idem, *La Russie*, 3:226–27; Novosel'skii, *Bor'ba*, 48–49.

197. Massa, *Short History*, 123, 142; Bussow, *Disturbed State*, 53; PSRL 14:68; Palitsyn, *Skazanie*, 114, 118; Belokurov, *Snosheniia*, 41–42; Skrynnikov, *Time of Troubles*, 31–32.

198. Popov, *Izbornik*, 330; Smirnov, *Vosstanie*, 224–26.

199. Skrynnikov, *Time of Troubles*, 32.

200. Bussow, *Disturbed State*, 58; Platonov, *Moscow and the West*, 38; Skrynnikov, *Smuta*, 26–27; idem, *Time of Troubles*, 22–23, 32. Skrynnikov erred in declaring that those foreign troops were brought to Moscow in order to protect the false tsar from boyar intrigue.

201. Massa, *Short History,* 123–24; Palitsyn, *Skazanie,* 113–14.
202. Skrynnikov, *Time of Troubles,* 37.
203. Margeret, *Russian Empire,* 72, 75, 87–89, 91; Kulakova, "Vosstanie," 41–42.
204. Skrynnikov, *Smuta,* 51.
205. Purchas, *Hakluytus Posthumus,* 14:189; Massa, *Short History,* 147; Palitsyn, *Skazanie,* 114.
206. RIB 13: col. 165; Bussow, *Disturbed State,* 56, 59; Purchas, *Hakluytus Posthumus,* 14:161; Massa, *Short History,* 142–43, 147; Howe, *False Dmitri,* 34, 41; Palitsyn, *Skazanie,* 114; *Reporte,* 12–12v.
207. Skrynnikov, *Time of Troubles,* 31; idem, *Samozvantsy,* 169–70. Cf. Margeret, *Russian Empire,* 75, 174 n. 283.
208. Massa, *Short History,* 148; Nemoevskii, "Zapiski," 119–20; Purchas, *Hakluytus Posthumus,* 14:187.
209. Margeret, *Russian Empire,* 71; Stanislavskii, *Grazhdanskaia voina,* 22; Perrie, *Pretenders,* 95. Cf. Belokurov, *Snosheniia,* 513.
210. Popov, *Izbornik,* 330; Margeret, *Russian Empire,* 70–71; SRIO 137:351–52; La Ville, *Discours sommaire,* 8.
211. Margeret, *Russian Empire,* 71.
212. On Tsarevich Petr's movements after receiving Dmitrii's letter, see chapter 18 below and Liubomirov, *Ocherk,* 323. Maureen Perrie ("Legends," 236–37) and Ruslan Skrynnikov (*Time of Troubles,* 37; *Smuta,* 29–30. 153) erroneously declared that Petr decided to travel to Moscow at that point.
213. PSRL 14:71; VBDM 226.
214. Nemoevskii, "Zapiski," 119–20.
215. *Novyi letopisets,* 78; Smirnov, *Vosstanie,* 369–70. Skrynnikov originally accepted this view (*Time of Troubles,* 24). He later came to accept Koretskii's notion of friendly relations between Dmitrii and Petr but still believed that Petr boldly demanded rewards from the impostor Otrepev (*Smuta,* 153).
216. Koretskii, *Formirovanie,* 256–57; Perrie, "Legends," 236–37; Skrynnikov, *Time of Troubles,* 24, 37; idem, *Smuta,* 29–30, 153.
217. Perrie, *Pretenders,* 97.
218. Smirnov, *Vosstanie,* 368.
219. Margeret, *Russian Empire,* 71.
220. Smirnov, *Vosstanie,* 224–27. Perhaps influenced by the story of Tsarevich Petr, it was also falsely claimed that Dmitrii—sensing danger—brought loyal streltsy from the southern frontier to Moscow by the spring of 1606. See Kulakova, "Vosstanie," 37.
221. Platonov, *Smutnoe vremia,* 120–33; Smirnov, *Vosstanie,* 88.
222. Koretskii, "K istorii formirovaniia," 92–93; idem, "Vosstanovlenie Iur'eva dnia," 118–30. Hellie accepted Koretskii's faulty theory (*Enserfment,* 107–8, 263).
223. Koretskii, *Formirovanie,* 249–57.
224. Ibid., 252–53; Skrynnikov, *Time of Troubles,* 24.
225. Dunning, "Cossacks," 63–64; Smirnov, *Vosstanie,* 365–70. In evaluating Tsarevich Petr, Koretskii relied far too much on testimony coerced from Petr by torture in 1607 and ignored the important testimony of Captain Margeret simply because that testimony did not agree with Koretskii's own view of Tsar Dmitrii's desperate situation in the spring of 1606. See VBDM 225–26; Perrie, *Pretenders,* 93–94; Margeret, *Russian Empire,* 70–71.
226. See *Pamiatniki russkogo prava,* 4:532–33; Koretskii, *Formirovanie,* 236, 238, 243–46, 249, 252–57; Andreev, "Svodnyi sudebnik," 638; Hellie, *Enserfment,* 107–8, 263; Nazarov, "Paleograficheskii analiz," 54–75.
227. See *Pamiatniki russkogo prava,* 4:480–81; Skrynnikov, *Samozvantsy,* 160–61; idem, *Smuta,* 15–16.
228. Culpepper, "Legislative Origins," 186; Skrynnikov, *Samozvantsy,* 160–62; idem, "Civil War," 63; idem, *Tsar' Boris i Dmitrii Samozvanets,* 560.
229. Skrynnikov, *Samozvantsy,* 161; idem, *Smuta,* 38–39. Cf. Bussow, *Moskovskaia khronika,* 353 n. 62.

230. *Pamiatniki russkogo prava,* 4:540–41; *Zakonodatel'nye akty,* 1:73–74; Koretskii, "Vosstanovlenie Iur'eva dnia," 121–22; Zimin, "Nekotorye voprosy," 99–100; Nazarov, "K istorii nachal'nogo perioda," 184–200.

231. Skrynnikov, *Smuta,* 18; idem, *Time of Troubles,* 25.

232. Culpepper, "Legislative Origins," 185; Hellie, *Enserfment,* 107.

233. *Zakonodatel'nye akty,* 1:74; Skrynnikov, *Time of Troubles,* 25–26; idem, *Smuta,* 17.

234. V. I. Koretskii, "Iz istorii zakreposhcheniia krest'ian v Rossii v kontse XVI–nachale XVII v.," *Istoriia SSSR,* 1957, no. 1:187; Paneiakh, "Iz istorii zakreposhcheniia," 168; Skrynnikov, *Smuta,* 16–17, 187; idem, *Time of Troubles,* 25–26.

235. Hellie, *Enserfment,* 326 n. 14, 328 n. 20.

236. Kulakova, "Vosstanie," 35; Skrynnikov, *Smuta,* 14–15, 37–39.

NOTES TO CHAPTER 13

1. Bussow, *Disturbed State,* 57–58; Margeret, *Russian Empire,* 72; Massa, *Short History,* 127–29.

2. RIB 13: cols. 857–58, 869; Platonov, *Times of Troubles,* 79–82; idem, *Moscow and the West,* 40–42; Skrynnikov, *Time of Troubles,* 38–43.

3. Kulakova, "Vosstanie," 39. Cf. Skrynnikov, *Boris Godunov,* 24–26.

4. Abramovich, *Kniaz'ia Shuiskie,* 117, 121, 131; Pokrovsky, *Brief History,* 1:74–75; Skrynnikov, *Smuta,* 44; Kulakova, "Vosstanie," 37, 39–41.

5. AI 2: no. 38; Baron, "Gosti Revisited," 11.

6. Bushkovitch, "Taxation," 398; Kulakova, "Moskvichi," 86–89.

7. See SGGD 2:217; AI 2: no. 56; Bussow, *Disturbed State,* 52; Baron, "Gosti Revisited," 11; Phipps, *John Merrick,* 62; Kulakova, "Vosstanie," 37–39.

8. Massa, *Short History,* 113; Kulakova, "Moskvichi," 88–89.

9. Massa, 119; Avrich, *Russian Rebels,* 33; Solov'ev, *Istoriia,* 4:471; Kulakova, "Vosstanie," 37.

10. Aleksandrenko, "Materialy," 257–58; Massa, *Short History,* 137; RIB 13: col. 747; Stadnitskii, "Dnevnik," 161; Kulakova, "Vosstanie," 37, 39.

11. Sokolova, *Russkie predaniia,* 60–63; Perrie, *Image,* 9–10, 25, 33, 56, 58–59, 79–80.

12. Massa, *Short History,* 147; Ul'ianovskii, "Russko-shvedskie otnosheniia," 66–67.

13. Massa, *Short History,* 114, 125; Kulakova, "Vosstanie," 39.

14. Bussow, *Disturbed State,* 58; Platonov, *Moscow and the West,* 38–39; Skrynnikov, *Smuta,* 27. Palitsyn (*Skazanie,* 112) and the Pinezhskii Chronicle (Kopanev, "Pinezhskii letopisets," 83) incorrectly estimated that six thousand Polish troops came to Moscow in the wedding party.

15. Skrynnikov, *Time of Troubles,* 32–33; idem, *Smuta,* 26–27, 51. The only evidence Skrynnikov could cite about Dmitrii being terrified of opposition at this time was testimony coerced from Dmitrii's secretary by Shuiskii's henchmen after the tsar was dead. See SGGD 2:298.

16. Margeret, *Russian Empire,* 87; Massa, *Short History,* 124; Palitsyn, *Skazanie,* 112; Platonov, *Moscow and the West,* 39; Skrynnikov, *Time of Troubles,* 35–36; Kulakova, "Vosstanie," 39.

17. Massa, *Short History,* 133, 148–49; Howe, *False Dmitri,* 41–42, 60; Platonov, *Moscow and the West,* 37–42; Brody, *Demetrius Legend,* 35–36; Skrynnikov, *Time of Troubles,* 35–36.

18. Massa, *Short History,* 132–33; Brody, *Demetrius Legend,* 35.

19. Bussow, *Disturbed State,* 59; Massa, *Short History,* 132.

20. Platonov, *Moscow and the West,* 39–43; idem, *Time of Troubles,* 82; Skrynnikov, *Time of Troubles,* 33–35.

21. Ul'ianovskii, "Pravoslavnaia tserkov'," 60–61; Skrynnikov, *Time of Troubles,* 33.

22. Perrie, *Pretenders,* 98.

23. Platonov, *Moscow and the West,* 40.

24. Skrynnikov, *Time of Troubles,* 33–35. Cf. SGGD 2:298.

25. MERSH 47:23; Belokurov, *Razriadnye zapisi,* 80; Massa, *Short History,* 132.

26. Massa, *Short History,* 126, 133; Skrynnikov, *Time of Troubles,* 33–34.

27. See, for example, Vovina, "Filaret," 59.

28. Kulakova, "Vosstanie," 35, 40–41; Skrynnikov, *Time of Troubles,* 35.

29. Howe, *False Dmitri,* 39; Massa, *Short History,* 133; *La légende,* 12; *Reporte,* F6; Brody, *Demetrius Legend,* 35.

30. Skrynnikov, *Time of Troubles,* 32–34.

31. Kulakova, "Vosstanie," 35, 40–41.

32. Bussow, *Disturbed State,* 58–59, 61–62; Skrynnikov, *Time of Troubles,* 35–36; Perrie, *Pretenders,* 103.

33. RIB 13: col. 165; Bussow, *Disturbed State,* 56, 59; Massa, *Short History,* 142–43, 147; Howe, *False Dmitri,* 34, 41; Palitsyn, *Skazanie,* 114; *Reporte,* 12–12v; Skrynnikov, *Smuta,* 51. Cf. Perrie, *Pretenders,* 102.

34. See Shlikhting, *Novoe izvestie,* 46; Perrie, *Image,* 93.

35. Massa, *Short History,* 133–35; Skrynnikov, *Time of Troubles,* 37.

36. Skrynnikov, *Smuta,* 31–32.

37. Platonov, *Moscow and the West,* 42; Skrynnikov, *Time of Troubles,* 31–32, 36.

38. Margeret, *Russian Empire,* 72, 75, 89, 91; Massa, *Short History,* 126; Bussow, *Disturbed State,* 62; Skrynnikov, *Smuta,* 32–33.

39. Bussow, *Disturbed State,* 55, 62; Massa, *Short History,* 135; Kulakova, "Vosstanie," 41–42; Skrynnikov, *Smuta,* 33–34.

40. Margeret, *Russian Empire,* 87–88; Massa, *Short History,* 138; Nemoevskii, "Zapiski," 75.

41. Skrynnikov, *Smuta,* 33.

42. Margeret, *Russian Empire,* xviii–xix; de Thou, *Histoire,* 14:494; Howe, *False Dmitri,* 44. There is no basis for the rumor Skrynnikov reported without citation (*Time of Troubles,* 38) that Margeret favored the coup against Dmitrii and "personally had ordered the interior guard to withdraw from the tsar's chambers, so that no more than thirty men were left." In fact, Margeret was devoted to Dmitrii.

43. Massa, *Short History,* 136–37; Skrynnikov, *Time of Troubles,* 37.

44. Margeret, *Russian Empire,* 70. Cf. Massa, *Short History,* 137; Palitsyn, *Skazanie,* 113.

45. RIB 13: cols. 581, 857–58, 869; Gnevushev, *Akty,* 1–3; Bussow, *Disturbed State,* 59–60, 63, 65; Palitsyn, *Skazanie,* 114–15.

46. Massa, *Short History,* 124, 134–35; Kulakova, "Vosstanie," 35, 40–41; Skrynnikov, *Smuta,* 31–34. Cf. Bussow, *Moskovskaia khronika,* 355 n. 63; Platonov, *Ocherki,* 223. Massa incorrectly estimated the number of conspirators at up to three thousand.

47. See, for example, MERSH 23:160; Platonov, *Time of Troubles,* 82; Skrynnikov, *Time of Troubles,* 17–18, 38, 42; Vovina, "Filaret," 59–60.

48. See, for example, Barsukov, *Rod,* 2:110; Gnevushev, *Akty,* 156–57; Platonov, *Ocherki,* 295 n. 89; Smirnov, *Vosstanie,* 224–27. Contrary to false reports, Princes Fedor and Petr Sheremetev did not join Shuiskii's conspiracy.

49. Skrynnikov, *Time of Troubles,* 32, 42. Cf. Platonov, *Time of Troubles,* 81; Barbour, *Dimitry,* 190–91.

50. Skrynnikov, *Time of Troubles,* 17–18.

51. Skrynnikov, *Smuta,* 26; idem, *Time of Troubles,* 13–14, 22–23. Cf. SGGD 2:262.

52. *Zapiski Zholkevskago,* cols. 171–72; Wielewicki, "Historici Diarii," 145.

53. Massa, *Short History,* 142; Pierling, *Rome,* 142; Santich, *Missio,* 141; Kulakova, "Vosstanie," 42; Skrynnikov, *Time of Troubles,* 32; Floria, "Rokosz," 69–81; Ul'ianovskii, "Rech' Pospolitaia," 78–93.

54. Turgenev, *Historica Monumenta,* 2:87–88; Skrynnikov, *Time of Troubles,* 27.

55. SRIO 137:322–23, 328; Pirling, *Dmitrii Samozvanets,* 380.

56. Dmitrievskii, *Arkhiepiskop Arsenii,* 114; Skrynnikov, *Smuta,* 31.

57. Nemoevskii, "Zapiski," 76–77; Skrynnikov, *Smuta,* 26; Kulakova, "Vosstanie," 43–44.

58. RIB 13: col. 747; Skrynnikov, *Smuta,* 35–36, 43, 46; Kulakova, "Vosstanie," 36, 42–43.

59. RIB 13: col. 748; Massa, *Short History,* 137; Pokrovsky, *Brief History,* 1:74–75; Kulakova, "Vosstanie," 38–39; Skrynnikov, *Smuta,* 26, 44; Baron, "Gosti Revisited," 11–12.

60. Bussow, *Disturbed State,* 59–60.

61. Massa, *Short History,* 135, 138; Kulakova, "Vosstanie," 40, 50.

62. Skrynnikov, *Smuta,* 34.

63. Massa, *Short History,* 137; Kulakova, "Vosstanie," 37, 50.

64. RIB 1: col. 423; 13: col. 746; Ustrialov, *Skazaniia,* 2:18, 59, 161; Massa, *Short History,* 137; Aleksandrenko, "Materialy," 257–58; Stadnitskii, "Dnevnik," 161; Abramovich, *Kniaz'ia Shuiskie,* 131.

65. Massa, *Short History,* 137; Nemoevskii, "Zapiski," 76–77; RIB 1: col. 423; Kulakova, "Vosstanie," 43–44.

66. RIB 13: cols. 747–48; Bussow, *Disturbed State,* 62; Kulakova, "Vosstanie," 39–40, 43, 50; Skrynnikov, *Smuta,* 35–36. Cf. Massa, *Short History,* 136–37.

67. Massa, *Short History,* 136; RIB 1: col 419; de Thou, *Histoire,* 14: 494; Skrynnikov, *Time of Troubles,* 38–39; idem, *Smuta,* 34, 35, 37.

68. Massa, *Short History,* 136; Kulakova, "Vosstanie," 40–41; Skrynnikov, *Smuta,* 34–36.

69. Bussow, *Disturbed State,* 69–70; Brody, *Demetrius Legend,* 36; Massa, *Short History,* 136, 139–40; Skrynnikov, *Time of Troubles,* 40, 49.

70. Massa, *Short History,* 141–42; Platonov, *Moscow and the West,* 43; Zhordaniia, *Ocherki,* 1:111–16, 211, 214–14, 225; Perrie, "Legends," 234–35.

71. RIB 13: col. 751; Nemoevskii, "Zapiski," 95–97; Massa, *Short History,* 140; Kulakova, "Vosstanie," 44; Skrynnikov, *Smuta,* 38.

72. Margeret, *Russian Empire,* 73; Howe, *False Dmitri,* 34, 41; Bussow, *Moskovskaia khronika,* 355 n. 64; Hirschberg, *Polska a Moskwa,* 59.

73. Howe, *False Dmitri,* 44; Massa, *Short History,* 135, 137–38; Bussow, *Disturbed State,* 162; Skrynnikov, *Smuta,* 34–35.

74. Massa, *Short History,* 137; Margeret, *Russian Empire,* 73. There is no truth to the rumor that the guards offered no resistance and actually parleyed with the assassins (Howe, *False Dmitri,* 44). Skrynnikov credited unreliable reports about the assassination and, as a result, confused some facts and the sequence of events that morning (*Time of Troubles,* 38–39; *Smuta,* 36). Bussow was completely mistaken about the "common multitude" being involved in the assassination (*Disturbed State,* 63–65).

75. Massa, *Short History,* 137–38; *Reporte,* 8v; *La légende,* 20.

76. Massa, *Short History,* 138.

77. Bussow, *Disturbed State,* 66; Massa, *Short History,* 138; Ustrialov, *Skazaniia,* 1:191. Skrynnikov (*Time of Troubles,* 34) incorrectly wrote that "Otrepev" was willing to repent.

78. Margeret, *Russian Empire,* 81–82, 87–91.

79. Ustrialov, *Skazaniia,* 1:191; Bussow, *Disturbed State,* 66; Skrynnikov, *Smuta,* 37–38. Mylnikov later received a large reward from Shuiskii; see Kulakova, "Moskvichi," 89. The traditional version of the assassination had dvorianin Ivan Voeikov or syn boiarskii Grigorii Valuev delivering the first blow. See Ustrialov, *Skazaniia,* 2:238; Skrynnikov, *Time of Troubles,* 40.

80. Massa, *Short History,* 138, 144.

81. Dunning, "Byla li krest'ianskaia voina," 31; Massa, *Short History,* 146–50; Skrynnikov, *Smuta,* 51; Perrie, *Pretenders,* 101–3.

82. Massa, *Short History,* 138; Ustrialov, *Skazaniia,* 1:191; Bussow, *Disturbed State,* 66–67; Kulakova, "Vosstanie," 43–44.

83. Bussow, *Disturbed State,* 76; Howe, *False Dmitri,* 46–47.

84. Ustrialov, *Skazaniia,* 2:238; Skrynnikov, *Smuta,* 38. Cf. Margeret, *Russian Empire,* 73. The "New Chronicle" (PSRL 14:69) incorrectly had the streltsy asking Marfa about the identity of the tsar before allowing the "impostor" to be killed. Skrynnikov (*Time of Troubles,* 40) incorrectly wrote that Marfa denounced the tsar as an impostor at this time. In fact, Marfa hesitated to denounce Tsar Dmitrii until after Vasilii Shuiskii succeeded in becoming tsar. See Perrie, *Pretenders,* 104.

85. Only at the end of May 1606 was Tsar Vasilii Shuiskii able to widely circulate Marfa's statement about having been coerced into recognizing the false tsar as her son. See AAE 2:111; SGGD 2:307, 312, 317; Massa, *Short History,* 150. See also Kleimola, "Canonization," 107–17.

86. Perrie, *Pretenders,* 103; Bercé, *Le roi caché,* 366–67. Cf. Massa, *Short History,* 147.

87. Timofeev, *Vremennik*, 83; RIB 13: cols. 568–69; Massa, *Short History*, 144.

88. Miller, *Istoricheskiia pesni*, 621; Uspenskij, "Tsar and Pretender," 273–74; Perrie, *Pretenders*, 99–100.

89. Aleksandrenko, "Materialy," 400, 535; Frantsev, "Istoricheskoe povestvovanie," 25, 31; *Moskovskaia tragediia*, 35–36; Purchas, *Hakluytus Posthumus*, 14:162; Uspenskij, "Tsar and Pretender," 276.

90. See Mousnier, *Assassination*, 97–99, 104.

91. Zguta, *Russian Minstrels*, 4–5, 8–9, 29–30.

92. Shlikhting, *Novoe izvestie*, 29–30; Rosovetskii, "Ustnaia proza," 91.

93. Rosovetskii, "Ustnaia proza," 91; Perrie, *Image*, 100–101.

94. Massa, *Short History*, 138. Cf. Margeret, *Russian Empire*, 73.

95. Ustrialov, *Skazaniia*, 1:347; Uspenskij, "Tsar and Pretender," 275; Perrie, *Pretenders*, 99.

96. Bussow, *Disturbed State*, 76–77; Ustrialov, *Skazaniia*, 1:196–97; Howe, *False Dmitri*, 47; RIB 13: cols. 59, 866; Massa, *Short History*, 142–43.

97. Ustrialov, *Skazaniia*, 2:238. Cf. Alekseeva et al., *Istoricheskie pesni*, 27–29.

98. Perrie, *Pretenders*, 99.

99. Miller, *Istoricheskiia pesni*, 585, 587–89, 591, 593, 595, 597, 601–2, 620, 624; Alekseeva et al., *Istoricheskie pesni*, 27–44.

100. Lotman and Uspenskij, "Role," 9.

101. Bussow, *Disturbed State*, 61, 66.

102. Ibid., 77; Skrynnikov, *Time of Troubles*, 44.

103. Several sources stated that the dead man was really a German (Bussow, *Disturbed State*, 78; PSRL 14:70; Bodianskii, "O poiskakh moikh," 5–6; Nemoevskii, "Zapiski," 119). Other sources identified him as a native of Prague (Ustrialov, *Skazaniia*, 1:213), a weaver from Poland (Massa, *Short History*, 157), a Lithuanian (RIB 13: cols. 584, 661), or a young Russian lord who resembled Dmitrii and had been much favored by the tsar (Margeret, *Russian Empire*, 77). Two veterans of Dmitrii's campaign for the throne declared that the tsar had two doubles: a man named Barkowski and a nephew of Prince Mosalskii (Pierling, *La Russie*, 3:345–46; SRIO 137:301). Another source claimed that Dmitrii had at least ten look-alikes (Massa, *Short History*, 158).

104. *Skazaniia Massy i Gerkmana*, 294.

105. Margeret, *Russian Empire*, 76–77. Cf. S.P. 91/1-f. 215.

106. Ustrialov, *Skazaniia*, 1:196–97; Massa, *Short History*, 156–58; Perrie, *Pretenders*, 112.

107. Margeret, *Russian Empire*, 75, 77; Nemoevskii, "Zapiski," 119; Skrynnikov, *Time of Troubles*, 46; Perrie, "Legends," 239–41; Dolinin, "K izucheniiu," 476. Bussow incorrectly claimed that the Poles were responsible for the rumor (*Disturbed State*, 78).

108. Bussow, *Disturbed State*, 78; Margeret, *Russian Empire*, 76; Hirschberg, *Polska a Moskwa*, 75.

109. SRIO 137:306; Perrie, *Pretenders*, 112.

110. Margeret, *Russian Empire*, 74; Massa, *Short History*, 144–45; Perrie, *Pretenders*, 115. Cf. Krejchi, *Great Revolutions Compared*, 10.

NOTES TO CHAPTER 14

1. RIB 13: col. 751; Massa, *Short History*, 139–42; Palitsyn, *Skazanie*, 265; Dmitrievskii, *Arkhiepiskop Arsenii*, 114; Smirnov, *Vosstanie*, 87; Kulakova, "Vosstanie," 44.

2. Margeret, *Russian Empire*, 74.

3. Nemoevskii, "Zapiski," 98; Skrynnikov, *Smuta*, 40.

4. RIB 13: cols. 160–61, 168–69, 172, 713–14.

5. Massa, *Short History*, 146; Bussow, *Moskovskaia khronika*, 356 n. 70; Skrynnikov, *Time of Troubles*, 43.

6. AAE 2:100–101, 106–15; SGGD 2:296–98, 302–4, 308–25; Massa, *Short History*, 143; Skrynnikov, *Time of Troubles*, 41, 46; Perrie, *Pretenders*, 101–3.

7. See, for example, Keenan, "Muscovite Political Folkways," 130–32, 138–45.

8. Skrynnikov, *Smuta*, 40; Nemoevskii, "Zapiski," 110. Perrie erred in stating that Ignatii was accused of circulating "proof" that Tsar Dmitrii was still alive (*Pretenders*, 110).

9. PSRL 14:69; Tatishchev, *Istoriia*, 6:298. One source incorrectly stated that Vasilii Shuiskii ordered the streltsy to suppress his opponents who called for the convocation of a zemskii sobor (Zolkiewski, *Expedition*, 47).

10. PSRL 34:211.

11. Kulakova, "Vosstanie," 48; Skrynnikov, *Smuta*, 43.

12. Skrynnikov, *Time of Troubles*, 42, 45; idem, *Smuta*, 51; "Tri gramoty," 3–4; *Vremennik Imperatorskago Moskovskago Obshchestva Istorii i Drevnostei*, 23 (1855):291.

13. Skrynnikov, *Smuta*, 40, 50; idem, *Time of Troubles*, 42, 44.

14. Margeret, *Russian Empire*, 78; Barsukov, *Rod Sheremetevykh*, 2:114. Platonov erred in identifying the Romanovs and Sheremetevs as parties to Shuiskii's conspiracy against Tsar Dmitrii (*Ocherki*, 287–94).

15. Margeret, *Russian Empire*, 74, 78–79; Skrynnikov, *Time of Troubles*, 46.

16. PSRL 14:69; Margeret, *Russian Empire*, 77. Cf. Rowland, "Muscovite Political Attitudes," 30–31.

17. Margeret, *Russian Empire*, 73, 77–78; RIB 13: cols. 541, 582; Palitsyn, *Skazanie*, 266; Timofeev, *Vremennik*, 153; Zolkiewski, *Expedition*, 47; Bennet, "Idea of Kingship," 114.

18. S.P. 91/1-f. 215; Popov, *Izbornik*, 329–30; PSRL 34:211; Tikhomirov, "Novyi istochnik," 100; idem, "Piskarevskii letopisets," 112–18; de Thou, *Histoire*, 14:500.

19. PSRL 14:69; AI 2:35; RIB 13: col. 582; Palitsyn, *Skazanie*, 115–16, 266; LaVille, *Discours sommaire*, 6; Timofeev, *Vremennik*, 100–102, 113, 133; Margeret, *Russian Empire*, 73–74, 77; Bussow, *Disturbed State*, 84; Zolkiewski, *Expedition*, 47.

20. Solov'ev, *Istoriia*, 4:458; Latkin, *Zemskie sobory*, 99.

21. See, for example, Cherepnin, *Zemskie sobory*, 153–54; Skrynnikov, *Time of Troubles*, 42–43.

22. Palitsyn, *Skazanie*, 115; Skrynnikov, *Smuta*, 43.

23. PSRL 34:211; LaVille, *Discours sommaire*, 6.

24. Timofeev, *Vremennik*, 101.

25. RIB 13: cols. 168–69, 227, 1295–96; Tikhomirov, "Novyi istochnik," 100; Belobrova, "K izucheniiu," 151; Skrynnikov, *Smuta*, 43–44. Cf. MERSH 35:55, 61.

26. SGGD 2:299, 304. Cf. AAE 2:213–14; PSRL 14:69.

27. RIB 13: cols. 544–45, 622.

28. See Kliuchevskii, *Boiarskaia duma*, 353–82; Platonov, *Time of Troubles*, 87–88; *Ocherki istorii SSSR*, 503; Crummey, "Constitutional Reform," 29–30, 33–35, 38–39.

29. Massa, *Short History*, 146; PSRL 34:211; Skrynnikov, *Time of Troubles*, 42–43. Cf. Cherepnin, *Zemskie sobory*, 153–54.

30. PSRL 14:69; LaVille, *Discours sommaire*, 6; Palitsyn, *Skazanie*, 115–16; Skrynnikov, *Smuta*, 41.

31. RIB 13: col. 65; Bussow, *Disturbed State*, 84; Solov'ev, *Istoriia*, 4:458.

32. Palitsyn, *Skazanie*, 115–16, 266; Margeret, *Russian Empire*, 74; LaVille, *Discours sommaire*, 6; Timofeev, *Vremennik*, 100–102; Zolkiewski, *Expedition*, 47; RIB 13: col. 582; *Istoriia krest'ianstva*, 2:433; Crummey, *Formation*, 220.

33. Margeret, *Russian Empire*, 74, 77; Timofeev, *Vremennik*, 153; Pokrovsky, *Brief History*, 1:75; Cherepnin, "Smuta," 101–3; Rowland, "Muscovite Political Attitudes," 204; Skrynnikov, *Time of Troubles*, 54; Perrie, *Pretenders*, 115.

34. Margeret, *Russian Empire*, 73; Massa, *Short History*, 145–46; RIB 13: col. 59. Bussow incorrectly wrote that the freeze occurred on the night of May 16–17 (*Disturbed State*, 62).

35. RIB 13: cols. 59–60, 656–57, 831; Bussow, *Disturbed State*, 77–78; Massa, *Short History*, 145; Hirschberg, *Polska a Moskwa*, 61; *Skazaniia Massy i Gerkmana*, 295–96; Uspenskij, "Tsar and Pretender," 275–76; Perrie, *Pretenders*, 100.

36. Margeret, *Russian Empire*, 75–77; Bussow, *Disturbed State*, 78; Massa, *Short History*, 156–58; PSRL 14:70; Nemoevskii, "Zapiski," 119; Dolinin, "K izucheniiu," 476.

37. Bussow, *Disturbed State*, 77; Margeret, *Russian Empire*, 73; Uspenskij, "Tsar and Pretender," 275; Perrie, *Pretenders*, 113; Skrynnikov, *Smuta*, 47–48.

38. Bussow, *Disturbed State*, 77–78; Nemoevskii, "Zapiski," 103–4; *Skazaniia Massy i Gerkmana*, 295–96; Ustrialov, *Skazaniia*, 1:194; Perrie, *Pretenders*, 100–101.

39. Nemoevskii, "Zapiski," 102; Margeret, *Russian Empire*, 77.

40. Platonov, *Ocherki*, 281; Skrynnikov, *Time of Troubles*, 44. Cf. M. A. Demidova, "Pis'ma S. F. Platonova S. D. Sheremetevu o Smutnom vremeni," *Arkhiv russkoi istorii*, part 3 (1993): 184.

41. It has long been erroneously believed that Shuiskii offered the patriarchate to Filaret in hopes of gaining Romanov support or as a reward for his participation in Tsar Dmitrii's assassination. See Platonov, *Ocherki*, 287–94; Skrynnikov, *Time of Troubles*, 45.

42. Khvalibog, "Donesenie," 3–4; Margeret, *Russian Empire*, 77; Platonov, *Ocherki*, 307; Smirnov, *Vosstanie*, 279–80; Skrynnikov, *Time of Troubles*, 45–46; idem, *Smuta*, 50–51.

43. Bussow, *Disturbed State*, 78; RIB 13: cols. 59, 831; Uspenskij, "Tsar and Pretender," 276.

44. Massa, *Short History*, 157–58; Uspenskij, "Tsar and Pretender," 275; Perrie, *Pretenders*, 101, 103, 113. Cf. Bercé, *Le roi caché*, 366–67.

45. Bussow, *Disturbed State*, 78; RIB 13: cols. 55–56, 656–57, 818–20; PSRL 14:69; Margeret, *Russian Empire*, 73; *La légende*, 24–25; *Reporte*, f 11v; Howe, *False Dmitri*, 63; Massa, *Short History*, 145.

46. Ustrialov, *Skazaniia*, 1:197.

47. Skrynnikov, *Time of Troubles*, 46.

48. Massa, *Short History*, 156, 159; Bussow, *Disturbed State*, 85–86.

49. RIB 13: cols. 892, 918; Margeret, *Russian Empire*, 74; Howe, *False Dmitri*, 237.

50. Skrynnikov, *Smuta*, 47; Massa, *Short History*, 146–50; AAE 2:100–101, 106–15; SGGD 2:296–325; Perrie, *Pretenders*, 105–6.

51. Massa, *Short History*, 146; Howe, *False Dmitri*, 53.

52. Massa, *Short History*, 156, 158; Perrie, "Legends," 241.

53. Margeret, *Russian Empire*, 77–78.

54. AAE 2:103; Skrynnikov, *Smuta*, 50–51.

55. Skrynnikov, *Time of Troubles*, 47.

56. AAE 2:104.

57. SGGD 2:310. Cf. Timofeev, *Vremennik*, 101–2.

58. RIB 13: col. 710; Skrynnikov, *Time of Troubles*, 47; RIB 31: col. 710; Koretskii, "Novye dokumenty," 81.

59. Skrynnikov, *Time of Troubles*, 44; idem, *Smuta*, 175.

60. Massa, *Short History*, 166; Skrynnikov, *Smuta*, 176.

61. Bussow, *Disturbed State*, 84; Stanislavskii, *Grazhdanskaia voina*, 24; RIB 13: col. 72; 18: cols. 23–24; Crummey, "Constitutional Reform," 29.

62. Gnevushev, *Akty*, 1–3; AAE 2:107–12; SGGD 2:300, 306–7; Massa, *Short History*, 146–49; Perrie, *Pretenders*, 101–4.

63. Purchas, *Hakluytus Posthumus*, 14:186; Zguta, "Witchcraft Trials," 189–94.

64. Margeret, *Russian Empire*, 73–74, 77.

65. Golubinskii, *Istoriia*, 120–21; Perrie, *Pretenders*, 105–6; Florinsky, *Russia*, 1:230–31.

66. Margeret, *Russian Empire*, 74; RIB 13: cols. 85, 154, 156, 172; Bussow, *Disturbed State*, 86; AAE 2:110–11; Thompson, "Legend," 48–49; Rudakov, "Razvitie," 254–57; Perrie, *Pretenders*, 105–6.

67. Margeret, *Russian Empire*, 74, 79; Bussow, *Disturbed State*, 85.

68. RIB 13: col. 85; Massa, *Short History*, 160–61; Skrynnikov, *Time of Troubles*, 47–48. Cf. Possevino, *Moscovia*, 58.

69. Bussow, *Disturbed State*, 86; Massa, *Short History*, 160–61; Skrynnikov, *Time of Troubles*, 48; idem, *Smuta*, 56.

70. RIB 13: col. 88.

71. Massa, *Short History*, 161. Although many scholars have credited at least parts of St. Dmitrii's hastily written official vita, the Russian Orthodox Church never formally accepted it due to its obvious political content and purpose. See *Zhitie*; Nikolaieff, "Boris Godunov," 283.

72. Margeret, *Russian Empire*, 77.

73. Platonov incorrectly placed this incident on Sunday, May 25, 1606 (*Ocherki*, 292–93). Cf. Howe, *False Dmitri*, 62; Smirnov, *Vosstanie*, 281.

74. Margeret, *Russian Empire*, 79; Hirschberg, *Polska a Moskwa*, 75.

75. Margeret, *Russian Empire*, 78–79; Platonov, *Ocherki*, 292–97; Skrynnikov, *Time of Troubles*, 49; idem, *Smuta*, 175; Kleimola, "Canonization," 114–15.

76. Massa, *Short History*, 161; Gnevushev, *Akty*, 4–5; Hirschberg, *Polska a Moskwa*, 75; PSRL 14:70; Belokurov, *Razriadnye zapisi*, 83–84, 139–41; *Boiarskie spiski*, 1:259; Smirnov, *Vosstanie*, 279; Skrynnikov, *Smuta*, 50, 55, 78, 175–76. Bogdan Belskii, for example, was demoted from his position as voevoda of Novgorod (a position he held until at least June 13, 1606) and sent to become voevoda of Kazan.

77. Khvalibog, "Donesenie," 3–4; Skrynnikov, *Smuta*, 50–51.

78. Skrynnikov, *Smuta*, 53–54; RIB 13: cols. 1314–15; Timofeev, *Vremennik*, 101–2.

79. See AAE 2:131, 137; RIB 13: cols. 96–101; Morozov, "Vazhnyi dokument," 162–68.

80. Ustrialov, *Skazaniia*, 1:214–15; 2:177–78; Perrie, *Pretenders*, 110, 115.

81. Margeret, *Russian Empire*, 75–76; Nemoevskii, "Zapiski," 119; Khvalibog, "Donesenie," 4; *Moskovskaia tragediia*, 71; Stadnitskii, "Dnevnik," 180; S.P. 91/1-f. 215.

82. SRIO 137:302; Skrynnikov, *Smuta*, 63–64; idem, *Time of Troubles*, 50. There is some evidence that Molchanov had been beaten for practicing sorcery during the reign of Tsar Boris (SRIO 137:368). Maureen Perrie was, unfortunately, tempted to credit Shuiskii's charges against both Molchanov and Tsar Dmitrii as sorcerers (*Pretenders*, 56, 119).

83. Khvalibog, "Donesenie," 3–4; Skrynnikov, "Civil War," 65. Massa (*Short History*, 144) incorrectly declared that Molchanov stole the royal scepter and golden crown. Bussow (*Disturbed State*, 87) incorrectly wrote that Prince Grigorii Shakhovskoi stole the state seal and fled from Moscow. See also Platonov, *Ocherki*, 318–19; Smirnov, *Vosstanie*, 99–105; Perrie, *Pretenders*, 113–14.

84. Margeret, *Russian Empire*, 78; Massa, *Short History*, 144.

85. Solov'ev, *Istoriia*, 4:466–67; Smirnov, *Vosstanie*, 105; Perrie, *Pretenders*, 117–18. Cf. Massa, *Short History*, 158.

86. Bussow incorrectly wrote (*Disturbed State*, 87–88) that Grigorii Shakhovskoi was Molchanov's companion on the journey from Moscow. (See Smirnov, *Vosstanie*, 100–105.) A number of scholars mistakenly credited Bussow on this point, resulting in considerable confusion. See, for example, Skrynnikov, *Time of Troubles*, 50; idem, *Smuta*, 65–67.

87. Margeret, *Russian Empire*, 76. Maureen Perrie (*Pretenders*, 114) incorrectly interpreted Margeret to mean that these stories of Tsar Dmitrii's escape were spread by three horsemen who fled from the Kremlin the night before the assassination.

88. An important contemporary English source (S.P. 91/1-f. 215) identified him as "Mulchan." Due to the use of a defective printed version of that document, many scholars believed the reference was to a man named "Mutcham." See Aleksandrenko, "Materialy," 262; Smirnov, *Vosstanie*, 553; Perrie, *Pretenders*, 115.

89. Massa, *Short History*, 156; Perrie, *Pretenders*, 111–12, 115.

90. SRIO 137:360. Cf. Bussow, *Disturbed State*, 100.

91. RIB 2: no. 217; Skrynnikov, *Samozvantsy*, 156.

92. Avrich (*Russian Rebels*, 19) was wrong on this point.

93. SRIO 137:368; Perrie, *Pretenders*, 119.

94. Smirnov, *Vosstanie*, 102 n. 6.

95. Massa, *Short History*, 119, 144; SRIO 137:302.

96. PSRL 14:66.

97. S.P. 91/1-f. 215; Nemoevskii, "Zapiski,"119.

98. Skrynnikov, *Smuta*, 64.

99. SRIO 137:313.

100. S.P. 91/1-f. 215; Smirnov, *Vosstanie*, 97; Perrie, "Legends," 240.

101. Gnevushev, *Akty*, 243. Cf. Skrynnikov, *Smuta*, 64, 80.

102. Bussow, *Disturbed State*, 87–88; S.P. 91/1-f. 215. Skrynnikov incorrectly wrote that Shakhovskoi and Molchanov traveled to Putivl together (*Time of Troubles*, 50; *Smuta*, 65–66).

103. *Razriadnaia kniga 1559–1605*, 302; Zolkiewski, *Expedition*, 47.

104. Belokurov, *Razriadnye zapisi*, 7, 30, 191; *Drevniaia Rossiiskaia Vivliofika*, 20:76; Platonov,

Ocherki, 302–3. Skrynnikov failed to note Grigorii Shakhovskoi's position of responsibility in Kursk during Tsar Dmitrii's reign and incorrectly denied that his father became a boyar (*Smuta*, 67).

105. Belokurov, *Razriadnye zapisi*, 80, 137.

106. Solov'ev, *Istoriia*, 4:468; Skrynnikov, *Smuta*, 78–79. Bussow (*Disturbed State*, 87) is unreliable on this topic.

107. Gnevushev, *Akty*, 1–3; Smirnov, *Vosstanie*, 98–101. Perrie incorrectly credited an English merchant's report that Molchanov "seduced" the courier, Gavrilo Shipov, into opposition to Shuiskii. See S.P. 91/1-f. 215; Perrie, *Pretenders*, 115.

108. PSRL 14:70; Bussow, *Disturbed State*, 88; S.P. 91/1-f. 215; *Boiarskie spiski*, 1:260; Ustrialov, *Skazaniia*, 1:79.

109. Smirnov, *Vosstanie*, 97–98; Perrie, *Pretenders*, 115–16. Belokurov (*Razriadnye zapisi*, 84) is not reliable on this issue.

110. Bussow, *Disturbed State*, 139; PSRL 14:70, 77; Massa, *Short History*, 149.

111. Bussow, *Disturbed State*, 88; Platonov, *Drevnerusskie skazaniia*, 390–94; Skrynnikov, *Smuta*, 79–81, 83, 132; idem, "Civil War," 64.

112. Skrynnikov, *Smuta*, 250–51; idem, "Civil War," 64. Cf. Massa, *Short History*, 149, 151.

113. Bussow, *Disturbed State*, 88; Nemoevskii, "Zapiski," 120. Captain Margeret, who was in Moscow at Tsar Vasilii's court until midsummer 1606, did not learn the truth about the seriousness of the rebellion before he left Russia. See Margeret, *Russian Empire*, xix, xxxiii–xxxv, 77.

114. Margeret, *Russian Empire*, 80.

115. Belokurov, *Razriadnye zapisi*, 157; AAE 2:137; Gnevushev, *Akty*, 243.

116. See, for example, AAE 2:129; S.P. 91/1-f. 215v; RIB 13: col. 484; Tikhomirov, "Novyi istochnik," 116.

117. Solov'ev, "Obzor sobytii," 11; Kliuchevskii, *Sochineniia*, 3:48; Platonov, *Time of Troubles*, 93–94; Smirnov, *Vosstanie*, 6–7, 88, 106–7, 137, 282–84; Eeckaute, "Les brigands," 188; Koretskii, *Formirovanie*, 259–62, 304, 309–10.

118. Skrynnikov, "Civil War," 66, 70, 77–78; idem, *Smuta*, 83, 250–51; Perrie, *Pretenders*, 111.

119. Belokurov, *Snosheniia*, 517; Skrynnikov, *Smuta*, 17–18; Miller, *Istoriia*, 2:193–94; Dmytryshyn et al., *Russia's Conquest*, 51–54. See also Tilly, *European Revolutions*, 187.

120. PSRL 14: 71, 73; RIB 13: cols. 108–9, 400; Popov, *Izbornik*, 332, 354; Koretskii, "Letopisets," 120–30; Pokrovsky, *Brief History*, 1:76; Vernadsky, *Tsardom*, 1:237–38; Avrich, *Russian Rebels*, 24, 30; Smirnov, *Vosstanie*, 6–8; Skrynnikov, *Time of Troubles*, 50–51, 55, 58.

121. Solov'ev, *Istoriia*, 4:391; Skrynnikov, *Smuta*, 250–51; Dunning, "Cossacks," 62, 71–72; Perrie, *Pretenders*, 111.

122. Avrich, *Russian Rebels*, 5–6; Nazarov, "Peasant Wars," 123–24; Skrynnikov, *Smuta*, 5–6, 79–83, 132–33.

123. Massa, *Short History*, 76, 151; Popov, *Izbornik*, 324; AAE 2:137; Belokurov, *Razriadnye zapisi*, 42, 117, 157, 173, 178; Piasetskii, *Istoricheskie ocherki*, 23; Smirnov, *Vosstanie*, 110–11; Skrynnikov, *Smuta*, 83; Dunning, "Byla li krest'ianskaia voina," 24.

124. Bussow, *Disturbed State*, 79–80, 83; RIB 13: cols. 108–9; Popov, *Izbornik*, 354; PSRL 34:214–15; Dunning, "Cossacks," 64–66; Skrynnikov, "Civil War," 64; idem, *Smuta*, 7–8, 79, 136, 145, 180–83, 251. Cf. Stanislavskii, *Grazhdanskaia voina*, 23–24, 29.

125. RIB 13: col. 484; Koretskii, "Letopisets," 120–30; PSRL 14:71; AAE 2: no. 60; Smirnov, *Vosstanie*, 106–7, 495; Vernadsky, *Tsardom*, 1:237–38; Hellie, *Slavery*, 574–76; Skrynnikov, *Time of Troubles*, 58.

126. Dunning, "Byla li krest'ianskaia voina," 23–24; idem, "Cossacks," 65; Skrynnikov, "Civil War," 66; Stanislavskii, *Grazhdanskaia voina*, 247.

127. Popov, *Izbornik*, 332; PSRL 14:70–71; AAE 2:137; RIB 13: cols. 99, 500; Smirnov, *Vosstanie*, 189–91; Avrich, *Russian Rebels*, 24.

128. PSRL 34:214–15; Belokurov, *Razriadnye zapisi*, 9–10; Avrich, *Russian Rebels*, 25–26; Kulakova, "Vosstanie," 49; Stanislavskii, "Novye dokumenty," 79; Koretskii, "Novye dokumenty," 68, 79–80; idem, "Novoe ob I. Bolotnikove," 101; idem, "K istorii vosstaniia Bolotnikova," 127–29; Indova et al., "Narodnye dvizheniia," 53–54, 83; Skrynnikov, "Civil War," 64, 67–68, 70; idem, *Smuta*, 79–83, 91–92, 108, 113, 131, 133.

129. Skrynnikov, "Civil War," 70. See also Zagorin, *Rebels*, 2:5, 53; Tilly, *European Revolutions*, 114; Scott, *Moral Economy*, 288–89; idem, "Everyday Forms," 13; Skocpol, *States and Social Revolutions*, 32.
130. Skrynnikov, "Civil War," 66, 70.
131. See, for example, Chistov, *Russkie legendy*, 52; Skrynnikov, *Smuta*, 39, 60.
132. Perrie, *Pretenders*, 111.
133. Koretskii, *Formirovanie*, 258–311, 366.
134. Skrynnikov, *Smuta*, 250–51; idem, "Civil War," 64.
135. Bacon, "Seditions," 79, 82, 85; Forster and Greene, *Preconditions*, 11, 13, 15–16; Bercé, *Revolt*, 72–73, 106, 127–28, 130, 221; Moote, "Preconditions," 155; Skocpol, *States and Social Revolutions*, 32; Zimmerman, *Political Violence*, 203; Gurr, *Why Men Rebel*, 207; Hagopian, *Phenomenon*, 11, 17, 40; Krejchi, *Great Revolutions Compared*, 14–15; Goldstone, *Revolution and Rebellion*, 24–25, 34, 37, 48, 67, 69–70, 82, 93, 107, 109, 133–34, 220, 222–24, 460, 464; Zagorin, *Rebels*, 2:2, 5; Tilly, *European Revolutions*, 189.
136. See Keenan, "Muscovite Political Folkways," 143.
137. See Stone, "Causal Stories," 293–94; Zimmerman, *Political Violence*, 213; Tilly, *European Revolutions*, 15.
138. Skrynnikov, *Smuta*, 51. Cf. Krejchi, *Great Revolutions Compared*, 10.
139. Perrie, "Popular Image," 279; idem, "Legends," 242; idem, "Folklore," 127–28, 133, 139. Cf. *Istoriia krest'ianstva*, 2:433.
140. Crummey, *Formation*, 220.
141. RIB 13: col. 622; Platonov, *Ocherki*, 325; Smirnov, *Vosstanie*, 164. Cf. Krejchi, *Great Revolutions Compared*, 15.
142. Gurr, *Why Men Rebel*, 121.
143. S.P. 91/1-f. 215; de Thou, *Histoire*, 14:495–96; Timofeev, *Vremennik*, 101–2; Howe, *False Dmitri*, 60; Ustrialov, *Skazaniia*, 1:215; Skrynnikov, *Time of Troubles*, 44–45; Perrie, *Pretenders*, 116.
144. Margeret, *Russian Empire*, 90.
145. S.P. 91/1-f. 215; Smirnov, *Vosstanie*, 90–91; Skrynnikov, *Smuta*, 64–65, 82. Cf. Bercé, *Revolt*, 113.
146. Ustrialov, *Skazaniia*, 1:215; Perrie, *Pretenders*, 116–17.
147. Sviatskii, *Istoricheskii ocherk*, 23, 41.
148. Zolkiewski, *Expedition*, 47; Timofeev, *Vremennik*, 101–2, 153; LaVille, *Discours sommaire*, 6–7; Palitsyn, *Skazanie*, 270.
149. RIB 13: cols. 173, 1300; Tikhomirov, "Novyi istochnik," 100; Belobrova, "K izucheniiu," 155.
150. Margeret, *Russian Empire*, 89; Timofeev, *Vremennik*, 101–2, 153; RIB 13: cols. 582, 622; Bennet, "Idea of Kingship," 114. Cf. RIB 13: col. 104.
151. Palitsyn, *Skazanie*, 266, 270; RIB 13: cols. 543–46; Bennet, "Idea of Kingship," 104–5.
152. Kimmell, *Revolution*, 12; Zimmerman, *Political Violence*, 208; Bacon, "Seditions," 85, 87; Skocpol, *States and Social Revolutions*, 11; Tilly, *European Revolutions*, 10; Forster and Greene, *Preconditions*, 16; Willner and Willner, "Charismatic Leaders," 97.
153. Perrie, *Pretenders*, 66, 69, 73–74, 78–79, 245.
154. Perrie, "Folklore," 131, 141. See also Field, *Rebels*, 10, 12–13, 24–25; Kivelson, "Devil Stole His Mind," 736, 745; Longworth, "Subversive Legend," 28.
155. Massa, *Short History*, 69–70, 76–77, 81–82; Timofeev, *Vremennik*, 84; Buganov, "Religious ideologies," 207; Siegelbaum, "Peasant Disorders," 227; Mousnier, *Peasant Uprisings*, 182; Perrie, *Pretenders*, 66–68, 245–46. See also Kivelson, "Devil Stole His Mind," 745–48, 755; Zagorin, *Rebels*, 1:145; Keep, "Emancipation," 48.
156. AAE 2:89–90, 92–93; SGGD 2:201; Perrie, "Legends," 227–28, 232, 243; idem, *Pretenders*, 64–65, 68–69, 79.
157. RIB 13: col 367; Timofeev, *Vremennik*, 84; Bussow, *Disturbed State*, 46; Pirling, *Dmitrii Samozvanets*, 159; Perrie, *Pretenders*, 65, 78–79, 83, 103; Uspenskij, "Tsar and Pretender," 211; Wada, "Inner World," 68.
158. Crummey, *Formation*, 220; Avrich, *Russian Rebels*, 17–18. See also Eskin, "Smuta i mestnichestvo," 268. Cf. Krejchi, *Great Revolutions Compared*, 10; Zimmerman, *Political Violence*, 203.

159. Perrie, *Pretenders,* 115; idem, "Legends," 239–40. Cf. Bennet, "Idea of Kingship," 1–2; Zimmerman, *Political Violence,* 208.
160. Bushkovitch, *Religion and Society,* 10, 74, 100–102, 106, 111.
161. SGGD 2:213–14; Perrie, "Legends," 234–36; Chistov, *Russkie legendy,* 46.
162. SRIO 137:306; Perrie, *Pretenders,* 111–12; Skrynnikov, *Smuta,* 152. Cf. Willner and Willner, "Charismatic Leaders," 95.
163. Stone, "Causal Stories," 281–83, 285, 293–295, 300.
164. See Bercé, *Revolt,* 32–33; Burke, *Popular Culture,* 152–53; Perrie, *Pretenders,* 245–46.
165. Billington, *Icon,* 199–200; Buganov, "Religious ideologies," 207; Bercé, *Revolt,* 120; Kimmell, *Revolution,* 222–23.
166. See Bercé, *Revolt,* 118, 124; Zagorin, *Rebels,* 1:149; Krejchi, *Great Revolutions Compared,* 15–16.
167. See Perrie, *Pretenders,* 157–207, 246; Massa, *Short History,* 144–45, 153; Skrynnikov, *Time of Troubles,* 60–71, 73–75, 80–82, 90–92, 96–100, 109–12, 177–78, 180–82, 194–95, 197, 201–3, 207–8, 223–28.

NOTES TO CHAPTER 15

1. S.P. 91/1-f. 215; Massa, *Short History,* 149; Popov, *Izbornik,* 331; Belokurov, *Razriadnye zapisi,* 8, 42, 178; RIB 13: col. 500; Smirnov, *Vosstanie,* 88–92.
2. Margeret, *Russian Empire,* 77; PSRL 14:71.
3. Massa, *Short History,* 151; Ustrialov, *Skazaniia,* 1:215; VBDM 208.
4. Petreius, *Istoriia,* 249; Popov, *Izbornik,* 331; Massa, *Short History,* 149, 151; Belokurov, *Razriadnye zapisi,* 8, 42, 178; *Boiarskie spiski,* 1:256; PSRL 14:70, 74; RIB 13: col. 99; Kulakova, "Vosstanie," 49. Massa incorrectly included Tula in the first wave of towns joining the rebellion. The exact timing of the rebellion in Novgorod Severskii is not known, but it may have occurred in mid-summer; see Skrynnikov, *Smuta,* 78.
5. Popov, *Izbornik,* 331.
6. Belokurov, *Razriadnye zapisi,* 8; *Boiarskie spiski,* 1:256; PSRL 14:65; Zimin, *Khrestomatiia,* 283; Skrynnikov, *Time of Troubles,* 15, 51.
7. VBDM 281; PSRL 14:71; RIB 13: col. 500; Massa, *Short History,* 151, 153.
8. Belokurov, *Razriadnye zapisi,* 42, 117, 173, 178; Piasetskii, *Istoricheskie ocherki,* 23.
9. Bussow, *Disturbed State,* 88; Dunning, "Cossacks," 57–74.
10. VBDM 373.
11. *Skazaniia Massy i Gerkmana,* 295; Ustrialov, *Skazaniia,* 1:214–15.
12. Bussow, *Disturbed State,* 87–88; Skrynnikov, *Smuta,* 66.
13. *Opis' arkhiva Posol'skogo prikaza,* 1:320.
14. Bussow, *Disturbed State,* 88; Skrynnikov, *Smuta,* 67–68.
15. VBDM 207–8; Skrynnikov, *Smuta,* 67. Cf. Howe, *False Dmitri,* 66.
16. SRIO 137:301, 306.
17. Pirling, *Dmitrii Samozvanets,* 402.
18. SRIO 137:301, 306, 312; Skrynnikov, *Smuta,* 70. Skrynnikov carefully deconstructed the legend of "Prince Vasilii Mosalskii" joining "Tsar Dmitrii" in Sambor (*Smuta,* 62–63).
19. SRIO 137:307; *Boiarskie spiski,* 1:259; Skrynnikov, *Smuta,* 63.
20. Skrynnikov, *Smuta,* 69–71, 74.
21. SRIO 137:360; Skrynnikov, *Smuta,* 68, 70–71.
22. Pirling, *Dmitrii Samozvanets,* 399–402; Pierling, *La Russie,* 3:344–45; Skrynnikov, *Smuta,* 76.
23. SRIO 137:307, 312.
24. A false rumor circulated in Moscow in late 1606 that Molchanov had arrived at the frontier with a large army. See Massa, *Short History,* 165.

25. Pirling, *Dmitrii Samozvanets,* 400; Skrynnikov, *Smuta,* 68–69.
26. SRIO 137:301–2, 306, 313, 360–61, 368.
27. See Howe, *False Dmitri,* 66; Smirnov, *Vosstanie,* 105.
28. Bussow, *Disturbed State,* 144; Likhachev, *Boiarskii spisok 1611g.,* 7.
29. Kliuchevskii, *Sochineniia,* 3:48; Platonov, *Ocherki,* 305; idem, *Smutnoe vremia,* 93; Smirnov, *Vosstanie;* Avrich, *Russian Rebels,* 10, 25; Eeckaute, "Brigands," 188.
30. Skrynnikov, "Civil War," 65; idem, *Smuta,* 75. Many scholars have erroneously credited Isaac Massa's faulty information. See, for example, Smirnov, *Vosstanie;* Perrie, *Pretenders,* 121; Koretskii, "O formirovanii," 128; idem, "Ivan Bolotnikov," 123–36; Skrynnikov, *Time of Troubles,* 52; Stanislavskii, *Grazhdanskaia voina,* 23.
31. Massa, *Short History,* 155; Bussow, *Disturbed State,* 91.
32. S.P. 91/1-f. 216.
33. Skrynnikov, *Smuta,* 74.
34. PSRL 14:71; Palitsyn, *Skazanie,* 116; VBDM 111; Massa, *Short History,* 155; Koretskii, "O formirovanii," 123–26; Skrynnikov, *Time of Troubles,* 52. Ivan Bolotnikov was not an ordinary slave or serf, as some writers, including Massa, thought. See, for example, Smirnov, *Vosstanie,* 138–40; Platonov, *Ocherki,* chapter 4.
35. Massa, *Short History,* 155; Skrynnikov, *Smuta,* 74.
36. S.P. 91/1-f. 216.
37. Bussow, *Disturbed State,* 91. Paul Avrich (*Russian Rebels,* 20) erroneously referred to him as a "helmsman" aboard a Turkish galley. Skrynnikov ("Civil War," 65) wrote that Bolotnikov was freed by Italians.
38. Massa, *Short History,* 155. Cf. Perrie, *Pretenders,* 121.
39. Skrynnikov, *Time of Troubles,* 52; Stanislavskii, *Grazhdanskaia voina,* 23.
40. Koretskii, "O formirovanii," 129–30.
41. Viktorov, *Krest'ianskie dvizheniia,* 6; Piontkovskii, "Istoriografiia," 118; *Istoriia krest'ianstva,* 2:434; Buganov, "Religious ideologies," 208; Avrich, *Russian Rebels,* 257–58; Stanislavskii, *Grazhdanskaia voina,* 23. Cf. Yaresh, "Peasant Wars," 254; Longworth, "Subversive Legend," 32; idem, "Peasant Leadership," 201–2; idem, "Last Great Cossack-Peasant Rising," 23. This faulty interpretation was due in part to the actual use of the cossack model of self-government in rebel-held territory during the Razin and Pugachev rebellions.
42. Bussow, *Disturbed State,* 91. For unclear reasons, Perrie questioned Bussow's story about Bolotnikov's journey to Sambor (*Pretenders,* 122).
43. Skrynnikov, *Smuta,* 76.
44. See VBDM 186–87; Smirnov, *Vosstanie,* 142–43; Avrich, *Russian Rebels,* 20.
45. Massa, *Short History,* 155.
46. Dmitrievskii, *Arkhiepiskop Arsenii,* 139.
47. Bussow, *Disturbed State,* 91–93, 100. Cf. Howe, *False Dmitri,* 66; Smirnov, *Vosstanie,* 105.
48. Skrynnikov, *Smuta,* 74, 76, 252–53. Massa's erroneous story about Bolotnikov's ten thousand cossacks may have been the result of confusion about the arrival from Ukraine in January 1607 of large numbers of Zaporozhian cossacks prepared to fight for Tsar Dmitrii and by Shuiskii propaganda about the rebels as foreign brigands. See Golobutskii, *Zaporozhskoe kazachestvo,* 153.
49. Margeret, *Russian Empire,* 79–80; Bussow, *Disturbed State,* 93.
50. Skrynnikov (*Smuta,* 82) continued to refer to Bezzubtsev as a sotnik (centurion), but that old and experienced military leader by 1606 had been promoted to the rank of golova (colonel). See RIB 1: col. 151; Anpilogov, "Novye materialy," 200. Cf. Smirnov, *Vosstanie,* 259.
51. Belokurov, *Razriadnye zapisi,* 152; AAE 2:137; PSRL 14:73; RIB 13: cols. 108–9, 400; Ustrialov, *Skazaniia,* 1:216. Cf. Bussow, *Disturbed State,* 88.
52. Skrynnikov, *Smuta,* 79; idem, "Civil War," 64.
53. See Bussow, *Disturbed State,* 53; PSRL 14:68; Palitsyn, *Skazanie,* 114, 118; Novosel'skii, *Bor'ba,* 48; Massa, *Short History,* 123.
54. Massa, *Short History,* 149. See also Anpilogov, *Novye dokumenty,* 320; *Boiarskie spiski,* 2:33, 51. A faulty source's claim that militiamen from the southern provinces refused to swear an oath to

Tsar Vasilii and left Moscow as an army may actually have been a reference to militiamen sent to Elets by Tsar Dmitrii who subsequently joined the rebellion against Shuiskii. See Skrynnikov, *Smuta*, 80–81, 83; Kulakova, "Vosstanie," 49; Platonov, *Drevnerusskie skazaniia*, 390–94.

55. Massa, *Short History*, 151–52, 215 n. 176; Skrynnikov, *Smuta*, 83.

56. Bussow, *Disturbed State*, 88.

57. Platonov, *Ocherki*, 248, 309; Smirnov, *Vosstanie*, 165–89; Ovchinnikov, "Nekotorye voprosy," 80; Koretskii, *Formirovanie*, 263–83, 290.

58. Skrynnikov, *Smuta*, 135–36.

59. Belokurov, *Razriadnye zapisi*, 157; AAE 2:137.

60. Kniaz'kov, "Materialy," 68–70.

61. Ibid., 71; Storozhev, "Desiatni," 131; Platonov, *Ocherki*, 248; Skrynnikov, *Smuta*, 136.

62. RGADA, fond 210 (Razriadnyi prikaz), opis' 4 (Dela desiaten'), kniga 223, listy 1–9 ob.; Skrynnikov, *Sotsial'no-politicheskaia bor'ba*, 141–42; idem, *Smuta*, 136.

63. RIB 13: cols. 108–9; Skrynnikov, *Smuta*, 137.

64. See Smirnov, *Vosstanie*, 166–68.

65. See, for example, Ovchinnikov, "Nekotorye voprosy," 80; Koretskii, *Formirovanie*, 282–83, 290.

66. S.P. 91/1-f. 216; AAE 2: no. 60; Ustrialov, *Skazaniia*, 1:216; Nemoevskii, "Zapiski," 177; Kniaz'kov, "Materialy," 71; VBDM 176, 183.

67. Belokurov, *Snosheniia*, 546; Skrynnikov, *Boris Godunov*, 113; Bushkovitch, *Merchants*, 15, 30–31, 94–101.

68. N. Veselovskii, *Pamiatniki*, 3:84–124; Smirnov, *Vosstanie*, 225, 231, 233–34.

69. See Smirnov, "Astrakhan'," 167–205; idem, *Vosstanie*, 213–16, 227–28; Platonov, *Ocherki*, 331–32.

70. PSRL 14:69; Popov, *Izbornik*, 330; Gnevushev, *Akty*, 202–3.

71. PSRL 14:71; Smirnov, *Vosstanie*, 223–25, 228.

72. Smirnov, *Vosstanie*, 250–52; Gnevushev, *Akty*, 206; Massa, *Short History*, 152. *Letopis' o mnogikh miatezhakh* (page 110) is to be preferred to the faulty text of PSRL 14:72. See Platonov, *Drevnerusskie skazaniia*, 311; Cherepnin, "Smuta," 110, 114–16; *Novyi letopisets*, 80.

73. Massa, *Short History*, 152; Smirnov, *Vosstanie*, 238; Savvinskii, *Istoricheskaia zapiska*, 117.

74. Smirnov, *Vosstanie*, 229, 235–39, 242–43.

75. Gnevushev, *Akty*, 161–64, 168, 180, 190–91; Smirnov, *Vosstanie*, 228.

76. See SGGD 2: no. 155.

77. There is great confusion in sources and historiography concerning Sheremetev's identification, location, and his official instructions. See Smirnov, *Vosstanie*, 224–27; Gnevushev, *Akty*, 156–57, 171; Popov, *Izbornik*, 330, 339–40.

78. Gnevushev, *Akty*, 161–62, 197–98, 203; VBDM 236; Skrynnikov, *Smuta*, 117, 222.

79. Massa, *Short History*, 152.

80. See Smirnov, *Vosstanie*, 231, 237.

81. Gnevushev, *Akty*, 169.

82. Ibid., 156, 162; Novosel'skii, *Bor'ba*, 56.

83. Gnevushev, *Akty*, 156–57, 161–64, 168, 190–91; SGGD 2: no. 155; Smirnov, *Vosstanie*, 227.

84. Massa, *Short History*, 152.

85. Kappeler, "Rolle," 254–55.

86. *Chronicle of the Carmelites*, 1:111–12; Skrynnikov, *Smuta*, 222.

87. See Perrie, *Pretenders*, 131–34, 174–81.

88. Massa, *Short History*, 152.

89. Ibid., 149; Perrie, *Pretenders*, 116.

90. See Skocpol, *States and Social Revolutions*, 25–27, 31–32; Zimmerman, *Political Violence*, 208, 213.

91. Stanislavskii, *Grazhdanskaia voina*, 24. See, for example, RGADA, fond 210 (Razriadnyi prikaz), opis' 4 (Dela desiaten'), kniga 98, listy 6ob, 9, 11ob, 12.

92. Platonov, *Drevnerusskie skazaniia*, 390–94; Kulakova, "Vosstanie," 49; Massa, *Short History*, 155; Skrynnikov, *Smuta*, 64, 80–81, 108.

93. Massa, *Short History*, 155; Skrynnikov, *Smuta*, 116.
94. de Thou, *Histoire*, 14:504.
95. Massa, *Short History*, 153, 155.
96. Margeret, *Russian Empire*, xix–xxi; Massa, *Short History*, 153; Zhordaniia, *Ocherki*, 1:258–60.
97. AAE 2: no. 70; AI 2: no. 67; RIB 35: nos. 51, 98; Bibikov, "Novye dannye," 7, 14; Smirnov, *Vosstanie*, 409–10.
98. Bussow, *Disturbed State*, 88–89; Nemoevskii, "Zapiski," 120; Skrynnikov, *Smuta*, 81; idem, *Time of Troubles*, 51.
99. AAE 2:270; RIB 35: no. 98.
100. Smirnov, *Vosstanie*, 406, 409.
101. Massa, *Short History*, 152. Cf. RIB 35: nos. 50–51.
102. SRIO 137:381; Bussow, *Moskovskaia khronika*, 141–42, 363 n. 90; Massa, *Short History*, 154–55; Roberts, *Early Vasas*, 453.
103. Belokurov, *Razriadnye zapisi*, 178.
104. Bussow, *Disturbed State*, 89.
105. Margeret, *Russian Empire*, 79–80; Smirnov, *Vosstanie*, 143–44; Skrynnikov, *Smuta*, 83. Cf. Nemoevskii, "Zapiski," 120.
106. Belokurov, *Razriadnye zapisi*, 178; Smirnov, *Vosstanie*, 143–44.
107. Margeret, *Russian Empire*, 80. Massa's estimate of 180,00 men is much too high and actually referred to a somewhat later stage in the civil war (*Short History*, 153).
108. Belokurov, *Razriadnye zapisi*, 42, 86, 184.
109. Skrynnikov, *Smuta*, 85, 89, 116.
110. Koretskii, "Novoe o krest'ianskom zakreposhchenii," 135.
111. SGGD 2: no. 149; Massa, *Short History*, 153. Avrich (*Russian Rebels*, 22–23) incorrectly identified Vorotynskii as Tsar Vasilii's brother-in-law. Bussow (*Disturbed State*, 89) incorrectly dated the start of the siege; it began in July, not August.
112. Margeret, *Russian Empire*, 79–80.
113. The vague chronology provided by Massa (*Short History*, 153) and Bussow (*Disturbed State*, 89) confused historians. See, for example, Kostomarov, *Smutnoe vremia*, 44.
114. Belokurov, *Razriadnye zapisi*, 85, 114; Margeret, *Russian Empire*, 79–80; Smirnov, *Vosstanie*, 149; Skrynnikov, *Smuta*, 85. A number of peasant war scholars incorrectly wrote that Pashkov might not have been the rebel commander who clashed with Vorotynskii before Elets; see, for example, Ovchinnikov, "Nekotorye voprosy," 72–75.
115. Belokurov, *Razriadnye zapisi*, 117, 156.
116. Ibid., 42, 85, 117; VBDM 127.
117. See, for example, Stanislavskii, *Grazhdanskaia voina*, 23; Koretskii, "O formirovanii," 130.
118. Belokurov, *Razriadnye zapisi*, 42, 86, 184, 206; Skrynnikov, *Smuta*, 77–78.
119. Bussow, *Disturbed State*, 93.
120. Belokurov, *Razriadnye zapisi*, 42, 86, 184, 206; Smirnov, *Vosstanie*, 145; Skrynnikov, *Smuta*, 85.
121. Skrynnikov, *Smuta*, 88.
122. PSRL 14:74; Popov, *Izbornik*, 331; Belokurov, *Razriadnye zapisi*, 42, 178; Skrynnikov, *Smuta*, 78.
123. Sviatskii, *Istoricheskii ocherk*, 41.
124. Piasetskii, *Istoricheskie ocherki*, 23; VBDM 281; RIB 13: col. 99; PSRL 14:70–71, 74; Belokurov, *Razriadnye zapisi*, 8, 9, 42, 84, 141, 178; Popov, *Izbornik*, 331, 335; AAE 2: nos. 74, 76, 81; *Akty Iushkova*, no. 271; Sukhotin, *Chetvertchiki*, 209; Massa, *Short History*, 167; Anpilogov, "O vosstanii," 93–94; Smirnov, *Vosstanie*, 96, 110, 163.
125. Belokurov, *Razriadnye zapisi*, 142, 213; PSRL 14:74; Popov, *Izbornik*, 331; Ovchinnikov, "Boiarskii spisok," 72; Smirnov, *Vosstanie*, 163. Cf. Skrynnikov, *Smuta*, 227.
126. Tikhomirov, "Novyi istochnik," 116.
127. Belokurov, *Razriadnye zapisi*, 8, 9, 85, 117, 141, 173, 184, 246; Smirnov, *Vosstanie*, 145; Skrynnikov, *Smuta*, 77.
128. Massa, *Short History*, 153.

129. Belokurov, *Razriadnye zapisi*, 8, 42, 117.
130. Ibid., 141, 156; Smirnov, *Vosstanie*, 146–49.
131. Belokurov, *Razriadnye zapisi*, 85; Skrynnikov, *Smuta*, 86, 108.
132. PSRL 14:71.
133. *Boiarskie spiski*, 1:41, 231; 2:79.
134. Belokurov, *Razriadnye zapisi*, 117, 156; Smirnov, *Vosstanie*, 149–50.
135. Koretskii, "Novoe o krest'ianskom zakreposhchenii," 148; Hirschberg, *Polska a Moskwa*, 80; Skrynnikov, *Smuta*, 90.
136. Belokurov, *Razriadnye zapisi*, 42, 178, 238; PSRL 34:244.
137. Skrynnikov, *Smuta*, 88; PSRL 34:244. On the damage caused by the severe freeze, see Massa, *Short History*, 146; Margeret, *Russian Empire*, 73.
138. PSRL 14:71; Belokurov, *Razriadnye zapisi*, 9, 42, 86, 184, 206.
139. VBDM 116; Skrynnikov, *Smuta*, 86–87.
140. See, for example, PSRL 14:71; Belokurov, *Razriadnye zapisi*, 9, 42; Smirnov, *Vosstanie*, 150–52. Some writers also confused events at Kromy with those at Elets; see, for example, Karamzin, *Istoriia*, 12:20; Solov'ev, *Istoriia*, 4:468.
141. *Boiarskie spiski*, 1:41, 231; Belokurov, *Razriadnye zapisi*, 9; Skrynnikov, *Smuta*, 91–92.
142. Belokurov, *Razriadnye zapisi*, 9, 12, 42, 46; SGGD 2: nos. 150–51; AAE 2: no. 60; Massa, *Short History*, 167; PSRL 14:73–74; Stanislavskii, "Novye dokumenty," 79; "Kostromskaia starina," 4–5.
143. Koretskii, *Formirovanie*, 268–71; idem, "Novoe ob I. Bolotnikove," 100–103.
144. Belokurov, *Razriadnye zapisi*, 8; Massa, *Short History*, 153; PSRL 14:71.
145. PSRL 34:244.
146. Zimin, "K istorii vosstaniia," 371. Ivan Smirnov thought the destruction of the supply train was actually a reference to a battle before Elets; see Bussow, *Moskovskaia khronika*, 359 n. 79.
147. PSRL 14:71; Belokurov, *Razriadnye zapisi*, 42, 156; Platonov, *Ocherki*, 321.
148. VBDM 116; Massa, *Short History*, 153; Bussow, *Disturbed State*, 89; Hirschberg, *Polska a Moskwa*, 80; Skrynnikov, *Smuta*, 86–87.
149. Smirnov, *Vosstanie*, 153, 155–56; Bussow, *Moskovskaia khronika*, 359 n. 79.
150. See Belokurov, *Razriadnye zapisi*, 156; PSRL 14:71; Skrynnikov, *Smuta*, 90.
151. Smirnov (*Vosstanie*, 153) incorrectly concluded that Bolotnikov was the commander of the rebel army at Elets. Platonov and others developed the erroneous idea that the rebel commander could not have been Pashkov, arguing that he joined the rebel cause only at a later time. See Platonov, *Ocherki*, 227, 326; Ovchinnikov, "O nachal'nom periode," 117; idem, "Nekotorye voprosy," 72–75.
152. PSRL 14:72; Koretskii, "Novye dokumenty," 67, 79; Bussow, *Moskovskaia khronika*, 359 n. 79; Skrynnikov, *Time of Troubles*, 53.
153. Belokurov, *Razriadnye zapisi*, 42; Smirnov, *Vosstanie*, 158.
154. Belokurov, *Razriadnye zapisi*, 156; Skrynnikov, *Smuta*, 93.
155. Massa, *Short History*, 153, 167; Bussow, *Disturbed State*, 89.
156. Belokurov, *Razriadnye zapisi*, 12, 46, 91, 118, 158; Sukhotin, *Chetvertchiki*, 266; Popov, *Izbornik*, 334; Massa, *Short History*, 167; Perrie, *Pretenders*, 124.
157. Smirnov, *Vosstanie*, 170–72.
158. Skrynnikov, *Smuta*, 93; Belokurov, *Razriadnye zapisi*, 156.
159. Platonov, *Ocherki*, 280, 323–27; Smirnov, *Vosstanie*, 164–65.
160. Skrynnikov, *Smuta*, 93.
161. PSRL 14:72, 74; Popov, *Izbornik*, 331; VBDM 110; Belokurov, *Razriadnye zapisi*, 7, 79, 83, 139.
162. Popov, *Izbornik*, 332; PSRL 14:74; Aleksandrov, "Pamflet," 119.
163. Popov, *Izbornik*, 331.
164. SGGD 2: nos. 150–51; AAE 2: nos. 60, 76; PSRL 14:73; *Akty Iushkova*, no. 272; Massa, *Short History*, 167; Popov, *Izbornik*, 331–32, 334; RIB 13: col. 99; Belokurov, *Razriadnye zapisi*, 42, 44, 89, 146, 185, 206, 213.
165. There is some confusion about when Shuiskii loyalists in Gremiachii were killed. See Koretskii, Solov'eva, and Stanislavskii, "Dokumenty," 39. Cf. Skrynnikov, *Smuta*, 225–26.

166. An example of the faulty Marxist interpretation of this phase of the civil war may be found in Nazarov, "Peasant Wars," 119.
167. Nemoevskii, "Zapiski," 120; Skrynnikov, *Time of Troubles*, 51.
168. Ustrialov, *Skazaniia*, 2:177; Stadnitskii, "Dnevnik," 171; Hirschberg, *Polska a Moskwa*, 76.
169. Hirschberg, *Polska a Moskwa*, 75–76; Margeret, *Russian Empire*, 76.
170. AAE 2:137; Bussow, *Disturbed State*, 89.
171. AAE 2:131.
172. Massa, *Short History*, 156–58. Cf. Perrie, *Pretenders*, 127.
173. Hirschberg, *Polska a Moskwa*, 79–80.
174. Belokurov, *Razriadnye zapisi*, 9, 156.
175. Ibid., 42; Platonov, *Ocherki*, 324–26.

NOTES TO CHAPTER 16

1. Tikhomirov and Floria, "Prikhodo-raskhodnye knigi," 339; Skrynnikov, *Smuta*, 101.
2. Belokurov, *Razriadnye zapisi*, 9, 88, 143, 145.
3. Ibid., 9, 88, 156, 173.
4. Ibid., 88, 145.
5. Ibid., 9; Stanislavskii, "Novye dokumenty," 77.
6. Belokurov, *Razriadnye zapisi*, 88, 145; Sukhotin, *Chetvertchiki*, 197.
7. Smirnov, *Vosstanie*, 160–61, 172; Avrich, *Russian Rebels*, 27. Reasons for the inaccurate legend include the use of a poorly informed and undated source concerning a defeat suffered by the boyars on the banks of the Oka followed by a massive retreat to Moscow as well as historians' frequent confusion of this battle with the siege of Kaluga in 1607. See VBDM 175; Ustrialov, *Skazaniia*, 2:100; Smirnov, *Vosstanie*, 162; Skrynnikov, *Smuta*, 102.
8. On Kaluga's ties to the southwest frontier, see Massa, *Short History*, 163.
9. Belokurov, *Razriadnye zapisi*, 9, 156; RIB 13: col. 99; Massa, *Short History*, 167; AAE 2: no. 60; SGGD 2: nos. 150–51; Smirnov, *Vosstanie*, 160; Skrynnikov, *Time of Troubles*, 53.
10. Belokurov, *Razriadnye zapisi*, 9, 155–56; Smirnov, *Vosstanie*, 161.
11. Faulty views of Bolotnikov's advance to Serpukhov may be found in Avrich, *Russian Rebels*, 27–28; Skrynnikov, *Time of Troubles*, 53. Those views were based on the misinterpretation of three laconic, vague, or confused sources; see VBDM 175; Massa, *Short History*, 155; Bussow, *Disturbed State*, 91.
12. Popov, *Izbornik*, 332; Belokurov, *Razriadnye zapisi*, 9, 156; Skrynnikov, *Smuta*, 107.
13. Bussow, *Disturbed State*, 91.
14. Koretskii mistakenly believed Pashkov himself went east from Tula to Riazhsk ("Novye dokumenty," 67, 79). Cf. Skrynnikov, *Smuta*, 101–2.
15. Skrynnikov, *Time of Troubles*, 52–53.
16. RIB 13: col. 99; PSRL 14:73.
17. VBDM 166–67; Hirschberg, *Polska a Moskwa*, 81. Several scholars incorrectly concluded that Bolotnikov, instead of Pashkov, occupied Serpukhov at this time; see, for example, Smirnov, *Vosstanie*, 173; Avrich, *Russian Rebels*, 27–28.
18. VBDM 271. Smirnov (*Vosstanie*, 173–74) incorrectly listed this as Bolotnikov's victory due to his use of an unreliable, later copy of relevant military records (Belokurov, *Razriadnye zapisi*, 9–10).
19. Belokurov, *Razriadnye zapisi*, 43, 89, 146.
20. *Opis' arkhiva Posol'skogo prikaza*, 1:320.
21. RIB 13: col. 99; Skrynnikov, *Smuta*, 104; idem, *Time of Troubles*, 52–53. Several scholars incorrectly listed this as Bolotnikov's defeat; see, for example, Smirnov, *Vosstanie*, 173–74; Avrich, *Russian Rebels*, 28. Avrich was also wrong about Skopin-Shuiskii rallying Ivan Shuiskii's retreating troops; those men were actually still near Kaluga at this time.

22. Belokurov, *Razriadnye zapisi*, 9, 88–89, 145–46; VBDM 264; Skrynnikov, *Smuta*, 105.
23. Bussow, *Disturbed State*, 90; RIB 13: cols. 99–100; Skrynnikov, *Smuta*, 98–100, 105. Smirnov mistook Kolomenskoe for Kolomna in his earlier work (*Vosstanie*, 178–79) but got it straight by 1961 (Bussow, *Moskovskaia khronika*, 361 n. 81). Scholars have often erred in estimating the timing of the first rebel approach to Moscow in part because they ignored the date of the earliest version of an important document that indirectly referred to rebels in the Moscow area. The earliest version of Archpriest Terentii's "vision tale" (used by Shuiskii propaganda and incorporated into "Inoe skazanie") was September 1606, not October. (See Skrynnikov, *Smuta*, 98–99; Koretskii, *Formirovanie*, 284.) Another factor leading to misdating the first rebel approach to the capital was an error in a Russian translation of an important Polish source which actually noted the rebel approach in September, not October—as many scholars long thought. See Hirschberg, *Polska a Moskwa*, 81; VBDM 166–67; Skrynnikov, *Smuta*, 99–100.
24. See Smirnov, *Vosstanie*, 175.
25. VBDM 167.
26. Belokurov, *Razriadnye zapisi*, 42.
27. VBDM 111; Skrynnikov, *Smuta*, 107–8.
28. Some vague or confused sources incorrectly placed Bolotnikov at the "siege" of Kolomna. See, for example, PSRL 14:72; Massa, *Short History*, 155; Belokurov, *Razriadnye zapisi*, 9, 10; Smirnov, *Vosstanie*, 177–79.
29. SGGD 2: nos. 150–51; AAE 2: no. 60; Belokurov, *Razriadnye zapisi*, 9–10, 89, 146; PSRL 14:72; Morozov, "Vazhnyi dokument," 166.
30. RIB 13: col. 99; VBDM 185.
31. Nemoevskii, "Zapiski," 178–79.
32. Smirnov, *Vosstanie*, 508. Cf. Skrynnikov, *Smuta*, 109–10. See also Floria, "Tri pis'ma," 165.
33. See AAE 2: no. 58; Smirnov, *Vosstanie*, 263; Skrynnikov, *Smuta*, 116.
34. Morozov, "Vazhnyi dokument," 166–68; Skrynnikov, *Smuta*, 109, 131.
35. PSRL 14:72; Popov, *Izbornik*, 332; VBDM 111; Skrynnikov, *Smuta*, 108–9; Kniaz'kov, "Materialy," 71. Many scholars incorrectly concluded that Pashkov only joined the rebel cause at this time, along with the Riazan area dvoriane. Some also incorrectly argued that Pashkov was no longer the senior voevoda when he was in the company of high-born Riazan lords. See, for example, Platonov, *Ocherki*, 227, 248; Smirnov, *Vosstanie*, 165–66, 170–71; Ovchinnikov, "O nachal'nom periode," 117; idem, "Nekotorye voprosy," 72–75; Koretskii, *Formirovanie*, 263–65, 282–83.
36. VBDM 208.
37. See Skrynnikov, *Smuta*, 107; Smirnov, *Vosstanie*, 176–79. Incorrect views of the two rebel commanders linking up at this time may be found in Zimin and Koroleva, "Dokument," 22; Ovchinnikov, "O nachal'nom periode," 116–20; PSRL 14:72; Belokurov, *Razriadnye zapisi*, 9, 10; Massa, *Short History*, 155.
38. Platonov, *Ocherki*, 267, 308–9; Smirnov, *Vosstanie*, 138–40, 165–89, 255–324; Koretskii, *Formirovanie*, 257–62, 266–80, 282–83, 290, 309–10; Ovchinnikov, "Nekotorye voprosy," 69–81. Cf. VBDM 381.
39. Smirnov, *Kratkii ocherk*, 72; Skrynnikov, "Civil War," 66; idem, *Smuta*, 130–34, 137.
40. Skrynnikov, *Smuta*, 79; Makovskii, *Pervaia krest'ianskaia voina*, 471.
41. Skrynnikov, *Smuta*, 132.
42. Ibid., 112–13, 131; idem, "Civil War," 64–66.
43. Morozov, "Vazhnyi dokument," 166; Dunning, "Byla li krest'ianskaia voina," 27–29; Skrynnikov, *Smuta*, 130–31, 250–51.
44. Skrynnikov, *Smuta*, 117.
45. Smirnov, *Vosstanie*, 190.
46. PSRL 34:214–15; Skrynnikov, *Smuta*, 113.
47. Bussow, *Disturbed State*, 91; Platonov, *Ocherki*, 327–28; Smirnov, *Vosstanie*, 189–91.
48. VBDM 198; "Kostromskaia starina," 4–5; AAE 2: nos. 58, 68. Chancellor Lew Sapieha's statement that these towns were taken by force is incorrect (SRIO 137:360).
49. Skrynnikov, *Smuta*, 117–18.

50. Belokurov, *Razriadnye zapisi,* 9; SRIO 137:360; PSRL 14:72; "Kostromskaia starina," 4–5; Smirnov, *Vosstanie,* 275; Skrynnikov, *Smuta,* 113, 117.

51. AAE 2: nos. 58, 60; AI 2: no. 75; SGGD 2: nos. 150–51; SRIO 137:360; PSRL 14:72; "Kostromskaia starina," 4–5; Massa, *Short History,* 167; Smirnov, *Vosstanie,* 189.

52. Skrynnikov, *Smuta,* 117–18.

53. AAE 2: no. 58; Smirnov, *Vosstanie,* 191.

54. VBDM 302; PSRL 34:214–15; Bibikov, "Novye dannye," 12–13.

55. SRIO 137:375; Ustrialov, *Skazaniia,* 2:176; Skrynnikov, *Smuta,* 118.

56. VBDM 167; PSRL 34:244; AI 2: no. 83; Belokurov, *Razriadnye zapisi,* 9; SRIO 137:380; Hirschberg, *Polska a Moskwa,* 81; Koretskii, "Novye dokumenty," 81.

57. PSRL 14:71.

58. *Akty Iushkova,* no. 269.

59. RIB 13: col. 1303.

60. Ustrialov, *Skazaniia,* 2:176.

61. Smirnov, *Vosstanie,* 402–3; Skrynnikov, *Smuta,* 177.

62. RIB 13: cols. 1292–93; Smirnov, *Vosstanie,* 411–14; Skrynnikov, *Smuta,* 176.

63. Miller, *Istoriia,* 2: prilozheniia, no. 70; Dmytryshyn et al., *Russia's Conquest,* 53–58.

64. SGGD 2: no. 151; AAE 2: no. 60; Smirnov, *Vosstanie,* 201–3.

65. AI 2: no. 67; RIB 35: nos. 50–51.

66. It is not likely that the cossack pretender Tsarevich Petr's activities in the summer of 1606 caused the central Volga region uprisings, but it is possible that they may have helped trigger some of them. See Aiplatov, "K voprosu," 144–46.

67. Belokurov, *Razriadnye zapisi,* 44; Popov, *Izbornik,* 333–34; AAE 2: nos. 60–61; SGGD 2: no. 151; PSRL 14:72–73; "Kostromskaia starina," 6; *Novyi Letopisets,* 83; *Pamiatniki istorii Nizhegorodskogo dvizheniia,* 3–4; Anpilogov, "O vosstanii," 91–93; Smirnov, "Vosstanie Bolotnikova i narody Povolzh'e," 24–48.

68. Skrynnikov, *Smuta,* 117.

69. See Belokurov, *Snosheniia,* 517; Miller, *Istoriia,* 2:193–94; Dmytryshyn et al., *Russia's Conquest,* 51–54; Tilly, *European Revolutions,* 187, 189.

70. Margeret, *Russian Empire,* 24, 47, 124 n. 67.

71. Buganov, "Religious ideologies," 217.

72. A. A. Geraklitov, "Arzamasskaia mordva," *Uchenye zapiski Saratovskogo gosudarstvennogo universiteta* 8 (1930), part 2:19, 24–25, 28, 42. Contrary to Platonov's assertion (*Ocherki,* 608 n. 104), many of the honey farmers were Russians.

73. Smirnov, *Vosstanie,* 353–54.

74. Emmausskii, "Iz istorii," 8–10.

75. Zimin, "Osnovnye etapy," 51. Cf. Margeret, *Russian Empire,* 124 n. 67.

76. Emmausskii, "Iz istorii," 26; Man'kov, "Pobegi," 54–58.

77. VBDM 207–10; Smirnov, *Vosstanie,* 354; Cherepnin, *Zemskie sobory,* 170; Nazarov and Floria, "Krest'ianskoe vosstanie," 351.

78. "Kostromskaia starina," 6; Skrynnikov, *Smuta,* 223–24.

79. Smirnov, *Vosstanie,* 359–60.

80. Popov, *Izbornik,* 352–53; Veselovskii, *Arzamasskie pomestnye akty,* no. 348.

81. Popov, *Izbornik,* 333–34.

82. Margeret, *Russian Empire,* 9, 47; Zimin, "Osnovnye etapy," 51.

83. Aiplatov, "K voprosu," 144–46; "Kostromskaia starina," 6.

84. *Novyi Letopisets,* 83.

85. PSRL 14:72; *Novyi Letopisets,* 30–31; Anpilogov, "O vosstanii," 92–93.

86. AAE 2: no. 60; Popov, *Izbornik,* 333; *Letopis' o mnogikh miatezhakh,* 313–14.

87. "Kostromskaia starina," 6–8.

88. AAE 2: no. 61; Smirnov, *Vosstanie,* 362–63; Avrich (*Russian Rebels,* 36) incorrectly wrote that the threat of interdiction forced the townspeople to renounce the rebellion.

89. See Hellie, *Enserfment,* 129; Avrich, *Russian Rebels,* 116–17.

90. PSRL 14:84.

91. Smirnov (*Vosstanie*, 192–201) listed seventy-one towns on the rebel side by October 1606. To his list should be added Astrakhan, Valuiki, Oskol, Trubchevsk, Borisov, and Popova Gora. (See Massa, *Short History*, 151; VBDM 281; SRIO 137:360; *Boiarskie spiski*, 1:256; Anpilogov, "O vosstanii," 91, 93–94.) Even though there are no documents to prove it, it is highly probable that the following towns also joined the rebellion by then: Donkov, Driskl, Efremov, Lebedian, Gorokhovets, Radoroshch, Brosovskii, Taletskii ostrog, Tarusa, Terek, Tetiushi, Kasimov, Kadom, Temnikov, and Tsivilsk.

92. Massa, *Short History*, 153; Ustrialov, *Skazaniia*, 1:80; Skrynnikov, *Smuta*, 108.

93. VBDM 105; Tikhomirov, "Novyi istochnik," 116. Koretskii and other peasant war scholars incorrectly interpreted this propaganda as the actual list of demands made by the revolutionary masses. See Koretskii, *Formirovanie*, 259. Cf. Skrynnikov, *Smuta*, 120, 134–35; Perrie, *Pretenders*, 125–26.

94. Massa, *Short History*, 155.

95. AAE 2: no. 58; VBDM 184.

96. RIB 13: cols. 101–5, 177–86. Platonov incorrectly credited the date of October 12, 1606 for the appearance of this vision (*Drevnerusskie skazaniia*, 72); Smirnov incorrectly dated its appearance between October 7 and October 12 (*Vosstanie*, 184–85).

97. RIB 13: cols. 72, 105, 177–78; Platonov, *Drevnerusskie skazaniia*, 72; Kopanev, "Novye spiski," 277–80; Smirnov, "O nekotorykh voprosakh," 127; Skrynnikov, *Smuta*, 98.

98. RIB 13: col. 104; Tikhomirov, "Novyi istochnik," 115; Vasenko, "Zametki," 266; Kusheva, "Iz istorii publitsistiki," 96–97; Platonov, *Drevnerusskie skazaniia*, 70–76; Smirnov, *Vosstanie*, 288–89; Koretskii, *Formirovanie*, 284; Skrynnikov, *Smuta*, 119.

99. Uspenskii, "Videniia," 134–35.

100. Margeret, *Russian Empire*, 27, 125 n. 75; Tikhomirov, *Rossiia*, 66–84.

101. Nemoevskii, "Zapiski," 37. A contemporary illustration of the rebel siege of Moscow that clearly shows the elaborate guliai gorod is located in Isaac Massa's "Album Amicorum" (The Hague: Koninklijke Bibliotheek, ms 78 H 56). See Figure 11 in this book. See also Duffy, *Siege Warfare*, 172; Razin, *Istoriia*, 3:78; Massa, *Short History*, 155; Hellie, *Enserfment*, 164; idem, "Warfare," 78–79. Construction of the guliai gorod was greatly facilitated by the immediate proximity of the *skorodom* ("quick house") district of the transriver "wooden town," where prefabricated houses were built and marketed. See Olearius, *Travels*, 112, 116.

102. Zimin and Koroleva, "Dokument," 30; Massa, *Short History*, 155. Cf. PSRL 14:71; Skrynnikov, *Smuta*, 110. Massa's claim (*Short History*, 153) that Tsar Vasilii's army was 180,000 strong at this time was a gross exaggeration.

103. Belokurov, *Razriadnye zapisi*, 89, 146; Skrynnikov, *Smuta*, 110–11. Contrary to Skrynnikov's assertion (*Time of Troubles*, 54), Skopin-Shuiskii did not abandon the pursuit of Bolotnikov to help out in this campaign against Pashkov. Skopin-Shuiskii had actually not been pursuing Bolotnikov at all and had, in fact, already defeated Pashkov at the Pakhra River almost a month earlier. A faulty source in military records led some scholars to believe that Pashkov and Bolotnikov had joined forces by this time. (See Belokurov, *Razriadnye zapisi*, 9–10; PSRL 14:72; Zimin and Koroleva, "Dokument," 22. Cf. Skrynnikov, *Smuta*, 107; Smirnov, *Vosstanie*, 176.) Some scholars confused the name of the village near which the battle of Troitskoe took place; see Ovchinnikov, "Nekotorye voprosy," 78–79.

104. Belokurov, *Razriadnye zapisi*, 89, 146; RIB 13: col. 99; Ovchinnikov, "Nekotorye voprosy," 78–79; Skrynnikov, *Time of Troubles*, 54.

105. PSRL 14:77.

106. VBDM 167. Skrynnikov (*Time of Troubles*, 54) incorrectly stated that Shuiskii's men were captured, beaten, and then sent home.

107. Hirschberg, *Polska a Moskwa*, 81.

108. VBDM 381; Koretskii, *Formirovanie*, 267.

109. Skrynnikov, *Smuta*, 112–13.

110. RIB 13:99–100; Skrynnikov, *Smuta*, 111–12. Various dates for the start of the siege may be found in surviving sources. For example, one source indicated that it began after October 1. Uncertainty about the date prompted some scholars not to date the siege at all or merely to write

"October" (e.g., Karamzin, *Istoriia*, 12:12; Smirnov, *Vosstanie*, 187–88). For a long time, historians used October 12 as the starting date (e.g., Platonov, *Ocherki*, 333 n. 103; Bestuzhev-Riumin, "Obzor sobytii," 251). That view was primarily based upon a misreading of Georg Peyerle's account (see Ustrialov, *Skazaniia*, 1:216; Smirnov, *Vosstanie*, 182–84); another influence was the false proclamation that Archpriest Terentii's "vision"—which included references to the rebel approach to Moscow— had occurred on October 12 (see RIB 13: cols. 101, 105; Platonov, *Drevnerusskie skazaniia*, 72). After rejecting October 12 as the date of the start of the siege, Ivan Smirnov unfortunately chose October 7 because of poor use of several sources. (See Smirnov, *Vosstanie*, 184–87. Cf. Skrynnikov, *Smuta*, 98–99; Smirnov, "O nekotorykh voprosakh," 128; Avrich, *Russian Rebels*, 28.) In favor of October 28 is its proximity to the timing of the battle of Troitskoe, after which the rebels approached Moscow very quickly (VBDM 167), and contemporary statements that the siege lasted five weeks and ended on December 2 (Belokurov, *Razriadnye zapisi*, 226, 229; Ustrialov, *Skazaniia*, 1:216–17).

111. There is considerable confusion about the timing of the arrival of Bolotnikov's army and the start of the siege. The problem has been mainly due to the use of poor sources that claimed that Bolotnikov joined Pashkov at Kolomna or that he marched straight from Kaluga to Moscow (see PSRL 14:72; Massa, *Short History*, 155, 161–62; Bussow, *Disturbed State*, 91; VBDM 175; Belokurov, *Razriadnye zapisi*, 9–10). Smirnov's mistake about Pashkov reaching the capital on October 7 led him to err about the arrival of Bolotnikov on October 28 (see Smirnov, *Vosstanie*, 185–88; Bussow, *Moskovskaia khronika*, 361 nn. 81–82; Koretskii, *Formirovanie*, 294). Aleksandr Zimin incorrectly wrote that the entire rebel army combined under Bolotnikov and arrived before Moscow on October 28 (Zimin and Koroleva, "Dokument," 22).

112. RIB 13: col. 99; VBDM 167; PSRL 14:71; Hirschberg, *Polska a Moskwa*, 81, 83; Smirnov, *Vosstanie*, 268.

113. RIB 13: cols. 400, 1303; SRIO 137:375.

114. S.P. 91/1-f. 215v; Bussow, *Disturbed State*, 90; SRIO 137:375; RIB 13: cols. 107–8; VBDM 117; Ustrialov, *Skazaniia*, 1:216–17; Skrynnikov, *Time of Troubles*, 54.

115. Skrynnikov, *Smuta*, 108.

116. Smirnov, *Vosstanie*, 506–7, 510–11.

NOTES TO CHAPTER 17

1. VBDM 111; Belokurov, *Razriadnye zapisi*, 10; Popov, *Izbornik*, 332; Tikhomirov, "Novyi istochnik," 116–17. Massa (*Short History*, 161) incorrectly reported that Bolotnikov was the commander of rebel forces at the start of the siege.

2. Massa, *Short History*, 162; Nemoevskii, "Zapiski," 177. See also Razin, *Istoriia*, 3:78; Gordon, *Cossack Rebellions*, 80–81, 226 n. 3; Le Vasseur, *Description*, 13.

3. RIB 13: cols. 100, 110.

4. Popov, *Izbornik*, 332; PSRL 14:72; Massa, *Short History*, 161–62; RIB 13: cols. 99–100. Smirnov (*Vosstanie*, 298–99) incorrectly reported that this rebel enclave was established at Kolomenskoe.

5. RIB 13: cols. 99–101; Belokurov, *Razriadnye zapisi*, 10, 43; Popov, *Izbornik*, 332; SRIO 137:360; Tikhomirov, "Novyi istochnik," 116–17; Bussow, *Moskovskaia khronika*, 138, 361 n. 81; Smirnov, *Vosstanie*, 298–99. Smirnov erred in identifying the location of Pashkov's camp at Kolomna.

6. See VBDM 181; Bussow, *Disturbed State*, 90; Ustrialov, *Skazaniia*, 1:217.

7. Bolotnikov did not reach Serpukhov and Moscow earlier then Pashkov, as some faulty sources and some scholars claimed (e.g., Smirnov, *Vosstanie*, 172–73); nor did he arrive with Pashkov. Many references to Bolotnikov reaching Serpukhov were really about Pashkov's army arriving there in September; Bolotnikov's army did not reach Serpukhov until late October. (See PSRL 34:214–15; Skrynnikov, *Smuta*, 113.) Bolotnikov did not arrive before Moscow three weeks after Pashkov, either; that erroneous suggestion by Ivan Smirnov was based upon a misinterpretation of "Inoe skazanie." (See RIB 13: cols. 99–100; Smirnov, *Vosstanie*, 181, 186–87, 299; Skrynnikov, *Smuta*, 115–16.)

Smirnov's suggestion was rejected by, among others, those still erroneously insisting that the two rebel armies joined before advancing against the capital; see Zimin and Koroleva, "Dokument," 22; Zimin, "Nekotorye voprosy," 111; Ovchinnikov, "O nachal'nom periode," 285–86.

8. RIB 13: col. 99. Smirnov (*Vosstanie*, 186–88) erred in interpreting this source and estimating the dates of the "three week" delay in fighting; see Skrynnikov, *Smuta*, 96–98. Even some scholars who were wrong about the timing of Bolotnikov's arrival understood that the reference in "Inoe skazanie" to a "three week" calm referred to the period from October 28 to mid-November; see Zimin, "Nekotorye voprosy," 111; Ovchinnikov, "Nekotorye voprosy," 75.

9. S.P. 91/1-f. 215v; Bussow, *Disturbed State*, 93.

10. Bussow, *Disturbed State*, 93.

11. See, for example, RIB 13: cols. 107, 111, 501, 584–85, 661; Popov, *Izbornik*, 332; AMG 1: no. 60; Sukhotin, *Chetvertchiki*, 210, 213, 231, 238; Ustrialov, *Skazaniia*, 1:173; Dmitrievskii, *Arkhiepiskop Arsenii*, 139; Massa, *Short History*, 155; Hirschberg, *Polska a Moskwa*, 103. See also Skrynnikov, *Smuta*, 78, 156. Cf. S.P. 91/1-f. 216; VBDM 176, 183.

12. Bussow, *Disturbed State*, 90. There is considerable confusion about where Pashkov moved to once he left Kolomenskoe. See, for example, Skrynnikov, *Smuta*, 116, 138; Nemoevskii, "Zapiski," 177; Koretskii, *Formirovanie*, 293.

13. S.P. 91/1-f. 215v; Bussow, *Disturbed State*, 90.

14. See, for example, Smirnov, *Vosstanie*, 106–9, 255–63; Koretskii, *Formirovanie*, 259–62, 309–10; Stanislavskii, *Grazhdanskaia voina*, 23; Avrich, *Russian Rebels*, 27; Makovskii, *Pervaia krest'ianskaia voina*, 468–72; Skrynnikov, *Time of Troubles*, 54–55; Platonov, *Ocherki*, 309; Kniaz'kov, "Materialy," 72.

15. Skrynnikov, *Smuta*, 131–32; idem, "Civil War," 66.

16. Margeret, *Russian Empire*, 79; Belokurov, *Razriadnye zapisi*, 9–10; Popov, *Izbornik*, 332; Bussow, *Disturbed State*, 88; Kulakova, "Vosstanie," 49; Skrynnikov, *Smuta*, 79–81, 83, 132–33.

17. Smirnov, *Vosstanie*, 260, 262; VBDM 111; Skrynnikov, *Smuta*, 133.

18. Bussow, *Disturbed State*, 93.

19. AAE 2: no. 60; PSRL 14:73; RIB 13: col. 400; Ustrialov, *Skazaniia*, 1:216; Smirnov, *Vosstanie*, 263, 266; Koretskii, *Formirovanie*, 259–62, 309–10; Skrynnikov, *Time of Troubles*, 54–55.

20. Belokurov, *Razriadnye zapisi*, 226, 229; Smirnov, *Vosstanie*, 267.

21. Skrynnikov, *Time of Troubles*, 52; Stanislavskii, *Grazhdanskaia voina*, 23; Koretskii, "O formirovanii," 129–30; Avrich, *Russian Rebels*, 257–58; *Istoriia krest'ianstva*, 2:434.

22. Skrynnikov, "Civil War," 66; Popov, *Izbornik*, 332.

23. Smirnov, *Vosstanie*, 257; VBDM 111.

24. AAE 2: no. 58; Smirnov, *Vosstanie*, 257.

25. Skrynnikov, "Civil War," 66. Cf. Smirnov, *Kratkii ocherk*, 72.

26. Smirnov, *Vosstanie*, 257–58; Popov, *Izbornik*, 332.

27. Floria, "Tri pis'ma," 165; Smirnov, *Vosstanie*, 259–63.

28. Skrynnikov, *Smuta*, 114–15; Ustrialov, *Skazaniia*, 1:216.

29. Tikhomirov, "Novyi istochnik," 116–17.

30. VBDM 185; Koretskii and Morozov, "Letopisets," 217.

31. Nemoevskii, "Zapiski," 179; SRIO 137:360; VBDM 112, 185; Popov, *Izbornik*, 332; Tikhomirov, "Novyi istochnik," 116–17; La Ville, *Discours sommaire*, 6; Koretskii and Morozov, "Letopisets," 217; Bussow, *Disturbed State*, 93; Massa, *Short History*, 162.

32. Bussow, *Disturbed State*, 94–95; La Ville, *Discours sommaire*, 6. Cf. Skrynnikov, *Smuta*, 114–15.

33. Massa, *Short History*, 161–62. Cf. *Istoriia krest'ianstva*, 2:436.

34. S.P. 91/1-f. 215v.

35. PSRL 14:71; Hirschberg, *Polska a Moskwa*, 81; Smirnov, *Vosstanie*, 402–3; Skrynnikov, *Smuta*, 177.

36. RIB 13: col. 100; Smirnov, *Vosstanie*, 208–9, 272; Skrynnikov, *Smuta*, 116.

37. *Boiarskie spiski*, 1:246–60; Skrynnikov, *Smuta*, 105, 116.

38. Massa, *Short History*, 155; Skrynnikov, *Smuta*, 121.

39. VBDM 184. Cf. Skrynnikov, *Smuta*, 124; Nemoevskii, "Zapiski," 177.

40. Nemoevskii, "Zapiski," 178; Smirnov, *Vosstanie*, 273; Avrich, *Russian Rebels*, 29.
41. RIB 13: cols. 106–7. Cf. Skrynnikov, *Smuta*, 128. "Inoe skazanie" exaggerated the number of soldiers reaching Moscow from the Northern Dvina region.
42. *Akty Iushkova*, no. 269.
43. PSRL 4:323; 14:84; RIB 13: cols. 107–8; AI 2: no. 83; Smirnov, *Vosstanie*, 272, 408; Skrynnikov, *Smuta*, 121.
44. Smirnov, *Vosstanie*, 292; Nemoevskii, "Zapiski," 177–78; VBDM 183. The Kasimov Tatar khan actually developed close ties to the rebels as they approached Moscow; see VBDM 207–10.
45. Hirschberg, *Polska a Moskwa*, 84.
46. Belokurov, *Razriadnye zapisi*, 43, 179. Massa (*Short History*, 162) mistakenly identified the commanders of this army as the tsar's brothers.
47. Belokurov, *Razriadnye zapisi*, 43; Massa, *Short History*, 162; Smirnov, *Vosstanie*, 272, 306.
48. Belokurov, *Razriadnye zapisi*, 43, 89, 146, 219.
49. RIB 13: col. 100; Belokurov, *Razriadnye zapisi*, 43; Smirnov, *Vosstanie*, 301–2.
50. RIB 13: col. 110; Massa, *Short History*, 162.
51. Hirschberg, *Polska a Moskwa*, 85; RIB 1: col. 121.
52. RIB 13: col. 100; Belokurov, *Razriadnye zapisi*, 10.
53. PSRL 34:244; Smith, *Peasant Farming*, 147; *Istoriia Moskvy*, 308; Skrynnikov, *Smuta*, 118–19.
54. S.P. 91/1-f. 215v; VBDM 175–77; SRIO 137:375.
55. Solov'ev, *Istoriia*, 4:470.
56. S.P. 91/1-f. 215v. Some of this information is missing from the flawed printed versions of the document used by previous scholars (e.g., Aleksandrenko, "Materialy," 261–63; Smirnov, *Vosstanie*, 553–55).
57. See Smirnov, *Vosstanie*, 137, 282–84; Nazarevskii, *Ocherki*, 10–11; Platonov, *Ocherki*, 334; Koretskii, *Formirovanie*, 259, 290, 304–6; Avrich, *Russian Rebels*, 30; Skrynnikov, *Time of Troubles*, 55.
58. Skrynnikov, "Civil War," 68–69; idem, *Smuta*, 134–35; Kopanev, "Pinezhskii letopisets," 85.
59. See AAE 2: no. 57–58. Cf. Skrynnikov, "Civil War," 69–70.
60. S.P. 91/1-f. 215v; Tikhomirov, "Novyi istochnik," 116. Cf. Skrynnikov, *Smuta*, 134–35.
61. S.P. 91/1-f. 215v.
62. Skrynnikov, "Civil War," 68–69; idem, *Smuta*, 134–35.
63. Bussow, *Disturbed State*, 94.
64. Skrynnikov, *Smuta*, 121–22; VBDM 275. In an earlier work, Skrynnikov (*Time of Troubles*, 55) recognized that the delegation was sent by Tsar Vasilii, but he later—incorrectly—declared that they were not stooges of Shuiskii.
65. S.P. 91/1-f. 215v; Skrynnikov, "Civil War," 69–70; idem, *Smuta*, 135; Perrie, *Pretenders*, 128.
66. Avrich, *Russian Rebels*, 30.
67. Tikhomirov, "Novyi istochnik," 116; S.P. 91/1-f. 215v; VBDM 184; Skrynnikov, *Smuta*, 120–21.
68. Bussow, *Disturbed State*, 94; Belokurov, *Razriadnye zapisi*, 10.
69. Belokurov, *Razriadnye zapisi*, 10.
70. Massa, *Short History*, 162; S.P.91/1-f. 215v; RIB 13: col. 101.
71. S.P. 91/1-f. 215v. Skrynnikov (*Smuta*, 118) erroneously claimed that the rebels had insufficient forces to capture Krasnoe selo and had no need to in any case because they had already surrounded Moscow.
72. Belokurov, *Razriadnye zapisi*, 46, 185.
73. See, for example, Platonov, *Ocherki*, 334–35; Smirnov, *Vosstanie*, 263, 295–302; Koretskii, *Formirovanie*, 259, 282–83, 290, 304; Avrich, *Russian Rebels*, 31–32; Skrynnikov, *Time of Troubles*, 55.
74. Skrynnikov, *Smuta*, 122.
75. Kleimola, "Genealogy," 289–93.
76. Skrynnikov, *Smuta*, 150.
77. Smirnov, *Vosstanie*, 293–94.
78. Ibid., 294–95; Skrynnikov, *Time of Troubles*, 55.

79. Nemoevskii, "Zapiski," 177; AAE 2: no. 58; Skrynnikov, *Smuta,* 122–23.
80. Koretskii, "Novye dokumenty," 70; Smirnov, *Vosstanie,* 260.
81. AAE 2: no. 58; PSRL 14:72; VBDM 200.
82. Smirnov, *Vosstanie,* 303; Skrynnikov, *Time of Troubles,* 53.
83. Skrynnikov, *Smuta,* 126–27, 137.
84. Koretskii, "Novye dokumenty," 70, 81.
85. Skrynnikov, *Smuta,* 127–28. Cf. VBDM 200; AAE 2: no. 58.
86. Nemoevskii, "Zapiski," 177–78.
87. AAE 2: no. 58.
88. Nemoevskii, "Zapiski," 177.
89. VBDM 183–84. On this occasion, at least, Tsar Vasilii was not one of the frightened ones; that is just a legend.
90. Popov, *Izbornik,* 332; Skrynnikov, *Smuta,* 175; *Akty Iushkova,* no. 273; Sukhotin, *Zemel'nye pozhalovaniia,* 81.
91. VBDM 282.
92. RIB 13: col. 100; Nemoevskii, "Zapiski," 177–78; VBDM 184. Skrynnikov (*Smuta,* 139) erroneously credited Shuiskii propaganda about rebel forces containing many coerced and reluctant soldiers. It is also unlikely, as Smirnov conjectured (*Vosstanie,* 273), that Ivan Shuiskii had returned from his recruiting campaign in time to participate in this battle.
93. Nemoevskii, "Zapiski," 178; VBDM 184; Ustrialov, *Skazaniia,* 2:176; Skrynnikov, *Smuta,* 124; Smirnov, *Vosstanie,* 315.
94. Margeret, *Russian Empire,* 46; Skrynnikov, *Time of Troubles,* 79. Smirnov (*Vosstanie,* 278) with reason suggested that there was less than total unanimity in Smolensk about supporting Tsar Vasilii. Certainly, Patriarch Hermogen's propaganda about all dvoriane, deti boiarskie, and lower status servicemen of Smolensk being loyal to Shuiskii (AAE 2: nos. 57–58) must be taken with a grain of salt.
95. PSRL 14:72; Mal'tsev, "Smolenskaia desiatnia," 339–41; idem, *Bor'ba,* 147–49; Vainberg, "Chelobitnye," 68, 70; VBDM 320–21.
96. Belokurov, *Razriadnye zapisi,* 10; Smirnov, *Vosstanie,* 275–56; Sedov, "Pomestnye oklady kak istochnik," 231.
97. PSRL 14:72. Lew Sapieha incorrectly dated Poltev's activities (SRIO 137:360).
98. The cossacks in Mozhaisk were part of Bolotnikov's army, but the assumption that all the rebels in that fortress were from the southern frontier (e.g., Koretskii, "Aktovye i letopisnye materialy," 58) is wrong. The local gentry and servicemen of Mozhaisk also joined the rebel cause, led by the wealthy and powerful Zekziulin. See *Boiarskie spiski* 1:325; 2:64; Skrynnikov, *Smuta,* 125.
99. VBDM 286; Zimin and Koroleva, "Dokument," 43.
100. PSRL 34:215; Skrynnikov, *Smuta,* 124.
101. VBDM 303.
102. Skrynnikov, *Smuta,* 125.
103. VBDM 277, 286; PSRL 14:72; Stanislavskii, *Grazhdanskaia voina,* 25.
104. AAE 2: no. 58; Belokurov, *Razriadnye zapisi,* 90; Mal'tsev, *Bor'ba,* 147; Vainberg, "Chelobitnye," 67; Smirnov, *Vosstanie,* 278–79.
105. VBDM 198; AAE 2: no. 58.
106. VBDM 277; Skrynnikov, *Smuta,* 126, 163–64, 175.
107. VBDM 132, 199–200, 243, 302; Nemoevskii, "Zapiski," 178.
108. S.P. 91/1-f. 215v; Massa, *Short History,* 162; Nemoevskii, "Zapiski," 178–79; VBDM 184–85, 201; AAE 2: no. 58; Skrynnikov, *Smuta,* 128–29. Kostomarov (*Smutnoe vremia,* 282) incorrectly claimed that Pashkov betrayed the rebel cause on November 26.
109. See Smirnov, *Vosstanie,* 305–8; Avrich, *Russian Rebels,* 33–34.
110. RIB 13: cols. 106, 108–9. Cf. Skrynnikov, *Smuta,* 128.
111. Zimin, "K izucheniiu," 206.
112. Smirnov, *Vosstanie,* 312–13. In addition to crediting the unreliable "Inoe skazanie," Smirnov incorrectly interpreted Massa's comments (*Short History,* 162) about Krasnoe selo as a rebel objective

and about battles on November 26 and 27 to mean that Pashkov succeeded in crossing the Iauza and reached Krasnoe selo. Smirnov also misinterpreted another source's comments about that village as a rebel goal (VBDM 184–85) to mean that Pashkov actually got there.

113. RIB 13: col. 106. "Inoe skazanie" did not mention a fierce struggle at Krasnoe selo, just a rebel approach.

114. Hirschberg, *Polska a Moskwa*, 85; Smirnov, *Vosstanie*, 315.

115. Nemoevskii, "Zapiski," 179; VBDM 185; RIB 13: col. 108. Platonov erred in dating the tsar's advance onto the battlefield as December 2 (*Ocherki*, 335). Massa's estimate of the size of the tsar's army at this time (*Short History*, 162) was a wild exaggeration.

116. VBDM 185; Nemoevskii, "Zapiski," 179.

117. RIB 13: cols. 109–10. Cf. Massa, *Short History*, 162; VBDM 185.

118. Smirnov, *Vosstanie*, 308–14.

119. SGGD 2: nos. 150–51; Bussow, *Disturbed State*, 94–95; Zimin, "K izucheniiu," 203–8; Koretskii, *Formirovanie*, 303; Platonov, *Ocherki*, 335. Smirnov's error about when Pashkov betrayed the rebels was due to a combination of his confusion about where Pashkov was on November 27 (erroneously placing him in Krasnoe selo), his use of an inaccurate source ("Inoe skazanie"), and his misinterpretation of Isaac Massa's account. "Inoe skazanie" did not actually date Pashkov's betrayal, and careful reading of Massa (*Short History*, 162) shows that he, like other sources, placed that betrayal at the beginning of December.

120. Hirschberg, *Polska a Moskwa*, 85; Ustrialov, *Skazaniia*, 1:217; RIB 1: col. 121.

121. AAE 2: no. 58; VBDM 200; Smirnov, *Vosstanie*, 314. Skrynnikov (*Smuta*, 142) claimed that those troops arrived in Moscow on November 29.

122. Belokurov, *Razriadnye zapisi*, 10; PSRL 14:72; Smirnov, *Vosstanie*, 315.

123. Nemoevskii, "Zapiski," 178.

124. PSRL 14:72; Koretskii, "Aktovye i letopisnye materialy," 58; Skrynnikov, *Smuta*, 142.

125. Belokurov, *Razriadnye zapisi*, 10, 43, 90; PSRL 14:72; Skrynnikov, *Smuta*, 142.

126. Massa, *Short History*, 162; Skrynnikov, *Smuta*, 141. "Inoe skazanie" (RIB 13: col. 110) incorrectly placed this siege at Kolomenskoe, an error credited by Smirnov (*Vosstanie*, 313) and others (e.g., Avrich, *Russian Rebels*, 34–35; Koretskii, "Novye dokumenty," 70).

127. Belokurov, *Razriadnye zapisi*, 10, 43, 90.

128. PSRL 14: 72–73; VBDM 185; Bussow, *Disturbed State*, 94–95; Massa, *Short History*, 162.

129. *Sbornik Mukhanova*, 273; PSRL 14:72; SGGD 2: nos. 150–51; AAE 2: no. 60; Nemoevskii, "Zapiski," 177; Smirnov, *Vosstanie*, 317–18; P. Sytin, *Proshloe Moskvy v nazvaniiakh ulits* (Moscow, 1946), 18, 65.

130. La Ville, *Discours sommaire*, 7; Bussow, *Disturbed State*, 95; Massa, *Short History*, 162; S.P. 91/1-f. 215v–216.

131. *Sbornik Mukhanova*, 273; Massa, *Short History*, 162; RIB 13: col. 110.

132. PSRL 14:72–73; VBDM 111; Skrynnikov, *Smuta*, 145. "Inoe skazanie" erroneously described a three-day siege of Kolomenskoe; see RIB 13: col. 109; Smirnov, *Vosstanie*, 313.

133. Popov, *Izbornik*, 332; VBDM 112.

134. RIB 1: col. 121; Ustrialov, *Skazaniia*, 1:217; Bussow, *Disturbed State*, 95; S.P.91/1-f. 216. Ivan Smirnov, confused about when Pashkov betrayed the rebels, erroneously regarded contemporary observations about that event's great significance as exaggerations. See Smirnov, *Vosstanie*, 313; Perrie, *Pretenders*, 130.

135. The faulty traditional view of Pashkov may be found in Smirnov, *Vosstanie*, 188, 282–84; 293–98; Koretskii, *Formirovanie*, 282–83, 289–92, 307–8.

136. Bussow, *Disturbed State*, 93; La Ville, *Discours sommaire*, 7; S.P.91/1-f. 215v–216; Floria, "Tri pis'ma," 165; Smirnov, *Vosstanie*, 293–94; Skrynnikov, *Smuta*, 137–39, 156; Perrie, *Pretenders*, 129–30.

137. Belokurov, *Razriadnye zapisi*, 157; Skrynnikov, *Smuta*, 135.

138. PSRL 14:72–73.

139. Bussow, *Disturbed State*, 95; Hirschberg, *Polska a Moskwa*, 86.

140. S.P.91/1-f. 216; Massa, *Short History*, 162.

141. RIB 13: col. 109.

142. Smirnov, *Vosstanie*, 261–62; Skrynnikov, *Smuta*, 137–39.

143. Smirnov (*Vosstanie*, 322) mistakenly believed the three-day siege of Zabore began on December 2 and ended on December 5.

144. VBDM 280.

145. Belokurov, *Razriadnye zapisi*, 117; Popov, *Izbornik*, 332; SGGD 2: nos. 150–51; PSRL 34:244; Skrynnikov, *Smuta*, 142. Because Tsar Vasilii's official proclamation about the victory over rebel forces mentioned the "capture" of rebel leaders Pashkov and "Mitka Buzzubtsev," some scholars mistakenly concluded that Bolotnikov's trusted lieutenant, Iurii Bezzubtsev, defected to Shuiskii. (See Kostomarov, *Smutnoe vremia*, 283; Platonov, *Ocherki*, 357.) Actually, Iurii retreated from Moscow with Bolotnikov; it was his son, Dmitrii (also a Putivl pomeshchik), who fell into the tsar's hands at this time. See Belokurov, *Razriadnye zapisi*, 10, 43; Anpilogov, *Novye dokumenty*, 165–66; idem, "Novye materialy," 199–202; Smirnov, *Vosstanie*, 319, 321–22; VBDM 202.

146. Belokurov, *Razriadnye zapisi*, 117; Smirnov, *Vosstanie*, 392; Zimin and Koroleva, "Dokument," 43; Stanislavskii, *Grazhdanskaia voina*, 24–25; idem, "Pervaia krest'ianskaia voina," 237; Massa, *Short History*, 162.

147. Popov, *Izbornik*, 332; SGGD 2: no. 150; Hirschberg, *Polska a Moskwa*, 86.

148. Sukhotin, *Chetvertchiki*, 71–72, 197, 208–38; VBDM 263–72; Smirnov, *Vosstanie*, 399–400; AMG 1: no. 60; Avrich, *Russian Rebels*, 35; Skrynnikov, *Smuta*, 175.

149. RIB 13: col. 110; Massa, *Short History*, 162.

150. Koretskii and Morozov, "Letopisets," 217.

151. Bussow, *Disturbed State*, 95; Massa, *Short History*, 162; Popov, *Izbornik*, 332; SRIO 137:360.

152. La Ville, *Discours sommaire*, 7; Tikhomirov, "Novyi istochnik," 116–17.

153. Massa, *Short History*, 163.

154. PSRL 4:323.

155. La Ville, *Discours sommaire*, 7.

156. Massa, *Short History*, 163.

157. Sukhotin, *Chetvertchiki*, 208–38; VBDM 263–72.

158. Bussow, *Disturbed State*, 106.

159. Skrynnikov, *Smuta*, 159.

NOTES TO CHAPTER 18

1. SGGD 2: nos. 150–51; VBDM 202–3. 393.

2. Skrynnikov, "Civil War," 67–68.

3. Belokurov, *Razriadnye zapisi*, 44; *Pamiatniki istorii Nizhegorodskago dvizheniia*, 3–4; Smirnov, "Vosstanie Bolotnikova i narody Povolzh'e," 45–48; Zimin and Koroleva, "Dokument," 37; Anpilogov, "O vosstanii," 92–93. One source incorrectly included troops from Murom in Pushkin's army and placed the expedition in 1607 (Popov, *Izbornik*, 333–34); that led to considerable confusion among historians.

4. Belokurov, *Razriadnye zapisi*, 44; Anpilogov, "O vosstanii," 93. The "New Chronicle" incorrectly listed Prince Ivan Vorotynskii as Tsar Vasilii's voevoda who advanced to Arzamas (PSRL 14:73); see Karamzin, *Istoriia*, 12: prim. 105. It is possible that Pushkin's force was the advance guard regiment of Vorotynskii's large army that Tsar Vasilii sent against Aleksin; see Artsybashev, *Povestvovanie*, 3, book 5:156 n. 865; Smirnov, *Vosstanie*, 363–64.

5. Popov, *Izbornik*, 333–34.

6. AAE 2: no. 61.

7. Liubomirov, *Ocherk*, 31–33; Skrynnikov, *Smuta*, 223–24.

8. *Akty Iushkova*, no. 268.

9. Koretskii, "Novye dokumenty," 76.

10. Zimin and Koroleva, "Dokument," 36.
11. Smirnov, *Vosstanie,* 294, 344–46.
12. Veselovskii, *Akty podmoskovnykh opolchenii,* 16–17.
13. VBDM 281.
14. *Akty Iushkova,* no. 269; AAE 2: nos. 60, 77; Liubomirov, *Ocherk,* 29, 33; RIB 35: no. 67; Smirnov, *Vosstanie,* 406–8.
15. SGGD 2:151; AAE 2: no. 60.
16. AAE 2: no. 70.
17. See, for example, Bussow, *Disturbed State,* 90.
18. AAE 2: no. 158; RIB 35: no. 98; Nikol'skii, *Kirillo-Belozerskii monastyr',* prilozhenie, CCXXXII, CCXXXVI, CCXLV, CCLX.
19. Bibikov, "Novye dannye," 7, 14, 22; Smirnov, *Vosstanie,* 410–11.
20. See Liubomirov, *Ocherk,* 33–34. Cf. Skrynnikov, *Smuta,* 177.
21. Liubomirov, *Ocherk,* 33; Sukhotin, *Chetvertchiki,* 71–72, 197, 209–10, 213–15, 224, 231, 238; AMG 1: no. 60.
22. RIB 13: col. 1303.
23. AAE 2: no. 70; AI 2: nos. 78, 97, 348; RIB 35: nos. 63–64; *Akty Iushkova,* no. 337. See also Smirnov, *Vosstanie,* 556, 561.
24. *Akty Iushkova,* no. 336; RIB 13: col. 1176; 35: nos. 59, 98; AAE 2: no. 158; Nikol'skii, *Kirillo-Belozerskii monastyr',* prilozhenie, CCXXXII, CCXLV; Bibikov, "Novye dannye," 7, 14.
25. VBDM 304.
26. Palitsyn, *Skazanie,* 202–3.
27. Massa, *Short History,* 168.
28. Veselovskii, *Arzamasskie pomestnye akty,* nos. 223, 337; Gnevushev, *Akty,* 257; Smirnov, *Vosstanie,* 398, 405; Skrynnikov, *Smuta,* 177.
29. Bibikov, "Novye dannye," 17–18; Gnevushev, *Akty,* 256.
30. Popov, *Izbornik,* 332; Belokurov, *Razriadnye zapisi,* 43. The "New Chronicle" erred in claiming that Bolotnikov did not have many rebel troops left after the siege of Moscow (PSRL 14:73).
31. PSRL 14:73; Massa, *Short History,* 163.
32. VBDM 279.
33. Bussow, *Disturbed State,* 95. "Inoe skazanie" incorrectly claimed that the inhabitants of Serpukhov refused to cooperate with Bolotnikov (RIB 13: col. 110).
34. Bibikov, "Novye dannye," 21; PSRL 14:73; VBDM 310.
35. Smirnov, *Vosstanie,* 328–33. Smirnov acknowledged the lack of Russian sources about Dmitrii Shuiskii's alleged defeat before Kaluga, incorrectly chalking it up to a cover-up by Tsar Vasilii's officials.
36. See Skrynnikov, *Smuta,* 163; Zimin, "K izucheniiu," 208; Smirnov, *Vosstanie,* 342; Bussow, *Moskovskaia khronika,* 363 n. 87.
37. See Hirschberg, *Polska a Moskwa,* 86–88; VBDM 168; SRIO 137:360; Avrich, *Russian Rebels,* 37; Skrynnikov, *Time of Troubles,* 57.
38. Skrynnikov, *Smuta,* 163; AI 2: no. 76; RIB 13: col. 1304.
39. *Sbornik Mukhanova,* 273; Belokurov, *Razriadnye zapisi,* 10; Skrynnikov, *Smuta,* 164.
40. Belokurov, *Razriadnye zapisi,* 89–90.
41. Ibid., 179, 246; PSRL 14:73.
42. Massa, *Short History,* 163; Bussow, *Disturbed State,* 95; Koretskii, "Novyi dokument," 318–19; RIB 13: col. 585; S.P. 91/1-f. 216.
43. PSRL 14:73; Belokurov, *Razriadnye zapisi,* 10–11, 156, 179, 246.
44. Very little is know about Vorotynskii's campaign. The "New Chronicle" incorrectly stated that he advanced against Aleksin from Arzamas (PSRL 14:73). In fact, he advanced from Moscow; see Smirnov, *Vosstanie,* 363.
45. Popov, *Izbornik,* 333; VBDM 112, 287–88, 291; PSRL 14:73. There is great confusion about the status of Aleksin in this period of the civil war. Massa (*Short History,* 167, 169) wrote that the rebels continued to hold Aleksin and resisted all attempts to take the town or to negotiate its sur-

render. However, it should be remembered that Massa also erred about other towns supposedly held by the rebels at this time (e.g., Kolomna and Pereiaslavl-Riazanskii). Smirnov erroneously claimed that the rebels held Aleksin throughout this period (*Vosstanie*, 342). In fact, Vorotynskii captured the town, and it remained loyal to Tsar Vasilii until early May, 1606, when it was reoccupied by rebel forces. See Skrynnikov, *Smuta*, 171, 203.

46. Popov, *Izbornik*, 334; PSRL 14:73; VBDM 116; Belokurov, *Razriadnye zapisi*, 206. Massa (*Short History*, 167) erred about Kashira remaining in rebel hands.

47. Stanislavskii, "Novye dokumenty," 79.

48. Belokurov, *Razriadnye zapisi*, 90, 143; *Boiarskie spiski*, 1:249; PSRL 14:73. Smirnov (*Vosstanie*, 334) confused events at Kaluga, incorrectly placing Khovanskii's arrival there before that of Mezetskii.

49. *Akty Iushkova*, no. 269; Nikol'skii, *Kirillo-Belozerskii monastyr'*, prilozhenie, CCXLV.

50. Belokurov, *Razriadnye zapisi*, 10–11; Bibikov, "Novye dannye," 15, 24; Smirnov, *Vosstanie*, 334; Skrynnikov, *Smuta*, 165.

51. Massa, *Short History*, 163; Petreius, *Istoriia*, 32; Bussow, *Disturbed State*, 95; RIB 13: col. 585; S.P. 91/1-f. 216; Laskovskii, *Materialy*, 1:34; Tikhomirov, *Rossiia*, 377–78.

52. Koretskii, "Novyi dokument," 319.

53. Bussow, *Disturbed State*, 95; Petreius, *Istoriia*, 32–33.

54. Bussow, *Disturbed State*, 95. Legend has it that the rebels were given three days to contemplate surrender. See Hirschberg, *Polska a Moskwa*, 88.

55. PSRL 14:73; Smirnov, *Vosstanie*, 410.

56. Massa, *Short History*, 164; Koretskii, "Novyi dokument," 318–19; VBDM 140.

57. Massa, *Short History*, 166; S.P. 91/1-f. 216.

58. Belokurov, *Razriadnye zapisi*, 11, 143, 214; RIB 13: col. 111.

59. Massa, *Short History*, 166.

60. Ibid., 164; Laskovskii, *Materialy*, 1:147–50; 192; PSRL 14:73; RIB 13: col. 113; Duffy, *Siege Warfare*, 172–73; Platonov, *Drevnerusskie skazaniia*, 65; Smirnov, *Vosstanie*, 336–38.

61. Massa, *Short History*, 164; RIB 13: col. 113; *Piskarevskii letopisets*, 125; Smirnov, *Vosstanie*, 338–39; PSRL 14:73; Skrynnikov, *Time of Troubles*, 56. This event occurred before the battles of Venev and Vyrkha. "Inoe skazanie" incorrectly placed it at the end of the siege of Kaluga in the spring of 1607. Cf. Kostomarov, *Smutnoe vremia*, 287, 292.

62. Belokurov, *Razriadnye zapisi*, 206; Massa, *Short History*, 166; PSRL 14:73; VBDM 169. "Inoe skazanie" incorrectly claimed that Prince Andrei Teliatevskii relieved Venev and put Khilkov to flight (RIB 13: col. 111). There were, in fact, rumors circulating at the time about Teliatevskii's advance with thirty thousand men.

63. PSRL 14:73; AAE 2: no. 76.

64. PSRL 14:74; Skrynnikov, *Smuta*, 175; Nikol'skii, *Kirillo-Belozerskii monastyr'*, prilozhenie, CCXXXII, CCXLV; Bibikov, "Novye dannye," 22.

65. Ovchinnikov, "Boiarskii spisok," 72.

66. Massa, *Short History*, 163, 166; Hirschberg, *Polska a Moskwa*, 94. Cf. Pierling, *La Russie*, 3:347.

67. AAE 2: no. 67; Skrynnikov, *Time of Troubles*, 57.

68. SRIO 137:380.

69. Massa, *Short History*, 166–67.

70. Skrynnikov, *Time of Troubles*, 56–57; idem, *Smuta*, 152–53; "Civil War," 75–76; Avrich, *Russian Rebels*, 39. Most scholars have accepted the idea that it was Bolotnikov's letter to Shakhovskoi during the siege of Moscow that stirred the latter to contact Tsarevich Petr, but Shakhovskoi actually contacted Petr during the summer of 1606. Two sources erred in dating his contact with Petr to early 1607 (Bussow, *Disturbed State*, 95–96; La Ville, *Discours sommaire*, 8). In fact, Shakhovskoi had been actively recruiting cossacks since the start of the rebellion, and he had been aware of Petr's activities since spring 1606. Petr himself got involved in the rebellion of Astrakhan during summer 1606 and by then was reportedly planning to march on Moscow in order to restore Tsar Dmitrii to the throne. (See Savvinskii, *Istoricheskaia zapiska*, 117; Berthold-Ignace, *Histoire*, 151–52.) Rumors circulated during the siege of Moscow that Tsarevich Petr was already one of the rebel leaders (Massa, *Short History*, 151; Hirschberg, *Polska a Moskwa*, 84).

71. Most of the details of Tsarevich Petr's life are taken from his coerced testimony after the rebel surrender of Tula in late 1607. See AAE 2: no. 81; Popov, *Izbornik*, 331.

72. Smirnov (*Vosstanie*, 367) wrote that Ileika became a cossack in 1603–4; see also Perrie, "Legends," 236. Skrynnikov (*Smuta*, 29) believed he joined the streltsy at that time. Petr did say that he had lived in the home of an Astrakhan strelets.

73. Gnevushev, *Akty,* 244; Kopanev, "Pinezhskii letopisets," 85.

74. Belokurov, *Snosheniia*, 447, 513; SRIO 137:351–52; Massa, *Short History*, 68.

75. Massa, *Short History,* 107; Skrynnikov, *Smuta*, 155.

76. Smirnov, *Vosstanie,* 221–22.

77. Stanislavskii, *Grazhdanskaia voina*, 9, 21; Skrynnikov, *Smuta*, 154, 219; VBDM 224–25.

78. Stanislavskii, *Grazhdanskaia voina*, 21–22; Smirnov, *Vosstanie*, 366; AAE 2:174. Cf. Margeret, *Russian Empire,* 71.

79. See, for example, Lesur, *Histoire,* 268–69; Koretskii, *Formirovanie*, 252–57.

80. Dunning, "Cossacks," 63–64; Smirnov, *Vosstanie*, 365–70.

81. Margeret, *Russian Empire,* 71; Stanislavskii, *Grazhdanskaia voina*, 22; Perrie, *Pretenders*, 95.

82. AAE 2:175.

83. See Nemoevskii, "Zapiski," 119; Margeret, *Russian Empire*, 71; SRIO 137:345, 351; Bussow, *Disturbed State*, 96; Bodianskii, "O poiskakh moikh," 3–6, 42–43; Kostomarov, *Smutnoe vremia*, 291–92; Tiumenev, "Peresmotr," 329; Chistov, *Russkie legendy,* 48; Perrie, "Popular Legends," 237–39; idem, *Pretenders,* 140–43.

84. See Smirnov, *Vosstanie,* 366–67; Koretskii, *Formirovanie*, 253. Cf. Stanislavskii, *Grazhdanskaia voina*, 22; Skrynnikov, *Smuta*, 28.

85. Smirnov, *Vosstanie,* 368.

86. Popov, *Izbornik,* 330.

87. Margeret, *Russian Empire,* 70–71; La Ville, *Discours sommaire*, 8; SRIO 137:351–52.

88. Smirnov, *Vosstanie,* 368; *Novyi Letopisets*, 78.

89. Margeret, *Russian Empire,* 71; AAE 2:175; Liubomirov, *Ocherk*, 323. Skrynnikov (*Time of Troubles,* 37; *Smuta*, 29–30, 153) and Maureen Perrie ("Popular Legends," 236–37) erred in claiming that Dmitrii actually invited Petr to Moscow.

90. Liubomirov, *Ocherk,* 323; Smirnov, *Vosstanie*, 370.

91. Popov, *Izbornik,* 331; PSRL 14:71; Massa, *Short History,* 148.

92. Margeret, *Russian Empire,* 71. Skrynnikov (*Smuta*, 29) confused the sequence of events on the Volga.

93. Smirnov, *Vosstanie,* 370. Cf. PSRL 14:71; Popov, *Izbornik*, 331; Margeret, *Russian Empire,* 71.

94. Smirnov, *Vosstanie,* 238; Savvinskii, *Istoricheskaia zapiska*, 117.

95. Berthold-Ignace, *Histoire,* 151–52.

96. VBDM 226; AAE 2: no. 81; Smirnov, *Vosstanie*, 370–71; Stanislavskii, *Grazhdanskaia voina,* 22. One faulty source claimed that Petr's men wintered on the Don; another faulty source claimed that they traveled to Voronezh. See PSRL 14:71; Popov, *Izbornik*, 331; VBDM 110.

97. Bussow, *Disturbed State,* 95–96. Ivan Smirnov questioned the traditional assumption that Shakhovskoi initiated contact with Petr; he plausibly suggested that Petr had on his own decided to join the rebellion against Shuiskii and may already have been on his way to Putivl hoping to rendezvous with Tsar Dmitrii when he met Shakhovskoi's courier. See Smirnov, *Vosstanie*, 373–74; Bussow, *Moskovskaia khronika*, 363 n. 89.

98. Belokurov, *Razriadnye zapisi,* 8; PSRL 14:74; Novombergskii, *Slovo i delo*, 12–13. Skrynnikov (*Smuta*, 158) erred in stating that Priiamakov-Rostovskii was executed later in Putivl.

99. *Boiarskie spiski,* 1:256.

100. Belokurov, *Razriadnye zapisi,* 8; Zimin, *Khrestomatiia*, 283; PSRL 14:74.

101. VBDM 265; Skrynnikov, *Smuta*, 155.

102. PSRL 14:74; Bussow, *Disturbed State*, 96; Skrynnikov, *Smuta*, 153; Stanislavskii, *Grazhdanskaia voina,* 22; Smirnov, *Vosstanie*, 240. Some scholars claimed Bussow's estimate of ten thouand men was too high (Smirnov, *Vosstanie*, 373; Platonov, *Ocherki*, 331).

103. Nazarov and Floria, "Krest'ianskoe vosstanie," 339; SRIO 137:330; Smirnov, *Vosstanie,* 371–72; Skrynnikov, *Smuta*, 153.

104. Nemoevskii, "Zapiski," 119–20; PSRL 34:214; VBDM 110, 243. Smirnov (*Vosstanie,* 371) and Skrynnikov (*Smuta,* 107) expressed some doubts about the accuracy of these sources.

105. Kostomarov, *Smutnoe vremia,* 291.

106. La Ville, *Discours sommaire,* 8; Koretskii, "Aktovye i letopisnye materialy," 57. Cf. Belokurov, *Razriadnye zapisi,* 84 n. 6.

107. See, for example, Skrynnikov, *Smuta,* 153–54; idem, *Time of Troubles,* 56–57.

108. Dunning, "Cossacks," 66–68.

109. PSRL 34:215; Skrynnikov, *Smuta,* 62–63, 156–57, 209, 211, 219–20, 229, 253; Nazarov and Floria, "Krest'ianskoe vosstanie," 339, 347. Skrynnikov plausibly conjectured that Teliatevskii headed Tsarevich Petr's boyar council.

110. Koretskii, *Formirovanie,* 268–75. Koretskii erred in claiming that Bolotnikov was involved in these decisions. See also SRIO 137:330, 345–46; AI 2: no. 75.

111. PSRL 14:74; VBDM 104.

112. Perrie, *Pretenders,* 136–38; Skrynnikov, *Smuta,* 157–58.

113. See, for example, PSRL 14:74; 34:211, 214; VBDM 104, 110, 131–32, 243.

114. Koretskii, "Aktovye i letopisnye materialy," 57.

115. PSRL 34:211.

116. VBDM 104; Skrynnikov, *Smuta,* 158–59. Lists of those supposedly executed in Putivl may be found in VBDM 110, 131–32, 243; PSRL 14:74; 34:211, 214; Gnevushev, *Akty,* 243–44; Koretskii, Solov'eva, and Stanislavskii, "Dokumenty," 38; Popov, *Izbornik,* 331. However, several of the voevodas listed (e.g., Saburov, Buinosov-Rostovskii, Priimakov-Rostovskii, Bakhteiarov-Rostovskii) had been killed earlier; see Belokurov, *Razriadnye zapisi,* 8; Smirnov, *Vosstanie,* 97–98.

117. Skrynnikov, *Smuta,* 159.

118. Dunning, "Cossacks," 67. In a similar way, Ukrainian cossacks in this period responded to Polish government terror against them by increasingly severe reprisals against captured officers and officials. See Gordon, *Cossacks Rebellions,* 198, 201.

119. Belokurov, *Razriadnye zapisi,* 84 n. 6.

120. Skrynnikov, *Smuta,* 156, 159–60.

121. PSRL 34:214; Skrynnikov, *Smuta,* 160. Cf. Gnevushev, *Akty,* 262.

122. PSRL 14:74; AAE 2: no. 81; Skrynnikov, *Smuta,* 154, 158.

123. Skrynnikov, *Smuta,* 158; Perrie, *Image,* 31–32, 62; idem, *Pretenders,* 137–38.

124. PSRL 14:74; 34:211; VBDM 104, 243; Popov, *Izbornik,* 331; Stanislavskii, "Novye dokumenty," 80–81; Skrynnikov, *Smuta,* 220–21.

125. PSRL 34:214; VBDM 132.

126. Rosovetskii, "Ustnaia proza," 90–93; Perrie, *Pretenders,* 125, 137–38; idem, *Image,* 62–65.

127. Gordon, *Cossack Rebellions,* 66–67, 80; Bercé, *Revolt,* 117–18, 127; Bracewell, *Uskoks,* 164–66, 168.

128. See, for example, Popov, *Izbornik,* 331; Sukhotin, *Chetvertchiki,* 266; Smirnov, *Vosstanie,* 250–52; Skrynnikov, *Smuta,* 220–21, 225–26.

129. Gnevushev, *Akty,* 262; Skrynnikov, *Smuta,* 159.

130. Stanislavskii, "Novye dokumenty," 80–81; idem, *Grazhdanskaia voina,* 22–23; Nazarov and Floria, "Krest'ianskoe vosstanie," 334.

131. Nazarov and Floria, "Krest'ianskoe vosstanie," 347; Skrynnikov, *Smuta,* 161.

132. SRIO 137:330, 345–46, 356–57; Skrynnikov, *Smuta,* 160, 191; Girshberg, *Marina Mnishek,* 49–50. Polish references to Petr's movements after departing Putivl are dated late December 1607 (New Style).

133. SRIO 137:356–57; Nazarov and Floria, "Krest'ianskoe vosstanie," 342; Skrynnikov, *Smuta,* 227.

134. Bodianskii, "O poiskakh moikh," 6; Girshberg, *Marina Mnishek,* 49–50.

135. PSRL 32:192; Skrynnikov, *Smuta,* 193, 197; idem, "Civil War," 75; Tikhomirov, "Novyi istochnik," 121.

136. Bodianskii, "O poiskakh moikh," 4–6; Skrynnikov, *Smuta,* 160. The improbable Belorussian legend of "Peter the Bear" was strongly influenced by folklore; see Perrie, "Popular Legends," 238–39. Nonetheless, some contemporaries and many scholars have seen it as a reference to Tsarevich Petr's

visit; see RIB 1: col. 122; Nazarov and Floria, "Krest'ianskoe vosstanie," 339; Girshberg, *Marina Mnishek,* 49–50; Liubovskii, "Litovskii Kantsler," 9–10; Skrynnikov, *Smuta,* 162 n. 23a. Maureen Perrie and a few others have unconvincingly argued against the identification of Peter the Bear with Tsarevich Petr; see Perrie, *Pretenders,* 141–43.

137. AI 2:101; Skrynnikov, *Smuta,* 191–92; Nazarov and Floria, "Krest'ianskoe vosstanie," 335–37, 340–41.

138. SRIO 137:380; PSRL 14:74; *Letopis' o mnogikh miatezhakh,* 116; Skrynnikov, *Smuta,* 153; Nazarov and Floria, "Krest'ianskoe vosstanie," 334, 339.

139. Belokurov, *Razriadnye zapisi,* 11; Bussow, *Disturbed State,* 96; Massa, *Short History,* 166–67; Smirnov, *Vosstanie,* 373, 386; Perrie, *Pretenders,* 144. One source incorrectly placed Petr in Kaluga at this time (AAE 2: no. 81); another source incorrectly dated his movement to Tula to a later time (PSRL 14:75); a third source incorrectly dated Petr's move to Tula to the end of 1606 (Massa, *Short History,* 155).

140. Popov, *Izbornik,* 332; Smirnov, *Vosstanie,* 374.

141. Bussow, *Disturbed State,* 96; Hellie, *Enserfment,* 158; Eaton, "Early Russian Censuses," 145–47; Shaw, "Southern Frontiers," 120; *Razriadnaia kniga 1559–1605,* 302; Kaiser, "Urban Identities," 210, 212–18, 224; French, "Early Town," 270–71; Tikhomirov, *Rossiia,* 385; Strumilin, *Istoriia chernoi metallurgii,* 48.

142. Gnevushev, *Akty,* 262. The actual path taken by Petr's army on its way from Putivl to Tula is not known. Petr's route shown on the map published in conjunction with *Ocherki istorii SSSR* and titled "Krest'ianskaia voina 1606–1607 gg. pod rukovodstvom I. Bolotnikova" is based upon conjecture, as is the grossly inaccurate route shown on the map found in Bussow, *Disturbed State,* 92.

NOTES TO CHAPTER 19

1. Belokurov, *Razriadnye zapisi,* 11; PSRL 14:73–74; Tikhomirov, "Novyi istochnik," 117. The "Belskii Chronicle" was mistaken about the names of the rebel commanders, the timing of the advance, and the point of origin of the relief force sent from Tula (PSRL 34:245). See also Massa, *Short History,* 166; SRIO 137:380.

2. Zimin, "K izucheniiu," 210; Smirnov, *Vosstanie,* 378; Skrynnikov, *Smuta,* 167. Avrich (*Russian Rebels,* 40) incorrectly dated the battle.

3. Belokurov, *Razriadnye zapisi,* 11, 44. "Inoe skazanie" incorrectly identified the commanders of both the rebel army and Shuiskii's forces at the battle of Vyrka (RIB 13: cols. 111–12).

4. PSRL 34:245; VBDM 105–6; Belokurov, *Razriadnye zapisi,* 11, 44, 157; RIB 13: col. 111; *Boiarskie spiski,* 1:257; Massa, *Short History,* 167. The "New Chronicle" incorrectly reported that Prince Mosalskii was killed in battle (PSRL 14:74). See also Longworth, *Cossacks,* 31–33; Gordon, *Cossack Rebellions,* 80–81; Le Vasseur, *Description,* 56.

5. PSRL 14:74; VBDM 106; Tikhomirov, "Novyi istochnik," 117.

6. Belokurov, *Razriadnye zapisi,* 11, 44.

7. Popov, *Izbornik,* 334; VBDM 113; Smirnov, *Vosstanie,* 380; Skrynnikov, *Smuta,* 223–24; Liubomirov, *Ocherk,* 31–33.

8. Belokurov, *Razriadnye zapisi,* 44, 185, 206; Popov, *Izbornik,* 334.

9. Popov, *Izbornik,* 334; Nazarov and Floria, "Krest'ianskoe vosstanie," 335; Stanislavskii, "Novye dokumenty," 75–76. Some sources incorrectly identified the rebel commander as Prince I. L. Mosalskii, who was actually the rebel voevoda in Riazhsk; see Skrynnikov, *Smuta,* 168.

10. *Boiarskie spiski,* 1:257; VBDM 113, 218; Massa, *Short History,* 167.

11. *Zakonodatel'nye akty,* 1:65–66, 75; Smirnov, *Vosstanie,* 417–19; Skrynnikov, *Smuta,* 178–84; Zimin, "Nekotorye voprosy," 101; Koretskii, *Formirovanie,* 332–33; Grekov, *Glavneishie etapy,* 80. Cf. Hellie, *Slavery,* 39–40, 575.

12. Paneiakh, *Kholopstvo v XVI–nachale XVII veka,* 235; idem, *Kholopstvo v pervoi polovine XVII v.,* 121.

13. Nazarov, "Bylo li podlinnym ulozhenie," 197–200; Hellie, *Muscovite Society*, 137–42; Smirnov, *Vosstanie*, 418–22; idem, "Zakony," 109–12; idem, "Novyi spisok," 72–87.

14. See, for example, Skrynnikov, *Time of Troubles*, 57–58; Hellie, *Enserfment*, 108–9.

15. Skrynnikov, *Smuta*, 178, 185–87; idem, *Time of Troubles*, 58; Smirnov, *Vosstanie*, 397, 404–6, 419–22; Hellie, *Enserfment*, 108–9; Culpepper, "Legislative Origins," 186–87. See also Man'kov, "Pobegi," 54; Cherepnin, "Iz istorii bor'by," 111.

16. Nazarov, "Bylo li podlinnym ulozhenie," 198; Grekov, *Krest'iane*, 2:350; Smirnov, "K kharakteristike politiki Lzhedmitriia II," 46; Koretskii, "Ob odnoi oshibke," 236.

17. Massa, *Short History*, 167.

18. Bussow, *Disturbed State*, 97–98. See also Tsvetaev, *Protestantstvo*, 53; Smirnov, *Vosstanie*, 382 n. 2.

19. See, for example, Bussow, *Moskovskaia khronika*, 367 n. 105.

20. Popov, *Izbornik*, 333; VBDM 112.

21. Zimin and Koroleva, "Dokument," 49–50; Massa, *Short History*, 168.

22. RIB 13: cols. 112–13; Popov, *Izbornik*, 332–33.

23. Bibikov, "Novye dannye," 9, 16. The "New Chronicle" incorrectly placed this campaign before the battle of Vyrka, which led some scholars astray; see PSRL 14:73; Karamzin, *Istoriia*, 12:31.

24. Massa, *Short History*, 169; *Boiarskie spiski*, 1:257; VBDM 286; Skrynnikov, *Smuta*, 169.

25. PSRL 14:73; Belokurov, *Razriadnye zapisi*, 157; VBDM 287–88, 291. Massa incorrectly identified the rebel commander defeating the tsar's troops as Tsarevich Petr (*Short History*, 169).

26. Bibikov, "Novye dannye," 9.

27. Popov, *Izbornik*, 334.

28. Massa, *Short History*, 167, 169; Popov, *Izbornik*, 334; Smirnov, *Vosstanie*, 386.

29. Massa, *Short History*, 165–66, 169.

30. Ibid., 165, 168–69, 172; Hirschberg, *Polska a Moskwa*, 96.

31. Skrynnikov, *Smuta*, 171.

32. Massa, *Short History*, 169–70. See also Smith, "Muscovite Logistics," 56–59.

33. Skrynnikov, *Smuta*, 175, 226.

34. PSRL 14:74; 34:245; Popov, *Izbornik*, 333.

35. Belokurov, *Razriadnye zapisi*, 44, 157; PSRL 34:245; Popov, *Izbornik*, 333–34; VBDM 112; RIB 13: col. 112; Bussow, *Disturbed State*, 98.

36. Belokurov, *Razriadnye zapisi*, 117, 157; Smirnov, *Vosstanie*, 320 n. 4, 392, 406, 410; Stanislavskii, *Grazhdanskaia voina*, 24–25; Zimin and Koroleva, "Dokument," 43; Bibikov, "Novye dannye," 16, 19. Isaac Massa incorrectly identified the "Zabore" cossacks as "Zaporozhian" cossacks. See Massa, *Short History*, 170; idem, *Kratkoe izvestie*, 170; *Skazaniia Massy i Gerkmana*, 245; *Rerum Rossicarum Scriptores Exteri*, 2:117; see also Bussow, *Disturbed State*, 106.

37. Russian sources about the battle of Pchelnia indicate only that it occurred in the "spring" (Popov, *Izbornik*, 333; Belokurov, *Razriadnye zapisi*, 11). Bussow's published account dated the battle May 13, but that was a New Style calendar mistake; other Bussow account manuscripts dated the battle May 1. (See Bussow, *Disturbed State*, 98, 213 n. 9.) Voevoda Boris Tatev was mortally wounded in the battle, and his death was recorded as May 3, 1607. (See PSRL 14:74; Gorskii, *Istoricheskoe opisanie*, 2:86.) By May 7, news of the battle reached Iaroslavl, and by May 9, Moscow was buzzing about it. See Hirschberg, *Polska a Moskwa*, 101; Zimin and Koroleva, "Dokument,"51.

38. Belokurov, *Razriadnye zapisi*, 157; PSRL 14:74; Tikhomirov, "Novyi istochnik," 117–18; Gorskii, *Istoricheskoe opisanie*, 2:86; Popov, *Izbornik*, 333; VBDM 112; Skrynnikov, *Smuta*, 171.

39. Hirschberg, *Polska a Moskwa*, 101; RIB 13: col. 112.

40. RIB 13: col. 112; Massa, *Short History*, 170.

41. Platonov, *Ocherki*, 609; Smirnov, *Vosstanie*, 391–92; Skrynnikov, *Smuta*, 170–71.

42. Smirnov, *Vosstanie*, 389–93; Hirschberg, *Polska a Moskwa*, 113; Massa, *Short History*, 170. It was erroneously reported that Teliatevskii only switched to the rebel side at this time.

43. Bussow, *Disturbed State*, 98; Popov, *Izbornik*, 333; VBDM 112–13.

44. Bussow, *Disturbed State*, 98–99; Massa, *Short History*, 170; Popov, *Izbornik*, 333; SRIO 137:380.

45. RIB 13: col. 114; Belokurov, *Razriadnye zapisi,* 157; Popov, *Izbornik,* 333.
46. Skrynnikov, *Smuta,* 171, 226; Popov, *Izbornik,* 335.
47. PSRL 14:74; Massa, *Short History,* 170–72; Zimin and Koroleva, "Dokument," 51; VBDM 293.
48. Massa, *Short History,* 170.
49. Platonov, *Ocherki,* 341; Smirnov, *Vosstanie,* 396–97.
50. Smirnov, *Vosstanie,* 404–6, 410–11.
51. Tikhomirov, "Novyi istochnik," 118.
52. Massa, *Short History,* 172; Smirnov, *Vosstanie,* 423–24.
53. Bussow, *Disturbed State,* 99; Zimin and Koroleva, "Dokument," 51. Massa (*Short History,* 170) incorrectly wrote that Bolotnikov retreated to Putivl.
54. On Albert Wandmann's activities, see Bussow, *Disturbed State,* 54, 106, 127, 129–30, 140; Stanislavskii, "Novye dokumenty," 78; Massa, *Short History,* 153, 170. Massa erred in naming the commanders Bolotnikov left in charge of Kaluga. One source claimed that most of the captured supplies were transferred to Tula by Bolotnikov (Hirshberg, *Polska a Moskwa,* 115); however, that is contradicted by another source (*Skazaniia Massy i Gerkmana,* 299).
55. Zimin and Koroleva, "Dokument," 26, 51.
56. Hirshberg, *Polska a Moskwa,* 101–2.
57. Massa, *Short History,* 164–65, 167.
58. Massa, *Short History,* 163, 166–67; Popov, *Izbornik,* 337; Belokurov, *Razriadnye zapisi,* 185, 206; PSRL 14:73–74; AAE 2: no. 76; Skrynnikov, *Smuta,* 203; Smirnov, *Vosstanie,* 294, 344–61, 397; Veselovskii, *Akty podmoskovnykh opolchenii,* 16–17.
59. Nazarov and Floria, "Krest'ianskoe vosstanie," 335–37, 339; Massa, *Short History,* 172–73. Massa and Skrynnikov (*Time of Troubles,* 57) incorrectly credited Shuiskii propaganda about the number of Polish subjects joining the rebels at this time.
60. See Smirnov, *Vosstanie,* 208–38, 463–64, 540–43; Skrynnikov, *Smuta,* 161, 180–81, 219. Cf. Ustrialov, *Skazaniia,* 1:219.
61. VBDM 117; Palitsyn, *Skazanie,* 108; Skrynnikov, *Smuta,* 180–81.
62. Miller, *Istoriia,* 2: prilozhenie, nos. 22, 70; Lantzeff and Pierce, *Eastward,* 129–30; Smirnov, *Vosstanie,* 556–61.
63. Hirshberg, *Polska a Moskwa,* 113; Floria, "Tri pis'ma," 166; Smirnov, *Vosstanie,* 424–27.
64. PSRL 14:75; Massa, *Short History,* 168; Hirshberg, *Polska a Moskwa,* 101–2; Smirnov, *Vosstanie,* 427–28.
65. Massa, *Short History,* 170–71; Tikhomirov, "Novyi istochnik," 120.
66. AAE 2: no. 73.
67. Massa, *Short History,* 168; Hirshberg, *Polska a Moskwa,* 101–2. Massa incorrectly dated the general mobilization, and another source misunderstood its purpose; see Smirnov, *Vosstanie,* 427–28.
68. Ustrialov, *Skazaniia,* 1:219; Smirnov, *Vosstanie,* 432; Massa, *Short History,* 172.
69. Nazarov and Floria, "Krest'ianskoe vosstanie," 347.
70. Liubomirov, *Ocherk,* 28, 31–33; Skrynnikov, *Smuta,* 175.
71. AAE 2: no. 77; RIB 35: no. 67; Popov, *Izbornik,* 335; Massa, *Short History,* 172; Belokurov, *Razriadnye zapisi,* 12; Bibikov, "Novye dannye," 17; Nikol'skii, *Kirillo-Belozerskii monastyr',* prilozhenie, CCXXXVI, CCLX, CCLXXVIII. Cf. Margeret, *Russian Empire,* 46, 47, 50, 139 n. 141.
72. Hirshberg, *Polska a Moskwa,* 102; Liubomirov, *Ocherk,* 29, 33; Smirnov, *Vosstanie,* 406–7.
73. Massa, *Short History,* 172.
74. Veselovskii, *Akty podmoskovnykh opolchenii,* 194; Nikol'skii, *Kirillo-Belozerskii monastyr',* prilozhenie, CCLX; Massa, *Short History,* 172.
75. Massa, *Short History,* 171–72; Bussow, *Disturbed State,* 99; VBDM 117, 178–79; *Istoriia krest'ianstva,* 436. Cf. Margeret, *Russian Empire,* 143 n. 159.
76. Ustrialov, *Skazaniia,* 1:219; VBDM 178–79; Popov, *Izbornik,* 336–37; Skrynnikov, *Smuta,* 226; Smirnov, *Vosstanie,* 450.
77. Popov, *Izbornik,* 335–36; Massa, *Short History,* 171; Belokurov, *Razriadnye zapisi,* 157; Skrynnikov, *Smuta,* 211.
78. Popov, *Izbornik,* 335–37; Belokurov, *Razriadnye zapisi,* 87–88, 117–18, 144–45, 157–58; Smirnov, *Vosstanie,* 435–36.

79. Massa, *Short History,* 171; *Sbornik Mukhanova,* 275; VBDM 216; AAE 2: no. 73; Belokurov, *Razriadnye zapisi,* 87–88, 118, 145, 157; Popov, *Izbornik,* 335. On the tsar's regiment, see also Hellie, *Enserfment,* 22–23; Keep, *Soldiers,* 20–22.

80. Massa (*Short History,* 171) probably erred in identifying Kriuk-Kolychev as the head of Shuiskii's army. See also Skrynnikov, *Smuta,* 175. Cf. Smirnov, *Vosstanie,* 435.

81. Massa, *Short History,* 171.

82. Hirschberg, *Polska a Moskwa,* 114.

83. Skrynnikov, *Smuta,* 161, 253.

84. Ibid., 211–12, 219.

85. VBDM 186; Bussow, *Disturbed State,* 99; Massa, *Short History,* 170. See also La Ville, *Discours sommaire,* 6–7.

86. Massa, *Short History,* 155; Belokurov, *Razriadnye zapisi,* 12.

87. Smirnov, *Vosstanie,* 395, 463–64.

88. Gnevushev, *Akty,* 262; PSRL 14:74; 34:211, 214; VBDM 104, 110, 131–32, 243; Stanislavskii, "Novye dokumenty," 80–81; idem, *Grazhdanskaia voina,* 22–23.

89. See Popov, *Izbornik,* 336; Skrynnikov, *Smuta,* 214–15; Smirnov, *Vosstanie,* 374.

90. Tikhomirov, "Novyi istochnik," 118; VBDM 106.

91. Stanislavskii, "Novye dokumenty," 77–78, 82.

92. Skrynnikov, *Smuta,* 220–21.

93. Smirnov, *Vosstanie,* 541–42; *Dokumenty i materialy,* 217.

94. Koretskii, "Novye dokumenty," 83; Smirnov, *Vosstanie,* 463–64; Iablochkov, *Dvorianskoe soslovie,* prilozhenie, 9.

95. Koretskii, Solov'eva, and Stanislavskii, "Dokumenty,"38–39; VBDM 106, 227; Iablochkov, *Dvorianskoe soslovie,* prilozhenie, 217. See also Skrynnikov, *Smuta,* 221; Berry and Crummey, *Rude and Barbarous Kingdom,* 283–84.

96. AAE 2:169; Skrynnikov, *Smuta,* 160–61; Nazarov and Floria, "Krest'ianskoe vosstanie," 347; Ustrialov, *Skazaniia,* 1:219.

97. Massa, *Short History,* 172. Cf. Smirnov, *Vosstanie,* 436–37; Skrynnikov, *Smuta,* 211.

98. Ustrialov, *Skazaniia,* 1:219.

99. Gnevushev, *Akty,* 161–62, 203.

100. Massa, *Short History,* 171.

101. Stanislavskii, "Novye dokumenty," 79; Geraklitov, "Materialy," 63; *Chronicle of the Carmelites,* 1:111–12. Smirnov (*Vosstanie,* 249–50) speculated that there had been class conflict developing in Tsaritsyn for several months but was unable to provide any convincing evidence.

102. SGGD 2: no. 153; Smirnov, *Vosstanie,* 479–80.

103. PSRL 14:89; VBDM 318–19; Burturlin, *Istoriia,* 2: prilozhenie, 56; Skrynnikov, *Smuta,* 222–23; *Letopis' o mnogikh miatezhakh,* 113; Geraklitov, "Materialy," 63; *Chronicle of the Carmelites,* 1:112; Berthold-Ignace, *Histoire,* 153, 160–61, 182–86; Smirnov, *Vosstanie,* 245–51, 253–54; Stanislavskii, "Novye dokumenty," 75–76, 79–80; Perrie, *Pretenders,* 132–34, 149.

104. Massa, *Short History,* 172.

105. Hirschberg, *Polska a Moskwa,* 114–15.

106. Massa, *Short History,* 172.

107. Nazarov and Floria, "Krest'ianskoe vosstanie," 342.

108. AAE 2: no. 74; Afremov, *Istoricheskoe obozrenie,* 159; Bussow, *Disturbed State,* 99; PSRL 14:75; VBDM 108; Tikhomirov, "Novyi istochnik," 120; Smirnov, *Vosstanie,* 437–39; Skrynnikov, *Smuta,* 212.

109. Smirnov, *Vosstanie,* 438; Bussow, *Moskovskaia khronika,* 367 n. 105; Tikhomirov, "Novyi istochnik," 120; AAE 2: no. 74; VBDM 217.

110. Popov, *Izbornik,* 335; VBDM 115; Tikhomirov, "Novyi istochnik," 120.

111. Belokurov, *Razriadnye zapisi,* 143; Afremov, *Istoricheskoe obozrenie,* 159.

112. PSRL 34:215.

113. Belokurov, *Razriadnye zapisi,* 45; PSRL 34:246. Skrynnikov (*Smuta,* 211) interpreted these sources to mean Bolotnikov had been demoted by Tsarevich Petr; but see Bussow, *Disturbed State,* 99.

114. Popov, *Izbornik,* 335; VBDM 115, 217; Tikhomirov, "Novyi istochnik," 120; Belokurov, *Razriadnye zapisi,* 45; PSRL 34:215, 246.

115. AAE 2: no. 74; Belokurov, *Razriadnye zapisi,* 45.

116. VBDM 115; Smirnov, *Vosstanie,* 442. Skrynnikov (*Smuta,* 212–13) incorrectly located Golitsyn's forces and the tactics employed by the tsar's voevoda during the battle.

117. Popov, *Izbornik,* 335; PSRL 14:75; Platonov, *Stat'i,* 424–25. One source incorrectly claimed 1,700 rebels crossed the Vosma, probably deriving that figure from military records concerning the number of prisoners taken in the battle; see Belokurov, *Razriadnye zapisi,* 45.

118. PSRL 14:75; Popov, *Izbornik,* 335; VBDM 115.

119. Bussow, *Disturbed State,* 99. Bussow identified the turncoat rebel commander as "Teletin," a completely unknown person. Several writers concluded that he mistakenly meant to identify Teliatevskii but correctly pointed out that the rebel commander did not, in fact, switch sides during the battle. See Smirnov, *Vosstanie,* 441–42; Kostomarov, *Smutnoe Vremia,* 294–95; Zimin, "K izucheniiu,"211–12; Skrynnikov, *Smuta,* 213–14.

120. See Smirnov, *Vosstanie,* 441–42; Bussow, *Moskovskaia khronika,* 364 n. 93; Skrynnikov, *Smuta,* 214.

121. Belokurov, *Razriadnye zapisi,* 45; Popov, *Izbornik,* 335; PSRL 14:75; AAE 2: no. 74; Bussow, *Disturbed State,* 99.

122. Popov, *Izbornik,* 335–36; VBDM 115, 217.

123. AAE 2: no. 74; VBDM 217; Belokurov, *Razriadnye zapisi,* 45; Smirnov, *Vosstanie,* 441–42.

124. Popov, *Izbornik,* 336; Skrynnikov, *Smuta,* 214–15. The "New Chronicle" did not mention the executions or the pardons but instead put the number of rebels captured alive at only three (PSRL 14:75). See also Smirnov, *Vosstanie,* 444.

125. PSRL 34:215; Smirnov, *Vosstanie,* 415; Skrynnikov, *Smuta,* 185.

NOTES TO CHAPTER 20

1. Belokurov, *Razriadnye zapisi,* 173; Popov, *Izbornik,* 336.

2. Afremov, *Istoricheskoe obozrenie,* 16, 162; Belokurov, *Razriadnye zapisi,* 158; Tikhomirov, "Novyi istochnik,"120–21; Bussow, *Disturbed State,* 99; Smirnov, *Vosstanie,* 444.

3. PSRL 34:246; Popov, *Izbornik,* 336; VBDM 116; Tikhomirov, "Novyi istochnik," 120–21; RGADA, fond 199 (Portfeli G. F. Millera), No. 150/4, list 10.

4. Belokurov, *Razriadnye zapisi,* 91.

5. Popov, *Izbornik,* 337; VBDM 117; AAE 2: no. 76; Belokurov, *Razriadnye zapisi,* 158.

6. Belokurov, *Razriadnye zapisi,* 118, 158; AAE 2: no. 76; PSRL 14:75; 34:247; Koretskii, "Aktovye i letopisnye materialy," 58. Cf. Smirnov, *Vosstanie,* 451–52.

7. Popov, *Izbornik,* 337; VBDM 117; *Sbornik Mukhanova,* 275.

8. Smirnov, *Vosstanie,* 449; Skrynnikov, *Smuta,* 216–17.

9. *Sbornik Mukhanova,* 275.

10. AAE 2: no. 76; Smirnov, *Vosstanie,* 340 n. 2, 344–45; Skrynnikov, *Smuta,* 224–25.

11. Bussow, *Disturbed State,* 99; *Akty Iushkova,* no. 272; Smirnov, *Vosstanie,* 345–46.

12. Gnevushev, *Akty,* 174; Berthold-Ignace, *Histoire,* 187–93; Perrie, *Pretenders,* 145–46.

13. *Chronicle of the Carmelites,* 1:111–12; Berthold-Ignace, *Histoire,* 194–95.

14. On Ivan-Avgust's plans at this point, see Pirling, *Iz Smutnago Vremeni,* 66; Smirnov, *Vosstanie,* 246–47, 249.

15. Popov, *Izbornik,* 339; Berthold-Ignace, *Histoire,* 195; Perrie, *Pretenders,* 147–48; Smirnov, *Vosstanie,* 247; Skrynnikov, *Smuta,* 223.

16. Iablochkov, *Dvorianskoe soslovie,* prilozhenie, 9; Smirnov, *Vosstanie,* 463–64; Skrynnikov, *Smuta,* 220.

17. Popov, *Izbornik,* 337; *Akty Iushkova,* no. 270.

18. Laskovskii, *Materialy*, 1:35–36; A. Kiparisova, *Tula* (Moscow, 1966), 15–18, 27; Smirnov, *Vosstanie*, 447–48; Kaiser, "Urban Identities," 210, 212, 214–18, 224.

19. See Belokurov, *Razriadnye zapisi*, 12; Popov, *Izbornik*, 336–37; VBDM 170; Bibikov, "Novye dannye," 17; Bussow, *Disturbed State*, 99; Ustrialov, *Skazaniia*, 1:219; Massa, *Short History*, 172; Dmitrievskii, *Arkhiepiskop Arsenii*, 138; Veselovskii, *Akty podmoskovnykh opolchenii*, 194; Nikol'skii, *Kirillo-Belozerskii monastyr'*, prilozhenie, CCXXXVI, CCLX, CCLXXVIII; Smirnov, *Vosstanie*, 433–34; Skrynnikov, *Smuta*, 218.

20. Popov, *Izbornik*, 337; VBDM 117; Nazarov and Floria, "Krest'ianskoe vosstanie," 339; Skrynnikov, *Smuta*, 218–19. See also Palitsyn, *Skazanie*, 108; Skrynnikov, *Rossiia v nachale XVII v.*, 180–81.

21. Popov, *Izbornik*, 337; Belokurov, *Razriadnye zapisi*, 158. Afremov (*Istoricheskoe obozrenie*, 163) erred in locating Tsar Vasilii's headquarters; see Smirnov, *Vosstanie*, 450.

22. Ustrialov, *Skazaniia*, 1:219; Popov, *Izbornik*, 336–37; VBDM 116–17; Belokurov, *Razriadnye zapisi*, 11, 87, 91, 145; Skrynnikov, *Smuta*, 217.

23. Hirschberg, *Polska a Moskwa*, 106; VBDM 170–71.

24. Popov, *Izbornik*, 337; VBDM 117.

25. See Massa, *Short History*, 173; Dmitrievskii, *Arkhiepiskop Arsenii*, 138–39; *Rerum Rossicarum Scriptores Exteri*, 2:155.

26. Popov, *Izbornik*, 337; VBDM 117, 124; Ustrialov, *Skazaniia*, 1:219; *Sbornik Mukhanova*, 275; Smirnov, *Vosstanie*, 451–52. One unreliable foreign source noted that Tsar Vasilii's initial failure to capture Tula prompted him to order the transfer of even more cannons from Moscow to the siege camp. See Floria, "Tri pis'ma," 169.

27. Nemoevskii, "Zapiski," 218.

28. Floria, "Tri pis'ma," 168–70; Hirschberg, *Polska a Moskwa*, 103, 105–6, 108.

29. Belokurov, *Razriadnye zapisi*, 158.

30. Bussow, *Disturbed State*, 103.

31. RGADA, fond 199 (Portfeli G. F. Millera), No. 150/4, list 10 ob.

32. Belokurov, *Razriadnye zapisi*, 12; Smirnov, *Vosstanie*, 455. Skrynnikov (*Smuta*, 225–26) conjectured that the execution of Shuiskii loyalists in Gremiachii during the summer of 1607 prompted Tsar Vasilii to order the town besieged. However, those executions probably occurred in 1606; see Koretskii, Solov'eva, and Stanislavskii, "Dokumenty," 39.

33. Belokurov, *Razriadnye zapisi*, 91; Smirnov, *Vosstanie*, 455.

34. Popov, *Izbornik*, 336–37; VBDM 116–17; Skrynnikov, *Smuta*, 226.

35. Palitsyn, *Skazanie*, 121; Hirschberg, *Polska a Moskwa*, 107. Military Affairs Office records (Belokurov, *Razriadnye zapisi*, 158–59) and the "New Chronicle" (PSRL 14:76) erred in identifying Urusov's destination as the Crimean peninsula.

36. Belokurov, *Razriadnye zapisi*, 46.

37. Bussow, *Disturbed State*, 103; PSRL 14:75–76.

38. Hirschberg, *Polska a Moskwa*, 107.

39. Ibid., 108; Tatishchev, *Istoriia*, 6:319–20.

40. Popov, *Izbornik*, 337; VBDM 117; PSRL 14:77; *Sbornik Mukhanova*, 275. See also Storozhev, "Desiatni," 77, 86; Smirnov, *Vosstanie*, 459. One source incorrectly identified Krovkov as a carpenter (RIB 13: col. 664).

41. Belokurov, *Razriadnye zapisi*, 12; Bibikov, "Novye dannye," 16.

42. Popov, *Izbornik*, 337; Bibikov, "Novye dannye," 16; Bussow, *Disturbed State*, 99.

43. Afremov, *Istoricheskoe obozrenie*, 167; Smirnov, *Vosstanie*, 461.

44. RGADA, fond 199, No. 150/4, listy 11ob-12; Popov, *Izbornik*, 337; VBDM 117–18; Belokurov, *Razriadnye zapisi*, 12; PSRL 14:77; Afremov, *Istoricheskoe obozrenie*, 167; Skrynnikov, *Smuta*, 231.

45. Hirschberg, *Polska a Moskwa*, 112.

46. Tatishchev, *Istoriia*, 6:319–20.

47. See for example, Massa, *Short History*, 172–73; Bussow, *Disturbed State*, 101; Ustrialov, *Skazaniia*, 2:21, 29; Savich, *Bor'ba*, 21–27; Kozachenko, *Razgrom*, 57–79.

48. The historians Shcherbatov, Karamzin, Kliuchevskii, and Platonov, among others, regarded the "second false Dmitrii" as a tool of Polish intervention in Russia, a view echoed by several Soviet scholars. See Ilovaiskii, *Smutnoe vremia*, 91, 291–92; [Shcherbatov], *Kratkaia povest'*, 85–86; Kliuchevskii, *Sochineniia*, 3:40; Bernadskii, "Konets," 83–133; Smirnov, *Vosstanie*, 458; Zimin, "Nekotorye voprosy," 101–2; Shepelev, *Osvoboditel'naia bor'ba*, 40–42; Tikhomirov et al., "Inostrannaia interventsiia," 269–70; Makovskii, *Pervaia krest'ianskaia voina*, 401–4; Perrie, *Pretenders*, 163–67.

49. See Platonov, *Ocherki*, 333–34; Smirnov, *Vosstanie*, 458; idem, "O nekotorykh voprosakh," 116–20.

50. AAE 2:183–84, 188–90. For useful reviews of the sources concerning the identity of the "second false Dmitrii," see Ilovaiskii, *Smutnoe vremia*, 289–92; Perrie, *Pretenders*, 157–65.

51. RIB 1: col. 514; Ustrialov, *Skazaniia*, 2:29; Howe, *False Dmitri*, 66.

52. *Novgorodskie letopisi*, 473–74; *Zapiski Zholkevskago*, prilozhenie, col. 192; PSRL 32:192; Bussow, *Disturbed State*, 101.

53. Palitsyn, *Skazanie*, 116; AAE 2:186, 192; PSRL 34:212; Bussow, *Disturbed State*, 101; Gnevushev, *Akty*, 29; Marchocki, *Historya*, 6.

54. RIB 1: col. 527; 16: cols. 435, 467; AAE 2:357; *Zapiski Zholkevskago*, prilozhenie, col. 192; Stadnitskii, "Dnevnik," 204; Jansson and Rogozhin, *England and the North*, 74, 90. See also Widekind, *Historia*, 212.

55. Skrynnikov, *Smuta*, 201–2; idem, "V to smutnoe vremia," 44–48. Cf. Dunning, "Skrynnikov," 80; Polikarpov, "V Rossii," 189.

56. Perrie, *Pretenders*, 158–60.

57. AAE 2:186. Cf. PSRL 14:89.

58. PSRL 34:212; VBDM 108–9; Marchocki, *Historya*, 6; Palitsyn, *Skazanie*, 116.

59. AAE 2:210; VBDM 108–9; RIB 1: col. 514; Forsten, "Politika Shvetsii," 339–40; *Zapiski Zholkevskago*, prilozhenie, col. 54; Ustrialov, *Skazaniia*, 2:29.

60. PSRL 14:89; Gnevushev, *Akty*, 29; AAE 2:192; Perrie, *Pretenders*, 157.

61. AI 2:231; AAE 2:210; *Zapiski Zholkevskago*, prilozhenie, col. 192; Forsten, "Politika Shvetsii," 339–40.

62. Perrie, *Pretenders*, 161–62, 165.

63. See Ustrialov, *Skazaniia*, 2:21, 29; Howe, *False Dmitri*, 66; RIB 1: col. 164; Platonov, *Moscow and the West*, 61; Smirnov, *Vosstanie*, 105; Margeret, *Russian Empire*, ix–x.

64. Bussow, *Disturbed State*, 101; Palitsyn, *Skazanie*, 116; AAE 2:186, 192; PSRL 34:212; Gnevushev, *Akty*, 29; Marchocki, *Historya*, 6.

65. PSRL 32:192; Bussow, *Disturbed State*, 101; Ustrialov, *Skazaniia*, 2:21, 29; Skrynnikov, *Smuta*, 194–96.

66. AZR 4:259–60; Maciszewski, *Polska a Moskwa*, 131–32.

67. PSRL 32:192; Ustrialov, *Skazaniia*, 2:21, 29; Marchocki, *Historya*, 6; Bussow, *Disturbed State*, 101; Ilovaiskii, *Smutnoe vremia*, 91, 291–92; Girshberg, *Marina Mnishek*, 49; Perrie, *Pretenders*, 163–65, 167.

68. Skrynnikov, *Smuta*, 190–93; idem, "Civil War," 76.

69. Perrie, *Pretenders*, 141–43, 163–65. Perrie's conclusions about the significance of the legend of "Peter the Bear" are contradicted by several contemporaries and many scholars; see, for example, RIB 1: col. 122; Nazarov and Floria, "Krest'ianskoe vosstanie," 339; Girshberg, *Marina Mnishek*, 49–50; Liubovskii, "Litovskii Kantsler," 9–10; Skrynnikov, *Smuta*, 162 n. 23a.

70. Bussow, *Disturbed State*, 94; Pirling, *Dmitrii Samozvanets*, 400; Skrynnikov, *Smuta*, 68–69.

71. Tikhomirov, "Novyi istochnik," 121; Girshberg, *Marina Mnishek*, 49–50; Solov'ev, *Istoriia*, 4:478–79; Nazarov and Floria, "Krest'ianskoe vosstanie," 332–33; Maciszewski, *Polska a Moskwa*, 116–33; Skrynnikov, *Smuta*, 190, 192–93; idem, "Civil War," 76.

72. AI 2:101; AZR 4:259–60; Nazarov and Floria, "Krest'ianskoe vosstanie," 335–37, 340–41; Skrynnikov, *Smuta*, 191–93.

73. Bussow, *Disturbed State*, 99–100; Tikhomirov, "Novyi istochnik," 121; VBDM 108–9; Platonov, *Ocherki*, 353; Skrynnikov, "Civil War," 76.

74. PSRL 32:192; *Novgorodskie letopisi*, 473–74; Bussow, *Disturbed State*, 101; *Zapiski*

Zholkevskago, prilozhenie, col. 192; Mal'tsev, "Barkulabovskaia letopis'," 317; Ustrialov, *Skazaniia,* 2:21, 29; Shepelev, *Osvoboditel'naia bor'ba,* 42. One of Tsar Vasilii's agents in 1609 misidentified the route the future "tsar" took and the towns he visited before declaring himself to be Tsar Dmitrii; see AI 2:231.

75. Bodianskii, "O poiskakh moikh," 6; PSRL 32:192; *Zapiski Zholkevskago,* prilozhenie, cols. 192–93; Bussow, *Disturbed State,* 101; Ustrialov, *Skazaniia,* 29–30; Marchocki, *Historya,* 6–8; Girshberg, *Marina Mnishek,* 53–54; Skrynnikov, *Smuta,* 194–95, 197, 206–7.

76. Bussow, *Disturbed State,* 101; PSRL 14:76; RIB 1: col. 123; Buturlin, *Istoriia,* 2: prilozh-enie, 53; Shepelev, *Osvoboditel'naia bor'ba,* 42; Skrynnikov, *Smuta,* 196–97. The "Barkulabovo Chronicle" erred in stating that the impostor declared himself to be "Tsar Dmitrii" in Popova Gora (PSRL 32:192); Bussow incorrectly had the impostor traveling to Putivl accompanied by Pan Miechowicki; M. Marchocki (*Historya,* 6–7) incorrectly identified the impostor's companions and erroneously wrote that Pan Ragoza accompanied him to Russia.

77. RIB 1: col 123; Bussow, *Disturbed State,* 101; Buturlin, *Istoriia,* 2: prilozhenie, 53; Skrynnikov, *Smuta,* 198, 200–201.

78. Bussow, *Disturbed State,* 101–2; PSRL 14:76; RIB 1: col. 124; Marchocki, *Historya,* 7; Buturlin, *Istoriia,* 2: prilozhenie, 90; Ilovaiskii, *Smutnoe vremia,* 92–93. See also Skrynnikov, *Smuta,* 206–7; Nazarov and Floria, "Krest'ianskoe vosstanie," 327–28, 339–40, 342–43, 349 n. 97; Perrie, *Pretenders,* 168–69.

79. RIB 1: cols. 123–24; 13: col. 558; Belokurov, *Razriadnye zapisi,* 13; PSRL 14:76; Marchocki, *Historya,* 6–7; Perrie, *Pretenders,* 169.

80. PSRL 32:192; Belokurov, *Razriadnye zapisi,* 13; Marchocki, *Historya,* 9; Skrynnikov, *Smuta,* 204, 207–8.

81. Buturlin, *Istoriia,* 2: prilozhenie, 90; Shepelev, *Osvoboditel'naia bor'ba,* 45; Skrynnikov, *Smuta,* 201; PSRL 32:192; Marchocki, *Historya,* 9.

82. Massa, *Short History,* 172; Maciszewski, "La noblesse," 23–48.

83. PSRL 14:76; Veselovskii, *D'iaki,* 455; idem, *Arzamasskie akty,* 386; Skrynnikov, *Smuta,* 228.

84. RIB 1: col. 121; Zolkiewski, *Expedition,* 120; Tikhomirov, "Novyi istochnik," 121; Stadnitskii, "Dnevnik," 212; Zimin, "Nekotorye voprosy," 104–5; Shepelev, "Mesto," 223–38; Ovchinnikov, "Nekotorye voprosy," 83; "O krest'ianskoi voine," 119; Makovskii, *Pervaia krest'ianskaia voina,* 445–50, 457–62; Skrynnikov, *Smuta,* 197, 199, 203, 229; Stanislavskii, *Grazhdanskaia voina,* 62–64.

85. RIB: cols. 127–28; Bussow, *Disturbed State,* 102–3; Platonov, *Ocherki,* 336, 358; Skrynnikov, *Smuta,* 207–8, 227–29; Avrich, *Russian Rebels,* 43. Bussow erred in dating the impostor's departure from Starodub.

86. PSRL 14:76; Stanislavskii, "Novye dokumenty," 79.

87. *Akty Iushkova,* no. 271; Belokurov, *Razriadnye zapisi,* 12; VBDM 219.

88. RIB 1: col. 125; Shepelev, *Osvoboditel'naia bor'ba,* 47; Skrynnikov, *Smuta,* 229.

89. PSRL 14:76; Hirschberg, *Polska a Moskwa,* 115–16; Skrynnikov, *Smuta,* 233. One source (VBDM 173) incorrectly reported that a truce was concluded as a result of this meeting.

90. Belokurov, *Razriadnye zapisi,* 12; PSRL 14:77; Popov, *Izbornik,* 333; VBDM 117–18; Tatishchev, *Istoriia,* 6:319–20; Skrynnikov, *Smuta,* 232–33.

91. RIB 1: col. 126.

92. See PSRL 14:75; Buturlin, *Istoriia,* 2: prilozhenie, 90; Shepelev, *Osvoboditel'naia bor'ba,* 47. Bussow (*Disturbed State,* 102) erred in dating Miechowicki's advance to Kozelsk.

93. Belokurov, *Razriadnye zapisi,* 12, 118, 158; PSRL 14:76; RIB 1:cols. 125–27.

94. Bussow, *Disturbed State,* 99–100; *Skazaniia Massy i Gerkmana,* 299–300. Cf. PSRL 14:77.

95. RGADA, fond 199 (Portfeli G. F. Millera), No. 150/4, listy 11ob-12; RIB 13: cols. 501, 1000; Bussow, *Disturbed State,* 99, 103. V. N. Tatishchev erred in dating the completion of the dam; see Smirnov, *Vosstanie,* 461.

96. Popov, *Izbornik,* 333; VBDM 118, 124; PSRL 14:77; RIB 13: cols. 587, 665; *Sbornik Mukhanova,* 276; Ustrialov, *Skazaniia,* 1:221; Bussow, *Disturbed State,* 99, 103.

97. Bussow, *Disturbed State,* 103.

98. Popov, *Izbornik,* 337–38; VBDM 118; Skrynnikov, *Smuta,* 237. The "Karamzin Chronograph"

erred in dating the surrender of Tula but correctly noted the contact between the townspeople and Tsar Vasilii two or three days before the surrender.

99. See, for example, PSRL 14:77; RIB 13: cols. 115, 501, 1000; Belokurov, *Razriadnye zapisi,* 12, 46, 88, 91, 118, 145, 158, 173, 226; SGGD 2: no. 154. See also Artsybashev, *Povestvovanie,* 3:166 n. 922; Platonov, *Ocherki,* 343 n. 112; Smirnov, *Vosstanie,* 480–81.

100. Massa, *Short History,* 173.

101. Koretskii, "Letopisets," 130; VBDM 223. Cf. Gnevushev, *Akty,* 171–72.

102. SGGD 2: no. 154; AAE 2: no. 81; RIB 13: cols. 587, 665; 35: no. 69; VBDM 222. Cf. Gnevushev, *Akty,* 171–72.

103. Smirnov, *Vosstanie,* 479–82.

104. Nemoevskii, "Zapiski," 217–18; VBDM 182; Hirschberg, *Polska a Moskwa,* 117; Smirnov, *Vosstanie,* 476.

105. PSRL 14:77; 34:247; Tikhomirov, "Novyi istochnik," 121; RIB 13: cols. 587, 665; Popov, *Izbornik,* 337–38; VBDM 118, 124; *Sbornik Mukhanova,* 276; Koretskii, "Novye dokumenty," 73.

106. Platonov, *Ocherki,* 324–25; Bykovskii, "Mnimaia 'izmena' Bolotnikova," 47–69; Skrynnikov, *Smuta,* 239.

107. Skrynnikov, *Smuta,* 236; Stanislavskii, *Grazhdanskaia voina,* 25.

108. Solov'ev, *Istoriia,* 4:479–80; Zimin, "I. I. Bolotnikov," 63–64.

109. See PSRL 34:247; VBDM 118; Skrynnikov, *Smuta,* 237–38.

110. Bykovskii, "Mnimaia 'izmena' Bolotnikova," 68; Zimin, "I. I. Bolotnikov," 63–64; Smirnov, *Vosstanie,* 489–91; idem, *Kratkii ocherk,* 149; Skrynnikov, *Smuta,* 237–39.

111. Makovskii, *Pervaia krest'ianskaia voina,* 395; Orlov, "Obsuzhdenie," 160–68. See also Koretskii, "Ivan Bolotnikov," 135–36.

112. Some variation of this version of the surrender of Tula was accepted by several nineteenth-century scholars; see for example, Kostomarov, *Smutnoe vremia,* 297; Solov'ev, *Istoriia,* 4:479–80; Karamzin, *Istoriia,* 12:39–40.

113. Bussow, *Disturbed State,* 103–4.

114. Hirschberg, *Polska a Moskwa,* 117.

115. *Skazaniia Massy i Gerkmana,* 298–300; VBDM 188.

116. Bussow, *Disturbed State,* 103–4; PSRL 34:247; RIB 13: col. 1300; *Skazaniia Massy i Gerkmana,* 300–302; Skrynnikov, *Smuta,* 235–36; Vernadsky, *Tsardom,* 1:240; Smirnov, *Vosstanie,* 478. Crummey (*Formation,* 223) erred in stating that rank-and-file rebels were executed or returned to slavery after the surrender of Tula.

117. Dmitrievskii, *Arkhiepiskop Arsenii,* 138–39; Bussow, *Disturbed State,* 103; *Zapiski Zholkevskago,* prilozhenie, cols. 195–96; RIB 1: cols. 122–23.

118. Skrynnikov, *Smuta,* 239. Cf. Gnevushev, *Akty,* 159, 197–98; Smirnov, *Vosstanie,* 484–85.

119. See RIB 13: col. 1300; Bussow, *Disturbed State,* 103.

120. PSRL 34:247; *Skazaniia Massy i Gerkmana,* 300–302; Bussow, *Disturbed State,* 104; RIB 13: col. 1300; Smirnov, *Vosstanie,* 478; Skrynnikov, *Smuta,* 235–37.

121. Koretskii, "Letopisets," 125–27; Stanislavskii, "Pervaia krest'ianskaia voina," 237; idem, *Grazhdanskaia voina,* 25.

122. Elias Herckman (*Skazaniia Massy i Gerkmana,* 304) erred in declaring that Shuiskii promised to set Bolotnikov and Tsarevich Petr free.

123. Massa, *Short History,* 173; Skrynnikov, *Smuta,* 237–38.

124. Massa, *Short History,* 173; La Ville, *Discours sommaire,* 9; RIB 13: col. 587; VBDM 118; *Sbornik Mukhanova,* 276.

125. *Skazaniia Massy i Gerkmana,* 304; Smirnov, *Vosstanie,* 490–91; Skrynnikov, *Smuta,* 237–39.

126. Dmitrievskii, *Arkhiepiskop Arsenii,* 138–39; RIB 1: cols 122–23; Smirnov, *Vosstanie,* 425.

127. See SGGD 2: no. 154; AAE 2: no. 81. There are a number of sources with the wrong date (e.g., RIB 35: no. 69; Bussow, *Disturbed State,* 103; *Sbornik Mukhanova,* 276; Popov, *Izbornik,* 338; Belokurov, *Razriadnye zapisi,* 12, 46, 173; RGADA, fond 199, No. 150/4, listy 11–12); see Smirnov, *Vosstanie,* 467 n. 2.

128. Popov, *Izbornik,* 338; RIB 13: col. 587; PSRL 14:77; 34:247; *Sbornik Mukhanova,* 276;

Gnevushev, *Akty,* 171–72; Ustrialov, *Skazaniia,* 1:221; Tikhomirov, "Novyi istochnik," 121; VBDM 118, 222–23; Massa, *Short History,* 173.

129. Bussow, *Disturbed State,* 104.

130. Gnevushev, *Akty,* 171–72, 181; SGGD 2: no. 154; La Ville, *Discours sommaire,* 9; RIB 13: cols. 587, 665, 1300; VBDM 182, 222; Nemoevskii, "Zapiski," 217–18.

131. *Rerum Rossicarum Scriptores Exteri,* 2:156–57; Bussow, *Disturbed State,* 104.

132. Bussow, *Disturbed State,* 103. Makovskii (*Pervaia krest'ianskaia voina,* 398) credited Bussow's story. Cf. Bykovskii, "Mnimaia 'izmena' Bolotnikova," 68.

133. PSRL 14:77; Bussow, *Disturbed State,* 104–5, 127, 136, 139. Bussow erred about Shakhovskoi's cleverness and his treatment by Shuiskii after Tula surrendered.

134. PSRL 14:77; 34:247; Solov'ev, *Istoriia,* 4:480, 703–4; Skrynnikov, *Smuta,* 240–41.

135. Bussow, *Disturbed State,* 105–6; Skrynnikov, *Time of Troubles,* 60–61, 68, 82. Bussow erroneously claimed that the four thousand cossacks sent to Kaluga had been prisoners in Moscow since December 1606; he also did not know that Bezzubtsev was their commander.

136. *Skazaniia Massy i Gerkmana,* 300–302; PSRL 34:247; Bussow, *Disturbed State,* 105; Koretskii, "Letopisets," 125–27; Smirnov, *Vosstanie,* 492; Skrynnikov, *Smuta,* 236; Stanislavskii, *Grazhdanskaia voina,* 25; Sedov, "Pomestnye oklady kak istochnik," 231.

137. Popov, *Izbornik,* 338; Bussow, *Disturbed State,* 105.

NOTES TO CHAPTER 21

1. Smirnov, *Vosstanie,* 455; Popov, *Izbornik,* 338; PSRL 14:75–76; Massa, *Short History,* 173; Belokurov, *Razriadnye zapisi,* 44–45; Bussow, *Disturbed State,* 105; Skrynnikov, *Smuta,* 230.

2. RIB 1: col. 127; Buturlin, *Istoriia,* 2:90.

3. RIB 1:127; Marchocki, *Historya,* 9; Shepelev, *Osvoboditel'naia bor'ba,* 48.

4. Piasetskii, *Istoricheskie ocherki,* 21–24; Platonov, *Time of Troubles,* 105.

5. *Akty Iushkova,* no. 272.

6. Ibid., no. 282; Veselovskii, *Akty podmoskovnykh opolchenii,* 16–17.

7. Smirnov, *Vosstanie,* 345–46, 405–6; Veselovskii, *Arzamasskie akty,* no. 337.

8. Sukhotin, *Zemel'nye pozhalovaniia,* 81; *Akty Iushkova,* no. 273; Skrynnikov, *Smuta,* 175.

9. Gnevushev, *Akty,* 180–81; Smirnov, *Vosstanie,* 238–39, 486.

10. Gnevushev, *Akty,* 168, 171; VBDM 361 n. 110; Smirnov, *Vosstanie,* 244–45, 248–50.

11. Kostomarov, *Smutnoe vremia,* 298. Cf. *Dokumenty i materialy,* 217; Smirnov, *Vosstanie,* 467.

12. Massa, *Short History,* 173.

13. RIB 13: col. 1314; Vasenko, "Novye dannye," 141, 144.

14. RGADA, fond 210 (Razriadnyi prikaz), opis' 4 (Dela desiaten'), no. 126; Sedov, "Pomestnye oklady kak istochnik," 231.

15. VBDM 186; Ustrialov, *Skazaniia,* 1:221; *Zapiski Zholkevskago,* prilozhenie, cols. 195–96; Platonov, *Ocherki,* 343; Smirnov, *Vosstanie,* 477; Bussow, *Disturbed State,* 104.

16. Dmitrievskii, *Arkhiepiskop Arsenii,* 138–39; *Skazaniia Massy i Gerkmana,* 304; *Zapiski Zholkevskago,* prilozhenie, cols. 195–96; RIB 1: cols. 122–23.

17. RIB 13: col. 115; Nemoevskii, "Zapiski," 218.

18. See Hirschberg, *Polska a Moskwa,* 128.

19. RIB 13: cols. 115, 1300; AAE 2: no. 81; VBDM 222–26; Smirnov, "Kogda byl kazen," 108–19; Zimin, "I. I. Bolotnikov i padenie Tuly," 63; Skrynnikov, *Smuta,* 235.

20. PSRL 34:215; Zimin, "I. I. Bolotnikov i padenie Tuly," 57; Cherepnin, *Zemskie sobory,* 157.

21. Massa, *Short History,* 173; Bussow, *Disturbed State,* 104; RIB 1: cols. 122–23; 13: cols. 115, 1300; *Zapiski Zholkevskago,* prilozhenie, cols.195–96; VBDM 118, 182; *Skazaniia Massy i Gerkmana,* 304; AI 2:231; Smirnov, *Vosstanie,* 481–82. One source incorrectly had Petr being impaled (Belokurov, *Razriadnye zapisi,* 226); another source incorrectly stated that he was killed by a blow to his forehead (Nemoevskii, "Zapiski," 217–18).

22. Bussow, *Disturbed State*, 104; Hirschberg, *Polska a Moskwa*, 128; VBDM 174–75; Skrynnikov, *Smuta*, 240.

23. Smirnov, *Vosstanie*, 489.

24. Bussow, *Disturbed State*, 104; *Skazaniia Massy i Gerkmana*, 304; RIB 1: cols. 122–23; VBDM 118; Skrynnikov, *Smuta*, 240–41; Smirnov ("Kogda byl kazen," 115–19) has a somewhat different, less plausible explanation for the timing of Petr's execution.

25. RIB 1: cols. 122–23, 13: cols. 115, 1300; VBDM 186; Massa, *Short History*, 174.

26. Dmitrievskii, *Arkhiepiskop Arsenii*, 138–39; Bussow, *Disturbed State*, 104.

27. La Ville, *Discours sommaire*, 6–7.

28. RIB 1: cols. 127–28; Massa, *Short History*, 172; Marchocki, *Historya*, 9–10; Shepelev, *Osvoboditel'naia bor'ba*, 50; Skrynnikov, *Smuta*, 207.

29. PSRL 14:77; Popov, *Izbornik*, 339; Girshberg, *Marina Mnishek*, 55–56; Smirnov, "Kogda byl kazen," 119. Bussow (*Disturbed State*, 107) was wrong about the timing and location of the arrival of reinforcements.

30. RIB 1: col. 128; Bussow, *Disturbed State*, 107–8.

31. PSRL 14:77; RIB 1: cols. 129–30; Bussow, *Moskovskaia khronika*, 367 n. 104; Skrynnikov, *Smuta*, 240. Bussow (*Disturbed State*, 107–8) erred about the timing of the battle of Briansk.

32. PSRL 14:79; Bussow, *Disturbed State*, 108.

33. RIB 1: cols. 125–30; PSRL 34:247; Bussow, *Disturbed State*, 107–8; Buturlin, *Istoriia*, 2:109–10; Shepelev, *Osvoboditel'naia bor'ba*, 46–50; Koretskii, *Formirovanie*, 344; Skrynnikov, *Smuta*, 239–40. There are some wildly exaggerated estimates of the number of cossacks in "Dmitrii's" army at this time; see, for example, Stanislavskii, *Grazhdanskaia voina*, 28.

34. Gnevushev, *Akty*, 180–81; Perrie, *Pretenders*, 180–81.

35. Skrynnikov, *Time of Troubles*, 63, 68. Bussow (*Disturbed State*, 107–8) erred about when and where Rozynski's forces arrived from Poland-Lithuania.

36. See, for example, Massa, *Short History*, 173; Platonov, *Time of Troubles*, 102, 105.

37. Stanislavskii, *Grazhdanskaia voina*, 27; Skrynnikov, *Time of Troubles*, 68–71; RIB 1: cols. 151, 164.

38. Tatishchev, *Istoriia*, 6:320; Palitsyn, *Skazanie*, 149; Stanislavskii, *Grazhdanskaia voina*, 25–27, 28.

39. See Solov'ev, *Istoriia*, 4:391; Kliuchevskii, *Sochineniia*, 3:48; Platonov, *Ocherki*, 305; Makovskii, *Pervaia krest'ianskaia voina*, 295–97; Nazarov, "O nekotorykh osobennostiakh," 120.

40. Dunning, "Cossacks," 57–74; Stanislavskii, *Grazhdanskaia voina*, 23–31; Veselovskii, *Arzamasskie akty*, 378–79. Cf. Pronshtein and Mininkov, *Krest'ianskie voiny*, 58. Tatishchev (*Istoriia*, 6:320) erred in declaring that peasants and slaves joining the rebel cause as cossacks were allowed to elect their own atamans.

41. *Zakonodatel'nye akty*, 1:76; Sukhotin, *Chetvertchiki*, 276–77; Smirnov, *Vosstanie*, 415–17; Skrynnikov, *Smuta*, 184–86; Paneiakh, *Kholopstvo v XVI-nachale XVII veka*, 213; Stanislavskii, *Grazhdanskaia voina*, 25, 30; Nosov, "Belozerskaia gubnaia izba," 52.

42. RGADA, fond 199 (Portfeli G. F. Millera), No. 150/4, list 14 ob; Petreius, *Istoriia*, 263; Tatishchev, *Istoriia*, 6:320; Buturlin, *Istoriia*, 2: prilozhenie, no. 7; Smirnov, *Vosstanie*, 458; Hellie, *Slavery*, 576.

43. AAE 2: no 87; Tikhomirov, "Novyi istochnik," 119; VBDM 106–7.

44. Bussow, *Disturbed State*, 108; Koretskii, *Formirovanie*, 347–51.

45. See Skrynnikov, "Civil War," 77; idem, *Smuta*, 205–6; Perrie, *Pretenders*, 173.

46. AI 2:260; Bussow, *Disturbed State*, 108, 120–21; Nikolai Iusupov, *O rode kniazei Iusupovykh*, 2 vols. (St. Petersburg, 1866–67), 2:120, 122; Bibikov, "Zemel'nye pozhalovaniia," 194; Smirnov, "K kharakteristike politiki Lzhedmitriia II," 43, 46, 48–49; Koretskii, "Ob odnoi 'oshibke'," 234, 237; idem, *Formirovanie*, 327, 348–50; Sedov, "Pomestnye oklady kak istochnik," 232.

47. Buturlin, *Istoriia*, 2: prilozhenie, 57–58; RIB 2: col. 218; VBDM 231; Perrie, *Pretenders*, 173–74.

48. Bussow, *Moskovskaia khronika*, 367 n. 106; Skrynnikov, *Time of Troubles*, 61, 64; Stanislavskii, *Grazhdanskaia voina*, 28, 30.

49. PSRL 14:79; Bussow, *Disturbed State*, 109–10.

50. Massa, *Short History*, 175; PSRL 14:79–80, 82; Skrynnikov, *Time of Troubles*, 64; Perrie, *Pretenders*, 186.

51. Massa, *Short History*, 175; Shepelev, *Osvoboditel'naia bor'ba*, 81.

52. Bussow, *Disturbed State*, 111; Buturlin, *Istoriia*, 2: prilozhenie, 69; Skrynnikov, *Time of Troubles*, 64–65; Perrie, *Pretenders*, 183.

53. PSRL 14:80; Bussow, *Moskovskaia khronika*, 396 n. 112. Bussow (*Disturbed State*, 110–11) erroneously claimed that the rebels could easily have captured Moscow at this time but that "Dmitrii" did not want his capital burned.

54. Bussow (*Disturbed State*, 110–11) incorrectly identified the defeated rebel commander as Jan-Piotr Sapieha, who actually joined the Tushino forces in August 1608; see Shepelev, *Osvoboditel'naia bor'ba*, 90.

55. PSRL 14:87; Bussow, *Disturbed State*, 113, 115; AAE 2:180; Palitsyn, *Skazanie*, 117, 119, 123; Hirschberg, *Polska a Moskwa*, 184; Skrynnikov, *Time of Troubles*, 68–70, 73; Perrie, *Pretenders*, 186–87. Sources disagree on the degree of complicity of the Mniszechs in their own "capture" by the rebels. Sources detailing Filaret's resistance to capture by the rebels, their humiliation of him, and his initial resistance to cooperating with the Tushino impostor (e.g., PSRL 14:82–83; Palitsyn, *Skazanie*, 123) should be taken with a grain of salt as Romanov-era propaganda intended to hide the new dynasty's support of the "second false Dmitrii" during the civil war.

56. PSRL 14:81; *Zapiski Zholkevskago*, 14–15; prilozhenie, cols. 47–56, 201–5; Hirschberg, *Polska a Moskwa*, 181–87; Stadnitskii, "Dnevnik," 180–82; SGGD 2: nos. 160, 164; Marchocki, *Historya*, 39; Bussow, *Disturbed State*, 112–13; idem, *Moskovskaia khronika*, 369 n. 113; Buturlin, *Istoriia*, 2: prilozhenie, 71–73; Ustrialov, *Skazaniia*, 2:21, 31–32; Perrie, *Pretenders*, 183–86.

57. Margeret, *Russian Empire*, xix–xx; RIB 1:col. 164; Platonov, *Moscow and the West*, 61; Howe, *False Dmitri*, 66.

58. Tikhomirov, "Novyi istochnik," 127; PSRL 14:77, 89; VBDM 229–31; AAE 2: no. 344; RIB 13: col. 228; Buturlin, *Istoriia*, 2: prilozhenie, 55–57; Smirnov, *Vosstanie*, 203–4, 253–54; idem, "Kogda byl kaznen,"116–17; Koretskii, *Formirovanie*, 344; Skrynnikov, *Time of Troubles*, 69–70, 77; Perrie, *Pretenders*, 131–34. 174–81.

59. Massa, *Short History*, 175; Bussow, *Disturbed State*, 108.

60. Bussow, *Disturbed State*, 110; Skrynnikov, *Time of Troubles*, 65, 67–68. Massa (*Short History*, 174) incorrectly referred to Jan-Piotr Sapieha as Grand Chancellor Lew Sapieha.

61. Bussow, *Disturbed State*, 114–15; Massa, *Short History*, 174–75; Shepelev, *Osvoboditel'naia bor'ba*, 105.

62. PSRL 14:81. Bussow (*Disturbed State*, 114–15) incorrectly estimated the size of Ivan Shuiskii's army at thirty thousand men.

63. PSRL 14:84; Palitsyn, *Skazanie*, 126–97; Massa, *Short History*, 175; Bussow, *Disturbed State*, 114–15; Skrynnikov, *Time of Trouble*, 76.

64. Platonov, *Time of Trouble*, 107; Skrynnikov, *Time of Troubles*, 72.

65. AI:2:131–33; AAE 2:180; Bussow, *Disturbed State*, 115–17; Popov, *Izbornik*, 354; PSRL 4:322–30; 5:66–72; 14:82–83; *Pskovskie letopisi*, 1:135–40; 2:267–73; Shepelev, *Osvoboditel'naia bor'ba*, 282; Liubomirov, "Novye materialy," 103–5; Skrynnikov, *Time of Troubles*, 67, 71. Massa (*Short History*, 175–77) merely repeated Shuiskii's false propaganda about the resistance of the population of Iaroslavl and the burning and looting of the town by rebel forces; Iaroslavl was actually initially enthusiastic about the Tushino impostor. In similar fashion, events in Pskov were falsely reported as a war between rich and poor that supposedly led to the massacre of many rich merchants and to the burning of the town; and peasant war scholars were quick to credit those lies. See Smirnov, *Vosstanie*, 205–6; Perrie, *Pretenders*, 190–92.

66. AAE 2: nos. 100, 116, 163; PSRL 14:86; Platonov, *Ocherki*, 282, 286–88, 307–8; Aiplatov, "K voprosu," 157–58; Anpilogov, "O vosstanii," 92–93; Keep, *Soldiers*, 78; Shepelev, *Osvoboditel'naia bor'ba*, 250–72; Nolde, *La Formation*, 1:55–57; Makovskii, *Pervaia krest'ianskaia voina*, 428–30.

67. PSRL 14:88; Platonov, *Ocherki*, 309–10; Skrynnikov, *Time of Troubles*, 67, 71–72; Anpilogov, "O vosstanii," 92.

68. PSRL 14:84, 86, 88; Aiplatov, "K voprosu," 158–59; Smirnov, *Vosstanie*, 296.

69. Bussow, *Disturbed State*, 113; RIB 13: cols. 391–92, 964–65; Palitsyn, *Skazanie*, 202–3.

70. Stanislavskii, *Grazhdanskaia voina*, 244.

71. Skrynnikov, *Time of Troubles*, 71.

72. Bussow, *Disturbed State*, 115–17; Massa, *Short History*, 175–76; Stanislavskii, *Grazhdanskaia voina*, 27–28. Cf. AAE 2:179–81.

73. Dunning, "Cossacks," 72–73; Platonov, *Time of Troubles*, 108–9; Zimin, "K istorii vosstaniia Bolotnikova," 364; Stanislavskii, *Grazhdanskaia voina*, 25–26, 28, 30–31, 244–45; idem, "Dokumenty," 295, 300, 304; PSRL 34:250; *Sbornik Khilkova*, 88; Veselovskii, *Arzamasskie akty*, 378–79.

74. Bussow, *Disturbed State*, 120; idem, *Moskovskaia khronika*, 372 n. 130; Kostomarov, *Smutnoe vremia*, 354. Massa (*Short History*, 176) erred in reporting that Vologda started the rebellion against the Tushino impostor.

75. AAE 2:179–81, 185–87, 191–92, 223–24, 230–31, 233–34; PSRL 14:86–87; SGGD 2:181–82; AI 2:144; Massa, *Short History*, 175–79; Bussow, *Disturbed State*, 116, 120–22; Shunkov, "Narodnaia bor'ba," 8; Platonov, *Ocherki*, 291–92, 297–306; Skrynnikov, *Time of Troubles*, 75; Stanislavskii, *Grazhdanskaia voina*, 27–28.

76. PSRL 14:88; Solov'ev, *Istoriia*, 4:530; Skrynnikov, *Time of Troubles*, 73–74. Tatishchev was arrested in Novgorod by Skopin-Shuiskii and beaten to death by a mob.

77. Massa, *Short History*, 176; PSRL 14:87; Platonov, *Time of Troubles*, 107.

78. Bussow, *Disturbed State*, 120. See also Kleimola, "Genealogy," 289–91.

79. Bussow, *Disturbed State*, 120; Skrynnikov, *Time of Troubles*, 77.

80. AI 2: no. 85/1; Smirnov, *Vosstanie*, 418; Paneiakh, *Kholopstvo v XVI-nachale XVII veka*, 238; Stanislavskii, *Grazhdanskaia voina*, 32.

81. SGGD 2:376; Roberts, *Early Vasas*, 453. Skrynnikov (*Time of Troubles*, 76) incorrectly wrote that the Swedes provided fifteen thousand troops to Tsar Vasilii.

82. Massa, *Short History*, 175, 179; Bussow, *Disturbed State*, 96–97, 115, 119–20, 122; Kostomarov, *Smutnoe vremia*, 380–97; Platonov, *Time of Troubles*, 110–11; Skrynnikov, *Time of Troubles*, 76–77, 80; Stanislavskii, "Dokumenty," 300–301; idem, *Grazhdanskaia voina*, 30. See also Howe, *False Dmitri*, 151–83.

83. RIB 1: col. 167; Bussow, *Disturbed State*, 126–27; PSRL 14:94; Kostomarov, *Smutnoe vremia*, 400–415; Platonov, *Time of Troubles*, 111–16; Skrynnikov, *Time of Troubles*, 80–83.

NOTES TO CHAPTER 22

1. *Zapiski Zholkevskago*, 15; Girshberg, *Marina Mnishek*, 147; Brown, "Muscovy," 60 n. 10; Platonov, *Time of Troubles*, 101–2; Davies, *God's Playground*, 341–43.

2. Roberts, *Early Vasas*, 453–54.

3. *Zapiski Zholkevskago*, 37; Medvedev, "Podgotovka," 72–90; Got'e, *Pamiatniki oborony Smolenska 1609–1611 gg.*

4. Hirschberg, *Polska a Moskwa*, 255–56; RIB 1: col. 184; Skrynnikov, *Time of Troubles*, 77–81; PSRL 4:326–28; 14:94; *Pskovskie letopisi*, 1:136–37.

5. Iakovlev, *Pamiatniki*, 47–49; SRIO 142:69; Platonov, *Ocherki*, 352; Stanislavskii, *Grazhdanskaia voina*, 32; Crummey, "Constitutional Reform," 29–40.

6. Bussow, *Disturbed State*, 129; Stanislavskii, *Grazhdanskaia voina*, 32; Skrynnikov, *Time of Troubles*, 82.

7. RIB 1: cols. 163–64; Skrynnikov, *Time of Troubles*, 82–83.

8. Bussow, *Disturbed State*, 129–31; PSRL 14:98; RIB 1: cols. 186, 198; Palitsyn, *Skazanie*, 205; Stadnitskii, "Dnevnik," 188–91; Perrie, *Pretenders*, 196–200.

9. PSRL 14:92–93, 96–97; *Skazaniia Massy i Gerkmana*, 313–14; Ikonnikov, *Kniaz' Skopin*, 229–30; Bibikov, "Opyt," 6–16. See also Miller, *Istoricheskiia pesni*, 541–84.

10. PSRL 14:97; Skrynnikov, *Time of Troubles*, 85–86.

11. Bussow, *Disturbed State*, 132–36; Howe, *False Dmitri*, 139–46, 151–81; Margeret, *Russian Empire*, xx; Zhordaniia, *Ocherki*, 1:264–67; Skrynnikov, *Time of Troubles*, 86–90; Perrie, *Pretenders*, 200. See also *Zakonodatel'nye akty*, 1: no. 64; 2:116–17.

12. PSRL 14:98–100; Popov, *Izbornik* 346; Bussow, *Disturbed State*, 144; Skrynnikov, *Time of Troubles*, 89–92; Baron, "Gosti Revisited," 11–13.

13. Belokurov, *Razriadnye zapisi*, 19; SGGD 2:388–89; Palitsyn, *Skazanie*, 207; Bussow, *Disturbed State*, 145; Skrynnikov, *Time of Troubles*, 92–93.

14. *Zapiski Zholkevskago*, 74–79, 85–86; PSRL 14:100; Palitsyn, *Skazanie*, 207; SRIO 142:93; RIB 13: cols 203, 1187; SGGD 2:388–90; AAE 2:277–78, 280; Bussow, *Disturbed State*, 145–47; Ustrialov, *Skazaniia*, 2:43; Iakovlev, *Pamiatniki*, 52–57; Tsvetaev, *K istorii Smutnogo vremeni*, 12–15; Skrynnikov, *Time of Troubles*, 93–95.

15. Platonov, *Time of Troubles*, 125; idem, *Stat'i*, 308–9; Latkin, *Zemskie sobory*, 115.

16. Solov'ev, *Istoriia*, 4:581.

17. SGGD 2:391–405; SRIO 142:93–109; Platonov, *Time of Troubles*, 125–26; Cherepnin, *Zemskie sobory*, 160–67.

18. *Zapiski Zholkevskago*, 79–85, prilozhenie, cols. 99–102; SGGD 2:452–63; *Pskovskie letopisi*, 2:273–75; Bussow, *Disturbed State*, 147–48; Baron, "Gosti Revisited," 12–13; Skrynnikov, *Time of Troubles*, 96–99, 177.

19. Bussow, *Disturbed State*, 146–47; PSRL 14:103; *Zapiski Zholkevskago*, 78–79, 86–89, 90–99; Ustrialov, *Skazaniia*, 2:47; MERSH 48:166; Skrynnikov, *Time of Troubles*, 99–100, 103–4, 108–9, 258–59. See also Tsvetaev, *Tsar Vasilii v Pol'she*.

20. RIB 1: col 691; 13:680–83; AI 2:355; AAE 2:301; Zhordaniia, *Ocherki*, 1:268–69, 283–89; Margeret, *Russian Empire*, xx–xxi, 99 n. 44; *Zapiski Zholkevskago*, 89–90; Ustrialov, *Skazaniia*, 2:46–47; SGGD 2:452–63; PSRL 14:102–3; AZR 4:327, 347; Solov'ev, *Istoriia*, 4:611, 626–27; Platonov, *Time of Troubles*, 128–30; Skrynnikov, *Time of Troubles*, 100–103, 106–11.

21. AAE 2:291–94; PSRL 14:104–5; Bussow, *Disturbed State*, 147–51; *Zapiski Zholkevskago*, 110–13; AI 2:364–65; Skrynnikov, *Time of Troubles*, 113–14, 122.

22. Bussow, *Disturbed State*, 152; PSRL 14:105, 112; *Zapiski Zholkevskago*, 113; Palitsyn, *Skazanie*, 215; Girshberg, *Marina Mnishek*, 269, 337; Skrynnikov, *Time of Troubles*, 114–15, 119; Perrie, *Pretenders*, 206–10; MERSH 45:177.

23. Skrynnikov, *Time of Troubles*, 115–19, 135–36; Platonov, *Time of Troubles*, 131–33; RIB 13: col. 210; Howe, *False Dmitri*, 204–5; Olearius, *Travels*, 190.

24. AI 2:358–59; Platonov, *Time of Troubles*, 133–34; Skrynnikov, *Time of Troubles*, 115–22. A sign of growing popular activism and of the increasing use of churches for political meetings and even ad hoc judicial proceedings during the final years of the Time of Troubles was the rapid growth in church architecture of attached (and larger) refectories. That practice ended abruptly during the reign of Tsar Aleksei—perhaps as an attempt to stifle unwanted popular activism. See Alexander Opolovnik et al., *The Wooden Architecture of Russia* (New York: Abrams, 1989), 18, 23.

25. Platonov, *Time of Troubles*, 134; Skrynnikov, *Time of Troubles*, 122, 184–86; Baron, "Gosti Revisited," 14–16.

26. Bogoiavlenskii and Riabinin, *Akty vremeni mezhdutsarstviia*, 6–7; AAE 2:305, 326–27; Stanislavskii, *Grazhdanskaia voina*, 35–36; idem, "Dokumenty," 298–99, 304–5; Skrynnikov, *Time of Troubles*, 122–24.

27. Bussow, *Disturbed State*, 161–65; Ustrialov, *Skazaniia*, 1:238; Zolkiewski, *Expedition*, 123–24; Margeret, *Russian Empire*, xx–xxi, 100 n. 48; Zhordaniia, *Ocherki*, 1:268–93; SGGD 2:605–6; Skrynnikov, *Time of Troubles*, 124–36.

28. PSRL 14:109–12; *Akty Iushkova*, no. 298; AMG 1:80–81; Sukhotin, *Chetvertchiki*, 311, 324; SGGD 2: no. 275; Cherepnin, *Zemskie sobory*, 173; Stanislavskii, *Grazhdanskaia voina*, 34–35; Skrynnikov, *Time of Troubles*, 138–42, 157–58; Sedov, "Pomestnye i denezhnye oklady," 226. The Poles were finally able to capture Smolensk because a traitor convinced them to concentrate their cannon fire on a weak section of the fortress wall that had been poorly constructed during wintertime. See Makovskii, *Razvitie*, 445.

29. AAE 2:279, 317; SGGD 2:560–61, 598; Widekind, *Historia,* 167–69, 201–3; Iakovlev, *Pamiatniki,* 74–76; Forsten, *Baltiiskii vopros,* 87, 148; Platonov, *Time of Troubles,* 174–76; Attman, *Struggle,* 186, 191, 193–94, 196, 200; Roberts, *Gustavus Adolphus,* 75–79; Stanislavskii, *Grazhdanskaia voina,* 39; Zhordaniia, *Ocherki,* 1:318, 363–65; MERSH 28:200–203; Skrynnikov, *Time of Troubles,* 142–53, 211, 216–17.

30. Liubimenko, "Project," 246–56; Dunning, "James I," 206–26; idem, "Letter," 94–108; Zhordaniia, *Ocherki,* 1:297–370; Purchas, *Hakluytus Posthumus,* 14:225–26; Phipps, *Sir John Merrick,* chapter 3; Fedorowicz, *England's Baltic Trade,* 27, 139, 151. There was even some brief discussion of a Habsburg candidate for tsar; see Liubimenko, "Project," 246; Liubomirov, *Ocherk,* 145; Skrynnikov, *Time of Troubles,* 215.

NOTES TO CHAPTER 23

1. See, for example, Platonov, *Time of Troubles,* 136–40; Zimin, "Nekotorye voprosy," 97–99; Koretskii, *Formirovanie,* 364–66; Makovskii, *Pervaia krest'ianskaia voina,* 295–97; Nazarov, "O nekotorykh voprosakh," 120; *Bol'shaia Sovetskaia Entsiklopediia,* s.v. "Krest'ianskaia voina nachala 17 v."; *Istoriia krest'ianstva,* 437–43; Crummey, *Formation,* 228.

2. AI 2:358–59; AAE 2:326–27; Platonov, *Time of Troubles,* 138; Skrynnikov, *Time of Troubles,* 159–60; Stanislavskii, "Dokumenty," 298–99, 304–5; idem, *Grazhdanskaia voina,* 29, 34–36, 39.

3. Dunning, "Cossacks," 70–71; Platonov, *Stat'i,* 308–9; Latkin, *Zemskie Sobory,* 115; Cherepnin, *Zemskie sobory,* 173–79; *Akty Iushkova,* no. 298; Stanislavskii, *Grazhdanskaia voina,* 34–35, 38–39; Skrynnikov, *Time of Troubles,* 157–62, 169–73; idem, *Minin i Pozharskii,* 207.

4. Iakovlev, *Pamiatniki,* 65–70; PSRL 14:112; Cherepnin, *Zemskie sobory,* 173–74.

5. Platonov, *Time of Troubles,* 138–40; Kazakov, "Bor'ba," 42; Zimin, "Nekotorye voprosy," 103; Shepelev, "Donskoe kazachestvo," 53–56; Stanislavskii, *Grazhdanskaia voina,* 38–39; Crummey, *Formation,* 228; idem, "Constitutional Reform," 30.

6. Kazakov, "Bor'ba," 42; Zimin, "Nekotorye voprosy," 103; Sakharov, *Obrazovanie,* 132.

7. Platonov, *Time of Troubles,* 139–40; idem, *Sotsial'nyi krizis,* 44–57.

8. Platonov, *Time of Troubles,* 140; idem, *Ocherki,* 378, 381–90; Zimin, "Nekotorye voprosy," 103; Longworth, *Cossacks,* 79; Hellie, *Enserfment,* 110; Crummey, *Formation,* 228; Stanislavskii, *Grazhdanskaia voina,* 38–39; Skrynnikov, *Time of Troubles,* 164–65.

9. PSRL 14:112; Stanislavskii, *Grazhdanskaia voina,* 36–39; Skrynnikov, *Time of Troubles,* 159–60; idem, *Minin i Pozharskii,* 207; Platonov, *Sotsial'nyi krizis,* 54.

10. Skrynnikov, *Time of Troubles,* 159; Pronshtein and Mininkov, *Krest'ianskie voiny,* 58; Dolinin, *Podmoskovnye polki.* Cf. Stanislavskii, *Grazhdanskaia voina,* 27–30, 42–43, 45, 243, 245; Dunning, "Cossacks," 72–73.

11. Stanislavskii, *Grazhdanskaia voina,* 28–29, 42–43, 245–46. Examples of cossacks receiving pomeste estates may be found in SGGD 2:595; Sukhotin, *Chetvertchiki,* 53, 270–72, 276, 307, 317.

12. Stanislavskii, *Grazhdanskaia voina,* 7–8, 23, 27–30, 36, 38, 43, 45, 243–47; idem, "Dvizhenie Zarutskogo," 307; Dunning, "Cossacks," 57–74; Yaresh, "Peasant Wars," 243–45, 254. See also Gordon, *Cossack Rebellions,* 85–86, 184–85, 188–90. Cf. Buganov, "Religious ideologies,"208; *Istoriia krest'ianstva,* 434.

13. Stanislavskii, *Grazhdanskaia voina,* 36, 42, 45; Gordon, *Cossack Rebellions,* 85–86, 89–96, 211–12.

14. See, for example, Popov, *Izbornik,* 351. See also Stanislavskii, *Grazhdanskaia voina,* 243–44.

15. Stanislavskii, *Grazhdanskaia voina,* 37–38.

16. Ibid., 35–38, 41; Platonov, *Sotsial'nyi krizis,* 51.

17. Tatishchev, *Istoriia,* 6:326; Stanislavskii, *Grazhdanskaia voina,* 256; idem, "Dokumenty," 295, 300, 304.

18. Stanislavskii, *Grazhdanskaia voina,* 31–32, 42, 45, 244–45.

19. PSRL 14:112–13; Skrynnikov, *Time of Troubles*, 165; Crummey, *Formation*, 228; Stanislavskii, *Grazhdanskaia voina*, 39–40.

20. Widekind, *Historia*, 292–93; Skrynnikov, *Time of Troubles*, 163–64; Orchard, "Election," 379–80.

21. PSRL 14:112; Skrynnikov, *Time of Troubles*, 164–65, 167–69.

22. Platonov, *Time of Troubles*, 140–41; Crummey, *Formation*, 228–29.

23. Veselovskii, *Akty podmoskovnykh opolchenii*, 36, 74–75; SGGD 2:594; Stanislavskii, *Grazhdanskaia voina*, 40–42; Sedov, "Pomestnye i denezhnye oklady," 226.

24. Skrynnikov, *Time of Troubles*, 172–76. Cf. Popov, *Izbornik*, 352.

25. Platonov, *Time of Troubles*, 145–46; AAE 2:243, 246; Iakovlev, *Pamiatniki*, 79–82; Bogoiavlenskii and Riabinin, *Akty vremeni mezhdutsarstviia*, 44–46.

26. PSRL 14:115, 118; AAE 2:346; Petreius, *Istoriia*, 297–99; Popov, *Izbornik*, 354; Widekind, *Historia*, 229–30, 355; *Pskovskie letopisi*, 1:139–40; 2:275; *Novgorodskie letopisi*, 474; Skrynnikov, *Time of Troubles*, 176–80; Perrie, *Pretenders*, 211–14; Stanislavskii, *Grazhdanskaia voina*, 35–36.

27. *Pskovskie letopisi*, 1:139; SGGD 2: no. 281; Popov, *Izbornik*, 352–53; Belokurov, *Razriadnye zapisi*, 277; Smirnov, *Vosstanie*, 351; Liubomirov, *Ocherk*, 101; Skrynnikov, *Time of Troubles*, 181–82. Cf. Proskuriakova, *Klassovaia bor'ba*.

28. Petreius, *Istoriia*, 298–99, 307–8; Widekind, *Historia*, 232; AI 2:401; Forsten, "Politika Shvetsii," 348–49; Perrie, *Pretenders*, 212–14.

29. SGGD 2: no. 277; PSRL 14:115; Popov, *Izbornik*, 354; *Novgorodskie letopisi*, 474; Perrie, *Pretenders*, 214 n. 51.

30. PSRL 14:115; AAE 2:342; Palitsyn, *Skazanie*, 219; RIB 1: col. 287; *Pskovskie letopisi*, 2:276; Popov, *Izbornik*, 354; Stanislavskii, *Grazhdanskaia voina*, 35; Perrie, *Pretenders*, 214–16. Unduly influenced by anti-Zarutskii propaganda (e.g., SGGD 2: no. 277), some scholars have mistakenly regarded Zarutskii as the mastermind behind the national militia's oath to the "third false Dmitrii"; see Zabelin, *Minin i Pozharskii*, 73; Liubomirov, *Ocherk*, 101.

31. Popov, *Izbornik*, 354; AAE 2:342–43, 346; SGGD 2: no. 281; Palitsyn, *Skazanie*, 220.

32. *Novgorodskie letopisi*, 474; *Pskovskie letopisi*, 1:140; 2:276–77; RIB 1: cols. 287–88; Popov, *Izbornik*, 354–55; Petreius, *Istoriia*, 299–300; Skrynnikov, *Time of Troubles*, 180–82, 224–25; Perrie, *Pretenders*, 216–17.

33. PSRL 14:118; SGGD 2:597; Perrie, *Pretenders*, 217–18.

34. Skrynnikov, *Time of Troubles*, 186–99; AAE 2:250, 297, 320, 348–50; *Pamiatniki istorii Nizhegorodskogo dvizheniia*, 428–29, 446–48; Popov, *Izbornik*, 353; Iakovlev, *Pamiatniki*, 93–95, 98–101; SGGD 2:281; Cherepnin, *Zemskie sobory*, 172; Stanislavskii, *Grazhdanskaia voina*, 42. See also Genkin, *Iaroslavskii krai*.

35. Skrynnikov, *Time of Troubles*, 200–208; AAE 2:355; SGGD 2:596, 604–7; Bogoiavlenskii and Riabinin, *Akty vremeni mezhdutsarstviia*, 54–56; *Pamiatniki istorii Nizhegorodskogo dvizheniia*, 165; Liubomirov, *Ocherk*, 93; Platonov, *Moscow and the West*, 47–48; Dunning, "James I," 208–9; Zhordaniia, *Ocherki*, 1:291–92, 308–12, 319–23, 327–47, 353–57, 362–67; Vernadsky, *Tsardom*, 1:268; Stanislavskii, *Grazhdanskaia voina*, 42–43; Kazakov, "Bor'ba,"52.

36. AAE 2:256, 279; DAI 1:288; *Pamiatniki istorii Nizhegorodskogo dvizheniia*, 254; Orchard, "Election," 378, 381–85; Skrynnikov, *Time of Troubles*, 210–17; idem, *Minin i Pozharskii*, 250–55.

37. Skrynnikov, *Time of Troubles*, 218–23; SGGD 2:605–6; RIB 1: cols. 295, 314; 2: cols. 223–29, 232–36, 243; Dmitrievskii, *Arkhiepiskop Arsenii*, 159–60; Zhordaniia, *Ocherki*, 1:269, 283–90; Margeret, *Russian Empire*, 37, 133 n. 115; Olearius, *Travels*, 190.

38. Palitsyn, *Skazanie*, 220–22; PSRL 14:121–23; 34:219–20; Liubomirov, *Ocherk*, 147–48; Stanislavskii, *Grazhdanskaia voina*, 47–58; idem, "Dvizhenie Zarutskogo," 308–12; Bernadskii, "Konets Zarutskogo," 83–88; Perrie, *Pretenders*, 218–20; Skrynnikov, *Time of Troubles*, 224–27.

39. Skrynnikov, *Time of Troubles*, 231–44, 258–62; PSRL 14:125–26; RIB 1: col. 337; Kazakov, "Bor'ba," 52.

40. Skrynnikov, *Time of Troubles*, 245–48; RIB 1: cols. 330, 337; AAE 2:369, 373; Palitsyn, *Skazanie*, 222–26; *Pamiatniki Nizhegorodskogo dvizheniia*, 124; Stanislavskii, *Grazhdanskaia voina*, 43–44.

41. RIB 1: cols. 326, 348, 352; *Pamiatniki Nizhegorodskogo dvizheniia,* 493; *Piskarevskii letopisets,* 139; Veselovskii, *Akty podmoskovnykh opolchenii,* 97; Howe, *False Dmitri,* 206–7; Stanislavskii, *Grazhdanskaia voina,* 44; Skrynnikov, *Time of Troubles,* 248–57.

42. Hirschberg, *Polska a Moskwa,* 363; DAI 1:291–94; PSRL 14:129; *Piskarevskii letopisets,* 140; Veselovskii, *Akty podmoskovnykh opolchenii,* 99; Platonov, *Time of Troubles,* 154–56; Skrynnikov, *Time of Troubles,* 264–67.

43. Platonov, *Sotsial'nyi krizis,* 152; Hirschberg, *Polska a Moskwa,* 363; Liubomirov, *Ocherk,* 165 n. 4; Orchard, "Election," 387–88; Almquist, "Nouveaux documents," 45; Stanislavskii, "Pravitel'stvennaia politika," 67.

44. Veselovskii, *Akty podmoskovnykh opolchenii,* 163; Skrynnikov, *Time of Troubles,* 258–64; Stanislavskii, *Grazhdanskaia voina,* 41–43, 251.

45. Orchard, "Election," 389; Skrynnikov, *Time of Troubles,* 267.

46. Orchard, "Election," 378–85, 388–90, 392, 402. Cf. Skrynnikov, *Minin i Pozharskii,* 250–55; idem, *Time of Troubles,* 211–17, 266–67.

47. Roberts, *Gustavus Adolphus,* 75–77; Orchard, "Election," 384–85.

48. SGGD 3:5–22; Almquist, "Nouveaux documents," 43; Orchard, "Election," 382, 386; Skrynnikov, *Time of Troubles,* 267.

49. Dunning, "Cossacks," 71; Platonov, *Time of Troubles,* 156–58; Skrynnikov, *Time of Troubles,* 266–76; Stanislavskii and Morozov, "Povest'," 89–96; Stanislavskii, *Grazhdanskaia voina,* 243.

50. Orchard, "Election," 390–92, 395.

51. *Novyi Letopisets,* 112; Kliuchevskii, *Sochineniia,* 3:60–61; Almquist, "Nouveaux documents," 50, 56–57.

52. Orchard, "Election," 391–92, 394–95.

53. Skrynnikov, *Time of Troubles,* 271–76; Orchard, "Election," 396.

54. Skrynnikov, *Time of Troubles,* 281. Cf. Crummey, *Formation,* 235; Dunning, "Letter," 105.

55. Barsukov, *Rod Sheremetevykh,* 311.

56. Palitsyn, *Skazanie,* 231–33; Almquist, "Nouveaux documents," 61–62; Platonov, *Time of Troubles,* 158–59; Skrynnikov, *Time of Troubles,* 276–77; Orchard, "Election," 396–401; Stanislavskii, *Grazhdanskaia voina,* 243.

57. Dunning, "Letter," 105–6; Almquist, "Nouveaux documents," 54–55; Skrynnikov, *Time of Troubles,* 279–81; Orchard, "Election," 400–401.

NOTES TO CHAPTER 24

1. Zimin, "Nekotorye voprosy," 107; Shapiro, "Historical Role," 30; Yaresh, "Peasant Wars," 258–59; Avrich, *Russian Rebels,* 50.

2. RIB 13: cols. 541–42, 547; Rowland, "Problem," 282–83; idem, "Limits," 132, 152; Keep, *Soldiers,* 19–20; Zhivov, "Religious Reform," 187–88; Cherniavsky, *Tsar and People,* 59; Billington, *Icon and Axe,* 200. Cf. Figarovskii, "Krest'ianskoe vosstanie," 195.

3. PSRL 5:63; Platonov, *Ocherki,* 175–76; Skrynnikov, *Time of Troubles,* 273–74, 280; Orchard, "Election," 397–98.

4. SGGD 1: no. 203; Belokurov, "Utverzhdenaia gramota," 36; PSRL 14:106–7; Bennet, "Idea of Kingship," 44–45; Perrie, *Image,* 110–11.

5. Belokurov, "Utverzhdenaia gramota," 41.

6. Dmitrievskii, *Arkhiepiskop Arsenii,* 172; Orchard, "Election," 390.

7. Palitsyn, *Skazanie,* 231–33, 235, 238; Timofeev, *Vremennik,* 165; PSRL 14:129; Belokurov, "Utverzhdenaia gramota," 41–43, 49–50; Bennet, "Idea of Kingship," 42–52; Rowland, "Problem," 226; Kondratieva and Ingerflom, "Bez Carja zemlja vdova," 257–66. Cf. SGGD 3:46–55, 70–87; Kivelson, *Autocracy,* 13.

8. Cherniavsky, *Tsar and People,* 59, 61, 71; Rowland, "Limits," 152.

9. Skrynnikov, *Time of Troubles*, 279, 284.
10. Platonov, *Time of Troubles*, 170; Tikhomirov, "Pskovskie povesti," 186.
11. Keep, "Regime," 343; Lapman, "Political Denunciations," 177.
12. Novombergskii, *Slovo i delo*, 4–7, 10–11, 16–17, 25–26, 36–40; Lapman, "Political Denunciations," 3–4, 163–64, 166; Kleimola, "Up through Servitude," 221; I. I. Polosin, "Igra v tsaria," *Izvestiia Tverskogo pedagogicheskogo instituta*, 1926, part 1:62–63; Keenan, "Reply," 204; Perrie, *Pretenders*, 234–36; Richard Hellie, "The Origins of Denunciation in Muscovy," *Russian History*, 24 (1997):13–14.
13. Lapman, "Political Denunciations," 5, 166, 177; Kleimola, "Duty to Denounce," 763, 770.
14. Lapman, "Political Denunciations," 143, 147–48.
15. Novombergskii, *Slovo i delo*, 1–2, 10, 18–22, 66–69, 428; Kleimola, "Duty to Denounce," 777; Lapman, "Political Denunciations," 4, 165–66.
16. Lapman, "Political Denunciations," 164–65; Perrie, *Pretender*, 234.
17. See Lapman, "Political Denunciations," 12–16.
18. Ibid., 214–15; Keenan, "Muscovite Political Folkways," 147.
19. Hellie, "Keenan's Scholarly Ways," 187–88. Cf. Lapman, "Political Denunciations," 177.
20. Lapman, "Political Denunciations," 63–64, 215.
21. Tikhomirov, "Pskovskie povesti," 186; Rowland, "Muscovite Political Attitudes," 226–27, 282–83; Crummey, *Formation*, 232, 238; Bushkovitch, *Religion and Society*, 131; N. S. Chaev, "Iz istorii krest'ianskoi bor'by za zemliu v votchinakh Antonieva-Siiskogo monastyria v XVII v.," *Istoricheskii arkhiv* 1 (1936): 32.
22. Platonov, *Time of Troubles*, 166–67, 169; idem, *Stat'i*, 395–406.
23. Kleimola, "Up through Servitude," 225; Keep, *Soldiers*, 19–21; Crummey, "Reconstitution," 192–97, 207–8.
24. Platonov, *Stat'i*, 402–6; Keep, *Soldiers*, 19–20; Skrynnikov, *Time of Troubles*, 279–81; Crummey, *Aristocrats and Servitors*, 108, 114, 178.
25. Kleimola, "Up through Servitude," 221, 223–25.
26. PSRL 5:63–64; Kleimola, "Up through Servitude," 225, 228; Hellie, *Enserfment*, 51–52; Crummey, "Crown and Boiars," 571–72.
27. Skrynnikov, *Time of Troubles*, 280–84. One reason Pozharskii was out of favor may have been his earlier willingness to consider a Swedish candidate for tsar; see Orchard, "Election," 402.
28. Massa, *Short History*, 185.
29. Platonov, *Time of Troubles*, 168–69; Figarovskii, "Krest'ianskoe vosstanie," 218; Crummey, *Formation*, 232; Skrynnikov, *Time of Troubles*, 284–85, 287.
30. Figarovskii, "Krest'ianskoe vosstanie," 196; Skrynnikov, *Time of Troubles*, 286–88; Hellie, *Enserfment*, 111–12; Stanislavskii, *Grazhdanskaia voina*, 245–48; idem, "Pravitel'stvennaia politika," 66–79.
31. Skrynnikov, *Time of Troubles*, 290–93. Cf. Stanislavskii, "Dokumenty," 285–307.
32. Platonov, *Ocherki*, 471–73, 506; Cherepnin, *Zemskie sobory*, 120–25, 220–29; Brown, "Zemskii Sobor," 80–82.
33. Veselovskii, *Akty podmoskovnykh opolchenii*, 129; Voskoboinikova, "K istorii finansovoi politiki russkogo gosudarstva," 156–61; Platonov, *Time of Troubles*, 172; Hellie, *Enserfment*, 240–41; Smith, *Peasant Farming*, 226; Keep, *Soldiers*, 80; Crummey, *Formation*, 234; Brown, "Zemskii Sobor," 82; Eaton, "Decline and Recovery," 223; Stevens, *Soldiers*, 19.
34. Hellie, *Enserfment*, 51–52; Platonov, *Stat'i*, 383–86; idem, *Time of Troubles*, 166–68, 170–73; Kliuchevskii, *Sochineniia*, 3:66–70, 88; 7:440–41; Mavrodin, "Soviet Historical Literature," 55. Cf. Weickhardt, "Political Thought," 321; Kivelson, *Autocracy*, 213–16.
35. Florinsky, *Russia*, 1:266–71; Rowland, "Muscovite Political Attitudes," 186, 188, 190, 220–22; idem, "Problem," 259–61, 276–77, 279, 282–83; Crummey, *Formation*, 205; Brown, "Zemskii Sobor," 79, 88–89. Cf. Kollmann, "Concepts," 38–39.
36. Crummey, *Formation*, 234–35.
37. Dunning, "Letter," 104–6.
38. Skrynnikov, *Time of Troubles*, 281–82, 288.

39. Ibid., 282–83; Stanislavskii, "Pravitel'stvennaia politika," 67.

40. Michael Roberts, *The Swedish Imperial Experience, 1560–1718* (Cambridge: Cambridge University Press, 1979), 9–12; idem, *Gustavus Adolphus*, 79–81; MERSH 28:203–4; Skrynnikov, *Time of Troubles*, 288, 293. The English merchant-diplomat John Merrick acted as mediator during peace talks between the Russians and the Swedes. See Phipps, *Sir John Merrick*, chapter 4.

41. Michael Roberts, ed., *Sweden's Age of Greatness, 1632–1718* (London: Macmillan, 1973), 4; idem, *Gustavus Adolphus*, 89–90. See also Artur Attman, *Swedish aspirations and the Russian market in the 17th century* (Göteborg, 1985).

42. Stanislavskii, *Grazhdanskaia voina*, 77.

43. Tkhorzhevskii, *Narodnye volneniia*, 44–76; Shepelev, "Mesto," 238; Dolinin, "K razboru," 138–46; Perrie, *Pretenders*, 227–28.

44. Massa, *Short History*, 184; PSRL 14:123, 128, 130, 132; AAE 3:39; Liubomirov, *Ocherk*, 163; Skrynnikov, *Time of Troubles*, 285–86; Stanislavskii, *Grazhdanskaia voina*, 49–76.

45. RIB 1: col. 317; PSRL 34:219; AAE 3:64; Kostomarov, *Smutnoe vremia*, 628–29; Perrie, *Pretenders*, 220–22.

46. Popov, *Izbornik*, 361; PSRL 14:134; 34:219; AAE 3:24, 39; AI 3:26, 412; SGGD 3:97; *Chronicle of the Carmelites*, 1:197; Bernadskii, "Konets Zarutskogo," 100–105; Skrynnikov, *Time of Troubles*, 285–86; Perrie, *Pretenders*, 222–23.

47. See, for example, Zimin, "Nekotorye voprosy," 104–5.

48. AI 3:411–12; Massa, *Short History*, 184; Skrynnikov, *Time of Troubles*, 285–86; Perrie, *Pretenders*, 220, 222–24; N. Veselovskii, *Pamiatniki*, 3:2, 24, 56–57.

49. PSRL 14:134; Massa, *Short History*, 184–85.

50. Popov, *Izbornik*, 361; AI 3:14, 17, 425, 430, 436; AAE 3:28–29; SGGD 3:97; PSRL 14:134; 34:219; Perrie, *Pretenders*, 221, 224.

51. AI 3:14–15, 411–13, 430–33, 435–36, 444–45, 447; Bernadskii, "Konets Zarutskogo," 106–23; Perrie, *Pretenders*, 224–26.

52. AI 3:19–20, 23, 25–26, 32, 448; Bernadskii, "Konets Zarutskogo," 123–33; Perrie, *Pretenders*, 226–27.

53. PSRL 14:134; 34:219.

54. Bussow, *Disturbed State*, 220 n. 18; Kostomarov, *Smutnoe vremia*, 635; Vernadsky, *Tsardom*, 1:284–85; Perrie, *Pretenders*, 227. Skrynnikov (*Time of Troubles*, 286) erred in claiming that Marina was incarcerated in Tula.

55. Perrie, *Pretenders*, 229.

56. Solov'ev, *Istoriia*, 5:115, 156–57, 248–54, 460–67, 471, 564–71; Troitskii, "Samozvantsy," 144–45; Chistov, *Russkie legendy*, 67–78; MERSH 2:2–4; Bercé, *Le roi caché*, 129; Stanislavskii, *Grazhdanskaia voina*, 193; Perrie, *Pretenders*, 229–33; R. G. Skrynnikov, *Likholet'e: Moskva v xvi–xvii vekakh* (Moscow: Moskovskii rabochii, 1989), 538–40.

57. Dunning, "Cossacks," 73; Longworth, *Cossacks*, 80–81; Skrynnikov, *Time of Troubles*, 279–82.

58. Stanislavskii, *Grazhdanskaia voina*, 45; Mavrodin, "Soviet Historical Literature," 55; Gordon, *Cossack Rebellions*, 141.

59. Massa, *Short History*, 183; Skrynnikov, *Time of Troubles*, 286–89.

60. AAE 3: nos. 44, 50, 64; Massa, *Short History*, 183; Platonov, *Time of Troubles*, 168–69; Keep, "Bandits," 201; Skrynnikov, *Time of Troubles*, 300–301. Cf. Stanislavskii, "Kazatskoe dvizhenie," 104–16.

61. AI 2:90; Hellie, *Enserfment*, 30,111; Skrynnikov, *Time of Troubles*, 286–87; Stanislavskii, *Grazhdanskaia voina*, 245; Gordon, *Cossack Rebellions*, 86, 89–91.

62. See, for example, Figarovskii, "Krest'ianskoe vosstanie," 194–218.

63. Stanislavskii, *Grazhdanskaia voina*, 243, 245–47; idem, "Pravitel'stvennaia politika," 66–79.

64. Skrynnikov, *Time of Troubles*, 287–90, 300–304; Stanislavskii, *Grazhdanskaia voina*, 93–151, 247–48; idem, "Vosstanie 1614–1615 gg," 111–26.

65. Skrynnikov, *Time of Troubles*, 289–99.

66. Stanislavskii, *Grazhdanskaia voina*, 245–48. Platonov (*Time of Troubles*, 165) wrongly credited the regime's sincerity about its offers of freedom and positions in state service to former serfs and

slaves among the cossacks. Stanislavskii ("Kazatskoe dvizhenie," 104–16) also initially credited the regime's sincerity but later changed his mind.

67. Skrynnikov, *Time of Troubles*, 299–304.

68. Solov'ev, *Istoriia*, 5:115, 156; Stanislavskii, *Grazhdanskaia voina*, 193; Chistov, *Russkie legendy*, 67–68; Skrynnikov, *Time of Troubles*, 303–5; MERSH 28:202; Perrie, *Pretenders*, 231.

69. Stanislavskii, *Grazhdanskaia voina*, 245–48; idem, "Pravitel'stvennaia politika," 66–79; Skrynnikov, *Time of Troubles*, 286–88; Crummey, *Formation*, 232. Cf. Gordon, *Cossack Rebellions*, 86.

70. Shaw, "Settlement," 232–56; Keep, *Soldiers*, 73–74.

71. Longworth, *Cossacks*, 80–82; Keep, *Soldiers*, 73; Dunning, "Cossacks," 73–74.

72. Crummey, *Formation*, 232; Keep, "Regime," 334–60; Dukes, *Making of Russian Absolutism*, 6–7.

NOTES TO CHAPTER 25

1. See, for example, Shapiro, "Historical Role," 27–29; Yaresh, "Peasant Wars," 258–59.

2. See, for example, Platonov, *Time of Troubles*, 166; Danilova, "K itogam," 64; Braudel, *Perspective of the World*, 444–51. Cf. Hellie, *Enserfment*, 107, 111, 237.

3. See, for example, Shapiro, "Historical Role," 27–28, 30; Yaresh, "Peasant Wars," 258–59; Zimin, "Nekotorye voprosy," 107; Mavrodin, "K voprosu," 85; Billington, *Icon*, 200; Avrich, *Russian Rebels*, 50.

4. Goldstone, *Revolution and Rebellion*, 27, 418–20, 450–54, 458.

5. Kivelson, *Autocracy*.

6. Kivelson, *Autocracy*, 3, 8, 20, 36–39, 151–53, 253–54, 261–62, 265, 276–77, 289 nn. 4, 16; Henshall, *Myth of Absolutism*.

7. Brewer, *Sinews of Power*, xvii–xxi, 3–24, 250–51.

8. Brown, "From Organic Society to Security State," 661–95.

9. Cherniavsky, *Tsar and People*, 59, 71; Rowland, "Muscovite Political Attitudes," 185–86, 217, 226–29; idem, "Problem," 259–61, 282–83; Kivelson, *Autocracy*, 278; Bushkovitch, "Formation," 363. See also RIB 13: cols. 541–42, 547.

10. Weickhardt, "Bureaucrats and Boiars," 331–34; Brown, "Muscovite Government Bureaus," 272; Hellie, *Enserfment*, 70; Kivelson, *Autocracy*, 229–30, 238; idem, "Devil Stole His Mind," 749–51; Crummey, *Formation*, 236–38.

11. Florovsky, "Problem," 11–15; Rowland, "Ivan the Terrible," 602.

12. See, for example, Rowland, "Muscovite Political Attitudes," 156–57; idem, "Problem," 281–82; idem, "Limits," 139.

13. Kivelson, *Autocracy*, 19, 26, 229; Weickhardt, "Political Thought," 329–30; Keep, *Soldiers*, 58; *Muscovite Law Code*, chapters 11 and 1.

14. Hellie, "Stratification," 119; idem, *Slavery*, 16; idem, "Warfare," 88; Crummey, *Formation*, 238–39; Eaton, "Decline," 234; Cracraft, "Empire Versus Nation," 527.

15. Wortman, *Scenarios of Power*.

16. Dukes, *Making of Russian Absolutism*, 5; Fuller, *Strategy and Power in Russia*.

17. Platonov, *Time of Troubles*, 166–68, 170–73; Hosking, *Russia*, 63.

18. Hellie, *Enserfment*, 103; Avrich, *Russian Rebels*, 50.

19. Goehrke, *Die Wüstungen*; Smith, *Peasant Farming*, 226.

20. Eaton, "Decline," 234; Hellie, "Foundations," 148, 150–52. On prices after the Time of Troubles, see Hellie, *The Economy and Material Culture of Russia*.

21. Eaton, "Decline," 220; idem, "Early Russian Censuses," 175, 212; Got'e, *Zamoskovnyi krai*, 156–68; Parker, *Europe in Crisis*, 23.

22. Hellie, *Enserfment*, 240–41; Eaton, "Early Russian Censuses," 182.

23. Eaton, "Early Russian Censuses," 186–87, 212.

24. Veselovskii and Iakovlev, *Pamiatniki*, 1:267.
25. Eaton, "Decline," 220–23; Hellie, *Enserfment*, 241. Cf. Kuznetsov, "K voprosu," 85–96.
26. Eaton, "Early Russian Censuses," 182.
27. Hellie, *Enserfment*, 241; idem, "Stratification," 119.
28. Eaton, "Decline," 223; Dukes, *Making of Russian Absolutism*, 5.
29. Keep, *Soldiers*, 58; idem, *Enserfment*, 240–41; idem, "Stratification," 119; Hosking, *Russia*, xxvii; Crummey, *Formation*, 239.
30. Hellie, "Foundations," 150–52; Eaton, "Decline," 234; Cracraft, "Empire Versus Nation," 527; Kleimola, "Up through Servitude," 225. See also Bushkovitch, "Towns," 215–32; Pipes, *Russia*, chapter 8; Baron, "The Weber Thesis and the Failure of Capitalism in Early Modern Russia," 321–36; Hittle, *The Service City*, chapters 2–3.
31. Pokrovsky, *Brief History*, 1:83; Zimin, "Nekotorye voprosy," 107; Yaresh, "Peasant Wars," 250, 252; Pronshtein, "Resolved and Unresolved Problems," 28. Cf. Makovskii, *Pervaia krest'ianskaia voina*, 295–97, 470–72, 477, 482.
32. See Bushkovitch, "Towns," 215–32; Crummey, *Formation*, 21–24.
33. Baron, "The *Gosti* Revisited," 9–10, 14–17.
34. Platonov, *Time of Troubles*, 166–72; idem, *Ocherki*, 291, 412, 430; Mavrodin, "Sovetskaia istoricheskaia nauka," 299, 318; Veselovskii, *Soshnoe pis'mo*, 1:318; Zimin, "Nekotorye voprosy," 106, 109; Zimin and Koroleva, "Dokument," 23–24, 28–29, 36–37; Gnevushev, "Zemlevladenie," 289. Cf. Hosking, *Russia*, 63–64.
35. See, for example, Kivelson, *Autocracy*, 7–8, 55, 216.
36. Stanislavskii, *Grazhdanskaia voina*, 248; Hellie, *Enserfment*, 52–53, 70–71, 73–74. Cf. Kivelson, *Autocracy*, 53–55.
37. Rowland, "Problem of Advice," 259–61, 276–77, 279, 282–83; idem, "Muscovite Political Attitudes," 186, 188, 190.
38. Hellie, *Enserfment*, 52; Cherepnin, *Zemskie sobory*, 229–38.
39. See Hellie, *Enserfment*, chapter 7; idem, *Muscovite Society*, 167–205; Kivelson, *Autocracy*, chapters 7 and 8.
40. Stanislavskii, *Grazhdanskaia voina*, 245; Hellie, *Enserfment*, 49; Bobrovskii, *Perekhod*, 61. Cf. Shaw, "Settlement," 248.
41. Crummey, *Formation*, 236–37; Keep, *Soldiers*, 80; Bobrovskii, *Perekhod*, 107; Hellie, *Enserfment*, 72–74, 165–71, 182, 216–17, 238–39. See also Stevens, *Soldiers on the Steppe*.
42. Skrynnikov, *Time of Troubles*, 279–82, 284–85, 287; Hellie, *Enserfment*, 53, 56–57, 209, 263; Stanislavskii, *Grazhdanskaia voina*, 248. Cf. Kivelson, *Autocracy*, 54; idem, "Devil Stole His Mind," 750.
43. Keep, *Soldiers*, 59; Hellie, *Slavery*, 38, 471; idem, "Warfare," 85; idem, *Enserfment*, 165.
44. Veselovskii, *Soshnoe pis'mo*, 2:188; Liubomirov, *Ocherk istorii*, 39; Hellie, *Enserfment*, 52–53, 59–63, 111; P. Smirnov, "Chelobitnyia," 9–10.
45. Keep, *Soldiers*, 49–50; Hellie, *Enserfment*, 65–67, 127, 171, 216–17; idem, *Slavery*, 78, 613; Shaw, "Settlement," 254–55.
46. Kivelson, *Autocracy*, 229; Hellie, *Enserfment*, 53, 129, 209; Keep, *Soldiers*, 74; Shaw, "Settlement," 254; Dunning, "Cossacks," 73–74; Zagorovskii, *Belgorodskaia cherta*, 29, 34; Davies, "Village into Garrison," 481–501.
47. Hellie, *Muscovite Society*, 167–205; Kivelson, *Autocracy*, 53, 55, 217–21. Cf. Hellie, *Enserfment*, 55–56, 70–73, 133, 138.
48. Hellie, *Enserfment*, 127.
49. Kivelson, *Autocracy*, 221, 227, 245–46.
50. Ibid., 221, 231; Zimin, "Osnovnye etapy," 50.
51. Kivelson, *Autocracy*, 248–54; Hellie, *Enserfment*, 134, 137, 139, 146; Hosking, *Russia*, 64. The most important concession by the central government as far as the gentry were concerned was the repeal of the statute of limitations for the recovery of fugitive peasants, a statute that in its various forms since the 1590s had worked to the disadvantage of the gentry and to the great advantage of the magnates. See *Muscovite Law Code*, chapter 11.

52. See Hellie, *Enserfment*, 53–58, 72, 247.

53. Platonov, *Time of Troubles*, 166–67, 169; idem, *Sochineniia*, 2 vols. (St. Petersburg, 1919), I: 395–406; Hosking, *Russia*, 63.

54. Kleimola, "Up through Servitude," 223–25; Hellie, *Enserfment*, 51–57, 73; idem, *Slavery*, 16; Crummey, "Origins," 46–75.

55. Crummey, "Crown and Boiars, 562–63, 571–72; idem, *Aristocrats and Servitors*.

56. Milov and Garskova, "A Typology," 375–90; I. L. Andreev, "Sil'nye liudi," 77–88; Hellie, *Enserfment*, 66–67, 73, 112–14; Kivelson, *Autocracy*, 53, 219–20, 231, 245–46, 250–51.

57. Platonov, *Time of Troubles*, 168; Hosking, *Russia*, 63.

58. See, for example, Avrich, *Russian Rebels*, 45, 50; Shapiro, "Historical Role," 27–28; Yaresh, "Peasant Wars," 258–59; Hellie, *Enserfment*, 107, 111, 237, 263.

59. Mavrodin, "Sovetskaia istoricheskaia nauka," 326 nn. 114–15; Zaozerskii, "K voprosu," 339. Cf. Figarovskii, "Krest'ianskoe vosstanie," 195.

60. See, for example, Mavrodin, "Sovetskaia istoricheskaia nauka," 297; Danilova, "K itogam," 64.

61. Shapiro, "Historical Role," 27–32, 43; Mavrodin, "Soviet Historical Literature," 43; Yaresh, "Peasant Wars," 250; Zimin, "Nekotorye voprosy," 102, 107; Makovskii, *Pervaia krest'ianskaia voina*, 49; Nazarov, "Peasant Wars," 115; Cherepnin, *Zemskie sobory*, 114, 132; L. V. Cherepnin, "Problema krest'ianskogo zakreposhcheniia v Rossii v osveshchenii burzhuaznoi istoriografii," in *Kritika burzhuaznykh kontseptsii istorii Rossii perioda feodalizma* (Moscow: AN SSSR, 1962), 73; Koretskii, "K istorii formirovaniia," 85.

62. Hellie, "Warfare," 84–85.

63. See, for example, Veselovskii, *Akty pisstsovogo dela*, 1: 184.

64. Hellie, *Enserfment*, 124; Veselovskii, *Soshnoe pis'mo*, 1: 319; B. F. Porshnev, "Sotsial'no-politicheskaia obstanovka v Rossii vo vremia Smolenskoi voiny," *Istoriia SSSR* 1:5 (Nov–Dec 1957), 121. Cf. Kahan, "Natural Calamities," 371.

65. Hellie, *Enserfment*, 111–12, 114, 133, 138, 140; A. E. Presniakov, "Moskovskoe gosudarstvo pervoi poloviny XVII veka," in *Tri veka*, 6 vols. (Moscow, 1912–13), 1: 60.

66. Hellie, *Enserfment*, 108–9; Smirnov, *Vosstanie*, 418–22; Skrynnikov, *Smuta*, 185–87; Nazarov, "Bylo li podlinnym ulozhenie," 197–200.

67. Ibid., 118–21.

68. Keep, "Regime," 337.

69. Hosking, *Russia*, xxii–xxiii, 63–64; Kivelson, *Autocracy*, 8–9; Billington, *Icon*, 123–27; Crummey, *Formation*, 235; Bushkovitch, *Religion & Society*, 111, 112.

70. Keep, "Regime"; Dukes, *Making of Russian Absolutism*, 26; Vernadsky, *Tsardom*, 1:308–10, 318.

71. Gorfunkel', "Rost," 237; Hellie, *Enserfment*, 68–69.

72. Hellie, *Enserfment*, 112, 237.

73. Andreev, "Sil'nye liudi," 77–88; Gnevushev, "Zemlevladenie," 286; Hellie, *Enserfment*, 69–70; Kivelson, *Autocracy*, 219.

74. Pipes, *Russia*, 226.

75. See Goldstone, *Revolution and Rebellion*, 418–20, 450–54, 458.

76. Vernadsky, *Tsardom*, 1:320–22; Billington, *Icon and Axe*, 125–26; Hellie, *Enserfment*, 55–56; Dukes, *Making of Russian Absolutism*, 25–26; Keep, "Regime," 337–38.

77. Hosking, *Russia*, 65; Vernadsky, *Tsardom*, 1:318, 413–15; Zguta, *Russian Minstrels*, 57–65.

78. Crummey, *Formation*, 235, 239–40; Hosking, *Russia*, 64–74; Pipes, *Russia*, 234–39.

79. Michels, *At War with the Church*.

80. Crummey, *Formation*, 234–35, 239–40; Vernadsky, *Tsardom*, 1:317; Keenan, "Muscovite Political Folkways," 154–56; idem, "Trouble with Muscovy," 114–16, 121; Billington, *Icon*, 123–26; Bushkovitch, "Formation," 369–74; idem, *Religion and Society*, 128, 131, 177; Rowland, "Problem," 271–72; idem, "Muscovite Political Attitudes," 226–27. See also Zhivov, "Religious Reform," 187, 195; Keenan, "Afterword," 200. Cf. Ziegler, *Black Death*, 267–69, 279.

81. Rowland, "Problem," 260, 271–73; Keenan, "Muscovite Political Folkways," 150; Iakovlev, "Bezumnoe molchanie," 651–78.

82. Rowland, "Problem," 272–73, 279–80; idem, "Ivan the Terrible," 602; idem, "Limits," 154–55.

83. Bushkovitch, "Formation," 374.
84. See Krom, "K voprosu o vremeni zarozhdeniia idei patriotizma v Rossii," 16–30. Cf. Dolinin, "Razvitie," 109–37.
85. Cherniavsky, *Tsar and People*, 112, 116.
86. Soloviev, *Holy Russia;* Cherniavsky, "Holy Russia," 617–37; idem, *Tsar and People*, 101–11.
87. Cherniavsky, *Tsar and People*, 111–12; Stief, *Studies*, 54. The term "Holy Russia" is found in the controversial writings attributed to Prince Andrei Kurbskii and supposedly composed in the late sixteenth century. (See Cherniavsky, *Tsar and People*, 103–4, 106–8.) However, Edward L. Keenan has argued that those works were actually generated in the decades following the Time of Troubles, and Daniel Rowland has commented on the remarkable similarity of the political ideas in Kurbskii's texts to tales about the Time of Troubles composed in the seventeenth century. In fact, Cherniavsky himself suspected that Kurbskii's use of the term "Holy Russia" meant that the writings attributed to him were composed after the Time of Troubles. See Keenan, *The Kurbskii-Groznyi Apocrypha;* Rowland, "Limits," 133 n. 24; Cherniavsky, *Tsar and People*, 110–11.
88. Cherniavsky, *Tsar and People*, 112–16.
89. Rowland, "Moscow," 597, 598, 605.
90. Kollmann, "Concepts,"40–42.
91. Cherniavsky, *Tsar and People*, 116.
92. Billington, *Icon and Axe*, 126; Zhivov, "Religious Reform," 187; Tsimbaev, "Rossiia i Russkie," 23–32.
93. Cherniavsky, *Tsar and People*, 112, 114, 116–17.
94. Kivelson, "Devil Stole His Mind," 756; idem, *Autocracy*, 253–54, 261–62, 265; Rowland, "Ivan the Terrible," 606.
95. Rowland, "Limits," 155.
96. Crummey, *Formation*, 240–41; Kivelson, *Autocracy*, 14–15, 165, 270; Cherniavsky, *Tsar and People*, 124; Rowland, "Ivan the Terrible," 605–6; Cracraft, "Empire Versus Nation," 524–25; Bushkovitch, "Formation," 374–75; Wortman, *Scenarios of Power;* Raeff, 181–250; Anisimov *The Reforms of Peter the Great*, viii, xi, 296.
97. Hosking, *Russia*, 69, 73–74; Pipes, *Russia*, 239; Cherniavsky, *Tsar and People*, 125–26.
98. See, for example, Kivelson, "Devil Stole His Mind"; idem, *Autocracy*, 19, 238–39. Cf. Weickhardt, "Political Thought," 316–22.
99. Kivelson, "Devil Stole His Mind," 742, 749–51, 755–56; Keep, "Regime," 337; Rowland, "Ivan the Terrible," 596, 605–6; Bennet, "Idea of Kingship," 211–13; Hellie, *Enserfment*, 247.
100. Hosking, *Russia*, xix–xx, xxiv–xxvii; Cherniavsky, *Tsar and People*, 118–20; Kivelson, "Devil Stole His Mind," 733–35; Rowland, "Ivan the Terrible," 596; Weickhardt, "Political Thought," 316; Bushkovitch, "Formation," 374–75.
101. Michael Cherniavsky, "Russia," in Orest Ranum, ed., *National Consciousness, History, and Political Culture in Early-Modern Europe* (Baltimore: Johns Hopkins University Press, 1975), 134–35; Tsimbaev, "Rossiia i Russkie," 23–32.
102. Rowland, "Problem of Advice," 272–73, 279–80; Cherniavsky, *Tsar and People*, 117–18; Billington, *Icon*, 197; Keenan, "Muscovite Political Folkways," 150, 154–55. See also Rowland, "Limits," 154–55; Buganov, "Religious ideologies," 206–12.
103. See, for example, Avrich, *Russian Rebels;* Smirnov et al., *Krest'ianskie voiny;* Buganov, *Krest'ianskie voiny;* idem, "Ob ideologii," 44–60; Mavrodin, "Sovetskaia istoriografiia," 53–82; Mavrodin et al., "Ob osobennostiakh," 69–79; Shapiro, "Historical Role," 27–47; Zimin, "Nekotorye voprosy," 97–113; Pronshtein, "Resolved and Unresolved Problems," 27–39.
104. See Khodarkovsky, "Razin Uprising," 1–19.
105. Longworth, "Last Great Cossack-Peasant Rising," 6–7, 17–21, 26; idem, "Peasant Leadership," 183–85.
106. Khodarkovsky, "Razin Uprising," 3, 7–8, 14–19; Avrich, *Russian Rebels*, 116–17, 252; Longworth, "Peasant Leadership," 184–85.
107. Khodarkovsky, "Razin Uprising," 4, 9, 11, 14–16, 18–19; Avrich, *Russian Rebels*, 1, 4–5, 20.
108. Avrich, *Russian Rebels*, 119, 246. Cf. Hellie, *Enserfment*, 128–29; Smirnov, *Vosstanie Bolotnikova*, 493.

109. Buganov, "Religious ideologies," 207, 212; Avrich, *Russian Rebels,* 120, 246.

110. Billington, *Icon,* 197; Cherniavsky, *Tsar and People,* 117–18; Keenan, "Muscovite Political Folkways," 150, 154–55; Kivelson, "Devil Stole His Mind."

111. The traditional view of Old Believer leadership in Russia's early modern rebellions may be found in V. G. Kartsov, *Religioznyi raskol kak forma antifeodal'nogo protesta v istorii Rossii,* vol. 1 (Kalinin, 1971): 76–101; Buganov, "Religious ideologies," 208–12; idem, *Krest'ianskie voiny,* chapter 4; Khodarkovsky, "Razin Uprising," 6–7; Longworth, "Subversive Legend," 21–22; idem, "Last Great Cossack-Peasant Rising," 12–13, 17; idem, "Peasant Leadership," 199. Cf. Druzhinin, *Raskol,* iii–ix, 85–86, 120, 219–20, 277–81.

112. Solov'ev, "Zametki," cols. 265–81; Kliuchevskii, *Sochineniia,* 3:27–28; Tikhomirov, "Samozvanshchina,"116–21; Troitskii, "Samozvantsy," 134–46; Longworth, "Pretender Phenomenon," 61–83; Perrie, *Pretenders.*

113. Crummey, *Formation,* 217. Cf. Perrie, *Pretenders,* 239–46; Uspenskij, "Tsar and Pretender," 260.

114. Kostomarov, *Bunt Sten'ki Razina,* 2: 356; Avrich, *Russian Rebels,* 251.

115. Longworth, "Subversive Legend," 22–25; idem, "Peasant Leadership," 188, 199, 201; Avrich, *Russian Rebels,* 121, 251; Raeff, "Pugachev's Rebellion," 195; Sokolova, *Russkie istoricheskie predaniia,* 164–65. See also Druzhinin, *Raskol,* 277–81.

116. Indova, Preobrazhenskii, and Tikhonov, "Narodnye dvizheniia," 88; Hellie, *Enserfment,* 261; Pushkin, *History of Pugachev,* 36, 105; idem, *The Poems, Prose, and Plays of Alexander Pushkin,* 741; Alexander, *Emperor of the Cossacks,* 203; Hosking, *Russia,* 115. See also Avrich, *Russian Rebels,* 258, 270.

117. Cherniavsky, *Tsar and People,* 126; Perrie, "Folklore," 141; Shapiro, "Resolved and Unresolved Problems," 42; Frierson, *Peasant Icons,* 33, 38, 44–47; Kornblatt, *Cossack Hero,* 5, 15–20, 25–26, 102–6, 144–48, 173.

BIBLIOGRAPHY

ARCHIVAL SOURCES

Koninklijke Bibliotheek [National Library of the Netherlands], Manuscript Division, The Hague:
  78 H 56 (Isaac Massa's Album Amicorum).
Public Record Office, London:
  State Papers Foreign 91/1 (Russia), fols. 215–16v ("The State of the Empire of Russia since the Death of the late pretended Demetry").
Rossiiskii gosudarstvennyi arkhiv drevnikh aktov (RGADA) [Russian State Archive of Ancient Acts], Moscow:
  fond 199, Portfeli G. F. Millera, No. 150/4 ("Istoriia tsaria Vasiliia Ivanovicha Shuiskago, V. N. Tatishchevym sochinennaia")
  fond 210, Razriadnyi prikaz, opis' 4, Dela desiaten', knigi 98, 124, 126, 130, 223.
  fond 214, Sibirskii prikaz, kniga 14.

PUBLISHED PRIMARY AND SECONDARY SOURCES

Abramovich, G. V., *Kniaz'ia Shuiskie i Rossiiskii tron.* Leningrad: Izdatel'stvo Leningradskogo universiteta, 1991.
———. "Novyi istochnik po istorii khlebnykh tsen v Rossii XVI v." *Istoriia SSSR,* 13 (March–April 1968): 116–18.
Absoliutizm v Rossii (XVII–XVIII vv.). Moscow: Nauka, 1964.
Adrianova-Peretts, V. P., ed. *Voinskie povesti drevnei Rusi.* Moscow-Leningrad: AN SSSR, 1949.
Afremov, Ivan. *Istoricheskoe obozrenie Tul'skoi gubernii.* Vol. 1. Moscow, 1850.
Aiplatov, G. N. "K voprosu ob uchastii trudovykh mass Mariiskogo kraia v krest'ianskoi voine v Rossii nachala XVII veka." *Trudy Mariiskogo nauchno-issledovatel'skogo instituta* 19 (1964): 137–72.
Akty feodal'nogo zemlevladeniia i khoziaistva. 4 vols. Moscow-Leningrad: AN SSSR, 1951–83.
Akty istoricheskie, sobrannye i izdannye Arkheograficheskoiu kommissieiu. 5 vols. and index. St. Petersburg, 1841–42.
Akty iuridicheskie, ili sobranie form starinnago deloproizvodstva. St. Petersburg: Izd. Arkheograficheskoi kommissii, 1838.
Akty Moskovskago gosudarstva, izdannye Imperatorskoiu Akademieiu Nauk. 3 vols. Edited by N. A. Popov. St. Petersburg, 1890–1901.

Akty, otnosiashchiesia k istorii Zapadnoi Rossii, sobrannye i izdannye Arkheograficheskoiu Kommissieiu. 5 vols. St. Petersburg, 1846–53.

Akty, sobrannye v bibliotekakh i arkhivakh Rossiiskoi imperii Arkheograficheskoiu ekspeditsieiu Imp. Akademii nauk. 4 vols. and index. St. Petersburg, 1836–38.

Akty XIII–XVII vv., predstavlennye v Razriadnyi prikaz predstaviteliami sluzhilykh familii posle otmeny mestnichestva. Edited by A. I. Iushkov. Moscow, 1898. ChOIDR 186.

Alef, Gustave. "Muscovite Military Reforms in the Second Half of the 15th Century." *FOG* 18 (1973): 73–108.

———. "The Origin of Muscovite Autocracy: The Age of Ivan III." Published as FOG 39 (1986).

Aleksandrenko, V. N. "Materialy po Smutnomu vremeni na Rusi XVII v." *Starina i Novizna* 14 (1911): 185–453, 524–45.

Aleksandrov, V. A. "Pamflet na rod Sukhotinykh (XVII v.)." *Istoriia SSSR,* 1971, no. 5: 114–22.

Alekseev, Iu. G., and A. I. Kopanev. "Razvitie pomestnoi sistemy v XVI v." In *Dvorianstvo i krepostnoi stroi Rossii XVI–XVIII vv.,* edited by N. I. Pavlenko, et al., 57–69. Moscow: Nauka, 1975.

Alekseeva, O. B., et al., eds. *Istoricheskie pesni XVII veka.* Moscow-Leningrad: Nauka, 1966.

Alexander, John T. *Emperor of the Cossacks.* Lawrence: Coronado Press, 1973.

Allen, W. E. D., ed. *Russian Embassies to the Georgian Kings, 1589–1605.* 2 vols. Cambridge: Cambridge University Press, 1970.

———. *The Ukraine: A History.* Cambridge: Cambridge University Press, 1940.

Almquist, H. "Nouveaux documents sur l'histoire de Russie en 1612–1613." *Le Monde oriental* 1 (1907): 36–65.

Alpatov, M. A. *Russkaia istoricheskaia mysl' i zapadnaia Evropa, XVII-pervaia chetvert' XVIII veka.* Moscow: Nauka, 1976.

Al'shits, D. N. *Nachalo samoderzhaviia v Rossii. Gosudarstvo Ivana Groznogo.* Leningrad: Nauka, 1988.

Anderson, Perry. *Lineages of the Absolutist State.* London: Verso, 1979.

Andreev, A. I. "Svodnyi Sudebnik." *Izvestiia Rossiiskoi Akademii nauk,* series 6, vol. 19 (1925): 621–44.

Andreev, I. L. "'Sil'nye liudi' Moskovskogo gosudarstva i bor'ba dvorian s nimi v 20–40-e gody XVII veka." *Istorii SSSR,* 1990, no. 5: 77–88.

Anisimov, Evgenii V. *The Reforms of Peter the Great: Progress through Coercion in Russia.* Armonk, N.Y.: M.E. Sharpe, 1993.

Anpilogov, G. N. "K voprosu o zakone 1592–1593 gg., otmeniavshem vykhod krest'ianam, i urochnykh letakh v kontse XVI–pervoi polovine XVII v." *Istoriia SSSR,* 1972, no. 5: 160–77.

———. *Novye dokumenty o Rossii kontsa XVI–nachala XVII v.* Moscow: Izd. Mosk. univ., 1967.

———. "Novye materialy o krest'ianskoi voine pod rukovodstvom I. Bolotnikova." *Voprosy istorii,* 1966, no. 12: 199–202.

———. "O vosstanii v Srednem Povolzh'e i g. Oskole v 1606–1609 gg." *Vestnik Moskovskogo universiteta,* series 9 (history), 1969, no. 2: 91–96.

Appleby, Andrew B. "Epidemics and Famine in the Little Ice Age." In Rotberg and Rabb, *Climate and History,* 63–84.

———. *Famine in Tudor and Stuart England.* Stanford: Stanford University Press, 1978.

Arnold, David. *Famine: Social Crisis and Historical Change.* Oxford: Basil Blackwell, 1988.

Aronovich, Ts. "Vosstanie Ivana Bolotnikova (1606–1607g.)." *Istoricheskii zhurnal,* 1937, no. 1 (January): 113–26.

Artsybashev, N. S. *Povestvovanie o Rossii.* 3 vols. Moscow, 1838–43.

Aston, Trevor, ed. *Crisis in Europe 1560–1660*. London: Routledge & Kegan Paul, 1965.

Attman, Artur. *The Bullion Flow Between Europe and the East 1000–1750*. Göteborg, 1981.

———. *The Struggle for Baltic Markets: Powers in Conflict, 1558–1618*. Göteborg, 1979.

———. *Swedish Aspirations and the Russian Market in the 17th Century*. Göteborg, 1985.

Auerbach, Ingre. "Der begriff 'Adel' im Russland des 16. Jahrhunderts." *Cahiers du Monde Russe et Soviétique* 34 (1993): 73–88.

Avrich, Paul. *Russian Rebels, 1600–1800*. New York: Schocken Books, 1972.

Bacon, Francis. "Of Seditions and Troubles." In Francis Bacon, *The Essayes or Counsels, Civill and Morall*, 76–90. London, 1625.

Bagalei, D. I. *Materialy dlia istorii kolonizatsii i byta stepnoi okrainy Moskovskago gosudarstva (Khar'kovskoi i otchasti Kurskoi i Voronezhskoi gub.) v XVI–XVIII stoletiiakh*. Khar'kov, 1886.

Bak, János M., and Gerhard Benecke, eds. *Religion and rural revolt*. Manchester: Manchester University Press, 1984.

Bakhrushin, S. V. *Nauchnye trudy*. 4 vols. in 5. Moscow: AN SSSR, 1952–59.

Barbour, Philip. *Dimitry Called the Pretender*. Boston: Houghton Mifflin, 1966.

Barezi, Bareze. *Discours merveilleux et veritable de la conqueste faite par le jeune Demetrius*. Paris, 1858.

Baron, Samuel H. "The *Gosti* Revisited." In *Explorations in Muscovite History*, 1–21. Great Yarmouth, Norfolk: Valorium, 1991.

———. "The Weber Thesis and the Failure of Capitalism in Early Modern Russia." *Jahrbücher für Geschichte Osteuropas* 18 (1970): 321–36.

Baron, Samuel H., and Nancy Shields Kollmann, eds. *Religion & Culture in Early Modern Russia and Ukraine*. De Kalb: Northern Illinois University Press, 1997.

Barsukov, Aleksandr. *Rod Sheremetevykh*. Vol. 2. St. Petersburg, 1882.

Beliaev, I. S. "Uglichskoe sledstvennoe delo 15 maia 1591 g." ChOIDR 220 (1907), book 1, part 4: 1–29.

Belobrova, O. A. "K izucheniiu 'Povesti o nekoei brani' i ee avtora Evstratiia." *Trudy Otdela Drevnerusskoi Literatury* 25 (1970): 150–61.

Belokurov, S. A., ed. *Razriadnye zapisi za Smutnoe vremia (7113–7121 gg.)* ChOIDR 221 (1907), book 2, part 1: 1–80.

———. *Snosheniia Rossii s Kavkazom, 1578–1613 gg.* ChOIDR, 1888, book 3, part 1: 1–584.

———. "Utverzhdenaia gramota ob izbranii na Moskovskoe gosudarstvo Mikhaila Fedorovicha Romanova." ChOIDR 218 (1906), no. 3: 1–110.

Belov, Evgenii. "O smerti tsarevicha Dimitriia." ZhMNP 168 (1873), part 1: 1–44; part 2: 277–320.

Bennet, Douglas. "The Idea of Kingship in 17th-century Russia." Ph.D. diss., Harvard University, 1967.

Bercé, Yves-Marie. *Revolt and revolution in early modern Europe*. Manchester: Manchester University Press, 1987.

———. *Le roi caché. Sauveurs et imposteurs. Mythes politiques populaires dans l'Europe moderne*. Paris: Fayard, 1990.

Bernadskii, V. N. "Konets Zarutskogo." *Uchenye zapiski Leningradskogo gosudarstvennogo pedagogicheskogo instituta imeni A.I. Gertsena* 19 (1939): 83–133.

Bernshtam, T. A. " Russian Folk Culture and Folk Religion." In *Russian Traditional Culture: Religion, Gender, and Customary Law*, edited by Marjorie Mandelstam Balzer, 34–47. Armonk, N.Y.: M. E. Sharpe, 1992.

Berry, Lloyd E., and Robert O. Crummey, eds. *Rude & Barbarous Kingdom: Russia in the Accounts of Sixteenth-Century English Voyagers*. Madison: University of Wisconsin Press, 1968.

Berthold-Ignace de Sainte-Anne. *Histoire de l'Etablissement de la Mission de Perse par les Pères Carmes-Déchaussés (de l'anée 1604 à 1612)*. Brussels, 1885.

Besançon, Alain. *Le tsarévitch immolé*. Paris: Librairie Plon, 1967.

Beskrovnyi, L. G. *Ocherki po istochnikovedeniia voennoi Rossii*. Moscow: Voenizdat, 1957.

Bestuzhev-Riumin, K. N. "Obzor sobytii ot smerti tsaria Ioanna Vasil'evicha do izbraniia na prestol Mikhaila Feodorovicha Romanova." *ZhMNP* 252 (1887): 49–112.

Bibikov G. "Novye dannye o vosstanii Bolotnikova." *Istoricheskii Arkhiv* 1 (1936): 5–24.

———. "Opyt voennoi reformy 1609–1610gg." *Istoricheskie zapiski* 19 (1946): 1–16.

———. "Zemel'nye pozhalovaniia v period krest'ianskoi voiny i pol'skoi interventsii nachala XVII v." *Uchenye zapiski Moskovskogo gorodskogo pedagogicheskogo instituta imeni V. P. Potemkina*, 2 (1941), part 1: 183–210.

Billington, James H. *The Icon and the Axe: An Interpretive History of Russian Culture*. New York: Knopf, 1966.

Blum, Jerome. *Lord and Peasant in Russia from the Ninth to the Nineteenth Century*. Princeton: Princeton University Press, 1961.

———. "Prices in Russia in the Sixteenth Century." *The Journal of Economic History* 16 (June 1956): 182–99.

Bobrovskii, P. O. *Perekhod Rossii k reguliarnoi armii*. St. Petersburg, 1885.

Bodianskii, O. "O poiskakh moikh v Poznanskoi publichnoi biblioteke." *ChOIDR*, 1846, book 1, part 1: 1–45.

Bodin, Jean. *The Six Bookes of a Commonwealth*. Cambridge: Harvard University Press, 1962.

Bogoiavlenskii, S. K., and I. S. Riabinin, eds. *Akty vremeni mezhdutsarstviia (1610–1613)*. Vol. 3 of *Smutnoe vremia Moskovskago gosudarstva 1604–1613 gg*. ChOIDR. Moscow, 1915.

Boiarskie spiski poslednei chetverti XVI–nachala XVII vv. i rospis' russkogo voiska 1604 g. 2 vols. Edited by S. P. Mordovina and A. L. Stanislavskii. Moscow: TsGADA, 1979.

Boldakov, I. M. *Sbornik materialov po russkoi istorii nachala XVII veka*. St. Petersburg: Izd. S. D. Sheremeteva, 1896.

Bol'shaia Sovetskaia Entsiklopediia. 3d ed. 31 vols. Moscow: Izd-vo "Sovetskaia entsiklopediia," 1970–81.

Bond, Edward, ed. *Russia at the Close of the Sixteenth Century*. London: Hakluyt Society, 1856.

Bonney, Richard, ed., *The Rise of the Fiscal State in Europe c. 1200–1815*. Oxford: Oxford University Press, 1999.

Bracewell, Catherine Wendy. *The Uskoks of Senj: Piracy, Banditry, and Holy War in the Sixteenth-Century Adriatic*. Ithaca: Cornell University Press, 1992.

Braudel, Fernand. *Capitalism and Material Life 1400–1800*. New York: Harper and Row, 1973.

———. *The Mediterranean and the Mediterranean World of Philip II*. 2 vols. New York: Harper and Row, 1975.

———. *The Perspective of the World*. New York: Harper & Row, 1984.

Brereton, Henry. *Newes of the present Miseries of Rushia: Occasioned by the late Warre in that Countrey*. London, 1614.

Brewer, John. *The Sinews of Power: War, Money and the English State, 1688–1783*. New York: Knopf, 1989.

Brody, Ervin C. *The Demetrius Legend and Its Literary Treatment in the Age of the Baroque*. Rutherford, N.J.: Fairleigh Dickenson Univ. Press, 1972.

Brown, Harold G. "From Organic Society to Security State: The War on Brigandage in France, 1797–1802." *Journal of Modern History* 69 (December 1997): 661–95.

Brown, Peter B. "Anthropological Perspective and Early Muscovite Court Politics." *Russian History* 16 (1989): 55–66.
———. "Muscovite Government Bureaus." *Russian History* 10 (1983): 269–330.
———. "Muscovy, Poland, and the Seventeenth-Century Crisis." *The Polish Review* 27, nos. 3–4 (1982): 55–69.
———. "The *Zemskii Sobor* in Recent Soviet Historiography." *Russian History* 10 (1983): 77–90.
Buganov, Viktor I. *Krest'ianskie voiny v Rossii XVII–XVIII vv.* Moscow: Nauka, 1976.
———. "Ob ideologii uchastnikov krest'ianskikh voin v Rossii." *Voprosy istorii* 1974, no. 1: 44–60.
———. "Religious ideologies in Russian popular movements in the seventeenth and eighteenth centuries." In Bak and Benecke, *Religion and rural revolt*, 206–13.
Burke, Peter. *Popular Culture in Early Modern Europe.* New York: Harper and Row, 1978.
Bushkovitch, Paul. "The Formation of a National Consciousness in Early Modern Russia." *Harvard Ukrainian Studies* 10 (December 1986): 355–76.
———. *The Merchants of Moscow 1580–1650.* Cambridge: Cambridge University Press, 1980.
———. *Religion and Society in Russia: The Sixteenth and Seventeenth Centuries.* New York: Oxford University Press, 1992.
———. "Taxation, Tax Farming, and Merchants in Sixteenth-Century Russia." *Slavic Review* 37 (1978): 381–98.
———. "Towns, Trade, and Artisans in Seventeenth Century Russia: The View from Eastern Europe." FOG 27 (1980): 215–32.
Bussow, Conrad. *The Disturbed State of the Russian Realm.* Translated and edited by G. Edward Orchard. Montreal: McGill-Queen's University Press, 1994.
———. *Moskovskaia khronika, 1584–1613.* Translated and edited by I. I. Smirnov. Moscow and Leningrad: AN SSSR, 1961.
Buturlin, D. *Istoriia Smutnago vremeni v Rossii v nachale XVII veka.* 3 vols. St. Petersburg, 1839–46.
Bykovskii, S. N. "Mnimaia 'izmena' Bolotnikova." *Problemy istochnikovedeniia* 8 (1936), part 2: 47–69.
Çambel, A. B. *Applied Chaos Theory: A Paradigm for Complexity.* Boston: Academic Press, 1993.
Camporesi, Piero. *Bread of Dreams: Food and Fantasy in Early Modern Europe.* Chicago: University of Chicago Press, 1989.
Chaev, N. S. "Moskva—tretii Rim' v politicheskoi praktike moskovskogo pravitel'stva XVI v.," *Istoricheskie zapiski* 17 (1945), 1–23.
Cheng, Roland Ye-lin, ed. *The Sociology of Revolution.* Chicago: Henry Regnery Co., 1973.
Cherepnin, L. V. "Iz istorii bor'by za krest'ian v Moskovskom gosudarstve v nachale XVII v." *Uchenye zapiski Instituta istorii RANION* 7 (1928): 100–116.
———. "'Smuta' i istoriografiia XVII veka." *Istoricheskie zapiski* 14 (1945): 81–128.
———. ed. *Voprosy metodologii istoricheskogo issledovaniia. Teoreticheskie problemy istorii feodalizma. Sbornik statei.* Moscow: Nauka, 1981.
———. *Zemskie sobory Russkogo gosudarstva XVI–XVII vv.* Moscow: Nauka, 1978.
Cherepnin, L. V., E. I. Indova, V. I. Koretskii, M. D. Kurmacheva, and A. A. Preobrazhenskii. *Krest'ianskie voiny v Rossii XVII–XVIII vekov: problemy, poiski, resheniia.* Moscow: Nauka, 1974.
Cherniavsky, Michael. "Holy Russia: A Study in the History of an Idea." *American Historical Review* 63 (April 1958): 617–37.
———. "Khan or Basileus: An Aspect of Russian Mediaeval Political Theory." In Cherniavsky, *The Structure of Russian History,* 65–79.

————. ed. *The Structure of Russian History*. New York: Random House, 1970.

————. *Tsar and People: Studies in Russian Myths*. New York: Random House, 1969.

Chernov, A. V. *Vooruzhennye sily Russkogo gosudarstva v XV–XVII vv*. Moscow: Voenizdat, 1954.

Chilli (Cilli), A. "Istoriia Moskovii." In *Maiak sovremennogo prosveshcheniia i obrazovannosti*, parts 17–18. St. Petersburg, 1841.

Chistov, K. V. *Russkie narodnye sotsial'no-utopicheskie legendy XVII–XIX vv*. Moscow: Nauka, 1967.

A Chronicle of the Carmelites in Persia, and the Papal Mission of the XVIIth and XVIIIth Centuries. 2 vols. London: Eyre and Spottiswoode, 1939.

Chteniia v Imperatorskom Obshchestve Istorii i Drevnostei Rossiiskikh pri Moskovskom Universitete. 264 vols. Moscow, 1845–1918.

Clark, Peter, ed. *The European Crisis of the 1590's*. London: George Allen & Unwin, 1985.

Cohn, Norman. *The Pursuit of the Millennium*. London: Paladin Books, 1970.

Cracraft, James. "Empire Versus Nation: Russian Political Theory under Peter I." *Harvard Ukrainian Studies* 10 (1986): 524–40.

————. "Opposition to Peter the Great." In *Imperial Russia, 1700–1917: State, Society, Opposition*, edited by Ezra Mendelsohn and Marshall Shatz, 22–36. De Kalb: Northern Illinois University Press, 1989.

Crummey, Robert O. *Aristocrats and Servitors: The Boyar Elite in Russia, 1613–1689*. Princeton: Princeton University Press, 1983.

————. "'Constitutional' Reform during the Time of Troubles." In *Reform in Russia and the U.S.S.R.: Past and Prospects*, edited by Robert O. Crummey, 28–44. Urbana: University of Illinois, 1989.

————. "Crown and Boiars under Fedor Ivanovich and Michael Romanov." *Canadian-American Slavic Studies* 6 (Winter 1972): 549–74.

————. *The Formation of Muscovy, 1304–1613*. London: Longman, 1987.

————. "Muscovy and the 'General Crisis of the Seventeenth Century.'" *Journal of Early Modern History* 2 (1998): 156–80.

————. "The Origins of the Noble Official: The Boyar Elite, 1613–1689." In *Russian Officialdom: The Bureaucratization of Russian Society from the Seventeenth to the Twentieth Century*, edited by Walter McKenzie Pinter and Don Karl Rowney, 46–75. Chapel Hill: University of North Carolina Press, 1980.

————. "The Reconstitution of the Boiar Aristocracy, 1613–1645." *FOG* 18 (1973): 187–220.

————. "Reform under Ivan IV: Gradualism and Terror." In *Reform in Russia and the U.S.S.R.: Past and Prospects*, edited by Robert O. Crummey, 12–27. Urbana: University of Illinois, 1989.

————. "The Silence of Muscovy." *The Russian Review* 46 (1987): 157–64.

Culpepper, Jack M. "The Legislative Origins of Peasant Bondage in Muskovy." *FOG* 14 (1969): 162–237.

d'Avity, Pierre. *Description générale de l'Europe, quatriesme partie du monde*, 3 vols. Paris, 1637.

Dal', Vladimir. *Tolkovyi slovar' zhivogo velikorusskogo iazyka*. 4 vols. Moscow: "Russkii iazyk," 1978–80.

Danilova, L. V. "Istoricheskie usloviia razvitiia russkoi narodnosti v period obrazovaniia i ukrepleniia tsentralizovannogo gosudarstva v Rossii." In *Voprosy formirovaniia russkoi narodnosti i natsii. Sbornik statei*, 106–54. Moscow-Leningrad: AN SSSR, 1958.

————. "K itogam izucheniia osnovnykh problem rannego i razvitogo feodalizma v Rossii." In *Sovetskaia istoricheskaia nauka ot XX k XXII s"ezdu KPSS. Istoriia SSSR. Sbornik statei*, 37–90. Moscow: AN SSSR, 1962.

Davies, Brian L. "Village into Garrison: The Militarized Peasant Communities of Southern Muscovy." *The Russian Review* 51 (October 1992): 481–501.

Davies, Norman. *God's Playground: A History of Poland.* Vol. 1. Oxford: Clarendon Press, 1982.

de Thou, Jacque-Auguste. *Histoire universelle.* 16 vols. London, 1734.

de Vries, Jan. "Measuring the Impact of Climate on History: The Search for Appropriate Methodologies." In Rotberg and Rabb, *Climate and History,* 19–50.

Demidova, N. F. *Sluzhilaia biurokratiia v Rossii XVII v. i ee rol' v formirovanii absoliutizma.* Moscow: Nauka, 1987.

D'iakonov, M. A. *Ocherki obshchestvennago i gosudarstvennago stroia drevnei Rusi.* St. Petersburg, 1912.

———. "Zapovednye i vykhodnye leta." *Izvestiia Petrogradskogo politekhnicheskogo instituta* 24 (1915): 1–20.

Dmitrievskii, A., ed. *Arkhiepiskop Elassonskii Arsenii i memuary ego iz Russkoi istorii.* Kiev: Tip. Imperatorskogo Universiteta sv. Vladimira, 1899.

Dmytryshyn, Basil, E. A. P. Crownhart-Vaughan, and Thomas Vaughan, eds. *Russia's Conquest of Siberia, 1558–1700.* Portland: Oregon Historical Society, 1985.

Dobrotvorskii, A. "Kto byl pervyi Lzhedmitrii?" *Vestnik Zapadnoi Rossii,* 2 (1886), book 6, part 2: 93–105; 3 (1886), book 7, part 2: 1–14.

Dokumenty i materialy po istorii Mordovskoi ASSR. Vol. 1. Saransk: AN SSSR, 1940.

Dolinin, N. P. "K izucheniiu inostrannykh istochnikov o krest'ianskom vosstanii pod rukovodstvom I. I. Bolotnikova 1606–1607 gg." In *Mezhdunarodnye sviazi Rossii do XVII v. Sbornik statei,* 462–90. Moscow: AN SSSR, 1961.

———. "K razboru versii pravitel'stva Mikhaila Romanova o I. M. Zarutskom." In *Arkheograficheskii ezhegodnik za 1962 g.,* 138–46. Moscow: AN SSSR, 1962.

———. *Podmoskovnye polki (kazatskie "tabory") v natsional'no-osvoboditel'nom dvizhenii 1611–1612 gg.* Khar'kov: Izd. Khar'kovskogo universiteta, 1958.

———. "Razvitie natsional'no-politicheskoi mysli v usloviiakh krest'ianskoi voiny i inostrannoi interventsii v nachale XVII veka." *Nauchnye zapiski Dnepropetrovskogo gosudarstvennogo universiteta* 40 (1951): 109–37.

Dopolneniia k Aktam Istoricheskim, sobrannye i izdannye Arkheograficheskoiu kommissieiu. 12 vols. St. Petersburg, 1846–72.

Downing, Brian. *The Military Revolution and Political Change.* Princeton: Princeton University Press, 1992.

Drevniaia Rossiiskaia Vivliofika, 2d ed. 20 vols. edited by N. Novikov. Moscow, 1788–91.

Druzhinin, V. G. *Raskol na Donu v kontse XVII veka.* St. Petersburg, 1889.

Dubrovskii, S. M. "Krest'ianskie voiny v Rossii XVII–XVIII veka." *Krest'ianskii Internatsional,* 1925, nos. 3–5 (March–May): 81–92.

Duffy, Christopher. *Siege Warfare: The Fortress in the Early Modern World, 1494–1660.* London: Routledge & Kegan Paul, 1979.

Duffy, Michael, ed. *The Military revolution and the state, 1500–1800.* Exeter: Exeter University Press, 1980.

Dukes, Paul. *The Making of Russian Absolutism, 1613–1801,* 2d ed. London: Longman, 1990.

———. "Russia and the 'General Crisis' of the Seventeenth Century." *The New Zealand Slavonic Journal,* new series, no. 2 (1974): 1–17.

Dunning, Chester. "Byla li v Rossii v nachale XVII veka krest'ianskaia voina?" *Voprosy istorii,* 1994, no. 9: 21–34.

———. "Cossacks and the Southern Frontier in the Time of Troubles." *Russian History* 19 (1992): 57–74.

―――. "Crisis, Conjuncture, and the Causes of the Time of Troubles." *Harvard Ukrainian Studies* 19 (1995): 97–119.

―――. "Does Jack Goldstone's Model of Early Modern State Crises Apply to Russia?" *Comparative Studies in Society and History* 39 (July 1997): 572–92.

―――. "James I, the Russia Company, and the Plan to Establish a Protectorate over North Russia." *Albion* 21 (Summer 1989): 206–26.

―――. "A Letter to James I Concerning the English Plan for Military Intervention in Russia." *The Slavonic and East European Review* 67 (1989): 94–108.

―――. "The Preconditions of Modern Russia's First Civil War." *Russian History* 25 (1998): 119–31.

―――. "R. G. Skrynnikov, the Time of Troubles, and the 'First Peasant War' in Russia." *The Russian Review* 50 (1991): 71–81.

―――. "The Use and Abuse of the First Printed French Account of Russia." *Russian History* 10 (1983): 357–80.

Eaton, Henry Lamar. "Decline and Recovery of the Russian Cities from 1500 to 1700." *Canadian-American Slavic Studies* 11 (Summer 1977): 220–52.

―――. "Early Russian Censuses and the Population of Muscovy, 1550–1650." Ph.D. diss., University of Illinois at Urbana-Champaign, 1971.

Eeckaute, Denise. "Les brigands en Russie du XVIIe au XIXe siècle: mythe et réalité." *Revue d'Histoire Moderne et Contemporaine* 12 (July–September 1965): 161–202.

Elliott, John. "Revolution and Continuity in Early Modern Europe." In Parker and Smith, *General Crisis*, 110–33.

Ellul, Jacques. *Autopsy of Revolution*. New York, 1971.

Emerson, Caryl. *Boris Godunov: Transpositions of a Russian Theme*. Bloomington: Indiana University Press, 1986.

Emerson, Caryl, and Robert William Oldani. *Modest Musorgsky and Boris Godunov*. Cambridge: Cambridge University Press, 1994.

Emmausskii, A. V. "Iz istorii bor'by za zemliu i krest'ian v Arzamasskom uezde v XVI–XVII vv." *Trudy Kirovskogo nauchno-issledovatel'skogo instituta kraevedeniia* 8 (1934), part 3.

Engels, Friedrich. *The Peasant War in Germany*. New York: International Publishers, 1926.

Eskin, Iu. M. "Smuta i mestnichestvo." *Arkhiv russkoi istorii*, part 3 (1993): 63–124.

―――. "Smuta i mestnichestvo." In *Realizm istoricheskogo myshleniia: Problemy otechestvennoi istorii perioda feodalizma*, 266–68. Moscow: Moskovskii gosudarstvennyi istoriko-arkhivnyi institut, 1991.

Esper, Thomas. "Military Self-Sufficiency and Weapons Technology in Muscovite Russia." *Slavic Review* 28 (1969): 185–208.

Fedorowicz, J. K. *England's Baltic Trade in the Early Seventeenth Century*. Cambridge: Cambridge University Press, 1980.

Fedotov, G. P. *St. Filipp, Metropolitan of Moscow—Encounter with Ivan the Terrible*. Belmont: Nordland, 1978.

Fenomenov, M. Ia. *Razinovshchina i Pugachevshchina*. Moscow: "Novaia Moskva," 1923.

Field, Daniel. *Rebels in the Name of the Tsar*. Boston: Houghton Mifflin, 1976.

Figarovskii, V. A. "Krest'ianskoe vosstanie 1614–1615 gg." *Istoricheskie zapiski* 73 (1963): 194–218.

Firsov, N. N. *Golod pred Smutnym vremenem v Moskovskom gosudarstve*. Kazan: Tip. Imperatorskago Universiteta, 1892.

―――. *Krest'ianskaia Revoliutsiia na Rusi v XVII veke*. Moscow: Gosudarstvennoe izdatel'stvo, 1927.

Fletcher, Giles. *Of the Russe Commonwealth*. London, 1591.

Flier, Michael S. "Breaking the Code: The Image of the Tsar in the Muscovite Palm Sunday Ritual." In *Medieval Russian Culture*, vol. 2, edited by Michael S. Flier and Daniel Rowland, 213–42. Berkeley: University of California Press, 1994.

———. "The Iconology of Royal Ritual in Sixteenth-Century Muscovy." In *Byzantine Studies: Essays on the Slavic World and the Eleventh Century*, edited by Speros Vryonis, Jr., 53–76. New Rochelle: Aristide Caratzas, 1992.

Floria, B. N. "Iz sledstvennogo dela Bogdana Bel'skogo." In *Arkheograficheskii ezhegodnik za 1985 god*, 304–5. Moscow: Nauka, 1986.

———. "Rokosz Sandomierski a Dymitr Samozwaniec." In *Odrodzenie i Reformacja w Polsce* 26 (1981): 69–81.

———. *Russko-pol'skie otnosheniia i politicheskoe razvitie Vostochnoi Evropy vo vtoroi polovine XVI–nachale XVII v.* Moscow: Nauka, 1978.

———. "Tri pis'ma o sobytiiakh Smuty." *Arkhiv russkoi istorii*, part 3 (1993): 161–76.

Florinsky, Michael T. *Russia: A History and an Interpretation.* 2 vols. New York: Macmillan, 1953.

Florovsky, Georges. "The Problem of Old Russian Culture." *Slavic Review* 21 (March 1962): 1–15.

Ford, Franklin. *Political Murder: From Tyrannicide to Terrorism.* Cambridge: Harvard University Press, 1985.

Forsten, G. V. *Baltiiskii vopros v XVI i XVII stoletiiakh (1544–1648).* Vol. 2. St. Petersburg, 1894.

———. "Politika Shvetsii v Smutnoe vremia." ZhMNP 261 (1889): 325–49; 265 (1889): 185–213; 266 (1889): 17–65.

Forster, Robert, and Jack P. Greene, eds. *Preconditions of Revolution in Early Modern Europe.* Baltimore: Johns Hopkins University Press, 1971.

Frantzev, V. A., ed. "Istoricheskoe i pravdivoe povestvovanie o tom, kak Moskovskii kniaz' Dimitrii Ioannovich dostig ottsovskago prestola." *Starina i Novizna* 15 (1911).

Freeze, Gregory L. ed., *Russia: A History.* Oxford: Oxford University Press, 1997.

French, R. A. "The early and medieval Russian town." In J. H. Bater and R. A. French, *Studies in Historical Geography*, vol. 2: 249–77. London: Academic Press, 1983.

Frierson, Cathy A. *Peasant Icons: Representations of Rural People in Late 19th Century Russia.* Oxford: Oxford University Press, 1993.

Fuller, William C., Jr., *Strategy and Power in Russia, 1600–1914.* New York: Free Press, 1992.

Genkin, L. B. *Iaroslavskii krai i razgrom pol'skoi interventsii v Moskovskom gosudarstve v nachale XVII veka.* Iaroslavl': Iaroslavskoe oblastnoe izdatel'stvo, 1939.

Geraklitov, A. "Materialy dlia istorii Saratovskogo Povolzh'e." *Trudy Saratovskoi uchenoi arkhivnoi komissii* 29 (1912): 62–83.

Girshberg [Hirschberg], Aleksandr. *Marina Mnishek.* Translated by Andrei Titov. Moscow, 1908.

Gnevushev, A. M., ed., *Akty vremeni pravleniia tsaria Vasiliia Shuiskago.* Vol. 2 of *Smutnoe vremia Moskovskago gosudarstva 1604–1613 gg.* ChOIDR 253. Moscow, 1915.

———. "Zemlevladenie i sel'skoe khoziaistvo v Moskovskom gosudarstve XVI–XVII vv." In M. V. Dovnar-Zapol'skii, ed., *Russkaia istoriia v ocherkakh i stat'iakh*, vol. 3: 267–311. Kiev: N. Ia. Ogloblin, 1912.

Goehrke, Carsten. *Die Wüstungen in der Moskauer Rus'.* Wiesbaden, 1968.

———. "Zur Problem von Bevölkerungsziffer und Bevölkerungsdichte des Moskauer Reiches im 16. Jahrhundert." FOG 24 (1978): 65–85.

Goldstone, Jack A. *Revolution and Rebellion in the Early Modern World.* Berkeley: University of California Press, 1991.

Golobutskii, V. A. *Zaporozhskoe kazachestvo.* Kiev: Gos. izd. polit. lit. SSSR, 1957.

Golubinskii, E. *Istoriia kanonizatsii sviatykh v Russkoi tserkvi.* 2d ed. Moscow: Univ. tip., 1903.
Golubtsov, I. A. "'Izmena' Nagikh." *Uchenye zapiski Instituta istorii RANION* 4 (1929): 55–70.
———. "'Izmena' Smol'nian pri B. Godunove i 'izvet' Varlaama." *Uchenye zapiski Instituta istorii RANION* 5 (1928): 218–51.
Golubtsov, V. V., and V. V. Rummel', *Rodoslavnyi sbornik russkikh dvorianskikh familii,* vol. 2. St. Petersburg, 1887.
Gordon, Linda. *Cossack Rebellions: Social Turmoil in the Sixteenth-Century Ukraine.* Albany: State University of New York Press, 1983.
Gorfunkel', A. Kh. "K voprosu ob istoricheskom znachenii krest'ianskoi voiny nachala XVII veka." *Istoriia SSSR,* 1962, no. 4:112–18.
———. "Perestroika khoziaistva Kirillo-Belozerskogo monastyria v sviazi s razvitiem tovarno-denezhnykh otnoshenii v XVI veke." *Uchenye zapiski Karelo-Finskogo pedagogicheskogo instituta* 2, part 1 (1955), Seriia obshchestvennykh nauk, 90–111.
———. "Rost zemlevladeniia Kirillo-Belozerskogo monastyria v kontse XVI i v XVII v." *Istoricheskie zapiski* 73 (1963): 219–48.
Gorskii, A. V. *Istoricheskoe opisanie Sviato-Troitskiia Sergievy lavry.* 2 vols. Moscow, 1873–79.
Got'e, Iu. V. *Pamiatniki oborony Smolenska 1609–1611 gg.* Vol. 6 of *Smutnoe vremia Moskovskago gosudarstva 1604–1613 gg.* Moscow, 1912. ChOIDR.
———. *Smutnoe vremia. Ocherk istorii revoliutsionnykh dvizhenii nachala XVII stoletiia.* (Moscow): Gosizdat, 1921.
———. *Zamoskovnyi krai v XVII veke.* Moscow: Sotsekgiz, 1937.
Gradostroitel'stvo Moskovskogo gosudarstva XVI–XVII vekov. Moscow: Stroiizdat, 1994.
Graham, Hugh. "Further Sources for the Rule of False Dmitrii I." In Lindsey Hughes, ed., *New Perspectives on Muscovite History,* 80–97. London: St. Martin's Press, 1993.
———. "A Note on the Identity of False Dmitrii I." *Canadian Slavonic Papers* 30 (September 1988): 357–62.
Grekov, B. D. *Glavneishie etapy v istorii krepostnogo prava v Rossii.* Moscow-Leningrad: Gos. sots-ek. izd., 1940.
———. "Iur'ev den' i zapovednye gody." *Izvestiia Akademii Nauk SSSR* 20 (1926): 67–84.
———. *Krest'iane na Rusi s drevneishikh vremen do XVII veka.* 2 vols. Moscow: Izd. Akad. Nauk SSSR, 1952–54.
Gurr, Ted Robert. *Why Men Rebel.* Princeton: Princeton University Press, 1970.
Hagopian, Mark N. *The Phenomenon of Revolution.* New York: Dodd, Mead & Co., 1975.
Hakluyt, Richard. *The Principal Navigations, Voyages, Traffiques, and Discoveries of the English Nation.* 12 vols. Glasgow: MacLehose, 1903–5.
Hale, J. R. *War and Society in Renaissance Europe, 1450–1620.* Baltimore: Johns Hopkins University Press, 1985.
Halperin, Charles. *Russia and the Golden Horde: The Mongol Impact on Medieval Russian History.* Bloomington: Indiana University Press, 1985.
Hellie, Richard. *The Economy and Material Culture of Russia, 1600–1725.* Chicago: University of Chicago Press, 1999.
———. "Edward Keenan's Scholarly Ways." *The Russian Review* 46 (1987): 177–90.
———. *Enserfment and Military Change in Muscovy.* Chicago: University of Chicago Press, 1971.
———. "The Foundations of Russian Capitalism." *Slavic Review* 26 (March 1967): 148–54.
———. *Readings for Introduction to Russian Civilization: Muscovite Society,* edited by Richard Hellie. Chicago: University of Chicago, 1967.
———. *Slavery in Russia, 1450–1725.* Chicago: University of Chicago, Press, 1982.

———. "The Stratification of Muscovite Society: The Townsmen." *Russian History* 5 (1978): 119–75.

———. "Warfare, Changing Military Technology, and the Evolution of Muscovite Society." In John A. Lynn, ed., *Tools of War: Instruments, Ideas, and Institutions of Warfare, 1445–1871*, 74–99. Urbana: University of Illinois Press, 1990.

———. "What Happened? How Did He Get Away with It? Ivan Groznyi's Paranoia and the Problem of Institutional Restraints." *Russian History* 14 (1987): 199–224.

———. "Why Did the Muscovite Elite Not Rebel?" *Russian History* 25 (1998): 155–62.

Henshall, Nicholas. *The Myth of Absolutism: Change & Continuity in Early Modern European Monarchy*. London: Longman, 1992.

Herberstein, Sigismund von. *Notes Upon Russia*. 2 vols. London: Hakluyt Society, 1851–52.

Hirschberg, Aleksander. *Dymitr Samozwaniec*. Lwów, 1898.

———, ed. *Polska a Moskwa w pierwszej polowie wieku XVII*. Lwów, 1901.

Hittle, J. Michael. *The Service City: State and Townsman in Russia, 1600–1800*. Cambridge: Harvard University Press, 1979.

Hobsbawm, Eric. *Bandits*. New York: Dell, 1969.

———. "The Overall Crisis of the European Economy in the Seventeenth Century." *Past & Present* 5 (1954): 33–53.

Horvath, Csaba A. "A Bolotnyikov-féle parasztháború ábrázolása az orosz történeti iro-dalomban." *Századok* 118 (1984): 998–1037.

Hosking, Geoffrey. *Russia: People and Empire, 1552–1917*. Cambridge: Harvard University Press, 1997.

Howe, Sonia E., ed. *The False Dmitri: A Russian Romance and Tragedy Described by British Eye-Witnesses, 1604–1612*. London: Williams and Norgate, 1916.

Hunt, Priscilla. "Ivan IV's Personal Mythology of Kingship." *Slavic Review* 52 (1993): 769–809.

Iablochkov, Mikhail Tikhonovich. *Dvorianskoe soslovie Tul'skoi gubernii*. Vol. 3. Moscow, 1901.

Iakovlev, A. I.. "Bezumnoe molchanie." In *Sbornik statei, posviashchennykh Vasiliiu Osipovichu Kliuchevskomu*, 651–78. Moscow: S. P. Iakovlev, 1909.

———. *Kholopstvo i kholopy v Moskovskom gosudarstve XVII v*. Vol. 1. Moscow-Leningrad: AN SSSR, 1943.

———, ed. *Novgorodskie zapisnye kabal'nye knigi 100–104 i 111 godov (1591–1596 i 1602–1603 gg.)*. Two parts. Moscow-Leningrad: Izd. Akad. Nauk SSSR, 1938.

———, ed. *Pamiatniki istorii Smutnogo vremeni*. Vol. 4 of *Pamiatniki Russkoi istorii*. Moscow: Klochkov, 1909.

Ikonnikov, V. S. *Kniaz' M. V. Skopin*. St. Petersburg, 1875.

———. *Neskol'ko zametok po voprosam Smutnago vremeni v Moskovskom gosudarstve*. Kiev: Tip. Imp. Universiteta, 1916.

Ilovaiskii, D. I. "Pervyi Lzhedimitrii." *Istoricheskii Vestnik* 12 (December 1891): 636–67.

———. *Smutnoe vremia Moskovskago gosudarstva*. Moscow, 1894.

Indova, E. I., A. A. Preobrazhenskii, and Iu. A. Tikhonov. "Narodnye dvizheniia v Rossii XVII–XVIII vv. i absoliutizm." In *Absoliutizm v Rossii (XVII–XVIII vv.)*, 50–91.

Ingerflom, K. S. "Samozvanstvo i kollektivnye predstavleniia o vlasti v russkoi istorii (XVII–XX vv.)." In *Realizm istoricheskogo myshleniia: Problemy otechestvennoi istorii perioda feodalizma*, 99–100. Moscow: Moskovskii gosudarstvennyi istoriko-arkhivnyi institut, 1991.

Ischboldin, Boris. *Essays on Tatar History*. New Delhi: New Book Society, 1963.

Istoriia krest'ianstva SSSR s drevneishikh vremen do Velikoi oktiabr'skoi sotsialisticheskoi revoliutsii. Vol. 2, *Krest'ianstvo v periody rannego i razvitogo feodalizma*. Moscow: Nauka, 1989.

Istoriia Moskvy. Vol. 1. Moscow: AN SSSR, 1952.

Istoriia SSSR s drevneishikh vremen do nashikh dnei. Vol. 2, *Bor'ba narodov nashei strany za nezavisimost' v XIII–XVII vv.* Edited by M. N. Tikhomirov et al. Moscow, 1966.

Ivanits, Linda J. *Russian Folk Belief.* Armonk, N.Y.: M. E. Sharpe, 1989.

Jansson, Maija, and Nikolai Rogozhin, eds. *England and the North: The Russian Embassy of 1613–1614.* Translated by Paul Bushkovitch. Philadelphia: American Philosophical Society, 1994.

Johnson, Chalmers. *Revolutionary Change.* Boston: Little, Brown, 1966.

Jütte, Robert. *Poverty and Deviance in Early Modern Europe.* Cambridge: Cambridge University Press, 1994.

Kahan, Arcadius. "Natural Calamities and Their Effect upon the Food Supply in Russia (An Introduction to a Catalogue)." *Jahrbücher für Geschichte Osteuropas* 16 (September 1968): 353–77.

Kaiser, Daniel. "Urban Identities in Sixteenth-Century Muscovy: The Case of Tula." In *Culture and Identity in Muscovy, 1359–1584,* edited by A. M. Kleimola and G. D. Lenhoff, 203–26. U.C.L.A. Slavic Studies, new series, vol. 3. Moscow: ITZ-Garant, 1997.

Kamen, Henry. *The Iron Century: Social Change in Europe 1550–1660.* London: Sphere Books, 1976.

Kappeler, Andreas. "Die Rolle der Nichtrussen der Mittleren Wolga in den russischen Volksaufständen des 17. Jhds." FOG 27 (1980): 249–68.

Karamzin, N. M. *Istoriia gosudarstva Rossiiskago.* 12 vols. St. Petersburg, 1818–29.

Kashtanov, S. M. "Diplomatika kak spetsial'naia istoricheskaia distsiplina." *Voprosy istorii* 40 (January 1965): 43–44.

Kazakov, N. I. "Bor'ba russkogo naroda s pol'sko-shvedskoi interventsiei v nachale XVII v. Minin i Pozharskii." In *Stranitsy boevogo proshlogo. Ocherki voennoi istorii Rossii,* 37–55. Moscow: Nauka, 1968.

Kedrov, S. *Zhizneopisanie sviateishogo Germogena, patriarkha moskovskogo i vseia Rossii.* Moscow: A. I. Snegirev, 1912.

Keenan, Edward L. "Afterword: Orthodoxy and Heterodoxy." In Baron and Kollmann, *Religion and Culture,* 199–206.

———. *The Kurbskii-Groznyi Apocrypha: The Seventeenth-Century Genesis of the "Correspondence" Attributed to Prince A.M. Kurbskii and Tsar Ivan IV.* Cambridge: Harvard University Press, 1971.

———. "Muscovite Political Folkways." *The Russian Review* 45 (1986): 115–81.

———. "Reply." *The Russian Review* 46 (April 1987): 199–209.

———. "The Trouble with Muscovy." *Medievalia et Humanistica* 5 (1974): 103–26.

Keep, J. L. H. "Bandits and the Law in Muscovy." *Slavonic and East European Review,* 35, no. 84 (December 1956): 201–22.

———. "Emancipation by the Axe? Peasant Revolts in Russian Thought and Literature." *Cahiers du Monde Russe et Soviétique* 23 (January-March 1982): 45–61.

———. "The Regime of Filaret, 1619–1633." *Slavonic and East European Review* 38 (June 1960): 334–60.

———. *Soldiers of the Tsar: Army and Society in Russia, 1462–1874.* Oxford: Clarendon Press, 1985.

Khodarkovsky, Michael. "The Stepan Razin Uprising: Was it a 'Peasant War?'" *Jahrbücher für Geschichte osteuropas* 42 (1994): 1–19.

Khvalibog (Chwalibog), G. "Donesenie G. Khvaliboga o lozhnoi smerti Lzhedimitriia." *Vremennik Imperatorskago Moskovskago Obshchestva Istorii i Drevnostei Rossiiskhik,* 23 (1855), part 3:3–5.

Kimmel, Michael S. *Absolutism and Its Discontents.* New Brunswick, N.J.: Transaction Books, 1988.

———. *Revolution: A Sociological Interpretation.* Philadelphia: Temple University Press, 1990.

Kirby, David. *Northern Europe in the Early Modern Period: The Baltic World 1492–1772.* New York: Longman, 1990.

Kivelson, Valerie A. *Autocracy in the Provinces: The Muscovite Gentry and Political Culture in the Seventeenth Century.* Stanford: Stanford University Press, 1996.

———. "The Devil Stole His Mind: The Tsar and the 1648 Moscow Uprising." *The American Historical Review* 98 (June 1993): 733–56.

———. "Merciful Father, Impersonal State: Russian Autocracy in Comparative Perspective." *Modern Asian Studies* 31 (1997): 635–63.

Kleimola, A. M. "The Canonization of Tsarevich Dmitrii: A Kinship of Interests." *Russian History* 25 (1998): 107–17.

———. "The Duty to Denounce in Muscovite Russia." *Slavic Review* 31 (1972): 759–79.

———. "Genealogy and Identity Among the Riazan' Elite." In *Culture and Identity in Muscovy, 1359–1584,* edited by A. M. Kleimola and G. D. Lenhoff, 284–302. U.C.L.A. Slavic Studies new series, vol. 3. Moscow: ITZ-Garant, 1997.

———. "Holding on in the 'Stamped-Over District'—The Survival of a Provincial Elite: Riazan' Landholders in the Sixteenth Century." *Russian History* 19 (1992): 129–42.

———. "Reliance on the Tried and True: Ivan IV and Appointments to the Boyar Duma, 1565–1584." *FOG* 46 (1992): 51–63.

———. "Up through Servitude: The Changing Condition of the Muscovite Elite in the Sixteenth and Seventeenth Centuries." *Russian History* 6 (1979): 210–29.

Klein, V. K., ed. *Uglichskoe sledstvennoe delo o smerti tsarevicha Dmitriia 15-go maia 1591 goda.* Moscow: Arkheologicheskii institut, 1913.

Klibanov, Aleksandr. "'Irreligiosity' in Seventeenth and Eighteenth Century Peasant Uprisings in Russia." In Bak and Benecke, *Religion and Rural Revolt,* 214–22.

Kliuchevskii, V. O. *Boiarskaia duma drevnei Rusi.* 4th ed. Moscow: Tip. A. I. Mamontova, 1909.

———. *Skazaniia inostrantsev o moskovskom gosudarstve.* Petrograd, 1918.

———. *Sochineniia.* 8 vols. Moscow: Gosudarstvennoe izdatel'stvo politicheskoi literatury, 1956–59.

Kniaz'kov, S. E. "Materialy k biografii Istomy Pashkova i istorii ego roda." In *Arkheograficheskii ezhegodnik za 1985 god,* 68–74. Moscow: Nauka, 1986.

Kobrin, V. B. *Vlast' i sobstvennost' v srednevekovoi Rossii.* Moscow, 1985.

Kollmann, Nancy Shields. *By Honor Bound: State and Society in Early Modern Russia.* Ithaca: Cornell University Press, 1999.

———. "Concepts of Society and Social Identity in Early Modern Russia." In Baron and Kollmann, *Religion and Culture,* 34–51.

———. *Kinship and Politics: The Making of the Muscovite Political System, 1345–1547.* Stanford: Stanford University Press, 1987.

———. "Pilgrimage, Procession, and Symbolic Space in Sixteenth-Century Russian Politics." In *Medieval Russian Culture,* vol. 2, edited by Michael S. Flier and Daniel Rowland, 163–81. Berkeley: University of California Press, 1994.

Kolycheva, E. I. *Agrarnyi stroi Rossii XVI veka.* Moscow: Nauka, 1987.

Kondratieva, Tamara, and Claudio-Sergio Ingerflom. "'Bez Carja zemlja vdova': Syncretisme dans le *Vremennik* d'Ivan Timofeev." *Cahiers du Monde Russe et Soviétique* 34 (1993): 257–66.

Kopanev, A. I. "Naselenie Russkogo gosudarstva v XVI v." *Istoricheskie zapiski* 64 (1959): 233–54.

———. "Novye spiski 'Povesti o videnii mekeony muzhu dukhovnu.'" *Trudy Otdela drevnerusskoi literatury* 16 (1960): 277–80.

———. "Pinezhskii letopisets XVII v." In *Rukopisnoe nasledie drevnei Rusi,* 57–91. Leningrad: Nauka, 1972.

———. "Zakonodatel'stvo o chernom krest'ianskom zemlevladenii XVI–XVII vv." In *Iz istorii feodal'noi Rossii: Stat'i i ocherki.* Leningrad, 1978.

Koretskii, V. I. "Aktovye i letopisnye materialy o vosstanii I. I. Bolotnikova." *Sovetskie arkhivy,* 1976, no. 5:45–58.

———. "Bor'ba krest'ian s monastyriami v Rossii XVI–nachala XVII v." In *Voprosy istorii religii i ateizma. Sbornik statei,* vol. 6: 169–215. Moscow: AN SSSR, 1958.

———. *Formirovanie krepostnogo prava i pervaia krest'ianskaia voina v Rossii.* Moscow: Nauka, 1975.

———. "Golod 1601–1603 gg. v Rossii i tserkov." In *Voprosy istorii religii i ateizma. Sbornik statei,* vol. 7:218–56. Moscow: AN SSSR, 1959.

———. "Ivan Isaevich Bolotnikov." *Voprosy istorii,* 1974, no. 5: 123–36.

———. "Iz istorii krest'ianskoi voiny v Rossii nachale XVII veka." *Voprosy istorii,* 1959, no. 3:118–37.

———. "Iz istorii zakreposhcheniia krest'ian v Rossii v kontse XVI–nachale XVII v. (o prakticheskoi realizatsii ukazov 1601–1602 gg.)." *Istoriia SSSR,* 1964, no. 3: 67–88.

———. "K istorii formirovaniia krepostnogo prava v Rossii." *Voprosy istorii,* 1964, no. 6:77–95.

———. "K istorii vosstaniia I. I. Bolotnikova." *Istoricheskii arkhiv,* 1956, no. 2: 126–45.

———. "K istorii vosstaniia Khlopka (Novye materialy)." In *Krest'ianstvo i klassovaia bor'ba v feodal'noi Rossii: Sbornik statei pamiati Ivana Ivanovicha Smirnova,* 209–22. Leningrad: Nauka, 1967.

———. "Letopisets s novymi izvestiiami o vosstanii Bolotnikova." *Istoriia SSSR,* 1968, no. 4: 120–30.

———. "Mazurinskii letopisets kontsa XVII v. i letopisanie Smutnogo vremeni." In *Slaviane i Rus',* 282–90. Moscow: Nauka, 1968.

———. "Novgorodskie dela 90-kh godov XVI v. so ssylkami na neizvestnye ukazy tsaria Fedora Ivanovicha o krest'ianakh." In *Arkheograficheskii ezhegodnik za 1966 god,* 306–30. Moscow: Nauka, 1968.

———. "Novoe ob I. I. Bolotnikove." *Sovetskie arkhivy,* 1967, no. 4: 100–103.

———. "Novoe o krest'ianskom zakreposhchenii i vosstanii I. I. Bolotnikova." *Voprosy istorii,* 1971, no. 5: 130–52.

———. "Novye dokumenty po istorii vosstaniia I. I. Bolotnikova." *Sovetskie arkhivy,* 1968, no. 6: 66–83.

———. "Novyi dokument po istorii Russkogo goroda vremeni krest'ianskoi voiny i pol'sko-shvedskoi interventsii." In *Arkheograficheskii ezhegodnik za 1964 god,* 316–32. Moscow: Nauka 1965.

———. "Ob odnoi 'oshibke' arkhivistov XVIII veke (Lzhedmitrii II i vopros o krest'ianskom vykhode)." In *Arkheograficheskii ezhegodnik za 1962 god,* 234–43. Moscow: Nauka, 1963.

———. "O formirovanii I. I. Bolotnikova kak vozhdia krest'ianskogo vosstaniia." In Smirnov et al., *Krest'ianskie voiny v Rossii XVII–XVIII vekov,* 122–47.

———. "Pravaia gramota ot 30 noiabria 1618 g. Troitse-Sergievu monastyriu (Iz istorii monastyrskogo zemlevladeniia XIV–XVI vv.)." *Zapiski otdela rukopisei biblioteki im. Lenina* 21 (1959): 173–217.

———. "Vosstanovlenie Iur'eva dnia v Rossii Lzhedmitriem I." In *Ezhegodnik po agrarnoi istorii Vostochnoi Evropy za 1960,* 118–30. Kiev, 1962.

———. *Zakreposhchenie krest'ian i klassovaia bor'ba v Rossii vo vtoroi polovine XVI v.* Moscow: Nauka, 1970.

Koretskii, V. I., and A. L. Stanislavskii. "Amerikanskii istorik o Lzhedmitrii I." *Istoriia SSSR* 14 (1969): 238–44.

Koretskii, V. I., and B. N. Morozov. "Letopisets s novymi izvestiiami XVI–nachala XVII v." In *Letopisi i khroniki: Sbornik statei, 1984 g.,* 187–218. Moscow: Nauka, 1984.

Koretskii, V. I., T. B. Solov'eva, and A. L. Stanislavskii, eds. "Dokumenty pervoi krest'ianskoi voiny v Rossii." *Sovetskie arkhivy,* 1982, no. 1: 34–41.

Kornblatt, Judith Deutsch. *The Cossack Hero in Russian Literature: A Study in Cultural Mythology.* Madison: The University of Wisconsin Press, 1992.

Kostomarov, Nikolai. *Bunt Sten'ki Razina.* St. Petersburg, 1872.

———. *Kto byl pervyi Lzhedimitrii? Istoricheskoe Issledovanie.* St. Petersburg, 1864.

———. *Smutnoe vremia Moskovskogo gosudarstva v nachale XVII stoletiia.* Vol. 2 of Nikolai Kostomarov, *Sobranie sochinenii.* St. Petersburg: Tip. M. M. Stasiulevicha, 1904.

"Kostromskaia starina." Published as *Sbornik, izdavaemyi Kostromskoi Uchenoi arkhivnoi komissiei,* part 3. Kostroma, 1894.

Kozachenko, A. I. *Razgrom pol'skoi interventsii v nachale XVII veka.* Moscow: Gos. izd. polit. lit., 1939.

Kozlov, S. A. "O poiavlenii russkogo kazachestva na Tereke." *Vestnik Leningradskogo universiteta,* series 2, 1988, no. 3: 92–95.

Kratkaia istoriia Astrakhanskoi Eparkhi. Astrakhan: Tip. P. Perova, 1886.

Krejchi, Jaroslav. *Great Revolutions Compared: The Search for a Theory.* Thetford, Norfolk: Wheatsheaf Books, 1983.

Krest'ianskie voiny v Rossii XVII–XVIII vekov: problemy, poiski, resheniia. Edited by L. V. Cherepnin, E. I. Indova, V. I. Koretskii, M. D. Kurmachev, and A. A. Preobrazhenskii. Moscow: Nauka, 1974.

Krom, M. M. "K voprosu o vremeni zarozhdeniia idei patriotizma v Rossii." In *Mirovospriiatie i samozoznanie russkogo obshchestva (XI–XX vv).* Sbornik statei, 16–30. Moscow, 1994.

Kulakova, I. P. "'Moskvichi torgovye liudi' kontsa XVI–nachala XVII v." In *Torgovlia i predprinimatel'stvo v feodal'noi Rossii,* 85–92. Moscow: Arkheograficheskii tsentr, 1994.

———. "Vosstanie 1606 g. v Moskve i votsarenie Vasiliia Shuiskogo." In *Sotsial'no-ekonomicheskie problemy istorii narodov SSSR: Sbornik statei,* 35–50. Moscow: Nauka, 1985.

Kulish, P. A. *Materialy dlia istorii vossoedineniia Rusi.* Part 1. Moscow, 1877.

Kusheva, E. N. "Iz istorii publitsistiki Smutnogo vremeni XVII veka." *Uchenye Zapiski Saratovskogo Gosudarstvennogo Universiteta* 5 (1926), part 2: 21–97.

———. "K istorii kholopstva v kontse XVI–nachale XVII vekov." *Istoricheskie zapiski* 15 (1945): 70–96.

Kuznetsov, V. I. "K voprosu ob evoliutsii sel'skikh poselenii v Rossii poslednei treti XVI–nachala XVII v." *Vestnik Moskovskogo Universiteta,* series 8, no. 5 (1986): 85–96.

Lacombe, Jacques. *Histoire des revolutions de l'empire de Russie.* Paris, 1760.

Ladokha, G. *Razinshchina i Pugachevshchina.* Moscow-Leningrad, 1928.

La légende de la vie et de la mort de Démétrius, dernier Grand-Duc de Moscovie. Amsterdam, 1606.

Lantzeff, George V., and Richard A. Pierce. *Eastward to Empire.* Montreal: McGill-Queen's University Press, 1973.

Lapman, Mark C. "Political Denunciations in Muscovy, 1600–1649." Ph.D. diss., Harvard University, 1982.

Larner, Christina. *Enemies of God: The Witch-hunt in Scotland.* Baltimore: Johns Hopkins University Press, 1981.

Laskovskii, F. *Materialy dlia istorii inzhenernogo iskusstva v Rossii.* 3 vols. St. Petersburg. 1858–65.

Latkin, Vasilii N. *Zemskie sobory Drevnei Rusi.* St. Petersburg, 1885.

La Ville, Pierre de. *Discours sommaire de ce qui est arrivé en Moscovie depuis le règne de Juan Vassilyvich Empereur, jusques a Vassily Juanouits Sousky.* Paris: A. Frank, 1859.

Le Roy Ladurie, Emmanuel. *Times of Feast, Times of Famine: A History of Climate Since the Year 1000.* Garden City: Doubleday, 1971.

Le Vasseur, Guillaume. *A Description of Ukraine.* Cambridge: Harvard Ukranian Research Institute, 1993.

Lerner, Robert E. "The Black Death and Western European Eschatological Mentalities." *The American Historical Review* 86 (June 1981): 533–52.

Lesur, Charles Louis. *Histoire des Kosaques,* 2 vols. Paris, 1814.

Letopis' o mnoghikh miatezhakh i o razorenii Moskovskago gosudarstva. Edited by N. I. Novikov. 2d ed. Moscow, 1788.

Levack, Brian P. *The Witch-Hunt in Early Modern Europe.* London: Longman, 1987.

Levesque, Pierre-Charles. *Histoire de Russie.* 8 vols. Hamburg, 1800.

Likhachev, N. P. *Boiarskii spisok 1611g.* St. Petersburg, 1895.

———. *Novoe rodoslovie kniazei Golitsynykh.* St. Petersburg, 1893.

Limonov, Iu. A. *Kul'turnye sviazi Rossii s evropeiskimi stranami v XVI–XVII vv.* Leningrad: Nauka, 1978.

Liubimenko, Inna. "A Project for the Acquisition of Russia by James I." *The English Historical Review* 29 (1914): 246–56.

Liubomirov, P. G. "Novye materialy dlia istorii Smutnogo vremeni." *Uchenye Zapiski Saratovskogo gosudarstvennogo universiteta* 5 (1926): 99–105.

———. *Ocherk istorii Nizhegorodskogo opolcheniia 1611–1613 gg.* Moscow: Sotsekgiz, 1939.

Liubovskii, M. "Litovskii Kantsler Lev Sapega o sobytiiakh Smutnago Vremeni." ChOIDR 197 (1901), book 2: 1–16.

Longworth, Philip. *The Cossacks.* London: Constable, 1969.

———. "The Last Great Cossack-Peasant Rising." *Journal of European Studies,* 1973, no. 3: 1–35.

———. "Peasant Leadership and the Pugachev Revolt." *The Journal of Peasant Studies* 2 (January 1975): 183–205.

———. "The Pretender phenomenon in eighteenth-century Russia." *Past & Present* 66 (1975): 61–83.

———. "The Subversive Legend of Stenka Razin." In *Rossiia/Russia; Studi i Ricerche a cura di Vittorio Strada,* no. 2 (1975): 17–40.

Lotman, Ju. M., and B. A. Uspenskij. "The Role of Dual Models in the Dynamics of Russian Culture (Up to the End of the Eighteenth Century)." In Lotman and Uspenskij, *Semiotics of Russian Culture,* 3–35.

———. *The Semiotics of Russian Culture.* Edited by Ann Shukman. Ann Arbor: Michigan Slavic Contributions, 1984.

Lur'e, S. S. "K voprosu o vosstanii Xhlopka." *Istoriia SSSR,* 1958, no. 4: 131–32.

———. "O date razgroma vosstaniia Khlopka." *Voprosy istorii,* 1963, no. 11: 209–11.

Macfarlane, Alan. *Witchcraft in Tudor and Stuart England.* New York, 1970.

Maciszewski, Jarema. "La noblesse polonaise et la guerre contre Moscou, 1604–18." *Acta Poloniae Historica* 17 (1968): 23–48.

———. *Polska a Moskwa, 1603–1618.* Warsaw: P. W. N., 1968.

MacKenzie, David, and Michael W. Curran. *A History of Russia, the Soviet Union, and Beyond,* 4th ed. Belmont, Ca.: Wadsworth, 1993.

Madariaga, Isabel de. "Autocracy and Sovereignty." *Canadian-American Slavic Studies* 16 (1982): 369–87.

Makarii (Metropolitan of Moscow). *Istoriia Russkoi tserkvi.* 2d ed. 13 vols in 12. St. Petersburg, 1883–1903.

Makkai, László. "Neo-Serfdom: Its Origin and Nature in East Central Europe." *Slavic Review* 34 (June 1975): 225–38.

Makovskii, D. P. *Pervaia krest'ianskaia voina v Rossii.* Smolensk: Moskovskii rabochii, 1967.

———. *Razvitie tovarno-denezhnykh otnoshenii v sel'skom khoziaistve Russkogo gosudarstva v XVI veke.* Smolensk: Smolenskii gos. ped. inst., 1963.

Mal'tsev, S., ed. "Barkulabovskaia letopis'." In *Arkheograficheskii ezhegodnik za 1960 god,* 291–320. Moscow: Nauka, 1962.

Mal'tsev, V. P. *Bor'ba za Smolensk (XVI–XVII vv.).* Smolensk: Smolenskoe oblastnoe gos. izd., 1940.

———. "Smolenskaia desiatnia 1606 g. kak pamiatnik rannego perioda krest'ianskoi voiny v Rossii nachala XVII." *Problemy istochnikovedeniia* 11 (1963): 338–45.

Man'kov, A. G. "Pobegi krest'ian v votchinakh Troitse-Sergieva monastyria v pervoi chetverti XVII veka." *Uchenye Zapiski Leningradskogo Gosudarstvennogo Universiteta* 80 (1941), Seriia istoricheskikh nauk, part 10: 45–74.

———. *Tseny i ikh dvizhenie v russkom gosudarstve XVI veka.* Moscow-Leningrad: AN SSSR, 1951.

Mansuy, Abel. *Le Monde slave et les classiques français aux XVIe–XVIIe siècles.* Paris: H. Champion, 1912.

March, George Patrick. "The Cossacks of Zaporozhe." Ph.D. diss., Georgetown University, 1965.

Marchocki, M. *Historya Wojny Moskiewskiéj.* Poznan, 1841.

Margeret, Jacques. *The Russian Empire and Grand Duchy of Muscovy: A Seventeenth-Century French Account.* Translated and edited by Chester S. L. Dunning. Pittsburgh: University of Pittsburgh Press, 1983.

———. *Sostoianie Rossiiskoi Derzhavy i Velikago Kniazhestva Moskovskago.* Translated and edited by Nikolai Ustrialov. St. Petersburg: Tip. Glavnago Upravleniia Putei Soobshcheniia, 1830.

Martin, John E. *Feudalism to Capitalism.* London: Macmillan, 1986.

Massa, Isaac. *Kratkoe izvestie o Moskovii v nachale XVII veka.* Translated by A. Morozov. Moscow: Gosudarstvennoe sotsial'no-ekonomicheskoe izdatel'stvo, 1937.

———. *A Short History of the Beginnings and Origins of These Present Wars in Moscow under the Reigns of Various Sovereigns down to the Year 1610.* Translated by G. E. Orchard. Toronto: University of Toronto Press, 1982.

Mavrodin, V. V. "K voprosu o roli klassovoi bor'by v istorii feodalizma v Rossii." *Vestnik Leningradskogo universiteta,* 1950, no. 2: 76–90.

———. "Sovetskaia istoricheskaia literatura o krest'ianskikh voinakh v Rossii XVII–XVIII vekov." *Voprosy istorii,* 1961, no. 5: 24–47.

———. "Sovetskaia istoricheskaia nauka o krest'ianskikh voinakh v Rossii." In Smirnov et al., *Krest'ianskie voiny v Rossii XVII–XVIII vv.,* 292–327.

———. "Sovetskaia istoriografiia krest'ianskikh voin v Rossii." In *Sovetskaia istoriografiia klassovoi bor'by i revoliutsionnogo dvizheniia v Rossii,* vol. 1, 53–82. Leningrad: Izd. Leningradskogo universiteta, 1967.

———. "Soviet Historical Literature on the Peasant Wars in Russia." *Soviet Studies in History* 1 (Fall 1962): 43–63.

Mavrodin, V. V., et al. "Ob osobennostiakh krest'ianskikh voin v Rossii." *Voprosy istorii,* 1956, no. 2: 69–79.

McNeill, William H. *Europe's Steppe Frontier, 1500–1800*. Chicago: University of Chicago Press, 1964.

Medvedev, P. A. "Podgotovka Smolenskoi oborony 1609 g." In *Istochnikovedcheskoe izuchenie pamiatnikov pis'mennoi kultury. Sbornik nauchnykh trudov*, 72–90. Leningrad: Gosudarstvennaia publichnaia biblioteka, 1990.

Mérimée, Prosper. *Épisode de l'histoire de Russie—les Faux Démétrius*. 2d ed. Paris: Calman-Lévy, 1889.

———. "Mémoires contemporains relatifs aux faux Démétrius." In Prosper Mérimée, *Mémoires historiques (inédits)*, 163–206. Paris: F. Bernouard, 1927.

Michels, Georg. *At War with the Church: Religious Dissent in Seventeenth-Century Russia*. Stanford: Stanford University Press, 1999.

Miklashevskii, I. N. *K istorii khoziaistvennago byta Moskovskago gosudarstva*, part 1. Moscow, 1894.

Miller, David R. "Creating Legitimacy: Ritual, Ideology, and Power in Sixteenth-Century Russia." *Russian History* 21 (1994): 289–315.

Miller (Müller), G. F. *Istoriia Sibiri*. 2 vols. Moscow-Leningrad: AN SSSR, 1937–41.

Miller, V. F. *Istoricheskiia pesni Russkago naroda XVI–XVII vv.* Petrograd: Tipografiia Imperatorskoi akademii nauk, 1915.

Milov, L. V., and I. M. Garskova. "A Typology of Feudal Estates in the First Half of the Seventeenth Century (Factor Analysis)." *The Russian Review* 47 (1988): 375–90.

Mironov, B. N. "Poverty of Thought or Necessary Caution?" *Russian History* 17 (Winter 1990): 427–35.

The Modern Encyclopedia of Russian and Soviet History, 55 vols. Edited by Joseph L. Wieczynski. Gulf Breeze: Academic International Press, 1976–93.

Moote, A. Lloyd. "The Preconditions of Revolution in Early Modern Europe: Did They Really Exist?" In Parker and Smith, *General Crisis*, 134–64.

Mordovtsev, D. *Samozvantsy i ponizovaia vol'nitsa*, 2 vols. St. Petersburg, 1867.

Morgan, E. D., and C. H. Coote, eds. *Early Voyages and Travels to Russia and Persia by Anthony Jenkinson and Other Englishmen*, 2 vols. London: Hakluyt Society, 1886.

Morozov, B. N. "Vazhnyi dokument po istorii vosstaniia Bolotnikova." *Istoriia SSSR*, 1985, no. 2: 162–68.

Morozova, L. E. "Boris Fedorovich Godunov." *Voprosy istorii*, 1998, no. 1: 59–81.

Moskovskaia tragediia, ili razskaz o zhizni i smerti Dimitriia. Translated by A. Braudo and I. Rostsius. St. Petersburg: Izd. S. D. Sheremeteva, 1901.

Moss, Walter G. *A History of Russia*, 2 vols. New York: McGraw-Hill, 1997.

Mousnier, Roland. *The Assassination of Henry IV*. Translated by Joan Spenser. New York: Charles Scribner's Sons, 1973.

———. *Les hierarchies sociales de 1450 à nos jours*. Paris, 1969.

———. *Peasant Uprisings in Seventeenth-Century France, Russia, and China, 1600–1800*. Translated by Brian Pearce. New York: Harper, 1970.

———. *La plume, la faucille, et le marteau*. Paris, 1970.

The Muscovite Law Code (Ulozhenie) of 1649, part 1. Edited and translated by Richard Hellie. Irvine, Ca.: Charles Schlacks, Jr., 1988.

Nazarevskii, A. A. *Ocherki iz oblasti russkoi istoricheskoi povesti nachala XVII veka*. Kiev:Izd. Kievskogo gosudarstvennogo universiteta, 1958.

Nazarov, V. D. "Bylo li podlinnym ulozhenie 9 marta 1607 goda?" *Voprosy istorii*, 1964, no. 12: 197–200.

———. "K istorii nachal'nogo perioda pervoi Krest'ianskoi voiny v Rossii." In *Genezis i razvitie feodalizma v Rossii: Problemy sotsial'noi i klassovoi bor'by*, 184–200. Leningrad: Izd. Leningradskogo universiteta, 1985.

———. "Klassovaia bor'ba gorozhan i pravitel'stvo Borisa Godunova." In *Goroda feodal'noi Rossii. Sbornik statei pamiati N. V. Ustiugova*, 216–38. Moscow: AN SSSR, 1966.

———. "'Novyi Letopisets' kak istochnik po istorii tsarstvovaniia Lzhedmitriia I." In *Letopisi i khroniki: Sbornik statei. 1973 g.*, 299–311. Moscow: Nauka, 1974.

———. "O datirovke 'Ustava ratnykh i pushechnykh del'." In *Voprosy voennoi istorii Rossii, XVIII i pervaia polovina XIX vekov*, 216–21. Moscow: Nauka, 1969.

———. "O nekotorykh osobennostiakh krest'ianskoi voiny nachala XVII v. v Rossii." In *Feodal'naia Rossiia vo vsemirno-istoricheskom protsesse: Sbornik statei, posviashchennyi L'vu Vladimirovichu Cherepninu*, 114–26. Moscow: Nauka, 1972.

———. "Paleograficheskii i tekstologicheskii analiz spiskov Svodnogo Sudebnika." *Vestnik Moskovskogo Universiteta*, series 9 (history), 1967, no. 1 (January-February): 54–76.

———. "The Peasant Wars in Russia and Their Place in the History of the Class Struggle in Europe." In *The Comparative Method in Soviet Mediaeval Studies*, 113–42. Moscow: AN SSSR, 1979.

———. "Zhalovannaia gramota Lzhedimitriia I Galitskomu Velikopustynskomu Avraam'evu monastyriu." In *Arkheograficheskii ezhegodnik za 1965 god*, 354–68. Moscow: Nauka, 1966.

Nazarov, V. D., and B. N. Floria. "Krest'ianskoe vosstanie pod predvoditel'stvom I. I. Bolotnikova i Rech' Pospolitaia." In *Krest'ianskie voiny v Rossii XVII–XVIII vv.*, 326–52.

Nechaev, V. N. *Bolotnikov: Epizod krest'ianskogo vosstaniia nachala XVII veka*. Moscow: Tip. Profizdata, 1931.

Nemoevskii (Niemojewski), S. "Zapiski Stanislava Nemoevskago (1606–1608)." In *Rukopisi slavianskie i russkie, prinadlezhashchie I. A. Vakhromeevu*, part 6. Edited by A. A. Titov. Moscow: A. Snegirev, 1907.

Nikitin, N. I. "K voprosu o sotsial'noi prirode pribornogo voiska." *Istoriia SSSR*, 1990, no. 2: 44–56.

Nikolaieff, A. M. "Boris Godunov and the Ouglich Tragedy." *The Russian Review* 9 (October 1950): 275–85.

Nikol'skii, Nikolai. *Kirillo-Belozerskii monastyr' i ego ustroistvo do vtoroi chetverti XVII veka (1397–1625)*. Vol. 1, part 2. St. Petersburg: Sinodal'naia tip., 1910.

Nolde, Boris. *La Formation de l'Empire Russe. Études, notes et documents*. 2 vols. Paris: Inst. d'Etudes Slaves, 1952–53.

Nosov, N. E. "Belozerskaia gubnaia izba v nachale XVII v." In *Voprosy sotsial'no-ekonomicheskoi istorii i istochnikovedeniia perioda feodalizma v Rossii. Sbornik statei k 70-letiiu A. A. Novosel'skogo*, 50–54. Moscow: AN SSSR, 1961.

Novgorodskie letopisi. St. Petersburg: Izd. Arkheograficheskoi kommissii, 1879.

Novombergskii, N. *Slovo i delo gosudarevy*. Vol. 1 of 2. Published as *Zapiski Moskovskago arkheologicheskago instituta*, vol. 14. Moscow, 1911.

Novosel'skii, A. A. *Bor'ba moskovskogo gosudarstva s Tatarami v pervoi polovine XVII veka*. Moscow-Leningrad: AN SSSR, 1948.

"Novyi dokument 1604 goda o Samozvantse." *Kievskaia Starina* 64 (January 1899), part 2: 8–13.

Novyi Letopisets, sostavlennyi v tsarstvovanie Mikhaila Feodorovicha, izdan po spisku Kniazia Obolenskago. Moscow, 1853.

"O krest'ianskoi voine v Russkom gosudarstve v nachale XVII veka (Obzor diskussii)." *Voprosy istorii*, 1961, no. 5: 102–20.

Obolenskii, K. M., ed. *Inostrannye sochineniia i akty, otnosiashchiesia do Rossii*. 4 vols. Moscow, 1847–48.

Obolenskii, M. A., ed. "Skazanie i povest', ezhe sodeiasia v Tsarstvuiushchem Grade, Moskve, i o Rastrige Grishke Otrep'eve, i o pokhozhdenii ego." ChOIDR, 1847, book 9, part 2:1–36.

Ocherki istorii SSSR. Period feodalizma. Konets XV v.–nachalo XVII v. Moscow: AN SSSR, 1955.

Olearius, Adam. *The Travels of Olearius in Seventeenth-Century Russia.* Translated and edited by Samuel H. Baron. Stanford: Stanford University Press, 1967.

Opis' arkhiva Posol'skogo prikaza 1626 g. 2 vols. Moscow: Izd. vostochnoi lit., 1977.

Orchard, G. Edward. "The Election of Michael Romanov." *The Slavonic and East European Review* 67 (July 1989): 378–402.

———. "The Frontier Policy of Boris Godunov." *The New Review: A Journal of East-European History* 8 (September 1969): 113–23.

Orlov, A. S. "Obsuzhdenie knigi D. P. Makovskogo 'Pervaia krest'ianskaia voina v Rossii'." *Voprosy istorii,* 1969, no. 9: 160–68.

Osipov, V. A. *Ocherki po istorii Saratovskogo kraia konets XVI i XVII vv.* Saratov: Izd-vo Saratovskogo universiteta, 1976.

Ostrowski, Donald. "The Mongol Origins of Muscovite Political Institutions." *Slavic Review* 49 (1990): 525–42.

Ovchinnikov, R. V. "Boiarskii spisok 1607 g." *Istoricheskii Arkhiv* 8 (1953): 71–79.

———. "Nekotorye voprosy krest'ianskoi voiny nachala XVII veka v Rossii." *Voprosy istorii,* 1959, no. 7: 69–83.

———. "O nachal'nom periode vosstaniia I. I. Bolotnikova." *Voprosy istorii,* 1955, no. 1: 116–20.

Paerle (Peyerle), Georg. "Zapiski Paerle o puteshestvii iz Krakova v Moskvu i obratno, s 19 marta 1606 goda do 15 dekabria 1608." In Ustrialov, *Skazaniia sovremennikov,* 1:153–234.

Palitsyn, Avraamii. *Skazanie Avraamiia Palitsyna.* Moscow and Leningrad: AN SSSR, 1955.

Pallott, Judith, and Denis J. B. Shaw. *Landscape and Settlement in Romanov Russia, 1613–1917.* Oxford: Clarendon Press, 1990.

Pamiatniki istorii Nizhegorodskago dvizheniia v epokhu Smuty i zemskago opolcheniia 1611–1612 gg. Published as *Deistviia Nizhegorodskoi gubernskoi uchenoi Arkhivnoi kommissii. Sbornik,* vol. 11 (1912).

Pamiatniki russkogo prava. Vol. 4, *Pamiatniki prava perioda ukrepleniia russkogo tsentralizovannogo gosudarstva XV–XVII vv.* Moscow: Gosiurizdat, 1956.

Paneiakh, V. M. "Iz istorii zakreposhcheniia krest'ian v kontse XVI–pervoi polovine XVII veka." *Istoriia SSSR,* 1981, no. 5: 164–73.

———. *Kabal'noe kholopstvo na Rusi v XVI veke.* Leningrad: Nauka, 1967.

———. *Kholopstvo v pervoi polovine XVII v.* Leningrad: Nauka, 1984.

———. *Kholopstvo v XVI–nachale XVII veka.* Leningrad: Nauka, 1975.

———. "K voprosu ob ukaze 1601 goda." *Problemy istochnikovedeniia* 9 (1961): 262–69.

———. "Materialy o prakticheskoi realizatsii ukaza 1601 goda." *Sovetskie arkhivy,* 1974, no. 4: 106–8.

———. "Zakreposhchenie krest'ian v XVI v.: Novye materialy, kontseptsii, perspektivy izucheniia." *Istoriia SSSR,* 1972, no. 1: 157–65.

Parker, Geoffrey. *Europe in Crisis, 1598–1648.* Glasgow: Fontana, 1979.

———. *The Military Revolution.* Cambridge: Cambirdge University Press, 1988.

Parker, Geoffrey, and Lesley M. Smith, eds. *The General Crisis of the Seventeenth Century.* London: Routledge & Kegan Paul, 1978.

Pavlov, A. P. *Gosudarev dvor i politicheskaia bor'ba pri Borise Godunove (1584–1605 gg.).* St. Petersburg: Nauka, 1992.

———. "Zemel'nye pereseleniia v gody oprichniny." *Istoriia SSSR,* 1990, no. 5, 89–104.

Pavlov-Sil'vanskii, N. P. *Sochineniia.* 3 vols. St. Petersburg: Tip. M. M. Stasiulevicha, 1909–10.

Perrie, Maureen. "Folklore as Evidence of Peasant Mentalité: Social Attitudes and Values in Russian Popular Culture." *The Russian Review* 48 (1989): 119–43.
——. *The Image of Ivan the Terrible in Russian Folklore.* Cambridge: Cambridge University Press, 1987.
——. "Jerome Horsey's Account of the Events of May 1591." *Oxford Slavonic Papers,* new series, 13 (1980): 28–49.
——. "The Popular Image of Ivan the Terrible." *The Slavonic and East European Review* 56 (April 1978): 275–86.
——. "'Popular Socio-Utopian Legends' in the Time of Troubles." *The Slavonic and East European Review* 60 (1982): 221–43.
——. *Pretenders and Popular Monarchism in Early Modern Russia: The False Tsars of the Time of Troubles.* Cambridge: Cambridge University Press, 1995.
Petreius, Peter. *Istoriia o Velikom Kniazhestve Moskovskom.* Translated by A. Shemiakin. Moscow, 1867.
——. *Reliatsiia Petra Petreia o Rossii nachala XVII v.* Edited by Iu. A. Limonov and V. I. Buganov. Moscow: AN SSSR, 1976.
Pfister, Christian. "The Little Ice Age: Thermal and Wetness Indices for Central Europe." In Rotberg and Rabb, *Climate and History,* 85–116.
Phipps, Geraldine M. *Sir John Merrick: English Merchant-Diplomat in Seventeenth Century Russia.* Newtonville: Oriental Research Partners, 1983.
Piasetskii, G. *Istoricheskie ocherki goroda Sevska i ego uezda.* Vol. 2 of *Sbornik Orlovskago tserkovnago istoriko-arkheologicheskago obshchestva.* Orel, 1906.
Picheta, V. I. *Istoriia krest'ianskikh volnenii v Rossii.* Minsk: Izd. "Beltrespechat'," 1923.
——. "Krest'ianskaia voina i bor'ba s inostrannoi interventsiei v nachale XVII veka." In *Protiv antimarksistskoi kontseptsii M. N. Pokrovskogo. Sbornik statei,* vol. 2: 91–139. Moscow-Leningrad: AN SSSR, 1940.
Pierling, Paul. *Dimitri dit le Faux et les Jésuites.* Paris: A Picard, 1913.
——. *Dimitri dit le Faux et Possevino.* Paris: Picard, 1914.
——. *Rome et Démétrius.* Paris, 1878.
——. *La Russie et le Saint-Siège: Études diplomatiques.* 3 vols. Paris: Plon, Nourrit, 1896–1901.
Piontkovskii, S. "Istoriografiia krest'ianskikh voin v Rossii: Marks, Engel's, Lenin i Stalin o krest'ianskikh voinakh." *Istorik Marksist,* 1933, no. 6: 80–119.
Pipes, Richard. *Russia Under the Old Regime.* New York: Scribners, 1974.
——. "Was There Private Property in Muscovite Russia?" *Slavic Review* 53 (1994): 524–30.
Pirling (Pierling), P. *Dmitrii Samozvanets.* Moscow: Sfinks, 1912.
——. *Iz Smutnago Vremeni: Stat'i i zametki.* St. Petersburg: A. S. Suvorin, 1902.
——. "Nazvannyi Dimitrii i Adam Vishnevetskii." *Russkaia Starina* 117 (1904), book 1 (January): 123–28.
——. "Nazvannyi Dimitrii i pol'skie ariane." *Russkaia Starina* 134 (1908): 1–10.
Piskarevskii letopisets. Edited by O. A. Iakovleva. Vol. 2 of *Materialy po istorii SSSR.* Moscow: AN SSSR, 1955.
Platon (Metropolitan of Moscow). *Kratkaia Tserkovnaia Rossiiskaia istoriia.* 2d edition. Vol. 2. Moscow, 1823.
Platonov, S. F. *Boris Godunov, Tsar of Russia.* Translated by L. Rex Pyles. Gulf Breeze: Academic International Press, 1973.
——. *Drevnerusskie skazaniia i povesti o Smutnom vremeni XVII veka, kak istocheskii istochnik.* St. Petersburg: Tip. M. Z. Aleksandrova, 1913.
——. *Moscow and the West.* Translated by Joseph Wieczynski. Hattiesburg, Miss.: Academic

International Press, 1972.

———. *Ocherki po istorii Smuty v Moskovskom gosudarstve XVI–XVII vv.* 3d ed. St. Petersburg: Bashmakov, 1910.

———. *Smutnoe vremia.* Prague: Plamia, 1924.

———. *Sotsial'nyi krizis Smutnogo vremeni.* Leningrad:Knigoizdatel'stvo "Put'" k znaniiu," 1924.

———. *Stat'i po Russkoi istorii.* 2d ed. St. Petersburg: Tip. M. A. Aleksandrov, 1912.

———. *The Time of Troubles.* Translated by John T. Alexander. Lawrence: University Press of Kansas, 1970.

Podorozhnyi, N. *Razgrom pol'skikh interventov v Moskovskom gosudarstve v nachale XVII veka.* Moscow: Gos. voennoe izd., 1938.

Poe, Marshall. "Elite Service Registry in Muscovy, 1500–1700." *Russian History* 21 (1994): 251–88.

———. "What Did Russians Mean When They Called Themselves 'Slaves of the Tsar'?" *Slavic Review* 57 (1998): 585–608.

Pokrovsky, M. N. *Brief History of Russia.* 2 vols. Translated by D. S. Mirsky. New York: International Publishers, 1933.

———. *Russkaia istoriia s drevneishikh vremen,* 3 vols. Moscow, 1920–23.

Polikarpov, V. V. "V Rossii grazhdanskuiu voinu nazyvaiut Smutoi." *Voprosy istorii,* 1994, no. 2: 189.

Polnoe sobranie russkikh letopisei. 40 vols. St. Petersburg/Leningrad and Moscow: Arkheograficheskaia komissiia, Nauka, and Arkheograficheskii tsentr, 1843–1995.

Polosin, I. I. *Sotsial'no-politicheskaia istoriia Rossii XVI–nachala XVII v.* Moscow: AN SSSR, 1963.

Popov, A. N., ed. *Izbornik slavianskikh i russkikh sochinenii i statei, vnesennykh v khrono-grafy russkoi redaktsii.* Moscow, 1869.

Possevino, Antonio. *Moscovia.* Translated by Hugh F. Graham. Pittsburgh: University of Pittsburgh Press, 1977.

Post, John D. *The Last Great Subsistence Crisis in the Western World.* Baltimore: Johns Hopkins University Press, 1977.

Presniakov, A. E. "Moskovskoe gosudarstvo pervoi poloviny XVII veka." In V. V. Kalesh, ed., *Tri veka. Rossiia ot smuty do nashego vremeni. Istoricheskii Sbornik,* vol. 1: 4–84. Moscow, 1912.

Prodan, David. "The Origins of Serfdom in Transylvania." *Slavic Review* 49 (Spring 1990): 1–19.

Pronshtein, A. P. "Reshennye i nereshennye voprosy istorii krest'ianskikh voin v Rossii." *Voprosy istorii,* 1967, no. 7: 151–61.

———. "Resolved and Unresolved Problems in the History of Peasant Wars in Russia." *Soviet Studies in History* 6, no. 3 (Winter 1967–68): 27–39.

Pronshtein, A. P., and N. A. Mininkov. *Krest'ianskie voiny v Rossii XVI–XVIII vekov i donskoe kazachestvo.* Rostov: Izd Rostovskogo universiteta, 1983.

Proskuriakova, G. V. *Klassovaia bor'ba v Pskove v period pol'sko-shvedskoi interventsii.* Leningrad: Leningradskii gosudarstvennyi pedagogicheskii institut, 1954.

Pskovskie letopisi. 2 vols. Edited by A. Nasonov. Moscow-Leningrad: AN SSSR, 1941–55.

Ptashitskii, S. L. "Despoty Zenovichi v kontse XVI i nachale XVII vekov." *Russkaia Starina* 21 (1878): 125–38; 22 (1878): 503–11.

———. "Perepiska litovskogo kantslera L'va Ivanovicha Sapega." ZhMNP 285 (January 1893): 194–223.

Purchas, Samuel. *Hakluytus Posthumus, or Purchas His Pilgrimes.* 20 vols. Glasgow: MacLehose, 1905–7.

Pushkarev, Sergei G. *Dictionary of Russian Historical Terms from the Eleventh Century to*

1917. New Haven: Yale University Press, 1970.

Pushkin, A. S. *Boris Godunov.* Chicago: Russian Language Specialities, 1965.

———. *History of Pugachev.* Ann Arbor: Ardis, 1983.

———. *The Poems, Prose, and Plays of Alexander Pushkin.* New York: Modern Library, 1936.

Raba, Joel. "The Authority of the Muscovite Ruler at the Dawn of the Modern Age." *Jahrbücher für Geschichte Osteuropas* 24 (1976): 321–44.

Rabb, Theodore K. *The Struggle for Stability in Early Modern Europe.* New York: Oxford University Press, 1975.

Raeff, Marc. "Pugachev's Rebellion." In Forster and Greene, *Preconditions,* 161–202.

———. *The Well-Ordered Police State: Social and Institutional Change through Law in the Germanies and Russia, 1600–1800.* New Haven: Yale University Press, 1983.

Razin, E. A. *Istoriia voennogo iskusstva.* 3 vols. Moscow: Voenizdat, 1955–61.

Razriadnaia kniga 1550–1636 gg. Vol. 2, parts 1–2. Moscow: AN SSSR, 1976.

Razriadnaia kniga 1559–1605 gg. Moscow: AN SSSR, 1974.

Razriadnye knigi 1598–1638 gg. 2 vols. Moscow: AN SSSR, 1974–76.

The Reporte of a bloudie and terrible massacre in the Citty of Mosco, with the fearfull and tragicall end of Demetrius the last Duke, before him raigning at this present. London, 1607.

Rerum Rossicarum Scriptores Exteri. 2 vols. St. Petersburg, 1851–68.

Riasanovsky, Nicholas. *A History of Russia,* 5th ed. New York: Oxford University Press, 1993.

Roberts, Michael. *The Early Vasas: A History of Sweden, 1523–1611.* Cambridge: Cambridge University Press, 1968.

———. *Essays in Swedish History.* London: Weidenfeld & Nicolson, 1967.

———. *Gustavus Adolphus: A History of Sweden 1611–1632.* Vol. 1. London: Longmans, Green and Co., 1953.

Rosovetskii, S. K. "Ustnaia proza XVI–XVII vv. ob Ivane Groznom-pravitele." *Russkii fol'klor* 20 (1981): 71–95.

Rotberg, Robert I., and Theodore K. Rabb, eds. *Climate and History: Studies in Interdisciplinary History.* Princeton: Princeton University Press, 1981.

Roth, Randolph. "Is History a Process? Nonlinearity, Revitalization Theory, and the Central Metaphor of Social Science History." *Social Science History* 16 (Summer 1992): 197–243.

Rowland, Daniel. "Biblical Military Imagery in the Political Culture of Early Modern Russia: The Blessed Host of the Heavenly Tsar." In *Medieval Russian Culture,* vol. 2, edited by Michael S. Flier and Daniel Rowland, 182–212. Berkeley: University of California Press, 1994.

———. "Did Muscovite Literary Ideology Place Limits on the Power of the Tsar (1540s–1660s)?" *The Russian Review* 49 (April 1990): 125–55.

———. "Ivan the Terrible as a Carolingian Renaissance Prince." *Harvard Ukrainian Studies* 19 (1995): 594–606.

———. "Moscow—the Third Rome or the New Israel?" *The Russian Review* 55 (October 1996): 591–614.

———. "Muscovite Political Attitudes as Reflected in Early Seventeenth-Century Tales about the Time of Troubles." Ph.D. diss., Yale University, 1976.

———. "The Problem of Advice in Muscovite Tales about the Time of Troubles." *Russian History* 6 (1979): 259–83.

Rozhdestvenskii, S. V., ed. *Akty vremeni Lzhedimitriia I-go, 1603–1606.* Vol. 1 of *Smutnoe vremia Moskovskago gosudarstva 1604–1613 gg.* ChOIDR. Moscow, 1918.

———. "Sel'skoe naselenie Moskovskago gosudarstva v XVI–XVII vekakh." In M. V. Dovnar-Zapol'skii, ed., *Russkaia istoriia v ocherkakhi stat'iakh*, vol. 3:34–84. Kiev: N. Ia. Ogloblin, 1912.

———. *Sluzhiloe zemlevladenie v Moskovskom gosudarstve XVI veke*. St. Petersburg, 1897.

Rozhkov, N. *Sel'skoe khoziaistvo moskovskoi Rusi v XVI veke*. Moscow: Universitetskaia tipografiia, 1899.

Rudakov, A. A. "Razvitie legendy o smerti tsarevicha Dimitriia v Ugliche." *Istoricheskie zapiski* 12 (1941): 254–83.

Rukopisnye nasledie Drevnei Rusi. Leningrad: Nauka, 1972.

Rusina, O. V. "Istorii vykhodzhennia Chernihovo-Sivershchyny do skladu Rosii." *Ukrain'skyi Istorychnyi Zhurnal*, 1989, no. 3, 91–100.

The Russian Primary Chronicle. Translated and edited by Samuel Hazzard Cross. Cambridge: Mediaeval Academy of America, 1953.

Russkaia istoricheskaia biblioteka. 2d ed. 39 vols. St. Petersburg-Leningrad, 1872–1927.

Russkii biograficheskii slovar', 25 vols. Moscow-St. Petersburg-Petrograd, 1896–1918.

Sakharov, A. M. *Obrazovanie i razvitie Rossiiskogo gosudarstva v XIV–XVII vv.* Moscow: Vysshaia shkola, 1969.

Santich, Jan Joseph. *Missio Moscovitica: The Role of the Jesuits in the Westernization of Russia, 1582–1689*. New York: Peter Lang, 1995.

Sapunov, B. V. "K voprosu o dostovernosti informatsii uglichskogo sledstvennogo dela." *Vspomogatel'nye istoricheskie distsipliny* 22 (1991): 157–74.

Savich, A. A. *Bor'ba russkogo naroda s pol'skoi interventsiei v nachale XVII veka*. Moscow: Gos. sots-ek. izd., 1939.

Savva, V. *Moskovskie tsari i Vizantiiskie vasilevsy*. Kharkov, 1901.

Savvinskii, I. *Istoricheskaia zapiska ob Astrakhanskoi eparkhii za 300 let ee sushchestvovaniia*. Astrakhan, 1903.

Sbornik Imperatorskago Russkago Istoricheskago Obshchestva. Vols. 137 and 142. Published as *Pamiatniki diplomaticheskikh snoshenii Moskovskago gosudarstva s Pol'sko-Litovskim gosudarstvom*, books IV–V. Edited by S. A. Belokurov. Moscow: 1912–13.

Sbornik Kniazia Khilkova. St. Petersburg, 1879.

Sbornik Mukhanova. 2d ed. Moscow, 1866.

Scott, James C. "Everyday Forms of Resistance." In *Everyday Forms of Peasant Resistance*, edited by Forrest D. Colburn, 3–33. Armonk, N.Y.: M. E. Sharpe, 1989.

———. *The Moral Economy of the Peasant*. New Haven: Yale University Press, 1976.

Sedov, P.V. "Pomestnye i denezhnye oklady kak istochnik po istorii dvorianstva v Smutu." *Arkhiv russkoi istorii*, part 3 (1993): 227–41.

———. "Pomestnye i denezhnye oklady v zhiletskom spiske pervogo podmoskovnogo opolcheniia 1611g." In *Realizm istoricheskogo myshleniia: Problemy otechestvennoi istorii perioda feodalizma*, 225–26. Moscow: Moskovskii gosudarstvennyi istoriko-arkhivnyi institut, 1991.

Semevskii, M. I. *Istoriko-iuridicheskie akty XVI i XVII vv*. St. Petersburg, 1892.

Seredonin, S. M. *Izvestiia inostrantsev o vooruzhennykh silakh Moskovskago gosudarstva*. St. Petersburg, 1891.

Shambinago, S. "Pis'ma koroliu Sigizmundu III o samozvantse." *Russkaia Starina*, 1908, no. 5: 439–50.

Shapiro, A. L. "The Historical Role of the 17th and 18th Century Peasant Wars in Russia." *Soviet Studies in History* 5, no. 2 (fall 1966): 27–47.

———. "Ob istoricheskoi roli krest'ianskikh voin XVII–XVIII vv. v Rossii." *Istoriia SSSR*, 1965, no. 5:61–80.

———. *Russkoe krest'ianstvo pered zakreposhcheniem (XIV–XVI vv.)* Leningrad: Leningradskii Universitet, 1987.

Shaum, M. "Tragoedia Demetrio-Moscovitica." Vol. 1 of Obolenskii, *Inostrannye sochi-neniia.*

Shaw, Denis J. B. "Settlement and Landholding on Russia's Southern Frontier in the Early Seventeenth Century." *The Slavonic and East European Review* 69 (April 1991): 232–56.

———. "Southern Frontiers of Muscovy, 1550–1700." In J. H. Bater and R. A. French, eds., *Studies in Russian Historical Geography,* vol. 1: 117–42. London: Academic Press, 1983.

Shchepkin, E. N. *Kratkie izvestiia o Lzhedimitrii I.* Odessa, 1900.

———. "Wer war Pseudodemetrius I.?" *Archiv für slavische Philologie* 20 (1898): 224–324; 21 (1899): 99–169, 558–606; 22 (1900): 321–432.

Shcherbatov, M. M. *Istoriia Rossiiskaia.* 7 vols. St. Petersburg, 1770–91.

[Shcherbatov, M. M.] *Kratkaia povest' o byvshikh v Rossii Samozvantsakh.* St. Petersburg, 1774.

Shepelev, I. S. "Donskoe i volzhsko-terskoe kazachestvo v klassovoi i natsional'no-osvo-boditel'noi bor'be v Russkom gosudarstve perioda krest'ianskoi voiny i pol'sko-shvedskoi interventsii." In *Iz istorii sotsial'no-ekonomicheskogo razvitiia i klassovoi bor'by v Nizhnem Povolzh'e,* 3–70. Volgograd: Volgogradskii pedagogicheskii insti-tut, 1972.

———. "Klassovaia bor'ba v russkom gosudarstve i ee osobennosti v period pol'sko-litovskoi i shvedskoi interventsii." In *Iz istorii klassovoi bor'by v dorevoliutsionnoi i sovetskoi Rossii,* 5–48. Volgograd: "Volgogradskaia pravda," 1967.

———. "K voprosu o klassovoi bor'be v russkom gosudarstve v gody pol'sko-litovskoi inter-ventsii (1608–1610gg.)." *Uchenye zapiski Piatigorskogo ped. inst.* 10 (1955): 277–322.

———. "Mesto i kharakter dvizheniia I. M. Zarutskogo v period krest'ianskoi voiny i pol'sko-shvedskoi interventsii (do ukhoda ego iz-pod Moskvy) 1606–1612 gg." *Trudy Leningradskogo Otdeleniia Instituta Istorii AN SSSR* 9 (1967): 223–38.

———. *Osvoboditel'naia i klassovaia bor'ba v Russkom gosudarstve v 1608–1610 gg.* Piatigorsk: Piatigorskii ped. inst., 1957.

Shevchenko, Igor. "A Neglected Byzantine Source of Muscovite Political Ideology." In Cherniavsky, *The Structure of Russian History,* 80–107.

Sheviakov, N. "K voprosu ob oprichnine pri Ivane IV." *Voprosy istorii* 31, no. 9 (1956): 71–75.

Shil', Mikhail. "Donesenie o poezdke v Moskvu pridvornago rimskago imperatora Mikhaila Shilia v 1598 godu." ChOIDR 1875 (April–June), book 2, part 4: 1–18.

Shlikhting, A. *Novoe izvestie o Rossii vremeni Ivana Groznogo.* Leningrad, 1934.

Shmidt, S. O. "Der Geschäftsgang in den russischen Zentralämtern der zweiten Hälfte des 16. Jahrhunderts." FOG 46 (1992): 65–86.

Shmurlo, E. *Kurs Russkoi istorii.* 3 vols. Prague: Cheskaia, 1931–35.

Shunkov, V. I. "Narodnaia bor'ba protiv pol'skikh i shvedskikh okkupantov v nachale XVII veka." *Istoricheskii zhurnal,* 1945, nos. 1–2: 3–8.

Shveikovskaia, Elena. "K kharakteristike mirovospriiatiia chernososhnykh krest'ian." *Istoriia SSSR,* 1992, no. 1: 75–86.

Siegelbaum, Lewis H. "Peasant Disorders and the Myth of the Tsar: Russian Variations on a Millenarian Theme." *The Journal of Religious History (Australia)* 10 (1979): 223–35.

Sinbirskii Sbornik. Moscow, 1845.

Sivkov, K. V. "Samozvanchestvo v Rossii v poslednei treti XVIII v." *Istoricheskie zapiski* 31 (1950): 80–135.

Skazaniia Massy i Gerkmana o Smutnom Vremeni v Rossii. St. Petersburg, 1874.

Skliar, I. M. "O nachal'nom etape Pervoi krest'ianskoi voiny v Rossii." *Voprosy istorii,* 1960, no. 6: 90–101.

Skocpol, Theda. *States and Social Revolutions*. Cambridge: Cambridge University Press, 1979.

Skripil', M. O. "Povest' ob Ulianii Osor'inoi." *Trudy otdela drevnerusskoi literatury* 6 (1948): 256–323.

Skrynnikov, R. G. *Boris Godunov*. Translated by Hugh Graham. Gulf Breeze, Fl.: Academic International Press, 1982.

———. "Boris Godunov i padenie Romanovykh v 1600 g." In *Iz istorii feodal'noi Rossii: Stat'i i ocherki*, 116–23. Leningrad: Nauka, 1978.

———. "Boris Godunov i tsarevich Dmitrii." *Trudy Leningradakogo otdeleniia instituta istorii* 12 (1971): 182–97.

———. "Boris Godunov's Struggle for the Throne." *Canadian-American Slavic Studies* 11 (1977): 325–53.

———. "The Civil War in Russia at the Beginning of the Seventeenth Century (1603–1607): Its Character and Motive Forces." In Lindsey Hughes, ed., *New Perspectives on Muscovite History*, 61–79. New York: St. Martin's Press, 1993.

———. "Glavnye vekhi razvitiia Russkogo dvorianstva v XVI–nachale XVII v." *Cahiers du Monde Russe et Soviétique* 34 (1993): 89–106.

———. *Ivan the Terrible*. Edited and translated by Hugh F. Graham. Gulf Breeze, Fla.: Academic International Press, 1981.

———. *Likholet'e: Moskva v xvi–xvii vekakh*. Moscow: Moskovskii rabochii, 1989.

———. *Minin i Pozharskii: Khronika Smutnogo vremeni*. Moscow: "Molodaia Gvardiia," 1981.

———. "Narodnye vystupleniia v 1602–1603 godakh." *Istoriia SSSR*, 1984, no. 2: 57–70.

———. "An Overview of the Reign of Ivan IV: What was the *Oprichnina?*" *Soviet Studies in History* 24 (1985): 62–82.

———. "Predvestniki pervoi krest'ianskoi voiny v Rossii." In *XXV Gertsenovskie chteniia. Istoricheskie nauki*, 54–56. Leningrad: Leningradskii gos. ped. inst., 1972.

———. "The Rebellion in Moscow and the Fall of the Godunov Dynasty." *Soviet Studies in History* 24 (Summer-Fall 1985): 137–54.

———. *Rossiia nakanune 'smutnogo vremeni'*. Moscow: Mysl', 1980.

———. *Rossiia posle oprichniny*. Leningrad: Izd. Leningradskogo Univ., 1975.

———. *Rossiia v nachale XVII v. "Smuta"*. Moscow: Mysl', 1988.

———. *Samozvantsy v Rossii v nachale XVII v.: Grigorii Otrep'ev*. Novosibirsk: Nauka, 1987.

———. *Sibirskaia ekspeditsiia Ermaka*. Novosibirsk: Nauka, 1982.

———. *Smuta v Rossii v nachale XVII v. Ivan Bolotnikov*. Leningrad: Nauka, 1988.

———. *Sotsial'no-politicheskaia bor'ba v Russkom gosudarstve v nachale XVII veka*. Leningrad: Izdatel'stvo Leningradskogo universiteta, 1985.

———. "Spornye problemy vosstaniia Bolotnikova." *Istoriia SSSR*, 1989, no. 5: 92–110.

———. *The Time of Troubles: Russia in Crisis, 1604–1618*. Translated by Hugh Graham. Gulf Breeze, Fla.: Academic International Press, 1988.

———. *Tsar' Boris i Dmitrii Samozvanets*. Smolensk: Rusich, 1997.

———. "V to smutnoe vremia. . . ." *Nauka i religiia*, 1988, no. 1: 44–48.

———. "Zapovednye i urochnye gody tsaria Fedora Ivanovicha." *Istoriia SSSR*, 1973, no. 1: 99–129.

———. "'Zemskaia' politika Borisa Godunova i bor'ba s golodom v nachale XVII v." In *Genezis i razvitie feodalizma v Rossii: Problemy sotsial'noi i klassovoi bor'by*, 164–84. Leningrad: Izdatel'stvo Leningradskogo universiteta, 1985.

Smirnov, I. I. "Astrakhan' i vosstanie Bolotnikova." *Istoricheskie zapiski* 22 (1947): 167–205.

———. "K istorii vosstaniia pod rukovodstvom Bolotnikova." *Voprosy istorii*, 1955, no. 10: 111–16.

———. "K kharakteristike politiki Lzhedmitriia II po krest'ianskomu voprosu." In *Voprosy sotsial'no-ekonomicheskoi istorii i istochnikovedeniia perioda feodalizma v Rossii*, 43–49. Moscow: AN SSSR, 1961.

———. "K kharakteristike vnutrennei politiki Lzhedmitriia I." *Uchenye Zapiski Leningradskogo Gosudarstvennogo Universiteta* 19 (1938), seriia istor. nauk, part 1: 186–207.

———. "Kogda byl kaznen Ileika Muromets?" *Istoriia SSSR*, 1968, no. 4: 108–19.

———. *Kratkii ocherk istorii vosstaniia Bolotnikova*. Moscow: Gos. izd. polit. lit., 1953.

———. "Novyi spisok Ulozheniia 9 Marta 1607g." *Istoricheskii Arkhiv*, 1949, no. 4: 72–87.

———. "O nekotorykh voprosakh istorii bor'by klassov v Russkom gosudarstve nachala XVII veka." *Voprosy Istorii*, 1958, no. 12: 116–31.

———. "Vosstanie Bolotnikova i narody Povolzh'e." *Zapiski Nauchno-issledovatel'skogo instituta pri Sovete Ministrov Mordovskoi ASSR* 9 (1947): 24–48.

———. *Vosstanie Bolotnikova 1606–1607*. Leningrad: Gospolitizdat, 1951.

———. "Zakony V. Shuiskogo o krest'ianakh i kholopakh i vosstanie Bolotnikova." *Voprosy istorii*, 1947, no. 5: 109–12.

Smirnov, I. I., A. G. Man'kov, E. P. Pod"iapol'skaia, and V. V. Mavrodin. *Krest'ianskie voiny v Rossii XVII–XVIII vv.* Moscow: Nauka, 1966.

Smirnov, P. P. "Chelobitnyia dvorian i detei boiarskikh vsekh gorodov v pervoi polovine XVII veke." ChOIDR. 254:3 (1915), part 1: 1–73.

———. *Goroda Moskovskogo gosudarstva v pervoi polovine XVII veka*. 2 vols. Kiev: Tip. A. I. Grosman, 1917–19.

———. *Posadskie liudi i ikh klassovaia bor'ba do serediny XVII veka*. 2 vols. Moscow-Leningrad: AN SSSR, 1947–48.

Smith, Dianne L. "Muscovite Logistics, 1462–1598." *The Slavonic and East European Review* 71 (1993): 35–65.

Smith, R. E. F. *Peasant Farming in Muscovy*. Cambridge: Cambridge University Press, 1977.

Smith, R. E. F., and David Christian, *Bread and Salt: A Social and Economic History of Food and Drink in Russia*. Cambridge: Cambridge University Press, 1984.

Smith, Thomas. *Sir Thomas Smithes Voiage and Entertainment in Rushia*. London, 1605.

Smuta v Moskovskom gosudarstve: Rossiia nachala XVII stoletiia v zapiskakh sovremennikov. Edited by A. I. Pliguzov and I. A. Tikhoniuk. Moscow: Sovremennik, 1989.

Sobieski, W. *Szkice Historyczne*. Warsaw, 1904.

Sobranie gosudarstvennykh gramot i dogovorov. 5 vols. St. Petersburg, 1813–94.

Sokolova, V. K. *Russkie istoricheskie predaniia*. Moscow: Nauka, 1970.

Solov'ev, S. M. *Istoriia Rossii s drevneishikh vremen*. 15 vols. Moscow: Sotsekgiz-Mysl', 1959–66.

———. "Obzor sobytii russkoi istorii ot konchiny tsaria Feodora Ioannovicha do vstupleniia na prestol doma Romanovykh." *Sovremennik* 13 (1849), no. 1, part 2: 1–36.

———. "Zametki o samozvantsakh v Rossii." *Russkii Arkhiv* 6 (1868): cols. 265–81.

Soloviev, Alexander V. *Holy Russia: The History of a Religious-Social Idea*. The Hague, 1959.

Sovetskaia voennaia entsiklopediia, 8 vols. Moscow: Voennoe Izdatel'stvo Ministerstva Oborony SSSR, 1976–80.

Sreznevskii, I. I. *Materialy dlia slovaria drevnerusskago iazyka po pis'mennym pamiatnikam*. 3 vols. St. Petersburg, 1893–1906.

Staden, Heinrich von. *The Land and Government of Muscovy*. Translated and edited by Thomas Esper. Stanford: Stanford University Press, 1967.

Stadnitskii (Stadnicki), M. "Dnevnik Martyna Stadnitskogo." *Russkii Arkhiv*, 1906, book 6, part 2: 129–222.

Stanishevskii, V. P. *Narodnoe dvizhenie v Smutnoe vremia*. Moscow, 1919.

Stanislavskii, A. L., ed. "Dokumenty o vosstanii 1614–1615 gg." In *Arkheograficheskii Ezhegodnik za 1980 god*, 285–307. Moscow: Nauka, 1981.

————. "Dvizhenie I. M. Zarutskogo i sotsial'no-politicheskaia bor'ba v Rossii v 1612–1613 gg." *Istoricheskie zapiski* 109 (1983): 307–38.

————. *Grazhdanskaia voina v Rossii XVII v. Kazachestvo na perelome istorii.* Moscow: Mysl', 1990.

————. "Kazatskoe dvizhenie 1615–1618 gg." *Voprosy istorii,* 1980, no. 1: 104–16.

————, ed. "Novye dokumenty o vosstanii Bolotnikova." *Voprosy istorii,* 1981, no. 7: 74–83.

————. "Pervaia krest'ianskaia voina v Rossii i pravitel'stvennaia politika po otnosheniiu k vol'nomy kazachestvy." In A. A. Preobrazhenskii, ed., *Problemy sotsial'no-ekonomicheskoi istorii feodal'noi Rossii,* 235–47. Moscow: Nauka, 1984.

————. "Pravitel'stvennaia politika po otnosheniiu k 'vol'nomu' kazachestvu (1612–1619 gg.)." *Istoriia SSSR,* 1984, no. 5: 66–79.

————. "Vosstanie 1614–1615 gg. i pokhod atamana Balovina." *Voprosy istorii,* 1978, no. 5: 111–26.

Stanislavskii, A. L., and B. N. Morozov. "Povest' o zemskom sobore 1613 goda." *Voprosy istorii,* 1985, no. 5: 89–96.

Steensgaard, Niels. "The Seventeenth-Century Crisis." In Parker and Smith, *General Crisis of the Seventeenth Century,* 26–56.

Stevens, Carol Belkin. *Soldiers on the Steppe: Army Reform and Social Change in Early Modern Russia.* DeKalb: Northern Illinois University Press, 1995.

Stief, Carl. *Studies in the Russian Historical Song.* Copenhagen: Rosenkilde and Bagger, 1953.

Stone, Deborah A. "Causal Stories and the Formation of Policy Agendas." *Political Science Quarterly* 104 (1989): 281–300.

Stone, Lawrence. *The Causes of the English Revolution, 1529–1642.* New York: Harper and Row, 1972.

Storozhev, V. N. "Desiatni i tysiachnaia kniga XVI veka." In *Opisanie dokumentov i bumag khraniashchikhsia v Moskovskom Arkhive Ministerstva Iustitsii,* book 8, part 3: 1–459. Moscow, 1891.

————. *Istoriko-iuridicheskie materialy izdavaemye Moskovskim Ministerstvom iustitsii.* Vol. 1, *Ukaznaia kniga pomestnago prikaza.* Moscow, 1889.

Strémooukhoff, Dimitri. "Moscow the Third Rome: Sources of the Doctrine." *Speculum* 28 (1953): 84–101.

Strumilin, S. G. *Istoriia chernoi metallurgii v SSSR.* Moscow, 1967.

Sukhorukov, V. D. *Istoricheskoe opisanie zemli voiska Donskogo.* 2d ed. Novocherkassk: Chastnaia Donskaia tip., 1903.

Sukhotin, L. M., ed. *Chetvertchiki Smutnago vremeni (1604–1617).* Moscow: Sinodal'naia Tipografiia, 1912.

————, ed. *Zemel'nye pozhalovaniia v Moskovskom gosudarstve pri tsare Vladislave, 1610–1611 gg.* Vol. 8 of *Smutnoe vremia Moskovskogo gosudarstva.* Moscow, 1911. ChOIDR.

Suvorin, A. S. *O Dimitrii Samozvantse.* St. Petersburg: A. S. Suvorin, 1906.

Sviatskii, D. *Istoricheskii ocherk gorodov Sevska, Dmitrovska i Komaritskoi volosti.* Orel, 1908.

Szeftel, Marc. "The Title of the Muscovite Monarch up to the End of the Seventeenth Century." *Canadian-American Slavic Studies* 13 (1979): 59–81.

Tallett, Frank. *War and Society in Early-Modern Europe, 1495–1715.* London: Routledge, 1992.

Tatishchev, V. N. *Istoriia Rossiiskaia.* 7 vols. Moscow-Leningrad: AN SSSR, 1962–68.

Thompson, A. H. "The Legend of Tsarevich Dimitry: Some Evidence of an Oral Tradition." *The Slavonic and East European Review* 46 (1968): 48–59.

Tikhomirov, M.N. *Klassovaia bor'ba v Rossii XVII v.* Moscow: Nauka, 1969.

———. "Maloizvestnye letopisnye pamiatniki XVI v." *Istoricheskie zapiski* 10 (1941): 84–94.

———. "Monastyr'-votchinnik XVI v." *Istoricheskie zapiski* 3 (1938): 130–60.

———. "Novyi istochnik po istorii vosstaniia Bolotnikova." *Istoricheskii Arkhiv* 6 (1951): 82–130.

———. "Piskarevskii letopisets kak istoricheskii istochnik o sobytiiakh XVI–nachala XVII v." *Istoriia SSSR*, 1957, no. 3: 112–22.

———. "Pskovskie povesti o krest'ianskoi voine v Rossii nachala XVII v." In *Iz istorii sotsial'no-politicheskikh idei. Sbornik statei*, 181–90. Moscow: AN SSSR, 1955.

———. *Rossiia v XVI stoletii.* Moscow: AN SSSR, 1962.

———. "Samozvanshchina." *Nauka i zhizn'*, 1969, no. 1: 116–21.

Tikhomirov, M. N., and B. N. Floria. "Prikhodo-raskhodnye knigi Iosifo-Volokolamskogo monastyria 1606/07 g." In *Arkheograficheskii ezhegodnik za 1966 god*, 331–83. Moscow: Nauka, 1968.

Tikhomirov, M. N., et al. "Inostrannaia interventsiia i bor'ba Rossii za nezavisimost'." In *Istoriia SSSR s drevneishikh vremen do nashikh dnei.* Vol. 2, *Bor'ba narodov nashei strany za nezavisimost' v XIII–XVII vv.* Moscow: Nauka, 1966.

Tilly, Charles. *European Revolutions, 1492–1992.* Oxford: Blackwell, 1993.

Timofeev, Ivan. *Vremennik Ivana Timofeeva.* Moscow and Leningrad: AN SSSR, 1951.

Tiumenev, A. I. "Peresmotr izvestii o smerti Tsarevicha Dimitriia." ZhMNP, new series, vol. 15 (1908): 93–135, 323–59.

Tkhorzhevskii, S. I. *Narodnye volneniia pri pervykh Romanovykh.* Petrograd: Izd. Seiatel', 1924.

Tomsinskii, S. G. *Krest'ianskie dvizheniia v feodal'no-krepostnoi Rossii.* Moscow: Zhurnal'no-gazetnoe ob"edinenie, 1932.

Treadgold, Donald. *The West in Russia and China.* 2 vols. Cambridge: Cambridge University Press, 1973.

Trevor-Roper, H. R. *The European Witch-Craze of the Sixteenth and Seventeenth Centuries and Other Essays.* New York: Harper and Row, 1968.

"Tri gramoty Lzhedimitriia I k koroliu pol'skomu Sigizmundu." *Vremennik Imperatorskago Moskovskago Obshchestva Istorii i Drevnostei* 23 (1855): 1–6.

Troitskii, S. M. "Samozvantsy v Rossii XVII–XVIII vekov." *Voprosy istorii*, 1969, no. 3: 134–46.

Tsimbaev, N. I. "Rossiia i Russkie (natsional'nyi vopros v Rossiiskoi imperii)." *Vestnik Moskovskogo Universiteta*, series 8 (history), 1993, no. 5: 23–32.

Tsvetaev, D. V. *K istorii Smutnogo vremeni. Sobranie dokumentov.* Vol. 1. Moscow, 1916.

———. *Protestantstvo i protestanty v Rossii do epokhi preobrazovanii.* Moscow, 1890.

———. *Tsar' Vasilii Shuiskii i mesta pogrebedeniia ego v Pol'she.* Vol. 1. Moscow-Warsaw, 1910.

Turgenev, A. I., ed. *Historica Rossiae Monumenta.* Vol. 2. St. Petersburg, 1842.

Ul'ianov, N. I., ed. *Krest'ianskaia voina v Moskovskom gosudarstve nachala XVII veka. Sbornik dokumentov.* Leningrad: Gosudarstvennoe sotsial'no-ekonomicheskoe izdatel'stvo, 1935.

Ul'ianovskii, V.I. "Pravoslavnaia tserkov' i Lzhedmitrii I." *Arkhiv russkoi istorii*, part 3 (1993): 29–62.

———. "Rech' Pospolitaia vo vneshnepoliticheskikh planakh Lzhedmitriia I." In *Rossiia ot Ivana Groznogo do Petra Velikogo*, 78–93. St. Petersburg, 1993.

———. "Russko-shvedskie otnosheniia v nachale XVII veka i bor'ba za Baltiku." *Skandinavskii sbornik* 33 (1990): 60–75

Urlanis, V. Ts. *Rost naselenie v Evrope.* Moscow: Statizdat, 1941.

Uspenskii, D. "Videniia smutnago vremeni." *Vestnik Evropy*, 1914, book 5: 130–48.

Uspenskij, B. A. "Tsar and Pretender: Samozvanchestvo or Royal Imposture in Russia as a Cultural-Historical Phenomenon." In Lotman and Uspenskij, *Semiotics of Russian Culture,* 259–92.

Ustrialov, N. G., ed. *Skazaniia sovremennikov o Dmitrii Samozvantse.* 2 vols. 3d ed. St. Petersburg, 1859.

Vainberg, E. I. "Chelobitnye Smolenskogo pomeshchika—uchastnika pokhoda protiv Bolotnikova." *Istoricheskii arkhiv* 8 (1953): 61–70.

Val'denberg, V. E. *Drevnerusskie ucheniia o predelakh tsarskoi vlasti.* Petrograd, 1916.

Vasenko, P. G. "Novye dannye dlia kharakteristiki patriarkha Germogena." ZhMNP, 1901, no. 7 (July): 138–45.

———. "Zametki k stat'iam o Smute, vkliuchennym v khronograf redaktsii 1617 goda." In *Sbornik statei po russkoi istorii posviashchennykh S. F. Platonovu,* 248–69. Petersburg: Ogni, 1922.

Vernadsky, George. "The Death of Tsarevich Dimitry: A Reconsideration of the Case." *Oxford Slavonic Papers* 5 (1954): 1–19.

———. *The Mongols and Russia.* New Haven: Yale University Press, 1953.

———. *Russia at the Dawn of the Modern Age.* New Haven: Yale University Press, 1959.

———. *The Tsardom of Moscow, 1547–1682.* 2 vols. New Haven: Yale University Press, 1969.

Veselovskii, N. I., ed. *Pamiatniki diplomaticheskikh i torgovykh snoshenii Moskovskoi Rusi s Persiei.* 3 vols. St. Petersburg, 1890–98.

Veselovskii, S. B., ed. *Akty pistsovogo dela.* 2 vols. Moscow: Sinodal'naia Tipografiia, 1913–17.

———, ed. *Akty podmoskovnykh opolchenii i zemskago sobora 1611–1613 gg.* Vol. 5 of *Smutnoe vremia Moskovskago gosudarstva 1604–1613 gg.* ChOIDR. Moscow, 1911.

———. *Arzamasskie pomestnye akty (1578–1618 gg.).* Vol. 4 of *Smutnoe vremia Moskovskago gosudarstva 1604–1613 gg.* ChOIDR 256. Moscow, 1916.

———. *D'iaki i pod'iachie XV–XVII vv.* Moscow: Nauka, 1975.

———. *Feodal'noe zemlevladenie v Severo-vostochnoi Rusi.* Moscow-Leningrad: AN SSSR, 1947.

———. *Issledovaniia po istorii oprichniny.* Moscow: AN SSSR, 1963.

———. "Iz istorii drevnerusskogo zemlevladeniia." *Istoricheskie zapiski* 18 (1946).

———. *Soshnoe pis'mo.* 2 vols. Moscow: Tip. G. Lissnera i D. Sovko, 1915–16.

Veselovskii, S. B., and A. I. Iakovlev, eds. *Pamiatniki sotsial'no-ekonomicheskoi istorii Moskovskogo gosudarstva XIV–XVII vv.* Vol. 1. Moscow, 1929.

Viktorov, V., ed. *Krest'ianskie dvizheniia XVII–XVIII vv. Sbornik dokumentov i materialov s primechaniiami.* Moscow: Kommunisticheskii universitet, 1926.

Vladimirskii-Budanov, M. F. *Obzor istorii russkago prava.* 6th ed. St. Petersburg, 1909.

Vlasov, V. G. "The Christianization of the Russian Peasants." In *Russian Traditional Culture: Religion, Gender, and Customary Law,* edited by Marjorie Mandelstam Balzer, 16–33. Armonk, N.Y.: M.E. Sharpe, 1992.

Vodarskii, Ia. E. *Naselenie Rossii za 400 let (XVI–nachalo XX vv.).* Moscow: "Prosveshchenie," 1973.

Von Loewe, Karl. "Juridical Manifestations of Serfdom in West Russia." *Canadian-American Slavic Studies* 6 (1972): 390–99.

Voskoboinikova, N. P. "K istorii finansovoi politiki russkogo gosudarstva v nachale XVII veka." *Istoriia SSSR,* 1986, no. 3, 156–61.

Vosstanie I. Bolotnikova: Dokumenty i materialy. Edited by A. I. Kopanev and A. G. Man'kov. Moscow: Izd-vo sotsial'no-ekon. lit-ry, 1959.

Vostokov, A. "Russkie sluzhiloe soslovie po desiatniam 1577–1608 gg." *Iuridicheskii vestnik* 28 (June–July 1888): 264–78.

Vovina, V. G. "Patriarkh Filaret (Fedor Nikitich Romanov)." *Voprosy istorii,* 1991, nos. 7–8: 53–74.
Wada, Haruki. "The Inner World of Russian Peasants." *Annals of the Institute of Social Science* 20 (1979): 61–94.
Waliszewski, K. *La Crise révolutionnaire, 1584–1614.* Paris: Plon-Nourrit, 1906.
Wallerstein, Immanuel. *The Modern World-System: Capitalist Agriculture and the Origins of the European World-Economy in the Sixteenth Century.* New York: Academic Press, 1974.
Weber, Max. "The Routinization of Charisma." In *The Sociology of Revolution,* edited by Roland Ye-lin Cheng, 269–77. Chicago: Henry Regnery Co., 1973.
Weickhardt, George G. "Bureaucrats and Boiars in the Muscovite Tsardom." *Russian History* 10 (1983): 331–56.
———. "Kotoshikhin: An Evaluation and Interpretation." *Russian History* 17 (1990): 127–54.
———. "Political Thought in Seventeenth-Century Russia." *Russian History* 21 (Fall 1994): 316–37.
———. "The Pre-Petrine Law of Property." *Slavic Review* 52 (1993): 663–79.
———. "Was There Private Property in Muscovite Russia?" *Slavic Review* 53 (1994): 531–38.
Widekind, J. *Historia belli Sveco-Moscovitici decennalis.* Stockholm, 1672.
Wielewicki, Jan. *Historici Diarii Domus professae Societatis Jesu Cracoviensis annos 1600–1608.* Published as *Scriptores Rerum Polonicarum* 10 (1886).
Willner, Ann Ruth, and Dorothy Willner. "The Rise and Role of Charismatic Leaders." In *The Sociology of Revolution,* edited by Roland Ye-lin Cheng, 194–204. Chicago: Henry Regnery Co., 1973.
Wortman, Richard S. *Scenarios of Power: Myth and Ceremony in Russian Monarchy.* Vol. 1, *From Peter the Great to the Death of Nicholas I.* Princeton: Princeton University Press, 1995.
Wright, William E. "Neo-Serfdom in Bohemia." *Slavic Review* 34 (June 1975): 238–52.
Yanov, Alexander. *The Origins of Autocracy: Ivan the Terrible in Russian History.* Berkeley: University of California Press, 1981.
Yaresh, Leo. "The 'Peasant Wars' in Soviet Historiography." *The American Slavic and East European Review* 16 (October 1957): 241–59.
Zabelin, I. *Minin i Pozharskii.* Moscow, 1883.
Zagorin, Perez. *Rebels and Rulers, 1500–1660.* 2 vols. Cambridge: Cambridge University Press, 1982.
Zagorovskii, V. P. *Belgorodskaia cherta.* Voronezh: Voronezhskii universitet, 1969.
Zakonodatel'nye akty russkogo gosudarstva vtoroi poloviny XVI–pervoi poloviny XVII veka. 2 vols. Edited by N. E. Nosov. Leningrad: Nauka, 1986–87.
Zaozerskii, A. I. "K voprosu o sostave i znachenii zemskikh soborov." ZhMNP (June 1909): 299–352.
Zapiski Getmana Zholkevskago o Moskovskoi voine. 2d ed. Edited by P. A. Mukhanov. St. Petersburg, 1871.
Zguta, Russell. *Russian Minstrels: A History of the Skomorokhi.* Oxford: Clarendon Press, 1978.
———. "Was there a Witch Craze in Muscovite Russia?" *Southern Folklore Quarterly* 41 (1977): 119–27.
———. "Witchcraft Trials in Seventeenth-Century Russia." *American Historical Review* 82 (1977): 1187–1207.
Zherbin, A. S., and I. P. Shakol'skii. "Krest'ianskaia voina v Finliandii v kontse XVI v." *Voprosy istorii,* 1981, no. 8: 76–90.
Zhitie Sviatago Dimitriia Tsarevicha. St. Petersburg, 1879.

Zhivov, Victor M. "Religious Reform and the Emergence of the Individual in Russian Seventeenth-Century Literature." In Baron and Kollmann, eds., *Religion and Culture*, 184–98.

Zhivov, Viktor M., and Boris A. Uspenskij. "Tsar' i Bog: Semioticheskie aspekty sakralizatsii monarkha v Rossii." In B. A. Uspenskij, ed., *Russkaia kul'tura i iazyka perevodimosti*, 47–153. Moscow: Nauka, 1987.

Zhordaniia, Givi. *Ocherki iz istorii franko-russkikh otnoshenii kontsa XVI i pervoi poloviny XVII v.* 2 vols. Tbilisi: Akademiia Nauk Gruzinskoi SSR, 1959.

Zhurnal Ministerstva Narodnago Prosveshcheniia. St. Petersburg, 1834–1917.

Ziegler, Philip. *The Black Death.* New York: Harper & Row, 1971.

Zimin, A. A. "I. I. Bolotnikov i padenie Tuly v 1607 g." In *Krest'ianskie voiny v Rossii XVII–XVIII vv.*, 52–64.

———, ed. *Khrestomatiia po istorii SSSR, XVI–XVII vv.* Moscow: Izdatel'stvo sotsial'no-ekonomicheskoi literatury, 1962.

———. "K istorii vosstaniia Bolotnikova." *Istoricheskie zapiski* 24 (1947): 353–85.

———. "K itogam izucheniia istorii pervoi krest'ianskoi voiny v Rossii." In *Ezhegodnik po agrarnoi istorii Vostochnoi Evropy 1971 g.*, 80–88. Vil'nius: Izd. "Mintis," 1974.

———. "K izucheniiu vosstaniia Bolotnikova." In *Problemy obshchestvenno-politicheskoi istorii Rossii i slavianskikh stran.* Moscow, 1963.

———. "K voprosu o zakreposhchenii krest'ianstva v 80–90e gody XVI v." In A. A. Preobrazhenskii, ed., *Problemy sotsial'no-ekonomicheskoi istorii feodal'noi Rossii*, 271–79. Moscow: Nauka, 1984.

———. "Nekotorye voprosy istorii krest'ianskoi voiny v Rossii v nachale XVII veka." *Voprosy istorii*, 1958, no. 3: 97–113.

———. *Oprichnina Ivana Groznogo.* Moscow: Mysl', 1964.

———. "Osnovnye etapy i formy klassovoi bor'by v Rossii kontsa XV–XVI veka." *Voprosy istorii* 40, no. 3 (1965): 38–52.

———. *Reformy Ivana Groznogo.* Moscow: Izdatel'stvo sotsial'no-ekonomicheskoi literatury, 1960.

———. "Smert' tsarevicha Dimitriia i Boris Godunov." *Voprosy istorii*, 1978, no. 9, 92–111.

———. *V kanun groznykh potriasenii. Predposylki pervoi krest'ianskoi voiny v Rossii.* Moscow: Mysl', 1986.

Zimin, A. A., and R. G. Koroleva. "Dokument Razriadnogo prikaza." *Istoricheskii arkhiv* 8 (1953): 21–60.

Zimmerman, Ekkart. *Political Violence, Crises, and Revolutions: Theories and Research.* Boston: G. K. Hall, 1983.

Zlotnik, Marc D. "Muscovite Fiscal Policy, 1462–1584." *Russian History* 6 (1979): 243–58.

Zolkiewski, Stanislas. *Expedition to Moscow.* Translated and edited by J. Giertych. London: Polonica, 1959.

INDEX

Abraham, 32
absolutism, 14, 19, 463. *See also* autocracy; fiscal-military state; tsar
Adriatic Sea, 82
Akinfiev, G., 148
Aksakov, M., 269, 334–35, 357
Alatyr, 287, 289, 322, 432
Aleksandrov, 403
Aleksandrov-Mosalskii, V., 341
Aleksei (tsar), 461, 465, 470, 473, 476
Aleksin, 186, 187, 191, 282, 300, 307, 321, 326–27, 344, 346–47, 348, 350, 360–61, 364, 416. *See also* sieges
Alferev, S., 344, 346
ambassadors: foreign, 217, 338, 345, 393, 423; Russian, 127, 214, 216, 336, 412. *See also* diplomacy
Antichrist, 201, 206, 236
Arabic, 78
Archangel Cathedral, 197, 199, 245, 248
Arians (Protestants), 132, 135, 517 n. 103
aristocrats, 23–24, 27, 29, 33–34, 36–37, 39, 49–50, 91, 94, 95, 157, 194, 204, 208, 212, 218, 219, 224, 244, 330, 343, 370, 391, 439, 441–42, 447, 462, 470–71, 476, 477, 480; in the civil war, 406, 429, 435, 437, 439; persecution of, 94, 194; plots by, 124, 174, 219, 393; and Romanov dynasty, 446, 447, 448, 449, 469, 470–71. *See also* boyars; courtiers
Arkhangelsk, 421, 451
Armenians, 346
armies, Russian, 23, 28, 30, 35, 36,

37–45, 46, 47, 48, 50, 154, 156; condition and morale, 49, 83, 87, 106, 150–51, 156, 159, 160, 164, 173, 178–79, 185–86, 281, 291, 348–49; hunger in, 150, 151, 156, 164, 186, 348, 349, 358–59, 368; modernization and reform of, 42, 47, 56, 219, 220, 409, 469; salaries, 40, 44, 82, 147, 148, 153, 167, 271, 282, 283, 311, 387, 398, 409, 417, 419, 440; of Tsar Boris, 93, 139, 143, 150, 151, 153, 158, 159, 160, 161, 163, 164, 165, 166, 171–72, 178, 216, 331; rebellion against Tsar Boris, 185–87, 190, 192, 272; of Tsar Dmitrii, 204, 211, 219; of Tsar Vasilii, 172, 176, 266, 270, 272–73, 276, 278–79, 280–83, 287–89, 295–96, 301–3, 322, 326–27, 329, 333, 341, 344, 348–49, 353, 357, 360, 362, 384–86, 392, 402–3, 409; of Tsar Mikhail Romanov, 453–56, 457, 469. *See also* rebel military forces
campaigns and battles: campaigns, 37, 40, 56, 105, 151, 154, 157–59, 161, 162–63, 211, 216, 221, 226, 275, 291, 293, 322, 323, 325, 331, 342, 346, 348, 352, 353, 355, 357, 389, 457; battles, 160–61, 163, 165–68, 273, 276, 278–79, 281, 283, 295–96, 303, 309, 313, 331, 344, 346–48, 350–51, 358, 361, 377, 384, 389, 391–92, 403, 409, 438, 452. *See also* sieges
officers: commanders (see also *voevodas*), 32, 33, 35, 36–37, 40, 45,

armies, Russian (continued)
85, 86, 89, 138, 144, 146, 149, 151,
156, 157, 158, 159, 160, 163, 164,
168, 169, 170, 171, 175, 177, 179,
180, 182, 183, 184, 189, 190, 191,
264, 266, 270, 272, 273, 274, 275,
277, 281, 293, 297, 303, 310, 311,
316, 327, 328, 329, 342, 345, 348,
353, 357, 358, 360, 362, 364, 366,
376, 416, 453, 456; frontier
commanders, 89, 143, 144, 146,
169–70, 171, 179, 180, 188, 352;
lower-ranking officers, 45, 148, 158,
170, 182, 266, 273, 275, 316, 318,
332, 336, 344, 409. See also rebel
commanders
organization of forces, 40, 45, 47,
100, 158, 159, 160, 164, 165, 166,
177, 187, 188, 272, 273, 275, 290,
293, 326, 346, 353, 357, 358;
detachments, 99, 102, 150, 153,
158, 160, 253, 266, 269, 271, 278,
314, 331, 357, 433, 440, 450, 453,
456; reinforcements, 149, 161, 163,
164, 170, 172, 176, 177, 180, 275,
283, 299, 307, 310, 311, 328, 339,
342, 344, 356, 362, 364, 376, 385;
tsar's regiment, 37, 42, 164, 172,
186, 281, 301, 302, 303, 311, 352,
353, 360, 361. See also garrisons;
gentry militia; Military Affairs Office
soldiers: absenteeism of, 40, 54, 55,
150–51, 272, 302, 324, 351, 352;
captives, 46, 144, 187, 284, 290,
295, 306, 309, 311, 312–13, 320,
326, 336, 337, 342, 347, 349, 354,
359, 363, 364, 377, 381, 453;
casualties, 161, 172, 178, 295, 314,
316, 328, 331, 342, 344, 346, 347,
350, 364, 368, 396; cavalry, 24, 30,
37, 39, 40, 41, 44, 47, 78, 150,
152–53, 166, 177, 283, 286, 288,
289, 324, 325, 358, 359, 360;
conscription of (see also recruits),
146, 148, 272, 302, 324, 354;
defection of, 182, 186, 190, 193,

299, 308, 309, 317, 318, 322, 329,
337, 339, 343, 345, 346, 347, 349,
355, 358, 362, 383, 391, 393, 412;
desertion of, 151, 163, 172, 179,
186, 277, 377, 379, 381, 403; foreign troops, 215, 220, 227, 232,
234, 235, 271, 364, 387, 394;
infantry, 24, 40, 44, 45, 77, 106,
137, 147, 149, 151, 155, 164, 165,
166, 167, 177, 220, 266, 268, 275,
276, 358, 469; foraging for food,
151, 164, 165, 172, 178, 275, 304,
398, 399, 410, 418, 427–28, 435;
low status soldiers, 1, 4, 24, 26, 39,
40, 42, 44, 47, 55, 69, 70, 71, 76,
86, 87, 93, 95, 105, 106, 109, 112,
117, 142, 144, 147, 149, 150, 151,
153, 154, 156, 158, 159, 161, 163,
165, 170, 174, 178, 185, 186, 187,
193, 199, 211, 220, 258, 262, 271,
272, 275, 279, 281, 283, 285, 286,
296, 300, 308, 310, 311, 319, 323,
324, 328, 348, 363, 389, 398, 419,
439; mobilization of, 40, 64, 146,
149, 150, 151, 153, 154, 156, 157,
158, 271, 275, 290, 300, 302, 313,
323, 351, 352, 409, 410, 419, 424;
non-Russian native troops (see also
Cheremis; Chuvashi; Kasimov
Tatars), 150, 154, 367, 437; on the
southern frontier, 24, 26, 83, 84, 87,
88, 105, 106, 142, 147, 185, 187,
253, 271, 300. See also artillery;
cossacks, fortress; cossacks, free; deti
boiarskie; dvoriane; garrisons; gentry;
gentry militia; harquebusiers; mercenary troops; rebel military forces;
slaves, military; streltsy
supplies and provisions, 35, 47, 51,
139, 150, 151, 154, 158, 159, 162,
163, 164, 172, 176, 189, 191, 192,
220, 227, 266, 272, 274, 275, 286,
290, 292, 293, 303, 304, 306, 307,
310, 313, 317, 327, 328, 340, 341,
342, 343, 344, 349, 350, 358, 367,
377, 378, 384, 389, 392, 398, 400,

427, 428, 429, 435, 438; food,
102, 153, 159, 262, 266, 272, 293,
327, 341, 368, 396, 400, 427–28,
429, 440; munitions (*see also*
gunpowder and lead), 148, 158,
177, 189, 191, 220, 301, 303, 318,
327, 329, 333, 344, 347, 350;
transportation by land, 35, 154, 166,
172, 176, 220, 297, 341, 343, 358;
transportation by water, 137, 220,
250, 331, 332, 346, 417. *See also*
food; grain; Military Affairs Office
tactics and strategy: ruses of war, 79,
93, 159, 178, 181, 187, 214, 292,
308, 311, 362, 383, 410, 413, 414,
429, 530 n. 98; strategy, 19, 138–39,
143, 144, 145, 148, 158, 160, 161,
163, 171, 173, 221, 269, 271, 272,
275, 276, 281, 284, 296, 310, 321,
342, 350, 386, 395, 403, 416;
tactics, 19, 30, 79, 94, 143, 158,
159, 160, 165, 166, 175, 177, 269,
275, 276, 281, 292, 293, 295, 313,
316, 319, 328, 329, 341, 342, 344,
346, 357, 406. *See also* armies,
Russian, officers; Military Affairs
Office; *voevodas*
weapons and armor: armor, 30, 54,
159, 199, 227; bows and arrows, 30,
40, 41, 152, 154, 159, 176, 177,
179, 352–53; firearms (*see also*
artillery; harquebuses), 40, 44, 81,
105, 159, 231, 415; spears, 155,
154, 159, 437; swords, 30, 40, 154,
159, 265; weapons mentioned, 44,
52, 54, 81, 86, 105, 139, 187, 227,
340, 350, 351, 357, 381
artillery, 42, 43, 44, 45, 146, 149, 154,
159, 163, 165, 166, 167, 170, 173,
177, 178, 189, 191, 193, 220, 221,
230, 245, 266, 279, 293, 301, 303,
314, 316, 318–19, 322, 327–28,
330, 333, 341, 344, 346, 347, 348,
349, 352, 357, 358, 364, 384, 392,
407, 415, 573 n. 26; artillerymen,
39, 44, 69, 146, 154, 171, 177, 268,

293, 328; siege guns, 44, 147, 150,
164, 177, 187, 191, 352, 357, 360,
361, 364, 384, 419; *voevoda* of, 188,
318, 352. *See also* armies, Russian,
campaigns and battles; fortifications;
fortresses; gunpowder and lead;
sieges
Arzamas, 287–89, 322, 397, 432
Asia, 28, 268, 421
assassinations, 14, 65, 96, 110, 197,
202–3, 207–8, 215, 218, 231–32,
237, 251, 252, 408, 409, 429, 436.
See also Dmitrii Ivanovich (pretender
and tsar), assassination of; plots and
conspiracies
assassins, 65, 109, 118, 129, 130, 136,
173, 180, 182, 197, 216, 232, 234,
235, 236, 242, 246, 344, 374
Assembly of the Land. See *zemskii sobor*
Astrakhan, 32, 74, 76, 84, 85, 192, 221,
222, 223, 261, 268, 269, 270, 287,
331, 332, 333, 334, 350, 355, 356,
362, 386, 389, 452–53, 557 n. 91.
See also cossacks, free; fortresses;
sieges; Terek cossacks
atamans. *See* cossacks, free
Augustus, 32
Austria, 21
autocracy, 11, 16, 28–34, 36, 39, 45, 49,
50, 70, 82, 89, 185, 209, 211, 242,
406, 490 n. 35, 512 n. 115;
Romanov era, 446, 449–50, 461,
463–64, 467–68, 476–77, 479. *See*
also government; political culture; tsar
Avrich, P., 11
Azov, 221, 334

Bakhteiarov-Rostovskii, A., 252, 253
Balakhna, 397
Balchik Island, 269, 350, 356, 386
Balkans, 82
Balovnia, M., 455
Baltic Sea, 46, 48, 344, 421, 451, 462
bandits and brigands, 15, 20, 22, 25, 26,
55, 63, 64, 70, 74, 78, 79, 82, 97,
99, 103, 104, 110, 222–23, 224,

bandits and brigands *(continued)*
264, 266, 267, 270, 271, 300, 305,
318, 321, 331, 332, 333, 351, 427,
430, 453, 454, 459. *See also*
cossacks, free
Basmanov, I., 104
Basmanov, P., 146, 149, 150, 158, 159,
161, 179, 180, 182, 183, 188, 189,
190, 191, 193, 197, 198, 208, 209,
210, 212, 216, 218, 219, 220, 231,
235, 237, 299
Bekbulatovich, S., 62, 92, 94, 181, 210,
219, 246
Belaia, 450
Beleshko (ataman), 143
Belev, 146, 277, 321, 366, 385
Belgorod, 84, 145, 148, 170, 252, 261, 324
bells, 162–63, 199, 234, 235, 242, 248,
292, 309, 319, 345
Belorussia *(see also* Poland), 165, 339,
370, 371, 372
Belorussians, 165, 187, 190, 196, 199,
221, 263, 339, 368, 371, 372, 375,
389
Belskii, B., 61, 92, 93, 96, 125, 132, 193,
195, 196, 200, 208, 209, 291, 414,
546 n. 76
Bernardine monastery, 263
Besputa River, 357
betrayal. *See* treason and betrayal
Bezobrazov, E., 376
Bezobrazov, I., 127, 216, 217
Bezzubtsev, Iu., 147, 174, 266, 274, 275,
301, 325, 336, 346, 380, 383, 384,
390, 394, 408, 419. *See also* rebel
commanders
Black Death, 107, 474
Blum, J., 22
bobyli, 54. *See also* peasants, landless
Bodyrin, F., 332
Bogoroditskii Molchinskii monastery, 336
Bolkhov, 227, 321, 366, 385, 389, 392,
432
Bolobanov, T., 339
Bolotnikov, Ivan, 2, 5, 6, 8, 112, 202,
260, 264–66, 267, 268, 273–77

passim, 281, 282, 284, 285, 295,
296, 299, 300, 301, 304, 305, 308,
312, 313, 317, 318, 321–30 *passim*,
335, 337, 338, 341, 343, 344, 345,
349, 353, 357, 360, 362, 364, 372,
374, 375, 378, 379, 380, 381, 382,
383, 384, 387, 388, 389, 411, 420,
429, 480. *See also* rebel commanders;
rebel military forces; sieges
Bolotnikov rebellion, 1, 2, 3, 6, 7, 8, 9,
71, 103, 223, 253, 254, 255, 261,
268, 284, 296, 299, 318, 336, 379,
384, 471, 478, 557 n. 91
Bordakovka, 274
Boris, Saint, 118
Borisov, 557 n. 91
Borovsk, 285, 321, 348, 402
boyar council, 33, 36, 48, 49, 61, 62, 64,
67, 92, 93, 94, 95, 126, 148, 157,
196, 197, 207, 209, 210, 211, 212,
233, 239, 240, 241, 242, 244, 247,
249, 252, 257, 264, 280, 342, 351,
401, 411, 412; rebel councils, 148,
172, 173, 185, 197, 335, 353. *See
also* boyars; court, tsar's; government
boyars, 24, 26, 32, 33, 34, 36, 37, 49, 50,
55, 60, 61, 62, 63, 64, 77, 91, 92,
93, 94, 95, 96, 99, 117, 125, 150,
157, 162, 164, 180, 181, 182,
192–212 *passim*, 214, 216, 218, 223,
226, 230, 232, 237, 239, 242, 243,
246, 247, 252, 257, 262, 263, 278,
286, 289, 306, 319, 320, 336, 353,
367, 390, 394, 404, 406, 409, 410,
411, 412, 414, 424, 425, 429, 438,
442, 446, 447, 455, 456, 535 n. 81;
conspirators among, 95, 125, 129,
130, 132, 157, 182, 190, 206, 217,
218, 220, 222, 223, 231, 237, 241,
243, 245, 247, 257, 351, 413, 425;
popular distrust of, 49, 332, 413;
punishment of, 103, 117, 211, 280,
336, 425. *See also* aristocrats; armies,
Russian, officers; boyar council;
court, tsar's; courtiers; government;
magnates; Votchina estates

Braudel, F., 20
bread and salt, 144, 163, 193, 196, 198,
  377, 378
Brewer, J., 19, 463
Briansk, 146, 149, 157, 164, 274, 330,
  339, 366, 375, 376, 377, 389, 391
bribery and corruption, 94, 117, 203,
  215, 286, 317, 412
Brosovskii, 557 n. 91
Brown, H., 463
Brown, P., 19
Buczynski, J., 127, 145, 204, 208, 211,
  217, 231
Buczynski, S., 204, 211
Budzilo, J., 375, 376, 377
Buinosov-Rostovskii, P., 334, 535 n. 81
Bulgakov, F., 357, 366
Bulgakov, S., 147
bureaucracy and bureaucrats, 19, 20, 28,
  29, 33, 35, 36, 45, 48, 49, 68, 91,
  92, 101, 117, 147, 158, 194, 197,
  199, 203, 210, 215, 227, 247, 267,
  279, 326, 353, 411, 412, 425, 430,
  450, 461, 464–45; clerical, 130, 472,
  476; rebel, 148, 165, 173, 375, 394;
  Romanov era, 454, 461, 462, 463,
  468, 470, 472, 476, 477; secretaries
  and clerks, 35, 86, 127, 158, 173,
  208, 211, 215, 232, 238, 251, 279,
  295, 306, 348, 353, 367, 371, 373,
  375, 425; state secretaries, 35, 208,
  210. See also government; Military
  Affairs Office; taxes; treasury, tsar's
Bushkovitch, P., 23, 475
Bussow, C., 218, 233, 252, 264, 302, 319,
  334, 335, 344, 374, 376, 378, 383
Buturlin, I., 63, 156, 331
Byzantine Empire, 31, 32; its influence on
  Russia, 31, 226, 474

Caesar, 32
Calvinists, 132, 135, 517 n. 103
capitalism, 7, 8, 14, 465, 467
Caspian Sea, 47, 268, 269, 332
Castile, 488 n. 4
Cathedral of the Annunciation, 292

Cathedral of the Archangel, 197, 199,
  245, 248
Cathedral of the Assumption, 234, 292
Catherine II (empress), 479
Catholic Church, 32, 107, 110, 132, 135,
  136, 201, 206, 213, 217, 221, 226,
  228, 232, 233, 263, 415. See also
  Jesuits; Poland; Poles
Caucasus Mountains, 85, 106, 153, 156,
  268, 331
Charles I (king), 423
Cheboksary, 287, 289
Chechersk, 339
Chemlyzhskii ostrog (fort), 162, 165
Cheremis (Mari), 47, 83, 84, 154, 287,
  289, 322, 352, 397, 448. See also
  armies, Russian, soldiers, non-Russian
  native troops
Cherkasskii, D., 394, 441, 450
Cherniavsky, M., 475
Chernigov, 135, 139, 144, 145, 146, 157,
  252, 374, 405, 457
Chertenok-Dolgorukii, A., 197
China, 462
Chistov, K., 9, 111
Chodkiewicz, J., 430, 436, 437, 438, 457.
  See also Polish military intervention
Chudinov-Akinfov, F., 356
Church, Russian Orthodox, 30, 31, 32,
  33, 34, 49, 64, 91, 94, 96, 100, 105,
  106, 113, 124, 125, 130, 180, 199,
  204, 206, 207, 212, 213, 214, 215,
  226, 228, 236, 237, 239, 246, 247,
  249, 292, 351, 415, 472–79 passim,
  490 n. 35; cathedrals, 197, 199, 228,
  234, 242, 245, 292; churches, 213,
  245, 247, 352, 416, 581 n. 24;
  clergy, 31, 32, 70, 91, 201, 204, 207,
  212, 213, 214, 215, 228, 242, 249,
  288, 292, 313, 397, 472; priests, 63,
  198, 199, 207, 213, 215, 233, 234,
  246, 263, 287, 292, 330; property
  of, 55, 213, 214, 312, 398, 442,
  472, 473; in Romanov era, 472, 473,
  476–77. See also monasteries; monks;
  Orthodox Christianity

Church, Russian Orthodox *(continued)*
hierarchy, 92, 126, 156, 180, 198,
203, 208, 212, 213, 214, 215, 226,
230, 247, 290, 430, 462; archbishops, 191, 192, 214, 312, 388, 452;
bishops, 99, 126, 127, 198, 199,
212, 214, 228, 230, 247, 292, 313,
351; metropolitans, 30, 32, 62, 214,
249, 352; patriarchs, 64, 96, 127,
130, 198, 207, 213, 214, 215, 240,
241, 244, 249, 313, 330, 352, 394,
406, 472. *See also* Hermogen; Ignatii;
Iov; Romanov, Fedor (Filaret)
Chuvashi, 83, 84, 154, 287, 288, 289,
322, 352, 397, 419, 435. *See also*
armies, Russian, soldiers, non-
Russian native troops
civil war, xi, xii, 11, 13, 14, 17, 19, 20,
21, 54, 106
civil war, Russia's first, xi, xii, 1, 2, 4, 5, 8,
10, 11, 12, 13, 15, 21, 22, 24, 25,
26, 27, 28, 33, 36, 40, 45, 46, 50,
60, 61, 65, 66, 69, 77, 78, 82, 84,
86, 91, 94, 96, 109, 110, 112, 113,
114, 115, 124, 138, 143; causes and
preconditions, 5, 12, 13, 14, 15, 16,
45, 48, 49, 66, 71, 73, 86, 90, 94,
95, 97, 108, 109–10, 243, 257;
impact of, 271, 325, 448, 460, 465,
466, 467, 471, 480; phases of, 196,
279, 281, 330, 335, 384, 386, 403,
406, 410, 429, 439, 443, 453, 459;
renewed civil war (1606–12), 138,
203, 225, 226, 242, 251, 255, 258,
260, 261, 264, 272, 273, 278, 279,
281; triggers of, 15, 22, 26, 28,
109–10, 148, 223, 238, 242, 243,
251, 253, 257, 258, 260
class war, 3, 4, 5, 6, 7, 14, 78, 102, 104, 111,
145, 174, 202, 223, 224, 254–55, 268,
284, 285, 354, 424, 428, 429, 430,
438, 446, 461, 471, 480. *See also* historiography, Marxist and Soviet; peasant wars; revolution, social
climate, 11, 17, 20, 21, 50, 54, 109, 243,
304, 393. *See also* little ice age

communications, 30, 85, 172, 175, 262,
269, 275, 285, 286, 287, 289, 301,
310, 400. *See also* bells; couriers; letters; roads
consciousness: elite, 11, 22, 26, 27, 111,
115, 240, 462, 474, 480;
gentry, 39, 191, 454, 468–70, 476;
peasant, 6, 53, 69, 115, 332; popular,
3, 11, 22, 26, 27, 49, 69, 71, 74, 93,
95, 99–100, 106, 107, 110, 111,
114–21 *passim*, 206, 259, 332, 445,
474–77, 478, 479, 480; rebel, 3, 4,
5, 10, 11, 12, 13, 104, 110, 114,
115, 116–17, 118, 120, 138, 255,
259, 280, 323; Russian Orthodox,
14, 32, 110, 111, 114, 115, 116,
117, 118, 119, 125, 218, 259, 475,
476, 479, 480. *See also* devil; God;
miracles; Orthodox Christianity;
Satan; sorcerers; witchcraft
coronations, 32, 61, 93, 94, 200, 214,
230, 246, 258
cossacks, fortress, 76, 79, 82, 83, 85, 86,
87, 142, 146, 147, 153, 156, 164,
166, 171, 177, 184, 253, 266, 267,
279, 300, 332, 391, 417, 426, 459.
See also armies, Russian, soldiers;
frontier, southern; garrisons;
investigations; rebel military forces
cossacks, free, 1, 4, 5, 6, 8, 9, 10, 24, 26,
55, 73, 78, 79, 80, 81, 82, 85, 86,
87, 88, 96, 106, 112, 117, 124, 137,
138, 139, 143, 144, 145, 153, 154,
156, 158, 163, 165, 167, 169, 170,
171, 174, 178, 179, 187, 188, 189,
190, 191, 196, 197, 199, 211, 221,
223, 247, 255, 262, 264, 266, 267,
269, 270, 285, 290, 295, 296, 300,
311, 317, 318, 319, 323, 330, 331,
332, 335, 336, 341, 344, 350, 354,
358, 362, 363, 370, 408, 417, 419,
424, 425, 426, 427, 428, 431, 434,
435, 439, 440, 441, 442, 448, 450,
452, 454–55, 456–58, 459, 469, 501
n. 67, 507 n. 136; banditry, 84, 85,
86, 430, 454; *chur* (young companion),

144, 145, 148, 163, 165; court and reign, 201–25; inner circle and allies, 127, 206, 210, 211, 212, 232, 238, 244, 249, 250, 252, 371, 441, 543 n. 103; and the church, 135, 175, 204, 206, 212, 213, 214, 336; foreign bodyguard, 215, 364, 383, 394; government policies of, 121, 131, 194, 201, 203, 204, 206, 209, 211, 212, 219, 220, 224, 225, 227, 233; marriage of, 214, 219, 221, 225, 226, 227, 228, 230, 234; opposition to, 110, 130, 201–2, 206, 212, 214, 222, 228, 231, 236, 237, 240, 243, 244, 246; popular support for, 111, 112, 113, 116, 118, 120, 129, 138, 144, 145, 148, 149, 162, 163, 169, 171, 174, 202, 218, 219, 225, 235, 236, 240, 252, 254, 255, 259, 261, 280, 445, 454; resurrections, 1, 4, 65, 96, 111, 114, 117, 118, 119, 121, 125, 137, 138, 144, 179, 191, 195, 199, 200, 202, 236, 237, 238, 243, 244, 251, 257, 259, 260, 262, 263, 264, 270, 280, 431–32, 453, 479. *See also* civil war, Russia's first, triggers of; pretenders
Dmitrii Ivanovich (second false, Tushino impostor), 380, 381, 383, 391, 405, 406, 410, 412, 413, 415, 417, 443, 574 n. 50; appearance on scene, 368–77; and cossacks, 374, 385, 389, 390, 391, 394, 399, 408, 417; court and courtiers of, 264, 371, 389–98 *passim*, 403, 406, 412, 414, 427; foreign mercenaries of, 364, 368–70, 371, 383, 394, 395; government policies, 375, 391, 394, 396, 397, 399. *See also* cossacks, free; Mniszech, Marina; pretenders; Tushino; Zarutskii, I.
Dmitrii Ivanovich (third false, Pskov pretender), 431, 432, 433, 434, 435. *See also* pretenders; Pskov
Dnepr River, 39, 78, 132, 137, 142
Dobrynichi, 165, 166, 167, 168, 171,

173, 174, 175, 179
documents, 93, 181, 201, 213, 214, 242, 250, 264, 305, 306, 337, 414, 479. *See also* bureaucracy and bureaucrats; communications; letters; propaganda and disinformation
Dolgorukii, G., 330
Dolgorukii, V., 312, 319, 352, 364
Domodedovo, 293
Domorocki, M., 160
Don cossacks, 85, 86, 134, 136, 137, 138, 145, 163, 174, 175, 177, 185–87, 193, 196, 214, 221, 264, 269, 270, 275, 334, 335, 355, 382, 390, 416, 417, 424, 452, 459, 475. *See also* cossacks, free
Don River, 78, 80, 84, 85, 87, 300, 333, 334, 459
dvoriane, 30, 37, 39, 42, 51, 55, 56, 77, 148, 149, 159, 170, 171, 173, 185, 187, 189, 190, 191, 194, 197, 234, 247, 250, 263, 264, 267, 278, 279, 285, 296, 308, 309, 310, 312, 316, 318, 334, 336, 337, 425, 437, 439; *dumnye*, 37, 188, 386, 447; Moscow, 42, 197, 242, 250, 281, 293, 302; *vybornye*, 42, 184, 185, 252, 284, 311. *See also* armies, Russian, officers; gentry; gentry militia; Pomeshchiki; Pomeste estates; *zhiltsy*
dynasty, Russia's old (Daniilovichi), 33, 90, 92, 93, 107, 108, 114, 116, 117, 119, 210, 270, 401, 441, 443, 445, 447, 450, 454, 464

economy (Russia's), 19, 20, 21, 29, 34, 36, 45, 50, 69, 71, 104, 325, 448, 465, 466, 467, 471, 487 n. 80; agricultural, 16, 17, 20, 51, 54, 55, 56, 59, 70, 71, 104, 288, 290, 352, 465; gentry, 54, 55, 150, 220, 469, 470; government interference in, 19, 29, 35, 36, 46, 465, 466; impact of civil war on, 325, 448, 465, 466, 467, 471; foreign trade, 227, 421, 423,

economy (Russia's) *(continued)*
451, 487 n. 80; internal trade and
markets, 16, 44, 58, 59, 94, 98, 144,
185, 234, 247, 269, 284, 289, 291,
305, 331, 398, 416, 417, 434; late
sixteenth-century crisis of, 15, 16,
21, 24, 28, 45, 48, 50, 53, 54, 70,
71, 93, 94, 96. *See also gosti*; merchants; prices in Russia; taxes
Efremov, 557 n. 91
Elagin, G., 331, 337
Elets, 84, 106, 171, 221, 234, 261,
266–67, 268, 272, 273, 274, 275,
276, 277, 278, 279, 300. *See also*
sieges
elites, 13, 14, 19, 21, 22, 23, 24, 25, 32,
33, 48, 49, 50, 95, 106, 109, 111,
112, 114, 117, 120, 181, 190, 191,
195, 203, 226, 227, 230, 242, 254,
270, 285, 304, 308, 337, 445, 454,
479; alienated, 49, 109, 114; intra-
elite rivalry, 21, 22, 24, 49, 50, 61,
90, 94, 209; marginal, 22, 24, 255;
provincial, 42, 89, 185, 386, 463,
468; ruling, 14, 19, 29, 32, 34, 36,
37, 39, 61, 77, 90, 94, 110, 158,
202, 209, 212, 242, 257, 289, 335,
447, 469, 476, 477, 479, 490 n. 35
Engels, F., 7
England, 21, 182, 421–3, 463
English Civil War (or Revolution), 14,
463
Englishmen, 154, 251, 402, 421, 423
enserfment, 3, 5, 15, 25, 26, 67–8, 69,
70, 71, 72, 76, 83, 84, 93, 100, 106,
111, 117, 142, 143, 147, 288, 343,
465, 470, 471, 477, 479. *See also*
peasants; serfdom
Epifan, 76, 276, 279, 318, 366, 385
estates (land), 23, 47, 50, 51, 55, 68, 91,
95, 139, 143, 178, 194, 209, 210,
220, 279, 288, 302, 309, 311, 318,
323, 324, 325, 343, 351, 354, 355,
426, 430, 432, 452; boyar, 49, 438;
church, 37, 49, 68, 100, 101, 311,
312; given as rewards, 309, 319, 336,

351. *See also* land and landholding;
Pomeste estates; Votchina estates
Eurasia, 17, 21
Europe and Europeans, 20, 21, 23, 28,
32, 34, 36, 39, 73, 82, 109, 122,
156, 202, 233, 421, 465, 474. *See
also* West (Western Europe)
Europe, Eastern, 17, 124, 134

False Dmitrii. *See* Dmitrii Ivanovich (pretender and tsar)
False Dmitrii, second. *See* Dmitrii
Ivanovich (Tushino impostor)
famines, 17, 20, 21, 107; Russian, 50, 53,
54, 55, 56, 58, 63, 288, 304, 430
Famine of 1601–3 (Great Famine), 1, 8,
21, 23, 25, 26, 27, 96–108, 109,
117, 125, 138, 139, 143, 144, 147,
150, 151, 154, 156, 159, 198, 225,
343, 468, 505 n. 74, 538 n. 178;
banditry in, 97, 102, 103, 104;
impact of, 96, 97, 104, 105, 106,
272, 507 n. 131; in Moscow, 99, 505
n. 89; prices during, 97, 98, 105,
400, 401, 505 n. 74
Fedor Fedorovich (cossack pretender),
222, 395
Fedor Ivanovich (tsar), 6, 14, 24, 57, 59,
60, 61, 62, 64, 65, 66, 67, 84, 90,
91, 92, 93, 131, 142, 147, 199, 222,
270, 331, 332, 334. *See also*
Godunov, Boris (tsar); Godunov,
Irina; regents of Tsar Fedor
Feodosiia, 91, 332
feudalism, 4, 6, 7, 8, 9, 111, 112, 220,
223, 264, 484 n. 5. *See also* historiography, Marxist and Soviet
Fiedler, F., 344
Field, D., 112
Finland, 21
Finland, Gulf of, 451
Finns, 47, 288, 289
First Peasant War. *See* peasant wars; historiography, Marxist and Soviet
fiscal-military state, 11, 19, 20, 21, 27,
28, 29, 34, 45, 46, 48, 73, 462, 463,

476. *See also* gunpowder revolution; military revolution; warfare

Flemings, 154

food, 86, 101, 109, 148, 153, 177, 178, 274, 286, 301, 304, 319, 350, 398, 417; fasting, 204, 292, 442; "unclean" food, 97, 206, 218, 378. *See also* armies, Russian, supplies and provisions; grain; liquor

forbidden years, 67, 76, 100. *See also* enserfment; peasants; serfdom

Foreign Affairs Office, 80

foreigners, 204, 206, 212, 234, 237, 238, 246, 248, 408, 415. *See also* mercenary troops; merchants

foreign military intervention, 2, 5, 6, 8, 10, 113, 123, 254, 371, 403, 404–23, 424, 425, 430, 433, 434, 439, 445, 447, 448, 450, 455, 464, 468, 472. *See also* national liberation movement; national militia; Polish military intervention; Swedish military intervention

fortifications, 39, 42, 45, 58, 69, 74, 84, 85, 144, 146, 149, 175, 176, 178, 268, 269, 293, 295, 297, 303, 311, 326, 327, 328, 340, 360, 363, 403, 409, 416; Moscow's, 292–93, 297, 303, 304. *See also* fortresses; military engineering; sieges

fortresses, 1, 35, 39, 42, 44, 58, 74, 84, 85, 87, 139, 143, 144, 146, 148, 149, 150, 159, 162, 170, 221, 261, 266, 267, 268, 269, 272, 273, 275, 277, 278, 280, 282, 285, 287, 290, 303, 310, 311, 327, 334, 340, 350, 352, 360, 363, 374, 391, 405, 419, 421, 434, 457, 581 n. 28. *See also* artillery; fortifications; garrisons; Kaluga; sieges; Smolensk; Tula

forts, 42, 77, 84, 85, 269, 271, 333

France, 21, 464

freedom, 73, 142, 203, 288, 381, 391, 411, 417, 424, 425, 440, 454, 456; cossack, 26, 79, 80, 86, 113, 426. *See also* consciousness; cossacks, free;

political culture

Frenchmen, 20, 130, 154, 237, 402, 464. *See also* Margeret, J.

French Revolution, 14, 463

frontier, southern, 1, 11, 15, 22, 23, 24, 25, 26, 36, 40, 42, 45, 47, 48, 54, 55, 58, 68, 73–90, 104, 109, 117, 137, 138, 144, 147, 156, 162, 163, 169, 171, 172, 173, 176, 184, 186, 190, 203, 221, 223, 224, 258, 261, 262, 264, 270, 276, 278, 280, 281, 286, 287, 288, 289, 290, 291, 340, 366, 452, 459, 469, 478; defense system (see also *zaseka*), 76, 85, 142, 184, 267, 277, 287; old frontier zone, 187, 191, 280, 300, 362; population of, 47, 72, 73, 74, 76, 85, 87, 89, 96, 118, 138, 139, 142, 143, 145, 147, 170, 184, 258; southwestern (*see also* Severia), 76, 138, 139, 142, 146, 148, 162, 172, 173, 176, 184, 253, 261, 272, 274, 280, 287, 291, 366, 386; towns of, 45, 74, 77, 82, 84–5, 89, 138, 145, 147, 169–70, 171, 179, 180, 184, 186, 187, 253, 254, 261, 266, 270, 358, 366, 432. *See also* cossacks, fortress; cossacks, free; Crimean Tatars; gentry, southern frontier; Tatars

frontiers, Russia's: borders to the west, 39, 44, 46, 80, 86, 126, 128, 132, 137, 138, 143, 150, 153, 156, 162, 163, 218, 262, 271, 285, 339, 345, 372, 373, 377, 402, 403, 421, 440, 457, 515 n. 32; eastern, 36, 47, 55, 74, 156, 184. *See also* frontier, southern; Russia

Galich, 397, 399

Gardie, J. de la, 409, 420, 421

garrisons, 40, 45, 73, 83, 138, 143, 144, 146, 147, 148, 149, 153, 156, 157, 161, 164, 173, 175, 180, 184, 191, 233, 261, 266, 268, 273, 275, 276, 277, 281, 282, 283, 285, 290, 291, 300, 310, 313, 325, 327, 350, 352,

historiography, xi, 3, 4, 5–11, 12, 13, 14, 15, 17, 19, 20, 21, 27, 58, 108, 109, 113, 258, 462, 485 n. 7; Marxist and Soviet, 4, 6, 7, 8, 9, 66, 67, 71, 103, 104, 107, 111, 112, 124, 128, 144, 148, 194, 201, 220, 223, 224, 255, 264, 265, 268, 279, 300, 305, 318, 332, 333, 374, 381, 390, 427, 443, 446, 455, 471, 477, 480, 484 n. 5

Hobsbawm, E., 55

Holy Roman Empire, 31

Holy Russia, 475, 476–77, 590 n. 87

honey farmers, 77, 139, 288, 289, 556 n. 72

honor and dishonor, 157, 183, 193, 203, 299, 317

horses, 30, 41, 44, 54, 57, 79, 97, 150, 152, 154, 159, 167, 191, 196, 197, 250, 286, 293, 304, 313, 341, 344, 352, 358, 374, 378, 398

Horsey, J., 66

Hosking, G., 477

Hungary, 21, 82, 265

Iadrin, 287, 289, 290

Iaik cossacks, 86, 269, 355. See also cossacks, free

Iaik River, 80, 85, 453

Iama, 421, 431, 451

Iaroslavl, 61, 276, 312, 342, 345, 388, 397, 398, 403, 416, 434, 435, 436, 437

Iatskii, V., 127, 128, 129

Iauza River, 303, 304, 306, 307, 312, 320

icons and holy relics, 199, 201, 236, 237, 246, 273, 336

Ignatii (Patriarch), 191, 207, 212, 214, 240, 249

imperialism, Russian, 16, 28, 29, 30, 31, 32, 34, 36, 45, 46, 48, 83, 84, 154, 477, 478. See also crusades; political culture; Russian state; tsar

impostor, 65, 120. See also pretenders

infantry: cossack, 137, 164, 167, 358; deti boiarskie, 77, 106, 147, 149,

166, 220, 266, 268, 275, 276, 469. See also harquebusiers; streltsy

intelligentsia, 480

investigations, 87, 147, 382, 401, 426, 446, 454–55, 501 n. 67. See also cossacks, fortress

Iosifo-Volokolamsk monastery, 286, 310, 311, 324, 325, 326

Iov (Patriarch), 62, 64, 91, 92, 99, 125, 126, 130, 174, 180, 198, 212, 213, 214, 240, 330

Ireland, 21

Irtysh River, 83

Ishterek (prince), 84, 173, 269, 452. See also Nogai Tatars

Isidor (Metropolitan), 214, 215

Islam, 82, 214, 221, 288

Israel, 32

Iurlov, T., 333

Ivan III (grand prince), 28, 29, 30, 31, 35, 36, 37, 39, 42, 46, 51, 94, 95, 226

Ivan IV (tsar), 1, 3, 17, 24, 31, 32, 34, 39, 42, 44–62 passim, 67, 76, 77, 80, 93, 94, 95, 112, 114, 117, 121, 123, 131, 132, 142, 182, 185, 191, 199, 212, 216, 220, 221, 227, 230, 242, 251, 270, 337, 338, 355, 356, 490 n. 35. See also crusades; oprichnina; terror; tyranny

Ivan Dmitrievich (little brigand), 414, 415, 430, 431, 433, 434, 435, 436, 437, 446, 448, 450, 452, 453, 457. See also Dmitrii Ivanovich (Tushino impostor); Mniszech, Marina; Zarutskii, I.

Ivan Ivanovich (son of Ivan IV), 61

Ivan-Avgust (cossack pretender), 356, 362–63, 386, 395. See also Astrakhan; pretenders

Ivangorod, 161, 421, 431, 451

Izmailov clan, 185, 306

Izmailov, A., 170, 173, 185, 197, 210, 330, 346

James I (king), 421, 423

Korela (town), 420, 451
Korela, A., 134, 136, 145, 175, 176, 178, 179, 187, 188, 193, 295, 328. *See also* Kromy; sieges
Koretskii, V., 8, 9, 103, 223, 224, 255, 308
kormlenie, 399, 427, 429
Korovin, Ilia. *See* Petr, tsarevich (cossack pretender)
Korovin, Ivan, 331
Kostomarov, M., 5
Kostroma, 345, 397, 400, 403, 434
Kotelnich, 287
Kotel River, 245
Kotly, 283, 299, 316
Kozelsk, 277, 321, 330, 346, 348, 366, 377, 385
Krapivna, 192, 264, 278, 364, 366, 385
Krasnoe Selo, 193, 293, 306, 307, 312, 313
Kremlin (citadel), 144, 363
Kremlin, Moscow, 126, 180, 198, 199, 206, 207, 209, 212, 213, 215, 216, 228, 232, 235, 236, 237, 243, 245, 248, 249, 264, 279, 280, 292, 304, 309, 401, 410, 415, 418, 436, 438, 439, 445, 453. *See also* court, tsar's; government; Moscow
Kriuk-Kolychev, I., 63, 233, 242, 310, 311–12, 313, 314, 316, 319, 352, 353, 383, 401
Kroma River, 188
Kromy, 84, 146, 149, 150, 164, 172, 173, 175, 178, 180; siege of, 176, 177, 182–93 *passim*, 196, 220, 272–79 *passim*, 281, 295, 299, 300, 328, 348. *See also* sieges
Kropotkin, S., 366
Krovkov, I., 367
Krupinov (renegade), 218
Krutitsa, 214, 243
Kurakin clan, 63
Kurakin, I., 192, 197
Kurmysh, 287, 289, 290, 432
Kursk, 84, 106, 148, 170, 171, 252, 261, 273
Kuzmin, S., 331

Ladoga, 421, 451
land and landholding: crown lands, 55, 87, 143, 262, 323, 428, 447; land, 22, 24, 25, 40, 53, 54, 77, 219, 288, 428; landholding, 22, 26, 37, 47, 51, 154, 219, 406, 470–71; land with peasant labor, 16, 24, 25, 40, 51, 55, 71, 77, 394; nontaxed lands, 68, 494 n. 56; state lands, 51, 142, 143, 149. *See also* estates; Pomeste estates; Votchina estates
Latin, 123, 251
laws, 47, 69, 90, 94, 204, 212, 224, 342–43, 391, 402, 471, 472
Lazarus, 134
Lebedian, 557 n. 91
legends, social utopian, 4, 9, 111, 112, 115, 120, 223, 255
Lenin, 4, 6, 7, 8
Leonid (monk), 127, 130
letters, 143, 179, 192, 198, 222, 244, 250, 251, 262, 265, 266, 268, 269, 273, 279, 280, 303, 304, 305, 306, 307, 330, 333, 351, 372, 374, 418, 429, 430, 434, 439. *See also* communications; documents; propaganda and disinformation
Lgov, 274
Liapunov, P., 184, 185, 187, 191, 279, 284, 306, 307, 308, 309, 310, 313, 317, 322, 323, 352, 357, 358, 366, 386, 398, 401–2, 408, 409, 410, 411, 415, 416, 417, 418, 419, 424, 425, 426, 428, 429, 430, 436. *See also* cossacks, free; Moscow, sieges of; national militia, first; Riazan
Liapunov, Z., 184, 185, 187, 191, 307, 410,
Likhvin, 277, 321, 366
liquor, 195, 196, 198, 239, 258, 507 n. 131
Lisowski, A., 400
Lithuania (*see also* Poland), 17, 39, 54, 127, 128, 135, 136, 139, 187, 405, 457
Lithuanians, 136, 221, 263, 339, 364, 395

little ice age, 17, 20, 21, 27, 46, 50, 54, 63, 97, 107, 275. *See also* climate
Livny, 84, 164, 261, 274, 275, 334
Livonia, 48, 220, 402, 405
Livonian War, 16, 21, 46, 48, 54, 58, 83
Livonians, 154
Lobnoe mesto, 242, 243. *See also* Red Square
Lodiagin, B., 144
looting. *See* plunder
Lunev (ataman), 174
Lvov, 134, 136
Lykov, B., 170, 173, 184, 191, 197, 208, 210, 357, 411

magnates, 49, 55, 56, 57, 68, 69, 101, 132, 270, 389, 454. *See also* aristocrats; boyars; *dvoriane*; Votchina estates
Makarii (Metropolitan), 32
Makovskii, D., 9
Malyi Iaroslavets, 285
Mankov, A., 23
Margeret, J., 130, 132, 157, 160, 165, 166, 167, 171, 178, 199, 204, 215, 219, 220, 222, 223, 232, 248, 249, 258, 271, 333, 371, 394, 409, 413, 418, 541 n. 42. *See also* mercenary troops
Mari. *See* Cheremis
Marx, K., 6
Mary (mother of Jesus), 292
Massa, I., 118, 159, 177, 178, 179, 218, 230, 232, 234, 235, 248, 261, 264, 265, 269, 319, 345, 346, 347, 348, 352, 355, 357, 379
master of the horse, 61, 413. *See* boyars; court, tsar's
Medyn, 285, 321
mercenary troops (European), 26, 55, 79, 130, 136, 144, 146, 148, 154, 157, 160–67 *passim*, 174, 187, 189, 190, 196, 198, 199, 211, 215, 218, 220, 221, 226, 227, 233, 234, 235, 263, 271, 304, 332, 339, 349, 350, 364, 368–75 *passim*, 377, 383, 385, 387, 389, 391, 393, 394, 395, 396, 398,

399, 402, 403, 408, 409, 413, 414, 418, 421, 435, 436, 521 n. 92. *See also* armies, Russian, soldiers; Dmitrii Ivanovich (pretender and tsar), campaign for the throne; Dmitrii Ivanovich (Tushino impostor); Polish military intervention; rebel military forces
merchants, 35, 58, 62, 98, 99, 136, 154, 156, 157, 194, 196, 207, 208, 226, 227, 233, 234, 235, 242, 243, 247, 268, 269, 284, 291, 305, 306, 325, 327, 331, 333, 397, 398, 400, 412, 416, 417, 434, 441, 467; elite, 69, 197, 226, 247, 410, 467; foreign, 48, 227, 234, 237, 251, 346, 400, 421; rich Russian (*see also gosti*), 193, 228, 327, 397, 417, 418. *See also* economy; Shuiskii, Vasilii
Merrick, J., 586 n. 40
Meshchovsk, 277, 321, 327, 330, 348, 376, 385
mestnichestvo, 157, 180, 183, 188, 328, 348
Mezetskii, D., 276, 310, 311, 326, 341, 342, 366
Miechowicki, M., 371, 372, 373, 374, 375, 377, 404
Mikhailov, 279, 329, 330, 342, 361, 437
Mikulin, G., 210
Military Affairs Office, 35, 49, 157, 158, 306, 353, 367; activities of, 35, 147, 148, 275, 295, 348, 351; intelligence gathering by (*see also* spies and agents), 35, 158, 165, 342; secretaries in, 158, 293, 348, 353, 367. *See also* armies, Russian; bureaucracy and bureaucrats; government; *voevodas*
military engineering, 146, 154, 166, 245, 293, 297, 328–9, 367–8; battering rams, 327, 328; dam construction, 369, 377, 378, 379; fortification construction, 39, 44, 69, 84, 166, 176, 269, 297, 328, 329, 376, 403; siege towers, 146, 245, 328, 329. *See also* armies, Russian, campaigns and

military engineering *(continued)*
  battles; fortifications; fortresses;
  guliai gorod; sieges
military revolution, 11, 19, 20, 28, 35,
  42, 44, 45, 160, 428, 463, 492 n.
  93. *See also* gunpowder revolution
millenarianism, 115
Minin, K., 433, 434, 435, 438, 439, 447,
  467. *See also* national militia, second;
  taxes
minstrels, 236, 237, 243, 473
miracles, 247, 259, 292. *See also* consciousness; Orthodox Christianity
Miracles (Chudov) monastery, 126
Mironov, B., 115
Mizinov, M., 377
Mniszech, J., 134, 135, 136, 137, 138,
  144, 145, 146, 148, 150, 160, 162,
  214, 221, 231, 238, 262, 264, 276,
  345, 394, 579 n. 55. *See also* Dmitrii
  Ivanovich (pretender and tsar)
Mniszech, Marina (tsaritsa), 214, 220,
  221, 226, 227, 228, 229, 230, 231,
  237, 238, 393, 394, 408, 414, 415,
  430, 431, 433, 437, 439, 445, 446,
  448, 450, 452, 453, 579 n. 55. *See
  also* Dmitrii Ivanovich (pretender
  and tsar); Dmitrii Ivanovich (second
  false, Tushino impostor); Ivan
  Dmitrievich; Tushino; Zarutskii, I
Mogilev, 372, 373
Molchanov, M., 204, 250, 251, 262, 263,
  264, 265, 269, 345, 371, 372, 394,
  401, 406, 546 n. 82. *See also*
  pretenders
Moldavia, 124
monarchism: naive, 6, 8, 9, 111, 112,
  113, 115, 255, 509 n. 28; popular,
  115, 117, 121. *See also* consciousness; political culture; tsar
monarchy, 13, 28, 35, 36; absolute, 16,
  21, 203; Russian monarchs, 32, 49,
  94. *See also* autocracy; political culture; monarchism; tsar
monasteries, 125, 126, 147, 154, 197,
  198, 213, 214, 270, 271, 272, 286,

297, 302, 303, 311, 316, 324, 325,
  336, 367, 383, 388, 398, 399, 410,
  433, 435, 472; abbots, 214; convent,
  92; elders, 214; estates and property
  of, 49, 100, 101, 143, 399; nuns in,
  212. *See also* Church, Russian
  Orthodox; fortresses; monks; *and
  listings of individual monasteries*
Monastyrevskii gorodok, 334
money (cash), 147, 150, 162, 167, 217,
  221, 262, 271, 273, 274, 286, 291,
  309, 311, 324, 325, 331, 398, 435,
  441. *See also* armies, Russian;
  rewards; taxes
Mongols, 29–30, 32, 35, 84, 94; khans
  and khanates, 29, 30, 32. *See also*
  Crimean Tatars; Golden Horde;
  Nogai Tatars; Tatars
monks, 96, 99, 110, 111, 118, 123, 125,
  126, 127, 147, 158, 173, 198, 199,
  202, 213, 215, 219, 233, 234, 244,
  270, 286, 311, 336, 378, 379, 412.
  See also Church, Russian Orthodox;
  monasteries
Moravsk, 143, 144, 274, 327
Mordvians (Mordva), 47, 154, 287, 288,
  289, 290, 386, 397, 419, 435. *See
  also* armies, Russian, soldiers, non-
  Russian native troops
Morozov clan, 63
Morozov, V., 188, 316, 318, 328
Mosalskii clan, 283, 335, 342, 371
Mosalskii, I. L., 361
Mosalskii, V. F., 366, 377
Mosalskii, V. M., 147, 148, 167, 173,
  197, 210, 227, 330, 335, 366, 377
Moscow, xi, 2, 28, 31, 32, 33, 37, 42, 44,
  45, 47, 48, 49, 65, 76, 84, 90, 99,
  119, 126, 146, 149, 150, 156, 157,
  158, 161, 164, 174, 180, 185, 186,
  189–99 *passim*, 202, 206, 213, 215,
  221, 223, 224, 226, 230, 233, 234,
  239, 242, 245, 246, 252, 254, 263;
  fortifications of, 292–93, 297, 302,
  303, 304; gates of, 234, 243, 295,
  297, 302, 303, 306, 308, 313, 316,

317, 394, 401, 453; Polish occupation of, 411, 413, 415, 424, 437,
438–39; roads to, 138, 172, 175,
191, 192, 247, 278, 280, 292, 293,
313, 348, 364, 388, 393, 396; region
of, 55, 101, 103, 273, 292, 350,
414, 417, 419, 428, 432, 438, 440;
streets of, 196, 234, 239, 279, 415;
suburbs of, 234, 280, 283, 291, 388,
419; transriver district (wooden
town, *zamoskvorech'e*), 293, 304, 557
n. 101. *See also* boyar council; court,
tsar's; government; Kremlin,
Moscow; Red Square
inhabitants of, 62, 99, 157, 182, 190,
192, 194, 199, 206, 213, 220,
227–37 *passim*, 240, 241, 245, 246,
257, 261, 282, 286, 291, 292, 297,
301–7 *passim*, 310, 313, 314, 319,
320, 339, 342, 348, 351, 392–93,
395, 401, 415, 418, 430, 457, 459,
505 n. 89; crowds, 194, 195, 198,
199, 200, 208, 235, 242, 245, 246,
247–8, 249, 292, 350, 387, 401,
410, 456–57; hungry, 99, 292, 301,
302, 304, 306, 310, 313, 314, 395,
401, 415, 430, 438, 505 n. 89;
streltsy, 146, 147, 148, 170, 216,
234, 284, 293, 301, 303, 304, 308,
309, 418; unrest, riots, and rebellion
of, 62, 64, 194, 195, 196, 197, 231,
234, 237, 239, 245, 246, 248, 249,
262, 270, 279, 304, 306, 307, 345,
414, 470, 476, 477, 478, 509 n. 28
sieges of: Bolotnikov's, 260, 281, 282,
283, 288, 290, 291, 292, 293, 296,
297–320, 321, 322, 324, 325, 330,
338, 346, 372, 429; Tushinite, 384,
392, 393, 394, 395, 396, 398, 401,
405, 408; by national militia, 417,
418, 419, 424, 430, 432, 435–36,
437, 438, 439, 440, 452; Polish,
456–57. *See also* council of seven;
Polish military intervention; sieges
Moskva River, 292, 312, 316
Mousnier, R., 17, 19

Mozhaisk, 285, 310, 311, 561 n. 98
Mstislavskii, F., 62, 92, 94, 157–67 *passim*, 171, 172, 175, 176, 177, 179,
180, 182, 183, 194, 195, 210, 216,
232, 242, 246, 248, 272, 273, 293,
295, 313, 328, 347, 353, 410, 411,
413, 418, 438, 439, 441, 442, 447,
450, 456. *See also* aristocrats; boyar
council; boyars; council of seven;
Polish military intervention; *voevodas*
Mstislavskii, I., 61, 62
Mtsensk, 278
Murom, 287, 290, 322, 331, 367, 397,
416, 417
Muscovite grand princes, 28, 29, 30, 31,
445. *See also* Ivan III; Vasilii II;
Vasilii III
Muscovy, xi, 28, 29, 30, 31, 33, 36
music and musical instruments, 160, 236,
243, 244, 358
muzhiki-sevriuki, 76, 142, 148, 163. *See
also* Komaritsk district; peasants;
Severia
Mylnikov (assassin, merchant), 235, 242,
306

Nagaia, Mariia (tsaritsa, nun Marfa), 61,
65, 66, 96, 182, 195, 208, 209, 216,
235, 247, 273. *See also* Dmitrii
Ivanovich; Nagoi clan
Nagiba, F., 331, 383, 384
Nagoi clan, 61, 62, 63, 64, 65, 67, 96,
125, 131, 132, 196, 209, 210, 211,
212, 216, 236, 249, 264, 273, 514
n. 21, 542 nn. 84–85. *See also* aristocrats; boyars; Dmitrii Ivanovich
Nagoi, A. F., 61, 63
Nagoi, G. F., 273
Nagoi, M. A., 272, 273, 274, 341
Nagoi, S., 127
Napoleonic regime, 464
Narva, 48, 220
national liberation movement, 399–442;
formation of, 399–403, 415–20;
partisan activity of, 419, 436, 438,
451; split in patriot forces, 432–33;

national liberation movement *(continued)*
new patriot movement, 433; unification of all patriot forces, 438
national militia (host), first, 416–31; commanders of 416, 418, 419, 421, 424–32 *passim*; cossacks in, 417, 419, 424–32 *passim*; council of the realm, 419, 425, 426, 427, 430; decree of June 30 (constitution), 425, 426; gentry in, 419, 424, 425, 426, 428, 430; government of, 419, 425, 426. *See also* Liapunov, P.; Polish military intervention; Pozharskii, D.; Swedish military intervention; Trubetskoi, D.; Zarutskii, I.
national militia, second, 433–42, 450; commanders of, 433, 434, 437; cossacks in, 438, 440, 450, 454; gentry in, 440. *See also* Minin, K.; Polish military intervention; Pozharskii, D.; Swedish military intervention; Trubetskoi, D.; Zarutskii, I.
Nazarov, V., 9
Nevskii, Aleksandr, 29, 61, 90, 242
Nikolskii, F., 372
Nikon (Patriarch), 473
Nizhnii Novgorod, 188, 269, 270, 287, 288, 289, 290, 291, 321, 322, 331, 342, 397, 403, 415, 416, 417, 430, 431, 433, 446. *See also* economy; fortresses; Shuiskii, Vasilii; sieges
nobles, 30, 37, 39, 44, 45, 48, 49, 91, 159, 185, 246, 267, 418, 434; lords, 190, 202, 279, 307, 322. *See also* aristocrats; boyars; *deti boiarskie, dvoriane*; gentry
Nogai Tatars (Horde), 84, 173, 269, 350, 366, 454. *See also* Ishterek (prince); Mongols; Tatars
non-Russian native subjects of the tsar, 47, 83–84, 150, 154, 214, 254, 270, 288, 289, 352, 367, 419, 435, 437, 448. *See also* Cheremis; Chuvashi; Kasimov Tatars; Mordvians; Ostiaks; Tatars
Northern Dvina River, 302, 313

Norway, 21
Novgorod, 37, 46, 99, 188, 190, 208, 214, 226, 227, 230, 233, 234, 242, 270, 273, 276, 291, 302, 303, 310, 312, 320, 396, 397, 400, 402, 419, 420, 421, 431, 432, 440, 451, 546 n. 76. *See also* fortresses; Swedish military intervention
Novgorod Severskii, 76, 139, 145, 146, 149, 150, 157, 158, 159, 160, 161, 163, 165, 167, 170, 179, 261, 274, 405
Novodevichii monastery, 316, 419
Novosil, 76, 275, 278

oaths, sacred: of loyalty to tsar, 144, 170, 171, 173, 183, 185, 192, 197, 198, 226, 247, 252, 253, 261, 265, 268, 271, 284, 287, 290, 291, 305, 318, 322, 327, 335, 337, 342, 343, 354, 397, 400, 411, 414, 415, 421, 432; of revenge, 253, 419; in testimony, 132, 382, 388. *See also* consciousness; Orthodox Christianity; tsar
Ob River, 83
Ododurov, I., 364, 366
Ododurov, S., 322, 342, 344
Odoev, 277, 366
Oka River, 76, 78, 142, 175, 184, 192, 250, 272, 276, 280, 281, 282, 283, 287, 288, 300, 327, 341, 346, 367, 402; frontier defense line, 193, 276, 305. *See also* armies, Russian, tactics and strategy; Crimean Tatars; frontier, southern; Tatars
okolnichii, 37, 61, 104, 146, 147, 148, 156, 172, 185, 188, 210, 233, 242, 310, 316, 319, 330, 346, 353. *See also* armies, Russian; boyar council; boyars; court, tsar's; *voevodas*
Old Believers, 474, 478
Old Testament, 32
oprichnina, 16, 46, 48, 49, 50, 53, 54, 60, 61, 62, 63, 93, 94, 183, 212, 227, 251. *See also* elites, intra-elite rivalry; Ivan IV; terror

419, 428, 432, 455, 463. *See also*
gentry; gentry militia; Pomeste estates
Pomeste estates, 37, 39, 40, 47, 49, 51,
53, 55, 77, 82, 101, 139, 143, 151,
178, 267, 288, 391, 425, 426, 430,
433. *See also* gentry; Pomeshchiki
Popova Gora, 274, 373, 557 n. 91
Populists, 480
Porkhov, 421, 451
posad, 58, 68, 144, 147, 149, 170, 171,
233, 312. *See also* economy;
merchants; towns
Posolskii prikaz, 80
poverty, 20, 22, 25, 93, 102, 243
Pozharskii, D., 184, 396, 416, 418–19,
424, 432–41 *passim,* 447, 449, 451,
455, 456, 457, 467, 585 n. 27. *See*
also cossacks, free; Moscow, sieges
of; national militia, first; national
militia, second; Polish military
intervention; Swedish military
intervention; *zemskii sobor*
pretenders, 2, 5, 111, 119, 120, 124, 134;
pretenderism, 115, 119, 121, 122,
135, 136, 138, 201, 222, 270, 332,
356, 389, 391, 395, 431, 453, 454,
479, 514 n. 19, 543 n. 103. *See also*
Dmitrii Ivanovich (pretender and
tsar); Dmitrii Ivanovich (Tushino
impostor); Dmitrii Ivanovich (Pskov
pretender); Fedor Fedorovich;
Ivan-Avgust; Ivan Dmitrievich;
Molchanov, M.; Petr, tsarevich
price revolution, 17, 23
prices in Russia, 16, 17, 20, 21, 22, 23,
25, 27, 46, 50, 53, 57, 58, 63, 74,
97, 98, 105, 150, 153, 286, 310,
378, 401, 465, 505 n 74. *See also*
economy; famines; sieges
Priimakov-Rostovskii, Iu., 334
prikaz, 35, 80, 216, 390. *See also* bureaucracy and bureaucrats; government
primët, 328
primogeniture, 33, 90
princes, 24, 32, 33, 36, 37, 49, 61, 62,
195, 207, 208, 212, 218, 252. *See*

also aristocrats
pristavstvo (cossack), 428
propaganda and disinformation: propaganda, 2, 66, 110, 111, 113, 123,
125, 127, 129, 130, 145, 162, 174,
175, 179, 197, 201, 202, 203, 213,
214, 216, 222, 223, 225, 228, 232,
236, 239, 241, 242, 247, 249, 250,
252, 254, 257, 259, 261, 263, 266,
280, 283, 285, 291, 292, 300, 303,
305, 308, 314, 318, 321, 322, 333,
336, 337, 338, 343, 345, 351, 354,
355, 359, 362, 370, 379, 380, 381,
382, 383, 387, 396, 415, 443, 454,
532 n. 5; disinformation, 93, 187,
214, 414, 429, 530 n. 98
property, 37, 142, 196, 210, 236, 242,
243, 254, 354, 362, 383–84, 391,
441. *See also* land and landholding;
Votchina estates
Propoisk, 373
Protestants, 204, 206, 213, 233, 435,
471–72
Prussia, 21
Pskov, 99, 188, 190, 226, 227, 233, 234,
273, 276, 291, 302, 303, 320, 397,
405, 421, 431, 432, 433, 435, 451.
See also Dmitrii Ivanovich (Pskov
pretender); fortresses; Swedish military intervention
Pugachev, E., 1, 2, 3, 119, 120, 122, 459,
478, 479, 480
punishment, 103, 117, 150–51, 211, 280,
324, 336, 351, 425; confiscation, 37,
54, 95, 96, 142, 151, 152, 213, 214,
242, 288, 324, 325, 351, 391, 398,
399, 408, 425, 438; exile, 61, 62,
64, 65, 94, 95, 96, 125, 197, 198,
199, 207, 210, 214, 219, 249, 252,
280, 291, 330, 383, 384, 535 n. 81;
prison, 87, 151, 289, 322; punitive
raids, 168, 178, 186, 259, 362, 386;
torture, 64, 86, 95, 96, 118, 125,
158, 169, 199, 201, 212, 232, 261,
277, 280, 306, 338, 345, 354, 355,
356, 362, 364, 370, 377, 380, 387,

rumors, 63, 65, 92, 93, 96, 99, 106, 125,
130, 182, 191, 206, 207, 213, 215,
217–23 *passim*, 230, 231, 237, 238,
243, 245, 247, 250, 251, 258, 259,
262, 263, 265, 270, 271, 276, 284,
320, 330, 345, 357, 364, 367, 379,
383, 386, 388, 432, 453, 549 n. 24,
565 n. 62
Rus, xi, xiI, 29, 30, 33, 36, 37, 118, 139,
401
Russia, 11, 32, 33, 116, 475, 479; central
(heartland), 11, 23, 26, 55, 58, 70,
73, 74, 76, 85, 87, 102, 138, 189,
190, 270, 272, 275, 276, 280, 281,
291, 300, 301, 352, 397, 398, 434,
459; frontier (*see* frontier, southern;
frontiers); north, 37, 190, 270, 286,
290, 291, 302, 307, 352, 388, 391,
395, 397–403 *passim*, 415, 417, 420,
421, 427, 432, 434, 435, 440, 450,
471; population of, 11, 16, 17,
20–26 *passim*, 46, 50, 54, 55, 58, 63,
74, 99, 466, 487 n. 75, 494 n. 56.
See also Russian state
Russia Company, 421
Russian people, 22, 26, 32, 33, 34, 36,
46–50 *passim*, 90–96 *passim*, 109,
113, 116, 162, 163, 202, 206, 230,
263, 290; children, 70, 97, 234, 305,
351, 393; patriotic, 415, 428, 442,
445, 447, 448, 450, 456, 472, 475,
477, 479, 480; woman, 97, 169,
177, 201, 212, 257, 271, 305, 336,
351, 352, 390, 393, 399; young
men, 21, 22, 23, 26, 42, 82, 86,
109, 293
Russian schism, 473–79 *passim. See also*
Church, Russian Orthodox; consciousness; Nikon; Orthodox
Christianity; political culture
Russian society, xii, 3, 4, 16, 19, 28, 31,
34, 35, 39, 71, 77, 95, 110, 144,
204, 206; status in, 39, 40, 42, 45,
49, 56, 69, 70, 77, 78, 82, 83, 87,
88, 159, 180, 183, 186, 188, 207,
236, 240, 257, 284, 299, 328, 348,

395, 399, 427, 434, 437, 439, 459,
502 n. 81; stratification of, 15, 16,
20, 22, 28, 35, 37, 45, 46, 53, 69,
70, 83, 220, 454, 461, 462, 464–65,
466, 467, 469, 473, 476. *See also*
consciousness; Orthodox
Christianity; political culture
Russian state, xii, 1, 11, 21, 31, 206; as
an empire, xi, 11, 28, 29, 30, 32, 36,
39, 45, 46, 47, 71, 461, 462, 464,
476, 479; expansion of, 11, 16, 18,
28, 32, 34–39 *passim*, 45, 46, 47, 73,
83, 96, 105, 147, 270, 286, 461,
463, 477, 485 n. 31; growth of state
power, 13–14, 17, 19, 20, 28, 46,
156, 476–77; as a service state, 16,
19, 20, 29, 32, 34, 50; unification
of, xi, 2, 28, 29, 30, 36, 37, 39, 42,
74, 90, 115. *See also* autocracy; fiscal-military state; imperialism,
Russian; Russia; tsar
Ruza, 285
Rylsk, 76, 146, 148, 168, 171, 261, 273
Ryndin, D., 375, 376
Rzhev, 285
Rzhevskii, A., 376

Saburov, M., 192, 331, 334
Saburov, Z., 183, 188, 362
St. George's Day, 9, 53, 67, 100, 223. *See
also* enserfment; peasants
Saltykov clan, 394
Saltykov, I., 419, 420
Saltykov, M. G., 185, 188, 191, 197, 210,
394, 406, 413, 418, 419. *See also*
council of seven; Moscow, sieges of;
Polish military intervention
Saltykov, M. M., 147, 148
Samara, 84, 85, 333
Sambor, 134, 135, 136, 262, 263, 264,
265, 273
Samoeds, 286
Samovsk district, 262, 274
Sandomierz, 134, 214
Sapieha, A., 339
Sapieha, J. P., 395, 396, 400, 403, 405,

Shuiskii, Vasilii (tsar) *(continued)*
357, 361–67 *passim,* 371, 374, 376,
377, 379, 381, 382, 385–88 *passim,*
391–95 *passim,* 398, 400–404, 408,
410–13 *passim,* 417, 471; and coconspirators, 208, 211, 215, 216, 221,
225, 226, 228, 230, 232, 233, 234,
240, 241, 242, 243, 247, 304, 389;
coup of, 258, 259, 265, 266, 268,
269; coups against, 401, 402, 410,
411; deposed, 410; rekindles civil
war, 242, 258–59. *See also* boyar
council; boyars; Dmitrii Ivanovich
(pretender and tsar), assassination of;
plots and conspiracies
Siberia, 47, 65, 83, 96, 105, 280, 286,
350, 417
sieges, 44, 146, 149, 150, 154, 158, 159,
161, 176–93 *passim,* 196, 220, 269,
272–79 *passim,* 283, 289, 290, 302,
303, 307, 310, 311, 321, 322,
327–34 *passim,* 343–49 *passim,*
358–64 *passim,* 366, 367, 368, 376,
377, 381, 383, 384, 397, 401, 403,
405, 407, 410, 412, 413, 416, 420,
421, 431, 450, 451, 581 n. 28. *See
also* artillery; fortresses; military
engineering; Moscow, sieges of; rebel
strongholds
Sienkiewicz (Pan), 372
Sigismund III (king), 124, 127, 128, 131,
134–37 *passim,* 216, 217, 220, 221,
227, 232, 233, 251, 262, 263, 272,
336, 339, 345, 350, 368, 371, 375,
393, 395, 403, 404, 405, 406,
409–16 *passim,* 419, 420, 421, 425,
438, 440, 450. *See also* Polish military intervention; Wladyslaw
Simonov monastery, 303, 304, 309, 412
sinklit, 33. *See also* boyar council
Sitskii clan, 394
skomorokhi, 236. *See also* minstrels
Skopin-Shuiskii, M., 233, 242, 283, 293,
303, 306, 307, 309, 312, 316, 317,
319, 328, 347, 348, 352, 353, 360,
361, 393, 394, 396, 400, 402, 403,

408, 409
Skrynnikov, R., 4, 10, 11, 16, 67, 68, 71,
91, 120, 126, 128, 130, 131, 162,
174, 201, 204, 208–14 *passim,* 217,
218, 227–33 *passim,* 284, 285, 302,
305, 308, 309, 337, 353, 361, 370,
371, 375, 381, 384, 426, 532 n. 5
Skuratov, M., 60
slavery, 24, 46, 55, 56, 57, 58, 71, 264,
265, 455, 456, 469, 476; slave laws,
26, 56, 69, 102–3, 186, 342–43,
402; slave raids, 16, 46
slaves, 3, 4, 8, 9, 15, 16, 26, 56, 57, 63,
68, 69, 70, 80, 88, 95, 96, 97, 101,
103, 112, 144, 163, 164, 188, 225,
254, 255, 272, 300, 305, 308, 318,
320, 331, 343, 359, 382, 390, 391,
395, 399, 406, 417, 424, 425, 426,
428, 448; agricultural, 101, 103;
contract, 15, 57, 69, 343; military, 4,
56, 57, 69, 70, 86, 98, 151, 153,
154, 156, 158, 163, 166, 186, 189,
255, 302, 311, 343, 391, 406, 469.
See also armies, Russian; laws
Slavs, 287
sluzhilie liudi po otechestvu, 39. *See also deti
boiarskie; dvoriane;* gentry; gentry
militia; Pomeshchiki; Pomeste estates
sluzhilie liudi po priboru, 39, 44. *See also*
armies, Russian, soldiers; garrison;
streltsy
Smirnov, I., 8, 251, 284, 285, 308, 314,
326, 388
Smith, R., 23
Smolensk, 39, 42, 46, 99, 135, 138, 139,
226, 227, 233, 234, 242, 270, 276,
285, 291, 301, 303, 307, 310, 311,
312, 314, 316, 326, 376, 391, 403,
405, 406, 407, 409, 410, 412, 413,
419, 421, 436, 450, 457, 561 n. 94,
581 n. 28. *See also* fortresses; Polish
military intervention; sieges
Socialist Revolutionaries, 480
Solovetskii monastery, 246
Solovev, S., 5, 131, 243, 304
sorcerers, 11, 108, 123, 124, 158, 201,

222, 236, 237; sorcery, 244, 245, 246, 251, 259, 378, 398, 479, 532 n. 5, 546 n. 82. *See also* witchcraft

sotniks (centurions), 45, 125, 143, 158, 160, 266, 267, 335. *See also* armies, Russian, officers

Soviet Union, xii, 480

Spain, 462, 488 n. 4

spies and agents, 95, 128, 158, 164, 182, 183, 281, 283, 316, 330, 331, 357, 362, 370, 372, 374, 376, 433, 441

Stalin, J., 8, 381

Stanislavskii, A., 4, 10, 79, 421, 426, 427, 451, 455

stanitsa (cossack settlement), 79

Staritsa, 285

Starodub, 76, 261, 372, 373, 374, 375, 389

Starovskii, I., 342, 364

steppe, 40, 55, 73, 74, 76, 77, 78, 79, 80, 83, 139, 159, 291, 333, 340. *See also* cossacks, free; Crimean Tatars; frontier, southern; Tatars

Stolbovo, Treaty of, 451, 586 n. 40

Stone, D., 114

streltsy, 44–45, 47, 64, 69, 99, 102, 104, 143, 144, 146, 147, 148, 149, 153, 157, 164, 166, 167, 170, 171, 191, 216, 231, 234, 235, 253, 268, 271, 276, 283, 284, 287, 293, 301, 302, 303, 304, 307, 308, 309, 313, 331, 376, 386, 417, 418, 432, 434, 437, 439, 440, 453, 455; Moscow, 146, 147, 148, 170, 216, 234, 284, 293, 301, 303, 304, 308, 309, 418; *streltsy prikaz*, 216. *See also* armies, Russian; harquebuses; harquebusiers

Sukin, V., 188

Sunbulov clan, 307

Sunbulov, G., 275, 279, 284, 307, 309, 322, 323, 352, 376, 401, 416

Sura River, 289

Sutupov, B., 147, 148, 173

Suzdal, 61, 188, 206, 322, 376, 397, 412, 417, 434

Sviatopolk (prince), 118

Sviazhsk, 269, 287, 290, 322, 333

Svodnyi sudebnik, 224

Sweden, 21, 44, 48, 134, 135, 143, 161, 209, 214, 220, 402, 420, 421, 440, 451, 455, 462; Swedish government, 213, 217, 272, 396, 401, 403, 405, 409, 451

Swedes, 44, 154, 397, 450, 455

Swedish military intervention, 397, 401, 420, 421, 431, 432, 433, 435, 436, 440, 443, 448, 450, 451, 453, 454. *See also* Gustav Adolf; Karl IX; Novgorod

syn boiarskii, 40, 56, 237, 331, 367, 375. *see also deti boiarskie*

tabor, 176

Taletskii ostrog, 557 n. 91

Talmud, 370

Tarnopol, 375

Tarusa, 432, 557 n. 91

Tatars, 16, 30, 31, 33, 36, 40, 42, 46, 47, 49, 58, 73, 74, 76, 78, 82, 84, 85, 106, 154, 168, 184, 187, 192, 214, 221, 287, 289, 322, 346, 360, 366, 386, 389, 397, 419, 435, 448. *See also* Crimean Tatars; frontier, southern; Golden Horde; Kasimov Tatars; Mongols; Nogai Tatars

Tatev, B., 170, 173, 184, 185, 197, 208, 210, 233, 303, 316, 328, 346, 347, 348

Tatev, I., 144

Tatishchev, M., 204, 218, 219, 233, 234, 235, 245, 401

Tatishchev, V., 5

taverns, 218, 250, 507 n. 131

taxes, 16, 17, 19, 20, 22, 25, 29, 30, 34, 35, 36, 45, 46, 48, 49, 50, 54, 55, 58, 59, 63, 70, 71, 91, 93, 94, 98, 100, 101, 106, 113, 142, 147, 174, 194, 203, 213, 214, 224, 271, 286, 287, 325, 352, 397, 433, 448, 449, 466, 494 n. 56, 538 n. 178; tax base, 15, 25, 51, 68; tax collectors, 29, 47, 48, 87, 101, 399; tax dodging, 57,

Velikie Luki, 273
Velikii Ustiug monastery, 324
Venev, 76, 267, 279, 300, 318, 325, 329, 342, 364
Venice, 265
Vereia, 285
Verevkin clan, 370, 375
Viatka, 207, 287
Viazma, 285, 311, 410, 450
villages, 70, 98, 148, 149, 151, 158, 162, 163, 191, 192, 282, 283, 285, 287, 291, 297, 299, 306, 309, 312, 324, 339, 346, 357, 360, 361, 364, 391, 396, 397, 398, 399, 400, 402, 433, 435, 466
Vishnevetskii clan, 132, 134, 135
Vishnevetskii, A., 128, 132, 134
Vladimir, 290, 312, 322, 397, 399, 412, 416, 417, 434
Vlasev, A., 208, 210
Voeikov, I., 542 n. 79
voevodas, 37, 143, 144, 145, 149, 150, 156, 157, 158, 160, 164, 167, 170, 173, 180, 188, 192, 203, 209, 210, 211, 252, 261, 263, 265, 266, 269, 274, 276, 279, 281, 283, 284, 289, 290, 291, 296, 303, 308, 309, 310, 313–14, 318, 321, 322, 323, 326, 328, 330, 335, 341, 342, 344, 352, 376, 397, 439. *See also* armies, Russian, campaigns and battles; armies, Russian, officers; garrisons; government; sieges; towns
Voguls, 286
Volga cossacks, 85, 86, 264, 269, 270, 331, 333, 334, 335, 350, 355, 356, 390, 417, 424, 459. *See also* cossacks, free; frontier, southern
Volga River, 47, 55, 79, 80, 83, 84, 85, 105, 142, 173, 191, 192, 222, 223, 261, 268, 269, 270, 281, 282, 287–89 *passim*, 300, 322, 331, 332, 333, 342, 350, 352, 355, 356, 362, 386, 395, 397, 417, 434, 448, 453, 556 n. 66
Volkhov River, 320
Vologda, 96, 397, 399–400, 416, 417,

434, 447
Volok Lamskii, 286, 310, 311, 438
Voronezh, 84, 164, 171, 452
Voronia River, 360, 361, 363, 364, 367
Vorontsov-Veliaminov, N., 144
Vorotynsk, 277, 432
Vorotynskii clan, 63
Vorotynskii, Iu., 274, 275, 277, 278, 279, 282, 293, 313
Vorotynskii, Ivan M., 273, 327, 344, 345, 348, 361, 411
Vorotynskii, Ivan V., 210
Vosma River, 357, 359, 360, 363
Votchina estates, 37, 47, 50, 139, 151. *See also* aristocracy; boyars
Vyborg, 402
Vyrka River, 341, 342, 343

Wandmann, A., 349, 570 n. 54
warfare, 17, 28, 30, 45, 46, 47, 49, 50, 58, 87, 143; cost of, 19, 20, 22, 23, 35, 45, 50, 94, 466; psychological, 79, 178, 292; steppe, 40. *See also* gunpowder revolution; military revolution
Warsaw, 162
weapons. *See* armies, Russian, weapons and armor; artillery; harquebuses
Weber, M., 29
West (Western Europe), 14, 15, 23, 28, 29, 35, 39, 166, 227, 421, 451, 463, 467; Westerners, 28, 44, 206; Western merchants, 48, 221, 227, 234, 237, 251, 400, 421
White Sea, 400, 421, 451
witchcraft, 95, 108, 125, 126, 131, 201, 236, 247, 250, 251, 436, 453. *See also* sorcerers
Wladyslaw (prince), 127, 216, 217, 232, 406, 410, 411, 412, 413, 438, 439, 440, 443, 450, 453, 456–57. *See also* Moscow, sieges of; Polish military intervention; Sigismund III
wooden town (*zamoskvorech'e*), 293, 304, 557 n. 101. *See* Moscow

Zabolotskii, 263, 266

Zabore, 297, 303, 304, 306, 314, 316,
317, 318, 319, 346, 347, 354. *See
also* cossacks, free; Moscow, sieges of
Zagorin, P., 15
Zagriazhskii, A., 148
Zakharin-Iurev, N. R., 61, 62, 67
zamoskvorech'e, 293. *See* Moscow
Zamoyski, J., 134
Zaporozhian cossacks, 78, 124, 134, 137,
145, 153, 154, 161, 163, 265, 273,
275, 276, 339, 342, 377, 385, 389,
411, 416, 437, 454, 517 n. 108. *See
also* cossacks, free; Ukraine
Zaporski, J., 187
Zaraisk, 279, 322, 416, 432
Zarutskii, I., 333, 372, 374, 375, 389,
390, 391, 394, 406, 411–17 *passim*,
424, 427–39 *passim*, 446, 450–54
passim. *See also* cossacks, free;
Dmitrii Ivanovich (Tushino impostor); Ivan Dmitrievich; Mniszech,
Marina; Moscow, sieges of; national
militia; Polish military intervention;
Tushino
zaseka (*zasechnaia cherta*), 74, 76, 79, 85,
360, 385. *See also* armies, Russian,
tactics and strategy; Crimean Tatars;
frontier, southern; steppe
Zasekin clan, 375
Zasekin, F., 335, 361–62
Zekziulin, P., 311
zemskii sobor (Assembly of the Land), 34,
92, 93, 181, 203, 207, 240, 241,
243, 388, 411, 412, 419, 431, 434,
435, 439–42, 443, 445, 448, 449,
450, 467, 468; cossacks and, 431,
439, 441, 442. *See also* government;
Orthodox Christianity; political
culture; Romanov, Mikhail; tsar
Zenowicz (Pan), 371, 372, 373, 339
zhiltsy, 42, 281, 293, 302. *See also
dvoriane*
Zimin, A., 8, 56, 66
Zmeev, Ia., 148
Zolkiewski, S., 216, 217, 404, 405, 409,
410, 411, 412, 413. *See also* Polish
military intervention
Zubtsov, 285
Zvenigorod, 285, 286